THE ENCYCLOPEDIA OF
SCIENCE FICTION AND FANTASY

VOLUME ONE

THE ENCYCLOPEDIA
OF SCIENCE FICTION
AND FANTASY

Through 1968

Compiled by DONALD H. TUCK

A bibliographic survey of
the fields of science fiction, fantasy,
and weird fiction through 1968

Volume 1:   WHO'S WHO, A–L

Advent:Publishers, Inc.

Chicago: 1974

For
AUDREY
and
MARCUS

Library of Congress Catalog Card Number: 73-91828

International Standard Book Number: 0-911682-20-1

FIRST EDITION, March 1974

Contents

    Comprising brief biographies (where available) of the personalities listed—authors, anthologists, editors, artists, etc.—together with information on series, hardbound books, and paperbacks as separate entries. In most cases all known forms and editions are included. Author entries include ones for Anonymous Anthologies and for the Creeps Library, as well as a number of magazines and newspapers that published or sponsored works that would otherwise be considered anonymous.

VOLUME 2 (in preparation)

WHO'S WHO AND WORKS, M–Z

LISTING BY TITLE
    Alphabetical coverage of all books, including paperbacks, and noted novels (not otherwise covered) as listed in the *WHO'S WHO*, with indication of the nature of each item.

VOLUME 3 (in preparation)

MAGAZINES
    Detailed discussion of each magazine of importance to the field, with checklists of issues. Included are some general magazines of interest and also some magazine chains.

PAPERBACKS
    Listed by Title, Author, and Publisher (including numbered series).

PSEUDONYMS
    Listed by pseudonym and by author's real name.

CONNECTED STORIES, SERIES, AND SEQUELS

GENERAL
    A coverage of other aspects of importance, including the more noted publishers and their title series (principally foreign language), films not covered in author entries, amateur magazines, etc.

Introduction

This encyclopedia is designed as a general reference work to cover all aspects relating to modern science fiction, fantasy, weird, and the associated "imaginative" fields.

The idea for such a volume was conceived in the early 1950's and it was first produced in 1954 in a limited duplicated edition as *A Handbook of Science Fiction and Fantasy*. A revised and enlarged second edition appeared in 1959. The sectional arrangement of this, the third edition, is the result of comment on the earlier editions and was adopted after evaluating the opinions of twelve enthusiasts. I feel the changes present all the information available in the best manner possible.

It is not my intention, however, to continually revise the known information every five years or so and then issue fresh editions. Because of the willingness of Advent:Publishers to produce this work in a commercial form, the opportunity has been taken to completely revise the second duplicated edition.

This new edition will thus remain the basic item for some time. It is anticipated, however, that the material presented will be updated periodically by the production of supplements containing four- or five-yearly accumulations of information.

The *WHO'S WHO AND WORKS* section will be the principal portion of the three volumes. It will present the biography of the person, where available, and will list his or her works as appropriate.

Fiction listings, if covering material prior to 1946, are often enlargements of the entries in *The Checklist of Fantastic Literature*, by E. F. Bleiler (Shasta, 1948), and hence this coverage can be considered as a sort of continuation to that book.

The basic idea of this section is to give the user some indication of the different forms in which a particular novel, collection, anthology, etc., has appeared. The original title and presentation of the item have been given as well as its appearances in other forms and editions. This therefore gives an indication of its availability—whether vintage or reasonably current, hard or soft cover. In a few cases the coverage may not be complete, mainly with the older popular fantastic adventure writers such as H. Rider Haggard and Jules Verne.

Pertinent nonfiction is often separately covered, or at least mentioned within the writer's biography.

Such subjects as flying saucers, ghosts, utopias, etc., are covered and a full list of these class entries as presented in the *GENERAL* section will be given in the Introduction there. The subjects of astronomy and space travel, however, are now only covered for writers primarily known for their work in the science fiction field or where it is felt a particular reference work is of value.

For *novels* the year 1945 (i.e., the end of World War II) has been taken as the limiting date for incorporation of the title as a separate entry, unless it has been reprinted since. There are some exceptions, such as a complete coverage of all the novels in *Famous Fantastic Mysteries* (which began in 1939), or where all the novels of a writer of importance are listed for the sake of completeness. This basis of selection notwithstanding, general biographic entries have been added for some older authors of fantasy interest, such as Fergus Hume, though they have not been reprinted since 1945. But in general this work does not cover old gothic novels, utopias, etc., *unless* such titles have been reprinted within the last two decades or so.

Some titles published before 1945 but omitted from the Bleiler *Checklist* have been added and are so noted. However, no attempt has been made to make this work complete in all such omitted titles.

An important feature of the *Encyclopedia* is the coverage given to foreign translations, which have been added as appropriate to the title entries or author biographies. This work can thus be used within such countries as Austria, France, Germany, Italy, Japan, Spain, and Sweden to determine whether any particular work has been translated into the language of that country. A brief picture of matters concerning science fiction, etc., for these and other countries is being compiled and will be given in the *GENERAL* section.

Although Canadian editions are often mentioned in the title coverage, this encyclopedia is by no means complete in that aspect.

The coverage of *collections* (stories by the one author) and *anthologies* (stories selected by a compiler from more than one author) has been chosen on an entirely different basis from that of novels. Although the basic publishing data for these classes of works is just as easy to obtain as for novels, the full listings of their contents are not. The only general source for such is the U.S. Library of Congress Card Catalogue, but even this is not consistent with the older works and since 1945 has not made full listings a general practice. Thus full listings are a most important feature of this encyclopedia, and some 1550 collections and 950 anthologies are covered. Such items go back to the 1890's; the early collections of Algernon Blackwood, Lord Dunsany, and others, as well as anthologies compiled by J. W. McSpadden, Ernest Rhys, and others, are covered.

Entries for novels and nonfiction items usually include brief descriptions, and sometimes relevant facts about their writing and history. Remarks on the quality of a work are only occasionally offered; however the term "classic" is employed where it is felt to be appropriate.

A recent source of book information for the science fiction enthusiast is *A Tale of the Future: 1664–1960*, by I. F. Clarke (The Library Association, London, 1961). This lists many books not covered in this encyclopedia because of my date limitation. Different in concept and layout from the Bleiler *Checklist*, as well as more recent, it is useful in that it gives a brief description of each title; however it is limited to the scope implied by its title (and even so has omissions), and covers only works from English publishers. Bradford Day's *The Supplemental Checklist of Fantastic Literature* (Science-Fiction and Fantasy Pubs., Denver, New York, 1963) is also a source of book information and lists some items not covered in this work.

All paperbacks will be listed in a separate section in Vol. 3; this will include many titles not considered to be of sufficient merit to be covered in the *WHO'S WHO* section. However, paperback editions of works covered in the *WHO'S WHO* section do have complete data presented, and reference to the *PAPERBACK* section should not normally be necessary.

All in all, the *Encyclopedia* is the culmination of over twenty years of work, and is an attempt to provide answers to all conceivable types of questions relevant to modern science fiction and fantasy. Many entries may lack encyclopedic completeness, but nevertheless some effort has been made to give an accurate, even if incomplete, answer. The authenticity of each particular fact, especially where it may appear to be questionable, has been checked to the best of my ability from those sources available to me.

Nevertheless, both my publisher and I would appreciate our attention being drawn to any particular aspect that may not be entirely accurate.

Donald H. Tuck
139 East Risdon Road
Lindisfarne, Tasmania 7015
Australia

November 1973

Acknowledgments

This encyclopedia is the "organisation" and "sifting" of pertinent material from many, many sources. As each of the previous editions has appeared, more reference material has become available and the field of willing helpers has ever widened. It is therefore to all these folk that I express my gratitude for all they have done to enable me to present such a comprehensive information coverage of the fields of science fiction and fantasy.

I first wish to place on record my thanks to Mr. Ron Graham of Sydney, Australia, for all the work he has done on this encyclopedia. He has provided a considerable amount of material over a number of years, and more recently has spent hours checking the final typescript, often with reference back to his outstanding collection. The improvement in accuracy of the information presented is due in a big way to Ron's scrutiny.

With this, the third edition, I would particularly thank Mr. Douglas Harding of Winnipeg, Canada. A noted book collector of many years standing, Doug has given me the contents of over 250 collections and anthologies, as well as drawing my attention to a number of books not covered in the Bleiler *Checklist of Fantastic Literature*.

I also express my appreciation for the work of Dr. Remsen T. Schenck of Bangor, Pennsylvania, who since December 1954 has continually forwarded to me a coverage of current U.S. material as well as giving me notes covering his own collection.

In this third edition a number of original biographies of contemporary figures are presented. My thanks are due to the persons concerned as well as Mr. James Sieger of Waukesha, Wisconsin, and Mr. Howard DeVore of Dearborn, Michigan, who both acted as intermediaries in obtaining this information. Mr. Sieger also continually supplied me with much information resulting from his own researches.

As the *Encyclopedia* is designed for use in Europe, South America, and Japan—besides the English-speaking world—I have naturally had considerable help from authorities in these areas. I therefore express a big "thank you" to the following:

Mr. Pierre Versins, formerly of Lausanne, Switzerland (for French material);

Dr. Antonio Dupla of Zaragoza, Spain (for Spanish, Italian, and South American material);

Messrs. Jakob Bleymehl of the Saar, the late Heinz Bingenheimer and his family, of Berlin [for his *Transgalaxis Catalogue* and associated material], Manfred Alex of Berlin, and Franz Rottensteiner of Austria (all for German material);

Messrs. Sam Lundwall, Roland Adlerberth, and Sture Sedolin of Sweden (for Scandinavian material); and

Messrs. Norio Itoh, Takumi Shibano, and Koichiro A. Noda of Tokyo (for Japanese material).

Also the following reference sources have been of great value: *Early Bird: A Short Handbook of Fantasy and SF in Belgium*, by Dany De Laet (1968); *Catalogo Generale della Fantascienza*, by Alfio Bertoni and Gianluigi Missiaja (1968), for Italian translations; and *100 Jaar S.F. in Nederland*, by D. Scheepstra (1967/68), for Dutch translations.

Further thanks are expressed to Dr. Dupla and Messrs. Versins and Rottensteiner for providing current material at the last minute and for earlier checking the authenticity of the major earlier draft.

One of the features of the *Encyclopedia* is its coverage of the story content of collections and anthologies. Besides those previously acknowledged, the following have been of particular help in this regard: G. Ken Chapman & Sons Ltd. of England; Messrs. Jock McKenna and David Cohen of Sydney, Australia; Mr. T.G.L. Cockcroft of Lower Hutt, New Zealand; Mr. John C. Nitka of Richmond Hill, New York; and Mr. Mark Owings of Bronx, New York.

The original basis of my paperback listing was given to me by Mr. Roger Dard of Perth, Australia, in 1954. Since then it has grown out of all recognition through natural expansion as well as help from many previously mentioned. Much of this as well as other information has been obtained by perusal of the catalogues of Fantast (Medway) Ltd., of Wisbech, England, as well as the columns of the late U.S. amateur magazine *Science-Fiction Times*, to both of which I acknowledge my indebtedness. The present layout results from perceptive comment by Mr. Robert Reginald of San Bernardino, California. I also wish to express my appreciation to this compiler for free use of his *Stella Nova: The Contemporary Science Fiction Authors* (1970), which, in particular, supplied me with many authors' pseudonyms and dates of birth not elsewhere obtainable.

I further express my thanks for the specific material provided upon request by the following: Mr. Gordon Rix of Vancouver, Canada, for a complete outline of Canadian magazines; the late Mr. Lewis D. Harrell of Birmingham, Alabama, for some important new information; Mr. Roy Hunt of Denver, Colorado, for clarifying some points on Sax Rohmer; Mr. I. L. Jacobs of National City, California, for giving a coverage of Mexican science fiction; the late Mr. Ted Carnell of London, and Mr. Don A. Wollheim of New York, who as editors clarified certain points; Mr. Al Lewis of Los Angeles for use of his Magazine Indexes; Mr. Ewan Hedger of the R.A.F., formerly in Cyprus, now in England, for certain British material; and Mr. George Locke of London, England, for many listings of collections covered in his *Ferret Fantasy's Christmas Annual For 1972*.

Many other persons also gave me corrections and pointed out items worthy of inclusion. They include:

Mr. Forrest J Ackerman of Los Angeles, California; Mr. William Austin of Seattle, Washington; the late Mr. Anthony Boucher of Berkeley, California; Mr. Robert Briney of Salem, Massachusetts; Mr. Milton Chambers of Hurstville, New South Wales, Australia; the late Mr. Basil Davenport of New York City; Mr. Ian Crozier of Melbourne, Australia; the late Mr. August Derleth of Sauk City, Wisconsin; the late Mr. Henry Eichner of Los Angeles; Mr. Geoffrey Farmer of Lindisfarne, Tasmania, Australia; Mr. Philip Harbottle of Wallsend-on-Tyne, England; Mrs. J. Joyce of Adelaide, Australia; Mr. Earl Kemp of El Cajon, California; Mr. Charles Mustchin of Coolangatta, Queensland, Australia; Mr. Frank Paccassi of Carmichael, California; Mr. Frank Parnell of Ipswich, England; Mr. Les Smith of Sydney, Australia; Mr. Graham Stone of Canberra Australia; and Mr. Stephen Takacs of New York City.

The following reference material has been freely used in the compilation of the *Encyclopedia*. All except the items restricted to the science fiction and fantasy fields were made available by the Chief Librarian of the University of Tasmania or the State Librarian of the State Library of Tasmania.

The British National Bibliography (1951–)
American Authors and Books (1962)
American Men of Science (1960)
Contemporary Authors (1962–)
The Cumulative Book Index (1929–)
The English Catalogue of Books (1900–1955)
Library of Congress Catalogue Cards
  (in book form)
The Author's and Writer's Who's Who (1960)
Who's Who (U.S. and British)
Who Was Who (U.S. and British)
A History of American Magazines, by F. L. Mott,
  Vol. 4, 1885–1905 (1957)
Twentieth Century Authors (and preceding similar
  volumes)

Pilgrims Through Space and Time,
  by J. O. Bailey (1946)
Checklist of Fantastic Literature,
  by E. F. Bleiler (1948)
The Tale of the Future, by I. F. Clarke (1961)
Index of the Weird and Fantastica in Magazines,
  by B. M. Day (1953)
Complete Checklist of Science-Fiction Magazines,
  by B. M. Day (1961)
*Index to the Science Fiction Magazines
  1926–1950*, by D. B. Day (1952)

Finally I express my deep thanks to Mr. Edward Wood, now of Hartford, Connecticut, both for his constructive suggestions and his continual encouragement. He also has had the onerous task of checking the final draft, and he has acted as my liaison with the Publisher, whose enquiring mind has also prevented many errors in producing the finished work.

Donald H. Tuck

System and Abbreviations

Indexing throughout the *Encyclopedia* is alphabetical word by word. Abbreviations such as "Dr." and "Mr." occurring in titles are alphabetized as if they were spelled out.

In the main *WHO'S WHO* section the full birth and death dates (where obtainable) are given for each person covered, followed by a brief biography which often covers general aspects of his or her career apart from the science-fiction and fantasy fields. Each person's material is then covered under the following headings, as appropriate:

Series / Fiction / Nonfiction / Anthologies / Artwork

The listings under these headings are as complete as possible within the scope of the compiler's knowledge.

The arrangement in the sections following the *WHO'S WHO* will be explained in the opening pages of each section.

ABBREVIATIONS

General

A	anthology
abr	abridged
Aust.	Australian
B.C.	Book Club
Brit.	British
C	collection(s)
¢	cents
ca.	*circa* (about)
contd	continued
D'day	Doubleday
ed.	edition
ext.	extract
FPCI	Fantasy Pub. Co. Inc. (Los Angeles)
frontis.	frontispiece
FSB	Four Square Book (became New English Library in 1968)
fy	fantasy
h	house name
IFA	International Fantasy Award
illus.—	illustrated (by)
lib.	library edition
n	novel(s)
nd	not dated (or unknown)
nn	not numbered
np	not priced (or unknown)
n'te	novelette(s)
pa	paperback, papercovered
pp.	pages (inclusive)
pseud.	pseudonym
rev.	revised
sf, s-f	science fiction
SF	Science Fiction (as part of title or name)
SFWA	Science Fiction Writers of America
S.J.	Sidgwick & Jackson
sr	serial (with number showing how many parts)

Magazines and Series published in English

AFR	*Avon Fantasy Reader*
Arg	*Argosy*
AS	*Amazing Stories*
ASF	*Analog Science Fiction / Science Fact* *Astounding Science Fiction* *Astounding Stories*
ASQ	*Amazing Stories Quarterly*
ASW	*All-Story Weekly* (including title changes)
BB	*Blue Book*
FA	*Fantastic Adventures*
Fan	*Fantastic* (including title changes)
F&SF	*The Magazine of Fantasy and Science Fiction*
FFM	*Famous Fantastic Mysteries*
FN	*Fantastic Novels*
FSM	*Fantastic Story Magazine*
FU	*Fantastic Universe*
Fut	*Future Science Fiction* (including title changes)
GSF	*Galaxy Magazine* *Galaxy Science Fiction*
NW	*New Worlds*
S&I	*Science and Invention*
SEP	*Saturday Evening Post*
SFA	*Science Fiction Adventures* (U.S. unless specified to be British)
SS	*Startling Stories*
SSS	*Super Science Stories*
2CSAB	*Two Complete Science Adventure Books*
TWS	*Thrilling Wonder Stories*
WS	*Wonder Stories*
WSQ	*Wonder Stories Quarterly*
WT	*Weird Tales*

General Note: The majority of the above abbreviations have come into use in the field gradually, and are therefore not entirely consistent. For most magazines other than the above, the first principal word of the title is given in full and the remainder omitted unless there would be ambiguity; for example, *Planet* means *Planet Stories*, but *Space SF* differs from *Space Stories*.

Foreign Language Publications (country of origin is always mentioned)

Danish:	F	Fremtidsromanen
	P	Planetbogerne
French:	A	Anticipation
	Classique SF	Les Classiques de la Science-Fiction
	Le RF	Le Rayon Fantastique
	PF	Presence du Futur
German:	*AW*	*Abenteuer im Weltenraum*
	L	*Luna-Weltall*
	T	*Terra*
	TE	*Terra Extra*
	TN	Terra Nova
	TS	*Terra Sonderband*
	UG	*Utopia-Grossband*
	UK	*Utopia-Kriminal*
	UTR	*Utopia-Taschenroman*
	UZ	*Utopia-Zukunftsroman*
	WF	*Der Weltraumfahrer*
Italian:	*Cosmo*	*I Romanzi di Cosmo Fantascienza*
	GRF	*Galassia Romanzi di Fantascienza*
	Urania	*I Romanzi di Urania* [later *Urania*—but do not confuse with original *Urania* magazine]
Swedish:	A	Atomböckerna (Lindqvists)
	JVM	*Jules Verne Magasinet*
	R	Rymdböckerna

ABBOT, ANTHONY (pseud) See OURSLER, (F.) F.

ABBOTT, EDWIN ABBOTT (20 Dec 1838–12 Oct 1926) English clergyman, educator, and Shakespearian scholar; Headmaster of the City of London School, 1865-89. Author of *Francis Bacon* (1885), *The Anglican Career of Newman* (1892), etc., also many works of New Testament criticism (1900-17).
Fiction
Flatland: A Romance of Many Dimensions (*A Square: Flatland*, Seely & Co., London, 1884, viii+100 pp., illus-author) (Roberts Bros., Boston, 1885, 155 pp.) (Little, Brown & Co., Boston, 1899, 155 pp.) (*Flachenland* [German], Reclam, 1929) (Dover, New York, 1952, 1955, 103 pp., $2.25, pa $1.00)
   A minor classic for mathematicians in which a "square" of the two-dimensional land "Flatland" describes how to recognise fellow inhabitants, etc. The Roberts Bros. edition appeared under the pseudonym "A. Square."
Square: Flatland, A See Flatland

ABDULLAH, ACHMED (12 May 1881–12 May 1945) Real name – Achmed Abdullah Nadir Khan el-Durani el-Iddrissyeh; born in Yalta, son of a Grand Duke, second cousin of Czar Nicholas II of Russia and the Princess Nurmahal. Educated at Eton, Oxford, and Univ. of Paris; served with the British Army in the Near East, India, China, and France before becoming a writer. He produced a vast amount of quick-moving and colourful fiction which included many fantasy tales for the early Munsey magazines. Later he had plays produced on Broadway and achieved fame in Hollywood with his scripts for *The Thief of Bagdad* (originally 1924) and *Lives of a Bengal Lancer*. Wrote his autobiography *The Cat Had Nine Lives* in 1933.
Fiction [Incomplete—other titles in Bleiler *Checklist*]
Alien Souls [C] (McCann, New York, 1922, 248 pp.) (Hutchinson, London, 1923, 287 pp., 7/6)
   15 stories: "Feud"; "Reprisal"; "The Home-Coming"; "The Dance on the Hill"; "The River of Hate"; "The Soul of a Turk"; "Morituri"; "The Jester"; "The Strength of the Little Thin Thread"; "Grafter and Master Grafter"; "The Logical Tale of the Four Camels"; "The Two-Handed Sword"; "Black Poppies"; "The Perfect Way"; "Tao."
Blue-Eyed Manchu, The ("The God of the Invincibly Strong Arms," 2nd Series *ASW*, sr6, 25 Mar 1916) (Shores, New York, 1917, 351 pp.) (Hutchinson, 1923, 286 pp., 7/6; 1924, 2/-)
   Oriental fantasy novelized from original serial appearance.
Mysteries of Asia [C] (P. Allan, London, 1934, 256 pp., 2/6)
   15 stories: "The Magic of the Cannibal"; "Sacrifice to the Black One"; "Serpent Gold"; "Mystery and a Mannikin"; "The Death Beam"; "Mermen of Sulaiman"; "The Dark Bungalow Ghost"; "The Krait"; "Her Blood for Hindu Goddess"; "The Haunted Carpet"; "The Ghosts of Rau Samandar"; "The Magic Horse of Afghan Glens"; "The Human Oil Curse"; "The Ebon Well"; "Ghostly Inheritance."
Red Stain, The ("The God of the Invincibly Strong Arms," 1st series *ASW*, sr6, 18 Sep 1915) (Hearst's International Library, New York, 1915, 309 pp., $1.25) (Simpkin, London, 1916, 309 pp., 6/-)
   Novelised from first appearance. A secret Asiatic Society tries to bring about a general revolt of East against West.
Steel and Jade [C] (Doran, New York, 1927, 319 pp., $2.00)
   12 stories: "Evening Rice"; "Flower of Deborah's Choosing"; "Godless Man"; "Lute of Jade"; "Matter of Face"; "Musa-of-the-

Seven-Goats"; "Mustaffa-of-the-Tricks"; "Road of His Feet"; "The Tale the Drum Told"; "The Way of the Grey Hills"; "When My Caravan Comes In"; "The Woman of the Benni Fukara."
Wings: Tales of the Psychic [C] (McCann, 1920, 239 pp.)
   12 stories (some from *ASW*, title story from *Munsey's Mag.*): "Disappointment"; "Fear"; "Krishnavana, Destroyer of Souls"; "Khizir"; "Light"; "The Man Who Lost Caste"; "Renunciation"; "Silence"; "Tartar"; "That Haunting Thing"; "To Be Accounted For"; "Wings."
Anthology
Fifty Enthralling Stories of the Mysterious East (Odhams, London, nd, 704 pp.)
   50 stories: "The Man With the Shaven Skull," S. Rohmer; "Out of the Jungle," H. S. Banner; "Footprints in the Jungle," W. S. Maugham; "One Way of Justice," M. Diver; "When I Was a Fakir," V. Ivanov; "The Frill," Pearl Buck; "The Rajah of Gool," H. Stacpoole; "The Sword of Ridicule," H. Peterson; "The Victor," D. Collins; "The Lagoon," J. Conrad; "Education Tells," Richard Carol; "Kin Yen, the Picture-Maker," E. Bramah; "The Traitor," K. Rhodes; "Story of the Baked Head," James Morier; "By Water," A. Blackwood; "The Head," Kathleen Wallace; "I See Death," Anthony Mills; "The Kiss of Fate," H. R. Haggard; "At Alexander's Palace," Harold Lamb; "The Justice of Suan Hli," R. Campbell; "The Dream of Akinosuké," L. Hearn; "Death in the Desert," Pierre Loti; "A Thug's First Victim," M. Taylor; "One–Not Two," A. Abdullah; "Cress," John Grant; "Cushy Ride," J. R. Holden; "No Ladies' Man," Dorothy Black; "Breath of Allah," S. Rohmer; "The Prison of Sunset," Sidney Denham; "Why They Do It," Jac. Marmur; "Huqm Chand, An Eastern Triangle," Afghan (pseud); "King of the Beggars," Richard Carol; "Pain Bestowing Consequences," Coutts Brisbane; "The Hut in the Paddy Fields," Reg. Campbell; "The Tryst," Dwan Sharar; "Once in Fifty Years," Glen Aldons; "East and West," Sir W. Scott; "The Lost Patrol," W. B. Bannerman; "Kali's Hand Strikes," M. E. Rutt; "The Tale of Philo," H. R. Haggard; "Cannon Ball Village," Anthony Mills; "A Romance of the Desert," Lady D. Mills; "The Toes of Abdul Fedullah," Murray Sanford; "The Amateur Sheik," John Grant; "Turbans and Termagants," John Hamilton; "The Throat of Green Jasper," Vincent Cornier; "The Slaver Is Ambushed," Rustam Khan-Urf; "The Love of Hermann Agha," W. G. Palgrave; "The Scarred Lover," Capt. Marryat; "The Golden Caravan," Sirdar Ikbal Ali Shah.

ABEL, R. COX
Fiction
Trivana 1 [pa] [with C. Barren] (Panther: 2077, 1966, 171 pp., pa 3/6)
   A utopia with some interesting ideas.

ABERNATHY, ROBERT (1924–) U.S. linguist and writer, resident in Tucson, Arizona. In 1945 he began graduate work in the Harvard Dept. of Slavic Languages, where he spent most of the next six years, obtaining his Ph.D. in 1951.
   His first sf story published was "Heritage" (*ASF*, Jun 1942), and from then to the '50s he appeared in a number of the sf magazines with such stories as "Saboteur of Space" (*Planet*, Spr 1944; *Tops in SF*, Fall 1953), "The Ultimate Peril" (*AS*, Mar 1950); "Heirs Apparent" (*F&SF*, June 1954); "Pyramid" (*ASF*, July 1954); and "Junior" (*GSF*, Jan 1956)—the last three of which have been anthologised.

ABRASHKIN, RAYMOND See WILLIAMS, J. (coauthor)

ACKERMAN, FORREST J (24 Nov 1916–) Noted U.S. sf and fantasy fan, world-wide authors' agent, film consultant, editor, and bookseller. Very philanthropic in fan fields, being noted for his promulgation of the hobby. He is a champion of Esperanto, has one of the world's most complete collections of sf, has had some sf published, and was also on the staff of the first fan magazine, *The Time Traveller*, and *Science Fiction Digest* in the early 1930s.
   He helped organize the Los Angeles Science Fantasy Society in 1934 (the oldest existing fan organization in the world) and origi-

nated the idea of the Fantasy Foundation to preserve sf and fantasy material for posterity. Popularly known as "Mr. Science Fiction," he is also called "4e" and "4SJ." He has written many film review columns for both sf and non-sf magazines as well as fan magazines like *Science-Fiction Times*.

He was to have been editor of the sf magazine *Sci-Fi* announced late in 1956, but this never appeared, as the publisher-to-be went bankrupt. Later, however, he edited *Famous Monsters of Filmland* for James Warren as a one-shot (appearing Jan 1958), and this sold so well that it has since become a regular magazine with its own fan following. Similar magazines, including *Spacemen*, have followed. As an authors' agent he has provided material for many foreign language publications as well as selecting the stories in *A Book of Weird Tales* [British one-shot magazine].

He has made selections from *Famous Monsters of Filmland* in a paper series from Paperback Publishers, New York: *Best From Famous Monsters of Filmland* (1964); *Son of Famous Monsters of Filmland* (1964), and *Famous Monsters of Filmland Strike Back* (1965). These, as well as the magazine, are banned in Australia.

ADAIR, HAZEL (pseud) See ADDIS, H. I.

ADAMS, GEORGE See ANDREAS, P. (co-author)

ADAMS, JOHN
Fiction
When the Gods Came (Badger: SF31, 1960, 142 pp., pa 2/-) (Arcadia, New York, 1967, 190 pp., $3.50)

ADAMS, W. S.
Fiction
Fourth Programme, The (Lawrence Wishart, London, 1955, 63 pp., illus—Gabriel, 5/-)
A broadcast by God, and how governments and churches react.

ADAMSKI, GEORGE (1891–) U.S. writer and lecturer, born in Poland; his family migrated to the U.S. in 1893. He served in the U.S. 13th Cavalry, 1913–19, then settled at Laguna Beach, Calif., and became a lecturer in philosophy and an ardent astronomer and photographer. He later moved to the slopes of Mt. Palomar where he installed a 15-inch telescope and a small observatory. He is noted for his books on the 'authenticity' of inhabitants from space visiting Earth in flying saucers.
Nonfiction
Behind the Flying Saucer Mystery [pa] (Paperback: 53-439, 1967, 159 pp., pa 60¢)
Flying Saucers Farewell (Abelard-Schuman, New York, 1961, 190 pp., $3.95)
A summary and interpretation of information received from the author's "interplanetary friends."
Flying Saucers Have Landed, The [with D. Leslie] (Werner Laurie, London, 1953, 232 pp., 13/6) (*Les soucoupes volantes ont atterri* [French], Ed. du Vieux Colombier, 1954) (*Fliegende Untertassen* [German], Europa-Verlag, 1954) (Panther: 663, 1957, 237 pp., pa 2/6)
The beginning chapters are similar to Keyhoe, Scully, and Heard, with general information on flying saucers; however, the last two chapters caused the sensation, for Adamski stated he had talked to a Venusian.
Inside the Flying Saucers [pa] See *Inside the Space Ships*
Inside the Space Ships (Abelard-Schuman, 1955, 256 pp., $3.50) (Arco, London, 1956, 236 pp., 16/-) (*Inside the Flying Saucers*, Paperback: 53-428, 1967, 192 pp., pa 60¢)
Written as fact, this is an extraordinarily persuasive picture of what the alleged Intelligences directing the "flying saucers" may both be and think of us.

ADDAMS, CHARLES SAMUEL (7 Jan 1912–) U.S. cartoonist, born in Westfield, N.J. Noted for his work in *The New Yorker*, in which he has appeared since 1935. His cartoon characters are of macabre interest and some have been transferred to the TV screen as the very successful series *The Addams Family*.

Artwork
Addams and Evil (Random, New York, 1947, unpaged, $2.75) (Random, Toronto, $3.50) (H. Hamilton, London, 12/6) (Simon & Schuster, New York, 1963, $3.95) **Introduction:** Wolcott Gibbs
Black Maria (Simon & Schuster, 1960, quarto, 96 pp., $3.95)
Charles Addams Mother Goose (Windmill Books, U.S.A., 1967, $4.95)
27 Mother Goose rhymes illustrated in the macabre.
Dear Dead Days (Putnam, New York, 1959, quarto, 126 pp., $3.95) (Longmans, Toronto, $3.95) (P. Hamlyn, London, 1960, quarto, 126 pp., 18/-) (Berkley: F1175, 1966, 124 pp., pa 50¢)
Macabre old-style presentation—called a "family album."
Drawn and Quartered (Random, 1942, 106 pp., $2.50) (Macmillan, Toronto, $2.75) (H. Hamilton, 1943, 112 pp., 12/6) (World, New York, 1944, $1.49) (Bantam: 37, 1946, 128 pp., pa 25¢) (Simon & Schuster, 1962, 112 pp., $3.95) **Introduction:** Boris Karloff
Groaning Board, The (Simon & Schuster, 1964, 88 pp., $3.95)
Homebodies (Simon & Schuster, 1954, quarto, 90 pp., $2.95) (Musson, Toronto, $3.75)
Monster Rally (Simon & Schuster, 1950, 91 pp., $2.95; 1962, $3.95) (Musson, Toronto, $3.50) (H. Hamilton, 1951, 91 pp., 15/-) **Foreword:** J. O'Hara
Nightcrawlers (Simon & Schuster, 1957, quarto, 96 pp., $3.95) (H. Hamilton, 1957, 18/-)

ADDEO, EDMOND G. See GARVIN, R. M. (coauthor)

ADDIS, HAZEL IRIS (Wilson) (Mrs. E. E. Addis) (1900–)
Fiction [as Hazel Adair, with R. Marriott]
Stranger From Space (Weidenfeld & Nicolson, London, 1953, 191 pp., illus—A. Hart, 10/6; 1955, 5/-)
The popular BBC serial in book form.

ADLER, ALLEN A. (25 Dec 1916–) U.S. writer, born into the famous Yiddish acting family created by Jacob P. Adler. He majored in English at New York University, wrote publicity for Ripley's "Believe It or Not," owned a New York theatre at 21, presented opera companies, and served in the U.S. Army Air Force during World War II—5th Air Force, Far Eastern Air Force, and 13th Bomber Command. He produced a revival of *Front Page* and has written both original stories and screen plays for the motion pictures, including conceiving the original story for *Forbidden Planet* [see STUART, W. J.].
Fiction
Mach 1: A Story of Planet Ionus (Farrar, Straus & Cudahy, New York, 1957, 212 pp., $3.00) (Ambassador, Toronto, $3.75) (*Terror on Planet Ionus*, Paperback: 52-941, 1966, 160 pp., pa 50¢) (*Projetto Mach 1* [Italian], *Urania*: 225, 1960)
A super torpedo boat is captured by a flying saucer, and its occupants undergo adventure on Saturn's moon Ionus.
Terror on Planet Ionus [pa] See *Mach 1*

ADLERBERTH, ROLAND (21 Sep 1923–) Swedish writer, book reviewer, and translator for the Swedish field. He found sf in early childhood via Swedish authors Ossian Elgström and Otto Witt, and later Jules Verne and H. G. Wells. He first met American sf in the anthology *Adventures in Time and Space*, by R. J. Healy and J. F. McComas. He has been a librarian, and is now a freelance writer, reviewer of sf and general material, and translator. His translations include a number of novels by R. A. Heinlein. He was on the Editorial Board of the late *Hapna*, the Swedish sf magazine, in its early years, and has edited four Verne novels, two of which were sf. He wrote the first article about sf in Sweden, "SF—Renaissance of the Adventure Novel," for *Bibliotek Bladet*, Sep 1951, following this with two others in later issues.

AHMED, ROLLO (deceased) Egyptian occultist; explored Asia and Europe, and also lived in the West Indies and South America.
Nonfiction
Black Art, The (Long, London, 1936) (Jarrolds, London, 1968, 320 pp., 32/6) (Paperback: 54-617, 1968, 318 pp., pa 75¢)
A collection of facts and fancies on magic from antediluvian days to modern black magic as practised in 1935.

AICHINGER, ILSE (Mme Gunther Eich) (1921–) German author, born in Vienna; during World War II had compulsory service in that city. Since 1950 she has been on the editorial staff of S. Fischer Verlag. In 1952 she received the Austrian Government Award for Literature and married the artist Gunther Eich. Besides the collection below she has written a novel and a play.

Fiction

Bound Man and Other Stories, The [C] [*Der Gefesselte Erzahlungen*, S. Fischer, Frankfurt-on-Main, 1953] (Secker & Warburg, London, 1955, 100 pp., 8/6, trans–E. Mosbacher) (Noonday, New York, 1956, 100 pp., $2.75)

12 off-trail fantasy stories: "The Bound Man"; "The Opened Order"; "The Advertisement"; "The Private Tutor"; "Angel in the Night"; "Story in a Mirror"; "Moon Story"; "Window Entertainment"; "Ghosts on the Lake"; "Speech Under the Gallows."

AICKMAN, ROBERT (FORDYCE) (27 Jun 1914–) British novelist, lecturer, broadcaster, and dramatic critic; born in London and educated at Highgate School, London. He has been film critic to *Jewish Monthly* and has been active in dramatics—Director and Chairman of the London Opera Society in 1954. A scholar on inland waterways, he has written two books on this subject as well as founding the Inland Waterways Association; he also has been Vice-President of the Railways Development Association. He has a considerable knowledge of the occult, and checked the hauntings at the famous Borley Rectory.

Fiction

Dark Entries [C] [pa] (Fontana: 981, 1964, 173 pp., pa 3/6)

5 curious and macabre stories: "The School Friend"; "Ringing the Changes"; "A Choice of Weapons"; "The View"; "Bind Your Hair."

Powers of Darkness [C] (Collins, London, 1966, 253 pp., 18/-) (Fontana: 1827, 1968, 190 pp., pa 5/-)

6 weird stories: "Your Tiny Hand Is Frozen"; "My Poor Friend"; "The Visiting Star"; "Larger Than Oneself"; "A Roman Question"; "The Wine-Dark Sea."

Sub Rosa [C] (Gollancz, London, 1968, 256 pp., 25/-)

8 strange stories: "Ravissante"; "The Inner Room"; "Never Visit Venice"; "The Unsettled Dust"; "The Houses of the Russians"; "No Stranger Than a Flower"; "The Cicerones"; "Into the Wood."

We Are for the Dark [C] See HOWARD, E. J. (coauthor)

Anthologies

Fontana Book of Great Ghost Stories, The [pa] (Fontana: 1055, 1964, 256 pp., pa 3/6)

11 stories and Compiler's Introduction: "The Travelling Grave," L. P. Hartley; "The Ghost Ship," R. Middleton; "Squire Toby's Will," J. S. Le Fanu; "The Voice in the Night," W. H. Hodgson; "Three Miles Up," Elizabeth J. Howard; "The Rocking-Horse Winner," D. H. Lawrence; "The Wendigo," A. Blackwood; "The Crown Derby Plate," Marjorie Bowen; "The Trains," R. Aickman; "The Old Nurse's Story," Mrs. Gaskell; "Seaton's Aunt," W. de la Mare.

Fourth Fontana Book of Great Ghost Stories [pa] (Fontana: 1635, 1967, 192 pp., pa 3/6)

11 stories and Compiler's Introduction: "The Accident," Ann Bridge; "Not on the Passenger List," Barry Pain; "The Sphinx Without a Secret," O. Wilde; "When I Was Dead," Vincent O'Sullivan; "The Queen of Spades," A. Pushkin; "Pargiton and Harby," Des MacCarthy; "The Snow," Hugh Walpole; "Carlton's Father," Eric Ambrose; "A School Story," M. R. James; "The Wolves of Cernogratz," Saki; "Mad Monkton," W. W. Collins.

Second Fontana Book of Great Ghost Stories, The [pa] (Fontana: 1227, 1966, 252 pp., pa 3/6)

12 stories with Compiler's Introduction: "Playing With Fire," Sir A. C. Doyle; "Man-Size in Marble," Edith Nesbit; "How Love Came to Professor Guildea," R. Hichens; "The Demon Lover," Eliz. Bowen; "A. V. Laider," Sir M. Beerbohm; "The Facts in the Case of M. Valdemar," E. A. Poe; "Our Distant Cousins," Lord Dunsany; "The Inner Room," R. Aickman; "Thurnley Abbey," P. Landon; "Nightmare Jack," J. Metcalfe; "The Damned Thing," A. Bierce; "Afterward," Edith Wharton.

Third Fontana Book of Great Ghost Stories, The [pa] (Fontana: 1465, 1966, 224 pp., pa 3/6)

10 stories with Compiler's Introduction: "Negotium Perambulans," E. F. Benson; "The End of the Flight," W. S. Maugham; "The Beckoning Fair One," O. Onions; "The Dream," A. J. Alan; "The Stranger," H. MacDiarmid; "The Case of Mr. Lucraft," Sir W. Besant & J. Price; "The Seventh Man," Sir A. Quiller-Couch; "No Ships Pass," Lady Eleanor Smith; "The Man Who Came Back," W. Gerhardi; "The Visiting Star," W. Aickmann.

AINSBURY, RAY (pseud) See VERRILL, A. H.

AINSWORTH, WILLIAM HARRISON (4 Feb 1805–3 June 1882) English author and editor. He was educated at Manchester Grammar School and, although articled to law, mainly led a life of literary activity. Noted for his editorship of *Bentley's Miscellany* (1840–42), *Ainsworth's Magazine* (1842–54), *New Monthly Magazine*, etc., he is also known for his historical romances. His first novel was *Rockwood* (1834); it was followed by some 40 others.

Fiction [Incomplete—other titles in Bleiler *Checklist*]

Auriol; or, The Elixir of Life (Routledge, London, 1898, 246 pp., illus.) (*The Elixir of Life*, FSB: 1576, 1966, 122 pp., pa 3/6)

This author's most important fantasy. The Routledge edition noted is that in the Bleiler *Checklist*. Presumably far earlier editions appeared, as G. Ken Chapman (bookseller) has ascribed editions in London in 1850, approx. 1865, 1879, and 1890.

Elixir of Life, The [pa] See *Auriol*

ALAN, A. J. English author who narrated mystery stories on the radio in pre-war years; a man of mystery whose identity has been carefully guarded. Some weird stories appear in his collection below, including "My Adventure in Norfolk," but his later works *A. J. Alan, His Second Book* (Hutchinson, 1932) and *The Best of A. J. Alan* (1954) appear to have none.

Fiction

Good Evening, Everyone! [C] (Hutchinson, London, 1928, 286 pp., 2/6)

15 stories: "My Adventure in Jermyn Street"; "The Dream"; "The Cabmen's Shelter"; "A Coincidence"; "The Diver"; "My Adventure in Dartmoor"; "The Hair"; "Charles"; "The Voice"; "An Impromptu Dance"; "The Photograph"; "A Foggy Evening"; "My Adventure in Norfolk"; "The First of April"; "The B.B.I."

ALBAN, ANTONY (Apparently pseud. of Anthony A. Thompson)

Fiction

Catharsis Central (Dobson, London, 1968, 192 pp., 21/-)

Inhabitants of advanced city have problems soothed by central robot—but murder causes disruption.

ALDISS, BRIAN W(ILSON) (18 Aug 1925–) English author, reviewer, and anthologist. He saw action in Burma and Sumatra in World War II, was a bookseller for eight years after the war, and since 1958 has been Literary Editor of *The Oxford Mail*.

He made his writing debut with "Criminal Record" (*Science-Fantasy*, July 1954), while he also won Third Prize in the *London Observer* [newspaper] science-fiction competition, selected stories from which were published as *AD 2500*. He has now become one of the foremost contemporary writers in the sf field, following continued success in both the British and American magazines. Voted by some as the most promising new author at the 1959 World SF Convention, he received a consolation "Hugo." He was the first President of the British Science Fiction Association, for a number of years from 1960.

His work is inclined to off-trail approaches to the various sf themes and he is at times controversial. More recently he has become very successful as an anthologist, while with Harry Harrison he edits the criticism and discussion magazine *SF Horizons*, two issues of which have so far appeared. In 1963 Margaret Mauson compiled a bibliography of his material: *Item Forty-Three—Brian Aldiss 1954–1962*.

Series

Hothouse Life on Earth in the far future. *F&SF*: "Hothouse" (Feb 1961); "Nomansland" (April 1961); "Undergrowth" (July 1961); "Timberline" (Sep 1961); "Evergreen" (Dec 1961).

Revised into continuity as *The Long Afternoon of Earth* (British title: *Hothouse*).

PEST Planetary Ecological Survey Team. *NW*: "Segregation" (July 1958) ([Italian] *GRF* 31, 1963); "Carrion Country" (Nov 1958). *AS*: "Tyrants' Territory" (March 1962).

Fiction

Age, An (*NW*, sr3, Oct 1967) (Faber, London, 1967, 224 pp., 21/-) (*Cryptozoic!*, Doubleday, New York, 1968, 240 pp., $4.50, and Doubleday Book Club, 1968, $1.70)

Time travel and political philosophy—man haunting the corridors of time burdened by real and imaginary phantoms.

Airs of Earth, The [C] (Faber, London, 1963, 256 pp., 18/-, jacket [wood engraving]: M. C. Escher) (SF Book Club [S.J.], 1965, 6/-) (FSB: 1325, 1965, 190 pp., pa 3/6) (*Airs de Terre* [French], Denoël: PF81, 1965, pa)

8 sf stories with Author's Introduction (5 from *NW*, 2 from *F&SF*): "A Kind of Artistry"; "How To Be a Soldier" ("Soldiers Running"); "Basis for Negotiation" (rev); " 'O Moon of My Delight!' " ("Moon of Delight"); "The International Smile"; "The Game of God" ("Segregation"); "Old Hundredth."

Best Science Fiction Stories of Brian Aldiss [C] (Faber, 1965, 253 pp., 21/-) (*Who Can Replace a Man?*, Harcourt, Brace & World, New York, 1966, 253 pp., $4.50, and Signet: P3311, 1967, 215 pp., pa 60¢)

14 stories and Introduction: "Who Can Replace a Man?"; "Not for an Age"; "Psyclops"; "Outside"; "Dumb Show"; "The New Father Christmas"; "Ahead" ("The Failed Men"); "Poor Little Warrior"; "Man on Bridge"; "The Impossible Star"; "Basis for Negotiation"; "Old Hundredth"; "A Kind of Artistry"; "Man in His Time."

Bow Down to Nul [pa] ("X for Exploitation," *NW*, sr3, Mar 1960) (Ace: D-443, 1960, 145 pp., pa 35¢ [with *The Dark Destroyers*]; F-382, 1966, pa 40¢) (*The Interpreter*, Digit: R506, 1961, 156 pp., 2/6; R766, 1963, pa 2/6; FSB:#1970, 1967, 126 pp., pa 3/6) (*Unter dem Terror fremder Sterne* [German], Zimmermann, 1962; *T*: 250, 1962; *Die Herrschaft der Null*, UZ: 553, 1967) (*Un despota sulla Terra* [Italian], Cosmo: 117, 1963)

The attempt of a despotic alien overlord to hoodwink his superior, in that he was not exploiting Earth.

Canopy of Time, The [C] (Faber, 1959, 222 pp., 15/-; 1966, 18/-) (SF B.C. [S.J.], 1961, 5/6) (FSB: 821, 1963, 191 pp., pa 2/6; 1078, 1964, pa 3/6)

Eleven sf stories arranged in sequence with connecting notes: "Three's a Cloud" ("Unbeaten Track"); "All the World's Tears"; "Who Can Replace a Man?"; "Blighted Profile"; "Judas Danced"; "O Ishrail!"; "Incentive"; "Gene Hive" ("Journey to the Interior"); "Secret of a Mighty City" ("Have Your Hatreds Ready"); "They Shall Inherit"; "Visiting Amoeba" ("What Triumphs"). Note: U.S. derivation of this book is *Galaxies Like Grains of Sand*.

Cryptozoic! See *Age, An*

Dark Light-Years, The (*Worlds of Tomorrow*, Apr 1964) —enlarged (Faber, 1964, 190 pp., 16/-) (Signet: D2497, 1964, 128 pp., pa 50¢) (FSB: 1437, 1966, 159 pp., pa 3/6)

Explorers encounter mentally remarkable but physically repulsive race possessing intricate code of social behaviour.

Earthworks ("Skeleton Crew," *Science-Fantasy*, Dec 1963) —enlarged (Faber, 1965, 155 pp., 16/-) (Doubleday, 1966, 154 pp., $3.50) (Doubleday B.C., 1966, $1.20) (Signet: P3116, 1967, 128 pp., pa 60¢) (FSB: 1741, 1967, 126 pp., pa 3/6)

Panoramic view of Earth in the future; Doubleday edition has minor changes compared with the Faber edition.

Equator [pa] See *Vanguard From Alpha*

Galaxies Like Grains of Sand [C] [pa] (Signet: S1815, 1960, 144 pp., pa 35¢) (*Das Ende aller Tage* [German], TS: 120, 1967, pa)

8 sf stories with subheadings and set into a cosmic pattern: The War Millennia: "Out of Reach." The Sterile Millennia: "All the World's Tears." The Robot Millennia: "Who Can Replace a Man?" The Dark Millennia: "O Ishrail!" The Star Millennia: "In-

centive." The Mutant Millennia: "Gene-Hive." The Megapolis Millennia: "Secret of a Mighty City." The Ultimate Millennia: "Visiting Amoeba."

Derived from *The Canopy of Time*, but with original interstitial sequences which the author intended to be included.

Greybeard (Faber, 1964, 237 pp., 18/-) (Harcourt, Brace & World, New York, 1964, 245 pp., $4.50) (Signet: P2689, 1965, 207 pp., 60¢) (SF B.C. [S.J.], 1965) (*Barbe-Grise* [French], Denoël: PF95, 1966, pa) (Panther: 24603, 1968, 219 pp., pa 5/-) (*Aufstand der Alten* [German], Heyne: 3107, 1967, pa)

Life in a future Britain with no children being born; the saga of a 50-year-old survivor (relatively young) and his adventures.

Hothouse See *Long Afternoon of Earth, The*

Interpreter, The [pa] See *Bow Down to Nul*

Long Afternoon of Earth, The (Signet: D2018, 1962, 192 pp., pa 50¢) (*Hothouse*, Faber, 1962, 253 pp., 16/-; SF B.C. [S.J.], 1963, 6/-; FSB: 1147, 1964, 206 pp., pa 3/6) (*Am Vorabend der Ewigkeit* [German], Heyne, 1964, pa)

The Hothouse Series in novel form. A vivid description of sentient man fighting to survive in Earth's far distant, bizarre, future. The paperback version is abridged by 8,000 words.

Male Response, The (Beacon: 305, 1961, 188 pp., pa 35¢) (Dobson, London, 1963, 224 pp., 16/-) (FSB: 1623, 1966, 174 pp., pa 3/6)

Slightly bawdy comedy of the goings-on in Umbalathorp in Africa when a super-computer is saved from a plane. Not really sf.

No Time Like Tomorrow [C] [pa] (Signet: S1683, 1959, 160 pp., pa 35¢)

12 fantasy and sf stories (6 from *Space, Time and Nathaniel*): "T"; "Not for an Age"; "Poor Little Warrior"; "The Failed Men"; "Carrion Country"; "Judas Danced"; "Psyclops"; "Outside"; "Gesture of Farewell"; "The New Father Christmas"; "Blighted Profile"; "Our Kind of Knowledge."

Non-Stop (*Science-Fantasy*, n'te, Feb 1956) (*Fahrt ohne Ende* [German], *T*: 2, 1957) —enlarged (Faber, 1958, 252 pp., 15/-; 1965, pa 7/6) (*Starship*, Criterion, New York, 1959, 256 pp., $3.50; Signet: S1779, 1960, 160 pp., pa 35¢; D2271, 1963, pa 50¢) (*Croisiere sans escale* [French], Denoël: PF29, 1959, pa) (SF B.C. [S.J.], 1960, 5/6) (Digit: R396, 1960, 160 pp., pa 2/6) (*Viaje al infinito* [Spanish], Nebula: 75, 1961, pa) (*Viaggio senza fine* [Italian], Cosmo: 128, 1963, pa)

A doomed world of warring "fantastic mutants" is studied and weighed in the balance; a neat variation of a starship's closed environment going awry. The German ed. has about 12 pages of new material added by the publisher and a completely different ending.

Primal Urge, The [pa] (Ballantine: F555, 1961, 191 pp., pa 50¢) (abr "Minor Operation," *NW*, sr3, June 1962) (Sphere: 10820, 1967, 191 pp., pa 5/-)

The use of an E.R. (Emotional Register) for sexual attraction has unexpected effects.

Report on Probability A (*NW*, Mar 1967) (Faber, 1968, 176 pp., 21/-)

A story of relative phenomena with watchers, watching watchers, watching watchers.

Saliva Tree and Other Strange Growths, The [C] (Faber, 1966, 232 pp., 18/-) (SF B.C. [S.J.], 1967) (Sphere: 10839, 1968, 253 pp., pa 5/-)

10 sf and fantasy stories: "The Saliva Tree" (*F&SF*, Sep 1965); "Danger: Religion" ("Matrix"); "The Source"; "The Lonely Habit"; "A Pleasure Shared"; "One Role With Relish"; "Legends of Smith's Burst"; "Day of the Doomed King"; "Paternal Case"; "The Girl and the Robot With Flowers."

Space, Time and Nathaniel [C] (Faber, 1957, 208 pp., illus—Jeni Turnbull, 12/6) (FSB: 1496, 1966, 159 pp., pa 3/6) (*L'espace, le temps et Nathanael* [French], Denoël: PF39, 1960, pa) (*Nathaniel* [and stories in that section], and *Espacio y tiempo* [remainder] [Spanish], Nebula: 80 and 84, 1962, pa)

14 sf stories: 1. Space: "T"; "Our Kind of Knowledge"; "Psyclops"; "Conviction." 2. Time: "Not for an Age"; "The Shubshub Race"; "Criminal Record"; "The Failed Men." 3. Nathaniel and Other People: "Supercity"; "There Is a Tide"; "Pogsmith"; "Outside"; "Panel Game"; "Dumb Show."

Starship See *Non-Stop*

Starswarm [C] [pa] (Signet: D2411, 1964, 159 pp., pa 50¢) (*Der Sternenschwarm* [German], Heyne: 3124, 1968, pa)

Chronicle type in 8 sections: *Sector Vermillion:* "A Kind of Artistry." *Sector Gray:* "Hearts and Engines" ("Soldiers Running"). *Sector Violet:* "The Underprivileged." *Sector Diamond:* "The Game of God" ("Segregation"). *Sector Green:* "Shards." *Sector Yellow:* "Legends of Smith's Burst." *Sector Azure:* "O Moon of My Delight" ("Moon of Delight"). *The Rift:* "Old Hundredth."

Vanguard From Alpha [pa] ("Equator," *NW*, sr2, Sep 1958) (Ace: D-369, 1959, 109 pp., pa 35¢; with *The Changeling Worlds*) (*Equator*, Digit: R533, 1961, 160 pp., pa 2/6; R695, 1963, 157 pp., pa 2/6) (*Feind aus dem Kosmos* [German], UZ: 315, 1962) (*Equateur* [French], Denoël: PF58, 1962, pa)

Spy and counterspy when the alien Rosks are granted bases on Earth. Note: The Digit edition also contains "Segregation"; the Denoël includes "Three's a Cloud," "Who Can Replace a Man?" "Gene Hive," "Secret of a Mighty City," and "Visiting Amoeba."

Who Can Replace a Man? [C] See *Best Science Fiction Stories of Brian Aldiss*

Anthologies

All About Venus [with Harry Harrison] [pa] (Dell: 0085, 1968, 219 pp., pa 60¢)

7 sf stories and 6 articles; foreword and titled introduction to each section; also bibliography of non-fiction used in compiling this book. 1. Clouded Judgments: "Destinies of the Stars" (art.), S. Arrhenius; "Last and First Men" (extract), O. Stapledon; "Pirates of Venus" (ext.), E. R. Burroughs; "Perelandra" (ext.), C. S. Lewis. 2. Venus Is Hell: "Exploring the Planets" (art., ext.), V. A. Firsoff; "The Big Rain," P. Anderson; "Intelligent Life in the Universe" (art.), Carl Sagan. 3. Big Sister: "Escape to Venus" (ext.), S. Makepeace Lott; "Sister Planet," P. Anderson; "Before Eden," A. C. Clarke. 4. The Open Question: "Some Mysteries of Venus Revealed" (art.), Sir Bernard Lovell; "Dream of Distance" (fragment), Anon.; "Venus Mystery for Scientists" (art.), John Davy. See also *Farewell Fantastic Venus*.

Best Fantasy Stories (Faber, 1962, 208 pp., 16/-)

10 stories and compiler's introductory essay: "The Jet-Propelled Couch," R. Lindner; "Baron Bagge," A. Lernet-Holenia; "Perforce to Dream," Michael Joyce; "Mummy to the Rescue," Angus Wilson; "In the Season of Cold Weather," R. Bradbury; "Incident on a Lake," J. Collier; "Cousin Len's Wonderful Adjective Cellar," J. Finney; "You Can't Have Them All," C. Beaumont; "The Story-Teller," Saki; "Intangibles, Inc.," B. W. Aldiss.

Best SF: 1967 See HARRISON, H. (coanthologist)

Farewell Fantastic Venus (with Harry Harrison) (MacDonald, London, 1968, 293 pp., 30/-)

Subtitled: A History of the Planet Venus in Fact and Fiction. 21 stories and articles: 1. Clouded Judgments: "A Trip to Venus" (1897), John Munro; "The Story of the Heavens" (1883) (article), Sir Robert Ball; "Honeymoon in Space" (1901), George Griffith. 2. Never-Fading Flowers: "The Destinies of the Stars" (1917), Svante Arrhenius; "Last and First Men" (1930) (extract), Olaf Stapledon; "Pirates of Venus" (1932) (extract), E. R. Burroughs; "Perelandra" (1943) (extract), C. S. Lewis. 3. Swamp and Sand: "Alchemy," J. and D. de Courcy; "The Man From Venus," F. R. Paul; "A City on Venus," Henry Gade; "Unveiling the Mystery Planet" (article), W. Ley. 4. Venus Is Hell: "Exploring the Planet" (art.), V. A. Firsoff; "The Big Rain," P. Anderson; "Intelligent Life in the Universe" (art.), Carl Sagan. 5. Big Sister: "Escape to Venus," S. Makepeace Lott; "Sister Planet," P. Anderson; "Before Eden," A. C. Clarke. 6. The Open Question: "Some Mysteries of Venus Resolved" (art.), Sir Bernard Lovell; "Dream of Distance" (art.), Anon.; "Venus Mystery for Scientists" (art.), John Davy. Stop Press: "Scientist Says Icecap on Venus Would Make Life Possible" (art.), Evert Clark [*N.Y. Times*, 9 March 1968].

See also *All About Venus*.

Introducing Science Fiction (Faber, 1964, 224 pp., 18/-; 1967, pa 6/-) (Queenswood, Toronto, $3.95)

12 stories with Compiler's Introduction, Glossary, and Recommended Reading; selected for general readers. "The Edge of the

Sea," A. Budrys; "Trouble With Time," A. C. Clarke; "Time in Advance," Wm. Tenn; "Arena," Fredric Brown; "Gesture of Farewell," B. W. Aldiss; "The Immortal Bard," I. Asimov; "The Cave," P. Schuyler Miller; "A Start in Life," A. Sellings; "The Happy Man," Gerald W. Page; "I Made You," W. M. Miller; "It's a Good Life," J. Bixby; "The Garden of Time," J. G. Ballard.

More Penguin Science Fiction [pa] (Penguin: #1963, 1963, 236 pp., pa 3/6; 1964, pa 3/6)

12 stories with Compiler's Introduction: "The Monkey Wrench," G. R. Dickson; "The First Men," Howard Fast; "Counterfeit," Alan E. Nourse; "The Greater Thing," Tom Godwin; "Built Up Logically," H. Schoenfeld; "The Liberation of Earth," Wm. Tenn; "An Alien Agony," Harry Harrison; "The Tunnel Under the World," Frederik Pohl; "The Store of the Worlds," R. Sheckley; "Jokester," I. Asimov; "Pyramid," R. Abernathy; "The Forgotten Enemy," A. C. Clarke.

Nebula Award Stories 1967 (with Harry Harrison) (Gollancz, London, 1967, 246 pp., 25/-) (*Nebula Award Stories 2*, Doubleday, 1967, 255 pp., $4.95) (Pocket Books: 75114, 1968, 244 pp., pa 75¢)

Second in the annual SFWA selections, with 11 stories: "The Secret Place," R. M. McKenna; "Light of Other Days," Bob Shaw; "Who Needs Insurance?" Robin S. Scott; "Among the Hairy Earthmen," R. A. Lafferty; "The Last Castle," J. Vance; "Day Million," F. Pohl; "When I Was Miss Dow," Sonya Dorman; "Call Him Lord," G. R. Dickson; "In the Imagicon," George H. Smith; "We Can Remember It for You Wholesale," P. K. Dick; "Man in His Time," B. Aldiss. Afterword: The Year in SF, listings of Nebula Awards and Roll of Honour. Note: First of this series was compiled by KNIGHT, D.

Penguin Science Fiction [pa] (Penguin: 1638, 1961, 236 pp., pa 3/6; 1638, 1966, pa 3/6)

12 stories with Compiler's Introduction: "Sole Solution," E. F. Russell; "Lot," Ward Moore; "The Short-Short Story of Mankind," J. Steinbeck; "Skirmish," C. D. Simak; "Poor Little Warrior," B. W. Aldiss; "Grandpa," J. H. Schmitz; "The Half Pair," B. Chandler; "Command Performance," W. M. Miller; "Nightfall," I. Asimov; "The Snowball Effect," Kath. MacLean; "The End of Summer," A. Budrys; "Track 12," J. G. Ballard.

Year's Best Science Fiction See HARRISON, H., as *Best SF: 1967*

Yet More Penguin Science Fiction [pa] (Penguin: 2189, 1964, 205 pp., pa 3/6; 1966, pa 3/6)

12 stories with Compiler's Introduction: "The Wall Around the World," T. R. Cogswell; "Protected Species," H. B. Fyfe; "Before Eden," A. C. Clarke; "The Rescuer," A. Porges; "I Made You," W. Miller; "The Country of the Kind," D. Knight; "Ms Found in a Chinese Fortune Cookie," C. M. Kornbluth; "The Cage," B. Chandler; "Eastward Ho!" W. Tenn; "The Window of Heaven," J. Brunner; "Common Time," J. Blish; "Fulfillment," A. E. van Vogt.

ALDRICH, THOMAS BAILEY (11 Nov 1836–19 Mar 1907) American editor, poet, novelist, dramatist and essayist. He was born in Portsmouth, N.H. His early literary prominence came through his poems; at the age of 19 he published his first book. He spent the first year of the American Civil War in the field as a correspondent for the New York *Tribune*. He edited the Boston magazine *Every Saturday* for nine years and then became the fourth editor of *Atlantic Monthly*, 1881-1890. He is chiefly remembered for *The Story of a Bad Boy* (1870) and the short story "Marjorie Daw" (1873).

Fiction [Incomplete—other titles in Bleiler *Checklist*]

Marjorie Daw and Other People [C] (J. R. Osgood, Boston, 1873, 272 pp.) (Houghton Mifflin, Boston, at least 19 printings to 1901, 272 pp. [some eds. 243 pp.]) (Riverside Press, Boston, 1882)

Fantasy, 9 stories: "Marjorie Daw"; "A Rivermouth Romance"; "Quite So"; "A Young Desperado"; "Miss Mehetabel's Son"; "A Struggle for Life"; "The Friend of My Youth"; "Mademoiselle Olympe Zabriski"; "Père Antoine's Date-Palm."

Marjorie Daw and Other Stories [C] (Houghton Mifflin, Boston, 1885, 287 pp.; 1894, 287 pp.; 1900) (D. Douglas, Edinburgh, 1894, 313 pp.)

Fantasy, 10 stories; same as *Marjorie Daw and Other People*

except omits 4th and 7th stories, and adds: "Our New Neighbours at Ponkapog"; "A Midnight Fantasy"; "The Little Violinist."
Marjorie Daw and Other Tales [C] (B. Tauchnitz, Leipzig, 1879, 296 pp.)

Fantasy, 8 stories; same as *Marjorie Daw and Other People* except omits 4th, 6th and 7th stories, and adds: "Our New Neighbours at Ponkapog"; "A Midnight Fantasy."

ALEXANDER, DAVID (21 April 1907–) U.S. writer born in Shelbyville, Kentucky, and educated at the University of Kansas. He started as advertising manager for a tourist bureau, then became Managing Editor and columnist for the *New York Morning Telegraph*, 1939–40. He served in the armed forces, 1943–45, then became a professional writer. He has had several stories in the sf magazines, and has won the Edgar Allan Poe Award and the Ellery Queen Award. He is a horse racing enthusiast.
Anthology
Tales for a Rainy Night [pa] (Crest: d557, 1962, 192 pp., pa 50¢)

Retitle of the 14th Mystery Writers of America anthology, with 18 stories ranging from comedy to horror: "Robert," S. Ellin; "The Human Chair," Edogawa Rampo; "Pressure," Morris Hershman; "The Murder of George Washington," Richard M. Gordon; "The Widow of Ephesus," Margaret Manners; "Lost Leader," Michael Gilbert; "Doctor's Orders," John F. Suter; "Walking Alone," Miriam A. deFord; "The Twenty Friends of William Shaw," Raymond E. Banks; "Inspector's Lunch," Donald A. Yates; "Reflections on Murder," Nedra Tyre; "West Riding in Maryland," Maurice Procter; "The Pink Caterpillar," Anthony Boucher; "Flash Attachment," Dell Shannon; "Death and the Compass," J. L. Borges; "Have You Lost Your Head?" Joseph Commings; "The Child Watcher," Ernest Harrison; "View From the Terrace," Mike Marmer.

ALEXANDER, LLOYD (30 Jan 1924–) U.S. author, born and brought up in Philadelphia, where he still lives. The purchase as a boy of a children's version of the King Arthur stories began an interest in tales of heroes which led him into the Mabinogion, the classic collection of Welsh legends. He served in the Army Combat Intelligence in World War II, and during that time was temporarily stationed in Wales. He is fluent in Spanish and French, and met his wife, Janine, while studying in Paris; he also taught himself Welsh. He is especially interested in cats (introduced into his Prydain Series in particular) and music. He has published ten adult books, of which the best known are *Fifty Years in the Doghouse*, *Park Avenue Vet* (with Dr. Louis J. Camuti), *My Love Affair With Music*, *Janine Is French*, *My Five Tigers*, and *Let the Credit Go*.
Series
Prydain Books: *The Book of Three*; *The Black Cauldron*; *The Castle of Llyr*; *Taran Wanderer*; *The High King*. Juveniles, covered below. There are also the two books *Coll and His White Pig* (1965) and *The Truthful Harp* (1967), from the same publisher, but which are primarily picture books and not part of the true chronicle.
Fiction
Black Cauldron, The (Holt, Rinehart & Winston, New York, 1965, 224 pp., $3.95, jacket–Evaline Ness)

2nd of Prydain Series: A council of warriors meets and determines to find and destroy the great black cauldron, chief implement of the evil powers of Arawn, Lord of the Land of Death.
Book of Three, The (Holt, Rinehart & Winston, New York, 1964, 217 pp., $3.75, jacket–Evaline Ness)

1st of Prydain Series: A chronicle of the hazardous journey of Taran, Assistant Pig-Keeper, through the land of Prydain.
Castle of Light, The (Holt, Rinehart & Winston, New York, 1966, 204 pp., $3.95, jacket–Evaline Ness)

3rd of Prydain Series: The heroes of Prydain set out on a mission to rescue the Princess Eilonwy from an evil enchantress.
High King, The (Holt, Rinehart & Winston, New York, 1968, 288 pp., $4.50; jacket–Evaline Ness)

5th and last of Prydain Series: The ultimate clash between the forces of good and evil to determine the fate of Prydain.
Taran Wanderer (Holt, Rinehart & Winston, New York, 1967, 256 pp., $4.50; jacket–Evaline Ness)

4th of Prydain Series: Taran learns life's hardest lesson—to accept failure.

ALEXANDER, SIGMUND B(OWMAN)
Fiction [One other fantasy: *The Veiled Beyond*, Cassell, New York, 1888]
10 of Us: Original Stories and Sketches [C] (Laughton MacDonald & Co., Boston, 1887, 167 pp.)

Fantasy, 10 stories or sketches (not known which): "The Modern Mephistopheles"; "Behind the Scenes"; "Out of the Sea"; "Love and Creed"; "A Dual Life"; "Society vs. Societies"; "The Living Dead"; "The Talisman"; "The Mystery of Death"; "The Little Model."

ALFVÉN, HANNES See JOHANNESSON, O. [pseud.]

ALGER, LECLAIRE GOWANS (1898–)
Fiction
Gaelic Ghosts: Tales of the Supernatural From Scotland [by Sorche Nic Leodhas] [C] (Holt, New York, 1964, 110 pp., illus– N. Hogrogian, $3.50; lib. $3.27) (Holt, Toronto, $4.50, $3.76) (Bodley Head, London, 1966, 189 pp., illus., 26/-)

ALLEN, DEXTER
Fiction
Jaguar and the Golden Stag (Coward, McCann, New York, 1954, 340 pp., $3.75) (Longmans, Toronto, $4.00)

Scholarly romance of ancient Mexico and the Aztecs.

ALLEN, EDWARD HERON
Fiction [as Christopher Blayre] [Another fantasy: *Some Women of the University*, 1934, limited ed.]
Purple Sapphire and Other Posthumous Papers, The. Selected from the unofficial records of the University of Cosmopoli by Christopher Blayre [C] (P. Allan, London, 1921, 210 pp., 7/6)

8 weird stories: "The Purple Sapphire"; "Aalila"; "Purpura Lapillus"; "The Thing That Smelt"; "The Blue Cockroach"; "The Demon"; "The Book"; "The Cosmic Dust."
Strange Papers of Dr. Blayre, The (P. Allan, 1932, 271 pp., 2/6)

12 weird stories (enlarged from *The Purple Sapphire*): "The Purple Sapphire"; "The House on the Way to Hell"; "Aalila"; "The Mirror That Remembered"; "Purpura Lapillus"; "Mane Pantea"; "The Thing That Smelt"; "The Blue Cockroach"; "The Man Who Killed the Jew"; "The Demon"; "The Book"; "The Cosmic Dust."

ALLEN, (CHARLES) GRANT (BLAIRFINDIE) (24 Feb 1848– 28 Oct 1899) Canadian novelist, philosopher and scientific writer. Born in Kingston, Canada, he graduated B.A. from Merton College in 1871. His serious novel *The Woman Who Did* (1895) brought him much criticism because of its sexual treatment, while his popular scientific work *Force and Energy* (1888), in which he gave his own statement on dynamics, did not get the scientific reception he expected.
Fiction [Incomplete—other titles in Bleiler *Checklist*]
Strange Stories [C] (Chatto & Windus, London, 1884, 356 pp.)

Fantasy, 16 stories: "The Reverend John Creedy"; "Dr. Greatrex's Engagement"; "Mr. Chung"; "The Curate of Churnside"; "An Episode in High Life"; "My New Year's Eve Among the Mummies"; "The Foundering of the 'Fortuna'"; "The Backslider"; "The Mysterious Occurrence in Piccadilly"; "Carvalho"; "Pausodyne"; "The Empress of Andorra"; "The Senior Proctor's Wooing"; "The Child of the Phalanstery"; "Our Scientific Observations on a Ghost"; "Ras Das of Cawnpore."
Twelve Tales [C] (G. Richards, London, 1899, 351 pp.)

Fantasy, 12 stories. Subtitled "With a Headpiece, a Tailpiece and an Intermezzo." Introduction. Headpiece: "A Confidential Communicator"; "The Reverend John Creedy"; "Frasine's First Communion"; "The Child of the Phalanstery"; "The Abbe's Repentance"; "Wolverden Tower"; "Janet's Nemesis." Intermezzo: "Langalula"; "The Curate of Churnside"; "Cecca's Lover"; "The Backslider"; "John Cann's Treasure"; "Ivan Greet's Masterpiece";

"The Churchwarden's Brother." Tailpiece: "A Matter of Standpoint."

ALLEN, HENRY M. See HOWELLS, W. D. (coanthologist)

ALLEN, HENRY WILSON
Fiction
Genesis Five (Morrow, New York, 1968, 256 pp., $5.95)
First person narrative, as by a Mongol, of Russian work on the creation of a superman in an Arctic laboratory.

ALLEN, M(ARION) C. (12 Dec 1914–) U.S. Baptist minister; born in Spartanburg, S.C., and now living in Kansas. He has contributed to religious journals and has written the book *A Voice Not Our Own* (1963).
Anthology
Shock! [pa] (Popular: SP375, 1965, 144 pp., pa 50¢)
10 weird stories: "The Destructors," Graham Greene; "Evening Primrose," John Collier; "Miriam," Truman Capote; "Earth to Earth," Robert Graves; "The Small Assassin," Ray Bradbury; "The Hunger," Charles Beaumont; "Thompson," George A. Zorn; "Suspicion," Dorothy L. Sayers; "You Can't Run Fast Enough," Arthur Kaplan; "The Man and the Snake," Ambrose Bierce.

ALLEN, THOMAS B. (TOM) U.S. writer, now managing editor of Chilton's Trade Book Division. He began his writing career on *The Sunday Herald*, Bridgeport, Connecticut, and later became a feature writer for the *New York Daily News*. He co-authored *Shadows in the Sea*, a book on sharks. He and his wife (who did many of the illustrations for the book below) live in Wayne, Pennsylvania, with their three children.
Nonfiction
Quest–A Report on Extraterrestrial Life, The (Chilton, Philadelphia, 1965, 325 pp., illus., $4.95)
An examination of the possibility of extraterrestrial life, well illustrated, with solid and significant reporting; deals also with man in space.

ALLIGHAN, HARRY (1898–) Journalist of 25 years experience in five countries; 14 years a resident of South Africa (as of 1960), and a skilled analyst of public affairs.
Fiction
Verwoerd–The End (Boardman, London, 1961, 228 pp., 18/-) (Smithers, Toronto, $4.25) (International Publications, New York, 1962, 228 pp., $4.50)
A history of South Africa 1960–85 showing how apartheid ends; political science fiction.

ALLINGHAM, CEDRIC (1922–)
Nonfiction
Flying Saucers From Mars (F. Muller, London, 1954, 143 pp., 10/6)
Author meets occupant of flying saucer which lands in Scotland, and presents new facts on the phenomena; book follows same line as Adamski.

ALLINGHAM, MARGERY (LOUISE) (Mrs. Phillip Youngman Carter) (20 May 1904–30 June 1966) British author who was educated in private schools and then practised writing under the tutelage of her father, writer Herbert John Allingham. She was particularly noted for her creation of the keen-witted, self-effacing Albert Campion, one of the best-loved fictional detectives. She began her own and Campion's career with *The Crime at Black Dudley* in 1928 (U.S.: *The Black Dudley Murder*, 1929). She wrote lighthearted thrillers, intellectual problem stories like *Death of a Ghost* (1934), and postwar novels of mature insight and powerful atmosphere like *Tiger in the Smoke* (1952).
Fiction
Mind Readers, The (Chatto Windus, London, 1965, 256 pp., 21/-) (Morrow, New York, 1965, 274 pp., $4.50) (Macfadden: 75-157, 1967, pa 75¢) (Penguin: C2779, 1968, 250 pp., pa 4/6)
Somewhat naive use of telepathy in a detective story of the self-effacing Mr. Campion.

ALLUM, TOM
Fiction
Boy Beyond the Moon See *Emperor of Space*
Emperor of Space (Blackie, London, 1959, 220 pp., 10/6) (*Boy Beyond the Moon*, Bobbs-Merrill, Indianapolis, 1960, 255 pp., illus.–J. Russel, $3.50)
Juvenile about convicts and a lad shanghaied by the frustrated inventor of a gravity-controlling space ship.

AMIS, KINGSLEY (WILLIAM) (16 Apr 1922–) British educator, author, critic, poet, playwright, and anthologist. He was educated at City of London School and St. John's Oxford–M.A. He served in the British Army 1942-45, and has been lecturer in English at University College of Swansea since 1949. Noted for his books *Lucky Jim* (1954, filmed in 1957) and *That Uncertain Feeling* (1955), he has also written verse and contributed to magazines such as *The Spectator* and *The Observer*. In 1959 he was invited to Princeton to take part in the Christian Gauss Seminars in Criticism, and he selected the field of science fiction; *New Maps of Hell* (covered below) is based on those lectures. Besides being on the Editorial Committee for the British SF Book Club, he has written some sf, and his novelette "Something Strange" (*Spectator*, 1960) was reprinted in *F&SF* (July 1961).
Nonfiction
New Maps of Hell (Harcourt, Brace, New York, 1960, 161 pp., $3.95) (Gollancz, London, 1961, 161 pp., 16/-) (Ballantine: 479K, 141 pp., pa 35¢) (SF B.C. [S.J.], 1962, 5/6) (*L'univers de la science fiction* [French], Payot, 1962) (FSB: 863, 1963, 141 pp., pa 2/6)
Based on the author's critical lectures on sf given at Princeton in 1959, this is a lucid and entertaining exposition of what he seeks in a sf story. His observations are impressively documented and shrewd; his main view on sf concerns its satiric quality. He concludes that sf is worthwhile and contains something of value, little of which is found elsewhere. (Refer: D. Knight, *F&SF*, June 1960, pp. 84-85; F. Pohl, *If*, July 1960, pp. 100-101; P. S. Miller, *ASF*, Aug 1960; F. Gale, *GSF*, Dec 1960; L. Flood, *NW*, April 1961; *Time*, 3 March 1960.)
Fiction
Anti-Death League, The (Gollancz, London, 1966, 325 pp., 30/-) (Doubleday, Toronto, $5.00) (Harcourt, Brace & World, New York, 1966, 307 pp., $5.95) (Ballantine: U6114, 1967, 317 pp., pa 75¢) (Penguin, 1968, 304 pp., pa 5/-)
Anthologies
Spectrum [with Robert Conquest] (Gollancz, London, 1961, 304 pp., 18/-) (Harcourt, New York, 1962, 304 pp., $4.50) (Doubleday, Toronto, $3.75) (SF B.C. [S.J.], 1962, 5/9) (Berkley: F733, 1963, 190 pp., pa 50¢) (Pan: M61, 1964, 317 pp., pa 5/-)
10 sf stories (US pa abr, omitting 5th, 6th, and 9th), with Introduction: "The Midas Plague," F. Pohl; "Limiting Factor," C. D. Simak; "The Executioner," A. Budrys; "Null-P," Wm. Tenn; "The Homing Instinct of Joe Vargo," Stephen Barr; "Special Flight," John Berryman; "Inanimate Objection," H. Chandler Elliott; "Pilgrimage to Earth," R. Sheckley; "Unhuman Sacrifice," Katherine MacLean; "By His Bootstraps," R. A. Heinlein.
Spectrum II [with Robert Conquest] (Gollancz, 1962, 271 pp., 18/-) (Harcourt, 1963, 271 pp., $4.50) (Doubleday, Toronto, $3.75) (SF B.C. [S.J.], 1963, 11/6) (Berkley: F950, 1964, 256 pp., pa 50¢) (Pan: M75, 1964, 286 pp., pa 5/-)
8 sf stories and Introduction (same contents in all editions): "Beyond Bedlam," Wyman Guin; "Bridge," J. Blish; "There Is a Tide," B. W. Aldiss; "Second Variety," P. K. Dick; "The Feeling of Power," I. Asimov; "Sense From Thought Divide," M. Clifton; "Resurrection," A. E. van Vogt; "Vintage Season," H. Kuttner.
Spectrum III [with Robert Conquest] (Gollancz, 1963, 272 pp., 21/-) (Harcourt, 1964, 272 pp., $4.50) (SF B.C. [S.J.], 1964, 10/6) (Berkley: X1108, 1965, 254 pp., pa 60¢) (Pan: M113, 287 pp., pa 5/-)
8 sf stories and Introduction: "Killdozer!" T. Sturgeon; "The Voices of Time," J. G. Ballard; "Call Me Joe," P. Anderson; "We Would See a Sign," Mark Rose; "Dreams Are Sacred," Peter Phillips; "Exploration Team," Murray Leinster; "Fondly Fahrenheit," Alfred Bester; "The Sentinel," Arthur C. Clarke.

Spectrum 4 [with Robert Conquest] (Gollancz, 1965, 320 pp., 21/-) (Harcourt, 1965, 320 pp., $4.50) (Berkley: S1272, 1966, 287 pp., pa 75¢) (Pan: M193, 1967, 335 pp., pa 5/-)

14 sf stories preceded by "Unreal Estates," a discussion of sf between the late C. S. Lewis, B. Aldiss, and K. Amis (from *SF Horizons*, No. 1, 1964): "Marching Morons," C. M. Kornbluth; "Gadget vs. Trend," Christopher Anvil; "Such Stuff," John Brunner; "The Sellers of the Dream," John Jakes; "The Large Ant," Howard Fast; "Barrier," Anthony Boucher; "The Great Nebraska Sea," Allen Danzig; "Compassion Circuit," John Wyndham; "A Planet Named Shayol," Cordwainer Smith; "Into the Shop," Ron Goulart; "The Secret Songs," F. Leiber; "Stranger Station," D. Knight; "Hot Planet," Hal Clement; "The Choice," W. Young.

Spectrum 5 [with Robert Conquest] (Gollancz, 1966, 272 pp., 21/-) (Harcourt, 1967, 303 pp., $4.50) (Berkley: S1595, 1968, 304 pp., pa 75¢) (Doubleday, Toronto, $4.25) (SF B.C. [S.J.], 1967, 8/-)

Introduction and 8 stories: "Student Body," F. L. Wallace; "Crucifixus Etiam," Walter M. Miller; "Noise Level," Raymond F. Jones; "Grandpa," James H. Schmitz; "Mother of Invention," Tom Godwin; "The Far Look," Theodore L. Thomas; "Big Sword," Paul Ash; "Commencement Night," Richard Ashby.

ANDERSON, ANDY (pseud) See ANDERSON, W. C.

ANDERSON, CHESTER (V. J.) U.S. poet, living in Greenwich Village.
Fiction
Butterfly Kid, The [pa] (Pyramid: X1730, 1967, 190 pp., pa 60¢)

The clever, glib story of how a pop group foils invaders by preventing them from putting 'reality pills' into New York's water supply.
Ten Years to Doomsday [with Michael Kurland] [pa] (Pyramid: R1015, 1964, 158 pp., pa 50¢) (*Dieci anni all'ora* [Italian], *Urania*: 365, 1965) (*Die Drohung aus dem All* [German], Winther, 1967, pa; *Terra Nova* No. 11, 1968)

The galaxy is about to be invaded, with Earth endeavouring to accelerate the technology of a certain planet.

ANDERSON, KAREN (KRUSE) (1932–) U.S. author, and wife (since 1953) of author Poul Anderson. She was born in Erlanger, Kentucky. While living in Washington, D.C., she founded the Red Circle, which is still active as the local scion of the Baker Street Irregulars. She is a member of such sf organisations as the Fantasy Amateur Press Association, and edited *Henry Kuttner: A Memorial Symposium* (duplicated, 1958, 33 pp., 40¢), in which this writer is discussed by noted authors, and a full bibliography of his works is given. She has published verse and fiction in *F&SF*, and edits the amateur magazine *Vorpal Glass*.

ANDERSON, POUL (WILLIAM) (25 Nov 1926–) U.S. science fiction and fantasy author, born in Bristol, Penna., of Scandinavian parents. One of the noted contemporary writers in the field, he first appeared in *ASF* with "Tomorrow's Children" (March 1947, with coauthor) while studying at the University of Minnesota. He financed his studies through writing, taking an honours degree in physics in 1948, but has since remained a writer. He has done historical and straight fiction as well as sf and fantasy, and because of his ancestry is extremely interested in Nordic writings. He now lives with his wife, Karen, and daughter, Astrid, near Berkeley, Cal.

Most of his sf works are of interest, and a number are set in his own Future History Series [see below]. Notable stories include "The Double-Dyed Villains" (1st of Wing Alak Series); "The Helping Hand" (*ASF*, May 1950); "Sister Planet" (*Satellite*, short novel, May 1959; also in *Get Out of My Sky* [Margulies], 1960, pa); "Epilogue" (*ASF*, short novel, Mar 1962); and the more recent long works "Outpost of Empire" (*GSF*, Dec 1967), "To Outlive Eternity" (*GSF*, sr2, June 1967), and "Satan's World" (*ASF*, sr4, May 1968). He has used the pseudonyms "Winston P. Sanders," inspired by Winnie the Pooh, and "A. A. Craig."

He won a Hugo in 1961 with "The Longest Voyage" (*ASF*, Dec 1960) [anthologized in *The Hugo Winners*, ed. by Asimov, 1962],

and a later one in 1964 with "No Truce With Kings" (*F&SF*, June 1963). He received the $2,000 Cock Robin Award for *Perish by the Sword* (Macmillan, 1959), a mystery and the first of his Trygve Yamamura Series. It was followed by "Stab in the Back" (*Saint Detective Mag.*, March 1960) and *Murder in Black Letter* (Macmillan, 1960). His historical novels of interest are *The Golden Slave* (1960), on the origin of the Aesir, and *Rogue Sword* (1960). A nonfiction paperback of interest, but little known, is *Thermonuclear Warfare* (Monarch, 1963).

He was Guest of Honour at the 1959 World SF Convention in Detroit, and served as chairman of the North California Chapter of the Mystery Writers of America in 1959.
Series
Alak, Wing. "The Double-Dyed Villains" (*ASF*, Sept 1949); "Enough Rope" (*ASF*, July 1953); "The Live Coward" (*ASF*, June 1956).
Flandry, Dominic. Space intelligence agent. [Stories marked "I" collected in *Agent of the Terran Empire*; "II" in *Flandry of Terra*.] "Ensign Flandry (*AS*, Oct 1966); "Tiger by the Tail" (*Planet*, Jan 1951, I); "Honorable Enemies" (*Future*, May 1951, I); "The Ambassadors of Flesh" (*Planet*, Sum 1954, in I as "The Warriors From Nowhere," the author's original title); "The Game of Glory" *Venture*, March 1958, II); "A Handful of Stars" (*AS*, June 1959); *We Claim These Stars* [pa], shorter version "Hunters of the Sky Cave" in I); "A Message in Secret" (*Fantastic*, Dec 1959; *Mayday Orbit* [pa] ; II); "A Plague of Masters" (*Fan*, sr2, Dec 1960; *Earthman, Go Home* [pa] ; II).
Future History. The future as it might happen, in the vein of Heinlein. The time chart presenting the date range for Series I was first presented in *SS*, Win 1954, p. 29. Titles in parentheses (...) are stories yet to be written; brackets [...] indicate author's original title, which may be used in any later reprinting.
Series I. "Marius" (*ASF*, Mar 1957); "Un-Man" (*ASF*, Jan 1953); "The Sensitive Man" (*FU*, Jan 1954); ("House in the Sky"); "The Big Rain" (*ASF*, Oct 1954); "Catalysis" (*If*, Feb 1956); ("Wolf"); "Quixote and the Windmill" (*ASF*, Nov 1950); ["Holmgang"] "Out of the Iron Womb" (*Planet*, Sum 1955); "Cold Victory" (*Venture*, May 1957); "The Snows of Ganymede" (*SS*, Win 1954); "The Troublemakers" (*Cosmos*, Sep 1953); "What Shall It Profit?" (*If*, June 1956); "Brake" (*ASF*, Aug 1957); ("Winter"); "Gypsy" (*ASF*, Jan 1950); "Entity" (*ASF*, June 1949, with John Gergen); "Star Ship" (*Planet*, Fall 1950); "The Acolytes" (*Worlds Beyond*, Feb 1951); "The Green Thumb" (*SFQ*, Feb 1953); "Virgin Planet" (*Venture*, Jan 1957, book); *Star Ways*.
Series II. [Not so formally organized as Series I, and subsumes a number of other series, *q.v.*] "Security" (*Space*, Feb 1953); "Sam Hall" (*ASF*, Aug 1953); "Duel on Syrtis" (*Planet*, March 1951); "Garden in the Void" (*GSF*, May 1952); ["The Big Hunt"] "War-Maid of Mars" (*Planet*, May 1952); Nicholas van Rijn Series; ["Collar of Iron"] "The Star Plunderer" (*Planet*, Sep 1952); ["Deus ex Machina"] "Lord of a Thousand Suns" (*Planet*, Sep 1951); Dominic Flandry Series; "A Twelvemonth and a Day" (*FU*, Jan 1960); Wing Alak Series; (. . . . . .); "The Chapter Ends" (*Dynamic*, Jan 1954). *Note:* Quite a number have been reprinted, with revisions.
Hoka [with G. R. Dickson]. Lovable intelligent bears. "Heroes Are Made" (*OW*, May 1951); "In Hoka Signo Vinces" (*OW*, June 1953); "The Adventure of the Misplaced Hound" (*Universe*, Dec 1953); "Yo Ho Hoka!" (*F&SF*, March 1955); "The Tiddlywink Warriors" (*F&SF*, Aug 1955); "Joy in Mudville" (*F&SF*, Nov 1955); "Undiplomatic Immunity" (*F&SF*, May 1957); "Full Pack (Hokas Wild)" (*F&SF*, Oct 1957). The stories up to "The Tiddlywink Warriors," plus one new one, "Don Jones," were collected in *Earthman's Burden*.
Matuchek, Stephen. Magic as a science. "Operation Afreet" (*F&SF*, Sep 1956); "Operation Salamander" (*F&SF*, Jan 1957); "Operation Incubus" (*F&SF*, Oct 1959).
Operation. See Matuchek, Stephen, Series.
Sky People, The. Re-emerging civilization. "The Sky People" (*F&SF*, March 1959); "Progress" (*F&SF*, Jan 1962).
Time Patrol. "Time Patrol" (*F&SF*, May 1955); "Delenda Est" (*F&SF*, Dec 1955); "Brave to Be a King" (*F&SF*, Aug 1959); "The Only Game in Town" (*F&SF*, Jan 1960). Published as *Guardians*

of Time, but in a different order.

Trader [or Nicholas van Rijn]. [Stories marked "I" collected in *Trader to the Stars* (which also includes two pages from "Margin of Profit"); "II" in *The Trouble Twisters*.] "Margin of Profit" (*ASF*, Sep 1956); "The Man Who Counts" (*ASF*, sr3, Feb 1958; *War of the Wing-Men*, pa); "Hiding Place" (*ASF*, March 1961; I); "Territory" (*ASF*, June 1963, I); "The Three-Cornered Wheel" (*ASF*, Oct 1963; II); "The Master Key" (*ASF*, July 1964; I); "Trader Team" (*ASF*, sr2, July 1965; "The Trouble Twisters" in II); "A Sun Invisible" (*ASF*, April 1966; II); "Supernova" (*ASF*, Jan 1967); "Satan's World" (*ASF*, sr4, May 1968).

Van Rijn, Nicholas. See Trader Series

Fiction

[A separate German title is *Rebellion auf der Venus* ("The Big Rain," *ASF*, Oct 1954), *UG*: 148, 1961; *TE*: 113, 1966.]

After Doomsday ("The Day After Doomsday," *GSF*, sr2, Dec 1961) (Ballantine: 579, 1962, 128 pp., pa 35¢) (*Die Untergang der Erde* [German], Goldmann, 1962, 1964 pa) (*Hanno distrutto la Terra* [Italian], *Urania*: 292, 1962) (Gollancz, London, 1963, 160 pp., 13/6) (Panther: 1798, 1965, 185 pp., pa 3/6) (*Apres L'Apocalypse* [French], Galaxie Bis: 2, 1966, pa; with *Trois mondes à conquerir* [*Three Worlds to Conquer*]).

After finding Earth devastated, a space crew wanders among alien worlds seeking other human survivors.

Agent of the Terran Empire [C] (Chilton, Philadelphia and New York, 1965, 198 pp., $3.95)

Four Dominic Flandry stories, as noted in the Series entry.

Brain Wave (Ballantine: 80, 1954, 139 pp., pa 35¢; 393K, 1960, 164 pp., pa 35¢; U2342, 1966, pa 50¢) (Heinemann, London, 1955, 212 pp., 10/6) (*Quoziente 100* [Italian], *Urania*: 108, 1955) ([Japanese], Gengen-sha: SF14, 1956; Hayakawa: 3036, 1962, pa) (*Hjernechock Fra Universet* [Danish], Skrifola: F5, 1957) (*Barrière mentale* [French], *Satellite*, sr2, Jan 1958) (*Die Macht des Geistes* [German], *UG*: 70, 1958) (Heyne: 3095, 1967, pa) (in *Treasury of Great SF*, ed. Boucher, 1959) (*Ik400* [Swedish], Wennerberg: R17, 1959, pa) (*Unter Kosmichen Nebeln* [German], Zimmermann, 1961) (*Panico en la Tierra* [Spanish], Cenit: 30, 1962, pa) (Mayflower: 0765, 1965, 159 pp., pa 3/6) (*Vlaag van verstand* [Dutch], Meulenhoff, Amsterdam. 1967)

Began as two-part serial in *Space SF*, Sep 1953, titled "The Escape," but not completed there. The Solar System leaves an inhibiting force field, and the IQ of all living creatures is raised with consequent turmoil.

Broken Sword, The (Abelard-Schuman, New York, 1954, 274 pp., $2.75)

A pleasing fairy-tale type.

Corridors of Time, The (*AS*, sr2, May 1965) (Doubleday, New York, 1965, 209 pp., $3.95) (Doubleday, Toronto, $4.75) (D'day SF B.C., 1965, $1.20) (Gollancz, 1966, 209 pp., 18/-) (Lancer: 73-505, 1966, 222 pp., pa 60¢) (SF B.C. [S.J.], 1967) (*Korridore der Zeit* [German], Heyne: 3115, 1968, pa) (Panther: 025693, 1968, 223 pp., pa 5/-)

Adventures in time.

Earthman, Go Home! [pa] ("A Plague of Masters," *Fantastic*, sr2, Dec 1960) (Ace: D-479, 1960, 110 pp., pa 35¢; with *To the Tombaugh Station*) (*Loro, i terrestri* [Italian], *Urania*: 279, 1962) (*Erdmenschen unerwünscht* [German], *T*: 340, 1964) (in *Flandry of Terra* [Anderson], 1965)

One of the Flandry Series, in which he breaks a government tyranny on Unan Besar, where antitoxin is necessary to survival.

Earthman's Burden [with Gordon R. Dickson] [C] (Gnome, New York, 1957, 185 pp., $3.00) (*Alexander Jones, Diplomat der Erde* [German], *T*: 382-3, 1965)

6 stories of the Hoka Series: the five to "The Tiddlywink Warriors" (with the first retitled "The Sheriff of Canyon Gulch"), and one new story, "Don Jones'"

Enemy Stars, The ("We Have Fed Our Sea," *ASF*, sr2, Aug 1958) (Lippincott, Philadelphia, 1959, 191 pp., $2.95) (Longmans, Toronto, $2.95) (D'day SF B.C., 1959, $1.20) (Berkley: G289, 1959, 142 pp., pa 35¢; F1112, 1965, pa 50¢) (*Die Söhne der Erde* [German], *TS*: 30, 1960)

A mobile-base star-ship breaks down, disabling the matter trans-

mitter through which crew members periodically change. The science of the novel is discussed by the author in an article, "Paper Spaceship," *New Frontiers* [amateur magazine], Jan 1960.

Ensign Flandry (*AS*, Oct 1966) (Chilton, 1966, 203 pp., $4.50) (Lancer: 73-677, 1967, 224 pp., pa 60¢) (*Dominic Flandry–Spion im All* [German], *TS*: 126, 1967, pa)

A story of Flandry at 19, upon the outset of his career in the Imperial Terran Navy, with the Merseian Empire bent on conquest.

Flandry of Terra [C] (Chilton, 1965, 225 pp., $3.95)

Three Flandry stories, as noted in the Series entry.

Guardians of Time [C] (Ballantine: 422K, 1960, 140 pp., pa 35¢) (Gollancz, 1961, 176 pp., 13/6) (SF B.C. [S.J.], 1962, 5/9) (*Hüter der Zeiten* [German], Goldmann, 1961, 1963 pa) (Pan: G660, 1964, 160 pp., pa 2/6) (*Guardianes del tiempo* [Spanish], Nebula: 102, 1964, pa) (*La patrouille du temps* [French], Gerard: Verviers 1965) (*Avontuur in het verleden* [Dutch], Spectrum, Utrecht & Antwerp, 1966)

4 sf stories of the Time Patrol Series (adventures of Manse Everard), in different order—"Delenda Est" removed to last.

High Crusade, The (*ASF*, sr3, July 1960) (Doubleday, 1960, 192 pp., $2.95; 'Dolphin': C351, 1962, pa 95¢) (Doubleday, Toronto) (*Kreuzzug nach fremden Sternen* [German], *UZ*: 298, 1961) (*Croaziata spaziale* [Italian], *Cosmo*: 105, 1962) (*Les croises du cosmos* [French], Denoël: PF57, 1962, pa) (Macfadden: 50-211, 1964, 160 pp., pa 50¢; 60-399, 1968, pa 60¢)

An English knight in the Middle Ages captures an alien space ship and sets out to conquer the stars. Entertaining.

Horn of Time, The [C] [pa] (Signet: P3349, 1968, 144 pp., pa 60¢)

6 sf stories (most revised): "The Horn of Time the Hunter" ("Homo Aquaticus," *AS*, Sep 1963); "A Man to My Wounding" ("State of Assassination"); "The High Ones"; "The Man Who Came Early"; "Marius"; "Progress."

Let the Spacemen Beware! [pa] ("A Twelvemonth and a Day," *FU*, Jan 1960) (Ace: F-209, 1963, 98 pp., pa 40¢; with *The Wizard of Starship Poseidon*) (*Raumfahrer, Vorsicht!* [German], *T*: 347, 1964)

Establishment of a refueling base on a world having ancient Celtic roots.

Makeshift Rocket, The [pa] ("A Bicycle Built for Brew," *ASF*, sr2, Nov 1958) (Ace: F-139, 1962, 97 pp., pa 40¢; with *Un-Man and Other Novellas* [Anderson]) (*Raumschiff Modell Eigenbau* [German], *UZ*: 585, 1968)

Outrageous adventure of a spaceship engineer endeavouring to escape from the wild Irish Expeditionaries in a spacecraft propelled by beer bubbles.

Mayday Orbit [pa] ("A Message in Secret," *Fan*, Dec 1959) (Ace: F-104, 1961, 126 pp., pa 40¢; with *No Man's Land*) (*Geheimagent auf Altai* [German], *T*: 226, 1962) (in *Flandry of Terra* [Anderson], 1965)

Flandry helps the down-trodden underground on Altai.

No World of Their Own [pa] ("The Long Way Home," *ASF*, sr4, April 1955) —abridged (Ace: D-110, 1955, 158 pp., pa 35¢ [with *The 1,000-Year Plan*]; D-550, 1962, pa 35¢) (*Die fremden Sterne* [German], K. G. Bewin, 1956; *T*: 65, 1959) (*Sin mundo propio* [Spanish], Cenit: 65, 1963, pa) (*Nessun mondo per loro* [Italian], *Cosmo*: 139, 1963)

The first starship returns to Earth and causes chaos to the complex galactic structure formed there during its 5,000-year absence.

Orbit Unlimited [pa] (Pyramid: G-615, 1961, 158 pp., pa 35¢; F-818, 1963, pa 40¢)

Rewritten from "Robin Hood's Barn" (*ASF*, Jan 1959); "The Burning Bridge" (*ASF*, Jan 1960); "Condemned to Death" (*FU*, Oct 1959). Political maneuvering and planetary adventure with colonists meeting problems of living on the large world Rustum.

Planet of No Return ("Question and Answer," *ASF*, sr2, June 1954) (Ace: D-199, 1956, 105 pp., pa 35¢; with *Star Guard*) (*Planet ohne Wiederkehr* [German], *Utopia Mag*: 12, 1958) (Dobson, London, 1966, 105 pp., 13/6)

Interstellar explorers interpret the contradictory behaviour of an unclassifiable alien race. This novel was to have been in a Twayne Triplet (book), in association with "Sucker Bait" by Isaac

Asimov and "Get Out of My Sky" by James Blish.

Shield (*Fan*, sr2, June 1962) —enlarged (Berkley: F743, 1963, 158 pp., pa 50¢) (Dobson, 1965, 158 pp., 15/-) (*Escudo invulnerable* [Spanish], Nebula: 112, 1965, pa) (*Der Ungreifbare* [German], *TS*: 93, 1965) (SF B.C. [S.J.], 1967)

Controlled atomic nuclei give a physicist super powers in an America after a future war.

Snows of Ganymede, The [pa]   (*SS*, Win 1955) (Ace: D-303, 1958, 96 pp., pa 35¢; with *War of the Wing-Men* [Anderson])

Intrigue and adventure in the terraforming of Ganymede.

Star Fox, The (Doubleday, 1965, 274 pp., $4.50) (D'day B.C., 1965, $1.20) (Gollancz, 1966, 274 pp., 18/-) (Signet: P2920, 1966, 207 pp., pa 60¢) (*Freibeuter im Weltraum* [German], TS: 116, 1966, pa) (SF B.C. [S.J.], 1967, 9/-) (Panther: 026312, 1968, 204 pp., pa 5/-)

Three novelettes from *F&SF*: "Marque and Reprisal" (Feb '65); "Arsenal Port" (Apr 1965); "Admiralty" (June 1965). Dramatic adventure fighting the non-human Aleriona.

Star Ways (Avalon, New York, 1956, 224 pp., $2.75) (Ryerson, Toronto, $2.75) (Ace: D-255, 1957, 143 pp., pa 35¢ [with *City Under the Sea*]; D-568, 1963, pa 35¢) (*Sternenwanderer* [German], *UG*: 77, 1958) (*I nomadi dell'infinito* [Italian], *Urania*: 183, 1958) (*La route etoilee* [French], Satellite 'Les Cahiers de la SF: 8,' 1959) (*Cita galactica* [Spanish], Cenit: 18, 1961, pa)

Romantic transgalactic tale of nomadic trading civilization encountering aliens bent on reshaping the Galaxy to their own ends.

Strangers From Earth [C] [pa] (Ballantine: 483K, 1961, 144 pp., pa 35¢) (*Extranjeros en la Tierra* [Spanish], Nebula: 88, 1963, pa) (Mayflower: 8345, 1964, 190 pp., pa 3/6) (*Die Sternzigeuner* [German], *T*: 376, 1965)

8 sf stories [foreign editions may be abridged]: "Earthman, Beware"; "Quixote and the Windmill"; "Gypsy"; "For the Duration"; "Duel on Syrtis"; "The Star Beast"; "The Disintegrating Sky"; "Among Thieves."

Three Hearts and Three Lions (*F&SF*, sr2, Sep 1953; also British ed. 1st Series) (Doubleday, 1961, 191 pp., $2.95, jacket—E. Gorey) (D'day B.C., 1961, $1.20) (Avon: G1127, 1962, 160 pp., pa 50¢)

Joyous blend of grand action fantasy with hero in a world of witches, dragons and fair maids, in a fight for Law against Chaos.

Three Worlds to Conquer [pa]   (*If*, sr2, Jan 1964) (Pyramid: R994, 1964, 143 pp., pa 50¢) (X1875, 1968, pa 60¢) (Mayflower: 8873, 1966, 142 pp., pa 3/6) (*Kontakt mit Jupiter* [German], Heyne: 3063, 1966, pa) (*Trois mondes à conquerir* [French], Galaxie Bis: 2, 1966, pa; with *Apres L'Apocalypse* [*After Dooms-Day*]).

Two interwoven stories of drama in the lives of a Ganymede colonist and a native of Jupiter, with both worlds well depicted.

Time and Stars [C] (Doubleday, 1964, 249 pp., $3.95) (Doubleday, Toronto, $4.75) (D'day B.C., 1964, $1.20) (Gollancz, 1964, 206 pp., 16/-) (Macfadden: 60-206, 1965, 190 pp., pa 60¢) (SF B.C. [S.J.], 1965, 6/-) (*Die Zeit und die Sterne* [German], *TS*: 103, 1965) (Panther: 2109, 1966, 169 pp., pa 3/6)

6 sf stories (British editions omit last story): "No Truce With Kings (*F&SF*, June 1963); "Turning Point" (*If*, May 1963); "Escape From Orbit" (*AS*, Oct 1962); "Epilogue" (*ASF*, Mar 1962); "The Critique of Impure Reason" (*If*, Nov 1962); "Eve Times Four" (*Fan*, April 1960).

Trader to the Stars [C]   (Doubleday, 1964, 176 pp., $3.50) (Doubleday, Toronto, $3.95) (D'day B.C., 1964, $1.20) (Gollancz, 1965, 176 pp., 15/-) (Berkley: F1284, 1966, 159 pp., pa 50¢) (*Die Sternenhändler* [German], Heyne: 3079, 1966, pa) (Panther: 2214, 1967, 144 pp., pa 3/6)

3 of the Trader (van Rijn) Series: "Hiding Place"; "Territory"; "The Master Key." Also 2-page quote from "Margin of Profit."

Trouble Twisters, The [C] (Doubleday, 1966, 189 pp., $3.95) (Gollancz, 1967, 191 pp., 21/-) (Berkley: X1417, 1967, 190 pp., pa 60¢) (*Die unsichtbare Sonne* [German], TS: 124, 1967, pa)

3 of the Trader Series adapted from *ASF* versions: "The Three-Cornered Wheel"; "A Sun Invisible"; "The Trouble Twisters" ("Trader Team").

Twilight World (Torquil, New York, 1961, 181 pp., $2.95) (D'day B.C., 1961, $1.20) (*Die Menscheit sucht Asyl* [German], Gold-

mann, 1961, 1963 pa) (Gollancz, 1962, 181 pp., 15/-) (SF B.C. [S.J.], 1963, 5/9) (Panther: 1676, 1964, 127 pp., pa 2/6) (*El crepusculo del mondo* [Spanish], Nebula: 108, 1965, pa) (*Na de derde wereldoorlog* [Dutch], Spectrum, Utrecht & Antwerp, 1965)

Novelisation of the *ASF* stories "Tomorrow's Children" (March 1947) and "Logic" (July 1947), with new final section. (Coauthor of first story is not credited.) The struggle of man to emerge from the chaos of an atomic war, and the colonisation of Mars.

Un-Man and Other Novellas [C] [pa]   (Ace: F-139, 1962, 158 pp., pa 40¢; with *The Makeshift Rocket* [Anderson]) (*UNO-Agent im Einsatz* [German; title story only], *UG*: 170, 1962; *TE*: 140; 1967)

3 sf novelettes from *ASF*: "Un-Man" (Jan 1953; in *All About the Future* [Greenberg], 1955); "Margin of Profit" (Sep 1956); "The Live Coward" (June 1956).

Vault of the Ages (Winston, Philadelphia, 1952, 210 pp., $2.00) (*La citta perduta* [Italian], *Urania*: 90, 1955) ([Japanese], Ginga-Shobo 'Adv in SF4,' 1956) (*Den Fortabte By* [Danish], Skrifola: F8, 1958, pa) (*Das Arkhiv in der Geisterstadt* [German], *T*: 537, 1967)

Juvenile; one of the *Adventures in SF* series. In a feudal future 500 years after atomic holocaust, a chief's son finds a time-vault.

Virgin Planet (*Venture*, n'te, Jan 1957) —enlarged (Avalon, 1959, 224 pp., $2.75) (Beacon: 270, 1960, 160 pp., pa 35¢) (*Planet der Amazonen* [German], *TS*: 38, 1960) (*Le Amazzoni* [Italian], *Urania*: 235, 1960) (*Planeta de mujeres* [Spanish], Galaxia: 13, 1964, pa) (Mayflower: 9336, 1966, 156 pp., pa 3/6)

A man lands on a planet occupied only by women descended from survivors of a space wreck 300 years earlier.

War of the Wing-Men [pa]   ("The Man Who Counts," *ASF*, sr3, Feb 1958) (Ace: D-303, 1958, 160 pp., pa 35¢ [with *The Snows of Ganymede* (Anderson)]; G-634, 1967, pa 50¢) (*Die Wing-Dynastie* [German], Zimmermann, 1959; *Die Rasse der Flügelmenschen*, *T*: 150, 1960) (*Guerra de los alados* [Spanish], Cenit: 60, 1963, pa)

Van Rijn and other Terrans land on the sea-world Diomedes in the midst of war between its winged races.

War of Two Worlds [pa]   ("Silent Victory," *2CSAB*, Win 1953) (Ace: D-335, 1959, 108 pp., pa 35¢; with *Threshold of Eternity*) (*Världar I Krig* [Swedish], Wennerberg: R19, 1959, pa) (*Dämonen des Weltalls* [German], *UG*: 131, 1960; *TE*: 107, 1966) (*La trois-ieme race* [French], Le Fleuve Noir: A150, 1960, pa)

Earth is occupied by Mars, and an Earthman seeks to liberate his world.

We Claim These Stars [pa]   ("A Handful of Stars," *AS*, June 1959) (Ace: D-407, 1959, 125 pp., pa 35¢ [with *The Planet Killers*]; G-697, 1967, pa 50¢) (*Schach dem Unbekannten* [German], *TS*: 41, 1960)

A Flandry story of interstellar intrigue.

World Without Stars [pa]   ("The Ancient Gods," *ASF*, sr2, June 1966) (Ace: F-425, 1966, 125 pp., pa 40¢) (*Gestrandet zwischen den Milchstrassen* [German], *T*: 547, 1967)

Group of future starmen marooned on a strange planet fight to survive and return home.

Nonfiction

Is There Life on Other Worlds? (Crowell-Collier: New York, 1963, 223 pp., illus., $4.95) (Collier-Macmillan, London, 1963, 223 pp., illus., 38/-) (Collier: 01625, 1968, 223 pp., pa 95¢)

New approaches to some of the problems of possible planetary types are presented. Besides airless, terrestrial, and Jovian gas-giant types, there are several intermediates and also the super-Jovian. Also discusses the "life zone" and the greenhouse effect.

ANDERSON, WILLIAM C(HARLES) ("ANDY") (7 May 1920–) U.S. Lieut. Colonel and author, born in La Junta, Colorado, and attended Boise Junior College, Fort Hays College, and Univ. of Maryland. He entered the U.S. Army Air Corps in 1941, and by 1963 was a command pilot, serving in the Office of Information under the Secretary of the Air Force. His first novel appeared under the name "Andy" from a specialist publisher.

Fiction

Adam M-1 (Crown, New York, 1964, 255 pp., $3.95) (Ambassador, Toronto, $5.00) (A. Redman, London, 1965, 155 pp., 21/-) (*Weltraum-Roboter* [German], Heyne: 3105, 1967, pa)

Human judgment and electronic reaction is combined in Adam M-1—the first Astrodynamically Designed Aerospace Man.

Five, Four, Three, Two, One—Pffff [pa] (Ace: D-467, 1960, 157 pp., pa 35¢)

Pandemonium on the Potomac (Crown, 1966, 245 pp., $2.95)

Father and daughter team from Venus, concerned with the atomic destruction on Earth, endeavour to destroy all countries including Russia.

Penelope (Crown, 1963, 215 pp., $3.95) (A. Redman, 1964, 215 pp., 21/-) (Pocket Books: 50126, 1965, 197 pp., pa 50¢)

A rollicking farce in the Thorne Smith tradition: a dedicated scientist with a knack for getting into trouble, and Penelope, a talking porpoise.

Valley of the Gods, The [as Andy Anderson] (Andoll Pub. Co., Baraboo, Wisconsin, 1957, $2.00, pa)

Girl and father, of telepathic race which replaced homo sapiens, wander through atomic war ruins; quite philosophical in viewing Man.

ANDREAS, PETER
Nonfiction

Between Heaven and Earth [with G. Adams] (Harrap, London, 1967, 160 pp., 21/-)

A resume of outstanding experiments and experiences in the realm of telepathy, clairvoyance, prediction, etc. A compilation, it does not attempt scientific criticism and evaluation.

ANDREWS, CHARLES M.
Anthology

Famous Utopias (Tudor: New York, 1901, 317 pp., later impressions)

The four classic utopias: Rousseau's *Social Contract*; More's *Utopia*; Bacon's *New Atlantis*; Campanella's *City of the Sun*.

ANDREWS, F(RANK) EMERSON (26 Jan 1902–) U.S. librarian, born Lancaster, Penna; B.A., Franklin & Marshall College, 1923. Director of Publications, Russell Sage Foundation, 1928-56, also Director of Philanthropic Research there, 1944-56; Director of Foundation Library Center in New York City since 1956.
Fiction

Grugan's God (Muhlenberg Press, Phila., 1955, 196 pp., $3.00)

ANDREZEL, PIERRE [pseud] See BLIXEN, K.

ANGELO (pseud)
Fiction

Dancing Imps of the Wine, The [C] (Hurst & Co., New York, 1880, 259 pp.)

Fantasy, 8 stories and 16 fables. *Stories:* "The Dancing Imps of the Wine"; "The Silver Fairy"; "The Skeleton on the Wall"; "A Christmas Story"; "A Frog Jubilee of Animals"; "The Feast of Flowers"; "The Four Angels: A Dream"; "The Haunted Castle." *Fables:* "The Rose and the Lily"; "The Pearl and the Diamond"; "Night and Day"; "The Fox and the Goose"; "The Cat and the Mouse"; "Light and Shadow"; "The Dog and the Cat"; "The Wind and the Air"; "The Butterfly and the Ants"; "The Peacock and the Canary-Bird"; "Winter and Spring"; "The Bear and the Bees"; "The Sun and the Snow"; "The Mirror and the Beauty"; "The Cloud and the Sunbeam"; "The Seasons." Described by bibliographer M. Owings as "horribly moralistic."

ANGELUCCI, ORFEO
Fiction

Son of the Sun (De Vorss, Los Angeles, 1959, 211 pp., $3.95)
Nonfiction

Secret of the Saucers, The (Ray Palmer Pubs., Amherst, Wisc., 1955, 167 pp., $3.00)

One of the books about contact with flying saucers; the author meets extradimensional beings from the destroyed planet Lucifer.

ANGOFF, CHARLES (22 April 1902–) U.S. literary figure, born in Russia, coming to the U.S.A. in 1908, naturalized in 1923; A.B.

Harvard University, 1923. He started as a news reporter in 1923, joined *American Mercury* and became managing editor in 1931, then editor in 1935. He later became editor of *American Spectator* and *North American Review*, and was executive editor of Mercury Publications, 1950-51. Since 1957 he has been professor of English at Fairleigh Dickinson University and co-editor of *Literary Review*. Uses pseudonym Richard W. Hinton.
Fiction

Adventures in Heaven [C] (Ackerman, New York, 1945, 120 pp., $2.00)

Fantasy, 21 stories: "Doctors in Heaven"; "Gift of Life"; "God Is Encouraged"; "God Repents"; "God's Felicity"; "Heaven and Hell"; "Jesus and the Little Girl"; "Love's Greatest Reward"; "Man's Greatest Dignity"; "Man's Work"; "One Woman to Another"; "Painter and the Little Boy"; "Power of Faith"; "Road to Heaven"; "Sacred and Profane Love"; "Scholar in Heaven"; "Substance of Things Hoped For"; "Three Dolls and a Woman"; "Two Women"; "Where Heaven Is"; "Wisdom of Woman."

ANONYMOUS
Fiction

Equality: or, a History of Lithconia ("The Temple of Reason," *Deist* [weekly newspaper], sr8, 15 May 1802) (Liberal Union, Philadelphia, 1837, 124 pp.,) (P. J. Mendum, Boston, 1863, 6 in. x 3¾ in., 82 pp., pa) (Prime Press 'American Utopia:2,' Philadelphia, 1947, 6½ in. x 4½ in., xxvii + 86 pp., $2.50)

Considered to be the first American Utopia. The author is not known with any certainty, but could be Dr. James Reynolds, who was a zealous liberal crusader.

ANONYMOUS ANTHOLOGIES
Fiction

Battle for the Pacific and Other Adventures at Sea, The (Harper, New York & London, 1908, 327 pp.)

Part I: The Dream of the Guns: "The Battle for the Pacific," Rowan Stevens; "The Bombardment of the Golden Gate," Yates Stirling Jr; "A Fight in the Fog," Y. Stirling Jr; "The Battle off the Hook," Y. Stirling Jr; "Harry Borden's Naval Monster," William J. Henderson; "The Cruise of a Commerce Destroyer," Y. Stirling Jr. *Part II: Strange Stories of the Sea:* "Private or Privateer?" George Ethelbert Walsh; "The Mutiny on the Swallow," Wm. J. Henderson; "The Scape-Goat of La Justicia," Harold Martin; "Captain Sampson's Queer Cargo," G. E. Walsh; "A Warm Corner in Sooloo," Owen Hall; " 'Cap'n il's' Closest Call," Kirk Munro; "My Borrowed Torpedo-Boat," Julian Ralph; "The Lost Voice," F. H. Spearman; "Joe Griffin's Great Jump," W. J. Henderson.

Bedside Tales of Mystery and Suspense [pa] (Panther: 1473, 1963, 126 pp., pa 2/6)

Weird, 7 stories: "The House in the Goblin Wood," J. D. Carr; "The Incredible Elopement of Lord Peter Wimsey," Dorothy L. Sayers; "The Romantic Young Lady," W. S. Maugham; "The Diamond Lens" Fitz-James O'Brien; "The Griffin and the Minor Canon," F. R. Stockton; "Exit Permit," Peter Cheyney; "The Good River," Pearl S. Buck.

Benn's Bedside Book [pa] (Ernest Benn, London, 1958, 319 pp., pa 3/6)

Anthology of 13 stories, 3 articles and 3 quizzes: "The Man Who Could Work Miracles," H. G. Wells: "Knole; the House," V. Sackville-West; "The Screaming Skull," F. M. Crawford; "Round the World in 80 Questions" [quiz]; "Without Cherry Blossom," P. Romanoff; two travel articles; "The Story of the Girl Who Answered No," C. G. Campbell; article; "The Upper Berth," F. M. Crawford; "The Spell of the Yukon," Robert W. Service; quiz; "The Walk," A. M. W. Stirling; "The Story of the Woman Who Was Stronger Than Man," C. G. Campbell; "The Truth About Pyecraft," H. G. Wells; "A Slave to the Work," 'Balaam'; quiz; "Man Overboard," F. M. Crawford; "Being Detectives," E. Nesbit.

Beyond [pa] (Berkley: F712, 1963, 160 pp., pa 50¢)

Fantasy, 9 stories from the extinct magazine *Beyond*, 1953-55: "The Watchful Poker Chip," R. Bradbury; "The Ghost Maker," F. Pohl; "Can Such Beauty Be?" Jerome Bixby; "The Real People,"

Algis Budrys; "The Beautiful Brew," James E. Gunn; "I'd Give a Dollar," Winston Marks; "The Root and the Ring," Wyman Guin; "Double Whammy," Fredric Brown; "Talent," Theodore Sturgeon.

Black Tales [pa] (Corgi: GN7272, 1965, 158 pp., pa 3/6)

Weird, 6 stories: "Mistrust," M. G. Lewis; "The Middle Toe of the Right Foot," A. Bierce; "Markheim," R. L. Stevenson; "Hop-Frog," E. A. Poe; "Rappaccini's Daughter," N. Hawthorne; "The Ghost Ship," R. Middleton.

Boys' World of Adventure, The (C. A. Pearson, London, 1937, 7½ in. x 10½ in., 160 pp., illus., 2/6)

Apparently an addendum to the weekly magazine *Scoops*, containing coloured plates and line drawings by "Drigin" and thirteen stories of which five were originally published in *Scoops*.

Century of Creepy Stories (Hutchinson, London, 1934, 15+1151 3/6, 5/-, 7/6) (Ryerson, Toronto)

Weird, 70 stories: "The Snow," "The Tarn," "A Little Ghost," "Mrs. Lunt," H. Walpole; "The Islington Mystery," "The Cosy Room," "Opening the Door," "Munitions of War," A. Machen; "The Red Turret," Flavia Richardson; "When Glister Walked," "Si Urag of the Tail," "The Great White Fear," "Boomerang," Oscar Cook; "The Apple Tree," "Telling," "The Cat Jumps," Elizabeth Bowen; "Crewe," "A Recluse," W. de la Mare; "Two Trifles," "The Smile of Karen," "John Gladwin Says . . .," O. Onions; "The Hanging of Alfred Wadham," E. F. Benson; "As in a Glass Dimly," "The Hospital Nurse," "The Lord-in-Waiting," Shane Leslie; "A Considerable Murder," B. Pain; "The Lovely Voice," "The Play-fellow," " 'God Grant That She Lye Still,' " "The Corner Shop," Lady C. Asquith; "Shall We Join the Ladies?" J. M. Barrie; "The Rocking-Horse Winner," "The Lovely Lady," D. H. Lawrence; "Rats," M. R. James; "The Killing-Bottle," "The Travelling Grave," "Visitor From Down Under," "The Cotillon," L. P. Hartley; "The Prince," "The Last Man In," W. B. Maxwell; "Dispossession," "Beauty and the Beast," C. H. B. Kitchin; "Those Whom the Gods Love . . .," "The Birthright," Hilda Hughes; "The Haunted Man and the Ghost's Bargain," C. Dickens; "The Villa Desiree," May Sinclair; "The Duenna," "The Unbolted Door," Mrs. Belloc Lowndes; "The Apparition of Mrs. Veal," D. Defoe; "The Lost Tragedy," D. Mackail; "Spinsters' Rest," C. Dane; "Circumstantial Evidence," E. Wallace; "A Descent Into the Maelström," "The Fall of the House of Usher," "The Black Cat," E. A. Poe; "Twelve O'Clock," C. Whibley; "The Amorous Ghost," Enid Bagnold; "Par-giton and Harby," D. MacCarthy; "The Country of the Blind," H. G. Wells; "The Spectre Bridegroom," W. Irving; "Mr. Tallent's Ghost," Mary Webb; "The Buick Saloon," Ann Bridge; "The Horns of the Bull," W. S. Morrison M.P.; "The Man Who Came Back," W. Gerhardi; "Our Feathered Friends," P. MacDonald; "The Stranger," Ambrose Bierce; "The Yellow Cat," M. Joseph; "My Adventure in Norfolk," A. J. Alan; "The Mysterious Mansion," H. de Balzac; "The Stranger," A. Blackwood.

Century of Ghost Stories (Hutchinson, London, 1936, 1013 pp., 3/6)

Ghost, 43 stories (many previously appearing in *Fifty Years of Ghost Stories*): "The Familiar," "Green Tea," J. S. Le Fanu; "The Saint and the Vicar," C. Binney; "The Tapestried Chamber," Sir W. Scott; "Gibbet Lane," A. Gittins; "The Old Nurse's Story," Mrs. Gaskell; "The Residence at Whitminster," "A Warning to the Curious," M. R. James; "The Haunted and the Haunters," Sir E. Bulwer-Lytton; "The Green Room," W. de la Mare; "Eveline's Visitant," Miss Braddon; "Afterward," Edith Wharton; "The Middle Toe of the Right Foot," A. Bierce; "Man Overboard!" F. M. Crawford; "As in a Glass Dimly," "The Lord-in-Waiting," S. Leslie; "Dracula's Guest," B. Stoker; "Expiation," "Pirates," E. F. Ben-son; "The Woman's Ghost Story," A. Blackwood; "Thurnley Ab-bey," P. Landon; "The Rosewood Door," O. Onions; "The Virgin of the Seven Daggers," V. Lee; "The Library Window," Mrs. Oli-phant; "The Song in the House," Ann Bridge; "The Operation," Violet Hunt; "The Sweeper," "The Running Tide," Ex-Private X; "Perez," W. L. George; "The Spectre of Tappington," R. H. Bar-ham; "The Phantom Coach," Amelia B. Edwards; "The Grey Champion," "Young Goodman Brown," N. Hawthorne; "The Dream Woman," W. W. Collins; "The Lifted Veil," G. Elliot; "The Werewolf," F. Marryat; "The Ghost-Seer," F. Schiller; "The Bota-

then Ghost," R. S. Hawker; "The Story of the Bagman's Uncle," C. Dickens; "John Charrington's Wedding," Evelyn Nisbit; "The Klausenburg," L. Tieck; "Berenice," E. A. Poe; "The Haunted Ships," A. Cunningham.

Century of Thrillers, A (Daily Express, London, 1934, 1087 pp., illus.)

Weird, 47 stories; Introduction by James Agate: "The Travel-ler's Story of a Terribly Strange Bed," "Mad Monkton," "The Biter Bit," Wilkie Collins; "The Adventure of the Speckled Band," A. C. Doyle; "The Mortal Immortal," Mary Shelley; "The Gentle-man From America," M. Arlen; "The Leech of Folkestone," "Jerry Jarvis's Wig," "The Spectre of Tappington," "Singular Passage in the Life of the Late Henry Harris, Doctor of Divinity," R. H. Barham; "The Ebony Box," Mrs. Henry Wood; "My Adventure at Chiselhurst," "The Hair," A. J. Alan; "The Gold Bug," "The Cask of Amontillado," "The Murders in the Rue Morgue," "The Mys-tery of Marie Roget," "The Pit and the Pendulum," "Berenice," "William Wilson," "The Masque of the Red Death," E. A. Poe; "Roger Malvin's Burial," "Dr. Heidegger's Experiment," "The Grey Champion," Nathaniel Hawthorne; "Wandering Willie's Tale," Sir W. Scott; "The Monkey's Paw," W. W. Jacobs; "Sir Dominick Sars-field," "Mr. Justice Harbottle," "Green Tea," J. S. Le Fanu; "The Birthday of the Infanta," O. Wilde; "The Trial for Murder," "The Story of the Bagman's Uncle," C. Dickens; "No. 1 Branch Line, the Signal-man," C. Dickens; "The Squire's Story," Eliz. Gaskell; "The Light-house on Shivering Sand," J. S. Fletcher; "Malachi's Cove," A. Trollope; "The Haunted and the Haunters," Lord Lytton; "The Story of the Greek Slave," F. Marryat; "The Woman's Ghost Story," "Secret Worship," A. Blackwood; "The Open Door," Mrs. Oliphant; "The Suitable Surroundings," "One of the Missing," "The Affair at Coulter's Notch," "A Tough Tussle," "A Horseman in the Sky," A. Bierce.

Century of Thrillers (President Press, New York, 1937, 3 volumes)

Vol. I (viii + 367 pp.; anonymous introduction): "Death & Co.," D. Hammett; "The Magic of Fear," E. Wallace; "Jewel Robbery at the Grand Metropolitan," A. Christie; "The Adventure of the Speckled Band," "The Adventure of the Blue Carbuncle," A. C. Doyle; "The Prussian Officer," D. H. Lawrence; "Tcheriapin," S. Rohmer; "The Queer Feet," G. K. Chesterton; "The Pavilion on the Links," R. L. Stevenson; "The Taipan," W. S. Maugham; "The Great Bear," E. P. Oppenheim; "The Squaw," B. Stoker; "Miss Bracegirdle Does Her Duty," S. Aumonier; "The Gold Bug," "The Cask of Amontillado," "Murders in the Rue Morgue," "The Mys-tery of Marie Roget," E. A. Poe.

Vol. II (vi + 373 pp.): "Locked Doors," M. R. Rinehart; "Pol-lock and the Porroh Man," H. G. Wells; "Adventure of the Three Lame Men," Ellery Queen; "Tale of the Piper," Donn Byrne; "A Gentleman for a Night," O. R. Cohen; "One of the Missing," "The Affair at Coulter's Notch," A. Bierce; "The Gentleman From America," M. Arlen; "Night," "The Drowned Man," G. de Mau-passant; "The Upper Berth," F. M. Crawford; "The Silent Bullet," A. B. Reeve; "When the World Was Young," J. London; "The Traveller's Story of a Terribly Strange Bed," "The Biter Bit," W. W. Collins; "The Doctor, His Wife, and the Clock," Anna K. Green; "Sir Dominick Sarsfield," "Green Tea," J. S. Le Fanu; "The Woman's Ghost Story," A. Blackwood; "The Knights of the Silver Dagger," A. Wolfe.

Vol. III (vi + 370 pp.): "The Lighthouse on Shivering Sand," "The Ivory God," J. S. Fletcher; "The Spectre of Tappington," R. H. Barham; "The Squire's Story," Eliz. Gaskell; "The Corpus Delicti," M. D. Post; "The Mortal Immortal," M. Shelley; "Diver's Drops," N. A. Temple Ellis; "The Story of the Bagman's Uncle," "A Madman's Manuscript," "The Trial for Murder," C. Dickens; "The Cards," Sydney Parkman; "The Birthday of the Infanta," O. Wilde; "The Last Leaf," O. Henry; "Roger Malvin's Burial," N. Hawthorne; "The Ebony Box," Mrs. Henry Wood; "Wandering Willie's Tale," "The Two Drovers," Sir W. Scott; "My Adventure at Chiselhurst," "The Hair," A. J. Alan; "The Thing in the Hall," E. F. Benson; "A Pair of Hands," Sir A. T. Quiller-Couch.

Come Not Lucifer (Westhouse, London, 1945, 267 pp., illus—R. A. Brandt, 12/6)

'A romantic anthology' of 12 stories: "King Pest," "The Case of

M. Valdemar," "The Black Cat," E. A. Poe; "Bartleby," H. Melville; "The Signalman," C. Dickens; "The Watcher," J. S. Le Fanu; "The Oath," H. de Balzac; "Torture by Hope," Villiers de L'Isle Adam; "The Pistol Shot," "The Queen of Spades," A. S. Pushkin; "Thrawn Janet," "A Lodging for the Night," R. L. Stevenson.

Destination: Amaltheia (Foreign Languages Pub. House, Moscow, *ca.* 1960, 420 pp.)

Sf, 7 stories (English translations of Russian material): "The Astronaut," Valentina Zhuravlyova; "Over the Abyss," A. Belayev; "The Maxwell Equations," A. Dnieprov; "The Valley of the Four Crosses," I. Zabelin; "The Golub-Yavan," K. Stanyukovich; "Flying Flowers," M. Vasilyev; "Destination: Amaltheia," A. & B. Strugatsky.

Dr. Jekyll and Mr. Hyde and Other Macabre Stories [pa] (Corgi: SN7049, 1964, 141 pp., pa 2/6)

Weird, 6 stories: "The Strange Case of Dr. Jekyll and Mr. Hyde," R. L. Stevenson; "Green Tea," J. S. Le Fanu; "The Boarded Window," A. Bierce; "The Upper Berth," F. M. Crawford; "A Terribly Strange Bed," Wilkie Collins; "The Facts in the Case of M. Valdemar," E. A. Poe.

Dr. Who Annual, The (World Distributors, Manchester, 1967, 93 pp.)

Juvenile—large-size miscellany of items by the 'Dr. Who Team': 8 stories, 2 strip stories, 5 games and puzzles, and 11 features.

Fairies Return, or New Tales for Old, The (P. Davies, London, 1934, 350 pp., 8/6)

Fantasy, 15 stories: "Jack the Giant Killer," A. E. Coppard; "Godfather Death," Clemence Dane; "The Fisherman and His Wife," E. M. Delafield; "Little Snow-White," Lord Dunsany; "Aladdin," Ann G. Keown; "Sindbad the Sailor," E. Linklater; "Ali Baba and the Forty Thieves," A. G. MacDonell; "Dick Whittington," E. Arnot Robertson; "Puss in Boots," Helen Simpson; "The Little Mermaid," Lady E. Smith; "Little Red Riding-Hood," E. Somerville; "Cinderella," R. Speaight; " 'O, If I Could But Shiver!' " Christina Stead; "The Sleeping Beauty," G. B. Stern; "Big Claus and Little Claus," R. J. Yeatman and W. C. Sellar.

Fantastic Annual—1969 (Odhams, London, 1968, 95 pp., 9/6)

Large-size juvenile collection of 8 cartoon stories and 4 articles. Covers adventures of 'X-Men' and includes "Iron Man Battles Invaders From Outer Space"; article on the conquest of space.

Fifty Strangest Stories Ever Told (Odhams, London, nd *ca.* 1930s, 704 pp., illus.)

Borderline, including some fantasy; not included in the Bleiler *Checklist*: "The Moonlight Sonata," A. Woolcott; "The Terrible Story of the 'Mary Russell,' " J. G. Lockhart; "The Death Trap," Carla Jenssen; "The Corpse Conductor," A. Munthe; "The Mountain of God," R. Courtney; "The Story of Kaspar Hauser," A. Lang; "The Siren and the Sorceress," W. Roughead; "Consolation," Mabel Smyth; "La Salpetriere," A. Munthe; "Eight Days in an English Snowdrift," Anon.; "Mysteries of the Elephant," C. Low; "The Moving Coffins," Sir A. E. Aspinall; "The Haunted Submarine," H. C. Bywater; "The Thugs," H. Lepper; "Marooned," J. G. Lockhart; "The Disappearance of Bathurst," S. Baring-Gould; "Smuggling Hashish," H. de Monfried; "The Celestial Fire," J. V. Trevor; "The Snail-Telegraph," S. Baring-Gould; "A Caucasian Riding-Lesson," S. Kournakoff; "Queer Happenings," Margery Lawrence; "The Tragedy of the Seven Hunters," J. G. Lockhart; "The Murder of the Countess Goerlitz," S. Baring-Gould; "Many Waters," N. Martin; "On 'Thirsty' Island," J. McLaren; "Three Crusoes in Epping Forest," Daniel Defoe; "The Case of the Poisoned Bun," M. Markey; "The Man in White," A. Lang; "Gripped by an Iceberg," F. K. Pease; "The Ordeal of Philip Stanfield," W. Roughead; "Across the Australian Desert," A. Lang; "In the Shadow of Death," De Valda; "Queer Disappearances," Margery Lawrence; "The Phantom Schooner," R. Huson; "Some English Eccentrics," J. Timbs; "The Dark Age Killer," E. T. Woodhall; "Si Urag of the Tail," O. Cook; "The Night of Witchcraft," R. Sabatini; "The Hell-Fire Monks of Medmenham," E. Bennett; "When Glister Walked," O. Cook; "Waltz Before Twilight," N. Straight; "Eastern Sorcery," A. Abdullah; "Man or Woman," "The Original Bluebeard," "A Murderer in the Force," H. Dearden; "The

Bogus Princess," Anon.; "The Musselburgh Miracle," J. May; "The Mystery of the Floating Bodies," "The Mystery of Orly Highway," H. Ashton-Wolfe; "The Devil's Hoofmarks," "Vampires in the Philippines," R. T. Gould; "Crime and the Supernatural," E. T. Woodhall.

Fifty Years of Ghost Stories (Hutchinson, London, 1935, 702 pp., 2/6) (Ryerson, Toronto, $1.00)

29 stories: "The Familiar," "Green Tea," J. S. Le Fanu; "The Saint and the Vicar," C. Binney; "The Tapestried Chamber," Sir W. Scott; "Gibbet Lane," A. Gittins; "The Old Nurse's Story," Mrs. Gaskell; "The Residence at Whitminster," "A Warning to the Curious," M. R. James; "The Haunted and the Haunters," Sir E. Bulwer-Lytton; "The Green Room," W. de la Mare; "Eveline's Visitant," Miss Braddon; "Afterward," Edith Wharton; "The Middle Toe of the Right Foot," A. Bierce; "Man Overboard!" F. M. Crawford; "As in a Glass Dimly," "The Lord-in-Waiting," S. Leslie; "Dracula's Guest," B. Stoker; "Expiation," "Pirates," E. F. Benson; "The Woman's Ghost Story," A. Blackwood; "Thurnley Abbey," P. Landon; "The Rosewood Door," O. Onions; "The Virgin of the Seven Daggers," Vernon Lee; "The Library Window," Mrs. Oliphant; "The Song in the House," Ann Bridge; "The Operation," Violet Hunt; "The Sweeper," "The Running Tide," Ex-Private X; "Perez," W. L. George.

Four-in-One Weird and Occult Shorts [pa] (Swan, London, *ca.* 1948, 144 pp., pa 9d)

Actually a restapling of four of Swan's 36-pp. booklets into one volume with a new title and cover:

Weird Story Magazine No. 2 (*ca.* 1947, 36 pp., 6d), 8 stories: "Death Was His Hobby," Tom Lawrence; "The Incident Is Closed," Anon.; "The Horror Undying," W. P. Cockcroft; "Invisible Filament," Bertha Low; "Obscene Parade," N. Wesley Firth; "Floating Hearse," R. Gilmour; "Arachne," Christine Gittins; "Prisoner," Rex Ernest.

Occult Shorts 2nd Collection (*ca.* 1945, 36 pp., 7d), 9 stories: "The Sack," Winifred M. Carnegie; "The Dancing Dolls," John Body; "The Black Caduceus," S. G. J. Ouseley; "The Hands," V. J. Hanson; "Self and Shadow," A. C. Bailey; "The Forbidden Village," W. P. Cockcroft; "Flashback," Henry Rawle; "Far Enough," Ian Avon; "Brain Storm," Anon.

Racing Shorts No. 1 (*ca.* 1947, 36 pp., 7d), 7 stories.

Detective Shorts No. 4 (*ca.* 1947, 36 pp., 7d), 6 stories.

Frozen Planet, The [pa] (Macfadden: 60-229, 1966, 160 pp., pa 60¢)

Sf, 5 novelettes: "The Quality of Mercy," D. Keyes; "Cinderella Story," Allen K. Lang; "The Frozen Planet," Keith Laumer; "Gleaners," C. D. Simak; "Growing Season," F. L. Wallace.

Georgian Stories—1924 (Chapman & Hall, London, 1924, vii+296 pp., 7/6)

14 stories, of which 4 are supernatural or fantasy: "Reparation," J. D. Beresford; "Tongues of Fire," Algernon Blackwood; "A Beautiful Superstition," Mrs. Belloc Lowndes; "My Son, My Son," St. John Lucas.

Ghost Stories and Other Queer Tales (Pearson, London, nd *ca.* 1935, 256 pp.)

Not listed in the Bleiler *Checklist*. 16 stories: "The Armless Man," W. G. Litt; "Terror by Night," Lewis Lister; "The Last Ascent," E. R. Punshon; "The Mailed Foot," Black & Blair-Staples; "The Pipers of Mallory," Theo Douglas; "The Jungle," Paul Eardley; "The Eighth Lamp," Roy Vickers; "The Unknown Quantity," E. R. Punshon; "The Tom-Tom Clue," Morgan & Jarvis; "The Case of Sir Alister Moeran," Strickland; "The Kiss," M. E. Royce; "The Goth," Roy Vickers; "The Tragedy at the 'Loup Noir,' " Stern; "The Haunted Chessmen," E. R. Punshon; "The Second Chance," Dayne; "The Man Who Got Back," Pollock.

Great Ghost Stories [pa] (New Era Library: 22, nd [pre-1950], 48 pp., pa 25¢)

6 stories, with introductory article "The Ghost Story": "The Damned Thing," A. Bierce; "The Mummy's Foot," T. Gautier; "An Ancient Haunted House," Pliny the Younger; "The Specter Bridegroom," W. Irving; "The Moon Slave," B. Pain; "The Ghost," Guy de Maupassant.

Great Short Stories—Ghost Stories (P. F. Collier & Son, New

York, nd, 428 pp.)

Not listed in the Bleiler *Checklist*. 18 stories: "La Morte Amoreuse," Theophile Gautier; "The Red Room," H. G. Wells; "The Phantom Rickshaw," R. Kipling; "The Roll Call of the Reef," A. T. Quiller-Couch; "The House and the Brain," E. Bulwer-Lytton; "The Dream Woman," W. W. Collins; "Green Branches," Fiona MacLeod; "A Bewitched Ship," W. C. Russell; "The Signal Man," C. Dickens; "The 4.15 Express," Amelia B. Edwards; "Our Last Week," Hugh Conway; "Thrawn Janet," R. L. Stevenson; "A Christmas Carol," C. Dickens; "The Spectre Bridegroom," W. Irving; "The Mysterious Sketch," Erckmann-Chatrian; "Mr. Higginbotham's Catastrophe," "The White Old Maid," N. Hawthorne; "Wandering Willie's Tale," Sir W. Scott.

Haunters and the Haunted and Other Ghost Stories, The [pa] (Corgi: SN1404, 1963, 158 pp., pa 2/6)

Weird, 8 stories with introductions on some, including first—noted as the complete version: "The Haunters and the Haunted, or, the House and the Brain," E. Bulwer-Lytton; "The Signalman," C. Dickens; "The Trial for Murder," C. Collins & C. Dickens; "The Watcher," J. S. Le Fanu; "The Dream Woman," Wilkie Collins; "What Was It?" Fitz-James O'Brien; "The Canterville Ghost," O. Wilde; "The Furnished Room," O. Henry.

Heart of the Serpent See *More Soviet Science Fiction* [Anonymous Anthologies]

Horror Omnibus (Grosset, New York, 1939, ix+354 pp., xiv+240 pp., $1.00)

Weird. Not listed in Bleiler *Checklist*. 2 novels: *Dracula*, Bram Stoker; *Frankenstein*, M. W. Shelley.

Laurie's Space Annual (Laurie, London, 1953, 96 pp., illus., quarto, 7/6) (Shakespeare, Sydney, 1953)

Juvenile. 4 stories: "Liaison Service," "A Matter of Salvage," S. J. Bounds; "The Best Holiday I Ever Had," John K. Cross; "Prison Trap," F. G. Rayer. 4 articles: "What Makes Rockets Rocket?" "And So to the Moon," "Adrift on the Sea of Space," R. F. Yates; "Gravity Is a Thing," Anon. 2 cartoon stories: "Death of a Planet," "The Dreaded Black Planet." Miscellaneous: "Saturn Facts"; "The British Interplanetary Society."

Macabre Mysteries and Horrors (K & G Publications, Herts. [England], 1966, 152 pp., 9/6)

7 stories: "The Vampyre," John Wm. Polidor; "Leixlip Castle," Charles R. Maturin; "The Queen of Spades," Alexander Pushkin; "Wicked Captain Walshawe of Wauling," "Schalken the Painter," "Dickon the Devil," J. Sheridan Le Fanu; "The Haunted House of Paddington," Charles Ollier.

Master Sea Stories (Clode, New York, 1929, 330 pp., $2.00)

17 stories, some of which are fantasy: "The Black Hour," A. Philips & G. Stair; "A Nightmare of the Doldrums," W. C. Russell; "The Fate of the *Alida*," L. Becke; "The Salvaging of the *Duncansey Head*," C. J. C. Hyne; "A Ride on a Whale," F. T. Bullen; "The Floating Beacon," Anon.; "False Colours," W. W. Jacobs; "The Strange Story of Emily Brand," A. H. Allen; "The Craft of Death," R. T. Rose; "The Derelict *Neptune*," M. Robertson; "Ms. Found in a Bottle," E. A. Poe; "The Haven of Dead Ships," S. Baxter; "The Fatal Repast," Anon.; "A Deal With Spain," J. A. Barry; "The Seeker," W. H. Holton; "A Cigar Cat," W. L. Auden; "J. Habakuk Jephson's Statement," A. C. Doyle.

Masters of Science Fiction [pa] (Belmont: 92-606, 1964, 157 pp., pa 50¢)

7 stories: "Service Call," P. K. Dick; "Path of Darkness," M. C. Pease; "Early Bird," E. F. Russell; "Forgive Us Our Debts," L. del Rey; "The Green Thumb," P. Anderson; "The Day of the Boomer Dukes," F. Pohl; "The Final Figure," S. Merwin, Jr.

Mindworm, The [pa] (Tandem: T118, 1967, 191 pp., pa 3/6)

Sf, 11 stories: "Not to Be Opened," Roger F. Young; "The Santa Claus Planet," F. M. Robinson; "The Mindworm," C. M. Kornbluth; "Process," A. E. van Vogt; "Contagion," Katherine MacLean; "Trespass," P. Anderson & G. R. Dickson; "To Serve Man," D. Knight; "Born of Man and Woman," R. Matheson; "The Fox in the Forest," R. Bradbury; "The Last Martian," F. Brown; "Two Face," F. B. Long.

Modern Ghosts (Harper, New York & London, 1890, xv+225 pp.)

7 stories, with introduction by George W. Curtis: "The Horla,"

G. de Maupassant (French); "Siesta," A. L. Kielland (German); "The Tall Woman," P. A. de Alarcón (Spanish); "On the River," G. de Maupassant (French); "Maese Perez, the Organist," G. A. Becquer (Spanish); "Fioraccio," G. Magherini-Graziani (Italian); "The Silent Woman," L. Kompert (German).

Molecule Monsters, The [pa] (Whitman Press, Sydney, 1950?, 32 pp., pa 8d)

4 stories: "The Molecule Monsters," O. J. Friend; "Galactic Heritage," F. B. Long; "The Impossible Highway," O. J. Friend; "Cables Parting!" [not sf] Steve Hail.

Moon Conquerors, The [pa] (Swan, London, 1943, 176 pp., pa 7d)

Actually a British edition of the U.S. magazine *Science Fiction Quarterly* (Sum 1940) in pa format: 4-7/8 in. x 7-1/4 in. with title and publisher on spine, trimmed edges. The cover is one-colour greyish blue; it is printed on cheap coloured paper, but one known copy shows no deterioration today. Contents: "The Moon Conquerors," R. H. Romans; "Space Ship Derby," M. Kaletsky; "Package of Power," D. C. Cooke; "Polar Doom," J. Coleridge; "The Gentle Brain," A. Allport; "Life Inside a Wall," H. Vincent.

More Soviet Science Fiction [pa] (*The Heart of the Serpent*, Foreign Languages Pub. House, Moscow, 1961, 267 pp., *ca*. $1.25 US) (Collier: AS295V, 1962, 190 pp., pa 95¢; O1647, 1967, 190 pp., pa 95¢) (*Das Herz der Schlange* [German], FLPH, 1962)

Stories translated by R. Prokofieva; FLPH book is designed by N. Grishin and has end flaps including author biographies; size 4-3/16 in. x 6-7/16 in. Collier edition has introduction by Isaac Asimov and omits many footnotes.

5 stories with emphasis on science: "The Heart of the Serpent," I. Yefremov (46,000 words—brilliant human-meets-alien theme), "Siema," A. Dnieprov; "The Trial of Tantalus," V. Saparin; "Stone From the Stars," Valentina Zhuravleva; "Six Matches," A. & B. Strugatsky.

More Tales of Terror and Surprise [pa] (Mitre: London, nd [1944], 127 pp., pa 1/6)

14 weird and mystery stories (6 new and 8 reprints): "Absolute Zero," Sidney Denham; "The Silent Ray," Arthur Armstrong; "William Wilson," E. A. Poe; "Vendetta," G. de Maupassant; "The Mysterious Mansion," H. de Balzac; "Prelude to Madness," Michael Hervey; "Third Finger Left Hand," Edward Martell; "The Trial for Murder," C. Dickens; "Venom," S. Denham; "The Cask of Amontillado," E. A. Poe; "The Werewolf," F. Marryat; "The Devil," G. de Maupassant; "The Mortal Immortal," Mary Shelley; "The Devil Has His Due," S. Denham.

New Tales of Horror (Hutchinson, London, 1934, 256 pp., 2/6) (Ryerson, Toronto, 85¢)

Weird, 30 stories: "A Double Return," "The Lost Club," A. Machen; "Love at First Sight," "The Luck of Keith-Martin," "The Amazing Hieroglyphs," "The Making of a Man," "The Murderer," "Wet Eyes and Sad Mouth," R. Middleton; "Medusan Madness," E. H. Visiak; "How Life Climbs," "The Globe of Gold-Fish," M. P. Shiel; "Scylla and Charybdis," J. Gawsworth; "The Truth," "Something for Arthur," "Madame Libismina," F. Carter; "The Dead Harlot," "A'body's Lassie," "Wound-Pie," "The Stranger," H. Macdiarmid; "The Ring of Fire," Sir D. Ross; "The House of Dust," H. De Hamel; "Effect and Cause," S. Graham; "Joshua Greenway," "The Cold-Meat Shop," E. H. W. Meyerstein; "Murderers' Corner," "Drink Monster," C. Duff; "The New War," H. Palmer; "Vision and Television," R. L. Megroz; "Mrs. Sayce's Guy," N. Barker; "Force of Habit," M. Magill.

Considered by some authorities to be Gawsworth's *Thirty New Tales of Horror*.

Now and Beyond [pa] (Belmont: B50-646, 1965, 157 pp., pa 50¢)

Sf, 8 stories: "The Turning Wheel," P. K. Dick; "Unreasonable Facsimile," L. del Rey; "Heav'n, Heav'n," E. F. Russell; "Venus Trap," R. Silverberg; "Telestassis," M. C. Pease; "Wapshot's Demon," F. Pohl; "The Case for Earth," E. F. Russell; "The Outcasts," George H. Smith.

Occult: A Collection of Stories of the Supernatural [pa] (Gerald Swan, London, 1945, 36 pp., pa 7d)

8 stories: "The Guide," Irene Amesbury; "Call of the Pool Goddess," John C. Craig; "The Room Without Windows," W. P. Cockroft; "The Bride of Yum-Chac," Henry Rawle; "The Fulfilment,"

Alexander O. Pearson; "Sir Rodney Keeps a Date," Andrew Ringwood; "The Window," Winifred M. Carnegie; "Binker's Ghost," A. C. Bailey.

One of Those Coincidences and Ten Other Stories by Julian Hawthorne and Others (Funk & Wagnall's, New York & London, 1899, 315 pp., illus.)

11 stories: "One of Those Coincidences," J. Hawthorne; "Francisco," W. L. Beard; "The Taper," L. Tolstoy; "How Viardeau Obeyed the Black Abbe," C. G. D. Roberts; "John Merrill's Experiment in Palmistry," Florence M. Kingsley; "The Strange Case of Esther Atkins," Mrs. L. E. L. Hardenbrook; "Jacob City," A. S. Clarke; "Selma the Soprano," Mabel Wagnalls; "At the End of His Rope," Florence M. Kingsley; "The Easter of La Mercedes," Mary C. Francis; "Romance of a Tin Roof and a Fire-Escape," Myrta L. Avary.

Pair From Space, A [pa] (Belmont: 92-612, 1965, 73 & 82 pp., pa 50¢)

Sf, 2 novels: "Giants in the Earth," J. Blish; "We, the Marauders," R. Silverberg.

Path Into the Unknown—The Best Soviet SF (MacGibbon & Kee, London, 1966, 191 pp., 26/-) (Delacorte, New York, 1968, 191 pp., $4.95) (SF B.C. [S.J.], 1968, 8/-) (Dell: 6862, 1968, 189 pp., pa 60¢)

8 stories (U.S. edition has introduction by J. Merril): "The Conflict," "Robby," Ilya Varshavsky; "Meeting My Brother," Vladislav Krapivin; "A Day of Wrath," Sever Gansovsky; "An Emergency Case," Arkady & Boris Strugatsky; "Wanderers and Travellers," A. Strugatsky; "The Boy," G. Gor; "The Purple Mummy," Anatoly Dneprov.

Premature Burial and Other Tales of Horror, The [pa] (Corgi: GN7509, 1966, 157 pp., pa 3/6)

Weird, 8 stories: "The Premature Burial," E. A. Poe; "I'll Kiss You Goodnight," F. H. Christian; "Thrawn Janet," R. L. Stevenson; "Cat," James Pearson; "The Flesh and the Devil," A. J. Ronald; "Sir Edmund Orme," Henry James; "A Dream of Crows," Richard Hengist; "Carmilla," Sheridan Le Fanu. First book publication for 2nd, 4th, 5th, and 7th stories.

Queer Stories From Truth (Cassel & Truth Pub. Ltd., London, 1921, 256 pp., 2/6)

This book is marked as being the 22nd of a series; this particular issue was the renewal after 5 years' suspension during World War I. It contains 4 weird stories (none of the series are listed in the Bleiler *Checklist*): "The Survivor," "The Crocodile God," "Johanna Goes First," Chris Newell; "Though One Rose Again—!" E. R. Punshon.

Satellite Series These paper-covered books were published by Jubilee Publications, Sydney, Australia. They had been originally compiled in the U.S. from *Orbit SF* Nos. 2, 4, 5 and *Possible Worlds of SF* [Conklin], 1951. The groups of stories were published as 4 titles, below (two others were novels).

Beyond the Stars and Other Stories [pa] (Satellite: 211, 1958, 114 pp., pa 2/-)

Sf, 7 stories: "Beyond the Stars" ("Space Rating"), John Berryman; "The Cold Equations," T. Godwin; "Limiting Factor," C. D. Simak; "Asleep in Armageddon," R. Bradbury; "Exploiters' End," James Causey; "Potential Enemy," M. Reynolds; "Century Jumper" ("A Traveler in Time"), A. Derleth.

Space Station 42 and Other Stories [pa] (Satellite: 212, 1958, 114 pp., pa 2/-)

Sf, 6 stories: "Space Station 42" ("Many Dreams of Earth"), C. E. Fritch; "Controlled Experiment," Chad Oliver; "Last of the Masters," P. K. Dick; "The Last Man" ("Noah"), Charles Beckham, Jr.; "Between Two Worlds" ("Aunt Else's Stairway"), Anthony Riker; "The Dreamer," ("The Enchanted Princess"), Jack Vance.

Sands of Mars and Other Stories, The [pa] (Satellite: 213, 1958, 114 pp., pa 2/-)

Sf, 6 stories: "The Sands of Mars" ("Enchanted Village"), A. E. van Vogt; "The Pillows," Margaret St. Clair; "Operation Zero" ("Intruder on the Run"), M. Lesser; "Adjustment Team," P. K. Dick; "Thinker, Mark VII" ("The Thinker and the Thought"), A. Derleth; "No More the Stars," I. E. Cox.

Planet of Doom and Other Stories [pa] (Satellite: 214, 1958, 114 pp., pa 2/-)

Sf, 8 stories: "Planet of Doom" ("Lilies of Life"), M. Jameson; "Lunar Escapade," H. B. Fyfe; "Retreat From Rigel" ("Tony and the Beetles"), P. K. Dick; "The Last War" ("The Butterfly Kiss"), A. D. Savage; "The Mating of the Moons," K. O'Hara; "The Image of the Gods," A. E. Nourse; "Place of Meeting," C. Beaumont; "Last Night of Summer," A. Coppel.

Science Fiction [pa] (International Storyteller Omnibus: 3, 1964, 174 pp., pa 5/-)

19 stories: "The Lady From Sirius," Eric Moore; "A Beautiful Sight to See," Barry Dixon; "Alien Fruit," Bennett Shann; " 'Holiday,' " Pamela Bernard; "The Hall of the Traitor," E. H. Crick; "The Long and Happy Life of Flaubus E. Munt," R. A. P. Pumphrey; "T.T.A.," Noel Ayliffe; "Reference Back," Frank E. Card; "Fred's Descendants," L. Davidson; ". . . And Bleep, Bleep to You," Cyril Bracegirdle; "They Who Must Hide," Mark Streeter; "The Last Silver Birch," James Gilfillan; "The Book of Sounds," Hugh C. Rae; "Many Years Ago," Donald Stark; "The Atomic Train," T. M. Curlow; "Congress of the Carnivores," K. Daly; "The Many Lives of Isidore," Brian Edginton; "Rhythm of the Rain," Allan Roe Stratton; "Escape to Paradise," Ronald Deacon.

Second Arrow Book of Horror Stories [pa] See *More Horror Stories* [Lee, Eliz.]

Second Century of Thrillers (Daily Express, London, *ca.* 1936)

Not listed in the Bleiler *Checklist* but a follow-on to this publisher's *A Century of Thrillers*.

41 stories: "The Taipan," W. S. Maugham; "Tale of the Piper," Donn Byrne; "The Lifted Veil," George Elliott; "Number 13," "Count Magnus," M. R. James; "The Queer Feet," G. K. Chesterton; "Pollock and the Porroh Man," H. G. Wells; "My Adventure in Norfolk," A. J. Alan; "Tcheriapin," S. Rohmer; "The Ivory God," J. S. Fletcher; "The Apparition of Mrs. Veal," D. Defoe; "The Thing in the Hall," E. F. Benson; "Night," "The Drowned Man," "Who Knows," G. de Maupassant; "Young Goodman Brown," N. Hawthorne; "The Ballad of Reading Gaol," O. Wilde; "The Tell Tale Heart," "The Fall of the House of Usher," "The Black Cat," "Ligeia," E. A. Poe; "The Squaw," B. Stoker; "A Pair of Hands," A. T. Quiller-Couch; "The Last Leaf," O. Henry; "The Well," W. W. Jacobs; "The Haunted Woman and the Ghost's Bargain," C. Dickens; "Moxon's Master," "The Middle Toe of the Right Foot," "The Damned Thing," A. Bierce; "The Beast With Five Fingers," W. F. Harvey; "The Upper Berth," "Man Overboard," F. M. Crawford; "Diver's Drops," N. A. Temple Ellis; "The Cards," Sydney Parkman; "The Knights of the Silver Dagger," Ashton Wolfe; "The Werewolf," F. Marryatt; "Schalken the Painter," "Carmilla," "The Familiar," J. S. Le Fanu; "Gabriel's Marriage," W. W. Collins; "The Sexton's Hero," Mrs. Gaskell.

Secret Temple and Other Tales, The (Sheldon Press, London, nd, 192 pp., front.—R. B. Ogle)

8 stories selected from *Boy's Torch Adventure Library* (not listed in the Bleiler *Checklist*): "The Secret Temple," R. J. McGregor; "The Torch," K. Hawkins; "The Bat," G. G. Barnes; "Rescue," P. J. Doherty; "The Crocodile Pool," V. M. Methly; "Ram Riley's Bridge," A. E. Southon; "The Witch Doctor," F. Featherstone; "The Lone Journey," M. I. Baumann.

Six Fingers of Time, The (Macfadden: 50-244, 1965, 128 pp., pa 50¢)

Sf, 6 novelettes from *GSF*: "The Six Fingers of Time," R. A. Lafferty; "A Pride of Islands," C. C. MacApp; "Sitting Duck," Daniel F. Galouye; "IOU," Edward Wellen; "To Each His Own," Jack Sharkey; "The Junkmakers," Albert Teichner.

Sometime, Never (Eyre & Spottiswoode, London, 1956, iii+224 pp., 12/6) (Ballantine, New York, 1957, 185 pp., $2.75, #215, pa 35¢; F657, 1962, pa 50¢; U2853, 1967, pa 50¢)

Sf and fantasy, 3 short novels: "Consider Her Ways," J. Wyndham (future matriarchy)[later title of a collection] ; "Envoy Extraordinary," W. Golding (barbarian genius sets Caesar's court on its heels); "Boy in Darkness," M. Peake (boy's nightmare adventures in a world like Wells' *Dr. Moreau*).

Soviet Science Fiction [pa] (*A Visitor From Outer Space*, Foreign Languages Pub. House, Moscow, *ca.* 1961, 202 pp., *ca.* $1.25

U.S.) (Colliers: AS279V, 1962, 189 pp., pa 95¢; 1965, pa 95¢; 01655, 1966, pa 95¢) (*Der Bote aus dem All* [German], FLPH, *ca.* 1962)

Stories translated by Violet L. Dutt. The FLPH book is designed by N. Grishin; end flaps include author biographies; size 5 in. x 7½ in.; Collier edition has Introduction by I. Asimov, and omits many footnotes. [See also *More Soviet Science Fiction*.] Six stories: "Hoity-Toity," A. Belayev; "Spontaneous Reflex," A. & B. Strugatsky; "A Visitor From Outer Space," "The Martian," A. Kazantsev; "Infra Draconis," G. Gurevich; "Professor Bern's Awakening," V. Savchenko.

Spooks and Spirits and Shadowy Shapes (Aladdin Books, New York, 1949, 167 pp., illus.–R. L. Doremus, $2.00) (Saunders, Toronto, $2.50)

Juvenile, 9 stories: "It Was So Spooky!" E. L. Brock; "The Friendly Ghost," Elizabeth Yates; "The Witch in the Wintry Woods," "Ghost in the Orchard," Aileen Fisher; "Thirteen Witches," Elizabeth Coatsworth; "The Ghost of Mad Maurice," R. D. McCrea; "The Floogles Are Detectives," Gertrude Crampton; "A Strange Surprise," Adele De Leeuw; "Shamus and the Black Cat," M. R. Walsh.

Spooks in Your Cupboard (Seven Seas, 1966, 260 pp., pa 3/6 Stg)

Weird, 10 stories: "The Trial for Murder," C. A. Collins & C. Dickens; "The Haunters and the Haunted, or The House and the Brain," E. Bulwer-Lytton; "The Signal-Man," C. Dickens; "Green Tea," Sheridan Le Fanu; "A Terribly Strange Bed," W. Collins; "The Canterville Ghost," O. Wilde; "Markheim," R. L. Stevenson; "The Great Keinplatz Experiment," Sir A. C. Doyle; "Wandering Willie's Tale," Sir W. Scott; "The Story of the Late Mr. Elvesham," H. G. Wells.

Stable for Nightmares, A [by J. Sheridan Le Fanu and Others] (New Amsterdam Book Co., New York, 1896, 256 pp., illus.)

11 stories: "Dickon the Devil," J. S. Le Fanu; "A Debt of Honor"; "Devereux's Dream"; "Catherine's Quest"; "Haunted"; "Pichon and Sons of the Croix Rousse"; "The Phantom Fourth"; "The Spirits Whisper"; "Dr. Feversham's Story"; "The Secret of the Two Plaster Casts"; "What Is It," F.-J. O'Brien.

Strange Happenings (Methuen, London, 1901, 309 pp., 6/-)

Not in the Bleiler *Checklist*. 18 stories, including some weird: "The First to Die," H. D. Lowry; "The Sequel," W. C. Russell; "The Philosopher's Son," "The Musical Mouse," W. E. Norris; "Selwyn Utterton's Nemesis," G. Allen; "The Wedding Dress," W. Beer; "The Three Spices," L. Cape Cornford; "The Silver Snake," Beatrice O'Connor; "The Bagman's Pony," M. Ross; "A Day of Solitude Royal," F. Hird; " 'Alter Idem,' " L. Galbraith; "At a Christmas Ball," Mrs. Fleming; "A Careful Mother," F. C. Philips; "An Honourable Precedent," H. B. Marriott-Watson; "A Lynching in Mesinee," H. Garland; "My Little Husband," F. C. Philips; "An Excellent Mystery," Francis Prevost; "The German Student's Romance," Clara Savile-Clark.

Strange Secrets Told by A. C. Doyle and Others (R. F. Fenno, New York, 1895, 287 pp.)

14 stories: "The Secret of Swalecliff Castle," F. Milford; "The Secret of the Mine," F. Talbot; "The Secret of Calverley Court," Gertrude Parsons; "The Secret of Cousin Geoffrey's Chamber," Hon. Mrs. Henry Clifford; "The Secret of Goresthorpe Grange," A. C. Doyle; "The Box With the Iron Clamps," Florence Marryat; "The Veiled Portrait," James Grant; "The Ghost of Lawford Hall," Walter Thornbury; "The Spectre Hand," James Grant; "A Coachful of Ghosts," Eleanor C. Price; "George Venn and the Ghost," Dutton Cook; "The Mystery in Daffodil Terrace," Percy Fitzgerald; "Why New Houses Are Haunted," Elwyn Keith; "A Very Queer Inn," M. B. Archer.

Tales for a Stormy Night (R. Clarke, Cincinnati, 1891, 279 pp.)

5 stories: "Ghosts," Tourgueneff; "A Miracle in Flanders," H. de Balzac; "The Venus of Isle," Merimee; "The Battle of Pere Fachaise," A. Daudet; "Farewell," Balzac.

Tales of Terror and the Unknown [pa] (Everybody's Books, London, 1944, 96 pp., pa 2/-)

No further data available.

Tales of the Supernatural [pa] (Pan: 22, 1947, 183 pp., pa 2/-; 1951, 186 pp., pa 2/-)

Weird, 8 stories (2nd edition has different cover): "The Haunted and the Haunters," E. Bulwer-Lytton; "The Horla," G. de Maupassant; "The Coffin-Maker," A. Pushkin; "The Shadow of a Shade," T. Hood; "Markheim," R. L. Stevenson; "The Haunted Doll's House," M. R. James; "Seaton's Aunt," W. de la Mare; "The Little Ghost," H. Walpole.

Tales of the Supernatural [pa] (Panther: 1397, 1962, 124 pp., pa 2/6)

Weird, 9 stories (no table of contents): "The Plattner Story," H. G. Wells; "The Yellow Cat," Michael Joseph; "Escort," Daphne du Maurier; "The Specter Bridegroom," Washington Irving; "Keeping His Promise," A. Blackwood; "The Corner Shop," Lady Cynthia Asquith; "The Brighton Monster," Gerald Kersh; "The Body-Snatcher," R. L. Stevenson [misspelt as Stephenson]; "Casting the Runes," M. R. James.

Tales of the Uncanny [pa] (Panther: 1454, 1962, 128 pp., pa 2/6)

Weird, 9 stories: "The Door in the Wall," H. G. Wells; "A Haunted Island," A. Blackwood; "A Man From Glasgow," W. S. Maugham; "The Playfellow," Lady Cynthia Asquith; "Mr. Humphries and His Inheritance," M. R. James; "The Celestial Omnibus," E. M. Forster; "The Ghost of a Hand," J. S. Le Fanu; "What Was It?" Fitz-James O'Brien; "A Tale of Negative Gravity," F. R. Stockton.

Terrible Tales (Brentano's, London & New York, nd, 193 pp.)

Not listed in Bleiler *Checklist*. Weird, 5 stories: "The Crystal Dagger"; "A Strange Bride"; "The Host of 'The Sun' "; "The Crazy Half-Heller"; "The Goldsmith of the Rue Nicaise."

Terrible Tales, French (W. W. Stebbings, London, 1891)

10 stories (no authors noted): "The Mysterious Sketch"; "The Weaver of Steinbach"; "The Lyons Courier"; "The Cabalist"; "The Citizen's Watch"; "A Science in the Desert"; "Cousin Elof's Dream"; "A Legend of Marseilles"; "The White and the Black"; "Lex Talionis."

Terrible Tales, German (W. W. Stebbings, London, 1891) (William Reeves, London, nd, viii+193 pp., 2/-)

5 stories and 1-p. preface: "The Crystal Dagger"; "A Strange Bride"; "The Host of 'The Sun' "; "The Crazy Half-Heller"; "The Goldsmith of the Rue Nicaise."

Terrible Tales, Italian (W. W. Stebbings, London, 1891, 181 pp.) (Wm. Reeves Co., nd, 181 pp.)

10 stories (no authors noted): "The Bridal Wreath"; "Domenico Matteo"; "The Betrothed"; "The Story of Lady Ermina"; "The Brigands"; "The Village Priest"; "Eurispe"; "Lanucci"; "The Lovers"; "The Unlucky Fortune."

Terrible Tales, Spanish (W. W. Stebbings, London, 1891, 178 pp.)

12 stories (no authors noted): "The Golden Bracelet"; "The Mirror of Friends"; "The Green Eyes"; "Josef Maria"; "The Passion Flower"; "The Thirteenth"; "The Effect of Being Undeceived"; "The White Doe"; "Maese Perez the Organist"; "Dorido and Clorinia"; "The Moonbeams"; "The Fountains of Spirit."

Thrillers (Clode, New York, 1929, 313 pp., $2.00)

Weird, 17 stories (only authors' surnames given): "The Horror of Johnson's Flats," Begbie; "Ferrier's Record," Swainson; "The Den of the Gray Wolf," Roberts; "The Treasure of Sacramento Nick," Boothby; "Aepyornis Island," "The Empire of the Ants," H. G. Wells; "The House of the Prodigal Sons," Martin; "My First Whale," Bullen; "Harun Pasha," S. Rohmer; "The Mystery of Sasassa Valley," "The American's Tale," A. C. Doyle; "The Killing of the Mammoth," Tukeman; "The Pilgrim Ship," Hyne; "The Man-Eater of Nagpore," Graydon; "The Cutting Off of the Queen Charlotte," Becke; "The Quest of the Golden Fleece," Clifford; "The Monster of Partridge Creek," Dupuy.

Thrills–Twenty Specially Selected New Stories of Crime, Mystery and Horror (Associated Newspapers, London, nd, 320 pp., illus.–N. Keane)

20 stories: "The Mysterious Fluid," O. Blakeston; "The Golden Gong," T. Burke; "The Haunted Bungalow," C. Duff; "How It Happened," J. Gawsworth; "The Unnecessary Undoing of Mr. Purgle," H. de Hamel; "Twopence for the Toll," K. Hare; "The Murder at the Fossicker's Club," "An Accident," E. Jepson; "Act

of God," P. Lindsay; "Blackmail," J. Lindsey; "A Modern Delilah," A. M. Ludovici; "The Vicar's Crime," G. R. Malloch; "Madrilene," F. Marsden; "The Divorce," E. H. W. Meyerstein; "Fifty Thousand Pounds," "The Kidnapped Collector," R. E. Page; "A Case for Deduction," M. P. Shiel & F. Armstrong; "The Count," Simon; "The Shop on the Corner," L. A. G. Strong; "The Cutting," E. H. Visiak.

Through the Forbidden Gates and Other Stories (Shortstory Publ. Co., Boston, 1903, 248 pp.)

20 stories: "Through the Forbidden Gates," Carroll Canington; "Margaret Kelly's Wake," S. C. Brean [noted as pseud. of E. Barnes]; "A Celestial Crime," Charles S. Pratt; "For the Sake of Lize," C. B. Lewis; "The Music of Money," Newt Newkirk; "The Diamond Drill and Mary," H. J. W. Dam; "Hans Kremler's Anniversary," Elisabeth F. Dye; "The Vase of the Mikado," A. Ernest B. Lane; "On Pigeon River," Jeanie Drake; "The Smile of Joss," William J. Neidig; "The King of the Subdivision," James O'Shaughnessy; "The Pillow of Justice," S. Innet; "The Lost Jurisdiction," Ellis Meredith; "The Diary of a White Kaffir," James O. Fagan; "The Statement of Jared Johnson," Geraldine Bonner; "The Levitation of Jacob," Clifford Howard; "The White Brick," F. E. Chase; "When Time Turned," Ethel Watts Mumford; "The Family Skeleton's Wedding Journey," Annie Fellows Johnston; "Missing," Mary Boardman Sheldon.

Time Untamed [pa] (Belmont: B50-781, 1967, 175 pp., pa 50¢)

Sf, 8 stories: "Sally," I. Asimov; "You'll Never Go Home Again," C. D. Simak; "The Eye of Tandyla," L. S. de Camp; "Tomorrow and Tomorrow," R. Bradbury; "The Hungry Eye," R. Bloch; "The Dark Room," T. Sturgeon; "The Eternal Eve," J. Wyndham; "I'm Looking for Jeff," F. Leiber.

Uncanny Stories (C. Pearson, London, 1916, 125 pp., 1/-; 3rd impression 1919)

Noted as being "The Uniform volume of More Uncanny Stories selected from the Novel Magazine." The Bleiler *Checklist* lists this as *Uncanny Tales*. Weird, 9 stories [most appearing in *Ghost Stories*]: "The Unknown Quantity," E. R. Punshon; "The Armless Man," W. G. Litt; "The TomTom Clue," O. Morgan & S. Jarvis; "The Case of Sir Alister Morran," Marg. Strickland; "The Kiss," M. E. Royce; "The Goth," R. Vickers; "The Last Ascent," E. R. Punshon; "The Terror by Night," L. Lister; "The Tragedy at the 'Loup Noir'," Gladys Stern.

Visitor From Outer Space, A See *Soviet Science Fiction*

Weird Tales—English (William Paterson, London, 1888, 256 pp., 1/-)

12 stories: "The Pythagorean," A. Stewart Harrison; "The Old Man's Tale About the Queer Client," Charles Dickens; "In Defence of His Right," Daniel Defoe; "Sixteen Days of Death," Anon.; "Adventure in a Forest," Tobias Smollett; "Cader Idris: The Chair of Idris," John Harwood; "A Skeleton in the House," Edmund Yates; "A Night With a Madman," "The Poisoned Mind," "A Dire Prediction," "The Postponed Wedding," Anon.; "Haunted House of Paddington," Charles Ollier.

Witches Three See PRATT, F.

World's Best Mystery Stories, The (United Press 'Home Entertainment Library,' Melbourne, 1935, illus.)

Weird, 43 stories (not listed in Bleiler *Checklist*): "The Taipan," W. S. Maugham; "Tale of the Piper," D. Byrne; "The Lifted Veil," G. Eliot; "Number 13," "Rats," "Count Magnus," M. R. James; "The Queer Feet," G. K. Chesterton; "Pollock and the Porroh Man," H. G. Wells; "My Adventure in Norfolk," A. J. Alan; "Tcheriapin," S. Rohmer; "The Ivory God," J. S. Fletcher; "The Apparition of Mrs. Veal," D. Defoe; "The Thing in the Hall," E. F. Benson; "Night," "The Drowned Man," "Who Knows," G. de Maupassant; "Young Goodman Brown," N. Hawthorne; "The Ballad of Reading Gaol," O. Wilde; "The Tell-Tale Heart," "The Fall of the House of Usher," "The Black Cat," "Ligeia," E. A. Poe; "The Squaw," B. Stoker; "A Pair of Hands," Sir A. T. Quiller-Couch; "The Last Leaf," O. Henry; "The Well," W. W. Jacobs; "The Haunted Man and the Ghost's Bargain," C. Dickens; "Moxon's Master," "The Middle Toe of the Right Foot," "The Damned Thing," A. Bierce; "The Beast With Five Fingers," W. F. ˙arvey; "The Upper Berth," "Man Overboard," F. M. Crawford;

"Diver's Drops," N. A. T. Ellis; "The Cards," S. Parkman; "The Knights of the Silver Dagger," A. Wolfe; "The Werewolf," F. Marryat; "Schalken the Painter," "Carmilla," "The Familiar," J. S. Le Fanu; "Gabriel's Marriage," W. Collins; "The Sexton's Hero," Mrs. Gaskell.

ANSTEY, F. (pseud) See GUTHRIE, T. A.

ANTON, LUDWIG (1872—?) German author.
Fiction
Interplanetary Bridges (*Brücken über den Weltraum*, Holzwarth, Düsseldorf, 1922) (Trans.—K. Schmidt) (*WSQ*, Win 1933)

One of the foreign works imported by H. Gernsback. Pioneer flight to Venus.

ANTONIORROBLES (pseud) See ROBLES, A.

ANVIL, CHRISTOPHER (pseud) See CROSBY, H. C.

APOLLINAIRE, GUILLAUME, (8 Aug 1880–9 Nov 1918) Controversial and brilliant French art critic, also highly regarded for his tales of sophisticated cruelty and the macabre, etc. He had some sf themes in the work below.
Fiction
Heresiarch and Co., The [C] (*L'heresiarque et Cie*, 1910 and later eds.) (Doubleday, New York, 1965, 183 pp., $3.95, trans.—R. I. Hall; Doubleday, Toronto, $5.00) (*The Wandering Jew and Other Stories*, R. Hart-Davis, 1967, 198 pp., 42/-)

Includes 2 stories of sf interest: "Remote Projection" (*F&SF*, July 1968); "The Disappearance of Honore Subrac."

APPEL, BENJAMIN (13 Sep 1907–) U.S. author, born in New York. He has been a professional writer since 1929, with some short stints as bank clerk, farmer, lumberjack, etc. He was an aviation mechanic during World War II and also served in government agencies. B.S. Lafayette College, 1929. He was Special Assistant to the U.S. Commissioner for the Philippines, 1945—46. As a writer he is noted for his novels of city life, ranging from *Brain Guy* (1943) to *The Raw Edge* (1958)—dealing with New York's waterfront.
Fiction
Funhouse, The [pa] (Ballantine: 345K, 1959, 157 pp., pa 35¢)

The Chief of Police of the Reservation (future U.S.) is called to find the detonator to blow up all nuclear bombs. Footnotes explaining the "Funhouse" (world outside the Reservation) culture and jargon are overdone.

APPLEMAN, M. J. See DEMAITRE, E. (coauthor)

APPLETON, VICTOR One of the pseudonyms used by the Stratemeyer Syndicate, which was begun by Edward Stratemeyer (d. 1930). Another was "Roy Rockwood"; both appeared on innumerable boys' books over the first quarter of the 20th century. The Appleton pseudonym was most noted for its use on the *Tom Swift* series; the first series was launched in 1910 and ran into the late 1930s, over 14 million copies being sold by Grosset & Dunlap Publishers (New York). The first 35 stories were written by Howard R. Garis; this became known only upon his decease.

Mrs. Harriet S. Adams (daughter of Edward Stratemeyer) as head of the Stratemeyer Syndicate instigated the second series in similar format in 1954. The Tom Swift and Ned Newton of the old series (as boys) continue in the new. Tom marries Mary Nestor and they have two children, Tom Swift, Jr., and Sandra. The older series was mainly "pseudo" science while the new has top scientists as consultants. (See article "The New Tom Swift," A. E. Svenson, *FU*, July 1959.) Some titles have appeared in French.
Series
Tom Swift. All titles are of the form *Tom Swift (and) . . .* ; and are listed in sequence of issue.
Series I Grosset & Dunlap, New York. [Probably began at 40¢, definitely being 40¢ in 1912; 50¢ from 1920's to 1935. Lengths 203-218 pp., mainly 216 pp.]

1910 *His Motor Cycle*; *His Motor Boat*; *His Airship*; *His Submarine Boat*; *His Electric Runabout*
1911 *His Wireless Message*; *Among the Diamond Makers*; *in the Caves of Ice*; *His Sky Racer*; *His Electric Rifle*
1912 *in the City of Gold*; *His Air Glider*; *in Captivity*; *His Wizard Camera*; *His Great Searchlight*

1913	*His Giant Cannon*	1914	*His Photo Telephone*
1915	*His Aerial Warship*	1916	*His Big Tunnel*
1917	*in the Land of Wonders*	1918	*His War Tank*
1919	*His Air Scout*	1920	*His Undersea Voyage*
1921	*Among the Fire Fighters*	1922	*His Electric Locomotive*
1923	*His Flying Boat*	1924	*His Great Oil Gusher*
1925	*His Chest of Secrets*	1926	*His Airline Express*
1927	*Circling the Globe*	1928	*His Talking Pictures*
1929	*His House on Wheels*	1930	*His Big Dirigible*
1931	*His Sky Train*	1932	*His Giant Magnet*
1933	*His Television Detector*	1934	*His Ocean Airport*
1935	*His Planet Stone*		

Series II Still published by Grosset & Dunlap, 95¢. Those marked by * have a British edition from Low, London, at 5/-. [1955-56, mainly 214 pp.; 1957-62, 188 pp.; 1962-68, 178 pp.]
1954 *His Flying Lab**; *His Jetmarine*; *His Rocket Ship*; *His Giant Robot**; *His Atomic Earth Blaster*
1955 *His Outpost in Space**
1956 *His Diving Seacopter*; *in the Caves of Nuclear Fire*; *on the Phantom Satellite*
1957 *His Ultrasonic Cycloplane*
1958 *His Deep-Sea Hydrodome*; *in the Race to the Moon*; *His Space Solartron*
1959 *His Electronic Retroscope*; *His Spectromarine Selector*
1960 *His Cosmic Astronauts*
1961 *His Visitor From Planet X*
1962 *His Triphibian Atomicar*; *His Electronic Hydrolung*; *His Megascope Space Prober* [First two, $1.00; hereon, $1.25]
1963 *His Repelatron Skyway*; *the Asteroid Pirates*
1964 *His Aquatomic Tracker*; *His 3-D Telejector*
1965 *His Polar-Ray Dynasphere*
1966 *His Sub-Ocean Geotron*; *the Mystery Comet*
1968 *His G-Force Inverter*

ARCH, E. L. (pseud) See PAYES, R. C.

ARCHER, RON (pseud) See WHITE, T. E. Used on *Lost in Space* [pa] with co-author VAN ARNAM, D.

ARDREY, ROBERT (1908–) U.S. playwright and journalist. His *African Genesis* (Atheneum, New York, 1961, 380 pp., $6.95) is a thought-provoking conjecture on man being descended from Cain, and covers some aspects important in sf, such as automatic hostility between men and aliens. (See P. S. Miller, *ASF*, April 1962, p. 157ff.)
Fiction
Thunder Rock [play] (Dramatists Play Service, New York, 1941)
World's Beginning (Duell, Sloan & Pearce, New York, 1944, 244 pp., $2.50) (Collins, Toronto, $3.00) (H. Hamilton, London, 1945, 204 pp., 8/-; 'Readers Union' ed., 1946, 204 pp., 5/-) (*Nu borjar världen* [Swedish], Natur & Kultur, 1946)
A chemical company formed on a just social basis gives the U.S. a new form of society.

ARISS, BRUCE WALLACE Jr (10 Oct 1911–) U.S. designer and illustrator.
Fiction
Full Circle (Avalon, New York, 1963, 224 pp., $2.95) (Burns, MacEachern, Toronto, $3.95)
A selected survival group causes discord in a future North America where a few Indian tribes survive.

ARLEN, MICHAEL (16 Nov 1895–23 June 1956) British novelist, born in Bulgaria as Dikran Kuyumjian. He became a British citizen in 1922, and served as public relations officer for the West Midlands area during World War II. More recently he was resident

in the U.S. His *The Green Hat* (1924), with its boyish unconventional heroine, was a huge success; others of his works include *Man's Mortality* (1933) and *The Flying Dutchman* (1939). His short story "The Gentleman From America" is probably his most noted fantasy story.
Fiction [Incomplete—other stories in Bleiler *Checklist*]
Ghost Stories [C] (Collins, London, 1930, 181 pp., 2/6)
7 stories selected from *May Fair* and *These Charming People*: "The Prince of the Jews"; "The Gentleman From America"; "To Lamoir"; "The Ghoul of Golders Green"; "The Ancient Sin"; "The Loquacious Lady of Lansdowne Passage"; "The Smell in the Library."
May Fair [C] (Collins, London, 1925, 320 pp., 7/6; 1931, 2/6) (Doran, New York, 1925, 369 pp., $2.50; limited autographed edition $5.00) (Grosset, New York, 1925, 75¢)
Prologue and 11 stories: "A Romance in Old Brandy"; "The Ace of Cads"; "Where the Pigeons Go to Die"; "The Battle of Berkeley Square"; "The Prince of the Jews"; "The Three-Cornered Moon"; "The Revolting Doom of a Gentleman Who Would Not Dance With His Wife"; "The Gentleman From America"; "To Lamoir"; "The Ghoul of Golders Green"; "Farewell, Farewell, These Charming People."
These Charming People (Collins, 1923, 265 pp., 1931, 2/-) (Doran, 1924, 302 pp.) (Grosset, 1928, 75¢) (*Blandat sällskap* [Swedish], Holgar Schildt, 1927)
15 stories: "The Ancient Sin"; "Cavalier of the Streets"; "Consuelo Brown"; "Hunter After Wild Beasts"; "Introducing a Lady of No Importance and a Gentleman of Even Less"; "Irreproachable Conduct of a Gentleman Who Once Refused a Knighthood"; "Loquacious Lady of Lansdowne Passage"; "Luck of Captain Fortune"; "Major Cypress Goes Off the Deep End"; "Man With the Broken Nose"; "Real Reason Why Shelmerdene Was Late for Dinner"; "Salute the Cavalier"; "Shameless Behaviour of a Lord"; "The Smell in the Library"; "When the Nightingale Sang in Berkeley Square."

ARMOUR, MARGARET
Anthology
Eerie Book, The (J. Schiells, London, 1898, 211 pp., illus.)
16 stories: "The Masque of the Red Death," E. A. Poe; "The Iron Coffin" (from *Faust*), G. M. Reynolds; "The Mother and the Dead Child," Hans C. Andersen; "Tregeagle" (from *Romance of W. England*), Robert Hunt; "The Dutch Officer's Story," Catherine Crowe; "The Cask of Amontillado," E. A. Poe; "Earl Beardie's Game at Cards," Anon.; "Frankenstein" (excerpt), M. W. Shelley; "The Garde Chasse," Cath. Crowe; "A Dream of Death," from the Danish; "A Mysterious Horseman," Rev. B. Saville; "The Blind Beggar of Odessa," Cath. Crowe; "The Story of Major Weir," R. Chambers; "Marshal Blücher," Rev. B. Saville; "Sir Huldbrand's Wife" (from *Undine*), F. H. de la Motte-Fouque; "The Masque" (excerpt from *Romance of Klosterstein*) T. De Quincy.

ARMSTRONG, ANTHONY (pseud) See WILLIS, A. A.

ARMSTRONG, MARTIN (DONISTHORPE) (2 Oct 1882–) British writer, born at Newcastle-on-Tyne. Termed by critics as an example and exponent of some of the finest qualities in British writing, he has been most versatile in many varieties of fiction, and has also been a serious poet. His better-known novels include *At the Sign of the Goat and Compasses* (1925), *Desert* (1926), *The Water Is Wide* (1927), and *A Case of Conscience* (1936).
Fiction
Bazaar and Other Stories, The [C] (J. Cape, London, 1924, 287 pp., 7/6; 1928, 3/6) (Knopf, New York, 1924, 287 pp., $2.50) (P. Smith, New York, *ca.* 1928, $1.00)
19 stories: "The Bazaar"; "The Birthday"; "Defensive Flank"; "Dog's Life"; "An Escape"; "Farmer Brock's Funeral"; "Helm Hall"; "In the Park"; "The Inn"; "Interview With a Genius"; "Little Miss Millett"; "The Materialist"; "Miss Webster's Dream"; "Mrs. Barber's Christmas"; "Mrs. Lovelace"; "Mrs. Symington at Home"; "Pursuit of the Swallow"; "Soft-Hearted Man"; "Symphony in G Minor."

Fiery Dive and Other Stories, The *[C]* *(Gollancz, London, 1929,* 283 pp., 7/6, limited autographed ed. 42/-; 1933, 3/6) (Harcourt, New York, 1930, 259 pp., $2.50)

6 stories: "The Fiery Dive"; "In the Wilds"; "Portrait of the Misses Harlowe"; "Saint Hercules"; "Sombrero"; "Widow of Ephesus."

General Buntop's Miracle and Other Stories [C] (Gollancz, 1934, 387 pp., 7/6) (Harcourt, 1934, 287 pp., $2.00) (McLeod, Toronto, $2.25)

16 stories: "Blind Victory"; "Drink, Dirty Creature!"; "Fizz"; "General Buntop's Miracle"; "Illumination"; "Katie Kennedy"; "Mary Ansell"; "Mr. Tucker and Miss Cribb"; "Mrs. Colenso's Daughter" "Mrs. Noah's Ark"; "Mrs. Vaudrey's Journey"; "Pipe-Smoker"; "Presence of Mind" (*Fan*, Oct 1962); "Pygmalion"; "Shepherd's Tale"; "Strange Encounter."

ARMSTRONG, TERENCE IAN FYTTON, See GAWSWORTH, J.

ARMSTRONG, WARREN (pseud) See BENNETT, W. E.

ARMYTAGE, W. H.
Nonfiction
Yesterday's Tomorrows (Routledge & Kegan Paul, London, 1968, 288 pp., 35/-)

Subtitled *A Historical Survey of Future Societies.* In forecasting the future, man mirrors his own wishes; they can be countries of imagination even springing from fears. The author shows how vision can refresh minds by arming them with ideas for man's future needs.

ARNE, AARON Pseudonym of Alf A. Jorgenson, Norwegian-born U.S. author living in Miami. Originally an electronics engineer, he spent some years working in Korea, Japan, and Canada. He retired in 1956 and began writing.
Fiction
Feet of Clay (Vantage, New York, 1958, 276 pp., $5.00)

Satan accuses the Lord Yahveh of breaking their agreement about the agnostic soul of Julian Jorgen.

ARNOLD, EDWIN LESTER (1887–1 Mar 1935) British author, son of the late Sir Edwin Arnold. After college he turned to cattle breeding in Scotland, then cultivation of unsurveyed forest in Travancore, India. He then returned to England and devoted himself to literary and journalistic work. A well-received novel was *The Constable of St. Nicholas.* A fantasy not covered below is *Lepidus the Centurion: A Roman of Today* (Crowell, New York, 1901).
Fiction
Gulliver of Mars (*Lieut. Gulliver Jones: His Vocation,* Brown Langham & Co., London, 1905, 301 pp., 6/-) (Ace: F-296, 1964, 224 pp., pa 40¢, jacket–F. Frazetta)

Rather dated adventure on Mars; might have given Burroughs the idea for his Martian series.
Lieut. Gulliver Jones: His Vocation See *Gulliver of Mars*
Phra the Phoenician (*The Wonderful Adventures of Phra the Phoenician,* Harper, New York, 1890, 329 pp.) (Burt, 189?, 415 pp., illus.–J. Watson Davis) (Chatto Windus, London, 1893, 347 pp., 3/6, illus.–H. M. Paget) (Putnam, New York & London, 1917, $2.50, illus.–H. M. Paget) (*FFM*, Sep 1945)

A man lives many lives through the ages before reuniting with his true love.
Story of Ulla and Other Tales, The [C] (Longmans Green, New York & London, 1895, 294 pp.)

Fantasy, 10 stories: "The Story of Ulla"; "The Vengeance of Dungarvan"; "A Dreadful Night"; "Rutherford the Twice-Born"; "A Stranger Woman"; "A Narrow Escape"; "That Baby of Meg's"; "A Fair Puritan"; "Meg of the Braids"; "Margaret Spens."
Wonderful Adventures of Phra the Phoenician, The See *Phra the Phoenician*

ARNOLD, FRANK EDWARD (1914–) British sf fan and author.
Fiction
Wings Across Time [pa] [C] (Pendulum 'Spacetime' Series 1,

London, 1946, 120 pp., pa 2/-)

Sf, 4 stories: "Wings Across Time" (*SFQ*, Win 1942); "The Mad Machines" ("City of Machines," *Tales of Wonder*, Sum 1939); "Endless Dimensions"; "The Twilight People" (*Comet*, Jan 1941).

ARNOLD, KENNETH (1915–) U.S. fire equipment salesman. While flying his own plane to rancher customers, on 24 June 1947 he sighted a chain of nine mysterious saucer-shaped objects. With the aid of R. A. Palmer he wrote about these and similar phenomena, thus starting the chain of "Flying Saucer" sightings.
Nonfiction
Coming of the Saucers, The [with R. A. Palmer] (Arnold, Idaho, 1952, 192 pp., illus., $4.00)

A documentary report on sky objects that have mystified the world.

ARTHUR, ROBERT (1 Nov 1909–) U.S. sf and fantasy writer; also radio and TV producer. He was born Robert Arthur Feder, which is still his legal name though he uses the Arthur surname for all purposes. Known as a master of chills and suspense on such programmes as *The Mysterious Traveler* and *Murder by Experts,* he has been a prominent writer in Hollywood. He married Joan Vatsek (1916–), who has had some stories published in *F&SF.* He was an oil operator 1929-36, joining MGM as a writer in 1937. He edited *The Mysterious Traveler Magazine* and wrote a number of stories for the sf magazines of the early 1940's. He also appeared in *Argosy* and is primarily remembered for the series given below.
Series
Morks, Murchison Originally published in *Argosy* [first printing noted]; only the reprinted stories are given: "Postpaid to Paradise" ("Postmarked for Paradise," 15 June 1940), *F&SF*, Win/Spr 1950; "Wilfred Weem, Dreamer" ("Just a Dreamer," 5 July 1941), *F&SF*, Aug 1951; "Obstinate Uncle Otis" (19 July 1941), *F&SF*, April 1958; "Mr. Milton's Gift" ("The Man With the Golden Hand," *BB*, 1953), *F&SF*, Nov 1958; "The Hero Equation" ("Don't Be a Goose," 3 May 1941), *F&SF*, June 1959; "The Devil's Garden" (1 Mar 1941), *F&SF*, Sep 1959.
Fiction
Ghosts and More Ghosts (Random, New York, 1963, 211 pp., illus–Irving Docktor, $3.95) (Random, Toronto, $4.95)

Juvenile, 10 stories (no dust jacket): "Footsteps Invisible"; "Mr. Milton's Gift" ("The Man With the Golden Hand"); "The Rose Crystal Bell" ("Ring Once for Death"); "The Stamps of El Dorado" ("Postpaid for Paradise"); "The Wonderful Day" ("Miracle on Main Street"); "Don't Be a Goose"; "Obstinate Uncle Otis"; "Do You Believe in Ghosts?" ("The Believers"); "Mr. Dexter's Dragon" ("The Book and the Beast"); "Hank Garvey's Daytime Ghost" ("Garvey's Ghost").
Anthologies
Davy Jones' Haunted Locker (Random, 1965, quarto, 204 pp., illus.–J. Cellini, $3.95, lib. $3.69)

Subtitled "Great Short Stories of the Sea." 15 stories and 1 verse: "On Board the Derelict," Young E. Allison; "Jabez O'Brien and Davy Jones' Locker," R. Arthur; "One August in the Red Sea," Lord Dunsany; "The Hemp," S. V. Benét; "Full Fathom Five," Wm. Shakespeare; "The Stone Ship," Wm. H. Hodgson; "The Voice in the Night," W. H. Hodgson; "The Roll-Call of the Reef," Arthur T. Quiller-Couch; "The Flying Dutchman," Auguste Jal; "Fire in the Galley-Stove," Wm. Outerson; "The Three Fishers," Charles Kingsley; "40 Singing Seamen," Alfred Noyes (verse); "2nd Night Out," Frank B. Long; "Ship-in-a-Bottle," P. Schuyler Miller; "The Phantom Ship," Frederick Marryat; "Anty Bligh," John Masefield.
Monster Mix [pa] (Dell: 5797, 1968, 284 pp., pa 60¢)

13 stories, with compiler's introduction (3¼ pp.): "The Day of the Dragon," Guy Endore; "Mrs. Amworth," E. F. Benson; "Daniel Webster and the Sea Serpent," S. V. Benét; "Creature of the Snows," Wm. Sambrot; "Aepyornis Island," H. G. Wells; "Fire in the Galley Stove," Wm. Outerson; "The Mannikin," Robert Bloch; "The Wendigo," Algernon Blackwood; "The Derelict," Wm. H. Hodgson; "The Ugly Bird," Manly W. Wellman; "Mimic," Donald A. Wollheim; "The Hoard of the Gibbelins," Lord Dunsany; "Footsteps Invisible," Robert Arthur.

ARTZYBASHEFF, BORIS (25 May 1899–) U.S. artist, born in Kharkov, Russia, and educated in St. Petersburg 1909-18. He came to the U.S. in 1919 and was naturalised in 1926. He is a painter of covers and illustrations for *Time*, *Life*, *Fortune*, etc., and many books including those of Edmund Wilson and Honore de Balzac. In the weird field he is particularly noted for his illustrations in C. Finney's *The Circus of Dr. Lao* (1935 ed., re-issued 1945).

ASBURY, HERBERT (1 Sep 1891–196?) U.S. biographer and historian. He was reared in strictest Puritanism but reacted against it in adolescence. His newspaper career was interrupted by World War I; he rose to 2nd lieut. of infantry but was badly gassed. He was on the staff of *Collier's* 1942-48. His special field was the portrayal of the shadier side of the past of the great American cities. His works included *The Life of Bishop Asbury* (biography of an ancestor, 1927); *The French Quarter* (1936); and *The Great Illusion: An Informal History of Prohibition* (1950). Of fantasy interest is *The Devil of Pei Ling* (Burt, New York, 1926) (also titled *The Crimson Rope*).
Anthology
Not at Night! (Macy-Macius, New York, 1928, 386 pp., $2.00)
Weird, 25 stories (originally published in *Not at Night*, *More Not at Night*, and *You'll Need a Nightlight* [see THOMSON, C. C.], prior to which all except "His Wife" appeared in *Weird Tales*): "The Purple Cincture," H. T. Rich; "The Horror at Red Hook," H. P. Lovecraft; "A Hand From the Deep," R. Poole; "The Tortoise-Shell Cat," Greye La Spina; "The House of Horror," S. Quinn; "The Coffin of Lissa," A. W. Derleth; "Swamp Horror," W. Smith & R. J. Robbins; "The Parasitic Hand," R. Anthony; "The Death Crescents of Koti," R. Poole; "The Beast," P. Benton; "His Wife," Zita I. Ponder; "Laocoon," B. Morgan; "The Life Serum," P. S. Powers; "The Girdle," J. McCord; "Bat's Belfry," A. W. Derleth; "The Sea-Thing," F. B. Long; "The Horror on the Links," S. Quinn; "The Experiment of Erich Weigert," S. P. Wright; "The Hooded Death," J. M. Nichols; "The Man Who Was Saved," B. W. Sliney; "The Plant-Thing," R. G. Macready; "Death Waters," F. B. Long; "Monsters of the Pit," P. S. Powers; "Four Wooden Stakes," V. Rowan (misspelt as "Roman"); "The Devil Bed," G. Dean.

ASCHER, EUGENE British author, has also written other paper-covered works.
Fiction
There Were No Asper Ladies [pa] See *To Kill a Corpse*
To Kill a Corpse [pa] (*There Were No Asper Ladies*, Mitre, 1946, 126 pp., pa 1/6) (*To Kill a Corpse*, WDL: M839, 1959, 160 pp., pa 2/-)
An unusual vampire story.

ASH, ALAN
Fiction
Conditioned for Space (Ward Lock, London, 1955, 192 pp., 10/6; #38, 1956, 194 pp., pa 2/6) (Digit: D478, 1961, 160 pp., pa 2/6; R754, 1963, 157 pp., pa 2/6) (*El planeta negro* [Spanish], Espacio: 1, 1962, pa)
A crashed pilot entombed in polar ice for 100 years is revivified with a changed form and undergoes various adventures.

ASHBY, WILLIAM ROSS (1903–) British M.A., M.D., Dip. Psychological Medicine; formerly Director of Research, Barnwood House, Gloucester; now Director of Burden Neurological Inst., Bristol. He contributes to psychiatric and neurological journals. His nonfiction works *Design for a Brain* (Wiley, 1952; Chapman Hall, 2nd ed., 1960) and *An Introduction to Cybernetics* (C. Hall, 1956) are of interest concerning the adaptive behaviour of the brain, etc.

ASHTON, FRANCIS LESLIE (1904–) British writer who, besides the novels below, wrote some sf stories for *Super Science* (2nd Series).
Fiction
Alas That Great City (Dakers, London, 1948, 395 pp., 9/6)

A follow-on to *The Breaking of the Seals* but not a sequel; adventure in Atlantis.
Breaking of the Seals, The (Dakers, 1946, 317 pp., 9/6)
A man is carried via a trance to a past age when a smaller satellite collided with Earth.
Wrong Side of the Moon, The [with Stephen Ashton] (Boardman, London, 1951, 191 pp., 8/6; #159, 1955, 190 pp., pa 2/-)
Power politics and the first attempt at space travel.

ASHTON, STEPHEN
Fiction
Wrong Side of the Moon, The See ASHTON, F.

ASIMOV, ISAAC (2 Jan 1920–) U.S. biochemist, science columnist, and sf author and anthologist. He was born in Petrovich, a suburb of Smolensk, U.S.S.R.; his family emigrated to the U.S. in 1923. He decided to study chemistry at Columbia University and became interested in sf, becoming quite prominent in fan affairs in the late 1930s. He obtained his B.A. in 1939, M.A. in 1941, and Ph.D. in 1948. After work as research chemist he became Associate Professor of Biochemistry at Boston University, and is now well known outside sf for his works on general science.
His first magazine appearance was with "Marooned Off Vesta" (*AS*, March 1939); his 20th year as a sf writer was celebrated by *Amazing* reprinting this story with a new sequel, "Anniversary," in May 1959. "Trends" was his first story for *ASF* (July 1939), and an indication of better things to come. He is mainly noted for his *Foundation* Series; another series of his stories gave the fundamental *laws of robotics*; and his own future history, in the vein of Heinlein, was presented in *TWS*, Win 1955, p. 63.
He has appeared in the juvenile sf field with the high-class *David Starr* Series written under the pseudonym "Paul French." More recently he had a murder mystery based on academic life: *The Death Dealers* (Avon, 1959, pa). In recent years he has written hardly any fiction but has concentrated on articles, first with a number in *ASF* and then with a monthly series in *F&SF* from Nov 1958. Since Feb 1959 he has been Contributing Science Editor to *F&SF*.
Probably his most noted article was "The Endochronic Properties of Resublimated Thiotimoline" (*ASF*, March 1948), concerning a rather odd compound, about which there have been some sequels. Among his general science books the following are of special interest: *The Intelligent Man's Guide to Science* (Basic Books, 1961, 2 volumes: Physical and Biological Sciences; Washington Square, 2 vols., 1968, pa), and *Asimov's Biographical Encyclopedia of Science and Technology* (Doubleday, 1964), the stories of over 1,000 great scientists. He has a nonfiction collaboration with W. Boyd: *Races and People* (1955).
S. Moskowitz's profile of Asimov appeared in *AS* (April 1962) and in *Seekers of Tomorrow* (1966), while the Oct 1966 *F&SF* was a special Asimov issue having a bibliography.
Series
Foundation All in *ASF*: "Foundation" (May 1942); "Bridle and Saddle" (June 1942); "The Big and the Little" (Aug 1944); "The Wedge" (Oct 1944); "Dead Hand" (April 1945); "The Mule" (sr2, Nov 1945); "Now You See It . . ." (Jan 1948); ". . . And Now You Don't" (sr3, Nov 1949). Published as the books *Foundation*; *Foundation and Empire*; *Second Foundation*.
Laws of Robotics Mostly incidents with Susan Calvin, robopsychologist. Includes all the stories listed in *I, Robot*, the first work to prominently portray the ideas in toto, and the later *Rest of the Robots*.
Starr, David Juvenile series under pseudonym "Paul French."
David Starr: Spaceranger (Doubleday, New York, 1952, $2.50; World's Work, England, 1953; [French], Fleuve Noir: A44, 1954; [Swedish], Sv. Läraretidn., 1958; [German], *T*, 277, 1963)
Lucky Starr and the Pirates of the Asteroids (Doubleday, N.Y., 1953, $2.50; World's Work, 1953; [French], Les Presses de la Cite, 1954; [German], *T*, 279, 1963)
Lucky Starr and the Oceans of Venus (Doubleday, N.Y., 1954, $2.50; [French], Les Presses de la Cite, 1955; [Spanish], Ed. Constancia, Mexico, 1955; [German], *T*, 282, 1963)

Lucky Starr and the Big Sun of Mercury (Doubleday, N.Y., 1956, $2.50; [Spanish], Nebulae: 43, 1957; [Swedish], Sv. Lära-retidn., 1959; [German], *T*, 285, 1963)

Lucky Starr and the Moons of Jupiter (Doubleday, N.Y., 1957, $2.75; [French], Les Presses de la Cite, 1958; [German], *T*, 287, 1963)

Lucky Starr and the Rings of Saturn (Doubleday, N.Y., 1958, $2.75; [German], *T*, 290, 1963)

Urth, Wendell Stories of eccentric future detective: "The Singing Bell" (*F&SF*, Jan 1955); "The Talking Stone" (*F&SF*, Oct 1955); "The Dying Night" (*F&SF*, July 1956). Included in *Asimov's Mysteries*.

Fiction

Asimov's Mysteries [C] (Doubleday, New York, 1968, xii+240 pp., $4.50) (D'day SF B.C., 1968, $1.70) (Rapp Whiting, London, 1968, 228 pp., 25/-)

14 sf mystery stories: "The Singing Bell"; "The Talking Stone"; "What's in a Name?"; "The Dying Night"; "Paté de Foie Gras"; "The Dust of Death"; "A Loint of Paw"; "I'm in Marsport Without Hilda"; "Marooned Off Vesta"; "Anniversary"; "Obituary"; "Star Light"; "The Key"; "The Billiard Ball."

Caves of Steel, The (*GSF* sr3, Oct 1953) (Doubleday, 1954, 224 pp., $2.95) (D'day SF B.C., 1954, $1.20) (Boardman, London, 1954, 224 pp., 9/6) (*Les villes d'acier* [French], *Galaxie* [mag], sr4, May 1954) (Signet: S1240, 1955, 189 pp., pa 35¢) (SF B.C. [S.J.], 1956, 4/6) (*Der Mann von druben* [German], AWA, 1956, 1958; Heyne, 1961, pa) (*Les caverns d'acier* [French, trans.–J. Brècard], Hachette: Le RF, 1956) (*Stalgrottorna* [Swedish], *Hapna*, sr7, Oct 1957) (Panther: 835, 1958, 189 pp., pa 2/6; 835, 1967, 206 pp., pa 5/-) ([Japanese], Hayakawa: 3016, 1959, pa) (Pyramid: F784, 1962, 189 pp., pa 40¢; X1824, 1968, pa 60¢) (*La metropoli sotterranea* [Italian], *Cosmo*, 116, 1963) (in *The Rest of the Robots*, 1964, 1967 [not in pa ed.]) (*Do stalen holen* [Dutch], Meulenhoff, Amsterdam, 1967)

A murder mystery combining robotics and sociology, with characters Lije Baley and R. Daneel Olivaw. *The Naked Sun* is a sequel. *Note:* The French magazine version is a poor translation—Hachette is more complete; the German translations are poor.

Currents of Space, The (*ASF*, sr3, Oct 1952) (Doubleday, 1952, 217 pp., $2.75) (D'day SF B.C., 1953) (Signet: 1082, 1953, 176 pp., pa 25¢) (Boardman, 1955, 217 pp., 9/6) ([Japanese], Muromachi-Shobo: SF1 (abr), 1955; Hayakawa: 3030, 1962 pa) (*Las corrientes del espacio* [Spanish], Nebula: 15, 1956, pa) (*Correnti dello spazio* [Italian], Biblioteca Economica Mondadori, nd) (Panther: 824, 1958, 192 pp., pa 2/6; 1964, pa 3/6; 1967, 205 pp., pa 5/-) (*Der fiebernde Planet* [German], Goldmann, 1960, 1962 pa) (in *Triangle* [Asimov], 1961) (Lancer: 74-816, 1963, 191 pp., pa 75¢; 72-104, 1966, pa 50¢; 73-703, 1968, pa 60¢) (*Les courants de l'espace* [French], Galaxie Bis: 3, 1967, pa)

A picture of the future of galactic civilization, with the struggle to save the planet Florina.

Earth Is Room Enough [C] (Doubleday, 1957, 192 pp., $2.95) (D'day, Toronto, $3.50) (D'day SF B.C., 1957) (Bantam: A1978, 1959, 166 pp., pa 35¢) (Panther: 1042, 1960, 176 pp., pa 2/6; 1967, pa 3/6) (*Con la tierra nos basta* [Spanish], Nebula: 92, 1963, pa) (*Geliebter Roboter* [German], Heyne: 3066, 1966, pa)

Sf, 15 stories and two verses: "The Dead Past"; "The Foundation of SF Success" (poem); "Franchise"; "Gimmicks Three"; "Kid Stuff"; "The Watery Place"; "Living Space"; "The Message"; "Satisfaction Guaranteed"; "Hell-Fire"; "The Last Trump"; "The Fun They Had"; "Jokester"; "The Immortal Bard"; "Someday"; "The Author's Last Ordeal" (poem); "Dreaming Is a Private Thing." *Note:* German ed. has only 10 stories, and Spanish may be abridged also.

Eight Stories From The Rest of the Robots [pa] See *Rest of the Robots, The*

End of Eternity, The (Doubleday, 1955, 191 pp., $2.95; 1966, 184 pp., $3.95) (D'day SF B.C., 1956) (*El fin de la eternidad* [Spanish], Nebula: 30, 1956, pa) (*La fine dell'eternitá* [Italian], *Urania*, 119, 1956) (Signet: S1493, 1958, 192 pp., pa 35¢) (*Am Ende der Ewigkeit* [German], *UG*, 73, 1958; *Das Ende der Ewigkeit*, Heyne: 3088, 1967, pa) (Panther: 881, 1959, 191 pp., pa 2/6; 1964, 207 pp., pa 3/6; 1965, 188 pp., pa 3/6; 24409, 1968, 189 pp., pa 5/-) (Lancer: 74-818, 1963, 176 pp., pa 75¢; 72-107, 1966, pa 50¢; 73-701, 1968, pa 60¢) (*La fin de l'éternité* [French], Denoël: PF105, 1967, pa) (*Het einde van de eeuwigheid* [Dutch], Bruna, Utrecht & Antwerp, 1967 [in *SF Omnibus*])

Intrigue within the 'Eternity' organization which ranges up and down the time stream.

Fantastic Voyage (Houghton Mifflin, Boston, 1966, 239 pp., $3.95) (Dobson, 1966, 211 pp., 21/-) (T. Allen, Toronto, $4.95) (D'day SF B.C., 1966, $1.20) (*SEP*, sr2, 20 Feb 1966 [abr.]) (Bantam: H3177, 1966, 186 pp., pa 60¢) (Corgi: GS7366, 1966, 186 pp., pa 3/6) (*Reisdoel: Menselijk brein* [Dutch], Bruna, Utrecht & Antwerp, 1967)

Novelisation of the film—a minisub in the bloodstream. *Film:* U.S., 20th Century Fox, 1966, screenplay by Harry Kleiner based on an original story by Otto Klement and J. L. Bixby (which Asimov's book follows). Generally well considered. Has appeared as a comic.

Foundation (Gnome, New York, 1951, 255 pp., $2.75) (Weidenfeld Nicolson, London, 1953, 256 pp., 10/6; 1955, 5/-) (abr: *The 1,000-Year Plan*, Ace: D-110, 1955, 160 pp., pa 35¢ [with *No World of Their Own*]; D-538, 1962, pa 35¢) ("Stiftelsen" [Swedish], *Hapna*, sr6, Sep 1955) (*Fondation* [French, trans.–J. Rosenthal], Hachette: Le RF, 1957; Denoël: PF89, 1966, pa; with sequels–Club du Livre d'Anticipation, 1965) (Panther: 1080, 1960, 189 pp., pa 2/6; 1965, pa 3/6; 1966, pa 3/6) (*Fundacion* [Spanish], Cenit: 23, 1961, pa; Nebula: 105, 1965 pa) (Doubleday 'Uniform Ed.,' 1963, 227 pp., $3.50) (in *The Foundation Trilogy* [Asimov], *ca.* 1964) (Avon: S224, 1966, 200 pp., pa 60¢; V2248, 1968, pa 75¢) (in *An Isaac Asimov Omnibus*, 1966) (*Der Tausendjahresplan* [German], Heyne: 3080, 1966, pa; other German, see *Foundation Trilogy*)

First book of the *Foundation* Series, covering the stories up to "The Wedge," under the headings The Psychohistorians; The Encyclopedists; The Mayors; The Traders; The Merchant Princes.

Foundation and Empire (Gnome, 1952, 247 pp., $2.75) (*The Man Who Upset the Universe*, Ace: D-125, 1955, 254 pp., pa 35¢; F-216, 1963, pa 40¢) ("Andra Stiftelsen" [Swedish], *Hapna*, sr, Sep 1955–Sep 1956) (*Fundacion e Imperio* [Spanish], Cenit: 26, 1962, pa) (Panther: 1355, 1962, 172 pp., pa 2/6; 1964, pa 3/6; 1965, pa 3/6) (Doubleday 'Uniform Ed.,' 1963, 227 pp., $3.50) (in *The Foundation Trilogy* [Asimov], *ca.* 1964) (Avon: S234, 1966, 224 pp., pa 60¢; V2236, 1968, pa 75¢) (in *An Isaac Asimov Omnibus*, 1966) (*Fondation et Empire* [French; trans.–J. Rosenthal] (with others), Club du Livre d'Anticipation, 1965; Denoël: PF92, 1966, pa) (*Der galaktische General* [German], Heyne: 3082, 1966, pa; other German, see *Foundation Trilogy*)

Second book of *Foundation* Series, containing "Dead Hand" and "The Mule."

Foundation Trilogy, The [C] (Doubleday SF B.C., *ca.* 1964, 227-227-225 pp., $2.20 [binding of 'Uniform Ed.']) (*Fondation, Fondation et Empire, Seconde Fondation* [French], Club du Livre d'Anticipation, Paris, 1965) (*An Isaac Asimov Omnibus*, Sidgwick & Jackson, London, 189-172-187 pp., 30/-)

The three works *Foundation, Foundation and Empire, Second Foundation*. The French set had later separate publication (the first only appearing before 1965). The 1966 appearance in German was in three Heyne paperbacks, but prior to this the series appeared in *TS* around early 1960 under the overall title "Der Tausendjahresplan," sectionalized as follows: "Terminus, der letzte Planet" (#22); "Der galaktische General" (#24); "Der Mutant" (#26); "Alle Wege führen nach Trantor" (#28).

I, Robot [C] (Gnome, 1950, 253 pp., $2.50; pa 35¢) (Grosset & Dunlap, New York, 1952, 253 pp., $1.00; introduction, G. Conklin) (Grayson, London, 1952, 224 pp., 8/6) (*Ich, der Robot* [German], Rauch, 1952; Weiss, 1959, pa) (SF B.C. [S.J.], 1954, 6/-) (*Jag, Robot* [Swedish], Eklund, 1954) (Signet: S1282, 1956, 192 pp., pa 35¢; S1885, 1961, pa 35¢; D2458, 1964, pa 50¢; P3540, 1968, pa 60¢) (*Yo, Robot* [Spanish], Nebula: 17, 1956, pa) (Digit: D164, 1958, 158 pp., pa 2/-) (Doubleday, 1963, 218 pp., $3.50) (D'day, Toronto, $4.00) (D'day SF B.C., 1963, $1.20) ([Japanese], Hayakawa: SF3055, 1963, pa) (*Ik, robot* [Dutch],

Spectrum, Utrecht & Antwerp, 1966) (Dobson, 1967, 218 pp., 21/-) (*Le Livre de Robots* [French; with *Rest of the Robots*], Ed. Opta 'Classiques SF' 7, 1967) (Panther: 025324, 1968, 206 pp., pa 5/-)

The Gnome paper edition is scarce; it was originally printed for U.S. troops in Korea and Germany. The Digit edition omits the last 2 stories. Sf, 9 stories covering "The Laws of Robotics" and featuring psychologist Susan Calvin: "Robbie" ("Strange Playfellow"); "Runaround"; "Reason"; "Catch That Rabbit"; "Liar"; "Little Lost Robot"; "(Paradoxical) Escape"; "Evidence"; "The Evitable Conflict." For other robot stories, see *The Rest of the Robots*.

Isaac Asimov Omnibus, An [C]   See *Foundation Trilogy, The*
Man Who Upset the Universe, The [pa]   See *Foundation and Empire*
Martian Way, The [C]   (Doubleday, 1955, 222 pp., $2.95) (D'day SF B.C., 1955, $1.15) (Signet: S1433, 1957, 159 pp., pa 35¢) (*Wasser für den Mars* [German], Goldmann, 1960, 1965 pa) (*En lo profundo* [Spanish], Nebula: 83, 1962, pa) (D. Dobson, 1964, 222 pp., 16/-) (Panther: 1799, 1965, 192 pp., pa 3/6; 1967, pa 3/6)

Sf, 4 stories: "The Martian Way" (*GSF*, Nov 1952); "Youth" (*Space SF*, May 1952); "The Deep" (*GSF*, Dec 1952); "Sucker Bait" (*ASF*, sr2, Feb 1954). *Note:* The 1st and 3rd have appeared in *Galaxie* [French]. "Sucker Bait" was intended to be part of a Twayne Triplet anthology around 1954, with "Get out of My Sky," J. Blish [became title for a Margulies anthology], and "Question and Answer" (*Planet of No Return*), P. Anderson.
Naked Sun, The (*ASF*, sr3, Oct 1956) (Doubleday, 1957, 187 pp., $2.95) (D'day SF B.C., 1957) (*Il sole nudo* [Italian], *Urania*: 161, 1957) (Bantam: A1731, 1958, 178 pp., pa 35¢) ([Japanese], Kodan-sha, 1958) (M. Joseph, London, 1958, 238 pp., 13/6) (*Mord I Universet* [Danish], Skrifola: P11, 1958, pa; double with *Not This August*, P21, 1958, pa) (SF B.C. [S.J.], 1959, 5/6) (Panther: 1016, 1960, 189 pp., pa 2/6; 1964 (2 ed), 202 pp., pa 3/6; 1965, pa 3/6; 1967, pa 5/-) (*Die nackte Sonne* [German], AWA, 1960; Heyne, 1962, pa; *Mord unter fremder Sonne, UG*: 174, 1962) (*El sol desnudo* [Spanish], Nebula: 65, 1960, pa) (Lancer: 72-753, 1964, 189 pp., pa 50¢; 72-108, 1966, 191 pp., pa 50¢; 73-702, 1968, pa 60¢) (in *The Rest of the Robots* 1964, 1967 [not in pa ed.])

Sequel to *The Caves of Steel*; Lije Baley and R. Daneel Olivaw investigate a murder on one of the Spacer worlds normally closed to Earthmen.
Nine Tomorrows [C]   (Doubleday, 1959, 236 pp., $3.50) (D'day SF B.C., 1959) (Bantam: A2121, 1960, 198 pp., pa 35¢) (*Nueve futuros* [Spanish], Nebula: 78, 1962, pa) (D. Dobson, 1963, 224 pp., 15/-) (SF B.C. [S.J.], 1964, 6/-) (*Unendlichkeit x 5* [German], TS: 109, 1966, pa) (Pan: M171, 1966, 251 pp., pa 5/-)

Sf, 9 stories and 2 poems: "Profession"; "The Feeling of Power"; "The Dying Night"; "I'm in Marsport Without Hilda"; "The Gentle Vultures"; "All the Troubles of the World"; "Spell My Name With an S" ("S as in Zebatinsky"); "The Last Question"; "The Ugly Little Boy" ("Lastborn"); "I Just Make 'Em Up, See!" (poem); "Rejection Slips" (poem). *Note:* Spanish has first 7 stories only; German has 1st, 5th, 6th, 7th and 9th—the 1st also appeared as part of *UZ*: 591, 1968.
1,000-Year Plan, The [pa]   See *Foundation*
Pebble in the Sky (Doubleday, 1950, 223 pp., $2.50) (*2CSAB*, abr., Win 1950) (Galaxy Novel: 14, 1953, 153 pp., pa 35¢) (*Tussen twee voetstappen* [Dutch], Servire, 's-Gravenhage, 1952) (*Cailloux dans le ciel* [French; trans.—A. Audiberti], Gallimard: Le RF, 1953) (*Paria dei cieli* [Italian], *Urania*: 20, 1953) (Bantam: A1646, 1957, 200 pp., pa 35¢; EP47, 1964, pa 45¢; FP47, 1968, pa 50¢) (Corgi: S583, 1958, 220 pp., pa 2/6) (*Radioaktiv* [German], Goldmann, 1960, 1964, pa) (in *Triangle* [Asimov], 1961) (Sidgwick & Jackson, London, 1968, 200 pp., pa 18/-)

Prepublication title was "Grow Old Along With Me." A modern man is cast into the far future and finds Earth about to rebel against its status as a pariah in the Galactic Empire.
Rebellious Stars, The [pa]   See *Stars Like Dust, The*
Rest of the Robots, The [C]   (Doubleday, 1964, 556 pp., $5.95)

(D'day SF B.C., 1964, $1.90) (*De nuevo los robots* [Spanish], Galaxia: 21, 1964, pa) (*Eight Stories From The Rest of the Robots*, Pyramid: R1283, 1966, 159 pp., pa 50¢; R1783, 1968, pa 50¢) (Dobson, 1967, 556 pp., 35/-) (French ed., see *I, Robot*) (Panther: 025944, 1968, 223 pp., pa 5/-)

10 robot stories (further to those in *I, Robot*), with the last two novels omitted from paperback. In four sections: I. The Coming of the Robots: "Robot AL-76 Goes Astray"; "Victory Unintentional." II. The Laws of Robotics: "First Law"; "Let's Get Together." III. Susan Calvin: "Satisfaction Guaranteed"; "Lenny"; "Galley Slave." IV. Lije Baley: *The Caves of Steel, The Naked Sun*.
Second Foundation   (Gnome, 1953, 210 pp., $2.75) (D'day SF B.C., 1954) (Avon: T232, 1958, 192 pp., pa 35¢; G1248, 1964, 191 pp., pa 50¢; S237, 1966, pa 60¢; 1968, pa 60¢) (Digit: D192, 1958, 160 pp., pa 2/-) ("Andra Stiftelsen" [Swedish], *Hapna*, sr7, Feb 1959) (*Fundacion segunda* [Spanish], Cenit: 28, 1962, pa; Nebula: 110, 1965, pa) (Doubleday 'Uniform Ed.,' 1963, 225 pp., $3.50) (in *The Foundation Trilogy* [Asimov], *ca.* 1964) (Panther: 1713, 1964, 187 pp., pa 3/6; 1965, pa 3/6; 17135, 1967, pa 5/-) (*Seconde Fondation* [French; trans.—J. Rosenthal] (with others), Club du Livre d'Anticipation, 1965; Denoël: PF94, 1966, pa) (in *An Isaac Asimov Omnibus*, 1966) (*Alle Wege führen nach Trantor* [German], Heyne: 3084, 1966, pa; other German, see *Foundation Trilogy*)

Third and last book of the *Foundation* Series, covering: "Now You See It . . ."; ". . . And Now You Don't."
Stars Like Dust, The ("Tyrann," *GSF*, sr3, Jan 1951) (Doubleday, 1951, 218 pp., $2.50) (D'day SF B.C., 1953) (*The Rebellious Stars*,Ace: D-84, 1954, 176 pp., pa 35¢; with *An Earth Gone Mad*) (*Världar I Krig* [Swedish], Lindqvist, 1954) (*Rebelion en la galaxia* [Spanish], Nebula: 20, 1956, pa) (Panther: 863, 1958, 191 pp., pa 2/6; 1964, 204 pp., pa 3/6; 1965, pa 3/6; 24417, 1968, 189 pp., pa 5/-) (*Sterne wie Staub* [German], Goldmann, 1960, 1963, pa) (in *Triangle* [Asimov], 1961) (Lancer: 74-815, 1963, 192 pp., pa 75¢; 72-103, 1966, pa 50¢; 73-704, 1968, pa 60¢)

Interstellar intrigue; generally recommended, though characterisation is weak.
Through a Glass, Clearly [C] [pa]   (FSB: 1866, 1967, 124 pp., pa 3/6)

Sf, 4 stories: "It's Such a Beautiful Day"; "Belief"; "Breeds There a Man . . . ?"; "The C-Chute."
Triangle [C]   (Doubleday, 1961, 516 pp., $3.95) (D'day SF B.C., 1961, $1.20) (D'day, Toronto, $4.50)

The three Trantorian Empire novels: *The Currents of Space*; *Pebble in the Sky*; *The Stars Like Dust. Note:* This is understood to be one of the few books that strictly had only a B.C. edition, as the trade edition differed only in the jacket.

Nonfiction

Asimov has had many books on biochemistry, anthropology, chemistry, physics, astronomy, mathematics., etc. since 1952. A listing is given in *F&SF*, Oct 1966. Later books of interest include *From Earth to Heaven* (Doubleday, 1966)—17 essays from *F&SF*; *Is Anyone There?* (Doubleday, 1967; Ace, 1968, pa)—37 articles mainly from sources outside sf; *Science, Numbers and I* (Doubleday, 1968)—essays from *F&SF*. He also assisted with a popular version of S. Dole's *Habitable Planets for Man* titled *Planets for Man* (1964).

Anthologies

Fifty Short Science Fiction Tales [with G. Conklin] [pa]   (Collier: AS516, 1963, 287 pp., pa 95¢; 01639, 1966, pa 95¢)

50 stories with separate introductions from both compilers: *Prelude:* "Ballade of an Artificial Satellite," Poul Anderson; "The Fun They Had," I. Asimov; "Men Are Different," Alan Bloch; "The Ambassadors," A. Boucher; "The Weapon," F. Brown; "Random Sample," T. P. Caravan; "Oscar," C. Cartmill; "The Mist," Peter Cartur; "Teething Ring," J. Causey; "The Haunted Space Suit," A. C. Clarke; "Stair Trick," Mildred Clingerman; "Unwelcome Tenant," Roger Dee; "The Mathematicians," Arthur Feldman; "The Third Level," J. Finney; "Beautiful, Beautiful, Beautiful!" Stuart Friedman; "The Figure," Edward Grendon; "The Rag Thing," D. Grinnell; "The Good Provider," Marion

Gross; "Columbus Was a Dope," R. A. Heinlein; "Texas Week," Albert Hernhuter; "Hilda," H. B. Hickey; "The Choice," W. Hilton-Young; "Not With a Bang," D. Knight; "The Altar at Midnight," C. M. Kornbluth; "A Bad Day for Sales," F. Leiber; "Who's Cribbing?" Jack Lewis; "Spectator Sport," J. D. MacDonald; "The Cricket Ball," Avro Manhatten; "Double-Take," W. K. Marks; "Prolog," J. P. McKnight; "The Available Data on the Worp Reaction," Lion Miller; "Narapoia," Alan Nelson; "Tiger by the Tail," A. E. Nourse; "Counter Charm," Peter Phillips; "The Fly," A. Porges; "The Business, As Usual," M. Reynolds; "Two Weeks in August," F. M. Robinson; "See?" Edward G. Robles, Jr., "Appointment at Noon," E. F. Russell; "We Don't Want Any Trouble," J. H. Schmitz; "Built Down Logically," Howard Schoenfeld; "An Egg a Month From All Over," Idris Seabright; "The Perfect Woman," R. Sheckley; "The Hunters," Walt Sheldon; "The Martian and the Magician," Evelyn E. Smith; "Barney," Will Stanton; "Talent," T. Sturgeon; "Project Hush," Wm. Tenn; "The Great Judge," A. E. van Vogt; "Emergency Landing," Ralph Williams; "Obviously Suicide," S. F. Wright; *Postlude:* "Six Haiku," Karen Anderson.

Hugo Winners, The (Doubleday, 1962, 318 pp., $4.50) (D'day, Toronto, $4.95) (Avon: S127, 1963, 320 pp., pa 60¢) (Dobson, 1963, 318, 18/-) (Penguin: #1905, 1964, 342 pp., pa 4/6; 1968, pa 5/-)

Sf, 9 stories, each winner of a Hugo Award (at a World SF Convention), and most capably introduced by the compiler: *1955:* "The Darfsteller," W. M. Miller; "Allamagoosa," E. F. Russell. *1956:* "Exploration Team," M. Leinster; "The Star," A. C. Clarke. *1958:* "Or All the Seas With Oysters," A. Davidson. *1959:* "The Big Front Yard," C. D. Simak; "The Hell-Bound Train," R. Bloch. *1960:* "Flowers for Algernon," D. Keyes. *1961:* "The Longest Voyage," P. Anderson.

Tomorrow's Children (Doubleday, New York, 1966, 431 pp., $4.95; lib. $5.70)

18 stories of fantasy and sf about children and young people, with Introduction: "No Life of Their Own," C. D. Simak; "The Accountant," R. Sheckley; "Novice," J. H. Schmitz; "Child of Void," Marg. St. Clair; "When the Bough Breaks," L. Padgett; "A Pail of Air," F. Leiber; "Junior Achievement," Wm. Lee; "Cabin Boy," D. Knight; "The Little Terror," W. F. Jenkins; "Gilead," Zenna Henderson; "The Menace From Earth," R. A. Heinlein; "The Wayward Cravat," Gertrude Friedberg; "The Father Thing," P. K. Dick; "Star, Bright," M. Clifton; "All Summer in a Day," R. Bradbury; "It's a Good Life," J. Bixby; "The Place of the Gods," S. V. Benét; "The Ugly Little Boy" ("Lastborn"), I. Asimov.

ASQUITH, (LADY) CYNTHIA (Mary Evelyn Charteris) (1887–31 Mar 1960) British author and anthologist of the weird; wife of Herbert Asquith (d. 1947). She was secretary to J. M. Barrie, 1918-37, and wrote a biography of Queen Elizabeth II.
Fiction
This Mortal Coil [C] (Arkham, Wis., 1947, 245 pp., $3.00, jacket –R. Clyne; 2,609 copies) (*What Dreams May Come*, J. M. Barrie, London, 1951, 254 pp., 10/6; Ambassador, Toronto, $2.25; FSB: 1283, 1965, 158 pp., pa 3/6)

Weird, 9 stories: "In a Nutshell"; "The White Moth"; "The Corner Shop"; " 'God Grante That She Lye Stille' "; "The Playfellow"; "The Nurse Never Told"; "The Lovely Voice"; "The First Night"; "The Follower." *Note:* British edition omits "The Nurse Never Told" and "The Follower" and adds "From What Beginnings?"

What Dreams May Come [C] See *This Mortal Coil*
Anthologies
Black Cap: New Stories of Murder and Mystery, The (Scribner, New York, 1928, 334 pp., $2.00) (Hutchinson, London, 1928, 318 pp., 7/6; 1929, 3/6; nd, 252 pp., pa)

Weird, 14 stories: "Shall We Join the Ladies?" J. M. Barrie (play); "The Killing-Bottle," L. P. Hartley; "An Unrecorded Instance," Mrs. B. Lowndes; "A Considered Murder," B. Pain; "The Tarn," H. Walpole; "The Islington Mystery," A. Machen; "Circumstantial Evidence," E. Wallace; "The Prince," W. B. Maxwell; "The Smile of Karen," O. Onions; "The Lovely Lady," D. H. Lawrence;

"The Hospital Nurse," S. Leslie; "Telling," Marj. Bowen; "Footprints in the Jungle," W. S. Maugham; "The Lovely Voice Lady," Cynthia Asquith.
Book of Modern Ghosts, A See *Second Ghost Book, The*
Ghost Book, The (Hutchinson, 1927, 318 pp., 7/6; #123, nd 1945?, 287 pp., pa 1/6) (Scribner, 1927, 327 pp., $2.00)

16 stories: "The Villa Desiree," May Sinclair; "Chemical," A. Blackwood; "The Duenna," Mrs. B. Lowndes; "A Visitor From Down Under," L. P. Hartley; "The Lost Tragedy," D. Mackail; "Spinster's Rest," C. Dane; "Mrs. Lunt," H. Walpole; "Munitions of War," A. Machen; "The Rocking-Horse Winner," D. H. Lawrence; " 'A Recluse,' " W. de la Mare; "The Corner Shop," C. L. Ray; "Two Trifles: 1. The Ether-Hogs; 2. The Mortal," O. Onions; "Twelve O'Clock," C. Whibley; "The Amorous Ghost," Enid Bagnold; "Mr. Tallent's Ghost," Mary Webb; "Pargiton and Harby," D. MacCarthy.
My Grimmest Nightmare (Allen Unwin, London, 1935, 210 pp., 5/-) (Nelson, Toronto, $1.50) (*Not Long for This World*, Telegraph, New York, 1936, 224 pp., $2.00)

22 stories: "The Follower," Cynthia Asquith; "To Be Let Furnished," Gabrielle Vallings; "Thunderbolt," Miranda Stuart; "By Water," A. Blackwood; "Not Long for This World," Inez Holden; "Jungle Night," R. A. Monson; "The Anonymous Gift," L. Vorley; " 'There Is One S.O.S.,' " S. E. Reynolds; "In the Jotunheim Mountains," J. B. Morton; "Dead Man's Room," E. Betts; "Incubus," Marj. Bowen; "Into the Enemy's Camp," H. Jay; "The Mask," H. de V. Stacpoole; "Behind the Wall," N. Streatfield; "The Mad Hatter," E. Middleton; "Six Months Ago," J. Laver; "Rendezvous With Fate," C. Madden; "Serenade for Baboons," N. Langley; "The Surprise Item," C. Spencer; "Split Second," Ann Knox; "The Blackmailers," A. Blackwood; "Room 2000 Calling," Theodora Benson.
Not Long for This World See *My Grimmest Nightmare*
Second Ghost Book, The (Barrie, London, 1952, 236 pp., 12/6) (*A Book of Modern Ghosts*, Scribner, 1953, 236 pp., $3.00) (Pan: 393, 1957, 222 pp., pa 2/-; G315, 1959, 223 pp., pa 2/6; 1961, pa 2/6; 1963, pa 2/6)

20 stories with Introduction by Elizabeth Bowen: "Captain Dalgety Returns," L. Whistler; "Christmas Meeting," Rosemary Timperley; "Danse Macabre," L. A. G. Strong; "The Memoirs of a Ghost," G. W. Stonier; "The Bewilderment of Snake McKoy," Nancy Spain; "A Story of Don Juan," V. S. Pritchett; "The Guardian," W. de la Mare; "Whitewash," Rose Macauley; "The Chelsea Cat," C. H. B. Kitchin; "W. S.," L. P. Hartley; "The Amethyst Cross," Mary Fitt; "Bomber's Night," Evelyn Fabyan; "Spooner," Eleanor Farjeon; "Autumn Cricket," Lord Dunsany; "The Restless Rest-House," J. Curling; "Back to the Beginning," J. Connell; "Possession on Completion," C. Brooks; "Hand in Glove," Eliz. Bowen; "The Lass With the Delicate Air," Eileen Bigland; "One Grave Too Few," C. Asquith.
Shudders (Scribner, 1929, 268 pp., $2.00) (Hutchinson, 1929, 287 pp., 7/6; 1931, 3/6)

15 stories: "The Travelling Grave," L. P. Hartley; "Those Whom the Gods Love," Hilda Hughes; "The Hanging of Alfred Wadham," E. F. Benson; "Crewe," W. de la Mare; "The Cosy Room," A. Machen; "The Snow," H. Walpole; "The Cat Jumps," Eliz. Bowen; "Rats," M. R. James; "The Stranger," A. Blackwood; "Dispossession," C. H. B. Kitchin; "The Lord-in-Waiting," S. Leslie; "The Last Man In," W. B. Maxwell; "The End of the Flight," W. S. Maugham; "Her Judgment Day," Mrs. B. Lowndes; "The Playfellow," Cynthia Asquith.
Third Ghost Book, The (J. Barrie, 1956, 302 pp., 15/-) (Pan: GP86, 1957, 253 pp., pa 2/6; 1960, pa 2/6; 2061, 1968, pa 5/-)

27 stories: "The Telephone," Mary Treadgold; "The Claimant," Eliz. Bowen; "Napoleon's Hat," Evelyn Fabyan; "The Bull," Rachael Hartfield; "The House That Wouldn't Keep Still," L. A. G. Strong; "The Doctor," Mary Fitt; "On No Account, My Love," Eliz. Jenkins; "The Ghost of My Valley," Lord Dunsany; "The Day of the Funeral," Mary Lane; "Take Your Partners," R. Blythe; "Someone in the Loft," L. P. Hartley; "Ringing the Changes," R. Aickman; "The Tower," Marghanita Laski; "I Became Bulwinkle," L. Curling; "Mrs. Smiff," C. Brooks; "Some-

body Calls," J. Laver; "Harry," Rosemary Timperley; "The Shades of Sleep," Ursula Codrington; "The Woman in Black," D. George; "A Laugh on the Professor," S. Leslie; "Poor Girl," Eliz. Taylor; "The House in the Glen," J. Connell; "The King of Spades," Nancy Spain; "The Uninvited Face," M. Asquith; "Animals or Human Beings," A. Wilson; "Remembering Lee," Eileen Bigland; "Who Is Sylvia?" Cynthia Asquith.

When Churchyards Yawn   (Hutchinson, 1931, 287 pp., 7/6) (Arrow: 679, 1963, 192 pp., pa 2/6)

15 stories: "The Apple Tree," Eliz. Bowen; "A Little Ghost," H. Walpole; "The Cotillon," L. P. Hartley; "The Buick Saloon," Mary O'Malley; "A Threefold Cord," A. Blackwood; "Opening the Door," A. Machen; "The Birthright," Hilda Hughes; "Beauty and the Beast," C. H. B. Kitchin; "As in a Glass Dimly," S. Leslie; "The Horns of the Bull," W. S. Morrison, M.P.; "The Man Who Came Back," W. Gerhardi; "The Unbolted Door," Mrs. B. Lowndes; " 'John Gladwin Says . . . ,' " O. Onions; "Our Feathered Friends," P. MacDonald; " 'God Grante That She Lye Stille,' " Cynthia Asquith. *Note:* Paper omits stories by Hughes and Kitchin.

ASTOR, W(ILLIAM) W(ALDORF) (31 Mar 1848–18 Oct 1919) American novelist and publisher, grandson of the first John Jacob Astor (founder of the famous family fortune). Following work in a law firm he became manager of his father's estate. He entered politics in 1877 as a member of the State Assembly and later the State Senate, but failed in his bids for Congress. He was U.S. minister to Italy 1882-1885. In the early 1890's he moved permanently to England. He bought the London *Pall Mall Gazette* in 1893, and the weekly *Observer* in 1911, but by 1914 he had sold all his publications.
Fiction
Pharaoh's Daughter and Other Stories [C]   (Macmillan, London, 1900, viii+235 pp.)

Fantasy, 12 stories (not in Bleiler *Checklist*): "Pharaoh's Daughter"; "The Ghosts of Austerlitz"; "Monsieur de Néron"; "The Romance of Cliveden"; "The Red Dwarf of Rabenstein"; "Forza del Destino"; "The Wrath of Cliveden Reach"; "Under the Black Flag"; "Bralantio's Love"; "Cliveden Lights and Shades"; "The Confession of Rui, the Priest"; "Madame Récamier's Secret."

ASTOUNDING SCIENCE FICTION [later *Analog Science Fiction/Science Fact*]   U.S. sf magazine. For anthologies entirely derived therefrom, see CAMPBELL, J. W. (Jr.).

ASTURIAS, MIGUEL ANGEL (1899–)   Spanish writer.
Fiction
Mulata [trans.-G. Rabassa]   (Delacorte, New York, 1967, 307 pp., $7.95) (S.J.R. Saunders, Toronto, $9.50) (*The Mulatta and Mr. Fly*, P. Owen, London, 1967, 304 pp., 42/-)

An amazing couple under various names in a fabulous adventure mingling science, sorcery, sociology, magic, etc. Recommended by J. Merril, *F&SF*, May 1968.
Mulatta and Mr. Fly, The   See *Mulata*

ATHELING, WILLIAM, JR. (pseud)   See BLISH, J. [nonfiction]

ATHERTON, GERTRUDE FRANKLIN (Horn) (30 Oct 1857–14 June 1948)   U.S. novelist with many works, from *The Doomswoman* (1892) to *The Horn of Life* (1942).
Fiction [all except *The White Morning* (1918)]
Bell in the Fog and Other Stories, The [C]   (Harper, New York & London, 1905, 300 pp.)

9 short stories (others not noted): "The Bell in the Fog"; "Crowned With One Crest"; "Death and the Countess"; "Death and the Woman"; "Greatest Good of the Greatest Number"; "Monarch of a Small Survey"; "Striding Place"; "Talbot of Ursula"; "Tragedy of a Snob."
Black Oxen   (Boni Liveright, New York, 1923, 346 pp.)

Somewhat dated; method of rejuvenation based on X-radiation of gonads working well on women (men not mentioned); psychological problems involved.
Foghorn, The [C]   (Houghton Mifflin, Boston & New York,

1934, 196 pp., $1.75) (Jarrolds, London, 1935, 191 pp., 6/-; 1937, 3/6)

4 stories: "Eternal Now"; "The Foghorn"; "Sacrificial Altar"; "Striding Place."

ATKINS, JOHN (ALFRED) (26 May 1916–)   British author and teacher, born in Carshalton, Surrey. B.A. (Hons) Bristol Univ. He started as a newspaperman, and later turned to teaching. After the war he organized a workers' educational association. He has written books on G. Orwell, A. Huxley, E. Hemingway; with J. B. Pick he wrote a whacky item of interest—*A Land Fit for Eros* (Arco, 1957). He taught in the Sudan 1951-55 and returned there in 1958.
Fiction
Tomorrow Revealed   (N. Spearman, London, 1955, 254 pp., 16/-) (Roy, New York, 1956, 254 pp., illus., $3.50) (Burns MacEachern, Toronto, $3.50) (*Les Memoires du Futur* [French], Denoël: PF27, 1958)

A monumental history of the world—a future man finds a library and from its contents reconstructs the history of the world and the planets, his source material being Wells, Heinlein, van Vogt, and numerous other present-day authors both sf and non-sf. The whole is skilfully woven into an almost believable history and, although wordy, is generally recommended. Compare *The Short History of the Future*, R. C. Churchill.

AUSTIN, F(REDERICK) BRITTEN (1885–)   British author educated at the Grocers' Company School, Hackney Downs. He enlisted in the London Rifle Brigade in 1914, was commissioned later that year, and was demobilised in Jan 1919 with the rank of Captain. He is noted for his vivid war stories and has also become known as a playwright.
Fiction [all except *Tomorrow* (1930)]
On the Borderland [C]   (Doubleday Page, New York, 1923, 379 pp., $2.00)

12 stories: "Buried Treasure"; "A Problem in Reprisals" "Secret Service"; "The Strange Case of Mr. Todmorden"; "Through the Gate of the Horn"; "The White Dog"; "A Point of Ethics"; "The Lovers"; "Held in Bondage"; "She Who Came Back"; "From the Depths"; "Yellow Magic."
Red Flag, The [C]   (Eyre Spottiswoode, London, 1932, 400 pp., 8/6) (Lippincott, Philadelphia, 1934, 400 pp., $2.50)

12 stories: "Danton Laughs"; "Divine Right Comes to Trial"; "Dragon Wakes"; "Evviva Garibaldi"; "Gladiator Revolts"; "In Ancient Egypt"; "In the Workers' Paradise"; "In the Year of Revolutions"; "In the Willow Pattern"; "Jacques Bonhomme Gets Angry"; " 'Viva la Commune!' "; "World Is Red."
Saga of the Sea, A [C]   (Macmillan, New York, 1929, 287 pp., $2.50) (Benn, London, 1929, 288 pp., 7/6; 1931, 3/6)

10 stories: "At Trafalgar"; "Beyond the Pillars of Melkart: B.C. 740"; " 'Blow the Man Down!' "; "Cleopatra at Actium"; "Mynheer Goes East"; "New Era Begins"; "Odysseus Goes Roving"; "Serene Republic"; "Through the Eyes of Columbus"; "Vikings Go South."
Thirteen [C]   (Doubleday Page, 1925, 340 pp., $2.00)

13 stories: "Affair of Honour"; "The Drum"; "Infernal Machine"; "Mother Sits by the Fire," "Nach Verdun!"; "One Beloved"; "Panzerkraftwagen"; "A Problem in Reprisals"; "Red Shawl"; "She Who Came Back"; "SOS"; "Through the Gate of the Horn"; "Under the Lens."
War God Walks Again, The [C]   (Doubleday Page, 1926, 274 pp., $2.00) (Williams & Northgate, London, 1926, 255 pp., 3/6)

6 stories: "A Battlepiece: New Style"; "A Battlepiece: Old Style"; "Goliath"; "In the China Sea"; "They Who Laughed"; "When the War God Walks Again."
When Mankind Was Young [C]   (Doubleday Page, 1927, 282 pp., $2.00)

10 stories: "Ariadne"; "Covered Wagon–2,000 B.C."; "Idyll of the Neolithic"; "In the Days of the Mammoth"; "In the Land of Osiris"; "Midsummer at Stonehenge"; "Rome Begins"; "Saga of the Vikings"; "Taming of the Brute"; "Where Paris Is."

AVALLONE, MICHAEL (ANGELO), Jr. (27 Oct 1924–) U.S. writer; he served in the U.S. Army in Europe 1943-46, becoming a sergeant and receiving a battle star. He has been a free-lance writer since, and was also editor of 27 publications in the men's magazine field 1955-59 and of *Third Degree*, the house organ of the Mystery Writers of America. His books include a series of "Ed Noon" novels as well as some of the U.N.C.L.E. books. He has used the pseudonyms Mark Dane and Steve Michaels; he wrote four stories in *Tales of the Frightened* magazine, including two as Mark Dane.
Fiction
Tales of the Frightened [C] [pa]   (Belmont: 90-297, 1963, 128 pp., pa 40¢; B50-736, 1965, pa 50¢) (Mayflower: 8474, 1964, 126 pp., pa 2/6; 1968, pa 3/6)
   26 stories (British edition is noted "recorded by Boris Karloff," and has no Table of Contents): "The Man in the Raincoat: The Story of Sylvester Dodge"; "The Deadly Dress: The Story of Dolores Martinez"; "The Hand of Fate: The Story of Vashtu Singh"; "Don't Lose Your Head: The Story of Henry Harper"; "Call at Midnight: The Story of John Le Grew"; "Just Inside the Cemetery: The Story of Arthur Wingate"; "The Fortune-Teller: The Story of the Gamboli Triplets"; "The Vampire Sleeps: The Story of Count Alexis"; "Mirror of Death: The Story of Celeste Collins"; "Never Kick a Black Cat: The Story of Felix Darnell"; "The Ladder: The Story of Gaspard and Francois"; "Nightmare!: The Story of John Day"; "Voice From the Grave: The Story of Martin Cable"; "Theda Is Death: The Story of Carlos Luga"; "The Barking Dog: The Story of Pedro and Tony"; "Defilers of the Tombs: The Story of Jonathan Jenkins"; "Terror in the Window: The Story of Barton Frisbee"; "Tom, Dick, and Horror: The Story of the Jones Brothers"; "Portrait in Hell: The Story of Robert Roeburne"; "The Graveyard Nine: The Story of the Ravenswood Ravens"; "Say Goodnight to Mr. Sporko: The Story of William Welles"; "Beware the Bird: The Story of Monah Trent"; "The Phantom Soldier: The Story of Captain Troy"; "Some Things Shouldn't Be Seen: The Story of Hugo James"; "You Can Take It With You: The Story of Danny Denning"; "Children of the Devil: The Story of Astra Vale."
Anthology
Edwina Noone's Gothic Sampler [under pseudonym] [pa] (Award: A199X, 1967, 159 pp., pa 60¢)
   8 stories: "The Silver Bullet," Phyllis A. Whitney; "The Bride Cried Murder," M. G. Eberhart; "The Blue, Blue Deeps," Virginia Coffman; "Death and the Maiden," V. P. Johns; "My True Love's Hair," Gladys Cuff; "Dead Mail," Natalie MacMurdy; "The Bedroom Bandit," Priscilla Dalton; "The Midnight Sadist," Edwina Noone; "The Swiss Peasant," Mary W. Shelley.

AVENEL, ANTHONY
Nonfiction
View From Orbit Two   (Laurie, London, 1957, 167 pp., illus., 18/-)
   A detached view of the Earth and the Universe from the orbit of Venus; the author also presents his views on evolution, disagreeing with generally accepted theory.

AXELROD, GEORGE (9 June 1922–) U.S. author, radio and TV script writer since 1947; the latter work has included sketches for comedians and the Celebrity Time series. He has also done some film work, and as a producer is noted for *The Seven Year Itch*. With Clinton Wilder he produced the play *Visit to a Small Planet*; his books include *Beggar's Choice* (1947) and *Blackmailer* (1952).
Fiction
Will Success Spoil Rock Hunter?   (Random, New York, 1956, 145 pp., $2.95) (Bantam, 1957, pa 35¢)
   Play in three acts, on the soul-vending theme with a demon-agent who takes the soul in 10% chunks; well worked out. *Film:* 20th Century Fox, 1957, in colour with Tony Randall and Jayne Mansfield; this has a new plot and is not fantasy.

AYCOCK, ROGER D(EE) (1914–) U.S. sf author, using the pseudonym "Roger Dee." He grew interested in the field from reading Tom Swift, E. R. Burroughs, etc. He was a postman in the Depression, and had three years in the U.S. Army Signal Corps in World War II. He started writing late in 1948, and his stories were soon accepted; he has had about 50 stories published in various sf magazines.
Fiction [as Roger Dee]
Earth Gone Mad, An [pa]   ("The Star Dice," *SS*, Nov 1952) (Ace: D-84, 1954, 144 pp., pa 35¢; with *The Rebellious Stars*) (*Follia planetaria* [Italian], *Urania*: 93, 1955) ([Japanese], Gengen-sha: SF5, 1956) (*Das Geheimnis der Würfe* [German], Zimmermann, 1957; *UK*: 27, 1958) (*Die Macht des Kyrill* [German], *UG*: 203, 1963)
   Man returns from exile to an Earth he never knew.

AYLESWORTH, JOHN B. (18 Aug 1938–) U.S. writer and producer.
Fiction
Fee, Fei, Fo, Fum [pa]   (Avon: G-1166, 1963, 158 pp., pa 50¢)
   Pill enlarges man to 350 feet tall–an updated Gulliver.

AYMÉ, MARCEL (28 Mar 1902–1967) French author. After working at a number of different trades he became a journalist for a radio-journal, etc. He was noted for his many works of romance. Besides the works below, his *The Transient Hour* has seen an English translation; the collection *The Proverb* (Bodley Head, 1961) includes some fantasy and points moral lessons. A short story of interest is "The Ubiquitous Wife" (*Story Mag*, Spr 1960; *F&SF*, Feb 1961).
Fiction
Across Paris and Other Stories [C] [trans.–N. Denny]   (Bodley Head, London, 1957, 254 pp., 15/-) (Ace [British]: H380, 1960, 187 pp., pa 2/6) (*The Walker Through Walls*, Berkley: F634, 1962, 191 pp., pa 50¢)
   Sf and fantasy, 12 stories: "Rue d'Evangile"; "The Wine of Paris"; "Martin the Novelist"; "The Dwarf"; "The State of Grace" (*F&SF*, Dec 1959); "The Seven-League Boots"; "Dermuche"; "The Walker-Through-Walls"; "A Roll of Daughters"; "The Picture-Well"; "Legend of Poldevia"; "Across Paris." *Note:* Berkley edition merely has title story first and then others in same order.
Fable and the Flesh, The   (*La vouivre*, Gallimard, Paris, 1943) (Bodley Head, 1949, 232 pp., 9/6) (Mayflower: 2450, 1965, 190 pp., pa 3/6)
   The story of Vouivre–The Lady of Serpents–and how her diadem causes upset to a French village.
Green Mare, The   (*La jument verte*, Gallimard, 1933, . . . , 1957) [Trans.–N. Denny] (Bodley Head, 1955, 234 pp., 12/6) (Harper, New York, 1955, 234 pp., $3.00) (Penguin: 1516, 1961, 237 pp., pa 2/6)
   A taunting satiric fantasy of French village life.
Second Face, The   (*La belle image*, Gallimard, 1941, 1946) (Bodley Head, 1951, 192 pp., 10/6) (Harper, 1952, 182 pp., $2.50)
   The consequences of having a new and more seductive face.
Walker-Through-Walls, The [C] [pa]   See *Across Paris and Other Stories*

AYRTON, MICHAEL (20 Feb 1921–) British painter, sculptor, author, theatre designer and illustrator. He has exhibited paintings throughout Europe, and was art critic of *The Spectator* 1944-46. Books he has illustrated include *The Human Age*, by W. Lewis, and *The Testament of Daedalus* (1962).
Fiction
Maze Maker, The   (Longmans, London, 1967, vi+282 pp., 30/-)
   The author haunted by the legend of the Greek craftsman Daedalus has written his 'life.' Ayrton invests the myth with a sense of reality—Daedalus, after losing Icarus, flew on to Cumae, built a temple to Apollo, constructed labyrinth fortifications for King Cocalus, etc.
Titivulus, or, The Verbiage Collector   (Reinhardt, London, 1953, 138 pp., illus., 12/6)
   A minor demon is given the dreary and thankless task of collecting in sacks all the negligences, pomposities and vanities of utterance throughout the world.

B

BABCOCK, DWIGHT V(INCENT) (1909–)
Fiction
Gorgeous Ghoul, The   (Knopf, New York, 1941, 276 pp., $2.00) (Ryerson, Toronto, $2.35) (United Authors, London, 1947, 256 pp., 7/6) (McLeod, Toronto, $1.25)

BADE, WILLIAM L(EMOINE) (5 April 1928–)   U.S. physicist. He was born in Lincoln, Neb.; took his Ph.D. at Nebraska Univ. 1954, where he was Assistant Professor of Physics until joining the research division of Avco in 1957. His specialty is theoretical physics. All his magazine stories are in the series below.
Series
Advent   "Advent" (*ASF*, Jan 1948); "New Lives for Old" (*ASF*, Feb 1948); "Lost Ulysses" (*ASF*, May 1949); "King of the Stars" (*SSS*, July 1950); "The Eight Hundredth Hundred-Day" (*Fantastic Worlds* [amateur mag.], Fall 1953).

BAERLEIN, HENRY PHILIP BERNARD (1875–)   British; translator of *Laugh and the Ghosts Laugh With You* [see FERNANDEZ FLOREZ, W.].

BAHNSON, AGNEW H., JR. (? –*ca*. June 1964)   U.S. writer, composer and part-time painter; son of a noted textile manufacturer (1915–). He sponsored gravitational research at North Carolina University. He was killed in a plane crash.
Fiction
Stars Are Too High, The   (Random, New York, 1959, 250 pp., $3.95) (Bantam: A2048, 1960, 183 pp., pa 35¢) (SF B.C. [S.J.], 1962, 5/6)
   Secretly built space ship is used by its inventors for pretending that Earth is being explored by aliens, so that mankind will unite.

BAILEY, CHARLES W(ALDO) (28 April 1929–)   U.S. writer; A.B. at Harvard, 1950. He began as a reporter for the Minneapolis *Star and Tribune*, then became a reporter for Cowles Publications in 1954.
Fiction
Seven Days in May   See KNEBEL, F.

BAILEY, J(AMES) O(SLER) (12 Aug 1903–)   U.S. English professor at the University of North Carolina. His M.A. thesis (1927) was "The Scientific Novels of H. G. Wells," from which grew his doctoral dissertation "Scientific Fiction in English, 1817–1914." He has been teaching at U. of N.C. since 1927, and obtained his Ph.D. there in 1934. He wrote texts for the U.S. Army.
Nonfiction
Pilgrims Through Space and Time   (Argus Books, New York, 1947, 341 pp., $5.00)
   Developed from the doctoral study mentioned above, this work traces sf through literature. It covers many of the old-time plots in the book field but fails to mention many of the magazine masters of sf like J. W. Campbell, L. S. de Camp, R. A. Heinlein, A. Merritt, S. G. Weinbaum, etc. Those that are selected, like E. E. Smith and G. O. Smith, do not have their best works mentioned. Nevertheless it is a good reference source for the older book field. The work classifies stories according to their settings and subjects, and in two parts traces the growth of sf through the centuries and then examines its common elements from an objective viewpoint.

BAILEY, PAUL DAYTON (1906–)   U.S. publisher and editor, born at American Fork, Utah; attended U. of Utah one year. He published the Eagle Rock *Press-Advertiser* 1938-45, and has been publisher and editor of Westernlore Press (books) since 1941.
Fiction
Deliver Me From Eva   (Murray Gee, Hollywood, 1946, 237 pp., $2.00)
   Hero's discovery that wife's father is a super-osteopath and can increase intelligence enormously, and the resultant misuses, etc.

BAIN, F(RANCIS) W(ILLIAM)
Fiction [Incomplete—other titles in Bleiler *Checklist*]
Digit of the Moon, A [C]   (Putnam, New York, 1905, 421 pp., illus.)
   Fantasy, 4 stories, each previously appearing from J. Parker, London, as noted: "Descent of the Sun" (1903, 109 ,pp.); "A Digit of the Moon" (1899, 122 pp.; Methuen, 1911, 118 pp.); "A Heifer of the Dawn" (1904, 75 pp.); "In the Great God's Hair" (1904, 89 pp.).

BAIN, WILLARD
Fiction
Informed Sources (Day East Received)   (Author, Corte Madera, Calif., 1967, mimeo, $3.00)
   24 hours of wire messages on the death of a legendary character named Robin the Cock. (See *F&SF*, Feb 1968.)

BAIR, PATRICK   British author; has had some radio plays broadcast by the BBC. His works include *Gargantua Falls* and *The Gypsum Flower*.
Fiction
Faster! Faster!   (Eyre Spottiswoode, London, 1950, 227 pp., 9/6) (Viking, New York, 1950, 251 pp., $3.00) (Collins, Toronto, $2.50)
   An allegory with civilisation represented by a train with humanity its passengers, with the object of going faster– faster–.

BAKER, BETTY
Anthology
Great Ghost Stories of the Old West   (Four Winds, New York, 1968, 126 pp., illus., $3.50; lib. $3.38)
   7 stories and 1 verse, with intro.: "The Strange Valley," T. V. Olsen; "The Phantom Mustang" (verse) S. Omar Barker; "The Trap," Clay Fisher; "The White Riders," Glenn R. Vernam; "Back Before the Moon," S. Omar Barker; "The Hexer," Thomas Thompson; "Johnny Who Rode the Ghost Train," Phoebe and Todhunter Ballard; "Ghost Wolf of Thunder Mountain," Will Henry.

BAKER, DENYS VAL (1917–)
Fiction
Return of Uncle Walter and Other Stories, The [C]   (Sampson Low Marston, London, 1948, viii+247 pp., 8/6)
   17 stories, several being fantasy (originally in U.S. and British pubs.): "The Return of Uncle Walter"; "A Man and a Trumpet"; "The Man From the Ministry"; "Escape"; "A Tale Washed Up by the Sea"; "Silence for His Lordship"; "The Woman on the Couch"; "The Last Day"; "The Mask of Carlton Smithers"; "My Uncle Who Paints Pictures"; "Evan the Prophet"; "Miss Meakin's Burglar"; "Memories of Michaelmas House"; "Beyond the Dump"; "The Way of the Healer"; "Seed Will Bear No Fruit"; "Child of Time."

BAKER, FRANK (22 May 1908–)   British novelist and dramatist. He began as an insurance clerk but through family interest in music took on secretarial work in a church music college. He started writing in 1935, and is most noted for his *Miss Hargreaves* (1946), which he wrote as a joke and which Margaret Rutherford turned into a hit.
Fiction
Allanayr   (Eyre Spottiswoode, London, 1941, 364 pp., 9/-) (Collins, Toronto, $2.00) (*Full Score*, Coward McCann, New York,

1942, 344 pp., $2.50)
Before I Go Hence (Dakers, London, 1946, 233 pp., 9/6) (Coward McCann, 1947, 248 pp., $2.75) (Longmans, Toronto, $3.25)
   Metaphysical type of time travel.
Birds, The (P. Davies, London, 1936, 246 pp., 7/6; 1938, 3/6) (rev., Panther: 1635, 1964, 224 pp., pa 3/6)
   Revolt of the birds. A sorry film of the same title is based on a story by Daphne Du Maurier.
Downs So Free, The (Dakers, 1948, 366 pp., 10/6)
   Poltergeists, mystics and yoga.
Embers: A Winter Tale (Coward McCann, 1946, 213 pp., $2.50) (Longmans, Toronto, $3.00) (Dakers, 1947, 232 pp., 7/6)
   Strange fantastic novel of death.
Full Score See *Allanayr*
Miss Hargreaves: A Fantasy (Eyre Spottiswoode, 1940, 311 pp., 9/-; 1943, 6/-) (Collins, Toronto, $2.00) (Coward McCann, 1941, 308 pp., $2.50) (Penguin: 783, 1950, 315 pp., pa 1/6) (Panther: #1959, 1965, 234 pp., pa 3/6)
   Two young men 'invent' an elderly poetess who takes on a semblance of life.
Mr. Allenby Loses the Way (Coward McCann, 1945, 262 pp., $2.75) (Longmans, Toronto, $3.50) (Boardman, London, 1946, 231 pp., 9/6)
   Humorous fantasy.
Sweet Chariot (Eyre Spottiswoode, 1942, 316 pp., 9/-) (Coward McCann, 1943, 335 pp., $2.50) (Longmans, Toronto, $3.00)
   Weird novel of the supernatural.
Talk of the Devil (Angus Robertson, London, 1956, 216 pp., 12/6) (Ryerson, Toronto, $2.50)

BAKER, GEORGE A. (1849–18 Sep 1906) U.S. lawyer and poet.
Fiction
Mrs. Hephaestus and Other Short Stories [C] (White Stokes & Allen, New York, 1887, 211 pp.)
   Fantasy, 6 stories and 1 play: "Mrs. Hephaestus"; "The Child of the Regiment"; "The Spirit of the Age"; "The Merman"; "The Invasion of Kleindorf"; "Labor Troubles on an Island"; "West Point" (play).

BAKER, ROBERT A(LLEN) (1921–)
Anthology
Stress Analysis of a Strapless Evening Gown, A (Prentice-Hall, New York, 1963, 188 pp., $3.95)
   32 pieces of technical fun, parodies, pastiches, etc., with compiler's introduction: "The Chisholm Effect," Francis P. Chisholm; "Body Ritual Among the Nacirema," Horace Miner; "Postal System Input Buffer Device," Robertson Osborne, Joe & Gil [J. Robertson & G. Osborne]; "Terns," F. E. Warburton; "The Bridge of San Luis Rey," Edwin B. Wilson; "Cosmic Gall," John Updike; "The Abominable Snowman," John Masters; "A Psychoanalysis of U.S. Missile Failures," S. A. Rudin; "Peniwisle," R. W. Payne; "Univac to Univac," Louis B. Salomon; "Saga of a New Hormone," Norman Applezweig; "Digging the Weans," Robert Nathan; "The Twenty-Third Psalm—Modern Versions," I—Alan Simpson & R. A. Baker, II—Lester del Rey; "Hiawatha's Lipid," Hugh Sinclair; "On the Nature of Mathematical Proofs," Joel Cohen; "A New Tool," Mo Twente; "Cosmic Sex and You," Nils Peterson (*F&SF*, Apr 1961); "Calling All Stars," Leo Szilard; "A Stress Analysis of a Strapless Evening Gown," Charles E. Siem; "Meihem in ce Klasrum," Dolton Edwards (*ASF*, Sep 1946); "A Report to the AMA," Frank Getlein; "Frieze," R. A. Baker; "The Chaostron," J. B. Cadwallader-Cohen, W. S. Zysiczk & R. R. Donnelly; "How Newton Discovered the Law of Gravitation," James E. Miller; "Mathmanship," Nicholas Vanserg; "Logarithmic and Arythmic Expression of a Physiological Function," R. Arnold Le Win; "Report of the Special Committee," Warren Weaver; "The Average Working Hours of a Scientist During Lifetime," S. Evershamen; "The Lab Coat as a Status Symbol," F. E. Warburton; "Principles of Research Administration or Eliza on the Radioactive Ice," Michael B. Shimkin; "Parkinson's Laws in Medical Research," C. Northcote Parkinson; "The Scientist as Seer," Rudolf B. Schmerl.

BALCHIN, (Brig.) NIGEL (MARTIN) (3 Dec 1908–17 May 1970) British author. As student at Cambridge he was Exhibitioner and Prizeman in Natural Science. He combined business and writing; during World War II he did scientific work for the Army, ending as Dep. Scientific Adviser to the Army Council. His writings run from *No Sky* (1933) to *The Fall of the Sparrow* (1955); he has also written under the pseudonym "Mark Spade." He wrote the Introduction for London Observer's *A.D. 2500*, and has been anthologised in *Fantasia Mathematica* (Fadiman, 1958).
Fiction
Kings of Infinite Space (Doubleday, New York, 1968, 264 pp., $4.95)
   A novel set in the future which asks probing questions as to the whys, wheres, and wherefores of the American space programme.

BALDWIN, (Mrs) ALFRED
Fiction
Shadow on the Blind and Other Ghost Stories, The [C] (Dent, London, 1895, 309 pp., illus.–J. Ayton Symington)
   9 stories: "The Shadow on the Blind"; "The Weird of the Walfords"; "The Uncanny Bairn: A Story of Second Sight"; "Many Waters Cannot Quench Love"; "How He Left the Hotel"; "The Real and the Counterfeit"; "My Next-Door Neighbour"; "The Empty Picture Frame"; "Sir Nigel Otterburne's Case."

BALDWIN, BEE New Zealand author
Fiction
Red Dust, The (Hale, London, 1965, 190 pp., 15/-) (T. Allen, Toronto, $3.25)
   Survivors of red dust epidemic struggle to live in New Zealand.

BALINT, EMERY U.S. writer and painter living in North Bronx, N.Y. His first novel was *Alpha*.
Fiction
Don't Inhale It (Gaer, New York, 1949, 223 pp., illus.–author, $2.75)
   A strange gas and its effects; a satire about a "divided" Earth.

BALL, BRIAN N(EVILLE) (19 June 1932–) British teacher, lecturer and free-lance writer.
Fiction
Sundog (Dobson, London, 1965, 215 pp., 16/-) (Corgi: GS7451, 1966, 190 pp., pa 3/6)
   Man is confined to his own solar system by aliens.
Timepiece (Dobson, London, 1968, 144 pp., 18/-)
   An ancient intergalactic ship and an eerie plunge into hyperspace.
Anthology
Tales of Science Fiction (H. Hamilton, London, 1964, 158 pp., 8/6) (Peacock: PK63, 1968, 173 pp., pa 4/-)
   9 stories selected for young people: "Hide and Seek," Arthur C. Clarke; "Return of the Moon Men," E. L. Malpass; "Life-Line," Robert A. Heinlein; "Escape Velocity," B. N. Ball; "Nothing Happens on the Moon," Paul Ernst; "Mr. Kowtshook," John Christopher; "Meteor," John Wyndham; "Allamagoosa," Eric F. Russell; "But Who Can Replace a Man?" Brian W. Aldiss.

BALL, JOHN (DUDLEY) (8 July 1911–) U.S. public relations consultant. He was born in Schenectady, N.Y.; has been a commercial pilot; was Music Editor for the Brooklyn *Eagle* 1946-50, columnist at the New York *World-Telegram*, then commentator at radio station WOL (Washington, D.C.); he is now in advertising and related fields. Another book to those below is *Spacemaster I* (1960).
Fiction
Operation Space See *Operation Springboard*
Operation Springboard (Duell, Sloan & Pearce, New York, 1958, 168 pp., $3.00) (Longmans, Toronto, $3.50) (*Operation Space*, Hutchinson, London, 1960, 208 pp., 10/6)
   Juvenile; U.S.-Soviet race to Venus using giant rocket-propelled flying boats—conditions on Venus unrealistically depicted.

BALLANTINE, IAN (15 Feb 1916–) U.S. publisher. He was born in New York; took B.A. at Columbia, 1938, and was a student at the London School of Economics 1938-39. He married in 1939 and has one son. He was general manager of Penguin Books 1939-45, and has been a director of Bantam Books 1945– and Ballantine Books 1952–. He has been a director of Trans-World Publishers Ltd., and was Instructor of Sociology at Columbia University.

BALLARD, J(AMES) G(RAHAM) (18 Nov 1930–) British author, born in Shanghai, the son of a Scottish doctor living in the American sector. Interned in a Japanese prisoner-of-war camp during World War II, he was repatriated to England in 1946. He was briefly at Leys School, Cambridge, before going to Cambridge to read medicine. Since then he has done some copywriting, has flown with the R.A.F.–having a tour of duty in Canada–, and worked as a script writer for a scientific film company before his present full-time writing. After winning the annual short story competition at Cambridge in 1951, he wrote his first novel and has since exploited his imagination in the field of science fiction and fantasy. He first appeared in *Science-Fantasy* with "Prima Belladonna" (Dec 1956), and thereafter appeared regularly in the British magazines. In recent years he has become noted for his controversial contributions and is considered by J. Merril and others as one of the most significant authors of today. His work since the mid-1960s has been experimental in style, quite provocative and unforgettable. While not liked by everyone, his fiction cannot be ignored; he has been compared with Conrad, Kafka, Bradbury and William Burroughs. His notions of "inner space" were so widely echoed that he himself stopped using the phrase. Brian Aldiss has summed up his writing: ". . . other writers are copying—Ballard is creating." His novelette "The Sound Sweep" has been commissioned by the BBC for an opera. Now a widower, he lives with his three children in a London suburb.

Series

Future crowded city life All in *New Worlds*: "Escapement" (Dec 1956); "Build-Up" (Jan 1956); "Manhole 69" (Nov 1957 [U.S., July 1960]); "Billenium" (Nov 1961).

Fiction

Billenium [C] [pa] (Berkley: F667, 1962, 159 pp., pa 50¢) ([German], selections in *UZ*: 403, 1964)

10 sf and fantasy stories (8 from *NW* and *Science-Fantasy*): "Billenium"; "The Insane Ones"; "Studio 5, the Stars"; "The Gentle Assassin"; "Build-Up"; "Now: Zero"; "Mobile"; "Chronopolis"; "Prima Belladonna"; "The Garden of Time."

Burning World, The [pa] (Berkley: F961, 1964, 160 pp., pa 50¢) (*The Drought*, J. Cape, London, 1965, 252 pp., 21/-; Penguin: 2753, 1968, 176 pp., pa 3/6) (*De brandende aarde* [Dutch], Meulenhoff, Amsterdam, 1967) (*Welt in Flammen* [German], Heyne: 3114, 1968, pa)

Nightmares of human perversion when a world-wide drought forces man to the sea to subsist by distillation. The British version is completely rewritten and expanded, having 42 titled chapters compared to 15 in the Berkley version.

Crystal World, The (J. Cape, 1966, 221 pp., 21/-) (Farrar, Strauss & Giroux, New York, 1966, 210 pp., $4.50) (D'day SF B.C., 1966, $1.20) (*La fôret de cristal* [French; trans.–C. Saunier], Denoël: PF98, 1967, pa) (Berkley: X1380, 1967, 160 pp., pa 60¢) (Panther: 24190, 1968, 175 pp., pa 5/-)

First half derived from "Equinox" (*NW*, sr2, May/June 1964) and second half from "The Illuminated Man" (*F&SF*, May 1964). Life in a crystallized pattern of "time-now," with its indication of embracing the world.

Day of Forever, The [C] [pa] (Panther: 2307, 1967, 141 pp., pa 3/6)

Sf, 10 stories: "The Day of Forever"; "Prisoner of the Coral Deep"; "Tomorrow Is a Million Years"; "The Man on the 99th Floor"; "The Waiting Grounds"; "The Last World of Mr. Goddard"; "The Gentle Assassin"; "The Sudden Afternoon"; "The Insane Ones"; "The Assassination of John Fitzgerald Kennedy Considered as a Downhill Motor Race."

Disaster Area, The [C] (J. Cape, 1967, 206 pp., 21/-)

Sf, 9 stories: "Storm Bird, Storm Dreamer"; "The Concentration City"; "The Subliminal Man"; "Now Wakes the Sea"; "Minus One"; "Mr. F is Mr. F"; "Zone of Terror"; "Manhole 69"; "The Impossible Man."

Drought, The See *Burning World, The*

Drowned World, The (*SFA* [Brit.], n'te, Jan 1962) Enlarged: (Berkley: F655, 1962, 158 pp., pa 50¢) (Gollancz, London, 1962, 175 pp., 15/-) (Melbourne *Herald*, sr6, 30 Mar 1963) (SF B.C. [S.J.], 1964, 6/-) (*Deserto d'acqua* [Italian], *Urania*: 311, 1963) (*Mundo sumergido* [Spanish], Galaxia: 20, 1964, pa) (*Le monde englouti* [French], Denoel: PF 74, 1964, pa) (Penguin: 2229, 1965, 171 pp., pa 3/6) (*The Drowned World & The Wind From Nowhere*, Doubleday, New York, 1965, 316 pp., $4.50; D'day SF B.C., 1965, $1.20) (Berkley: F1266, 1966, 158 pp., pa 50¢)

Vivid outline of Earth's changed ecology with high and stagnant oceans pushing men to the poles; the adventures of a man being lured into a strange hypnotic state.

Four-Dimensional Nightmare, The [C] (Gollancz, 1963, 208 pp., 16/-) (SF B.C. [S.J.], 1964, 6/-) (Penguin: 2345, 1965, 223 pp., pa 3/6) (*Cauchemar à quatre dimensions* [French], Denoël: PF82, 1965, pa)

Sf and fantasy, 8 stories: "The Voices of Time"; "The Sound-Sweep"; "Prima Belladonna"; "Studio 5, the Stars"; "The Garden of Time"; "The Cage of Sand"; "The Watch-Towers"; "Chronopolis." *Note:* Italian *Urania*: 371, 1965, published a collection called "The Watching Towers" which presumably included some of these stories or those in *Passport to Eternity*.

Impossible Man, The [C] [pa] (Berkley: F1204, 1966, 160 pp., pa 50¢)

Sf, 9 stories: "The Drowned Giant"; "The Reptile Enclosure"; "The Delta at Sunset"; "Storm-Bird, Storm-Dreamer"; "The Screen Game"; "The Day of Forever"; "Time of Passage"; "The Gioconda of the Twilight Noon"; "The Impossible Man."

Overloaded Man, The [C] [pa] (Panther: 2336, 1967, 158 pp., pa 3/6)

Sf, 10 stories: "Now: Zero"; "The Time-Tombs"; "Thirteen to Centaurus"; "Track 12"; "Passport to Eternity"; "Escapement"; "Time of Passage"; "The Venus Hunters"; "The Coming of the Unconscious"; "The Overloaded Man."

Passport to Eternity [C] [pa] (Berkley: F823, 1963, 160 pp., pa 50¢)

Sf, 9 stories: "The Man on the 99th Floor"; "Thirteen to Centaurus"; "Track 12"; "The Watch-Towers"; "A Question of Re-Entry"; "Escapement"; "The Thousand Dreams of Stellavista"; "The Cage of Sand"; "Passport to Eternity."

Terminal Beach [C] (Gollancz, 1964, 221 pp., 18/-; Penguin: 2499, 1966, 224 pp., pa 4/6) (Berkley: F928, 1964, 160 pp., pa 50¢)

Contents differ. British edition (12 stories): "Terminal Beach"; "A Question of Re-Entry"; "The Drowned Giant"; "End Game"; "The Illuminated Man"; "The Reptile Enclosure"; "The Delta at Sunset"; "Deep End"; "The Volcano Dances"; "Billenium," "The Gioconda of the Twilight Moon"; "The Lost Leonardo."

U.S. edition (9 stories): "End Game"; "The Subliminal Man"; "The Last World of Mr. Goddard"; "The Time-Tombs"; "Now Wakes the Sea"; "The Venus Hunters" ("The Encounter"); "Minus One"; "The Sudden Afternoon"; "Terminal Beach" (*NW*, Mar 1964).

Voices of Time, The [C] [pa] (Berkley: F607, 1962, 158 pp., pa 50¢; 1243, 1966, pa 50¢)

Sf, 7 stories (all from *NW* and *Science-Fantasy*): "The Voices of Time"; "The Sound Sweep"; "The Overloaded Man"; "Zone of Terror"; "Manhole 69"; "The Waiting Grounds"; "Deep End."

Wind From Nowhere, The [pa] ("Storm-Wind," *NW*, sr2, Sep 1961) Enlarged: (Berkley: F600, 1962, 160 pp., pa 50¢; F1198, 1966, pa 50¢) (*Il vento dal nulla* [Italian], *Urania*: 288, 1962) (*Der Sturm aus dem Nichts* [German], Heyne, 1964, pa) (*The Drowned World & The Wind From Nowhere*, Doubleday, 1965, 316 pp., $4.50; D'day SF B.C., 1965, $1.20) (Penguin: 2591, 1967, 186 pp., pa 4/-)

Effective story of a world-wide disastrous wind (over 200 mph) and how some manage to survive.

BALLOU, ARTHUR U.S. business consultant. He was born in the Boston area and has lived there all his life; he is married and has four children.
Fiction
Marooned in Orbit (Little, Brown; Boston, 1968, 183 pp., $4.50)
 Disabled spacecraft circling the moon; rescue performed by U.S. astronaut in another ship.

BALMER, EDWIN (26 July 1883–21 Mar 1959) U.S. author and editor. He was born in Chicago, and took his B.A. at Northwestern Univ. in 1902, and M.A. at Harvard, 1903. In 1909 he married his first wife, Kath. MacHarg (d. 1925). He was editor of *Red Book* 1927-49, and was a member of some literary societies. His books (solo) ran from *Waylaid by Wireless* (1909) to *In His Hands* (1954). He wrote others with William MacHarg 1910-17 (some of their detective stories appeared in *Amazing Stories* 1926-27 and *Amazing Detective Tales* in 1930), and with Philip Wylie 1932-56. He wrote many short stories and plays and also wrote for motion pictures.
Fiction
After Worlds Collide See WYLIE, P. (co-author)
When Worlds Collide See WYLIE, P. (co-author)

BANGS, JOHN KENDRICK (17 May 1862–21 Jan 1922) U.S. humorist, editor and lecturer. He graduated from Columbia University in 1883, and was on the staff of *Harper's Magazine* 1888-99. In 1899 he was briefly editor of *Munsey's Weekly* and then became editor of *Harper's Weekly* (1899-1903), *New Metropolitan Magazine* (1903-04), and *Puck*. After 1907 he devoted himself to free-lancing. His stories are mainly humour with a slight fantastic flavour; of his 30 or so volumes of verse and humour to 1910, *A House-Boat on the Styx* is the most notable.
Fiction [Covers most collections; for novels see Bleiler *Checklist*]
Bicyclers and Three Other Farces, The [C] (Harpers, New York, 1896, 176 pp., illus.)
 4 stories: "The Bicyclers"; "A Dramatic Evening"; "The Fatal Message"; "A Proposal Under Difficulties."
Bikey the Skicycle and Other Tales of Jimmieboy [C] (Riggs, New York, 1902, 321 pp., illus.)
 13 stories: "Bikey the Skicycle"; "The Imp of the Telephone"; "Caught in Toy Town"; "Totherwayville, the Animal Town"; "An Electrical Error"; "In the Brownie's House"; "Jimmieboy"; "And Something"; "Jimmieboy's Fire Works"; "High-Jinks in the Barn"; "Jimmieboy's Valentine"; "The Magic Sled"; "The Stupid Little Apple Tree."
Dreamers: A Club, The [C] (Harper, New York & London, 1899, 246 pp., illus.)
 13 stories: "Being the Contribution of Mr. Bedford Parke"; "Dolly Visits Chicago"; "Dreamers Discuss a Magazine Poem"; "The Idea"; "In Which Harry Snobbe Recites a Tale of Gloom"; "In Which Mince-Pie Is Responsible for a Remarkable Coincidence"; "In Which Thomas Snobbe, Esq. of Yonkers, Unfolds a Tale"; "In Which Yellow Journalism Creeps In"; "Involvular Club, or, The Return of the Screw"; "Lang Tammas and Drumsheugh Swear Off"; "Likewise Mr. Billy Jones"; "Mystery of Pinkham's Diamond Stud"; "Salvation of Findlayson."
Enchanted Type-Writer, The [C] (Harper, New York & London, 1899, 171 pp., illus.–P. Newell)
 10 stories: "The Discovery"; "Mr. Boswell Imparts Some Late News of Hades"; "From Advance Sheets of Baron Munchausen's Further Recollections"; "A Chat With Xanthippe"; "The Editing of Xanthippe"; "The Boswell Tours: Personally Conducted"; "An Important Decision"; "A Hand-Book to Hades"; "Sherlock Holmes Again"; "Golf in Hades."
Ghosts I Have Met [C] (Harper, New York, 1898, 191 pp.)
 7 stories: "Ghosts That Have Haunted Me"; "The Mystery of My Grandmother's Hair Sofa"; "The Mystery of Barney O'Rourke"; "The Exorcism That Failed"; "Thurlow's Christmas Story"; "The Dampmere Mystery"; "Carleton Barker, First and Second."
House-Boat on the Styx, A (Harper, New York & London, 1896, 1902, 1913, 171 pp., illus.) ([Swedish], 1917)
 A sort of conventional conversation piece about famous charac-

ters—Napoleon, Cleopatra, Sherlock Holmes, etc.—who have a social club on the House-Boat; sequel is *The Pursuit of the House-Boat*.
Inventions of an Idiot, The [C] (Harper, New York & London, 1904, 185 pp.)
 Fantasy, 12 stories: "The Culinary Guild"; "A Suggestion for the Cablecars"; "The Transatlantic Trolley Company"; "The Incorporation of the Idiot"; "University Extension"; "Social Expansion"; "A Beggar's Hand-Book"; "Progressive Waffles"; "A Clearing-House for Poets"; "Some Electrical Suggestions"; "Concerning Children"; "Dreamaline." Considered by bibliographer M. Owings to be quite good, though not as science-fictional as some titles appear to indicate.
Mr. Munchausen [C] (Noyes Platt, Boston, 1901, 180 pp., illus.–P. Newell)
 15 stories: "Adventure in the Desert"; "Baron as a Runner"; "Decoration Day in the Cannibal Islands"; "He Tells the Twins of Fireworks"; "I Encounter the Old Gentleman"; "Lucky Stroke"; "Mr. M. Meets His Match"; "Mr. M's Adventure With a Shark": "Poetic June-Bug, Together With Some Remarks on the Gillyhooly Bird"; "Saved by a Magic Lantern"; "Some Hunting Stories for Children"; "Sporting Tour of Mr. M."; "Story of Jang"; "Three Months in a Balloon"; "Wriggletto."
Olympian Nights [C] (Harper, New York & London, 1902, 224 pp.)
 Fantasy, 12 stories: "I Reach Mount Olympus"; "I Seek Shelter and Find It"; "The Elevator Boy"; "I Summon a Valet"; "The Olympian Links"; "In the Dining Room"; "Oescalapius, M.D."; "At the Zoo"; "Some Account of the Palace of Jupiter"; "An Extraordinary Interview"; "A Royal Outing"; "I Am Dismissed."
Over the Plum Pudding [C] (Harper, New York & London, 1901, 244 pp., illus.)
 11 stories: "Affliction of Baron Humpfelhimmel"; "Amalgamated Brotherhood of Spooks"; "Bills, M.D."; "Flunking of Watkin's Ghost"; "Glance Ahead: Being a Christmas Tale of A.D. 3568"; "Great Composer"; "Hans Pumpernickel's Vigil"; "How Fritz Became a Wizard"; "Loss of the 'Gretchen B' "; "Rise and Fall of the Poet Gregory"; "Unmailed Letter: Being a Christmas Tale of Some Significance."
Pursuit of the House-Boat, The (Harper, New York, 1897, 204 pp.)
 Sequel to *A Houseboat on the Styx*; more of the same.
Water Ghost of Harrowby Hall, The [C] (Harper, New York, 1894, 296 pp., illus.)
 8 stories: "The Water Ghost of Harrowby Hall" (*AFR*: 16, 1951); "The Spectre Cook of Bangletop"; "The Speck on the Lens"; "A Midnight Visitor"; "A Quicksilver Cassandra"; "The Ghost Club"; "A Psychical Prank"; "The Literary Remains of Thomas Bragdon."

BANISTER, MANLY (MILES) (1914–) U.S. author. He wrote for radio and advertising, and then served with the Marines in the Pacific in World War II. He contributed to *Weird Tales* and also *Beyond* and *Galaxy*. His second novel appeared in *Amazing* [see below], while his first (not sf) was published in 1939. Recent novels of interest are "Magnanthropus" (*Fan*, sr2, Sep 1961; [German], *T*: 424, 1965) and "Seed of Eloraspon" (*Fan*, sr2, Oct 1964). He published a fantasy satire, *Egoboo*, on his own Nekronomantikon Press.
Fiction
Conquest of Earth ("The Scarlet Saint," *AS*, sr4, Jan 1956 [not in Apr]) (Avalon, New York, 1957, 224 pp., $2.75) (Ryerson, Toronto, $3.00) (*Los hermanos azules* [Spanish], Cenit: 16, 1961, pa) (Airmont: SF 7, 1964, 128 pp., pa 40¢)
 Man gradually realizing his own powers seeks to rid the universe of the alien Trisz.

BANKS, RAYMOND E. (1918?–) U.S. industrial account executive for scientific instruments; took B.A. in English from UCLA, and is a war veteran. He always wanted to write, and in 1946 he was *Esquire*'s Discovery of the Month with a fantasy story. Following this he was unsuccessful with a novel but did have a radio play on the NBC network. He began writing in earnest late in 1952 for the sf magazine market and has had over 30 stories published in many magazines, including *ASF, F&SF* and *GSF.*

BARBER, MARGARET (1869–1901)
Fiction [as Michael Fairless]
Complete Works of Michael Fairless, The [C] (Duckworth, London, 1931, 356 pp., 10/6, 5/-) (Dutton, New York, 1932, 356 pp., $2.50)
5 stories or groups: "The Road-Mender" (Duckworth, 1902, 158 pp.); "The Gathering of Brother Hilarius"; "The Grey Brethren"; "Four Stories Told to Children"; "Tonseul, an unfinished story"; Letters.

BARBEY D'AUREVILLY, JULES (AMÉDÉE) (1801–1899) One other fantasy: *Bewitched* (Harper, New York & London, 1928).
Fiction

Diaboliques, Les [C] ([French], 1874) (Elek, London, 1947, 250 pp., illus.–Dodie Masterman, 12/6) (Saunders, Toronto, $2.75)
6 stories, with Introduction by Peter Quennell: "The Crimson Curtain"; "The Greatest Love of Don Juan"; "Happiness in Crime"; "Beneath the Cards of a Game of Whist"; "At a Dinner of Atheists"; "Woman's Revenge." Not all fantasy.

BARCLAY, ALAN (pseud) See TAIT, GEORGE B.

BARDENS, D(ENNIS)
Nonfiction
Ghosts and Hauntings (Zeus, London, 1965, 255 pp., illus., 25/-) (FSB: 1610, 1967, 256 pp., pa 5/-) (Taplinger, New York, 1968, 255 pp., illus., $5.95)

BARFIELD, (ARTHUR) OWEN (9 Nov 1898–) English lawyer and author.
Fiction
Silver Trumpet, The (Eerdmans, New York, 1968, $4.95)

BARGONE, CHARLES See FARRERE, C.

BARING, MAURICE (27 Apr 1874–15 Dec 1945) British diplomat and author; fourth son of the First Lord Revelstoke. He was educated at Eton and Trinity College, Cambridge. He entered diplomatic service in 1898 and resigned in 1904; he was a newspaper correspondent in various countries for *The Morning Post* and *The Times.* Besides various volumes of poems, parodies and critical essays, he wrote on Russia, and produced some fiction and other works such as *Sarah Bernhardt* (1933).
Fiction
Glass Mender and Other Stories, The [C] (J. Nisbet, London, 1910, 260 pp., illus.) (Heinemann, London, 1926, 210 pp.)
11 stories: "The Glass Mender"; "The Blue Rose"; "The Story of Vox Angelica and Lieblich Gedacht"; "The Vagabond"; "The Minstrel"; "The Hunchback, the Pool, and the Magic Ring"; "The Silver Mountain"; "The Ring"; "The Merchant's Daughter"; "The Cunning Apprentice"; "Orestes and the Dragon"; "The Wise Princess."

Half a Minute's Silence and Other Stories [C] (Doubleday Page, New York, 1925, 204 pp., $2.00) (Heinemann, 8/6)
25 stories: "The Alternative"; "The Antichrist"; "Brass Ring"; "Chun Wa"; "Cricket Match"; "Dirge in Marriage"; "Dr. Faust's Last Day"; "Fete Galante"; "Flute of Chang Laing"; "The Garland"; "Governor's Niece"; " 'Habent Sua Fata Libelli' "; "Half a Minute's Silence"; "The Ikon"; "The Island"; "Luncheon-Party"; "Man Who Gave Good Advice"; "Pogrom"; "Police Officer"; "Prodigal Who Came Back Too Late"; "Russalka"; "Shadow of a Midnight"; "The Thief"; "Venus"; " 'What Is Truth?' "

BARING-GOULD, SABINE (28 Jan 1834–2 Jan 1924) British author. He wrote over 50 books of fiction but was probably better

known for his other writings, such as *The Book of Were Wolves* (1865), *Historic Oddities and Strange Events* (1889-90), and *Strange Survivals* (1892). Many of his best books were about Devon, Cornwall, and the West Country.
Fiction [One other fantasy–*The Crock of Gold* (1899)]
Book of Ghosts, A [C] (Putnam, New York, 1904, 383 pp., illus.–D. Murray Smith) (Methuen, London, 1904, 392 pp., 6/-)
21 stories: "Jean Brishon"; "Pomps and Vanities"; "McAlister"; "The Leaden Ring"; "The Mother of Pansies"; "The Red Haired Girl"; "A Professional Secret"; "H.P."; "Glamr"; "Colonel Halifax's Ghost Story"; "The Merewigs"; "The 'Bold Venture' "; "Mustapha"; "Little Joe Gander"; "A Dead Finger"; "Black Ram"; "A Happy Release"; "The 9.30 Up-Train"; "On the Leads"; "Aunt Joanna"; "The White Flag."

BARJAVEL, RENÉ (1911–) French sf author with a number of original stories in the French magazine *Anticipation* and other series.
Fiction
Ashes, Ashes (*Ravage*, Denoël, Paris, 1943) Trans.–D. Knight: (Doubleday, New York, 1967, 215 pp., $3.95)
Unconnected cataclysms occur, electrical forces disappear, and a rural haven develops in France.

BARKER, GRAY
Nonfiction
They Knew Too Much About Flying Saucers (Univ. Books, 1956, 256, $3.50) (Laurie, London, 1958, 256 pp., 18/-) (*The Unidentified*, Badger: SS3, 1960, 156 pp., pa 2/6) (Tower: 43-817, 1967, 190 pp., pa 60¢)
Tells of the three men in black suits who go around hushing up saucer researchers and pledging them to secrecy; gives a picture of life in the inner circles of saucer devotees.
Unidentified, The [pa] See *They Knew Too Much About Flying Saucers.*

BARKER, SHIRLEY (4 Apr 1911–1965) U.S. librarian, author and poet. She was at the New York Public Library 1940-53, and then became a professional writer. Her verse includes *The Dark Hills Under.*
Fiction
Peace, My Daughters (Crown, New York, 1949, ix+248 pp., $3.00) (Ambassador, Toronto, $3.50) (Allen, London, 1952, xii+263 pp., 10/6)
The Devil in 17th Century Salem—deftly written, poignant and gripping.
Swear by Apollo (Random, New York, 1958, 306 pp., $3.95)

BARLOW, JAMES (1 Dec 1921–) British novelist; educated at Leamington Spa, Stoke-on-Trent and North Wales. In 1940 he became a gunnery instructor in the R.A.F., but TB ended his service career. While in hospital he began to write technical articles for *Flight* and *Aeroplane.* Later he wrote for *Punch* (1948-53); then his novels appeared, beginning with *The Protagonists* (1956), *One Half of the World* (1957), and *The Man With Good Intentions.* It was not until *The Patriots* (1960) that the critics and public took notice—he was a rating inspector in Birmingham at that time. His *Term of Trial* (1961) was made into a very successful film in 1962, starring Sir Laurence Olivier and Sarah Miles. He does extensive research for all his books—nine months for *The Hour of Maximum Danger*, on communist espionage, which was written as a warning but seems more of a prophecy. *The Patriots* was a selection of the Book Society and was to be published in ten foreign countries. Mr. Barlow is married and has three children.
Fiction
One Half of the World (Cassell, London, 1957, 215, 13/6) (Harper, New York, 1957, 277 pp., $3.50)
Britain is ruled by a regime of Marxist outlook; a detective regains his faith in God and humanity and comes into direct conflict with the regime's principles.

BARNARD, MARJORIE FAITH See ELDERSHAW, M. B.

BARNES, ARTHUR K(ELVIN) (1911-1969) U.S. writer. He was born in Bellingham, Wash., but spent most of his life in the Los Angeles area. He graduated from UCLA and was a Phi Beta Kappa. He was a free-lance writer, and also served in the military (OTC) in peacetime. He was a member of Peter Pan Country Club and American Contract Bridge Club. He wrote all kinds of fiction, including detective, horror, sports, adventure and sf. His first sf appearance was "Lord of the Lightning" (*WS*, Dec 1931); a short novel of interest is "Fog Over Venus" (*TWS*, Win 1945; *FSM*, Spr 1955).
Series
Carlyle, Gerry "The Hothouse Planet" (*TWS*, Oct 1937; *SS*, Sep 1949); "The Dual World" (*TWS*, June 1938); "Satellite Five" (*TWS*, Oct 1938); "The Energy Eaters"* (*TWS*, Oct 1939; *SS*, Sep 1950); "The Seven Sleepers"* (*TWS*, May 1940); "Trouble on Titan" (*TWS*, Feb 1941; *FSM*, Fall 1954); "Siren Satellite" (*TWS*, Win 1946). Five stories published as *Interplanetary Hunter*.
   * Collaborations with H. Kuttner, bringing in 'Tony Quade.'
Fiction
Interplanetary Hunter (Gnome, New York, 1956, 231 pp., illus.–Emsh, $3.00) ([German], 3 parts: *Jagd im Weltall, Jenseits des Mondes, Almussens Komet*; *UZ*: 106, 107, 111; 1957, 1958) (*Caceria interplanetaria* [Spanish], Nebula: 95, 1964, pa)
   The zoological exploits of Carlyle and Strike, adapted from the original stories: 1. Venus ("Hothouse Planet"); 2. Jupiter ("Satellite Five"); 3. Neptune ("Siren Satellite"); 4. Almussen's Comet ("The Seven Sleepers"); 5. Saturn ("Trouble on Titan").

BARNHOUSE, PERL T.
Fiction
My Journeys With Astargo (Bell, Denver, 1952, 212 pp.)
   A 40-credit tour of many worlds. See extended review in D. Knight's *In Search of Wonder* (2nd Ed., 1967).

BARR, DENSIL N.
Fiction
Man With Only One Head, The (Rich Cowan, London, 1955, 192 pp., 9/6) (Digit: R558, 1962, 156 pp., pa 2/6)
   Similar to Pat Frank's *Mr. Adam*, in that a world catastrophe results in only one man being fertile; a World Federation is formed with much subsequent intrigue.

BARR, ROBERT (1850–1912) A fantasy besides those below is *From Whose Bourne* (Stokes, New York & London, 1896).
Fiction
Face and the Mask, The [C] (Hutchinson, London, 1894, 3/6) (Stokes, New York, 1895, 250 pp., illus.–A. Hencke)
   Mixed, 24 stories, some fantasy: "The Woman of Stone"; "The Chemistry of Anarchy"; "The Fear of It"; "The Metamorphoses of Johnson"; "The Reclamation of Joe Hollends"; "The Typewritten Letter"; "The Doom of London" (*F&SF*, July 1954); "The Predicament of de Plonville"; "A New Explosive"; "The Great Pegram Mystery"; "Death Cometh Soon or Late"; "High Stakes"; " 'Where Ignorance Is Bliss' "; "The Departure of Cub M'Lean"; "Old Number Eighty-Six"; "Playing With Marked Cards"; "The Bruiser's Courtship"; "The Raid on Mellish"; "Striking Back"; "Crandall's Choice"; "The Failure of Bradley"; "Ringamy's Convert"; "A Slippery Customer"; "The Sixth Bench."
In a Steamer Chair and Other Shipboard Stories [C] (Cassell, London, 1892, 278 pp.) (Stokes, New York, 1892, 278 pp.)
   Mixed, 13 stories, some fantasy: "In a Steamer Chair"; "Mrs. Tremain"; "Share and Share Alike"; "An International Row"; "A Ladies' Man"; "A Story for the Reformation of Poker Players"; "The Man Who Was Not on the Passenger List"; "The Terrible Experience of Plodkins"; "A Case of Fever"; "How the Captain Got His Steamer Out"; "My Stowaway"; "The Purser's Story"; "Miss McMillan."

BARR, TYRONE C. British author.
Fiction
Last 14, The [pa] See *Split Worlds*
Split Worlds [pa] (Digit: D248, 1959, 156 pp., pa 2/-; R563,

1962, 160 pp., pa 2/6) (Chariot: CB150, 1960, 156 pp., pa 50¢) (*Abschied von der Erde* [German], *UG*: 172, 1962)
   Manned space station "The Wheorld" with 14 crew members stays in space after the world commits suicide, and lands five years later. Sensational and slightly sexy, with implausible selection of crew.

BARRETT, CHARLES LEE, M.D. (1909–) U.S. physician and surgeon, graduate of Western Reserve School of Medicine, Cleveland, 1933; licenced to practice in 1933; member of American Fracture Association. He is a notable collector and prominent sf fan, having probably the world's largest collection of pulp magazines of all kinds. He was founder of the annual Midwestcon regional sf convention in Ohio.

BARRETT, WILLIAM E(DMUND) (16 Nov 1900–) U.S. author and book reviewer. He was born in New York City and educated at Manhattan College; he was President of the Colorado Author's League 1943-44, and lecturer at U. of Colorado 1939-57. He has contributed to *SEP*, *Red Book*, etc., with book reviews in the Boston *Transcript* and the Boston *Post*; he has had a number of novels published, beginning with *Flight From Youth* (1940).
Fiction
Edge of Things, The [C] (Doubleday, New York, 1959, 336 pp., $3.95) (Heinemann, London, 1961, 285 pp., 18/-)
   3 stories involving aviation: "Flight From Youth"; "Velma"; "The Blue Sleep."
Fools of Time, The (Doubleday, 1963, 309 pp., $4.50) (D'day, Toronto, $4.95) (Heinemann, 1964, 309 pp., 25/-) (Cardinal: 50003, 1964, 309 pp., pa 50¢) (*De grote verleiding* [Dutch], Fontein, Utrecht, 1964) (*Serum 223* [German], Herder, 1966)
   The Russians have an immortality serum which is partly derived from cancer; the novel has some flaws in its reasoning.

BARRIE, SIR JAMES MATTHEW (9 May 1860–19 June 1937) British dramatist and novelist; M.A. Edinburgh, 1882. He was a free lance for many years, then made his name as a playwright in the early 1900s with *Quality Street*, *The Admirable Crichton* (1903), and *Peter Pan* which still lives and was based on his friend W. E. Henley's daughter Wendy, who died as a child. *Peter Pan* was filmed as a silent in 1925, and in 1953 RKO remade it in colour, produced by Walt Disney.
Fiction [Incomplete—other titles in Bleiler *Checklist*]
When Wendy Grew Up (Dutton, New York, 1958, 32 pp., $2.00)
   "An afterthought" to *Peter Pan*; a final scene performed only once (in 1908).

BARRINGER, D(ANIEL) MOREAU (1900–)
Fiction
And the Waters Prevailed (Dutton, New York, 1956, 188 pp., illus.–P. A. Hutchinson, $3.00) (Smithers, Toronto, $3.50)
   The life of a small Stone Age youth who has a keen mind.

BARRON, D(ONALD) G(ABRIEL) (1922–) English author and architect.
Fiction
Zilov Bombs, The (A. Deutsch, London, 1962, 173 pp., 16/-) (W. W. Norton, New York, 1963, 173 pp., $3.95) (Collins, Toronto, $4.25) (*100.000 degrés à Londres* [French], Laffont, 1964) (Pan: G698, 1965, 125 pp., pa 2/6)
   Thriller with England as a Soviet puppet and the underground seeking clean nuclear bombs.

BARROWS, (RUTH) MARJORIE U.S. editor of children's books; born in Chicago. She was Associate Editor of *Compton's Pictured Encyclopedia*, 1920; Associate Editor (1922-31) and Editor (1931-38) of *Child Life*; and Co-Editor for Consolidated Book Publishers, 1943-48.
Anthology
Science Fiction and Reader's Guide—Vol. 16 of *The Children's Hour* (Spencer Press, New York, 1954, 376 pp., $120 the set of 16 vols.; *not* released separately)

8 stories and 1 article: "What Time Is It?" "Adventure on Mars," R. M. Elam; "Mars and Miss Pickerell," Ellen MacGregor; "The Star Ducks," Bill Brown; "Lancelot Biggs on Saturn," N. S. Bond; "The Truth About Pyecraft," H. G. Wells; "The Black Pits of Luna," R. A. Heinlein; "Is There Life on the Moon?" H. P. Wilkins (art.); "Trail to the Stars," Capt. B. Leyson. Plus Reader's Guide, Glossary, etc.

BARTER, ALAN FRANK (20 Aug 1933–) English schoolmaster and anthologist.
Anthology
Untravelled Worlds [with R. Wilson] (Macmillan, London, 1966, 168 pp., pa 7/6)
Subtitled: "An Anthology of Science Fiction." 12 stories with compilers' foreword: "Impostor," P. K. Dick; "Meteor," J. Wyndham; "The Windows of Heaven," Anon.; "The Veldt," R. Bradbury; "Creature of the Snows," Wm. Sambrot; "Grenville's Planet," M. Shaara; "The Gentleman Is an EPWA," C. Jacobi; "Summertime on Icarus," A. C. Clarke; "One for the Books," R. Matheson; "Bitter End," E. F. Russell; "The Cricket Ball," Avro Manhattan; "The Fun They Had," I. Asimov.

BARTH, JOHN (27 May 1930–) U.S. prof. of English at Pennsylvania State Univ.; married with three children. Books previous to his 4th (below) were *The Floating Opera* (1956), *End of the Road* (1958) and *The Sot-Weed Factor* (1961)–a send-up of historical fiction.
Fiction
Giles Goat-Boy (Doubleday, New York, 1966, xxxi + 710 pp., $6.95) (Secker Warburg, London, 1967, 710 pp., 42/-) (Penguin: 2728, 1967, 813 pp., pa 8/6)
A boy brought up with goats matures into his full manhood as he meets the modern multiversity of the world.

BARTHELME, DONALD U.S. editor, born in Texas, now living in New York City. He has worked as a newspaper reporter, a magazine editor, and a museum director. He served in the U.S. Army in Korea and Japan. His fiction has appeared in *The New Yorker*, *Contact*, *New World Writing*, *Harper's Bazaar* and other magazines. He became managing editor of the art-literary review *Location* (1965), but more recently became a full-time writer.
Fiction
Come Back, Dr. Caligari [C] (Little, Brown; Boston, 1964, 183 pp., $4.95) (Little, Toronto, $6.00) (Eyre Spottiswoode, London, 1966, 183 pp., 18/-) (Anchor: A470, 1965, 138 pp., pa 95¢)
Strictly, not sf or fantasy, but some stories are surrealistic and might suit 'way out' interests: "The Big Broadcast of 1938"; "Will You Tell Me?"; "For I'm the Boy Whose Only Joy Is Loving You."

BARTLETT, LANDELL U.S. author of the scarce booklet below; around 1957 he was trying to compile an anthology of stories on Venus but it was never published.
Fiction
Vanguard of Venus, The (Gernsback, 1928, 24 pp., front.–R. E. Lawlor, 5¾ x 8¾ in.)
Noted booklet sent free upon request with special coupon from *Amazing Stories* (started in Sep 1928 issue); Gernsback wanted to find where his readers lived, for circulation purposes. It is now quite scarce.

BARUCH, HUGO (1907–)
Fiction
Out of My Mind [as Jack Bilbo] [C] (The Modern Art Gallery, London, 1946, large size, 124 pp., illus.–author, 12/6)
20 stories, supposedly spontaneously composed—some fantasy, some 'true strange,' some just gory; with Introduction: "The Strange Story of an Hors D'Oeuvre"; "The Strange Story of the Cold Lover"; "The Strange Story of the Three Warnings of Death"; "The Strange Story of a Toad"; "The Strange Story of Hen Schultze's Mistake"; "The Strange Story of a Wireless Headache"; "The Strange Story of the Miracle of the Mediterranean";

"The Strange Story of the Mad Gardener"; "The Strange Story of the Invisible Torture"; "The Strange Story of Four Cheeky Fellows"; "The Strange Story of the One-Two Music Teacher Who Killed My Shadow"; "The Strange Story of the Suicide Machine"; "The Strange Story of the Crying Madonna"; "The Strange Story of the Human Piano"; "The Strange Story of the Sighing Well"; "The Strange Story of Vampires Over London"; "The Strange Story of the Unexpected Visitor"; "The Strange Story of Three Chinamen"; "The Strange Story of a Cup of Coffee"; "Directions to the Psychiatrists in the Event of My Going Mad."

BARZMAN, BEN U.S. author; born in Toronto, Canada, of Russian ancestry; attended Reed College, Portland, Oregon. He has written film scripts in both Hollywood and England. His films include *He Who Must Die* and *Give Us This Day*. He has been living in France since 1950.
Fiction
Echo X [pa] See *Twinkle, Twinkle, Little Star*
Out of This World See *Twinkle, Twinkle, Little Star*
Twinkle, Twinkle, Little Star (Putnam, New York, 1960, 261 pp., $3.95) (D'day SF B.C., 1960, $1.20) (*Out of This World* Collins, London, 1960, 320 pp., 15/-; Collins, Toronto, $3.50; Fontana: 681, 1963, 255 pp., pa 5/-) (*Fran En Annan Värld* [Swedish], Berghs, 1960) (*Echo X*, Paperback: 52-130, 1962, 252 pp., pa 50¢; 52-329, 1964, pa 50¢; 54-684, 1968, pa 75¢)
Inventors on Earth contact a twin Earth which sends people practically identical to those on this Earth, with consequent mix-up.

BASHFORD, SIR HENRY HOWARTH (1880–16 Aug 1961) British novelist and physician; medical officer with the English Post Office (1933-43) and medical advisor to the Treasury (1943-45).
Fiction
Happy Ghost and Other Stories, The [C] (Harper, New York, 1925, 280 pp., $2.50) (Heinemann, London, 1925, 280 pp., 7/6)
20 stories: "Back to the Trees"; "Before Dinner"; "Bishop's Move"; "The Brink"; "Crossing the Bridge"; "The Escape"; "Farquarson"; "Father Prescott's Creed"; "Gardener of Eden"; "Gentleman Upstairs"; "God and the Bud Openers"; "Good Beds for Gentlemen"; "The Happy Ghost"; "Human Factor"; "Last of the Aristocrats"; "Maud"; "The Miracle"; "Mr. Curgenven-Curgenven"; "Mr. Parchester and the Gods"; "Waiter Whose Hand Shook."

BATEMAN, FREDERICK See SOAL, S. G. (co-author)

BATEMAN, ROBERT (MOYES CARRUTHERS) (21 June 1922–) British radio figure and author. He was born in Manchester, and educated in Australia and England with college in England and Scotland. He served in the Merchant Navy in World War II, and has been a member of the BBC since 1949, being Sports Editor and News Film Commentator since 1956. Besides revising *The Hands of Orlac* (1961), he has written books on philately and amateur movies.
Fiction
When the Whites Went (Dobson, London, 1963, 183 pp., 15/-) (Walker, New York, 1964, 183 pp., $3.75) (Digit: R854, 1964, 158 pp., pa 2/6)
Negroes, the only survivors in England of a deadly disease, battle to live.

BATES, ARLO (16 Dec 1850–24 Aug 1918) American novelist, poet and teacher. He was born at East Machias, Maine. Following education at Washington Academy, he obtained his B.S. in 1876, then M.A. in 1879 from Bowdoin College (which also conferred an honorary Litt.D. on him in 1894). He was editor of the Boston *Sunday Courier* 1880-1893, which was also his most productive literary period. Later he wrote poetry, of which most is forgotten, and as Professor of English at Massachusetts Institute of Technology produced many textbooks which are still of use.

Fiction
Intoxicated Ghost and Other Stories, The [C] (Houghton Mifflin, Boston & New York, 1908, 303 pp.)

Weird, 9 stories: "The Intoxicated Ghost"; "A Problem in Portraiture"; "The Knitters in the Sun"; "A Comedy in Crape"; "A Meeting of the Psychical Club"; "Tim Calligan's Grave-Money"; "Miss Gaylord and Jenny"; "Dr. Polnitzski"; "In the Virginia Room."

BATES, HARRY (1900–) U.S. editor and author. He worked at a variety of jobs, including acting and writing a one-act play (*Philly*) which was produced, until he became editor of several Clayton magazines. These included *Astounding Stories* (later *Astounding Science Fiction*, now *Analog Science Fiction/Science Fact*) and its companion *Strange Tales*. His story "Farewell to the Master" (*ASF*, Oct 1940) was the basis for the film *The Day the Earth Stood Still* (1951). Other notable stories include: "A Matter of Size" (*ASF*, Apr 1934); "Alas, All Thinking" (*ASF*, June 1935); "The Experiment of Dr. Sarconi" (*TWS*, July 1940). In 1953 he appeared in the short-lived *Science Fiction Plus*.
Series
Carse, Hawk [by Anthony Gilmore, pseudonym of Bates and D. W. Hall] "Hawk Carse" (*ASF*, Nov 1931); "The Affair of the Brains" (*ASF*, Mar 1932); "The Bluff of the Hawk" (*ASF*, May 1932); "The Passing of Ku Sui" (*ASF*, Nov 1932); "The Return of Hawk Carse" (*AS*, Aug 1942, by Bates only). Published as *Space Hawk*.
Fiction
Space Hawk [as Anthony Gilmore] (Greenberg, New York, 1952, 274 pp., $2.75) (Ambassador, Toronto, $3.25) (*Il falco degli spazi* [Italian], *Urania*: 36, 1954) (*Der Unsichtbare Asteroid* and *Rivalen im All* [German, 2 parts], AWA, 1954; *T*: 216, 218, 1962)

The swashbuckling *Hawk Carse* series.

BATES, HERBERT ERNEST (16 May 1905–) English writer, born at Rusden, Northampton. His first novel, *The Two Sisters* (1926), was published when he was 21. By 1941, when he joined the R.A.F., he had had 18 volumes of fiction and other works published. He was the first short-story writer commissioned by the British government to write about the R.A.F.; his work appeared under the pseudonym "Flying Officer." He has written further novels since the war.
Fiction
Seven Tales and Alexander [C] (Scholastic Press, London, 1929, 166 pp., 7/6; 1,000 copies) (Viking, New York, 1930, 201 pp., $2.00)

Fantasy, 8 stories: "Alexander"; "The Barber"; "The Child"; "A Comic Actor"; "The Peach-Tree"; "A Tinker's Donkey"; "The King Who Lived on Air"; "Lanko's White Mare."

BATES, RALPH (3 Nov 1899–) English novelist. He served as a private for the last years of World War I and then in 1923 went to live in Spain, remaining there until the end of the Spanish Civil War. He also lived for a time in Mexico, and has written many forceful novels of Spain and Mexico. He was adjunct professor of literature at New York U. for several years from 1948.
Fiction
Miraculous Horde and Other Stories, The [C] (J. Cape, London, 1939, 315 pp., 7/6) (Nelson, Toronto) (*Sirocco and Other Stories*, Random, New York, 1939, 388 pp., $2.50)

Fantasy of 8 stories: "Monastery With Curled Clouds"; "The Miraculous Horde"; "Jarama Ballad"; "Brunette Ballad"; "The Yoke"; "43rd Division"; "The Haunted Man"; "Burning Corn." The *Cumulative Book Index* says both titles are the same book; hence "Sirocco" may be an added story or a retitled one.
Sirocco and Other Stories [C] See *Miraculous Horde, The*

BATTEAU, DWIGHT W. (25 Sep 1916–) U.S. scientist (Sc.D.); has often contributed nonfiction to *ASF*.
Nonfiction
Stupidtheorems (Author, Mass., 1966, $2.00)

Mathematical theorems, information theory basics, and meaning theory concepts translated into English.

BAUER, WOLFGANG
Fiction
Golden Casket, The [with Herbert Franke] [C] (Harcourt Brace & World, New York, 1964, viii+391 pp., illus., $7.50) (Longmans, Toronto, $9.50) (Allen & Unwin, London, 1965, viii+391 pp., 40/-)

Translated by Christopher Levenson from the German original (*Chinese Die Goldene Truhe*, Carl Hauser, Munich) with introduction by H. Franke; English versions had the benefit of supervision and advice from Arthur Waley; illustrated by Chinese woodcuts contemporary to the stories. From the vast treasure house of Chinese narrative literature this is a selection of 46 novellas from over two millennia. Chronologically arranged, they throw light on the development of Chinese social and moral history; from archaic and heroic harshness they lead to love as the favourite theme, and also cover supernatural and religious influences.

BAUM, L(YMAN) FRANK (5 May 1856–6 May 1919) U.S. author, the first great creator of purely American fairy tales, inventing wondrous countries such as Mo, Yew, Ix and Merryland. He is most noted, however, for his *Oz* books. Martin Gardner's article on Baum's life "The Royal Historian of Oz" (*F&SF*, sr2, Jan 1955) was later enlarged by Gardner and Nye as *The Wizard of Oz and Who He Was* (Michigan State Univ. Press, 1957, $3.75). A further fantasy was *The Master Key: An Electrical Fairy Tale* (Bowen-Merrill, Indianapolis, 1901).
Series
Oz Oz was one of the wondrous countries invented by Baum. The series began with *The Wonderful Wizard of Oz* (1900), followed by a sequel *The Marvellous Land of Oz* (1904), and quite a number more until 1921. Various other authors took over the series, with Jack Snow writing the last ones including the 40th volume *Who's Who in Oz* (1954), which summarizes the 39 plots and discusses the many aspects of the series. MGM's famous film was *The Wizard of Oz* (1939), starring Judy Garland as Dorothy, Bert Lahr (Cowardly Lion), Ray Bolger (Scarecrow), and Jack Haley (Tin Woodman); this was preceded by three relative failures —in 1910 by Selig Pictures; in 1914 by Oz Film Company (Baum's own company); and in 1925 by Chadwick Pictures (with Larry Semon as the Scarecrow).
Fiction
Surprising Adventures of the Magical Monarch of Mo, The (U.S.A., 1900) (Dover: T1892, 1968, 237 pp., illus., pa $2.00)

This was first published in Oct 1900, a month after the author's *Wonderful Wizard of Oz*, when he didn't know which book would sell the best. The public gave its answer and the "Oz" series followed. *The Monarch of Mo* consists of 14 episodes which have a quaint turn-of-the-century charm and mirror a happier, more innocent era—kings battle dragons, princes go on conquests, and princesses are bewitched. The Dover edition includes 15 full-page colour plates and more than 100 line drawings from the first two editions.

BAXTER, JOHN Australian free-lance journalist living in Sydney, becoming a script writer with Commonwealth Film Unit in mid-1966. He has been a sf writer since 1963, appearing in *New Worlds*, *Science-Fantasy* and *Analog* magazines, and the *New Writings in SF* series (compiled by E. J. Carnell). He has written extensively on the cinema and is co-editor of the magazine *Film Digest*.
Fiction
God Killers, The [pa] See *Off-Worlders, The*
Off-Worlders, The [pa] ("The God Killers," *NW*, sr2, June 1966; Horwitz: PB345, 1968, 127 pp., pa 55¢) (Ace: G-588, 1966, 127 pp., pa 50¢; with *The Star Magician*)

Adventure on a backward farming-society world with old science forbidden.
Anthology
Pacific Book of Australian Science Fiction [pa] (Angus & Rob-

ertson 'Pacific 92,' Sydney, 1968, 180 pp., pa $1.00)

12 stories and Compiler's Introduction: "Burning Spear," Kit Denton; "It Could Be You," Frank Roberts; "The Evidence," Lee Harding; "An Ounce of Dissension," Martin Loran (pseud.); "The Weather in the Underworld," Colin Free; "All My Yesterdays," Damien Broderick; "Final Flower," Stephen Cook; "For Men Must Work," Frank Bryning; "Beach," John Baxter; "All Laced Up," Bertram Chandler; "Strong Attraction," Ron Smith; "There Is a Crooked Man," Jack Wodhams.

BAXTER, (Mrs) MARIA
Nonfiction (?)
My Saturnian Lover (Vantage, New York, 1958, 72 pp., $2.50)

Flying saucer type; author describes her awareness of Alyn, a mysterious young man (from Saturn) who has contact with people of other worlds.

BAYLDON, ARTHUR ALBERT
Fiction
Tragedy Behind the Curtain and Other Stories, The [C] (S. D. Townsend, Sydney, 1910, 209 pp.)

Fantasy, 18 stories (not in Bleiler *Checklist*): "The Tragedy Behind the Curtain"; "Document Found in a Mirror"; "Dr. Grahame's Great Experiments: Part I – In the Haunted House"; "Dr. Grahame's Great Experiments: Part II – Between Two Worlds"; "Benson's Flutter for a Fortune"; "Thirst!"; "The Triumph of Faith"; "Jennie"; "Ned's Return"; "An Experience of Old Yorkie's"; "Little Paul"; "Waiting"; "A Pawn of Fate's"; "A Study in White and Yellow"; "His Invisible Enemy"; "The Romance of a Moth"; "The Poet's Vision"; "The Philosopher's Dream."

BAYLISS, ALFRED EDWARD MacDUFF (1892–) British schoolmaster and author; educated at Westminster and Univ. of London. He contributed to *The Schoolmaster* (1929-34), and has written numerous Certificate English and other textbooks as well as a number of plays for boys.
Anthology
Science in Fiction [with J. C. Bayliss] (Univ. London 'Pilot Book,' 1957, 191, 4/3, no dust-jacket)

A selection meant presumably to liven up high-school English. It contains one complete short story–"The Star," H. G. Wells– and 11 episodes (titled by the compilers, but not given here) from books: Clarke's *Prelude to Space*; Lucian's *True Story*; Swift's *Third Voyage of Gulliver*; Doyle's *The Lost World*; Mercier's *Journal of the Year 2440*; Lewis' *Out of the Silent Planet*; Wells' *The Food of the Gods*; Seamark's *The Avenging Ray*; Verne's *20,000 Leagues Under the Sea*; Wyndham's *The Day of the Triffids*; and Northrup/Pseudoman's *Zero to Eighty*.

BAYLISS, JOHN CLIFFORD (4 Oct 1919–) British civil servant; born Wotton-under-Edge, Gloucester, son of A. E. M. Bayliss; M.A., St. Catherine's College, Cambridge. Has worked at Macmillan and in the Colonial Office.
Anthology
Science in Fiction See BAYLISS, A. E. M. (co-anthologist)

BEAGLE, PETER S(OYER) (29 Apr 1939-) U.S. author. He was born and brought up in the Bronx, and graduated from U. of Pittsburgh in 1959. He lived in Paris, travelled in France, Italy and England, and then spent a year at Stanford U. on a writing fellowship. He now lives in Santa Cruz, Calif.
Fiction
Fine and Private Place, A (Viking, New York, 1960, 272 pp., $3.95) (Dell: Delta 2530, 1960, 272 pp., pa $1.85) (Corgi: GN1273, 1963, 222 pp., pa 3/6)

A different type of "ghost" story in the escape from reality of hermit-like Mr. Rebeck living in a mausoleum in the Yorkchester cemetery.
Last Unicorn, The (Viking, New York, 1968, 218 pp., $4.95) (Bodley Head, London, 1968, 218 pp., 25/-)

A touching fairy tale, the story of a quest–by a unicorn–for her lost fellows.

BEARDSLEY, AUBREY (VINCENT) (1872–16 Mar 1898) British draughtsman, artist and writer, particularly remembered in the weird and fantasy field for his art work. He first worked as a clerk, drawing in his spare time. He had a very eventful life but was most unhappy at being linked with Oscar Wilde, as public opinion reacted against him also. He began working for *Pall Mall Magazine* and *Pall Mall Budget* in 1892, later being art editor for some journals, and was elected a member of the New English Art Club in 1893. In spite of TB he was brilliant, prolific, and vastly influential. He is primarily remembered for his illustrations for such books as *Le Mort d'Arthur* (1893), *Salome* (1894), and *Rape of the Lock* (1896). Collections of his works include: *An Album of Fifty Drawings* (1896); *The Early Works of Aubrey Beardsley* (1899)–with many of his early famous paintings; *The Best of Beardsley* (Spring Books, London, *ca.* 1950, quarto)–150 examples of his art; *The Art of Aubrey Beardsley* (Modern Library). A bibliography of his work was produced by E. A. Gallatin and published by the Grolier Society. A more recent work was *Beardsley*, by Stanley Weintraub (W. H. Allen, London, 1967, 35/-).

BEATTY, JEROME, JR.
Fiction
Matthew Looney's Invasion of the Earth (W. R. Scott, New York, 1965, 155 pp., $3.25; lib. $3.50) (S. J. R. Saunders, Toronto, $4.25)

Juvenile.

BEAUMONT, CHARLES (pseud) See NUTT, C.

BEBBINGTON, W(ILLIAM) G(EORGE) British poet. His works include *Introducing Modern Poetry*, *Poems for Everyone*, and a selection of narrative poems, *A Tale Told*.
Anthology
Fancy Free (Allen Unwin, London, 1949, 131 pp., 6/-; school ed. 3/-)

Fantasy, 9 stories with compilers' foreword and notes on authors: "Uncle Arthur," John Pudney; "A Horseman in the Sky," A. Bierce; "The Truth About Pyecraft," H. G. Wells; "The Dancers," Eric Linklater; "The Ghost Ship," Richard Middleton; "How Jembu Played for Cambridge," Lord Dunsany; "Wottie," A. J. Alan; "Over the Side," W. W. Jacobs; "The Celestial Omnibus," E. M. Forster.

BECHDOLT, JOHN ERNEST (JACK) (1884–) U.S. journalist. He was with the Seattle *Post-Intelligencer* 1906-16; he then moved to New York to work as a reader at Munsey Publications. After a year he changed to free-lancing; his first novel was *The Torch*.
Fiction [Incomplete—other titles in Bleiler *Checklist*]
Torch, The (*Arg*, sr5, 24 Jan 1920) (Prime, Philadelphia, 1948, 299 pp., illus.–Tschirky, $2.50) (*FN*, Apr 1951)

Adventure in the New York of 3050 A.D. after a world catastrophe.

BECK, CALVIN (THOMAS) (1930–) U.S. sf and fantasy fan, quite prominent in post-war fan activities. At one time he was endeavouring to publish an anthology of fan fiction.
Anthology
Frankenstein Reader, The [pa] (Ballantine: F680, 1962, 159 pp., pa 50¢)

Weird, 11 stories: "The Middle Toe of the Right Foot," A. Bierce; "The Four-Fifteen Express," Amelia B. Edwards; "Passeur," R. W. Chambers; "The Isle of Voices," R. L. Stevenson; "The Ghost of Fear," H. G. Wells; "The Trial for Murder," C. Dickens; "The Dead Valley," R. A. Cram; "The Thing in the Hall," E. F. Benson; "A Pair of Hands," Sir A. T. Quiller-Couch; "The Ghost Ship," R. Middleton; "On the Staircase," Katharine F. Gerould.

BECK, (Mrs.) LILY ADAMS (? –3 Jan 1931) British novelist and mystic. The daughter of Admiral John Moresby, she had her first acquaintance with the Orient when he was stationed there. After World War I she made her home in British Columbia but travelled widely. She is primarily noted for her best sellers of 1924 and 1925, *The Divine Lady* (about Nelson and Lady Hamilton) and *Glorious Apollo* (a fictional study of Byron). She was thoroughly versed in Oriental doctrine and was a very fine writer of this class of story; she claimed she never knew weariness of mind and body. Besides her own name she used the pseudonyms E. Barrington and L. Moresby.

Fiction [Collections only; see Bleiler *Checklist* for novels]
Dreams and Delights [C]   (Dodd Mead, New York, 1926, 317 pp., $2.50) (Benn, London, 1932, 288 pp., 7/6)

11 stories: "V. Lydiat"; "The Bride of a God"; "The Sea of Lilies"; "The Beloved of the Gods"; "The Hidden One"; "The Marriage of the Princess"; "The Wisdom of the Orient"; "Stately Julia"; "The Island of Pearls"; "The Wonderful Pilgrimage to Amarnath"; "The Man Without a Sword."

Ninth Vibration and Other Stories, The [C]   (Dodd Mead, 1922, 333 pp., $2.50) (Unwin, London, 1928, 280, 7/6) (Benn, 1930, 288 pp., 3/6)

8 stories: "The Ninth Vibration"; "The Interpreter"; "The Incomparable Lady"; "The Hatred of the Queen"; "Fire of Beauty"; "The Building of the Taj Mahal"; "How Great Is the Glory of Kwannon!"; "Round-Faced Beauty."

Openers of the Gate, The [C]   (Cosmopolitan, New York, 1930, 368 pp., $2.50)

10 occult stories: "The Openers of the Gate"; "Lord Killary"; "How Felicity Came Home"; "Waste Manor"; "The Mystery of Iniquity"; "Many Waters Cannot Quench Love"; "The Horoscope"; "The Thug"; "Hell"; "The Man Who Saw."

Perfume of the Rainbow and Other Stories, The [C]   (Dodd Mead, 1923, 324 pp., $2.00) (Benn, 1931, 288 pp., 7/6; 1932, 3/6)

16 stories: "The Man and the Lesser Gods"; "Juana"; "The Courtesan of Vaisali"; "The Flute of Krishna"; "The Emperor and the Silk Goddess"; "The Loveliest Lady of China"; "The Ghost Plays of Japan"; "The Marvels of Xanadu"; "From the Ape to Buddha"; "The Sorrow of the Queen"; "The Perfect One"; "The Way of Attainment"; "The Day Book of a Court Lady of Old Japan"; "The Courtesan Princess"; "The Happy Solitudes"; "The Desolate City."

BECKE, LOUIS (1855–1913)
Fiction
Strange Adventure of James Shervington and Other Stories, The [C] (T. F. Unwin, London, 1902, 319 pp., 6/-; 1926, 319 pp.) (Lippincott, Philadelphia, 1926, 319 pp., $2.00)

Fantasy, 9 stories: "The Strange Adventure of James Shervington"; "'Pig-Headed' Sailor Men"; "The Flemmings"; "'Flash Harry' of Savaii"; "Concerning 'Bully' Hayes"; "Amona; the Child; and the Beast"; "The Snake and the Bell"; "South Sea Notes"; "Apinoka of Apamama."

BECKER, KURT (1915–)
Fiction
Countdown (Benziger, New York, 1958, 179 pp., $2.95)

BECKFORD, WILLIAM (1 Oct 1760–2 May 1844) British gentleman of means, and writer of oriental tales and travel books. He is particularly noted for the fantasy *Vathek*, which appeared as two stories, the trilogy being completed by the late C. A. Smith as "The Third Episode of Vathek" (no further information). A biography of this writer is *Beckford*, G. Chapman (1952).
Fiction [all except *The Vision, Liber Veritatis* (1930)]
Episodes of Vathek, The [Trans.–Sir Frank T. Marzials] (Stephen Swift, London, 1912, 368 pp., 21/-) (Chapman & Dodd 'Abbey Classics,' 1922, 226 pp.) ([with *Vathek*; Editor–G. Chapman], Constable, London, 1929, 2 vols., 31/6, 1,000 copies)

Further adventures of Vathek.
History of the Caliph Vathek, The See *Vathek*
Vathek: An Arabian Tale (R. Bentley, London, 1834, 150 pp.) (*The History of the Caliph Vathek*, Sampson Low, London, 1881, 189 pp.) (Greening, London, 1905, 280 pp., illus.–W. S. Rogers, 1/6, 2/-) (*The Episodes of Vathek* and *Vathek*, Constable 1929

[see above]) (Trans.–H. B. Grimsditch; Nonesuch, London, 1929, 172 pp., illus.–M. V. Dorn, 17/6, 1550 copies of which 500 sold by Random in U.S.) ([Swedish], Wahlstrom & Widstrand, 1927) (in *Shorter Novels of the 18th Century* [Henderson], 1948) (Lane, London, 1953, 125 pp., illus.–Charles W. Stewart, 12/6) (Folio Society, London, 1958, 128 pp., illus.–Edward Bawden; foreword–Grimsditch) (FSB: 1575, 1966, 123 pp., pa 3/6) (in *Three Gothic Novels* [Bleiler], 1966, pa)

This was originally written in French, beginning in 1782, and was to have been published first in that language. However, Rev. Samuel Henley translated it and published it in 1786 as "An Arabian Tale From an Unpublished Manuscript," suppressing Beckford's name. Of a number of 1787 French editions, that of Lausanne is considered the first. The early editions are poor translations; Grimsditch made a fresh one from the definitive 1815 text. The bibliography above is not complete.

The story itself is considered a fantasy classic, and is noted for its remarkable knowledge of the East by one who had never travelled there—it is rich in description and teeming in imagination.

BEECHING, JACK
Fiction
Dakota Project, The (Cape, London, 1968, 256 pp., 25/-)
A man seeks to learn the true nature of a scientific project.

BEERBOHM, SIR MAX (24 Aug 1872–20 May 1956) British caricaturist and writer, educated at Charterhouse and Merton College, Oxford. He soon made a reputation as an essayist of wit and polish, and succeeded G. B. Shaw as dramatic critic of *The Saturday Review*. From 1910 he lived at Rapallo, Italy. He was knighted in 1939. His nickname 'The Incomparable Max' was given him by Shaw because of his taste in dress, in which he rivalled an 18th Century beau. His books of essays, etc., started with *The Works of Max Beerbohm* (1896), and with his drawings appeared regularly. He had only one work of fantasy interest.
Fiction
Seven Men [C] (Heinemann, London, 1919, 218 pp.) (Knopf, New York, 1920, 238 pp., illus.) (Armed: c-67, nd, pa) (Penguin: 1010, 1954, 185 pp., pa 2/-)

5 stories: "A. V. Laider"; "Enoch Soames"; "Hilary Maltby and Stephen Braxton"; "James Pethel"; "'Savonarola' Brown." Editions of 1949 and later, including paper editions titled *Seven Men and Two Others*, also contain: "Felix Argallo and Walter Ledgett" (from *A Variety of Things*).

BELAYEV, ALEXANDER (1884–1942) Russian author. He was confined to bed for years by tuberculosis of the spine. He studied law, attended the conservatoire, worked on newspapers and periodicals, and was deeply interested in science and technical problems. He produced many sf books, of which only two have seen English translation (see below); he has had some short stories in recent Russian anthologies published in English—"Over the Abyss" in *Destination: Amaltheia* and "Hoity-Toity" in *Soviet Science Fiction*.
Fiction
Amphibian, The (Foreign Languages Publishing House, Moscow, nd–late '50s, 285 pp., *ca.* $1.00)

Originally written in 1928. It is similar to Wells' *The Island of Dr. Moreau*, but set in Argentina with the creation of weird life forms including a man with gills. It was filmed as *The Amphibian Man*, in colour, directed by Gennady Kazansky and produced by Lenfilm.
Struggle in Space, The [1928; trans.–A. Parry] (Arfor, U.S.A., 1965, 116 pp., $4.95)

Death rays, evil Americans, and the conquest of the U.S.A.

BELING, MABEL ASHE
Fiction
Wicked Goldsmith: Tales of Ancient India, The [C] (Harper, New York & London, 1941, 144 pp., illus.–Owen Smith, $1.75) (Musson, Toronto, $2.50)

Fantasy, 7 stories with Introduction and Afterword: "For the Arm of Parvati"; "Always Look at Your Coachman's Feet"; "Half a God, and All a Hero"; " 'This Hound Hath Loved Me' "; "Markanda"; "The Wicked Goldsmith"; "The Abbot Whose Prayer Was Answered"; "About the Indian Epics" (afterword).

BELL, ERIC TEMPLE (7 Feb 1883–20 Dec 1960) U.S. mathematician and author, better known in the sf field for his fiction under the pseudonym "John Taine." He was born in Aberdeen Scotland. As a schoolboy he was influenced by a mathematics teacher of rare distinction, E. M. Langley of Bedford, and later became a research mathematician. He went to the U.S. in 1902, took his master's degree at U. of Washington in 1908 and a doctorate from Columbia in 1912. He taught at U. of Washington until 1926. He then became Professor of Mathematics at California Institute of Technology in 1927; he retired from there in 1953. He became noted outside his profession for his books on mathematics for the intelligent layman; the most notable were *Men of Mathematics* (1937), *The Development of Mathematics* (1940) and *Mathematics, Servant of Science* (1952). He was a member of many learned societies.

Under the by-line "John Taine" he was noted for many novels in the late 1920's and 1930's. Some first appeared in magazines; most have appeared as books. Fiction that was never in book form was "Twelve Eighty-Seven" (*ASF*, sr5, May 1935) and "Tomorrow" (*Marvel*, Apr/May 1939).
Fiction
Before the Dawn (Williams Wilkins, Baltimore, 1934, 247 pp., $2.00) (in *Portable Novels of Science* [Wollheim], 1945) (*FFM*, Feb 1946)

A time-viewing device graphically portrays Earth in the saurian age, ending with a fight of the giants.
Cosmic Geoids and One Other, The (FPCI, Los Angeles, 1949, 179 pp., illus./jacket–Lou Goldstone, $3.00; 1950, $3.00) (*Spaceway*, sr3, Dec 1954)

The novel is "Stapledonian"—good but not readily readable. The one other is "Black Goldfish" (*Fantasy Book*, sr2, No. 4, 1948), a poor type of "Kelleryarn." *Note:* Printings after the first edition contain no interior illustrations.
Crystal Horde, The ("White Lily," *ASQ*, Win 1930) (Fantasy Press, Reading, 1952, 254 pp., $3.00) (*L'orda di cristallo* [Italian], Fantascienza: 6, 1962, pa) (*Seeds of Life & White Lily*, Dover: T1626, 1966, 367 pp., pa $2.00; Peter Smith [rebind], 1967, $4.00)

Magnificent science-horror type, though science is somewhat dated.
Forbidden Garden, The (Fantasy, Reading, 1947, 278 pp., illus.–A. J. Donnell, $3.00)

Mystery in the quest for soil from a remote part of Asia; a mixture of many factors, but not up to Taine's usual standard of plausibility.
G.O.G. 666 (Fantasy, Reading, 1954, 256 pp., $3.00) (Rich Cowan, London, 1955, 224 pp., 10/6; 1957, 6/6) (Arrow: 705, 1963, 192 pp., pa 2/6)

Communism, intrigue in the U.S.A., etc.; GOG is a Russian genetic experiment that is half ape, half brain.
Gold Tooth, The (Dutton, New York, 1927, 436 pp.) (Burt, New York, 1929, 441 pp., 75¢)
Greatest Adventure, The (Dutton, 1929, 258 pp., $2.50) (*FFM*, June 1944) (Ace: D-473, 1960, 256 pp., pa 35¢) (with *The Time Stream*, Dover: T1180, 1964, 532 pp., pa $2.00)

Adventure in the Antarctic where evolution runs wild with the creation of amazing denizens.
Green Fire (Dutton, 1928, 313 pp., $2.00) (FPCI, 1952, 313 pp., $3.00)

Taine's variation on the mad scientist theme—the story of the terrible days in the summer of 1990. It has been produced as a play. The 2nd edition is a photolithographic copy of the 1st.
Iron Star, The (Dutton, 1930, 356 pp., $2.50) (*FFM*, Sep 1943) (FPCI, 1951, 312 pp., $3.00)

An immense metallic meteorite causes hallucinations; long exposure reverses evolution in the individual–turning man into ape.

Purple Sapphire, The (Dutton, 1924, 325 pp.) (*FFM*, Aug 1948) (with *The Time Stream*, Dover: T1180, 532 pp., pa $2.00)

Adventure in the depths of Tibet in the search for the sapphire.
Quayle's Invention (Dutton, 1927, 451 pp.)

Process for electrically precipitating gold from sea-water, and the subsequent intrigue.
Seeds of Life (*ASQ*, Fall 1931) (Fantasy, Reading, 1951, 255 pp., $2.75) (Galaxy Novel: 13, 1953, 174 pp., pa 35¢) (Rich Cowan, London, 1955, 192 pp., 8/6) (*Germes de vie* [French], Hachette Le RF, 1953) (Panther: 784, 1959, 156 pp., pa 2/6) (*L'uomo che visse nel futuro* [Italian], Biblioteca Economica Mondadori) (with *White Lily*, Dover, 1966, 367 pp., pa $2.00; Peter Smith [rebind], 1967, $4.00)

A scientist produces a superman.
Singer, The [by "J.T."] (Gorham Press, Boston, 1916, 166 pp.)

A book of poetry, not listed in the Bleiler *Checklist*, and given here for interest: "J.T." is an old pseudonym for "James Temple." Contains: "The Singer" and *Shorter Jets:* "Remark"; "Love in 1915"; "Werther Exhumed"; "William in Belgium"; "Ballad of England's Secret"; "David in Heaven"; "War-Poetry"; "A Quarter of a Century of Song"; "The Advancement of Learning"; "The Giant"; "Flowers"; "The Last Stand."

"The Singer" is partly fantasy and "England's Secret" completely. The title poem was done as a lampoon. The book is copyrighted by Richard C. Badger, probably a further pseudonym.
Time Stream, The (*WS*, sr4, Dec 1931) (Buffalo Book Co., Buffalo, 1946, 251 pp., $3.00) (*Le flot du temps* [French], Gallimard Le RF, 1957) (with *The Greatest Adventure* and *The Purple Sapphire*, Dover: T1180, 532 pp., pa $2.00)

One of the first novels to develop the idea of time as a flowing stream; high class but involved.
White Lily See *Crystal Horde, The*

BELL, NEIL (pseud) See SOUTHWOLD, S.

BELL, NORMAN
Fiction
Weightless Mother, The (Follett, New York, 1967, 144 pp., illus.–W. T. Mars, $3.50)

Juvenile.

BELL, PAUL W. See ROBINETT, R. F. (co-author)

BELL, ROBERT Note: *Contemporary Authors* lists two writers of this name, neither of whom acknowledges the work herewith.
Fiction
In Realms Unknown (Vantage, New York, 1954, 194 pp., $3.00)

Two men embark upon years of strange adventure as they fly to the Moon.

BELLAMY, EDWARD (26 Mar 1850–22 May 1898) U.S. author and social reformer; he studied in Schenectady and Germany. He was admitted to the bar in 1871 but became Associate Editor of the Springfield *Union* and then an editorial writer for the New York *Evening Post*. His first works were light fiction, e.g. *Dr. Heidenhoff's Process* (1880). He later wrote *Looking Backward, 2000-1887* (1888), which became the most popular of the American utopian romances and has been translated into many other languages; this has kept his name alive today. The sequel, *Equality* (1897; Judd, Sydney, 1932), and his attempts as writer, lecturer and politician to promote his communistic theories under the title "Nationalism" are, however, almost forgotten. A biographical study is *Edward Bellamy*, by Arthur E. Morgan (Columbia, 1944).
Fiction [Incomplete—other titles in Bleiler *Checklist*]
Blindman's World and Other Stories, The [C] (Houghton Mifflin, Boston & New York, 1898, 415 pp.)

15 stories: "The Blindman's World"; "An Echo of Antietam"; "The Old Folks' Party"; "The Cold Snap"; "Two Days' Solitary Imprisonment"; "A Summer Evening's Dream"; "Pott's Painless Cure"; "A Love Story Reversed"; "Deserted"; "Hooking Watermelons"; "A Positive Romance"; "Lost"; "With the Eyes Shut"; "At Pinney's Ranch"; "To Whom This May Come."

Looking Backward, 2000-1887 (Ticknor, Boston, 1888, 470 pp.) (W. Reeves, U.S., 1889, 247 pp.) ([French], Dentu, Paris, 1890) ([German], Wigand, Leipzig, 1890; Mensch & Arbeit, Zurich, 1947) ([Swedish], Björcke Börjesson, 1919) (Routledge, London, nd, 156 pp., pa np) (Judd Pub. Co., Sydney, 1932, 220 pp., pa 2/-) (Foulsham 'Pilgrim Lib.,' 1927, 188 pp., 1/6; 1945, 4/6) (World, New York, 1945, 311 pp., 49¢; 1950, 318 pp., $1.00) (Packard Univ. Classic, 1946, 233 pp., $1.25) (Dolphin: C55, nd, 234 pp., pa 95¢) (Signet: CD26, 1960, 222 pp., pa 50¢) (Lancer: 13-440, 1968, 349 pp., pa 60¢) (also several Spanish eds. and one Argentine)

Some of the printings of one of the first sf novels of any historical significance. A magically preserved survivor of the 19th century converses with dwellers in the communistic utopia of the Year 2000. *Note:* The Signet edition has an interesting introduction by Erich Fromm which helps explain the tremendous influence this book has had.

BELLAMY, FRANCIS RUFUS (24 Dec 1886–)   U.S. literary figure, born in New Rochelle. He was editor of *Outlook* 1927-32, *New Yorker* 1933, *Fiction Parade* 1935-38, and has been president of University Publishers Inc. since 1958.
Fiction
Atta   (A. A. Wyn, New York, 1953, 216 pp., $3.00) (Copp, Toronto) (Ace: D-79, 1954, 179 pp., pa 35¢; with *The Brain Stealers*)

A man hit by lightning becomes a half inch tall and makes friends with Atta, a warrior ant.

BELLAMY, HANS SCHINDLER (1901–)
Nonfiction
Atlantis Myth, The   (Faber, London, 1948, 168 pp., maps, 10/6)
An exhaustive analysis of the legend of Atlantis, with good argument for it.
Moons, Myths and Man   (Faber, 1936, 351 pp., 7/6; 2nd ed., 1949, 312 pp., illus., 16/-) (Ryerson, Toronto, 1936, $2.50) (Harper, New York, 1938, 351 pp., illus., $3.00)
Relates Hans Hoerbiger's Cosmic Ice Theory to various mythological themes.

BELLER, WILLIAM (STERN) (28 Aug 1919–)   U.S. aerodynamicist and engineer. He was born in Cleveland, Ohio; his original surname was Hyman. An aerodynamicist with Hughes Aircraft Co., he has instructed in mathematics and mechanical engineering. He has worked in public relations and has been Senior Editor of *Missiles and Rockets* from 1960.
Nonfiction
Satellite! See BERGAUST, E. (co-author)

BENEDICT, STEWART H(URD) (17 Dec 1924–)   U.S. author, born in Mineola and educated at Drew U. (A.B.) and Johns Hopkins (M.A.). He has been a college instructor in German, humanities and English; he became a free-lance writer in 1964.
Anthology
Tales of Terror and Suspense [pa]   (Dell: 8466, 1963, 288 pp., pa 45¢)
Weird, 13 stories and compiler's introduction: "Mademoiselle de Scuderi" [trans. and abr.–W. E. Reichert], E. T. A. Hoffmann; "Mateo Falcone," Prosper Mérimée; "A Descent Into the Maelstrom," Edgar A. Poe; "Mr. Justice Harbottle" [abr.], J. Sheridan Le Fanu; "The Traveller's Story of a Terribly Strange Bed," Wilkie Collins; "The Squaw," Bram Stoker; "The Hand," Guy de Maupassant; "The Adventure of the Speckled Band," Sir Arthur C. Doyle; "The Strange Ride of Morrowbie Jukes," Rudyard Kipling; "The Lodger," Marie B. Lowndes; "The Escape," Hereward Carrington; "The Vanishing Lady," Alexander Woolcott; "The Small Assassin," Ray Bradbury.

BENEFIELD, (JOHN) BARRY (1883–)
Fiction
Eddie and the Archangel Mike (Reynal & Hitchcock, New York, 1943, 310 pp., $2.50) (McClelland, Toronto, $3.00) (Armed: 710,

ca. 1944, 320 pp., pa) (*Texas, Brooklyn and Heaven*, World, New York, 1948, 310 pp., $1.00; McClelland, Toronto, $1.29)
Paths cross for a man and a girl running from life, with numerous odd and fantastic events.
Texas, Brooklyn and Heaven See *Eddie and the Archangel Mike*

BENET, LAURA
Fiction
Goods and Chattels [C]   (Doubleday, New York, 1930, 223 pp., $2.00)
Fantasy, 15 stories: "Always Keep a Butterfly"; "The Blue Village"; "Eccentric Is the Manner"; "The Girl Who Wanted a Career"; "Goods and Chattels"; "The Harvest"; "The Lake and the Mountain"; "The Magic Balloon"; "Mr. Windsor's Back Door"; "Never Rent Eyes"; "Run, Sheep, Run"; "The Saint's Three Sticks"; "Subject to the Power"; "Toxberry Tadpoles"; "The Wind That Worked Itself Up."

BENÉT, STEPHEN VINCENT (22 July 1898–13 March 1943)   U.S. poet and author; B.A. (1919), M.A. (1920), Yale; he was awarded a Guggenheim fellowship in 1926. He wrote some fine fantasy stories which originally appeared in non-fantasy magazines; these included "The King of the Cats"; "The Devil and Daniel Webster"; "Daniel Webster and the Sea Serpent"; "Johnny Pye and the Fool Killer"; "Doc Mellhorn and the Pearly Gates." Other stories not covered in the collections below were "A Tooth for Paul Revere" (*Atlantic*, Dec 1937) and "Mr. Penny and the Rhine Maiden" (*Delineator* June 1932). His *John Brown's Body* (1928) and *Western Star* (1943, posthumously published) both received Pulitzer poetry prizes. In 1940 RKO made a notable film of *The Devil and Daniel Webster*.
Fiction
Devil and Daniel Webster, The   (*SEP*, 24 Oct 1936) (Readers League of America, New York, 1937, 61 pp.) (in *Thirteen O'Clock* [Benét] and *Twenty-Five Short Stories* [Benét]; *Speak of the Devil* [North], 1945)
Some appearances of this noted novelette.
Johnny Pye and the Fool Killer   (*SEP*, 18 Sep 1937) (Countryman Press, Vermont, 1938, 78 pp., illus.–Charles Child, $3.50) (in *Tales Before Midnight* [Benét] and *Twenty-Five Short Stories* [Benét]) (*Fan*, May/June 1953)
First book edition autographed by the author.
Last Circle, The [C]   (Farrar Strauss, New York, 1946, 309 pp., $3.00) (Oxford, Toronto, $3.50) (Heinemann, London, 1948, 288 pp., 10/6)
15 stories (fy = fantasy) and verse: "The Bishop's Beggar"; "The Captives"; "The Minister's Books" (fy); "The Angel Was a Yankee" (fy); "As It Was in the Beginning"; "The Three Fates"; "A Gentleman of Fortune"; "Famous"; "Good Picker"; "The Prodigal Children"; "This Bright Dream"; "William Riley and the Fates" (fy); "The Danger of Shadows"; "The Gold Dress" (fy); "The Land Where There Is No Death."
Poems: "Annotated Edition"; "If This Should Change"; "To the People of France"; "Song for Three Soldiers"; "Remarks From a Back-Row Seat by an Amateur Propagandist"; "Tuesday, 11th May 1940"; "With a Gift of Crystal Candlesticks"; "Today I Saw You Smiling"; "For Us"; "Thirty-Five"; "For You"; "Little Testament."
Selected Works of Stephen Vincent Benét [C]   (Farrar Rinehart, New York, 1942, $5.00) (*The Stephen Vincent Benét Pocket Book*, Pocket Books: 360, 1946, x+414 pp., pa 25¢)
Edited and with introduction by Robert Van Gelder. Paper ed. has 18 stories (many fantasy) and 33 poems (not listed): "The Devil and Daniel Webster"; "Jacob and the Indians"; "Johnnie Pye and the Fool-Killer"; "A Tooth for Paul Revere"; "Freedom's a Hard-Bought Thing"; "O'Halloran's Luck"; "The Last of the Legions"; "Doc Mellhorn and the Pearly Gates"; "The Curfew Tolls"; "The King of the Cats"; "By the Waters of Babylon"; "A Death in the Country"; "No Visitors"; "Everybody Was Very Nice"; "Glamour"; "The Story About the Anteater"; "All Around the Town"; "Schooner Fairchild's Class."

Short Stories of Stephen Vincent Benét – A Selection, The [C] (Armed: C-77, *ca.* 1944, 320 pp., pa)

Fantasy, 13 stories from the Farrar & Rinehart book editions: *Stories of American History:* "Jacob and the Indians"; "A Tooth for Paul Revere"; "The Devil and Daniel Webster"; "Freedom's a Hard-Bought Thing"; "O'Halloran's Luck"; "The Die-Hard"; "Johnny Pye and the Fool-Killer." *Fantasies and Prophecies:* "The Curfew Tolls"; 'The King of the Cats"; "Doc Mellhorn and the Pearly Gates"; "The Last of the Legions"; "Into Egypt"; "By the Waters of Babylon."

Stephen Vincent Benét Pocket Book, The [C] [pa] See *Selected Works of Stephen Vincent Benét*

Tales Before Midnight [C] (Farrar Rinehart, New York, 1939, 274 pp., $2.50)

12 stories, many fantasy: "Into Egypt"; "Johnny Pye and the Fool Killer"; "O'Halloran's Luck"; "Jacob and the Indians"; "The Die-Hard"; "Doc Mellhorn and the Pearly Gates" (*SEP*, 24 Dec 1938); "The Story About the Ant-Eater"; "A Life at Angelo's"; "Too Early Spring"; "Schooner Fairchild's Class"; "Among Those Present"; "The Last of the Legions." This collection is also Part 2 of *Twenty-Five Short Stories.*

Thirteen O'Clock [C] (Farrar Rinehart, 1937, 305 pp., $2.50) (Heinemann, 1938, 352 pp., 7/6; 1939, 344 pp., 3/6)

Subtitled "Stories of Several Worlds"—13 stories, many fantasy: "By the Waters of Babylon" ("The Place of the Gods," *SEP*, 31 July 1937); "Blood of the Martyrs"; "The King of the Cats (*Golden Book*, Feb 1932); "Story of Angela Poe"; "Treasure of Vasco Gomez"; "Curfew Tolls"; "Sobbin' Women"; "The Devil and Daniel Webster"; "Daniel Webster and the Sea Serpent" (*SEP*, 22 May 1937); "Glamour"; "Everybody Was Very Nice"; "Death in the Country"; "Blossom and Fruit." This collection is also Part 1 of *Twenty-Five Short Stories.*

Twenty-Five Short Stories [C] (Sun Dial, New York, 1943, 274 pp., $1.49)

Many stories are fantasy. Consists of: Part 1—*Thirteen O'Clock* and Part 2—*Tales Before Midnight* (see both for listings).

BENJAMIN, LEWIS SAUL (30 Mar 1874–Jan 1932) U.S. anthologist of folk stories, under the pseudonym Lewis Melville.
Anthologies [as Lewis Melville with Reginald Hargreaves (not credited in Bleiler)]
Great English Short Stories (Viking, New York, 1930, 1047 pp., $5.00) (Harrap, London, 1931, 1047 pp., 8/6)

82 stories arranged chronologically by author's birth, from Barnabe Riche (*ca.* 1540) to Aldous Huxley (1894–). Many stories are fantasy or weird, including some by D. Defoe, Sir W. Scott, R. H. Barham, Lord Lytton, J. S. Le Fanu, W. Collins, H. G. Wells, etc.
Great German Short Stories (Liveright, New York, 1929, 1012 pp., $3.00) (Benn, London, 1929, 1012 pp., 8/6)

50 stories arranged roughly chronologically, with many anonymous; includes selections from Johann Wolfgang von Goethe, E. T. A. Hoffman, Albert von Chamisso, the Grimm brothers and Theodor Körner.

BENNETT, ALFRED GORDON (11 Dec 1901–) British author, F.R.S.A. (London). He was a reporter with the Liverpool *Daily Post*; founder and chairman of Pharos Books Ltd.; and assisted in founding the Warrington Art Theatre. He is a Fellow of the British Inst. Cinematography, founding member of the Inst. Amateur Cinematographers, and member of the Associate Inst. of Journalists. He produced and directed war-time training documentaries 1943-44, and has contributed articles, fiction and poetry to British, U.S. and other publications.
Fiction
Demigods, The (Jarrolds, London, 1939, 284 pp., 8/6; 1940, 4/6, 3/6) (*Les demi-dieux* [French], Hachette Le RF, 1951) (*Sconfitta dei semidei* [Italian], *Urania:* 28, 1953) (Rich Cowan, London, 1955, 368 pp., 12/6)

Giant ants directed by a brain control the world.
Whom the Gods Destroy [pa] (Pharos Books, N. Wales, 1946, 100 pp., pa 2/-)

Oriental fantasy.

Nonfiction
Focus on the Unknown (Rider, London, 1953, 206 pp., illus., 16/-) (Library Pub., New York, 1954, 257 pp., illus., $3.95)

Analytical studies of natural and supernatural phenomena—mermaids, giant insects, deep-sea monsters, witch-doctors, etc.

BENNETT, GEOFFREY British author
Fiction
This Creeping Evil (by "Sea-Lion" [pseud.], Hutchinson, London, 1950, 176 pp., 8/6) (Arrow: 693, 1963, 190 pp., pa 2/6)

Horror yarn.

BENNETT, GEORGE U.S., chairman of the English Department at Exeter Academy.
Anthology
Great Tales of Action and Adventure [pa] (Dell: LB126, 1959, 256 pp., pa 35¢)

12 stories selected to be suitable for literature classes. The 4 sf and fantasy stories are: "Leiningen Versus the Ants," C. Stephenson; "The Pit and the Pendulum," E. A. Poe; "Rescue Party," A. C. Clarke; "August Heat," W. F. Harvey.

BENNETT, GERTRUDE (BARROWS) (18 Sep 1884–Sep 1939?) U.S. fantasy author. She was born in Minneapolis and brought up in the midst of books, but was forced to leave school at the end of the grammar grades and go to work. At the turn of the '20s she took up writing to support herself and her infant daughter after her husband had been drowned. Using the pseudonym Francis Stevens she wrote only 11 stories, but of quite high quality. Of the four short stories only "The Elf-Trap" has been reprinted (*Arg*, 5 July 1919; *FN*, Nov 1949); novels not later reprinted were "The Labyrinth" (*ASW*, sr3, 27 July 1918), "Avalon" (*Arg*, sr4, 16 Aug 1919), "Sunfire" (*WT*, sr2, July 1923). No further original stories appeared after "Sunfire." She suddenly disappeared in California in September 1939 and has never been traced.
Fiction
Citadel of Fear, The [n] (*Arg*, sr7, 14 Sep 1918) (*FFM*, Feb 1942)

Powers from the lost city of an ancient race endeavour to make their mark on the outside world.
Claimed (*Arg*, sr3, 6 Mar 1920) (*FFM*, Apr 1941) (Avalon, New York, 1966, 192 pp., $3.25)

Evil sea forces fight a despotic collector of statuettes.
Heads of Cerberus, The (*Thrill Book*, sr5, 15 Aug 1919) (Polaris, Reading, 1952, 191 pp., $3.00)

The book edition was the first of Eshbach's limited editions of old fantasy classics. The story is good satire even if dated, and a worthy collector's item.
Serapion [n] (*Arg*, sr4, 19 June 1920) (*FFM*, July 1942)

Intrigue with a man having two personalities.

BENNETT, JOHN (14 May 1865–28 Dec 1956) U.S. author.
Fiction
Doctor to the Dead, The [C] (Rinehart, New York, 1946, 260 pp., $2.50)

Grotesque legends and folk tales of old Charleston: "The House of the Doctor to the Dead" (etching); "The Doctor to the Dead"; "The Death of the Wandering Jew"; "Madame Margot"; "The Black Constable"; "Tales From the Trapman Street Hospital"; "The Thirsty Dead"; "The Little Harlot and Her Broken Pitcher"; "The Army of the Dead"; "All God's Chillun Had Wings"; "The Measure of Grief"; "The Enchanted Cloak"; "The Young Wife Whose Vine Meloned Before the Fence"; "Death and the Two Bachelors"; "When the Dead Sang in Their Graves"; "Rolling Rio and the Grey Man, or, The Gift of Strength"; "The Remember Service"; "A Young Girl's Virtue Preserved by the Devil"; "Crook-Neck Dick"; "Louie Alexander"; "The Apothecary and the Mermaid"; "The Man Who Wouldn't Believe He Was Dead"; "Daid Aaron I"; "Daid Aaron II"; "Buried Treasure, or, The Two Bold Fishermen."

BENNETT, KEM (1919–) British author and translator. He has contributed to such varying markets as MGM and *SEP*, and also translates plays from French. He has had some short stories published in *F&SF*: "The Soothsayer" (Aug 1952); "Rufus" (Feb 1956). His wife is Gillian, daughter of Joan Grant (author of *Winged Pharaoh*, etc.).

Fiction

Fabulous Wink, The See *Wink, The*
Wink, The (Hart-Davis, London, 1951, 227 pp., 10/6) (Clarke Irwin, Toronto, $2.25) (*The Fabulous Wink*, Pellegrini Cudahy, New York, 1951, 244 pp., $3.00)

Noted light fantasy of a plaster saint that winked; satire on the materialistic phonies of all religions.

BENNETT, MARGOT (1912–) British mystery writer, born in Scotland. She is noted for her intricate puzzles combining sharp wit and shrewd insight into character. She has contributed to the BBC and has appeared in *F&SF*: "An Old-Fashioned Poker for My Uncle's Head" (1946; May 1954).

Fiction

Long Way Back, The (Bodley Head, London, 1954, 206 pp., 10/6) (Coward McCann, New York, 1955, 248 pp., $3.50) (SF B.C. [S.J.], 1956, 4/6)

In the future a small expedition from Africa visits Great Britain to see if man still exists there.

BENNETT, W(ILLIAM) E(DWARD) (1898–)

Fiction

Authentic Shudder, The [by Warren Armstrong] (Elek, London, 1965, 176 pp., 18/-) (Day, New York, 1967, 192 pp., $3.95) (Longmans, Toronto, $4.95)

BENOIT, PIERRE (6 July 1886–3 Mar 1962) French novelist. He was much travelled and placed his colourful romances in widely diverse locales. He regularly produced more than a novel a year, but is mainly noted for the one below, which some authorities consider to be plagiarised from an H. R. Haggard theme. [See D. Richardson, *Science Fiction Advertiser* (fan magazine), Jan 1952.] He was a member of the French Academy from 1931.

Fiction

Atlantida See *L'Atlantide*
L'Atlantide (Michel Pub. Co., Paris, 1919, 350 pp.) (*Adventure*, sr2, 3 Aug 1920) (*The Queen of Atlantis* [trans.–A. Chambers], Hutchinson, London, 1920, 286 pp., 8/6; #359, nd [*ca*. 1930], 128 pp., pa 6d) (*Atlantida* [trans.–Mary C. Tongue & Mary Ross], Duffield, New York, 1920, 303 pp., $2.00) (*Atlantis* [Swedish], Ahlen & Söner, 1933) (*L'Atlantida* [Spanish], –) (Ace: F-281, 1964, 192 pp., pa 40¢)

A Haggard type of fantastic adventure. *Films:* French, 1929, silent; German, UFA, 1933, with Brigitte Helm; U.S., United Artists, 1948, as *Siren of Atlantis* with Maria Montez as Antinea and Pierre Aumont as the hapless French officer who murdered his best friend—the picture was hammy and a financial flop.

Queen of Atlantis, The See *L'Atlantide*

BENSEN, D(ONALD) R. (3 Oct 1927–) U.S. editor, born in Brooklyn, graduated A.B. Columbia in 1950. He was production manager at Wilfred Funk Inc. 1951-52; assistant editor at People's Book Club 1952-56; editor of Pyramid Books from 1957 to 1967, adding many sf and fantasy works of note to its list. In Sep 1967 he became executive editor at Berkley Books.

Anthologies

Unknown, The [pa] (Pyramid: R851, 1963, 192 pp., pa 50¢, illus.–Edd Cartier)

Fantasy, 11 stories all originally in *Unknown (Worlds)*, with foreword by I. Asimov and compiler's introduction: "The Misguided Halo," Henry Kuttner; "Prescience," N. S. Bond; "Yesterday Was Monday," T. Sturgeon; "The Gnarly Man," L. S. de Camp; "The Bleak Shore," Fritz Leiber; "Trouble With Water," H. L. Gold; "Doubled and Redoubled," Malcolm Jameson; "When It Was Moonlight," Manly W. Wellman; "Mr. Jinx," Robert Arthur; "Snulbug," A. Boucher; "Armageddon," F. Brown.

Unknown Five, The [pa] (Pyramid: R962, 1964, 190 pp., pa

50¢, illus.–E. Cartier & J. Schoenherr) ([German], Ullstein: PB No. 1183, 1968 [*Kriminalmagazin*: 11])

Fantasy, 5 stories and compiler's introduction [all but the first story originally appeared in *Unknown (Worlds)*; the first was purchased for it but never published]: "Author! Author!" Isaac Asimov; "The Bargain," Cleve Cartmill; "The Hag Seleen," Theodore Sturgeon; "Hell Is Forever," Alfred Bester; "The Crest of the Wave," Jane Rice.

BENSON, A(RTHUR) C(HRISTOPHER) (24 Apr 1862–17 June 1925) British essayist, poet and scholar. He was the oldest surviving son of Edward White Benson (Archbishop of Canterbury), and brother of Edward F. and Robert H. Benson. After schooling at King's College, Cambridge, he went into teaching and became house master at Eton in 1892. In 1903 he went to Cambridge, primarily to join Viscount Esher in editing the diaries of Queen Victoria. He is noted primarily for his poems ("Land of Hope and Glory" being best known), essays and biographies. A nervous invalid much of his life, he never married.

Fiction

Basil Netherby [C] (Hutchinson, London, 1926, 211 pp., 6/-)

Not listed in Bleiler. Two brilliant novelettes of the supernatural: "Basil Netherby"; "The Uttermost Farthing."

Child of the Dawn, The (E. Smith, London, 1911, 328 pp., 7/6) (Putnam, New York, 1912, 396 pp.) (Falcon's Wing, Indian Hills, Colorado, 1957, 314 pp., $3.95)

A story of immortality.

Hill of Trouble and Other Stories, The [C] (Isbister, London, 1903, 298 pp., 6/-)

12 stories, including some fantasy: "The Hill of Trouble"; "The Grey Cat"; "The Red Camp"; "The Light of the Body"; "The Snake, the Leper, and the Grey Frost"; "Brother Robert"; "The Closed Window"; "The Brothers"; "The Temple of Death"; "The Tomb of Heiri"; "Cerda"; "Linus."

Isles of Sunset, The [C] (Isbister, 1904, 318 pp., 6/-; 1905, 307 pp.)

7 stories: "The Isles of Sunset"; "The Waving of the Sword"; "Renatus"; "The Slype House"; "Out of the Sea"; "Paul the Minstrel"; "The Troth of the Sword."

Paul the Minstrel and Other Stories [C] (E. Smith, London, 1911, 458 pp., 7/6) (Putnam, New York, 1912, 443 pp.)

19 stories: those in *The Isles of Sunset* and *The Hill of Trouble*.

BENSON, E(DWARD) F(REDERICK) (24 July 1867–29 Feb 1940) British author; third son of E. W. Benson–Archbishop of Canterbury. He worked at Athens for the British Archaeological Society (1892-95) and later in Egypt for the Hellenic Society. In 1893 his society novel *DoDo* brought him to the front among writers of clever fiction; this was followed by other stories whose subjects were drawn from modern Greece. Of his many weird and fantasy stories, he is best remembered for "Caterpillars" (often anthologised; *FFM*, June 1947) and "Mrs. Amworth" (typical vampire type), while in general fiction he was noted for his gentle satires centered around the heroine Lucia.

Fiction [Incomplete—other titles in Bleiler *Checklist*]

Countess of Lowndes Square and Other Stories [C] (Cassell, London, 1920, 311 pp., 8/6)

14 stories: "The Ape"; "Blackmailer of Park Lane"; "Case of Frank Hampden"; "Countess of Lowndes Square"; "Dance on the Beefsteak"; "False Step"; "In the Dark"; "Mrs. Andrew's Control"; "The Oriolists"; "Philip's Safety Razor"; "Puss-Cat"; "There Arose a King"; " 'Through' "; "Tragedy of Oliver Bowman."

More Spook Stories [C] (Hutchinson, London, 1934, 288 pp., 7/6; 1935, 2/6)

Weird, 13 stories: "The Step"; "Bed by the Window"; "James Lamp"; "The Dance"; "The Hanging of Alfred Wadham"; "Pirates"; "The Wishing Well"; "The Bath Chair"; "Monkeys"; "Christopher Comes Back"; "The Sanctuary"; "Thursday Evenings"; "The Psychical Mallards."

Room in the Tower and Other Stories, The [C] (Mills Boon, London, 1912, 338 pp., 6/-; 1914, 296 pp., 1/-) (Knopf, London, 1929, 320 pp., 5/-)

17 stories: "At Abdul Ali's Grave"; "Between the Lights"; "The Bus-Conductor"; "The Cat"; "Caterpillars"; "Confession of Charles Linkworth"; "Dust-Cloud"; "Gavon's Eve"; "The House With the Brick-Kiln"; "How Fear Departed From the Long Gallery"; "The Man Who Went Too Far"; "Other Bed"; "Outside the Door"; "The Room in the Tower"; "Shootings of Achnaleish"; "Terror by Night"; "The Thing in the Hall."

Spook Stories [C] (Hutchinson, 1928, 288 pp., 7/5; 1929, 3/6; 1933, 2/-)

12 stories: "Reconciliation"; "The Face"; "Spinach"; "Bagnell Terrace"; "A Tale of an Empty House"; "Naboth's Vineyard"; "Expiation"; "Home Sweet Home"; " 'And No Bird Sings' "; "The Corner House"; "Corstophine"; "The Temple."

Visible and Invisible [C] (Hutchinson, 1923, 288 pp., 7/6; 1925, 2/6) (Doran, New York, 1924, 298 pp.)

12 stories: " 'And the Dead Spake' "; " 'The Outcast' "; "The Horror-Horn"; "Machaon"; "Negotium Perambulans"; "At the Farmhouse" (*FFM*, Dec 1946); "Inscrutable Decrees"; "The Gardener"; "Mr. Tilby's Seance"; "Mrs. Amworth" (*FFM*, June 1950); "In the Tube"; "Roderick's Story" (*FFM*, Apr 1946).

BENSON, R(OBERT) H(UGH) (18 Nov 1871–19 Oct 1914) British novelist; like his brothers Edward and Arthur, a prominent literary figure. After Eton, he studied theology at Cambridge U. and was ordained a priest in the Church of England in 1895; he transferred to the Roman Catholic Church in 1903. He began to write intense and historical fiction, with others on modern life. Probably his best known works are *Come Rack! Come Rope!* (1912) and *Oddsfish* (1914). His *Lord of the World* (1908) is an apocalyptic novel with the R.C. church driven to Palestine. He died of pneumonia at the age of 43.

Fiction [Incomplete—other titles in Bleiler *Checklist*]

Light Invisible, The [C] (Isbister, London, 1903, 250 pp., 3/6) (Hutchinson, London, 1906, 250 pp.) (Pitman, London, 1911, 250 pp., 3/6) (Burns & Oates, London, nd, 250 pp., 3/6)

Weird, 15 stories with author's preface and pictorial cover: "The Green Robe"; "The Watcher"; "The Blood Eagle"; "Over the Gateway"; "Poena Damni"; " 'Consolatrix Afflictorum' "; "The Bridge Over the Stream"; "In the Convent Chapel"; "Under Which King"; "With Dyed Garments"; "Unto Babes"; "The Traveller"; "The Sorrows of the World"; "In the Morning"; "The Unexpected Guest."

BENSON, STELLA (6 Jan 1892–6 Dec 1933) British novelist, short story writer, poet and dramatist; wife of J. C. O'Gorman Anderson. She was noted for such novels as *The Far-Away Bride* (1930) and collections such as *The Awakening* (1925) and *Christmas Formula* (1932); she also wrote travel and poetry books. She died in China.

Fiction [one other fantasy—*Living Alone* (1919)]

Collected Short Stories [C] (Macmillan, London, 1936, 303 pp., 7/6) (Macmillan, Toronto, $2.00)

13 stories: "The Awakening"; "Christmas Formula"; "Desert Islander"; "A Dream"; "Hairy Carey's Son"; "Hope Against Hope"; "Man Who Fell in Love With the Co-operative Stores"; "Man Who Missed the Bus"; "On the Contrary"; "Out-Islander Come In"; "Story Coldly Told"; "Submarine"; "Tchotl."

BENSON, THEODORA (1906–)
Fiction
Man From the Tunnel and Other Stories, The [C] (Gollancz, London, 1950, 271 pp., 10/6) (Longmans, Toronto, $2.50) (Appleton, New York, 1951, 271 pp., $3.00)

Fantasy, 21 stories: "The Man From the Tunnel"; "The Lion and the Prey"; "The Funeral Feast"; "The Childishness of Mr. Mountfort"; "A Nice Fright"; "Not by Bread Alone"; "The Man With the Phoney Tin Foot"; "The White Sea Monkey"; "Harry Was Good to the Girls"; "Shakespeare's Elderly Bore"; "The White Cock"; "In the Fourth Ward"; "The Frog and the Lion"; "Door Marked Exit"; "The Bones of A. T. Stewart"; "Yes-Girl"; "Tomorrow Is Another Day"; "A Long Time Ago"; "The Golden Fish."

BENTLEY, JOHN
Fiction
Where Are the Russians? (Doubleday, New York, 1968, $4.95)

Americans and Russians race to make the first Moon landing.

BENTLIF, SYD
Anthology
Horror Anthology [pa] (Mayflower: 3720, 1965, 126 pp., pa 3/6)

Weird, 9 stories: "Left Luggage," Elizabeth J. Howard; "Silence," E. A. Poe; "The Dwarf," R. Bradbury; "The Nice Boys," Isabel Colegate; "The Tell-Tale Heart," E. A. Poe; "The Uncommon Prayer Book," M. R. James; "It's a Good Life," J. Bixby; "The Terror of the Twins," A. Blackwood; "Marmalade Wine," Joan Aiken.

BENWELL, GWEN
Nonfiction
Sea Enchantress—The Tale of the Mermaid and Her Kin [with Arthur Waugh] (Hutchinson, London, 1961, 287 pp., 35/-)

Strange and varied are the people of the sea—mermen, tritons, etc., but the most fascinating of all is the mermaid. Does she exist? 15 chapters trace the origin of the mermaid through the ancient world and classical times to the 19th century, and in folklore from the church in England, Ireland, Wales and Scotland, etc. Select bibliography (1¾ pp.) and index (5 pp.).

BERCKMANN, EVELYN (DOMENICA) (18 Oct 1900–) U.S. author and musician. She was born in Philadelphia, educated at Columbia U., N.Y., and now resides in England. She is unmarried. She uses the pseudonym Joanna Wade; her novels include *The Beckoning Dream*; *The Strange Bedfellow*, etc.

Fiction
Evil of Time, The (Dodd Mead, New York, 1954, 197 pp., $2.75) (Dodd, Toronto, $3.00) (Eyre Spottiswoode, London, 1955, 187 pp., 9/6)

Red Badge prize-winning novel—ruin, death and decay in an old German castle.

Heir of Starvelings, The (Eyre Spottiswoode, London, 1968, 255 pp., 25/-)

A modern gothic novel: a girl becomes nursemaid-teacher to an odd child in an old house with an aura of evil.

BERESFORD, ELIZABETH
Fiction
Sea Green Magic (R. Hart-Davis, London, 1968, 156 pp., 21/-)

Juvenile fantasy in the E. Nesbit tradition—Johnny finds an odd bottle which has a djinn who can make magic at the drop of a hat.

BERESFORD, J(OHN) D(AVYS) (17 Mar 1873–1 Feb 1947) British novelist and architect. He first achieved prominence with a trilogy about the life of an architect—*The Early History of Jacob Stahl* (1911). In the fantasy field his *The Hampdenshire Wonder* is considered a classic.

Fiction [Incomplete—other titles in Bleiler *Checklist*]

Hampdenshire Wonder, The (Sidgwick Jackson, London, 1911, 412 pp., 6/-) (Secker, London, 1926, 256 pp., 3/6) (Eyre Spottiswoode 'Century Library 10,' London, 1948, 235 pp., 6/-)

A noted British classic, and an excellent mutant novel.

Meeting Place and Other Stories, The [C] (Faber, London, 1929, 410 pp., 7/6)

26 stories, some of fantasy interest (not mentioned in Bleiler *Checklist*): "The Meeting Place"; "End of Phipson"; "The Three Cases"; "Justice: An Impartial Comment"; "The Air of Paris"; "The Gambler"; "Verity"; "Tops and Bottoms"; "The Hands of Serge David"; "Professional Pride"; "Love of Youth"; "The Man Who Hated Flies"; "Ways of Escape"; "The Wind and Mr. Tittler"; "Laughter and Tears"; "The Marionettes"; "The Devil's Own Luck"; "Common Humanity"; "The Artificial Mole"; "The Champion"; "The Clever Mr. Fall"; "The Trap Without a Bait"; "The

Last Tenants"; "Illusion"; "The Indomitable Mrs. Garthorne"; "The Summary." Conclusion: A Few Words of Advice to the English Writer of Short Stories.
Nineteen Impressions [C] (Sidgwick Jackson, 1918, 226 pp., 6/-)

17 stories: "Ashes of Last Night's Fire"; "The Contemporaries"; "The Criminal"; "Cut-Throat Farm"; "Empty Theatre"; "The Escape"; "Flaws in the Time Scheme"; "Force Majeure"; "Great Tradition"; "Instrument of Destiny"; "Little Town"; "Lost in the Fog"; "Lost Suburb"; "Man in the Machine"; "The Misanthrope"; "Power o' Money"; "Powers of the Air."
Signs and Wonders [C] (Putnam, New York, 1921, 151 pp.) (Golden Cockerel, Berkshire, 1921, 151 pp., 5/-)

17 stories: "Appearance of Man"; "As the Crow Flies"; "The Barrage"; "The Barrier"; "The Cage"; "The Convert"; "Difference of Temperament"; "Enlargement"; "Hidden Beast"; "The Introvert"; "The Miracle"; "Negligible Experiment"; "Night of Creation"; "Perfect Smile"; "Reference Wanted"; "Signs and Wonders"; "Young Strickland's Career."

BERGAUST, ERIK R. (23 Mar 1925–) Noted U.S. writer on rocketry. He was born in Oslo, Norway; B.S. in chemistry 1943. He was in the Norwegian Resistance Movement 1943-44 and the Norwegian Exile Army 1944-45. He was an aviation editor and also manager of an aircraft company. He came to the U.S.A. in 1949 and was naturalised in 1956. He has become a consultant in guided missile work for U.S. companies; he has edited in this field for *American Aviation* and became managing editor of *Missiles and Rockets*. His books on space travel and rocketry include *Satellite!* [with W. Beller] (Hanover House, 1956; D'day SF B.C., 1957; Bantam, 1957, pa); *Rockets Around the World* (Putnam, 1958); *Rocket to the Moon* [with S. Hull] (Van Nostrand, 1959); *The Next 50 Years in Space* (Macmillan, 1964); and *Mars, Planet for Conquest* (Putnam, 1967). He also wrote a biography of Wernher Von Braun, *Reaching for the Stars* (Doubleday, 1960, 407 pp., $4.95).

BERGER, YVES (1936–) French author, born in Avignon. He taught English in French schools and wrote literary criticism for the Paris *Weekly Express*. He is an editor for the Bernard Grasset publishing house.
Fiction
Garden, The (*Le Sud*; trans.–R. Baldick) (G. Braziller, New York, 1963, 226 pp., $4.00)

An alternate-time story set in Virginia of the 1840's.

BERGEY, EARLE K. (? –1952) U.S. artist predominantly remembered for his covers on the Standard magazines. He painted all the covers for *Strange Stories* and then began working for the associated *Startling Stories*, *Thrilling Wonder Stories* and *Captain Future*. Later he did some for *Fantastic Story Magazine*; his last covers for Standard were in 1952. He also did two covers for *Future SF* in 1950 and a few paperback books. Although he continued a trend begun by H. W. Brown, his predecessor with Standard, Bergey more than any other artist came to be identified with the type of cover showing "Guy, Gal and Goon" or "Bug-Eyed Monster."

BERGIER, JACQUES (1912–) See PAUWELS, L. (co-author)

BERGQUIST, N. O.
Nonfiction
Moon Puzzle, The (Sidgwick Jackson, London, 1954, 378 pp., illus., 16/-)

A revival of the classical theory that the Pacific Ocean was formed when the Earth gave birth to the Moon.

BERNA, PAUL (1913–) French author.
Fiction
Continent in the Sky (*Le continent du ciel*, Editions-Genérale Publicité, Paris, 1955) (Bodley Head, London, 1959, 170 pp., illus.–J. Duchesne, 10/6) (Abelard-Schuman, New York, 1963, 192 pp., $3.50)

Sequel to *Threshold of the Stars* but not as good. A young French lad is caught up in space intrigue with an English-American syndicate.
Threshold of the Stars (*La porte des étoiles*, Bibliotheque Rouge et Or: 74, Paris, 1954) (Bodley Head, 1958, 163 pp., illus.–G. Spence, 12/6; 1967, 163 pp., 13/6) (Abelard-Schuman, 1961, 176 pp., $3.00)

Won the 1955 Grand Prix Litteraire du Salon de L'Enfance. The adventures of a group of children whose parents work in a secret French space-flight base—the Moon is to be given an atmosphere. Sequel is *Continent in the Sky*.

BERNANOS, GEORGES (20 Feb 1888–5 July 1948)
Fiction
Star of Satan, The (Trans.–H. L. Binsse; Lane, London, 1927, 339 pp., 7/6) (Trans.–Pamela Morris; Macmillan, New York, 1940, 348 pp., $2.50; Macmillan, Toronto, $2.75; Lane, 1940, 336 pp., 8/6) (*Under the Sun of Satan*, Pantheon, New York, 1949, 252 pp., $3.00)

A weird novel.
Under the Sun of Satan See *Star of Satan, The*

BERNARD, CHRISTINE British anthologist.
Anthologies
Armada Ghost Book, The [pa] (Armada: C197, 1967, 159 pp., illus.–G. D'Achille, pa 2/6)

Juvenile, 11 stories with editor's introduction: "Sandy MacNeil and His Dog," S. N. Leodhas; "School for the Unspeakable," M. W. Wellman; "The House of the Nightmare," E. L. White; "The Story of the Inexperienced Ghost," H. G. Wells; "The Giant Bones," S. N. Leodhas; "Prince Godfrey Frees Mountain Dwellers and Little Shepherds From a Savage Werewolf and Witches," Halina Gorska; "The Water Ghost of Harrowby Hall," J. K. Bangs; "The Red Room," H. G. Wells; "Spooks of the Valley," Louis C. Jones; "The Lads Who Met the Highwayman," S. N. Leodhas; "A Pair of Hands," Sir A. Quiller-Couch.
Fontana Book of Great Horror Stories, The [pa] (Fontana: 1232, 1966, 221 pp., pa 3/6)

14 stories: "The Squaw," B. Stoker: "No Stronger Than a Flower," R. Aickman; "Tarnhelm," H. Walpole; "The Gypsy," Agatha Christie; "A Case of Eavesdropping," A. Blackwood; "The Pond," N. Kneale; "William and Mary," R. Dahl; "The Two Vaynes," L. P. Hartley; "The Next in Line," R. Bradbury; "In the Steam Room," Frank Baker; "The Interlopers," Saki; "The Cat Jumps," Elizabeth Bowen; "The Boarded Window," A. Bierce; "Marmalade Wine," Joan Aiken.
Second Armada Ghost Book [pa] (Armada: C253, 1968, 126 pp., pa 2/6)

9 stories and introduction: "The Ghost That Didn't Want to Be a Ghost," Sorche Nic Leodhas; "The Keepers of the Wall," W. C. Dickinson; "Fiddler, Play Fast, Play Faster," Ruth Sawyer; "The Magic Shop," H. G. Wells; "Mr. Fox," traditional; "His Own Number," W. C. Dickinson; "The Man Who Walked Widdershins Round the Kirk," S. N. Leodhas; "The Flowering of the Strange Orchid," H. G. Wells; "The Ugly-Wuglies," Edith Nesbit.
Third Fontana Book of Great Horror Stories [pa] (Fontana: 1702, 1968, 188 pp., pa 3/6)

11 stories: "Green Fingers," R. C. Cook; "The Specialty of the House," Stanley Ellin; "The Room in the Tower," E. F. Benson; "The Academy," David Ely; "Cut-Throat Farm," J. D. Beresford; "The Romance of Certain Old Clothes," Henry James; "Poison," Roald Dahl; "Lucky's Grove," H. R. Wakefield; "Housebound," P. Chetwynd-Hayes; "The Shuttered Room," H. P. Lovecraft & A. Derleth; "At the End of the Passage," R. Kipling.

BERNARD, RAFE British author. Besides the novel below, he more recently wrote one of the TV 'Invader' stories as *The Halo Highway* (Corgi, 1967, pa).
Fiction
Wheel in the Sky, The (Ward Lock, London, 1954, 192 pp., 9/6; 1955, 6/-; #26, 1955, 193 pp., pa 2/-) (*El planeta artificial* [Span-

ish], *Futuro*: 33, 1954) (*La ruota nei cielo* [Italian], *Cosmo*: 4, 1957)

Construction of space station, with murder, intrigue, and a girl.

BERNARD, Dr. RAYMOND   Probably a pseudonym. Author of works on geriatrics, fluoridation, yoga, the Dead Sea Scrolls, the "real" Christ, etc.
Nonfiction
Hollow Earth, The   (Fieldcrest Pub. Co., New York, 1964, 105 pp., mimeo, 8½ x 11, illus., $3.50)

A serious exposition (wrong scientifically) that Earth is hollow with great opening at the poles and that the interior has a central sun, like Burroughs' Pellucidar. It is supposedly based on Admiral Byrd's flight beyond the Pole in 1947 (actually in 1926); it also quotes from similar earlier works. (See P. S. Miller, *ASF*, Apr 1965.)

BERNERI, MARIE LOUISE   (1918–13 Apr 1949)   Italian journalist. She was born in Florence; later she and her family fled from the Fascists, and she spent 11 years in Paris, and came to England in 1937. A political journalist, she was joint editor of anarchist periodicals published in Britain: *Spain and the World* (1937-39), *War Commentary* (1939-45) and *Freedom* (1945 until her death). She was particularly interested in the practical aspects of social revolution; she travelled extensively and was fluent in four languages.
Nonfiction
Journey Through Utopia   (Routledge & K. Paul, London, 1950, 339 pp., 16/-) (Beacon, Boston, 1951, 339 pp., $3.75)

A critical assessment of the most important (not necessarily the most famous) utopias, including many with no English version. This book is somewhat more readable and broader than G. Negley's *The Quest for Utopia*. The author has excerpted and discussed the early classical utopias (running back to 900 B.C.—the presumed date of Lycurgus' Spartan state), with a running commentary showing them in relation to the thought of their times. Only the "positive" utopias are accepted, though the "negative" ones (such as A. Huxley's *Brave New World* or G. Orwell's *1984*) are covered by Negley. The two works duplicate each other with relatively few of the more important works, mainly More's *Utopia*, Bacon's *New Atlantis*, and Wells' *Modern Utopia*. The Berneri work has a good bibliography and index.

BERNSTEIN, MOREY   (1920?–)   U.S. amateur hypnotist who caused quite a stir with the book below.
Nonfiction (?)
Search for Bridey Murphy, The   (Doubleday, New York, 1956, 256 pp., $3.75; 1965, 308 pp., $4.95) (Hutchinson, London, 1956, 256 pp., 15/-) (*A la recherche de Bridey Murphy* [French], Laffont, 1956) (Pocket Books: GC37, 1958, 324 pp., pa 50¢)

A documentation of the case for ESP and parapsychology, recounting prenatal memory experiments in which the author hypnotised a woman (Ruth Simmons) and supposedly took her back not merely to childhood, but to a former life in Ireland from 1798 to 1864. It became a best seller and started a wave of parlour hypnosis. An authoritative work to dispell the unease and hysteria resulting from this book is *A Scientific Report on the Search for Bridey Murphy* by Dr. Milton V. Kline et al. (Julian, New York, 1956, $3.50); an article was "Bridey Murphy: An Irishman's View," W. B. Ready (*F&SF*, Aug 1956). The 1965 Doubleday edition has additional material by William Barker.

BERRILL, N(ORMAN) J(OHN)   (28 Apr 1903–)   U.S. science writer. He was born in Bristol, England, and educated at Bristol U. (B.Sc. 1924) and U. London (Ph.D. 1929, D.Sc. 1931). He began as a lecturer at Swarthmore College, and then was professor of zoology at McGill U., Montreal, 1928-65 and U. Hawaii 1964-65. Other works besides the one below include *The Living Tide* (Premier, 1957, pa) and *You and the Universe* (Premier, 1959, pa).
Nonfiction
Man's Emerging Mind   (Dodd Mead, New York, 1955, 308 pp., $4.00) (Premier: d50, 1957, 240 pp., pa 50¢) (D. Dobson, Lon-

don, 1958, xii+308 pp., 21/-) (Scientific Book Guild, London, 1961, 308 pp., np)

Subtitled "Man's progress through time–his contact with trees, ice, flood, atoms and the universe." Covers the evolution of man and his mind through the ages.

BERRY, BRYAN   (1930–)   British author. He became interested in sf when he was 11, and was very active in the sf field in the early 1950's. He first worked in a publisher's office writing advertising copy, and was also a staff writer for an agency and subeditor for an international literary monthly; he collaborated with the editor of *Nature* on educational film strip scripts. He began free-lancing around 1952. He wrote many paperback novels for Hamilton Publishers. His first three short stories submitted in the U.S.A. were all printed in one issue of *Planet* (Jan 1953). He also had two novels in *2CSAB*: "Mission to Marakee" (Sum 1953) [retitle of "Aftermath"] and "World Held Captive" (Spr 1954). His "Rolf Garner" novels were of good quality. Other novels not listed below include *Aftermath* (*Authentic*: 24, 1952; [German], K. G. Bewin, 1955, Lehning, 1958, pa); *Dread Visitor* (Panther, 1952, pa); *Return to Earth* (Hamilton, nd, pa; [German], *UG*: 22, 1955).
Series
Venus Trilogy [as Rolf Garner]: *Resurgent Dust*; *The Immortals*; *The Indestructible* [covered below].
Fiction
And the Stars Remain [pa]   (Panther: nn, 1952, 112 pp., pa 1/6) (Atlas: SFL7, 1956, 114 pp., pa 2/-) (*Tödliche Grenze im All* [German], W. Riedel, 1955; *T*: 158, 1960)

In reaching for the stars Earthmen and Martians learn of the Master Planners.
Born in Captivity   (Hamilton, London, 1952, 198 pp., 8/6; Panther: nn, pa 2/-)

The future after World War III; a couple's adventures after killing a state official.
From What Far Star?   (Hamilton, 1953, 143 pp., 6/-; Panther: 40, pa 1/6) (Atlas: SFL3, 1955, 114 pp., pa 2/-) (*Weltraumspione am Werk* [German], K. G. Bewin, 1954; *Gyrotaxi 430 verschwunden*, *L*: 47, 1959)

An alien race endangers Earth.
Immortals, The [as Rolf Garner]   (Hamilton, 1953, 159 pp., 6/-; Panther: 78, pa 1/6)

Second in trilogy—the discovery of science on Venus.
Indestructible, The [as Rolf Garner]   (Hamilton, 1954, 159 pp., 6/-; Panther: 104, pa 1/6)

Last in trilogy—the remnants of Earth's population freed from tyranny.
Resurgent Dust [as Rolf Garner]   (Hamilton, 1953, 160 pp., 6/-; Panther: 68, pa 1/6)

First in trilogy—mankind on Venus after the destruction of life on Earth.
Venom Seekers, The   (Hamilton, 1953, 160 pp., 6/-; Panther: 57, pa 1/6) (*In der Ewigkeit verschollen* [German], Zimmermann, 1957; *T*: 32, 1958)

A man goes back in time for a weapon to save mankind.

BERRY, CHARLES W.
Nonfiction
Arthurian Reverie, An   (Buckley Press, London, 1939, 171+xxiii pp., illus., 6/-)

Essentially an Encyclopedia of Arthurian Legend, with foreword by Arthur C. R. Carter (2½ pp.), intro. (1½ pp.) and preface (3½ pp.). Contents: *Arthur:* Authorities, Birth, Merlin, Battles, Peace, Names, etc., The Exodus. *Interesting Notes:* The Round Table, Persons, Places, and Arthurian Literature. *Arthurian Legend in the Spanish Peninsula. Arthurian Legend in Italy.* Index (21 pp.). The author at the time of writing this 'Reverie' was "Knight-Remembrancer" of "The Knights of the Round Table" and all proceeds from the sale of the volume were to be devoted to the "Knights Benevolent Fund" of that society.

BERTIN, JOHN U.S. author. The story below was his only appearance.
Fiction
Brood of Helios (*WS*, sr3, May 1932) (Arcadia House, New York, 1966, 189 pp., $3.25)
Time travel to four million years in the future.

BESANT, (SIR) WALTER (14 Aug 1836–9 June 1901) British novelist and miscellaneous writer. He was born in Portsmouth, and educated at King's College, London, and Christ's College, Cambridge. He wrote a number of novels, first in collaboration with James Rice and then alone; many were historical. He edited *Once a Week* until 1881, and was also one-time editor of *The Author*, first published in 1890. He was knighted in 1895.
Fiction [with James Rice] [Incomplete—other titles, alone and in collaboration, in Bleiler *Checklist*]
Case of Mr. Lucraft and Other Tales, The [C] (Dodd Mead, New York, 1888, 367 pp.) (Chatto Windus, London, 1888, 367 pp.; 1895, 367 pp.) *Note:* The Bleiler *Checklist* gives the Dodd, Mead as the first edition; actually the first was in London, 1876, 2 vols., with a new edition in 1877–the publisher is not known.
Part I – From the Supernatural: "The Case of Mr. Lucraft"; "The Mystery of Joe Morgan"; "An Old, Old Story"; "Lady Kitty"; "The Old Four Poster"; "My Own Experience."
Part II – From Fairyland: "Titania's Farewell."
Part III – From Fact: "On the Goodwin"; "Edelweiss"; "Love Finds the Way"; "The Death of Samuel Peckwick"; "When the Ship Comes Home."

BESSAND-MASSENET, PIERRE French writer.
Fiction
Amorous Ghost (*Magie Rose*, Librairie Plon, Paris, 1956) Trans.– Hugh Shelley: (Elek, London, 1957, 126 pp., 10/6)
A 20th century Paris student encounters a phantom courtesan of the early 19th century.

BEST, HERBERT (1894–)
Fiction
Twenty-Fifth Hour, The (Random, New York, 1940, 321 pp., $2.50) (Macmillan, Toronto, $2.25) (J. Cape, London, 1940, 285 pp., 8/-) (Nelson, Toronto, $2.50) (*FFM*, Aug 1946)
A graphic novel of soldiers in war-torn Europe and pestilence in the U.S.

BESTER, ALFRED (18 Dec 1913–) U.S. sf author and book reviewer. B.Sc. in science and fine arts, U. of Pennsylvania. He became a professional writer after winning the *Thrilling Wonder Stories* amateur contest with "The Broken Axiom" (Apr 1939). He followed with such stories as "Voyage to Nowhere" (*TWS*, July 1940), "The Probable Man" (*ASF*, July 1941), "Adam and No Eve" (*ASF*, Sep 1941), and the novel "Hell Is Forever" in *Unknown Worlds* (Aug 1942). He has written scenarios for comic books and comic strips. Postwar, his novels (covered below) have been landmarks in the sf field. He now writes mainly for TV. From Oct 1960 to July 1962 he was book reviewer for *F&SF*; his idea of a composite sf author was in the Mar 1961 column. His U. of Chicago lecture "SF and the Renaissance Man" was published in *The Science Fiction Novel* (1959) [see SYMPOSIA]. A non-sf novel of interest, *Who He?* (Dial, 1953), was retitled for its appearance in U.S. and British paperback as *The Rat Race* (Berkley: G-19, 1956, 255 pp., pa 35¢; Panther: 947, 1959, 223 pp., pa 2/6).
Fiction
Dark Side of the Earth, The [C] [pa] (Signet: D2474, 1964, 160 pp., pa 50¢)
Sf, 7 stories: "Time Is the Traitor"; "The Men Who Murdered Mohammed"; "Out of This World"; "The Pi Man"; "The Flowered Thundermug"; "Will You Wait?"; "They Don't Make Life Like They Used To."
Demolished Man, The (*GSF*, sr3, Jan 1952) (Shasta, Chicago, 1953, 250 pp., $3.00) (Sidgwick Jackson, London, 1953, 224 pp., 9/6) (Signet: 1105, 1954, 175 pp., pa 25¢; S1593, 1958, pa 35¢; D2679, 1965 pa 50¢) (SF B.C. [S.J.], 1954, 6/-) (D'day SF B.C.,

1955, 185 pp., $1.15) (*L'homme demoli* [French], Denoël: PF9, 1955, pa) (*Ensam Mot Universum* [Swedish], Lindqvist, 1955) (*El hombre demolido* [Spanish (Argentine)], Minotaur: 6, 1956, pa) (Panther: 933, 1959, 189 pp., pa 2/6; 1962, pa 2/6) (*Sturm aufs Universum* [German], Goldmann, 1960; 1962, pa) (*L'uomo disintegrato* [Italian], *Urania*: 312, 1963)
Won the 1953 Hugo award for novels and the 2nd International Fantasy Award in 1954. The New York *Herald Tribune* summarized it: "A subtle and more complex whydunit."
Starburst [C] [pa] (Signet: S1524, 1958, 160 pp., pa 35¢; D2672, 1965, pa 50¢) (Sphere, 1968, 158 pp., pa 5/-)
Sf, 11 stories: "Disappearing Act"; "Adam and No Eve"; "Star Light, Star Bright"; "The Roller Coaster"; "Oddy and Id" ("The Devil's Invention"); "The Starcomber" ("5,271,009"); "Travel Diary"; "Fondly Fahrenheit"; "Hobson's Choice"; "The Die-Hard"; "Of Time and Third Avenue."
Stars My Destination, The (*GSF*, sr4, Oct 1956) (*Tiger! Tiger!* Sidgwick Jackson, London, 1956, 232 pp., 12/6; Penguin: SF2620, 1967, 249 pp., pa 4/6) (Signet: S1389, 1956, 197 pp., pa 35¢; S1931, 1961, pa 35¢) ("Jusqu'aux étoiles," [French], *Galaxie*, sr2, July 1958) (*Terminus les étoiles* [French], Denoël: PF22, 1958, pa) (*Tiger! Tiger!* SF B.C. [S.J.], 1958, 5/6) ([Japanese], Kodan-sha: SF5, 1958) (*Tigermannen* [Swedish], *Galaxy* [Swedish ed.], sr5, July 1959) (Panther: 973, 1959, 192 pp., pa 2/6) (in *A Treasury of Great SF* [Boucher], 1959) (*Die Rache des Kosmonauten* [German], Heyne, 1965, pa)
Action packed story of the unique man who possesses secrets vital to Earth in a war of the outer and inner planets. It was mooted to appear in *F&SF* as "The Burning Spear." Although Denoël's French edition was printed in April 1958, it was released only after publication in *Galaxie*.
Tiger! Tiger! See *Stars My Destination, The*

BETHURUM, TRUMAN (1898–)
Nonfiction (?)
Aboard a Flying Saucer (De Corss: Los Angeles, 1954, 192 pp., $3.00)
One of the numerous 'flying saucer' expositions; the author meets the crew of a saucer from the planet 'Clarion.'

BEUF, CARLO (MARIA LUIGI) (1893–)
Fiction
Innocence of Pastor Muller, The (Duell Sloan, New York, 1951, 156 pp., illus.–author, $2.50) (Collins, Toronto, $3.50)
A remarkably off-trail absurd but touching satire about a device that photographs thoughts.

BEYER, W(ILLIAM) G(RAY) Erstwhile U.S. author. He worked his way through an electrical engineering course at Drexel Institute by making and selling primitive radio receivers; he then spent 30 or so years on such jobs as taxi driving, selling, railroading, and police work. He recently became captain in charge of Philadelphia police radio and several other communications and technical services. Other than his *Minions* series, his only sf story was "Let 'Em Eat Space" (*Arg*, n'te, 4 Nov 1939; *Fan*, Feb 1963).
Series
Minions *Minions of the Moon* (*Arg*, sr 3, 22 Apr 1939; book; *2CSAB*, Sum 1952); "Minions of Mars" (*Arg*, sr5, 13 Jan 1940); "Minions of Mercury" (*Arg*, sr5, 31 Aug 1940); "Minions of the Shadow" (*Arg*, sr5, 20 Sep 1941).
Fiction
Minions of the Moon (*Arg*, sr3, 22 Apr 1939) (Gnome, New York, 1950, 190 pp., $2.50) (abr., *2CSAB*, Sum 1952)
Light adventure with good characterisation of the being "Omega."

BEYNON, JOHN (pseud) See HARRIS, J. B.

BIEMILLER, CARL LUDWIG (16 Dec 1912–)
Fiction [juvenile]
Magic Ball From Mars, The (Morrow, New York, 1953, 127 pp., illus.–K. Voute, $2.50) (McLeod, Toronto, $3.00)

For 8-12 years old; typical flying saucer from Mars—boy befriends Martian. Sequel is *Starboy*.

Starboy ("Johnny and the Boy From Space," *Jack and Jill* sr?) (Holt, New York, 1956, 158 pp., $2.50)

Sequel to *The Magic Ball From Mars*; a Martian and his son holiday on Earth and are met by bureaucracy.

BIER, JESSE (18 July 1925–) U.S. scholar, born in Hoboken, N.J. He studied at several colleges, obtaining his M.A. and Ph.D. at Princeton. He has been a college instructor since 1952, and Associate Professor of English at Montana State U. since 1959.

Fiction

Hole in the Lead Apron, A [C] (Harcourt, New York, 1964, 248 pp., $4.50)

Includes 2 fantasies: "Father and Son" (alternate history of Germany at end of World War II), and "Migdone" (ghost and psychiatric). Other stories of marginal interest.

BIERCE, AMBROSE (24 June 1842–1914) U.S. satirist, story-writer and poet. In boyhood he read widely from his father's library. In 1861 he volunteered for the Union Army and served throughout the Civil War, being severely wounded twice and breveted as a major for bravery. He started in journalism as editor of the San Francisco *News Letter*; in 1872 he went to London, where his caustic humor was soon revealed in the periodical *Fun* and other works, and he became famous as "Bitter Bierce." He returned to San Francisco and remained for 25 years, writing for *The Wasp* and *The Argonaut* and conducting the notable weekly column "Prattle" in the *Examiner*. He went to Mexico in 1913 and never returned; his death was reported in 1914.

Throughout the 1880's he wrote many short stories without once finding an editor willing to publish them; eventually his collection *Tales of Soldiers and Civilians* was financed in 1891 by a San Francisco merchant. It later saw many editions as *In the Midst of Life*. The listing below is complete for fantasy except for the scarce *A Horseman in the Sky* . . . [see the Bleiler *Checklist*]. Bierce's collected works were published in Chicago 1909-12, and his *Collected Writings* contains much of interest. *The Monk and the Hangman's Daughter* (Avon, 1955, pa) includes "An Occurrence at Owl Creek Bridge" and "The Damned Thing", both of which are often anthologised. His *Devil's Dictionary* has recently reappeared as *The Enlarged Devil's Dictionary* (Gollancz, 1968, 30/-); this is a compilation of sweeping and shallow witticisms. Biographies of Bierce include: *The Devil's Lexicographer*, Paul Fatout (Oklahoma, 1951)—strong in fresh material on Bierce's peculiar life but weak in any comprehension of his fiction; *Ambrose Bierce: A Biography*, Carey McWilliams (Archon, 1967, $12.00); *Ambrose Bierce*, Richard O'Connor (Gollancz, 1968, 42/-).

Fiction

Can Such Things Be? [C] (Cassell, New York, 1893, 320 pp.) (Neale, Washington, 1903, 320 pp.) (in *The Collected Writings of Ambrose Bierce*, 1946)

42 stories: "Arrest"; "At Old Man Eckerts' "; "Baby Tramp"; "Baffled Ambuscade"; "Beyond the Wall"; "Charles Ashmore's Trail"; "Cold Greeting"; "The Damned Thing"; "Death of Halpin Frayser"; "Diagnosis of Death"; "Difficulty of Crossing a Field"; "Fruitless Assignment"; "Haita the Shepherd"; "Haunted Valley"; "Inhabitant of Carcosa"; "Isles of Pines"; "John Bartine's Watch"; "John Nortonson's Funeral"; "Jug of Sirup"; "The Man With Two Lives"; "The Middle Toe of the Right Foot"; "Moonlit Road"; "Moxon's Master"; "Night Doings at Deadman's"; "One of Twins"; "One Summer Night"; "Other Lodgers"; "Present at a Hanging"; "Psychological Shipwreck"; "Realm of the Unreal"; "Resumed Identity"; "Secret of Macarger's Gulch"; "Spook House"; "Staley Fleming's Hallucination"; "The Stranger"; "Thing at Nolan"; "Three and One Are One"; "Tough Tussle"; "Two Military Executions"; "Unfinished Race"; "Vine on a House"; "Wireless Message."

Collected Writings of Ambrose Bierce, The [C] (Citadel, New York, 1946, 810 pp., $4.00; 1963, pa $2.75) (McLeod, Toronto, $4.75)

His collected works, with introduction "Ambrose Bierce, Portrait of a Misanthrope," C. Fadiman:

In the Midst of Life—Tales of Soldiers and Civilians. Soldiers: "A Horseman in the Sky"; "An Occurrence at Owl Creek Bridge"; "Chickamauga"; "A Son of the Gods"; "One of the Missing"; "Killed at Resaca"; "The Affair at Coulter's Notch"; "The Coup de Grace"; "Parker Adderson, Philospher"; "An Affair of Outposts"; "The Story of a Conscience"; "One Kind of Officer"; "One Officer, One Man"; "George Thurston"; "The Mocking-Bird." Civilians: "The Man Out of the Nose"; "An Adventure at Brownville"; "The Famous Gilson Bequest"; "The Applicant"; "A Watcher by the Dead"; "The Man and the Snake"; "A Holy Terror"; "The Suitable Surroundings"; "The Boarded Window"; "A Lady From Redhorse"; "The Eyes of the Panther."

The Devil's Dictionary.

Can Such Things Be?: "The Death of Halpin Frayser"; "The Secret of Macarger's Gulch"; "One Summer Night"; "The Moonlit Road"; "A Diagnosis of Death"; "Moxon's Master"; "A Tough Tussle"; "One of Twins"; "The Haunted Valley"; "A Jug of Sirup"; "Staley Fleming's Hallucination"; "A Resumed Identity"; "A Baby Tramp"; "The Night Doings at 'Deadman's' "; "Beyond the Wall"; "A Psychological Shipwreck"; "The Middle Toe of the Right Foot"; "John Mortonson's Funeral"; "The Realm of the Unreal"; "John Bartine's Watch"; "The Damned Thing"; "Haita the Shepherd"; "An Inhabitant of Carcosa"; "The Stranger."

Fantastic Fables: "Fables From *Fun*"; "Aesopus Emendatus"; "Old Saws With New Teeth"; "Fables in Rhyme."

The Monk and the Hangman's Daughter.

Negligible Tales: "A Bottomless Grave"; "Jupiter Doke, Brigadier-General"; "The Widower Turmore"; "The City of the Gone Away"; "The Major's Tale"; "Curried Cow"; "A Revolt of the Gods"; "The Baptism of Dobsho"; "The Race at Left Bower"; "The Failure of Hope and Wandel"; "Perry Chumly's Eclipse"; "A Providential Intimation"; "Mr. Swiddler's Flip-Flap"; "The Little Story."

The Parenticide Club: "My Favorite Murder"; "Oil of Dog"; "An Imperfect Conflagration"; "The Hypnotist."

Eyes of the Panther: Tales of Soldiers and Civilians [C] (Cape 'Travellers' Library,' London, 1928, 282 pp., 3/6)

Not listed in the Bleiler *Checklist*, but can be considered as an edition of *In the Midst of Life* . . . Contains 24 stories, with introduction by Martin Armstrong: "The Affair at Coulter's Notch"; "The Applicant"; "The Boarded Window"; "Chickamauga"; "Coup de Grace"; "The Curried Cow"; "Eyes of the Panther"; "George Thurston"; "Horseman in the Sky"; "The Imperfect Conflagration"; "Killed at Resaca"; "The Man and the Snake"; "Mr. Swiddler's Flip-Flap"; "The Mocking-Bird"; "An Occurrence at Owl Creek Bridge"; "One Kind of Officer"; "One of the Missing"; "Parker Adderson. Philosopher"; "A Providential Intimation"; "A Shipwrecollection"; "Son of the Gods"; "The Story of a Conscience"; "Suitable Surroundings"; "A Watcher by the Dead."

Fantastic Fables [C] (Putnam, New York & London, 1899, 194 pp.) (Knickerbocker, New York, 1899) (in *The Collected Writings of Ambrose Bierce*, 1946)

No further information available.

Ghost and Horror Stories of Ambrose Bierce (edited by E. F. Bleiler) [C] (Dover, New York, 1964, 199 pp., pa $1.00)

24 stories and compiler's introduction—biography and critique of Bierce's work: "The Death of Halpin Frayser"; "Moxon's Master"; "Beyond the Wall"; "The Damned Thing"; "A Watcher by the Dead"; "An Occurrence at Owl Creek Bridge"; "The Ways of Ghosts"; "Some Haunted Houses"; " 'Mysterious Disappearances' "; "The Man and the Snake"; "The Suitable Surroundings"; "The Eyes of the Panther"; "The Famous Gilson Bequest"; "An Adventure at Brownville"; "An Inhabitant of Carcosa"; "The Secret of Macarger's Gulch"; "The Moonlit Road"; "The Haunted Valley"; "A Jug of Sirup"; "The Night Doings at 'Deadman's' "; "The Middle Toe of the Right Foot"; "John Bartine's Watch"; "The Stranger"; "Visions of the Night."

In the Midst of Life: Tales of Soldiers and Civilians [C] (*Tales of Soldiers and Civilians*, E. L. G. Steele, San Francisco, 1891, 300 pp.) (Putnam, New York, 1898, 362 pp.) (Chatto Windus, London, 1910, 244 pp.; 'Phoenix,' 1930, 244 pp., 3/6; 1941, 244 pp.,; 'Phoenix 6,' 1950, 244 pp., 6/-) (Boni Liveright, New York, 1918, 403 pp., $2.00) (Modern Library, New York, 1927, 403 pp., 95¢) (Penguin: 199, 1939, 215 pp., pa 1/-) (*Tales of Soldiers and Civilians*, Limited Edition Club, New York, 1943, 222 pp., illus.—P. Landaire, $10.00; Hermitage, New York, 1943, $3.50) (in *The Collected Writings of Ambrose Bierce*, 1946) (Signet: CP160, 1961, 256 pp., pa 60¢)

Contents of many of these differ considerably; those known are covered separately herewith:

Steele, 1891. 19 stories: "The Affair at Coulter's Notch"; "The Boarded Window"; "Chickamauga"; "Coup de Grace"; "Haita the Shepherd"; "The Heiress From Redhorse"; "The Holy Terror"; "Horseman in the Sky"; "Inhabitant of Carcosa"; "Killed at Resaca"; "The Man and the Snake"; "The Middle Toe of the Right Foot"; "An Occurrence at Owl Creek Bridge"; "One of the Missing"; "Parker Adderson, Philosopher"; "Son of the Gods"; "Suitable Surroundings"; "A Tough Tussle"; "A Watcher by the Dead."

Modern Library, 1927 [this could be a reprint of Boni Liveright 1918 edition]. 26 stories: "The Adventure at Brownville" [with I. L. Peterson]; "The Affair at Coulter's Notch"; "The Affair of Outposts"; "The Applicant"; "The Boarded Window"; "Chickamauga"; "Coup de Grace"; "Eyes of the Panther"; "The Famous Gilson Bequest"; "George Thurston"; "The Holy Terror"; "Horseman in the Sky"; "Killed at Resaca"; "The Lady From Redhorse"; "The Man and the Snake"; "The Man Out of the Nose"; "The Mocking-Bird"; "An Occurrence at Owl Creek Bridge"; "One Kind of Officer"; "One of the Missing"; "One Officer, One Man"; "Parker Adderson, Philosopher"; "Son of the Gods"; "The Story of a Conscience"; "Suitable Surroundings"; "A Watcher by the Dead."

Chatto, 1950 [this may cover older editions from the same publisher]. 21 stories: *The Suitable Surroundings:* "The Night"; "The Day Before"; "The Day After." *Soldiers:* "A Horseman in the Sky"; "An Occurrence at Owl Creek Bridge"; "Chickamauga"; "A Son of the Gods"; "One of the Missing"; "Killed at Resaca"; "The Affair at Coulter's Notch"; "A Tough Tussle"; "The Coup de Grace"; "Parker Adderson, Philosopher."

Signet, 1961. 26 stories: *In the Midst of Life. Tales of Soldiers:* The 10 stories listed in Chatto 1950 under *Soldiers* plus "An Affair of Outposts." *Tales of Civilians:* "A Watcher by the Dead"; "The Man and the Snake"; "A Holy Terror"; "The Suitable Surroundings"; "An Inhabitant of Carcosa"; "The Boarded Window"; "The Middle Toe of the Right Foot"; "A Lady From Redhorse"; "Haita the Shepherd"; "The Damned Thing"; "The Eyes of the Panther."

Tales from *Can Such Things Be?* "The Death of Halpin Frayser"; "Jupiter Doke, Brigadier General"; "The Major's Tale"; "The Night-Doings at 'Deadman's.' "

Extracts from *The Devil's Dictionary.* Afterword by Marcus Cunliffe. Selected Bibliography. A Note on the Text.

Tales of Soldiers and Civilians [C]   See *In the Midst of Life*

BIGGLE, LLOYD JR. (17 Apr 1923–) U.S. author, born in Waterloo, Iowa. Writing and music were early interests; he won several writing awards while in high school, and also first prize in a national contest for musical composition. He entered Wayne U., Detroit, in 1941 to major in music, but his education was interrupted by war service 1943-46, when he was a communications sergeant with the 102nd Infantry Division in Europe. Upon returning to Wayne U. he switched from music to English, receiving an A.B. Degree with High Distinction in 1947. He entered U. of Michigan for graduate study in music and took his M.M. Degree (Music Literature) in 1948 and Ph.D. (Musicology) in 1953. From 1948-51 he taught Music Literature and Music History at U. of Michigan. He left teaching for business, but began writing seriously about 1954. He was married in 1947 to Hedwig Janiszewski, violinist, and has two children.

Since his first appearance in the sf field ("Gypped," *GSF*, July 1956) he has sold some three dozen sf stories and appeared in a variety of magazines. He occasionally uses musical themes in his stories, e.g. "The Tunesmith" (*If*, Aug 1957), "Gypped," "Spare the Rod" (*GSF*, Mar 1958), "Still, Small Voice" (*ASF*, Apr 1961).

He has written many mystery stories, appearing in *Ellery Queen's Mystery Magazine*, etc.

Fiction

All the Colors of Darkness (Doubleday, New York, 1963, 210 pp., $3.95) (D'day SF B.C., 1964, $1.20) (D. Dobson, London, 1964, 210 pp., 16/-) (Paperback: 52-514, 1965, 176 pp., pa 50¢; 53-746, 1968, pa 60¢) (*Für Menschen verboten* [German], 1964, 1964 pa) (*Tuti i colori del buio* [Italian], *Urania*: 335, 1964) (SF B.C. [S.J.], 1965, 6/-) (Penguin: 2387, 1966, 204 pp., pa 4/-)

Intrigue with aliens when matter transmitters are brought into operation on Earth.

Angry Espers, The [pa]   ("A Taste of Fire," *AS*, Aug 1959) (Ace: D-485, 1961, 136 pp., pa 35¢; with *The Puzzle Planet*) (*Die Unbesiegbaren* [German], *TS*: 47, 1961) (Hale, London, 1968, 192 pp., 18/-)

An Earthman fights his way out of a planet of espers. *Note:* The Ace edition has some revisions and cuts restored.

Fury Out of Time, The (Doubleday, 1965, 257 pp., $4.50) (D'day, Toronto, $4.95) (Dobson, 1966, 257 pp., 21/-) (Berkley: X1393, 1967, 223 pp., pa 60¢) (*De tijdcapsule* [Dutch], Spectrum, Utrecht & Antwerp, 1967) (Sphere: 16519, 1968, 192 pp., pa 5/-)

Interesting story of the path of a time capsule and the adventure in time of a grounded flyer.

Rule of the Door and Other Fanciful Regulations, The [C] (Doubleday, 1967, 206 pp., $3.95) (*Verbrechen in der Zukunft* [German], Goldmann: 098, 1968, pa)

9 stories: "The Rule of the Door"; "Petty Larceny"; "On the Dotted Line"; "Judgment Day"; "Secret Weapon" ("Bridle Shower"); "The Perfect Punishment" ("Pariah Planet"); "A Slight Case of Limbo"; "D.F.C." ("Cronius of the D.F.C."); "Wings of Song."

Still, Small Voice of Trumpets, The (Doubleday, 1968, 189 pp., $4.50)

A bureau dedicated to spreading universal self-rule use trumpets to aid their task on the planet Kurr. Enlarged from "Still Small Voice," *ASF*, n'te, Apr 1961.

Watchers of the Dark (Doubleday, 1966, 228 pp., $4.50) (D'day SF B.C., 1966, $1.20) (*Spiralen aus dem Dunkel* [German], Goldmann: 096, 1968, pa) (Chapp & Whiting, London, 1968, 228 pp., 21/-)

A secret mental weapon threatens the Galaxy.

BILBO, JACK (pseud) See BARUCH, H.

BINDER, EANDO Pseudonym for BINDER, E. A. and BINDER, O. O.

BINDER, EARL ANDREW (1904–) U.S. author; older brother of Otto, with whom he formed the writing team known as Eando Binder. Fans since 1926, their first story appeared in 1932. The collaboration ceased about 1940. (For full coverage of fiction, see BINDER, O. O.)

BINDER, JACK U.S. artist, brother to Earl and Otto. He illustrated the *Captain Marvel* comic strip (written by Otto) and also did some illustrations for *Thrilling Wonder Stories* in 1939.

BINDER, OTTO OSCAR (26 Aug 1911–) U.S. sf author. He was born in Bessemer, Michigan, the son of an iron worker, and brother of Earl and Jack. He married Ione Frances Turek, author of children's books, in 1940. He was a librarian, and a manuscript reader at Otis Adelbert Kline Literary Agency 1936-38. He was a freelance writer 1932-36 and 1939-59, Editor-in-Chief of *Space World* 1960-62, and Publisher from 1962. His column "Our Space Age" has been published in 25 U.S. and 11 foreign newspapers through the Bell-McClure Syndicate.

Earl and Otto Binder, both fans since 1926, wrote in collaboration as "Eando Binder." They first appeared with "The First Martian" (*AS*, Oct 1932). "Eando Binder" wrote many stories up to the postwar years, although Earl dropped out of the collaboration about 1940. The pair used many pseudonyms, of which one of the more noted was "Gordon A. Giles." Otto wrote few stories postwar, but did have some in *Science Fiction Plus*. In recent years he has been writing science-fact articles and juvenile science books, as well as editing *Space World* (nonfiction).

Besides the works below, the following stories are of probable interest: "After an Age" (*AS*, Nov 1942; [Swedish], *Jules Verne Magasinet*, Nos. 20-46, 1944); "Spawn of Eternal Thought" (*ASF*, sr2, Apr 1936); "The Impossible World" (*SS*, Mar 1939); "Five Steps to Tomorrow" (*SS*, July 1940; [Swedish], *JVM*, Nos. 1-7, 1940); "The Chessboard of Mars" (*TWS*, June 1937; *Wonder Story Annual*, 1951); "The Time Cheaters" (*TWS*, Mar 1940); "The Teacher From Mars" (*TWS*, Feb 1941; *My Best SF Story* [Margulies], 1949); "Dawn to Dusk" (*WS*, sr3, Nov 1934).

Series

Link, Adam Sentient robot. All in *Amazing Stories*: "I, Robot" (Jan 1939; Apr 1961); "The Trial of Adam Link, Robot" (July 1939); "Adam Link in Business" (Jan 1940); "Adam Link's Vengeance" (Feb 1940); "Adam Link, Robot Detective" (May 1940); "Adam Link, Champion Athlete" (July 1940); "Adam Link Fights a War" (Dec 1940); "Adam Link in the Past" (Feb 1941); "Adam Link Faces a Revolt" (May 1941); "Adam Link Saves the World" (Apr 1942). The first 6 stories and the final one were revised into continuity as *Adam Link–Robot*. "Adam Link in the Past" appeared as an Australian paper-covered item *ca*. 1950. The first 3 stories appeared in Gaines' comic *Weird Science-Fantasy* in 1954. The 1st, 2nd, 4th, 5th and 7th appeared in *JVM* [Swedish], 1940-42.

Via [as "Gordon A. Giles"] All in *TWS*: (Mars) "Via Etherline" (Oct 1937); "Via Asteroid" (Feb 1938; *FSM*, Fall 1951); "Via Death" (Aug 1938; *FSM*, Win 1952). (Venus) "Via Venus" (Oct 1939); "Via Pyramid" (Jan 1940); "Via Sun" (Mar 1940). (Mercury) "Via Mercury" (Oct 1940); "Via Catacombs" (Nov 1940); "Via Intelligence" (Dec 1940). (Jupiter) "Via Jupiter" (Jan 1942–as Eando Binder).

York, Anton Immortal man (and wife). All in *TWS*: "Conquest of Life" (Aug 1937; *SS*, May 1949); "Life Eternal" (Feb 1938); "The Three Eternals" (Dec 1939; Whitman [Australian], 1951, pa); "The Secret of Anton York" (Aug 1940). Published as *Anton York, Immortal*.

Fiction

Adam Link–Robot [pa] (Paperback: 52-847, 1965, 174 pp., pa 50¢; 53-763, 1968, pa 60¢)
7 stories of the series.

Anton York, Immortal [pa] (Belmont: B50-627, 1965, 158 pp., pa 50¢)
The series under one cover.

Avengers Battle the Earth-Wrecker, The [pa] (Bantam: F3569, 1967, 122 pp., pa 50¢)

Enslaved Brains (*WS*, sr3, July 1934; *FSM*, Win 1951) (Avalon, New York, 1965, 192 pp., $3.25)

Lords of Creation (*Arg*, sr6, 23 Sep 1939) (Prime, Philadelphia, 1949, 232 pp., $3.00) (*Antarkta* [German], *UG*: 87, 1958)
Adventure and intrigue on a future Earth with dominating Overlords.

Nonfiction

What We Really Know About Flying Saucers [pa] (Gold Medal, 1967, pa 75¢)

BINGENHEIMER, HEINZ (1923–17 Aug 1964) German bibliographer and organiser of the book service "Transgalaxis" (now being run by his widow and son). This service published a catalogue of German sf and also circulates a regular news sheet on the latest published German material. Bingenheimer worked with Jakob Bleymehl on a revised and enlarged edition of the catalogue.

Nonfiction

Katalog der deutschsprachigen utopisch-phantastischen Literatur (Transgalaxis, abgeschlossen 1959, 124 pp., DM7.50)
A listing of German sf by author, covering books and the various magazine series 1460-1960. Original titles of translated material are given in most cases; publishers and fan magazine information are given at the end. Although in German, it can be readily used by any bibliographer.

BINGHAM, CARSON (pseud) See CASSIDAY, B.

BIRCH, A(LBERT) G.

Anthology

Moon Terror, The (Popular Fiction Pub. Co., Indianapolis, 1927, 192 pp., $1.50)
Weird, 4 stories from *Weird Tales*: "The Moon Terror," A. G. Birch (sr2, May 1923); "Ooze," A. M. Rud (Mar 1923, Jan 1952); "Penelope," V. Starrett (May 1923); "An Adventure in the Fourth Dimension," Farnsworth Wright (Oct 1923).

BIRKIN, CHARLES LLOYD (24 Sep 1907–) British author. He used the pseudonym "Charles Lloyd" on a number of stories published in the prewar P. Allan *Creeps Library* book series. In the 1960's he returned to the weird field as both writer and anthologist.

Fiction

Dark Menace [C] [pa] (Tandem: T199, 1968, 188 pp., pa 3/6)
Weird, 13 stories: "Dark Menace"; " 'Happy As Larry' "; "S.O.S."; "The Jungle"; "T-I-M"; "The Life Giver"; " 'Don't Ever Leave Me' "; "The Yellow Dressing Gown"; "Waiting for Trains"; "The Lord God Made Them All"; "The Accessory"; "Simple Simon"; "Siren Song."

Devil's Spawn [C] (P. Allan, London, 1936, 252 pp., 5/-)
Not in Bleiler *Checklist*. Weird, 16 stories: "Old Mrs. Strathers"; "Shelter"; "The Cockroach"; "The Terror on Tobit"; "The Last Night"; "An Eye for an Eye"; "Henri Larne"; "Havelock's Farm"; "The Harlem Horror"; "A Poem and a Bunch of Roses"; "Obsession"; "The Happy Dancers"; "The Actor's Story"; "Special Diet"; "Premiere" (from *The Sketch*); "Angela."

Kiss of Death, The [C] [pa] (Tandem: T2, 1964, 234 pp., pa 3/6; T2, 1967, 192 pp., pa 3/6)
Weird, 15 stories (14 in 2nd ed., omitting "Lighten Our Darkness"), with introduction by D. Wheatley: "The Kiss of Death"; "The Hens"; "Les Belles Dames sans Merci"; " 'The New Ones' "; "The Mouse Hole"; "Fairy Dust"; " 'Some New Pleasures Prove' "; "The Kennel"; "Mon Ami, Pierrot"; "The Mutation"; "Lighten Our Darkness"; "Fine Needlework"; "The Hitch"; "The Three Monkeys"; "Malleus Maleficarum."

My Name Is Death and Other New Tales of Horror [c] [pa] (Panther: 2150, 1966, 139 pp., pa 3/6)
Weird, 8 stories: "My Name Is Death"; "Kitty Fisher"; "King of the Castle"; "Parlez Moi d'Amour"; "Who's Your Lady Friend?"; "The Finger of Fear"; "Hosanna!"; "Hard to Get."

Smell of Evil, The [C] [pa] (Tandem: T28, 1965, 189 pp., pa 3/6)
Weird, 8 stories; introduction by D. Wheatley: "The Smell of Evil"; "Text for Today"; "The Godmothers"; "Green Fingers"; "Ballet Negre"; "The Lesson"; " 'Is Anyone There?' "; "The Serum of Doctor White"; " 'Dance Little Lady' "; "Little Boy Blue"; "The Cornered Beast"; "The Interloper"; "The Cross."

Where Terror Stalked [C] [pa] (Tandem: T80, 1966, 192 pp., pa 3/6)
Weird, 13 stories: "Where Terror Stalked"; "Old Mrs. Strathers"; "New Faces"; "Paris Pilgrimage"; "Obsession"; "The Harlem Horror"; " 'Bring Back My Bonny' "; "Softly . . . Softly"; "The Belt"; "Shelter"; "The Orphanage"; " 'Gran' "; "No More for Mary."

Anthologies

Haunted Dancers, The [pa] See *Tandem Book of Ghost Stories*

Tandem Book of Ghost Stories, The [pa] (Tandem: T52, 1965, 192 pp., pa 3/6) (*The Haunted Dancers*, Paperback: 52-472, 1967, 159 pp., pa 50¢)
12 stories: "Lost, Strayed, Stolen," M. F. K. Fisher; "Florinda," Shamus Frazer; "Dead Men's Bones," Edith Olivier; "The Third Coach," H. R. Wakefield; "Last Time Lucky," P. M. Hubbard; "Cold in the Night," Marguerite Steen; "Zara and Zita," C. Birkin; "Out of the Earth," Flavia Richardson; "Sophy Mason Comes Back," E. M. Delafield; "The Haunted Dancers," A. Mayse; "The Yew Tree," Shamus Frazer; "No Ships Pass," Lady Eleanor Smith.

Tandem Book of Horror Stories, The [pa] (Tandem: T49, 1965,

192 pp., pa 3/6) (*The Witch Baiter*, Paperback: 52-468, 1967, 159 pp., pa 50¢)

11 stories: "The Puppets," Francis King; "Old Man's Beard," H. R. Wakefield; "The Cyclops Ju Ju," Shamus Frazer; "Arabesque: The Mouse," A. E. Coppard; "Thirty," Guy Preston; "The Medicine Cupboard," C. Birkin; "Dorner Cordaianthus," Hester Holland; "The Witch Baiter," R. Anthony; "Cold Blood," George Langelaan; "The Fifth Mask," Shamus Frazer; "Lord Mount Prospect," John Betjeman.

Witch Baiter, The [pa]   See *Tandem Book of Horror Stories, The*

BISHOP, WILLIAM HENRY (1847–26 Sep 1928) American novelist, born in Hartford, Conn. A further fantasy to the collections below was *The Garden of Eden, U.S.A.* (C. H. Kerr, Chicago, 1895).
Fiction
Anti-Babel and Other Such Doings [C]   (Neale, New York, 1919, 251 pp.)

Fantasy, 8 stories: " 'Anti-Babel' "; "The Man Who Made Believe He Had Failed"; "The Bric-a-Brac Mission"; "The Last of the Fairy Wands"; "Insects I Have Met"; " 'Aleck,' a Sort of Ghost Story"; "Yessamina"; "The Cruise of a Drifted Boat."
Choy Susan and Other Stories [C]   (Houghton Mifflin, Boston & New York, 1885, 349 pp.)

Fantasy, 7 stories: "Choy Susan"; "The Battle of Bunkerloo"; "Deodand"; "Braxton's New Art"; "One of the 30 Pieces"; "McIntyre's False Face"; "Miss Calderon's German."

BISHOP, ZEALIA BROWN (REED) U.S. author; wife of D. W. Bishop of Highland View Farm, near Kansas City. A pupil of H. P. Lovecraft, at his urging she wrote the stories in the collection below, all being considered genuine contributions to the Cthulhu Mythos. She has had published many more romantic stories than weird, contributing to *Life Story* and *The Kansas Magazine*, and also writing a historical series.
Fiction
Curse of Yig and Others, The [C]   (Arkham, Wisconsin, 1953, 175 pp., $3.00, jacket–R. Clyne; 1217 copies)

Weird, 3 stories and 2 profiles: "The Curse of Yig" (*WT*, Nov 1929; *AFR*: 14, 1950); "Medusa's Coil" (*WT*, Jan 1939); "The Mound (*WT*, Nov 1940). *Profiles:* "H. P. Lovecraft: A Pupil's View"; "A Wisconsin Balzac: A Profile of August Derleth." With bibliographies of book publications of these two authors, but not magazine printings.

BIXBY, JEROME (LEWIS) (11 Jan 1923–) U.S. sf editor and author. He is also a concert pianist and has done some illustrations. He edited *Planet Stories* Sum 1950 to July 1951, and began its companion *Two Complete Science Adventure Books*. He did some writing, and became assistant to Sam Mines on the Standard sf magazines until 1952, when he returned to freelancing. From March to July 1953 he was on the staff of *Galaxy* under H. L. Gold. Besides sf, he has written adventure and westerns, and has had over a thousand stories published. His screenplays include *It–The Vampire From Outer Space* and *The Curse of the Faceless Men*.
Fiction
Devil's Scrapbook [C] [pa]   (Brandon: 625, 1964, 158 pp., pa 60¢)

19 stories: "Lust in Stone"; "The Best Lover in Hell"; "Sin Wager"; "Spell of the Witch Wife"; "The Dirtiest Story in Hell"; "The Last Wish"; "A Doll, a Gypsy Curse and Murder"; "The Oldest Story in Hell"; "The Demon and the Well-Heeled Satyr"; "The Strange Habits of Robert Prey"; "The Love Jug"; "Heavenly Nymph on Hell's Island"; "The Shangri-La Caper"; "Jungle Sin"; "The Saddest Story in Hell"; "Kiss of Blood"; "The Marquis' Magic Potion"; "Tabu Cave Goddess"; "The Mortal and the Goddess."
Space by the Tale [C] [pa]   (Ballantine: U2203, 1964, 159 pp., pa 50¢)

Sf, 11 stories: "The Draw"; "The Young One"; "Laboratory"; "The Good Dog"; "One Way Street"; "Small War"; "Trace";

"Angels in the Jets"; "The Battle of the Bells"; "The Magic Typewriter"; "The Bad Life."

BLACK, DOROTHY
Fiction
Candles in the Dark   (Cassell, London, 1954, 190 pp., 9/6)
Romantic adventure after the bombing of New York.

BLACK, WILLIAM (15 Nov 1841–10 Dec 1898) Scottish novelist. Born at Glasgow and educated at private schools, he tried his hand at landscape painting, and then began to write criticism, essays and poetry for the *Glasgow Weekly Citizen*. His first novel, *James Merle* (1864), was a failure. His wife died in 1866. From 1870 he spent some years in editorial work, then became successful as a novelist, and remarried. He is mainly remembered for his descriptive detail and stories with settings in the mountains and along the Scottish coast. A fantasy besides that below is *The Strange Adventures of a Phaeton* (Macmillan, London, 1878).
Fiction
Magic Ink and Other Stories, The [C]   (Harper, New York, 1892, 258 pp.)

Weird, 3 stories: "The Magic Ink"; "A Hallowe'en Wraith"; "Manciebel: A Tale of Stratford-on-Avon."

BLACKBURN, JOHN (FENWICK) (26 June 1923–) British author; born in Northumberland, son of a clergyman; B.A. U. of Durham, member of the Crime Writer's Association. He has had a number of occupations ranging from lorry driver and merchant seaman to council school teacher. He was Director of Red Lion Books 1952-59. Since 1954 he has been dealing in second-hand books. He is married. His brother is the poet, Thomas Blackburn. A further novel (non-sf) is *Broken Boy*.
Fiction
Children of the Night   (J. Cape, London, 1966, 192 pp., 18/-) (Panther: 24689, 1968, 158 pp., pa 5/-)

Mystery-horror involving humans who have lived 7 centuries, telepathy, and a desire to bring about Judgment Day.
Nothing But the Night   (J. Cape, London, 1968, 192 pp., 21/-)

Murders form a bizarre jigsaw puzzle, which an occultist helps to solve.
Scent of New-Mown Hay, A   (Secker Warburg, London, 1958, 221 pp., 13/6) (Mill-Morrow, New York, 1958, 224 pp., $3.50) (*La morte viene col vento* [Italian], *Urania*: 212, 1959) (Penguin: 1615, 1961, 191 pp., pa 2/6) (Digit: R846, 1964, 158 pp., pa 2/6) (*Une odeur de foin coupé* [French], Fayard, 1964, pa) (*De dood heeft geen aangezicht* [Dutch], Spectrum, Utrecht & Antwerp, 1964) (NEL: 2056, 1968, 160 pp., pa 6/-)

Escaped Nazi mycologist, one of Himmler's confederates, out to devastate the world with a parasitic mutant fungus.
Sour Apple Tree, A   (M. S. Mill, New York, 1959, 189 pp., $3.50)

Mad-scientist type; a series of inexplicable murders in the search for an English traitor.

BLACKWOOD, ALGERNON (1869 – 10 Dec 1951) British author of ghost and fantasy stories. When 20 he emigrated to Canada; he later became a reporter with the *New York Sun* and then the *New York Times*. He led a varied life and did not settle down to writing until he was 36. In his occult investigator "John Silence" (other books besides this title) he created a masterly character who has maintained his popularity against even Dion Fortune's "Doctor Tavener" and Seabury Quinn's "Jules de Grandin." He has many outstanding novels not in the listing below, which covers primarily his collections. Of his fantasy short stories, probably the most noted are "The Wendigo" (*FFM*, June 1944) and "The Willows" (*FFM*, Apr 1946). Many of his stories have been reprinted in weird and fantasy anthologies. Recent writings reprinted include *The Collected Essays, Journalism and Letters* (Harcourt, 4 vol., 1968, v. 3 $7.95, others $8.95). French collections in recent years include *Elève de quatrième . . . dimension* (Denoël: PF91, 1966, pa) and *Migrations* (Denoël: PF101, 1967, pa).
Fiction
Ancient Sorceries and Other Stories [C] [pa]   (Penguin: 2904,

1968, 203 pp., pa 5/-)

6 stories: "The Empty House"; "A Haunted Island"; "Keeping His Promise"; "A Case of Eavesdropping"; "Ancient Sorceries"; "The Nemesis of Fire."

Ancient Sorceries and Other Tales [C]   (Collins 'Kingsway Classics,' London & Glasgow, nd [1927?], 251 pp., 3/6)

6 stories: "Ancient Sorceries"; "The Willows"; "The Return"; "Running Wolf"; "The Man Whom the Trees Loved"; "The Man Who Played Upon the Leaf."

Centaur, The   (Macmillan, London, 1911, 347 pp., 6/-) (Penguin: 166, 1938, 280 pp., pa np)

Fantastic adventure.

Dance of Death and Other Tales, The [C]   (Dial, New York, 1928, 223 pp., $2.00) (Jenkins, London, 1927, 224 pp., 5/-) (Pan: G645, 1963, 126 pp., pa 2/6)

6 stories: "The Dance of Death"; "A Psychical Invasion"; "The Old Man of Visions"; "The South Wind"; "The Touch of Pan"; "The Valley of Beasts."

Day and Night Stories [C]   (Dutton, New York, 1917, 228 pp.) (Cassell, London, 1917, 332 pp., 6/-)

15 stories: "Bit of Wood"; "By Water"; "Cain's Atonement"; "Desert Episode"; "Egyptian Hornet"; "H.S.H."; "Initiation"; "Occupant of the Room"; "Other Wing"; "Touch of Pan"; "The Tradition"; "Transition"; "The Tryst"; "Victim of Higher Space"; "Wings of Horus."

Doll and One Other, The [C]   (Arkham, Wisconsin, 1946, 138 pp., $1.50; 3,490 copies)

2 novels: "The Doll"; "The Trod." Both supernatural horror.

Empty House, The [C]   (E. Nash, London, 1906, 316 pp., 6/-; 1915, 324 pp., 3/6; 1930, 314 pp., 7/6) (?, New York, 1917) (Richards, London, 1948, 316 pp., 7/6)

10 stories: "The Empty House"; "A Haunted Island"; "A Case of Eavesdropping"; "Keeping His Promise"; "With Intent to Steal"; "The Wood of the Dead"; "Smith: An Episode in a Lodging House"; "A Suspicious Gift"; "The Strange Adventures of a Private Secretary in New York"; "Skeleton Lake: An Episode in Camp."

In the Realm of Terror [C]   (Pantheon, New York, 1957, 312 pp., $3.95)

8 stories: "The Willows"; "The Man Whom the Trees Loved"; "The Wendigo"; "A Haunted Island"; "A Psychical Invasion"; "Smith: An Episode in a Lodging House"; "The Empty House"; "The Strange Adventures of a Private Secretary in New York."

Incredible Adventures [C]   (Macmillan, London, 1914, 368 pp., 6/-)

5 stories: "The Damned"; "Descent Into Egypt"; "Regeneration of Lord Ernie"; "The Sacrifice"; "Wayfarers."

Insanity of Jones and Other Tales, The [C] [pa]   See *Tales of Terror and the Unknown*

John Silence [C]   (E. Nash, London, 1908, 390 pp., 6/-; 1910, 398 pp., 2/-; 1914, 3/6; 1922, 400 pp., 3/6) (Unwin, London, 1928, 318 pp., 2/6) (Nash Grayson, London, 1929, 390 pp.) (Richards, London, 1942, 1943, 1947, 390 pp., 7/6)

5 stories: "A Psychical Invasion"; "Ancient Sorceries"; "The Nemesis of Fire"; "Secret Worship"; "The Camp of the Dog." Other 'John Silence' stories include "A Victim of Higher Space" (*AFR*: 18, 1952).

Listener and Other Stories, The [C]   (E. Nash, 1907, 350 pp., 6/-; 1914, 3/6; 1922, 3/6; 1931, 7/6)

9 stories: "Dance of Death"; "Insanity of Jones"; "The Listener"; "Max Hensig—Bacteriologist and Murderer"; "May Day Eve"; "Miss Slumbubble—and Claustrophobia"; "Old Man of Visions"; "The Willows"; "The Woman's Ghost Story."

Lost Valley and Other Stories, The [C]   (E. Nash, 1910, 328 pp., 6/-; 1914, 3/6) (Vaughan Gomme, New York, 1914, 328 pp., illus.—W. G. Robertson) (Grayson, London, 1936, 328 pp., 2/6)

10 stories: "Carlton's Drive"; "Eccentricity of Simon Parnacute"; "The Lost Valley"; "The Man From the 'Gods' "; "The Man Who Played Upon the Leaf"; "Old Clothes"; "Perspective"; "Price of Wiggin's Orgy"; "Terror of the Twins"; "The Wendigo."

Pan's Garden: A Volume of Nature Stories [C]   (Macmillan, London, 1912, 530 pp., illus.—W. G. Robertson, 6/-)

15 stories: "The Man Whom the Trees Loved"; "The South Wind"; "The Sea Fit"; "The Attic"; "The Heath Fire"; "The Messenger"; "The Glamour of the Snow"; "The Return" "Sand"; "The Transfer"; "Clairvoyance"; "The Golden Fly"; "Special Delivery"; "The Destruction of Smith"; "The Temptation of Clay."

Selected Short Stories of Algernon Blackwood [C] [pa]   (Armed: s26, nd, pa)

7 stories: "The Willows"; "The Wendigo"; "A Psychical Invasion"; "The Woman's Ghost Story"; "Max Hensig"; "The Wood of the Dead"; "The Listener."

Selected Tales of Algernon Blackwood [C]   (Penguin: 393, 1948, 173 pp., pa 1/6) (J. Baker, London, 1964, 281 pp., 25/-)

6 stories: "The Empty House"; "Strange Adventures of a Private Secretary"; "Keeping His Promise"; "The Woman's Ghost Story"; "Ancient Sorceries"; "The Camp of the Dog."

Shocks [C]   (Dutton, New York, 1936, 300 pp., $2.00) (Grayson, 1935, 300 pp., 7/6; 1936, 3/6; 1938, 2/6)

15 stories: "Adventure of Tornado Smith"; "Adventure of Miss De Fontenay"; "Chemical"; "Colonel's Ring"; "Dr. Feldman"; "Elsewhere and Otherwise"; "Full Circle"; "Hands of Death"; "Land of Green Ginger"; "The Man Who Lived Backwards"; "Revenge"; "Shocks"; "The Stranger"; "The Survivors"; "Threefold Cord."

Short Stories of A. Blackwood [C]   (Harrap, London, 1930, 284 pp., 6/-; 2/6)

10 stories and introduction by F.H.P.: "The Regeneration of Lord Ernie"; "The Sacrifice"; "Chinese Magic"; "Land of Green Ginger"; "The Stranger"; "First Hate"; "The Olive"; "Two in One"; "Dream Trespass"; "Cain's Atonement."

Strange Stories [C]   (Heinemann, London, 1929, 745 pp., 7/6; 1931, 3/6)

24 stories: "The Man Whom the Trees Loved"; "Sea Fit"; "The Glamour of the Snow"; "The Tryst"; "Transistion"; "The Occupant of the Room"; "The Wings of Horus"; "By Water"; "Malahide and Forden"; "Alexander Alexander"; "The Man Who Was Milligan"; "The Little Beggar"; "The Pikestaffe Case"; "Accessory Before the Fact"; "The Deferred Appointment"; "Ancient Lights"; "The Goblin Collection"; "Running Wolf"; "The Valley of the Beasts"; "The Decoy"; "Confession"; "A Descent Into Egypt"; "The Willows"; "Ancient Sorceries."

Tales of Algernon Blackwood [C]   (M. Secker, London, 1938, 704 pp., 8/6) (Dutton, 1939, 684 pp., $2.50)

21 stories: "Ancient Sorceries"; "The Camp of the Dog"; "Case of Eavesdropping"; "The Dance of Death"; "The Empty House"; "The Insanity of Jones"; "Keeping His Promise"; "The Listener"; "The Man From the 'Gods' "; "Max Hensig—Bacteriologist and Murderer"; "May Day Eve"; "Nemesis of Fire"; "The Psychical Invasion"; "Secret Worship"; "Strange Adventures of a Private Secretary"; "Suspicious Gift"; "The Wendigo"; "The Willows"; "With Intent to Steal"; "The Woman's Ghost Story"; "The Wood of the Dead."

Tales of Terror and the Unknown [C] [pa]   (Dutton: D166, 1965, 381 pp., pa $1.75) (*The Insanity of Jones and Other Tales*, Penguin: 2527, 1966, 365 pp., pa 5/-)

Weird, 11 stories (in chronological sequence as written between 1906-10): "The Willows"; "The Woman's Ghost Story"; "Max Hensig"; "The Listener"; "The Old Man of Visions"; "May Day Eve"; "The Insanity of Jones"; "The Dance of Death"; "Miss Slumbubble"; "The Wendigo"; "The Camp of the Dog."

Tales of the Uncanny and Supernatural [C]   (P. Nevil, London, 1949, 426 pp., 12/6)

22 stories: "The Doll"; "Running Wolf"; "Little Beggar"; "The Occupant of the Room"; "The Man Whom the Trees Loved"; "Valley of the Beasts"; "The South Wind"; "The Man Who Was Milligan"; "The Trod"; "Terror of the Twins"; "Deferred Appointment"; "Accessory Before the Fact"; "Glamour of the Snow"; "House of the Past"; "The Decoy"; "The Tradition"; "Touch of Pan"; "Entrance and Exit"; "Pikestaff Case"; "Empty Sleeve"; "Violence"; "The Lost Valley."

Ten Minute Stories [C]   (Dutton, 1914, 271 pp.) (Murray, London, 1914, 280 pp., 6/-)

29 stories: "Accessory Before the Fact"; "Ancient Light"; "De-

ferred Appointment"; "Dream Trespass"; "Entrance and Exit"; "Faith Cure on the Channel"; "Goblin Collection"; "Her Birthday"; "House of the Past"; "If the Cap Fits—"; "Imagination"; "The Impulse"; "The Invitation"; "Jimbo's Longest Day"; "The Lease"; "Let Not the Sun—"; "News vs. Nourishment"; "Pines"; "The Prayer"; "Second Generation"; "The Secret"; "Strange Disappearance of a Baronet"; "Two in One"; "Up and Down"; "Violence"; "The Whisperers"; "Wind"; "Winter Alps"; "You May Telephone From Here."

Tongues of Fire and Other Sketches [C] (Jenkins, London, 1924, 311 pp., 7/6; 1926, 2/6; 1929, 1/-) (*Tongues of Fire and Other Stories*, Dutton, 1925, 288 pp.)

20 stories: "Alexander Alexander"; "Continuous Performance"; "Falling Glass"; "Laughter of Courage"; "Little Beggar"; "Lost!"; "Malahide and Forden"; "Man of Earth"; "Man Who Was Milligan"; "Nephele"; "The Olive"; "Open Window"; "Other Woman"; "Petershin and Mr. Snide"; "Picking Fir-Cones"; "Pikestaffe Case"; "Playing Catch"; "S.O.S."; "Spell of Egypt"; "Tongues of Fire"; "World-Dream of McCallister."

Willows and Other Queer Tales, The [C] (Collins 'Pocket Classics,' London, 1932, 318 pp., illus., 2/-; 1934, 1/3)

11 stories: "The Willows"; "Ancient Sorceries"; "The Return"; "Running Wolf"; "The Man Whom the Trees Loved"; "The Man Who Played Upon the Leaf"; "The Tryst"; "By Water"; "The Occupant of the Room"; "The Decoy"; "Dream Trespass."

Wolves of God and Other Fey Stories [with Wilfred Wilson] [C] (Dutton, 1921, 320 pp.; 1925, 288 pp.) (Cassell, 1921, 328 pp., 8/6)

15 stories: "Wolves of God"; "Chinese Magic"; "Running Wolf"; "First Hate"; "Tarn of Sacrifice"; "The Valley of the Beasts"; "The Call"; "Egyptian Sorcery"; "The Decoy"; "The Man Who Found Out"; "Empty Sleeve"; "Wireless Confusion"; "Confession"; "The Lane That Ran East and West"; "'Vengeance Is Mine.'"

BLAINE, JOHN (pseud) See GOODWIN, H. L. or HARKINS, P. J.

BLAIR, ERIC ARTHUR (1903–20 Jan 1950) Noted author under the pseudonym "George Orwell." He was born in India and educated at Eton. He served in Burma with the Indian Imperial Police, was a school-teacher, and fought in the Spanish Civil War; he was in the Home Guard during World War II. He joined the *Tribune* staff in 1943, and later contributed to *The Observer*. Besides the two novels covered below, he had a number of other controversial books. A recommended book on his life is *George Orwell*, by Laurence Brander (Longmans Green, New York, 1955, 212 pp., $2.75).

Fiction [as George Orwell]

Animal Farm (Secker Warburg, London, 1945, 9+91 pp., 6/-) (Harcourt, New York, 1946, 118 pp., $1.75) (S. J. R. Saunders, Toronto, 89¢) (*Les animaux partout* [French], Odile Pathé, 1947) (*Boerderij der dieren* [Dutch], Phoenix, Bussum, 1947; Arbeiderspers, Amsterdam, 1956) ([Japanese], Osaka Kyōiku Tosho, 1949; Kokusai Bunka Kenhyū-jo, 1958; Nan'un-dô, 1958) (Penguin: 838, 1951, 120 pp., pa 1/6; 1954, pa 2/-; 1959, pa 2/6); 1968, pa 3/-) (S. Warburg, special ed., 1954, illus.—John Halas & Joy Batchelor, 12/6) (Harcourt, special ed., 1954, 160 pp., illus.—Halas & Batchelor, $3.00) (Signet: 1289, 1956, 128 pp., pa 25¢; CP121, 1962, pa 60¢; CT304, 1966, pa 75¢) (*Farm der Tiere* [German], S. Fischer, 1958) (Longmans Green, 'Heritage of Literature': B45, London, 1960, xxiii+112 pp., 4/9, introduction and notes by Laurence Brander) (*Djurfarmen* [Swedish], Biblioteksförlaget, 1961; Aldus-Bonnier, 1964) (*La republique des animaux* [French], Gallimard, 1964)

The noted satire on dictatorship based on the rebellion of farm animals. *Film:* British cartoon by Louis de Rochemont, with colour animation by John Halas and Joy Batchelor. The special book edition has some of this work as illustrations.

1984 (Harcourt, 1949, 314 pp., $3.00) (S. Warburg, 1950, 312 pp., 10/-) (Signet: 798, 1950, 237 pp., pa 25¢; CP100, 1961, 267 pp., pa 60¢; CT311, 1966, pa 75¢) (*1984* [French], Gallimard 'La Meridienne,' 1950) (*1984* [German], Diana, 1950, 1961) (*1984*

[Dutch], Arbeiderspers, Amsterdam, 1950; 1955; 1963) ([Japanese], Bungei Shunjū Shinsha, 1950; abr., Suppan Kyôdô-Sha, 1958) ([Spanish], Destino, 1950) ([Argentine], Kraft, 1950) (Penguin: 972, 1954, pa 2/-; 1959, pa 2/6; 1962, pa 2/6; 1967, pa 4/-) (*Nittonhundraattiofyra* [Swedish], Bonnier, 1949; Aldus-Bonnier, 1961)

Novel of a future world in which socialism is extrapolated to a very logical conclusion. *Film:* Associated British, 1955, starring Edmond O'Brien and Jan Sterling, directed by Michael Anderson. A dramatisation was on BBC TV in the late 1950's, and received considerable criticism.

BLAISDELL, ELINOR (Mrs. Melrich Vonelm Rosenberg) (1904–) U.S. author and anthologist. She wrote a psychological horror novel, *Nightmare* (Corgi, 1964, pa), the Lancer edition of which (1967) was noted as being by Anne Blaisdell.

Anthology

Tales of the Undead (T. Crowell, New York, 1947, 372 pp., $3.50) (Oxford, Toronto, $3.50)

Weird, 23 stories, many reprinted from *Weird Tales*: "Carmilla," J. S. Le Fanu; "Brother Lucifer," C. W. Whipple; "The Metronome," A. W. Derleth; "Uncanonized," S. Quinn; "The Feast in the Abbey," R. Bloch; "Clay-Shuttered Doors," Helen R. Hull; "Amour Dure," Vernon Lee; "School for the Unspeakable," M. W. Wellman; "The Adventure of the German Student," Washington Irving; "The Tomb," H. P. Lovecraft; "Second Night Out," F. B. Long; "Clarimonde," T. Gautier; "The Seed From the Sepulchre," C. A. Smith; "For the Blood Is Life," F. M. Crawford; "The Story of Ming-Y," L. Hearn; "The Quick and the Dead," V. Starrett; "Satan's Circus," Eleanor Smith; "Miss Mary Pask," Edith Wharton; "Septima," Muriel Schwob; "Count Magnus," M. R. James; "And He Shall Sing," H. R. Wakefield; "Doom of the House of Duryea," Earl Pierce; "The Room in the Tower," E. F. Benson.

BLAKE, THOMAS

Fiction

UN Confidential—A.D. 2000 (Vantage, New York, 1968, 86 pp., $2.50)

BLAMIRES, HARRY (6 Nov 1916–) British author and lecturer. M.A., University College, Oxford, 1939. Lecturer in English at King Alfred's College, Winchester, from 1948.

Fiction

Blessing Unbounded: A Vision (Longmans, London & New York, 1955, 185 pp., 12/6 & $2.75) (Longmans, Toronto, $2.25)

Ironic novel of the journey to 'the Kingdom of Heaven.'

Cold War in Hell (Longmans Green, London, 1955, 198 pp., 10/6) (Longmans Green, New York, 1956, 207 pp., $2.50)

The story of a Trip to Hell on a return ticket; sequel to *Devil's Hunting Ground*.

Devil's Hunting Ground (Longmans Green, 1954, 162 pp., 9/6)

A visualisation of the subtle torments of Hell; sequel is *Cold War in Hell*.

BLAKEBOROUGH, RICHARD (? –1918)

Fiction

Hand of Glory and Further Grandfather's Tales, The [Editor—J. Fairfax-Blakeborough] [C] (G. Richards, London, 1924, 268 pp., 7/6) (*Legends of Highwaymen and Others*, Stokes, New York, 1924, 269 pp.)

16 Yorkshire Legends, with preface: "The Hand of Glory: A Thrilling Legend of Stagecoach Days"; "The Wraith of Little Smeaton Hall"; "The Mystery of Anngrove Hall"; "Abbas: The Cross-Roads Spectre"; "The Highwayman of Leeming Lane"; "The Wicked Giant of Penhill"; "The Maid of the Golden Shoon"; "Elphi the Dwarf and Siba the Good"; "The Giant's Japstone"; "'T' Hunt o' Yatton Brig"; "Auld Nan of Sexhow"; "The Coach Ghost"; "Bonny Bona"; "'Swift Nick,' the Highwayman"; "The Story of Dick Turpin"; "Pennock's Curse."

Legends of Highwaymen and Others [C] See *Hand of Glory, The*

BLATCHFORD, ROBERT
Fiction [Another fantasy is *The Sorcery Shop* (Clarion, London, 1907)]
Fantasias [C] (Clarion, London, 1895, 170 pp.)
    22 stories: "Dreams"; "Bob's Fairy"; "Force and Cunning"; "Buffalo"; "Caught"; "Cuffy"; "Romeo"; "The Studio"; "Pride and a Fall"; "Ali's Luck"; "Posterity"; "Whitewash"; "Il Penseroso"; "Moonshine"; "A Genial Savage"; "Robin Hood's Bay"; "Chetham College"; "Culture"; "Poetry"; "February Filldyke"; "Three Baby Buntings"; "My Sister."

BLAUSTEIN, ALBERT PAUL (12 Oct 1921–) U.S. professor of law. An anthology apparently sub-edited by G. Conklin is covered in Conklin's entry; Blaustein assisted Basil Davenport in compiling *Deals With the Devil*, *Invisible Men* and *Famous Monster Tales*.
Anthology
Human and Other Beings [as Allen DeGraeff] [pa] See CONKLIN, G.

BLAVATSKY, H(ELEN) P(ETROVNA) (HAHN-HAHN) (30 July 1831–8 May 1891) Noted U.S. figure, founder of the Theosophical Society in New York in 1875. She was born at Ekaterinoslav (now Dniepropetrovsk). In 1856, in the course of extensive travels, she succeeded in entering the forbidden land of Tibet. Much of her later work was done in India, supposedly the home of her ancient mystical creed. There she manifested her psychic powers, without, however, satisfying an investigator from the Society for Psychical Research. Her works included *Isis Unveiled* (1877), *The Secret Doctrine* (1888), *Key to Theosophy* and *Voice of the Silence* (1889).
Fiction
Nightmare Tales [C] (Theosophical Pub. Soc., New York, 1892, 133 pp., illus.) (Theosophical Pub. Co., London, 1892, 133 pp., illus.)
    5 stories: "A Bewitched Life"; "The Cave of the Echoes"; "The Luminous Shield"; "From the Polar Lands"; "The Ensouled Violin."

BLAYRE, CHRISTOPHER (pseud) See ALLEN, E. H.

BLEILER, E(VERETT) F(RANKLIN) (1920–) Noted U.S. anthologist who for a period compiled with T. E. Dikty the annual *Best Science-Fiction Stories* and *Year's Best Science Fiction Novels*; later both were combined and continued by T. E. Dikty alone. He is best known for editing *The Checklist of Fantastic Literature*, a mammoth compilation of science fiction, fantasy and weird books. The only reference work of its type, it involved some seven years of research and lists over 5,000 books. He joined Dover Publications in 1955 and was elected Executive Vice-President in 1967, remaining managing editor and head of the publishing company. He has been responsible for editing some Wells' and other collections.
Anthologies [all with co-anthologist T. E. Dikty]
Best Science Fiction Stories, The See *Best Science-Fiction Stories 1950, The*
Best Science Fiction Stories: Second Series, The See *Best Science-Fiction Stories 1951, The*
Best Science Fiction Stories: Third Series, The See *Best Science-Fiction Stories 1952, The*
Best Science Fiction Stories: Fourth Series, The See *Best Science-Fiction Stories 1953, The*
Best Science Fiction Stories: Fifth Series, The See *Best Science-Fiction Stories 1954, The*
Best Science-Fiction Stories 1949, The (F. Fell, New York, 1949, 314 pp., $2.95) (in *Science Fiction Omnibus* [Bleiler & Dikty], 1952)
    12 stories: "Mars Is Heaven!" R. Bradbury; "Ex Machina," L. Padgett; "The Strange Case of John Kingman," M. Leinster; "Doughnut Jockey," Eric Fennell; "Thang," Martin Gardner; "Period Piece," J. J. Coupling; "Knock," F. Brown; "Genius," P. Anderson; "And the Moon Be Still as Bright," R. Bradbury; "No Connection," I. Asimov; "In Hiding," Wilmar H. Shiras; "Happy Ending," H. Kuttner.

Best Science-Fiction Stories 1950, The (F. Fell, 1950, 347 pp., $2.95) (McLeod, Toronto) (*The Best Science Fiction Stories*, Grayson, London, 1951, 256 pp., 8/6) (in *Science Fiction Omnibus* [Bleiler & Dikty], 1952)
    13 stories (British edition has 8 stories, marked †): "Private Eye,"† H. Kuttner; "Doomsday Deferred,"† W. F. Jenkins; "The Hurkle Is a Happy Beast," T. Sturgeon; "Eternity Lost,"† C. D. Simak; "Easter Eggs,"† R. S. Carr; "Opening Doors,"† Wilmar H. Shiras; "Five Years in the Marmalade," R. W. Krepps; "Dwellers in Silence," R. Bradbury; "Mouse,"† F. Brown; "Refuge for To-night,"† R. M. Williams; "The Life-Work of Professor Muntz,"† M. Leinster; "Flaw," J. D. MacDonald; "The Man," R. Bradbury.
Best Science-Fiction Stories 1951, The (F. Fell, 1951, 352 pp., $2.95) (McLeod, Toronto) (*The Best Science Fiction Stories: Second Series*, Grayson, London, 1952, 240 pp., 9/6)
    18 stories (British edition, 14 stories marked †): "The Santa Claus Planet,"† (new) F. M. Robinson; "The Gnurrs Come From the Voodvork Out,"† R. Bretnor; "The Mindworm,"† C. M. Kornbluth; "The Star Ducks,"† Bill Brown; "Not To Be Opened,"† Roger F. Young; "Process,"† A. E. van Vogt; "Forget-Me-Not," W. F. Temple; "Contagion,"† Katherine MacLean; "Trespass,"† P. Anderson & G. Dickson; "Oddy and Id," ("The Devil's Invention") A. Bester; "To Serve Man,"† D. Knight; "Summer Wear,"† L. S. de Camp; "Born of Man and Woman,"† R. Matheson; "Fox in the Forest,"† ("To the Future") R. Bradbury; "The Last Martian,"† F. Brown; "The New Reality," C. L. Harness; "Two Face,"† F. B. Long; "Coming Attraction," F. Leiber. Some stories were also reprinted in *Frontiers in Space* [Bleiler], 1955, pa.
Best Science-Fiction Stories 1952, The (F. Fell, 1952, 288 pp., $2.95) (McLeod, Toronto) (*The Best Science Fiction Stories: Third Series*, Grayson, 1953, 256 pp., 9/6)
    18 stories (British edition, 16 stories marked †): "The Other Side,"† W. Kubilius; "Of Time and Third Avenue,"† A. Bester; "The Marching Morons,"† C. M. Kornbluth; "A Peculiar People,"† Betsy Curtis; "Extending the Holdings,"† D. Grinnell; "The Tourist Trade,"† W. Tucker; "The Two Shadows,"† W. F. Temple; "Balance,"† J. Christopher; "Brightness Falls From the Air,"† I. Seabright; "Witch War,"† R. Matheson; "At No Extra Cost,"† ("Unknown Quantity") Peter Phillips; "Nine-Finger Jack,"† A. Boucher; "Appointment in Tomorrow,"† F. Leiber; "The Rats,"† A. Porges; "Men of the Ten Books,"† J. Vance; "Dark Interlude," M. Reynolds & F. Brown; "The Pedestrian," R. Bradbury; "Generation of Noah,"† W. Tenn. Some stories were also reprinted in *Frontiers in Space* [Bleiler], 1955, pa.
Best Science-Fiction Stories 1953, The (F. Fell, 1953, 279 pp., $3.50) (McLeod, Toronto) (*The Best Science Fiction Stories: Fourth Series*, Grayson, 1955, 239 pp., 9/6)
    15 stories (British edition, 13 stories marked †) and Introduction by A. Bester: "The Fly," A. Porges; "Ararat,"† Zenna Henderson; "Counter-Transference,"† W. Temple; "The Conqueror,"† M. Clifton; "Machine,"† J. Jakes; "The Middle of the Week After Next,"† M. Leinster; "The Dreamer,"† A. Coppel; "The Moon Is Green,"† F. Leiber; "I Am Nothing,"† E. F. Russell; "Command Performance,"† W. M. Miller; "Survival,"† J. Wyndham; "Game for Blondes,"† J. D. MacDonald; "The Girls From Earth,"† F. Robinson; "Lover, When You're Near Me," R. Matheson; "Fast Falls the Eventide,"† E. F. Russell. Some stories were also reprinted in *Frontiers in Space* [Bleiler], 1955, pa.
Best Science-Fiction Stories 1954, The (F. Fell, 1954, 316 pp., $3.50) (McLeod, Toronto) (*The Best Science Fiction Stories: Fifth Series*, Grayson, 1956, 207 pp., 10/6)
    13 stories (British edition, 10 stories marked †) and Introduction, "Icon of the Imagination," F. Leiber: "DP!"† J. Vance; "The Big Holiday,"† F. Leiber; "The Collectors,"† G. R. Dewey & G. Dancy; "One in Three Hundred," J. T. McIntosh; "Wonder Child,"† J. Shallit; "Crucifixus Etiam," († as "The Sower Does Not Reap") W. Miller; "The Model of a Judge,"† W. Morrison; "The Last Day,"† R. Matheson; "Time Is the Traitor," A. Bester; "Lot,"† W. Moore; "Yankee Exodus,"† Ruth Goldsmith; "What Thin Partitions,"† M. Clifton & A. Apostolides; "A Bad Day for Sales," F. Leiber. Includes index to all stories in the series, 1949–1954.

Castle of Otranto, Vathek, and The Vampyre, The [pa] (Dover, 1966, 291 pp., pa $2.00)

Trio of Gothic novels, as noted.

Category Phoenix See *Year's Best Science-Fiction Novels 1953*

Frontiers in Space [pa] (Bantam: 1328, 1955, 166 pp., pa 25¢)

14 stories selected from *The Best Science-Fiction Stories 1951, 1952* and *1953*: "Oddy and Id," A. Bester; "Process," A. E. van Vogt; "The Star Ducks," Bill Brown; "To Serve Man," D. Knight; "The Fox in the Forest," R. Bradbury; "Nine-Finger Jack," A. Boucher; "Dark Interlude," M. Reynolds & F. Brown; "Generation of Noah," W. Tenn; "The Rats," A. Porges; "Ararat," Zenna Henderson; "The Moon Is Green," F. Leiber; "Survival," J. Wyndham; "Machine," J. Jakes; "I Am Nothing," E. F. Russell.

Imagination Unlimited (Farrar Strauss, New York, 1952, 430 pp., $3.50) (British edition in two titles: *Imagination Unlimited*, Bodley Head, London, 1953, 175 pp., 8/6, and Mayflower: 3985, 1964, 190 pp., pa 3/6, marked †; *Men of Space and Time*, Bodley Head, 1953, 221 pp., 8/6, marked ††) (Berkley: G-233, 1959, 152 pp., pa 35¢, 7 stories marked *)

13 sf stories: "What Dead Men Tell,"†* T. Sturgeon; "Referent,"†* R. Bradbury; "Blind Man's Buff,"† M. Jameson; "Pressure,"† R. Rocklynne; "The Xi Effect,"† P. Latham; "Old Faithful,"† R. Z. Gallun; "Alas, All Thinking,"†† H. Bates; "Dune Roller,"††* Julian May; "Employment,"††* L. S. de Camp; "Dreams Are Sacred,"††* P. Phillips; "Hold Back Tomorrow,"†† K. Neville; "Berom,"†† J. Berryman; "The Fire and the Sword,"†† F. Robinson.

Men of Space and Time See *Imagination Unlimited*

Science Fiction Omnibus (Garden City, New York, 1952, 341 pp., $2.95)

The Best Science-Fiction Stories 1949 and *1950* bound in one cover.

Three Gothic Novels See *Castle of Otranto, The*

Year's Best Science Fiction Novels, The See *Year's Best Science Fiction Novels 1952*

Year's Best Science Fiction Novels: Second Series, The See *Year's Best Science Fiction Novels 1954*

Year's Best Science Fiction Novels 1952 (F. Fell, 1952, 351 pp., $3.50) (*The Year's Best Science Fiction Novels*, 1954, 263 pp., 9/6)

5 novels (British edition, 4 novels marked †): "Izzard and the Membrane,"† W. M. Miller; ". . . And Then There Were None,"† E. F. Russell; "Flight to Forever,"† P. Anderson; "The Hunting Season,"† F. Robinson; "Seeker of the Sphinx," A. C. Clarke.

Year's Best Science Fiction Novels 1953 (F. Fell, 1953, 315 pp., $3.50) (*Category Phoenix*, Bodley Head, 1955, 192 pp., 9/6)

5 novels (British edition, 3 novels marked †): "Firewater,"† W. Tenn; "Category Phoenix,"† B. Ellanby; "Surface Tension,"† J. Blish; "The Gadget Had a Ghost," M. Leinster; "Conditionally Human," W. Miller.

Year's Best Science Fiction Novels 1954 (F. Fell, 1954, 317 pp., $3.50) (*The Year's Best Science Fiction Novels: Second Series*, Grayson, 1955, 240 pp., 10/6)

5 novels (British edition, 4 novels marked †): "The Enormous Room,"† H. L. Gold & R. W. Krepps; "Assignment to Aldebaran,"† K. F. Crossen; "The Oceans Are Wide,"† F. M. Robinson; "The Sentimentalists,"† M. Leinster; "Second Variety," P. K. Dick.

Nonfiction

Checklist of Fantastic Literature, The (Shasta, Chicago, 1948, 455 pp., $6.00)

The only source book of its type for the collector, giving an almost complete listing of all science fiction, fantasy and weird books. Over 5,000 titles are listed by name and author. However, there is no determination of the degree of fantasy for each, and naturally, as in any work like this, there are some omissions.

BLISH, JAMES (BENJAMIN) (23 May 1921–) U.S. science fiction author. He was trained as a zoologist at Rutgers University, and spent two years in the Army as a medical laboratory technician. While doing post-graduate work at Columbia U. he switched to literature. He has worked with trade papers and also

has been a teacher and a public relations counsellor. His former wife, Virginia Kidd, also a professional writer, helped him on much of his work. He is now married to Judith Ann Lawrence, an illustrator; they live in England.

Blish is noted for his *Okie* series, which was published in 1970 as the omnibus *Cities in Flight*. The most noted story of his "pantropy" series (collected as *The Seedling Stars*) is "Surface Tension," originally in *GSF*, Aug 1952; further appearances include *Year's Best SF Novels* [Bleiler], 1953, *Six Great Short Novels of SF* [Conklin], 1953 pa, *Second Galaxy Reader* [Gold], 1954, *Category Phoenix* [Bleiler], 1955, and of course the author's *Best SF Stories*, 1965. Other noted stories include: "There Shall Be No Darkness" (*TWS*, Apr 1950; *Witches Three* [Anon.], 1952; *Zacherley's Vulture Stew* [Zacherley], 1960, pa); "Beep" (*GSF*, Feb 1954; *Stories for Tomorrow* [Sloane], 1954; *Space Police* [Norton], 1956); "Get Out of My Sky" (*ASF*, sr2, Jan 1957; *Get Out of My Sky*, anthology [Margulies], 1960, pa)—this was to have appeared in a Twayne Triplet anthology, with "Question and Answer" [*Planet of No Return*], P. Anderson, and "Sucker Bait," I. Asimov.

Mr. Blish edited the sf magazine *Vanguard Science Fiction* for its one issue (June 1958), which was quite favourably received. He was book reviewer for *Science-Fiction Times* [amateur magazine] April 1956–October 1957, and has done considerable reviewing for various professional and amateur magazines. The following articles are of note: "Science in Science Fiction" (*SFQ*, 4 parts, May 1951–May 1952); "Our Inhabited Universe" (*TWS*, series, June 1951–Dec 1952). He was Guest of Honour at the 1960 World SF Convention. His best critical writings have been published as *The Issue at Hand* (1964) and *More Issues at Hand* (1970) [as William Atheling, Jr.]. His novel on Roger Bacon is *Doctor Mirabilis* (Faber, 1964).

Series

Okie. Self-contained cities roving through space. "Okie" (*ASF*, Apr 1950); "Bindlestiff" (*ASF*, Dec 1950); "Sargasso of Lost Cities" (*2CSAB*, Spr 1953); "Earthman, Come Home" (*ASF*, Nov 1953). All combined as *Earthman, Come Home*. This and other works in the same background were collected in the omnibus *Cities in Flight* (1969), consisting of *They Shall Have Stars* (*Year 2018!*), *A Life for the Stars*, *Earthman, Come Home*, and *The Triumph of Time*.

Pantropy. See *The Seedling Stars*

Fiction

Best Science Fiction Stories of James Blish [C] (Faber, London, 1965, 224 pp., 18/-)

7 stories: "There Shall Be No Darkness"; "Surface Tension"; "Testament of Andros"; "Common Time"; "A Work of Art"; "Tomb Tapper"; "The Oath."

Black Easter ("Faust Aleph Null," *If*, sr3, Aug 1967) (Doubleday, New York, 1968, 165 pp., $3.95)

A magician unleashes Hell upon the Earth.

Case of Conscience, A (*If* n'te, Sep 1953) —enlarged (Ballantine: 256, 1958, 192 pp., pa 35¢; U2251, 1966, 188 pp., pa 50¢) (Faber, 1959, 208 pp., 15/-; 1966, 21/-) (*Un cas de conscience* [French], Denoël: PF30, 1959, pa) (SF B.C. [S.J.], 1959, 5/6) (*Guerra al grande nulla* [Italian], Urania: 226, 1960; 474, 1967) (Penguin: 1809, 1963, 192 pp., pa 3/-)

Fascinating study of the society of the planet Lithia, ruled absolutely by evolution and reason, and the religious questions raised by its existence. Received the Hugo Award in 1959.

Clash of Cymbals, A See *Triumph of Time, The*

Duplicated Man, The [with R. W. Lowndes] (*Dynamic SF*, Aug 1953) (Avalon, New York, 1959, 222 pp., $2.95) (Airmont: SF8, 1964, 128 pp., pa 40¢)

Quite complicated; interplay of duplicates of Paul Danton against the background of a cold war between Earth and Venus.

ESP-er [pa] See *Jack of Eagles*

Earthman, Come Home (Putnam, New York, 1955, 239 pp., $3.50) (T. Allen, Toronto, $3.75) (*Il ritorne dall'infinito* [Italian], Urania: 97, 1955) (Faber, 1956, 256 pp., 12/6; 1965, 18/-) (D'day SF B.C., 1956) (slightly abr: Avon: T225, 1958, 191 pp., pa 35¢; S218, 1966, 254 pp., pa 60¢) (SF B.C. [S.J.], 1958, 5/6) (*Stadt* *zwischen den Planeten* [German], Goldmann, 1960; 1963, pa) (Mayflower: 2205, 1963, 222 pp., pa 3/6) (*La Terre est une idee* [French], Denoël: PF103-4, 1967, pa)

The *Okie* series written into continuity.

Fallen Star, The See *Frozen Year, The*

Frozen Year, The (Ballantine, 1957, 155 pp., $2.75; #197, 1957, pa 35¢) (*The Fallen Star*, Faber, 1957, 224 pp., 15/-; FSB: 340, 1961, 156 pp., pa 2/6)

Written as a 'contemporary novel'; an expedition to the North Pole in 1958 seeks evidence that the asteroids were once a planet; scientific and technical problems are well worked out.

Galactic Cluster [C] (Signet: S1719, 1959, 176 pp., pa 35¢; D2790, 1965, pa 50¢) (Faber, 1960, 233 pp., 15/-) (SF B.C. [S.J.], 1961, 5/6) (*Terre, il faut mourir* [French], Denoël: PF50, 1961, pa) (FSB: 889, 1963, 128 pp., pa 2/6; 2229, 1968, pa 3/6) (*Grupo galáctico* [Spanish], Galaxia: 15, 1964, pa)

Sf, 8 stories [British book ed. has 5 stories, marked †, plus short novel "Beanstalk"; British pa has 5 stories, marked *]: "Tomb Tapper"; "King of the Hill"; "Common Time"†*; "A Work of Art" ("Art Work")†*; "To Pay the Piper"†*; "Nor Iron Bars (including "Detour to the Stars")*; "Beep"†*; "This Earth of Hours"†. The French edition follows the U.S.

Giants in the Earth See *Titans' Daughter*

Jack of Eagles ("Let the Finder Beware," *TWS*, Dec 1949) —enlarged (Greenberg, New York, 1952, 246 pp., $2.75) (Galaxy SF Novel: 19, 1954, 128 pp., pa 35¢) (*Mondi invisibili* [Italian], *Urania*; 47, 1954) (Nova: NS4, 1955, 159 pp., pa 2/-) (*ESP-er*, Avon: T-268, 1958, 190 pp., pa 35¢; S337, 1968, 176 pp., pa 60¢) (*L'asso di coppe* [Italian], *GRF*: 8, 1961) (*Terras letzte chance* [German], Zimmermann, 1962; *Der Psi-Mann*, *T*: 253-4, 1962)

Psychic supernatural abilities based on power fantasies.

Life for the Stars, A (*ASF*, sr2, Sep 1962) (Putnam, 1962, 188 pp., $3.50) (Longmans, Toronto, $4.25) (Avon: H107, 1963, 143 pp., pa 45¢; G1280, 1966, 144 pp., pa 50¢) (Faber, 1964, 147 pp., 15/-) (*Villes nomades* [French], Denoël: PF99, 1967, pa)

Subtitled "Cities in Flight 2"; this runs parallel to *Earthman, Come Home*, with a youth impressed into the take-off of the city of Scranton.

Mission to the Heart Stars (Putnam, 1965, 158 pp., $3.75) (Faber, 1965, 135 pp., 13/6)

Juvenile.

Night Shapes, The [pa] (Ballantine: F647, 1962, 125 pp., pa 50¢) (FSB: 942, 1963, 125 pp., pa 2/6; 1305, 1965, pa 3/6)

An entertaining African adventure, but generally not considered science fiction.

Seedling Stars, The (Gnome, New York, 1956, 185 pp., $3.00) (*Il seme fra le stelle* [Italian], *Urania*: 189, 1958) (Signet: S1622, 1959, 158 pp., pa 35¢; D2549, 1964, pa 50¢) (*Auch sie sind Menschen* [German], Goldmann, 1960; 1962, pa) (*Semailles humaines* [French], Galaxie Bis: 6, 1968, pa)

"Pantropy" and man's survival as planned mutants on utterly alien worlds. Consists of following stories welded into continuity: "Seeding Programme" ("A Time to Survive," *F&SF*, short novel, Feb 1956); "The Thing in the Attic" (*If*, n'te, July 1954); "Surface Tension" (combination of "Surface Tension," *GSF*, Aug 1952, and "Sunken Universe," *SSS*, n'te, May 1942 and Nov 1950 [under pseud. "Arthur Merlyn"]); "Watershed" (*If*, May 1955).

So Close to Home [C] [pa] (Ballantine: 465K, 1961, 142 pp., pa 35¢; 632, 1962, pa 35¢)

Sf, 10 stories: "Struggle in the Womb" ("Battle of the Unborn"); "Sponge Dive"; "One-Shot"; "The Box"; "First Strike"; "The Abattoir Effect" (original); "The Oath"; "FYI"; "The Masks"; "Testament of Andros."

Star Dwellers, The (*Boys' Life* [abr], sr3, ?, 1961) (Putnam, 1961, 192 pp., $3.50) (Avon: F122, 1962, 128 pp., pa 40¢; G1268, 1965, pa 50¢) (Faber, 1962, 153 pp., 13/6) (*Das Zeichen des Blitzes* [German], Goldmann, 1963; 1965, pa)

Two cadets and a noted trouble shooter endeavour to contact "energy" creatures in space; well-written, and different.

Star Trek [C] [pa] (Bantam: F3459, 1967, 136 pp., pa 50¢)

7 stories of the TV series, adapted by J. Blish: "Charlie's Law"; "Dagger of the Mind"; "The Unreal McCoy"; "Balance of Terror";

"The Naked Time"; "Miri"; "The Conscience of the King."

Star Trek Two [C] [pa] (Bantam: F3439, 1968, 122 pp., pa 50¢)

8 stories of the TV series adapted by Blish, with original authors noted: "Arena" (Gene L. Coon); "A Taste of Armageddon" (R. Hamner & G. L. Coon); "Tomorrow Is Yesterday" (D. C. Fontana); "Errand of Mercy" (G. L. Coon); "Court Martial" (D. M. Mankiewicz & S. W. Carabatsos); "Operation–Annihilate!" (S. W. Carabatsos); "The City on the Edge of Forever" (H. Ellison); "Space Seed" (C. Wilber & G. L. Coon).

They Shall Have Stars (Faber, 1956, 181 pp., 12/6; 1965, 18/-; Avon: S210, 1966, 159 pp., pa 60¢; V2216, 1967, pa 75¢; NEL: 2303, 1968, pa 5/-) (*Year 2018!* Avon: T193, 1957, 159 pp., pa 35¢; FSB: 954, 1964, 159 pp., pa 2/6; 1306, 1965, 159 pp., pa 3/6) (*Aux hommes, les étoiles* [French], Denoël: PF80, 1965, pa)

The story of the "Bridge" (*ASF*,n'te, Feb 1952) and the anti-agathic drugs ("At Death's End," *ASF*, May 1954) in the time preceding *Earthman, Come Home*. The Avon edition includes a chronology of the author's originally planned *Cities in Flight*.

Titans' Daughter [pa] (Berkley: G507, 1961, 142 pp., pa 35¢; F1163, 1966, pa 50¢) (FSB: 912, 1963, 142 pp., pa 2/6; 1307, 1965, pa 3/6) (*I tetraploidi* [Italian], *GRF*: 27, 1963) (*Die Tochter des Giganten* [German], *UZ*: 384, 1964)

Novel in 2 parts. First part was originally "Beanstalk" (*Future Tense* [Crossen], 1952), then retitled "Giants in the Earth," *SFS*, Jan 1956; *Galactic Cluster* [Blish] [only in British ed.]; *A Pair From Space* [Anon.], 1965 pa. Second part is a new story, a hard-science novel of intrigue around tetraploid giantism. In the pa ed. the author acknowledges the help of his wife, Virginia Kidd.

Torrent of Faces, A [with Norman L. Knight] (Doubleday, 1967, 270 pp., $4.95) (D'day SF B.C., 1968, $1.70) (Faber, 1968, 270 pp., 25/-) (Ace: A29, 1968, 286 pp., pa 75¢)

A sort of sequel to Knight's "Frontier of the Unknown" and "Crisis in Utopia"; in process of writing since 1948. Portions have appeared in sf magazines: "The Shipwrecked Hotel" (*GSF*, Aug 1965); "The Piper of Dis" (*GSF*, Aug 1966); "To Love Another" (*ASF*, April 1967). The technical details of 28th Century Earth as a utopia with 1,000 billion people. Although logical and fascinating, the story doesn't generate tension.

Triumph of Time, The (Avon: T279, 1958, 158 pp., pa 35¢; S221, 1966, pa 60¢; 1968, pa 60¢) (*A Clash of Cymbals*, Faber, 1959, 197 pp., 13/6; 1965, 18/-) (*Guerra al grande nulla* [Italian], *Urania*: 226, 1960) (*Il trionfo del tempo* [Italian], *Cosmo*: 87, 1961) (*El triunfo del tiempo* [Spanish], Cenit: 64, 1964 pa) (*Un coup de cymbales* [French], Denoël: PF106, 1968, pa)

The concluding *Okie* book; heavy-science story of Amalfi's city and the world of He fighting the end of the Universe.

Vanished Jet, The (Weybright & Talley, New York, 1968, $4.50)

Juvenile.

VOR [pa] (Avon: T238, 1958, 159 pp., pa 35¢; S313, 1967, pa 60¢) (Corgi: S681, 1959, 156 pp., pa 2/6)

Expansion of "The Weakness of RVOG" (*TWS*, Feb 1949, with D. Knight). An invulnerable robot comes to Earth and must be destroyed, otherwise its masters will destroy Earth itself.

Warriors of Day, The [pa] ("Sword of Xota," *2CSAB*, Sum 1951) (Galaxy SF Novel: 16, 1953, 125 pp., pa 35¢) (*I guerri del planeta giorne* [Italian], *GRF*: 4, 1960) (Lancer: 73-580, 1967, 160 pp., pa 60¢)

Welcome to Mars! ("The Hour Before Earthrise," *If*, sr3, July 1966) (Putnam, New York, 1967, 160 pp., $3.75) (Faber, 1967, 160 pp., 16/-)

A lad uses a unique method to go to Mars, and then struggles to survive there.

Year 2018! [pa] See *They Shall Have Stars*

Nonfiction

Issue at Hand, The [as William Atheling, Jr.] (Advent, Chicago, 1964, 136 pp., $5.00; 1967, pa $1.95)

13 chapters of serious criticism of sf, from reviews originally in the amateur magazines—Redd Bogg's *Skyhook*, Larry Shaw's *Axe*, Richard Bergeron's *Warhoon*, and Dick Lupoff's *Xero*. A good picture of sf writing.

Anthology

New Dreams This Morning [pa] (Ballantine: U2331, 1966, 190 pp., pa 50¢)

Sf, 8 stories with Compiler's Preface: "Dreaming Is a Private Thing," I. Asimov; "A Work of Art," "The Dark Night of the Soul" ("The Genius Heap"), J. Blish; "Portrait of the Artist," H. Harrison; "The Country of the Kind," D. Knight; "With These Hands," C. M. Kornbluth; "A Master of Babylon" ("Music Master of Babylon"), E. Pangborn; "A Man of Talent" ("The Man With Talent"), R. Silverberg.

BLISS, DOUGLAS PERCY (1900–)
Anthology
Devil in Scotland, The (MacLehouse, London, 1934, 107 pp., illus., 8/6) (Macmillan, New York, 1934, 107 pp., illus., $3.25)

4 great Scottish stories of diabolerie, with Introduction "The Devil and His Folk in Scottish Life and Literature": "Tam O'Shanter," R. Burns; "Wandering Willie's Tale," Sir Walter Scott; "Thrawn Janet" and "The Tale of Tod Lapraik," R. L. Stevenson.

BLIXEN, KAREN (Karen Christence Dinesen, Baroness Blixen-Finecke) (17 April 1885–7 Sep 1962). Danish author, under the pseudonyms "Isak Dinesen" and "Pierre Andrezel." She is particularly noted for her first collection *Seven Gothic Tales* which shows a strong influence of 18th Century writers. Her next, *African Farm* (1937), was based on 18 years of living in East Africa. Other works followed. Her friend Parmenia Migel recently wrote a book on her life titled *Titania* (M. Joseph, 1967, 30/-).

Fiction
Angelic Avengers, The [as Pierre Andrezel] (Putnam, London, 1947, 303 pp., 10/6) (Random, New York, 1947, 304 pp., $3.00) (Ace: K167, 1963, 252 pp., pa 50¢)

Romantic atmosphere to disguise a political message.
Last Tales [as Isak Dinesen] [C] (Putnam, London, 1957, 405 pp., 18/-) (FSB: 1797, 1967, 223 pp., pa 7/6)

12 stories, many of a fantasy nature. *Chapters from the novel 'Albondocani'*: "The Cardinal's First Tale"; "The Cloak"; "Night Walk"; "Of Hidden Thoughts and of Heaven"; "Tales of Two Old Gentlemen"; "The Cardinal's Third Tale"; "The Blank Page." *New Gothic Tales*: "The Caryatides"; "Echoes." *New Winter's Tales*: "A Country Tale"; "Copenhagen Season"; "Converse at Night in Copenhagen."
Seven Gothic Tales [as Isak Dinesen] [C] (H. Smith & R. Haas, New York, 1934, 420 pp., $2.50; new ed., 1934, $7.50) (Putnam, London, 1934, 522 pp., 7/6; 1936, 3/6) (*Sju romantiska berättelser* [Swedish], Bonnier, 1934) (Modern Library, New York, 1939, 420 pp., 95¢) (Macmillan, Toronto, $1.25) (Armed: 687, nd, pa) (Penguin: #1952, 1963, 364 pp., pa 5/-)

Supernatural, 7 stories: "The Roads Around Pisa"; "The Old Chevalier"; "The Monkey"; "The Deluge at Norderney"; "The Supper at Elsinore"; "The Dreamers"; "The Poet."
Winter's Tales [as Isak Dinesen] [C] (Putnam, London, 1942, 313 pp., 8/6; 1945; 1949, 292 pp., 6/-) (Random, New York, 1943, 313 pp., $2.50) (Random, Toronto, $3.25) (World, New York, 1944, 313 pp., $1.00) (Ryerson, Toronto, $1.69) (Armed: 802, nd, pa) (Dell: D191, 1957, 287 pp., pa 35¢)

Weird, 11 stories: "The Sailor-Boy's Tale"; "The Young Man With the Carnation"; "The Pearls"; "The Invincible Slave-Owners"; "The Heroine"; "The Dreaming Child"; "Alkmene"; "The Fish"; "Peter and Rosa"; "Sorrow-Acre"; "A Consolatory Tale."

BLOCH, ROBERT (5 April 1917–) U.S. writer of weird fiction, scenarioist, and copywriter. He became interested in *Weird Tales* in 1932 and wrote his first fan letter to H. P. Lovecraft, beginning a friendship whose influence and inspiration Bloch has freely acknowledged. He began to write for the fan field in 1934, with the short stories "Lilies" and "The Black Lotus" being accepted by W. Crawford, and later by Farnsworth Wright for *Weird Tales*. He has been a frequent contributor to the fan field, including articles on fantasy films in which he has always been interested. Forced to work in other fields in the early 1940's, he turned to advertising. In 1944 he wrote a 39-episode radio horror show, "Stay Tuned for Terror," which was broadcast widely throughout the continental U.S., Hawaii and Canada. After his very successful short story "Yours Truly, Jack the Ripper," broadcast over 20 times and often reprinted, he wrote his first novel *The Scarf*.

With the decline of the weird market, he has appeared mainly in *Fantastic* in recent years. Although he has written some sf, he personally doesn't favour it. He took over the fan column "Fandora's Box" in *Imagination* from Mari Wolf in June 1956, and edited, with W. Tucker, Gnome Press's short-lived *Science-Fiction World* [fan magazine]. His short story "That Hell-Bound Train" (*F&SF*, Sep 1958) won the 1959 Hugo for the best short story; it was later reprinted in *The Hugo Winners* [Asimov], 1962. His lecture at the University of Chicago on "Imagination and Modern Social Criticism" was published in *The Science Fiction Novel* (1959) [see *SYMPOSIA*]. The Ace Double D-265, 1958, contains his novel *Shooting Star* backed with 7 crime stories of which the last two are fantasy. He had one booklet in the *American Fiction* Series titled *Sea-Kissed* which is listed under this Series entry. Recent magazine novels of interest have been "This Crowded Earth" (*AS*, Oct 1958) and "Sneak Preview" (*AS*, Nov 1959).

Following the success of Bloch's novel *Psycho*, which was made into a notable even if controversial film by Alfred Hitchcock in 1960, he moved to Hollywood. (The film version of *Psycho* was scripted by Joseph Stefano.) Bloch has since written teleplays and screenplays as well as a number of other thrillers like *The Couch*, *The Dead Beat*, *Firebug*, and *Terror* (on Thuggee). Sam Moskowitz's profile " "Psycho"-logical Bloch" appeared in *AS*, Dec 1962, and was a chapter in his *Seekers of Tomorrow* (1966).

Series
Feep, Lefty. All in *Fantastic Adventures*: "Time Wounds All Heels" (Apr 1942); "Gather 'Round the Flowing Bowler" (May 1942); "The Pied Piper Fights the Gestapo" (June 1942); "The Weird Doom of Floyd Scrilch" (July 1942); "The Little Man Who Wasn't All There" (Aug 1942); "Son of a Witch" (Sep 1942); "Jerk the Giant Killer" (Oct 1942); "The Golden Opportunity of Lefty Feep" (Nov 1942); "Lefty Feep and the Sleepy-Time Gal" (Dec 1942); "Lefty Feep Catches Hell" (Jan 1943); "Nothing Happens to Lefty Feep" (Feb 1943); "The Chance of a Ghost" (Mar 1943); "Lefty Feep and the Racing Robot" (Apr 1943); "Genie With the Light Brown Hair" (May 1943); "Stuporman" (June 1943); "The Goon From Rangoon" (July 1943); "You Can't Kid Lefty Feep" (Aug 1943); "A Horse on Lefty Feep" (Oct 1943); "Lefty Feep's Arabian Nightmare" (Feb 1944); "Lefty Feep Does Time" (Apr 1944); "Lefty Feep Gets Henpecked" (Apr 1945); "Tree's a Crowd" (July 1946). A number appeared in the Swedish *Jules Verne Magasinet*, 1944–46.

Fiction
Atoms and Evil [C] [pa] (Gold Medal: s1231, 1962, 160 pp., pa 35¢) (Muller: GM638, 1963, 160 pp., pa 2/6)

13 stories, mostly from the sf magazines: "Try This for Psis"; "Comfort Me, My Robot"; "Talent"; "The Professor Plays It Square"; "Block That Metaphor"; "Wheel and Deal"; "You Got to Have Brains"; "You Could Be Wrong"; "Egghead"; "Dead-End Doctor"; "Change of Heart"; "Edifice Complex"; "Constant Reader."
Blood Runs Cold [C] (Simon & Schuster, New York, 1961, 246 pp., $3.50, jacket—Tony Palladino) (Popular: K18, 1963, 206 pp., pa 40¢) (Corgi: SC7021, 1964, 127 pp., pa 3/6)

17 stories reprinted from many magazines, including *Playboy* and *Ellery Queen's Mystery* (British pa, 13 stories, marked †): "The Show Must Go On"†; "The Cure"; "Daybroke"†; "Show Biz"; "The Masterpiece"; "I Like Blondes"†; "Dig That Crazy Grave!"; "Where the Buffalo Roam"†; "Is Betsy Blake Still Alive?"†; "World of Honor"†; "Final Performance"†; "All on a Golden Afternoon"; "The Gloating Place"†; "The Pin"†; "I Do Not Love Thee, Dr. Fell"†; "The Big Kick"†; "Sock Finish"†.
Bogey Men [C] [pa] (Pyramid: F839, 1963, 159 pp., pa 40¢)

Weird, 10 stories, finishing with profile " "Psycho"-logical Bloch," S. Moskowitz: "A Matter of Life"; "The Model Wife"; "Broomstick Ride"; "The Skull of the Marquis de Sade"; "Memo to a Movie-Maker"; "The Thinking Cap"; "The Shoes"; "The Man Who Collected Poe"; "The Ghost Writer"; "The Man Who Murdered Tomorrow."

Chamber of Horrors [C] [pa] (Award: A187X, 1966, 139 pp., pa 60¢)

Weird, 12 stories: "The Living End"; "The Head Hunter"; "Impractical Joker"; "Pride Goes–"; "The Screaming People"; "Fat Chance"; "The Unpardonable Crime"; "Method for Murder"; "Two of a Kind"; "Untouchable"; "Beelzebub"; "Frozen Fear."

Horror-7 [C] [pa] (Belmont: 90-275, 1963, 125 pp., pa 40¢) (Horwitz: PB160, 1963, 130 pp., pa 4/-) (FSB: 1196, 1964, 125 pp., pa 2/6; 1967, pa 3/6)

7 stories: "Enoch"; "The Strange Flight of Richard Clayton"; "The Opener of the Way"; "Return to the Sabbath"; "The Mandarin's Canaries"; "The Shambler From the Stars"; "The Secret of Sebek."

House of the Hatchet, The [pa] See *Yours Truly, Jack the Ripper*
Living Demons, The [C] [pa] (Belmont: B50-787, 1967, 156 pp., pa 50¢)

Weird, 12 stories, with introduction by author: "Life in Our Time"; "The Indian Spirit Guide"; "Lucy Comes to Stay"; "The Plot Is the Thing"; "Underground"; "The Beasts of Barsac"; "Philtre Tip"; "The Unspeakable Betrothal"; "Black Bargain"; "Girl From Mars"; "Beauty's Beast"; "Tell Your Fortune."

More Nightmares [C] [pa] (Belmont: L92-530, 1962, 173 pp., pa 50¢)

Weird, 10 stories: "That Hell-Bound Train"; "The Feast in the Abbey"; "Slave of the Flames"; "One Way to Mars"; "The Cheaters"; "The Fiddler's Fee"; "Mother of Serpents"; "Waxworks"; "Seal of the Satyr"; "The Dark Demon."

Night Walker [with S. Stuart] [pa] (Award: A124F, 1964, 139 pp., pa 50¢) (Brown Watson: R913, 1965, 156 pp., pa 3/6)

Nightmares [C] [pa] See *Pleasant Dreams*
Opener of the Way, The [C] (Arkham, Wis., 1945, 309 pp., $3.00, 2065 copies)

Weird, 21 stories and introduction: "The Cloak"; "Beetles"; "The Fiddler's Fee"; "The Mannikin"; "The Strange Flight of Richard Clayton"; "Yours Truly, Jack the Ripper"; "The Seal of the Satyr"; "The Dark Demon"; "The Faceless God"; "The House of the Hatchet"; "The Opener of the Way"; "Return to the Sabbath"; "The Mandarin's Canaries"; "Waxworks"; "The Feast in the Abbey"; "Slave of the Flames"; "The Shambler From the Stars"; "Mother of Serpents"; "The Secret of Sebek"; "The Eyes of the Mummy"; "One Way to Mars."

Pleasant Dreams [C] (Arkham, 1960, 233 pp., $4.00, 2000 copies) (*Nightmares*, Belmont: 233, 1961, 140 pp., pa 35¢) (*Pleasant Dreams & Nightmares*, Whiting & Wheaton, London, 1967, 239 pp., 21/-) (German selection: *16 Gruselgeschichten*, Heyne, 1964, pa)

Weird, 15 stories (pa has 10, marked †; remainder appear in other pa collections): "Sweets to the Sweet"; "The Dream Makers"; "The Sorcerer's Apprentice"†; "I Kiss Your Shadow"†; "Mr. Steinway"†; "The Proper Spirit"†; "Catnip"†; "The Cheaters"; "Hungarian Rhapsody"†; "The Light-House"†; "The Hungry House"†; "The Sleeping Beauty"†; "Sweet Sixteen"†; "That Hell-Bound Train"; "Enoch."

Scarf, The (Dial, New York, 1947, 247 pp., $2.50) (*The Scarf of Passion*, Avon Monthly Novel: 9, 1948, 126 pp., pa 35¢; Avon: 211, 1949, 154 pp., pa 25¢; 494, 1952, pa 25¢) (Gold Medal: d1727, 1967, 160 pp., pa 50¢)

Bloch's first book novel; recommended horror type.

Scarf of Passion, The [pa] See *Scarf, The*
Skull of the Marquis de Sade [C] [pa] (Pyramid: R1247, 1965, 157 pp., pa 50¢)

Weird, 7 stories (5 from *WT*): "The Skull of the Marquis de Sade"; "A Quiet Funeral"; "The Weird Tailor"; "The Man Who Knew Women"; " 'Lizzie Borden Took an Axe . . .' "; "The Devil's Ticket"; "The Bogey Man Will Get You."

Tales in a Jugular Vein [C] [pa] (Pyramid: R1139, 1965, 144 pp., pa 50¢ 10 stories (mysteries taken from contemporary detective magazines): "Sabbatical"; "Double-Cross"; "The Past Master"; "Terror Over Hollywood"; "A Home Away From Home"; "Rhyme Never Pays"; "Night School"; "Pin-Up Girl"; "Founding Fathers"; "The Deadliest Art."

This Crowded Earth & Ladies' Day [C] [pa] (Belmont: B60-080,

1968, 172 pp., pa 60¢)
Two short novels; first-named from *AS*, Oct 1958.

Yours Truly, Jack the Ripper [C] [pa] (Belmont: L92-527, 1962, 189 pp., pa 50¢) (*The House of the Hatchet*, Tandem: T19, 1965, 190 pp., pa 3/6)

Weird, 9 stories (selected from *Pleasant Dreams* and *The Opener of the Way*) with introduction: "Sweets to the Sweet"; "The Dream-Makers"; "Yours Truly, Jack the Ripper"; "The Eyes of the Mummy"; "The Mannikin"; "The House of the Hatchet"; "The Cloak"; "Beetles"; "The Faceless God."

Nonfiction
Eighth Stage of Fandom, The (Advent, Chicago, 1962, 176 pp., $5.00; pa $1.95)

A selection of fan writing (from both fanzines and prozines) published specially for the 1962 World SF Convention. Essays include "Gafia House"; "McGuffey's First SF Reader"; "The Demolished Fan"; "How to Attend an SF Convention"; "From Hubbub Horizontal." Poems include "Non-Lewis Carol."

BLOW, ERNEST J. South African author.
Fiction
Appointment in Space [pa] (Consul: 1270, 1963, 221 pp., pa 2/6)

A group make and take an amazing spaceship to Mars and have adventures there.

BOARDMAN, TOM (THOMAS VOLNEY) Jr. (20 Dec 1930–) British editor, publisher and anthologist. He was born in New York State and was brought to England two months later. He was educated in England, the U.S.A., and Argentina. In 1949 he worked in publishing, but in 1951 returned to the U.S. to join the Army. He came back to England in 1954 and continued his publishing career, and is now editor and publisher of the house bearing his name, and sales manager for a publishing group. He and his wife live in Berkshire and have two children. Mr. Boardman was the first reviewer in Britain to have a regular monthly column on sf books (in *Books and Bookmen*); he has been literary adviser on sf to three publishers, and in 1962 was Guest of Honour at the British SF Convention. He is co-founder of *S.F. Horizons*, the first professional magazine of sf criticism and comment. Other interests are golf, cooking, and jazz.
Anthologies
ABC of Science Fiction, An [pa] (FSB: 1652, 1966, 205 pp., pa 3/6) (Avon: V2258, 1968, 223 pp., pa 75¢)

26 stories with brief Introduction: "Let's Be Frank," B. Aldiss; "Pattern," Fredric Brown; "The Awakening," A. C. Clarke; "I Do Not Hear You, Sir," A. Davidson; "Day at the Beach," Carol Emshwiller; "The King of the Beasts," P. J. Farmer; "Homey Atmosphere," D. F. Galouye; "Mute Milton," H. Harrison; "The Conquest of the Moon," Washington Irving; "In the Bag," L. M. Janifer; "Maid to Measure," Damon Knight; "X Marks the Pedwalk," F. Leiber; "No Moon for Me," W. M. Miller, Jr.; "Family Resemblance," A. E. Nourse; "Final Exam," Chad Oliver; "The Bitterest Pill," F. Pohl; "He Had a Big Heart," F. Quattrocchi; "Love Story," E. F. Russell; "The Fence," C. Simak; "Project Hush," Wm. Tenn; "The Finer Breed," Helen M. Urban; "Harrison Bergeron," K. Vonnegut, Jr.; "Close Behind Him," J. Wyndham; "Three Limericks," B. T. H. Xerxes; "Thirty Days Had September," Robert F. Young; "The Great Slow Kings," R. Zelazny.

Connoisseur's Science Fiction [pa] (Penguin: 2223, 1964, 234 pp., pa 3/6)

10 stories with Compiler's Introduction: "Disappearing Act," A. Bester; "The Wizards of Pung's Corner," F. Pohl; "Tomorrow and Tomorrow and Tomorrow," K. Vonnegut; "Mr. Costello, Hero," T. Sturgeon; "Quit Zoomin' Those Hands Through the Air," J. Finney; "Build-Up," J. G. Ballard; "The Fun They Had," I. Asimov; "Diabologic," E. F. Russell; "Made in U.S.A.," J. T. McIntosh; "The Waveries," F. Brown.

Science Fiction Horizons No. 1 (Dobson, London, 1968, 189 pp., 21/-)

Foreword and 10 stories: "Subversive," M. Reynolds; "Game for Motel Room," F. Leiber; "Comic Inferno," B. W. Aldiss;

"After a Few Words," Seaton McKettrig; "Period of Gestation," Thom Keyes; "My Son the Physicist," I. Asimov; "The Shipwrecked Hotel," J. Blish & N. L. Knight; "Not Me, Not Amos Cabot," H. Harrison; "The Transfinite Choice," D. I. Masson; "The Big Cow-Pat Boom," D. Knight.

Unfriendly Future, The [pa] (FSB: 1347, 1965, 173 pp., pa 3/6)
Sf, 6 stories with Compiler's Introduction: "Russkies Go Home!" M. Reynolds; "The Food Goes in the Top," Will Worthington; "Danger: Religion!" B. W. Aldiss; "Rescue Operation," H. Harrison; "The Hades Business," Terry Pratchett; "The Seed of Violence," Jay Williams.

BOGGON, MARTYN
Fiction
Inevitable Hour, The [pa] (Tandem: T169, 1968, 188 pp., pa 3/6)
An armaments millionaire holds a nation to ransom during the carnage of a thermonuclear war, but murder strikes within his chosen group.

BOILEAU, PIERRE (28 April 1906–) French author. He and T. Narcejac form a noted French thriller writing team. They began with stories in the Simenon tradition, and are now noted for their crisp studies of character leading to homicidal impulses. Their *Spells of Evil* (Hamilton, 1961) covers the effects of black magic on a veterinary surgeon.
Fiction
Evil Eye, The [with T. Narcejac] (*Le Mauvais oeil*, Denoël: Paris, 1956) (Hutchinson, London, 1959, 207 pp., 12/6) (FSB: 349, 1961, 128 pp., pa 2/6)
Weird mystery and suspense. The Hutchinson edition includes another story not by Boileau.
Choice Cuts (A. Barker, London, 1966, 207 pp., 21/-) (Bantam: S3578, 1968, 198 pp., pa 75¢) (Panther: 24700, 1968, 191 pp., pa 5/-)
Macabre—surgeon passes parts of condemned criminal to various recipients who are each driven to suicide.

BOISGILBERT, EDMUND (pseud) See DONNELLY, I.

BOK, HANNES (VAJN) (2 July 1914–11 April 1964) U.S. artist and author, and a keen astrologer. A pupil of Maxfield Parrish, he was noted for his quite distinctive style of artwork. He first appeared professionally in *Weird Tales* with illustrations after editor F. Wright had liked his work in his close friend Ray Bradbury's amateur magazine *Futuria Fantasia*. He later did covers for *Weird Tales* (Dec 1939–March 1942), *Stirring Science Stories* (April 1941), and other magazines into 1942. He returned to the field in 1950 with covers on *Imagination* and *Other Worlds*. After painting all the covers for *Fantasy Fiction (Magazine)* and some for *Fantastic Universe* (Oct 1956–Jan 1957), he left the field and concentrated mainly on astrology.
A follower of A. Merritt, he completed that writer's *The Black Wheel* and *The Fox Woman* and also illustrated them. In his own right he has written the novels "Starstone World" (*SFQ*, Sum 1942), "The Sorcerer's Ship" (*Unknown*, Dec 1942), and "The Blue Flamingo" (*SS*, Jan 1948). At the time of his death he was working on a collection of masks intended for museum use and a series of illustrations in colour for the *Rubaiyat* of Omar Khayyam. More recently the Bokanalia Foundation was formed, with Emil Petaja as chairman. By mid-1968 it had produced *Bokanalia Memorial Folder* No. 1 (15 drawings), No. 2 (15 drawings), and No. 3 (12 drawings, with 5 new), at $3.00 each, as well as some other memorial material.

BOLAND, (BERTRAM) JOHN (12 Feb 1913–) British author, born in Birmingham, the son of a manufacturer. He has had widely varied experience—deck hand, lumberjack, commercial traveller, etc., and lived and worked in the U.S., Canada, and Alaska as well as throughout Europe. He has contributed several hundred stories to various newspapers and periodicals, including some sf to *New Worlds*, 1957–58. Nonfiction works include *New Writer's Guide*

to *Short Story Writing* and *Free-Lance Journalism*. Besides some TV scripts he did the film scripts for "The Golden Fleece" and "The Stone Desert." He was Chairman of the Birmingham Writers' Group, Vice-Chairman (1956–57) and Chairman (1958–60) of Writer's Summer School, and has been connected with other such groups.
Fiction
No Refuge (M. Joseph, London, 1956, 254 pp., 12/6) (Mayflower: 6458, 1963, 191 pp., pa 3/6)
Two robbers crashland in 'Yademos,' a Utopian country north of Greenland; there is much sociological discussion, with justice finally being meted out.
Operation Red Carpet (Boardman, London, 1959, 192 pp., 10/6)
Borderline sf; set in future with Russia trying to conquer Britain by novel means.
White August (M. Joseph, 1955, 239 pp., 12/6) (*Sneeuw in augustus* [Dutch], Elsevier, Amsterdam, 1956) (Brown Watson, 1956, 189 pp., pa 2/6) (*La morte bianca* [Italian], *Urania*: 109, 1955) (*Den Hvide Dod* [Danish], Skrifola: P13, 1958, pa) (*Weisser August* [German], *T*: 108, 1960) (Mayflower: 9514, 1963, 192 pp., pa 3/6) (Arcadia, New York, 1966, 188 pp., $2.95)
Terrifying possibilities of man trying to control the weather; wireless waves bury Britain under snow.

BOLITHO, (HENRY) HECTOR (28 May 1897–) British author, born in New Zealand but resident in England since 1922. Fellow of both Royal Society of Arts and Royal Society of Literature; founder and first editor of *R.A.F. Journal*. His works include *The Island of Wonder* (1920) and many books on British royalty. His "The House on Half Moon Street" has often been produced as a play.
Fiction
House on Half Moon Street and Other Stories, The [C] (Cobden-Sanderson, London, 1935, 303 pp., 7/6) (Appleton-Century, New York, 1936, 303 pp., $2.00)
14 stories: "The Albatross"; "Blood Will Out"; "Boy Who Was Mad"; "Cracky Miss Judith"; "Crying Grate"; "Dirge"; "Duke of Ethirdova"; "Empty Clothes"; "The House on Half Moon Street"; "Long Journey"; "Mr. and Mrs. Perry"; "Taureke's Eyes"; "Yellow Glove"; "Young Canadian."

BOND, J. HARVEY (pseud) See WINTERBOTHAM, R.

BOND, NELSON S(LADE) (23 Nov 1908–) U.S. author. He was born in Scranton and spent his war-time boyhood in several cities including Washington, D.C. The depression forced him to abandon intentions of being an engineer. He first wrote publicity articles and then his fiction began to sell through the help of his agent, August Lenniger. In recent years he has been very active in the Roanoke Community Theatre.
An early notable story was "Mr. Mergenthwirker's Lobblies" (*Scribner's Magazine*, Nov 1937); this became the title of a radio series, saw a number of reprintings, and was enlarged into a play. Probably his most anthologised story has been "Conqueror's Isle" (*BB*, June 1946). He was a regular contributor to *Blue Book*, 1942–51, notably with the various series covered below. In later years he has branched into televison. Stories of interest include: "Sons of the Deluge" (*AS*, sr2, Jan 1940; *Jules Verne Magasinet* [Swedish], sr7, No. 1, 1940); "Gods of the Jungle" (*AS*, sr2, June 1942); "That Worlds May Live" (*AS*, April 1943; *JVM*, No. 2–19, 1945). The Australian *American Science Fiction Magazine* had an issue devoted to Bond's stories titled *The Monster* (No. 9, Feb 1953). A nonfantasy play was *State of Mind* (S. French, 1957), and another work is the reference catalogue *The Postal Stationery of Canada* (Herman Hirst, 1953).
Series
Biggs, Lancelot. "F.O.B. Venus" (*FA*, Nov 1939); "Lancelot Biggs Cooks a Pirate" (*FA*, Feb 1940); "The Madness of Lancelot Biggs" (*FA*, Apr 1940); "Lancelot Biggs, Master Navigator" (*FA*, May 1940); "The Genius of Lancelot Biggs" (*FA*, June 1940); "Honeymoon in Bedlam" (*WT*, Jan 1941); "The Downfall of Lancelot Biggs" (*WT*, Mar 1941); "Where Are You, Mr. Biggs?" (*WT*,

Sep 1941); "The Ghost of Lancelot Biggs" (*WT*, Jan 1942); "The Return of Lancelot Biggs" (*AS*, May 1942); "The Love Song of Lancelot Biggs" (*AS*, Sep 1942); "Mr. Biggs Goes to Town" (*AS*, Oct 1942); "The Ordeal of Lancelot Biggs" (*AS*, May 1943). Lancelot Biggs also appears in "The Scientific Pioneer Returns" (*AS*, Nov 1940). All the above stories appeared in *Lancelot Biggs: Spaceman*, most in revised form, while the first five, the seventh, and the last two appeared in the Swedish *JVM*, 1941–44.

Hank, Horse-Sense. "The Scientific Pioneer" (*AS*, Mar 1940); "The Scientific Pioneer Returns" (*AS*, Nov 1940); "Horse-Sense Hank Does His Bit" (*AS*, May 1942); "Horse-Sense Hank in the Parallel Worlds" (*AS*, Aug 1942).

Lobblies, The. "Mr. Mergenthwirker's Lobblies" (*Scribner's Magazine*, Nov 1937); "Tell Me About Tomorrow" (*Arg*, 13 Dec 1941); "Miracles Made Easy" (*Arg*, 15 Apr 1942); "Don't Fool With Phantoms" (*Arg*, Dec 1942).

McGhee, Squaredeal Sam. Tall stories [† = not sf]. "One's Got to Be Best"† (*BB*, Mar 1943); "Nothing in the Rules" (*BB*, Aug 1943); "The Masked Marvel" (*BB*, Dec 1943); "Music's Got Charms"† (*BB*, Nov 1945); "The Gripes of Wraith" (*BB*, Aug 1946); "Knights Must Fall"† (*BB*, Jan 1947); "A Matter of a Pinion" (*BB*, Mar 1948); "Daze Without End" (*BB*, Nov 1948); "Strikes to Spare" (*BB*, May 1949); "Black Magic" (*BB*, Feb 1951).

Meg the Priestess. "The Priestess Who Rebelled" (*AS*, Oct 1939); "The Judging of the Priestess" (*FA*, Apr 1940); "Magic City" (*ASF*, Feb 1941).

Pending, Pat. Screwy inventions, devised by 'Pat Pending.' "The Bacular Clock" (*BB*, July 1942); "Pat Pending's Periscoop" (*BB*, Jan 1943); "Miracular and Importulant" (*BB*, Apr 1943); "The Masked Marvel" (*BB*, Dec 1943); "Pat Pending's Invisibelt" (*BB*, Jan 1944); "Pat Pending Returns" (*BB*, June 1945); "Magnifular and Marvaceous" (*BB*, Apr 1946); "The Greater Gizmo" (*BB*, May 1946); "Pat Pending, Detectivator" (*BB*, Oct 1946); "Double Trouble for Pat Pending" (*BB*, Apr 1947); "Much Ado About Pending" (*BB*, Aug 1948); "Lighter Than You Think" (*FU*, Aug 1957).

Fiction

Exiles of Time (*BB*, May 1940) (Prime, Philadelphia, 1949, 183 pp., $3.00) (Paperback: 52-804, 1965, 159 pp., pa 50¢) (*Im Zeitexil* [German], *T*: 516, 1967)

A well-written interpretation of the Twilight of the Gods.

Lancelot Biggs: Spaceman [C] (Doubleday, New York, 1950, 224 pp., $2.50) ("The Adventures of Lancelot Biggs," *Sunday Telegraph* [Sydney], supplement, 16 Apr 1950, 23 pp.) (Young Moderns Edition, 1951?) (*De zonderlinge aventuren van Lancelot Biggs, ruimtevaarder* [Dutch], Servire, 's-Gravenhage, 1952) (D'day SF B.C., 1953?) (*Lancelot Biggs wundersame Weltraumfahrten* [German], Weiss, 1953; Heyne, 1961, pa)

Sf, 13 stories—the Lancelot Biggs series. All the stories except "The Genius . . ." and "The Return . . ." were revised from their original appearance. The Australian newspaper supplement has only the first five episodes.

Mr. Mergenthwirker's Lobblies and Other Fantastic Tales [C] (Coward-McCann, New York, 1946, 243 pp., $2.75) ([Spanish], Hispano Americana) (Title story only, S. French, New York, nd [late 1940's], 85 pp., pa $1.00)

Sf and fantasy, 13 stories: "Mr. Mergenthwirker's Lobblies"; "The Magic Stair-Case"; "The Remarkable Talent of Egbert Haw"; "Johnny Cartwright's Camera"; "The Master of Cotswold"; "The Einstein Inshoot"; "The Fountain"; "Dr. Fuddle's Fingers"; "Conqueror's Isle"; "Socrates of the South Forty"; "The Bacular Clock"; "Union in Gehenna"; "The Bookshop."

Nightmares and Daydreams [C] (Arkham, Wisconsin, 1968, 269 pp., $5.00; 2,000 copies)

Sf and fantasy, 15 stories (all from *Blue Book* except marked †): "To People a New World"; "A Rosy Future for Roderick"; "The Song"; "Petersen's Eye"; "The Abduction of Abner Green"; "Bird of Prey"; "The Spinsters"; "The Devil to Pay"; " 'Down Will Come the Sky' "†; "The Pet Shop"; "Al Haddon's Lamp"†; "Last Inning"; "The Dark Door"; "Much Ado About Pending"; "Final Report"† [verse].

No Time Like the Future [C] [pa] (Avon: T80, 1954, 221 pp., pa 25¢) (*Ningún tiempo como el futuro* [Spanish], Nebula: 62, 1959, pa) (*Insel der Eroberer* [German], Heyne, 1964, pa)

Sf and fantasy, 12 stories (German abr.): "Vital Factor . . ."; "The Voice From the Curious Cube"; "Button, Button"; "Conqueror's Isle"; "Life Goes On"; "Uncommon Castaway"; "The Cunning of the Beast"; "The Last Outpost"; "And Lo! The Bird"; "This Is the Land"; "The World of William Gresham"; "The Silent Planet."

31st of February, The [C] (Gnome, New York, 1949, 272 pp., $3.00; 1949, pa 35¢)

Fantasy, 13 stories: "The Sportsman"; "The Mask of Medusa"; "My Nephew Norvell"; "The Ring"; "The Gripes of Wraith"; "The Cunning of the Beast"; "The Five Lives of Robert Jordan"; " 'Take My Drum to England' "; "Saint Mulligan"; "The Monster From Nowhere"; "The Man Who Walked Through Glass"; "The Enchanted Pencil"; "Pilgrimage" ("The Priestess Who Rebelled"). The Gnome pa edition was printed for the U.S. Army overseas and is scarce.

BONE, J(ESSE) F(RANKLIN) (15 June 1916–) U.S. veterinarian and author, born in Tacoma, Washington. He received his D.V.M. in 1950, and M.S. in 1953 from Oregon State College. He is a Professor of Veterinary Medicine and now lives in Corvallis, Oregon. His first story was "Survival Type" (*GSF*, Mar 1957); he has contributed regularly to the sf magazines since. His stories include the short novel "Second Chance" (*Satellite*, Feb 1959).

Fiction

Lani People, The [pa] (Bantam: J2363, 1962, 152 pp., pa 40¢) (Corgi: SS1181, 1962, 152 pp., pa 2/6) (*Il popolo dei Lani* [Italian], *Cosmo*: 151, 1963)

The exploitation of an alien race looking like humans but having tails.

BONESTELL, CHESLEY (1887?–) U.S. artist, noted for his astronomical paintings. He studied architecture at Columbia under Frank D. Sherman, from whom he learnt perspective, shades and shadows, and stereotomy. He became interested in the art side of architectural draftsmanship. After World War I he worked in London as a special artist on *Illustrated London News* and London evening papers, returning to New York in 1927. He has worked in Hollywood where his almost photographic technique has been of much use.

In the 1940's he became prominent for his astronomical artwork in *Life* (29 May 1944 and later) and *Coronet*. Then he entered the sf field with the *ASF* cover "The Sun With Mercury in Transit" (Oct 1947), the first of a number which appeared to Dec 1954. *F&SF* also used many of his covers from Dec 1950–Feb 1959; other appearances included *Mechanix Illustrated* and *Collier's*. The largest amount of his work in a single volume is that in *The Conquest of Space* (with W. Ley, 1949). His work is also featured in C. Ryan's compilations *Across the Space Frontier* (1952) and *Conquest of the Moon* (1953), as well as in K. Heuer's *The End of the World* (1953, retitled 1957). His most recent work with W. Ley is *Beyond the Solar System* (1964); *Rocket to the Moon* (Children's Press, 1968) is a juvenile. The Hayden Planetarium in 1967-68 displayed 39 of his paintings. A bibliography of Bonestell's astronomical artwork was compiled by R. T. Gallant of Canada and presented in his amateur magazine *Scientillo*, Winter 1961.

BONFIGLIOLI, KYRIL British editor of *Science-Fantasy*, beginning when Roberts & Vinter Ltd., London, took over its publishing in 1964. He edited this magazine from its June/July 1964 issue through to Feb 1966, and continued when the title was changed to *Impulse*, through to Sep 1966. Bonfiglioli operates an art gallery in Oxford and lectures in antiquities and medieval art.

BOOTHBY, GUY (NEWELL) (13 Oct 1867–26 Feb 1905) Australian novelist. He was born in Adelaide, but educated in England. After a short period of writing melodrama in his home city, he resettled in England in 1894. He wrote over 50 sensational novels, many dealing with life in Australia, and some being best-sellers of their time. His most noted character was 'Dr. Nikola' and his most popular book was *A Bid for Fortune, or, Dr. Nikola's Vendetta* (Ward Lock, 1895).

BORDERLINE Books below contain selections from *Borderline* magazine.
Nonfiction
Strange Horizons (Paperback: 52-490, 1967, 171 pp., pa 50¢)
   24 articles, including: "I Ching—The Book of Changes!"; "The Great Sir William Crookes Scandal"; "Aleister Crowley"; "Krishna Venta and the Fountain of the World."
Strange, Stranger, Strangest (Paperback: 52-930, 1966, 158 pp., pa 50¢)

BORGES, JORGE LUIS (1899–) Argentinian writer, born of Scottish forebears in Buenos Aires. He was educated in Europe and returned to the Argentine in 1921. Usually considered as a scholarly and brilliant poet, he is primarily an essayist and short story writer. He is now recognised as one of the most intriguing literary minds of our time. An able and gifted linguist, he has translated many writers and has an intimate knowledge of the literatures of France, Germany, England, Spain and the U.S.A., as well as his native South America. In 1955 he was elected Director of the Argentine National Library. In 1961 he and Samuel Beckett shared the Formentor Prize (First International Publishers Award). Among his translated works is *Dreamtigers* (Univ. Texas Press, 1964).
Fiction
Ficciones [Editor and translator: A. Kerrigan] [C] (Weidenfeld Nicolson, London, 1962, 174 pp., 21/-) (Grove, New York, 1962, 174 pp., $3.50; 1963, pa $2.45) (*Fictions*, Jupiter: J7, 1966, 159 pp., pa 6/6)
   Collection of 17 stories with a "parallel paths in time" theme (British pa, 16 stories omitting 4th from last); introduction by Anthony Kerrigan: *I. The Garden of Forking Paths:* "Prologue"; "Tlön, Uqbar, Orbis Tertius"; "The Approach to Al-Mûtasin"; "Pierre Menard—Author of Don Quixote"; "The Circular Ruins"; "The Babylon Lottery"; "An Examination of the Work of Herbert Quain"; "The Library of Babel"; "The Garden of Forking Paths." *II. Artifices:* "Prologue"; "Funes, the Memorious"; "The Form of the Sword"; "Theme of the Traitor and Hero"; "Death and the Compass"; "The Secret Miracle"; "Three Versions of Judas"; "The End"; "The Secret of the Phoenix"; "The South."
Fictions [pa] See *Ficciones*
Labyrinths [Editors: D. A. Yates & J. E. Irby] [C] (New Directions, New York, 1962, 248 pp., $5.50; NDP186, 1964, 260 pp., pa $1.90) (McClelland, Toronto, 1964, pa $2.30) ([German], Hanser, 1968)
   In sections, with Preface (6 pp.) by Andre Maurois and Introduction (9 pp.) by J. E. Irby, plus an 'Elegy,' a Chronology and a Bibliography of Borges. *23 Stories:* "Tlön, Uqbar, Orbis Tertius"; "The Garden of Forking Paths"; "The Lottery in Babylon"; "Pierre Menard, Author of 'Quixote' "; "The Circular Ruins"; "The Library of Babel"; "Funes the Memorious"; "The Shape of the Sword"; "Theme of the Traitor and the Hero"; "Death and the Compass"; "The Secret Miracle"; "Three Versions of Judas"; "The Secret of the Phoenix"; "The Immortal"; "The Theologians"; "Story of the Warrior and the Captive"; "Emma Zanz"; "The House of Asterion"; "Deutsches Requiem"; "Averroes' Search"; "The Zahir"; "The Waiting"; "The God's Script." *10 Essays:* "The Argentine Writer and Tradition"; "The Wall and the Books"; "The Fearful Sphere of Pascal"; "Partial Magic in the 'Quixote' "; "Valery as Symbol"; "Kafka and His Precursors"; "Avatars of the Tortoise"; "The Mirror of Enigmas"; "A Note on (toward) Bernard Shaw"; "A New Refutation of Time." *8 Parables:* "Inferno I, 32"; "Paradiso XXXI, 108"; "Ragnarok"; "Parable of Cervantes and the Quixote"; "The Witness"; "A Problem"; "Borges and I"; "Everything and Nothing."

BORGESE, ELIZABETH MANN (1918–) One of Thomas Mann's three daughters. She has had some sf short stories published, including "Twin's Wail" (*Star SF No. 6* [Pohl], 1959), "For Sale, Reasonable (*F&SF*, July 1959), and "True Self" (*GSF*, Oct 1959).

BORN, FRANZ
Nonfiction
Jules Verne: The Man Who Invented the Future (Scholastic: T838, 1968, pa 50¢)
   Juvenile.

BORODIN, GEORGE (pseud) See SAVA, G.

BOSLEY, KEITH
Fiction
Tales From the Long Lakes [C] (Gollancz, London, 1966, 144 pp., illus.–R. Kennedy, 21/-)
   Juvenile; stories from the great Finnish saga, the *Kalevala*. Easily assimilated episodes told by Great Uncle Erkki to a group of children.

BOSTON, (Mrs) L(UCY) M(ARIA) (1892–)
Fiction [juvenile]
Children of the Green Knowe (Faber, London, 1954, 157 pp., illus.–Peter Boston, 10/6; 1963, pa 5/-) (Harcourt Brace, New York, 1955, 157 pp., illus.–P. Boston, $2.75)
   Time interplay in an ancient house between a lonely modern child and a family of three children who died in the Great Plague.
Chimneys of Green Knowe (Faber, 1958, 186 pp., illus., 13/6; 1964, pa 6/-) (*Treasure of Green Knowe*, Harcourt, 1958, 185 pp., illus., $3.00)
   Second in series.
Enemy at Green Knowe, An (Faber, 1964, illus., 15/-) (Harcourt, 1964, 156 pp., illus., $3.25)
   Fifth of series.
River at Green Knowe, The (Faber, 1959, 3-144 pp., illus., 13/6) (Harcourt, 1959, 153 pp., illus., $2.00)
   Third of series.
Stranger at Green Knowe, A (Faber, 1961, 158 pp., illus., 13/6) (Harcourt, 1961, 158 pp., illus., $3.00)
   Fourth of series.
Treasure of Green Knowe See *Chimneys of Green Knowe*

BOUCHER, ANTHONY (pseud) (21 Aug 1911–29 April 1968) U.S. author, editor, and book reviewer. His real name was William Anthony Parker White, but he used "Boucher" for all his writings except for some early work as "H. H. Holmes" and certain book reviewing. Before entering the sf field he was noted for his detective writings, and was a well-known anthologist in that field with *Great American Detective Stories*; *Four-and-Twenty Bloodhounds* (Simon & Schuster, 1950); *The Pocket Book of True Crime Stories* (nonfiction, Pocket Books, 1943).
   His first story in the fantasy field was "Snulbug" (*Unknown*, Dec 1941); others followed in both *Unknown* and *ASF*. In the latter his "The Barrier" (Sep 1942) and "The Chronokinesis of Jonathan Hull" (June 1946) were notable; *ASF* also published "Q.U.R." (Mar 1943) and a sequel under the H. H. Holmes by-line. With J. F. McComas as co-editor, he began the noted *Magazine of Fantasy and Science Fiction* in 1949. He became sole editor from Sep 1954, but was forced to leave because of ill health in April 1958; he also did the book reviews for *F&SF* in this period. Boucher and McComas also compiled regular anthologies from the magazine, with Boucher alone doing them from the 4th to the 8th Series (R. P. Mills then continuing them).
   As a book reviewer Boucher covered sf and fantasy for the *San Francisco Chronicle* 1946-47, the *Chicago Sun-Times* 1949-50, the *New York Herald Tribune* 1951-68 (as H. H. Holmes), the *New York Times* (also till his death), and *Ellery Queen's Mystery Magazine*. He wrote the Introduction for *The Science-Fictional Sherlock Holmes* (Council of Four, 1960) in which he also had two stories; this was also published in *New Frontiers* [fan magazine], Aug 1960, and *The Baker Street Journal*, July 1960.
   His death was a great loss to all science fiction, fantasy, and detective fiction enthusiasts.

Fiction

Far and Away [C] (Ballantine, New York, 1955, 166 pp., $2.00; #109, pa 35¢)

Sf and fantasy, 11 stories: "The Anomaly of the Empty Man"; "The First"; "Balaam"; "They Bite"; "Snulbug"; "Elsewhen"; "Secret of the House"; "Sriberdegibit"; "Star Bride"; "Review Copy"; "The Other Inauguration."

Rocket to the Morgue [as H. H. Holmes] (Duell, Sloan & Pearce, New York, 1942, 279 pp., $2.00). [As Boucher]: (Dell: 591, 1952, 223 pp., pa 25¢) (Pyramid: X1681, 1967, pa 60¢)

A good detective novel which includes a number of sf authors as characters and is written around the Mañana Literary Society.

Anthologies

Best From Fantasy and Science Fiction, The [with J. F. McComas] (Little, Brown; Boston, 1952, 214 pp., $2.75)

19 stories: "Huge Beast," C. Cartmill; "John the Revelator," O. La Farge; "Gavagan's Bar," L. S. de Camp & F. Pratt; "The Friendly Demon," D. Defoe; "Old Man Henderson," K. Neville; "The Threepenny Piece," J. Stephens; "No-Sided Professor," M. Gardner; "The Listening Child," I. Seabright; "Dress of White Silk," R. Matheson; "The Mathematical Voodoo," H. Nearing; "The Hub," P. MacDonald; "Built Down Logically," H. Schoenfeld; "The Rat That Could Speak," C. Dickens; "Narapoia," A. Nelson; "Postpaid to Paradise," R. Arthur; "In the Days of Our Fathers," W. McClintic; "Barney," W. Stanton; "The Collector," H. F. Heard; "Fearsome Fable," B. Elliott.

Best From Fantasy and Science Fiction, Second Series, The [with J. F. McComas] (Little, Brown; 1953, 270 pp., $3.00)

18 stories: "Budding Explorer," R. Robin; "The Shout," R. Graves; "The Tooth," G. G. Dewey; "Ugly Sister," J. Struther; "The Black Ball," L. S. de Camp & F. Pratt; "The Third Level," J. Finney; "Ransom," H. B. Fyfe; "The Desrick on Yandro," M. W. Wellman; "The Soothsayer," Kem Bennett; "The Hyperspherical Basketball," H. Nearing; "Come On, Wagon," Zenna Henderson; "Stair Trick," Mildred Clingerman; "Hobson's Choice," A. Bester; "Hole in the Moon," I. Seabright; "The Cheery Soul," Elizabeth Bowen; "The Earlier Service," Marg. Irwin; "Jizzle," J. Wyndham; "Letters to the Editor," R. Goulart.

Best From Fantasy and Science Fiction, Third Series, The [with J. F. McComas] (Doubleday, New York, 1954, 252 pp., $3.25, jacket–C. Bonestell) (D'day SF B.C., 1954) (Ace: D-422, 1960, 256 pp., pa 35¢; G-712, 1968, pa 50¢)

16 stories: "Attitudes," P. J. Farmer; "Maybe Just a Little One," R. Bretnor; "The Star Gypsies," Wm. L. Gresham; "The Untimely Toper," L. S. de Camp & F. Pratt; "Vandy, Vandy," M. W. Wellman; "Experiment," Kay Rogers; "Lot," Ward Moore; "Manuscript Found in a Vacuum," P. M. Hubbard; "The Maladjusted Classroom," H. Nearing; "Child by Chronos," C. L. Harness; "New Ritual," I. Seabright; "Devlin," W. B. Ready; "Captive Audience," Ann W. Griffith; "Snulbug," A. Boucher; "Shepherd's Boy," Richard Middleton; "Star Light, Star Bright," A. Bester.

Best From Fantasy and Science Fiction, Fourth Series, The (Doubleday, 1955, 250 pp., $3.50, jacket–Mel Hunter) (D'day SF B.C., 1955) (Ace: D-455, 1960, 255 pp., pa 35¢; G-713, 1968, pa 50¢)

15 stories and 1 poem, with compiler's Introduction: "Fondly Fahrenheit," A. Bester; "I Never Ast No Favors," C. M. Kornbluth; "Heirs Apparent," R. Abernathy; "$1.98," A. Porges; "The Immortal Game," P. Anderson; "All Summer in a Day," R. Bradbury; "The Accountant," R. Sheckley; "Brave New Word," J. F. McComas; "My Boy Friend's Name Is Jello," A. Davidson; "The Test," R. Matheson; "Careless Love," Albert C. Friborg; "Bulletin," Shirley Jackson; "Sanctuary," D. F. Galouye; "Misadventure," Lord Dunsany; "The Little Black Train," M. W. Wellman; "The Foundation of Science Fiction Success" (poem), I. Asimov.

Best From Fantasy and Science Fiction, Fifth Series, The (Doubleday, 1956, 256 pp., $3.50, jacket–Lowell Hess) (D'day, Toronto, $4.00) (D'day SF B.C., 1956) (Ace: F-105, 1961, 254 pp., pa 40¢; G-714, 1968, pa 60¢)

16 stories, 2 poems, and 4 vignettes, with compiler's Introduction: "Imagine: a Proem," Fredric Brown; "You're Another," D. Knight; "This Earth of Majesty," A. C. Clarke; "Birds Can't Count," Mildred Clingerman; "The Golem," A. Davidson; "Pot-

tage," Zenna Henderson; "The Vanishing American," C. Beaumont; "Created He Them," Alice E. Jones. *Four vignettes:* "Too Far," F. Brown; "A Matter of Energy," J. Blish; "Nellthu," A. Boucher; and "Dreamworld," I. Asimov. "One Ordinary Day, With Peanuts," Shirley Jackson; "The Short Ones," R. E. Banks; "The Last Prophet," M. Clingerman; "Botany Bay," P. M. Hubbard; "A Canticle for Leibowitz," W. M. Miller, Jr.; "Lament by a Maker" (poem), L. S. de Camp; "Pattern for Survival," R. Matheson; "The Singing Bell," I. Asimov; "The Last Word," Chad Oliver & C. Beaumont.

Best From Fantasy and Science Fiction, Sixth Series, The (Doubleday, 1957, 255 pp., $3.50, jacket–Dick Shelton) (D'day, Toronto, $4.00) (D'day SF B.C., 1957) (Ace: F-131, 1962, 254 pp., pa 40¢)

15 stories, with compiler's Introduction: "The Cosmic Expense Account," C. M. Kornbluth; "Mr. Sakrison's Halt," Mildred Clingerman; "The Asa Rule," Jay Williams; "King's Evil," A. Davidson; "The Census Takers," F. Pohl; "The Man Who Came Early," P. Anderson; "Final Clearance," Rachel Maddux; "The Silk and the Song," C. L. Fontenay; "The Shoddy Lands," C. S. Lewis; "The Last Present," Will Stanton; "No Man Pursueth," Ward Moore; "I Don't Mind," Ron Smith; "The Barbarian," P. Anderson; " 'And Now the News . . . ,' " T. Sturgeon; "Icarus Montgolfier Wright," R. Bradbury.

Best From Fantasy and Science Fiction, Seventh Series, The (Doubleday, 1958, 264 pp., $3.75) (D'day SF B.C., 1958, $1.65) (Ace: F-162, 1962, 252 pp., pa 40¢)

15 stories, with compiler's Introduction: "The Wines of Earth," Idris Seabright; "Adjustment," Ward Moore; "The Cage," A. B. Chandler; "Mr. Stilwell's Stage," A. Davidson; "Venture to the Moon" (6 short shorts), A. C. Clarke; "Expedition," F. Brown; "Rescue," G. C. Edmondson; "Between the Thunder and the Sun," Chad Oliver; "A Loint of Paw," I. Asimov; "The Wild Wood," Mildred Clingerman; "Dodger Fan," W. Stanton; "Goddess in Granite," Robert F. Young; "Ms. Found in a Chinese Fortune Cookie," C. M. Kornbluth; "Journey's End," P. Anderson; "The Big Trek," F. Leiber.

Best From Fantasy and Science Fiction, Eighth Series, The (Doubleday, 1959, 240 pp., $3.75) (D'day SF B.C., 1959, $1.20) (Ace: F-217, 1963, 224 pp., pa 40¢)

15 stories, 2 Feghoot episodes, and 7 poems, with compiler's Introduction: "Ministering Angels," C. S. Lewis; "Backwardness," P. Anderson; "The Wait," Kit Reed; "The Up-To-Date Sorcerer," I. Asimov; "A Deskful of Girls," F. Leiber; "Eripmav," D. Knight; "Poor Little Warrior!" B. W. Aldiss; "The Omen," Shirley Jackson; "Gil Braltar," J. Verne; "The Grantha Sighting," A. Davidson; "Theory of Rocketry," C. M. Kornbluth; "A New Lo!" Ron Goulart; "Gorilla Suit," John Shepley; "Captivity," Zenna Henderson; "The Men Who Murdered Mohammed," A. Bester. "Through Time and Space With Ferdinand Feghoot" (2 episodes), G. Briarton. *Verse:* "Origin of the Species," Karen Anderson; "Epithalamium," Doris P. Buck; "The Watchers" and "The Better Bet," A. Brode; "Ye Phantasie Writer and His Catte" and "Valise Macabre," Winona McClintic; "In Memoriam: Henry Kuttner," K. Anderson.

Treasury of Great Science Fiction, A (Doubleday, 1959, 2 vols, 527 & 522 pp., $5.95 for set) (D'day SF B.C., 1960, $2.20)

Vol. I. "Before the Curtain," Editor, and 12 stories: *Re-Birth*, J. Wyndham; "The Shape of Things to Come," R. Deming; "Pillar of Fire," R. Bradbury; "Waldo," R. Heinlein; "The Father-Thing," P. K. Dick; "The Children's Hour," H. Kuttner & C. L. Moore; "Gomez," C. M. Kornbluth; "The (Widget), the (Wadget) and Boff," T. Sturgeon; "Sandra," G. P. Elliott; "Beyond Time and Space," J. T. Rogers; "The Martian Crown Jewels," P. Anderson; *The Weapon Shops of Isher*, A. E. van Vogt. *Vol. II.* 12 stories: *Brain Wave*, P. Anderson; "Bullard Reflects," M. Jameson; *The Lost Years*, Oscar Lewis; "Dead Center," Judith Merril; "Lost Art," G. O. Smith; "The Other Side of the Sky," A. C. Clarke; "The Man Who Sold the Moon," R. A. Heinlein; "Magic City," N. S. Bond; "The Morning of the Day They Did It," E. B. White; "Piggy Bank," H. Kuttner; "Letters From Laura," Mildred Clingerman; *The Stars My Destination*, A. Bester.

BOULLE, PIERRE (20 Feb 1912–) French writer, born in Avignon. He was trained as an engineer, but in 1936 went to Malaya as a rubber planter. During World War II he served with the Free French Mission and later with the Special Force, Calcutta; he infiltrated as a guerilla into Indochina where he was captured in 1943 and escaped in 1944. Postwar he returned to Malaya and then went to the Cameroons. He now resides in Paris. His first novel published in France was the tremendously successful *The Bridge Over the River Kwai*, later made into the Academy Award winning film.

Fiction

Garden on the Moon, The (*Le jardin de Kanashima*, Julliard, Paris, 1964) (Vanguard, New York, 1965, 315 pp., $4.95) (S. Warburg, London, 1965, 316 pp., 25/-) (Signet: P3031, 1966, 255 pp., pa 60¢)

Peenemünde V-2 scientist turns his attention to spaceflight; an interesting depiction of growth among four nations, with integration into past and future U.S. history.

Monkey Planet See *Planet of the Apes*

Planet of the Apes (Vanguard, 1963, 246 pp., $4.50) (*Monkey Planet*, S. Warburg, 1964, 223 pp., 18/-; Penguin: 2401, 1966, 174 pp., pa 3/6) (Signet: D2547, 1964, 128 pp., pa 50¢; P3399, 1968, 128 pp., pa 60¢; T3423, 1968, pa 75¢) ([German], Goldmann, 1965) (*De apenplaneet* [Dutch], Bruna, Utrecht, 1967)

The narrator, part of an expedition to Betelgeuse, finds humans are but mindless beasts on a planet run by great apes. He proves his intelligence and foments a revolt. *Film: Planet of the Apes*, Arthur Jacobs Production for 20th Century Fox, 1967, starring Charlton Heston, Maurice Evans and Kim Hunter, with screenplay by Michael Wilson and Rod Serling. It is generally true to the story and was well received.

Time Out of Mind and Other Stories [C] [trans.–X. Fielding & E. Abbott] (S. Warburg, 1966, 254 pp., 25/-) (Vanguard, 1966, 352 pp., $5.95)

9 stories, of which the 2nd and 7th are not sf or fantasy and the last is marginal: "Time Out of Mind"; "The Man Who Picked Up Pins"; "The Miracle"; "The Perfect Robot"; "The Enigmatic Saint"; "The Lunians"; "The Diabolical Weapon"; "The Age of Wisdom"; "The Man Who Hated Machines."

BOUNDS, SYDNEY J. (1920–) British author. Closely connected with sf in his youth, he first wrote for pleasure. He studied electrical engineering, and in World War II served with the R.A.F. as an electrician and instrument repairer. He was then a sub-station assistant on London Transport's Underground system until 1951, when he became a professional writer. His literary ventures cover a wide field but he prefers sf. He has one novel other than those covered below—*Dimension of Horror* (Hamilton, 1953, 6/-, pa 1/6).

Fiction

Moon Raiders, The (Foulsham, London, 1955, 160 pp., 8/6) (Digit, 1958, 158 pp., pa 2/-) (*Los comandos de la luna* [Spanish], Nebula: 61, 1959, pa)

Earth secret service agents are shanghaied to the Moon by invaders who have been stealing U235.

Robot Brains, The [pa] (Digit, 1956, 160 pp., pa 2/-; R521, 1961, pa 2/6) (*Cerebros infernales* [Spanish], Espacio: 16, 1962, pa) (Digit: R819, 1964, 158 pp., pa 2/6) (Arcadia, New York, 1967, 191 pp., $3.50)

Evil brains (*not* robotic!), time travellers from Earth's future, endeavour to alter their time by preventing research in ours.

World Wrecker, The (Foulsham, 1956, 159 pp., 8/6) (Digit: R885, 1964, 158 pp., pa 2/6)

Mad scientist type—rocks in a 'sub-energy' state are placed under cities and explode when they return to normal.

BOUSFIELD, H(ENRY) T(HOMAS) W(ISHART)

Fiction

God With Four Arms and Other Stories, The [C] (Rich Cowan, London, 1939, 248 pp., 7/6; 1942, 4/-) (S. J. R. Saunders, Toronto, $2.00)

Fantastic short stories (no further information).

Vinegar—and Cream [C] (J. Murray, London, 1941, 275 pp., 8/6)

Fantasy, 20 stories and 1 verse: "The Unselfish Mother"; "Why Not?"; "The Kingdom of Albert Smith"; "The Last Ghost"; "Fat Girl"; "Death and the Duchess"; "Magazines!"; "According to Plan"; "The Identical Twin"; "Albert Mansions"; "Stink and Yap"; "The Impossible Adventure"; "Poison Pen"; "Susannah the Second"; "The Man Who Took Too Much Trouble"; "The Haunted Ghost"; "The Pearls That Failed"; "All Is Vanity"; " 'Poor Little Rich Girl' "; "Should a Woman Tell?"; "The End of the Honeymoon" (verse).

BOUTELL, CLARENCE BURLEY (1908–) See NORTH, S. (co-anthologist)

BOVA, BEN(JAMIN WILLIAM) (8 Nov 1932–) U.S. editor, writer, and executive. He took a degree in journalism from Temple U., Philadelphia, and did graduate work at Georgetown U.'s School of Foreign Service. After some newspaper and magazine work he was a technical editor for Project Vanguard with the Martin Co., and later directed a technical publishing company. He became a technical communications executive at Avro-Everett Research Laboratories. Author of the popular technical work *The Milky Way Galaxy* (Holt, 1961), he also had a series of articles on the possibility of extra-terrestrial life and planetary engineering in *Amazing Stories* from June 1962. A story of interest was the short novel "The Dueling Machine" [with Myron R. Lewis] in *ASF*, May 1963. He became editor of *Analog* after the death of John W. Campbell in 1971.

Fiction

Out of the Sun (Holt, New York, 1968, 188 pp., $2.95)

A scientist stakes his life on his theory of fighter plane disintegration.

Star Conquerors (Winston, Philadelphia, 1959, 216 pp., $2.50) (*Bezwinger der Galaxis* [German], *T*: 443, 1966)

Juvenile—one of the Adventures in SF series. Earth's star watchers fight interstellar war with the mysterious Masters.

Star Watchman (Holt, Rinehart, Winston; New York, 1964, 224 pp., $3.50) (*Der Mann von der Sternenwache* [German], *T*: 446 & 447, 1966)

A young officer on a frontier planet endeavours to negotiate a truce with the humanoid Komani.

Weathermakers, The (expanded from *ASF*, Dec 1966) (Holt, 1967, 250 pp., $3.95; lib. $3.59) (*Projekt Tornado* [German], TN: 32, 1968, pa)

Scientists fight 'the establishment' to retain weather control programme in civilian hands.

BOVET, RICHARD

Nonfiction

Pandaemonium, or The Devils Cloyster (Hand & Flower Press, Aldington, Kent, 1951, xxviii+191 pp., 30/-)

Introduction (12 pp.), and Notes by Montague Summers. First published in London in 1684, this is an important book in the subject of occult research (only 9 copies of the original are known). One of the original title pages states the contents and purpose of the book as:

Giving a brief account of

Part 1.

1. The Fall of Angels, The Seduction of the Human Race & Their Impieties before the Flood.

2. The Idolatry of the first ages after the Flood; That Defections of Devil Worship was a great step to Infernal Confederacies.

3. Heathen and Idol Priests given to Magic and Divination.

4. Arguments proving the existence of Witchcraft.

5. A Dissertation on Witches and Witchcraft, the character of a Witch & origin of their powers.

6. Examples of Witchcraft, and familiarity with Devils amongst the Ancient Druids, Sybils, Vestal Virgins and Heathen Priests.

7. Confederacies of several Popes, and Roman Priests with the Devil.

Part 2.

Evidence of Apparitions; Spirits; Witches; Demons, Spectres, etc. never before printed, Plus Two Poems, One to King William III & One to Admiral Russell.

BOWDEN, PHIL and ETTA
Fiction
Mercy Island (Vantage, New York, 1965, 281 pp., $5.00)

BOWEN, ELIZABETH (7 Jan 1899–22 Feb 1973) One of the foremost British novelists and short story writers, and a popular touring lecturer and perceptive critic. Her works include *The Hotel* (1927) and *The Death of the Heart* (1938). She was married in 1923 to Alan Charles Cameron. She was not in the public eye in recent years, but her *Afterthoughts* (Longmans, 1962) is a collection of miscellaneous essays of interest to her followers.
Fiction
Cat Jumps and Other Stories, The [C] (Gollancz, London, 1934, 285 pp., 7/6)
   12 stories: "The Apple-Tree"; "The Cat Jumps"; "The Disinherited"; "Firelight in the Flat"; "Good Girl"; "Her Table Spread"; "Last Night in the Old Home"; "Little Girl's Room"; "Man of the Family"; "Maria"; "The Needlecase"; "The Tommy Crans." Many stories later appeared in *Look at All Those Roses.*
Demon Lover and Other Stories, The [C] (J. Cape, London, 1945, 192 pp., 7/6; Clarke, Irwin, Toronto, $2.25) (*Ivy Gripped the Steps*, Knopf, New York, 1946, 233 pp., $2.50) ([Swedish], Bonnier, 1947)
   12 stories: "Careless Talk"; "The Cheery Soul" (*F&SF*, Apr 1952); "The Demon Lover"; "Green Holly"; "Happy Autumn Fields"; "In the Square"; "Inherited Clock"; "Ivy Gripped the Steps"; "Mysterious Kôr"; "Pink May"; "Songs My Father Sang Me"; "Sunday Afternoon."
Encounters [C] (Sidgwick Jackson, London, 1923, 203 pp., 5/-; 1949, 178 pp., 7/6) (Boni Liveright, New York, 1924, 203 pp., $2.00) (Ace [British]: H457, 1961, 125 pp., pa 2/6)
   14 stories: "Breakfast"; "Daffodils"; "The Return"; "The Confidante"; "Requiescat"; "All Saints"; "The New House"; "Lunch"; "The Lover"; "Mrs. Windermere"; "The Shadowy Third"; "The Evil That Men Do—"; "Sunday Evening"; "Coming Home." The S.J. 1949 edition and the paper edition have an author's preface telling how she wrote her early stories.
Ivy Gripped the Steps [C] See *Demon Lover and Other Stories, The*
Joining Charles and Other Stories [C] (Constable, London, 1929, 216 pp., 6/-) (Dial, New York, 1929, 302 pp., $2.50)
   11 stories: "Aunt Tatty"; "The Cassowary"; "The Dancing-Mistress"; "Dead Mabelle"; "Foothold"; "Joining Charles"; "The Jungle"; "Mrs. Moysey"; "Shoes: An International Episode"; "Telling"; "Working Partv."
Look at All Those Roses [C] (Gollancz, 1941, 263 pp., 7/6) (Knopf, 1941, 329 pp., $2.50) (J. Cape, London, collected edition, 1967, 222 pp., pa 25/-)
   1941 editions, 19 stories: "The Apple-Tree"; "The Cat Jumps"; "The Disinherited"; "Easter Egg Party"; "Girl With the Stoop"; "Her Table Spread"; "Last Night in the Old Home"; "Look at All Those Roses"; "Love"; "Love Story"; "The Needlecase"; "Number 16"; "Oh Madam . . ."; "Queer Heart"; "Reduced"; "Summer Night"; "Tears, Idle Tears"; "The Tommy Crans"; "Walk in the Woods."
   1967 edition, 14 stories: "Reduced"; "Tears, Idle Tears"; "A Walk in the Woods"; "A Love Story"; "Look at All Those Roses"; "Attractive Modern Homes"; "The Easter Egg Party"; "Love"; "No. 16"; "A Queer Heart"; "The Girl With the Stoop"; "Unwelcome Idea"; "Oh, Madam . . ."; "Summer Night."
   Includes many stories from *The Cat Jumps and Other Stories.*
Stories by Elizabeth Bowen [C] [pa] (Vintage: K79, 1959, 306 pp., pa $1.25)
   Preface (6 pp.) and 18 stories: "Coming Home"; "The Storm"; "The Tommy Crans"; "Her Table Spread"; "The Disinherited"; "The Easter Egg Party"; "Number 16"; "Reduced"; "Look at All Those Roses"; "A Love Story"; "Summer Night"; "Songs My Father Sang Me"; "The Inherited Clock"; "Sunday Afternoon" "The Demon Lover"; "Ivy Gripped the Steps"; "The Happy Autumn Fields"; "Mysterious Kôr."

BOWEN, JOHN (GRIFFITH) (5 Nov 1924–) British author, born in Calcutta; M.A. (Oxon). He has contributed to BBC radio and television and also commercial television. Some of his works are *The Truth Will Not Help Us*, *The Centre of the Green*, and *The Mermaid and the Boy*.
Fiction
After the Rain (Faber, London, 1958, 203 pp., 15/-) (Ballantine: 248K, 1959, 158 pp., pa 35¢; U2248, 1965, pa 50¢) (Penguin: 1634, 1961, 144 pp., pa 2/6) (*Le grande pluie* [French], Mercure de Paris, 1964) (Panther: 2241, 1967, 140 pp., pa 3/6) (Random, New York, 1968, $4.50)
   A cataclysm, and the behaviour of people as they struggle and scheme to survive. The story was adapted by the author as a stage-play. After being a hit on the London stage, it was on Broadway in December 1967 and closed after only 64 performances.

BOWEN, MARJORIE (pseud) See LONG, G. M. V.

BOWLES, PAUL (FREDERIC) (30 Dec 1910–) U.S. writer and musician; born in Jamaica, Long Island. He spent 15 years in Paris from 1931 devoting himself to music and music criticism. He went to Mexico for a period in 1941 on a Guggenheim fellowship, and composed the opera *The Wind Remains*. He has lived in the native quarter of Tangier, and now lives at times on his own island at Ceylon. He has contributed to many U.S. magazines, and his works include *The Sheltering Sky* and *Let It Down*.
Fiction
Delicate Prey and Other Stories, The [C] (Random, New York, 1950, 307 pp., $3.00) (Signet: 1296, 1956, 192 pp., pa 25¢)
   A highly praised collection of weird, almost Gothic, short stories. 17 stories: "At Paso Rojo"; "Pastor Dowe at Tacate"; "Call at Corazon"; "Under the Sky"; "Señor Ong and Señor Ha"; "The Circular Valley"; "The Echo"; "The Scorpion"; "The Fourth Day Out From Santa Cruz"; "Pages From Cold Point"; "You Are Not I"; "How Many Midnights"; "A Thousand Days for Mokhtar"; "Tea on the Mountain"; "By the Water"; "The Delicate Prey"; "A Distant Episode."

BOYD, HALBERT J(OHNSTON) (1872–?) Another title on lines similar to that below is *Strange Tales of the Western Isles* (1930).
Fiction
Strange Tales of the Borders, Old and New [C] (Moray Press, Edinburgh, 1948, 238 pp., 8/6)
   Weird, 16 stories (first 10 based on legends, 11th partly so, remainder fiction): "The Duel of the Dowie Dens of Yarrow"; "The Wicked Laird of Buckholm"; "A Night in Hermitage"; "The Deil of Littledean"; "Raeburn's Meadow"; "Canobie Dick"; "The Treasure of the Tribune"; "The Murder Moss"; "The Fanatic"; "Spot"; "Sandybed Pool"; "The Return"; "The Rat Man"; "Happy Valley"; "The Gift of the Goddess"; "The Iconoclast."

BOYD, JOHN (pseud) See UPCHURCH, B. D.

BOYD, LYLE G. See BOYD, WILLIAM CLOUSER

BOYD, WILLIAM CLOUSER (4 Mar 1903–) Professor of Immunochemistry, Boston University. He and his wife, Lyle G. Boyd, use the pseudonym Boyd Ellanby for stories written in collaboration. Both were born in Missouri, and both majored in English Literature, while W. C. Boyd also majored in organic chemistry. He has studied at various universities, as well as the School of Oriental Studies in Cairo, Egypt, and has had some technical books published. He collaborated with I. Asimov on *Races and People* (1955). Under the Boyd Ellanby pseudonym their first appearance was the short novel "Category Phoenix" (*GSF*, May 1952), since anthologised. About 15 sf stories have since been published, including such novels as "The Pattern" (*SFS*, Mar 1955) and "The Star Lord" (*Imagination*, June 1953).

BOYLE, VIRGINIA FRAZIER (1863–13 Dec 1938)
Fiction
Devil Tales [C] (Harper, New York & London, 1900, 210 pp.)

Weird, 10 stories using Negro dialect: "Old Cinder Cat"; " 'A Kingdom for Micajah' "; "The Devil's Little Fly"; "Asmodeus in the Quarters"; "The Taming of Jezrul"; "Dark er de Moon"; "The Other Maumer"; "Stolen Fire"; "The Black Cat"; " 'Liza."

BOYS' LIFE (editors of)
Anthology
Boys' Life Book of Outer Space Stories, The (Random, New York, 1964, 182 pp., $1.95)

Sf, 10 stories (first from *TWS*, Feb 1949; rest from *Boys' Life*): "The Man," Ray Bradbury; "A New Game," A. M. Lightner; "Tiger by the Tail," Gene L. Henderson; "The Smallest Moon," Don Wilcox; "Space Lane Cadet," Wm. F. Halstead III; "Load of Trouble," Edward W. Wood; "Best Friend," A. M. Lightner; "The Terrible Intruders," James V. Hinrichs; "The Samaritan," Richard Harper; "Quads From Mars," William W. Greer.

BRACKETT, LEIGH (DOUGLAS) (7 Dec 1915–) U.S. author, wife of sf author Edmond Hamilton. An avid reader in her youth, she always wanted to write. As a sf writer she is particularly noted for her colourful adventure stories set on other planets. She mainly appeared in *Planet Stories* and the Standard magazines, but also had some work in *Astounding Science Fiction*, including "Sorcerer of Rhiannon" (Feb 1942). She has written only a few original sf stories since the mid-50's, but has concentrated on other fields of fiction, where she has written five novels (one under a pseudonym). These include the notable suspense novel *An Eye for an Eye* (Doubleday, 1958); the earlier *The Tiger Amongst Us* was about juvenile delinquency. She is also the author and co-author of some movie scripts. She lives in Kinsman, Ohio, but often works in Hollywood.
Series
N'Chaka. All in *Planet Stories*: "Queen of the Martian Catacombs" (Sum 1949); "Enchantress of Venus" (Fall 1949); "Black Amazon of Mars" (Mar 1951).
Fiction
Alpha Centauri or Die! [pa] ("Teleportress of Alpha," *Planet*, Win 1954-55) –enlarged: (Ace: F-187, 1963, 121 pp., pa 40¢; with *Legend of Lost Earth*)

Spacemen fighting for the freedom of space against invincible robots.
Big Jump, The [pa] (*Space Stories*, Feb 1953) (Ace: D-103, 1955, 131 pp., pa 35¢; with *Solar Lottery*; G-683, 1967, 128 pp., pa 50¢) ([Japanese], Gengen-sha: SF19, 1957) (*Der grosse Sprung* [German], *T*: 112, 1960)

One man returns from the first expedition to another sun; the hero attempts to find the facts behind the man's silence.
Coming of the Terrans, The [C] [pa] (Ace: G-669, 1967, 157 pp., pa 50¢)

Sf, 5 'Martian' novelettes: (1998) "The Beast Jewel of Mars"; (2016) "Mars Minus Bisha"; (2024) "The Last Days of Shandakor"; (2031) "Purple Priestess of the Mad Moon"; (2038) "The Road to Sinharat."
Enchantress of Venus [n] (*Planet*, Fall 1949) (in *Giant Anthology of Science Fiction* [Margulies], 1954, and pa retitle *Race to the Stars*, 1958) (*Revolte der Verlorenen* [German], *UZ*: 95, 1957)

Typical colourful adventure on Venus.
Galactic Breed, The [pa] See *Starmen, The*
Long Tomorrow, The (Doubleday, New York, 1955, 222 pp., $2.95) (D'day SF B.C., 1956) (*La citta proibita* [Italian], *Urania*: 122, 1956) (*Vejen Til I Morgen* [Danish], Skrifola: F13, 1958, pa) (*Am Morgen einer anderen Zeit* [German], *UG*: 110, 1959; *TE*: 86, 1966) (Ace: F-135, 1962, 223 pp., pa 40¢) (Mayflower: B57, 1962, 223 pp., pa 3/6)

Atomic war decentralizes the U.S. so that there are no cities or towns; the hero searches for a legendary last settlement.
Nemesis From Terra, The [pa] See *Shadow Over Mars*
People of the Talisman [pa] ("Black Amazon of Mars," *Planet*, Mar 1951) –revised: (Ace: M-101, 1964, 128 pp., pa 45¢; with *The Secret of Sinharat* [Brackett])

Eric John Stark acquires a stolen talisman from a dying friend.

Secret of Sinharat, The [pa] ("Queen of the Martian Catacombs," *Planet*, Sum 1949) (Ace: M-101, 1964, 95 pp., pa 45¢; with *People of the Talisman* [Brackett]) (*Krieg der Unsterblichen* [German], *UZ*: 579, 1968)

Precedes *People of the Talisman*. Stark endeavours to prevent Martian villages being subjugated by the army for which he is a mercenary.
Shadow Over Mars [pa] (*SS*, Fall 1944) (World Distributors, 1951, 128 pp., pa 1/6) (*FSM*, Mar 1953) (*The Nemesis From Terra*, Ace: F-123, 1961, 120 pp., 40¢; with *Collision Course*) (*E su Marte dominerai* [Italian], *Cosmo*: 111, 1962)

Love, intrigue and adventure on the Red Planet.
Starmen, The ("The Starmen of Llyrdis," *SS*, Mar 1951) (Gnome, New York, 1952, 213 pp., $2.75) (*La legge dei Vardda* [Italian], *Urania*: 26, 1953) (Museum, London, 1954, 168 pp., 8/6) (*The Galactic Breed*, Ace:D-99, 1955, 168 pp., pa 35¢; with *Conquest of the Space Sea*) (*Das Schiff von Orthis* [German], *T*: 117, 1960)

Space-opera, with only one race being able to stand up to the rigours of interstellar travel.
Sword of Rhiannon ("Sea-Kings of Mars," *TWS*, June 1949) (Ace: D-36, 1953, 187 pp., pa 35¢, with *Conan the Conqueror*; F-422, 1967, 128 pp., pa 40¢) (Boardman, London, 1956, 208 pp., 9/6) (*La Spada di Rhiannon* [Italian], *Urania*: 131, 1956) (*Das Vermächtnis der Marsgötter* [German], *UG*: 46, 1957) (*La porte vers l'infini* [French], Le Fleuve Noir: A92, 1957)

Fantastic adventure on Mars when Matt Carse finds himself in ancient times fighting wizardry.

BRADBURY, EDWARD P. (pseud) See MOORCOCK, M.

BRADBURY, RAY(MOND DOUGLAS) (22 Aug 1920–) U.S. sf and fantasy author. He was born in Waukegan, Illinois; his family moved to Arizona, and then to Los Angeles in 1934. Here he joined the Los Angeles Science Fantasy Society and eventually produced four issues of his own fan magazine *Futuria Fantasia*, illustrated by Hannes Bok. Although he is now a noted figure in the field, it took him many years to become an accepted writer. For a number of years he sold newspapers. He made his professional debut with "The Pendulum" (*SSS*, Nov 1941, in collaboration with H. Hasse), while his first solo story was "The Piper" (*TWS*, Feb 1943). His fifth sale was to *Weird Tales* ("The Candle," Nov 1942), initiating a long series of appearances in that magazine, but it was probably his "The Million Year Picnic" (*Planet*, Sum 1946) that really showed he had "arrived." The latter was the forerunner to his many stories with Martian settings which culminated in his *The Martian Chronicles*. Many of Bradbury's stories have appeared in magazines outside the sf and fantasy field, such as *Collier's*, *Mademoiselle* and *Maclean's Magazine* [Canadian]; a number were reprinted in Martha Foley's *Best American Short Stories* annuals.

Bradbury is noted for his essentially simple plots in which his power of writing sustains complete interest, basically through emotional levels. Most of his stories are short; a longer one of interest is "The Creatures That Time Forgot" (*Planet*, Fall 1946). In 1954 he received two important literary prizes: a $1,000 award from the National Institute of Arts and Letters for his contribution to American literature in *The Martian Chronicles*, and the Commonwealth Club of California's second annual gold medal for *Fahrenheit 451*.

He has had a profound effect on contemporary music; the BBC has presented a symphony based on *Fahrenheit 451* and the Charles Hamm chamber opera based on "A Scent of Sarsaparilla"; others are being worked up. In the comics field he first appeared in March 1953 *Vault of Horror*, and soon followed this with works in *Weird Science*, etc.

He has mainly concentrated on script writing in Hollywood in recent years, with such works as *It Came From Outer Space*; *The Beast From 20,000 Fathoms* (from his short story "The Fog," in *SEP*); R. Manvell's *The Dreamer*; and Huston's film *Moby Dick*.

Lately he has emerged as a playwright-producer. In October 1964, he presented at the Coronet Theatre in Los Angeles a programme entitled "The World of Ray Bradbury–Three Fables of the Future." These were staged against stunning projected backgrounds and punctuated by some of the most imaginative sound effects used on the stage. After a successful run, this trilogy was followed by "The Wonderful Ice Cream Suit," another trilogy of plays in a nostalgic vein. Bradbury later opened at the Orpheum Theatre, off Broadway, New York.

The first comprehensive bibliography of his writings was *The Ray Bradbury Review*, compiled and published by William F. Nolan in 1961. An appreciation and bibliography (also two short stories) appeared in the May 1963 *F&SF*. Sam Moskowitz's profile of Bradbury was first published in *AS*, Oct 1961, and repeated in Moskowitz's *Seekers of Tomorrow* (1966). Nolan has a more recent bibliography in his *Three to the Highest Power* (1968, pa).

A non-sf Bradbury work of interest is *Dandelion Wine* (1957, 1959 pa, 1964 pa, 1965 pa, 1967 pa, 1968 pa).

Fiction

Autumn People, The [C] [pa] (Ballantine: U2141, 1965, 188 pp., pa 50¢)

Comic-book versions (most by W. Wood) of stories adapted from appearances in E.C. comics: "There Was an Old Woman"; "The Screaming Woman"; "Touch and Go"; "The Small Assassin"; "The Handler"; "The Lake"; "The Coffin"; "Let's Play Poison."

Dark Carnival [C] (Arkham, Wisconsin, 1947, 313 pp., $3.00, jacket–Burrows; 3,112 copies) (H. Hamilton, London, 1948, 271 pp., 9/-; 1951, 5/-)

Weird, 27 stories (British, 20 stories, marked †): "The Homecoming"†; "Skeleton"†; "The Jar"†; "The Lake"†; "The Maiden"; "The Tombstone"†; "The Smiling People"†; "The Emissary"†; "The Traveller"†; "The Small Assassin"†; "The Crowd"†; "Reunion"; "The Handler"†; "The Coffin" ("Wake for the Dead"); "Interim"; "Jack-in-the-Box"; "The Scythe"; "'Let's Play Poison'"†; "Uncle Einar"†; "The Wind"†; "The Night"†; "There Was an Old Woman"†; "The Dead Man"†; "The Man Upstairs"†; "The Night Sets"; "Cistern"†; "The Next in Line"†.

Day It Rained Forever, The [C] See *Medicine for Melancholy, A*

Fahrenheit 451 (expansion of "The Fireman," *GSF*, Feb 1951) (Ballantine, New York, 1953, 199 pp., illus.–Joe Mugnani, $2.50; #41, pa 35¢; 382K, 1960, 147 pp., pa 45¢; F676, 1962, pa 50¢; U2138, 1963, pa 50¢; U2843, 1967, pa 50¢; U5060, 1967, pa 60¢; 70002, 1968, pa 50¢) (Hart-Davis, London, 1954, 158 pp., 9/6) (Special edition bound in asbestos—200 copies ca. 1954, $4.00 [probably Ballantine text]) (SF B.C. [S.J.], 1955, 4/6) (*Fahrenheit 451* [French], Denoël: PF8, 1955) (*Fahrenheit 451* [German], Ullstein Taschenbuch, 1956; Die Arche, 1962; Heyne: 3112, 1967, pa) ([Japanese], Gengen-sha: SF7, 1956) (Corgi: T389, 1957, 157 pp., pa 2/-; SS821, 1960, 159 pp., pa 2/6; YS1367, 1963, 126 pp., pa 3/-; GS7186, 1965, 158 pp., pa 3/6; GS7654, 1967, pa 3/6) (*Fahrenheit 451* [Swedish], Norstedt, 1958) ([Argentine], Minotauro: 11, 1958, pa) (Doubleday [Simon & Schuster], 1967, 191 pp., $1.20)

One of Bradbury's few long sf works, of a future time when all books are burnt. *Note:* Only the U.S. 1953 editions and the 1967 D'day include two short stories, "The Playground" and "And the Rock Cried Out." The D'day also has a new Introduction. *Film:* 1967; Director, Francois Truffaut; starring Julie Christie and Oskar Werner.

Golden Apples of the Sun [C] (Doubleday, New York, 1953, 250 pp., $3.00) (Hart-Davis, 1953, 192 pp., illus., 10/6) (Bantam: A1241, 1954, 200 pp., pa 35¢; J2306, 1961, 169 pp., pa 40¢; H3357, 1967, pa 60¢; in *Twice 22* [D'day], 1966) (Corgi: 1241, 1956, 189 pp., pa 2/-; SS820, 1960, pa 2/6; GS7130, 1964, 169 pp., pa 3/6; 1966, pa 3/6) (*Les Pommes Dorées du Soleil* [French], Denoël: PF15, 1956, pa) (*Solen Gyllene Applen* [Swedish], Norstedt, 1958) ([Argentine], Minotauro: 17, 1961, pa [abr]) ([Japanese], Hayakawa: 3032, 1962, pa)

Fantasy, 22 stories, many from slick magazines: "The Fog Horn"; "The Pedestrian"; "The April Witch"; "The Wilderness"; "The Fruit at the Bottom of the Bowl"; "Invisible Boy"; "The Flying Machine"; "The Murderer"; "The Golden Kite, the Silver Wind"; "I See You Never"; "Embroidery"; "The Big Black and White Game"; "A Sound of Thunder"; "The Great Wide World Over There"; "Powerhouse"; "En la Noche"; "Sun and Shadow";

"The Meadow"; "The Garbage Collector"; "The Great Fire"; "Hail and Farewell"; "Golden Apples of the Sun." *Note:* British edition has 20 stories, omitting "The Big Black and White Game" and "The Great Fire."

Illustrated Man, The [C] (Doubleday, 1951, 256 pp., $3.50; 1958, 241 pp., $2.95) (D'day, Toronto, $3.50) (Hart-Davis, 1952, 192 pp., 12/6) (Bantam: 991, 1952, 246 pp., pa 25¢; 1282, 1954, 196 pp., pa 25¢; F2588, 1963, 186 pp., pa 50¢; H3484, 1967, pa 60¢) (*L'homme illustré* [French], Denoël: PF3, 1954, pa) (Corgi: 1282, 1955, 246 pp., pa 2/-; SS818, 1960, pa 2/6; YS1349; 1963, 186 pp., pa 3/-; GS7184; 1965, pa 3/6) ([Argentine], Minotauro: 4, 1955, pa) (*Don Illustrerede Mand* [Danish] (8 stories) and *Yderste Nat* (7 stories), Skrifola: P1 & P7, 1957 & 1958, pa) ([Japanese], Hayakawa: 3024, 1960, pa) (*Den Illustrerade Mannen* [Swedish], Norstedt, 1961) (*Der illustrierte Mann* [German], Diogenes, 1962)

Sf, 18 stories with Prologue and Epilogue: "The Veldt"; "Kaleidoscope"; "The Other Foot"; "The Highway"; "The Man"; "The Long Rain" ("Death-by-Rain"); "The Rocket Man"; "The Fire Balloons" ("In This Sign"); "The Last Night of the World"; "The Exiles"; "No Particular Night or Morning"; "The Fox and the Forest"; "The Visitor"; "The Concrete Mixer"; "Marionettes, Inc."; "The City" ("Purpose"); "Zero Hour"; "The Rocket" ("Outcast to the Stars"). *Note:* British edition has 16 stories: omits "The Rocket Man," "The Fire Balloons," "The Exiles," "The Concrete Mixer," and adds "Usher II" and "The Playground."

Machineries of Joy, The [C] (Simon & Schuster, New York, 1964, 255 pp., $4.50) (Hart-Davis, London, 1964, 239 pp., 21/-) (Bantam: H2988, 1965, 213 pp., pa 60¢) (*Les machines a bonheur* [French], Denoël: PF84-85, 1965 pa) (*Glädjens mekanismer* [Swedish], Norstedt, 1965) (Corgi: GN7489, 1966, 213 pp., pa 3/6)

21 stories, most from *Playboy* and pre-1963 *SEP*; reasonably straight fiction about dark corners of tormented people's minds: "The Machineries of Joy"; "The One Who Waits" [sf]; "Tyrannosaurus Rex"; "The Vacation" [sf]; "The Drummer Boy of Shiloh"; "Boys! Raise Giant Mushrooms in Your Cellar!" [sf]; "Almost the End of the World" [sf]; "Perhaps We Are Going Away"; "And the Sailor, Home From the Sea"; "El Dia de Muerte"; "The Illustrated Woman"; "Some Live Like Lazarus"; "A Miracle of Rare Device"; "And So Died Riabouchinska"; "The Beggar on O'Connell Bridge"; "Death and the Maiden"; "A Flight of Ravens"; "The Best of All Possible Worlds"; "The Lifework of Juan Diaz"; "To the Chicago Abyss" [sf]; "The Anthem Sprinters."

Martian Chronicles, The [C] (Doubleday, 1951, 222 pp., $2.50; 1958, $2.95) (D'day, Toronto, $3.50) (*The Silver Locusts*, Hart-Davis, 1951, 232 pp., 12/6) (Bantam: 886, 1951, 200 pp., pa 25¢; 1261, 1954, 181 pp., pa 25¢; A1885, 1959, pa 35¢; F2438, 1962, pa 50¢; H3243, 1967, pa 60¢) (D'day SF B.C., 1953) (SF B.C. [S.J.], 1953, 6/-) (*Chroniques Martiennes* [French], Denoël: PF1, 1954) ([Argentine], Minotauro: 1, 1955, pa) (*The Silver Locusts*, Corgi: 886, 1956, 256 pp., pa 2/-; SS819, 1960, 221 pp., pa 2/6; YS1350, 1963, 181 pp., pa 3/-; GS7185, 1965, pa 3/6) ([Japanese], Gengen-sha: SF10, 1956) (abr, *Kroniker fra Mars* [Danish], Skrifola: F1, 1957, pa) (*Invasion Pa Mars* [Swedish], Norstedt, 1961) (*Cronacche Marziane* [Italian], Biblioteca Economica Mondadori, nd)

The Martian short stories welded into continuity (interim bits italicized): *"Rocket Summer"*; "Ylla"; "The Summer Night" ("The Spring Night") "The Earth Men"; *"The Taxpayer"*; "The Third Expedition" ("Mars Is Heaven"); *"...And the Moon Be Still as Bright"*; *"The Settlers"*; "The Green Morning"; *"The Locusts"*; "Night Meeting"; *"The Shore"*; *"Interim"*; *"The Musicians"*; "Way in the Middle of the Air"; *"The Naming of Names"*; "Usher II" ("Carnival of Madness") *"The Old Ones"*; "The Martian"; *"The Luggage Store"*; "The Off Season"; *"The Watchers"*; "The Silent Towns"; "The Long Years" ("Dwellers in Silence"); "There Will Come Soft Rains"; "The Million Year Picnic." *Note:* The British edition (*The Silver Locusts*) omits "Usher II" and includes "The Fire Balloons." The SF B.C. [S.J.] omits "Usher II" and

includes "The Wilderness" and "The Fire Balloons."
Medicine for Melancholy, A [C] (Doubleday, 1958, 240 pp., $3.75) (*The Day It Rained Forever*, Hart-Davis, 13/6; SF B.C. [S.J.], 1960, 254 pp., 5/6) (Bantam: A2069, 1960, 183 pp., pa 35¢; F2637, 1963, pa 50¢; H3398, 1967, pa 60¢) (in *Twice 22*, D'day, 1966) (*Un remède à la mélancolie* [French], Denoël: PF49, 1960, pa) ([Japanese], Hayakawa Shobō: Tales of Menace 5, 1961, pa) (*The Day It Rained Forever*, Penguin: 1878, 1963, 233 pp., pa 3/6) (*Medicina contra la melancolia* [Spanish], Galaxia: 30, 1965, pa)

About half are fantasy. U.S. editions have 22 stories; all British eds. have 23, marked †, plus others listed below: "In a Season of Calm Weather."†; "The Dragon"†; "A Medicine for Melancholy"; "The End of the Beginning"†; "The Wonderful Ice Cream Suit"†; "Fever Dream"†; "The Marriage Mender"†; "The Town Where No One Got Off"†; "A Scent of Sarsaparilla"†; "Icarus Montgolfier Wright"†; "The Headpiece"†; "Dark They Were, and Golden-Eyed" ("The Naming of Names")†; "The Smile"†; "The First Night of Lent"; "The Time of Going Away"†; "All Summer in a Day"; "The Gift"†; "The Great Collision of Monday Last"; "The Little Mice ("Mice")†; "The Shore Line at Sunset"†; "The Strawberry Window"†; "The Day It Rained Forever"†. Stories only in British editions: "Referent"; "Almost the End of the World"; "Here There Be Tygers"; "Perchance to Dream"; "The Sunset Harp"; "And the Rock Cried Out."
October Country, The [C] (Ballantine, 1955, 306 pp., $3.50; F139, 1956, 276 pp., pa 50¢; F580, 1962, pa 50¢; U2139, 1964, pa 50¢; 72138, 1968, 277 pp., pa 75¢) (Hart-Davis, 1956, 306 pp., 15/-) (*Le pays d'Octobre* [French], Denoël: PF20, 1957, pa) (*Oktoberlandet* [Swedish], Norstedt, 1958) (Ace [British]: H422, 1961, 142 pp., pa 2/6) (FSB: H422, 1963, 158 pp., pa 2/6; 1233, 1965, pa 3/6)

Weird, 19 stories, of which 15 originally appeared in *Dark Carnival* (British pa has 13 stories—12 marked †, and "The Traveller"): "The Dwarf"†; "The Next in Line"; "The Watchful Poker Chip of H. Matisse"†; "Skeleton"†; "The Jar"†; "The Lake"; "The Emissary"†; "Touched With Fire"†; "The Small Assassin"; "The Crowd"; "Jack-in-the-Box"; "The Scythe"†; "Uncle Einar"†; "The Wind"†; "The Man Upstairs"; "There Was an Old Woman"†; "The Cistern"; "Homecoming"†; "The Wonderful Death of Dudley Stone"†.
R Is for Rocket [C] (Doubleday, 1962, 233 pp., $2.95; 1963 & 1964, $2.95) (D'day, Toronto, $3.50) (Bantam: F2915, 1965, 184 pp., pa 50¢; FP164, 1967, pa 50¢; FP4078, 1968, pa 50¢) (Hart-Davis, London, 1968, 21/-)

17 stories, mostly reprinted from previous collections: "R Is for Rocket"; "Frost and Fire." From *The Illustrated Man*: "The Rocket"; "The Rocket Man"; "The Long Rain"; "The Exiles." From *Golden Apples of the Sun*: "The Fog Horn"; "The Golden Apples of the Sun"; "A Sound of Thunder." From *A Medicine for Melancholy*: "The End of the Beginning"; "The Strawberry Window"; "The Dragon"; "The Gift." From *The October Country*: "Uncle Einar." From *New Tales of Space and Time* (Healy, 1951): "Here There Be Tygers." From *Dandelion Wine*: "The Time Machine"; "The Sound of Summer Running" (2 episodes).
"S" Is for Space [C] (Doubleday, 1966, 239 pp., $3.50; lib. $4.25) (Hart-Davis, 1963, 21/-)

Sf, 16 stories and Introduction: "Chrysalis"; "Pillar of Fire"; "Zero Hour"; "The Man"; "Time in Thy Flight"; "The Pedestrian"; "Hail and Farewell"; "Invisible Boy"; "Come Into My Cellar"; "The Million-Year Picnic"; "The Screaming Woman"; "The Smile"; "Dark They Were and Golden Eyed" ("The Naming of Names"); "The Trolley"; "The Flying Machine"; "Icarus Montgolfier Wright."
Silver Locusts, The [C] See *Martian Chronicles, The*
Small Assassin, The [C] [pa] (Ace [British]: H521, 1962, 144 pp., pa 2/6) (FSB: 1234, 1965, 144 pp., pa 3/6)

Weird, 13 stories, many from *The October Country*: "The Small Assassin"; "The Next in Line"; "The Lake"; "The Crowd"; "Jack-in-the-Box"; "The Man Upstairs"; "The Cistern"; "The Tombstone"; "The Smiling People"; "The Handler"; "Let's Play 'Poison' "; "The Night"; "The Dead Man."

Something Wicked This Way Comes (Simon & Schuster, New York, 1962, 317 pp., $4.95) (Hart-Davis, 1963, 250 pp., 18/-) (Bantam: H2630, 1963, 215 pp., pa 60¢; S3408, 1967, pa 75¢) (*La foire aux ténèbres* [French], Denoël: PF71-72, 1964, pa) (*Oktoberfolket* [Swedish], Norstedt, 1964) (Corgi: GN7114, 1965, 215 pp., pa 3/6)

Two young lads spy on the horror of Cooger & Dark's Carnival when it appears at a country town; some sketches are good Bradbury but the whole is not consistent.
Switch on the Night (Pantheon, New York, 1955, illus.–S. Gekiere, $2.50) (Hart-Davis, 1955, illus.–Gekiere, 8/6) (McClelland, Toronto, $2.95)

Juvenile (suitable for 3–6 years), written for his own child; why not to be afraid at night.
Tomorrow Midnight [C] [pa] (Ballantine: U2142, 1966, 188 pp., pa 50¢)

8 stories in cartoon form: "Punishment Without Crime"; "I, Rocket"; "King of the Grey Spaces"; "The One Who Waits"; "The Long Years"; "There Will Come Soft Rains"; "Mars Is Heaven"; "Outcast of the Stars."
Twice 22 [C] (Doubleday, 1966, 406 pp., $4.95) (D'day, Toronto, $5.95) (D'day SF B.C., 1966, $1.90)

44 stories—the two collections *Golden Apples of the Sun* and *A Medicine for Melancholy*.
Vintage Bradbury, The [C] [pa] (Vintage: V-294, 1965 v+329 pp., pa $1.45)

26 stories or selections, mostly reprints from other collections, with Introduction by Gilbert Highet: "The Watchful Poker Chip of H. Matisse"; "The Veldt"; "Hail and Farewell"; "A Medicine for Melancholy"; "The Fruit at the Bottom of the Bowl"; "Ylla" ("I'll Not Ask for Wine," *Maclean's Mag*, 1950); "The Little Mice" ("The Mice," *Escapade*, 1955); "The Small Assassin"; "The Anthem Sprinters" ("The Queen's Own Evaders," *Playboy*, 1963); "And the Rock Cried Out"; "Invisible Boy"; "Night Meeting"; "The Fox and the Forest"; "Skeleton"; "Kaleidoscope"; "Sun and Shadow"; "The Illustrated Man"; "The Fog Horn"; "The Dwarf"; "Fever Dream"; "The Wonderful Ice Cream Suit" ("The Magic White Suit," *SEP*, 1958); "There Will Come Soft Rains." Selections from *Dandelion Wine*: "Illumination"; "Dandelion Wine"; "Statues" ("A Weather of Statues," 1957); "Green Wine for Dreaming."
Anthologies
Circus of Dr. Lao and Other Improbable Stories, The [pa] (Bantam: A1519, 1956, 210 pp., pa 35¢)

Fantasy, 12 stories and compiler's Introduction: "The Circus of Dr. Lao," Charles G. Finney; "The Pond," Nigel Kneale; "The Hour of Let-Down," E. B. White; "The Wish," R. Dahl; "The Summer People," Shirley Jackson; "Earth's Holocaust," Nathaniel Hawthorne; "Buzby's Petrified Woman," L. Eiseley; "The Resting Place," O. La Farge; "Threshold," H. Kuttner; "Greenface," J. H. Schmitz; "The Limits of Walter Horton," J. S. Sharnik; "The Man Who Vanished," R. M. Coates.
Timeless Stories for Today and Tomorrow [pa] (Bantam: A994, 1952, 306 pp., pa 35¢; H2343, 1961, 258 pp., pa 60¢; H3358, 1967, pa 60¢)

Weird, 26 stories with compiler's Introduction: "The Hour After Westerly," R. M. Coates; "Housing Problem," H. Kuttner; "The Portable Phonograph," W. Van Tilburg Clark; "None Before Me," Sidney Carroll; "Putzi," L. Bemelmans; "The Demon Lover," Shirley Jackson; "Miss Winters and the Wind," Christine N. Govan; "Mr. Death and the Redheaded Woman," ("The Rider on the Pale Horse") Helen Eustis; "Jeremy in the Wind," Nigel Kneale; "The Glass Eye," J. K. Cross; "Saint Katy the Virgin," J. Steinbeck; "Night Flight," Josephine W. Johnson; "The Cocoon," John B. L. Goodwin; "The Hand," W. H. Smitter; "The Sound Machine," R. Dahl; "The Laocoön Complex," J. C. Furnas; "I Am Waiting," C. Isherwood; "The Witnesses," Wm. Sansom; "The Enormous Radio," John Cheever; "Heartburn," Hortense Calisher; "The Supremacy of Uruguay," E. B. White; "The Pedestrian," R. Bradbury; "A Note for the Milkman," S. Carroll; "The Eight Mistresses," Jean Hrolda; "In the Penal Colony," F. Kafka; "Inflexible Logic," Russell Maloney.

BRADDOCK, JOSEPH (1902–) British poet, interested in psychical research and the occult. He was educated at Uppingham School and St. John's College, Cambridge. His varied interests also include natural history and travel. His autobiography is *Bright Ghost: Recollections of a Georgian Boyhood.*
Nonfiction
Haunted Houses (Batsford, London, 1956, 218 pp., illus.–Felix Kelly, 21/-) (Clarke Irwin, Toronto, $4.50)
 Noteworthy book on the supernormal, with unusually macabre pictures.

BRADDON, RUSSELL (25 Jan 1921–) Australian journalist and writer, educated at Sydney U. (B.A., 1940). He joined an Army artillery unit in 1941, took part in the Malayan Campaign, and was captured by the Japanese in 1942. He spent the remainder of the war in Changi prison camp, where Sydney Piddington, Braddon, and room-mate Ronald Searle began experiments with telepathy. Braddon later managed the Piddingtons on their world tour demonstrating telepathy. He later took up writing. Amongst others he wrote the biographies *The Piddingtons; Cheshire, V.C.; Nancy Wake;* and *Joan Sutherland.* His novels include *Those in Peril; Out of the Storm; Gabriel Comes to Twentyfour;* and *The Proud American Boy.*
Fiction
Year of the Angry Rabbit, The (Heinemann, London, 1964, 181 pp., 18/-) (Collins, Toronto, $4.25) (Pan: X625, 1967, 159 pp., pa 3/6) (*Australian Women's Weekly,* sr, 21 Oct–4 Nov 1964) (*Het jaar van het boze konijn* [Dutch], Spectrum, Utrecht & Antwerp, 1967)
 Giant rabbits can wipe out civilization; Australia has the virus to kill them.

BRADFORD, J. S.
Fiction
Even a Worm (A. Barker, London, 1936, 220 pp., 2/6) (*FFM,* June 1945)
 All living creatures revolt against man without individually expecting to survive.

BRADFORD, ROARK (21 Aug 1896–13 Nov 1948) U.S. novelist and short story writer, and Sunday Editor of the New Orleans *Times-Picayune.* Besides his works below, he is noted for *Let the Band Play Dixie* (1934) and *The Three-Headed Angel* (1937). He wrote the play *How Come Christmas* (1934). The Bleiler *Checklist* does not list one book which is apparently fantasy: *This Side of Jordan* (Harper, 1929; Heinemann, 1930).
Fiction
John Henry [C] (Harper, New York & London, 1931, 225 pp., illus.–J. J. Lankes (woodcuts), $2.50)
 25 stories: "Back of Town"; "Bend Your Back and Sing"; "The Birth of John Henry"; "The Black River Country"; "Coonjine"; "Doing for His Woman"; "Down the Road"; "Fourteen-Thirty-Six"; "Hand in Hand"; "The How Long Song"; "John Henry Lays His Burden Down"; "John Henry's Last Go Round"; "John Henry's Pathway"; "Julie Anne"; "Lord, My Burden"; "Man's Ever Burden"; "No Rest for the Weary Burden"; "Poor Selma"; "The Poor Selma 'Gris Gris' "; "Ring, Steel, Ring"; "Roll, You Wheelers"; "Shoulder Your Load and Walk"; "Stacker Lee"; "The Way With Women"; "Woman on My Weary Mind." Dramatised by the author in 1940 with music by Jacques Wolfe.
Ol' King David an' the Philistine Boys [C] (Harper, New York & London, 1930, 227 pp., illus.–A. B. Walker, $2.50)
 25 Biblical fantasies: "Business of the Lord"; "Christmas Gift!"; "Country Boy"; "Daniel in the Lions' Den"; "Elijah and the Meal Barrel"; "Elijah's Chariot Ride"; "Frustrating Satan"; "Futile Sin"; "Good-Looking Esther"; "Humility of Old King Nebuchadnezzar"; "Jonah and That Whale"; "Last Romance of King Ahab"; "Little David and His Mouth Harp"; "Lord's Way With Women"; "Naboth's Vineyard"; "Old Witch Woman"; "Parable of the Good Samaritan"; "Parable of the Prodigal Son"; "Regeneration of Baldwin Country"; "Saturday Afternoon Miracles"; "Subtle Ways of the Lord"; "Tentacles of Sin"; "Throw Down

Jezebel"; "Widow Woman Named Ruth"; "Wild-Oat Harvest of Old King David."
Ol' Man Adam an' His Chillun [C] (Harper, New York, 1928, 264 pp., illus.–A. B. Walker, $2.50) (Heinemann, London, 1930, 7/6) (Armed: i-244, nd, pa) (Military: M638, 1944, 187 pp., pa 25¢)
 32 Biblical fantasies: "Adulteration of Old King David"; "All About the Potiphar Scandal"; "Balaam and His Talking Mule"; "Battling With Baal"; "Big Lodge"; "Crossing Jordan"; "Esau"; "Eve and That Snake"; "The Fortune-Teller"; "Green Pastures"; "Little David"; "Little Isaac"; "Manna of the Lord"; "Mantle of Saul"; "Mrs. Lot"; "Nigger Deemus"; "Old King Pharaoh's Daughter"; "Old Man Job"; "Populating the Earth"; "Preliminary Motion in Judge Pilate's Court"; "Romance and Education of Moses"; "Romance and Marriage of Abraham"; "Samson, Strong Boy"; "Sin"; "Steamboat Days"; "Strategem of Josua"; "Sun Trick"; "Trick Boys"; "The Understanding"; "Wisdom of Solomon"; "Wrestling Jacob"; "Younger Generation." Dramatised by Marc Connelly as *Green Pastures* (1930).

BRADLEY, MARION ZIMMER (3 June 1930–) U.S. sf author. She discovered sf when she was 16. When she began writing she collected many rejection slips before her first acceptance in 1953. Besides being an active sf fan, she is a member of the Circus Fans of America and has doubled as a target for a carnival knife-thrower. She is keen on Tolkien. She is married to Walter Breen, a sf fan and noted coin-collecting authority; she has one son.
Series
Darkover. In chronological order (all published by Ace; see entries): *Star of Danger; The Bloody Sun; The Door Through Space; Falcons of Narabedla; The Sword of Aldones; The Planet Savers.*
Fiction
Bloody Sun, The [pa] (Ace: F-303, 1964, 191 pp., pa 40¢) (*Die blutige Sonne* [German], Pebel: 238, 1966, pa)
 A man returns to his home planet, Darkover, and endeavours to find his background.
Colors of Space, The [pa] (Monarch: 368, 1963, 124 pp., pa 35¢) (*Das Rätsel der achten Farbe* [German], *UZ:* 426, 1965)
 Color-blind aliens with a star drive produced from distinctively-colored material.
Dark Intruder and Other Stories, The [C] [pa] (Ace: F-273, 1964, 124 pp., pa 40¢; with *Falcons of Narabedla* [Bradley])
 Sf, 7 stories, with Introduction: "The Dark Intruder"; "Jackie Sees a Star"; "Exiles of Tomorrow"; "Death Between the Stars"; "The Crime Therapist"; "The Stars Are Waiting"; "Black and White."
Door Through Space, The [pa] (enlargement of "Bird of Prey," *Venture,* May 1957) (*Raubvogel der Sterne* [German], Zimmermann, 1959; *T:* 147, 1960) (Ace: F-117, 1961, 132 pp., pa 40¢; with *Rendezvous on a Lost World*) (*La puerta del espacio* [Spanish], Galaxia: 34, 1965, pa)
 Intrigue on the planet Wolf—an intelligence agent renews a feud and finds a plot to destroy Terran control.
Falcons of Narabedla [pa] (*OW,* May 1957) (Ace: F-273, 1964, 127 pp., pa 40¢; with *The Dark Intruder* [Bradley])
 A man is flung into the future where the ruling race controls by using the mental powers of psionic mutants.
Planet Savers, The [pa] (*AS,* Nov 1958) (*Dr. Allisons zweites Ich* [German], *UZ:* 236, 1960) (Ace: F-153, 1962, 91 pp., pa 40¢; with *The Sword of Aldones* [Bradley])
 Two personalities in one body, with the task of obtaining help from an alien race to save the planet Darkover. *Note:* The German edition began as an abridgement of the original but then added entirely new chapters (pp. 35-49) not by the author.
Seven From the Stars [pa] (*AS,* Mar 1960) (Ace: F-127, 1961, 120 pp., pa 40¢; with *Worlds of the Imperium*) (*Erde, der verbotene Planet* [German], *UG:* 139, 1961)
 Alien castaways on Earth, and an unknown menace.
Star of Danger [pa] (Ace: F-350, 1965, 160 pp., pa 40¢) (*Die Krafte der Comyn* [German], *UZ:* 520, 1967)
 Hero in furious combat with aliens, etc., to decide the fate of Terrans on Darkover.
Sword of Aldones, The [pa] (Ace: F-153, 1962, 164 pp., pa 40¢;

with *The Planet Savers* [Bradley]) (*Odio cósmico* [Spanish], Cenit: 45, 1963, pa)

Further involved intrigue on Darkover.

BRADLEY, WILLIS T. U.S. translator who produced a modern rendering of Jules Verne's *Journey to the Center of the Earth* (Ace, 1956, pa; Wyn, 1956).

BRAMAH, ERNEST (pseud) See SMITH, ERNEST B.

BRAMWELL, JAMES
Nonfiction
Lost Atlantis (Cobden-Sanderson, London, 1937, 288 pp., 7/6) (Oxford, Toronto, $2.50) (Harper, New York, 1938, 23+288 pp., $2.75)

A scholarly discussion on the Atlantis myth, dealing with many books on the subject and presenting fairly and impartially the various views, from Plato to Ignatius Donnelly and Lewis Spence. With 18-p. introduction and endcovers comprising a map showing places mentioned and probable locations of Atlantis and Antilla.

BRANDEIS, JULIAN W(ALTER) (1875– ?)
Fiction
Outstanding Exploits and Experiences of Munchausen, M.D., The (Quip, New York, 1924, 229 pp., $1.90)

A novel.

BRANDT, C. A. (1879–1947) U.S. book reviewer, born in Germany. He was an authority on science fiction in all languages, and became associated with the development of *Amazing Stories*. By the mid-1920's he had amassed a unique collection of science-fantasy in various languages, and through this met Hugo Gernsback, founder and editor of *Amazing Stories*, who made him Literary Editor of that magazine soon after it began. He selected reprints, etc., and introduced many new writers who later became big names in the field. He left *Amazing* late in 1931 to be Literary Editor of *Wonder Stories* and *Wonder Stories Quarterly*, but soon returned to *Amazing* as assistant to T. O'Conor Sloane. Primarily remembered for his book reviewing, he retired when *Amazing* was bought by Ziff-Davis in 1938. Before his decease he was planning a new magazine.

BRANLEY, FRANKLYN M(ANSFIELD) (1915–) U.S. associate astronomer of the Hayden Planetarium. Besides one juvenile novel in the sf field he has written some nonfiction of interest, including *Experiments in the Principles of Space Travel* (Crowell, 1955) and *Exploring by Satellite* (Crowell, 1957).
Fiction
Lodestar: Rocket Ship to Mars (Crowell, New York, 1951, 248 pp., $2.50) (Heinemann, London, 1952, 213 pp., 10/6) (Ambassador, Toronto, $3.25) (*Raketen Till Mars* [Swedish], Lektyr, 1953)

Juvenile—the first rocket trip to Mars; technically of much interest, but weak in characterisation.

BRAY, JOHN FRANCIS U.S. champion of the American labour movement. Born in the U.S., he was brought up in England by an aunt following the death of his father. His experiences in the hard times of the mid-19th century caused him to be one of the founders of the Leeds Working Men's Association—his *Labour's Wrongs and Labour's Remedy* was a pioneering work of early English socialism. When it was criticized as being too Utopian, he answered by writing the book below. When he returned to America in 1842 the manuscript was lost and only came to light in 1937.
Nonfiction
Voyage From Utopia to Several Unknown Regions of the World, A (Lawrence & Wishart, London, 1957, 192 pp., 21/-)

A depiction of the world of a century ago through the eyes of an imaginary visitor from Utopia. Edited and with introduction (24 pp.) by M. F. Lloyd-Pritchard, and preface (2 pp.) by author.

BREBNER, WINSTON (1924?–) U.S. author.
Fiction
Doubting Thomas (Rinehart, New York, 1956, 210 pp., $3.00) (Clarke Irwin, Toronto) (Hart-Davis, London, 1958, 182 pp., 12/6)

An unabashed glimpse of a future hell ruled by a vast computer and its human arm.

BREDESON, LENORE
Anthologies
More From One Step Beyond [pa] (Citadel, 1961, 123 pp., pa $1.00) (Digit: R552, 1961, 156 pp., pa 2/6; R676, 1963, 158 pp., pa 2/6)

Fantasy, 5 stories from the U.S. TV series *Alcoa Presents*: "Message From Clara," Larry Marcus; "If You See Sally," Howard Rodman; "The Trap," "Reunion," and "To Know the End," L. Marcus.
One Step Beyond [pa] (Citadel, New York, 1961, 122 pp., pa $1.00) (Digit: R468, 1961, 156 pp., pa 2/6)

Fantasy, 5 stories from the U.S. TV series *Alcoa Presents*, with Foreword by Collier Young (producer of *One Step Beyond*): "Make Me Not a Witch," Gail Ingram; "Bride Possessed," Merwin Gerard & Larry Marcus; "The Aerialist," "The Hand," and "The Vision," Larry Marcus.

BRENNAN, JOSEPH P(AYNE) (20 Dec 1918–) U.S. author and poet. Born in Bridgeport, Conn., he was reared and still lives at New Haven, where he works in the Yale Library. He has had two books of poetry published: *Heart of Earth* (1950) and *The Humming Stair* (1953), while both poetry and prose have appeared in such periodicals as *The New York Times*, *Coronet* and *Esquire*. He edits two "little magazines": *Macabre* (weird and supernatural prose and poetry) and *Essence* (poetry semi-annual).
Fiction
Dark Returners, The [C] (Macabre House; New Haven, Conn., 1959, 70 pp., $3.00; 150 copies autographed)

9 stories: "Disappearance"; "Goodbye, Mr. Bliss"; "The Corpse of Charlie Rull"; "The Impulse to Kill"; "The Pool"; "Daisy Murdock"; "The Fete in the Forest"; "Curb Service"; "The Pavilion."
Nightmare Need [C] (Arkham, Wis., 1964, 69 pp., $3.50, jacket—F. Utpatel)

57 macabre verses, of which about 20 are reprinted from previous works. The selections are well regarded by R. A. Lowndes (*Mag Horror*, Aug 1965), and include: "The Guest"; "The Old Man"; "The Snow Wish"; "Grandmother's Parlour"; "An Hour After Midnight"; "Confederate Cemetery 1961"; "The Silent Noises"; "Epitaph."
Nine Horrors and a Dream [C] (Arkham, Wis., 1958, 120 pp., $3.00; 1,336 copies) (Ballantine: 587, 1962, 121 pp., pa 35¢)

Weird, 10 stories (4 marked † originally published in *WT*): "Slime"†; "Levitation"; "The Calamander Chest"†; "Death in Peru"; "On the Elevator"†; "The Green Parrot"†; "Canavan's Back Yard"; "I'm Murdering Mr. Massington"; "The Hunt"; "The Mail for Juniper Hill."
Scream at Midnight [C] (Macabre, New Haven, 1963, $3.50; 150 copies)

9 stories: "The Horror at Chilton Castle"; "The Midnight Bus"; "The Vampire Bat"; "The Seventh Incantation"; "Killer Cat"; "The Dump"; "The Tenants"; "The Man Who Feared Masks"; "The Visitor in the Vault."
Nonfiction
Lovecraft Bibliography, A (Biblio Press, Washington, 1953, $1.00)

A follow-on to A. Derleth's *H.P.L.: A Memoir*, including a number of items omitted from or not in print at the time of that book. It lists other Lovecraft works (books, etc.), mentioning *The Cats of Ulthor*; and gives a listing of pseudonyms (though incomplete in comparison with some other sources) for Lovecraft's many writings in amateur press periodicals. [Reviewed in *Destiny* (fan magazine), Spr 1953.]

BRENT, LORING (pseud) See WORTS, G. F.

BRETNOR, REGINALD C. (1911–) U.S. author. He was born in Siberia, and brought to California in 1919. During World War II and for some time after, he worked for the OWI and the U.S. Dept. of State writing material connected with Japan. His fiction has been published in a wide range of magazines, such as *Harper's*, *The Pacific Spectator*, *Esquire*, etc. His long interest in the 'why' of science fiction resulted in his book *Modern Science Fiction*. He has also appeared with a number of stories in the field, such as "The Gnurrs Come From the Voodvork Out" (*F&SF*, Win-Spr 1950). Under the pseudonym "Grendel Briarton" he has been writing the 'Ferdinand Feghoot' vignettes (fantastic, with a punning punch line), which have appeared in *F&SF* since May 1956 (almost continuously from Jan 1959 to Jan 1964). Some of the 'Feghoots' use puns submitted by readers.

Fiction

Through Space and Time With Ferdinand Feghoot [As Grendel Briarton] [C] (Paradox Press; Berkeley, Calif., 1962, illus.–Bruce Ariss, $1.25)

A collection of 50 Feghoot puns—45 from *F&SF* and 5 original.

Nonfiction

Modern Science Fiction: Its Meaning and Its Future (Coward-McCann, New York, 1953, 294 pp., $3.75) (Longmans Green, Toronto)

An outstanding symposium analyzing the birth and growth of the science fiction field, in three sections. *Science Fiction Today:* "The Place of Science Fiction," J. W. Campbell, Jr.; "The Publishing of Science Fiction," A. Boucher; "Science Fiction in Motion Pictures, Radio and Television," Don Fabun. *Science Fiction as Literature:* "A Critique of Science Fiction," F. Pratt; "Science Fiction and the Main Stream," Rosalie Moore; "Imaginative Fiction and Creative Imagination," L. S. de Camp. *Science Fiction, Science, and Modern Man:* "Social Science Fiction," I. Asimov; "Science Fiction: Preparation for the Age of Space," A. C. Clarke; "Science Fiction and Sanity in an Age of Crisis," Philip Wylie; "Science Fiction, Morals, and Religion," Gerald Heard; "The Future of Science Fiction," R. Bretnor.

BRETT, LEO (pseud) See FANTHORPE, R. L.

BREUER, MILES J(OHN) (1889–1947) U.S. medical doctor, born in Chicago of Czechoslovak descent. His father was a physician and so were two daughters; his only son was killed in a mountain climbing accident when 18. Breuer was educated in the public schools of Crete, Nebraska, and later at U. of Texas and Rush Medical College. He served in the Medical Corps in World War I as a lieutenant, and then practised medicine as an internist in Lincoln, Nebraska. His writings on tuberculosis became internationally recognised. He was also a keen amateur photographer. He died in California after several years of illness.

In the sf field he is noted for his exceptionally fine short stories in the early 1930's. He first appeared in *Amazing Stories* with "The Man With the Strange Head" (Jan 1927). Notable stories include "The Appendix and the Spectacles" (*AS*, Dec 1928)—which had some sequels—and was written because he did not agree with the ideas expressed in Bob Olsen's *Four Dimensional* series; "The Gostak and the Doshes" (*AS*, Mar 1930; *Great Science Fiction by Scientists* [Conklin], 1962); and "The Fitzgerald Contraction" (*Science Wonder*, Jan 1930) and its sequel. Probably his most famous work is the novel "Paradise and Iron" (*ASQ*, Sum 1930). Two authors with whom he collaborated were Clare W. Harris ("A Baby on Neptune," *AS*, Dec 1929), and Jack Williamson ("Birth of a New Republic," *ASQ*, Win 1931; "The Girl From Mars," SF Series No. 1, 1929).

BRIARTON, GRENDEL (pseud) See BRETNOR, R. G.

BRIDGE, ANN (pseud) See O'MALLEY, M. D.

BRIGGS, PHILIP
Fiction
Escape From Gravity (Lutterworth, London, 1955, 192 pp., 6/-)

Juvenile—a sixth form student discovers a new planet; his trip there and adventures.

BRIGHOUSE, HAROLD (26 July 1882–25 July 1958) English novelist and dramatist. In his early years he worked in the cotton trade. He wrote over 50 plays, of which *Hobson's Choice* was first produced in 1916. He served in R.A.F. Intelligence in World War I, and was chairman of the Authors' Society dramatic committee 1930-31.

Fiction

Six Fantasies [C] (S. French, New York, 1931, 155 pp., $1.50)

6 fantasy stories (not in Bleiler *Checklist*): "The Exiled Princess"; "The Ghost in the Garden"; "The Romany Road"; "Cupid and Psyche"; "The Oracles of Apollo"; "The Ghosts of Windsor Park."

BRIGHT, MARY CHAVELITA DUNNE (14 Dec 1860–13 Aug 1945) English novelist, dramatist and translator. She was born Mary Dunne in Melbourne, Victoria, Australia. She first intended to be an artist, but became a writer when family affairs prevented the necessary course of study. Married three times, her books include *Keynotes* (1893), under the pseudonym "George Egerton," describing the intricacies of married life. She was a founder of the Irish Genealogical Research Society.

Fiction [as George Egerton]

Fantasias [C] (J. Lane, London & New York, 1897, 156 pp., 3/6)

6 stories: "The Star Worshipper"; "The Elusive Melody"; "The Mandrake Venus"; "The Futile Quest"; "The Kingdom of Dreams"; "The Well of Truth."

BRINEY, ROBERT E(DWARD) (2 Dec 1933–) Noted U.S. sf fan; part-owner of Advent:Publishers. Mathematician and computer expert.

Anthology

Shanadu (SSSR Pubs., Tonawanda, 1953, 101 pp., $1.50)

3 stories: "Quest of the Veil," Eugene DeWeese; "The Fire-Born," Toby Duane [pseud. of W. Paul Ganley]; "The Black Tower," Brian J. McNaughton & Andrew Duane [latter is pseud. of R. E. Briney]. An integrated fantasy anthology which was announced as the first of a series.

BRINTON, HENRY (27 July 1901–) British author and lecturer, born at Wolverhampton, Staffordshire. He has spent a number of years in social and political work, and is a member of the Royal Astronomical Society.

Fiction

Purple-6 (Hutchinson, London, 1962, 207 pp., 15/-) (Nelson Foster & Scott, Toronto, $3.25) (Walker, New York, 1962, 207 pp., $3.95) (Arrow: 701, 1963, 191 pp., pa 2/6) (Avon: S135, 1963, 192 pp., pa 60¢)

A drama of people knowing an atomic holocaust is coming.

BRODERICK, DAMIEN Australian freelance writer living in Melbourne; works occasionally as a journalist.

Fiction

Man Returned, A [C] [pa] (Horwitz: PB216, 1965, 130 pp., pa 4/6)

12 stories, some fantasy. No table of contents, but list is on back cover: "The Howling Sky"; "The Disposal of Man"; "A Question of Conscience"; "All My Yesterdays"; "Children of Tantalus"; "Little Tin God" (from *Man Junior*); "A Man Returned" (from *Man*); "Requiem in Heaven"; "I Remember Man"; "Darkness Changeling"; "There Was a Star"; "Every Little Star" ("Casanova Mark II," *Man*).

BROMFIELD, HELEN WARD

Fiction

Dragon Tales [C] (Commercial Press, Shanghai, 1923, viii+239 pp.)

13 stories set in China (listed in Bleiler, but very scarce): "The Silkworm"; "The Jazz Lady"; "The Philosopher"; "On Liping Road"; "The Grief of Ah Nam"; "Pak-Ling"; "Dorothea"; "The

Native Born"; "Peking Amber Beads"; "The Night of the Moon-quake"; "The Autumn Fan"; "If I Were King"; "Sonia's Hands."

BROMFIELD, LOUIS (27 Dec 1896–19 Mar 1956) U.S. novelist. He served with the French Army in World War I, receiving the Croix de Guerre. His first published novel was *The Green Bay Tree* (1924); he won the 1926 Pulitzer Prize with *Early Autumn*. He is noted for his farming activities (at Malabar) as well as his writing. His early works are considered his best, though many comparatively recent ones, such as *The Rains Came* and *Mrs. Parkington*, have appeared as films.
Fiction
Strange Case of Miss Annie Spragg, The (Stokes, New York, 1928, 314 pp., $2.50) (Cape, London, 1928, 7/6) (Grosset, New York, 1930, 75¢, $1.00) (Penguin: 19, 1935, 255 pp., pa 6d; 1959, 240 pp., pa 2/6) ([Swedish], Bonnier, 1951) (Berkley: G-36, 1956, 219 pp., pa 35¢)
A noted reincarnation novel.

BRONOWSKI, J(ACOB) (18 Jan 1908–) Polish-English statistician, born in Lodz. He took his M.A. and Ph.D. and became a Senior Lecturer at University College, Hull, 1934-42. He was seconded to government service in 1942, and later to UNESCO. He was Visiting Professor to Mass. Inst. of Technology in 1953, and is a director for the National Coal Board. Besides being a BBC radio panelist, he has written an opera that has been broadcast, numerous papers in mathematics, and a book on William Blake.
Nonfiction
Common Sense of Science, The (Harvard U., Cambridge, 1953, 154 pp., $2.00)
A brief and admirably written book on the historic development of scientific thinking, the factors which distinguish contemporary attitudes in science, and possible trends to come.

BRONTE, CHARLOTTE (21 Apr 1816–31 Mar 1855) English author, the oldest of the three famous Bronte sisters. Her early life was spent as a teacher, but she was unhappy in that occupation and became a governess. She wrote *Jane Eyre* (1847), now considered an immortal novel. A fantasy not covered below is *Villette, by Currer Bell* (Harper, New York & London, 1900).
Fiction
Legends of Angria [C] (Oxford, London, 1933, 322 pp., illus., 16/-) (Yale U., 1933, 332 pp., $3.50)
Compiled from the earlier writings of Charlotte Bronte by Fennie E. Ratchford and others: "Caroline Vernon"; "Green Dwarf"; "Mina Laury."
Twelve Adventurers and Other Stories, The [C] (Hodder & Stoughton, London, 1925, 214 pp., 10/6; 1,000 copies) (Doran, New York, 1925, 224 pp., $3.00)
Fantasy, 13 'Angria' stories: "The 12 Adventurers"; "An Adventure in Ireland"; "The Search After Happiness"; "The Adventures of Ernest Alembert"; "Albion and Marina"; "The Rivals"; "The Fairy Gift"; "Love and Jealousy"; "Napoleon and the Spectre"; "The Tragedy and the Essay"; "A Peep into a Picture Book"; "Mina Laury–I"; "Mina Laury–II."

BROOK-ROSE, CHRISTINE
Fiction
Such (M. Joseph, London, 1966, 194 pp., 25/-)
The protagonist dies but comes into contact with 'something'; upon revival both his real and 'death' worlds interpenetrate.

BROOKE, (BERNARD) JOCELYN (30 Nov 1908–) British writer, born at Sandgate, Kent, the son of a wine merchant. He has been a poet and has worked at various jobs in the book trade. He joined BBC in 1949 for a year and has been a professional writer since.
Fiction
Image of a Drawn Sword, The (Lane, London, 1950, 9+183 pp., 8/6) (Knopf, New York, 1951, 242 pp., $2.75)
Strange fantasy of the fourth dimension.
Scapegoat, The (Lane, 1949, 128 pp., 7/6) (Harper, New York,

1950, 209 pp., $2.50)
Haunting psychological fantasy.

BROOKINS, DEWEY C. (4 June 1904–) U.S. naval inspector and newspaper columnist.
Fiction
Flying High (Vantage, New York, 1965, 91 pp., $2.50)

BROOKS, WALTER ROLLIN (9 Jan 1886–17 Aug 1958) U.S. editor and author, born at Rome, N.Y. Besides his entertaining juvenile series below, *To and Again* (1927) is of fantasy interest.
Series
Freddy. *Freddy and the Space Ship* (1953); *Freddy and the Men From Mars* (1954); *Freddy and the Baseball Team From Mars* (1955). Juvenile books.
Fiction
Jimmy Takes Vanishing Lessons (Knopf, New York, 1965, illus.– D. Bolognese, $2.95; lib. $2.99)
Juvenile.

BROPHY, BRIGID (ANTONIA) (12 June 1929–) British author, born in London, daughter of writer John Brophy. She was educated at St. Paul's Girls School and St. Hugh's College, Oxford. She is now Mrs. Michael Levy. Her first novel is of fantastic nature; others in general fiction include *The Crown Princess* and *The King of a Rainy Country*.
Fiction
Hackenfeller's Ape (Hart-Davis, London, 1953, 122 pp., 9/6) (Random, New York, 1954, 177 pp., $2.75) (Secker, London, 1964, 160 pp., 18/-) (Penguin: 2560, 1968, 121 pp., pa 3/6) (*De aap van Hackenfeller* [Dutch], Contact, Amsterdam, 1967)
Novel tale on thoughts of apes.

BROSTER, D(OROTHY) K(ATHLEEN) (1877–7 Feb 1950) British author, noted for such novels as *The Flight of the Heron*, etc. She has written some fiction of weird interest, including her much anthologised "Couching at the Door." She also wrote *World Under Snow* (Heinemann, 1935) with G. Forester.
Fiction
Couching at the Door [C] (Heinemann, London, 1942, 136 pp., 6/-)
Weird, 5 stories: "Couching at the Door"; "The Pestering"; "From the Abyss"; "Juggernaut"; "The Pavement."

BROUGHTON, RHODA (29 Nov 1840–5 June 1920) English author. She was a niece by marriage of J. S. Le Fanu, who encouraged her and as an editor bought her first novel. In the 1870's she was a noted writer of three-volume novels, but she disliked length and padding and as soon as she was successful she began to write novelettes and short stories.
Fiction
Tales for Christmas Eve [C] See *Twilight Stories*
Twilight Stories [C] (*Tales for Christmas Eve*, R. Bentley, London, 1873, 216 pp.,; ? 1879) (Home & Van Thal, London, 1947, 99 pp., 6/-)
Weird, 5 stories with Introduction by H. Van Thal (1947 ed.): "The Truth, the Whole Truth, and Nothing But the Truth"; "The Man With the Nose" (*F&SF*, Oct 1954); "Behold It Was a Dream!"; "Poor Pretty Bobby"; "Under the Cloak."

BROWN, ALEC Understood to be a pseudonym of a well known British writer.
Fiction
Angelo's Moon (Bodley Head, London, 1955, 221 pp., 9/6) (*Un sepolcro sulla Luna* [Italian], *Urania*: 124, 1956)
A scientist changes economics in Hypolitania, an underground city-state in Africa.

BROWN, ALICE (5 Dec 1857–21 June 1948) American novelist, born in Hampton Falls, N.H. She never married. She was a teacher for some years until 1885, when she joined the staff of *Youth's Companion*. Her first novel was *My Love and I* (1886). In 1914 she won the $10,000 Winthrop Ames Prize for the play *Children of Earth*.

Fiction [Incomplete—other titles in Bleiler *Checklist*]
Flying Teuton and Other Stories, The [C] (Macmillan, New York, 1918, 321 pp., $1.50)

Fantasy, 12 stories: "The Flying Teuton"; "The Island"; "The Empire of Death"; "The Man and the Militant"; "A Citizen and His Wife"; "The Torch of Life"; "The Tryst"; "Waves"; "The Flags on the Tower"; "The Trial at Ravello"; "The Mid-Victorian"; "Father Nemesis."

BROWN, CHARLES BROCKDEN (17 Jan 1771–22 Feb 1810) U.S. author, considered to be America's first professional man of letters. Born into a Quaker family in Philadelphia, he was a frail youth but precocious in mind. He entered a law office at 16 but conceived a strong distaste and left 4 years later. He commenced writing—in those days not considered a serious profession—and in 1798 his first novel, *Wieland*, was published. *Ormond, Arthur Mervyn* and *Edgar Huntley* followed [all listed in Bleiler *Checklist* as of fantasy interest], and then he became editor of *Monthly Magazine & American Review*. This ceased in 1800 and he went into business with his two brothers as a mercantile shipping firm, but it dissolved six years later through losses by storm and the depredations of the warring French and British against their ships. In 1809 he was elected an honorary member of the New York Historical Society in recognition of the value of his *American Register*.
Fiction
Arthur Mervyn (S. G. Goodrich, Boston, 1827, 2 vol.) (Holt Rinehart & Winston, New York, 1962, 430 pp., pa $1.75; P. Smith, Mass., 1963, $3.75)

Subtitled "Memoirs of the Year 1793."
Novels (Kennikat, New York, 1963, 6 vol., $45)

Omnibus.
Ormond; or, the Secret Witness (S. G. Goodrich, 1827, 256 pp.) (Haffner: 24, 1962, 242 pp., pa $2.75)
Wieland, or the Transformation (1798) (S. G. Goodrich, 1827, 5+227 pp.) (Doubleday 'Dolphin C320,' 1962, 276 pp., pa 95¢) (Haffner: 17, 1958, 351 pp., pa $1.95)

A Gothic-like tale of terror and the supernatural—a searching and original study of mania and remorse, foreshadowing Poe and Hawthorne.

BROWN, FREDRIC (29 Oct 1906–11 Mar 1972) U.S. author, born in Cincinnati. He attended Hanover College, Indiana. For a number of years his home was in Milwaukee, Wis., where he worked for the *Milwaukee Journal*. Later he lived in New York City and in Taos, New Mexico, after having given up journalism to devote himself completely to writing. He was primarily noted for his detective novels, the first of which, *The Fabulous Clipjoint*, won the Edgar Award of the Mystery Writers of America. It was followed by more than a dozen unusually successful mysteries, including *The Deep End*, *The Screaming Mimi*, and *Here Comes a Candle*. He wrote one serious novel, *The Office* (Dutton, 1958), based on his early memories.

In the sf field he was noted for his humourous fiction as well as some vignettes. He is particularly remembered for the short story "The Star-Mouse" (*Planet*, Spr 1942), the novel *What Mad Universe*, and the weird novelette "Come and Go Mad" (*WT*, July 1949). A Japanese collection is *Come and Go Mad* (Hayakawa 'Tales of Menace 7,' 1962, pa; 12 stories). He often collaborated with Mack Reynolds.
Fiction
Angels and Spaceships [C] (Dutton, New York, 1954, 224 pp., $2.75) (D'day SF B.C., 1954, 186 pp., $1.15) (Gollancz, London, 1955, 224 pp., 10/6) (*Star Shine*, Bantam: 1423, 1956, 135 pp., pa 25¢) (FSB: 709, 1962, 160 pp., pa 2/6)

Sf, 17 stories (vignettes marked †): "Pattern"†; "Placet Is a Crazy Place"; "Answer"†; "Etaoin Shrdlu"; "Preposterous"†; "Armageddon"; "Politeness"†; "The Waveries"; "Reconciliation"†; "The Hat Trick"; "Search"†; "Letter to a Phoenix"; "Daisies"†; "The Angelic Angleworm"; "Sentence"†; "The Yehudi Principle"; "Solipsist"†.

Daymares [C] [pa] (Lancer: 73-727, 1968, 317 pp., pa 60¢)

Sf, 7 novelettes: "Gateway to Darkness" (*SSS*, Nov 1949); "Daymare" (*TWS*, Fall 1943); "Come and Go Mad" (*WT*, July 1949); "The Angelic Angleworm" (*Unknown*, Feb 1943); "The Star Mouse" (*Planet*, Feb 1942); "Honeymoon in Hell" (*GSF*, Nov 1950); "Pi in the Sky" (*TWS*, Win 1945).
Honeymoon in Hell [C] [pa] (Bantam: A1812, 1958, 170 pp., pa 35¢; J2650, 1963, 150 pp., pa 40¢) ([Japanese], Sōgan-sha, 1961) (*Luna de miel en el infierno* [Spanish], Nebula: 79, 1962 [abr]) (*Lune de miel en enfer* [French], Denoël: PF75, 1964, pa)

Sf, 21 stories: "Honeymoon in Hell"; "Too Far"; "Man of Distinction"; "Millennium"; "The Dome"; "Blood"; "Hall of Mirrors"; "Experiment"; "The Last Martian"; "Sentry"; "Mouse"; "Naturally"; "Voodoo"; "Arena"; "Keep Out"; "First Time Machine"; "And the Gods Laughed"; "The Weapon"; "A Word From Our Sponsor"; "Rustle of Wings"; "Imagine."
Lights in the Sky Are Stars, The (Dutton, 1953, 254 pp., $3.00) (D'day SF B.C., 1954, $1.15) (*Project Jupiter*, Boardman, London, 1954, 222 pp., 9/6; Digit: D173, 1958, 156 pp., pa 2/-; R828, 1964, 160 pp., pa 2/6) (Bantam: 1285, 1955, 149 pp., pa 25¢; J2578, 1963, pa 40¢) (*Lockende Sterne* [German], UG: 86, 1958) ([Japanese], Kōdan-sha, 1958) (*Mot Stjärnorna* [Swedish], Wennerberg: R16, 1959, pa)

Space travel after Earth's near companions have been reached; intrigue behind an attempt to visit the moons of Jupiter.
Martians, Go Home (*ASF*, Sep 1954) —enlarged (Dutton, 1955, 189 pp., $2.75) (D'day SF B.C., 1956, $1.15) (Bantam: A1546, 1956, 159 pp., pa 35¢) (*Martiens, go home* [French], Denoël: PF17, 1957) ([Japanese], Hayakawa: 3003, 1958, pa) (*Marciano ¡vete a casa!* [Spanish], Nebulae: 48, 1958, pa) (*Marziani, Andate a Casa!* [Italian], GRF: 2, 1960) (*Die grünen Teufel vom Mars* [German], Heyne, 1965, pa; T: 548, 1967)

The prankish capers in the ultimate invasion of Earth by the little green men of Mars.
Mind Thing, The [pa] (*FU*, sr, Mar 1960, 1 part only) (Bantam: A2187, 1961, 149 pp., pa 35¢) (*Gli strani suicidi di Bartlesville* [Italian], Urania: 296, 1962) (*La mente asesina de Androméda* [Spanish], Nebula: 94, 1963, pa) (*Der Unheimlicher aus dem All* [German], Heyne, 1965, pa)

Reminiscent of Clement's *Needle*; a fugitive from another world takes possession of mind after mind in search of one to help him get home.
Nightmares and Geezenstacks [C] [pa] (Bantam: J2296, 1961, 137 pp., pa 40¢) (Corgi: SS1167, 1962, 137 pp., pa 2/6) (*Fantômes et farfafouilles* [French], Denoël: PF65, 1963, pa) (*Alpträume* [German], Heyne, 1965, pa; Hunna-V, 1963)

47 pieces—38 vignettes and 9 short stories (3 in collaboration with Mack Reynolds): "Nasty"; "Abominable"; "Rebound"; "Nightmare in Gray"; "Nightmare in Green"; "Nightmare in White"; "Nightmare in Blue"; "Nightmare in Yellow"; "Nightmare in Red"; "Unfortunately"; "Granny's Birthday"; "Cat Burglar"; "The House"; "Second Chance"; "Great Lost Discoveries: I. Invisibility"; "Great Lost Discoveries: II. Invulnerability"; "Great Lost Discoveries: III. Immortality"; "Dead Letter"; "Recessional"; "Hobbyist"; "The Ring of Hans Carvel"; "Vengeance Fleet"; "Rope Trick"; "Fatal Error"; "The Short Happy Lives of Eustace Weaver" (Parts I, II, III); "Expedition"; "Bright Beard"; "Jaycee"; "Contact"; "Horse Race"; "Death on the Mountain"; "Bear Possibility"; "Not Yet the End"; "Fish Story"; "Three Little Owls"; "Runaround"; "Murder in Ten Easy Lessons"; "Dark Interlude" [with M. Reynolds]; "Entity Trap"; "The Little Lamb"; "Me and Flapjack and the Martians" [with M. Reynolds]; "The Joke"; "Cartoonist" [with M. Reynolds]; "The Geezenstacks"; "The End."
Project Jupiter See *Lights in the Sky Are Stars, The*
Rogue in Space (Dutton, 1957, 189 pp., $2.75) (Smithers, Toronto, $3.25) (Bantam: A1701, 1957, 163 pp., pa 35¢) (*Il vagabundo dello spazio* [Italian], Urania: 170, 1958) (*Ein zelgänger des Alls* [German], TS: 75, 1963)

Interplanetary crime and a sentient asteroid. Rewrite of "Gateway to Darkness" (*SSS*, Nov 1949, also in *Daymares* [Brown], 1968, pa) and "Gateway to Glory" (*AS*, Oct 1950).

Space on My Hands [C] (Shasta, Chicago, 1951, 224 pp., $2.50) (Bantam: 1077, 1953, 239 pp., pa 25¢) (Corgi: 1077, 1953, 239 pp., 2/-) (*Une étoile m'a dit* [French], Denoël: PF2, 1954) (*Amo del espacio* [Spanish], Nebulae: 21, 1956, pa) (*Sehnsucht nach der Erde* [German], TS: 94, 1965)

Sf and fantasy, 9 stories: "Knock"; "Nothing Sirius"; "The Star Mouse" "Something Green"; "Crisis, 1999"; "Pi in the Sky"; "All Good BEMs"; "Daymare"; "Come and Go Mad."

Star Shine [C] [pa] See *Angels and Spaceships*

What Mad Universe (*SS*, Sep 1948) —enlarged (Dutton, 1949, 255 pp., $2.50) (Bantam: 835, 1950, 199 pp., pa 25¢; 1253, 1954, 183 pp., pa 25¢) (Boardman, 1951, 223 pp., 8/6; #154, 1954, 192 pp., pa 2/-) (*Assurdo universo* [Italian], *Urania*: 25, 1953) (*L'univers en folie* [French], Hachette, Le RF, 1953) ([Japanese], Gen-gen-sha: SF3, 1956) (*Universo de locos* [Spanish], Nebulae: 18, 1956, pa) (*Das andere Universum* [German], *TS*: 6, 1958) (*Vilken Vanvettig Värld* [Swedish], Wennerberg: R14, 1959, pa)

Notable satire on sf, with the hero finding himself on an alternate Earth—similar in some ways, but oh so diverse in others.

Anthology

Science Fiction Carnival [with Mack Reynolds] (Shasta, 1953, 315 pp., illus., $3.50) (Bantam: A1615, 1957, 167 pp., pa 35¢)

Sf, 13 humorous stories (pa ed., 10 stories, marked †): "The Wheel of Time"†, R. Arthur; "SRL Ad," R. Matheson; "A Logic Named Joe"†, M. Leinster; "Simworthy's Circus"†, Larry Shaw; "The Well-Oiled Machine"†, H. B. Fyfe; "Venus and the Seven Sexes," Wm. Tenn; "The Swordsman of Varnis"†, C. Jackson; "Paradox Lost"†, F. Brown; "Muten"†, E. F. Russell; "The Martians and the Coys"†, M. Reynolds; "The Ego Machine"†, H. Kuttner; "The Cosmic Jackpot"†, G. O. Smith; "The Abduction of Abner Green," N. S. Bond.

BROWN, HARRISON SCOTT (26 Sep 1917–) U.S. professor of nuclear studies and also a noted geochemist; compiler of *A Bibliography on Meteorites* (U. Chicago, 1953).

Fiction

Cassiopeia Affair, The See ZERWICK, C. (co-author)

Nonfiction

Challenge of Man's Future, The (Viking, New York, 1954, 290 pp., illus., $3.75) (Macmillan, Toronto, $4.25) (Secker Warburg, London, 1954, 290 pp., illus., 21/-)

World-wide conservation problem—review of each element in the population versus resources; suggested alternatives for the future.

Next Hundred Years, The [with James Bonner & John Weir] (Viking, 1957, 193 pp., $3.95)

A sober, factual documentation of our future giving facts, figures and serious extrapolations; the closing chapters go a bit beyond Huxley's *Brave New World*.

BROWN, HOWARD V. (5 July 1878–?) U.S. artist. He studied at Chicago's Art Institute. His paintings were accepted by the National Academy and also were featured by the International Exhibition of American Illustrators. He travelled extensively in South America. He had covers of importance on almost every major pre-war national American magazine. He appeared in *Electrical Experimenter* around 1916-17 where his portrayals of future inventions proved very popular. However, he is more directly remembered in the sf field for his covers on the Tremaine *Astounding Stories* (as *ASF* was then known) from Jan 1934–Nov 1938. He followed these with many covers for the Standard magazines.

BROWN, JAMES GOLDIE (21 May 1901–) New Zealand literary figure.

Anthology

From Frankenstein to Andromeda: An anthology of science fiction (Macmillan, London, 1966, 150 pp., pa 7/6)

15 stories or selections from noted novels: "Moxon's Master," Ambrose Bierce; "There Will Come Soft Rains," Ray Bradbury; "Report on the Nature of the Lunar Surface," John Brunner; "The Curse," "The Deep Range" (n'te), Arthur C. Clarke; "The Lost World" (selection), A. C. Doyle; "A for Andromeda" (selec-

tion), F. Hoyle & J. Elliot; "The Dancing Partner," Jerome K. Jerome; "The Ruum," Arthur Porges; "The Adventures of Baron Munchausen" (selections), Rudolf Raspe; "Frankenstein, or, the Modern Prometheus" (selection), Mary Shelley; "A Journey to the Centre of the Earth" (selection), Jules Verne; "The Star," "The War of the Worlds" (selection), H. G. Wells; "The Day of the Triffids" (selection), John Wyndham.

BROWN, ROSEL GEORGE (15 Mar 1926–Nov 1967) U.S. author. She was married and had two children; she died in New Orleans. She had her B.A. from Sophie Newcomb and her M.A. from U. of Minnesota, both in ancient Greek; her main interest was Greek historians, particularly Thucydides. She worked as a welfare visitor for the State of Louisiana for three years. She wrote about 20 stories in the sf field, taking three years to make her first sale ("From an Unseen Censor," *GSF*, Sep 1958).

Fiction

Earthblood See LAUMER, K. (co-author)

Galactic Sybil Sue Blue [pa] See *Sibyl Sue Blue*

Handful of Time, A [C] [pa] (Ballantine: F703, 1963, 160 pp., pa 50¢)

Sf, 12 stories: "Lost in Translation"; "Step IV"; "A Little Human Contact"; "Signs of the Time"; "Of All Possible Worlds"; "Just a Suggestion"; "Save Your Confederate Money, Boys"; "Visiting Professor"; "Car Pool"; "Fruiting Body"; "Smith's Revenge"; "The Devaluation of the Symbol."

Sybil Sue Blue (Doubleday, New York, 1966, 183 pp., $3.95) (*Galactic Sybil Sue Blue*, Berkley: X1503, 1968, 158 pp., pa 60¢)

A 'swinging mama' policewoman, skilled with the rabbit punch and wielding her stiletto heel, rounds up the benzale pushers from Radix.

BROWN, SLATER (1896–)

Fiction

Spaceward Bound (Prentice-Hall, New York, 1955, 213 pp., $2.75; 'Magic Windows' ed. 1956, $2.82, for schools)

Juvenile—youths banding together to achieve spaceflight and to found a better world; educational in its way.

BROWNE, HOWARD (15 Apr 1908–) U.S. author and editor. He was with Ziff-Davis 1942–47 as Managing Editor of *Amazing Stories* and *Fantastic Adventures*, and Editor of *Mammoth Detective* and *Mammoth Mystery*. He left to write full-time in Hollywood but returned in 1950 to take over the editorship of *AS* and *FA* from R. A. Palmer. He planned to publish *AS* large-size, but the Korean War forced the idea to be dropped. Later he began the digest-sized *Fantastic*, allowing *FA* to cease, and eventually changed *AS* to this size also. Just prior to leaving for Hollywood under a five-year contract to Warner Bros. he announced the new magazine *Dream World*, which lasted three issues.

Under the pseudonym "John Evans" he has established a reputation as a writer of outstanding mystery-suspense novels. He has written some sf and fantasy, much of it under pseudonyms. Novels of note include "Forgotten Worlds" (*FA*, May 1948, as Lawrence Chandler); "The Man From Yesterday" (*FA*, Aug 1948, as Lee Francis); "Twelve Times Zero" (*If*, Mar 1952), as well as his Burroughs-type novel *Warrior of the Dawn*.

Fiction

Return of Tharn (*AS*, sr3, Oct 1948) (Grandon, Providence, 1956, 253 pp., $2.00; 500 copies)

Sequel to *Warrior of the Dawn*—further prehistoric adventures.

Warrior of the Dawn: The adventures of Tharn (*AS*, sr2, Dec 1942) (Reilly Lee, Chicago, 1943, 11+286 pp., $1.00) ([Swedish], *JVM*, #18–#38, 1944)

Prehistoric adventures; sequel is *Return of Tharn*.

BROWNE, REGINALD

Fiction

School in Space (Swan, London, 1946, 189 pp., 5/-)

Juvenile—schoolboys go to Venus and have strange adventures there.

BROWNELL, GERTRUDE HALL (8 Sep 1863 – ?) Author of some fantasy under her maiden name.
Fiction [as Gertrude Hall]
Foam of the Sea and Other Tales [C] (Robert Bros., Boston, 1895, 299 pp.)
    Fantasy, 6 stories: "Foam of the Sea"; "In Batlereagh House"; "Powers of Darkness"; "The Late Returning"; "The Wanderers"; "Garden Deadly."
Hundred and Other Tales, The [C] (Harper, New York & London, 1889, 255 pp., illus.)
    Fantasy, 5 stories: "The Hundred"; "The Passing of Spring"; "Paula in Italy"; "Dorastus"; "Chloe, Chloris, and Cytherea."

BROYLES, L(LOYD) D(OUGLAS) (3 Feb 1931–) U.S. payroll clerk and sf fan. He became interested in the field in 1951. His first publishing venture was the work below.
Nonfiction
Who's Who in Science Fiction Fandom 1961 (published by the compiler, Waco, Texas, 1961, 39 pp., photolith, 50¢)
    A directory of about 250 fans, collectors and professionals in the field, with brief biographies on each. However, it omits many notable persons.

BRUCKNER, K(ARL) (1906–)
Fiction
Hour of the Robots, The (*Nur Zwei Roboter?* [German], Verlag für Jugend und Volk, Vienna, 1963) Trans.–F. Labb: (Burke, London, 1964, 187 pp., 15/-) (Ambassador, Toronto, $3.50)
    Juvenile. Russians steal U.S. plans for a robot and build 'Natasha' as successfully as the U.S. 'William'; both become more than pawns.

BRULLER, JEAN (26 Feb 1902–) French author, formerly an electrical engineer, later a painter of considerable reputation. He uses the pseudonym "Vercors" which originated from his code name as a member of the French resistance in World War II. He is noted for his *The Silence of the Sea*; *The Insurgents* (London, 1957) is of fantasy interest.
Fiction
Borderline See *You Shall Know Them*
Murder of the Missing Link, The [pa] See *You Shall Know Them*
Sylva (Editions Bernard Grasset, Paris, 1961) –[Trans.–Rita Barisse] (Hutchinson, London, 1962, 208 pp., 16/-) (Putnam, New York, 1962, 256 pp., $4.00) (Longmans, Toronto, $4.95) (Crest: d586, 1963, 175 pp., pa 50¢) (Macmillan, 1964, 212 pp., pa $2.50)
You Shall Know Them (*Les animaux denatures*, Albin Michel, Paris, 1952) –[Trans.–Rita Barisse] (Little Brown, Boston, 1953, 249 pp., $3.50) (McClelland, Toronto, $4.00) ([Japanese], Kakusui-sha, 1953) (*Borderline*, Macmillan, London, 1954, 231 pp., 11/6) (Pocket Books: 1038, 1955, 196 pp., pa 25¢) (*The Murder of the Missing Link*, Pocket Books: 1206, 1958, 196 pp., pa 25¢) (*Das Geheimnis der Tropi* [German], ? (Austria), 1959) (Popular: 60-2202, 1967, 191 pp., pa 60¢)
    A notable work. A race of missing links is discovered in New Guinea, and the murder of one produces great ramifications—is it Man or Animal?

BRUNDAGE, MARGARET U.S. artist. She is famous for her artwork on *Weird Tales*, where her paintings of lightly-clad curvy women were covers from 1932 to 1945 (continuously from June 1933–Aug/Sep 1936).

BRUNNER, JOHN (KILIAN) (HOUSTON) (24 Sep 1934–) British author. He read Wells' *War of the Worlds* and *The Time Machine* at a very early age and became a confirmed sf addict. He made his way via science fiction to an interest in science itself. He was educated at Cheltenham College. Soon after leaving school, at the end of 1951, he sold a novel to a pocket book firm and followed this with one short and one novel sold to the U.S. magazines during the sf boom. After National Service as a Pilot Officer in the Secretarial Branch of the R.A.F., he began writing steadily

and is now one of the more prominent writers in the British sf field. He is interested in the potentialities of sf as a literary genre; other interests include folk music and playing the guitar. Married in 1958, he lives in London. He toured Europe with a nuclear disarmament exhibition in 1959. Some of his early stories appeared under the name K. H. Brunner; he has also used the pseudonym "John Loxmith" in magazines, and more recently "Keith Woodcott" and "Trevor Staines"; however, John Brunner is his usual writing name. A novel not yet published in book form is "Crack of Doom" (*NW*, sr2, Sep 1962, as K. Woodcott).
Series
Society of Time. All in *SFA* [Brit.] : "Spoil of Yesterday" (Mar 1962); "The Word Not Written" (May 1962); "The Fullness of Time" (July 1962).
    Published as *Times Without Number*.
Fiction
Altar on Asconel, The [pa] (*If*, sr2, Apr 1965) (Ace: M-123, 1965, 143 pp., pa 45¢; with *Android Avenger*)
    A trainee priest fights for his home planet against a fanatical cult.
Astronauts Must Not Land, The [pa] (Ace: F-227, 1963, 148 pp., pa 40¢; with *The Space-Time Juggler* [Brunner]) (*Atteraggio prohibito* [Italian], *Urania*: 330, 1964) (*Angeles o monstruos* [Spanish], Infinitum: 9, 1965, pa) (*Ungeheuer am Himmel* [German], T: 434, 1966)
    First spaceship returns with crew turned to monsters; intrigue develops.
Atlantic Abomination, The [pa] (Ace: D-465, 1960, 128 pp., pa 35¢; with *The Martian Missile*)
    The revival of a monstrous inhuman creature from the ocean depths causes world upheaval.
Bedlam Planet [pa] (Ace: G-709, 1968, 159 pp., pa 50¢)
    The efforts of colonists from Earth to survive and prosper on the planet Asgard.
Born Under Mars [pa] (*AS*, sr2, Dec 1966) (Ace: G-664, 1967, 127 pp., pa 50¢)
    Vivid depiction of a Martian way of life and how this downtrodden race fights back.
Brink, The (Gollancz, London, 1959, 192 pp., 12/6)
    A colonel intuitively recalls bombers sent on mission to Moscow after a Russian rocket had penetrated the U.S. defence system.
Castaways' World [pa] (Ace: F-242, 1963, 127 pp., pa 40¢; with *The Rites of Ohe* [Brunner]) (*Flucht vor der Nova* [German], T: 445, 1966)
    Fight for survival of two refugee parties under different leadership on a vicious world.
Catch a Falling Star [pa] (Ace: G-761, 1968, 158 pp., pa 50¢)
    Retitling and revision of *The 100th Millennium*.
Day of the Star Cities, The [pa] (Ace: F-361, 1965, 158 pp., pa 40¢) (*Transit ins All* [German], Goldmann, 1967; #080, 1967, pa)
    Alien cities appear on Earth after atomic destruction.
Dreaming Earth, The [pa] ("Put Down This Earth," *NW*, sr3, Jun 1961) (Pyramid: F829, 1963, 159 pp., pa 40¢) (*La Tierra sonadora* [Spanish], Cenit: 70, 1963, pa) (*Träumende Erde* [German], Pabel: 302, 1967, pa)
    Action-packed story of a 21st Century U.S. where a strange new drug causes vanishings.
Echo in the Skull [pa] (*Science-Fantasy*, Aug 1959) (Ace: D-385, 1959, 94 pp., pa 35¢; with *Rocket to Limbo*) (*Echo aus dem All* [German], T: 403, 1965)
    Sally Ercott "remembers" impossible experiences in other worlds, and with the help of an inventor clears up the mystery.
Endless Shadow [pa] ("The Bridge to Azrael," *AS*, Feb 1964) (Ace: F-299, 1964, 97 pp., pa 40¢; with *The Arsenal of Miracles*)
    Transport bridge system between planets.
Enigma From Tantalus [pa] (*AS*, sr2, Oct 1964) (Ace: M-115, 1965, 102 pp., pa 45¢; with *Repairmen of Cyclops* [Brunner])
    An alien life form that can assume any human shape and face.
Father of Lies [pa] (*Science-Fantasy*, Apr 1962) (Belmont: B50-081, 1968, pa 60¢; with *Mirror Image*)
I Speak for Earth [as Keith Woodcott] [pa] (Ace: D-498, 1961, 120 pp., pa 35¢; with *Wandl the Invader*) (*Ich spreche für die Erde*

[German], *T*: 247, 1962)

A combination of six personalities in one body form a human being to act as emissary to the Federation of Worlds.

Into the Slave Nebula [pa] (Lancer: 73-797, 1968, 176 pp., pa 60¢)

Retitling and revision of *Slavers of Space*.

Ladder in the Sky [as Keith Woodcott] [pa] (Ace: F-141, 1962, 137 pp., pa 40¢; with *The Darkness Before Tomorrow*) (*Der Ring des terror* [German], TN: 33, 1968, pa)

Young thief caught up in a revolt is "possessed" and undergoes superman-type adventures.

Listen, the Stars! [pa] (*ASF*, July 1962) (Ace: F-215, 1963, 96 pp., pa 40¢; with *The Rebellers*) (*El mensajero de los astros* [Spanish], Galaxia: 5, 1964, pa) (*Die Sternelauscher* [German], *T*: 428, 1965)

Psionic mystery with "stardroppers" that pick up sounds, etc., out of the depths of space.

Long Result, The (Faber, London, 1965, 204 pp., 18/-) (Ballantine: U2329, 1966, 190 pp., pa 50¢) (*Botschaft aus dem All* [German], Goldmann, 1967, #078, 1967, pa) (Penguin: 2804, 1968, 186 pp., pa 4/-)

Intrigue and murder aimed against Earth's control of a new offshoot planet with an expanding technology.

Martian Sphinx, The [as Keith Woodcott] [pa] (Ace: F-320, 1965, 149 pp., pa 40¢)

A United Nations group from Earth solve the enigma of aliens on Mars.

Meeting at Infinity [pa] (Ace: D-507, 1961, 155 pp., pa 35¢; with *Beyond the Silver Sky*)

Fascinating intrigue with Earth traders having franchises on other worlds, and a woman kept alive by an imported miraculous device.

No Future in It [C] (Gollancz, 1962, 192 pp., 15/-) (*Anfrage an Pluto* [German], Goldmann, 1963, #065, 1966, pa) (SF B.C. [S.J.], 1964, 6/-) (Doubleday, New York, 1964, 181 pp., $3.50) (D'day, Toronto, $4.00) (*Stimulus* [French], Denoël: PF77, 1964, pa) (Panther: 1840, 1965, 192 pp., pa 3/6)

Sf, 11 stories: "Report on the Nature of the Lunar Surface"; "No Future in It"; "Puzzle for Spacemen"; "Windows of Heaven"; "Elected Silence"; "Stimulus"; "Iron Jackass"; "Badman"; "Out of Order"; "Protect Me From My Friends"; "Fair."

No Other Gods But Me [C] [pa] (Compact: F317, 1966, 159 pp., pa 3/6)

3 stories: "No Other Gods But Me" (based on "A Time to Rend," *Science-Fantasy*, Dec 1956); "The Man From the Big Dark" (*SFA*, June 1958); "The Odds Against You" ("Against the Odds," *If*, Aug 1965).

Not Before Time [C] [pa] (FSB: 2138, 1968, 128 pp., pa 3/6)

Sf, 10 stories: "Prerogative"; "Fair Warning"; "The Warp and the Woof-Woof"; "Singleminded"; "A Better Mousetrap"; "Coincidence Day"; "Seizure"; "Treason Is a Two-Edged Sword"; "Eye of the Beholder"; "Round Trip."

Now Then [C] [pa] (Mayflower: 6500, 1965, 143 pp., pa 3/6) (Avon: S323, 1968, 160 pp., pa 60¢)

Sf, 3 novelettes: "Some Lapse of Time" (*Science-Fantasy*, Feb 1963); "Imprint of Chaos" (*Science-Fantasy*, Aug 1960); "Thou Good and Faithful" (*ASF*, Mar 1953 [as John Loxmith]).

100th Millennium, The [pa] ("Earth Is But a Star," *Science-Fantasy*, June 1958) (Ace: D-362, 1959, 110 pp., pa 35¢; with *Edge of Time*) (Revised as *Catch a Falling Star*, 1968)

A future man strives to save his decadent Earth from final catastrophe.

Out of My Mind [C] [pa] (Ballantine: U5064, 1967, 220 pp., pa 60¢) (FSB: 2102, 1968, 128 pp., pa 3/6)

Sf. Contents of U.S. and British editions differ substantially.

U.S., 13 stories: *Past:* "Fair Warning"; "The Nail in the Middle of the Hand." *Present:* "Orpheus's Brother"; "Prerogative"; "Such Stuff"; "The Totally Rich." *Future:* "See What I Mean!"; "The Fourth Power"; "The Last Lonely Man"; "Singleminded"; "A Better Mousetrap"; "Eye of the Beholder"; "Round Trip."

British, 10 stories (with no divisions): "The Fourth Power"; "The Man Who Played the Blues"; "Orpheus's Brother"; "Such Stuff"; "When Gabriel—"; "The Nail in the Middle of the Hand"; "The Last Lonely Man"; "Whirligig"; "See What I Mean!"; "The Totally Rich."

Planet of Your Own, A [pa] ("The Long Way to Earth," *If*, Mar 1966) (Ace: G-592, 1966, 99 pp., pa 50¢; with *The Beasts of Kohl*)

Fascinating depiction of the work of a planetary supervisor on a world growing exotic pelts.

Productions of Time, The [pa] (*F&SF*, sr2, Aug 1966) (Signet: P3113, 1967, 139 pp., pa 60¢)

A sadistic playwright thrusts a group of actors into an experiment in programmed perversion. *Note:* The Signet version is badly edited and not done with the author's approval.

Psionic Menace, The [as Keith Woodcott] [pa] ("Crack of Doom," *NW*, sr2, Sep 1962) (Ace: F-199, 1963, 108 pp., pa 40¢; with *Captives of the Flame*) (*Ruf des Todes* [German], *UZ*: 386, 1964)

A telepathic screaming promises the end of the universe.

Quicksand (Doubleday, 1967, 240 pp., $4.50) (D'day SF B.C., 1968, $1.70)

A psychiatrist in a mental hospital—who are insane or controlled?

Repairmen of Cyclops, The [pa] (*Fan*, sr2, Jan 1965) (Ace: M-115, 1965, 150 pp., pa 45¢; with *Enigma From Tantalus* [Brunner])

Fast-moving intrigue on a somewhat backward planet which has limb grafting.

Rites of Ohe, The [pa] (Ace: F-242, 1963, 129 pp., pa 40¢; with *Castaways' World* [Brunner]) (*Die Sitten der Oheaner* [German], *T*: 407, 1964)

An immortal investigates a disappearance and finds the secret of an alien race.

Sanctuary in the Sky [pa] (Ace: D-471, 1960, 122 pp., pa 35¢; with *The Secret Martians*) (*Asyl zwischen den Sternen* [German], *UG*: 204, 1963)

Intrigue by aliens of different races in the control of a way station, a huge synthetic world.

Secret Agent of Terra [pa] (Ace: F-133, 1962, 127 pp., pa 40¢; with *The Rim of Space*) (*Geheimagentin der Erde* [German], *TS*: 82, 1964)

An agent of the Corps Galactica helps a primitive human-seeded world against usurpers.

Skynappers, The [pa] (Ace: D-457, 1960, 117 pp., pa 35¢; with *Vulcan's Hammer*)

Intergalactic underground kidnaps an Earthman to help in their struggle against tyranny by using a giant computer, Solver.

Slavers of Space [pa] (Ace: D-421, 1960, 118 pp., pa 35¢; with *Dr. Futurity*) (*Bürger der Galaxis* [German], *TS*: 39, 1960) (Revised as *Into the Slave Nebula*, 1968)

By luck and pluck an inexperienced youth uncovers the conspiracy behind the production of androids.

Space-Time Juggler, The [pa] ("The Wanton of Argus," *2CSAB*, Sum 1953) (Ace: F-227, 1963, 84 pp., pa 40¢; with *The Astronauts Must Not Land* [Brunner])

Sword and sorcery, with two men moving human pieces in the feudal society of a far planet.

Squares of the City, The [pa] (Ballantine: U6035, 1965, 319 pp., pa 75¢)

Political machinations in a large Latin-American city; based on a famous chess game of Steinitz-Tchidorin (Havana), 1892. Not considered sf by some.

Stand on Zanzibar (Doubleday, 1968, 507 pp., $6.95)

Overpopulation and social conflicts arising from present trends; intrigue in an African state in a nightmarish future world.

Super Barbarians, The [pa] (Ace: D-546, 1962, 160 pp., pa 35¢) (*Los super bárbaros* [Spanish], Cenit: 53, 1963, pa)

Earthmen on their conquerors' home planet eventually turn the tables.

Telepathist See *Whole Man, The*

Threshold of Eternity [pa] (*NW*, sr3, Dec 1957) (Ace: D-335, 1959, 148 pp., pa 35¢; with *The War of Two Worlds*) (*Al borde de la nada* [Spanish], Cenit: 10, 1961, pa) (*Der grosse Zeitkrieg* [German], *TS*: 77, 1963)

Three persons from different time eras become involved in a colossal war.

Times Without Number [pa] (Ace: F-161, 1962, 139 pp., pa 40¢; with *Destiny's Orbit*) (*Sturz in die Wirklichkeit* [German], *UZ*: 527, 1967) (*Hot rijk van de tijd* [Dutch], Meulenhoff, Amsterdam, 1967)

The "Society of Time" series—three sections with original titles. Interesting variations on the theme that nothing in time should be tampered with.

To Conquer Chaos [pa] (*NW*, sr3, Aug 1963) (Ace: F-277, 1964, 192 pp., pa 40¢) (*Die Wächter der Sternen Station* [German], *TS*: 102, 1965)

Survival around a sterile area, and an expedition to an old research station.

Whole Man, The (Ballantine: U2219, 1964, 188 pp., pa 50¢) (*Telepathist*, Faber, 1965, 239 pp., 18/-; SF B.C. [S.J.], 1966; Penguin: 2715, 1968, 190 pp., pa 4/-) (*Beherrscher der Träume* [German], Goldmann, 1966, #068, 1966, pa)

Rewrite of the following: "City of the Tiger" (*Science-Fantasy*, Dec 1958; *FU*, Nov 1959); "The Whole Man" (*Science-Fantasy*, Apr 1959; "Curative Telepath," *FU*, Dec 1959). Telepathy with its faults and compensations.

World Swappers, The [pa] (Ace: D-391, 1959, 153 pp., pa 35¢ [with *Siege of the Unseen*]; G-649, 1967, 153 pp., pa 50¢) (*Ein Planet zu verschenken* [German], *TS*: 63, 1962) (*Comerciantes en mundos* [Spanish], Cenit: 58, 1963, pa)

Intricate story with mankind preserving individuality on colonised worlds, and a scheme to use Earth's surplus population as an unconscious fifth column.

BRUNNER, ROBERT K(ENDRICK) (1888–)
Anthology
Shocking Tales (Wyn, New York, 1946, 323 pp., $2.95) (Ambassador, Toronto, $3.75)

31 stories, in sections: *Caustic Tales:* "The Widow of Ephesus," Petronius; "Wakefield," N. Hawthorne; "The Adopted Son," G. de Maupassant; "Mrs. Fonss," J. P. Jacobsen. *Cynical Tales:* "The Shadow," H. C. Andersen; "The Desire To Be a Man," Auguste V. De L'Isle Adam; "Lord Arthur Savile's Crime," O. Wilde; "A Friend in Need," W. S. Maugham. *Cruel Tales:* "The Parricide's Tale," C. R. Maturin; "Torture by Hope," A. V. De L'Isle Adam; "El Verdugo," H. de Balzac; "El Cabecilla," A. Daudet. *Crime Tales:* "Prologue" from Thomas de Quincey's essay *Murder Considered as One of the Fine Arts*; "Happiness in Crime," J. A. B. d'Aurevilly; "A Jolly Fellow," G. de Maupassant; "The Blind Spot," Saki; "The Gioconda Smile," A. Huxley; "A Rose for Emily," W. Faulkner; "The Quick and the Dead," O. Cameron. *Tales of Vengeance:* "The Cask of Amontillado," E. A. Poe; "A Vendetta," G. de Maupassant; "The Reconciliation," H. G. Wells. *Tales of Jealousy:* "The Pearl of Toledo," P. Merimee; "The Revolt of a Sheep," H. de Balzac; "The Man With the Dogs," G. de Maupassant. *Tales of Frenzy:* "The Tell-Tale Heart," E. A. Poe; "Sleepy," A. Chekhov; "The Abyss," L. Andreyev. *Tales of Obsession:* "The Crucifix," A. Von Chamisso; "The Oval Portrait," E. A. Poe; "The Doctor's Heroism," A. Villiers De L'Isle Adam.

BRUSS, B. R. French author who has had many novels in the Fleuve Noir *Anticipation* series.

BRUSSOF, VALERY (13 Dec 1873–9 Oct 1924) Russian poet and short-story writer. His name is also rendered Valery Yakovlevich Bryusov. He was born in Moscow and died there. He edited *The Scales* and the literary section of *Russkaja Myslj*. He was noted for his verse, and his complete works were published from the Russian in 1925 in 12 volumes. A weird near-Gothic adventure under the by-line Valeri Briussov was *The Fiery Angel, a 16th Century Romance* (Cayme Press, London, 1930).
Fiction
Republic of the Southern Cross and Other Stories, The [C] (Constable, London, 175 pp., 5/-) (McBride, New York, 1919, 175 pp.)

Fantasy, 9 stories with intro.—Stephen Graham: "The Republic

of the Southern Cross"; "The Marble Bust"; "For Herself or for Another"; "In the Minor"; "Protection"; "The 'Bemol' Shop of Stationery"; "Rhea Silvia"; "Eluli, Son of Eluli"; "In the Tower." This includes 6 stories from *The Axis of the Globe* [translated title], a collection of the early 1900's. D. A. Wollheim reprinted "The Republic of the Southern Cross" in his anthology *Terror in the Modern Vein* (Hanover House, 1955; *More Terror in the Modern Vein*, Digit, 1961, pa).

BRYAN, P(ATRICK) H(ENRY) H(AMILTON)
Fiction
Barford Cat Affair, The (Abelard-Schumann, New York, 1958, 152 pp., $2.75)

The cats retaliate when the the "housekeepers" of the English city of Barford resolve to destroy them.

BRYANT, PETER (pseud) See GEORGE, P.

BRYNING, FRANK (1907–) Australian sf author, born in Melbourne. He was office boy, clerk, salesman, and free-lance journalist; he became Associate Editor of *Rydge's Business Journal*, Sydney, in 1934. Various positions in trade and business journalism followed, and since May 1950 he has been Editor of *Architecture, Building, Engineering*, Brisbane, the building industry journal of Queensland. He has been a sf fan since 1929. His first story appeared in the Australian *Pocket Book Weekly*: "Miracle in the Moluccas" (Apr 8, 1950). Many of his stories then appeared in *The Australian Magazine* [denoted by *A.M.* below] and later in *The Australian Journal*. All of these have since been reprinted in *Fantastic Universe*; some fit into the following series. Pressure of work has prevented him from writing for a number of years.
Series
Buckley, Joan. Telepathic daughter of Dr. Eliz. Buckley. *FU*: "Coming Generation" (July 1955; formerly "The Gambler," *A.M.*, 5 Oct 1954); "Daughter of Tomorrow" (Nov 1957; *A.M.*, 8 Feb 1955); "Infant Prodigy" (Nov 1955); "Consultant Diagnostician" (Dec 1955).
Gale, Vivienne. Blonde girl doctor on satellite space stations. *FU*: "Operation in Free Orbit" (Feb 1955; formerly "Operation in Free Flight," *A.M.*, Mar 1952); "Action–Reaction" (Mar 1955; *A.M.*, June 1952); "Space Doctor's Orders" (May 1955; *A.M.*, Jan 1953); "–And a Hank of Hair" (*Au. J.*, May 1956).

BRYUSOV, VALERY See BRUSSOF, V.

BUCHAN, JOHN (20 Aug 1875–11 Feb 1940) First Baron Tweedsmuir; Scottish Government official, novelist, essayist, biographer and historian. He was called to the bar in 1901. He was a war correspondent and saw service in France. After serving 1927–35 as a member of Parliament for the Scottish Universities, he was Governor General of Canada 1935–40. He died at Montreal. He was noted for fiction such as *Prester John* (1910); *The 39 Steps* (1915); *The Gap in the Curtain* (1932). He also wrote biographies of Sir Walter Raleigh (1911) and others, and many books about World War I including a comprehensive set of four volumes. A book about this author is *John Buchan* by Janet A. Smith (Hart-Davis, 1965, 63/-).
Fiction [Incomplete—other titles in Bleiler *Checklist*]
Gap in the Curtain, The [C] (Hodder Stoughton, London, 1932, 315 pp., 7/6; 1934, 3/6) (Houghton, New York, 1932, 313 pp., $2.50) (Nelson, London, 1934, 299 pp., 4/6, 2/-; 1935, 1/-)

6 stories, interconnected: "Whitsuntide at Flambard"; "Mr. Arnold Tavanger"; "The Rt. Hon. David Mayot"; "Mr. Reginald Daker"; "Mr. Robert Goodeve"; "Captain Charles Ottery."
Grey Weather [C] (J. Lane, London, 1899, 298 pp., 6/-)

15 stories, many of fantasy flavour: "At the Article of Death"; "At the Rising of the Waters"; "Ballad for Grey Weather"; "The Black Fishers"; "Comedy in the Full Moon"; "Earlier Affection"; "The Herd of Standlan"; "Journey of Little Profit"; "The Moor-Song"; "Oasis in the Snow"; "Politics and the May Fly"; "Prester John"; "A Reputation"; "Streams of Water in the South"; "Summer Weather."

Moon Endureth; Tales and Fancies, The [C] (Blackwood, Edinburgh, 1912, 324 pp., 6/-) (Sturgis Walton, New York, 1912, 298 pp., $1.25) (Hodder Stoughton, nd, 269 pp.)

Contents of British and U.S. editions differ slightly: "From the Pentlands Looking North and South–The Company of the Marjolane"; "Avignon, 1759–A Lucid Interval"; "The Shorter Catechism (revised version)–The Lemnian"; "Atta's Song–Space"; "Stocks and Stones–Streams of Water in the South"; "The Gipsy's Song to the Lady Cassilis–The Grove at Ashtaroth"; "Wood Magic–The Riding of Ninemileburn"; "Plain Folk–The Kings of Orion"; "Babylon–The Green Glen"; "The Wise Years–The Rime of True Thomas."

Runagates Club, The [C] (Houghton Mifflin, Boston & New York, 1928, 306 pp., $2.50) (Hodder Stoughton, 1928, 331 pp., 7/6; 1930, 3/6) (Nelson, 1930, 320 pp., 4/6, 2/-; 1931, 1/-)

12 stories and Preface: "The Green Wildebeast: Sir Richard Hannay's Story"; "The Frying Pan and the Fire: The Duke of Beerminster's Story–1. The Frying Pan, 2. The Fire"; "Dr. Sartius: Mr. Palliser Yeate's Story"; "The Wind in the Portico: Mr. Henry Nightingale's Story"; " 'Devus' Johnson: Lord Samancha's Story"; "The Loathly Opposite: Major Oliver Pugh's Story"; "Sing a Song of Sixpence: Sir Edward Leithen's Story"; "Ship to Tarshesh: Mr. Ralph Collatt's Story"; "Skule Skerry: Mr. Anthony Hurrell's Story"; "Terdebant Manus: Sir Arthur Warcliff's Story"; "The Last Crusade: Mr. Francis Martendale's Story"; "Fullcircle: Mr. Martin Peckwether's Story."

Watcher by the Threshold, The [C] (Blackwood, Edinburgh, 1915, 334 pp., 1/-; 1921) (Doran, New York, 1918, 13+319 pp., $1.40) (Digit: R613, 1962, 157 pp., pa 2/6)

8 stories (Digit edition 5 stories–first four and the last): "No Man's Land" (*FFM*, Dec 1949); "The Far Islands"; "The Watcher by the Threshold"; "The Outgoing of the Tide"; "The Rime of True Thomas"; "Basilissa"; "Divus Johnston"; "The King of Ypres."

BUCK, PEARL S(YDENSTRICKER) (Mrs. Richard John Walsh) (26 June 1892–6 Mar 1973) U.S. author. Born in the U.S., she lived forty years in China as the wife of an agricultural missionary. She taught English literature at U. of Nanking and other universities. She was noted for *The Good Earth* (1931) and other works on China, for which she won a Nobel Prize for Literature in 1938. She devoted her last years to humanitarian causes, such as finding permanent homes for abandoned Asian-American children.

Fiction

Command the Morning (J. Day, New York, 1959, 317 pp., $4.50) (Longmans, Toronto, $5.25) (*Ik ontbied de morgenstond* [Dutch], Meulenhoff, Amsterdam, 1967) (Pan: G561, 1963, 238 pp., pa 2/6)

Borderline sf: interpretation of the complicated motives behind a team building the atomic bomb.

BUCKNER, ROBERT (28 May 1906–) U.S. author. Originally a Virginian, he now lives in Palm Springs, Calif. In 1936 he embarked for Hollywood on leave of absence from his newspaper, and stayed as a film writer (*Yankee Doodle Dandy*; *Knute Rockne*) and producer (*Life With Father*; *Mission to Moscow*). His first sale to *SEP* was the novel below.

Fiction

Moon Pilot See *Starfire*

Starfire [pa] ("Moon Pilot," *SEP*, sr3, 19 Mar 1960) (Permabook: M4185, 1960, 139 pp., pa 35¢) (*Moon Pilot*, Permabook: M241, 1962, pa 35¢)

A burlesque on the space race; the spacecraft is not at all feasible. The second edition appeared because of the film. *Film*: As *Moon Pilot*, Walt Disney production in Technicolor, starring Tom Tryon, Brian Keith and Edmond O'Brien, and introducing Dany Saval.

BUDRYS, ALGIS [ALGIRDAS] (JONAS) (9 Jan 1931–) U.S. sf author and editor. He was born in Prussia and came to the U.S. in 1936. He holds a captain's commission in the Lithuanian Army, and was assistant to his father, the U.S. representative of the Lith-

uanian government-in-exile. He was a clerk with American Express Co. 1950-51, then Assistant Editor at Gnome Press in 1952, and Assistant Editor at Galaxy Pubs. in 1953. From 1954-57 he freelanced. He was on the editorial staff of Royal Publications 1958-61, and was Editor-in-Chief of Regency Books from Oct 1961 to late 1963, when he became Editorial Director of Playboy Press (the book publishing side of *Playboy* magazine). Since Feb 1965 he has been doing the book reviews for *Galaxy* and these are generally highly regarded. He is one of the more noted contemporary sf writers.

Fiction

Amsirs and the Iron Thorn, The [pa] ("The Iron Thorn," *If*, sr4, Jan 1967) –enlarged: (Gold Medal: d1852, 1967, 159 pp., pa 50¢) (*Iron Thorn*, Gollancz, London, 1968, 189 pp., 21/-)

Survival on a future Mars, with the protagonist discovering his original heritage.

Budrys' Inferno [C] [pa] (Berkley: F799, 1963, 160 pp., pa 50¢) (*The Furious Future*, Gollancz, London, 1964, 191 pp., 15/-; Panther: 2019, 1966, 174 pp., pa 3/6) (*Die sanfte Invasion* [German], Goldmann, 1965; 1965 pa)

Sf, 9 stories with Author's Introduction: "Silent Brother"; "Between the Dark and the Daylight"; "And Then She Found Him"; "The Skirmisher"; "The Man Who Tasted Ashes"; "Lower Than Angels"; "Contact Between Equals"; "Dream of Victory"; "The Peasant Girl."

Falling Torch, The [pa] (Pyramid: G-416, 1959, 158 pp., pa 35¢; F693, 1962, pa 40¢; F1028, 1964, 148 pp., pa 40¢; X1837, 1968, pa 60¢) (*La forcia cadente* [Italian], *GRF*: 38, 1964) (*Exil auf Centaurus* [German], *TS*: 99, 1965)

Rewritten from: "Falling Torch" (*Venture*, Jan 1958); "The Man Who Did Not Fit" (*ASF*, Mar 1959); "Hot Potato" (*ASF*, July 1957). The exiled Earth Government sends the President's son to Earth to act as liaison with the underground. Future politics, but is nevertheless quite similar to the present.

False Night [pa] (Lion: 230, 1954, 127 pp., pa 25¢)

Remnants of the human race attempt to recivilize after a world catastrophe. Chapter 6 was originally "Ironclad" (*GSF*, Mar 1954). It is understood that the publisher seriously abridged the author's draft for this edition; the full story was later published as *Some Will Not Die*.

Furious Future, The See *Budrys' Inferno*

Iron Thorn See *Amsirs and the Iron Thorn, The*

Man of Earth [pa] ("The Man From Earth," *Satellite*, Oct 1956) –revised: (Ballantine: 243, 1958, 144 pp., pa 35¢) (*Auf Pluto gestrandet* [German], *UG*: 112, 1960)

Adventures of a financial sharper in a remade body who is shanghaied to Pluto.

Rogue Moon [pa] (*F&SF*, st n, Dec 1960) –enlarged: (Gold Medal: s1057, 1960, 176 pp., pa 35¢; L1474, 1964, pa 45¢) (Muller: GM540, 1962, 173 pp., pa 2/6) (*Projekt Luna* [German], Heyne, 1965, pa) (Hodder: 04455, 1968, 159 pp., pa 3/6)

Dramatic use of matter transmission to conquer an alien deathtrap on the Moon. The characterisation is extremely good, and this is considered by many to be one of the best novels of 1960.

Some Will Not Die [pa] (Regency: RB110, 1961, 159 pp., pa 50¢) (Mayflower: 8103, 1964, 159 pp., pa 3/6)

The full version of *False Night* (which see).

Unexpected Dimension, The [C] (Ballantine: 388K, 1960, 159 pp., pa 35¢) (Gollancz, 1962, 159 pp., 15/-) (SF B.C. [S.J.], 1963, 5/9) (Panther: 1649, 1964, 124 pp., pa 2/6) (*Dimension inesperada* [Spanish], Galaxia: 39, 1965, pa)

Sf, 7 stories: "The End of Summer"; "The Distant Sound of Engines"; "Never Meet Again"; "The Burning World"; "First to Serve"; "Go and Behold Them"; "The Executioner."

Who? (Pyramid: G-339, 1958, 157 pp., pa 35¢) (*Zwischen Zwei Welten* [German], *WF*: 3, 1958) (Badger: SF28, 1960, 142 pp., pa 2/-) (*¿Quien?* [Spanish], Cenit: 1961, pa) (Gollancz, 1962, 176 pp., 15/-) (Penguin: 2217, 1964, 159 pp., pa 3/6) (*¿Quien?* [Spanish], Nebula: 104, 1964, pa) (Lancer: 73-810, 1968, 191 pp., pa 60¢)

Expansion of short story ("Who?" *FU*, Apr 1955). The Russians return a man who purports to be a Western scientist whose injuries have been repaired by a miraculous triumph of prosthetics, which renders him unidentifiable. A remarkable study of thought processes in espionage and counter-espionage.

BUEDELER, WERNER (1928–) German writer, widely known in Europe for his work in astronomy, nuclear physics and related fields. He founded the Association of German Science Writers in 1953. "Satellites of the Future," an excerpt from his book *Operation Vanguard* (Deutsche, 1956; Burke, 1957), was published by *FU* in July 1958. Another popular nonfiction work that has been translated is *To Other Worlds* (Burke, 1954).

BULGAKOV, MIKHAIL (AFANAS'EVICH) (1891–Mar 1940) Prolific Russian dramatist; 36 plays are attributed to him.
Fiction
Heart of a Dog, The [Trans.–M. Glenny] (Harcourt, New York, 1968, 146 pp., $3.95, pa $1.45) (Harvill, 1968, 21/-) ([Trans.–M. Ginsburg], Grove, 1968, 123 pp., $3.95)
Master and Margarita, The [Trans.–Mirra Ginsburg] (Grove, New York, 1967, 402 pp., $5.95; pa 95¢) ([Trans.–Michael Glenny], Harper, 1967, 394 pp., $5.95; Collins, 1967, 445 pp., 30/-)
A reconstruction of the Passion, with Pilate as a civilized protagonist, and an intriguing fantasy of the Devil in modern Moscow.

BULL, RANDOLPH C. British anthologist. Besides the works herewith he also compiled *Great Tales of Detection* (1960).
Anthologies
Great Tales of Mystery (Weidenfeld Nicolson, London, 1960, 272 pp., illus., 12/6) (*Great Tales of Terror*, Panther: 1489, 1963, 224 pp., pa 3/6)
11 stories, many weird: "The Purloined Letter," E. A. Poe; "The Biter Bit," W. W. Collins; "The Adventure of the Sussex Vampire," A. C. Doyle; "The Absent-Minded Coterie," R. Barr; "The Lenton-Croft Robberies," A. Morrison; "The Queer Feet," G. K. Chesterton; "The Blue Sequin," R. Austin Freeman; "The Tragedy at Brookbend Cottage," E. Bramah; "The Level Crossing," F. W. Crofts; "The Treasure Hunt," E. Wallace; "The Appalling Politician," L. Charteris.
Great Tales of Terror See *Great Tales of Mystery*
Perturbed Spirits (A. Barker, London, 1954, 287 pp., 12/6; D20, 1968, 191 pp., pa 2/6)
Ghost, 16 stories (pa ed, 14 stories, omitting 13th and 14th): "The Demoiselle D'Ys," R. W. Chambers; "Wolverden Tower," G. Allen; "The Dead Valley," R. A. Cram; "The Corpse Light," D. Donovan; "The Death Mask," H. D. Everett; "The Invisible Eye," Erckmann-Chatrian; "The Man With the Nose," Rhoda Broughton; "Ghost of Honour," Pamela Hansford-Johnson; "The Derelict," W. H. Hodgson; "Vera," Villiers de l'Isle Adam; "The Devil of the Marsh," H. B. Marriott-Watson; "The Unquiet Grave," F. M. Mayor; "Mortmain," J. Metcalfe; "The Haunted Station," Hume Nisbet; "The Lost Room," F.-J. O'Brien; "The Fireplace," H. S. Whitehead.
Upon the Midnight (MacDonald, London, 1957, 288 pp., 15/-)
Weird, 16 stories: "The Voice in the Night," W. H. Hodgson; "The White Wolf of Kostopchin," Sir G. Campbell; "The Demon King," J. B. Priestley; "The Parlour Car Ghost," A Lady; "The Middle Bedroom," H. De Vere Stacpoole; "Dog or Demon," T. Gift; "A Little Place off the Edgware Road," G. Greene; "The Murder of the Mandarin," A. Bennett; "The Four Fifteen Express," Amelia B. Edwards; "A Life Watch," Georgina C. Clark; "Decay," John Moore; "Awake, Asleep, Awake," J. J. Curle; "The Flagstone," N. Edwards; "The Messenger," R. W. Chambers; "Nightly She Sings," Clemence Dane; "The Squire's Story," Eliz. C. Gaskell.

BULLETT, GERALD W(ILLIAM) (30 Dec 1908–)
Fiction [Incomplete—other titles in Bleiler *Checklist*]
Baker's Cart and Other Tales, The [C] (J. Lane, London, 1925, 313 pp., 7/6) (Doubleday Page, New York, 1926, ix+301 pp., $2.00)
Fantasy, 13 stories: "The Baker's Cart"; "Simpson's Funeral"; "The Bending Sickle"; "Attitudes"; "Mrs. Pusey's Chickens";

"The Renewal of Youth"; "Summer's End"; "Last Days of Binnacle"; "Three Sundays"; "The Sunflowers"; "Queer's Rival"; "The Dark House"; "Prentice."
Street of the Eye and Nine Other Tales, The [C] (J. Lane, London, 1923, viii+307 pp., 7/6) (Boni & Liveright, New York, 1923, viii+307 pp., $2.00)
10 stories (one in parts), some fantasy: "The Street of the Eye"; "Sleeping Beauty"; "The Enchanted Moment"; "The Mole"; "A Sensitive Man"; "Miss Lettice"; "Wedding-Day"; "Dearth's Farm"; "The Ghost"; "The House at Maadi: Pt. 1. An Afternoon in April; Pt. 2. Sheila Dryle; Pt. 3. Sheila Fairfield; Pt. 4. Evening of the Same Day."

BULMER, (HENRY) KENNETH (14 Jan 1921–) British sf author. Born in London, he was interested in the genre from his early youth. He served with the Royal Corps of Signals 1939-45, editing a service magazine in Africa, Sicily and Italy. As a leading figure in the British fan field, he was official British delegate to the 1955 World SF Convention at Cleveland, U.S.A. His first appearance as a writer was in the early 1950's, when he had a number of novels published in the Hamilton 'Panther' (pa) series [some covered below]. Since then he has had over 70 stories published, primarily in the British magazines. Some paperback appearances in the early 1950's were under pseudonyms—George Newnes Ltd. (associated with the Pearson 'Tit-Bits' SF Library) published a number of his titles under the name "Philip Kent"; he also wrote two of the three titles by "Karl Maras." He collaborated with John Newman under the name "Kenneth Johns" to write numerous science articles featured in *New Worlds* for a number of years. Other Bulmer pseudonyms include Nelson Sherwood and Ernest Corley. Besides the novels below, other works of interest include "Wisdom of the Gods" (*Nebula*, sr4, July 1958), "Castle of Vengeance" (*Science-Fantasy*, short novel, Nov 1959), an interesting trilogy beginning with "Mission One Hundred" (*NW*, Sep 1957), and—under the pseudonym Nelson Sherwood—"Trial" (*SFA* [Brit.], Nov 1961) and "Scarlet Denial" (*SFA* [Brit.], May 1962).
Series
Earth-Shurilala-Takkat. Space war. "Unreluctant Tread" (*NW*, Feb 1958); "Space Command" (*NW*, Aug 1958); "The Aztec Plan" (*SFA* [Brit.], Jan 1961)
Fiction
Behold the Stars [pa] (Ace: M-131, 1965, 120 pp., pa 45¢; with *Planetary Agent X*) (Mayflower: 0529, 1966, 126 pp., pa 3/6) (*Transit zu den Sternen* [German], *T*: 530, 1967)
Matter transmission and the worries of meeting an alien race.
Beyond the Silver Sky [pa] (*Science-Fantasy*, Oct 1960) (Ace: D-507, 1961, 100 pp., pa 35¢; with *Meeting at Infinity*) (*Die Wassermenschen von Nablus* [German], *T*: 252, 1962)
Humanity as an underwater civilization fights to survive and return to its original heritage.
Challenge [pa] (Curtis Warren, 1954, 160 pp., pa 1/6)
The voyage of the spaceship *Challenge* to Saturn.
Changeling Worlds, The [pa] (Ace: D-369, 1959, 145 pp., pa 35¢; with *Vanguard From Alpha*) (Digit: D466, 1961, 156 pp., pa 2/6; R758, 1963, 159 pp., pa 2/6) (*Verbotene Welten* [German], Zimmermann, 1960; *UZ*: 272, 1961)
Culture of star-roving billionaires supported by certain worlds, one of which has a revolution.
City Under the Sea [pa] ("Green Destiny," *NW*, sr3, Mar 1957) (Ace: D-255, 1957, 175 pp., pa 35¢; with *Star Ways*) (*Verte destinee* [French], Le Fleuve Noir: A125, 1958, pa) (*Sklaven der Tiefe* [German], Zimmermann, 1959; *T*: 176, 1961) (*Gli schiavi degli abissi* [Italian], *Urania*: 214, 1959) (Digit: R505, 1961, 158 pp., pa 2/6)
Intrigue and adventure under the sea.
Cybernetic Controller [with A. V. Clarke] [pa] (Hamilton, 1952, 112 pp., pa 1/6) (*Das Robotgehirn* [German], *UG*: 8, 1954)
Man's revolt against scientific segregation brings death to the Overlords.
Cycle of Nemesis [pa] (Ace: G-680, 1967, 190 pp., pa 50¢)
An extra-terrestrial monster from the past awakens and assaults the world of today.

Defiance [pa] (Digit: R666, 1963, 160 pp., pa 2/6) (*Forschungs-kreuzer Saumarez* [German], *TS*: 45, 1961; *TE*: 156, 1967)

Some adventures of the Terran Survey Corps on other worlds.

Demons, The [pa] See *Demons' World*

Demons' World [pa] (Ace: F-289, 1964, 139 pp., pa 40¢; with *I Want the Stars*) (*The Demons*, Compact: F277, 1965, 184 pp., pa 3/6) (*Im Reich der Dämonen* [German], *TS*: 110, 1966)

The life of a small foraging race on a planet with much larger people; dramatic denouement.

Doomsday Men, The (*If*, short novel, Nov 1965) —enlarged: (Doubleday, New York, 1968, 207 pp., $4.50) (R. Hale, London, 1968, 191 pp., 19/-)

Freedom and free choice disappear in a future megalopolis.

Earth Gods Are Coming, The [pa] ("Of Earth Foretold," *SFA* [Brit.], May 1960; Digit: R539, 1961, 160 pp., pa 2/6; R681, 1963, pa 2/6) (Ace: D-453, 1960, 107 pp., pa 35¢; with *The Games of Neith*) (*Die Propheten der Erde* [German], *T*: 270, 1963)

Earth uses android missionaries to give a religion to natives.

Earth's Long Shadow [pa] See *No Man's World*

Empire of Chaos (Panther: 69, 1953, 158 pp., pa 1/6; Hamilton, 6/-) (*Welt des Schreckens* [German], Bewin, 1957; *UTR*: 11, 1959)

Illegal trafficking in space, and danger to the Galaxy.

Encounter in Space [pa] (Panther: 29, 1952, 128 pp., pa 1/6) (*Begegnung im All* [German], *UZ*: 115, 1958)

Terran ships battle alien 'sharks' in and out of hyperspace in a struggle to bring sanity to the Universe.

Fatal Fire, The [pa] (*NW*, sr3, July 1960) (Digit: R597, 1962, 160 pp., pa 2/6) (*Das Verhängnisvolle Feuer* [German], *UZ*: 443, 1965)

Intrigue in the 21st Century with its three classes, and a trio after power.

Galactic Intrigue (Panther: 60, 1953, 160 pp., pa 1/6; Hamilton, 6/-) (*Zwischenfall auf Luralve* [German], *T*: 42, 1958)

An interplanetary struggle for a matter transmitter.

Key to Irunium, The [pa] (Ace: H-20, 1967, 138 pp., pa 60¢; with *The Wandering Tellurian*)

A Borgia-like countess from another dimension menaces Earth.

Key to Venudine, The [pa] (Ace: H-65, 1968, 122 pp., pa 60¢; with *Mercenary From Tomorrow*)

Knighthood is in flower on the parallel world of Fezius, but with a difference. A sequel to *The Key to Irunium*.

Land Beyond the Map [pa] ("The Map Country," *Science-Fantasy*, Feb 1961) —enlarged: (Ace: M-111, 1965, 136 pp., pa 45¢; with *Fugitive of the Stars*) (*Weigweiser ins Grauen* [German], *UZ*: 458, 1965)

Fascinating adventure in an extradimensional land.

Million Year Hunt, The [pa] (Ace: F-285, 1964, 133 pp., pa 40¢; with *Ship to the Stars*) (*Die letzte Hoffnung* [German], *UZ*: 487, 1966)

A citizen of a small planet has adventures with a parasite.

No Man's World [pa] ("Earth's Long Shadow," *SFA* [Brit.], Nov 1960; Digit: R572, 1962, 159 pp., pa 2/6) (Ace: F-104, 1961, 128 pp., pa 40¢; with *Mayday Orbit*) (*Der grosse Blitz* [German], *T*: 388, 1965)

Intrigue on a forbidden central planet with its arsenal of space-war factories. *Note:* Digit ed. also contains Bulmer's short story "Strange Highway" (*Science-Fantasy*, Apr 1960).

Of Earth Foretold [pa] See *Earth Gods Are Coming, The*

Secret of ZI, The [pa] (Ace: D-331, 1958, 161 pp., pa 35¢; with *Beyond the Vanishing Point*) ("The Patient Dark," *NW*, sr3, July 1959) (Digit: R515, 1961, 156 pp., pa 2/6) (*Il segreto di ZI* [Italian], *Cosmo*: 48, 1960) (*Freiheit für die Erde* [German], *T*: 394, 1965)

Efforts of Earth's underground to throw off the invader's yoke.

Space Salvage [pa] (Panther: 37, 1953, 143 pp., pa 1/6) (*Todesfalle Jupiter* [German], *UG*: 21, 1955)

Space wreckers start an interstellar war.

Space Treason [with A. V. Clarke] [pa] (Panther, 1952, 112 pp., pa 1/6) (*Rebellen des Weltraums* [German], *TS*: 30, 1960)

Rival powers struggle to dominate space.

Stars Are Ours, The (Panther: 48, 1953, 158 pp., pa 1/6; Hamilton, 6/-) (*Die Sterne gehören uns* [German], *UG*: 18, 1955) (Atlas: SFL6, 1956, 114 pp., pa 2/-) (*Nuestras son las estrellas* [Spanish], Futuro: 34, 1954, pa)

In the days of the robots an unseen danger menaces mankind.

To Outrun Doomsday [pa] (Ace: G-625, 1967, 159 pp., pa 50¢)

Lost on a planet of programmed chaos, Jack Waley has to change a whole world's luck to save his own neck.

Wind of Liberty, The [pa] (*SFA* [Brit.], May 1961) (Digit: R607, 1962, 159 pp., pa 2/6)

Colonies fight for liberty. *Note:* Digit ed. also has short story "Don't Cross a Telekine."

Wizard of Starship Poseidon, The [pa] (Ace: F-209, 1963, 124 pp., pa 40¢; with *Let the Spacemen Beware!*) (*Der Hexer der Poseidon* [German], *UZ*: 422, 1965)

Frustrated scientist helps cashiered nephew to hijack a Navy payroll, and other events ensue.

World Aflame [pa] (Panther: 159, 1954, 144 pp., pa 1/6; Hamilton, 6/-)

A shadow people subtly different from normal mankind cause a terrified world.

Worlds for the Taking [pa] (Ace: F-396, 1966, 159 pp., pa 40¢)

Episodic adventures of members of the Terran Corps who move planets.

Nonfiction

True Book About Space Travel, The [by Kenneth Johns] See NEWMAN, J. (co-author)

BULWER-LYTTON, EDWARD GEORGE (25 May 1803–18 Jan 1873) Lord Lytton, First Baron Lytton; British novelist, playwright and statesman. He entered the House of Commons in 1831, was Colonial Secretary 1858-59, and was raised to the Upper House in 1866. As an author, his *Pelham* (1828) first brought him to popularity. He wrote some noted historical novels, such as *The Last Days of Pompeii* (1834) and *Rienzi* (1835), while probably his best book is *The Caxtons* (1850). He wrote a number of novels of interest in the sf & fantasy field (see the Bleiler *Checklist*), of which the most noted are *The Coming Race* (1870; French, 1888; Spanish–Grifón, 1954; German–Geering, 1960), and *The Haunted and the Haunters; or, The House and the Brain* (book appearance, 1905). The latter is a novelette and a classic story of its type; it is reprinted in many weird anthologies.

BUNCH, DAVID R. U.S. author, and Federal employee at the Aeronautical Chart and Information Center in St. Louis. He graduated from U. of St. Louis with an M.A. in English. His first writing experience was with literary quarterlies. "Routine Emergency" (*If*, Dec 1957) was the first of a number of appearances in the sf magazines. He is principally noted for his many short stories of a mechanized future society, 'Moderan.'

BUNIN, IVAN A(LEXSIEEVICH) (1870–?)

Fiction [One other: *The Gentleman From San Francisco* (Knopf, New York, 1934, 313 pp.]

Dreams of Chang, The [C] (Knopf, New York, 1923, 313 pp., $2.50) (M. Secker, London, 1924)

Translated from the Russian; not listed in the Bleiler *Checklist*. 15 stories, mystical in approach with 3 (marked †) supernatural: "The Dreams of Chang"; "A Compatriot"; "Brethren"; "Gautami"; "The Son"; "Light Breathing"; "An Evening in Spring"; "The Sacrifice"†; "Aglaia"†; "The Grammar of Love"; "A Night Conversation"; "A Goodly Life"; " 'I Say Nothing' "; "Death"†; "The Gentleman From San Francisco."

BURDETT, OSBERT (29 Sep 1885–21 Nov 1936) British author. He was born in London, took his B.A. in 1907, and was a lecturer on literature. He edited the 'Makers of the Modern Age' series, and has written critical works on William Blake (1926), W. E. Gladstone (1927), and the Brownings (1928, rev. 1933).

Fiction

Very End and Other Stories, The [C] (Scholartis, London, 1929, 178 pp., 1,960 copies, 7/6; 100 copies signed and in buckram, 30/-)

Includes 2 fantasy stories (with others): "The Very End"; "The Propheteer."

BURDICK, EUGENE L(EONARD) (1 Jan 1918–26 July 1965) U.S. political scientist. He came to prominence after he and William Lederer wrote *The Ugly American* (1958), an indictment of U.S. foreign policy in Southeast Asia. He taught at U. of California at Berkeley. He wrote some other novels and one work of nonfiction.

Fiction
Fail-Safe [with J. H. Wheeler] (*SEP*, sr3, 13 Oct 1962) (McGraw-Hill, New York, 1962, 286 pp., $4.95) (*Fail-Safe, Point-limite* [French], Laffont, 1962) (Hutchinson, London, 1963, 256 pp., 16/-) (Dell: 2459, 1963, 285 pp., pa 75¢) (*Fataal Alarm* [Dutch], Kroonder, Bussum, 1963) (Pan: X388, 1965, 205 pp., pa 3/6)

A warning of the future when a mechanical or electrical accident can precipitate a war: a flight of U.S. bombers mistakenly pass the "fail-safe" point and head for Moscow. This is said to have been conceived by Wheeler as a short story in 1958, but in early 1963 Peter Bryant brought a law suit against this work, alleging it to be a copy of his *Two Hours to Doom*.

BURGEL, BRUNO H. (1875–?) German author of sf and popular treatises on astronomy in the 1920's. His autobiography *Vom Arbeiter zum Astronomen* (1919) traces his career from lowly beginnings to a position of responsibility in adult education. A work in English translation is *Oola-Boola's Wonder Book* (1932); the story below was imported by H. Gernsback.

Fiction
Cosmic Cloud, The [Trans. from German–K. Schmidt & F. Pratt] (novel, *WSQ*, Fall 1931)

The effect on the world when it passes through a cosmic cloud.

BURGER, DIONYS Dutch physics lecturer and writer, now retired. Born in the Netherlands, he studied mathematics and physics at U. of Amsterdam and U. of Utrecht. He graduated from the latter, and taught physics for many years. He now writes articles for the scientific journals; he has written a book about Galileo.

Fiction
Sphereland (*Bolland; een roman van gekromde ruimten en uitdijend heelal;* ... [Dutch], Blommendaal, 's-Gravenhage, 1957) ([Trans.–C. J. Rheinboldt], Crowell, New York, 1965, 208 pp., $4.95; 'Apollo': A184, 1968, pa $1.95)

A fantasy about curved space and the expanding universe—an entertaining sequel to Abbott's *Flatland*, and written in the same vein.

BURGESS, ANTHONY (25 Feb 1917–) British novelist and critic. He was educated at Xaverian College, Manchester, and attended Manchester U. He served in the Army 1940-46. He lectured at Birmingham U. Extra-Mural Dept, 1946-48; was with the Ministry of Education 1948-50; then was English master, Bunbury Grammar School, 1950-54, and Education Officer in Malaya and Brunei, 1954-59. He has written numerous books since 1956. He has used the pseudonyms Joseph Kell and John B. Wilson.

Fiction
Clockwork Orange, A (Heinemann, London, 1962, 196 pp., 16/-) (W. W. Norton, New York, 1962, 184 pp., $3.95; N224, 1963, pa 95¢) (Pan: X321, 1964, 189 pp., pa 3/6) (Ballantine: U5032, 1965, 191 pp., pa 60¢)

A vicious young criminal is experimentally "rehabilitated" by mental conditioning. Questions of moral justification are posed.
Wanting Seed, The (Heinemann, 1962, 285 pp., 18/-) (Norton, 1963, 285 pp., $3.95) (Ballantine: U5030, 1964, 223 pp., pa 60¢) (Pan: X384, 1965, 206 pp., pa 3/6)

The far future with population explosion and no space; a society in which teeth are atavistic, procreation is prohibited or rationed, etc.

BURGESS, ERIC (30 May 1920–) British rocket engineer, born at Stockport, Cheshire, now living in Northridge, Calif., U.S.A. He

is F.F.A.S. and M.I.Ae.S. He was Chairman of the Council of the British Interplanetary Society, 1946-47. He has been Senior Systems Engineer at Telecomputing Corp., Los Angeles, since 1956, and contributes to many learned aeronautical journals. His non-fiction on space travel, etc., includes: *Rocket Propulsion* (Chapman Hall, [2nd ed.] 1954); *Frontier to Space* (Chapman Hall, 1955; Macmillan 1955); *An Introduction to Space Travel* (Hodder & Stoughton, 1956); *Guided Weapons* (Chapman Hall, 1957; Macmillan, 1957); *Satellites and Spaceflight* (Chapman Hall, 1957; Macmillan, 1958); *Assault on the Moon* (Hodder & Stoughton, 1966).

BURKE, JOHN FREDERICK (8 Mar 1922–) British author, editor and public relations man. Born at Rye, Sussex, he was educated at Holt High School, Liverpool. He was associate editor at Museum Press 1953-56, then production manager 1956-57. He became editorial manager of the Books for Pleasure Group, London, 1957-58; then changed to public relations and publications executive at Shell International Petroleum, 1959-63, London. He has been London story editor for 20th Century Fox since 1963. He won the Atlantic Award in Literature from Rockefeller Foundation with the socialistic satire *Swift Summer* (Laurie, 1949). He has written some radio plays and helped translate some Danish works; he is a member of Crime Writers' Association. In the sf field he has had a number of stories published in the British magazines, mainly under the name "Jonathan Burke" around the mid 1950's, as well as many novels in the Hamilton 'Panther' series, of which some are covered below.

Fiction
Alien Landscapes [C] (Museum, London, 1955, 160 pp., 8/6)
Sf, 6 stories: "Stand In"; "Once Upon a Time"; "For You, the Possessed"; "The Censors"; "An Apple for the Teacher"; "The Old Man of the Stars."
Dark Gateway (Hamilton, London, 1954, 223 pp., 8/6; Panther: 94, 1954, pa 2/-) (*Tor der Dämonen* [German], Bewin, 1954; *T*: 280, 1963)
A gateway in Wales to another dimension leads to conflict.
Deep Freeze (Panther: 182, 1955, 144 pp., pa 1/6; Hamilton, 6/-)
Only women survive on an alien world, and form a feminist government.
Dr. Terror's House of Horrors [pa] (Pan: G692, 1965, 159 pp., pa 2/6) (*Die Todeskarten des Dr. Schreck* [German], Heyne: 428, 1967, pa)
Echoing Worlds, The [pa] (Panther: 103, 1954, 159 pp., pa 1/6; Hamilton, 6/-) (*Die letzte Schlacht* [German], Bewin, 1954; "Schlacht im Weltenraum," *L*: 7, 1955) (Atlas: SFL1, 1955, 114 pp., pa 2/-)
A parallel universe and the danger of an invasion from Earth.
Exodus From Elysium [C] [pa] (Horwitz: PB238, 1965, 130 pp., pa 4/9)
Sf, 4 stories [no table of contents]: "The Robot Wife"; "All Mad, Except Me"; "The Entity Strikes Twice"; "Exodus From Elysium" [short novel].
Hotel Cosmos (Panther: 135, 1954, 142 pp., pa 1/6; Hamilton, 6/-) (*Hotel Cosmos* [German], Zimmermann, 1960; *T*: 163, 1960)
A detective tracks down a criminal from Urania.
Pattern of Shadows (Museum, 1954, 128 pp., 7/6) (Horwitz: PB233, 1965, 128 pp., pa 4/9)
Adventure and a future dictatorship when the Interplanetary Federation controls space travel.
Pursuit Through Time (Ward Lock, London, 1956, 187 pp., 10/6; 1957, 6/6) (Digit: R612, 1962, 159 pp., pa 2/6)
Journey back in time from 1996 to prevent the rise of a dictator.
Revolt of the Humans (Panther: 192, 1955, 141 pp., pa 1/6; Hamilton, 6/-) (*Revolte der Menschheit* [German], *UG*: 38, 1956; *TE*: 134, 1967) (*La rivolta degli uomini* [Italian], *Cosmo*: 17, 1958)
Mankind fights for freedom.
Twilight of Reason (Panther: 118, 1954, 159 pp., pa 1/6; Hamilton, 6/-) (*Parasiten* [German], *UG*: 16, 1955; *TE*: 133, 1967)
Evolutionary retrogression and the loss of intelligence.

Anthologies

Hammer Horror Omnibus, The [pa] (Pan: X520, 1966, 331 pp., pa 3/6)

4 stories from Hammer horror films: "The Gorgo"; "The Curse of Frankenstein"; "The Revenge of Frankenstein"; "The Curse of the Mummy's Tomb."

Second Hammer Horror Film Omnibus, The [pa] (Pan: M223, 1967, 349 pp., pa 5/-)

4 novels written from films: "The Reptile"; "Dracula—Prince of Darkness"; "Rasputin—The Mad Monk"; "The Plague of the Zombies."

Tales of Unease [pa] (Pan: X482, 1966, 271 pp., pa 3/6)

Weird, 21 stories: "The Sound and the Silence," D'Arcy Niland; "The Other Woman," R. A. Hall; "Such a Good Idea," Andrea Newman; "The Skylight," Penelope Mortimer; "Rendezvous," J. Christopher; "Red Rubber Gloves," Christine Brook-Rose; "Superstitious Ignorance," Michael Cornish; "Sheela-Na-Gig," B. S. Johnson; "Gone Is Gone," Joan Fleming; "A Pleasure Shared," B. Aldiss; "Black Goddess," Jack Griffith; "Reflections of Truth," John Kippax; "Short Circuit," C. E. Maine; "The Appointment," John Marsh; "Watch Your Step," Cressida Lindsay; "Janus," Paul Tabori; "The Voice," Marten Cumberland; "A Mistake of Creation," Kate Barlay; "Out of the Country," Jeffry Scott; "End of the Road," Alex Hamilton; "The Practical Joke," Dell Shannon.

BURKE, THOMAS (1886–22 Sep 1945) British writer of fiction and essays; born in London. He created the character 'Quong Lee, Chinatown philosopher' in *Limehouse Nights*, and in that book and others he popularized the Limehouse district of London. Besides the works below he wrote the autobiographical novel *The Wind and the Rain* (1924), the fantasy *The Bloomsbury Wonder* (1929), and also *Nights in Town* (1925) and *Victorian Grotesque* (1941) covering aspects of London at night and the mysteries of its music halls, respectively. A collection is *The Best Short Stories of Thomas Burke*, edited by J. Gawsworth (Phoenix, London, 1950, 256 pp., 8/6; McBride, New York, $2.50).

Fiction

Dark Nights [C] (Jenkins, London, 1944, 154 pp., 7/6; 1948, 5/-)

A quite scarce work, not listed in the Bleiler *Checklist*. 12 stories: "The Beautiful Doll"; "The Black Stick"; "The Bloomsbury Wonder"; "Estella and Dolores"; "The Message of Chan-Hsu-Tsiaman"; "A Mysterious Disappearance"; "A Proud Mother"; "The Purple Star"; "Roses Round the Door"; "Sonata in Scarlet"; "Sweet and Low"; "The Yellow Box."

East of Mansion House [C] (Doran, New York, 1926, 270 pp., $2.00) (*Whispering Windows*, Cassell, London, 1928, 269 pp.; 1930, 2/6)

12 stories: "Adventure"; "Crash!"; "Dow"; "Dream of Ah Lum"; "Johnny"; "The Pash"; "The Purse"; "Spot of Water"; "Tablets of the House of Li"; "Top of the Stairs"; "Uncle Reuben"; "White Wings."

Limehouse Nights [C] (Grant Richards, London, 1916, 311 pp., 6/-) (McBride, New York, 1917, 311 pp., $2.00; 1926, 277 pp., illus.—M. Blaine, $5.00; 1935, 277 pp., illus.—Blaine, $1.00) (Grosset, New York, 1930, 311 pp., $1.00) (McLeod, Toronto, $1.25) (Digit: R486, 1961, 156 pp., pa 2/6)

14 stories (Digit ed. has no title page): "The Chink and the Child"; "The Father of Yoto"; "Gracie Goodnight"; "The Paw"; "The Cue"; "Beryl, the Croucher and the Rest of England"; "The Sign of the Lamp"; "Tai Fu and Pansy Greers"; "The Bird"; "Gina of the Chinatown"; "The Knight-Errant"; "The Gorilla and the Girl"; "Ding-Dong-Dell"; "Old Joe."

More Limehouse Nights, [C] (Doran, New York, 1921, 282 pp., $1.90) (Burt, New York, 1923, 75¢) (Little Brown, Boston, 1931, $2.00)

18 stories: "The Affair at the Warehouse"; "Big Boy Blue"; "Bluebell"; "The Cane"; "Dumb Wife"; "Family Affair"; "Game of Poker"; "Good Samaritans"; "Heart of a Child"; "Katie the Kid"; "Little Flowers of Frances"; "Mazurka"; "Miss Plum-Blossom"; "Perfect Girl"; "Scarlet Shoes"; "Song of Ho Ling"; "Twelve Golden Curls"; "Yellow Scarf."

Night Pieces: Eighteen Tales [C] (Constable, London, 1935, 311

pp., 7/6; 1938, 2/6) (Macmillan, Toronto, $2.00) (Appleton-Century, New York, 1936, 309 pp., $2.50) (Ryerson, Toronto)

18 stories: "Black Courtyard"; "Events at Wayless-Wagtail"; "Father and Son"; "Funspot"; "Gracious Ghosts"; "Hollow Man"; "Horrible God"; "Jack Wapping"; "Johnson Looked Back"; "Lonely Inn"; "Man Who Lost His Head"; "Miracle in Suburbia"; "Murder Under the Crooked Spire"; "One Hundred Pounds"; "Two Gentlemen"; "Uncle Ezekiel's Long Sight"; "The Watcher"; "Yesterday Street."

Pleasantries of Old Quong [C] (Constable, London, 1931, 279 pp., 7/6) (*Tea-House in Limehouse*, Little, Boston, 1931, 263 pp., $2.00)

Neither title listed in the Bleiler *Checklist*. 16 stories: "The Sweet Enemy"; "The Ministering Angel"; "The Faultless Painter"; "The Shadow and the Bone"; "The Silver Star"; "The Case of Valentine Thrill"; "We Are the Music Makers"; "The Yellow Imps"; "The Obscenity of Glam's Fang"; "The Beautiful End"; "John Brown's Body"; "Desirable Villa"; "The Secret of Francesco Shedd"; "The Hands of Mr. Otternole"; "An Angel Unawares"; "Hotel Cote D'Azur."

Tea-House in Limehouse [C] See *Pleasantries of Old Quong*
Whispering Windows [C] See *East of Mansion House*

BURKETT, WILLIAM R., Jr. (31 Aug 1943–) U.S. author and newspaperman. He was born in Georgia and now lives at Neptune Beach, Florida. His main interests are writing and hunting.
Fiction
Sleeping Planet (*ASF*, sr3, July 1964) (Gollancz, London, 1965, 297 pp., 18/-) (Doubleday, New York, 1965, 297 pp., $4.95) (SF B.C. [S.J.], 1966) (*Die Schlafende Welt* [German], *TS*: 118, 1967) (Paperback: 54-445, 1967, 285 pp., 75¢) (Panther: 23704, 1968, 285 pp., pa 5/-)

Aliens take over Earth by putting everyone into a coma, but a few do not succumb and eventually they cause the invaders to leave.

BURKS, ARTHUR J. (13 Sep 1898–) U.S. author. He made the army his career, working his way to a commission and then becoming aide to General Smedley D. Butler in 1924; he resigned in 1928. At the outbreak of World War II he joined the Marine Corps and supervised the basic training of about one third of the marines engaged in the war. He retired in the rank of Lieutenant Colonel. He is widely travelled and wrote much sf in the pre-war years, being featured primarily in *Weird Tales* and *ASF*. Some of his works are "Earth—the Marauder" (*ASF*, sr3, July 1930); "Manape the Mighty" (*ASF*, June 1931) and sequel; "West Point of Tomorrow" (*TWS*, Sep 1940); "Survival" (*Marvel*, Aug 1938) and sequel "Exodus" (*Marvel*, Nov 1938); "The Far Detour" (*SFQ*, Win 1942); "The Room of Shadows" (*WT*, May 1936; *Magazine of Horror*, Spr 1967); "My Lady of the Tunnel" (*ASF*, Nov 1933; *Startling Mystery*, Fall 1967).
Series
McNab, Josh. All in *ASF*: "Hell-Ship" (Aug 1938); "The First Shall Be Last" (Jan 1939); "Follow the Bouncing Ball" (Mar 1939); "Done in Oil" (June 1939).
Fiction
Black Medicine [C] (Arkham, Wis., 1966, 308 pp., $5.00; 2,000 copies)

Weird, 16 stories (15 from *WT* 1924-28, last from *Strange Tales*, Nov 1931): *Strange Tales of Santo Domingo* (6 stories): "A Broken Lamp Chimney"; "Desert of the Dead"; "Daylight Shadows"; "The Sorrowful Sisterhood"; "The Phantom Chibo"; and "Faces." "Three Coffins"; "When the Graves Were Opened"; "Vale of the Corbies"; "Voodoo"; "Luisma's Return"; "Thus Spake the Prophetess"; "Black Medicine"; "Bells of Oceana"; "The Ghosts of Steamboat Coulee"; "Guatemozin the Visitant."

Great Amen, The (Egmont Press, New York, 1938, 231 pp., $2.50)

Weird adventure.

Great Mirror, The [pa] (*SFQ*, Sum 1942) (Swan, London, 1952, 128 pp., pa 1/-)

Tibetan lamas steal the Great Mirror from the Martians.

Look Behind You [C] [pa] (Shroud, New York, 1954, 73 pp., illus., pa [wraps] photolith $1.00; 650 copies)

Weird, 6 stories: "All the Lights Were Green"; "The Kindness of Maracati"; "Our Daily Tuesday"; "Ye Impys of Helle"; "Look Behind You"; "The Chosen of the Gods."

BURLAND, COTTIE
Nonfiction
North American Indian Mythology (Paul Hamlyn, London, 1968, 141 pp., illus., 17/6)

A very broad survey of the various groups of North American Indians, outlining the principal deities and heroes of their mythology, etc. Covers races ranging from the Eskimo to the Apache and Navajo.

BURMAN, BEN (LUCIEN) (12 Dec 1896–) U.S. journalist and novelist. He was a graduate of Harvard (1920), and was a war correspondent in World War II with the Free French and the British 8th Army. His fiction includes *Blow for a Landing* (1938); *Big River to Cross* (1940); and *Rooster Crows for a Day* (1945). His *Mississippi* (1929) was filmed as *Heaven on Earth* (1931) and his *Steamboat Round the Bend* (1933) was filmed in 1935 starring Will Rogers.
Fiction
High Water at Catfish Bend (Messner, New York, 1952, 121 pp., illus.–Alice Cuddy, $2.75) (Copp, Toronto, $3.50)

Floods on the Mississippi cause all the animals to invade New Orleans and force the engineers to institute flood control.
Owl Hoots Twice at Catfish Bend (Taplinger, New York, 1961, 115 pp., illus.–A. Cuddy, $2.95) (Burns MacEachern, Toronto, $3.75) (Prentice-Hall, London, 1962, 115 pp., illus.–A. Cuddy, 10/6)

Third allegory of the animals on the Mississippi.
Seven Stars for Catfish Bend (Funk & Wagnalls, New York, 1956, 133 pp., illus.–A. Cuddy, $2.75) (Ryerson, Toronto, $3.25)

Second allegory of the animals on the Mississippi.

BURNETT, HALLIE (SOUTHGATE) U.S. literary figure; wife of Whit Burnett since 1942. She was co-editor of *Story* 1942-65, has taught literature and creative writing, and has worked with the Book-of-the-Month Club and Prentice-Hall.
Anthologies
19 Tales of Terror See BURNETT, W. (co-anthologist)
Things With Claws See BURNETT, W. (co-anthologist)

BURNETT, WHIT (14 Aug 1899–) U.S. journalist, editor and author. He married Martha Foley in 1930; they were later divorced, and in 1942 he married Hallie Southgate. He has been editor of several newspapers, including the Paris edition of the New York *Herald-Tribune*. He was founding editor with Martha Foley of the magazine *Story* in 1931; Martha left in 1941. Begun in Vienna, the magazine was transferred to New York in 1933. Burnett has written some novels and compiled anthologies both alone and with his wife Hallie.
Anthologies
Flying Yorkshireman, The (Harper, New York, 1938, 273 pp., $2.50) (H. Hamilton, London, 1938)

5 novelettes (from *Story* magazine) and a note by W. Burnett and Martha Foley: "The Flying Yorkshireman," Eric Knight; "Snow in Summer," H. Hull; "Season of Celebration," A. Maltz; "Turnip's Blood," Rachel Maddux; "The Song the Summer Evening Sings," I. J. Kapstein.
19 Tales of Terror [with Hallie Burnett] [pa] (Bantam: A1550, 1956, 229 pp., pa 35¢)

Weird, 19 stories: "Return of the Griffins," A. E. Shandeling; "The White Quail," J. Steinbeck; "The Two Bottles of Relish," Lord Dunsany; "Paul's Tale," Mary Norton; "Lord Mountdrago," W. S. Maugham; "The Cat," Gloria N. Biggs; "The Young Man With the Carnation," I. Dinesen; "The Foot of the Giant," R. W. Cochran; "I Am Edgar," J. Wexler; "The Calling Cards," I. Bunin; "The Night of the Gran Baile Mascara," W. Burnett; "The Screen," May Sarton; "Totentanz," A. Wilson; "The Salamander," W. B.

Seabrook; "The Murder on Jefferson Street," Dorothy C. Fisher; "John Duffy's Brother," F. O'Brien; "Forever Florida," Felicia Gizycka; "The Blond Dog," L. C. Stoumen; "The Childish Thing," J. Metcalfe.
Seas of God (Lippincott, Philadelphia, 1944, 585 pp., $3.00) (Longmans, Toronto, $1.49) (World, New York, 1946, $1.49)

49 great stories of the human spirit: *1. God's Lonely Man:* "In Memory of L.H.W.," Dorothy C. Fisher; "A Fallen King," Selma Lagerlof; "A Weary Hour," T. Mann; "The Road to Jerusalem," L. Douglas; "God's Lonely Man," T. Wolfe; "Where Love Is," L. Tolstoy; "Solitude," H. D. Thoreau. *2. The Vineyard:* "The Story of the Stranger," J. Cournos; "Father Andrea," Pearl Buck; "The Death of Kristin Lavransdatter," S. Undset; "A Peculiar Gift," S. Asch; "Redemption," M. Brod; "The New Order," P. Van Paassen. *3. Shadows of Childhood:* "The Little Black Boys," Clare Laidlaw; "Martyr," Martha Foley; "The Office Puppet," F. Werfel; "Holy Day in Persia," Nellie Mar Yohannan; "Shadows From Childlife," Olive Schreiner; "Dark Spring," Mary B. Post. *4. Through a Glass Darkly:* "The Death of Mrs. Folger," S. Anderson; "The Votive Offering," A. Strindberg; "Mr. Onion," D. Burnet; "My Father's Religion," C. Day; "God on Friday Night," I. Shaw; "By the Breath of God," M. Komroff; "The Atheist's Mass," H. de Balzac. *5. The Inward Vision:* "The Snows of Kilimanjaro," E. Hemingway; "A Still Moment," Eudora Welty; "Sherrel," W. Burnett; "Between Two Worlds," W. Beck; "The Black Monk," A. Chekhov; "Barren to the Stars," Hallie Southgate; "Fern," Jean Toomer; "A Story Told to the Dark," R. M. Rilke. *6. City of God:* "The Builders: On Parables. The City Coat of Arms. The Great Wall of China," F. Kafka; "On the Road to Rome," A. Huxley; "The Refugee From Judea," Wm. Zukerman. *7. The Green Bough:* "The Barefoot Saint," S. V. Benét; "The Vigil of Brother Fernando," Joan Vatsek; "Bontshe the Silent," I. Peretz; "The Wonderful White Paper," Ruth Domino; "Many Mansions," Mary Webb; "The Captive," L. Pirandello; "The Green Bough," Mary Austin. *8. Testament:* "Leaning on the Everlasting Arms," Wm. Saroyan; "The Last Mass," Glennyth M. Woods; "Over Arras," A. de St. Exupery; "Five Lie Dying," L. Paul; "Testament: From Three–A Man Outside Jerusalem, The Mother of Judas, Matthew," K. Gibran.
Things With Claws [with Hallie Burnett] [pa] (Ballantine: 466K, 1961, 159 pp., pa 35¢; U2816, 1965, pa 50¢)

10 stories: "The Birds," Daphne Du Maurier; "The Cats," T. K. Brown III; "The Cocoon," J. L. B. Goodwin; "Baby Buntings," R. Squires; "The Red Rats of Plum Fork," Jesse Stuart; "Butch," Oreste F. Pucciani; "Salamander," W. B. Seabrook; "Return of the Griffins," A. E. Shandeling; "Congo," S. Cloete; "The Cat Man," B. Liggett.
Two Bottles of Relish (Dial, New York, 1943, 395 pp., illus.–C. Petrina, $3.00) (Longmans, Toronto, $4.00)

Weird, 17 stories: "The Camel," Lord Berners; "Pecos Bill and the Willful Coyote," W. C. White; "Two Bottles of Relish," Lord Dunsany; "The Portable Mrs. Tillson," W. Cook; "Mr. Sycamore," R. Ayre; "John Duffy's Brother," F. O'Brien; "Foot of the Giant," R. W. Cochran; "That's What Happened to Me," M. Fessier; "The Man Fish of North Creek," T. Fenstad; "No Dawn," W. A. Krauss; "Horse in the Apartment," F. Eisenberg; "Harold Peavey's Fast Cow," G. Cronyn; "The Night Before," G. Gerould; "The Arbutus Collar," J. Digges; "The Night of the Gran Baile Mascara," W. Burnett; "A Carp's Love," A. Chekhov; "Congo," S. Cloete.

BURR, FRANK U.S. pastor and author. Born in Rock Rapids, Iowa, he took his B.A. at Drake University. He is now pastor of the Congregational Church, United Church of Christ, in Humboldt, Iowa. He is married with two children; his main hobby is golf.
Fiction
Genial Ghost, The (Vantage, New York, 1964, 157 pp., $3.50)

A satire on the U.S. political scene; a ghost becomes mayor and is nominated for election as governor of the state.

BURRAGE, A(LFRED) M(cLELLAND) (1889–) British author. He wrote *Seeker to the Dead* (Swan, 1942) as well as those below.

Fiction

Between the Minute and the Hour [C] (H. Jenkins, London, 1967, 221 pp., 21/-)

Subtitled "Stories of the Unseen." 14 stories (1-p. preface—A. Skene): "Between the Minute and the Hour"; "The Hawthorn Tree"; "Playmates"; "The Affair at Paddock Cross"; "The Waxwork"; "The Ivory Cards"; "The Green Scarf"; "The Captain's Watch"; "Smee"; "The Oak Saplings"; "One Who Saw"; "The Garden in Glenister Square"; "The Gamblers' Room"; "Browdean Farm."

Some Ghost Stories [C] (C. Palmer, London, 1927, 276 pp., 7/6)

13 stories: "Playmates"; "The Room Over the Kitchen"; "The Green Scarf"; "The Wrong Station"; "The Gamblers' Room; "The Summer-House"; "The Yellow Curtains"; "Nobody's House" (*FFM*, Oct 1951); "Between the Minute and the Hour"; "Footprints"; "Browdean Farm"; "Furze Hollow"; "Wrastler's End."

Someone in the Room [by Ex-Private X] [C] (Jarrolds, London, 1931, 285 pp., 7/6)

Weird, 14 stories: "The Sweeper"; "The Blue Bonnet"; "The Waxwork"; "Through the Eyes of a Child"; "The Running Tide"; "The Strange Case of Dolly Frewan"; "The Oak Saplings"; "The Cottage in the Wood"; "Smee"; "The Case of Mr. Ryalstone"; "Someone in the Room"; "The Shadowy Escort"; "Mr. Garshaw's Companion"; "One Who Saw."

BURRAGE, A(THOL) HARCOURT
Fiction

Hurtlers Through Space (F. Warne, London, 1951, 255 pp., 7/-)

Juvenile—a youth helps to thwart the world domination plans of some scientists based in the Amazon Valley.

BURROUGHS, EDGAR RICE (1 Sep 1875–19 Mar 1950) U.S. author, noted throughout the world for his Tarzan stories, though he also wrote much other fantastic adventure. He was educated at several private schools, served a brief term with the U.S. Cavalry, and then was at various times a gold miner, policeman, and storekeeper, among other occupations. For a while he was a department manager at Sears, Roebuck & Co. in Chicago.

Not being a business success, he put his dreams to paper. His first story, *The Outlaw of Torn*, was not then accepted. He continued writing, however, and his "Under the Moons of Mars" was published as a serial in *All-Story Magazine* in 1912 under the pseudonym "Norman Bean" (which he had intended to be "Normal Bean)." His next published story was *Tarzan of the Apes* under his own name, and numerous other Tarzan stories soon followed. Seldom has a writer so captured the world's imagination; *Tarzan* appeared in hard covers from McClurg in 1914 and eventually was published in more than 60 languages. It was only natural that Tarzan be filmed, and since the first *Tarzan of the Apes* there have been about 30 different films up to the present day, with many notable actors in the title roles. Tarzan has also been in comic strips, on radio, and more recently in TV series. Burroughs' stories are not noted for their literary quality, but nevertheless hold a fascination all their own. He is considered by some to be one of the most underestimated writers of his day.

In 1931 Burroughs formed his own publishing company at Tarzana (Calif.), named of course after his own famous character. During the war years he witnessed the bombing of Hawaii, and was an accredited war correspondent to the *Los Angeles Times*, spending four years in the Pacific theatre.

Many bibliographies and criticisms of Burroughs' works have been published in recent years. B. M. Day published his *Edgar Rice Burroughs Biblio* in 1956 (29 pp., 50¢; revised 1962, 48 pp., $1.10); it was also part of *Bibliography of Adventure* (1964) with other author bibliographies. The notable *A Golden Anniversary Bibliography of Edgar Rice Burroughs* by Rev. H. Heins (Grant, 1964, $10.00) is now a collector's item. It is one of the most comprehensive works of its type ever to appear; it gives all kinds of data on Burroughs and his works as well as a big section of illustrations from both dust-jackets and the s-f magazines. Sam Moskowitz's profile of Burroughs appeared in *Satellite* (Oct 1958), *Science-Fantasy* (June 1960) and also his book *Explorers of the In-*

finite (World, 1963). Then Richard A. Lupoff appeared with *Edgar Rice Burroughs: Master of Adventure* (Canaveral Press, New York, 1965, 296 pp., $7.50), which is essentially a running chronicle of Burroughs' writings shown against the popular fiction of his time. *The Big Swingers* by R. W. Fenton (Prentice-Hall, 1967) is a sort of double-viewed biography covering Burroughs' life and the presentation of *Tarzan* from both the film and related angles.

There have been a number of fan groups devoted to Burroughs' writings as well as a number of amateur magazines; these include *Erbania*, published in Blackpool, England, for at least 9 issues (Apr 1956–Mar 1960), and *ERB-dom* currently published in the U.S. by C. Cazedessus. Also continuing is Vernell Coriell's *Burroughs Bulletin*. The Rev. D. Richardson is a noted Burroughs collector and bibliographer.

Many Tarzan novels have been translated, and this character has also been plagiarised in some foreign countries. In the U.S. a series of five 'Tarzan' novels by Barton Werper (pseud.) were discontinued after an injunction against them was obtained by the Burroughs estate. At one time R. A. Palmer endeavoured to get support for having the 'John Carter' (Martian) novels continued by another writer.

A considerable resurgence of interest in Burroughs' works began in the 1960's, with Canaveral Press (U.S.) publishing both reprint book editions and newly discovered manuscripts, while both Ace and Ballantine pocket book publishers have also covered (and duplicated) many of his titles. The most recent original work was *I Am a Barbarian* (E. R. Burroughs Inc., 1967, $6.00, 2,000 copies) —a thoroughly researched historical novel recreating the decadent era of the Roman Caesars.

Series

Martian (mainly John Carter). *A Princess of Mars*; *The Gods of Mars*; *The Warlord of Mars*; *Thuvia, Maid of Mars*; *The Chessmen of Mars*; *The Mastermind of Mars*; *A Fighting Man of Mars*; *Swords of Mars*; *Synthetic Men of Mars*; *John Carter of Mars*; *Llana of Gathol*; "Skeleton Men of Jupiter."

Pellucidar (mainly David Innes). *At the Earth's Core*; *Pellucidar*; *Tanar of Pellucidar*; *Tarzan at the Earth's Core*; *Back to the Stone Age*; *Land of Terror*; *Savage Pellucidar*.

Tarzan. The following alphabetical listing gives a brief coverage; these titles are not included in the regular *Fiction* section, with the exception of one title with a brief appearance of Tarzan. The position of the story in the series is given thus: [T8]; then follows the original magazine serialisation, the first U.S. and British book publication dates, and all known appearances after World War II (excluding the Grosset reprint editions which usually followed the U.S. appearance, and the Grosset 'Madison Square' reprints in 1943). More complete bibliographic detail is given in Heins' *Golden Anniversary Bibliography*. A number of Tarzan stories appeared as U.S. "Big Little Books" and "Better Little Books"; these are now collector's items.

Beasts of Tarzan, The [T4] (*All-Story Cavalier* sr5, 16 May 1914; McClurg, 1916; Cazenove, 1916; Methuen, 1918; Goulden, 1951, pa (2 ed); FSB, 1960, pa; Ace, 1963, pa; Ballantine, 1963, pa (2 ed); Dragon, 1967, pa)

Eternal Lover, The [T3] See *Fiction* section

Jungle Tales of Tarzan, The [T7] ("New Stories of Tarzan," *BB*, 12 titled chapters from Sep 1916; McClurg, 1919; Methuen, 1919; Pinnacle, 1954, pa; *Tarzan's Jungle Tales*, FSB, 1961 pa, 1964 pa, 1967 pa; Ballantine, 1963, pa (2 ed))

"New Stories of Tarzan" See *Jungle Tales of Tarzan*

Official Guide of the Tarzan Clans of America [T24] (Booklet given upon joining. Now scarce.)

"Quest of Tarzan, The" See *Tarzan and the Castaways*

"Red Star of Tarzan, The" See *Tarzan and the Forbidden City*

Return of Tarzan, The [T2] (*New Story Mag*, sr7, June 1913; McClurg, 1915; Cazenove, 1915; Methuen, 1918; Armed: o-22, nd, pa; Goulden, 1951, pa (2 ed); FSB, 1959, pa (2 ed); 1960 pa, 1961 pa; Ballantine, 1963, pa (2 ed), 1967 pa; Dragon, 1967, pa)

Son of Tarzan, The [T5] (*All-Story*, sr6, 4 Dec 1915; McClurg, 1917; Methuen, 1919; C. A. Ransom, 1929, pa; Pinnacle, 1953, pa; FSB, 1959 pa, 1962 pa, 1964 pa; Ace, 1963, pa; Ballantine, 1963, pa (2 ed); Dragon, 1967, pa)

Tarzan and the Ant Men [T11] (*Arg All-Story*, sr7, 2 Feb 1924; McClurg, 1924; Methuen, 1925; Pinnacle, 1953, pa; FSB, 1959 pa, 1964 pa, 1967 pa; Ballantine, 1963, pa (2 ed); Dragon, 1967, pa)
Tarzan and the Castaways [T28] ("The Quest of Tarzan," *Arg*, sr3, 23 Aug 1941; Canaveral, 1965; Ballantine, 1965, pa; FSB, 1966 pa, 1967 pa) The book edition also contains "Tarzan and the Champion" and "Tarzan and the Jungle Murders."
"Tarzan and the Champion" [T26] (*BB*, Apr 1940; in *Tarzan and the Castaways*)
Tarzan and the City of Gold [T18] (*Arg*, sr6, 12 Mar 1932; Burroughs, 1933; Lane, 1936; Goulden, 1950 pa, 1951 pa, 1952 pa; FSB, 1961 pa, 1964 pa, 1967 pa; Ace, 1963, pa; Ballantine, 1964, pa)
"Tarzan and the Elephant Men" See *Tarzan the Magnificent*
Tarzan and the Forbidden City [T23] ("The Red Star of Tarzan," *Arg*, sr6, 19 Mar 1938; Burroughs, 1938; Methuen, 1952; Goulden, 1950 pa, 1952 pa; Ballantine, 1963, pa; FSB, 1965 pa, 1968 pa)
Tarzan and the Foreign Legion [T29] (Burroughs, 1947; Allen, 1949; Goulden, 1950 pa, 1952 pa; Pinnacle, 1958, pa; FSB, 1964 pa; Ballantine, 1964, pa)
Tarzan and the Golden Lion [T10] (*Arg All-Story*, sr7, 9 Dec 1922; McClurg, 1923; Methuen, 1924; Pinnacle, 1952, pa; FSB, 1960 pa, 1961 pa, 1964 pa; Ballantine, 1963, pa (2 ed))
"Tarzan and the Immortal Men" See *Tarzan's Quest*
Tarzan and the Jewels of Opar [T6] (*All-Story*, sr5, 18 Nov 1916; McClurg, 1918; Methuen, 1919; Goulden, 1951, pa (2 ed); FSB, 1959 pa, 1962 pa, 1964 pa, 1968 pa; Ace, 1963 pa; Ballantine, 1963, pa (2 ed); House of Greystoke, 1964, pa; Dragon, Part 1, Part 2, 1967, pa)
"Tarzan and the Jungle Murders" [T27] (*Thrilling Adventures*, June 1940; in *Tarzan and the Castaways*)
Tarzan and the Leopard Men [T20] (*BB*, sr6, Aug 1932; Burroughs, 1935; Lane, 1936; Goulden, 1950 pa, 1952 pa; FSB, 1961 pa, 1964 pa, 1967 pa; Ballantine, 1964, pa)
Tarzan and the Lion Man [T19] (*Liberty*, sr9, 11 Nov 1933; Burroughs, 1934; Goulden, 1950, pa; Ace, 1963, pa; Ballantine, 1964, pa; FSB, 1965, pa)
Tarzan and the Lost Empire [T14] (*BB*, sr5, Oct 1928; Metropolitan, 1929; Cassell, 1931; Goulden, 1949 pa, 1950 pa, 1951 pa, 1952 pa; Pinnacle, 1958, pa; Dell, 1951, pa; Ace, 1962, pa; Ballantine, 1963, pa (2 ed); FSB, 1964 pa, 1965 pa)
Tarzan and the Madman [T30] (Canaveral, New York, 1964, 236 pp., illus.—R. Crandall, $3.50; Ballantine, 1965, pa; FSB, 1966 pa, 1967 pa) A newly discovered manuscript.
Tarzan and the Tarzan Twins See *Tarzan Twins, The*
Tarzan at the Earth's Core [T15] (*BB*, sr7, Sep 1929; Metropolitan, 1930; Methuen, 1938; Wren, 1941, pa; Goulden, 1949 pa, 1951 pa, 1952 pa; FSB, 1959 pa, 1962 pa, 1964 pa, 1967 pa; Canaveral, 1962, 301 pp., $3.50; Ace, 1963 pa, 1968 pa; Ballantine, 1964, pa)
"Tarzan, Guard of the Jungle" See *Tarzan the Invincible*
Tarzan, Lord of the Jungle [T13] (*BB*, sr6, Dec 1927; McClurg, 1928; Cassell, 1928; Goulden, 1949, pa (2 ed); Pinnacle, 1953 pa, 1958 pa; Ballantine, 1963, pa (2 ed); FSB, 1963 pa, 1965 pa)
Tarzan of the Apes [T1] (*All-Story*, Oct 1912; McClurg, 1914; Methuen, 1917; Armed: m-16, nd, pa; Goulden, 1951, pa (2 ed); FSB, 1959 pa, 1961 pa, 1964 pa, 1967 pa; Ballantine, 1963 pa (2 ed), 1966 pa; Dragon, 1967, pa)
Tarzan the Invincible [T16] ("Tarzan, Guard of the Jungle," *BB*, sr7, Oct 1930; Burroughs, 1931; Lane, 1933; Goulden, 1949 pa, 1952 pa; Pinnacle, 1958, pa; Ace, 1963, pa; Ballantine, 1964, pa; FSB, 1964 pa, 1967 pa)
Tarzan the Magnificent [T25] ("Tarzan and the Magic Men," *Arg*, sr3, 19 Sep 1936, and "Tarzan and the Elephant Men," *BB*, sr3, Nov 1937; Burroughs, 1939; Methuen, 1940; Goulden, 1950 pa, 1952 pa; FSB, 1959 pa (2 ed), 1960 pa, 1964 pa, 1967 pa; Horwitz [Australian], 1961 pa; Ballantine, 1964 pa)
Tarzan the Terrible [T9] (*Arg All-Story*, sr7, 12 Feb 1921; McClurg, 1921; Methuen, 1921; Pinnacle, 1953, pa; FSB, 1960 pa, 1961 pa, 1964 pa; Ballantine, 1963, pa (2 ed))
Tarzan the Untamed [T8] (*Red Book*, sr6, Mar 1919, and "Tarzan and the Valley of Luna," *All-Story*, sr5, 20 Mar 1920; McClurg, 1920; Methuen, 1920; Goulden, 1951 pa, 1952 pa; FSB, 1959 pa, 1962 pa, 1964 pa; Ballantine, 1963, pa (2 ed))
Tarzan Triumphant [T17] ("The Triumph of Tarzan," *BB*, sr6, (Oct 1931; Burroughs, 1932; Lane, 1934; Goulden, 1950 pa (2 ed), 1952 pa; FSB, 1961, pa; Ace, 1963, pa; Ballantine, 1964, pa)
Tarzan Twins, The [T12] (Volland, 1927; Collins, 1930; *Tarzan and the Tarzan Twins*, Canaveral, 1963, 192 pp., jacket & illus.—R. G. Krenkel, $3.50) The Canaveral ed. also contains "Tarzan and the Tarzan Twins With Jad-Bal-Ja the Golden Lion" [T21], which was written in 1928 but not published until 1936 (by Whitman); this is very scarce.
Tarzan's Jungle Tales See *Jungle Tales of Tarzan*
Tarzan's Quest [T22] ("Tarzan and the Immortal Men," *BB*, sr6, Oct 1935; Burroughs, 1936; Methuen, 1938; Goulden, 1949 pa (2 ed), 1952 pa; FSB, 1960 pa, 1962 pa, 1964 pa, 1967 pa; Ballantine, 1964, pa; Dragon, 1967, pa) *Note:* "The Quest of Tarzan" is a different story.
Venusian (mainly Carson Napier). *Pirates of Venus*; *Lost on Venus*; *Carson of Venus*; *Escape on Venus*; "The Wizard of Venus" [see *Tales of Three Planets*].
Fiction [excluding the Tarzan series]
At the Earth's Core (*All-Story*, sr4, 4 Apr 1914) (*New York Evening World*, sr, 8 to 13 June 1914) (McClurg, Chicago, 1922, 277 pp., illus.—M. A. Donohue; Grosset, New York, 1923, *ca.* 1940, 277 pp., 75¢) (Methuen, London, 1923, 209 pp., illus.—J. A. St. John, 7/6; 1924 (2 ed), 2/6; 1926, 183 pp., 2/-; 1932, 1/-; 1937, 2/6) (*Pluck* [British boys' weekly], sr11, 31 Mar 1923) ("Lost Inside the Earth," *Modern Mechanics & Invention*, sr3, Feb 1929) (Ace: F-156, 1962, 142 pp., pa 40¢; G-733, 1968, pa 50¢) (Canaveral, New York, 1962, 159 pp., jacket & illus.—M. Blaine, $2.75; 1963, $2.95) (in *Three Science Fiction Novels* [Burroughs], 1963) (*Au coeur de la Terre* [French], Ed. Opta, 'Classique SF6,' 1966 [with *Pellucidar*])
1st of Pellucidar series; the discovery of this strange inner world of cave men and savage reptiles.
Back to the Stone Age ("Seven Worlds to Conquer," *Arg*, sr6, 9 Jan 1937) (Burroughs, Tarzana, 1937, 318 pp., illus.—J. C. Burroughs, $2.00; Grosset, 1939, 75¢) (Ace: F-245, 1963, 221 pp., pa 40¢; G-737, 1968, pa 50¢) (Canaveral, 1963, 318 pp., jacket—S. Sigaloff [based on original], illus.—J. C. Burroughs, $3.50)
5th of Pellucidar series.
Beyond the Farthest Star [pa] (Ace: F-282, 1964, 125 pp., pa 40¢)
The title story (*BB*, Jan 1942) and its unpublished sequel "Tangor Returns." A fighter pilot is translated to a world where war is continuous. See also *Tales of Three Planets*.
Beyond Thirty & The Man-Eater "Beyond Thirty" (*All Around Mag*, Feb 1916; Anon Pub. [L. A. Eshbach], 1955, 57 pp., offset, $3.00, 300 copies; *The Lost Continent*, Ace: F-235, 1963, 123 pp., pa 40¢) and "The Man-Eater" (*New York Evening World*, sr6, 15 to 20 Nov 1915; Anon Pub. [L. A. Eshbach], 1955, 50 pp., offset, $3.00, 300 copies) (*Beyond Thirty & The Man-Eater*, Science-Fiction & Fantasy Publications, New York, 1957, 229 pp., $3.00; 1962, $4.00)
Originals of both are very rare. In the first a young American has adventures in Europe and Asia, which have been isolated from the Western Hemisphere for 200 years. The second is a Tarzan type which Burroughs referred to as "Ben, King of Beasts."
Carson of Venus (*Arg*, sr6, 8 Jan 1938) (Burroughs, 1939, 312 pp., illus.—J. C. Burroughs, $3.00; 1948, $1.00) (Goulden: 9, 1950, 136 pp., pa 1/6; 1951, pa 1/6; 1952, pa 2/-) (Canaveral, 1963, 312 pp., illus.—J.C.B., $3.50) (Ace: F-247, 1963, 192 pp., pa 40¢) (FSB: 1726, 1967, 155 pp., pa 3/6)
3rd of Venusian series.
Cave Girl, The (*All-Story*, sr3, July 1913, and "The Cave Men," *All-Story*, sr4, 31 Mar 1917) (McClurg, 1925, 323 pp., front.—J. A. St. John, $2.00; Grosset, 1926, 75¢) (Methuen, 1927, 250 pp., 7/6; 1928, 2/6; 1934; 1935, 1/-) (Dell: 320, 1949, 240 pp., pa 25¢) (Pinnacle: 35, 1954, 153 pp., pa 2/-) (Canaveral, 1962, 323 pp., jacket & illus.—R. G. Krenkel, $2.75; 1963, $2.95) (Ace: F-258, 1964, 224 pp., pa 40¢)

A stone-age cave girl helps a civilized man to become a mighty cave man.

Chessmen of Mars, The (*Arg*, sr7, 18 Feb 1922) (McClurg, 1922, 375 pp., illus., $1.90; Grosset, 1924, 75¢; Burroughs, 1948, $1.00) (Methuen, 1923, 243 pp., illus.–J. A. St. John, 7/6; 1924, 2/6; 1938, 2/-; 1935, 1/-; 1951, 243 pp., 7/-) (Pinnacle: 36, 1954, 151 pp., pa 2/-) (in *Three Martian Novels* [Burroughs], 1962, 1963) (FSB: 661, 1962, 205 pp., pa 2/6; 1964, pa 2/6; #1403, 1965, pa 3/6) (Ace: F-170, 1962, 256 pp., pa 40¢) (Ballantine: F776, 1963, 220 pp., pa 50¢)

5th of Martian series; the game of Jetan (Martian chess) with living pieces.

Escape on Venus (Burroughs, 1946, 347 pp., illus.–J. C. Burroughs, $2.00) (Canaveral, 1963, 347 pp., illus.–J.C.B. [5 of originals], $3.50) (Ace: F-268, 1964, 254 pp., pa 40¢) (FSB: 1660, 1966, 222 pp., pa 3/6)

4th of the Venusian series—novelisation of the four novelettes from *FA*: "Slaves of the Fish Men" (Mar 1941); "Goddess of Fire" (July 1941); "The Living Dead" (Nov 1941); "War on Venus" (Mar 1942). J. A. St. John illustrated the magazine stories with both covers and interiors for each instalment.

Eternal Lover, The (*All-Story*, 7 Mar 1914, and "Sweetheart Primeval," *All-Story*, sr4, 23 Jan 1915) (*New York Evening World*, 13 to 18 Apr 1914 and 12 to 17 July 1915) (McClurg, 1925, 316 pp., front.–J. A. St. John, $2.00; Grosset, 1927, and *ca.* 1940, 75¢) (Methuen, 1927, 248 pp., 7/6; 1928, 2/6; 1935, 2/-) (Pinnacle: 28, 1953, 152 pp., pa 2/-) (*The Eternal Savage*, Ace: F-234, 1963, 192 pp., pa 40¢)

Romance of a stone-age cave man and a modern girl. Tarzan is a minor character, and his son Jack makes his first appearance.

Eternal Savage, The [pa] See *Eternal Lover, The*

Fighting Man of Mars, A (*BB*, sr6, Apr 1930) (Metropolitan Books, New York, 1931, 319 pp., front.–H. Hutton, $2.00; Grosset, 1932, and *ca.* 1940, 75¢; Burroughs, 1948, $1.00) (Lane, London, 1932, 304 pp., 7/6; 1933, 2/-; 1936, 2/6) (Pinnacle: 33, 1954, 154 pp., pa 2/-; 1955, pa 2/-) (Canaveral, 1962, 249 pp., jacket & illus.–M. Blaine, $2.75; 1963, $2.95) (Ace: F-190, 1963, 253 pp., pa 40¢) (Ballantine: U2037, 1964, 192 pp., pa 50¢) (Dover: T1140, 1964, 356 pp., illus.–Schoonover, pa $1.75, with *A Princess of Mars*) (FSB: 1638, 1966, 192 pp., pa 3/6)

7th of the Martian series.

Gods of Mars, The (*All-Story*, sr5, Jan 1913) (*New York Evening World*, 31 Jan to 5 Feb 1916) (McClurg, 1918, 1919, 348 pp., $1.35; Grosset, 1919, and *ca.* 1940, 75¢; Burroughs, 1948, $1.00) (Methuen, 1920 [4 ed], 233 pp., 6/-; 1930, 2/-; 1935, 1/-; 1942, 3/6; 1952, 246 pp., 7/-) (*Prinsessan av Mars befras* [Swedish], Hökerberg, 1924) (Pinnacle: 30, 1953, 160 pp., pa 2/-) (FSB: 353, 1961, 192 pp., pa 2/6; 1962, pa 2/6) (Canaveral, 1962, 348 pp., illus.–L. Ivie, $2.75; 1963, $2.95) (Ballantine: F702, 1963, 190 pp., pa 50¢; U2032, 1964, pa 50¢) (FSB: 1199, 1964, 192 pp., pa 3/6) (Dragon: D77, 1968, 153 pp., pa 2/6)

2nd of the Martian series.

John Carter of Mars [C] (Canaveral, 1964, 208 pp., illus.–R. Crandall, $3.50) (Ballantine: U2041, 1965, 191 pp., pa 50¢) (FSB: 1758, 1968, 126 pp., pa 3/6)

10th and 12th of the Martian series: "John Carter and the Giants of Mars" (*AS*, Jan 1941, Apr 1961), and "Skeleton Men of Jupiter" (*AS*, Feb 1943, Jan 1964). These are poorer stories than the earlier ones; the latter was the starting novelette for a proposed new novel.

Jungle Girl ("The Land of Hidden Men," *BB*, sr5, May 1931) (Burroughs, 1932, 318 pp., illus.–S. O. Burroughs, $2.00; Grosset, 1933, and *ca.* 1940, 75¢) (Odhams, London, 1933, 248 pp., illus.–S. O. Burroughs, 7/6) (Collins, London, 1950, 248 pp., 4/6) (*The Land of Hidden Men*, Ace: F-232, 191 pp., pa 40¢)

An American explorer discovers an ancient civilization in Cambodia.

Lad and the Lion, The (*All-Story*, sr3, 30 June 1917) (Burroughs, 1938, 317 pp., illus.–J. C. Burroughs, $2.00; Grosset, 1939, 75¢) (Canaveral, 1964, 317 pp., illus.–J. C. Burroughs, $3.50) (Ballantine: U2048, 1964, 192 pp., pa 50¢)

Desert adventure of a royal youth and a lion.

Land of Hidden Men, The [pa] See *Jungle Girl*

Land of Terror (Burroughs, 1944, 319 pp., jacket–J. C. Burroughs, $2.00) (Canaveral, 1963, 319 pp., illus.–R. G. Krenkel, $3.50) (Ace: F-256, 1964, 175 pp., pa 40¢; G-738, 1968, pa 50¢)

6th of Pellucidar series.

Land That Time Forgot, The [Trilogy from *BB* (see below)] (McClurg, 1924, 422 pp., illus.–J. A. St. John, $2.00; Grosset, 1925, 75¢, and *ca.* 1940, 75¢ [no illus.]) (Methuen, 1925 279pp., 7/6; 1926, 2/6; 1928, 2/-; 1937, 2/6) (Canaveral, 1962, 318 pp., jacket & illus.–M. Blaine, $2.75; 1963, $2.95) (in *The Land That Time Forgot & The Moon Maid*, Dover: T358, 1963, 552 pp., illus.–J. A. St. John [repro. of originals], $3.75, pa $2.00)

The original three novelettes were: "The Land That Time Forgot" (*BB*, Aug 1918; *AS*, Feb & Mar 1927; Ace: F-213, 1963, 126 pp., pa 40¢); "The People That Time Forgot" (*BB*, Oct 1918; *AS*, Mar 1927; Ace: F-220, 1963, 124 pp., pa 40¢); "Out of Time's Abyss (*BB*, Dec 1918; *AS*, Apr 1927; Ace: F-233, 1963, 125 pp., pa 40¢).

Llana of Gathol (Burroughs, 1948, 317 pp., illus.–J. C. Burroughs, $2.00) (Ballantine: F762, 1963, 191 pp., pa 50¢; U2040, 1965, pa 50¢) (FSB: 1746, 1967, 191 pp., pa 3/6)

11th of the Martian series—compilation of 4 novelettes from *AS*: "The City of Mummies" (Mar 1941); "Black Pirates of Barsoom" (June 1941); "Yellow Men of Mars" (Aug 1941); "Invisible Men of Mars" (Oct 1941). J. A. St. John illustrated the magazine stories with both covers and interiors for each instalment.

Lost Continent, The [pa] See *Beyond Thirty*

Lost on Venus (*Arg*, sr7, 4 Mar 1933) (*The Passing Show* [British weekly], illus.–F. Matania, sr10, 2 Dec 1933) (Burroughs, 1935, 318 pp., illus.–J. A. St. John, $2.00; 1940, 75¢; 1948, $1.00; Grosset, 1936, 1940, 75¢) (Methuen, 1937, 275 pp., 7/6; 1938, 2/6; 1941, 380 pp., 3/-) (Pinnacle: 23, 1953, 136 pp., pa 2/-) (Ace: F-221, 1963, 192 pp., pa 40¢) (in *The Pirates of Venus & Lost on Venus*, Dover: T1053, 1963, 340 pp., illus.–F. Matania, pa $1.75) (Canaveral, 1963, 318 pp., illus.–J. A. St. John, $3.50) (FSB: 1215, 1965, 190 pp., pa 3/6)

2nd of Venusian series.

Mad King, The ("The Mad King," *ASW*, 21 Mar 1914, and "Barney Custer of Beatrice," *ASW*, sr3, 7 Aug 1915) (McClurg, 1926, 365 pp., $2.00; Grosset, 1927, and *ca.* 1940, 75¢) (Ace: F-270, 1964, 255 pp., pa 40¢)

Adventure and intrigue in a mythical European kingdom—not sf.

Man-Eater, The See *Beyond Thirty & The Man-Eater*

Man Without a Soul, The See *Monster Men, The*

Master Mind of Mars, The (*AS Annual*, 1927) (McClurg, 1928, 312 pp., illus.–J. A. St. John, $2.00; Grosset, 1929, 75¢; Burroughs, 1948, $1.00) (Methuen, 1939, 216 pp., 3/6; 1952, 142 pp., 7/6) (Pinnacle: 38, 1955, 158 pp., pa 2/-) (in *Three Martian Novels* [Burroughs], 1962, 1963) (FSB: 751, 1962, 144 pp., pa 2/6; #1216, 1964, pa 3/6; 1965, pa 3/6) (Ace: F-181, 1963, 159 pp., pa 40¢) (Ballantine: U2036, 1963, 160 pp., pa 50¢)

6th of the Martian series.

Monster Men, The ("A Man Without a Soul," *All-Story*, Nov 1913) (McClurg, 1929, 304 pp., $2.00; Grosset, 1930, 75¢) (Canaveral, 1962, 188 pp., illus.–M. Blaine, $2.75; 1963, $2.95) (Ace: F-182, 1963, 159 pp., pa 40¢)

A brilliant and mad professor produces synthetic life on a Java Sea island. *Note:* "The Man Without a Soul" was a retitling of "The Return of the Mucker" [see *The Mucker*].

Moon Maid, The [Trilogy from *ASW* (see below)] (McClurg, 1926, 412 pp., illus.–J. A. St. John, $2.00; Grosset, 1927, and *ca.* 1940, 75¢) (*The Moon Men*, Canaveral, 1962, 375 pp., illus.–M. Blaine, $2.75; 1963, $2.95) (Ace, see below) (in *The Land That Time Forgot & The Moon Maid*, Dover: T358, 1963, 259 pp., illus.–J. A. St. John, $3.75, pa $2.00)

The original trilogy was: *The Moon Maid* (*Arg-ASW*, sr5, 5 May 1923; "Conquest of the Moon," *Modern Mechanics & Invention*, sr4, Nov 1928; Ace: F-157, 1963, 176 pp., pa 40¢; G-475, 1968, pa 50¢); *The Moon Men* (*Arg-ASW*, sr4, 21 Feb 1925; Ace: F-159, 1963, 222 pp., pa 40¢ [combined with "The Red Hawk"]; G-748, 1968, pa 50¢); and "The Red Hawk" (*Arg-ASW*, sr3, 5 Sep 1925;

included in *The Moon Men*, Ace, 1963, 1968). Ace published the original magazine version; the McClurg and Grosset editions were slightly abridged.

Moon Men, The See *Moon Maid, The*

Mucker, The (*All-Story*, sr4, 24 Oct 1914, and "The Return of the Mucker," sr5, 17 June 1916) (*New York Evening World*, 5 to 10 Apr 1915 and "The Man Without a Soul" ["Return of the Mucker"], 7 to 11 Dec 1916) (McClurg, 1921, 414 pp., illus.–J. A. St. John, $1.90; 1922, $1.90; Grosset, 1922, and *ca.* 1940, 75¢) ([Part I only], Methuen, 1921, 201 pp., 6/-; 1923, 2/6; 1925, 6/-; 1928, 2/-) ([Part II], *The Man Without a Soul*, Methuen, 1922, 209 pp., 6/-; 1927, 2/-; 1939, 3/6) (Canaveral, 1963, 414 pp., $3.50) (Ballantine: U6039, 1966, 320 pp., pa 75¢)

The far-flung adventures of a Chicago hoodlum.

Out of Time's Abyss [pa] See *Land That Time Forgot, The*

Pellucidar (*All-Story Cavalier*, sr5, 1 May 1915) (McClurg, 1923, 322 pp., illus.–J. A. St. John, $1.75; Grosset, 1924, and *ca.* 1940, 75¢) (Methuen, 1924, 253 pp., 7/6; 1925, 2/6; 1935, 213 pp., 1/-, 2/6) (Pinnacle: 39, 1955, 159 pp., pa 2/-) (Ace: F-158, 1962, 160 pp., pa 40¢; G-734, 1968, pa 50¢) (Canaveral, 1962, 180 pp., illus.–M. Blaine, $2.75; 1963, $2.95) (in *Three Science Fiction Novels* [Burroughs], Dover, 1963, pa) ([French], Ed. Opta, 'Classique SF6,' 1966 [with *At the Earth's Core*])

2nd of the Pellucidar series.

People That Time Forgot, The [pa] See *Land That Time Forgot, The*

Pirates of Venus (*Arg*, sr6, 17 Sep 1932) (*Passing Show* [British weekly], sr9, illus.–F. Matania, Sep 1933) (Burroughs, 1934, 314 pp., illus.–J. A. St. John, 193?, $2.00; Grosset, 1935, and *ca.* 1940, 75¢; Burroughs, *ca.* 1940, 75¢, 1948 $1.00) (Lane, 1935, 312 pp., 7/6; 1937, 3/6; 1948, 3/6) (Pinnacle: 34, 1954, 153 pp., pa 2/-) (Canaveral, 1962, 314 pp., illus.–J. A. St. John, $2.75; 1963, $2.95) (Ace: F-179, 1963, 173 pp., pa 40¢) (FSB: 820, 1963, 159 pp., pa 2/6; #1217, 1964, pa 3/6; 1965, pa 3/6) (in *Pirates of Venus & Lost on Venus*, Dover: T1053, 1963, 340 pp., illus.–F. Matania, pa $1.75)

1st of the Venusian series.

Princess of Mars, A ("Under the Moons of Mars," by Norman Bean, *All-Story*, sr6, Feb 1912) (*New York Evening World*, 3 to 8 Jan 1916) (McClurg, 1917, 326 pp., illus.–F. E. Schoonover, $1.35; Grosset, 1918, and *ca.* 1940, 75¢; Burroughs, 1948, $1.00) (Methuen, 1919 (2 ed), 252 pp., 6/-; 1920 (7 ed), 2/-; 1930, 2/-; 1936, 1/-; 1942, 3/6; 1952, 7/6) (*Prinsessan Av Mars* [Swedish], Hökerberg, 1924) (*Eine Mars-prinzessin* [German], Dieck, 1925) ("Carter of the Red Planet," *Modern Mechanics & Invention*, sr4, Apr 1929) (Goulden: 6, 1948, 127 pp., pa 1/6 (2 ed); 1952, pa 2/-) (FSB: 306, 1961, 161 pp., pa 2/6; 1962, pa 2/6; #1401, 1965, pa 3/6) (Oxford Univ. Press, 1962, 120 pp., pa 3/-) (Ballantine: F701, 1963, 159 pp., pa 50¢; U2031, 1963, pa 50¢) (in *A Princess of Mars & A Fighting Man of Mars*, Dover: T1140, 1964, 356 pp., illus., pa $1.75) (Dragon: D76, 1968, 156 pp., pa 2/6)

1st of the Martian series.

Savage Pellucidar (Canaveral, 1963, 274 pp., illus.–J. A. St. John, $3.50) (Ace: F-280, 1964, 221 pp., pa 40¢; G-739, 1968, pa 50¢)

7th in the Pellucidar series. From novelettes in *AS*: "The Return to Pellucidar" (Feb 1942); "Men of the Bronze Age" (Mar 1942); "Tiger Girl" (Apr 1942); "Savage Pellucidar" (Nov 1963).

Swords of Mars (*BB*, sr6, Nov 1934) (Burroughs, 1936, 315 pp., illus., $2.00; Grosset, 1937, 75¢; Burroughs, *ca.* 1940 (2 ed), 75¢; 1948 $1.00) (Ballantine: F728, 1963, 191 pp., pa 50¢; U2038, 1965, pa 50¢) (FSB: 1676, 1966, 191 pp., pa 3/6)

8th of the Martian series.

Synthetic Men of Mars (*Arg*, sr6, 7 Jan 1939) (Burroughs, 1940, 315 pp., illus.–J. C. Burroughs, $2.00; 1949, $1.00) (Methuen, 1941, 251 pp., 7/6; 1942, 4/6; 1951, 7/-) (Ballantine: F739, 1963, 160 pp., pa 50¢; U2039, 1965, pa 50¢) (FSB: 1153, 1964, 160 pp., pa 3/6)

9th of the Martian series.

Tales of Three Planets [C] (Canaveral, 1964, 283 pp., illus.–R. Krenkel, $3.50)

3 stories: "Beyond the Farthest Star" & sequel [as one story]; "The Resurrection of Jimber-Jaw" (*Arg*, 20 Feb 1937); "The

Wizard of Venus" [previously unpublished adventure of Carson Napier].

Tanar of Pellucidar (*BB*, sr6, Mar 1929) (Metropolitan Books, 1930, 312 pp., front.–P. F. Berdanier, $2.00; Grosset, 1931, and *ca.* 1940, 75¢) (Methuen, 1939, 274 pp., 7/6; 1940, 4/-) (Pinnacle: 29, 1953, 154 pp., pa 2/-) (Canaveral, 1962, 245 pp., illus.–M. Blaine, $2.75; 1963, $2.95) (Ace: F-171, 1962, 224 pp., pa 40¢; G-735, 1968, pa 50¢) (in *Three Science Fiction Novels* [Burroughs], 1963, pa) (*Tanar de Pellucidar* [French], Ed. Opta, 'Classique SF9,' 1967; with *Tarzan at the Earth's Core*)

3rd of the Pellucidar series.

Three Martian Novels [C] (Dover: T39, 1962, 499 pp., illus.–J. A. St. John, pa $1.75; 1963, $1.85)

3 novels: *Thuvia, Maid of Mars*; *The Chessmen of Mars*; *The Master Mind of Mars*.

Three Science Fiction Novels [C] (Dover: T1051, 1963, 433 pp., illus.–St. John, pa $2.00)

3 novels: *At the Earth's Core*; *Pellucidar*; *Tanar of Pellucidar*.

Thuvia, Maid of Mars (*All-Story*, sr3, 8 Apr 1916) (McClurg, 1920, 256 pp., $1.75; 1921, $1.75; Grosset, 1921 $1.00, 1922 75¢, *ca.* 1940 75¢; Burroughs, 1948, $1.00) (Methuen, 1921, 218 pp., 6/-; 1922, 2/6; 1928, 2/-; 1936, 2/6; 1940, 4/-; 1951, 7/-) (Pinnacle: 25, 1953, 136 pp., pa 2/-) (FSB: 613, 1962, 127 pp., pa 2/6; 1964, pa 2/6; #1402, 1965, pa 3/6) (in *Three Martian Novels* [Burroughs], 1962, pa; 1963, pa) (Ace: F-168, 1962, 143 pp., pa 40¢) (Ballantine: F770, 1963, 158 pp., pa 50¢; U2034, 1965, pa 50¢)

4th of the Martian series.

Warlord of Mars, The (*All-Story*, sr4, Dec 1913) (McClurg, 1919, 296 pp., $1.40; Grosset, 1920 $1.00, 1922 75¢, *ca.* 1940, 75¢; Burroughs, 1948, $1.00) (Methuen, 1920, 221 pp., 6/-; 1921, 2/6; 1930, 2/-; 1935, 1/-; 1951, 7/-) (Pinnacle: 26, 1953, 152 pp., pa 2/-) (FSB: 367, 1961, 128 pp., pa 2/6; #1232, 1965, 160 pp., pa 3/6) (Ballantine: F711, 1963, 158 pp., pa 50¢; U2033, 1965, pa 50¢)

3rd of the Martian series.

BURROUGHS, JOHN COLEMAN (28 Feb 1913–) U.S. author and artist, third child (younger son) of Edgar Rice Burroughs. He illustrated 13 titles, starting with his father's *The Oakdale Affair* and *The Rider* in 1937 and continuing through to the final *Llana of Gathol* from Tarzana. Besides the story below, he teamed with his elder brother Hulbert to write the following: "The Man Without a World" (*TWS*, June 1939) and sequel "The Lightning Men" (*TWS*, Feb 1940); and "The Bottom of the World" (*SS*, Sep 1941), for which he did 7 interior illustrations.

Fiction

Treasure of the Black Falcon [pa] (Ballantine: U6085, 1967, 253 pp., pa 75¢)

Fantastic adventure on the Atlantic Ocean floor in an area inhabited by aliens.

BURROUGHS, WILLIAM S(EWARD) (5 Feb 1914–) U.S. author, graduate from Harvard University; grandson of the adding machine inventor. He is noted for his *Naked Lunch*, a once-banned classic written in a private kind of gibberish derived from 15 years as a drug addict. He uses the pseudonym "William Lee" (but this is not the contributor to *ASF* of recent years.)

Fiction

Dead Fingers Talk (J. Calder, London, 1963, iv+215 pp., 25/-) (Tandem: T55, 1966, 224 pp., pa 3/6)

Constructed from the author's earlier *The Naked Lunch*, *The Soft Machine* and *The Ticket That Exploded*, with some new material—the world of junkies seen through their depraved and distorted eyes—utterly depressing and nauseating.

Nova Express (Grove, New York, 1964, 187 pp., $5.00; 'Evergreen BC102,' 1965, 155 pp., pa 95¢) (J. Cape, London, 1966, 187 pp., 25/-) (Panther: 23771, 1968, 157 pp., pa 5/-)

Displays a conviction that the universe is foul and so is everyone in it. The galaxy's Nova Police are fighting the Nova Mob and need to be as foul.

Soft Machine, The (Grove, New York, 1966, 182 pp., $5.00)

(Calder, London, 1968, 188 pp., 42/-, illus.—O. J. McCaffery)

A not-too-far-future with an irresponsible society—sex, drugs, death and violence, and also BEM's and metal monsters.

Ticket That Exploded, The (Grove, 1967, 217 pp., $5.00; 'Evergreen B164,' 1968, pa $1.25) (Calder & Boyars, London, 1968, 217 pp., 42/-)

BURT, MICHAEL (1900–) British author. He has written a trilogy with Roger Poynings, a novelist, as the protagonist who solves mysteries mixed with supernatural aspects, which are treated both humorously and seriously. The set has appeared also in Argentina (Emecé, 1952). Another book with fantasy overtones is *The House of Sleep* (1945).

Fiction

Case of the Angels' Trumpets, The (Ward Lock, London, 1947, 255 pp., 9/6; 1949, 254 pp., 5/-)

Second of the Poynings trilogy, dealing with witches and gnosticism.

Case of the Fast Young Lady, The (Ward Lock, 1942, 384 pp., 8/6; 1944, 5/-)

First of the Poynings trilogy, dealing with occultism.

Case of the Laughing Jesuit, The (Ward Lock, 1948, 256 pp., 9/6)

Last of the Poynings trilogy, dealing with satanism.

BURTON, ELIZABETH (1908–) British author, born in Cairo, Egypt, and educated privately in Canada and Italy. She has been a correspondent for the *Windsor Star* (Ontario, Canada), and has written such works as *The Elizabethans at Home* as well as six novels (five under a pseudonym).

Fiction [as "Susan Alice Kerby"]

Miss Carter and the Ifrit (Hutchinson, London, 1945, 160 pp., 8/6)

A woman and a djinn from the Arabian Nights.

Mr. Kronion (Laurie, London, 1949, 223 pp., 8/6) (Smithers, Toronto, $2.50)

Visit of Jupiter to modern Britain.

Roaring Dove, The (Dodd Mead, New York, 1948, 260 pp., $3.00) (Dodd, Toronto, $3.25)

A comedy about an imaginary utopian civilization.

BURTON, MAURICE (28 Mar 1898–) British scientist, educated at King's College, London; D.Sc., F.Z.S., F.R.S.A. He was Assistant Keeper and then Deputy Keeper at the Dept. of Zoology of the British Museum of Natural History; he retired in 1958. He has been Science Editor for *Illustrated London News*, a correspondent for *Nature*, etc., and is noted for his numerous works on animals, etc.

Nonfiction

Animal Legends (Puller, London, 1955, 215 pp., illus.—Jane Burton, 15/-) (S. J. R. Saunders, Toronto, $3.35) (Coward-McCann, New York, 1957, 318 pp., illus.—G. T. Hartmann, $4.95)

Although not considered as good as W. Ley's or R. Carrington's books on this subject, it has interesting material on such possible fantasies as sea serpents, snowmen, and jumping snakes.

BURTON, SAMUEL HOLROYD

Anthology

Science Fiction (Longmans, London, 1967, 245 pp., 7/-)

BURTT, J. LEWIS U.S. author, prominent in *Amazing Stories* in the early 1930's.

Series

Lemurian Documents. All in *AS*: 1. "Pygmalion" (Jan 1932); 2. "The Gorgons" (Mar 1932); 3. "Daedalus and Icarus" (May 1932); 4. "Phaeton" (June 1932); 5. "The Sacred Cloak of Feathers" (July 1932); 6. "Prometheus" (Sep 1932).

BUSH, LUCIUS

Fiction

Peek at Heaven, A (Exposition, New York, 1964, 186 pp., $3.50)

BUSHNESS, GEORGE H(ERBERT) (1896–)

Fiction

Handful of Ghosts [C] [pa] (St. Andrew's Univ. Press, Scotland, 1946, 59 pp., pa 2/-)

Supernatural tales told at meetings of the St. Andrew's University Celtic Society.

BUSSON, BERNARD French journalist.

Nonfiction

Last Secrets of the Earth, The [with G. Leroy] (*Les Derniers Secrets de la Terre*, La Table Ronde, Paris, 1955) (W. Laurie, London, 1956, 176 pp., 18/-) (Putnam, New York, 1957, $3.50)

Two young French journalists discuss mysteries; these include flying saucers, the coelacanth, the Abominable Snowman, active volcanoes, subterranean rivers, and the Antarctic.

BUTLER, I.

Nonfiction

Horror Film, The [pa] (Zwemmer, London, and Barnes, New York, 1967, 176 pp., pa $2.25)

BUTLER, JOAN Pseudonym of Robert William Alexander (1905–). A further novel, *Stormy Weather*, is a weird concerning the capers of an Egyptian mummy.

Fiction

Deep Freeze (Stanley Paul, London, 1952, 256 pp., 10/6; 1953, 6/-)

Space to Let (Paul, London, 1955, 192 pp., 9/6; 1957, 6/6)

Typical Butler humour with slight sf theme.

BUTLER, SAMUEL (4 Dec 1835–18 June 1902) English author, born at Langar, Nottinghamshire, son of Rev. Thomas Butler and grandson of Samuel Butler, Bishop of Lichfield. He was educated at Shrewsbury and St. John's College, Cambridge. He wished to be a painter and refused the church career for which he was intended. After some differences with his father on this question he emigrated to New Zealand in 1859. There he managed a sheep run and successfully wrote various articles relating to Darwin, including "Darwin Among the Machines" (1863), which was the germ of his well-known work *Erewhon*. He returned to London where he lived the rest of his life, making annual excursions to North Italy and Sicily. He studied painting seriously and exhibited regularly at the Royal Academy. Many of his writings gave his views on the Darwinian theories of evolution; later he was interested in the Homeric question—whether Homer wrote *The Iliad* and *The Odyssey*. His most important work is considered to be the autobiographical *The Way of All Flesh* (published posthumously, 1903); *Erewhon* and sequel are notable in the field of Utopian fantasy. He also wrote topographical books on the Alps and a biography of his grandfather.

Fiction

Erewhon, or, Over the Range (1872) (D. Bogue, London, 1880, 244 pp.) (Richards, London, 1901, 342 pp., 6/-) (De La More Press, London, 1906, 342 pp., 6/-) (Fifield, London, 1908, 376 pp., 2/6) (*Erewhon* [French], Gallimard, 1920) (J. Cape, London, 1924, 324 pp., 7/6) (*Erewhon & Erewhon Revisited*, Dent 'Everyman's Library': 881, 1932, 389 pp.; 1959, xvi+391 pp., 8/6; Modern Library, New York, 1933, 622 pp.; Dutton, 1959) (Penguin: 20, 1936, 256 pp., pa 6/-; 1954, 217 pp., pa 2/-) (*Landet Ingenstans* [Swedish], Natur & Kultur, 1957) (in *The Essential Samuel Butler*, 1950) (Signet: CD41, 1961, 250 pp., pa 50¢) (Collier: HS16, 1961, pa 65¢) (Airmont: CL130, 1967, 192 pp., pa 50¢)

A noted Utopian classic: a civilization in New Zealand which has advanced beyond the use of machinery. Sequel is *Erewhon Revisited*.

Erewhon Revisited Twenty Years Later (Richards, 1901, 350 pp., 6/-) (Fifield, 1908, 350 2/6) (? , London, 1923) (*Erewhon & Erewhon Revisited* [see *Erewhon*]) (*Nouveaux Voyages en Erewhon* [French], Gallimard, 1924)

The sequel to *Erewhon*; generally considered to be not as good.

Essential Samuel Butler, The [C] (Dutton, New York, 1950, 544 pp., $3.75) (Cape, London, 1950, 544 pp., 12/6) (Clarke Irwin, Toronto, $2.75)

Contains *Erewhon* [but not its sequel], a long Introduction by G. H. D. Cole, and multitudinous excerpts from one of the most stimulating minds of the 19th Century.

BUTLER, WILLIAM (1929–) U.S. author, born in Oregon and growing up near San Francisco. He studied music and worked in radio in Berkeley and New York City. Deciding ultimately to devote his life to writing, he went to Japan and worked as a cartoonist for a Tokyo paper and taught English in Kita Kyushu. His first novel was *The Ring in Meiji* (1965). He now (1968) lives in Kamakura, Japan.

Fiction

Butterfly Revolution, The (Putnam, New York, 1967, 217 pp., $4.95) (Ballantine: U6099, 1967, 221 pp., pa 75¢) (Panther: 2286, 1967, 158 pp., pa 3/6)

A chilling tale of terror and upheaval in a world without adults.

BUTTERWORTH, OLIVER (1915–) U.S. teacher, born in Hartford, Conn. He studied at Dartmouth (A.B. 1937), Harvard, and Middlebury College (M.A. 1947). He was a schoolteacher in Connecticut, and has been English teacher at Hartford College for Women since 1947.

Fiction

Enormous Egg, The (Little Brown, Boston, 1956, 187 pp., $2.95)
Juvenile.

BUZZATI, DINO (1906–) Italian author. He has written some fantasy in his own language, and is noted for his children's book *Invasion of the Bears of Sicily*. He has been translated into German, a collection being *Eine Frau von Welt* (Goldmann, 1966).

Fiction

Catastrophe [C] (Calder & Boyars, London, 1965, viii+139 pp., 30/-)

15 stories (first 14 translated from Italian by Judith Landry, 15th by Cynthia Jolly): "The Collapse of the Baliverna"; "Catastrophe"; "The Epidemic"; "The Landslide"; "Just the Very Thing They Wanted"; "Oversight"; "The Monster"; "Seven Floors"; "The March of Time"; "The Alarming Revenge of a Domestic Pet"; "And Yet They Are Knocking at Your Door"; "Something Beginning With 'L' "; "The Slaying of the Dragon"; "The Opening of the Road"; "The Scala Scare."

Larger Than Life [Trans.–Henry Reed] (Secker Warburg, London, 1962, 155 pp., 15/-) (Walker, New York, 1967, 154 pp., $3.95)

Research on an elaborate machine complex duplicating and surpassing the human brain, and programmed with a woman's personality traits.

BYLISE, MARGUERITE

Fiction

Earth Eagles (Holt, New York, 1948, $2.50)
An appealing novel about the ghost of a racehorse.

BYNNER, EDWIN L(ASSETER) (1842–4 Sep 1893) U.S. novelist, born in Brooklyn. His works include *Nimport* (1877); *Damen's Ghost* (1881); *Penelope's Daughters* (1887); *The Begum's Daughter* (1890).

Fiction

Chase of the Meteor, The [C] (Little Brown, Boston, 1891, 13+ 209 pp., illus.)

Fantasy, 9 stories: "Black Beard's Last Struggle"; "The Chase of the Meteor"; "Cruise in a Soap Bubble"; "The Discontented Dowager"; "The Extra Train"; "Hercules-Jack"; "Jammer's Ghost"; "Our Special Artist"; "The Tramp's Dinner Party."

BYRNE, DONN (20 Nov 1889–18 June 1928) Irish-American novelist and short-story writer. Born in Brooklyn, he grew up in County Antrim, Ireland. He received his M.A. from University College, Dublin. At first his literary attempts were unsuccessful. He went to New York and worked on the staffs of the *New Standard* and the *Century* dictionaries. He burst into literary prominence with his *Messer Marco Polo* in 1920.

Fiction

Changeling and Other Stories [C] (Century, New York, 1923, 418 pp., $2.00)

Fantasy, 14 stories: "Changeling"; "The Barnacle Goose"; "Belfasters"; "The Keeper of the Bridge"; "In Praise of Lady Margery Kyteler"; "Reynardine"; "Dramatis Personae"; "Wisdom Buildeth Her House"; "The Parliament at Thebes"; "Delilah"; "Now It Was Dusk"; "A Quatrain of Ling Tai Fu's"; " 'Irish' "; "By Ordeal of Justice."

BYRNE, STUART J(AMES) U.S. author of Scotch-Irish descent. He has travelled through most parts of South and Central America and has worked in Guam. He first appeared in *Amazing Stories* with "Music of the Spheres" (Aug 1935), and returned after the war with "Prometheus II" (*AS*, Feb 1948) and sequels. His later novels have tended to be Shaverish in outlook. He has been Executive Vice-President of the Science Fantasy Writers of America Association. He has written a new Tarzan novel which, because of copyright difficulties, may never be published.

Series [as "John Bloodstone"]

Flannigan, Michael. All in *AS*: "The Land Beyond the Lens" (Mar 1952); "The Golden Gods" (Apr 1952); "Return of Michael Flannigan" (Aug 1952).

CABELL, JAMES BRANCH (14 Apr 1879–5 May 1958) U.S. novelist. He was born in Richmond, Va., and graduated from William and Mary College in 1898. Except for three years as a reporter on the *New York Herald*, he worked and lived in his home town. His long writing career embraced over 50 books, beginning with *The Eagle's Shadow* (1904), and includes fantasy novels, essays, history and autobiography. Probably his major achievement is *Biography in the Life of Manuel*, 21 volumes dealing with the poetic, chivalrous and gallant attitudes; it is in the form of a fantasy novel (each book being a chapter of the whole) set in Lichfield, a fictitious Virginian city, and in Poictesme, a fictitious land in the south of France. His most famous fantasy, *Jurgen*, was suppressed for a time. He also wrote a number of genealogical works on his ancestry and other Virginia families. During his time he was both extravagantly praised and utterly disliked. A recent book about Cabell and his writings is *The Dream and the Reality* by Desmond Tarrant (U. of Oklahoma Press, 1967).

Series

Biography of Manuel, The. [With thanks to James N. Hall and *Kalki* (1967).] This list shows the order in which the volumes should be read, not the order in which they were written or published:

Beyond Life: Dizain des Demiurges (McBride, 1919; republished in the Kalki and Storisende editions, and by the Modern Library). A non-fiction (or nearly non-fiction) prologue to the work as a whole.

Figures of Earth: A Comedy of Appearances (McBride, 1921; republished in the Storisende edition and presumably in the Kalki edition). The story of Dom Manuel himself.

The Silver Stallion: A Comedy of Redemption (McBride, 1926; republished in the Storisende and Kalki editions). The story of the growth of the legend of Manuel the Redeemer.

The Witch Woman. This book was never published as such. It was planned as ten episodes in the life of Ettarre, the witchwoman of the title, who also appears elsewhere in the Biography. Only three of these episodes were published, in separate volumes, as follows: *The Music From Behind the Moon* (John Day Co.,

1926; included in Vol. IV, *Domnei*, of the Storisende edition); *The White Robe* (McBride, 1928; included in Vol. XVIII, *Townsend of Lichfield*, of the Storisende edition); *The Way of Ecben* (McBride, 1929; included in Vol. XVIII, *Townsend of Lichfield*, of the Storisende edition). See entry in *Fiction* section below.

Domnei: A Comedy of Woman-Worship (originally published as *The Soul of Melicent*, 1913; revised edition, McBride, 1920; republished in the Storisende and Kalki editions).

Chivalry: Dizain des Reines (originally published in 1909; revised edition, McBride, 1921; Storisende and Kalki editions).

Jurgen: A Comedy of Justice (McBride, 1919; Storisende and Kalki editions, and several modern paperback editions).

The Line of Love: Dizain des Mariages (originally published by Harpers, 1905; revised edition, McBride, 1921; Storisende and Kalki editions).

The High Place: A Comedy of Disenchantment (McBride, 1923; Storisende and Kalki editions).

Gallantry: Dizain des Fetes Galantes (originally published in 1907; revised edition, McBride, 1922; Storisende and Kalki editions).

Something About Eve: A Comedy of Fig-Leaves (McBride, 1927; Storisende and Kalki editions).

The Certain Hour: Dizain des Poetes (McBride, 1916; Storisende and Kalki editions).

The Cords of Vanity: A Comedy of Shirking (originally published in 1909; revised edition, McBride, 1920; Storisende and Kalki editions).

From the Hidden Way: Dizain des Echoes (originally published in 1916; revised edition, McBride, 1924; *Ballades From the Hidden Way*, revised excerpts, Crosby Gaige, 1928; Storisende).

The Jewel Merchants (McBride, 1921; included in Vol. XIII, *From the Hidden Way*, of the Storisende edition).

The Rivet in Grandfather's Neck: A Comedy of Limitations (McBride, 1915; Storisende and Kalki editions).

The Eagle's Shadow: A Comedy of Purse-Strings (originally published in 1904; revised edition, McBride, 1923; Storisende). This is Cabell's first published work, although *The Line of Love* was written earlier.

The Cream of the Jest: A Comedy of Evasions (originally published in 1917; revised edition, McBride, 1922; Storisende, Kalki and Modern Library editions).

The Lineage of Lichfield (McBride, 1922; included in Vol. XVI, *The Cream of the Jest*, of the Storisende edition). This is the genealogy of the descendants of Dom Manuel, from Poictesme to Lichfield.

Straws and Prayer Books: Dizain des Diversions (McBride, 1924; Storisende and Kalki editions). Mostly non-fiction; the Epilogue to the Biography.

Other volumes only for the completist:

Townsend of Lichfield: Dizain des Adieux (McBride, 1930). This was the title selected by Cabell for a novel which was never written. Instead the title was used to collate several of the shorter works of the Biography, as well as the famous Colophon to *The Way of Ecben* which led many critics to conclude that Cabell was abandoning writing entirely, instead of just saying farewell to Dom Manuel.

Preface to the Past (McBride, 1931; Kalki). A collection of the prefaces and author's notes from the various volumes of the Storisende edition, republished in the Kalki edition for the benefit of those not fortunate enough to have acquired the deluxe edition.

Sonnets From Antan (Fountain Press, 1930; included in Vol. XVIII, *Townsend of Lichfield*, of the Storisende edition).

Fiction [Incomplete—other titles in Bleiler *Checklist*]
Devil's Own Dear Son, The (Farrar Strauss, New York, 1949, 27+209 pp., $2.75) (Clarke Irwin, Toronto, $3.00) (J. Lane, London, 1950, 198 pp., 8/6)

Fantasy of the Son of the Prince of Hell—titillating conversation with sundry shades and demons.
Jurgen (McBride, New York, 1919, 9+368 pp., $2.50) (J. Lane, London, 1921, 325 pp.) ([German], Insel, 1922) (Grosset, New York, 1929, 368 pp., $1.00) (Lane 'Week-End Library' 43, 1932, 352 pp., 3/6) (Modern Library, New York, 1934, 368 pp., 95¢)

(Penguin: 268, 1940, 247 pp., pa 1/-) (Penguin [U.S.]: 601, 1946, 375 pp., pa 25¢) (Bodley Head [Lane], 1949, 326 pp., 6/-) ([Swedish], Wahlström & Widstrand, 1949) (Crown 'Xanadu' Library, 1962, 368 pp., pa $1.45, Introduction—B. R. Redman) (Avon: VS7, 1964, 287 pp., pa 75¢)

Above are some of the appearances of this famous novel which was originally suppressed for some 20 months in 1920-21. A middle-aged pawnbroker and would-be poet rides into the past on a centaur.
Witch-Woman, The [C] (Farrar Strauss, 1948, 160 pp., $2.50)

Subtitled "A Trilogy About Her." This is a reprint of the only three stories written of a projected ten; the fourth was to have been "The 31st of February." The stories are: "The Way of Ecben" (a beautiful fantasy); "The Music Behind the Moon" (a mortal's tampering with the book of the Norns); "The White Robe" (wherein a lycanthrope happens to be a bishop).

CADE, C(ECIL) MAXWELL
Nonfiction
Other Worlds Than Ours (Museum, London, 1966, 248 pp., illus., 30/-) (Burns MacEachern, Toronto, $6.50)

A consideration of the problem of life in the Universe, taking account of such factors as genius, astrology, flying saucers, etc.

CADELL, (Mrs.) ELIZABETH (1903–)
Fiction
Brimstone in the Garden (Morrow, New York, 1950, 264 pp., $3.00)

An English village is subjected to a summer's haunting by two soul-catching demons and a wistful ghost.
Crystal Clear See *Journey's Eve*
Journey's Eve (Hodder & Stoughton, London, 1953, 254 pp., 10/6) (*Crystal Clear*, Musson, Toronto, $2.50, & Morrow, 1953, 250 pp., $3.00)

Not out-and-out fantasy, but has a sub-plot involving ESP; otherwise a beautiful, deft and charming novel of light love and British humour.

CAIDIN, MARTIN (14 Sep 1927–) U.S. scientist and writer on aviation. He became Associate Editor of *Air News* and *Air Tech* at 16. He founded Martin Caidin Associates Inc., a radio and TV service network in the aerospace field, and was consultant on atomic warfare for the New York Civil Defense Commision 1950-62.

He has written much popular nonfiction, including *Rockets and Missiles—Past and Future* (McBride, 1954); *Rockets Beyond Earth* (McBride [2nd ed.], 1954; Arco, 1955); *Worlds in Space* (Holt, 1954; Sidgwick Jackson, 1954); *Vanguard* (Dutton, 1957); *Spaceport U.S.A.* (Dutton, 1959); *War for the Moon* (Dutton, 1959); *Man Into Space* (Pyramid, 1961, pa); *The Moon: New World for Men* (Bobbs-Merrill, 1963); *The Man-In-Space Dictionary* (Dutton, 1963, $6.95—1900 terms pertinent to the field).
Fiction
Four Came Back (D. McKay, New York, 1968, 275 pp., $5.50)

Eight people in a space station become involved in human conflict, and then with a plague from space.
God Machine, The (Dutton, New York, 1968, 316 pp., $5.95)

An electronic brain decides to take over the world.
Last Fathom, The (Meredith Press, New York, 1967, 312 pp., $5.95)

American and Soviet nuclear submarines, and a critical event in the deepest reaches of the sea.
Long Night, The (Dodd Mead, New York, 1956, 242 pp., $3.00)

Sf inspired by research on the Hamburg firestorm ("The Night Hamburg Died," by Caidin, *Arg*, June 1956) and similar to Wylie's *Tomorrow*.
Marooned (Dutton, New York, 1964, 378 pp., $4.95) (Clarke Irwin, Toronto, $6.00) (Hodder Stoughton, London, 1964, 378 pp., 25/-) (Bantam: S2965, 1965, 314 pp., pa 75¢) (Corgi: FN7217, 1965, 314 pp., pa 5/-) (*S.O.S. Mercury VII* [French], Stock, 1965) (*Gemini roept Mercury* [Dutch], West-Friesland, Hoorn])

A rescue in space, written as a follow-on to contemporary rocket orbiting.

No Man's World (Dutton, 1967, 414 pp., $5.95) (Clarke Irwin, Toronto, $7.25)

Battle for the Moon in 1971, after Russia has been there three years.

CAILLOIS, ROGER French literary figure associated with the U.N.E.S.C.O.; he wrote the Preface to Jan Potocki's *Saragossa Manuscript* when it was revived around 1960.
Anthology
Dream Adventure: A Literature Anthology, The (Orion, New York, 1963, 285 pp., $5.95)

Fantasy, including the following: "A Wild Surmise," H. Kuttner & C. L. Moore; "The Door in the Wall," H. G. Wells; "An Occurrence at Owl Creek Bridge," A. Bierce; "Tale of the Ragged Mountains," E. A. Poe; some short Chinese fantasies; an extract from Apuleius and another from Marco Polo; further stories by J. L. Borges, R. Kipling, W. S. Maugham, T. Gautier, Nabokov, and K. S. Gjalski (a Croatian writer).

CALDECOTT, SIR ANDREW (26 Oct 1884–14 July 1951) British author and civil servant; M.A. Oxon, L.L.D. Ceylon. From 1907-35 he held various appointments in the Malayan Civil Service and was later Governor of Hong Kong and of Ceylon. Knighted in 1935, he received the C.B.E. in 1926 and K.C.M.G. in 1937. As an author, he wrote many weird and ghost stories in the older tradition. Another work is *History of Jelebu*.
Fiction
Fires Burn Blue [C] (E. Arnold, London, 1948, 222 pp., 8/6) (Longmans, New York, 1949, 222 pp., $2.75) (Longmans, Toronto, $2.25)

Ghost, 13 stories: "An Exchange of Notes"; "Cheap and Nasty"; "Grey Brothers"; "Quintet"; "Authorship Disputed"; "Final Touches"; "What's in a Name?"; "Under the Mistletoe"; "His Name Was Legion"; "Tall Tales But True"; "A Book Entry"; "Seeds of Remembrance"; "Seated One Day at the Organ."
Not Exactly Ghosts [C] (E. Arnold, 1946, 213 pp., 7/6) (Longmans Green, 1947, 213 pp., $2.50) (Longmans, Toronto, $2.25)

Weird, 12 stories: "A Room in a Rectory"; "Branch Line to Benceston"; "Sonata in D Minor"; "Autoepitaphy"; "The Pump in Thorp's Spinney"; "Whiffs of the Sea"; "In Due Course"; "Light in the Darkness"; "Decastroland"; "A Victim of Medusa"; "Fits of the Blues"; "Christmas Reunion."

CALDER-MARSHALL, ARTHUR (19 Aug 1908–)
Fiction
Scarlet Boy, The (Hart-Davis, London, 1961, 222 pp., 16/-) (Corgi: SN1161, 1962, 190 pp., pa 2/6)

The ghost of a boy found hanged proves very elusive; the story fails, however, either as a character study or a psychic problem.

CALDWELL, (JANET MIRIAM) TAYLOR (HOLLAND) (7 Sep 1900–) U.S. author. She was born in Manchester, England, and was brought to the U.S.A. when six years old; she was educated at U. of Buffalo, N.Y. (A.B. 1931). She was Secretary of Board of Special Inquiry, U.S. Dept. of Immigration and Naturalization. Her second husband, Marcus Reback (married 1931) is her agent and researcher, but is not a collaborator as mentioned in some references. Since her first novel, *Dynasty of Death* (1938), she has written many notable novels, including *This Side of Innocence*.
Fiction
Devil's Advocate, The (Crown, New York, 1952, 375 pp., $3.50) (Macfadden: 75-126, 1964, 349 pp., pa 75¢; 75-184, 1967, pa 75¢)

A political revolution in the U.S. in 1970.
Dialogues With the Devil (Collins, London, 1968, 224 pp., 21/-)

A sequence of deadly serious dialogues between the Archangel Michael and the Mover of the Underworld—along the lines of C. S. Lewis' *The Screwtape Letters* and C. E. S. Wood's *Heavenly Discourse*. A dramatisation of crucial universal issues of today ranging across the entire cosmos from Earth to planets yet unknown.
Your Sins and Mine (Gold Medal: 156, 1956, 140 pp., pa 25¢) (Muller: GM156, 1956, 140 pp., pa 2/-; nn, nd, 140 pp., pa 3/-)

(Caxton, Caldwell (Idaho), 1959, 181 pp., $3.00) (Copp, Toronto, $3.50)

An apocalyptic novel, well received in some religious circles. The Earth refuses to bring forth its fruits.

CALHOUN, MARY
Fiction
Goblin Under the Stairs, The (Morrow, New York, 1968, illus.–J. McCaffery, $3.32)

Juvenile fantasy.

CALISHER, HORTENSE (1911–)
Fiction
Journey From Ellipsia (Little Brown, Boston, 1965, 375 pp., $5.95) (S. Warburg, London, 1966, 375 pp., 30/-)

The story of a visitor 'Eli' to Earth from Ellipsia (where ellipsoidal creatures inhabit an ellipsoidal planet, and there are no pronouns but *we* and *our*), with a reciprocal visit by an academic. Recommended by J. Merril.

CALVINO, ITALO (1923–) Italian author, born at San Remo. He has had five books published in English. He won the Premio Riccione of Italy for *The Path to the Nest of Spiders*, based on war experiences.
Fiction
Cosmicomics (*Le Cosmicomiche*, Guilio Einaudi, Turin, 1965) Trans.–W. Weaver: (Harcourt Brace, New York, 1968, 153 pp., $3.95) (J. Cape, London, 1968)

12 stories (theories on the evolution of the universe narrated by "Ofwfg"): "The Distance of the Moon"; "At Daybreak"; "A Sign in Space"; "All at One Point"; "Without Colours"; "Games Without End"; "The Aquatic Uncle"; "How Much Shall We Bet"; "The Dinosaurs"; "The Form of Space"; "The Light Years"; "The Spiral."

CAMERON, ALISTAIR Canadian sf fan.
Nonfiction
Fantasy Classification System (Canadian SF Association, 1952, quarto, 52 pp., $1.00 mimeo; 500 copies)

A well-thought-out production giving a comprehensive index for the various classifications within the field of fantasy.

CAMERON, ELEANOR (BUTLER) (23 Mar 1912–) U.S. librarian and author; now Mrs. Ian Stuart Cameron. Born in Canada, she studied at U. of California-Los Angeles. She has been a librarian since 1930, becoming research librarian for an advertising agency in 1942. Noted for her juvenile series below, she has also written the suspenseful mystery *The Terrible Churnadryne* (Little Brown, 1960).
Series
Mushroom Planet. Juvenile book series for 8-12 years old, published by Little, Brown (Boston). *Wonderful Flight to the Mushroom Planet* (1954); *Stowaway to the Mushroom Planet* (1956); *Mr. Bass's Planetoid* (1958); *Mystery for Mr. Bass* (1960); *Time and Mr. Bass* (1967).

CAMERON, IAN [pseud] See PAYNE, D. G.

CAMPBELL, CLYDE CRANE [pseud] See GOLD, H. L.

CAMPBELL, Sir GILBERT E., Bart.
Fiction [Incomplete—other titles in Bleiler *Checklist*]
Wild and Weird: Tales of Imagination and Mystery [C] (Ward Lock, London, 1889, 162+144+175 pp.)

14 stories: *Part I—Russia:* "Nepimoff's Father"; "The Thief's Taper"; "The White Wolf of Kostopchin"; "The Midnight Skater." *Part II—England:* "The Warning of the Sword"; "A Day's Shooting–"; "What Was It?"; "The Ghost at the Proscenium"; "The Lady Isopel"; "48, Fernvalley Terrace, N--." *Part III—Italy:* "The Evil Eye"; "The Marble Faun"; "From the Grave"; "The Green Staircase."

CAMPBELL, HERBERT J. (BERT) (1925–) British sf editor and author, and chemical research worker. He started his career in chemistry and became a noted research worker; he was elected Fellow of The Chemical Society and of The Royal Horticultural Society. From writing science articles he branched into fiction, and then became Technical Editor of *Authentic Science Fiction*. He was Editor from Dec 1952 to Jan 1956 and developed the magazine considerably, but with an unusually strong bias for science articles. He resigned because of the pressure of his research work. He wrote a number of novels which appeared in *Authentic* and in the Hamilton 'Panther' book series; a number of these saw translation into German and Italian. He edited a collection, *Sprague de Camp's New Anthology*.

Fiction
Beyond the Visible (Hamilton, Stafford, 1952, 192 pp., 8/6; 189 pp., pa 2/-) (*Die unsichtbare Gefahr* [German], Rappen, 1953; *UG*: 11, 1954)
   Similar in nature to E. F. Russell's *Sinister Barrier*.

Anthologies
Authentic Book of Space (Hamilton, London, 1954, 8½ x 11 in., 102 pp., 5/-)
   Foreword by A. C. Clarke, numerous articles, and the following stories: "Explorers of Mars," W. F. Temple; "Death Rides the Spaceways," F. J. Ackerman; "The Blue Cloud," Mary Dogge; "Old Growler Space Ship No. 2213" [cartoon], John J. Deegan; "Playmate," Leslie A. Crouch; "Our Friends the Aliens," H. K. Bulmer. A good value for its price.
Tomorrow's Universe (Hamilton, 1953, 224 pp., 8/6; Panther: 101, pa 2/-)
   Sf, 8 stories: "Heritage," C. L. Harness; "It Pays to Advertise," K. Neville; "Ticking His Life Away," Thelma D. Hamm; "M33 in Andromeda," A. E. van Vogt; "The Immortal," R. Rocklynne; "The Shore of Tomorrow," C. Oliver; "The Soaring Statue," L. S. de Camp; "Exterran," M. Lesser.

CAMPBELL, J(OHN) RAMSEY (4 Jan 1946–) British author and tax officer. He was born in Liverpool, and studied at St. Edward's College there. He has been an Inland Revenue Tax Officer since 1962.

Fiction
Inhabitant of the Lake and Less Welcome Tenants, The [C] (Arkham, Wis., 1964, 207 pp., $4.00, jacket–F. Utpatel; 2,000 copies)
   Weird, 10 stories with Author's Introduction: "The Room in the Castle"; "The Horror From the Bridge"; "The Insects From Shaggai"; "The Render of the Veils"; "The Inhabitant of the Lake"; "The Plain of Sound"; "The Return of the Witch"; "The Mine on Yuggoth"; "The Will of Stanley Brooke"; "The Moon Lens."

CAMPBELL, JOHN S(COTT) U.S. sf author. His "The Invulnerable Scourge" was recently reprinted (*WS*, Nov 1930; *Famous SF*, Spr 1968).

Fiction
Beyond Pluto [n] (*WSQ*. Sum 1932) (*FSM*, Fall 1951) (*Die vergessene Stadt* [German], *UG*: 135, 1960)
   An exploration party discovers superior beings with a city on Earth.

CAMPBELL, JOHN W(OOD) Jr. (8 June 1910–11 July 1971) U.S. sf editor and author. He first appeared in the field with "When the Atoms Failed" (*AS*, Jan 1930) while a student at Massachusetts Institute of Technology, and immediately followed this with his 'Arcot, Morey and Wade' series. He later changed his writing style and gained new popularity as "Don A. Stuart" in *Astounding Stories* (*ASF*). As Stuart he wrote "Who Goes There?" (Aug 1938) which was later the basis of the film *The Thing*. Under another pseudonym, "Karl van Campen," he wrote the controversial "The Irrelevant" (*ASF*, Dec 1934). Under his own name he wrote a series of articles on the planets for *ASF* (June 1936–Nov 1937).
   Effective October 1937 he became editor of *Astounding* (now *Analog*) and remained there to his death. With the March 1938

issue he changed the title from *Astounding Stories* to *Astounding Science-Fiction*. He soon made the magazine the leader in the field, with its zenith probably being in the early 1940's. Around this time he introduced such writers as Isaac Asimov, Robert Heinlein, Lester del Rey, Theodore Sturgeon, and A. E. van Vogt to sf; on the art side he featured many astronomical covers on *ASF* and introduced artists such as Hubert Rogers, Edd Cartier and Chesley Bonestell.
   Through the years, however, Campbell received considerable criticism for fostering L. Ron Hubbard's 'Dianetics' when this science was originated, for supporting the 'Dean Drive' (rejected by the U.S. Patent Office), for his bias toward publishing 'psi'-type stories, and for changing the title of his magazine in 1960 to *Analog Science Fiction/Science Fact*. Nevertheless the magazine always remained among the best in the field, winning the Hugo Award for best sf magazine in 1955, 1956, 1957, 1961, 1962, 1964, and 1965, and sharing the first such award with *Galaxy Science Fiction* in 1953.
   Sam Moskowitz's profile on Campbell was published in *Amazing* in Aug 1963 (also in *Seekers of Tomorrow* [Moskowitz], 1966), but this essentially reviews only his fiction. It is rather ironical that Campbell made his name as a writer with the heavy-science type of story, a class of writing which he made obsolete by his stories under the "Don A. Stuart" byline and by his editorship of *Astounding/Analog*.
   In March 1939 he introduced *Unknown* (later *Unknown Worlds*) as a companion to *Astounding*, and this became noted for its own particular style of fantasy. It ceased publication in 1943 because of the wartime paper shortage.
   Campbell wrote one of the first books on atomic power, *The Atomic Story* (1947). He was written up in *SEP* (8 Oct 1960), but this article was not very science-fictional in its implications. He always showed his interest in fan activities, and was guest of honour at a number of World SF Conventions, namely Philadelphia (1947), San Francisco (1954), and London (1957).

Series
Arcot, Morey and Wade. Future inventions. "Piracy Preferred" (*AS*, June 1930); "Solarite" (*AS*, Nov 1930); "The Black Star Passes" (*ASQ*, Fall 1930); "Islands of Space" (*ASQ*, Spr 1931); "Invaders From the Infinite" (*ASQ*, Spr/Sum 1932). Published as the books *The Black Star Passes*, *Islands of Space*, and *Invaders From the Infinite*.
Machine [as Don A. Stuart]. All in *ASF*: "The Machine" (Feb 1935); "The Invaders" (June 1935); "Rebellion" (July 1935). All contained in *Cloak of Aesir*.
Penton and Blake. Interplanetary adventurers. All in *TWS*: "The Brain Stealers of Mars" (Dec 1936; *WS Annual*, 1952); "The Double Minds" (Aug 1937; *FSM*, Win 1954); "The Immortality Seekers" (Oct 1937); "The Tenth World" (Dec 1937); "The Brain Pirates" (Oct 1938). Published as *The Planeteers*.

Fiction
Black Star Passes, The (Fantasy, Reading, 1953, 254 pp., $3.00) ([German], 3 stories: *Der Luftpirat*, *Raumschiff Solarit*, *Der Schwarze Stern*, *UZ*: 82, 84, 85, 1957) (Ace: F-346, 1965, 223 pp., pa 40¢)
   The first 3 stories in the 'Arcot, Morey and Wade' series.
Cloak of Aesir [C] (Shasta, Chicago, 1952, 254 pp., $3.00)
   Sf, 7 stories: "Forgetfulness"; "The Escape"; *The Story of the Machine:* "The Machine," "The Invaders," "Rebellion"; *The Story of Aesir:* "Out of Night," "Cloak of Aesir."
Incredible Planet, The (Fantasy, 1949, 344 pp., $3.00, jacket–Donnell) (*Der Unglaubliche Planet* [German], Rauch, 1952; *Einsam leuchten die Sterne* & *Das Unendliche Atom*, *UG*: 115, 116, 1960) (*Avventura nell'iperspazio* & *L'atomo infinito* [Italian], *Urania*: 40, 42, 1954)
   High-class space opera. Originally written as 3 novelettes: "The Incredible Planet"; "The Interstellar Search"; "The Infinite Atom." Sequels to *The Mightiest Machine*, they were not accepted by Tremaine for *ASF*.
Invaders From the Infinite (Fantasy Press, 1961, 300 copies; Gnome, New York, 1961, 189 pp., $3.00) (Burns MacEachern, $3.50) (Ace: M-154, 1966, 192 pp., pa 45¢)

Third volume of 'Arcot, Morey and Wade' series, revised from magazine appearance. Old-fashioned melodrama with the trio helping a race of superdogs.

Islands of Space (Fantasy, 1956 [released 1957], 224 pp., $2.50) (*Kosmiche Kreuzfahrt* [German], Zimmermann, 1960; *T*: 152, 1960; *TE*: 143, 1967) (Ace: M-143, 1966, 191 pp., pa 45¢)

Second volume of the 'Arcot, Morey and Wade' series.

Mightiest Machine, The (*ASF*, sr5, Dec 1934) (Hadley, Providence [R.I.], 1947, 228 pp., illus.–R. Pailthorpe, $3.00) (*I figli di Mu* [Italian], *Urania*: 87, 1955) (*Das unglaubliche System* [German], Zimmermann, 1960; *T*: 187, 1961) (*La machine suprême* [French], Hachette Le PF 110, 1962) (Ace: F-364, 1965, 220 pp., pa 40¢)

A product of Campbell in his space-opera days, and good for its type. Extraction of energy from the Sun, and meeting with other beings. Three sequels were written but were rejected by F. O. Tremaine of *ASF*. These were published in *The Incredible Planet*.

Moon Is Hell, The [C] (Fantasy, 1950, 256 pp., $3.00; 'Golden SF Library,' 1956, $1.00) (*Martirio lunare* [Italian], *Urania*: 30, 1953) (*Gefangene des Mondes* [German], *UG*: 57, 1957) ([Japanese], Hayakawa: 3041, 1962, pa)

Gripping and factual novel of survival on the Moon while awaiting a rescue party. The U.S. edition alone contains the further story "The Elder Gods" (*Unknown*, Oct 1939, by "Don A. Stuart").

Planeteers, The [C] [pa] (Ace: G-585, 1966, 150 pp., pa 50¢; with *The Ultimate Weapon* [Campbell])

The 5 stories of the 'Penton and Blake' series.

Thing & Other Stories, The [British pa] See *Who Goes There?*

Thing From Outer Space, The [British pa] See *Who Goes There?*

Ultimate Weapon, The [pa] ("Uncertainty," *AS*, sr2, Oct 1936) (Ace: G-585, 1966, 106 pp., pa 50¢; with *The Planeteers* [Campbell])

Aliens from Mira seek to take the Solar System, but an "ultimate weapon" is designed to save Earth.

Who Goes There? [C] (Shasta, 1948, 1951, 230 pp., $3.00) (*The Thing & Other Stories*, Kemsley: CT408, 1952, 190 pp., pa 1/6) (*Le ciel est mort* [French], Denoël: PF6, 1955, pa) (*Das Ding aus einer anderen* [German], Weiss, 1958; title story and "Twilight" only, *T*: 529, 1967) (*The Thing From Outer Space*, Tandem: T75, 1966, 220 pp., 3/6)

Sf, 7 stories: "Who Goes There?"; "Blindness"; "Frictional Losses"; "Dead Knowledge"; "Elimination"; "Twilight"; "Night." Weiss [German] edition: "Who Goes There?"; "Twilight"; "The Story of Aesir."

"Who Goes There?" also appeared as "The Thing From Another World" (*American SF Series* [Australian], No. 5, 1952) and as "The Thing" (Sydney *Daily Mirror*, sr5, Mar 1962). The film of this story is covered as *The Thing* (GENERAL).

Who Goes There? & Other Stories [C] [pa] (Dell: D150, 1955, 254 pp., pa 35¢)

Sf, 6 stories: "Who Goes There?"; "Twilight"; "Night"; "Blindness"; *The Story of Aesir: I.* "Out of Night"; *II.* "Cloak of Aesir."

Nonfiction

Atomic Story, The (H. Holt, New York, 1947, vi+297 pp., $3.00) (Oxford, Toronto, $3.50) (U.S. pa, *ca.* 1948, 25¢)

History of nuclear research up through the first atomic bombs.

Collected Editorials From Analog [selected by Harry Harrison] (Doubleday, New York, 1966, 248 pp., $4.95)

31 editorials from *ASF*, Nov 1943–Dec 1965; representative of Campbell on science, medicine, politics, logic, civil rights, psi, etc.

Anthologies

Analog Anthology (Dobson, London, 1965, 799 pp., 30/-) (SF B.C. [S.J.], 1966)

26 stories from *Prologue to Analog*; *Analog 1*; *Analog 2*. One of the best book bargains in many years.

Analog 1 (Doubleday, New York, 1962, 219 pp., $3.95) (D'day, Toronto, $4.75) (D'day SF B.C., 1963, $1.20) (Paperback: 52-293, 1964, 160 pp., pa 50¢) (in *Analog Anthology*) (Panther: 2256, 1967, 169 pp., pa 3/6)

Sf, 8 stories and compiler's introduction: "Monument," Lloyd Biggle Jr.; "The Plague," Teddy Keller; "Remember the Alamo!" T. R. Fehrenbach; "The Hunch," Christopher Anvil; "Barnacle Bull," Winston P. Sanders; "Join Our Gang?" Sterling E. Lanier; "Sleight of Wit," G. R. Dickson; "Prologue to an Analogue," Leigh Richmond.

Analog 2 (Doubleday, 1964, 275 pp., $4.50) (D'day, Toronto, $5.00) (D'day SF B.C., 1964, $1.20) (Paperback: 52-509, 1965, 207 pp., pa 50¢) (in *Analog Anthology*) (Panther: 2254, 1967, 218 pp., pa 3/6)

Sf, 8 stories and compiler's preface: "The Weather Man," T. L. Thomas; "Good Indian," M. Reynolds; "Blind Man's Lantern," Allen K. Lang; "Junior Achievement," Wm. Lee; "Novice," J. H. Schmitz; "Ethical Quotient," J. T. Phillifent; "Philosopher's Stone," C. Anvil; "The Circuit Riders," R. C. FitzPatrick.

Analog 3 (Doubleday, 1965, 269 pp., $4.50) (Dobson, 1966, 296 pp., 21/-) (Panther: 025952, 1968, 219 pp., pa 5/-)

Sf, 8 stories with compiler's introduction: "Hilifter," G. R. Dickson; "Not in the Literature," C. Anvil; "Sonny," Rick Raphael; "The Trouble With Telstar," John Berryman; "New Folks' Home," C. D. Simak; "Industrial Revolution," Winston P. Sanders; "A World by the Tale," Seaton McKettrig; "Thin Edge," Jonathan B. MacKenzie.

Analog 4 (Doubleday, 1966, 224 pp., $4.50) (Dobson, 1968, 224 pp., 25/-)

Sf, 7 stories and compiler's introduction: "Subjectivity," Norman Spinrad; "The Permanent Implosion," Dean McLaughlin; "Sunjammer," P. Anderson; "A Day in the Life of Kelvin Throop," R. A. J. Phillips; "Genus Traitor," M. Reynolds; "A Case of Identity," R. Garrett; "The Mary Celeste Move," F. Herbert.

Analog 5 (Doubleday, 1967, 242 pp., $4.95) (Dobson, 1968, 242 pp., 25/-)

Sf, 9 stories and compiler's introduction: "Mission 'Red Clash'," Joe Poyer; "Coincidence Day," J. Brunner; "Computers Don't Argue," G. R. Dickson; "Balanced Ecology," J. H. Schmitz; "The Adventure of the Extraterrestrial," M. Reynolds; "Fighting Division," R. Garrett; "Overproof," Jonathan B. MacKenzie; "Countercommandment," Patrick Meadows; "Say It With Flowers," W. P. Sanders.

Analog 6 (Doubleday, 1968, 313 pp., $4.95)

Sf, 13 stories, 1 article, and compiler's introduction: "Prototaph," K. Laumer; "Bookworm, Run!" Vernor Vinge; "The Easy Way Out," L. Correy; "Giant Meteor Impact" (article), J. E. Enever; "Early Warning," R. S. Scott; "Call Him Lord," G. R. Dickson; "CWACC Strikes Again," H. Dempsey; "Stranglehold," C. Anvil; "The Message," P. Anthony & F. Hall; "Light of Other Days," B. Shaw; "Something to Say," J. Berryman; "Letter From a Higher Critic," S. Robb; "Not a Prison Make," J. P. Martino; "10.01 A.M.," A. B. Malec.

Astounding Science Fiction Anthology, The (Simon & Schuster, New York, 1952, 585 pp., $3.95) (D'day SF B.C., 1953, $1.90) (*The First Astounding Science Fiction Anthology*, Grayson, London, 1954, 240 pp., 9/6—7 stories marked *1*) (*The Second Astounding Science Fiction Anthology*, Grayson, 1954, 224 pp., 9/6—7 stories and 1 article marked *2*) (Berkley: G-41, 1956, 188 pp., pa 35¢; F-875, 1964, 192 pp., pa 50¢; X1490, 1967, pa 60¢—8 stories marked *p1*) (*Astounding Tales of Space and Time*, Berkley: G-47, 1957, 189 pp., pa 35¢; F-951, 1964, 190 pp., pa 50¢—7 stories marked *p2*) (*The First Astounding Science Fiction Anthology*, FSB: 1166, 1964, 320 pp., pa 5/-—11 stories marked *p3*) (*The Second Astounding Science Fiction Anthology*, FSB: 1211, 1965, 320 pp., pa 5/-—12 stories marked *p4*)

Sf, 22 stories and 1 article in Simon & Schuster edition (other editions as noted): "Blowups Happen" (*1,p3*), R. A. Heinlein; "Hindsight" (*p2,p3*), Jack Williamson; "Vault of the Beast" (*2,p1,p3*), A. E. van Vogt; "The Exalted" (*p3*), L. S. de Camp; "Nightfall" (*p1,p4*), I. Asimov; "When the Bough Breaks" (*p1,p3*), L. Padgett; "Clash by Night" (*p3*), L. O'Donnell; "Invariant" (*1,p1,p3*), J. Pierce; "First Contact" (*1,p1,p3*), M. Leinster; "Meihem in ce Klasrum" (article) (*2,p3*), Dolton Edwards; "Hobbyist" (*1,p2,p3*), E. F. Russell; "E for Effort" (*2,p2,p3*), T. L. Sherred; "Child's Play" (*1,p4*), Wm. Tenn; "Thunder and Roses" (*1,p2,p4*), T. Sturgeon; "Late Night Final" (*2,p2,p4*), E. F. Russell; "Cold War" (*2,p1,p4*), K. Neville; "Eternity Lost" (*p1,p4*), C. D. Simak;

"The Witches of Karres" (*1,p4*), J. H. Schmitz; "Over the Top" (*p1,p4*), L. del Rey; "Meteor" (*p4*), W. T. Powers; "Last Enemy" (*p4*), H. B. Piper; "Historical Note" (*2,p2,p4*), M. Leinster; "Protected Species" (*2,p4*), H. B. Fyfe.

Astounding Tales of Space and Time [pa] See *Astounding Science Fiction Anthology, The*

First Astounding Science Fiction Anthology, The See *Astounding Science Fiction Anthology, The*

Prologue to Analog (Doubleday, 1962, 308 pp., $3.95) (D'day SF B.C., $1.20) (in *Analog Anthology*) (Panther: 2255, 1967, 236 pp., pa 5/-)

Sf, 10 stories (selected from 1950-60) and compiler's introduction: "Belief," I. Asimov; "Pandora's Planet," Christopher Anvil; "Sound Decision," R. Garrett & R. Silverberg; "Omnilingual," H. B. Piper; "Triggerman," J. F. Bone; "A Filbert Is a Nut," Rick Raphael; "Business as Usual, During Alterations," Ralph Williams; "Pushbutton War," Joseph P. Martino; "We Didn't Do Anything Wrong, Hardly," Roger Kuykendall; "Minor Ingredient," E. F. Russell.

Second Astounding Science Fiction Anthology, The See *Astounding Science Fiction Anthology, The*

CAMPBELL, REGINALD (JOHN)

(1867–1 Mar 1956) British religious figure. He entered the Congregational ministry in 1895 and was ordained into the Church of England in 1916. He served as Vicar and Chancellor in Christchurch, Westminster, and finally Chichester, and was Canon Emeritus of Chichester after 1946. He had many publications, mainly of a religious nature.

Fiction

Abominable Twilight, The (Cassell, London, 1948, 232 pp., 8/6)
A woman with a split personality, with one side predominantly in a twilight world.

Death by Apparition (Cassell, 1949, 249 pp., 8/6)
Weird—a man being haunted by his own ghost.

CANNAN, GILBERT

Fiction

Windmills, A Book of Fables [C] (M. Secker, London, 1915, 201 pp., 5/-)
4 fantasy satires: "Samways Island"; "Ultimus"; "Gynecologia"; "Out of Work." Events about an imaginary nation 'Fatland'; not listed in the Bleiler *Checklist*.

CANNING, JOHN (1920–)

Nonfiction

50 Great Ghost Stories (Odhams, London, 1966, 495 pp., jacket & illus.–'Eisner,' 25/-) (Taplinger, New York, 1967, 496 pp., illus., $5.95)
50 stories, with Editor's Note (1¼ pp.): "Ghosts of Ancient Egypt," Frank Usher; "Chased by a Prehistoric Horseman," J. Wentworth Day; "Hauntings Royal," "The Phantoms of Littlecote," F. Usher; "Phantom Lovers," Vida Derry; "The White Lady of Berlin," Michael & Mollie Hardwick; "School for Ghosts," "Vengeful Ghosts," Vida Derry; "Pearlin Jean," M. & M. Hardwick; "Child Ghosts," Vida Derry; "The Club of Dead Men," J. W. Day; "A Piece of Black Velvet," M. & M. Hardwick; "The Ghost in Two Halves," "The Ghosts of Nance," "The Haunting of Itchell's Manor," Ronald Seth; "The Brown Lady of Raynham," F. Usher; "The Return of Richard Tarwell," R. Seth; "Ghosts of Old France," F. Usher; "The Spirit of Sergeant Davies," M. & M. Hardwick; "The Haunting at Hinto Ampner," F. Usher; "The Drunk Who Lost His Way," "Radiant Boys," R. Seth; "The Ghost of Garpsdal," M. & M. Hardwick; "Mischief Among the Dead," F. Usher; "The Whiskered Sailor of Portsmouth," M. & M. Hardwick; "The Reverend John Jones and the Ghostly Horseman," " 'Steer Nor'West,' " R. Seth; "The Haunted House at Hydesville," M. & M. Hardwick; "The Guardian Ghost," R. Seth; "Charles Kean's Ghost Story: 'Nurse Black,' " "Ghosts of the Mutiny," "The Artists' Ghost Story," M. & M. Hardwick; "Phantoms of the East," Vida Derry; "The Fur-Trader's Corpse and the Gold-Miners' Vengeance," F. Usher; "The Coach Calls for George Mace," R. Seth; "Shades of Murder," F. Usher; "Black Shuck–the Dog of Death,"

J. W. Day; "The Strange Haunting at Ballechin," F. Usher; "The Amherst Mystery," M. & M. Hardwick; "Glamis, the Haunted Castle," Tony Parker; "The Horror at No. 56 Berkeley Square," R. Seth; "The Bird of Lincoln's Inn," T. Parker; "The Ghosts of Versailles," "A Bargain With a Ghost," F. Usher; "Ghostly Cavalry Charge and the Spectres of Crecy," J. W. Day; "The Mystery of Borley," F. Usher; "The Ghostly Trapper of Labrador," J. W. Day; "The Sceptic's Tale," R. Miller; "Brighton Ghost," F. Usher.

CANTOR, HAL

Anthology

Ghosts and Things [pa] (Berkley: F666, 1962, 160 pp., pa 50¢)
Weird, 11 stories: "The Romance of Certain Old Clothes," Henry James; "Caterpillars," E. F. Benson; "Markheim," R. L. Stevenson; "The Ghost Ship," R. Middleton; "The Novel of the White Powder," A. Machen; "The Night-Doings at 'Deadman's,' " A. Bierce; "Running Wolf," A. Blackwood; "The Music on the Hill," Saki; "Phantas," O. Onions; "The House," A. Maurois; "The Lovely House," Shirley Jackson.

CANTRIL, HADLEY

Nonfiction

Invasion From Mars, The (Princeton Univ. Press, 1940, 228 pp., $2.50) (Oxford Univ., 1940, 15/6) (Harper: TB1282, 1966, vxi+ 224 pp., pa $1.95)
A study of the psychology of panic as evidenced during the Orson Welles broadcast in 1938 of H. G. Wells' *War of the Worlds*; includes complete script of the broadcast. The 1966 pa ed. has a new preface.

CAPEK, KAREL (9 Jan 1890–25 Dec 1938)

Czech author. He studied philosophy and received his doctorate in Prague in 1915. After the independence of Czechoslovakia he allied himself to the theatrical world; with his brother Joseph he managed a theatre. His first books were collaborations with his brother, the pair being noted for their verse play *The Insects* (1920). About the same time Karel, alone, achieved international success with his drama *R.U.R.*, which first opened in Prague 26 Jan 1921; from this comes the word "robot." A further collaboration with his brother was the fantasy play *Adam the Creator*, which was first produced in 1927.

Capek is remembered as one of the European authors who wrote about the evils of "scientific barbarism" which could be seen in the rise of Nazism and Fascism. Sam Moskowitz's profile of Capek was published in *Fantastic*, July 1960 (*Science-Fantasy*, Apr 1961) and also in *Explorers of the Infinite* (World, 1963). His widow was Olga Scheinpflugova, a leading actress of the Prague National Theatre; she died on 13 Apr 1968, about 65 years of age.

Fiction

Absolute at Large, The (Macmillan, New York, 1927, 293 pp., $2.50) (Macmillan, London, 1927, 7/6; 1930, 3/6) (Allen Unwin, London, 1944, 168 pp., 7/6) (*La fabrique d'absolu* [French], Nagel, 1945)
Atomic devices are sold to anyone who will pay, bringing overproduction and war with the world destroying itself. (Abridged in *Century of Great Short SF Novels* [Knight], 1965.)

Fairy Tales, With One Extra as a Makeweight by Joseph Capek [C] (H. Holt, New York, 1933, 288 pp., illus.–J. Capek, $1.00) (Allen Unwin, London, 1934, 249 pp., 5/-)
Fantasy, 10 stories of which 4th is by Joseph Capek: "A Long Tale About a Cat"; "The Dogs' Tale"; "The Birds' Tale; "The First Bandits' Tale"; "The Water-Sprites' Tale"; "The Second Bandits' Tale"; "The Tramps' Tale"; "The Long Police Tale"; "The Postmen's Tale"; "A Long Tale for Doctors."

Krakatit: An Atomic Fantasy [Trans.–L. Hyde] (Macmillan, New York, 1925, 408 pp., $2.50) (Bles, London, 1925, 416 pp., 7/6) (*Krakatit* [Swedish], Geber, 1926) (Allen Unwin, London, 1948, 294 pp., 9/6) (Arts Inc., New York, 1951, 294 pp., $2.50) (*Krakatit* [German], A. Cassirer, 1952; Weiss, 1959)
Though dated, it is generally recommended. A queer inventor comes up with a marvelous explosive, and blows up everything. The story has been filmed.

Makropoulos Secret, The (Luce, Boston, 1925, 165 pp., $2.50)

A woman who has lived 300 years and others seek an elixir for longer life, but she convinces them that immortality is a frightful vacuum. It was originally written as a play and produced in 1923.
Meteor (G. Allen, London, 1935, 256 pp., 7/6) (Putnam, New York, 1935, 256 pp., $2.00) (*Meteor* [Swedish], Geber, 1935) (in *Three Novels* [Capek], 1948)

Considered one of this author's best fantasies.
R.U.R. A Fantastic Melodrama (*R.U.R.* [German], ? , 1922) (Doubleday 'Theatre Guild Version,' New York, 1923, 187 pp.) (*R.U.R.* [French], Cahiers dramatiques: 21, 1 Oct 1924; in *Quatre pas dans l'etrange* [Gallet], 1961) (*R.U.R.* [Swedish], Radiorjanits Teaterbibliotek, 1934) (in *Science Fiction Thinking Machines* [Conklin], 1954) (in *Treasury of SF Classics* [Kuebler], 1954) (*R.U.R. & The Insects* [with J. Capek], Oxford: PB34, 1961, 177 pp., pa 9/6)

"Rossum's Universal Robots"—artificially produced workers become emotionally advanced and cast off the rule of man, and then ruthlessly exterminate the human race. The play was first produced in Prague 26 Jan 1921, and opened in New York and London 9 Oct 1922. It is one of the most frequently anthologised plays ever written. It introduced the word "robot" into the English language. *Film:* Italian, 1958.
Tales From Two Pockets [C] [Trans.– P. Selver] (Faber, London, 1932, 287 pp., 7/6; 1935, 3/6) (Macmillan, New York, 1943, 215 pp.) (G. Allen, 1943, 215 pp., 7/6) ([Japanese], Shisei-dô, 1960)

26 stories: "Attempt at Murder"; "The Clairvoyant"; "Confessional"; "The Coupon"; "Disappearance of an Actor"; "Disappearance of Mr. Hirsch"; "Discharged"; "Epic Exploit of Jaraj Cup"; "Farm Murder"; "The Fortune-Teller"; "Giddiness"; "Misadventures of a Matrimonial Swindler"; "Mr. Havlena's Verdict"; "Musical Conductor's Story"; "The Needle"; "Oplatka's End"; "Ordinary Murder"; "Proof Positive"; "Secrets of Handwriting"; "Selvin Case"; "Stamp Collection"; "Stolen Murder"; "Stolen Papers—139/vii Sect. C"; "Strange Experiences of Mr. Janik"; "There Was Something Shady About the Man"; "Troubles of a Carpet Fancier."
Three Novels [C] [Trans.–M. R. Weatherall] (Allen Unwin, 1948, 469 pp., 12/6) (Wyn, New York, 1949, 469 pp., $3.00)

3 novels: *Hordubal* (G. Allen, 1934); *Meteor*; *The Ordinary Life* (G. Allen, 1936).
War With the Newts (*Valka S. Mloky*, Dr. Borovny, Prague, 1936) (*Oorlog met de salamanders* [Dutch], Van Holkema en Warendorf, Amsterdam, 1937) ([Trans.–M. & R. Weatherall], Putnam, New York, 1939, 348 pp., $3.00) (Nelson, Toronto) (*Salamanderkriget* [Swedish], Geber, 1936) ([Spanish], Revista de Occidente, 1945) ([Japanese], Sekai Bunka-sha, 1953; San'ichi Shobô, 1956) (*Die Krieg mit den Molchen* [German], V. Aufbau, 1954; Weiss, 1967) (Bantam: A1292, 1955, 236 pp., pa 35¢; FC46, 1963, pa 50¢; QC250, 1965, pa $1.25) (*La guerre des Salamandres* [French], Les Editeurs français réunis, 1960) (Berkley: S1404, 1967, 241 pp., pa 75¢)

Intelligent giant newts become "civilized"; a noted work.

CAPES, BERNARD
Fiction [Incomplete—other titles in Bleiler *Checklist*]
At a Winter's Fire [C] (Doubleday, New York, 1899, 303 pp.) (Pearson, London, 1899, 303 pp., 6/-)

Fantasy, 11 stories, some of which were originally published in *Cornhill Magazine*, *Macmillan's*, *Lippincott's* and *Pearson's Magazine*: "The Moon Stricken"; "Jack and Jill"; "The Vanishing House"; "Dark Dignum"; "William Tyrwhitt's 'Copy' "; "A Lazy Romance"; "Black Venn"; "An Eddy on the Floor"; "Dinah's Mammoth"; "The Black Reaper"; "A Voice From the Pit."
From Door to Door [C] (Stokes, New York, 1900, 318 pp.)

Mixed, 17 stories: *Fantasies:* "The Sword of Corporal Lacoste"; "An Ugly Customer"; "The Cursing-Bell (A Dream Story)"; "A Coward"; "The Foot of Time"; "The Meek Shall Inherit the Earth." *Romances:* "The Chapter's Doom"; "Jemmy Jessama, the Runner." *Whimsies:* "The Scatterling and the Aurelian"; "The Writer and the Prince"; "Solomon's Seal." *Levities:* "A True Prin-

cess"; "The Widow's Clock"; "Above Proof"; "Doña Pollonia's Corset"; "The Lady-Killer"; "A Doll and a Moral."
Plots [C] (Methuen, London, 1902, 308 pp., 6/-)

Mixed, assorted themes, with fantasies: "The Accursed Cordonnier"; "The Devil's Fantasia"; "The Green Bottle"; "Plots."

CAPLIN, ALFRED G(ERALD) (1909–) See CAPP, AL

CAPON, (HARRY) PAUL (18 Dec 1912–) British author and film director. He was born at Kenton Hall, Suffolk, and educated at St. George's School, Harpenden. He was Technical Director of the Soviet Film Agency 1941-44, Supervising Editor for Walt Disney Production Ltd. 1955-57, and is now head of the Film Division, Independent Television News. He first wrote detective stories but branched into the sf field in the 1950's; he has published over 30 novels.
Fiction
Down to Earth (Heinemann, London, 1954, 196 pp., 12/-) (Digit: R842, 1964, 158 pp., pa 2/6)

Last of trilogy which begins with *The Other Side of the Sun*. Gangster-type intrigue.
Flight of Time (Heinemann, 1960, 166 pp., illus.–Marina Hoffer, 12/6)

Juvenile.
Into the Tenth Millennium (Heinemann, 1956, 196 pp., 12/-; 1958, 280 pp., 5/-) (Brown-Watson: R895, 1965, 224 pp., pa 3/6)

Time-travel for 8,000 years by suspended animation; an ideal future world with everyone happy. Not convincing.
Lost: a Moon See *Phobos, the Robot Planet*
Other Half of the Planet, The (Heinemann, 1952, 255 pp., 12/6; 1954, 6/-)

Second of trilogy which begins with *The Other Side of the Sun*. Adventure on Antigeos.
Other Side of the Sun, The (Heinemann, 1950, 321 pp., 10/6) (*Naar de tegenpool der aarde* [Dutch], 's-Gravenhage, 1954)

Journey to Antigeos, a planet directly opposite Earth on the other side of the Sun, and having the ideal state. It was a serial on BBC radio. First of a trilogy; sequels are *The Other Half of the Planet* and *Down to Earth*.
Phobos, the Robot Planet (Heinemann, 1955, 178 pp., 10/6) (*Lost: a Moon*, Bobbs-Merrill, Indianapolis, 1956, 222 pp., $2.75) (*Månen Som Kom Bort* [Swedish], Wennerberg: R2, 1957) (Digit: R887, 1965, 160 pp., pa 2/6)

Juvenile—Phobos is a giant computer whose curiosity causes him to kidnap some people, using a flying saucer.
Wonderbolt, The (Ward Lock, London, 1955, 206 pp., 9/6)

Juvenile—cloak-and-dagger work to secure a dangerous meteorite.
World at Bay, The (Heinemann, 1953, 199 pp., 12/-) (Winston, Philadelphia, 1954, 210 pp., $2.00) ([Japanese], GingaShobo 'Adv. in SF': 12, 1956) (*Schwarzen Stern Nero* [German], *UG*: 122, 1960) ([French] ?) (Digit: R863, 1964, 158 pp., pa 2/6)

Juvenile—invasion by villainous aliens in miniature space stations. The Winston edition is one of the Adventures in SF series.

CAPOTE, TRUMAN (30 Sep 1924–) U.S. author. He has earned his living by dancing on a river cruise, painting on glass, working as office boy for the *New Yorker*, and writing speeches. He won an O. Henry Prize at 19. His collection *A Tree of Night* (1950) contains 8 nebulous and haunting stories of which two were O. Henry Award winners. Recently reprinted was his "Master Misery" (1949; *F&SF*, July 1962).
Fiction
Other Voices, Other Rooms (Random, New York, 1948, 231 pp., $2.75) (Random, Toronto, $3.25) (Heinemann, London, 1948, 192 pp., 7/6) (Ace [British], pa) (Penguin: 2135, 1964, 173 pp., pa 3/6)

Strange and eerie psychological novel.
Tree of Night, A [C] (Random, New York, 1949, 209 pp., $2.75) (Random, Toronto, $3.25) (Heinemann, 1950, 209 pp., 8/6)

CAPP, AL (1909–) The better-known pseudonym of U.S. cartoonist Alfred Gerald Caplin. His most famous strip is *Li'l Abner*, which has been syndicated world-wide. Some strips have been published by Ballantine, and a genuine sf adventure "The Time Capsule" appeared in *Satellite* (Aug 1957). Other works include *The Life and Times of the Shmoo* (1948, pa), *Fearless Fosdick* (1956), and *Al Capp's Bald Iggle* (1956, pa).

CAPPS, CARROLL M. (1917?–15 Jan 1971) U.S. science-fiction author, better known under his pseudonym "C. C. MacApp." He became quite prominent with his first appearance, "A Pride of Islands" (*If*, n'te, May 1960); most of his stories appeared in *If* or *Galaxy*. A short novel of interest is "Prisoners of the Sky" (*If*, Feb 1966).
Series [as C. C. MacApp]
Gree. Despotic alien invaders. In *If*: "Gree's Commandos" (Feb 1965); "Gree's Hellcats" (Apr 1965); "No Friend of Gree" (June 1956); "Gree's Damned Ones" (Sep 1965); "Enemies of Gree" (Sep 1966); "The Sign of Gree" (Nov 1966); "A Beachhead for Gree" (Feb 1967). In *Worlds of Tomorrow*: "Like Any World of Gree" (Mar 1966). A number of these have been published in Italian in *Urania*.
Fiction [as C. C. MacApp]
Omha Abides [pa] (Paperback: 52-649, 1968, 160 pp., pa 50¢)
A computer and Amerind-like Terrans work to overthrow alien invaders. A novelization of stories from *Worlds of Tomorrow*: "Under the Gaddyl" (Apr 1964); "Trees Like Torches" (May 1966).

CARDIFF, IRA D.
Nonfiction
Million Years of Progress, A (Pageant, New York, 2nd ed. 1955, 146 pp., $2.50)
An outline of some highlights, scientific and social, in the history of Man leading to the advancement of civilization.

CARLSON, ESTHER (ELIZABETH) (3 Dec 1920–) U.S. author and secretary. She has worked as a secretary, in courts 1940-45, and in Belmont public schools since 1945. Her novel *Moon Over the Back Fence* (Doubleday, 1947) has fantasy overtones, being about a little girl and her imaginary companion, "Uncle George." She has had a fantasy series in *F&SF*.
Series
Abercrombie, Dr. Aesop. All in *F&SF*: "Heads You Win" (Apr 1953); "Night Life" (Dec 1953); "Somewhere East of Rudyard" (Feb 1954).

CARLTON, MARY SHAFFER
Fiction
Golden Phoenix, The (Vantage, New York, 1958, 69 pp., $2.50)
Story of a visit to another planet; rather Utopian.

CARMER, CARL
Fiction
Screaming Ghost & Other Stories, The [C] (Knopf, New York, 1956, 146 pp., $3.00)
No further information.

CARNELL, EDWARD JOHN [TED] (8 Apr 1912–23 Mar 1972) British editor, anthologist, and book agent. He was a prewar sf fan and a founding member of the firm later known as H. M. Johnson (sf specialist) in Liverpool. He was Publicity Director and Editor for the British Interplanetary Society. In 1940 he joined the Royal Artillery as a gunner, but transferred to combined operations in 1941, and spent four years as an observer with Naval Bombardment on Mediterranean commando raids and major invasions.

In 1946 he began *New Worlds*, one of the first British postwar sf magazines, but its publisher, Pendulum Publications, failed after only three issues. Carnell also edited some paperback items for this firm. In 1949, with the backing of British fandom, he formed Nova Publications to again produce *New Worlds*. He edited *New Worlds*, *Science-Fantasy* and *Science Fiction Adventures* (the last began as a reprint of U.S. material and changed to original) for

Nova for some time. *SF Adventures* ceased publication early in 1963, and through lack of sales the other two ceased early in 1964, only to be taken over by a different publisher and editors. However, Carnell continued to the end of his life as editor of the *New Writings in SF* anthology series which has appeared quarterly from Dobson with a paper edition following from Corgi.

He was a representative of certain U.S. sf book publishers; was SF Editor for the Museum Press when this firm had a 'Science Fiction Club'; and was a member of the Adjudicating Panel of the International Fantasy Award. He was a member of the Selection Committee of the (British) Science Fiction Book Club since its inception (Dr. J. G. Porter and Kingsley Amis were his last co-selectors). Always interested in fan affairs, Carnell attended the 7th and 14th World SF Conventions at Cincinnati (1949) and New York (1956), respectively; he was Chairman of the 15th World Convention in London in 1957.
Anthologies
Best From New Worlds Science Fiction, The [pa] (Boardman: 163, 1955, 190 pp., pa 2/-)
Sf, 8 stories, with Introduction by J. Wyndham (J. B. Harris) and Foreword by E. J. Carnell: "Jetsam," A. B. Chandler; "Crossfire," J. White; "Ship From the Stars," Peter Hawkins; "Robots Don't Bleed," J. W. Groves; "The Hard Way," Alan Barclay; "The Broken Record," J. T. McIntosh; "Rockets Aren't Human," E. C. Tubb; "Unknown Quantity," Peter Phillips.
Gateway to the Stars (Museum, London, 1955, 192 pp., 9/6)
Sf, 9 stories: "Stitch in Time," J. T. McIntosh; "Only an Echo," A. Barclay; "Conspiracy," J. Christopher; "Stranger From Space," Gene Lees; "Never on Mars," J. Wyndham; "Assisted Passage," J. White; "Circus," P. Hawkins; "Unfortunate Purchase," E. C. Tubb; "Operation Exodus," Lan Wright.
Gateway to Tomorrow (Museum, 1954, 192 pp., 9/6) (Panther: 1460, 1963, 160 pp., pa 2/6)
Sf, 10 stories: "Dumb Martian," J. Wyndham; "Hide and Seek," A. C. Clarke; "Home Is the Hero," E. C. Tubb; "Lost Memory," Peter Phillips; "Of Those Who Came," George Longdon; "The Bliss of Solitude," J. T. McIntosh; "Finishing Touch," A. B. Chandler; "The Drop," J. Christopher; "Emergency Working," E. R. James; "Life Cycle," Peter Hawkins.
Jinn and Jitters [pa] (Pendulum, 1946, 116 pp., pa 2/-)
Fantasy, 5 stories: "Jinn and Jitters," H. S. W. Chibbett; "See?" H. S. W. Chibbett; "McGinty's Imp," A. Devereux; "Bottled Spirit," H. S. W. Chibbett; "You Can Be a Ghost!" W. P. Cockcroft.
Lambda 1 & Other Stories [pa] (Berkley: F883, 1964, 175 pp., pa 50¢) (Penguin: 2275, 1965, 206 pp., pa 3/6) (*Die Phase des Schreckens* [German], Pabel: 277, 1967, pa [first 2 and last 2 stories of U.S. ed.])
U.S.—7 stories, all from *NW*, with Foreword: "Lambda 1," Colin Kapp; "Basis for Negotiation," Brian W. Aldiss; "Quest," Lee Harding; "All Laced Up," George Whitley; "Routine Exercise," Philip E. High; "Flux," Michael Moorcock; "The Last Salamander," John Rackham.
British—8 stories: "Lambda 1," C. Kapp; "Tee Vee Man," A. Hargreaves; "Beyond the Reach of Storms," Donald Malcolm"; "Quest," L. Harding; "All Laced Up," G. Whitley; "Routine Exercise," P. High; "Flux," M. Moorcock; "The Last Salamander," J. Rackham.
New Writings in SF 1 (D. Dobson, London, 1964, 190 pp., 16/-) (Corgi: GS7083, 1964, 190 pp., pa 3/6) (Bantam: F3245, 1966, 147 pp., pa 50¢)
5 stories and Foreword: "Key to Chaos" (n'te), Edward Mackin; "Two's Company," John Rankine; "Man on Bridge," B. W. Aldiss; "Haggard Honeymoon," Joseph Green & James Webbert; "The Sea's Furthest End," Damien Broderick.
New Writings in SF 2 (D. Dobson, 1964, 191 pp., 16/-) (Corgi: GS7125, 1965, 191 pp., pa 3/6) (Bantam: F3379, 1966, 150 pp., pa 50¢)
8 stories and Foreword: "Hell-Planet" (n'te), J. Rackham; "The Night-Flame," Colin Kapp; "The Creators," Joseph Green; "Rogue Leonardo," G. L. Lack; "Maiden Voyage," John Rankine; "Odd Boy Out," Dennis Etchison; "The Eternal Machines," Wm. Spencer; "A Round Billiard Table," Steve Hall.

New Writings in SF 3 (D. Dobson, 1965, 188 pp., 16/-) (Corgi: GS7199, 1965, 189 pp., pa 3/6) (Bantam: F3380, 1967, 168 pp., pa 50¢)

8 stories and Foreword: "The Subways of Tazoo" (n'te), Colin Kapp; "The Fiend" (*Playboy*, 1964), Frederik Pohl; "Manipulation," John Kingston; "Testament," John Baxter; "Night Watch," James Inglis; "Boulter's Canaries," Keith Roberts; "Emreth," Dan Morgan; "Spacemaster," James H. Schmitz.

New Writings in SF 4 (D. Dobson, 1965, 186 pp., 16/-) (Corgi: GS7262, 1965, 186 pp., pa 3/6) (Bantam: F3763, 1968, 154 pp., pa 50¢)

7 stories and Foreword: "High Eight" (n'te), David Stringer; "Star Light," Isaac Asimov; "Hunger Over Sweet Waters," Colin Kapp; "The Country of the Strong," Dennis Etchison; "Parking Problem," Dan Morgan; "Sub-Lim," Keith Roberts; "Bennie the Faust," Wm. Tenn.

New Writings in SF 5 (Dobson, 1965, 190 pp., 16/-) (Corgi: GS7329, 1966, 190 pp., pa 3/6)

7 stories and Foreword: "Potential" (n'te), Donald Malcolm; "The Liberators," Lee Harding; "Takeover Bid," John Baxter; "Acclimatization," David Stringer; "The Expanding Man," R. W. Mackelworth; "Treasure Hunt," Joseph Green; "Sunout," Eric C. Williams.

New Writings in SF 6 (Dobson, 1965, 190 pp., 16/-) (Corgi: GS7383, 1966, 190 pp., pa 3/6)

7 stories and Foreword: "The Inner Wheel" (n'te), Keith Roberts; "Horizontal Man," Wm. Spencer; "The Day Before Never," Robert Presslie; "The Hands," John Baxter; "The Seekers," E. C. Tubb; "Atrophy," Ernest Hill; "Advantage," John Rackham.

New Writings in SF 7 (Dobson, 1966, 190 pp., 16/-) (Corgi: GS7469, 1966, 190 pp., pa 3/6)

7 stories and Foreword: "Invader" [n'te in Sector General series], James White; "The Man Who Missed the Ferry," Douglas R. Mason; "The Night of the Seventh Finger," Robert Presslie; "Six Cubed Plus One," John Rankine; "Coco-Talk," Wm. F. Temple; "A Touch of Immortality," R. W. Mackelworth; "Man-scarer," Keith Roberts.

New Writings in SF 8 (Dobson, 1966, 188 pp., 16/-) (Corgi: GS7564, 1966, 188 pp., pa 3/6)

6 stories and Foreword: "The Pen and the Dark," Colin Kapp; "Spacemen Live Forever," Gerald W. Page; "The Final Solution," R. W. Mackelworth; "Computer's Mate," John Rackham; "Tryst," John Baxter; "Synth," Keith Roberts.

New Writings in SF 9 (Dobson, 1966, 187 pp., 16/-) (Corgi: GS7650, 1967, 187 pp., pa 3/6)

7 stories and Foreword: "Poseidon Project," J. Rackham; "Folly To Be Wise," Douglas R. Mason; "Gifts of the Gods," Arthur Sellings; "The Long Memory," Wm. Spencer; "Guardian Angel," Gerald W. Page; "Second Genesis," Eric F. Russell; "Defense Mechanism," Vincent King.

New Writings in SF 10 (Dobson, 1967, 189 pp., 16/-) (Corgi: GS7722, 1967, 189 pp., pa 3/6)

7 stories and Foreword: "The Imagination Trap," Colin Kapp; "Apple," John Baxter; "Robot's Dozen," G. L. Lack; "Birth of a Butterfly," Joseph L. Green; "The Affluence of Edwin Lollard," T. M. Disch; "A Taste for Dostoevsky," B. W. Aldiss; "Image of Destruction," John Rankine.

New Writings in SF 11 (Corgi: GS7803, 1967 [actually 1968], 190 pp., pa 3/6) (Dobson, 1968, 190 pp., 16/-)

9 stories and Foreword: "The Wall to End the World," Vincent King; "Catharsis," John Rackham; "Shock Treatment," Lee Harding; "Bright Are the Stars That Shine, Dark Is the Sky," Dennis Etchison; "There Was This Fella . . .," Douglas R. Mason; "For What Purpose?" W. T. Webb; "Flight of a Plastic Bee," John Rankine; "Dead to the World," H. A. Hargreaves; "The Helmet of Hades," Jack Wodhams.

New Writings in SF 12 (Corgi: 07878, 1968, 188 pp., pa 3/6) (Dobson, 1968, 188 pp., 18/-)

6 stories and Foreword: "Vertigo," James White; "Visions of Monad," M. John Harrison; "Worm in the Bud," John Rankine; "They Shall Reap," David Rome; "The Last Time Around," Arthur Sellings; "The Cloudbuilders," Colin Kapp.

New Writings in SF 13 (Corgi: 08037, 1968, 190 pp., pa 3/6) (Dobson, 1968, 190 pp., 18/-)

8 stories and Foreword: "The Divided House," J. Rackham; "Public Service," S. J. Bounds; "The Ferryman on the River," David Kyle; "Testament," Vincent King; "The Macbeth Expiation," M. John Harrison; "Representative," David Rome; "The Beach," John Baxter; "The City, Dying," Eddy C. Bertin.

No Place Like Earth (Boardman, London, 1952, 255 pp., 9/6) (SF B.C.[S.J.], 1954, 6/-) (Boardman: 140, 1954, 192 pp., pa 2/-) (Panther: 1252, 1961, 190 pp., pa 2/6) (*Roboter bluten nicht . . .* [German], *UZ*: 449, 1965)

Sf, 10 stories [1954 pa has 7 stories marked †; 1961 pa is complete; German has 5 stories marked *]: "Time to Rest" & "No Place Like Earth" [as one story]†, J. Beynon; "Breaking Strain"†, A. C. Clarke; "Survival"†*, J. Wyndham; "The Two Shadows"†, W. F. Temple; "Unknown Quantity," P. Phillips; "Balance"†, J. Christopher; "Robots Don't Bleed"*, J. W. Groves; "Castaway"*, George Whitley; "Machine Made"†*, J. T. M'Intosh; "Chemical Plant"†*, I. Williamson.

Weird Shadows From Beyond [pa] (Corgi: GS7208, 1965, 157 pp., pa 3/6)

10 stories (6 from *Science-Fantasy*) with compiler's Introduction: "Danse Macabre," Mervyn Peake; "Blood Offering," John Kippax; "Same Time, Same Place," M. Peake; "Master of Chaos," Michael Moorcock; "Wednesday's Child," Wm. Tenn; "Dial 'O' for Operator," Robert Presslie; "The Flowers of the Forest," B. W. Aldiss; "Fresh Guy," E. C. Tubb; "The Garden of Paris," Eric Williams; "The Graveyard Reader," T. Sturgeon.

CARPENTER, ELMER J.
Fiction
Moonspin [pa] (Flagship: 00715, 1967, 159 pp., pa 60¢)

The Reds control Earth's climate and a spaceman endeavours to counteract this.

CARPENTER, (Rev.) WILLIAM BOYD Bishop of Ripon.
Fiction
Twilight Dreams [C] (Macmillan, London & New York, 1893, 225 pp., 4/6)

Fantasy, 12 stories, not in Bleiler *Checklist*: "The Ministry of the Graces"; "The Story of a Poet"; "The Land and Sea"; "The Angel of the Beautiful"; "The Seeker for the Sun"; "Old Adam"; "A Little Child Shall Lead Them"; "The Sin of the Red Angel"; "The Lost Pearl"; "Mervan's Dream"; "The Skeleton in the Cupboard"; "Dives Dreams."

CARR, CHARLES
Fiction
Colonists of Space (Ward Lock, London, 1954, 192 pp., 9/6; 1955, 6/-; #25, 1955, pa 2/-) (*I coloni dello spazio* [Italian], Cosmo: 11, 1958) (*Colonizadores del espacio* [Spanish], Nebula: 50, 1958, pa) (Digit: R617, 1962, 158 pp., pa 2/6)

Space ship exploration for a new world to colonize. Sequel is *Salamander War*.

Salamander War (Ward Lock, 1955, 190 pp., 9/6) (*Le orribile salamandre* [Italian], Urania: 123, 1956) (*La guerra de las salamandras* [Spanish], Nebula: 34, 1957, pa) (Digit: R616, 1962, 160 pp., pa 2/6)

Conflict on the nonrotating planet 'Bel' between humans and the salamanders on the hot side. Sequel to *Colonists of Space*.

CARR, J(OHN) D(ICKSON) (1906–) U.S.-British writer of detective fiction. He was born in the U.S.A. but lived in England until 1948, when he returned to the U.S. He is brother of Robert S. Carr. He first came to notice with *It Walks By Night* (1930). Recently he has been writing 4–6 novels per year under his own name and under the name "Carter Dickson"; an older pseudonym was "Carr Dickson." He has often been called the king in his field; J. B. Priestley said that Carr has "a sense of the macabre that lifts him high above the average run of detective story writers."

Besides his fiction he wrote the biography *The Life of Sir Arthur Conan Doyle* (1949), and in collaboration with Adrian Conan

Doyle (Sir Arthur's youngest son) he has written further adventures of the immortal Holmes—*The Exploits of Sherlock Holmes* (1954). Three detective novels have Scotland Yard as a background from its founding to the opening of the 20th Century: *Fire, Burn!* (set in 1829, covered below), *Scandal at High Chimneys* (set in 1865), and *The Witch of Low Tide* (Edwardian times) (Hamilton, 1961). His two weird stories in *Department of Queer Complaints* were reprinted in *F&SF*.

Fiction

Burning Court, The (H. Hamilton, London, 1937, 318 pp., 7/6; 1938, 3/6) (Harper, New York, 1937, 304 pp., $2.00) (Musson, Toronto, $2.25) (Popular, 1944, 221 pp., pa 25¢) (H. Hamilton, 1949, 208 pp., 6/-) (Guild, 1952, 192 pp., pa 2/-) (*Detective Book*, ? 1952) (*Svart Sabbat* [Swedish], Bonnier, 1953) (Bantam: 1207, 1954, 215 pp., pa 25¢; J2706, 1963, pa 40¢)

A murder mystery with inexplicable happenings, set in the present day.

Department of Queer Complaints [as Carter Dickson] [C] (Heinemann, London, 1940, 238 pp., 7/6) (Morrow, New York, 1940, 241 pp., $2.00) (Ryerson, Toronto, $2.35) (Pan: X208, 1963, 223 pp., pa 3/6)

Contents include 2 weird stories: "New Murders for Old" (*F&SF*, Jan 1957; *F&SF* [Australian], #12, 1958); "Blind Man's Hood" (*F&SF*, Jan 1955; *Best Ghost Stories* [Ridler], 1945, 1960).

Devil in Velvet, The (H. Hamilton, 1951, 352 pp., 12/6) (Harper, 1951, vii+335 pp., $3.00) (Bantam: A1009, 1952, 378 pp., pa 35¢; F2052, 1960, 312 pp., pa 50¢; S3637, 1968, pa 75¢) (Penguin: 1252, 1956, 352 pp., pa 3/6)

Time-travel detective novel in which Nicholas Fenton of the 20th Century returns to Restoration London as his own ancestor.

Fear Is the Same [as Carter Dickson] (Morrow, 1956, 284 pp., $3.50) (Bantam: A2000, 1959, 199 pp., pa 35¢) (World Distributors: HN847, 1959, 257 pp., pa 2/6)

Borderline time-travel—historical mystery set in 1795.

Fire, Burn! (H. Hamilton, 1956, 287 pp., 13/6) (Harper, 1957, 265 pp., $3.50) (Bantam: A1847, 1959, 214 pp., pa 35¢; S3638, 1968, pa 75¢) (Penguin: 1622, 1961, 269 pp., pa 3/6; C1622, 1965, pa 3/6) ([Swedish], S. Bergström, nd)

Fast-moving historical mystery in which a modern Scotland Yard superintendent is transferred to old Scotland Yard at the time of its creation.

CARR, ROBERT S(PENCER) (1909–) U.S. author, brother of John Dickson Carr. His writing career began at 15 with a sale to *Weird Tales*. When 17, his novel *The Rampant Age* became a bestseller and brought a Hollywood contract and sales to the "slick" magazines. His second novel was *The Bells of St. Ivan's*. He has worked in a biological research laboratory.

Fiction

Beyond Infinity [C] (Fantasy Press, Reading, 1951, 236 pp., $2.75) (Dell: 781, 1954, 223 pp., pa 25¢)

Sf, 4 stories: "Morning Star" (*SEP*, 6 Dec 1947); "Mutation"; "Those Men From Mars" ("Easter Eggs," *SEP*, 24 Sep 1949; *Best SF Stories 1950* [Dikty]); "Beyond Infinity."

Room Beyond, The (Appleton-Century, New York, 1948, 427 pp., $3.00)

Fantasy novel.

CARR, TERRY (GENE) (19 Feb 1937–) U.S. science fiction writer and editor, born in California. A former sf fan, he began writing in recent years and has had a number of stories in the sf magazines. After being on the staff of a literary agency he became an editor with Ace Books in 1964. He edited the Ace Specials which gained considerable critical acclaim.

Fiction

Invasion From 2500 [as Norman Edwards (pseud. with T. E. White)] [pa] (Monarch: 453, 1964, 126 pp., pa 40¢)

An invasion where the intruders can anticipate all opposition movements—time travel philosophy.

Warlord of Kor [pa] (Ace: F-177, 1963, 97 pp., pa 40¢; with *The Star Wasps*)

Expeditionary corps on a distant world interrogates alien race to learn of the past.

Anthologies

New Worlds of Fantasy [pa] (Ace: A-12, 1967, 253 pp., pa 75¢, illus.–K. Freas)

15 stories and introduction: "Divine Madness," R. Zelazny; "Break the Door of Hell," J. Brunner; "The Immortal," J. L. Borges; "Narrow Valley," R. A. Lafferty; "Comet Wine," Ray Russell; "The Other," Katherine MacLean; "A Red Heart and Blue Roses," Mildred Clingerman; "Stanley Toothbrush," Terry Carr; "The Squirrel Cage," T. M. Disch; "Come Lady Death," P. S. Beagle; "Nackles," Curt Clark; "The Lost Leonardo," J. G. Ballard; "Timothy," K. Roberts; "Basilisk," A. Davidson; "The Evil Eye," Alfred Gillespie.

Science Fiction for People Who Hate Science Fiction (Doubleday, New York, 1966, 190 pp., $3.95) (Funk Wagnalls, New York, 1968, pa 95¢)

9 stories with introduction by compiler: "The Star," Arthur C. Clarke: "A Sound of Thunder," Ray Bradbury; "The Year of the Jackpot," R. A. Heinlein; "The Man With English," H. L. Gold; "In Hiding," Wilmar H. Shiras; "Not With a Bang," Damon Knight; "Love Called This Thing," Avram Davidson with Laura Goforth; "The Weapon," Fredric Brown; "What's It Like Out There?" Edmond Hamilton.

World's Best Science Fiction: 1965 [pa] See WOLLHEIM, D. A. (co-anthologist)

CARRINGTON, HEREWARD (1880–) U.S. writer noted for works on psychic phenomena, etc. Born on Jersey in the Channel Islands; after obtaining his Ph.D. he went to America in 1899. He was editor of Street & Smith's novels 1906-07, and has worked for radio. He has contributed scientific articles to various magazines, encyclopedias, etc. He is a member of the Society for Psychical Research. A work not covered below is *The Phenomena of Astral Projection* [with S. J. Muldoon] (1951). He has used the pseudonym Hubert Lavington.

Nonfiction

Case for Psychic Survival, The (Citadel, New York, 1958, 157 pp., $3.50) (McLeod, Toronto, $4.00)

Brief record of a new departure in psychic research: the use of psychological personality tests on medium Eileen Garrett.

Haunted People [with Nandor Fodor] (Dutton, New York, 1952, 225 pp., $3.50) (Signet: T3726, 1968, pa 75¢)

A notable omnibus account of all historic cases of poltergeists and allied phenomena, including many detailed histories.

Invisible World, The (Beechhurst, New York, 1949, 128 pp., $2.50) (Rider, London, 1949, 128 pp., 9/6) (Smithers, Toronto, $3.25)

Famous book on psychic phenomena, dealing with ghosts and giving possible explanations.

Mysterious Psychic Phenomena (Christopher, New York, 1955, $3.00)

Written only for the absolute novice; contains little of interest except advice on "How to go to a Medium."

Psychic Oddities (Rider, London, 1952, 183 pp., 16/-)

Subtitled "Fantastic and bizarre events in the life of a psychical observer."

Anthology

Week-End Book of Ghost Stories (Ives Washburn, New York, 1953, 280 pp., $3.50)

20 stories: "Up the Garret Stairs," J. deLavigne; "The Open Window," Saki; "The Ghost-Extinguisher," G. Burgess; "The Bottle Party," J. Collier; "The Escape," H. Carrington; "The Shell of Sense," O. H. Dunbar; "Courage," F. Reid; "The Spiritualist's Tale," J. L. Ford; "My Own True Ghost Story," R. Kipling; "August Heat," W. F. Harvey; "The Red Lodge," H. R. Wakefield; "Couching at the Door," D. K. Broster; " 'The Monkey's Paw'," W. W. Jacobs; "The Mysterious Villa," Anon.; "Clarimonde," T. Gautier; "The Rescue at Sea," Anon.; "Let Me Go," L. A. G. Strong; "The Miracle," H. Carrington; "The Amorous Ghost," Enid Bagnold; "A Psychical Invasion," A. Blackwood.

CARRINGTON, RICHARD (10 June 1921–) Noted British scientist; Fellow of Royal Anthropological Institute, Royal Geographic Society and Zoological Society. He has written many nonfiction books in these fields, such as *A Guide to Earth History*, *East From Tunis*, *Elephants*, *The Tears of Isis*.

Nonfiction

Mermaids and Mastodons (Rinehart, New York, 1957, 251 pp., $3.95) (Chatto, London, 1957, 257 pp., illus., 25/-) (Clarke Irwin, Toronto, $4.75) (Grey Arrow: 40, 1960, 256 pp., illus., pa 5/-)

Covers the same ground as W. Ley in such works as *Dragons in Amber* and *Salamanders*, etc., but nevertheless stands in its own right. In parts: legendary animals (mermaid, kraken, etc.), with origins explained by an ingenious combination of legends and the psychology of folklore; extinct animals (mammoth, chirotherium, etc.) and the science of ichnology; "living fossils" (coelacanth, peripatus, ginkgo, marsupials and monotremes); animals recently extinct (quagga, passenger pigeon, Steller's sea cow) or threatened with extinction (the Javan rhinoceros, the notornis of New Zealand).

CARROLL, LEWIS Better known name of Charles Lutwidge Dodgson (27 Jan 1832–14 Jan 1898), British author and mathematician. He was the eldest of 11 children, of very religious parents. He matriculated at Christ Church College, Oxford, in 1850; after obtaining his B.A. he became a lecturer in mathematics there, and held that position until 1881. He had conceived of *Alice's Adventures Underground* by 1862, and it appeared in 1865 as *Alice's Adventures in Wonderland*; six years later *Through the Looking Glass* appeared. Carroll was considered an interesting but erratic genius, and was also noted for his mathematical texts, which, however, have not lived like his *Alice*. This has seen innumerable book editions; two film versions include Paramount's in 1933 and Walt Disney's (RKO Radio) in 1951.

Fiction [Incomplete—other titles in Bleiler *Checklist*]

Complete Works of Lewis Carroll, The [C] (Modern Library, New York, 1936, 1287 pp., $2.45)

Usually not dated but has been reissued post-war. Contains: I. *Alice's Adventures in Wonderland*; II. *Through the Looking Glass*; III. *Sylvie and Bruno*; IV. *Sylvie and Bruno Concluded*; V. *Verse*: "The Hunting of the Snark"; "Early Verse" (21 poems; "Puzzles From Wonderland"; "Prologues to Plays"; "Phantasmagoria" (this plus 15 others); "College Rhymes and Notes by an Oxford Chiel" (7); "Acrostics, Inscriptions, and Other Verse" (27); "Three Sunsets & Other Poems" (13); "Stories" (5); "A Miscellany" (25).

CARROLL, TED

Fiction

White Pills, a novel (Crown, New York, 1964, 191 pp., $3.95)

CARSON, ROBIN Author, born in Stockholm, Sweden, in the 1900's; apparently now living in the U.S.A.

Fiction

Pawn of Time (Holt, New York, 1957, 442 pp., $4.95)

Heitman Urban of modern New York lands in Venice in 1521 and becomes a swashbuckling noble. An entertaining long novel (200,000 words) covering many aspects of this historical era. It took several years to write.

CARTER, ANGELA

Fiction

Magic Toyshop, The (Heinemann, London, 1967, vi+200 pp., 25/-)

A girl becomes entrapped in a Gothic dream world with curious events and music.

CARTER, BRUCE (pseud) See HOUGH, R. A.

CARTER, JOHN FRANKLIN (27 Apr 1897–) U.S. political journalist and writer of detective fiction. His life up till his graduation from Yale in 1920 is described in his informal autobiography *The Rectory Family*; at Yale in this period were S. V. Benét, Thornton Wilder and Thomas Coward (who became his publisher). He spent

some time as a secretary in political positions, and started to write for reasons of health. Under the pseudonym "Jay Franklin" he wrote the notable syndicated column "We, the People" and other items, while as "Diplomat" he wrote between 1930 and 1935 a series of unusual and amusing detective stories about the character Dennis Tyler.

Fiction [as Jay Franklin]

Champagne Charlie (Duell Sloan Pearce, New York, 1950, 3+190 pp., $2.50) (Collins, Toronto, $3.00)

Amusing fantasy of a man endowed with a miraculous power.

Rat Race, The (*Collier's*, ?, 1947) (FPCI, Los Angeles, 1950, 371 pp., $3.00, jacket–J. Gaughan) (Galaxy Novel, No. 10, 1952, 160 pp., pa 35¢)

A political fantasy in which the hero's mind switches bodies.

CARTER, LIN(WOOD VROOMAN) (9 June 1930–) U.S. sf and fantasy author. Before writing professionally he was an enthusiast with many articles in the sf amateur magazines, e.g., a series on the books of H. P. Lovecraft. He has completed certain fragments of Robert E. Howard's writings (see Howard, *Conan* and *King Kull* series). He had a series of articles on various aspects of science fiction fandom in *If* from April 1966 through to May 1968.

Series

Thongor. Barbarian adventurer: *Wizard of Lemuria*; *Thongor of Lemuria*; *Thongor Against the Gods*; *Thongor in the City of Magicians*; *Thongor at the End of Time*.

Fiction

Conan See HOWARD, R. E.

Conan of the Isles See HOWARD, R. E.

Conan the Wanderer See HOWARD, R. E.

Destination: Saturn See WOLLHEIM, D. A. (as co-author David Grinnell)

Flame of Iridar, The [pa] (Belmont: B50-759, 1967, 99 pp., pa 50¢; with *Peril of the Starmen*)

King Kull See HOWARD, R. E.

Man Without a Planet, The [pa] (Ace: G-606, 1966, 113 pp., pa 50¢; with *Time to Live*)

Intrigue and adventure in a future galactic empire.

Star Magicians, The [pa] (Ace: G-588, 1966, 124 pp., pa 50¢; with *The Off-Worlders*)

Sorcery and adventure in the service of a barbaric overlord.

Thief of Thoth, The [pa] (Belmont: 00809, 1968, 85 pp., pa 50¢; with *And Others Shall Be Born*)

Thongor Against the Gods [pa] (Paperback: 52-586, 1967, 157 pp., pa 50¢)

Third of Thongor series; Thongor searches for his love, kidnapped by powerful enemies.

Thongor at the End of Time [pa] (Paperback: 53-780, 1968, 158 pp., pa 60¢)

Fifth of Thongor series.

Thongor in the City of Magicians [pa] (Paperback: 53-665, 1968, 160 pp., pa 60¢)

Fourth of Thongor series. Thongor defeats the mighty magicians of Zaar, the Black City.

Thongor of Lemuria [pa] (Ace: F-383, 1966, 127 pp., pa 40¢)

Second of Thongor series. Fantastic adventure, with Thongor rising to become Sark (king) of Patanga.

Tower at the Edge of Time [pa] (Belmont: 00804, 1968, 141 pp., pa 50¢)

Wizard of Lemuria, The [pa] (Ace: F-326, 1965, 127 pp., pa 40¢)

First of Thongor series. With the aid of a magician Thongor conquers in fighting the Dragon Kings.

CARTIER, EDD U.S. artist, born in North Bergen, N.J. He graduated from Pratt Institute as Bachelor of Fine Arts. He was drawn into science fiction artwork by J. W. Campbell. He served as a combat infantryman in the U.S. Army during World War II, and was wounded at Bastogne in the Battle of the Bulge. After the war he returned to sf, but in 1954 left free-lance illustrating and is now a staff artist preparing flexographic art. He is married, with two sons.

Although Cartier began his sf illustrating for *Astounding Sci-*

ence *Fiction*, he became the mainstay in *Unknown*, to which his distinctive style was eminently suited. He even had some covers before *Unknown* changed to non-illustrative covers with only a story line-up. Cartier has also done some illustrations for other magazines and for some Fantasy Press books.

CARTMELL, V(AN) H(ENRY) (1896–)
Anthology
Golden Argosy, The   See GRAYSON, C. (co-anthologist)

CARTMILL, CLEVE (1908–11 Feb 1964) U.S. author. He was born in Platteville, Wis., attended elementary schools in the Midwest, and went to California in 1927. He was an accountant, newspaperman, radio operator, and professional writer. He was co-inventor of the Blackmill system of high-speed typography. He was married, with one son. As a science fiction writer Cartmill was noted for describing the atomic bomb a year before it was used, in the story "Deadline" (*ASF*, Mar 1944). He had the following novels in *Unknown*: "Bit of Tapestry" (Dec 1941), "Prelude to Armageddon" (Apr 1942), "Hell Hath Fury" (Aug 1943).
Series
Space Salvage. All in *TWS*: "Salvage" (Aug 1949); "High Jack and Dame" (Oct 1949); "Thicker Than Water" (Dec 1949); "Dead Run" (Feb 1950); "Little Joe" (Apr 1950); "No Hiding Place" (June 1950).

CASELEYR, CAMILLE AUGUSTE MARIE (22 Sep 1909–) Australian writer and teacher, better known under his writing pseudonym "Jack Danvers." Born in Antwerp, Belgium, he studied at the U. of Antwerp. He served in the Belgian Army (field artillery) 1931-33. He was with the BBC 1941-43, and was then Territorial Agent in the Belgian Congo 1943-49. Coming to Australia, he worked with the Victorian State Rivers Commission 1951-53 and since then has been a school teacher in Australia. He is now an Australian citizen. His *The Living Come First*, prior to the book below, was a thriller set on a cattle station in South Australia.
Fiction
End of It All, The (Heinemann, London, 1962, 231 pp., 18/-) (*La lurga ombra della fine* [Italian], *Urania*: 308, 1963)
   Attempts of people to survive in Australia after fatal epidemic begins.

CASEWIT, CURTIS W. (21 Mar 1922–) U.S. author, born in Mannheim, Germany. Before the war he studied in three foreign countries, and speaks fluent French, Italian and German, and good Spanish and Schweizerdeutsch (Swiss dialect). During World War II he was an interpreter for the British Army. He came to the U.S.A. in 1948, and is now book buyer for a large store in Denver, Colo. He also teaches fiction and short-story writing at night. He is also a free-lance writer and has contributed to some 40 magazines. He has reviewed adventure, mystery and sf for magazines and newspapers, for which he won a Mystery Writers Association Award. He won the Colorado Authors League Award for the best novel of 1960 by a Colorado author. His wife, Charlotte Fischer-Lamberg, is also a writer.
Fiction
Peacemakers, The (Avalon, New York, 1960, 224 pp., $2.95) (*Der Diktator* [German], *UZ*: 460, 1965) (Digit: R704, 1963, 191 pp., pa 2/6) (Macfadden: 60-321, 1968, 143 pp., pa 60¢)
   After World War III, a former army sergeant strives to be dictator in post-nuclear-war wreckage; a well-written depiction of two future societies.

CASEY, KENT   Pseudonym of Kenneth McIntosh
Series
Dr. von Theil and Sgt. John West. All in *ASF*: "Flareback" (Mar 1938); "Static" (May 1938); "The Ceres Affair" (Oct 1938); "Thundering Peace" (Dec 1939).
Pvt. Kelton. All in *ASF*: "Good Old Brig!" (July 1938); " 'They Had Rhythm!' " (Dec 1938); "Star Crash" (Mar 1939); "Melody and Moons" (May 1939).

CASOLET, JACQUES
Fiction
Theory of Flight (No publisher noted, *ca.* 1958, pa probably 35¢)
   An odd item appearing in the U.S., subtitled "a theoretical science novel." It is narrated by a French-Canadian (fictitious name) who goes to Quebec, builds a flying saucer, and then visits "Earthal," a hidden planet diametrically opposite Earth, which proves to be the source of flying saucers.

CASSIDAY, BRUCE (BINGHAM) (25 Jan 1920–) U.S. writer and editor. A graduate of U.C.L.A., after college he served in the U.S. Air Force during World War II in Tunisia, Algeria, Italy and Puerto Rico. He has been a radio announcer, radio script writer and newsreel caption writer. He was editor of Popular Publications 1946-49, Farrell Publications 1950-53, and has been Fiction Editor of *Argosy* since 1954. As a writer he uses the pseudonyms Max Day and Carson Bingham; under the latter he wrote the novelisation of the film *Gorgo* (U.S. pa).

CASTERET, NORBERT
Fiction
Mission Underground [Trans. & adapted from French—Antonia Rudge] (Harrap, London, 1968, 140 pp., illus.–H. Johns, 16/-)
   An eminent French scientist makes a craft capable of drilling to 13,000 metres, and four go on a dangerous mission.

CASTILLA, CLYDE ANDRE
Fiction
Shara-Li (Clear Thoughts, Hollywood, Cal., 1958, 100 pp., $2.50)
   The projection of a young Atlantean of 27,000 years ago into a modern body, and his tale of what happened to Atlantis. Old-fashioned. Review by P. S. Miller, *ASF*, Sep 1960.

CASTLE, J(EFFERY) LLOYD (1898–) British aircraft designer, born at Surbiton, Surrey; B.Sc., educated at Epsom and the Royal Military Academy, Woolwich. He is assistant designer for Hawker Aircraft Ltd, contributes to *Newnes Aircraft Engineering*, and is a member of the British Interplanetary Society.
Fiction
Satellite E One (Eyre Spottiswoode, London, 1954, 192 pp., 9/6) (Dodd Mead, New York, 1954, 223 pp., $3.00) (McClelland, Toronto, $2.25) (D'day SF B.C., 1955) (Bantam: A1766, 1958, 164 pp., pa 35¢) (*Satélite T-1* [Spanish], Nebula: 23, 1956, pa) (*Raumstation E1* [German], Goldmann, 1960, 1964 pa) (Consul: 1140, 1963, 157 pp., pa 2/6)
   Well-written novel on the various problems in setting up the first Earth satellite; the problems are treated factually rather than theoretically.
Vanguard to Venus (Dodd Mead, 1957, 212 pp., $3.00) (D'day SF B.C., 1957) (*Expedición a Venus* [Spanish], Nebula: 57, 1959, pa) (*Avanguardia su Venere* [Italian], Cosmo: 63, 1960) (*Raumschiff Omega* [German], Goldmann, 1960, 1965 pa)
   Flying saucer pilots are "Venutians" and descended from the Egyptians who colonized Venus about 4182 B.C.

CAYCE, EDGAR   Dr. Gina Cerminara's *Many Mansions: The Edgar Cayce Story* (Signet: Q3307, 1967, 240 pp., pa 95¢) is an interpretation of Cayce's discoveries. It covers all levels of human experience and offers proof that each soul lives more than once, while the case histories given show astounding accuracy in cures prescribed by Cayce for people he had not seen.

CERF, BENNETT (ALFRED) (25 May 1898–27 Aug 1971) U.S. publisher, lecturer, columnist and TV panelist. He founded Random House and was its chairman from 1965. He compiled *Out on a Limerick* (Cassell, 1962)—over 300 of the world's best printable limericks.
Anthologies
Famous Ghost Stories (Modern Library, New York, 1944, 361 pp., $1.25; P21, 1963, pa 95¢) (Vintage: V-140, *ca.* 1960, 361 pp., pa $1.25)
   15 stories and compiler's introduction; following the stories is

"The Current Crop of Ghost Stories" (7 vignettes): "The Haunted and the Haunters," E. Bulwer-Lytton; "The Damned Thing," A. Bierce; "The Monkey's Paw," W. W. Jacobs; "The Phantom 'Rickshaw," R. Kipling; "The Willows," A. Blackwood; "The Rival Ghosts," B. Matthews; "The Man Who Went Too Far," E. F. Benson; "The Mezzotint," M. R. James; "The Open Window," Saki; "The Beckoning Fair One," O. Onions; "On the Brighton Road," R. Middleton; "The Considerate Hosts," T. McClusky; "August Heat," W. F. Harvey; "The Return of Andrew Bentley," A. Derleth & M. Schorer; "The Supper at Elsinore," I. Dinesen.

Stories Selected From The Unexpected [pa] See *The Unexpected*
Unexpected, The [pa] (Bantam: 502, 1948, 273 pp., pa 25¢) (*Stories Selected From The Unexpected*, Bantam: FP30, 1963, 184 pp., pa 50¢; omits 3 stories marked †)

Weird, 20 stories with compiler's introduction: "Salesmanship," Mary E. Chase; "The Storm," McKnight Malmar; "Back for Christmas"†, J. Collier; "The Thousand Dollar Bill," Manuel Komroff; "Two Thanksgiving Day Gentlemen," O. Henry; "Exchange of Men," Joseph Cross; "A Horseman in the Sky," A. Bierce; "Two Bottles of Relish," Lord Dunsany; "Final Break," Ian S. Thomason; "Addio," Thomas Beer; "Suspicion," Dorothy L. Sayers; "Gavin," John Van Druten; "Mammon and the Archer," O. Henry; "Clay Shuttered Doors"†, Helen R. Hull; "The Interlopers," Saki; "Yours Truly, Jack the Ripper"†, R. Bloch; "Adam and Eve and Pinch Me," A. E. Coppard; "Revelations in Black," Carl Jacobi; "The Price of the Head," John Russell; "The Chaser," John Collier.

CERF, CHRISTOPHER BENNETT (19 Aug 1941–) U.S. editor, at Random House. Son of Bennett Cerf.
Anthology
Vintage Anthology of Science Fantasy, The [pa] (Vintage: V326, 1966, 310 pp., pa $1.65)

20 stories and introduction: "The Great Automatic Grammatisator," Roald Dahl; "An Egg a Month From All Over," Idris Seabright; "There Will Come Soft Rains," R. Bradbury; "And Now the News," T. Sturgeon; "No-Sided Professor," M. Gardner; "Random Quest," John Wyndham; "The Rocket of 1955," C. M. Kornbluth; "Something for Nothing," R. Sheckley; "The Death of the Sea," Jose M. Gironella; "The Red White and Blue Rum Collins," John C. M. Brust; "Pie in the Sky," Wm. Styron; "The Analogues," D. Knight; "Immortality," F. Brown; "Shadow Show," C. D. Simak; "Chronopolis," J. G. Ballard; "Or All the Seas With Oysters," A. Davidson; "Patent Pending," A. C. Clarke; "I Kill Myself," Julian Kawalec; "The Men Who Murdered Mohammed," A. Bester; "A Canticle for Leibowitz," W. M. Miller Jr.

CERMINARA, GINA
Nonfiction
Many Mansions: The Edgar Cayce Story See CAYCE, E.

CHALKER, JACK (LAURENCE) (17 Dec 1944–) U.S. publisher and editor of the Anthem Series and Mirage Press since 1961. His own nonfiction publications from Anthem include *The New H. P. Lovecraft Bibliography* (1961); *In Memoriam: Clark Ashton Smith* (1963) and *Mirage on Lovecraft* (1965). He lives in Baltimore.
Nonfiction
Index to the Science-Fantasy Publishers, The See OWINGS, M. (co-compiler)

CHAMBERLAIN, ELINOR (21 June 1901–) U.S. author, born in Muskegon, Michigan, the daughter of a manufacturer. She married and divorced William R. Kuhns. She has lived in Peking and was an instructor of English in Manila 1923-26. She has been a semiprofessional dancer. She is M.S., Columbia, 1954, and was a librarian 1954-56.
Fiction
Snare for Witches (Dodd Mead, New York, 1948, 240 pp., $2.50)

Borderline—a 1663 New England community obsessed with a witchcraft craze.

CHAMBERLAIN, WILLIAM U.S. author. He has written many

stories of military life and action.
Fiction
China Strike [pa] (Fawcett Gold Medal: d1783, 1967, 191 pp., pa 50¢)

A U.S. strike force attacks a Chinese Communist nuclear base to destroy cobalt bombs that could wreck the world.
Red January [pa] (Paperback: 52-501, 1964, 158 pp., pa 50¢)

U.S. Army raiders strike into Cuba to destroy Soviet missiles about to be used by the U.S.S.R. for nuclear blackmail.

CHAMBERS, ROBERT W(ILLIAM) (26 May 1965–13 Dec 1933) U.S. author, born in Brooklyn, N.Y. He attended Brooklyn Polytechnic Institute and after graduation decided to follow his artistic bent; he later went to Paris where he studied art at the Julien Academy and was an exhibitor in the Paris Salon in 1889. Upon returning to New York he became a top-flight illustrator, with his work appearing in *Life*, *Truth*, and *Vogue*, the leaders of the day. His book *In the Quarter*, using background material from the Bohemian life of Paris, was printed in 1894 (the first printing did not list the author). His second book, *The King in Yellow*, was such an immediate and resounding success that he gave up art completely and devoted his full time to writing. By the time of his death he had published 72 books of all kinds—fantasy, biography, historical novels, and sports, and also plays and books of verse. His writing technique was to work on three or four books at one time.
Fiction [Incomplete—other titles in Bleiler *Checklist*]
King in Yellow, The [C] (F. T. Neely, New York, 1895, 316 pp.) (Chatto Windus, London, 1895, 316 pp.) (Constable, London, 1916, 1919, 312 pp.) (Appleton-Century, New York, 1938, xiv+274 pp., $2.00) (Ryerson, Toronto, $2.25) (Ace: M-132, 1965, 253 pp., pa 45¢)

Fantasy, 10 stories [reprintings in *FFM* noted]: "The Repairer of Reputations"; "The Mask" (Dec 1943); "In the Court of the Dragon"; "The Yellow Sign" (Sep 1943); "The Demoiselle D'Ys" (Nov 1942); "The Prophets' Paradise"; "The Street of the Four Winds; "The Street of the First Shell; "The Street of Our Lady of the Fields"; "Rue Barree." There were three U.S. editions in 1895, and all early editions are now collector's items.
Maker of Moons, The [C] (*English Illustrated Magazine* [title story only], July 1896) (Putnam, New York, 1896, 401 pp., $1.50) (Putnam, London, 1896, 410 pp., 6/-) (Title story only: Shroud, Buffalo, 1954, 82 pp., pa $1.00; 1,025 copies)

8 stories: "The Maker of Moons"; "The Silent Land"; "The Black Water"; "In the Name of the Most High"; "The Boy's Sister"; "The Crime"; "A Pleasant Evening"; "The Men at the Next Table." The Shroud edition omits the last two chapters of the story to make it fantastic, and includes a brief essay on Chambers by Ken Krueger.
Mystery of Choice, The [C] (Appleton, New York, 1897, 288 pp.)

7 stories: "The Purple Emperor"; "Pompe Funèbre"; "The Messenger" (*FFM*, Apr 1948); "The White Shadow"; "Passeur"; "A Matter of Interest"; "Envoi."
Police!!! [C] (Appleton, 1915, 293 pp., illus.–H. Hutt)

6 stories: "The Third Eye"; "The Immortal"; "The Ladies of the Lake"; "One Over"; "Un peu d'Amour"; "The Eggs of the Silver Moon." Sf hilariously funny and beautifully written.
Slayer of Souls, The (Doran, New York, 1920, 301 pp., $1.75) (Hodder Stoughton, London, 1920, 301 pp., 8/6) (*FFM*, May 1951)

Sorcery attempts to control a girl's life and defeat the world; highly melodramatic and well written.
Tracer of Lost Persons, The (*Idler*, sr7, Oct 1906) (Appleton, New York & London, 1906, 293 pp., illus.)

Connected series.
Tree of Heaven, The [C] (Appleton, New York, 1907, 325 pp.) (Constable, London, 1908, 332 pp., 6/-)

10 stories: "The Carpet of Belshazzar"; "The Sign of Venus"; "The Case of Mr. Helmer"; "The Tree of Dreams"; "The Bridal Pair"; "Ex Curia"; "The Golden Pool"; "Out of the Depths"; "The Swastika"; "The Ghost of a Chance."

CHANDLER, A(RTHUR) BERTRAM (28 Mar 1912–) British science fiction author and merchant marine officer. He spent his early years in tramp steamers on the Indian coast; after some work ashore he joined a liner company, and eventually became chief officer on a passenger liner between England and Australia. Since the mid-1950's he has been engaged with an Australian/New Zealand shipping line in the Australian coastal trade; he makes his home in Sydney.

During World War II he visited John W. Campbell in New York, and was invited to write for *Astounding Science Fiction*. His first sale to *ASF* was "This Means War" (May 1944); others followed in the same magazine, including "Giant Killer" (Oct 1945), "Special Knowledge" (Feb 1946; *Planet ohne Umkehr* [German], *UG*: 150, 1961), and "Drift" (June 1957). In the 1950's he wrote many neat short stories which were a feature in the U.S. and British (Nova) magazines. In the last few years he has concentrated more on novels. Many of his stories have been based on his experience at sea. Many of his early stories are noted for his (fictional) Mannschen Drive and Ehrenhaft faster-than-light drive. His most recent series gives a realistic picture of the colonisation of the Rim Worlds at the fringe of our galaxy.

Chandler often uses the pseudonym "George Whitley"; the protagonist in "Special Knowledge" is one George Whitley. The Feb 1953 *SF Adventures* was mostly Chandler, having the novel "Farewell to the Lotus" under his own name and the novelette "Final Voyage" under the Whitley pseudonym. He has had a number of stories published in the Australian *Man* where the pseudonym "Andrew Dunstan" has been used. Short novels of interest include "No More Sea" (*AS*, Jan 1959) and "The Winds of If" (*AS*, Sep 1963).

Series

Rim Worlds. "To Run the Rim" (*AS*, Jan 1959; expansion: *The Rim of Space*); "Chance Encounter" (*NW*, Mar 1959); "The Man Who Could Not Stop" (*F&SF*, May 1959; author's title, "Edge of Night"); "Wet Paint" (*AS*, May 1959); "Forbidden Planet" (*FU*, July 1959); "The Key" (*Fan*, July 1959); "The Outsiders" (*ASF*, Aug 1959); "When the Dream Dies" (*AS*, Feb 1961; expansion: *Rendezvous on a Lost World*). Some published as *Beyond the Galactic Rim*.

Fiction

Alternate Martians, The [pa] (Ace: M-129, 1965, 129 pp., pa 45¢; with *Empress of Outer Space* [Chandler])
Fantastic adventures on the Mars of another era.

Beyond the Galactic Rim [C] [pa] (Ace: F-237, 1963, 114 pp., pa 40¢; with *The Ship From Outside* [Chandler])
Sf, 4 Rim Worlds stories: "Forbidden Planet"; "Wet Paint"; "The Man Who Could Not Stop"; "The Key."

Bring Back Yesterday [pa] (Ace: D-517, 1961, 173 pp., pa 35¢; with *The Trouble With Tycho*) (*Im Zeitkreis gefangen* [German], *T*: 331, 1964)
Terran spaceman becomes involved in a vicious time cycle caused by an aberrant Mannschen Drive unit.

Coils of Time, The [pa] (*Star Weekly* [Toronto newspaper supplement], 7 Nov 1964) (Ace: M-107, 1964, 128 pp., pa 45¢; with *Into the Alternate Universe* [Chandler]) (*Sprung in die Zeit* [German], *UZ*: 538, 1967)
Adventures in time.

Contraband From Otherspace [pa] ("Edge of Night," *If*, sr2, Sep 1966) (Ace: G-609, 1967, 104 pp., pa 50¢; with *Reality Forbidden*) (*Das Wrack aus der Unendlichkeit* [German], TN: 18, 1968, pa)
Grimes and his Rim Worlds crew use a space derelict to save humans in another dimension.

Deep Reaches of Space, The (Revision of "Special Knowledge," *ASF*, Feb 1946) (H. Jenkins, London, 1964, 190 pp., 12/6) (*Der Mann, der zu den Sternen flog* [German], *T*: 465, 1966) (Mayflower: #1885, 1967, 128 pp., pa 3/6)
World War II merchant marine officer has his mind switched with an officer of the space force of tomorrow.

Empress of Outer Space [pa] (Ace: M-129, 1965, 127 pp., pa 45¢; with *The Alternate Martians* [Chandler]) (*Die Kaiserin der Galaxie* [German], *T*: 498, 1967)

Based on the Fearn *Golden Amazon* theme—action-packed adventure with the Empress fighting a despot.

False Fatherland [pa] ("Spartan Planet," *Fan*, sr2, Mar 1968) (Horwitz: PB374, 1968, 161 pp., pa 65¢)
Grimes comes to the planet Sparta where most men have never seen a woman—and he has some in his crew.

Glory Planet (Avalon, New York, 1964, 190 pp., $2.95) (Ryerson, Toronto)
Colonists isolated on Venus fight each other with a Mississippi-type river boat, etc.

Hamelin Plague, The [pa] (Monarch: 390, 1963, 126 pp., pa 35¢)
Mutant rats begin to take over the world, but a sonic ray saves man.

Into the Alternate Universe [pa] (Ace: M-107, 1964, 128 pp., pa 45¢; with *The Coils of Time* [Chandler]) (*Im Spalt zwischen den Universen* [German], *UZ*: 518, 1967)

Nebula Alert [pa] (Ace: G-632, 1967, 121 pp., pa 50¢; with *The Rival Rigelians*)

Rendezvous on a Lost World [pa] ("When the Dream Dies," *AS*, Feb 1961) (Ace: F-117, 1961, 124 pp., pa 40¢; with *The Door Through Space*) (*Die Welt der Roboter* [German], *T*: 263, 1963)
Adventure on one of the lost Rim Worlds where the crew of the *Lucky Lady* encounter self-perpetuating robots and a feudal society.

Rim of Space, The (Avalon, 1961, 220 pp., $2.95) (Ryerson, Toronto, $3.25) (Ace: F-133, 1962, 128 pp., pa 40¢; with *Secret Agent of Terra*) (*Am Rande der Milchstrasse* [German], *T*: 214, 1962) (*I fuorilegge dell'universo* [Italian], *Cosmo*: 110, 1962)
Expansion of "To Run the Rim" (*ASF*, n'te, Jan 1959); Derek Calver joins the Rim Runners and sees many planets, succeeds the captain of the ship, but is then forced to sacrifice it.

Road to the Rim, The [pa] (Ace: H-29, 1967, 117 pp., pa 60¢; with *The Lost Millennium*)
An early adventure of Grimes when he is forced to fight for the Rim World Navy in taking over a hijacked space ship.

Ship From Outside, The [pa] (enlargement of "Familiar Pattern," *ASF*, Aug 59, as G. Whitley) (Ace: F-237, 1963, 108 pp., pa 40¢; with *Beyond the Galactic Rim* [Chandler])
Search of Derek Calver for a ship from another galaxy; with female intrigue.

Space Mercenaries [pa] (Ace: M-133, 1965, 131 pp., pa 45¢; with *The Caves of Mars*)
Sequel to *Empress of Outer Space* with the Empress and her husband blockade-running through the Halicheki bird-people.

CHAPELA, E. SALAZAR Spanish author.
Fiction
Naked in Piccadilly [Trans.–Patricia Crampton] (*Desnudo en Piccadilly*, Editorial Losada: Buenos Aires, 1959) (Abelard-Schuman, London, 1961, 285 pp., 18/-) (FSB: 1559, 1966, 253 pp., pa 5/-)
A man changed by an explosion assumes a new name and has a love affair with his original wife; a lighthearted fantasy but rarely explores comic heights. Can be compared with G. M. Glaskin's *A Change of Mind*, but not as good.

CHAPIN, MAUD LOUISE HUDNUT
Fiction
Lost Star and Other Stories, The [C] (Falmouth Pub. House, Portland [Maine], 1948, 78 pp.)
Fantasy, 12 stories, not in Bleiler *Checklist*: "The Lost Star"; "The Prior"; "The Diet of Worms"; "The Bagpipes"; "Ad Astra"; "The Dryad"; "All Souls"; "The Rivals"; "The Leech"; "The Iconoclast"; "The Last Hansom"; "The Shadow."

CHAPPELL, CONNERY
Fiction
Arrival of Master Jinks, The (Falcon, London, 1949, 220 pp., 8/6)
Fantasy.

CHARBONNEAU, LOUIS (HENRY) (20 Jan 1924–) U.S. author. Born in Detroit, he lived there until 1952, and since then in

Los Angeles. He was in the U.S. Army Air Force in England 1943-46, meeting his wife there and marrying in 1945. He took his B.A. in 1948 and M.A. in 1950 at U. of Detroit, and taught English there for four years. He has been an advertising agency copywriter; since 1959 he has been with the *Los Angeles Times*. He sold quite a number of radio plays in 1948-53; his first novel was *No Place on Earth*, and two others (non-sf) followed in 1959.

Fiction

Antic Earth See *Down to Earth*

Corpus Earthling [pa] (Zenith: ZB-40, 1960, 160 pp., pa 35¢) (*La invasión invisible* [Spanish], Cenit: 22, 1961, pa) (Digit: R753, 1963, 159 pp., pa 2/6)

Prepublication title was "The Alien Mind"; intrigue with discovery of Martians inhabiting human bodies.

Down to Earth [pa] (Bantam: F3442, 1967, 187 pp., pa 50¢) (*Tod eines Roboters* [German], Goldmann, 1967, 1967 pa) (*Antic Earth*, H. Jenkins, London, 1967, 221 pp., 20/-; SF B.C. [S.J.], 1968)

A family in an emergency landing station faces an unseen menace.

No Place on Earth (Doubleday, New York, 1958, 184 pp., $2.95) (D'day, Toronto, $3.50) (D'day SF B.C., 1959, $1.20) (Crest: s342, 1959, 160 pp., pa 35¢) (*Flucht zu den Sternen* [German], Goldmann, 1960) (*Orrendo futuro* [Italian], *Urania*: 244, 1960) (*No hay lugar en la Tierra* [Spanish], Cenit: 27, 1962, pa) (H. Jenkins, 1966, 188 pp., 18/-) (Doubleday, 1966, 183 pp., $3.95)

A young man imprisoned in a tomb-like cell undergoes a relentless inquisition—an excellent study of a man's will.

Psychedelic-40 (Bantam: F2929, 1964, 184 pp., pa 50¢) (*The Specials*, H. Jenkins, 1965, 191 pp., 15/-; SF B.C. [S.J.], 1966) (*Die Wunderdroge* [German], Goldmann, 1965, 1965 pa)

Adventure in a world where drugs are used for social control.

Sensitives, The [pa] (Bantam: H3759, 1968, 204 pp., pa 60¢)

Based on an original movie script by Deane Romano.

Sentinel Stars, The [pa] (Bantam: J2686, 1963, 156 pp., pa 40¢) (Corgi: GS1480, 1964, 156 pp., pa 3/-)

One human against the world-wide organization that smoothly operates future society.

Specials, The See *Psychedelic-40*

CHARKIN, PAUL (20 July 1907-) British.

Fiction

Living Gem, The (Digit: R782, 1963, 159 pp., pa 2/6)

Alien overlords and a sort of philosopher's stone, in a future society of free love, etc.

CHARLES-HENNEBERG, N. See HENNEBERG, C.

CHARLOT, JEAN (8 Feb 1898) American artist, born in Paris. He was mural painter for the Mexican Government 1921-24, and staff artist in Yucatan for the Carnegie Institute 1926-30. He painted some 40 murals in the U.S.A. and Mexico, and has been an art teacher since.

Fiction

Dance of Death (Sheed & Ward, New York, 1951, $2.50)

50 drawings and captions; superlative macabre humour.

CHARTERIS, LESLIE (12 May 1907-) Naturalised U.S. author, born Leslie Charles Bowyer Yin (not Lin) in Singapore. In his youth he went around the world three times. He attended Cambridge, but after a year there his keen interest in crime fiction led him to become a writer, though he also had to work at various jobs. He came to the U.S. in 1932. Charteris is noted worldwide for his *Saint* novels; these have now sold over 22 million copies, been made into 10 films (most starring George Sanders), and some have been sold for a BBC TV series. His *The Second Saint Omnibus* (Crime Club, 1951) contains the two Saint stories which are fantasy: "The Darker Drink" (*TWS*, Oct 1947; *F&SF*, Oct 1952) and "The Man Who Liked Ants" (1937; *F&SF*, June 1953). Another story of interest is "Fish Story" (1953; *F&SF*, June 1954). The Bleiler *Checklist* mentions his *The Last Hero* (Hodder & Stoughton, 1930) as a fantasy.

Anthology

Saint's Choice of Impossible Crime, The [pa] (Bond-Charteris, 1945, 125 pp., pa 25¢)

Sf, 5 stories (all from *TWS* and *SS* except Charteris' own story): "The Gold Standard," L. Charteris; "The Impossible Highway," O. J. Friend; "Plants Must Slay," F. B. Long; "Daymare," F. Brown; "Trophy," H. Kuttner.

CHARTERS, DAVID WILTON (1900-)

Fiction

Grotto (Pageant, New York, 1955, 211 pp., $3.50) (Smithers, Toronto, $4.00)

CHASE, ADAM (pseud) See FAIRMAN, P. W., or LESSER, M.

CHASE, JAMES HADLEY (1906-) Better-known name of British author René Raymond. Educated at King's Rochester. He was formerly editor of the *R.A.F. Journal*. He is noted for suspense novels, of which he has written over 46. He resides in Paris.

Fiction

Miss Shumway Waves a Wand (Jarrolds, London, 1944, 169 pp., 8/6; 1947, 6/-) (*Miss Shumway jette un sort* [French], Gallimard Série Noire: 16, 1948) (Panther: 1116, 1960, 224 pp., pa 2/6)

Entertaining and rollicking fantasy.

CHATRIAN, ALEXANDRE (1826-1890) See ERCKMANN, EMILE (co-author)

CHEEVER, JOHN (27 May 1912-) U.S. author. He was born in Quincy, Mass., studied at Thayer Academy, and is a member of the Nat. Inst. of Arts and Letters. He is noted for *The Way People Live* (1942); his *The Wapshot Chronicle* (1957) won the 1958 National Book Award.

Fiction

Enormous Radio and Other Stories, The [C] (Funk & Wagnalls, New York, 1953, 237 pp., $3.50) (Gollancz, London, 1953, 237 pp., 12/6) (Berkley: G-119, 1958, 190 pp., pa 35¢)

14 stories, some fantasy: "Goodbye, My Brother"; "The Pot of Gold"; "O City of Broken Dreams"; "The Children"; "Torch Song"; "The Cure"; "The Hartleys"; "The Summer Farmer"; "The Superintendent"; "The Enormous Radio" (also in R. Bradbury's *Timeless Stories for Today and Tomorrow*); "The Season of Divorce"; "Christmas Is a Sad Season for the Poor"; "The Sutton Place Story"; "Clancy in the Tower of Babel."

CHENEY, D(AVID) (MacGREGOR)

Fiction

Son of Minos (Biblo & Tannen, New York, 1965, 238 pp., $3.50)

CHESNEY, WEATHERBY (pseud) See HYNE, C. J. C.

CHESTER, MICHAEL (ARTHUR) (23 Nov 1928-) U.S. physicist and engineer, born in New York City. B.A. in physics, U. of California 1952. He has been a physicist and engineer for various aircraft companies, and for Lockheed since 1957.

Fiction

Mystery of the Lost Moon, The (Putnam, New York, 1962, 127 pp., illus.—C. Geer, $2.75) (Longmans, Toronto, $2.75)

Juvenile.

CHESTER, WILLIAM L. (1907-) U.S. author, noted for his adventure-fantasy series covered below.

Series

Kioga. All in *BB*: "Hawk of the Wilderness" (sr7, Apr 1935; [see below]); "Kioga of the Wilderness" (sr7, Oct 1936); "One Against the Wilderness" (sr6, Mar 1937)—6 n'te covering his youth; "Kioga of the Unknown Land" (sr6, Mar 1938).

Fiction

Hawk of the Wilderness (*BB*, sr7, Apr 1935) (Harper, New York & London, 1936, 308 pp., $2.00; Grosset & Dunlap, *ca.* 1938, 308 pp., 50¢) (Hodder, London, 1937, 3/6) (Ace: G-586, 1966, 287 pp., pa 50¢)

Fantastic adventure on an island above the Arctic circle. The Grosset ed. jacket reprints one of Herbert M. Stoops' *BB* covers. *Film:* Republic serial, *ca*. 1938, starring Herman Brix; converted to U.S. TV movie *ca*. 1967.

CHESTERTON, G(ILBERT) K(EITH) (29 May 1874–14 June 1936) English journalist and author. Educated at St. Paul's, he left to study art. He found his bent was journalism, in which he went through the usual apprenticeship. His revolt against the trend of writing of the 19th Century was exemplified in many volumes (1901-05); he became noted for his literary criticism of such writers as Browning and Dickens. He began as an orthodox liberal but later reacted against socialism, like Belloc and others, and propagated the Distributist theories with which his name is associated. His first noted work was *The Napoleon of Notting Hill* (1904). His *The Club of Queer Trades* (1905; Darwen Finlayson, 1960) foreshadowed his success in detective fiction which came with the 'Father Brown' stories (1911-27). These have since been collected and most are available in paper editions; one has been filmed.
Fiction [Incomplete—other titles in Bleiler *Checklist*]
Flying Inn, The (J. Lane, London, 1914, 320 pp., 6/-) (Dodd Mead, New York, 1914, $2.00) ([Swedish], Geber, 1922) (Methuen, London, 1925, 282 pp., 3/6; 1941, 5/-; 1949) (Sun Dial, New York, *ca*. 1930, 320 pp., $1.00) (in *G. K. Chesterton Omnibus*, 1936) (Sheed, New York, 1955, 320 pp., $3.50) (Penguin: 1338, 1958, 288 pp., pa 2/6)
Socio-allegorical. A fantastic satire on a joyless Mohammedan supremacy in England when all inns are suppressed.
G. K. Chesterton Omnibus, A [C] (Methuen, 1936, 726 pp., 3/6; 1947; 1949, 10/6; 1953)
Three novels: *The Napoleon of Notting Hill*; *The Man Who Was Thursday*; *The Flying Inn*.
Man Who Knew Too Much, The [C] (Harper, New York, 1922, 365 pp., $2.00) (Cassell, London, 1922, 304 pp., 7/6; 1933, 3/6) (Burt, New York, 1930, 365 pp., 75¢) (Darwen Finlayson, London, 1961, 190 pp., 12/6)
13 stories (Darwen Finlayson ed. has only 8, marked †): "The Bottomless Well"†; "The Face in the Target"†; "The Fad of the Fisherman"†; "Five of Swords" [Cassell ed. only]; "The Fool of the Family"†; "Garden of Smoke"; "The Hole in the Wall"†; "The Soul of the Schoolboy"†; "Temple of Silence"; "Tower of Treason"; "Trees of Pride"; "The Vanishing Prince"†; "The Vengeance of a Statue"†.
Man Who Was Thursday, The (Dodd Mead, 1908, 281 pp., $2.75) (Modern Library, New York, 1917, 281 pp., 95¢) (*Der Mann der Donnerstag War* [German], Drei Masten Verlag, 1925; Fischer, ?, pa) (*Le nommé Jeudi* [French], Gallimard, 1926) (Arrowsmith, London, 1930, 3/6) (in *G. K. Chesterton Omnibus*, 1936, 2/6) (Penguin: 95, 1937, 184 pp., pa 6d; 1958, 188 pp., pa 2/6) (Armed: 984, nd, pa) (*FFM*, Mar 1944) (? , Bristol, 1947) (Dent, London, [5th] 1949, 192 pp., 5/-) (Capricorn: CAP27, New York, 1960, 192 pp., pa $1.15)
A nightmare of anarchistic intrigue and conspiracy.
Napoleon of Notting Hill, The (J. Lane, 1904, 300 pp., illus.–W. G. Robertson, 6/-; 1922, 301 pp., 7/-; 1928; 1937, 300 pp., 3/6; 1949, 6/-) (*Le Napoléon de Notting Hill* [French], Gallimard, 1912) (in *G. K. Chesterton Omnibus*, 1936) (Penguin: 550, 1946, pa 1/6) (Devin-Adair, New York, 1949, 200 pp., $2.50) (World Distributors: H947, 1960, 192 pp., pa 1/6)
Fantastic dream-history of civil wars between the suburbs of London.
Tales of the Long Bow [C] (Cassell, 1925, 309 pp., 7/6) (Dodd Mead, 1925, 218 pp., $2.00) (Sheed, 1956, 219, $3.00) (Darwen Finlayson, 1962, 191 pp., 12/6)
8 stories: "The Unpresentable Appearance of Colonel Crane"; "The Improbable Success of Mr. Owen Hood"; "The Unobtrusive Traffic of Captain Pierce"; "The Elusive Companion of Parson White"; "The Exclusive Luxury of Enoch Oates"; "The Unthinkable Theory of Professor Green"; "The Unprecedented Architecture of Commander Blair"; "The Ultimate Ultimatum of the League of the Long Bow."

CHETWYND, BRIDGET
Fiction
Future Imperfect (Hutchinson, London, 1946, 174 pp., 9/6; 1948, 6/-)
Women run future world, and men cannot keep up to them politically and professionally.

CHEVALIER, HAAKON (MAURICE) (10 Sep 1902–) U.S. author, born in Lakewood, N.Y. He studied at Stanford U. 1918-20, A.B. U. of California 1923, A.M. 1925, Ph.D. 1929. He was Professor of French at U. Calif. 1929-46 and has been French interpreter for the U.N. and the War Crimes Trials. His book below is probably only his second, but since 1934 he has translated many works.
Fiction
Man Who Would Be God, The (Putnam's, New York, 1959, 449 pp., $4.95) (Longmans, Toronto, $5.75)
Brilliant physicist co-ordinating a super-bomb project becomes convinced that only he can save the world from atomic suicide.

CHILTON, CHARLES (FREDERICK WILLIAM) (1927–) British radio producer and amateur astronomer. Besides writing scripts for TV, he contributes to the London newspapers. He wrote the popular Western *Riders of the Range* series for boys, after which the *Jet Morgan* trilogy (books below) was written for the BBC.
Fiction
Journey Into Space (Jenkins, London, 1954, 220 pp., 9/6) (*Sprong in het heelal; operatie Luna* [Dutch], Elsevier, Amsterdam, 1957, 1962 pa) (Pan: 437, 1958, 189 pp., pa 2/-) (*Mission dans l'espace* [French], Le Fleuve Noir: A132, 1959) (*Viaggio nello spazio* [Italian], Cosmo: 27, 1959) (Digit: R811, 1963, 160 pp., pa 2/6)
There were three different radio serials under this title, on the adventures of 'Jet Morgan' and comrades. The first (book above) covered the trip to the Moon, time travel, and flying saucers; it ran 20 weeks on the BBC.
Red Planet, The (Jenkins, 1956, 208 pp., 10/6; 1958, 6/-) (*Sprong in het heelal; de rode planeet* [Dutch], Elsevier, Amsterdam, 1958, 1962 pa) (Pan: G274, 1960, 185 pp., pa 2/6) (Digit: R770, 1963, 158 pp., pa 2/6)
Second of trilogy. Jet Morgan has further adventures, going to Mars and combatting the Martians who plan to invade Earth.
World in Peril, The (Jenkins, 1960, 222 pp., 12/6; 1962, 7/6) (Pan: G579, 1962, 191 pp., pa 2/6) (*Sprong in het heelal; Aanval op de aarde* [Dutch], Elsevier, Amsterdam, 1962 pa)
Third of trilogy. Jet Morgan foils the Martian plot to use a giant asteroid to invade Earth.

CHRIST, HENRY (IRVING) (1 Oct 1915–) U.S. English instructor, born in Brooklyn, A.B. and B.S. at City College of New York. He teaches English in a New York high school.
Anthology
Short Stories [with Jerome Shostak] (Oxford Book Co., New York, 1948, 429 pp., $2.08)
A general fiction anthology for high school students. One section covers weird stories, etc.: *Part II: Stories of Suspense and Terror:* "The Waxwork," A. M. Burrage; "The Open Window," Saki; "The Inexperienced Ghost," H. G. Wells; "August Heat," W. F. Harvey; "A Struggle for Life," T. B. Aldrich; "Dr. Heidegger's Experiment," N. Hawthorne.

CHRISTIE, AGATHA (MARY CLARISSA) (nee MILLER) (1890–) English detective writer, born in Torquay, Devon. She was tutored at home by her mother until age 16. Her first marriage was to Arch Christie, 1914-28, ending in divorce; she married Max Mallowen, an archaeologist, in 1930. She studied singing. She began writing during World War I and her first novel, *The Mysterious Affair at Styles*, was published in 1920. She has been consistently on best-seller lists; her 50th novel, *A Murder Is Announced*, appeared in 1950. Recently she has become a successful modern dramatist. One of her hit plays was *Witness for the Prosecution*, built up from the short story in the collection below (the only straight crime story in it). "The Fourth Man" from the same book is the only fantasy in the American collection *The Witness for the Prosecution* (Dodd Mead, 1948).

Fiction

Hound of Death and Other Stories, The [C] (Odhams—for Crime Club, London, 1933, 247 pp., 7/6) (Collins, London, 1936, 3/6) (Pan: G377, 1960, 219 pp., pa 2/6) (Fontana: 970, 1966, 190 pp., pa 3/6)

12 stories: "The Hound of Death"; "The Red Signal"; "The Fourth Man" (*F&SF*, Sep 1955); "The Gypsy"; "The Lamp"; "Wireless"; "The Witness for the Prosecution"; "The Mystery of the Blue Jar"; "The Strange Case of Sir Arthur Carmichael"; "The Call of Wings" (*F&SF*, June 1952); "The Last Seance"; "S.O.S."

CHRISTIE, ROBERT

Fiction

Inherit the Night (Farrar Rinehart, New York, 1949, 409 pp., $3.00) (Clarke Irwin, Toronto, $3.25) (R. Hale, London, 1951, 408 pp., 12/6; 1952, 6/-)

Borderline allegory; lost-race story.

CHRISTOPHER, JOHN (pseud) See YOUD, C. S.

CHURCHILL, R(EGINALD) C(HARLES) (9 Feb 1916–) British author. He was born at Bromley, Kent, and was educated (M.A.) at Downing College, Cambridge. He has been a teacher, and since 1943 has been an Examiner in Education for the Oxford and Cambridge Joint Board. He has contributed to many learned journals such as *Library World*, *Spectator* and *New English Review*, and has also written many works on English literature, e.g., *English Literature of the 18th Century* and *Shakespeare and His Betters*.

Fiction

Short History of the Future, The (Werner Laurie, London, 1955, 192 pp., 12/6) (*Welt wohin?* [German], Diana, 1956)

A history of the period 1967-6601 is built up from the novels of G. Orwell, G. Frankau, A. Huxley, K. Vonnegut, D. Karp, R. Bradbury, etc., each of which envisages future societies; a time-line has been produced and the various novels have been correlated. Compare *Tomorrow Revealed* by J. A. Atkins.

CHURCHWARD, JAMES (1854–4 Jan 1936) U.S. author, born in England. He is noted for his books alleging the reality of the legendary continent of Mu.

Nonfiction

Children of Mu, The (Washburn, New York, 1931; Spearman, 1959; Paperback, 1968, pa)

Second of Mu works. The colonization of Earth by explorers and adventurers of Mu.

Cosmic Forces of Mu, The (Baker & Taylor, 1934-35 [2 vols.]; Paperback, 1968, pa [2 vols.: *Cosmic Forces of Mu* and *The Second Book of the Cosmic Forces of Mu*])

Fourth of Mu works. It is not strictly of a piece with the other three, as it contains more of the author's beliefs than prevail in the earlier books.

Lost Continent of Mu, The (Rudge, New York, 1926; Spearman, London, 1959; Crown 'Xanadu,' 1962, pa; Paperback, 1968, pa)

First of Mu works. The prehistoric civilization of Mu.

Sacred Symbols of Mu, The (Washburn, 1933; Spearman, 1960; Paperback, 1968, pa)

Third of Mu works. The origin of all religions of Mu.

Second Book of the Cosmic Forces of Mu, The See *Cosmic Forces of Mu, The*

CLAIR, COLIN

Nonfiction

Unnatural History: An Illustrated Bestiary (Abelard-Schuman, New York, 1967, 256 pp., illus., $5.95)

Compilation of classical and medieval writings on real and imaginary animals from the hippopotamus to the hippogriff.

CLARENS, CARLOS

Nonfiction

Horror Movies—An Illustrated Survey See *Illustrated History of the Horror Film, An*

Illustrated History of the Horror Film, An (Putnam, New York, 1967, 256 pp., illus., $6.95) (Capricorn 'Giant 295,' 1967, 256 pp., 48 illus., pa $2.75) (*Horror Movies—An Illustrated Survey*, Secker & Warburg, London, 1968, 264 pp., 63/-)

A readable reference volume giving a chronological history of the horror film and some attempt to understand horror film interest; it devotes some space to the sf film.

CLARK, BARRETT HARPER (28 Aug 1890–5 May 1953) U.S. dramatic critic and editor, born in Toronto. He attended U. of Chicago and then became an actor. He was noted for his writings, compilations, and translations in the field of drama, and was the author of *Eugene O'Neill* (1925; rev. 1947). He also did radio work and was director of the Dramatists Play Service.

Anthology

Great Short Stories of the World [with M. Lieber] (McBride, New York, 1925, 1072 pp., $5.00) (Heinemann, London, 1927, 1072 pp.) (Garden City, New York, 1938)

No further information; probably numerous stories with a few fantasy.

CLARK, CURT

Fiction

Anarchaos [pa] (Ace: F-421, 1967, 143 pp., pa 40¢)

Drama and intrigue on the lawless world where the only crime is to be killed.

CLARK, JOHN D(RURY) U.S. physical chemist, born in Fairbanks, Alaska. He was educated at U. of Alaska 1925-27, Cal. Inst. Tech. 1927-30 (B.S.), U. of Wisconsin 1930-32 (M.S.), and Stanford 1932-34 (Ph.D.). From 1934 to 1949 he worked in industry; since 1949 he has been at the U.S. Naval Air Rocket Test Station, Dover, N.J., where he is now head of the Propellants Division. He was one of the developers of "Amphigel" (not the sulfa drugs as stated on the jacket of *The Petrified Planet*). He is a specialist in rocket propellants and has developed a new and highly successful type of high-energy liquid monopropellant. As a fantasy fan, he helped revive the *Conan* series of R. E. Howard.

Anthology

Petrified Planet, The (Twayne, New York, 1952, 263 pp., $2.95)

3 novels, written independently but all based on science outlined by Clark in an introduction [edited anonymously]: "The Long View," F. Pratt (*SS*, Dec 1952); "Uller Uprising," H. B. Piper (*Space SF* sr2, Feb 1953); "Daughters of Earth," J. Merril.

CLARK, RONALD (WILLIAM) (2 Nov 1916–) British free-lance writer.

Fiction

Queen Victoria's Bomb (Cape, London, 1967, 256 pp., 25/-) (Morrow, New York, 1968, 234 pp., $4.95)

A 19th Century scientist discovers fission and builds a Bomb; it is kept in reserve, and misfortune attends attempts to use it in the Crimean and Zulu wars.

CLARKE, ARTHUR C(HARLES) (16 Dec 1917–) British author of science fiction and of nonfiction on space flight, underwater research, etc. He was born at Minehead, Somerset, and lived on a farm in his youth. He entered the Civil Service in 1936 as an auditor. In his war service with the R.A.F., 1941-46, he was a technical officer on the first experimental trials of GCA (Ground Controlled Approach) radar. He was demobilized as Flight-Lieutenant. After the war he obtained first class honours in Physics and in Pure and Applied Mathematics at Kings College, London. He was Assistant Editor of *Science Abstracts* 1949-50, and then became a full-time writer. Since 1954 he and his partner, Mike Wilson, have been engaged in underwater photography along the Great Barrier Reef of Australia, and the coast of Ceylon; this work has been the basis of such books as *The Coast of Coral*. Clarke has lived in Ceylon since 1954.

He wrote numerous papers on electronics, applied mathematics, astronomy and astronautics for learned journals such as *Electronic Engineering, Wireless World, Journal of the B.I.S.*, etc. It is of considerable interest that his article "Extra-Terrestrial Relays" (*Wireless World*, Oct 1945) was the first publication of the idea that satellites would make global TV possible; he proposed the use of three in the 24-hour orbit. By now he has written about 200 articles for such periodicals as *Reader's Digest, New York Times, Harper's Magazine*, and *Playboy*.

Clarke began fiction writing for W. Gillings' *Fantasy*, and when this magazine ceased, some of his stories appeared in *Astounding Science Fiction*, notably "Loophole" (Apr 1946) and "Rescue Party" (May 1946). He has since appeared in most magazines in the field, mainly with sf but also a little fantasy. His nonfiction works *Interplanetary Flight* and *The Exploration of Space* were among the best of their type in the pre-Sputnik era. For a number of years he concentrated on nonfiction about underwater research, but has recently returned with new science fiction. He worked with Stanley Kubrick on the screenplay of the film *2001: A Space Odyssey*, and simultaneously wrote the book version.

Clarke was Chairman of the British Interplanetary Society 1946-47 and 1950-53; he also chaired the International Astronautical Congress, London, 1951, and the Symposium on Space Flight, Hayden Planetarium, New York, 1953. He is a member of many learned societies. He was Guest of Honour at the World SF Convention, New York, 1956. He won the 1956 Hugo for best short story with his controversial "The Star" (*Infinity*, Nov 1955; *The Hugo Winners* [Asimov], 1962), and he received the 1962 Kalinga Award for the 'popularisation of science' at New Delhi in Sep 1962. Sam Moskowitz's profile of Clarke was published in *AS* (Feb 1963) and was a chapter in *Seekers of Tomorrow* [Moskowitz] (1966).

Fiction

Across the Sea of Stars [C] (Harcourt, New York, 1959, 584 pp., $3.95) (Longmans, Toronto, $4.50) (D'day SF B.C., 1959, $1.90)

Omnibus of 2 novels and 18 short stories, with introduction by C. Fadiman: I. *Expedition to Earth:* "The Sentinel"; "Inheritance"; "Encounter at Dawn"; "Superiority"; "Hide and Seek"; "History Lesson"; " 'If I Forget Thee, Oh Earth . . .' "; "Breaking Strain." II. *Tales From the White Hart:* "Silence Please"; "Armaments Race"; "The Pacifists"; "The Next Tenants"; "The Reluctant Orchid." III. *Reach for Tomorrow:* "Rescue Party"; "Technical Error"; "The Fires Within"; "Time's Arrow"; "Jupiter Five." IV. *Childhood's End.* V. *Earthlight.*

Against the Fall of Night (*SS*, Nov 1948) (Gnome, New York, 1953, 223 pp., $2.75) (Permabook: 310, 1954, 160 pp., pa 25¢) (Pyramid: G554, 1960, 159 pp., pa 35¢; F754, 1962, pa 40¢; X1703, 1967, pa 60¢) (in *The Lion of Comarre & Against the Fall of Night*)

A richly imaginative fantasy of man seeking the stars. Campbell rejected it for *ASF*, but it was later very well received in *SS*. Clarke began writing it in 1937, and more recently revised it as *The City and the Stars*.

Arthur C. Clarke Omnibus, An [C] (Sidgwick & Jackson, London, 1965, 596 pp., 30/-) (Ambassador, Toronto, 1965, $7.50)

Two novels and a collection: *Childhood's End; Prelude to Space; Expedition to Earth.*

Arthur C. Clarke Second Omnibus, An [C] (Sidgwick & Jackson, London, 1968, 30/-)

Three novels: *A Fall of Moondust; Earthlight; Sands of Mars.*

Childhood's End (Extension of "Guardian Angel," *NW*, Win 1950; *FFM*, Apr 1950 [revised by J. Blish]) (Houghton Mifflin, New York, 1953, 214 pp., $2.00; Ballantine: 33, 1953, 214 pp., pa 35¢; 398K, 1960, pa 35¢; U2111, 1963, pa 50¢; U5066, 1967, 222 pp., pa 60¢) (Sidgwick Jackson, London, 1954, 253 pp., 10/6) (SF B.C. [S.J.], 1955, 4/6) (*Mot Nya Världar* [Swedish], Eklund, 1955; *Hapna*, sr2, Sep 1956) (*Les enfants d'Icare* [French], Gallimard: Le RF, 1956) (Pan: 369, 1956, 189 pp., pa 2/-; G463, 1961, pa 2/6; G643, 1963, pa 2/6; X573, 1966, pa 3/6) (*El fin de la infancia* [Spanish], Porrua, ?) (*A Idada do Ouro* [Portuguese], Livros de Brasil, ?) (*Det Tavse Arhundrede* [Danish], Skrifola: P8, 1958, pa) (in *Across the Sea of Stars* [Clarke], 1959) (*Die letzte Generation* [German], Weiss, 1960; Goldmann:

070, 1966, pa) (*Le guide del Framonto* [Italian], Biblioteca Economica Mondadori, nd, pa) (Harcourt Brace, New York, 1963, 216 pp., $4.50) (Longmans, Toronto, 1963, $5.59) (in *Arthur C. Clarke Omnibus*, 1965) (*Het einde van het begin* [Dutch], Bruna, Utrecht & Antwerp, 1967 [in *SF Omnibus*])

An alien race dominates Man for his own good and his future evolution. Rather different from Clarke's usual works.

City and the Stars, The (Harcourt Brace, 1956, 310 pp., $3.75; Harbrace: HPL1, 1966, 221 pp., pa 75¢; Harcourt, 1967, 310 pp., $4.95) (Muller, London, 1956, 256 pp., 13/6) (D'day SF B.C., 1956, 184 pp., $1.15) (Signet: S1464, 1956, 191 pp., pa 35¢; D1858, 1961, pa 50¢: P3429, 1968, pa 60¢) (Corgi: G443, 1957, 319 pp., pa 3/6; GS933, 1960, 283 pp., pa 3/6; FS7295, 1965, 254 pp., pa 5/-) (*La citta e le stelle* [Italian], *Urania*: 158, 1957) (*Die Sieben Sonnen* [German], Goldmann, 1960, 1962 pa) (in *From the Ocean, From the Stars* [Clarke], 1961) (*La cité et les astres* [French], Gallimard: Le RF95, 1962) (Gollancz, 1968, 255 pp., 25/-)

Complete rewriting and expansion of *Against the Fall of Night*. A lad in the far future discovers what lies outside the completely self-sufficient City of Diaspar.

Deep Range, The (enlargement of "The Deep Range," *Star SF Stories No. 3* [Pohl], 1954) (Harcourt Brace, 1957, 238 pp., $2.95) (Longmans, Toronto, $4.50) (Muller, 1957, 224 pp., 13/6) (*In den Tiefen des Meeres* [German], Weiss, 1957; Goldmann, 1962, pa) (Signet: S1583, 1958, 175 pp., pa 35¢; D2528, 1964, pa 50¢) ([Japanese], Hayakawa: 3023, 1960, pa) (SF B.C. [S.J.], 1960, 5/6) (in *From the Ocean, From the Stars* [Clarke], 1961) (*I guardiani del mare* [Italian], *Urania*: 278, 1962) (Gollancz, 1968, 224 pp., 25/-)

Deep-sea farming of the future, with a former spaceman retrained as a submarine warden for whales.

Dolphin Island ("People of the Sea," *Worlds of Tomorrow*, sr2, Apr 1963) (Holt Rinehart Winston, New York, 1963, 187 pp., $3.50; lib. bdg. $3.27) (Gollancz, London, 1963, 186 pp., 12/6) (*Le porte dell'oceano* [Italian], *Urania*: 373, 1965) (*L'ile des dauphins* [French], Laffont, 1966) (Berkley: F1495, 1968, 143 pp., pa 50¢) (Dragon: D88, 1968, 126 pp., pa 2/6)

Juvenile. A teenage orphan stows away on a hovercraft; when it is wrecked at sea he is rescued by dolphins.

Earthlight (enlargement of n'te, *TWS*, Aug 51) (Muller, 1955, 222 pp., 10/6) (Ballantine, 1955, 155 pp., $2.75; #97, pa 35¢; 249, 1957, pa 35¢; F698, 1963, pa 50¢; U2824, 1965, pa 50¢) (*Claro de tierra* [Spanish], Nebulae: 33, 1956, pa) ([Japanese], Gengensha: SF11, 1956) (Pan: 420, 1957, 158 pp., pa 2/-; G641, 1963, pa 2/6; X574, 1966, pa 3/6) (*Um die Macht auf dem Mond* [German], Weiss, 1957; *T*: 540, 541, 1967) (*Ombre sulla Luna* [Italian], *Urania*: 145, 1957) ([French], ?) (in *Across the Sea of Stars* [Clarke], 1959)

On the Moon in the 22nd Century; a well-written melodramatic plot with Moon conditions faithfully detailed.

Expedition to Earth [C] (Ballantine, 1953, 167 pp., $2.00; #52, pa 35¢; 472K, 1961 pp., pa 35¢; U2112, 1965, pa 50¢) (Sidgwick Jackson, 1954, 167 pp., 8/6) (*Expedición a la Tierra* [Spanish], Nebulae: 8, 1955, pa) (Corgi: S650, 1959, 192 pp., pa 2/6) (in *Across the Sea of Stars* [Clarke], 1959) (*Verbannt in die Zukunft* [German], Goldmann, 1960, 1965 pa) (in *An Arthur C. Clarke Omnibus*, 1965) (selected stories in *Prelude to Mars* [Clarke], 1965) (Pan: X462, 1966, 174 pp., pa 3/6) (Sphere: 23973, 1968, 174 pp., pa 5/-)

Sf, 11 stories: "Second Dawn"; " 'If I Forget Thee, Oh Earth . . .' "; "Breaking Strain"; "History Lesson"; "Superiority"; "Exile of the Eons"; "Hide and Seek"; "Expedition to Earth" (British ed.: "Encounter in the Dawn"); "Loophole"; "Inheritance"; "The Sentinel." *Note: Across the Sea of Stars* has only 8 of these stories, and *Prelude to Mars* about 4.

Fall of Moondust, A (Gollancz, 1961, 224 pp., 16/-) (Harcourt, 1961, 248 pp., $2.95) (Reader's Digest Condensed Book, Vol. 4, 1961; related Dutch edition, 1962) (*Polvere di luna* [Italian], *Urania*: 281, 1962) (*Im Mondstaub Versunken* [German], Goldmann, 1962, 1964 pa) (*S.O.S. Lune* and *Naufrages de la Lune* [French], Le Fleuve Noire: A206, A207, 1962, trans.—B. R.

Bruss) (Dell: 2463, 1963, 240 pp., pa 50¢) (SF B.C. [S.J.], 1963, 5/9) (Pan: X280, 1964, 206 pp., pa 3/6) (*Scheepsramp op de maan* [Dutch], Spectrum, Utrecht & Antwerp, 1964) (*Naufragio en el mar Selenita* [Spanish], Nebula: 100, 1964, pa)

Rescue of people in a tourist cruiser on the Moon, sunk to the bottom of a "sea" of lunar dust. Plausible and well characterised.

From the Ocean, From the Stars [C]   (Harcourt Brace & World, 1961, 515 pp., $4.50) (D'day SF B.C., 1962, $1.90)

Omnibus of 2 novels and 24 stories: I. *The Deep Range*; II. *The Other Side of the Sky* [same contents and order as book]; III. *The City and the Stars*.

Glide Path (Harcourt Brace, 1963, 229 pp., $4.50) (Longmans, Toronto, $5.50) (Dell: 2919, 1965, 224 pp., pa 50¢)

Not sf, but a readable story on aeronautics and radar.

Islands in the Sky (Sidgwick Jackson, 1952, 190 pp., illus.– Quinn, 8/6) (Winston, Philadelphia, 1952, 209 pp., $2.00) (abr., *Popular Science*, June 1953) (*Iles de l'espace* [French], Le Fleuve Noir: A35, 1954, pa) (*Isole cosmiche* [Italian], *Urania*: 54, 1954) (*Ilmojen Saaret* [Finnish], ? , 1954) ([Japanese], GingaShobo 'Adv. in SF: 2,' 1955) ([Argentine], Minotauro: 5, 1956, pa) (*Aventyr Pa Rymdstationerna* [Swedish], Eklund, 1957) (*Inseln im All* [German], AWA, 1958; Goldmann, 1962, pa) (Signet: S1769, 1960, 127 pp., pa 35¢; KD510, 1965, 157 pp., pa 50¢) (*L'isola nel cielo* [Italian], Fantascienza: 7, 1962, pa) (Digit: R802, 1963, 158 pp., pa 3/-)

A boy wins a stay on a space station circling the Earth. The Winston ed. (in the *Adventures in SF* series) has a short introduction by Clarke, while the original British ed. does not.

Lion of Comarre and Against the Fall of Night, The (Harcourt, New York, 1968, x+214 pp., $4.75)

The first appearance in hardcover of *The Lion of Comarre* (from *TWS*, Aug 1949)—a man escapes from a city where dreams give the heart's desire. For other appearances of *Against the Fall of Night* see its own entry.

Master of Space [pa]   See *Prelude to Space*

Nine Billion Names of God, The [C]   (Harcourt, 1967, 288 pp., $4.75)

Sf, 21 stories and introductions: "The Nine Billion Names of God"; "I Remember Babylon"; "Trouble With Time"; "Rescue Party"; "The Curse"; "Summertime on Icarus"; "Dog Star"; "Hide and Seek"; "Out of the Sun"; "The Wall of Darkness"; "No Morning After"; "The Possessed"; "Death and the Senator"; "Who's There?"; "Before Eden"; "Superiority"; "A Walk in the Dark"; "The Call of the Stars"; "The Reluctant Orchid"; "Encounter at Dawn"; " 'If I Forget Thee, Oh Earth . . .' "

Other Side of the Sky, The [C]   (Harcourt Brace, 1958, 245 pp., $3.95) (Longmans, Toronto, $4.50) (Signet: S1729, 1959, 1959, 158 pp., pa 35¢; D2433, 1964, 160 pp., pa 50¢) (Gollancz, 1961, 245 pp., 15/-; 1963, 16/-) (*Die andere Seite des Himmels* [German], Goldmann, 1961, 1963 pa) (in *From the Ocean, From the Stars* [Clarke], 1961) (SF B.C. [S.J.], 1962, 5/6) (Corgi: YS1289, 1963, 158 pp., pa 3/-; GS7531, 1966, 1966, pa 3/6) (Harbrace: HPL25, 1968, 248 pp., pa 75¢)

Sf, 24 stories: "The Nine Billion Names of God"; "Refugee."

The Other Side of the Sky (6 stories, all in *London Evening Standard*, 1957; first 3, *Infinity*, Sep 1957; second 3, Oct 1957; *Hapna* [Sweden], sr6, Nov 1958): "Special Delivery"; "Feathered Friend"; "Take a Deep Breath"; "Freedom of Space"; "Passer-By"; "The Call of the Stars."

"The Wall of Darkness; "Security Check"; "No Morning After."

Venture to the Moon (6 stories, all in *London Evening Standard*; 2 each in *F&SF* Dec 1956, Jan & Feb 1957 [Australian *F&SF*, #11, 12, 13, 1957-58]; all in *Best From F&SF, 7th Series* [Boucher], 1958): "The Starting Line"; "Robin Hood F.R.S."; "Green Fingers"; "All That Glitters"; "Watch This Space"; "A Question of Residence."

"Publicity Campaign"; "All the Time in the World"; "Cosmic Casanova"; "The Star"; "Out of the Sun"; "Transience"; "The Songs of Distant Earth." The German ed. omits "The Star," "The Nine Billion Names of God," and "Refugee."

Prelude to Mars [C]   (Harcourt Brace & World, 1965, 497 pp., $4.95) (D'day SF B.C., $1.90)

Omnibus binding of: *Prelude to Space*; *Sands of Mars*; 8 stories selected from *Tales From the White Hart*; and 8 stories from both *Expedition to Earth* and *Reach for Tomorrow*.

Prelude to Space (Galaxy Novels: 3, 1951, 160 pp., pa 25¢) (Sidgwick Jackson, 1953, 176 pp., 9/6) (Gnome, 1954, 191 pp., $2.50) (Ballantine: 68, 1954, 166 pp., pa 35¢) (Pan: 301, 1954, 156 pp., pa 2/-) (*Preludio allo Spazio* [Italian], *Urania*: 19, 1953) (*Die Erde lasst uns los* [German], Weiss, 1954) (*Preludio al espacio* [Spanish], Nebulae: 25, 1956, pa) ([Portuguese], Bestseller, ?) (*Prelude a l'espace* [French], La Fleuve Noir: A133, 1959) (*Marchen Mod Stjernerne* [Danish], Skrifola: 'Lommeromanen' P18, 1959, pa) (*Master of Space*, Lancer: 72-610, 1961, 158 pp., pa 50¢) (FSB: 755, 1962, 159 pp., pa 2/6; 2147, 1968, pa 3/6) (in *An Arthur C. Clarke Omnibus*, 1965) (in *Prelude to Mars* [Clarke], 1965)

Realistic narration of the months of preparation before the take-off of the first moon rocket. The Lancer and FSB eds. have a new preface.

Reach for Tomorrow [C]   (Ballantine, 1956, 166 pp., $2.00; #135, pa 35¢; U2110, 1963, pa 50¢) (5 stories in *Across the Sea of Stars* [Clarke], 1959) (*Demain, moisson d'etoiles* [French], Denoël: PF36, 1960, pa) (Gollancz, 1962, 166 pp., 15/-) (selected stories in *Prelude to Mars* [Clarke], 1965)

Sf, 12 stories: "Rescue Party"; "A Walk in the Dark"; "The Forgotten Enemy"; "Technical Error"; "The Parasite"; "The Fires Within"; "The Awakening"; "Trouble With the Natives"; "The Curse"; "Time's Arrow"; "Jupiter Five"; "The Possessed."

Sands of Mars (Sidgwick Jackson, 1951, 219 pp., 10/6) (Gnome, 1952, 216 pp., $2.75) (*Le sabbie di Marte* [Italian], *Urania*: 1, 1952) (*In het zand van Mars* [Dutch], Pax, 's-Gravenhage, 1952) (D'day SF B.C., 1953) (*Projekt Morgenrote* [German], Weiss, 1953; Goldmann, 1963, pa) (Corgi: T43, 1954, 251 pp., pa 2/-; S564, 1958, pa 2/6) (Pocket Books: 989, 1954, 217 pp., pa 25¢) (*Las arenas de Marte* [Spanish], Nebula: 5, 1955, pa) ([Japanese], Muro-machi Shobô, 1955; Hayakawa: 3025, 1961, pa) (*Les sables de Mars* [French], Fleuve Noir, 1958 [not a series]) ([Yugoslavian], ?) (*Piaski Marsa* [Polish], Wiedza Powszechna, 1957) (Permabooks: M4149, 1959, 217 pp., pa 35¢) (Pan: X281, 1964, 207 pp., pa 3/6) (in *Prelude to Mars* [Clarke], 1965) (Harcourt, 1967, 218 pp., $4.50)

An easy-flowing novel of the exploitation of Mars' natural resources, and the finding of some native inhabitants.

Tales From the White Hart [C]   (Ballantine: 186, 1957, 151 pp., pa 35¢; 539, 1961, pa 35¢; U2113, 1966, pa 50¢) (5 stories in *Across the Sea of Stars* [Clarke], 1959) (*In het Witte Hert* [Dutch], Elsevier, Amsterdam, 1962, pa) (8 stories in *Prelude to Mars* [Clarke], 1965)

Fantasy, 15 stories—tall tales told by the bar character Harry Purvis: "Silence Please"; "Big Game Hunt"; "Patent Pending"; "Armaments Race"; "Critical Mass"; "The Ultimate Melody"; "The Pacifist"; "The Next Tenants"; "Moving Spirit"; "The Man Who Ploughed the Sea"; "The Reluctant Orchid"; "Cold War"; "What Goes Up"; "Sleeping Beauty"; "The Defenestration of Ermintrude Inch."

Tales of Ten Worlds [C]   (Harcourt Brace, 1962, 245 pp., $3.95) (Longmans, Toronto, $4.95) (Gollancz, 1963, 245 pp., 16/-) (SF B.C. [S.J.], 1964, 6/-) (Dell: 8467, 1964, 224 pp., pa 50¢) (*Unter den Wolken der Venus* [German], Goldmann, 1963; 083, 1967, pa) (Pan: X424, 1965, 204 pp., pa 3/6)

Sf, 15 stories: "I Remember Babylon"; "Summer on Icarus" ("The Hottest Piece of Real Estate in the Solar System"); "Out of the Cradle, Endlessly Orbiting . . ."; "Who's There?"; "Hate"; "Into the Comet"; "An Ape About the House"; "Saturn Rising"; "Let There Be Light"; "Death and the Senator"; "Trouble With Time"; "Before Eden"; "A Slight Case of Sunstroke"; "Dog Star"; "The Road to the Sea" ("The Seeker of the Sphinx," n'te, 2CSAB, Spr 1951; *Best SF 1952* [Bleiler])

2001: A Space Odyssey (New American Library, New York, 1968, 221 pp., $4.95) (Signet: Q3580, 1968, 221 pp., pa 95¢) (Hutchinson, London, 1968, 224 pp., 25/-) (Arrow: 153, 1968, 256 pp., pa 5/-)

Based on the screenplay by S. Kubrick and Clarke. Discovery of a strange monolith on the Moon causes a spacecraft to be sent on a mission to Saturn. *Film:* MGM, 1967, produced and directed by Stanley Kubrick, and starring Keir Dullea and Gary Lockwood, with Hal the Computer, in Panavision. One of the most noteworthy sf films ever produced.

Nonfiction

Not covered below are the following on underwater research, etc.: *Boy Beneath the Sea* (Harper, 1958, juvenile); *The Challenge of the Sea* (Holt Rinehart Winston, 1960; Muller, 1961); *The Coast of Coral* (Harper, 1956; Muller, 1956); *The First Five Fathoms* (Harper, 1960); *Indian Ocean Adventure* (Harper, 1961; Barker, 1962); *Indian Ocean Treasure* [with Mike Wilson] (Harper, 1964); *The Reefs of Taprobane* (Harper, 1957; Muller, 1957); *The Treasure of the Great Reef* (Harper, 1964); *Voice Across the Sea* (Muller, 1958; Harper, 1959), a review of the submarine cable from its infancy to the present day.

Challenge of the Space Ship, The (Harper, New York, 1959, 212 pp., illus., $3.50) (Muller, London, 1960, ix+213 pp., illus., 15/-) ([German], Econ Verlag, 1960?) (Ballantine: F528, 1961, 189 pp., pa 50¢)

Fact and speculation on subjects such as why aliens haven't come to Earth, what a summer-resort satellite may be like, whether climate control is feasible, how to travel between the stars, and UFO's. 20 articles reprinted from *Holiday, Harper's, Coronet, F&SF, J. of B.I.S.*, etc.

Coming of the Space Age, The (Meredith, New York, 1967, 302 pp., $6.95)

A collection of articles, diaries, fiction, etc., forming a literary exhibit of the birth of space flight. 36 selections including autobiographies of Tsiolkovsky, Oberth and Goddard; articles by Dornberger and Von Braun; a thoughtful visionary speech by O. Stapledon to the B.I.S.; and a discussion by C. S. Lewis and S. Moskowitz on "God in Space" and "Space, God and Science Fiction."

Exploration of Space, The (Temple, London, 1951, 198 pp., illus.–L. Carr & R. A. Smith, 12/6; 1955, 8/6) (Harper, 1952, 198 pp., illus., $3.50; rev. 1959, 200 pp., illus., $4.00) (Ambassador, Toronto, 1952, $3.25) (Cardinal: C135, 1954, 210 pp., pa 35¢) (Pelican: A434, 1958, 192 pp., pa 3/6) (Premier: d102, 1961, 192 pp., pa 50¢; R228, 1964, 183 pp., pa 60¢) (German, French, Japanese, Swedish, Yugoslavian, Spanish, Danish, Italian, Dutch, Brazilian, and Polish editions)

A layman's introduction to interplanetary flight; though it is not highly technical, the science is accurate. It won the 1952 International Fantasy Award for nonfiction, and was a joint selection of the U.S. Book-of-the-Month Club.

Exploration of the Moon, The (Muller, 1954, 112 pp., illus.–R. A. Smith, 18/-; 1956, 10/6) (Harper, 1955, 112 pp., illus.–Smith, $2.50) (Saunders, Toronto, $2.25)

A step-by-step account of lunar colonisation. The colour plates of the British ed. are black & white in the U.S. ed.

Going Into Space See *Young Traveller in Space, The*

Interplanetary Flight (Temple, 1950, xiii+164 pp., 8/6; rev., 1960, viii+144 pp., 12/6) (Harper, 1951, $2.50; rev. 1960, viii+144 pp., $3.50) (Canadian, Italian and Spanish editions)

Clarke's notable first book on space flight. Semitechnical, with mathematical appendix.

Making of a Moon, The (Muller, 1957, 182 pp., illus., 21/-) (Harper, 1957, 205 pp., illus., $3.50; rev. 1958, 205 pp., illus., $3.50)

A comprehensive coverage of artificial satellites and the satellite programme.

Man and Space (*Life* Book, 1964, 1965, 200 quarto to Science Library subscribers)

Popular and up-to-date coverage, well illustrated.

Profiles of the Future (Gollancz, 1962, 223 pp., 21/-) (Harper Row, New York, 1963, 234 pp., $3.95) (Bantam: H2734, 1964, 235 pp., pa 60¢) (Pan: XP54, 1964, 223 pp., pa 3/6) (*Profil du futur* [French], Ed. Retz "Encyclopedie Planète: 7," 1964)

An enquiry into the limits of the possible, reprinting material from such magazines as *Holiday, Horizon, Science Digest*, etc.

Promise of Space, The (Harper & Row, New York, 1968, $7.50)

Scottie Book of Space Travel, The [pa] See *Young Traveller in Space, The*

Voices From the Sky (Harper & Row, 1965, 243 pp., $3.95) (Gollancz, 1966, 241 pp., 25/-) (Longmans, Toronto, $4.95) (Pyramid: X1688, 1967, 205 pp., pa 60¢)

Short articles from various sources, e.g. *Rogue, Playboy, New York Times.* Arranged in groups—going into space, communication satellites, comments on fan mail, etc.

Young Traveller in Space, The (Phoenix, London, 1954, 72 pp., illus., 7/6) (*Going Into Space*, Harper, 1954, 117 pp., illus., $2.50; Trend Book: 50, Los Angeles, 1957, 128 pp., pa 75¢) (*The Scottie Book of Space Travel*, Scottie: JS7, 1957, 126 pp., pa 2/6)

Juvenile; nontechnical discussion of the possibilities of interplanetary travel and the problems of building and basing a space ship. The U.S. paper ed. has some illustrations different from the British original.

Anthology

Time Probe (Delacorte, New York, 1966, 242 pp., $4.95) (Dell: 8925, 1967, 238 pp., pa 75¢) (Gollancz, 1967, 242 pp., 21/-)

Sf, 11 stories and introduction, "Science and Science Fiction": "And He Built a Crooked House," R. A. Heinlein; "The Wabbler," M. Leinster; "The Weather Man," T. L. Thomas; "The Artifact Business," R. Silverberg; "Grandpa," J. H. Schmitz; "Not Final!" I. Asimov; "The Little Black Bag," C. M. Kornbluth; "The Blindness," P. Latham; "Take a Deep Breath," A. C. Clarke; "The Potters of Firsk," J. Vance; "The Tissue-Culture King," Julian Huxley.

CLARKE, I(GNATIUS) F(REDERIC) (1918–) English lecturer, head of the General Studies Dept., Royal College of Science and Technology. He graduated from Liverpool U. with a degree in English Literature. During World War II he was an officer in the artillery, and later in intelligence. He is married, with 3 children. At the age of 11 he read his first sf story—Wells' *War of the Worlds*—and became an ardent follower of the genre. After five years' research he compiled his *Tale of the Future*.

Nonfiction

Tale of the Future, The (Library Association, London, 1961, 165 pp., 4 illus., 20/-)

Subtitled "From the Beginning to the Present Day: A Checklist of those satires, ideal states, imaginary wars and invasions, political warnings and forecasts, interplanetary voyages and scientific romances—all located in an imaginary future period—that have been published in the U.K. between 1644 and 1960."

Part 1. Chronological list: alphabetical within each year of publication, giving publisher, pages, and short-sentence description. *Part 2.* Short-title index. *Part 3.* Author index. *Part 4.* Bibliography.

This volume gives quite good leads to collectors on many sf works, but is not complete even within the limits of its selection. It is of value for books not within the scope of this *Encyclopedia* and enlarges on the entries in the Bleiler *Checklist* in that it briefly states what the books are about.

Voices Prophesying War 1763-1984 (Oxford Univ. Press, London, 1966, 254 pp., illus.–35 pp., 42/-)

Political and technical prophecy in stories of war-to-come is traced from Napoleonic times to the present. The coverage runs through such books as Chesney's *The Battle of Dorking* (1871) and Wells' *The War of the Worlds* (1898) to *On the Beach* and *Fail-Safe.* Although the book is provocative, it is valuable only to those directly interested in the subject.

CLARKE, JOAN

Fiction

Happy Planet, The (J. Cape, London, 1963, 192 pp., illus.–A. Maitland, 15/-) (Clarke Irwin, Toronto, $3.25) (Lothrop, New York, 1965, 254 pp., illus., $3.50)

Juvenile.

CLARKE, T. E. B.

Fiction

World Was Mine, The (Bodley Head, London, 1964, 224 pp., 18/-)

Time-travel—a divorced unsuccessful civil servant is knocked unconscious in 1962 and finds himself in 1928, a young man but with a fading memory.

CLARKSON, HELEN Understood to be a pseudonym of an established U.S. author.
Fiction
Last Day, The (Dodd 'Torquil,' New York, 1959, 183 pp., $3.50) (Dodd, Toronto, $4.00)

Woman's view of atomic war and its aftermath; an isolated island community copes with fall-out, etc. In the tradition of *Shadow on the Hearth* by J. Merril.

CLASON, CLYDE
Fiction
Ark of Venus (Knopf, New York, 1955, 181 pp., $2.00)

Juvenile—the adventures of 18-year-old Tal Roberts fighting for survival on Venus.

CLAUDY, CARL (13 Jan 1879–1957) U.S. author. He wrote some sf for boys which was published in *American Boy*. Two of the four novels below were reprinted in *Year After Tomorrow* [del Rey], 1954, which also has Claudy's "Tongue of Beast" (an Alan Kane and Ted Dolliver story).
Fiction [all juvenile]
Blue Grotto Terror, The (*American Boy*, ?) (Grosset, New York, 1934, 234 pp., illus.–A. C. Valentine, 50¢)

The story of a fantastic explosive known as "X."
Land of No Shadow, The (*American Boy*, ?) (Grosset, 1933, 214 pp., illus.–A. C. Valentine, 50¢) (in *Year After Tomorrow* [del Rey], 1954)

A Dr. Arronson story; a trip to the 4th dimension.
Mystery Men of Mars, The (*American Boy*, ?) (Grosset, 1933, 216 pp., illus.–A. C. Valentine, 50¢) ("The Master Minds of Mars," in *Year After Tomorrow* [del Rey], 1954)

Alan Kane and Ted Dolliver have adventures with Dr. Lutyens on Mars.
Thousand Years a Minute, A (*American Boy*, ?) (Grosset, 1933, 216 pp., illus.–A. C. Valentine, 50¢)

Time travel to a million years ago; battling prehistoric animals.

CLAYTON, RICHARD (HENRY MICHAEL) (11 Aug 1907–) British author. After education at Oxford (M.A.) he joined the Indian Civil Service. In World War II he became a staff lieutenant in Intelligence. He later worked at Whitehall, being Controller of Enemy Property in 1957. Under the pseudonym "William Haggard" he writes highly original thrillers, half sinister and half satire, which have been successful in both Britain and the U.S.
Fiction
Slow Burner [as William Haggard] (Cassell, London, 1958, 192 pp., 12/6) (Little, Boston, 1958, 192 pp., $3.00) (Corgi: S669, 1959, 223 pp., pa 2/6) (Penguin: 2233, 1965, 159 pp., pa 3/6) (Signet: D2773, 1965, 143 pp., pa 50¢)

Detective story with slight sf content: an intrigue about "slow" atomic power.

CLEARY, JON (22 Nov 1917–) Australian writer and journalist, born in Sydney. He worked at a number of jobs, including commercial artist, but has been a full-time writer and journalist since 1945. He has done film scripts for MGM, Warner, and Ealing, and also TV scripts in the U.S. and England. His *A Flight of Chariots* (Collins, London, 1964, 21/-) is an astronautic novel set in the present day.

CLEATOR, P(HILIP) E(LIABY) (1908–) British author, and a founder of the British Interplanetary Society. He wrote *Rockets Through Space* (Simon & Schuster, 1936), one of the few prewar books on rocketry; this was followed postwar by *Into Space* (Unwin, 1953; Crowell, 1954) and, more recently, *Introduction to Space Travel* (Putnam, 1961; Museum, 1961?). Other nonfiction works are *The Robot Era* (Unwin, 1955; Crowell, 1956)—a discussion of the effects of automation; and *The Past in Pieces* (1958), on archaeology.

CLEMENS, SAMUEL LANGHORNE (30 Nov 1835–21 Apr 1910) U.S. author, better known as Mark Twain. Although born

in a Florida crossroads town, he was raised in the river town of Hannibal, Missouri, the steamboat stop above St. Louis. In his early years he worked as a printer and reporter. His first book covered folklore of the frontier: *The Celebrated Jumping Frog of Calaveras County and Other Sketches* (1867). After his marriage in 1870 he had his most productive years, and wrote his masterpieces *The Adventures of Tom Sawyer* (1876), *Life on the Mississippi* (1883), and *The Adventures of Huckleberry Finn* (1885), really all parts of one masterwork. At the height of his popularity he wrote *A Connecticut Yankee in King Arthur's Court* (1889). Through personal misfortunes which had an impact on his writing he did not produce many other works of note before his death.
Fiction [as Mark Twain] [Incomplete—other titles in the Bleiler *Checklist*]
Connecticut Yankee in King Arthur's Court, A (C. L. Webster, New York, 1889, 575 pp.) (Harper, New York & London, 1889, 433 pp.; 1930, 510 pp.) ([German], C. Stephenson, 1923) (Heritage, New York, 1942, 319 pp., $3.75) (Armed: e-139, nd, pa) (Pocket Books: 497, 1948, 360 pp., pa 25¢) (Modern Library, New York, 1949, 450 pp., $1.25) (Royal Giant, nd, 218 pp., pa 50¢) ([Japanese], Okakura Shobō, 1951) (Cardinal: C107, 1954, 360 pp., pa 35¢) (in *Stories of Scientific Imagination* [Gallant], 1954) (Washington: W150, 1960, 360 pp., pa 35¢; RE301, 1964, pa 75¢) (*Ein Yankee am Hofe König Arthurs* [German], Heyne, 1961, pa) (Signet: CD158, 1963, 334 pp., pa 50¢)

Twain's noted transplanting of a modern man into the past. A very revealing story that can be read as a lighthearted burlesque or as a devastating satire on American society, etc. *Films:* Three versions: 1. Fox, 1921, silent; 2. Fox, 1931, with Will Rogers; 3. Paramount, 1949, with Bing Crosby and Rhonda Fleming.
Extract From Captain Stormfield's Visit to Heaven (Harper, New York & London, 1909, 120 pp., frontis.) (in *The Mysterious Stranger* [Twain], 1922) (in *Report From Paradise* [Twain], 1952)

Noted fantasy.
Mysterious Stranger and Other Stories, The [C] (Harper, New York & London, 1922, 323 pp., $2.25) (Armed: n-1, nd, pa)

7 stories: "A Fable"; "Extract From Captain Stormfield's Visit to Heaven"; "Horse's Tale"; "Hunting of the Deceitful Turkey"; "McWilliamses and the Burglar Alarm"; "My Platonic Sweetheart"; "The Mysterious Stranger."
Report From Paradise [C] (Harper, New York, 1952, 94 pp., $2.00)

2 stories: "Captain Stormfield's Visit to Heaven" (expanded version, prepared by Dixon Wecter); "Letter From the Recording Angel" (previously unpublished satire).

CLEMENT, HAL (pseud) See STUBBS, H. C.

CLIFFORD, Sir HUGH C(HARLES) (5 Mar 1866–18 Dec 1941) English writer and statesman; G.C.M.G. 1921, C.B.E. 1925. He joined the Malay States Civil Service as a cadet in 1883 and served throughout Malaya for 10 years, including the time of the Pahang Rebellion. He was a governor in West African states 1912-1925 and also in Ceylon and elsewhere. His writings were based on his experiences, and include a dictionary of the Malay language. A fantasy besides that below is *The Downfall of the Gods* (Dutton, New York, 1911).
Fiction
Further Side of Silence, The [C] (Doubleday Page, New York, 1916, 405 pp., 95¢; 1917, 405 pp.; 1927, 405 pp., $3.50)

19 stories and 1 poem set in Malaya in the last quarter of the 19th century, telling of the beliefs and adventures of the natives: "The Further Side of Silence"; "The Were-Tiger"; "The Experiences of Raja Haji Hamid"; "Droit Du Seigneur"; "In the Valley of the Telom"; "The Inner Apartment"; "The Ghoul"; "A Malayan Prison"; "He of the Hairy Face"; "The Flight of Chep, the Bird"; "A Daughter of the Muhammadans"; "The Lone-Hand Raid of Kulop Sumbing"; "The Flight of the Jungle Folk"; "One Who Had Eaten My Rice"; "At a Malayan Court"; "The Amok of Dato' Kaja Biji Derja"; "A Malayan Actor-Manager"; "Tukang Burok's Story"; "In Chains"; "L'Envoi" (poem).

CLIFTON, MARK (1906–1963) U.S. science fiction author. He was trained as a teacher, but then spent 25 years in industry in various phases of personnel work during which he personally compiled 200,000 case histories, using a variant of the Kinsey approach. He thus arrived at some interesting conclusions regarding human beings, which formed the basis of most of his science fiction. He began writing sf as a sideline in the early 1950's.
Series
Joey (later **Bossy**). All in *ASF*: "Crazy Joey" (Aug 1953, with A. Apostolides); "Hide! Hide! Witch!" (Dec 1953, with A. Apostolides); "They'd Rather Be Right" (sr 4, Aug 1954, with F. Riley; book ed. below).
Kennedy, Ralph. "What Thin Partitions" (*ASF*, Sep 1953, with A. Apostolides); "Sense From Thought Divide" (*ASF*, Mar 1955); "Remembrance and Reflection" (*F&SF*, Jan 1958); "How Allied" (*ASF*, Mar 1957); "Pawn of the Black Fleet" (*AS*, Jan 1962; *When They Come From Space*). The first four titles are from Alexander Pope's *Essay on Man* Vol. I, pp. 225-6.
Fiction
Eight Keys to Eden (Doubleday, New York, 1960, 187 pp., $2.95) (D'day SF B.C., 1960, $1.20) (*Das Berg aus Quarz* [German], Goldmann, 1961, 1964 pa) (Gollancz, London, 1962, 187 pp., 16/-) (Ballantine: F639, 1962, 160 pp., pa 50¢) (SF B.C. [S.J.], 1963, 8/6) (Pan: X353, 1965, 173 pp., pa 3/6) (*Las ocho llaves del Eden* [Spanish], Galaxia: 35, 1965, pa)
Future civilization with a class of supermen "Extrapolators," one of whom endeavours to solve the peculiar problem of the planet Eden.
Forever Machine, The [with F. Riley] See *They'd Rather Be Right*
McKenzie's Experiment [in German] [C] (Goldmann, 1962, 1964 pa)
7 stories: "Crazy Joey"; "Hide! Hide! Witch!"; "The Kenzie Report"; "What Now, Little Man?" "We Are Civilized"; "Clerical Error"; "What Have I Done?" [None of the original co-authors were credited.]
They'd Rather Be Right [with Frank Riley] (*ASF*, sr4, Aug 1954) (Gnome, New York, 1957, 189 pp., $3.00) (*The Forever Machine*, Galaxy SF Novels: 35, 1959, 159 pp., pa 35¢) (*Computer der Unsterblichkeit* [German], *TS*: 119, 1967)
Winner of the 1955 Hugo for the best novel. Bossy, the supercomputer, offers immortality and is forced to go underground.
When They Come From Space ("Pawn of the Black Fleet," *AS*, sr2, Jan 62) —enlarged: (Doubleday, 1962, 192 pp., $2.95) (D'day SF B.C., 1962, $1.20) (D'day, Toronto, $3.50) (*Vennero dalla spazio* [Italian], *Urania*: 113, 1962) (Dobson, London, 1963, 184 pp., 15/-) (Macfadden: 40-105, 1963, 144 pp., pa 40¢; 50-341, 1967, pa 50¢) (FSB: 1128, 1964, 192 pp., pa 3/6)
A joyous comedy of bureaucracy; Ralph Kennedy becomes the "extraterrestrial psychologist" dealing with an alien invasion.

CLINGERMAN, MILDRED (McELROY) (14 Mar 1918–) U.S. author, born in Allen, Oklahoma. She married Stuart K. Clingerman in 1937 and has a son and a daughter; her husband is a construction superintendent. She likes to garden and cook and occasionally write; she collects Victorian travel journals and books of all kinds, especially those by or about Kenneth Grahame. She has had over a dozen stories in *F&SF*, where she first appeared with "Minister Without Portfolio" (Feb 1952).
Fiction
Cupful of Space, A [C] [pa] (Ballantine: 519K, 1961, 142 pp., pa 35¢)
Sf and fantasy, 16 stories (including 11 from *F&SF* and 2 from *Collier's*): "First Lesson"; "Stickeney and the Critic"; "Stair Trick"; "Minister Without Portfolio"; "Birds Can't Count"; "The Word"; "The Day of the Green Velvet Cloak"; "Winning Recipe"; "Letters From Laura"; "The Last Prophet"; "Mr. Sakrison's Halt"; "The Wild Wood"; "The Little Witch of Elm Street"; "A Day for Waving"; "The Gay Deceiver" (new); "A Red Heart and Blue Roses" (new).

CLINTON, EDWIN M. (1926–) U.S. author and technical writer.

Active in fan circles, he has been a director of the Los Angeles Science Fantasy Society. Stories under his own name have appeared in the sf magazines, and he used the pseudonym "Anthony More" for the collection covered below.
Fiction
Puzzle Box [as "Anthony More"] (Trover Hall, San Francisco, 1946, 111 pp., jacket–St. Crain, $1.75; 2,000 copies)
Fantasy, 6 stories: "Puzzle Box"; "Footsteps"; "Nightmare"; "The Last Message"; "Seven Sapphires"; "Five Strands of Yellow Hair." This book was a promising start to a proposed series from this publisher, but nothing else appeared.

CLOUGH, BEN C.
Anthology
American Imagination at Work: Tall Tales and Folk Tales, The (Knopf, New York, 1947, 707 pp., $6.00)
A notable compilation of folk lore. It includes several fine and memorable tales of witchcrafts and special providences, of strange deliverances and improbable animals, of murder and sudden death, of the supernatural and of marvels.

CLOUKEY, CHARLES U.S. science fiction author, pseudonym of Charles Cloutier, youthful genius who died around the age of 20. He is remembered for stories from his first, "Sub-Satellite" (*AS*, Mar 1938; Dec 1967), through his 'Paradox' series (see *CONNECTED STORIES* section), to his final novel "The Swordsman of Saarvon" (*AS*, sr3, Aug 1932).

CLOUSTON, J(OSEPH) STORER (23 May 1870–23 June 1944) British author. Born in Cumberland, he was called to the bar in 1895. He was associated with the Orkney Islands in many capacities–Convenor, Chairman of Orkney Harbour Commissioners. He wrote a number of works, including several plays.
Fiction [Incomplete—other titles in Bleiler *Checklist*]
Tales of King Fido [C] (Mills & Boon, London, 1909, 185 pp., 1/-)
Fantasy, 9 stories: "My Introduction to King Fido"; "His Majesty's Laureate"; "The Hereditary Cleaner"; "The Baroness Lotta"; "A Harmless Exaggeration"; "The Experts"; "His Majesty's Head"; "The Martyr"; "His Majesty's Excuse."

CLYNE, RONALD U.S. artist. He began working on dust jackets for Arkham House, and also designed Arkham's colophon. Some of his jackets were selected for showing in the first annual exhibition of the Book Jacket Designer's Guild in 1948. Since then he worked for other publishers and published an art folio on Wallace Smith.

COATES, JOHN (1912–)
Fiction
Here Today (Methuen, London, 1949, 264 pp., 10/6) (Macmillan, New York, 1950, 263, $2.75)
Current English life, and time travel. The fantasy aspect is not very strong.

COATES, ROBERT (MYRON) (6 Apr 1897–) U.S. novelist. He was born in New Haven, Conn., graduated from Yale (B.A.) in 1916, and went to Europe in 1921 for five years. He has worked on the staff of *The New Yorker* in many capacities, and now contributes to this magazine and others. As a writer he is distinguished not only for his mainstream fiction but also for his crime and fantasy works. His novels run from *The Eater of Darkness* (1929) to *The Wisteria Cottage* (1948; reprinted as *The Night Before Dying*). Stories in *F&SF* were "Return of the Gods" (Win-Spr, 1950) and "A Parable of Love" (Sep 1957).
Fiction
Eater of Darkness, The (Macauley, New York, 1929, 238 pp., $2.50) (Putnam's 'Capricorn': CAP18, New York, 1959, 238 pp., pa $1.15)
This has been called "the first Dadaist novel," although that ancestor of surrealism had faded out some years earlier. It is a burlesque, by exaggeration, of the mad-scientist thriller of the day,

with its international criminal of many names whose "Dead Plane" can see through solid objects and fry the brains of its victims.

Hour After Westerly and Other Stories, The [C] (Harcourt Brace, New York, 1957, 216 pp., $3.50) (Longmans, Toronto, $4.00)

15 stories from *The New Yorker*: "In a Foreign City"; "The Reward"; "The Law"; "A Friendly Game of Cards"; "An Autumn Fable"; "The Hour After Westerly"; "The Storms of Childhood"; "The Need"; "The Decline and Fall of Perry Whitman"; "Accident at the Inn"; "The Man Who Vanished"; "Will You Wait?"; "A Parable of Love"; "Rendezvous"; "The Oracle."

COBB, IRVIN S(HREWSBURY) (23 June 1876–10 Mar 1944) American humorist and novelist. He began as a cub reporter, and later was a lecturer and war correspondent. He was traveling and even acting at the age of 60. He wrote millions of words—essays, articles, etc., many for syndicated columns. He wrote his first short story when he was 37. A fantasy besides the collection below is *The Escape of Mr. Trimm* (Doran, New York, 1913).

Fiction

Faith, Hope and Charity [C] (Bobbs Merrill, Indianapolis, 1934, 318 pp., $2.00)

Fantasy, 15 stories: "Ace, Deuce, Tenspot, Joker"; "At the Feet of the Enemy"; "Balm of Gilead"; "Bird in the Hand"; "Cabbages and Kings"; "Crime of the Century"; "Detail of the Depression"; "Faith, Hope and Charity"; "January Thaw"; "Lightnings of the Lord"; "Masterpiece"; "Moral Leopard"; "Nothing to Write About"; "Queer Creek"; "We Can't All Be Thoroughbreds."

COBLENTZ, STANTON A(RTHUR) (24 Aug 1896–) U.S. author and poet, one of the earliest sf magazine writers. He studied law at U. of California, but a year short of completion he turned to literature and in 1919 received his M.A. in English. In the early 1920's he wrote book reviews for some New York metropolitan newspapers. In 1933 he founded *Wings: A Quarterly of Verse*, which he edited until 1960; he has been connected with the Avalon Arts Academy and was co-editor of *Different*. His first volume of verse, *The Thinker and Other Poems*, was published in 1923; his first prose book, *The Decline of Man*, appeared in 1925. Numerous other works have followed through the years, including *The Literary Revolution*. Nonfiction works include *From Arrow to A-Bomb* (P. Owen, 1956), *Demons, Witchdoctors and Modern Man* (T. Yoseloff, New York, 1965, 485 pp., $7.50)–a cross-cultural technique of solving modern-age problems, and *Ten Crises in Civilization* (Follet, 1965; Muller, 1965); *Youth Madness* was a title in the British Utopian *American Fiction* series (pa).

Coblentz entered the sf field in the late 1920's with the novels *The Sunken World* and *The Blue Barbarians*. He is particularly noted for his satirical novels, such as *Hidden World* and *Lord of Tranerica*. Many of his novels appeared in the old sf quarterlies and later saw book editions; those not so far reprinted are "Reclaimers of the Ice" (*ASQ*, Spr 1930) and "The Man From Tomorrow" (*ASQ*, Spr-Sum 1933). His verse has appeared in many magazines, including *Famous Fantastic Mysteries*; a recent collection is *Atlantis and Other Poems* (Wings, 1960).

Fiction

After 12,000 Years (*ASQ*, Spr 1929) (FPCI, Los Angeles, 1950, 295 pp., $3.00)

One of Coblentz's better sf novels; a "sleeper awakes" theme, in a future world of organized insects.

Blue Barbarians, The (*ASQ*, Sum 1931) (Avalon, New York, 1958, 223 pp., $2.75)

Our society is belaboured in a burlesque about the businessmen's culture of Venus. The science doesn't hold together, but the satire is typical of Coblentz.

Crimson Capsule, The (Avalon, 1967, 190 pp., $3.25)

Suspended animation with a new type of life in a far future.

Day the World Stopped, The (Avalon, 1968, 189 pp., $3.50)

Hidden World ("In Caverns Below," *WS*, sr3, Mar 1935; *FSM*, Fall 1950) (Avalon, 1957, 224 pp., $2.75) (Airmont: SF6, 1964, 127 pp., pa 40¢)

A Coblentz satire describing an underground civilization with peculiar ways.

Into Plutonian Depths [pa] (*WSQ*, Spr 1931) (Avon: 281, 1950, 159 pp., pa 25¢)

Adventure among the "people" of Pluto.

Last of the Great Race, The (Arcadia, New York, 1964, 192 pp., $2.95)

Refugees from Mu are revived, and cause trouble in New York.

Lizard Lords, The (Avalon, 1964, 192 pp., $2.95)

Superlizards kidnap humans, who find two factions on the planet Drumgrade.

Lord of Tranerica (*Dynamic SF*, Feb 1939) (Avalon, 1966, 190 pp., $3.25)

A satire on dictatorship.

Lost Comet (Arcadia, 1964, 188 pp., $2.95)

Superinventor intends to use Earth's heat to reclaim the Arctic for man.

Moon People (Avalon, 1964, 191 pp., $2.95)

Inhabitants on the other side of the Moon have racial segregation and dry war.

Next Door to the Sun (Avalon, 1960, 224 pp., $2.95) (Ryerson, Toronto, $3.00)

After a poor start, this gives a delicious satire about the morals, manners and politics of a lost tribe from Earth living under a Plastidome on Mercury.

Pageant of Man, The (Wings, New York, 1936, 319 pp., $2.50)

Not in the Bleiler *Checklist*. A protest against the iniquities of the world; recommended by C. A. Brandt.

Planet of Youth, The (*WS*, Oct 1932) (*Tales of Wonder*, Win 1938) (FPCI, 1952, 71 pp., $1.50)

A novelette of the first real estate boom on Venus.

Runaway World, The (Avalon, 1961, 224 pp., $2.95) (Ryerson, Toronto, $3.25)

A wandering planet, Orcus, nearly wrecks Earth, and then is settled by half the human race; raiding for women follows.

Shadows on a Wall (Poetic Pubs., New York, 1930, 83 pp., $1.00)

A book of poems.

Sunken World, The (*ASQ*, Sum 1928; Fall 1934) (FPCI, 1949, 184 pp., $3.00; 1950, $2.50) (Kemsley: CT402, 1951, 190 pp., pa 1/6)

Coblentz's first published sf novel; adventure in the city of Atlantis.

Under the Triple Suns (Fantasy, Reading, 1955, 224 pp., $3.00) (*Un pianeta e tre stelle* [Italian], *Urania*: 111, 1955)

The settling of an extrasolar planet by a few survivors, after the Earth's end.

When the Birds Fly South (Wings, 1945, 223 pp., $2.50; 1951, $1.49)

A lost-race novel set in Afghanistan. An explorer marries a native girl, and finds himself alone when the people vanish for the winter.

Wonder Stick, The (Cosmopolitan, New York, 1929, 309 pp., illus.–S. Glenckoff, $2.00)

Well-written prehistoric type.

Anthology

Unseen Wings (Beechhurst, New York, 1948, 282 pp., $4.50)

Supposedly high-class verse anthology which follows the style of *The Haunted Hour* (M. Widdemer) and *Dark of the Moon* (A. Derleth). However, it has many flaws, omitting many noted names; it makes up slightly by including some of last century's classic British and U.S. writers.

COCKBURN, CLAUD (12 Apr 1904–) British author. He won a travelling fellowship of Queen's College, Oxford. He was a correspondent of *The Times* in New York and Washington (1929-32), and diplomatic and foreign correspondent of *The Daily Worker* (1935-46). He has been a regular contributor of humor to *Punch*, from which his "The Incredulity of Colonel Mumph" was reprinted in *F&SF* (Apr 1956).

Fiction

Overdraft on Glory [as James Helvick] (Boardman, London, 1955, 285 pp., 12/6) (Lippincott, Philadelphia, 1955, 320 pp., $3.95)

An unconventional story explaining why the crash of a jet plane on its first flight, July 13, 1910, has not come down through history.

COCKCROFT, THOMAS [TOM] G. L. New Zealand collector and bibliographer of weird fiction. He contributed verse and drawings to *The Acolyte* and also contributed to *The Shuttered Room and Other Pieces* (H. P. Lovecraft). He is an authority on Lovecraft, C. A. Smith, and some other writers. He has published the following of interest to bibliographers: *The Tales of Clark Ashton Smith: A Bibliography* (1951), *Index to the Verse in Weird Tales* (1960), and the notable two-part work below.

Nonfiction

Index to the Weird Fiction Magazines: Index by Author (Published by the compiler, Lower Hutt, N.Z., 1964, 100 pp., 17/6)

The following magazines are indexed: *Weird Tales, Strange Tales, Strange Stories, Strange Tales* (English), *The Thrill Book, Oriental Stories, The Magic Carpet* and *Golden Fleece*.

Index to the Weird Fiction Magazines: Index by Title (Published by the compiler, Lower Hutt, N.Z., 1962, 6¾ x 9¾ in., lithographed, 17/6)

This and the later volume (see above) satisfy a big need in the weird field. The compiler acknowledges the work of earlier enthusiasts.

CODY, C. S. (pseud.) See WALLER, L.

COFFIN, LEWIS
Fiction

Fog Boat, The [with Manning Long] (Lothrop Lee Shepard, New York, 1957, 128 pp., illus.–G. Miret, $2.75)

Juvenile, revivifying old myths of the sea and creating new ones.

COGGINS, JACK (BANHAM) (10 July 1911–) U.S. artist. He was born in London, the son of a career soldier. He has been a marine painter, war illustrator, and commercial writer. He was an artist and correspondent with *Yank* during World War II. He is now an art teacher. In the sf field Coggins became prominent with his illustrations for the nonfiction books *Rockets, Jets, Guided Missiles and Spaceships*; *By Space Ship to the Moon* and *All About Rockets and Jets* [all with text by F. Pratt]. He has done many fine covers for sf magazines, principally *Galaxy* and *F&SF*. His work generally depicts space ships in various locations.

COGSWELL, THEODORE R. (10 Mar 1918–) U.S. author and college instructor, born in Coatesville, Penna. He was an ambulance driver in the Spanish Republican Army 1937-39, and served in the U.S. Army Air Force as a statistical control officer 1942-46, in India, Burma and China. He took his B.A. at U. of Colorado in 1948, and his M.A. at U. of Denver 1948-49. He taught at U. of Minnesota 1949-53, and returned to U. of Colorado for postgraduate study 1956-57. He was assistant professor of English at Ball State Teachers College, Muncie, Indiana, 1958-65, and since 1965 has been with the English faculty at Keystone Junior College, La Plume, Pennsylvania. He was married in 1948 and has two daughters.

While teaching at U. of Minnesota he met Poul Anderson and Gordon Dickson, who urged him to write. He first appeared with "The Specter General" (*ASF*, June 1952), which created much interest. He has since written about 30 stories both sf and fantasy, including the short novel "The Other Cheek" (*SFA*, May 1953), has had a number of stories anthologised, and has written some sf and fantasy ballads.

Fiction

Third Eye, The [C] [pa] (Belmont: B50-840, 1968, 175 pp., pa 50¢)

16 stories (4th omitted from table of contents): "No Gun to the Victor" ("Deconditioned Response"); "Mr. Hoskin's Heel"; "The Cabbage Patch"; "Limiting Factor"; "Disassembly Line"; "A Spudget for Thwilbert"; "Training Device"; "Impact With the Devil"; "Machine Record"; "One to a Customer"; "The Man Who Knew Grodnik"; "Lover Boy"; "The Other Cheek"; "Minimum Sentence"; "The Short Count"; "Conventional Ending."

Wall Around the World, The [C] [pa] (Pyramid: F-703, 1962, 160 pp., pa 40¢) (*Die Mauer um die Welt* [German], *T*: 296, 1963 [abr.])

Sf and fantasy, 10 stories, with introduction by A. Boucher and F. Pohl: "The Masters"; "The Specter General"; "Wolfie"; "Emergency Rations"; "The Burning"; "Thimgs"; "Test Area"; "Prisoner of Love"; "Invasion Record"; "The Wall Around the World" (*Beyond*, st n, Sep 1953).

COHN, EMIL BERNHARD (1881–1948) German writer.
Fiction

Stories and Fantasies From the Jewish Past [Trans. from German—Charles Reznikoff] [C] (Jewish Pub. Soc. of America, Philadelphia, 1951, 262 pp., $3.00)

Fantasy, 10 stories: "The Given Years"; "Simha of Worms"; "Rabbi and Emperor"; "The Remains of Virtue"; "The Legend of Rabbi Akiba"; "Honi Ha-Meaggel"; "The Rebellious Tree"; "Rabban Gamaliel"; "The Waters of Shiloah"; "It Looks Like Justice."

COHN, VICTOR (4 Aug 1919–) U.S. writer. He is an able interpreter of the worlds of science and medicine, with articles in general magazines for which he does much research. He is Vice President of the National Association of Science Writers, and the American Association for the Advancement of Science has twice awarded him the annual George Westinghouse Prize for newspaper science writing. He is married, with three children.

Nonfiction

1999: Our Hopeful Future (Bobbs-Merrill, Indianapolis, 1956, 205 pp., illus., $3.75)

The author opens a vista that looks like a reckless pipe dream, but points out that most of it is already on the drawing board or in the laboratory.

COLBY, C(ARROLL) B(URLEIGH) (7 Sep 1904–) U.S. author, adventurer, and freelance artist. He was born in Claremont, N.H., and studied at Boston School of Practical Art. He was editor of *Air Trails* and *Air Progress* 1937-43, and aviation editor of *Popular Science* 1943-46. He is now a member of the Adventurers Club of New York and many professional writers' associations, including the Company of Military Historians. He is also a Lieut. Colonel in the Civil Air Patrol (U.S. Air Force auxiliary) and a Special Game Protector for the State of New York. Author of the syndicated newspaper column "Adventure Today," he has written or compiled over 70 books, including *Strangely Enough* (Popular Lib.).

Nonfiction

Weirdest People in the World [pa] (Popular: SP385, 1965, 143 pp., pa 50¢)

A collection of brief tales about inexplicable events, supposedly true, and including many concerning ghosts.

COLE, BURT (1930–)
Fiction

Subi: The Volcano (Macmillan, New York, 1957, 220 pp., $3.75) (W. H. Allen, London, 1958, 240 pp., 13/6; 1960, 6/-)

A moving novel of world war in the 1960's; "future" fiction rather than science fiction.

COLE, EVERETT B. (1910–) U.S. professional soldier, a signal maintenance and property officer at Fort Douglas, Utah. His first science fiction story was "Philosophical Corps" (*ASF*, Mar 1951), the first of a noted series (covered below). A more recent novel in *ASF* was "The Best Made Plans" (sr2, Nov 1959).

Series

Philosophical Corps. All in *ASF*: "Philosophical Corps" (Mar 1951); "These Shall Not Be Lost" (Jan 1953); "Exile" (Jan 1954); "Fighting Philosopher" (Apr 1954); "The Players" (Apr 1955); "Millennium" (May 1955); "Final Weapon" (June 1955); "The Missionaries" (May 1956).

Fiction

Philosophical Corps, The (Gnome, New York, 1962, 187 pp., $3.00)

Rewritten from "Fighting Philosopher," "Philosophical Corps," and "The Players."

COLE, WALTER R(ANDALL) (19 Apr 1933–) U.S. science fiction and fantasy bibliographer, formerly on the staff of *Science-Fiction Times* (amateur magazine).
Nonfiction
Checklist of Science Fiction Anthologies, A (Published by compiler, New York, 1964, xvi+374 pp., $7.50)
Checklist covers anthologies published in English 1927-63, but omits the purely weird or fantastic ones. It indexes 227 books containing nearly 2,700 stories, with listings by anthology titles, authors, story titles, etc.

COLEMAN, JAMES NELSON
Fiction
Seeker From the Stars [pa] (Berkley: X1438, 1967, 159 pp., pa 60¢)
Aliens help control Earth factions, but another alien enters the picture.

COLES, CYRIL HENRY See COLES, MANNING

COLES, MANNING Combined pseudonym of Cyril Henry Coles (11 June 1899) and Adelaide F. O. Manning, a neighbour with whom he collaborated in writing from 1936 until her death in 1959. Coles was born in London. He served in World War I in British Intelligence. During the Depression he travelled the world, spending some time in Victoria, Australia, where amongst other things he wrote a column a day for a Melbourne newspaper. Upon his return to England the writing partnership began; the success of their first novel, *Drink to Yesterday* (1940) was the forerunner of many more. The pair also used the pseudonym "Francis Gaite."
Fiction
Brief Candles (Doubleday, New York, 1954, 252 pp., $3.00)
Quiet farce of two Victorian ghosts at large in Paris; sequel is *Happy Returns*.
Come and Go (as Francis Gaite: Hodder & Stoughton, London, 1958, 192 pp., 12/6) (as Manning Coles: Doubleday, 1958, 236 pp., $3.75)
A follow-on to *Brief Candles* and *Happy Returns*. A distant cousin is rescued from an overbearing aunt, saved from various perils, and delivered to a beautiful damsel.
Family Matter See *Happy Returns*
Far Traveller, The (Doubleday, 1956, 224 pp., $3.00)
The ghost of a drowned man portrays his descendant for a British film company.
Happy Returns (Doubleday, 1955, 224 pp., $3.00) (*Family Matter*, Hodder & Stoughton, 1956, 192 pp., 10/6)
The spectral Victorian brothers of *Brief Candles* have further zany exploits; a later book is *Come and Go*.

COLLIER, JOHN (3 May 1901–) British author. His first writings were verse, at the age of 19. He later won *This Quarter*'s prize for English poetry, and was poetry editor of *Time and Tide* for several years. His scholarly interests are shown in his editing of *John Aubrey* the 17th Century autobiographer. Collier's first novel was *His Monkey Wife* (1930); a later non-fantasy was *Defy the Foul Fiend* (1934). His most notable collection is *Fancies and Goodnights*, which won the 1952 International Fantasy Award. Two of his stories were reprinted in *F&SF*: "After the Ball" (Nov 1959) and "Man Overboard" (Mar 1960). His noted short stories "Green Thoughts" and "Thus I Refute Beelzy" originally appeared in *Harper's* (May 1931) and *Atlantic* (Oct 1940). He has often been anthologised. A German collection is *Mitternachtsblaue Geschichten* (Rowohlt, 1967).
Fiction
Devil and All, The [C] (Nonesuch Press, London, 1934, vi+125 pp., 12/6; 1,000 signed by author)
6 stories: "Possession of Angela Bradshaw"; "The Right Side"; "Halfway to Hell"; "After the Ball"; "The Devil, George and Rosie"; "Hell Hath No Fury."
Fancies and Goodnights [C] (Doubleday, New York, 1951, 364 pp., $4.00) (Bantam: A1106, 1953, 506 pp., pa 35¢; F1703, 1956, 375 pp., pa 50¢; SC91, 1963, 418 pp., pa 75¢) (abr. as *Of*

Demons and Darkness, Corgi: FS7126, 1965, 303 pp., pa 5/-)
Weird, 50 stories, including nearly all those in *Presenting Moonshine* and *The Touch of Nutmeg*, and 17 never before published in book form (the British *Of Demons and Darkness* contains the first 37 stories plus the introduction from the 1963 Bantam edition): "Bottle Party"; De Mortuis"; "Evening Primrose"; "Witch's Money"; "Are You Too Late, Or Was I Too Early?"; "Fallen Star"; "The Touch of Nutmeg Makes It"; "Three Bears Cottage"; "Pictures in the Fire"; "Wet Saturday"; "Squirrels Have Bright Eyes"; "Halfway to Hell"; "The Lady on the Grey"; "Incident on a Lake"; "Over Insurance"; "Old Acquaintance"; "The Frog Prince"; "Season Mists"; "Great Possibilities"; "Without Benefit of Galsworthy"; "The Devil, George, and Rosie"; "Ah, the University"; "Back for Christmas"; "Another American Tragedy"; "Collaboration"; "Midnight Blue"; "Gavin O'Leary"; "If Youth Knew If Age Could"; "Thus I Refute Beelzy"; "Special Delivery"; "Rope Enough"; "Little Memento"; "Green Thoughts"; "Romance Lingers, Adventure Lives"; "Bird of Prey"; "Variation on a Theme"; "Night! Youth! Paris! and the Moon"; "The Steel Cat"; "Sleeping Beauty"; "Interpretations of a Dream"; "Mary"; "Hell Hath No Fury"; "In the Cards"; "The Invisible Dove-Dancer of Strathpeen Island"; "The Right Side"; "Spring Fever"; "Youth From Vienna"; "Possession of Angela Bradshaw"; "Cancel All I Said"; "The Chaser." This won the first International Fantasy Award in 1952, and also won the Edgar award of the Mystery Writers of America.
Full Circle, A Tale (Appleton, New York, 1933, 290 pp., $2.00) (*Tom's A-Cold*, Macmillan, London, 1933, 320 pp., 7/6; 1936, 3/6)
A gloomy picture of England reduced by war to primitive savagery, and the development of a new civilization.
Green Thoughts (W. Jackson, London, 1932, 56 pp., 10/6, 550 copies)
Green Thoughts and Other Strange Tales [C] [pa] (Armed: 871, nd, 287 pp., pa)
Weird, 24 stories, Armed Services edition: "Green Thoughts"; "The Touch of Nutmeg Makes It"; "De Mortuis"; "Wet Saturday"; "Little Memento"; "Mary"; "Midnight Blue"; "Back for Christmas"; "Evening Primrose"; "The Frog Prince"; "Rope Enough"; "The Chaser"; "The Devil, George and Rosie"; "Halfway to Hell"; "Possession of Angela Bradshaw"; "The Right Side"; "Another American Tragedy"; "Bird of Prey"; "Thus I Refute Beelzy"; "Night! Youth! Paris! and the Moon!"; "Variation on a Theme"; "Old Acquaintance"; "Ah, the University"; "Hell Hath No Fury."
His Monkey Wife, or Married to a Chimp (Davies, London, 1930, 274 pp., 7/6) (Appleton, New York, 1931, 301 pp., $2.00) ([German], Tauchnitz: 4994, 1931) (Hart-Davis 'Uniform Edition,' London, 1957, 185 pp., 13/6) (Doubleday, 1957, $3.75) (D'day, Toronto, $4.25)
The hero is engaged to a modern young lady but fails to see her glaring flaws or the virtues of his pet, an adoring chimpanzee.
No Traveller Returns (White Owl, London, 1931, 62 pp., 210 copies)
A fantasy apparently not later reprinted. Some copies were specially signed, including a number on vellum.
Of Demons and Darkness [pa] See *Fancies and Goodnights*
Pictures in the Fire [C] (Hart-Davis 'Uniform Edition Vol. 3,' 1958, 190 pp., 13/6) ([Japanese], Hayakawa 'Tales of Menace': 6, 1961, pa)
23 stories: "Interpretation of a Dream"; "And Who, With Eden ..."; "Little Memento"; "Are You Too Late, or Was I Too Early?"; "Think No Evil"; "Incident on a Lake"; "Old Acquaintance"; "Mademoiselle Kiki"; "Without Benefit of Galsworthy"; "Spring Fever"; "Back for Christmas"; "Pictures in the Fire"; "Romance Lingers, Adventure Lives"; "The Steel Cat"; "In the Cards"; "Wet Saturday"; "Season of Mists"; "Over Insurance"; "De Mortuis"; "Ah, the University"; "Three Bears Cottage"; "Gavin O'Leary"; "The Tender Age."
Presenting Moonshine [C] (Viking, New York, 1941, 327 pp., $2.50) (Macmillan, Toronto, $3.00) (Macmillan, London, 1941, 359 pp., 8/6) (Hart-Davis 'Uniform Edition,' 1957, 192 pp., 13/6)
Weird, 24 stories: "Another American Tragedy"; "Bird of

Prey"; "Bottle Party"; "The Chaser"; "Collaboration"; "The Devil, George, and Rosie"; "Evening Primrose"; "Frog Prince"; "Green Thoughts"; "Halfway to Hell"; "If Youth Knew If Age Could"; "The Invisible Dove-Dancer of Strathpeen Island"; "Mary"; "Night! Youth! Paris! and the Moon"; "Old Acquaintance"; "Possession of Angela Bradshaw"; "Right Side"; "Rope Enough"; "Sleeping Beauty"; "Special Delivery"; "Squirrels Have Bright Eyes"; "Thus I Refute Beelzy"; "Variation on a Theme"; "Witch's Money."

Tom's A-Cold See *Full Circle*

Touch of Nutmeg and Other Unlikely Stories, The [C] (Readers Club, New York, 1943, 247 pp., $2.00) (*Un Rien de Muscade* [French], Hachette, 1949)

Weird, 26 stories: "After the Ball"; "Ah, the University"; "Another American Tragedy"; "Back for Christmas"; "Bird of Prey"; "The Chaser"; "De Mortuis"; "The Devil, George, and Rosie"; "Evening Primrose"; "Frog Prince"; "Great Possibilities"; "Green Thoughts"; "Halfway to Hell"; "Hell Hath No Fury"; "Little Memento"; "Mary"; "Midnight Blue"; "Night! Youth! Paris! and the Moon"; "Old Acquaintance"; "Possession of Angela Bradshaw"; "Right Side"; "Rope Enough"; "Thus I Refute Beelzy"; "The Touch of Nutmeg Makes It"; "Variations on a Theme"; "Wet Saturday."

Variation on a Theme (Grayson, London, 1935, 64 pp., illus., 10/6)

First publication of this story, later reprinted in collections.

COLLINS, CHARLES M.
Anthologies

Feast of Blood, A [pa] (Avon: S277, 1967, 190 pp., pa 60¢)

Introduction "Images of the Vampire," by compiler, and Bibliography of Gothic Items. 9 stories: "The Mysterious Stranger" (1860), Anon. [from the German]; "The Vampyre" (1819), Dr. John W. Polidor; "Dracula's Guest" (1914), Bram Stoker; "Wake Not the Dead" (*ca.* 1800), Johann L. Tieck; "Revelations in Black" (1933), Carl Jacobi; "Schloss Wappenberg" (1948), D. Scott-Moncrieff; "The Room in the Tower" (1912), E. F. Benson; "Blood Son" (1951), Richard Matheson; "A Rendezvous in Averoigne" (1931), Clark A. Smith.

Fright [pa] (Avon: G1178, 1963, 141 pp., pa 50¢)

Weird, 6 stories with compiler's introduction and foreword to first story: "The Forest Warden," E. T. A. Hoffman; "Schalken the Painter," Joseph S. Le Fanu; "Podolo," L. P. Hartley; "Glamour," Seabury Quinn; "Clay," C. Hall Thompson; "The Horror at Red Hook," H. P. Lovecraft.

COLLINS, ERROL
Fiction [juvenile]

Mariners of Space (Lutterworth, London, 1949, 240 pp., 5/-) (*Krieg zwischen den Welten* and *Flucht zur Erde* [German], *UG*: 12, 13, 1954)

Interplanetary war and adventure in 2000 AD.

Submarine City (Lutterworth, 1949, 247 pp., 5/-)

International pirates capture a submarine city in the Atlantic.

COLLINS, GILBERT (1890-) British author. After working in the British Civil Service and serving in the British Army in World War I, he spent 1919-22 in the British Consular Service in China. Since 1922 he has been a journalist and has travelled throughout Europe. He wrote light verse for *Punch* (1913-19); it was collected as *Sidelights of Song*. He has also written detective thrillers such as *Death Meets the King's Messenger* and straight thrillers such as *Horror Comes to Thripplands*.
Fiction

Starkenden Quest, The (McBride, New York, 1925, 13+316 pp., $2.00) (Duckworth, London, 7/6) (*FFM*, Oct 1949)

A strange country and an intrigue between two brothers, one enslaved by drugs.

Valley of Eyes Unseen, The (Duckworth, 1923, 327 pp., 7/6) (McBride, 1924, 327 pp., $2.00) (*FFM*, Feb 1952)

Adventure in finding the secret of Lost Tibet's phantom valley. It was rewritten five times before publication.

COLLINS, HUNT (pseud) See HUNTER, E.

COLLINS, VERE HENRY
Anthologies

Ghosts and Marvels (Oxford U. Press "World Classics," 1924, 506 pp., 2/-, 3¾ x 6 in.; 1927)

Subtitled: A selection of uncanny tales from Daniel Defoe to Algernon Blackwood. 15 stories and introduction by M. R. James: "Mrs. Veal," D. Defoe; "Wandering Willie's Tale," Sir W. Scott; "The Werewolf," F. Marryat; "The Haunted and the Haunters; or, The House and the Brain," Lord Lytton; "Young Goodman Brown," N. Hawthorne; "Ligeia," E. A. Poe; "A Strange Event in the Life of Schalken the Painter," J. S. Le Fanu; "The Lifted Veil," G. Eliot; "The Open Door," Mrs. Oliphant; "The Body-Snatcher," R. L. Stevenson; "The Monkey's Paw," W. W. Jacobs; "The Crystal Egg," H. G. Wells; "Ancient Sorceries," A. Blackwood; "The Moon-Slave," B. Pain; "Casting the Runes," M. R. James.

More Ghosts and Marvels (OUP "Worlds Classics," 1929, 498 pp., 2/-, 3¾ x 6 in.)

Subtitled: A selection of uncanny tales from Sir Walter Scott to Michael Arlen. 20 stories: "The Tapestried Chamber," Sir W. Scott; "The Botathen Ghost," R. S. Hawker; "The Facts in the Case of M. Valdemar," E. A. Poe; "The Old Nurse's Story," Mrs. Gaskell; "No. 1 Branch Line: The Signalman," C. Dickens; "Squire Toby's Will," J. S. Le Fanu; "The Lady in the Mirror," G. MacDonald; "The Case of Mr. Lucraft," Sir W. Besant & J. Rice; "The Great Good Place," H. James; "The Upper Berth," F. M. Crawford; "The Novel of the White Powder," A. Machen; "The Door in the Wall," H. G. Wells; "Negotium Perambulans," E. F. Benson; "Running Wolf," A. Blackwood; "Venus," M. Baring; "The Bureau d'Echange de Maux," Lord Dunsany; "Loquier's Third Act," Katharine F. Gerould; "Nightmare Jack," J. Metcalfe; "Where Their Fire Is Not Quenched," May Sinclair; "The Ancient Sin," M. Arlen.

COLLINS, (WILLIAM) WILKIE (8 Jan 1824-23 Sep 1889) British author. His godfather was Sir David Wilkie, the painter. Apprenticed to the tea business, he deserted it to study law, and was called to the bar in 1851. While articled to the tea firm he wrote a novel secretly, and upon its success and his friendship with Charles Dickens he adopted writing as a career. In 1855 he began writing stories for *Household Words*, which was edited by Dickens. His flair was for mystery novels and he was recognised as a master of the involved plot. After his first novel, *Hide and Seek* (1854), he became particularly noted for his dramatic *The Woman in White* (1860), which has been often reprinted and was eventually filmed, and for *The Moonstone* (1868), which was based on a contemporary murder case and also has been often reprinted. A fantasy besides those below was *The Haunted Hotel: A Mystery of Modern Venice* (Lovell, New York, 1887).
Fiction

After Dark and Other Stories [C] (Tauchnitz, Leipzig, 1856, 377 pp.) (? , London, 1864) (Harper, New York, 1873, 536 pp., illus.) (Chatto Windus, London, 1894, 392 pp.) (other London editions, 1900, 1902, 1904)

The Bleiler *Checklist* notes the Harper edition as the first. Contents of the editions vary; the following is for Chatto Windus 1894. 7 stories: "Leaves From Leah's Diary"; "The Traveller's Story: A Terribly Strange Bed"; "The Lawyer's Story: A Stolen Letter"; "The French Governess' Story: Sister Rose"; "The Angler's Story: The Lady of Glenwith Grange"; "The Nun's Story: Gabriel's Marriage"; "The Professor's Story: The Yellow Mask."

Ghost's Touch and Other Stories, The [C] (Harper, New York, 1885, 198 pp.) (*The Ghost's Touch*, Lovell, New York, 1885, 116 pp.)

Harper ed. has 3 stories: "The Ghost's Touch"; "My Lady's Money"; "Percy and the Prophet." Lovell ed. has 3 stories, omitting "My Lady's Money" and adding "Our Last Walk."

Tales of Suspense [edited by Robert Ashley & H. Van Thal] [C] (Folio Society, London, 1954, illus.–Anne Scott)

No further information.

COLVIN, IAN G. (23 Nov 1912–) British author. He was born in London, the son of author Ian Duncan Colvin. He studied at the Sorbonne and other colleges. He has been a journalist and leader writer with the *Daily Telegraph* since 1933.
Fiction
Domesday Village (Falcon, London, 1948, 126 pp., 7/6)
Brief novel of the socialised Britain of 1986.

COLVIN, JAMES (pseud) See MOORCOCK, M.

COLWELL, EILEEN
Anthology
Hallowe'en Acorn, A (Bodley Head, London, 1966, 95 pp., 10/6)
Juvenile, 17 stories and poems, those given as Anon. being traditional: "Hallowe'en Party," Eileen Colwell; "The Witch in the Forest," Anon.; "Teeny-Tiny," Joseph Jacobs; "Rhyme," "Peeping Jane," Anon.; "The Witch," Caron Rock; "The Wee Ghostie," Alison Uttley; "Jorinda and Joringel," Anon.; "Spells," Leonard Clark; "Biddy and the Hallowe'en Cat," Anon.; "The Clock That Wasn't There," E. Colwell; "The Hare," Walter de la Mare; "Childe Roland," Anon.; "Brer Rabbit and the Spewter Slutter Ghost," Joel C. Harris; "The Fairy Ointment," "Three Little Ghostesses," Anon.; "The King of the Cats," J. Jacobs.

COMPTON, D(AVID) G(UY) (9 Aug 1930–) British author and playwright.
Fiction
Farewell, Earth's Bliss (Hodder Stoughton, London, 1966, 191 pp., 18/-)
Mars becomes a dumping ground for Earth's misfits.
Quality of Mercy: A Novel of 1979, The (Hodder, 1965, 157 pp., 16/-)
Thriller based on the population explosion.
Silent Multitude, The (Hodder, 1967, 190 pp., 21/-)
Four people are alone in an evacuated city of the near future—a masterpiece of urban planning—and each awaits its disintegration.
Synthajoy (Hodder, 1968, 190 pp., 25/-) (Ace: H-86, 1968, 189 pp., pa 60¢)
A novel set within a mind that is being reshaped by machine.

COMYNS, BARBARA (IRENE VERONICA) (nee BAYLEY) (27 Dec 1912–) British author. She was born at Bidford-on-Avon, and was educated mostly by governesses. She worked in commercial art studios before her marriage to Richard Comyns-Carr; they live in Spain. She has contributed to *Lilliput*. Her earlier novels were *Sisters by a River* and *Our Spoons Come From Woolworths*.
Fiction
Vet's Daughter, The (Heinemann, London, 1959, 190 pp., 13/6)
The story of a strange case of levitation, based on an Edwardian newspaper account.
Who Was Changed and Who Was Dead (J. Lane, London, 1954, 146 pp., 8/6)
Macabre.

CONDON, RICHARD (THOMAS) (18 Mar 1915–) U.S. author and film publicist, born in New York City. On Broadway he co-produced *Twentieth Century* and *Stalag 17* with José Ferrer, 1951-52. He has been a publicist for the U.S. film industry for over 20 years.
Fiction
Manchurian Candidate, The (McGraw-Hill, New York & Toronto, 1959, 311 pp., $4.50) (Pan: X156, 1962, 272 pp., pa 3/6) (Signet: T1826, 1960, 351 pp., pa 75¢)
A fertile hybrid between sf and a suspense thriller, with good characterisation. A U.S. soldier is hypnotised by the Communists in Korea and turned into a Communist time-bomb. His former commander struggles to de-fuze him.

CONGDON, DON U.S. author's agent (with Harold Matson Agency) and anthologist. His mainstream anthologies include *The Wild Sweet Wine* and *Sensual Love*.

Anthologies
Alone By Night [with Michael Congdon] [pa] (Ballantine: 563, 1961, 144 pp., pa 35¢; U2852, 1967, pa 50¢)
Weird, 11 stories: "Sweets to the Sweet" [witch], R. Bloch; "The Strange Children" [ghost], Elisabeth S. Holding; "The Likeness of Julie" [succubus], Logan Swanson; "It Will Come to You" [ghoul], Frank B. Long; "A Gnome There Was" [gnome], H. Kuttner; "Nightmare at Twenty Thousand Feet" [gremlin], R. Matheson; "In the Midst of Death" [phantom], Ben Hecht; "Gabriel-Ernest" [werewolf], Saki; "Baynter's Imp" [imp], A. Derleth; "Enoch" [fiend], R. Bloch; "For the Blood Is Life" [vampire], F. Marion Crawford.
Stories for the Dead of Night [pa] (Dell: B107, 1957, 288 pp., pa 35¢; 8925, 1967, 240 pp., pa 50¢)
Weird, 20 stories: "The Shadow," B. Hecht; "Miss Gentilbelle," Charles Beaumont; "The Chaser," J. Collier; "Taboo," G. Household; "Revenge," Sam'l Blas; "The Pit," Gwyn Jones; "The Man From the South," R. Dahl; "Sredni Vashtar," Saki; "The Demon Lover," Elizabeth Bowen; "Silver Circus," A. E. Coppard; "Palace of Sleep," Anna Kavan; "The Woman at Seven Brothers," W. D. Steele; "A Journey," Edith Wharton; "The Lottery," Shirley Jackson; "Two Bottles of Relish," Lord Dunsany; "The Proof," J. Moore; "The Turn of the Tide," C. S. Forester; "The Tell-Tale Heart," E. A. Poe; "The Middle Toe of the Right Foot," A. Bierce; "The Illustrated Man," R. Bradbury.
Tales of Love and Horror [pa] (Ballantine: 522K, 1961, 144 pp., pa 35¢)
Weird, 12 stories: "No Such Thing as a Vampire," R. Matheson; "The Love Letter," Jack Finney; "The Horsehair Trunk," Davis Grubb; "Lucia's Kiss," Roderick MacLeish; "The Sign of Scorpio," Charles Mergendahl; "Clay-Shuttered Doors," Helen R. Hull; "Various Temptations," Wm. Sansom; "The Nature of the Evidence," May Sinclair; "Tactical Exercise," Evelyn Waugh; "The Illustrated Woman," Ray Bradbury; "The Shout," R. Graves; "Not Far Away, Not Long Ago," J. Collier.

CONGDON, MICHAEL See CONGDON, D. (co-anthologist)

CONKLIN, (EDWARD) GROFF (6 Sep 1904–20 July 1968) U.S. anthologist. He burst into the science fiction field in 1946 with his superb anthology *The Best of Science Fiction*. Thereafter he compiled nearly forty anthologies in both the sf and fantasy fields, all of which are recommended. He wrote general articles outside the field, and was book editor for Robert McBride & Co., and later was scientific researcher for the N. W. Ayer & Son advertising agency. He edited the Grosset & Dunlap SF series (books) of the early 1950's, and also author collections of T. Sturgeon (*A Way Home*) and E. A. Poe (*Ten Great Mysteries*). He did the book reviews for *Galaxy Science Fiction* from the first issue (Oct 1950) through to Oct 1955. He was Editorial and Writing Consultant to the American Diabetes Association, Consultant Science Fiction Editor for Collier Books, and for the last three years prior to his death, Science Editor for the *American Heritage Dictionary of the English Language*. He left a widow, his second wife.
Anthologies
Adventures in Dimension See *Science Fiction Adventures in Dimension*
Another Part of the Galaxy [pa] (Gold Medal: d1628, 1966, 224 pp., pa 50¢)
Sf, 6 stories and introduction: "The Red Hills of Summer," E. Pangborn; "Big Sword," Paul Ash; "First Lady," J. T. McIntosh; "Insidekick," J. F. Bone; "The Live Coward," P. Anderson; "Still Life," E. F. Russell.
Best of Science Fiction, The (Crown, New York, 1946, 785 pp., $3.50) (Crown 'Bonanza,' 1963, 440 pp., pa $1.95)
Sf, 40 stories, with preface "Concerning Science Fiction," J. W. Campbell, and compiler's introduction (pa ed., 22 stories marked †, with new introduction): *I. The Atom:* "Solution Unsatisfactory," A. MacDonald; "The Great War Syndicate" (abr.), F. Stockton; "The Piper's Son"†, L. Padgett; "Deadline"†, C. Cartmill; "Lobby"†, C. D. Simak; "Blowups Happen," R. A. Heinlein; "Atomic Power," D. A. Stuart. *II. The Wonders of the Earth:*

"Killdozer"†, T. Sturgeon; "Davy Jones' Ambassador"†, R. Z. Gallun; "Giant in the Earth"†, M. Colladay; "Goldfish Bowl"†, A. MacDonald; "The Ivy War"†, D. H. Keller; "Liquid Life," R. M. Farley. *III. The Superscience of Man:* "A Tale of the Ragged Mountains," E. A. Poe; "The Great Keinplatz Experiment," A. C. Doyle; "The Remarkable Case of Davidson's Eyes," H. G. Wells; "The Tissue-Culture King," Julian Huxley; "The Ultimate Catalyst," J. Taine; "The Terrible Sense"†; C. Peregoy; "A Scientist Divides," D. Wandrei. *IV. Dangerous Inventions:* "Tricky Tonnage"†, M. Jameson; "The Lanson Screen," A. L. Zagat; "The Ultimate Metal," N. Schachner; "The Machine"†, D. A. Stuart. *V. Adventures in Dimension:* "Short-Circuited Probability"†, N. L. Knight; "The Search"†, A. E. van Vogt; "The Upper Level Road," W. Van Lorne; "The 32nd of May"†, P. Ernst; "The Monster From Nowhere"†, Nelson Bond [error in first printing credited this to D. Wandrei]. *VI. From Outer Space:* "First Contact"†, M. Leinster; "Universe"†, R. A. Heinlein; "Blind Alley"†, I. Asimov; "En Route to Pluto"†, W. West; "The Retreat to Mars," C. B. White; "The Man Who Saved the Earth," A. Hall; "Spawn of the Stars," C. W. Diffin; "The Flame Midget"†, F. B. Long; "Expedition"†, A. Boucher; "The Conquest of Gola," Leslie F. Stone; "Jackdaw"†, R. Rocklynne. One of the best sf anthologies, and widely recommended.

Big Book of Science Fiction, The (Crown, 1950, 545 pp., $3.50) (Berkley: G53, 1957, 187 pp., pa 35¢; F975, 1964, pa 50¢)

Sf, 32 stories (pa, 10 stories marked †) and compiler's introduction: *I. Inventions, Dangerous and Otherwise:* "Mr. Murphy of New York," Thomas McMorrow; "The Diminishing Draft," W. Kaempffert; "Peacebringer" ("Sword of Peace"), Ward Moore; "A Matter of Form," H. L. Gold. *II. Wonders of Earth and of Man:* "The Planetoid of Doom," M. Colladay; "One Leg Too Many," W. Alexander; "Man With the Strange Head," M. J. Breuer; "Defense Mechanism," Katherine MacLean; "Margin for Error," L. Padgett. *III. From Outer Space:* "Isolationist," M. Reynolds; "Nobody Saw the Ship"†, M. Leinster; "Mewhu's Jet"†, T. Sturgeon; "The Outer Limit," Graham Doar; "Rat Race," Dorothy & John de Courcy; "Dear Devil," E. F. Russell. *IV. Adventures in Dimension:* "Emergency Landing," Ralph Williams; "The Ship That Turned Aside," Green Peyton (Wertenbaker); "Manna," Peter Phillips; "The Long Dawn," N. Loomis; "E for Effort," T. L. Sherred. *V. Far Travelling:* "The Roger Bacon Formula"†, F. Pratt; "The Wings of Night"†, L. del Rey; "Desertion"†, C. D. Simak; "Contact, Incorporated" ("Action on Azura"), Robertson Osborne; "Arena"†, F. Brown; "Culture," Jerry Shelton. *VI. World of Tomorrow:* "In the Year 2889," J. Verne; "Forever and the Earth"†, R. Bradbury; "The Miniature"†, J. D. MacDonald; "Sanity"†, F. Leiber; "The Only Thing We Learn"†, C. M. Kornbluth; "Not With a Bang," D. Knight.

Br-r-r! [pa] (Avon: T-289, 1959, 192 pp., pa 35¢)

Weird, 10 stories: "It," T. Sturgeon; "Nursery Rhyme," C. Beaumont; "Doomsday Deferred," W. F. Jenkins; "Warm, Dark Places," H. L. Gold; "Legal Rites," I. Asimov & F. Pohl; "An Egyptian Hornet," A. Blackwood; "White Goddess," Idris Seabright; "The Handler," R. Bradbury; "The Sound Machine," R. Dahl; "The Worm," D. H. Keller.

Crossroads in Time [pa] (Permabook: P254, 1953, 312 pp., pa 35¢)

Sf, 16 short stories and 2 novelettes: "Assumption Unjustified" (n'te), H. Clement; "The Eagles Gather," J. E. Kelleam; "The Queen's Astrologer," M. Leinster; " 'Derm Fool'," T. Sturgeon; "Courtesy," C. D. Simak; "Secret," Lee Cahn; "Thirsty God," Marg. St. Clair; "The Mutant's Brother," F. Leiber; "Student Body," F. L. Wallace; "Made in U.S.A." (n'te), J. T. M'Intosh; "Technical Advisor," Chad Oliver; "Feedback," Kath. MacLean; "The Cave," P. S. Miller; "Vocation," G. O. Smith; "The Time Decelerator," A. MacFadyen, Jr.; "Zen," J. Bixby; "Let There Be Light," H. B. Fyfe; "The Brain," W. Norbert.

Dimension 4 [pa] (Pyramid: F-973, 1964, 159 pp., pa 40¢)

Sf, 4 short novels with introductory remarks on each: "Won't You Walk?" Theodore Sturgeon (*ASF*, Jan 1956); "Sense of Proportion," E. C. Tubb (*Nebula*, Nov 1958); "Trojan Horse Laugh," John D. MacDonald (*ASF*, Aug 1949); "Some Day We'll Find

You," Cleve Cartmill (*ASF*, Dec 1942).

Elsewhere and Elsewhen [pa] (Berkley: S1561, 1968, 253 pp., pa 75¢)

Sf, 9 stories with compiler's introduction: *Elsewhen:* "Shortstack," Walt & Leigh Richmond; "How Allied," M. Clifton; "The Wrong World," J. T. McIntosh; "World in a Bottle," A. K. Lang. *Elsewhere:* "Think Blue, Count Two," Cordwainer Smith; "Turning Point," P. Anderson; "The Book," M. Shaara; "Trouble Tide," J. H. Schmitz; "The Earthman's Burden," D. E. Westlake.

Enemies in Space [pa] See *Invaders of Earth*

Fifty Short Science Fiction Tales [pa] See ASIMOV, I. (co-anthologist)

Five-Odd [pa] (Pyramid: R-1056, 1964, 188 pp., pa 50¢)

Sf, 5 stories with brief introduction [no authors credited on contents page]: "The Dead Past," Isaac Asimov (*ASF*, Apr 1956); "Something Strange," Kingsley Amis (*F&SF*, July 1961); "Unit," J. T. McIntosh (*NW*, Feb 1957); "Gone Fishing," James H. Schmitz (*ASF*, May 1961); "Big Ancestor," F. L. Wallace (*GSF*, Nov 1954).

5 Unearthly Visions [pa] (Gold Medal: d1549, 1965, 175 pp., pa 50¢; D1868, 1967, pa 50¢)

Sf, 5 stories with introductory paragraph on each: "Legwork," Eric F. Russell (*ASF*,Apr 1956); "Conditionally Human," Walter M. Miller, Jr. (*GSF*, Feb 1952); "Stamped Caution," Raymond Z. Gallun (*GSF*, Sep 1953); "Dio," Damon Knight (*Infinity*, Sep 1957); "Shadow World," Clifford D. Simak (*GSF*, Sep 1957).

Four for the Future [pa] (Pyramid: G-434, 1959, 160 pp., pa 35¢; F-743, 1962, pa 40¢) (Consul: N1018, 1961, 174 pp., pa 2/6)

Sf, novelettes: "Enough Rope," Poul Anderson (*ASF*, July 1953); "The Claustrophile," T. Sturgeon (*GSF*, Aug 1956); "The Children's Hour," H. Kuttner (*ASF*, Mar 1944); "Plus X," Eric F. Russell (*ASF*, June 1956).

Giants Unleashed (Grosset & Dunlap, New York, 1965, 248 pp., $2.95; lib. bdg. $3.19) (Tempo: T111, 1966, 248 pp., pa 50¢)

Sf, 12 stories with compiler's introduction, "The Non-Limitation of Intelligence": "Microcosmic God," Theodore Sturgeon; "Commencement Night," Richard Ashby; "Deep Range," Arthur C. Clarke; "Machine Made," J. T. McIntosh; "Trip One," Edward Grendon; "Venus Is a Man's World," Wm. Tenn; "Goodbye, Ilha!" Lawrence Manning; "Misbegotten Missionary," Isaac Asimov; "The Ethical Equations," Murray Leinster; "Misfit," Robert A. Heinlein; "Genius," Poul Anderson; "Basic Right," Eric Frank Russell.

Graveyard Reader, The [pa] (Ballantine: 257, 1958, 156 pp., pa 35¢; U2822, 1965, pa 50¢)

Weird, 12 stories: "The Screaming Woman," R. Bradbury; "A Bottomless Grave," A. Bierce; "The Cart," R. Hughes; "The Graveyard Rats," H. Kuttner; "Skin," R. Dahl; "Night Court," M. E. Counselman; "Free Dirt," C. Beaumont; "Listen, Children, Listen," W. West; "Special Delivery," J. Collier; "The Child That Loved a Grave," F.-J. O'Brien; "The Outsider," H. P. Lovecraft; "The Graveyard Reader," T. Sturgeon.

Great Science Fiction About Doctors [with Noah D. Fabricant] [pa] (Collier: AS518, 1963, 412 pp., pa 95¢; 01895, 1965, pa 95¢)

Sf, 18 stories with compilers' introduction, and introductory remarks on each story: "The Man Without and Appetite," Miles J. Breuer; "Out of the Cradle, Endlessly Orbiting," Arthur C. Clarke; "The Brothers," Clifton Dance Jr., "The Great Keinplatz Experiment," Sir Arthur Conan Doyle; "Compound B," David H. Fink; "Rappaccini's Daughter," Nathaniel Hawthorne; "The Psychophonic Nurse," David H. Keller; "The Little Black Bag," C. M. Kornbluth; "Ribbon in the Sky," Murray Leinster; "Mate in Two Moves," Winston K. Marks; "Bedside Manner," Wm. Morrison; "The Shopdropper," Alan Nelson; "Family Resemblance," Alan E. Nourse; "Facts in the Case of M. Valdemar," E. A. Poe; "Emergency Operation," Arthur Porges; "A Matter of Ethics," J. R. Shango; "Bolden's Pets," F. L. Wallace; "Expedition Mercy," J. A. Winter. This pair also compiled *Great Detective Stories About Doctors* (Collier, 1965, pa).

Great Science Fiction by Scientists [pa] (Collier: AS218, 1962, 313 pp., pa 95¢; 01903, 1966, pa 95¢)

16 stories, with compiler's introduction and introductory prefaces: "What If . . .," I. Asimov; "The Ultimate Catalyst," Eric T. Bell; "The Gostak and the Doshes," M. J. Breuer; "Summertime on Icarus" ("The Hottest Piece of Real Estate in the Solar System"), A. C. Clarke; "The Neutrino Bomb," Ralph S. Cooper; "Last Year's Grave Undug" (new), Chan Davis; "The Gold-Makers," J. B. S. Haldane; "The Tissue-Culture King," Julian Huxley; "A Martian Adventure," ("At the Perihelion"), W. Ley; "Learning Theory," James McConnell; "The Mother of Necessity," Chad Oliver; "John Sze's Future" (new), John R. Pierce; "Kid Anderson," Robert S. Richardson; "Pilot Lights of the Apocalypse," Louis N. Ridenour; "Grand Central Terminal," Leo Szilard; "The Brain," Norbert Wiener.

Great Stories of Space Travel [pa] (Tempo: T39, 1963, 256 pp., pa 50¢)

Sf, 11 stories with compiler's introduction and opening paragraph on each: *The Solar System:* "The Wings of Night," Lester del Rey; "The Holes Around Mars," Jerome Bixby; "Kaleidoscope," Ray Bradbury; "I'll Build Your Dream Castle," Jack Vance. . . . *And Beyond the Solar System:* "Far Centaurus," A. E. van Vogt; "Propagandist," Murray Leinster; "Cabin Boy," Damon Knight; "A Walk in the Dark," Arthur C. Clarke; "Blind Alley," Isaac Asimov; "The Helping Hand," Poul Anderson; "Allamagoosa," Eric F. Russell.

Human and Other Beings [pa] [by Allen DeGraeff (pseud. of A. P. Blaustein), Conklin sub-editing] (Collier: AS567, 1963, 319 pp., pa 95¢)

Sf, 16 stories, with introduction "Science Fiction and Ideas" by G. Conklin, and preface by DeGraeff: "Dark Interlude," F. Brown & M. Reynolds; "Love," "Honor," Richard Wilson; "Double Dome," Raymond E. Banks; "Way in the Middle of the Air," "The Other Foot," Ray Bradbury; "The Vilbar Party," Evelyn E. Smith; "Made in U.S.A.," J. T. McIntosh; "The NRACP," George P. Elliott; "The Big Stink," Theodore R. Cogswell; "Down Among the Dead Men," William Tenn; "All the Colors of the Rainbow," Leigh Brackett; "The World of Myrion Flowers," F. Pohl & C. M. Kornbluth; "My Lady Greensleeves," Frederik Pohl; "Holdout," Robert Sheckley; "Test Piece," Eric F. Russell.

In the Grip of Terror [pa] (Permabooks: P117, 1951, 364 pp., pa 25¢)

Weird, 22 stories: "The Last Kiss," M. Level; "The Illustrated Man," R. Bradbury; "The Upturned Face," S. Crane; "The Incredible Elopement of Lord Peter Wimsey," Dorothy Sayers; "The Horror Horn," E. F. Benson; "Night Drive," W. F. Jenkins; "In the Vault," H. P. Lovecraft; "The Diary of a Madman," G. de Maupassant; "The Tool," W. F. Harvey; "Bianca's Hands," T. Sturgeon; "The Cross of Carl," W. Owen; "Hathor's Pets," Margaret St. Clair; "A Terribly Strange Bed," W. Collins; "The Well," W. W. Jacobs; "Revenge," W. Blas; "The Pit and the Pendulum," E. A. Poe; "Macklin's Little Friend," H. Wandrei; "The Easter Egg," H. H. Munro; "Problem in Murder," H. L. Gold; "The Moth," H. G. Wells; "A Resumed Identity," A. Bierce; "Bubbles," W. D. Steele.

Invaders of Earth (Vanguard, New York, 1952, 333 pp., $3.75) (Weidenfeld Nicolson, London, 1953, 256 pp., 10/6; 1955, 5/- [14 stories marked †]) (Pocket Books: 1074, 1955, 257 pp., pa 25¢ [15 stories marked p1]) (Digit: R562, 1962, 160 pp., pa 2/6 [8 stories marked p2]) (*Enemies in Space*, Digit: R577, 1962, 159 pp., pa 2/6; R833, 1964, pa 2/6 [6 stories marked p3]) (Tempo: T6, 1962, 382 pp., pa 50¢ [17 stories marked p4]) (*Invasores de la Tierra* [Spanish], *Galaxia*: 29, 1964 [not known which stories])

Sf, 22 stories, 'idea' series: *Prologue: The Distant Past:* "This Star Shall Be Free" †,p1,p2,p4, M. Leinster. *I. The Immediate Past:* "Castaway" †,p2,p4, R. M. Williams; "Impulse" †,p1,p2,p4, E. F. Russell; "Top Secret" p1,p4, David Grinnell; "An Eel by the Tail" †,p1,p2, Allen K. Lang; "A Date to Remember" p4, W. F. Temple; "Storm Warning" †,p1,p2, D. A. Wollheim; "Child of the Void" †,p2,p4, Margaret St. Clair; "Tiny and the Monster" p1,p4, T. Sturgeon; "The Discord Makers" p1,p4, M. Reynolds; "Pen Pal" p1, Milton Lesser; "Not Only Dead Men" †,p2,p4, A. E. Van Vogt. *II. The Immediate Future:* "Enemies in Space" (1907), †,p2, Karl Grunert; "Invasion From Mars" (radio script), †,p1,p3,p4, Howard Koch; "Minister Without Portfolio"

p1,p4, Mildred Clingerman; "The Waveries" †,p3,p4, F. Brown; "Crisis" p1,p4, Edward Grendon; "Angel's Egg" †,p1,p3,p4, E. Pangborn; " 'Will You Walk a Little Faster?' " p1,p4, Wm. Tenn; "The Man in the Moon" †,p2, Henry Norton; "Pictures Don't Lie" †,p1,p3,p4, Katherine MacLean. *Epilogue: The Distant Future:* "The Greatest Tertian" (new), †,p1,p3,p4, A. Boucher.

Omnibus of Science Fiction, The (Crown, 1952, 562 pp., $3.50) (D'day SF B.C., 1953) (*Strange Travels in Science Fiction*, Grayson, London, 1953, 256 pp., 9/6 [13 stories marked 1]) (*Strange Adventures in Science Fiction*, Grayson, 1954, 240 pp., 9/6 [9 stories marked 2]) (*Science Fiction Omnibus*, Berkley: G31, 1956, 187 pp., pa 35¢; F851, 1963, pa 50¢ [11 stories marked p])

Sf, 43 stories, with compiler's introduction: *I. Wonders of the Earth and of Man:* "John Thomas's Cube" 1, John Leimert; "Hyperpilosity," L. S. de Camp; "The Thing in the Woods," F. Pratt & B. F. Ruby; "And Be Merry," Kath. MacLean; "The Bees From Borneo," Will H. Gray; "The Rag Thing," D. Grinnell; "The Conqueror," M. Clifton. *II. Inventions, Dangerous and Otherwise:* "Never Underestimate . . ." 2, T. Sturgeon; "The Doorbell" 2, D. H. Keller; "A Subway Named Mobius" 1,p, A. J. Deutsch; "Backfire," R. Rocklynne; "The Box" 2, J. Blish; "Zeritsky's Law," A. Griffith; "The Fourth Dynasty," R. R. Winterbotham. *III. From Outer Space:* "The Color Out of Space" 1,p, H. P. Lovecraft; "The Head Hunters," Ralph Williams; "The Star Dummy" 1,p, A. Boucher; "Catch That Martian" 2, D. Knight; "Shipshape Home" 1, R. Matheson; "Homo Sol" p, I. Asimov. *IV. Far Travelling:* "Alexander the Bait," Wm. Tenn; "Kaleidoscope" 1,p, R. Bradbury; " 'Nothing Happens on the Moon' " 1, Paul Ernst; "Trigger Tide," Wyman Guin; "Plague" 2,p, M. Leinster; "Winner Lose All," J. Vance; "Test Piece" p, E. F. Russell; "Environment" 2, C. S. Geier. *V. Adventures in Dimension:* "High Threshold" 1, Alan E. Nourse; "Spectator Sport" 2,p, J. D. MacDonald; "Recruiting Station" 2, A. E. van Vogt; "A Stone and a Spear" 1, R. F. Jones; "What You Need," L. Padgett; "The Choice" 2, W. Hilton-Young. *VI. Worlds of Tomorrow:* "The War Against the Moon," A. Maurois; "Pleasant Dreams" 1, Ralph Robin; "Manners of the Age" 1, H. B. Fyfe; "The Weapon" 1,p, F. Brown; "The Scarlet Plague" 1, J. London; "Heritage," R. Abernathy; "History Lesson" p, A. C. Clarke; "Instinct" p, L. del Rey; "Counter Charm," Peter Phillips.

Operation Future [pa] (Permabooks: M-4022, 1955, 356 pp., pa 35¢)

Sf, 17 shorts and 2 novelettes, with compiler's introduction: "The Education of Drusilla Strange" (n'te), T. Sturgeon; "C/o Mr. Makepeace," P. Phillips; "Technical Slip," J. Beynon; "Short in the Chest," Idris Seabright; "Cure for a Ylith," M. Leinster; "Exposure," E. F. Russell; "Worrywart," C. D. Simak; "Day Is Done," L. del Rey; "Quit Zoomin' Those Hands Through the Air," J. Finney; "Hilda," H. B. Hickey; "Blood's a Rover" (n'te), C. Oliver; "Call Me Adam," W. K. Marks; "Special Delivery," D. Knight; "The Garden in the Forest," Robert F. Young; "The Sorcerer's Apprentice," M. Jameson; "Games," Kath. MacLean; "The Holes Around Mars," J. Bixby; "Project," L. Padgett; "The Fun They Had," I. Asimov.

Possible Worlds of Science Fiction (Vanguard, 1951, 372 pp., $2.95) (Grayson, 1951, 254 pp., 9/6, jacket–M. Marriott [13 stories marked †]) (Berkley: G-3, 1955, 189 pp., pa 35¢; G-471, 1960, 188 pp., pa 35¢; X1633, 1968, pa 60¢ [10 stories marked p])

Sf, 22 stories, 'idea' series, with compiler's introduction: *I. The Solar System:* "Operation Pumice" †, R. Z. Gallun; "The Black Pits of Luna," R. A. Heinlein; "Enchanted Village" †,p, A. E. van Vogt; "Lilies of Life" †,p, M. Jameson; "Asleep in Armageddon" †,p, R. Bradbury; "Not Final" †,p, I. Asimov; "Cones," F. B. Long; "Moon of Delirium" †, D. L. James; "Completely Automatic," T. Sturgeon; "The Day We Celebrate," N. S. Bond; "The Pillows" †,p, Margaret St. Clair; "Proof," H. Clement. *II. The Galaxy:* "Propagandist" †,p, M. Leinster; "In Value Deceived" p, H. B. Fyfe; "Hard-Luck Diggings" †, J. Vance; "Space Rating" †,p, J. Berryman; "Contagion," Kath. MacLean; "Limiting Factor" †,p, C. D. Simak; "Exit Line" †, S. Merwin; "Second Night of Summer," J. H. Schmitz; "A Walk in the Dark," A. C. Clarke; "The Helping Hand" †,p, P. Anderson. *Note:* A few of these were later included in the Australian 'Satellite Series' (see *ANONY-MOUS ANTHOLOGIES*).

Science Fiction Adventures in Dimension (Vanguard, 1953, 354 pp., $2.95) (*Adventures in Dimension*, Grayson, 1955, 240 pp., 10/6 [13 stories marked †]) (Berkley: F1053, 1965, 174 pp., pa 50¢ [12 stories marked p])

Sf, 23 stories, 'idea' series, with compiler's introduction (not in pa): *I. Time Tales. Present to Future:* "Yesterday Was Monday" p, T. Sturgeon; "Ambition" p, Wm. L. Bade; "The Middle of the Week After Next" p, M. Leinster; ". . . And It Comes Out Here" p, L. del Rey. *Present to Past:* "Castaway," A. B. Chandler; "The Good Provider," Marion Gross; "Reverse Phylogeny" †, Amelia R. Long; "Other Tracks" p, Wm. Sell. *Past to Present:* " 'What So Proudly We Hail . . .' " †, Day Keene; "Night Meeting" †,p, Ray Bradbury. *Future to Present:* "Perfect Murder," H. L. Gold; "The Flight That Failed" †,p, E. M. Hull; "Endowment Policy" †,p, L. Padgett; "Pete Can Fix It" †, R. F. Jones. *II. Parallel Worlds:* "The Mist" †,p, Peter Cartur; "The Gostak and the Doshes" †, M. J. Breuer; "What If" †,p, I. Asimov; "Ring Around the Redhead" †, J. D. MacDonald; "Tiger by the Tail" †,p, A. E. Nourse; "Way of Escape" †, W. F. Temple; "Suburban Frontiers," Roger F. Young; "Business of Killing" p, F. Leiber; "To Follow Knowledge" †, F. B. Long.

Science Fiction Adventures in Mutation (Vanguard, 1955, 316 pp., $3.75) (Berkley: F1096, 1965, 174 pp., pa 50¢ [14 stories marked p])

Sf, 20 stories, 'idea' series, with compiler's introduction: "Chain of Command" p, S. Arr [S. A. Rynas]; "Battle of the Unborn" p, J. Blish; "The Hungry Guinea Pig," M. J. Breuer; "Keep Out" p, F. Brown; "The Small World of M-75," Ed M. Clinton; "Limiting Factor" p, T. R. Cogswell; "The Lysenko Maze" p, D. Grinnell; "The Patient" p, E. Mayne Hull; "Cold War" p, H. Kuttner; "Skag With the Queer Head" p, M. Leinster; "Veiled Island," E. McDowell; "Experiment Station" ("The First"), Kris Neville; "Family Resemblance" p, A. E. Nourse; "And Thou Beside Me" p, M. Reynolds; "This One's on Me" p, E. F. Russell; "The Age of Prophecy," Margaret St. Clair; "The Love of Heaven" p, T. Sturgeon; "The Impossible Voyage Home," F. L. Wallace; "The Conspirators" p, James White; "The Better Choice" (new) p, S. F. Wright. Bibliography of mutation stories.

Science Fiction Galaxy, The [pa] (Permabooks: P67, 1950, 242 pp., pa 35¢)

Sf, 12 stories and compiler's introduction: *Worlds of Tomorrow:* "The Machine Stops," E. M. Forster; "Easy as A.B.C.," R. Kipling. *Wonders of the Earth:* "The Derelict," W. H. Hodgson; "The Fires Within," A. C. Clarke. *Dangerous Inventions:* "A Child Is Crying," J. D. MacDonald; "Quis Custodiet . . . ?" Margaret St. Clair. *Other Dimensions:* "The Life Work of Professor Muntz," M. Leinster; "The Appendix and the Spectacles," M. J. Breuer. *From Outer Space:* "Death From the Stars," A. R. Hilliard; "The Hurkle Is a Happy Beast," T. Sturgeon. *Far Travelling:* "King of the Gray Spaces," R. Bradbury; "The Living Galaxy," L. Manning.

Science Fiction Oddities [pa] (Berkley: S1311, 1966, 256 pp., pa 75¢)

19 stories and brief introduction: "People Soup," Alan Arkin; "What Is This Thing Called Love?" I. Asimov; "Callahan and the Wheelies," Stephen Barr; "Mrs. Poppledore's Id," R. Bretnor; "The Teeth of Despair," A. Davidson & S. Klein; "The Galactic Calabash," G. C. Edmondson; "Space-Crime Continuum," H. F. Ellis; "The Chessplayers," C. L. Harness; "What's the Name of That Town?" R. A. Lafferty; "Rump-Titty-Titty-Tum-TAH-Tee," Fritz Leiber; "Rundown," Robert Lory; "The Trouble With H.A.R.R.I.," Edward Mackin; "The Water Eater," W. K. Marks; "A Pride of Carrots," R. Nathan; "The Terra-Venusian War of 1979," Gerard E. Neyroud; "The Coffin Cure," A. E. Nourse; "On Camera," John Novotny; "See No Evil," John R. Pierce; "Punch," F. Pohl.

Science Fiction Omnibus [pa] See *Omnibus of Science Fiction*

Science-Fiction Terror Tales (Gnome, New York, 1955, x+262 pp., $3.50) (Pocket Books: 1045, 1955, 262 pp., pa 25¢) ([Japanese], Gegensha & Tokyo-Life-sha, 1957 [omits 1st, 3rd & last]; Hayakawa: 3043, 1962, pa)

15 stories and compiler's introduction: "Punishment Without Crime," R. Bradbury; "Arena," F. Brown; "The Leech," R. Sheckley; "Through Channels," R. Matheson; "Lost Memory," P. Phillips; "Memorial," T. Sturgeon; "Prott," Margaret St. Clair; "Flies," I. Asimov; "The Microscopic Giants," Paul Ernst; "The Other Inauguration," A. Boucher; "Nightmare Brother," A. E. Nourse; "Pipeline to Pluto," M. Leinster; "Impostor," P. K. Dick; "They," R. A. Heinlein; "Let Me Live in a House," Chad Oliver.

Science Fiction Thinking Machines (Vanguard, 1954, 367 pp., $3.50) (*Selections From Science Fiction Thinking Machines*, Bantam: 1352, 1955, 183 pp., pa 25¢; EP63, 1964, 201 pp., pa 45¢ [12 stories marked †])

Sf, 'idea' series, 18 stories and 2 plays, with compiler's introduction: *I. Robots:* "Automata: I," S. F. Wright; "Moxon's Master," A. Bierce; "Robbie" ("Strange Playfellow")†, I. Asimov; "The Scarab," R. Z. Gallun; "The Mechanical Bride" (TV script), F. Leiber; "Virtuoso"†, Herbert Goldstone; "Automata: II," S. F. Wright; "Boomerang" ("A Great Deal of Power")†, E. F. Russell; "The Jester"†, Wm. Tenn; "R.U.R." (play), K. Capek; "Skirmish" ("Bathe Your Bearings in Blood")†, C. D. Simak; "Soldier Boy," M. Shaara; "Automata: III," S. F. Wright; "Men Are Different" (new)†, Alan Bloch. *II. Androids:* "Letter to Ellen"†, Chan Davis; "Sculptors of Life," W. West; "The Golden Egg"†, T. Sturgeon; "Dead End"†, Wallace MacFarlane. *III. Computers:* "Answer," H. Clement; "Sam Hall"†, P. Anderson; "Dumb Waiter"†, W. M. Miller; "Problem for Emmy"†, Robert S. Townes.

Selections From Science Fiction Thinking Machines See *Science Fiction Thinking Machines*

Seven Come Infinity [pa] (Gold Medal: d1752, 1966, 288 pp., pa 50¢) (Coronet: 02880, 1967, 288 pp., pa 3/6)

Sf, 7 stories with preface: "The Golden Bugs," C. D. Simak; "Special Feature," Charles V. DeVet; "Panic Button," E. F. Russell; "Discontinuity," R. F. Jones; "The Corianis Disaster," M. Leinster; "The Servant Problem," Wm. Tenn; "Rite of Passage," Chad Oliver.

Seven Trips Through Time and Space [pa] (Gold Medal: R1924, 1968, 256 pp., pa 60¢)

Sf, 7 stories and compiler's introduction: "Flatlander," Larry Niven; "The Crime and the Glory of Commander Suzdac," Cordwainer Smith; "Overproof," J. B. MacKenzie; "Poor Planet," J. T. McIntosh; "Shamar's War," K. Neville; "The Tactful Saboteur," F. Herbert; "Ministry of Disturbance," H. B. Piper.

17 × Infinity [pa] (Dell: 7746, 1963, 272 pp., pa 50¢) (Mayflower: 7746, 1963, 272 pp., pa 3/6)

SF, 17 stories and compiler's introduction: "The Simian Problem," Hollis Alpert; "Strikebreaker," I. Asimov; "Come Into My Cellar," Ray Bradbury; "Ms Fnd in a Lbry," Hal Draper; "Cato the Martian," Howard Fast; "The Spaceman Cometh," Henry G. Felsen; "The Machine Stops," E. M. Forster; "Frances Harkins," Richard Goggin; "The Day They Got Boston," Herbert Gold; "A-W-F, Unlimited," Frank Herbert; "As Easy as A.B.C.," "MacDonough's Song," Rudyard Kipling; "Silenzia," Alan Nelson; "What to Do Until the Analyst Comes," Frederik Pohl; "Short in the Chest," Idris Seabright; "The Last of the Spode," Evelyn E. Smith; "Never Underestimate," Theodore Sturgeon; "Brooklyn Project," Wm. Tenn.

6 Great Short Novels of Science Fiction [pa] (Dell: D9, 1954, 384 pp., pa 35¢)

Sf, 6 novels and compiler's introduction: "The Blast," Stuart Cloete (*Collier's*, sr2, 12 Apr 1947); "Coventry," R. A. Heinlein (*ASF*, July 1940); "The Other World," M. Leinster (*SS*, Nov 1949); "Barrier," A. Boucher (*ASF*, Sep 1942); "Surface Tension," J. Blish (*GSF*, Aug 1952); "Maturity," T. Sturgeon (*ASF*, Feb 1947).

Six Great Short Science Fiction Novels [pa] (Dell: C111, 1960, 350 pp., pa 50¢)

Sf, 6 novels and compiler's introduction: "Galley Slave," I. Asimov (*GSF*, Dec 1957); "Project Nursemaid," J. Merril (*F&SF*, Oct 1955); "Final Gentleman," C. D. Simak (*F&SF*, Jan 1960); "Chain Reaction," A. Budrys (*ASF*, Apr 1957; as John A. Sentry); "Rule Golden," D. Knight (*SFA*, May 1954); "Incommunicado," Katherine MacLean (*ASF*, June 1950).

Strange Adventures in Science Fiction See *Omnibus of Science Fiction*

Strange Travels in Science Fiction See *Omnibus of Science Fiction*

Supernatural Reader, The [with Lucy Conklin (wife)] (Lippincott, Philadelphia, 1953, 349 pp., $3.95) (Longmans, Toronto, $4.50) (Cassell, London, 1956, 349 pp., 16/-) (World Distributors: M706, 1958, 252 pp., pa 2/6 [19 stories marked †]) (Collier: AS392X, 1962, 352 pp., pa 95¢; 01911, 1966, pa 95¢; 01911, 1968, pa 95¢)

Weird, 27 stories: "The Angel With Purple Hair"†, H. Paul; "For the Blood Is Life"†, F. M. Crawford; "The Stranger"†, R. Hughes; "Mrs. Manifold," S. Grendon; "Piffingcap"†, A. E. Coppard; "Shottle Bop," T. Sturgeon; "Gabriel-Ernest"†, H. H. Munro; "The Lost Room"†, F.-J. O'Brien; "The Traitor"†, J. H. Hart; "Angus MacAuliffe and the Gowden Touch," C. R. Tanner; "Are You Rundown, Tired—," B. Rosmond & L. M. Lake; "The Nature of the Evidence," May Sinclair; "Tree's Life"†, Mary E. Counselman; "The Pavilion"†, E. Nesbit; "Pick-up for Olympus" (new)†, E. Pangborn; "The Swap," H. F. Heard; "The Tombing Day" (new)†, R. Bradbury; "Minuke"†, N. Kneale; "Bird of Prey"†, J. Collier; "The Thing in the Cellar"†, D. H. Keller; "Devil's Henchman"†, W. Jenkins; "Lost Hearts," M. R. James; "Thirteen at Table"†, Lord Dunsany; "Lights"†, P. Fisher; "The Silver Highway," H. Lawlor; "The Moonlit Road"†, A. Bierce; "The Curate's Friend"†, E. M. Forster.

13 Above the Night [pa] (Dell: 8741, 1965, 286 pp., pa 60¢)

Sf, 13 stories with compiler's introduction: "Founding Father," J. F. Bone; "Mating Call," Frank Herbert; "Nice Girl With Five Husbands," F. Leiber; "Prone," M. Reynolds; "The Education of Tigress Macardle," C. M. Kornbluth; "Now Inhale," E. F. Russell; "The Back of Our Heads," Stephen Barr; "Button, Button," I. Asimov; "The Deep Down Dragon," Judith Merril; "The Kappa Nu Nexus," A. Davidson & M. Klass; "Idiot Solvant," G. R. Dickson; "Counter Security," J. White; "The Dreistein Case," J. Lincoln Paine.

13 Great Stories of Science Fiction [pa] (Gold Medal: s997, 1960, 192 pp., pa 35¢; k1243, 1962, pa 40¢; d1444, 1964, pa 35¢) (Coronet: 2382, 1967, 192 pp., pa 3/6)

13 stories and compiler's introduction: "The War Is Over," A. Budrys; "The Light," P. Anderson; "Compassion Circuit," J. Wyndham; "Volpla," W. Guin; "Silence, Please!" A. C. Clarke; "Allegory," W. T. Powers; "Soap Opera," A. Nelson; "Shipping Clerk," W. Morrison; "Technological Retreat," G. C. Edmondson; "The Analogues," D. Knight; "The Available Data on the Worp Reaction," L. Miller; "The Skills of Xanadu," T. Sturgeon; "The Machine," R. Gehman.

Treasury of Science Fiction, A (Crown, 1948, 517 pp., $3.50) (Berkley: G63, 1957, 186 pp., pa 35¢; F1047, 1965, pa 50¢ [8 stories marked †])

30 stories (25 from *ASF*) and compiler's introduction: *I. The Atom and After:* "The Nightmare," Chan Davis; "Tomorrow's Children," P. Anderson & F. N. Waldrop; "The Last Objective," Paul Carter; "Loophole"†, A. C. Clarke; "The Figure," Edward Grendon. *II. The Wonders of the Earth:* "The Great Fog"†, H. F. Heard; "The Chrysalis," P. S. Miller; "Living Fossil," L. S. de Camp; "N Day," P. Latham. *III. The Superscience of Man:* "With Folded Hands"†, J. Williamson; "No Woman Born," C. L. Moore; "With Flaming Swords," C. Cartmill; "Children of the Betsy B," M. Jameson. *IV. Dangerous Inventions:* "Child's Play," Wm. Tenn; "The Person From Porlock," R. F. Jones; "Juggernaut"†, A. E. van Vogt; "The Eternal Man," D. D. Sharp. *V. Adventures in Dimension:* "Mimsy Were the Borogoves"†, L. Padgett; "Time and Time Again," H. B. Piper; "Housing Shortage," H. Walton; "Flight of the Dawn Star," R. M. Williams; "Vintage Season," L. O'Donnell. *VI. From Outer Space:* "Of Jovian Build," O. J. Friend; "Wings Across the Cosmos," P. Cross; "The Embassy," M. Pearson; "Dark Mission," L. del Rey. *VII. Far Travelling:* "The Ethical Equations"†, M. Leinster; "It's Great to Be Back"†, R. A. Heinlein; "Tools," C. D. Simak; "Rescue Party"†, A. C. Clarke.

12 Great Classics of Science Fiction [pa] (Gold Medal: d1366, 1963, 192 pp., pa 50¢; d1669, 1966, pa 50¢)

Sf, 12 stories and compiler's introduction: "Due Process," Algis Budrys; "Earthmen Bearing Gifts," Fredric Brown; "Things," Zenna Henderson; "The Top," George S. Albee; "My Object All Sublime," Poul Anderson; "Human Man's Burden," Robert Sheckley; "On the Fourth Planet," J. F. Bone; "The Ballad of Lost C'Mell," Cordwainer Smith; "Thirty Days Had September," Robert F. Young; "The Cage," Bertram Chandler; "Star-Crossed Lover," Wm. W. Stuart; "Immortality . . . for Some," J. T. McIntosh.

Twisted [pa] (Belmont: L92-535, 1962, 189 pp., pa 50¢; B50-771, 1967, pa 50¢) (Horwitz: PB153, 1963, 130 pp., pa 4/- [10 stories marked †]) (FSB: 1379, 1965, 189 pp., pa 3/6)

Weird, 15 stories: "The Playground"†, R. Bradbury; "The Other Hand"†, George Langelaan; "The Thing in the Cellar"†, D. H. Keller; "The Diary of a Madman"†, Guy de Maupassant; "The Upturned Face"†, Stephen Crane; "The Little Man Who Wasn't Quite"†, Wm. W. Stuart; "Night Drive"†, W. F. Jenkins; "The Song of Marya"†, W. M. Miller; "Mrs. Manifold"†, Stephen Grendon; "A Holy Terror," A. Bierce; "Impulse"†, E. F. Russell; "Brenda," Margaret St. Clair; "The Tell-Tale Heart," E. A. Poe; "The Shunned House," H. P. Lovecraft; "The World Well Lost," T. Sturgeon.

Worlds of When [pa] (Pyramid: F-733, 1962, 159 pp., pa 40¢)

Sf, 5 short novels and compiler's introduction: "Transfusion," Chad Oliver (*ASF*, June 1959); "Bullet With His Name," F. Leiber (*GSF*, July 1958); "Death and the Senator," A. C. Clarke (*ASF*, May 1961); "Farmer," M. Reynolds (*GSF*, June 1961); "Rations of Tantalus," Margaret St. Clair (*FU*, July 1954).

CONNELL, ALAN Australian science fiction author. He lived in Sydney before the war, and had some notable stories in the sf magazines: "The Reign of the Reptiles" (*WS*, Aug 1935; *FSM*, Win 1951); "Dream's End" (*WS*, Dec 1935; *FSM*, Sum 1951); "Espionage in Space" (*Planet*, Win 1941). He also wrote a paperback trilogy for Currawong Publishing Co., Sydney, in the early 1940's: *Lords of the Serpent Land, Prisoners of Serpent Land* and *Warriors of Serpent Land*. A collection of his works was considered at one time by the Australian Futurian Press, Sydney.

CONNINGTON, J. J. (pseud) See STEWART, A. W.

CONQUEST, (GEORGE) ROBERT (ACKWORTH) (15 July 1917—) British poet, author and lecturer. He was born at Malvern, and was educated (B.A.) at Magdalene College, Oxford, and U. of Grenoble. He was in the Foreign Service 1945-56, during which he was First Secretary of H. M. Legation in Sofia, and was with the U.K. delegation to the U.N. He is O.B.E., and a Fellow of the London School of Economics. A number of his poems have been published, and he has contributed to *The Spectator* and *Guardian*; he was Literary Editor of the former, 1962-63. He wrote *Courage of Genius* (1962), which deals poignantly with Boris Pasternak and the political censorship of *Doctor Zhivago*.

Fiction

World of Difference, A (Ward Lock, London, 1955, 192 pp., 10/6; 1956, 6/6) (Ballantine: U2213, 1964, 192 pp., pa 50¢)

A rather involved plot of a future world where an atomic war has fizzled out and the search is on for a photon drive to reach the stars.

Anthologies

Spectrum . . . [series] See AMIS, K. (co-anthologist)

CONRAD, EARL

Fiction

Da Vinci Machine: Tales of the Population Explosion, The [C] (Fleet, New York, 1968, 189 pp., $5.95)

16 stories: "The Proof Was in Drinkwater's Pudding"; "Thermidor"; "The Two by Fours"; "Jacob Wrestles With the Angel"; "The Cosmic Megillah"; "Hodson's Caper"; "The Ecstasy Machine"; "Maturation of the Aborigines"; "Upshaw's Upset"; "The Feasibility Plan"; "Medical Chart of Stephen Payne"; "The Da Vinci Machine"; "Ook, Ook, Ook"; "Report on the Condition of Poetry, Circa A.D. 2022"; "Origins of Pill and Hammer"; "Made He a Rib."

CONRAD, JOSEPH (6 Dec 1856–3 Aug 1924) British novelist, born Josef Teodor Konrad Korzeniowski in the Ukraine. When 17 he found his way to Marseilles, served in French ships, and by 1884 had worked up to being a master in the British merchant service. He became a British subject. He started to write during a period of ill health; his first work, *Almayer's Folly* (1895), was recognised as something new in English fiction, the product of a rare temperament and unusual experiences expressed with a fastidious choice of phrase. This was followed by many others up to 1904, ending his "first period" with the writing of *Nostromo*. His "second period" started with *The Secret Agent* (1907) and went to *The Rover* (1925). This was considered by many of his admirers to be not as creative as his first period, but nevertheless there was a great vogue for his works in both the U.S. and Britain. A recent critical survey by Jocelyn Baines (McGraw-Hill, 1960) covers both his life and writings.

Fiction

Set of Six, A [C] (Methuen, London, 1908, 310 pp.) (Doubleday Page, New York, 1915, 356 pp.)

6 stories: "Gaspar Ruiz"; "The Informer"; "The Brute"; "An Anarchist"; "The Duel"; "Il Conde."

Shadow Line, The (Dent, London, 1917, 227 pp., 5/-) (Doubleday, New York, 1917, $1.90, $2.50)

Tales of Hearsay [C] (Doubleday Page, New York, 1925, 120 pp.)

4 stories: "The Warrior's Soul"; "Prince Roman"; "The Tale"; "The Black Mate."

Tales of Unrest [C] (Scribner's, New York, 1898, 3+348 pp.)

5 stories: "Karain: A Memory"; "The Idiots"; "An Outpost of Progress"; "The Return"; "The Lagoon."

CONSTANCE, ARTHUR

Nonfiction

Inexplicable Sky, The (Werner Laurie, London, 1956, 308 pp., illus., 21/-) (Citadel, New York, 1956, 287 pp., $2.95) (Ambassador, Toronto, $4.75)

This covers strange phenomena over and above UFO's and flying saucers—items such as mysterious showers of objects and creatures, and other 'Fortean' occurrences. The author challenges modern materialistic science and confronts it with a cosmos "alive with intelligence."

COOK, FRED U.S. sf enthusiast.

Nonfiction

Index to the Wonder Group (published by the compiler, Michigan, 1966, 239 pp., $5.00)

Coverage runs from *Science Wonder Stories*, June 1929, through *Thrilling Wonder Stories*, *Startling Stories*, and others of the Standard Magazines group, to the "Treasury" reprint issues of 1964 and 1965. The magazines are covered alphabetically with a running account of the rise and fall of each, then a checklist of issues, contents listings and author indexes. The coverage cuts across the Day *Index to the Science Fiction Magazines* and the newer M.I.T. *Index*.

COOK, W. PAUL (1881– 22 Jan 1948) U.S. author and publisher who worked in the background of the weird & fantasy field. Through nearly 50 years he was friendly with many amateur and advanced journalists, principally Rheinhart Kleiner, Ernest Edkins, boyhood chum Edward Cole, and H. P. Lovecraft—for whom he wrote a fine appreciation in *Beyond the Walls of Sleep*. Mirage Press recently reissued his writings on Lovecraft as *H.P.L.: A Portrait* (1968). Cook's publications have long since become collector's items: *The Monadnock Monthly* (1901-13), *The Vagrant* (15 issues, 1923-27), and *The Ghost* (5 issues, 1943-47), which printed much fine material. These, as well as his volumes of *Told in Vermont* (descriptive poetry) and his vocation as foreman of printers on the *Athol Transcript* and *Driftwind Presses* marked W. Paul Cook as a professional who did much to encourage amateur work in these fields.

COOMBS, CHARLES IRA (27 June 1914–) U.S. author, born in Los Angeles, the son of a building contractor. B.A., U. of California, 1939. He has been a full-time writer since 1946 and has written many teen-age books for Lantern Press. He is West Coast movie and TV representative for *Boys' Life*. His nonfiction of popular interest includes *Rockets, Missiles and Moons* (Morrow, 1957), *Skyrocketing into the Unknown* (Morrow, 1954), and *Survival in the Sky* (Morrow, 1956; R. Hale, London, 1957, Badger, 1959, pa).

Fiction (juvenile)

Celestial Space, Inc. (Westminster, Philadelphia, 1954, 190 pp., illus., $2.75) (Ryerson, Toronto, $3.25)

Youthful hero obtains "legal" monopoly on 100 light years of space by Earth.

Mystery of Satellite 7 (Westminster, 1958, 160 pp., $2.95) (Tempo: T9, 1962, 192 pp., pa 50¢)

Exciting story of Project Argus; a satellite is put into orbit by communications companies.

COON, CARLETON S(TEVENS) (23 June 1904–) U.S. anthropologist, born at Wakefield, Mass. He took his Ph.D. at Harvard in 1928, and taught there 1935-48, becoming Professor of Anthropology. He then was Professor at U. of Pennsylvania 1948-53.

Nonfiction

Story of Man, The (Knopf, New York, 1954, xii+437 pp., $6.75)

Subtitled: "From the First Human to Primitive Culture and Beyond—The adventures and misadventures of Mankind from the Pliocene to the Iron Curtain." It is generally conceded to be one of the best general accounts on Neolithic Man; it also gives views on various controversial subjects.

COON, HORACE C. (1897–10 Dec 1961) U.S. author. His books included *Money to Burn* (1938), *American Tel and Tel* (1939), and *Triumph of the Eggheads* (1955).

Fiction

43,000 Years Later [pa] (Signet: S1534, 1958, 143 pp., pa 35¢) (Panther: 975, 1959, 157 pp., pa 2/6)

An exploratory expedition from "The Great Galaxy" visits Earth 43,000 years after its destruction by atomic war.

COONEY, MICHAEL

Fiction

Doomsday England (Cassell, London, 1967, 183 pp., 21/-) (Corgi: 08032, 1968, 221 pp., pa 5/-)

A brilliant spy melodrama in which the Queen's investigators are licensed to massacre in a rather different England.

Ten Years to Oblivion (Cassell, 1968, 167 pp., 18/-)

COOPER, COLIN

Fiction

Thunder and Lightning Man, The (Faber, London, 1968, 182 pp., 25/-)

A man claims to be in touch with aliens en route to Earth.

COOPER, EDMUND (30 Apr 1926–) British author, educated at Manchester Grammar School and Didsbury Training College. He had literary aspirations early in life but didn't then fulfil them, leaving school at 15 to be a labourer, becoming a public servant at 16, and at 17 training for the sea. At 16 he proposed to a schoolmistress who was then 20; she advised him to continue his education; they were married when he was 19. He became a teacher but disliked it and decided to be a writer. He appeared with one story in *Authentic* (Sep 1954), and then had five stories in *Fantastic Universe* (1956-59). He has also contributed to the BBC, *Everybody's*, the *SEP*, etc. He wrote the story for the film *The Invisible Boy* (MGM, 1957, produced by Nicholas Nayfack), which included the character Robbie the Robot who originally appeared in *Forbidden Planet*.

Fiction

All Fool's Day (Hodder Stoughton, London, 1966, 192 pp., 16/-) (Walker, New York, 1966, 191 pp., $3.50) (Berkley: X1469, 1967, 176 pp., pa 60¢) (Hodder: 02860, 1967, 192 pp., pa 3/6)

In 1971 certain sunspots produce killing radiation; those immune are psychopaths and eccentrics.

Deadly Image (Ballantine: 260, 1958, 190 pp., pa 35¢) (*The Uncertain Midnight*, Hutchinson, London, 1958, 224 pp., 13/6) (Panther: 988, 1959, 192 pp., pa 2/6) (*Pygmalion 2113* [French], Denoël: PF32, 1959, pa) ([Japanese], Hayakawa: 3019, 1960, pa) (*Uomini e androidi* [Italian], *Urania*: 227, 1960) (*Aufstand der Roboter* [German] (slightly abr.), Heyne, 1961; *T*: 524, 1967)

A decadent future society dependent on androids finds them about to take over.

Far Sunset, A (Hodder, 1967, 189 pp., 18/-; 04364, 1967, pa 3/6) (Walker, 1967, 189 pp., $3.95) (Berkley: X1607, 1968, 160 pp., pa 60¢) (*Unter den Strahlen von Altair* [German], Heyne: 3118, 1968, pa)

The sole survivor of an Earth expedition to Altair seeks to bring some technology into the lives of the natives.

Five to Twelve (Hodder, 1968, 187 pp., 21/-)

Side effects of future birth control cause women to outnumber men; they are reduced to chattels, and rebellion follows.

News From Elsewhere [C] [pa] (Mayflower: 6304, 1968, 128 pp., pa 3/6)

Sf, 8 stories (no table of contents): "The Menhir"; "M81: Ursa Major"; "The Enlightened Ones"; "Judgment Day"; "The Intruders"; "The Butterflies"; "The Lizard of Woz"; "Welcome Home."

Seed of Light (Hutchinson, 1959, 224 pp., 15/-) (Ballantine: 327, 1959, 159 pp., pa 35¢) (Panther: 1094, 1960, 189 pp., pa 2/6) (*Equazione tempo* [Italian], *Urania*: 234, 1960) (*Die Söhne des Alls* [German], Heyne, 1965, pa)

Ten survivors from Earth travel in a starship to find a virgin planet for their descendants.

Tomorrow Came [C] [pa] (Panther: 1511, 1963, 123 pp., pa 2/6) (*Als die Ufos Kamen* [German], *T*: 396, 1965 [probably abr.])

Sf, 12 stories: "Welcome Home"; "Death Watch"; "Piccadilly Interval"; "The Mouse That Roared"; "Nineteen Ninety-Four"; "When the Saucers Came"; "The First Martian"; "The Lizard of Woz"; "The Life and Death of Plunky Goo"; "Judgment Day"; "Vertical Hold"; "The Doomsday Story."

Tomorrow's Gift [pa] (Ballantine: 279K, 1958, 164 pp., pa 35¢) (Digit: D280, 1959, 160 pp., pa 2/-) (*Endstation Zukunft* [German], *TS*: 85, 1964)

Sf, 10 stories: "Tomorrow's Gift"; "A Question of Time"; "The Butterflies"; "Repeat Performance"; "Brain Child" ("Invisible Boy," *SEP*, 23 June 1956); "Falcon Chase"; "The Jar of Latakia"; "M81—Ursa Major" ("The End of the Journey," *FU*, Feb 1956); "The Enlightened Ones"; "The Intruders."

Transit (Faber, London, 1964, 232 pp., 18/-) (Lancer: 74-758, 1964, 159 pp., pa 50¢; 73-690, 1967, 287 pp., pa 60¢) (*Pas de quatre* [French], Denoël: PF79, 1964, pa) (FSB: 1391, 1965, 190 pp., pa 3/6) (*Die Welt der zwei Monde* [German], Heyne, 1965, pa)

A dramatic fight for survival against aliens on an unknown planet.

Uncertain Midnight, The See *Deadly Image*

Voices in the Dark [C] [pa] (Digit: D349, 1960, 157 pp., pa 2/-; R663, 1963, pa 2/6)

15 stories, not all sf or fantasy (no contents page): *The Voice of Innocence:* "The Unicorn"; "Six Eggs for Mafeking"; "The Boy David." *Laughter Below:* "The Mouse That Roared"; "I Am a Ghost"; "Nineteen Ninety-Four." *The Voice of Love:* "Sentimental Journey"; "Burnt Umber"; "The Miller's Daughter." *Impossible Echoes:* "When the Saucers Came"; "The Lions and the Harp"; "The First Martian." *The Fatal Voice:* "Duet for One Finger"; "So I Never Left Home"; "The Last Act."

COOPER, MERIAN C. See WALLACE, E. (co-author)

COOPER, SUSAN British author. A former feature writer for the London *Sunday Times*, she married an American scientist in 1963 and moved to Massachusetts. She has also written a book for children.
Fiction
Mandrake (Hodder Stoughton, London, 1964, 253 pp., 18/-)

("The Angry Earth," *Melbourne Herald*, sr6, 24 Oct 1964) (Penguin: 2491, 1966, 238 pp., pa 4/-)

An anthropologist returns from Brazil to England in 1973, and finds it under the control of Mandrake, Minister of Planning.

COPPARD, A(LFRED) E(DGAR) (4 Jan 1878–13 Jan 1957) British author of short stories, including many fantasies. He engaged in many occupations, principally accountancy, before he started to write at the age of 40. His first book was *Adam and Eve and Pinch Me* (1921). Some of his fantasy stories are in his *Collected Tales*, and most of them are included in the Arkham collection *Fearful Pleasures* (1946). The short story "The King of the World" was reprinted in *FFM* (Jan 1951).
Fiction [Incomplete—other titles in Bleiler *Checklist*]
Adam and Eve and Pinch Me [C] (Golden Cockerell Press, Berkshire, 1921, 140 pp., 4/6) (Knopf, New York, 1921, 140 pp.; 1922, 331 pp., $2.50) (Cape, London, 1926, 224 pp., 3/6)

First edition has 12 stories: "Adam and Eve and Pinch Me"; "The Angel and the Sweep"; "Arabesque: The Mouse"; "Communion"; "Dusky Ruth"; "King of the World"; "Marching to Zion"; "Piffingcap"; "Princess of Kingdom Come"; "The Quiet Woman"; "The Trumpeters"; "Weep Not My Wanton."

The 1922 and 1926 editions add 9 more stories: "Broadsheet Ballad"; "The Cherry Tree"; "Clorinda Walks in Heaven"; "Cotton"; "Craven Arms"; "Elixir of Youth"; "Felix Tingler"; "The Hurly Burly"; "Pomona's Babe."

Black Dog and Other Stories, The [C] (Cape, 1923, 294 pp., 7/6; 1926, 3/6) (Knopf, 1923, 294 pp., $2.50) (in *Fares Please! An Omnibus* [Coppard])

18 stories: "The Black Dog"; "Alas, Poor Bollington!"; "The Ballet Girl"; "Simple Simon"; "The Tiger"; "Mordecai and Cocking"; "The Man From Kilsheelan"; "Tribute"; "The Handsome Lady"; "The Fancy Dress Ball"; "The Cat, the Dog, and the Bad Old Dame"; "The Wife of Ted Wickham"; "Tanil"; "The Devil in the Churchyard"; "Huxley Rustem"; "Big Game"; "The Poor Man"; "Luxury."

Clorinda Walks in Heaven [C] (Golden Cockerell, 1922, 130 pp., 6/6)

9 stories: "The Hurly-Burly"; "Clorinda Walks in Heaven"; "The Cherry Tree"; "The Elixir of Youth"; "Felix Tingler"; "Craven Arms"; "A Broadsheet Ballad"; "Cotton"; "Pomona's Blade."

Collected Tales of A. E. Coppard, The [C] (Knopf, 1948, 532 pp., $5.00)

38 stories selected from those written 1921-28: "The Higgler"; "The Cherry Tree"; "The Poor Man"; "The Ballet Girl"; "Arabesque: The Mouse"; "Alas, Poor Bollington"; "Dusky Ruth"; "The Old Venerable"; "Adam and Eve and Pinch Me"; "The Presser"; "The Green Drake"; "Abel Staple Disapproves"; "Purl and Plain"; "A Broadsheet Ballad"; "Silver Circus"; "Luxury"; "The Fair Young Willowy Tree"; "My Hundredth Tale"; "Ring the Bells of Heaven"; "Nixey's Harlequin"; "Judith"; "Father Raven"; "The Man From Kilsheelan"; "Olive and Camilla"; "Clorinda Walks in Heaven"; "Doe"; "Fine Feathers"; "Christine's Letter"; "Ahoy, Sailor Boy!"; "Ninepenny Flute"; "A Little Boy Lost"; "The Little Mistress"; "Fishmonger's Fiddle"; "The Hurly Burly"; "The Field of Mustard"; "The Third Prize"; "The Watercress Girl"; "Fifty Pounds."

Crotty Shinkwin (Golden Cockerell for Waltham Saint Lawrence, Reading [Berkshire, England], 1932, 67 pp., illus.—Robert Gibbings [wood engravings], quarto, 21/-; 500 copies) (Random, New York, 1932, as above, $6.50) (in *Fearful Pleasures* [Coppard], 1946, 1951)

Dark-Eyed Lady, The [C] (Methuen, London, 1947, 247 pp., 9/6)

14 stories: no further information.

Dunky Fitlow [C] (Cape, 1933, 320 pp., 7/6; limited autographed edition, 21/-)

15 stories: "Abel Staple Disapproves"; "Ahoy, Sailor Boy!"; "Beauty Spot"; " 'Cheefoo' "; "Corridors"; "Crotty Shinkwin"; "Doe"; "Dunky Fitlow"; "Grroggo's Chimney"; "Joggy Foggy Due"; "The Perfect Fool"; "Poste Restante"; "The Smith of

Pretty Peter"· "Vincent's Pride"; "The Watchman."
Fares Please! An Omnibus [C] (Cape, London, 1931, 13+884 pp., 7/6)

Binding of the collections *The Black Dog*, *The Field of Mustard*, and *Silver Circus*.
Fearful Pleasures [C] (Arkham, Wisconsin, 1946, xiii+301 pp., $3.00; 4,033 copies) (P. Neville, London, 1951, 284 pp., 11/6)

Weird, 22 stories, with Foreword: "Adam and Eve and Pinch Me"; "Clorinda Walks in Heaven"; "The Elixir of Youth"; "Simple Simon"; "Old Martin"; "The Bogie Man"; "Polly Morgan"; "The Gollan"; "The Post Office and the Serpent"; "Crotty Shinkwin"; "Ahoy, Sailor Boy!"; "Gone Away"; "Rocky and the Bailiff"; "Ale Celestial?"; "The Fair Young Willowy Tree"; "Father Raven"; "The Drum"; "Cheese"; "The Homeless One"; "The Kisstruck Bogie"; "The Tiger"; "The Gruesome Pit." Selected by A. Derleth as all of Coppard's stories in the province of the weird and terrible.
Field of Mustard: Tales, The [C] (Cape, 1926, 320 pp., 7/6; 1931, 3/6) (Knopf, 1927, 309 pp., $2.50) (in *Fares Please! An Omnibus* [Coppard])

11 stories: "The Field of Mustard"; "Fifty Pounds"; "The Truant Hart"; "Olive and Camilla"; "The Man From the Caravan"; "The Funnel"; "Christine's Letter"; "The Bogey Man"; "The Old Venerable"; "Judith"; "The Two Wretches."
Fishmonger's Fiddle: Tales [C] (Knopf, 1925, 320 pp., $2.50) (Cape, 1925, 320 pp., 7/6; 1929, 3/6)

17 stories: "Old Martin"; "The Little Mistress"; "Willie Waugh"; "The Higgler"; "Italian Whirligig"; "The Jewel of Jeopardy"; "Alice Brady"; "The Watercress Girl"; "At Laban's Well"; "A Wildgoose Chase"; "Dumbledon Donkey"; "A Three-Handed Reel"; "The Snare"; "Fishmonger's Fiddle"; "A Little Boy Lost"; "A Diversion With Thomas"; "Mr. Lightfoot in the Green Isle."
Lucy in Her Pink Jacket [C] (P. Nevil, London, 1954, 207 pp., 11/6)

18 stories: "The Gentle Amanda"; "Pastoral Symphony"; "Stupid! Stupid!"; "Commentary by Dixon"; "To My Little Marisco"; "Deep and Dirty"; "The Three Windows"; "Rabsky and the Peri"; "Nancy Doo"; "The Cheat"; "Enobarbus Cotman"; "The Lion and Lord B"; "Chasewood's Legacy"; "Song in a Quiet World"; "Startup"; "She Don't Answer"; "Fatnose Charley"; "Lucy in Her Pink Jacket."
Ninepenny Flute, The [C] (Macmillan, London, 1937, 305 pp., 7/6) (Macmillan, Toronto, $2.00)

21 stories of fantasy interest: "The Abbotts"; "All the World a Stage"; "The Badge"; "The Chronicles of Andrew"; "The Deserter"; "The Good Samaritans"; "Gudgeon and the Squirrel"; "Half-yard Ham"; "Hannibal's Bust"; "His Worship Receives"; "Jack the Giant Killer"; "Jove's Nectar"; "The Landmark"; "Life Is Like That"; "The Ninepenny Flute"; "The Philosopher's Daughter"; "Six Sad Men"; "Sofa One, Sofa Two"; "Some Talk of Alexander"; "Speaking Likenesses"; "Were Deceivers Ever."
Nixey's Harlequin [C] (Cape, 1931, 296 pp., 7/6, limited autographed edition 31/6; 1934, 2/6) (Knopf, 1932, 270 pp., $2.50) (Nelson, Toronto, 1934, $1.00)

10 stories: "Count Stefan"; "Dark Knowledge"; "The Gollan"; "The Green Drake"; "The Idle Frumkin"; "The Limping Lady"; "My Hundredth Tale"; "Nixey's Harlequin"; "The Post Office and the Serpent"; "Wilt Thou Leave Me Thus?"
Silver Circus: Tales [C] (Cape, 1928, 288 pp., 7/6; 1931, 3/6) (Knopf, 1929, 272 pp., $2.50) (in *Fares Please! An Omnibus* [Coppard])

16 stories: "Silver Circus"; "Darby Dallow Tells His Tale"; "That Fellow Tolstoy"; "Rifki"; "The Ape and the Ass"; "The Martyrdom of Solomon"; "Fine Feathers"; "The Almanac Man"; "A Looking Glass for Saint Luke"; "The Birthday Party"; "The Third Prize"; "The Presser"; "Adolf Plumflower"; "Purl and Plain"; "Faithless Phoebe"; "Polly Morgan."

COPPEL, ALFRED (9 Nov 1921–) U.S. author, born in Oakland, California, the son of Alfredo José de Marini y Coppel. He attended Menlo College and Stanford U. until World War II, when he became a cadet, a fighter pilot, and in 1945 a general's aide-de-camp.

He began writing in 1947, and though sf has been only part of his output, he has had over 50 sf stories in various magazines. He is married. One of his interests is sports car racing.
Fiction
Dark December (Gold Medal: s989, 1960, 208 pp., pa 35¢) ([Japanese], Hayakawa: 3031, 1962, pa) (H. Jenkins, London, 1966, 176 pp., 12/6) (*Nach der Stunde Null* [German], Heyne: 3078, 1966, pa)

A well-written story of survival after an atomic war, depicting realistic situations when a fighter pilot tries to trace his family.
Rebel of Rhada, The [as Robert Cham Gilman] (Harcourt, New York, 1968, 192 pp., $3.75)

Juvenile—tale of treachery and treason at a galactic empire outpost 10,000 years in the future.

COPPER, BASIL
Fiction
Not After Nightfall [C] [pa] (FSB: 1845, 1967, 190 pp., pa 5/-)

Weird, 8 stories: "The Spider"; "Camera Obscura"; "The Cave"; "The Grey House"; "Old Mrs. Cartwright"; "Charon"; "The Great Vore"; "The Janissaries of Emilion."

CORELLI, MARIE (1864–24 Apr 1924) British novelist, originally known as Mary (or Minnie) Mackay. She adopted her pseudonym as a musician; she was a brilliant pianist and was preparing for a concert career when a "psychical experience" turned her into a writer in 1885. Her first seven novels, from *A Romance of Two Worlds* (1886) to *The Life Everlasting* (1911) dealt with "spirit power and universal love." Her first substantial success was *Thelma* (1887), her great popularity began with *Barabbas* (1894), and her unique appeal to "royalty and servant girls" was evident with *The Sorrows of Satan* (1895). She produced 28 novels in all, but her popularity waned greatly in her latter years of writing.
Fiction [Incomplete—other titles in Bleiler *Checklist*]
Barabbas: A Dream of the World's Tragedy (Lippincott, Philadelphia, 1894, 317 pp.) (Methuen, London, 1894-5?, 465 pp., 1961, 12/6) ([Swedish], Skoglund, 1894)
Life Everlasting, The (Hodder Stoughton, London, 1911, 439 pp., 6/-) (Doran, New York, 1911) (Grosset, New York, 1920, 439 pp., 75¢) (Burt, New York, 1931, 439 pp., 75¢) (Methuen, 1953, 448 pp., 8/6)

A famous psychological semi-fantasy.
Love of Long Ago and Other Stories, The [C] (Doubleday Page, New York & Toronto, 1921, 295 pp.)

Fantasy, 15 stories: "The Love of Long Ago"; "Brown Jim's Problem"; "The Boy: An Episode"; "Claudia's Business"; "Rejected: The Story of a Picture"; " 'Sunny': A Red Cross Incident"; "The Panther: A Conquest of Heredity"; "The Stepping-Star"; "Why She Was Glad"; "The Sculptor's Angel: The Story of a Love Miracle"; "Lolita: A Love Episode"; "The Trench Comrade"; "The Signal"; "The Mystic Tune: An Idyll of the Hebrides"; " 'Lead, Kindly Light'."
Song of Miriam, The [C] (Munro, New York, 1898, 193 pp.)

Fantasy, 13 stories: "Angel's Wickedness"; "The Distant Voice"; "Lady With the Carnations"; " 'Mademoiselle Zephyr' "; "Nehemiah P. Hoskins, Artist"; "Old Bundle"; "One of the World's Wonders"; "Silence of the Maharajah"; "The Song of Miriam"; "Soul of the Newly-Born"; " 'Three Wise Men of Gotham' "; "Tiny Tramps"; "The Withering of a Rose."
Ziska, the Problem of a Wicked Soul (Stone Kimball, New York, 1897, 315 pp.) (Arrowsmith, Bristol, 1897, 365 pp.; 1911, 240 pp., 1/-; 1923, 365 pp., 3/6) ([Swedish], Skoglund, 1898) (Methuen, 1960, 192 pp., 8/6)

A brilliant novel of reincarnation and romance.

COREY, PAUL (FREDERICK) (8 July 1903–) U.S. free-lance writer.
Fiction
Planet of the Blind, The (R. Hale, London, 1968, 190 pp., 18/-)

A man with normal vision is marooned on a planet of blind people with superior technology.

CORLEY, DONALD
Fiction
House of Lost Identity, The [C] (McBride, New York, 1927, 324 pp.) (G. Harrup, London, 1927, 326 pp., 10/-)
11 weird stories with 2½-p. introduction by J. B. Cabell: "The House of Lost Identity"; "The Price of Reflection"; "The Daimyo's Bowl"; "Figs"; "The Manacles of Youth"; "The Ghost-Wedding"; "The Glass Eye of Throgmorton"; "The Legend of the Little Horses"; "The Tale That the Ming Bell Told"; "The Book of Debts"; "Song of the Tombelaine."

CORREY, LEE (pseud) See STINE, G. H.

CORWIN, NORMAN (LEWIS) (3 May 1910–) U.S. radio dramatist and novelist. He spent 10 years in newspaper work; from 1936 he was with the Columbia Broadcasting network directing dramatic programmes and writing plays (many published). From 1941 he presented the noted programmes "26 by Corwin," etc. He left Columbia in 1948, and in 1949 joined the U.N. as Chief of Special Projects in Radio. A selection of his plays was published in an Armed Services paper edition.
Fiction
Dog in the Sky (Simon & Schuster, New York, 1952, 156 pp., $3.00)
Juvenile—a young boy sets out to locate Curgatory, where his dog went after being run over.

CORY, CHARLES B(ARNEY) (31 Jan 1857–29 July 1921) U.S. ornithologist, born in Boston. He was curator of the Boston Society of Natural History until 1905, then continued this work elsewhere. He wrote many books on birds, covering them for a number of the states of the U.S.A.
Fiction
Montezuma's Castle and Other Weird Tales [C] (Author's edition [press of Rockwell & Churchill, Boston], 1899, 233 pp., illus.) (R. S. Mighill, New York, 1899, 233 pp., illus.)
Very scarce. 16 stories: "Montezuma's Castle"; "The Amateur Championship"; "The Tragedy of the White Tanks"; "Too Close for Comfort"; "The Strange Powder of Yon Yon Priests"; "An Aztec Mummy"; "A Lesson in Chemistry"; "An Interesting Ghost"; "The Mound of Eternal Silence"; "The Story of a Bad Indian"; "A Queer Coincidence"; "The Story of an Insane Sailor"; "The Elixir of Life"; "The Voodoo Idol"; "An Arizona Episode"; "One Touch of Nature."

CORY, HOWARD L. (pseud) See JARDINE, J. O.

COST, MARCH (pseud) See MORRISON, P.

COULSON, JUANITA (12 Feb 1933–) U.S. fan and housewife, living in Indiana. She and her husband Robert publish the long-lived fanzine Yandro.
Fiction
Crisis on Cheiron [pa] (Ace: H-27, 1967, 129 pp., pa 60¢; with The Winds of Gath)
Famine faces the Centaur world unless its ecology can be returned to normal.
Singing Stones, The [pa] (Ace: H-77, 1968, 132 pp., pa 60¢; with Derai)
A planet is enslaved because of its mind-stimulating gems.

COUNCIL OF FOUR (Denver) Pseudonym for the following U.S. persons: Tom Walker, Archangel; Chuck Hansen, Recording Angel; Roy Hunt, Chief Prophet; Bob Peterson, Mammon; Ellis Mills, plain member; Norm Metcalf, Archangel-in-Exile. The group began with four members.
Anthology
Science-Fictional Sherlock Holmes, The (Council of Four, Denver [printed by Grandon Co.], 1960, 137 pp., offset, $3.00, 1,000 copies; 1968, $4.00)
Sf, 7 stories and introduction "Sherlock Holmes and Science Fiction," by A. Boucher (also published in the amateur magazines

New Frontiers, Aug 1960, and Baker Street Journal, July 1960): "The Martian Crown Jewels," P. Anderson; "Half a Hoka—Poul Anderson," G. R. Dickson [article: fictional biography of P. Anderson]; "The Adventure of the Misplaced Hound," P. Anderson & G. R. Dickson; "The Anomaly of the Empty Man," A. Boucher; "The Greatest Tertian," A. Boucher; "The Adventure of the Snitch in Time," M. Reynolds & A. Derleth; "The Adventure of the Ball of Nostradamus," M. Reynolds & A. Derleth; "The Return," H. B. Piper & J. J. McGuire.

COUNSELMAN, MARY ELIZABETH (1911–) U.S. author and poet. She has spent most of her life in Gadsden, Alabama, and still lives there on a houseboat. She wrote many stories for Weird Tales from 1933, including "The Black Stone Statue" (Dec 1937; AFR: 3, 1947), "The Cat-Woman" (Oct 1933; AFR: 8, 1948), and "The Three Marked Pennies" (Aug 1934). Some of her stories have been anthologised, and she had some verse in A. Derleth's Dark of the Moon (1947).
Fiction
Half in Shadow [C] [pa] (Consul: 788, 1964, 189 pp., pa 3/6)
Weird, 14 stories: "The Three Marked Pennies"; "Cordona's Skull"; "The Lens"; "The Black Stone Statues"; "Mommy"; "The Green Window"; "A Death-Crown for Mr. Hapworthy"; "The Prism of Truth"; "Something Old"; "The Unwanted"; "The Tree's Wife"; "The Bonan of Baladewa"; "The Monkey Spoons"; "Gleason's Calendar."

COUNTESS OF MUNSTER, THE
Fiction
Ghostly Tales [C] (Hutchinson, London, 1896, 320 pp., illus.—Fred Hyland)
Not in Bleiler Checklist. 11 stories: "A Double"; "The Ghost of My Dead Friend" (from Strand); "The Tyburn Ghost"; "The Bruges Ghost"; "The Page Boy's Ghost"; "Aunt Jean's Story"; "Only a Cat"; "The Leather Box"; "Saved"; "A 'Mauvais Quart D'heure' "; "A Mysterious Visitor."

COURY, PHIL U.S. buyer for an aircraft corporation. Born in Barnsdall, Oklahoma, he attended Oklahoma schools and Air Force technical schools. In World War II he served four years in the U.S. Army Air Force, and saw the atomic desolation caused to Hiroshima and Nagasaki. His book below is a vehicle for his views on a future U.S.
Fiction
Anno Domini 2,000 (Vantage, New York, 1959, 147 pp., $2.95)
An American runs for the Senate on a platform contrary to the trend of the times; an outline of a quite socialistic U.S. of 40 years hence.

COVE, JOSEPH WALTER (1891–) British author who writes under the pseudonym "Lewis Gibbs." A work older than the one below was Parable for Lovers (1934).
Fiction [as Lewis Gibbs]
Late Final (Dent, London, 1951, 216 pp., 9/6; 1954, 6/-) (Digit: R487, 1961, 156 pp., pa 2/6)
After World War III a man returns to devastated England.

COWIE, DONALD
Fiction
Rape of Man, or, The Zoo Let Loose, The (Tantivy Press, Malvern, 1947, 222 pp., 12/6)
Fantasy satire—the animals unite against man.

COWLES, FREDERICK I(GNATIUS) (1900–) British author, a Fellow of the Royal Society of Literature. He is an honorary member of the Institut Litteraire et Artistique de France, which in 1936 awarded him its Silver Laureate Medal.
Fiction
Horror of Abbot's Grange, The [C] (Muller, London, 1936, 256 pp., 3/6) (Saunders, Toronto, $1.25)
Ghost, 20 stories (not in the Bleiler Checklist): "The Horror of Abbot's Grange"; "The House on the Marsh"; "Room for One";

"The New Inn"; "Terrible Mrs. Greene"; "The Mandarin's Chair"; "The Castle in the Forest"; "The Bell"; "One Side Only"; "Guardians of the Dead"; "The Unfinished Tower"; "The Headless Leper"; "The Pink Columbine"; "Passenger From Crewe"; "The Ring"; "Eyes for the Blind"; "Treasure Trove"; "The Limping Ghost"; "The Thing From the Sea"; "The Haunted Church."
Night Wind Howls, The [C] (Muller, 1938, 315 pp., 7/6)

Ghost, vampire, etc., 24 stories: "Rendezvous"; "The House of the Dancer"; "Wood Magic"; "Twisted Face"; "June Morning"; "The Witch-Finder"; "The Florentine Mirror"; "The Vampire of Kaldenstein"; "Lavender Love"; "The Mask of Death"; "King of Hearts"; "Voodoo"; "The Little Saint of Hell"; "Confession"; "The Lamasery of Beloved Dreams"; "The Cadaver of Bishop Louis"; "Out of the Darkness"; "The Lover of the Dead"; "The Caretaker"; "Gypsy Violin"; "Death in the Well"; "Retribution"; "Lady of Lyonnesse"; "Rats."

COWPER, RICHARD (pseud) See MURRY, M.

COX, DONALD (WILLIAM) (16 Apr 1921–) U.S. author and lecturer. Born in Rutherford, N.J., he studied at Montclair State College and at Columbia U., receiving his M.A. in 1947 and Ed.D. in 1948. He was a professor of education, and in 1957-58 Manager of Public Relations for Project Vanguard. He is now a free-lance author and lecturer.
Nonfiction
Spacepower: What It Means to You [with M. Stoiko] (Winston, Philadelphia, 1958, xxiv+262 pp., $4.50) (D'day SF B.C., 1958, 240 pp., $1.90)

Deals mostly with the social and political aspects of space travel.

COX, ERLE (15 Aug 1873–20 Nov 1950) Australian author, educated at Melbourne Church of England Grammar School. He entered journalism on the literary staff of *The Argus*, and became dramatic critic and reviewer for both *The Argus* and *Australasian*, 1918-46. He contributed short stories to *The Lone Hand* (winning its short story competition in 1910) and to other general magazines. He is primarily noted for his *Out of the Silence*, generally rated one of the world's sf classics. *Out of the Darkness* was the title of a book review he did for *Australasian*, and many readers mistook this for the title of a novel by him.
Fiction
Fool's Harvest (Robertson Mullen, Melbourne, 1939, 194 pp., 6/-; pa 2/-)

Future invasion of Australia.
Missing Angel, The (Robertson Mullen, 1947, 298 pp., 10/6)

A humorous fantasy in the *Unknown* manner.
Out of the Silence (*Argus*, sr?, 1919) (Vidler, Melbourne, 1925) (Hamilton, London, 1925, 1927, 319 pp., 3/6) (Robertson Mullen, 1928, 320 pp., 6/-; [4th], 1932, 6/-, 4/6; 1947, 416 pp., 10/6) (Rae D. Henkle, New York, 1928, 310 pp., $2.00) (*La sphère d'or* [French], Librairie des Champs-Elysées, Le Masque: 30, 1929)

One of sf's classics: an omnipotent woman from a past super-race endeavours to take control of Australia. *Note:* The only post-war edition (R. Mullen, 1947) is now out of print, but for many years was the main swap item between Australian and overseas collectors. The novel has also been translated into Russian.

COX, IRVING E(NGLAND) (1917–) U.S. author, born in Philadelphia. He took his B.A. at Whittier College, Calif., and returned there after the war for his M.A. and teaching credentials. During the war years he worked in transportation, mainly handling explosives for the Pacific theatre. He became interested in semantics and this led him to an interest in sf. He has been teaching since 1946, principally at Long Beach. His first published sf story was "Hell's Pavement" (*ASF*, Dec 1951), and he has since appeared in most sf magazines. His novels include "Apprentice to the Lamp" (*Rocket*, Sep 1953) and "One of Our Cities Is Missing" (*AS*, Apr 1958). He also writes short detective fiction and hopes to do long historical fiction.

COX, LUTHER
Fiction
Earth Is Mine, The (Exposition, New York, 1968, 171 pp., $6.00)

A race of supermen evolved from a former Earth civilization live on an 'opposite' Earth.

COXON, M. See HINE, M.

COYE, LEE BROWN (24 July 1907–) U.S. sculptor and artist, born in Syracuse. He did much work for *Weird Tales*, including the department "Weirdisms" and covers from July 1945 on. He has also illustrated a number of weird works, including one by Lovecraft and some Derleth anthologies. He has had numerous one-man exhibitions.

COZZENS, JAMES GOULD (19 Aug 1903–) U.S. author, born in Chicago. He published his first novel while still in college. He has lived in Cuba and Europe. Among his best-known novels are *The Last Adam, The Just and the Unjust, Guard of Honor*, and the more recent *By Love Possessed*; he won a Pulitzer Prize in 1949.
Fiction
Castaway (Random, New York, 1934, 9+181 pp., $1.75) (Longmans, London, 1934, 182 pp., 6/-) (Armed: s4, nd, pa) (Bantam: A1007, 1952, 121 pp., pa 25¢) (Corgi: 1007, 1952, 121 pp., pa 2/-) (Modern Library: P17, nd, 182 pp., pa 95¢–with one nonfantasy story)

A notable psychological novel of the terror in a man's mind.

CRAIGIE, DAVID (pseud) See CRAIGIE, DOROTHY M.

CRAIGIE, DOROTHY M. British author who writes under the pseudonym "David Craigie."
Fiction [as David Craigie; all juvenile]
Dark Atlantis (Heinemann, London, 1952, 221 pp., illus.–author, 9/6) (Macmillan, New York, 1953, 221 pp., $2.00)

Deep-sea diving, strange frogmen, and giant snails in a drowned continent.
Voyage of the Luna I, The (Eyre Spottiswoode, London, 1949, 272 pp., illus., 6/-; 1954, 5/-)

Two children make the first Moon flight; readable by adult standards.

CRAM, RALPH ADAMS (16 Dec 1863–22 Sep 1942) British architect and author; Litt.D., Princeton 1910; Williams 1928; LL.D., Yale 1915, Notre Dame 1925. He was a member of many learned societies in both arts and architecture. He wrote many works on architecture and religion as well as fiction.
Fiction
Black Spirits and White: A Book of Ghost Stories [C] (Stone Kimball, Chicago, 1895, 150 pp.) (Chatto, London, 1896, 160 pp., 1/6)

6 stories and Postscript: "No. 252 Rue M. Le Prince"; "In Kropfsberg Keep"; "The White Villa"; "Sister Maddelena"; "Notre Dame Des Eaux"; "The Dead Valley"; "Postscript." Weird stories of extraordinary merit.

CRAMP, LEONARD G. (1919–) British illustrator and UFO enthusiast. He is a technical illustrator for an engineering firm. He belongs to the Interplanetary Society and has formed the Isle of Wight UFO Investigation Society.
Nonfiction
Piece for a Jigsaw (Somerton, Cowes, 1967, 388 pp., illus: 100 drawings and 58 plates, 27/6)

A lengthy exposition of how unidentified flying objects (flying saucers) could work—a mixture of facts, hearsay, evidence and drawings with theory.
Space, Gravity and the Flying Saucer (Werner Laurie, London, 1954, 182 pp., 10/6)

Introduction by D. Leslie. The author gives a theory of the motive power of flying saucers based on a thorough study of the subject, and also gives reasons for his belief that Adamski's photographs are authentic.

CRANDALL, REED U.S. artist. He is best known for his protracted work on the comic book, radio and movie serial character "Blackhawk" during the 1940's and 1950's. He later became an artist for the E.C. comics.

CRANE, ROBERT (pseud) See GLEMSER, B.

CRANE, WALTER B(EVERLY)
Fiction
Odd Tales [C] (Witmark & Sons, Chicago & London, 1900, 106 pp.)
    Fantasy, 13 stories: "Mrs. Vane Flutterby's Photograph"; "Triplets"; "Bob Hervier's Typewriter"; "His Wife or His Life"; "La Vague"; "Miss Santa Claus"; "Jockey Atkins"; "A Pair of Boots"; "The Fate of Gigi"; "An Infamous Conspiracy"; "The Eight-Day Clock"; "The Baron Du Rhem"; "The Last Tone."

CRAWFORD, F(RANCIS) MARION (2 Aug 1854–9 Apr 1909) American author, born in Italy. The cosmopolitanism of his work is attributable to his early training in many places. He became a Sanskrit scholar, and then in 1882 produced his first novel, *Mr. Isaacs*. After further world travelling he settled in Italy, and wrote many historical works on that country. Among the most noted of his novels are *A Roman Singer* (1884), *A Tale of a Lonely Parish* (1886), *Paul Patoff* (1887), *The Witch of Prague* (1891), *Via Crucis* (1899), *In the Palace of the King* (1900) and *The White Sister* (1909). He has often appeared in weird anthologies, where probably his most noted work is "The Upper Berth."
Fiction [Incomplete—other titles in Bleiler *Checklist*]
Uncanny Tales [C] See *Wandering Ghosts*
Upper Berth, The [C] (Putnam, New York & London, 1894, 145 pp.)
    2 fantasies: "The Upper Berth"; "By the Waters of Paradise."
Wandering Ghosts [C] (Macmillan, New York, 1911, 302 pp., $1.50) (*Uncanny Tales*, Unwin, London, 1911, 307 pp., 6/-; 1917, 254 pp., 1/-)
    Weird, 7 stories: "The Dead Smile"; "The Screaming Skull"; "Man Overboard!"; "For the Blood Is Life"; "The Upper Berth"; "By the Waters of Paradise"; "The Doll's Ghost" (*F&SF*, Apr 1952)

CRAWFORD, JOSEPH H. Jr. (1932–) U.S. sf collector. He was born in Providence, R.I., where he still resides; he graduated from La Salle Academy in 1949, and took a B.A. in Political Science at Providence College, 1953. He was in the U.S. Army 1955-57, and is now a credit adjuster for a local department store. He was first attracted to sf in 1943 via *FFM* and is now a collector; he is also interested in classical and contemporary music.
Nonfiction (compiled with others)
333. A Bibliography of the Science-Fantasy Novel (Grandon, Providence, 1953, 79 pp., $2.00, jacket–Hunt)
    A pamphlet giving short synopses of (obviously) 333 books considered outstanding, covering U.S. books before 1951 and some British. It has some notable omissions but is a recommended aid for the collector.

CRAWFORD, WILLIAM L. (1911–) U.S. editor and publisher who became noted in the early 1930's through his ventures in the sf field. He edited and published *Marvel Tales* and *Unusual Stories* (setting the type himself, etc.) but was unable to give them newsstand distribution. Although amateurish in appearance, these magazines printed some notable material and are now collector's items. In the same period he published the paper-covered items *The Shadow Over Innsmouth*, by H. P. Lovecraft, *Mars Mountain*, by Eugene George Key, and *The White Sybil*, by C. A. Smith (which also contained "Men of Avalon," by D. H. Keller) (40 pp., 15¢); these did not sell well at the time but are now in demand by collectors. His editions usually ran 400 copies for books and 1,000 copies for magazines. After printing *Fantasy Magazine* from late 1935 to Jan 1937 (following on from Ruppert) he left the field. He returned after the war, and his first venture was *The Garden of Fear*, a paper-covered anthology which he anonymously edited. He

was the main force behind Fantasy Publishing Co. Inc., Los Angeles. After producing a considerable number of books, as well as two magazines, FPCI went into recess in the late 1950's, but recently returned to publishing. A further venture of the late 1940's which presented only a few works was Griffin Publishing Co. With others, including his wife Margaret Crawford, he used the pseudonym "Garret Ford" in editing the FPCI magazines *Fantasy Book* and *Spaceway*, and also the anthology *Science and Sorcery* selected from the former.
Anthologies
Garden of Fear, The [pa] (Crawford, Los Angeles, 1945, 79 pp., pa 25¢)
    Weird, 5 stories (first 4 from *Marvel Tales*) [no compiler given]: "The Garden of Fear," R. E. Howard; "The Man With the Hour Glass," L. A. Eshbach; "Celephais," H. P. Lovecraft; "Mars Colonizes," M. J. Breuer; "The Golden Bough," D. H. Keller.
Machine God Laughs, The (Griffin, Los Angeles, 1949, 134 pp.)
    3 stories [no compiler given]: "The Machine God Laughs," F. Pragnell (*Fantasy Book*, sr3, No. 2, 1948); "Star of the Undead," P. D. Lavond (*FB*, No. 2, 1948); "Crusader," B. Wells (*FB*, No. 5, 1949 [as Gene Ellerman]).
Science and Sorcery [compiled by Garret Ford] (FPCI, Los Angeles, 1953, 327 pp., illus.–A. L. Walter, $3.00)
    Sf, 15 stories: "Scanners Live in Vain," Cordwainer Smith; "The Little Man on the Subway," I. Asimov & J. MacCreigh; "What Goes Up," A. Coppel; "Kleon of the Golden Sun," E. E. Repp; "How High on the Ladder?" L. Paige; "Footprints," R. E. Gilbert; "The Naming of Names," R. Bradbury; "The Eyes," H. Hasse; "The Scarlet Lunes," S. A. Coblentz; "Demobilization," G. Cowie; "Voices From the Cliff," J. M. Leahy; "The Lost Chord" (new), S. Moskowitz; "The Watchers," R. H. Deutsch; "The Peaceful Martian," J. T. Oliver; "Escape to Yesterday" (new), A. J. Burks. All the reprints except the Repp and Paige stories are from *Fantasy Book*.
Double Bindings Omnibus bindings by the publisher (FPCI–W. L. Crawford). Where both sections have the same author they are listed under that author; these are *From Death to the Stars*, by L. R. Hubbard, and *Strange Worlds* by R. M. Farley [R. S. Hoar].
    Fantasy Twin (FPCI, Los Angeles, 1953, 503 pp., $3.50)
        The Undesired Princess, L. S. de Camp, and *The Dark Other*, S. G. Weinbaum.
    Quadratic (FPCI, 1953, 580 pp., $3.50)
        Worlds of Wonder O. Stapledon, and *Murder Madness*, M. Leinster [W. F. Jenkins].
    Science-Fantasy Quintet (FPCI, 1953, $3.50)
        The Radium Pool, E. E. Repp, and *Triton*, L. R. Hubbard.

CREASEY, JOHN (27 Sep 1908–) British author. His first book was published in 1932 after he had collected 700 rejection slips for works from novels to epic poems. He is now noted for his thrillers, some of which have sold up to 500,000 copies. In the early 1960's he was still working 14 hours per day as he did in his lean years. Of more than 370 books then published, many fell into the crime series: "Dr. Palfrey" (20); "Inspector West" (28); "The 'Toff' " (40); " 'Department Z' " (32). The Palfrey series has many novels of sf nature, including *The Blight* (Walker, 1968) and *The Depths* (Berkley, 1968, pa).
Fiction
Flood, The (Hodder & Stoughton, London, 1956, 191 pp., 10/6; 1958, pa 2/6) (Walker, New York, 1960, 191 pp., $4.50?)
    A super-scientist and assistant create floods, the giant *octi*, etc., with the aim of making a new Eden. A Dr. Palfrey novel.

CREEPS LIBRARY A book series from Philip Allan (London) around 1932-36. Among other works, it included a number of anonymous anthologies.
    The following works are covered in Author entries:
Abdullah, (Sheik) Achmed: *Mysteries of Asia* [C] (1935)
Allen, E. H. [as Christopher Blayre]: *The Strange Papers of Dr. Blayre* [C] (1932)
Birkin, C. L.: *Devil's Spawn* [C] (1936) [used pseud. C. Lloyd in the anthologies]

Hamilton, E.: *Horror on the Asteroid* [C] (1936)
Lewis, L. A.: *Tales of the Grotesque* [C] (1936)
Robbins, C. A.: *The Three Freaks* (1934)
The following works are not covered in this *Encyclopedia*:
Meik, Vivian: *The Curse of Red Shiva* (1936); *Devil Drums* (1933); *Veils of Fear* (1934)

Anthologies [all weird; all listed as Anonymous in Bleiler *Checklist*]

Creeps (P. Allan, 1932, 248 pp., 2/6) (in *Creeps Omnibus*, 1935)
9 stories: "Silent, White and Beautiful," T. Robbins; "The Red Lodge," H. R. Wakefield; "The Ghost Table," E. O'Donnell; "Spurs," T. Robbins; "He Cometh and He Passeth By," H. R. Wakefield; "The Charnel House," P. Murray; "A Wager and a Ghost," E. O'Donnell; "The Last Night," C. Lloyd; "Cockcrow Inn," T. Robbins.

Creeps Omnibus (P. Allan, 1935, 638 pp., 3/6) (S. J. R. Saunders, Toronto, $1.00)
Contains all stories of *Creeps*, *Shudders* and *Shivers* in the order within entries.

Horrors (P. Allan, 1933, 252 pp., 2/6)
12 stories: "Doctor Browning's Bus," E. S. Knights; "The Ever-Turning Dynamos," A. Govan; "The Doll's House," H. Gorst; "Special Diet," C. Lloyd; "Meshes of Doom," N. Kelvington; "Unburied Bane," N. Dennett; "The Mystery of the Locked Room," E. O'Donnell; "Doctor Fawcett's Experiment," R. F. Broad; "Without a Hitch," Pamela James; "Lover's Meeting," J. Ratho; "A Poem and a Bunch of Roses," C. Lloyd; "Dark Seance," G. Benwood.

Monsters (P. Allan, 1934, 236 pp., 2/6; 1937, 1/-)
12 stories: "The Two Old Women," V. Meik; "Harvest," T. Leaf; "The Confession," K. Ingram; "The Round Graveyard," E. K. Allan; "The Interrupted Honeymoon," G. Benwood; "Blood for a Tiger," Phyllis Stone; "The Caretaker's Story," Edith Olivier; "A Lover Came to Sunnamees," G. Preston; "The Haunted Telephone," E. O'Donnell; "The Yellow Cat," M. Joseph; "The 'Locum'," K. Ingram; "The Cockroach," C. Lloyd.

Nightmares (P. Allan, 1933, 255 pp., 2/6)
12 stories: "High Tide," Hester Gaskell; "The Curse," R. Aggett; "Hangman's Cottage," P. Murray; "The Escape," J. Ratho; "The Wimpus," T. Robbins; " 'Is It True?'," Sonja Converse; "The Headless Leper," F. Cowles; " 'The Happy Dancers'," C. Lloyd; "The End of the Holiday," V. A. Chappell; "Binkie," A. C. S. Tibbett; "The Haunted Bungalow," B. L. Milne; "The Woollen Helmet," P. Erroll.

Panics (P. Allan, 1934, 241 pp., 2/6; 1937, 1/-)
12 stories: "The Night Nurse's Story," Edith Olivier; "Aceldama," G. W. Jaggard; "Shelter," C. Lloyd; "The Blazing Crystals," A. Govan; "Death in Hyde Park," E. K. Allan; " '?'," J. R. Warren; "The Psyche," F. Graves; "Fog," J. Ratho; "A Very Potent Poison," H. Johnson; "The Menthir," N. Dennett; "In the Interests of Science," E. O'Donnell; "Reprieve," K. Ingram.

Powers of Darkness (P. Allan, 1934, 243 pp., 2/6)
10 stories: "The Two Bottles of Relish," Lord Dunsany; "The Coat," A. E. D. Smith; "Obsession," C. Lloyd; "The Third Time," K. Ingram; "The Guillotine," J. H. Turner; "The Mutineers," Cicely Fox-Smith; "November the Thirteenth," R. Thorndike; "The Miniature in Black," L. A. Westney; "The Temple Servant," E. R. Mourroughs; "A Nice Cup of Tea," Maureen E. Shaw.

Quakes (P. Allan, 1933, 253 pp., 2/6; 1937, 1/-)
13 stories: "The Incredible," Mirabel Cobbold; "B72," Phyllis Stone; "The Man in the Mirror," P. B. Barry; "Old Mrs. Strathers," C. Lloyd; "The Spirit of Higgins," H. Glyn-Ward; "Littlesmith," Hester Gorst; "The Terror by Night," Ismay Trimble; "The People of the Darkness," D. Newton; "Death Is Avenged," A. J. Woodgate; "The Actor's Story," C. Lloyd; "Dead Men's Bones," Edith Olivier; "The Cupboard of Dread," E. O'Donnell; "Queer," C. Cullum.

Shivers (P. Allan, 1932, 254 pp., 2/6) (in *Creeps Omnibus*, 1935)
9 stories: "The 17th Hole at Duncaster," H. R. Wakefield; "An Eye for an Eye," C. Lloyd; "Wild Wullie the Waster," T. Robbins; "The Death Mask," Mrs. Everett; "The Ghost in the Ring," E. O'Donnell; "The Poplar Tree," P. Murray; "And He Shall Sing . . . ," H. R. Wakefield; "Who Wants a Green Bottle?" T. Robbins; "The Tank of Death," E. O'Donnell.

Shudders (P. Allan, 1932, 254 pp., 2/6) (in *Creeps Omnibus*, 1935)
11 stories: "Of Persons Unknown," H. R. Wakefield; "Toys," T. Robbins; "Accusing Shadows," E. O'Donnell; "Professor Pownall's Oversight," H. R. Wakefield; "The Harlem Horror," C. Lloyd; "The Trunk," P. Murray; "The Third Coach," H. R. Wakefield; "The Crimson Blind," Mrs. Everett; "The Haunted Spinney," E. O'Donnell; "The Patch," P. Murray; "That Dieth Not," H. R. Wakefield.

Tales of Death (P. Allan, 1936, 254 pp., 2/6)
11 stories: "An Appointment With Death," E. H. Bidlake; "The Hut," O. Blakeston; "The Return," M. Critchley; "Swift Death," S. Darcy; "The Devil-Plant," M. Ellison; "Kismet," C. Knight; "Down-Draught to Hell," H. B. Lancaster; "The Graverhouse Affair," S. G. MacDonell; "Lost With All Hands," R. P. Morrison; "The Cottage," W. J. Pollock; "Lion of Bengal," H. Wilson.

Tales of Dread (P. Allan, 1936, 248 pp., 2/6)
9 stories: "Babysphere Number 7," F. H. Sibson; "Angela," C. Lloyd; "The Green Taxi," Anne Edgar; "The Secret of the Graves," O. Blakeston; "The Silver Lady," S. Denham; "The Dead Watch," D. Lord; "Dispossessed," H. Markham; "The Tiger," Francis Bruguire; "The False Trail," K. Ingram.

Tales of Fear (P. Allan, 1935, 243 pp., 2/6)
12 stories: "The Road," Vera A. Gadd; "Bitten by a Spider," P. Clark; "The Silent Inn," G. W. Lewis; "Many Cats and One Tale," W. A. C. Chadwick; "The Horror in the Pond," A. D. Avison; "Adventure Without Asking," O. Blakeston; "The Thing From the Pit," A. S. Aylmer; "Lonely Cottage," Tilly Scard; "The Figure at the Window," Helen Adad; "A Journey by Train," H. L. Lawrence; "Hillmount," Vera A. Gadd; "The Snake," Chrystabel Earle.

Terrors (P. Allan, 1933, 252 pp., 2/6; 1937, 1/-)
11 stories: "The Terror on Tobit," C. Lloyd; "Thirty," G. Preston; "The Westerdale's Tow," F. H. Sibson; "Waxworks," A. de Lorde; "The Man With the Flayed Face," Phyllis Stone; "The Muffler," Ursula Gwynne; "The Terror of Stranger Island," Marjory Lawrence; "Blue Black Hair," Pamela James; "Arabella Goes North," J. Ratho; "Spider's Web," P. Stone; "The Mystery of Beechcroft Farm," E. O'Donnell.

Thrills (P. Allan, 1935, 249 pp., 2/6; 1937, 1/-)
14 stories: "The Confession," T. Robbins; "The Kosso," W. F. Temple; "A Fishing Story," H. R. Wakefield; "Henri Lorne," C. Lloyd; "They Come for Their Own," A. H. Claxton; "I Am Smith," E. F. Henry; "The House With No Road," J. A. Hopson; "The Queer People," E. Reed; "The Divine Spark," Catherine Clark; "Ashes for Ashes," R. A. P. Crawshay; "Death of a Poacher," H. R. Wakefield; "A Bed for the Poacher," G. A. Archard; "Passing of a Terror," K. Ingram; "Doctor Horder's Room," P. Carleton.

CRISP, CASSIUS
Fiction

Enchanted Ghost and Other Stories, An [C] (F. Sackett, New York, 1900, 165 pp.)
Fantasy, 5 stories: "Paul Stoddard's Romance"; "An Enchanted Ghost"; "The Hunt for the Golden Buck"; "Ruth"; "The Valley Tragedies."

CRISP, FRANK R(OBSON) (30 Nov 1915–) British author and businessman, born at Durham. He served in the British Merchant Navy, and is now director of a London catering service.
Fiction

Ape of London, The (Hodder & Stoughton, London, 1959, 192 pp., 12/6)
Terror attacks helpless people in southern Britain in the summer of 1963.

Night Callers, The (J. Long, London, 1960, 184 pp., 11/6) (Nelson, Toronto, $2.50) (Panther: 1276, 1961, 156 pp., pa 2/6)
A thriller with a sf motive, concerning a mysterious crystal and the odd events caused by an invasion of creatures from Ganymede.

CRISPIN, EDMUND (pseud) See MONTGOMERY, R. B.

CROMPTON, RICHMAL (pseud) See LAMBOURN, R. C.

CRONIN, BERNARD CHARLES (18 Mar 1884–) Australian novelist. He worked on the land until 1913 although he had previously won the Fink Scholarship and was Dux and Gold Medallist 1901. He founded certain clubs in Melbourne, including the Society of Australian Authors, of which he was president 1927-34. From 1918 to date he has written many books of all types, some under pseudonyms. He is known in the science fiction field under the pseudonym "Eric North." Many of his stories were published in the Australian *Bulletin* and the Melbourne *Herald* (newspaper) before overseas appearances.
Fiction [as Eric North]
Ant Men, The (Winston, Philadelphia, 1955, 216 pp., $2.00, jacket–P. Blaisdell) (*Deserto dei mostri* [Italian], *Urania*: 114, 1956) ([Japanese], GingaShobō, 'Adv. in SF': 14, 1956) (Macfadden: 60-277, 1967, 175 pp., pa 60¢)
Juvenile, one of the *Adventures in Science Fiction* series—ants of high intelligence.
Green Flame, The [n] (*Melbourne Herald*, sr, 1924) (*Toad*, Hodder Stoughton, London, 1929, 320 pp., 7/6) (*Arg*, sr4, 24 Feb 1940) (*A. Merritt's Fantasy*, July 1950)
A man can set water afire with a small but potent pellet.
Three Against the Stars [n] ("The Satyr," *Melbourne Herald*, sr, 1924) (*Arg*, sr5, 2 July 1938) (*FN*, May 1950)
Menacing invaders from another dimension fill Earth with fear.
Toad See *Green Flame, The*

CROSBY, HARRY C. U.S. author, better known under the pseudonym Christopher Anvil. He has written many stories for the sf magazines in the last decade, most of which have been published in *ASF*.
Series [as Christopher Anvil]
Pandora. All in *ASF*: "Pandora's Planet" (Sep 1956); "Pandora's Envoy" (Apr 1961); "The Toughest Opponent" (Aug 1962).
Fiction [as Christopher Anvil]
Day the Machines Stopped, The [pa] (Monarch: 478, 1964, 124 pp., pa 40¢)

CROSS, JOHN KEIR (1914–) British author and BBC writer. He was responsible for the radio scripting of *The Kraken Wakes*, *The Einstein Way*, etc.; he often uses the pseudonym Stephen Macfarlane.
Fiction
Angry Planet, The (P. Lunn, London, 1945, 200 pp., illus., 8/6) (Coward McCann, New York, 1946, 239 pp., $2.50) (*Vi Landade Pa Mars K1* [Swedish], Raben & Sjögren, 1947)
The chronicle of the first Martian expedition; sequel is *SOS From Mars*.
Flying Fortunes in an Encounter With Rubberface, The (F. Muller, London, 1952, 219 pp., 9/6) (*The Stolen Sphere*, Dutton, New York, 1953, 220 pp., $2.75)
Juvenile—plots and counterplots in launching an Earth satellite space station.
Other Passenger, The [C] (Westhouse, London, 1944, 11+274 pp., illus.–B. Angrave, 12/6) (Lippincott, Philadelphia, 1946, 320 pp., $2.75) (Longmans, Toronto, $3.00) (Ballantine: 480K, 1961, 159 pp., pa 35¢ [9 stories marked †])
18 stories, mainly fantasy: "The Glass Eye"†; "Petronella Pan"; "The Last of the Romantics"†; "Clair de Lune"†; "Absence of Mind"; "Hands"†; "Another Planet"; "Liebestraum"; "Miss Thing and the Surrealist"†; "Valdemosa"; "Amateur Gardening"; "The Little House"†; "Esmeralda"; "Music When Soft Voices Die"†; "Cyclamen Brown"; "Couleur de Rose"; "The Lovers"†; "The Other Passenger"†. *Note:* Only the Westhouse edition has the eight surrealistic colour plates.
Other Side of Green Hills See *Owl and the Pussycat, The*
Owl and the Pussycat, The (P. Lunn, 1946, 158 pp., illus., 7/6) (*Other Side of Green Hills*, Coward McCann, New York, 1947, 190 pp., $2.50; Longmans, Toronto, $3.00)

Juvenile—a strange fantasy of conflict between good and evil.
Red Journey Back See *SOS From Mars*
SOS From Mars (Hutchinson, London, 1954, 216 pp., 7/6) (*Red Journey Back*, Coward McCann, 1954, 252 pp., illus.–R. Jacques, $2.75; McGraw, Toronto, $1.65)
Sequel to *The Angry Planet*; the chronicles of the second and third Martian expeditions.
Stolen Sphere, The See *Flying Fortunes in an Encounter With Rubberface, The*
Anthologies
Best Black Magic Stories (Faber, London, 1960, 3+269 pp., 16/-; pa 6/-)
Weird, 13 stories and compiler's introduction: "The Earlier Service," Margaret Irwin; "The Lady on the Grey," J. Collier; "A Room in Leyden" ("Singular Passage in the Life of the Late Henry Harris, Doctor in Divinity, as Related by His Friend Thomas Ingoldsby"), R. H. Barham; "Mothering Sunday," J. K. Cross; "The Snake," D. Wheatley; "The Hill," R. E. Roberts; "Casting the Runes," M. R. James; "More Sinned Against," J. Wyndham; "The Haunted and the Haunters," Lord Lytton; "Homecoming," R. Bradbury; "Couching at the Door," Dorothy K. Broster; "A Way of Thinking," T. Sturgeon; "The Black Mass," J.-K. Huysman; "Envoi."
Best Horror Stories (Faber, 1956, 300 pp., 15/-; 1962, pa 6/-)
Weird, 16 stories and compiler's introduction: "Skeleton," R. Bradbury; "A Watcher by the Dead," A. Bierce; "Raspberry Jam," Angus Wilson; "Berenice," E. A. Poe; "August Heat," W. F. Harvey; "Lot No. 249," A. C. Doyle; "The Lovers," J. K. Cross; "The Mark of the Beast," R. Kipling; "The End of the Party," Graham Greene; "Heartburn," Hortense Calisher; "Bartleby," Herman Melville; "Our Feathered Friends," Philip MacDonald; "Thrawn Janet," R. L. Stevenson; "Mars Is Heaven," R. Bradbury; "Oh Whistle, and I'll Come to You, My Lad," M. R. James; "A Rose for Emily," Wm. Faulkner.
Best Horror Stories 2 (Faber, 1965, 270 pp., 18/-)
Weird, 15 stories and compiler's introduction: "The Professor's Teddy Bear," T. Sturgeon; "The Last Chukka," Alec Waugh; "The Boarded Window," A. Bierce; "The Flowers in the Forest," B. W. Aldiss; "The Thing on the Doorstep," H. P. Lovecraft; "How to Make a Foon," Spike Mulligan; "Brown God in the Beginning," Angus Stewart; "Skin to Love," Christianna Brad; "The Glass Eye," J. K. Cross; "The Treasure of Abbot Thomas," M. R. James; "Evening Primrose," J. Collier; "The House of Desolation," Alan Griff; "Making Sure of a Little One," Derek Ingrey; "The Derelict," Wm. H. Hodgson; "Thurnley Abbey," P. Landon.

CROSS, POLTON (pseud) See FEARN, J. R.

CROSSEN, KENDELL FOSTER (1910–) U.S. author. He did work in various fields before he became a radio writer and newspaperman in 1939. He has written a great deal for the pulp detective market and has had a number of mystery novels published under his own name and the pseudonym "M. E. Chaber." Other pennames he has used are Christopher Monig, Richard Foster, Bennet Barlay, Kent Richard, and H. C. R. Lorac, but only Foster and Monig have been used for sf. In the sf field he wrote a number of space-adventure stories, often humorous, for the Standard magazines in the early 1950's. Novels include "Passport to Pax" (*SS*, July 1952) and "Things of Distinction" (*SS*, Mar 1952). Besides sf anthologies he edited the mystery anthology *Murder Cavalcade* (1953).
Series
Draco, Manning. All in *TWS*: "The Merakian Miracle" (Oct 1951); "The Regal Rigellian" (Feb 1952); "The Polluxian Pretender" (Oct 1952); "The Caphian Caper" (Dec 1952); "Assignment to Aldebaran" (Feb 1953); "Whistle Stop in Space" (Aug 1953); "Mission to Mizar" (Nov 1953); "The Agile Algolian" (Win 1954). The first four appeared as *Once Upon a Star*.
Fiction
Once Upon a Star (Holt, New York, 1953, 237 pp., $2.95) (Clarke Irwin, Toronto, $3.75)
The first four "Manning Draco" series stories connected to form

a novel; the rollicking adventures of a salesman with alien races.

Rest Must Die, The [as Richard Foster] [pa] (Gold Medal: s853, 1959, 176 pp., pa 35¢) (Muller: 'GM' 462, 1960, 160 pp., pa 2/-)

Well-written story of the fight for survival in New York's underground transit system after the city is H-bombed.

Year of Consent [pa] (Dell: 32, 1954, 224 pp., pa 25¢)

One man's fight against the mechanical brain that dominates the U.S. and allied countries.

Anthologies

Adventures in Tomorrow (Greenberg, New York, 1951, 278 pp., $3.50) (Ambassador, Toronto, $4.50) (Bodley Head, London, 1953, 240 pp., 10/6) (Belmont: B75-215, 1968, 236 pp., pa 75¢) (Israeli edition—understood to be the first U.S. sf ever translated into Hebrew)

Sf, 15 stories and introduction "Houyhnhnms & Co.": *I. Atomic Age:* "Flying Dutchman," W. Moore; "The Mute Question," F. J. Ackerman; "The Portable Phonograph," W. V. T. Clark; "There Will Come Soft Rains," R. Bradbury. *II. Galactic Age:* "Automaton," A. E. van Vogt; "Restricted Clientele," K. F. Crossen; "Christmas on Ganymede," I. Asimov; "Shambleau," C. L. Moore. *III. Stellar Age:* "Memory," T. Sturgeon; "Exiled From Earth," S. Merwin; "Retreat to the Stars," L. Brackett; "Voice of the Lobster," H. Kuttner. *Note:* The British ed. omits the Asimov and Moore stories.

Future Tense (Greenberg, 1952, 364 pp., $3.50) (Bodley Head, 1954, 216 pp., 10/6 [7 stories marked †])

Sf, 14 reprints and new stories: *Reprints:* "Plagiarist"†, P. Phillips; "The Ambassadors"†, A. Boucher; "Dream's End"†, H. Kuttner; "We the People," W. Moore; "Throwback"†, Miriam A. deFord; "Things of Distinction"†, K. F. Crossen; "Scarlet Dream," C. L. Moore. *New:* "Cyclops," H. F. Heard; "The Battle of the S . . S," B. Elliott; "The Island of Five Colors," M. Gardner; "Baby Killers," R. B. Elliott; "Beanstalk"†, J. Blish; "Incubation"†, J. D. MacDonald; "Love Story," C. Monig. *Note:* "Beanstalk" later appeared as "Giants in the Earth," *SF*, Jan 1958, and (enlarged) as *Titans' Daughter*.

CROSSLAND, JOHN R. See PARRISH, J. M. (co-anthologist)

CROSSLEY-HOLLAND, KEVIN
Fiction
Green Children, The (Seabury Press, U.S.A., 1968, not paged, illus.–Marggret Gordon, $4.50)

Juvenile—retelling of a 700-year-old legend of two children emerging through a cave from a world below.

CROWCROFT, PETER (1925–) British author. He was born at Watford, England, of Anglo-Russian parents, and educated at University College, London. During World War II he served in Combined Operations. He has been an auctioneer, motorcycle racer, and accountant, and has built a yacht.
Fiction
Fallen Sky, The (P. Nevil, London, 1954, 222 pp., 11/6)

A few survivors strive for existence in the ruins of London.

CROWE, Mrs. CATHERINE (STEVENS) (*ca.* 1799-1876) Renowned English novelist and writer on the supernatural. She is remembered for her Gothic romance *Susan Hopley*, which had a pirated editon, while her *The Night Side of Nature* (1848 or earlier) is an oft-reprinted book still much sought after. Other books of interest include *Ghosts and Family Legends* (Newby, 1858) and *Light and Darkness* (Routledge, 1856).

CROWLEY, ALEISTER (1875–1947) British disciple of the occult. He squandered his money in his early years, and then lived as a "master of the Black Arts." John Symonds has written the full-length biography *The Great Beast: The Life of Aleister Crowley* (Rider, 1951), as well as the later *The Magic of Aleister Crowley* (Muller, 1958, 8 plates).
Fiction
Moonchild: A Prologue (Mandrake, London, 1929, 335 pp., 10/6)

A lovely innocent woman is caught in the war between the forces of good and evil. A forerunner to D. Wheatley's novels of this type.

Strategem and Other Stories, The [C] (Mandrake, 1929, 140 pp., 3/6)

3 stories: "The Stratagem"; "The Testament of Magdalene Blair"; "His Secret Sin."

CRUMP, I(RVING) (1887–)
Fiction
Og, Son of Og (Dodd Mead, New York, 1965, 211 pp., $3.25)

Juvenile.

CUMMINGS, M(ONETTE) A.
Fiction
Exile and Other Tales of Fantasy [C] [pa] (Flagship: 00864, 1968, 160 pp., pa 60¢)

Sf, 14 stories: "Exile" (short novel); "There Were Giants"; "Don't You Remember?"; "Buy Me a Woofl"; "Specimen"; "What Happened to Tuesday?"; "Get Rich Quick"; "To Change the Past"; "Moon Down"; "Aliens Aren't Wanted"; "Little Old Lady"; "The Girl With the Green Glass Eyes"; "Full Moon"; "The Cat Who Liked Thrillers."

CUMMINGS, RAY(MOND) (KING) (30 Aug 1887–23 Jan 1957) U.S. science fiction author. He was born in New York City. He was a freshman at Princeton U., but then went with his family to Puerto Rico and lived on orange plantations. Later, with his family, he worked at oil wells in Wyoming and placer mines in British Columbia and Alaska. In the late 1920's he was an editor of house organs for Thomas A. Edison, and during this time he wrote "The Girl in the Golden Atom." This story was an instant success when published in *All-Story Weekly*. It began his career as a writer— mainly in the sf field—and was the forerunner of the many 'journey into atomic smallness' stories with which his name will always be associated. Another of his early stories began the popular *Tubby* series.

Cummings had many notable stories in the general fiction magazines in the 1920's, and he also appeared in the sf magazines through to the 1950's and had over 30 years of writing in the field, a tenure exceeded only by Murray Leinster (W. F. Jenkins). Although his later works varied greatly in quality, his stories brought new conceptions into science fiction, especially in the early years. His daughter Betty was his companion in the latter years of his life. A mistake of interest occurred on one of his works when the Canadian firm of Duchess credited its paperback edition of his *Brigands of the Moon* to John W. Campbell, Jr. His fiction listed below is primarily sf, but the following weird stories are of interest: "The Other Man's Blood" (*ASW*, 18 Oct 1919; *FFM*, Dec 1940), and "The Dead Who Walk" (*Strange Tales*, Sep 1931; *Magazine of Horror*, Apr 1968).
Series
Crimes of the Year 2000. In *Detective Fiction Weekly*: "Crimes of the Year 2000" (1935; *FFM*, Dec 1941); "No. 2, The Television Alibi" (1935; *FFM*, June 1942). There may be others.

Matter, Space and Time trilogy (some sections of this were themselves series). "The Girl in the Golden Atom" (*ASW*, 15 Mar 1919; *FFM*, Sep/Oct 1939; *FN*, June 1951; *Famous SF*, Win 1966/67); "People of the Golden Atom" (*ASW*, sr6, 24 Jan 1920; *FN*, Sep 1940); "The Princess of the Atom" (*Arg*, sr6, 14 Sep 1929); "The Fire People" (*Arg*, sr5, 21 Sep 1922); "The Man Who Mastered Time" (*Arg*, sr5, 12 July 1924); "The Shadow Girl" (*Arg*, sr4, 22 June 1922; *SFQ*, Spr 1942); "The Exile of Time" (*ASF*, sr4, Apr 1931). All have appeared in book form.

Robot Saga. All in *TWS*: "Decadence" (Dec 1941); "Fugitive" (Feb 1942); "Regeneration" (Apr 1942).

Tama. Both in *Arg*: "Tama of the Light Country" (sr3, 13 Dec 1930); "Tama, Princess of Mercury" (sr4, 27 June 1931). Both have appeared in pa editions.

Tubby. "The Man Who Discovered Nothing" (*ASW*, 10 Jan 1920; *Avon SF Reader*, No. 2, 1951); "The Light Machine" (*Arg*, 19 June 1920); "The Time Professor" (*Arg*, 9 Jan 1921); "The Gravity Professor" (*Arg*, 7 May 1921; in *Every Boy's Book of SF*

[Wollheim], 1951); "The Thought Machine" (*Arg*, 26 May 1923); "The Three-Eyed Man" (*Arg*, 7 July 1923; *AFR*, No. 14, 1950); "Around the Universe" (*S&I*, sr6, July 1923; *AS*, Oct 1927; *Future Fiction*, Dec 1941); "The Space-Time-Size Machine" (*TWS*, Oct 1937); "The Man Who Saw Too Much" (*TWS*, Oct 1938); "World Upside Down" (*TWS*, Dec 1940); "Up an Atom" (*SS*, Sep 1941); "Tubby–Time Traveller" (*TWS*, Dec 1942); "Tubby–Atom Smasher" (*TWS*, Aug 1943); "Battle of the Solar System" (*TWS*, Spr 1944); "The Gadget Girl" (*TWS*, Fall 1944); "Tubby–Master of the Atom" (*TWS*, Fall 1946).

Fiction

Beyond the Stars [pa] (*Arg*, 11 Feb 1928; *Future Fiction*, Feb 1942) (Ace: F-248, 1963, 160 pp., pa 40¢)

The Earth is an atom in a greater universe, and a space ship enlarges to travel into 'bigness.'

Beyond the Vanishing Point [pa] (*ASF*, n'te, Mar 1931) (Ace: D-331, 1958, 95 pp., pa 35¢; with *The Secret of ZI*)

Variation on the 'Golden Atom' theme; adventures in a microworld in a gob of gold.

Brand New World, A [pa] (*Arg*, sr6, 22 Sep 1928) (*FFM*, Sep 1942) (Ace: F-313, 1964, 158 pp., 40¢) (*Der rote Wahnsinn* [German], *UZ*: 433, 1965)

The visiting world "Xenephrene" causes world-wide disaster and threatens invasion.

Brigands of the Moon (*ASF*, sr4, Mar 1930) (McClurg, Chicago, 1931, 386 pp., $2.00) (*SFQ*, Fall 1942) (Duchess, nd, 191 pp., pa 25¢ [credited to J. W. Campbell]) (Ace: D-324, 1958, 224 pp., pa 35¢) (*Banditen vom Mond* [German], *UG*: 114, 1960; *Raub auf Sternenstrassen*, Zimmermann, 1961) (Consul: 1481, 1966, 191 pp., pa 3/6)

A typical space-opera; sequel was *Wandl the Invader*.

Exile of Time (*ASF*, sr4, Apr 1931) (Avalon, New York, 1964, 192 pp., $2.95) (Ace: F-343, 1965, 157 pp., pa 40¢)

An evil crippled genius uses a time shuttle between centuries for his own purposes.

Explorers Into Infinity ("Explorers Into Infinity" and "The Giant World," *WT*, sr3, Apr 1927, and sr3, Jan 1928, respectively) (Avalon, 1965, 192 pp., $3.25)

An old scientist and his sons see a beautiful girl in peril in the macro-world, and attempt her rescue.

Girl in the Golden Atom, The (Harper, New York, 1923, 341 pp.)

This edition is the original story with its sequel "The People of the Golden Atom" [check the *Matter, Space and Time* trilogy]. It is the story that made Cummings famous, and from which he made many variations in later years.

Insect Invasion, The (*Arg*, sr5, 16 Apr 1932) (Avalon, 1967, 191 pp., $3.25)

Into the Fourth Dimension [n] (*S&I*, sr9, Sep 1926) (*SFQ*, Win 1941/42) (*SFQ* [British], as pa, 1943)

Man on the Meteor, The [pa] (*S&I*, sr9, Jan 1924) (*Future Fiction*, Oct 1941) (Swan, nd, 125 pp., pa 1/-) (*Im Banne des Meteors* [German], *WF*: 7, 1958)

A noted novel about life on a meteor.

Man Who Mastered Time, The (*Arg*, sr5, July 1924) (McClurg, 1929, 351 pp., $2.00) (Burt, New York, 1930, 75¢) (*FN*, Mar 1950) (Ace: D-173, 1956, 172 pp., pa 35¢; with *Overlords From Space*) (*Le Maitre du temps* [French], Hachette: Le RF, 1958, pa)

Part of the *Matter, Space and Time* trilogy. One of this author's best, with an ingenious time travel theme and good adventure.

Princess of the Atom, The (*Arg*, sr6, 14 Sep 1929) (Avon: FN1, 1950, 158 pp., pa 25¢) (Boardman, London, 1951, 191 pp., 8/6)

Dianne of the atom world, raised on Earth, returns to her world with Earthmen to remove a despot.

Sea Girl, The (*Arg*, sr6, 2 Mar 1929) (McClurg, 1930, 310 pp., $2.00) (Burt, 1932, 75¢)

A vast undersea civilization seeks to conquer dry-land dwellers.

Shadow Girl, The (*Arg*, sr4, 22 June 1929) (*SFQ*, Spr 1942) (Swan, London, 1947, 186 pp., 5/- [unauthorised edition]) (*Schatten der Zukunft* [German], *UZ*: 203, 1960) (Ace: D-535, 1962, 159 pp., pa 35¢) (*Enigma!* [Spanish], Cenit: 39, 1962, pa)

A romance in time.

Tama of the Light Country [pa] (*Arg*, sr3, 13 Dec 1930) (Ace:

F-363, 1965, 124 pp., pa 40¢)

Girls are kidnapped from Earth and have adventures on Mercury.

Tama, Princess of Mercury [pa] (*Arg*, sr4, 27 June 1931) (Ace: F-406, 1966, 128 pp., pa 40¢)

Tarrano the Conqueror (*S&I*, sr14, July 1925) (McClurg, 1930, 345 pp., $2.00) (Burt, 1931, 75¢) (*Tarrano el conquistador* [Spanish], Novelas y Cuentos: 137, 1931) (*Tarrano* [French], Hachette: Le RF 115, 1963, pa)

A terrifying despot and interplanetary war in 2400 A.D.

Wandl the Invader [pa] (*ASF*, sr4, Feb 1932) (*SFQ*, Spr 1943) (Ace: D-497, 1961, 135 pp., pa 35¢; with *I Speak for Earth*) (*Invasion* [Spanish], Cenit: 31, 1962, pa)

Sequel to *Brigands of the Moon*: Earth is saved from an invading planetoid peopled by insectlike workers and malignant giant brains.

CUMMINS, HARLE OWEN

Fiction

Welsh Rarebit Tales [C] (Mutual Book Co., Boston, 1902, 173 pp., illus.–R. E. Owen)

15 stories: "The Man Who Made a Man"; "In the Lower Passage"; "The Fool and His Joke"; "The Man and the Beast"; "At the End of the Road"; "The Space Annihilator"; "A Question of Honor"; "The Wine of Pantinelli"; "The Strangest Freak"; "The False Prophet"; "A Study in Psychology"; "The Painted Lady and the Boy"; "The Palace of Sin"; "The Man Who Was Not Afraid"; "The Story the Doctor Told."

CUPPY, WILL(IAM) (JACOB) (23 Aug 1884–19 Sep 1949) U.S. critic and humorist. He took his Ph.B. at U. of Chicago in 1907, was a lieutenant in World War I, and then joined the editorial staff of the New York *Herald Tribune*. His books include *How to Be a Hermit* (1929), *How to Tell Your Friends From Apes* (1931), *How to Become Extinct* (1941), and *The Decline and Fall of Practically Everybody* (1948).

Anthology

World's Great Mystery Stories (World 'Tower Book,' Cleveland, 1943, 299 pp., 49¢)

18 stories, many weird: "A Rose for Emily," W. Faulkner; "The Adventure of the Clapham Clock," Agatha Christie; "A Message to Laura," Francis B. Young; "Suspicion," Dorothy L. Sayers; "The Fiend of the Cooperage," A. C. Doyle; "Miss Mary Pask," Edith Wharton; "The Signal-Man," C. Dickens; "The Cosy Room," A. Machen; "A Bird in the Hand," I. S. Cobb; "The Listener," A. Blackwood; "A Short Trip Home," F. S. Fitzgerald; "The Magic of Fear," E. Wallace; "The Door in the Wall," H. G. Wells; "The Interruption," W. W. Jacobs; "The Dream Woman," W. Collins; "The Boarded Window," A. Bierce; "Vain Oblations," Katharine F. Gerould; "Who Do You Think Did It?, or, The Mixed-Up Murder Mystery," S. Leacock.

CURRY, JANE LOUISE

Fiction

Sleepers, The (Harcourt Brace & World, New York, 1968, 255 pp., illus.–G. Floyd, $4.50)

CURTIS, JEAN-LOUIS French author.

Fiction

Neon Halo, The (*Un saint au neon*, Denoël: PF 13, 1956) [Trans.–Humphrey Hare]: (Secker Warburg, London, 1958, 248 pp., 15/-) (SF B.C. [S.J.], 1960, 5/6)

CURTIS, PETER (pseud) See LOFTS, N.

CURTIS, RICHARD (23 June 1937–) U.S. free-lance writer and editor.

Anthology

Future Tense [pa] (Dell: 2769, 1968, 220 pp., pa 60¢)

Sf, 10 stories with introduction "On Prediction," by I. Asimov: "The Land Ironclads," H. G. Wells; "New York A.D. 2660," Hugo Gernsback; "Billenium," J. G. Ballard; "The Lysenko Maze,"

David Grinnell; "QRM—Interplanetary," George O. Smith; "With These Hands," C. M. Kornbluth; "Politics," M. Leinster; "The Day Rembrandt Went Public," Arnold M. Auerbach; "Solution Unsatisfactory," R. A. Heinlein; "Security Check," Arthur C. Clarke.

CUSACK, FRANK Australian lecturer in humanities at Bendigo Institute of Technology (1967). He fills in his spare time with writing, broadcasting, gemmology, nature photography and research into the history of goldfields.
Nonfiction
Australian Ghost Stories (Heinemann, Melbourne, 1967, 177 pp., $4.50) (Pacific: 101, 1968, 177 pp., pa 80¢)
   Australia has had things that go bump in the night—the first story is about Fisher's Ghost, the wraith of Frederick George James Fisher, murdered at Campbelltown in 1826. Ghosts seem to shun modern Australia, though it is recorded that a sobbing headless figure awoke a camping party at Berrima at Easter, 1961. This book was launched at the Princess Theatre (Melbourne), where the ghost of the opera singer Fredrici is said to walk.

CYRANO DE BERGERAC, SAVINIEN (6 Mar 1619–28 July 1655) French writer and famed swordsman. His noted science fiction classics *The Voyages to the Moon and the Sun* influenced many later writers, but because of their atheistic nature were both originally considerably censored. The original manuscript of only . . . *The Moon* survives. Of his serious works, some plays are still in use, *The Death of Agrippina* being the most noted. Moskowitz's profile of Cyrano was published in *Satellite* (Mar 1959) and *Science-Fantasy* (Feb 1960).
Fiction
Voyages to the Moon and the Sun (Routledge, London, 1923, 329 pp., illus.) (Dutton, New York, 1923, $3.00) ([Trans.—R. Aldington], Orion, New York, 1962, 301 pp., illus., $6.00)
   The above editions are a combination of the stories which appeared in France in 1657 and 1662 (in English in 1659 and 1683). A German edition of one appeared in 1913, and from Heyne in 1962. Both have also seen Japanese (1952) and Spanish editions. They are noted primarily for the historic value in their scientific and satiric ideas.
   The Moon: After misadventures, the traveller eventually lands on the Tree of Life in the Garden of Eden, and meets Adam, Eve, Enoch, Elijah and St. John. The Lunarian civilization outside the Garden is depicted with its fantastic inventions, etc.
   The Sun: The traveller uses a concave glass machine to escape from prison, and is drawn to the Sun. There he finds civilized birds, and meets Campanella and discusses utopias with him.

D

DAGMAR, PETER
Fiction
Sands of Time, The (Digit: R696, 1963, 155 pp., pa 2/6) (Arcadia, New York, 1967, 191 pp., $3.25)

DAHL, ROALD (13 Sep 1916–) U.S. mystery writer, born in Wales of Norwegian parentage. He worked in Newfoundland and Tanganyika before joining the R.A.F. in 1939. Injuries invalided him to service in Washington. He is married to actress Patricia Neal; they have two daughters. His first full-length book was *Over to You* (1946), a collection of flying stories. He also sold a fantasy

script to Walt Disney Studios which was later made into a children's book, *The Gremlins* (1943).
Fiction
Kiss, Kiss [C] (Knopf, New York, 1960, 309 pp., $3.95) (McClelland, Toronto, $4.50) (M. Joseph, London, 1960, 255 pp., 15/-) ([Japanese], Hayakawa 'Tales of Menace 1,' 1961, pa) (Dell: F128, 1961, 288 pp., pa 50¢; 4572, 1965, 223 pp., pa 60¢) (*Puss puss* [Swedish], Bonnier, 1961) (Penguin: 1832, 1962, 233 pp., pa 3/6; 1966, pa 4/6) (*Kusschen, Kusschen* [German], Ruwolt, 1962)
   11 off-trail stories (science-fantasy denoted by †): "The Landlady"; "William and Mary"†; "The Way Up to Heaven"; "Parson's Pleasure"; "Mrs. Boxby and the Colonel's Coat"; "Royal Jelly"†; "Georgy Porgy"; "Genesis and Catastrophe"; "Edward the Conqueror"; "Pig"†; "The Champion of the World."
Someone Like You [C] (Knopf, 1953, 359 pp., $3.50) (Secker Warburg, London, 1954, 256 pp., 12/6) (*Nagon Som Du* [Swedish], Bonnier, 1955, 1964) (Dell: F139, 1961, 320 pp., pa 50¢; 8116, 1965, 253 pp., pa 60¢) (FSB: 1229, 1965, 252 pp., pa 3/6)
   18 stories (most from such periodicals as *The New Yorker* and *Harper's*, 1948-53): "Taste"; "Lamb to the Slaughter"; "Man From the South"; "The Soldier"; "My Lady Love, My Dove"; "Dip in the Pool"; "Galloping Foxley"; "Skin"; " 'Poison' "; "The Wish" (horror); "Neck"; "The Sound Machine" (sf); "Nunc Dimittis"; "The Great Automatic Grammatisator" (sf); *Claud's Dog*: 1. "The Rat-Catcher" (horror); 2. "Rummins" (horror); 3. "Mr. Hoddy"; 4. "Mr. Feasey." The stories other than horror and sf are mainly suspense mysteries; the volume won the Edgar award of the Mystery Writers of America.
Sometime Never (Scribner's, New York, 1948, 244 pp., $2.75) (S. J. R. Saunders, Toronto, $3.00) (Collins, London, 1949, 255 pp., 8/6)
   A fighter pilot meets gremlins and visits their city.

DAHLGREN, (Mrs.) MADELEINE (VINTON) (13 July 1825–28 May 1898) American poet and novelist. Daughter of Samuel Vinton, a U.S. Congressman for 20 years, she acted as his hostess in Washington following the death of her mother. These surroundings gave atmosphere for some of her writings. She was married twice, but in her later years was mainly occupied with Catholic missionary activities and her 'literary' salon. Another fantasy besides the collection below was *South-Mountain Magic* (J. R. Osgood, Boston, 1882).
Fiction
Woodley Lane Ghost and Other Stories, The [C] (Drexel Biddle. Philadelphia, 1899, 474 pp.)
   Fantasy, 24 stories: "The Woodley Lane Ghost"; "The Miser's Last Christmas"; "Who Was She?" "My Dread Secret"; "The Amulet Ring"; "A Night's Adventure"; "A Sublime Sacrifice"; "A Reminiscence"; "Earth-Bound"; "The Fatal Boots"; "My First Patient"; "The Faithful Slave"; "A Murder Mystery"; "The Judge's Dream"; "Before the War"; "A Murillo"; "My Moufflon"; "Wilful Betty"; "How Not to Propose"; "The Trouble of a Double"; "His Plural Wives"; "The Poor Author"; "A Harmless Lunatic"; "Leap Year and Coincidence."

DAKERS, ELAINE (KIDNER) British author (Mrs. Andrew Dakers).
Fiction [as Jane Lane]
State of Mind, A (Muller, London, 1964, 204 pp., 18/-)
   A post-nuclear-war society at the end of this century, with everything state-controlled—even life itself.

DALE, HARRISON (CLIFFORD) (1885–)
Anthologies
Great Ghost Stories (Jenkins, London, 1929, 399 pp., 7/6; 1931, 3/6)
   15 stories: "Wandering Willie's Tale," Sir W. Scott; "The Old Nurse's Story," Mrs. Gaskell; "What Was It?" F.-J. O'Brien; "The Haunted and the Haunters," E. Bulwer-Lytton; "Madam Crowl's Ghost," J. S. Le Fanu; "The Cedar Closet," L. Hearn; "Thrawn Janet," E. L. Stevenson; "Teig O'Kane and the Corpse," trans.–

Dr. D. Hyde; "The Lady's Maid's Bell," Edith Wharton; "The Upper Berth," F. M. Crawford; "The Mummy's Foot," T. Gautier; "Maese Perez, the Organist," G. A. Becquer; "The Tall Woman," P. de Alarcon; "The Corpse the Blood-Drinker," trans.–G. Soulie; "The Story of Ming-Y," L. Hearn.

More Great Ghost Stories (Jenkins, 1932, 396 pp., 7/6)

13 stories and Introduction "Anthologists and Other Ghouls": "In Defense of His Right," D. Defoe; "Peter Rugg, the Missing Man," Wm. Austin; "The Botathen Ghost," R. S. Hawker; "Young Goodman Browne," N. Hawthorne; "The Signal-Man," C. Dickens; "The Familiar," J. S. Le Fanu; "The Phantom Regiment," J. Grant; "The Open Door," Mrs. Oliphant; "Though One Rose From the Dead," W. D. Howells; "Afterward," Edith Wharton; "In the Blackfriars Wynd," H. Pease; "Thurnley Abbey," P. Landon.

DALLAS, PAUL V. Author, born in Plymouth, England. After schooling in England, France, Malta and the U.S., he was employed variously as lumberjack, civil engineer, hotel clerk, drawing instructor, salesman and window displayman. He now lives in a small town in New York State.

Fiction

Lost Planet, The (Winston, Philadelphia, 1956, 209 pp., $2.00, jacket–Schomburg) (*Il pianeta sperduto* [Italian], Fantascienza: 8, 1962, pa)

Juvenile, one of the *Adventures in SF* series. Intrigue between Earth and Poseida, which is inhabited by amphibious octopi.

DANE, CLEMENCE (pseud) (1888–28 Mar 1965) British novelist and dramatist; her real name was Winifred Ashton. She began as a teacher and became an actress. Her health collapsed because of war work in World War I, and during her recovery she wrote her first novel, *Regiment of Women* (1917). Her third book, *Legend* (1919), was rewritten as the very successful play *A Bill of Divorcement* (1921) in which Katharine Cornell made her name. She usually alternated between plays and fiction, and was considered one of the foremost modern women writers in English. For a time she edited the 'Novels of Tomorrow' series for the publisher Michael Joseph; these began in 1955 and ceased as such in 1957.

Fiction [Incomplete—other titles in Bleiler *Checklist*]

Babyons, The [C] (Heinemann, London, 1927, 380 pp.,; 1929, 3/6; 1931, 2/6) (Doubleday Doran, New York, 1929, 4 vol.. $5.00; 1929, 378 pp., $2.50)

4 stories, being chronicles of a family: "Third Person Singular" (*FFM*, Oct 1946); "Midsummer Men"; "Creeping Jenny"; "Lady Babyon."

Anthology

100 Enchanted Tales (M. Joseph, London, 1937, 685 pp., 8/6) (S. J. R. Saunders, Toronto, $2.50)

Selected from the fairy tales of the Brothers Grimm, Hans Andersen, Nathaniel Hawthorne, etc.

DANIEL, GLYN EDMUND (23 Apr 1914–) British archaeologist, M.A., Ph.D. He was educated at St. Johns' College, Cambridge, where he was a Research Fellow 1938-45, Fellow and Lecturer from 1945, and Steward 1945-55. The editor of *Antiquity*, he has written various works on archaeology, etc.

Nonfiction

Myth or Legend? [with others] (Macmillan, New York, 1955, 125 pp., illus., $2.50) (G. Bell, London, 1955, 10/6) (Clarke Irwin, Toronto, $2.10)

Analyses of the possible truth behind legends; recommended by A. Boucher.

DANIEL, HOWARD

Nonfiction

Devils, Monsters and Nightmares (Abelard-Schuman, London, 1964, 67+304 pp., 8½ in. x 11¼ in., 55/-)

Text, then plates (photos and drawings). An exploration of demonology in art, ranging from American Indian masks to Van Cleeve's "Last Judgment," etc.

DANVERS, JACK (pseud) See CASELEYR, C. A. M.

DANZIGER, GUSTAF ADOLF DE CASTRO (1859–4 Mar 1959) U.S. writer, poet and philosopher. He mastered 14 languages, and was the U.S. Consul General to Madrid in the administration of Theodore Roosevelt. He knew Mark Twain and H. P. Lovecraft. As Adolphe de Castro he contributed to *Weird Tales*: "The Last Test" (Nov 1928) and "The Electric Executioner" (Aug 1930). He also collaborated with A. Bierce on "The Monk and the Hangman's Daughter." For 20 years he was a familiar figure in Los Angeles fantasy circles, attending special meetings of the LASFS and the various conventions in the area. He died peacefully just after his 100th birthday.

DARAUL, ARKON Author of nonfiction works such as *Secret Societies* (Tandem: T37, 1965, pa) covering the Rosicrucians, Thuggee, the tongs of China, and other societies.

Nonfiction

Witches and Sorcerers [pa] (Tandem: T35, 1965, 224 pp., illus., pa 5/-)

An account of the uses of witchcraft and magic in the last 2,500 years.

DARE, MARCUS PAUL (1902–)

Fiction

Unholy Relics and Other Uncanny Tales [C] (Arnold, London, 1947, 184 pp., 7/6) (Longmans, New York, 1947, 184 pp., $2.50) (Longmans, Toronto, $2.25)

Weird, 13 stories: "Abbot's Magic"; "The Beam"; " 'Borgia Pomade' " "Bring Out Your Dead"; "Demoniac Goat"; "Fatal Oak"; "Forgotten Italian"; "Haunted Drawers"; "Haunted Helmet"; " 'A Nun's Tragedy' "; "Nymph Still Lives"; "Officer's Coat"; "Unholy Relics."

DARK, JAMES Australian author of mystery/sensational thrillers, such as *Havoc* and *Impact* for the Australian pulp market.

Fiction

Horror Tales [C] [pa] (Horwitz: PB138, 1963, 130 pp., pa 3/9)

Horror, 6 stories [no table of contents]: "The Creep"; "The Flare"; "Perkins and the Pilot"; "The Flashing Scar"; "Man on the Run"; "Fattened Calf."

Terrifying Tales [C] [pa] (Horwitz: PB129, 1962, 130 pp., pa 3/9)

Horror, 7 stories: "Shadow Men"; "Dogged"; "Hanging On"; "The Flying Fix"; "Dead on Time"; "A Small Grave Matter"; "Mad to Start."

DARWIN, Sir CHARLES (GALTON) (19 Dec 1887–31 Dec 1962) Distinguished British mathematical physicist, and grandson of his namesake famous for *The Origin of Species*. He worked with Rutherford at U. of Manchester, then served as an officer in France in World War I, receiving the Military Cross. After being a Fellow of Christ's College, Cambridge, and Professor of Natural Philosophy at U. of Edinburgh, he became the fourth Director of the National Physical Laboratory in 1936. He did much war work, and postwar he did much to enlarge the work of the N.P.L. He was very interested in scientific problems of national importance, and after his retirement in 1949 he spent two years writing the book below.

Nonfiction

Next Million Years, The (Hart-Davis, London, 1952, 210 pp., 15/-) (Doubleday, New York, 1952, 210 pp., $2.75) (Clarke Irwin, Toronto, $3.50)

A book of prophecy. Although a fountain of plot ideas for the sf writer, it does not encompass space flight or the tremendous potential of future inventions, and hence is unduly pessimistic from the sf angle.

DAUMAL, RENÉ French writer.

Fiction

Mount Analogue (*Le Mont Analogue* [French], Gallimard, Paris, 1952) (Pantheon, New York, 1960, 157 pp., $3.00)

An unfinished work written in 1943, concluding with notes on what the author was trying to do. An expedition of queerly assorted intellectuals is trying to climb the highest mountain on Earth —one which is enveloped in a sort of geometric warp and has its own fauna, etc. A surrealistic fantasy.

DAVENPORT, BASIL (7 Mar 1905–7 Apr 1966) U.S. anthologist. He took his B.A. at Yale in 1926, and M.A. at Oxford; he spent a year teaching Greek at Rutgers. During World War II he was in the Counter-Intelligence Corps in the U.S., England, France and Germany. He was one of the judges of the Book of the Month Club, and also told some ghost stories on radio. Besides the works below, he compiled a collection of O. Stapledon, *To the End of Time*, and wrote introductions for *Islandia*, by A. T. Wright, and for *The Science Fiction Novel* (symposium, Advent, 1959).

Nonfiction
Inquiry Into Science Fiction (Longmans Green, New York, 1955, 87 pp., $2.50) (Longmans, Toronto, $2.75)

Chapters: 1. "What Is Science Fiction?"; 2. "Space Operas, Mad Scientists and Bug-Eyed Monsters"; 3. "Scientific Science Fiction"; 4. "Speculative Science Fiction"; 5. "Science Fiction and the Emotions"; 6. "The Future of Science Fiction." Suggested reading for those interested in the field as such.

Anthologies
Deals With the Devil (Dodd Mead, New York, 1958, 332 pp., $4.00) (Dodd, Toronto, $4.50) (Ballantine: 326K, 1959, 160 pp., pa 35¢; U2828, 1966, pa 50¢ [12 stories marked †]) (Faber, London, 1959, 328 pp., 18/-)

Weird, 25 stories: "The Brazen Locked Room," I. Asimov; "The Trammel," Miriam A. DeFord; "Impact With the Devil," T. R. Cogswell; "Doctor Faustus," Anon. [*ca*. 1590]; "The Devil and Mr. Chips" ("The Rat That Could Speak"), C. Dickens; "Sir Dominick's Bargain"†, J. S. Le Fanu; "Enoch Soames"†, M. Beerbohm; "A Deal With the Devil"†, Lord Dunsany; "Satan and Sam Shay"†, R. Arthur; "The Legend of Mont St. Michel," Guy de Maupassant; "The Tinker of Tamlacht," S. MacManus; "The Devil and Simon Flagg"†, A. Porges; "The Devil and the Old Man"†, J. Masefield; "Devil-Puzzlers," F. B. Perkins; "Threshold"†, H. Kuttner; "The Three Wishes," V. Randolph; "Nellthu"†, A. Boucher; "Threesie"†, T. R. Cogswell; "A Bargain in Bodies," M. Schere; "Caveat Emptor," L. S. de Camp & F. Pratt; "Hell-Bent"†, F. McCormack; "The Devil and Daniel Webster," S. V. Benét; "The Countess Kathleen O'Shea," Anon. [Irish folk tale]; "The Devil, George and Rosie"†, J. Collier; "The Devil Was Sick"†, B. Elliott.

Famous Monster Tales (Van Nostrand, New York, 1967, 201 pp., $4.75)

Weird, 13 stories with foreword—Clifton Fadiman: "Smoke Ghost," Fritz Leiber; "The Phantom Farmhouse," Seabury Quinn; "The Horror of the Heights," Arthur C. Doyle; "The Thing on Outer Shoal," P. Schuyler Miller; "The Outsider," H. P. Lovecraft; "Second Night Out," Frank B. Long; "It," Theodore Sturgeon; "The Dancing Partner," Jerome K. Jerome; "The Damned Thing," Ambrose Bierce; "Skeleton," Ray Bradbury; "The Thing in the Pond," Paul Ernst; "Negotium Perambulans," E. F. Benson; "The 51st Dragon," Heywood Broun.

Ghostly Tales To Be Told (Dodd Mead, 1950, xvii+317 pp., $3.00) (Dodd, Toronto, $3.50) (Faber, 1952, 320 pp., 15/-; 1963, pa 7/6)

16 stories of pure horror picked for reading aloud: "The Wendigo," A. Blackwood; "August Heat," W. F. Harvey; "Count Magnus," M. R. James; "Where Angels Fear," Wade Wellman; "The House of the Nightmare," E. White; "The Screaming Skull," F. M. Crawford; "The Monkey's Paw," W. W. Jacobs; "The Gentleman From America," M. Arlen; "The White Powder," A. Machen; "Couching at the Door," Dorothy K. Broster; "The Yellow Wall Paper," Charlotte P. Gilman; "Johnson Looked Back," T. Burke; "Where Their Fire Is Not Quenched," May Sinclair; "Moonlight Sonata," A. Woollcott; "Captain Murderer," C. Dickens; "The Refugee," Jane Rice.

Invisible Men [pa] (Ballantine: 401K, 1960, 158 pp., pa 35¢; U2842, 1966, pa 50¢)

Sf and fantasy, 11 stories: "The Weissenbroch Spectacles," L. S. de Camp & F. Pratt; "The Shadow and the Flash," J. London; "The New Accelerator," H. G. Wells; "Invisible Boy," R. Brad-

bury; "The Invisible Prisoner," M. LeBlanc; "Love in the Dark," H. L. Gold; "What Was It?" F.-J. O'Brien; "The Invisible Dove Dancer of Strathpeen Island," J. Collier; "The Vanishing American," C. Beaumont; "Shottle Bop," T. Sturgeon; "The Invisible Man Murder Case," H. Slesar.

Tales To Be Told in the Dark (Dodd Mead, 1953, 335 pp., $3.00) (Dodd, Toronto, $3.50) (Faber, 1953, 288 pp., 15/-; 1967, pa 7/6) (Ballantine: 380K, 1960, 159 pp., pa 35¢; U2807, 1965, pa 50¢)

Weird, 13 stories arranged for telling aloud (U.S. pa, 10 stories marked †): "The Beast With Five Fingers"†, W. F. Harvey; "By One, By Two, and By Three"†, S. Hall; "Sredni Vashtar"†, Saki; "The Black Seal," A. Machen; "Two Bottles of Relish"†, Lord Dunsany; "The Book"†, Marg. Irwin; "Thus I Refute Beelzy"†, J. Collier; "The Whippoorwill," J. Thurber; "The White People," A. Machen; "Mujina"†, L. Hearn; "The Open Window"†, Saki; *Two Anecdotes*: "Closed Cabinet"†, "Closed Cabinet, Retold," Anonymous.

13 Ways to Dispose of a Body (Dodd Mead, 1966, 277 pp., $4.00) (Faber, 1967, 277 pp., 25/-)

13 stories, many weird, and compiler's introduction (2½ pp.): "Being a Murderer Myself," Arthur Williams; "The Best of Everything," Stanley Ellin; "The Corpus Delicti," Melville Davisson Post; "De Mortuis," John Collier; "Earth to Earth," Robert Graves; "The Duchess at Prayer," Edith Wharton; "The Hole in the Wall," G. K. Chesterton; "The Man With Copper Fingers," Dorothy Sayers; "The Night I Died," Cornell Woolrich; "The October Game," Ray Bradbury; "Out of This Nettle," Robert Twohy; "The Two Bottles of Relish," Lord Dunsany; "Love Lies Bleeding," Philip MacDonald.

DAVENTRY, LEONARD (JOHN) (7 Mar 1915–) British author. He was born in Brixton, London, the son of an Army captain. He left school at 13 and is mostly self-educated. He served in the British Army 1932-41, and is presently a supplier of vegetables to caterers.

Fiction
Man of Double Deed, A (Gollancz, London, 1965, 176 pp., 15/-) (Doubleday, New York, 1965, 191 pp., $3.95) (D'day, Toronto, $3.00) (SF B.C. [S.J.], 1966) (D'day SF B.C., 1966, $1.20) (Pan: X650, 1967, 174 pp., pa 3/6) (Berkley: X1491, 1967, 159 pp., pa 60¢)

Telepathic vigil-keepers vs. juvenile delinquents in 2090—a century after a nuclear war.

DAVID-NEEL, ALEXANDRA (MARIE LOUISE) (24 Oct 1868– 8 Sep 1969) The first European woman to be honoured with the rank of Lama in Tibet (before 1932). A further work is *Initiations and Initiates in Tibet* (Rider, 2nd ed., 1958; Univ. Books, 1959).

Nonfiction
Magic and Mystery in Tibet (Lane, London, 1931, 320 pp., 15/-) (Kendall, New York, 1932, 320 pp., illus., $3.75) (Univ. Books, New York, 1958, 320 pp., illus., $6.00)

An important reference work on Tibet when first published. It covers the powers of Tibetan mystics and psychic phenomena in Tibet; these are not considered miracles in that country. Its original publication preceded J. B. Rhine and his experiments in ESP by five years.

DAVIDSON, AVRAM A. (23 Apr 1923–) U.S. author and editor. He was born in Yonkers, N.Y., and attended four colleges. He served with the U.S. Navy 1941-45 and was later attached to the U.S. Marines in the South Pacific and China; he fought with the Israeli Army 1948-49.

He first appeared in the science fiction field with the short story "My Boy Friend's Name Is Jello" (*F&SF*, July 1954) and has since had over 30 stories in *F&SF*, *Galaxy* and *If*. He won first place in the 12th Annual *EQMM* Contest. His most notable story is "Or All the Seas With Oysters" (*GSF*, May 1958), which won the 1958 Hugo Award for best short story and was reprinted in *The Hugo Winners* [Asimov] in 1962. He was Executive Editor for *The Magazine of Fantasy and Science Fiction* from Apr 1962 to Nov

1964; he left to write full time. He is married, has one son, and now lives in Mexico. A number of his works have been translated, especially into German. He wrote the factual collection *Crimes and Chaos* (Regency, 1963, pa), has won the Edgar award of the Mystery Writers of America, and has recently begun work on a cycle of novels around the title *Vergil Magus*.

Fiction

Clash of Star-Kings [pa] (Ace: G-576, 1966, 105 pp., pa 50¢; with *Danger From Vega*)

Mysterious events among the native Aztecs in Mexico, with supernatural overtones.

Enemy of My Enemy [pa] (Berkley: X1341, 1966, 160 pp., pa 60¢)

A refugee pirate is changed so he can take sanctuary in an alien environment.

Joyleg [pa] See MOORE, W.

Kar-Chee Reign, The [pa] (Ace: G-574, 1966, 138 pp., pa 50¢; with *Rocannon's World*)

Humanity reduced to savagery rebels against the monstrous scavengers from space.

Masters of the Maze [pa] (Pyramid: R-1208, 1965, 156 pp., pa 50¢) (*Wachters van het web* [Dutch], Meulenhoff, Amsterdam, 1967)

A mystical maze short-circuits space and time, and gives entry to an infinite variety of universes and probabilities.

Mutiny in Space [pa] ("Valentine's Planet," *Worlds of Tomorrow*, Aug 1964) (Pyramid: R-1069, 1964, 158 pp., pa 50¢)

After a mutiny, loyal crewmen endeavour to survive on a planet with a matriarchal feudal system.

Or All the Seas With Oysters [C] [pa] (Berkley: F639, 1962, 176 pp., pa 50¢)

Sf, 17 stories: "Or All the Seas With Oysters"; "Up the Close and Doun the Stair"; "Now Let Us Sleep"; "The Grantha Sighting"; "Help! I Am Dr. Morris Goldpepper"; "The Sixth Season"; "Negra Sum"; "My Boy Friend's Name Is Jello"; "The Golem"; "Summerland"; "King's Evil"; "Great Is Diana"; "I Do Not Hear You, Sir!"; "Author, Author"; "Dagon"; "The Montavarde Camera"; "The Woman Who Thought She Could Read."

Rogue Dragon [pa] (*F&SF*, July 1965) —Enlarged: (Ace: F-353, 1965, 142 pp., pa 40¢)

Intrigue in the far future when Earth is a hunting world for dragons.

Rork! [pa] (Berkley: F1146, 1965, 144 pp., pa 50¢) (Rapp Whiting, London, 1968, 142 pp., 18/-)

Frontier adventure story on an alien planet.

Sources of the Nile, The [n] (*F&SF*, n'te, Jan 1961) (in *Tomorrow X 4* [Knight], 1964, pa)

What Strange Stars and Skies [C] [pa] (Ace: F-330, 1965, 188 pp., pa 40¢)

Sf, 14 stories with author's introduction: "What Strange Stars and Skies"; "The Bounty Hunter"; "The Ogre"; "Fair Trade"; "Love Called This Thing"; "Faed-Out"; "The Lineaments of Gratified Desire"; "The Teeth of Despair"; "Jury-Rig"; "Miss Buttermouth"; "Where Do You Live, Queen Esther?"; "Mr. Stilwell's Stage"; "The Unknown Law"; "The Singular Events Which Occurred in the Hovel on the Alley off of Eye Street."

Anthologies

Best From Fantasy and Science Fiction, 12th Series, The (Doubleday, New York, 1963, 225 pp., $3.95) (D'day SF B.C., 1963, $1.20) (Ace: G-611, 1967, 254 pp., pa 50¢) (Panther: 2275, 1967, 176 pp., pa 3/6)

Sf and fantasy, 14 stories: "Test," Theodore L. Thomas; "Please Stand By," Ron Goulart; "Who's in Charge Here?" J. Blish; "Three for the Stars," Jos. Dickinson; "When Lilacs Last in the Dooryard Bloomed," Vance Aandahl; "Landscape With Sphinxes," Karen Anderson; "My Dear Emily," Joanna Russ; "The Gumdrop King," Will Stanton; "The Golden Horn," Edgar Pangborn; "The Singular Events Which Occurred in the Hovel on the Alley off Eye Street," A. Davidson; "A Kind of Artistry," B. W. Aldiss; "Two's a Crowd," Sasha Gilien; "The Man Without a Planet," Kate Wilhelm; "The Garden of Time," J. G. Ballard; "Hop-Friend," Terry Carr.

Best From Fantasy and Science Fiction, 13th Series, The (Doubleday, 1964, 255 pp., $4.50) (D'day SF B.C., 1964, $1.20) (Gollancz, 1966, 255 pp., 21/-) (Ace: H-26, 1967, 256 pp., pa 60¢) (Panther: 026185, 1968, 219 pp., pa 5/-)

Sf and fantasy, 13 stories: "The Golden Brick," P. M. Hubbard; "Peggy and Peter Go to the Moon," Don White; "Now Wakes the Sea," J. G. Ballard; "Green Magic," Jack Vance; "Captain Honario Harpplayer, R.N.," Harry Harrison; "Treaty in Tartessos," Karen Anderson; "Hunter, Come Home," Richard McKenna; "McNamara's Fish," Ron Goulart; "Nina Sol," Felix Marti-Ibanez; "They Don't Make Life Like They Used To," A. Bester; "What Strange Stars and Skies," A. Davidson; "Eight O'Clock in the Morning," Ray Nelson; "Deluge," Zenna Henderson.

Best From Fantasy and Science Fiction, 14th Series, The (Doubleday, 1965, 251 pp., $4.50) (D'day SF B.C., 1965, $1.20) (Gollancz, 1966, 251 pp., 21/-) (Ace: A-17, 1968, 255 pp., pa 75¢)

Sf and fantasy, 17 stories: "Sacheverell," A. Davidson; "Trade-In," Jack Sharkey; "The Illuminated Man," J. G. Ballard; "Bulletin From the Trustees of the Institute of Advanced Research," Wilma Shore; "Automatic Tiger," Kit Reed; "The Court of Tartary," T. P. Caravan; "Touchstone," Terry Carr; "Thaw and Serve," Allen K. Lang; "Nada," Thomas M. Disch; "Into the Shop," Ron Goulart; "A Rose for Ecclesiastes," Roger Zelazny; "Olsen and the Gull," Eric St. Clair; "Dark Conception," Louis J. A. Adams; "The Compleat Consumators," A. E. Nourse; "The House by the Crab Apple Tree," S. S. Johnson; "The Girl With the Hundred Proof Eyes," Ron Webb; "Fred One," James Ransom.

DAVIES, HUGH SYKES Welsh novelist and broadcaster. He has been a Fellow of St. John's and a lecturer at Cambridge U., teaching English since 1933 except for the war years, when he was with the Ministry of Food. His early novels included *No Man Pursues* and *Full Fathom Five*, and he has published a book on the use of English: *Grammar Without Tears*.

Fiction

Papers of Andrew Melmoth, The (Methuen, London, 1960, 237 pp., 16/-) (Morrow, New York, 1961, 221 pp., $3.50)

A quiet and subtle story about a study of rats and the discovery that they are about to evolve further than humans.

DAVIES, L(ESLIE) P(URNELL) (20 Oct 1914–) British freelance writer.

Fiction

Alien, The (Jenkins, London, 1968, 183 pp., 20/-)

Doctors find a strange human and keep him under surveillance.

Artificial Man, The (H. Jenkins, London, 1965, 188 pp., 15/-) (Doubleday, New York, 1967, 191 pp., $3.95) (D'day SF B.C., 1967, $1.20) (*L'homme artificiel* [French], Denoël: PF102, 1967, pa) (*Der Mann aus der Zukunft* [German], Goldmann: 090, 1968, pa) (Mayflower: 113087, 1968, 170 pp., pa 3/6)

An artificial man is kept in a village environment to prevent him from knowing his origin. Film: *Project X*, British, 1968, starring Christopher George and Greta Baldwin; considered above average.

Grave Matter, A (Doubleday 'Crime Club,' New York, 1968, 190 pp., $3.95)

The discovery of the remains of two small children in an English village unfolds a story of horror, greed and murder.

Lampton Dreamers, The (Jenkins, 1966, 192 pp., 18/-) (Doubleday, 1967, 188 pp., $3.95)

The same unpleasant dreams are dreamt by different people.

Man Out of Nowhere [pa] (Mayflower: 112625, 1968, 175 pp., pa 3/6)

Four different people identify an amnesia victim as being four different persons.

Paper Dolls, The (H. Jenkins, London, 1964, 224 pp., 15/-) (Doubleday 'Crime Club,' 1966, 216 pp., $2.95) (Signet: P3027, 1966, 176 pp., pa 60¢) (Mayflower: 6840, 1967, 157 pp., pa 3/6)

A story of the English countryside with mutant telepaths, superstitious farmers and remote-control murders.

Psychogeist (Jenkins, 1966, 191 pp., 15/-) (Doubleday, 1967, 191 pp., $3.95) (D'day SF B.C., 1967, $1.70) (Mayflower: 7175, 1967, 188 pp., pa 5/-) (Tower: 44-115, 1968, 218 pp., pa 75¢)

A man's alter ego has adventures in the caverns of the Lost Moon.
Twilight Journey (Jenkins, 1967, 191 pp., 18/-) (Doubleday, 1968, $4.50) (SF B.C. [S.J.], 1968)
A scientist seeks an antidote to his method of feeding dreams to a patient.

DAVIES, VALENTINE
Fiction
It Happens Every Spring (Farrar Strauss, New York, 1949, 224 pp., $2.50) (Clarke Irwin, Toronto, $3.50)
Brisk and delightful, if superficial, fantasy based on the popular movie.
Miracle on 34th Street (Harcourt Brace, New York, 1947, 120 pp., $1.75) (McLeod, Toronto, $2.25) (Pocket Books: 903, 1952, x+117 pp., pa 25¢)
Delightful fantasy about Santa Claus.

DAVIS, (Dr. HORACE) CHAN(DLER) (12 Aug 1926–) U.S. mathematician, born in Ithaca, N.Y. He became a sf enthusiast in 1940, and first planned to be a chemist. He sold a number of short stories to *ASF* 1946-48, of which "Letter to Ellen" (June 1947) is probably the most noted. He was then a mathematician returning from service in the U.S. Naval Reserve for graduate study at Harvard, where he obtained his Ph.D. in 1950. He has remained in mathematics and is now Associate Editor of the learned journal *Mathematical Reviews*. His fiction was primarily of the sociological/political type; he has not written any stories since 1954.

DAVIS, RICHARD
Anthology
Tandem Horror 2 [pa] (Tandem: T198, 1968, 192 pp., pa 3/6)
13 stories and editor's introduction: "Working for Miss Arethusa," Angus Janes; "The Dooley Street Centre-Forward," Robin Smyth; "Reply Guaranteed," J. Ramsey Campbell; "Ice in Their Laughter," Rosemary Timperley; "Dead on His Feet," Julia Burley; "The Forgiver," Walter Harris; "The Inheritance," Simon Pilkington; "I'm Not Mad Yet," Elizabeth Fancett; "From Our Special Correspondent," D. E. Piper; "The Stocking," J. R. Campbell; "The Lady by the Stream," Richard Davis; "Voices in the Night," Rosemary Timperley; "The Last Bus," Michel Parry.

DAVIS, RICHARD HARDING (18 Apr 1864–11 Apr 1916) American journalist and novelist, born in Philadelphia. He was correspondent for the New York *Sun* and *Harper's Weekly*, and also had articles in *Scribner's Magazine*. His books ran from *Gallegher and Other Stories* (1891) to *Notes of a War Correspondent* (1910).
Fiction
Vera, the Medium (Scribners, New York, 1911, 215 pp., illus.)
2 fantasy novels: "Vera, the Medium" (originally 1908; Scribners, 1910); "Miss Civilization."

DAVIS, ROBERT HOBART ("BOB") (23 Mar 1869–11 Oct 1942) Noted U.S. editor. He was educated in public school at Carson City, and as a youth was a compositor on the Carson *Appeal*. He became a reporter for the San Francisco newspapers *Examiner*, *Call* and *Chronicle*. After being with the New York *Journal* and *American* 1895-1903, he joined the editorial staff of Frank A. Munsey Co. He was the first Managing Editor of *All-Story Magazine*, *Scrap Book*, *The Cavalier* and numerous other magazines. He collaborated on some books with Perley Poore Sheehan, and wrote many books, such as *Bob Davis Abroad*. His "Bob Davis Reveals" column for the New York *Sun* ran for 17 years until his death. An amateur photographer, he took more than 3,000 portraits of prominent people, and interviewed Mussolini in 1926.
His importance to the science fiction and fantasy field lies in the fact that as a Munsey editor he published many notable stories which have an important place in the background of the genre. He fostered such authors as G. A. England, R. Cummings, O. A. Kline and E. R. Burroughs.

DAWSON, ARNOLD
Anthology
Tales That Enthrall (Richard, London, 1930, 256 pp., 2/-)
29 stories: "A Romance of the Desert," Al-Asma'I; "The Three Rings," G. Boccaccio; "Kirk Alloway Witches," R. Burns; "Dream Children," C. Lamb; "El Verdugo" ("The Executioner"), H. de Balzac; "The Shot," A. Pushkin; "A Tale of Terror," T. Hood; "The Lost Hand of Zaleukos," W. Hauff; "The Haunted and the Haunters; or, The House and the Brain," Lord Lytton; "A True Story," B. Disraeli; "The Wicked Prince," H. Andersen; "The Mummy's Foot," T. Gautier; "The Masque of the Red Death," E. A. Poe; "The Moss-Rose," G. Murray; "The Passage of the Red Sea," H. Murger; "A Terribly Strange Bed," W. W. Collins; "Journalism in Tennessee," M. Twain; "Our New Neighbours at Ponkapog," T. B. Aldrich; "Tennessee's Partner," B. Harte; "After Twenty Years," O. Henry; "The Pearl of Love," H. G. Wells; "Arvie Aspinall's Alarm Clock," H. Lawson; "A Christmas Criminal," E. Nesbit; "Many a Tear," M. P. Shiel; "The Mother Stone," J. Galsworthy; "The Wag," H. Barbusse; "The Opening of the Door," M. P. Willcocks; "A Love Tale of Two Common People," J. Corrie; "The Soul of Ivan the Peasant," A. Neveroff.

DAWSON, BASIL
Fiction
Dan Dare on Mars (Hulton, London, 1956, 176 pp., frontis., 7/6)
Juvenile—space-opera.

DAWSON, EMMA FRANCES (1851–6 Feb 1926) American poet and short-story writer.
Fiction
Itinerant House and Other Stories, An [C] (William Doxey, San Francisco, 1897, xii+320 pp., illus.—Ernest C. Peixotto)
10 stories with 1½-p. preface (reprints from *The Argonaut*, *The Wasp* and various journals, with 6th and 9th original): "An Itinerant House"; "Singed Moths"; "A Stray Reveler"; "The Night Before the Wedding"; "The Dramatic in My Destiny"; "A Gracious Visitation"; "A Sworn Statement"; "The Second Card Wins"; "In Silver Upon Purple"; "Are the Dead Dead?"

DAY, BRADFORD M(ARSHALL) (20 Sep 1916–) U.S. science fiction fan, bibliographer, publisher and specialty dealer. He was born in Marblehead, Mass. He produced a number of issue listings of magazines in the field, culminating in *The Complete Checklist* (covered below). He produced the following works coverages: *Edgar Rice Burroughs Biblio* (1956, 29 pp., 50¢; rev. 1962, 48 pp., $1.10) and *Talbot Mundy Biblio* (1956, 28 pp., 50¢). He trades under the name Science-Fiction and Fantasy Publications, and has the Woodhaven Bookland book store.
Nonfiction
Bibliography of Adventure: Mundy, Burroughs, Rohmer, Haggard (Woodhaven Bookland, Denver, N.Y., 1964, 126 pp., mimeo, $3.25)
A binding of the four individual bibliographies, presenting biographical sketches and extensive but incomplete listings of the authors' published books and magazine fiction.
Complete Checklist of Science-Fiction Magazines, The (Science-Fiction & Fantasy Pubs., Woodhaven, N.Y., 1961, 63 pp., lithographed, $1.10)
The most complete issue listing so far made of all magazines relating to the field. It covers many foreign magazines. Magazine titles are not cross-indexed; changed titles are mentioned only with the original magazine. It lists a considerable number of quite borderline magazines, and in this regard is far more embracing than the MAGAZINE section of this *Encyclopedia*.
Index on the Weird and Fantastica in Magazines, An (Published by the compiler, New York, 1953, 162 pp., quarto, mimeo, $2.00)
A story listing, issue by issue, for *Weird Tales*, *Golden Fleece*, *Strange Tales*, *Oriental Stories*, *Magic Carpet*, *Tales of Magic and Mystery*, *Thrill Book*, and *Strange Stories*. Next is a listing of only the fantasy stories in *Complete Stories*, *Romance Magazine*, *Popular Magazine*, *The Idler*, *Blue Book Magazine*, the Munsey periodicals such as *All-Story Magazine* and *The Argosy*, with a further

listing of others including *Cosmopolitan*, *Thrilling Adventures* and *Top-Notch*. It concludes with a Checklist of Fantastic Magazines which was brought up to date in *The Complete Checklist of S-F Magazines*.

Supplemental Checklist of Fantastic Literature, The (Science-Fiction and Fantasy Pubs., Denver, N.Y., 1963, 155 pp., quarto, mimeo, $5.50; 403 copies)

A supplement to the Bleiler *Checklist of Fantastic Literature*, covering some omissions and updating it to 1963. It covers some material not presented in this *Encyclopedia*.

Anthology

Past and Future and The Last Generation (Published by the compiler, 1954, 51 pp., quarto, mimeo, pa 50¢)

3 stories: "Henry Fitzowen" (1798), Nathan Drake; "A Tale of the Future" [new], B. M. Day; "The Last Generation" (1908), James E. Flecker.

DAY, DONALD B(RYNE) (1909–) Noted U.S. science fiction fan and publisher. Born in Syracuse, N.Y., he went to Oregon in 1919 and has lived in Portland since 1923. He graduated from high school in 1927, worked at various occupations, and since 1940 has been a postal clerk. He has been a reader and collector of sf and fantasy for around 40 years, and began compiling his *Index to the SF Magazines* in 1935. He has been an active fan in local and national affairs since 1946, and was Chairman of the 8th World SF Convention (Norwescon) in Portland in 1950. For three years he edited the very high-class amateur magazine *The Fanscient*. His Perri Press, which was founded for publication of the *Index* (below), has become established as a spare-time offset and letter-press printing shop of five presses, with a regular business location and a partner.

Nonfiction

Index to the Science Fiction Magazines: 1926-50 (Perri Press, Oregon, 1952, 184 pp., quarto, photolith, $6.50; 1968, $10.00)

An enormous compilation listing stories by author (with pseudonyms) and by title (giving the page number of each story in the magazines). It covers 58 different magazines and is the basic bibliographic source for the science fiction collector. The continuation of this work (1951-1965) was edited by Norman Metcalf.

DAY, Mrs. FRANK R. (Emily Foster Day)

Fiction

Princess of Manoa and Other Romantic Tales From the Folk-Lore of Old Hawaii, The (Paul Elder & Co., San Francisco & New York, 1906, xiv+85 pp., illus.–D. Howard Hitchcock [sepia prints mounted])

9 stories: "The Princess of Manoa"; "The Well of Last Resource"; "A King's Ransom"; "The Story of the Eight Islands"; "The Forest of Haina Kolo"; "The Magic Arrow"; "The Island of Demons"; "The Maid of the Twilight"; "The Culprit Star." An unusual book, printed on brown paper by Tomoye Press, New York.

DAY, JAMES WENTWORTH (21 Apr 1899–) British author. He did an extramural course at Cambridge University. From 1922-39 he worked on various British journals in editing and other capacities; he also has contributed to numerous British newspapers and magazines. His books, covering many diverse phases of sports and adventure, include *Life of Sir Malcolm Campbell* (1931), *The Dog in Sport* (1938), *Marshland Adventures* (1950), *Poison on the Land* (1957) and *A Ghost Hunter's Game Book* (1958).

Nonfiction

Here Are Ghosts and Witches (Batsford, London, 1954, 171 pp., illus.–M. Ayrton, 12/6) (Clarke Irwin, Toronto, $2.65)

A record of haunting and witchcraft in England.

DAY, (GERALD WILLIAM) LANGSTON

Fiction

Deep Blue Ice, The (Cresset, London, 1960, 285 pp., 16/-)

A mountaineer revives after 60 years buried in a glacier.

Magic Casements [C] (Rider, London, 1951, 200 pp., illus.–A. Ogden, 12/6)

A series of 10 enchanting fables ranging from the days of Atlan-

tis to modern times; e.g., "The Three Bounties of Bacchus," about ancient Rome.

DE BERARD, FREDERICK B.

Anthologies [Incomplete—other titles in Bleiler *Checklist*]

Classic Library of Famous Literature: Vol. 4, Wonder (Bodleian Society, New York, 1902, 306 pp., illus.)

5 stories with 'Critical Analysis of Selections' and 'Biographical Dictionary of Authors,' both by the compiler: "Undine," Baron Friedrich De La Motte Fouque; "Rip Van Winkle," Washington Irving; "The Coming of Arthur" (extract from *Idylls of the King*), Alfred, Lord Tennyson; "Sintram," Baron F. De La Motte Fouque; "The Passing of Arthur" (extract from *Idylls of the King*), Tennyson.

Classic Library of Famous Literature: Vol. 5, Weird Tales (Bodleian Society, New York, 1902, 250 pp., illus.)

5 stories and one verse with 'Critical Analysis' and 'Biographical Dictionary' by the compiler: "The House and the Brain," Edward Bulwer-Lytton; "The Strange Case of Dr. Jekyll and Mr. Hyde," "Markheim," R. L. Stevenson; "The Were-Wolf," Clemence Housman; "The Wondersmith," Fitz-James O'Brien; "The Rime of the Ancient Mariner" (verse), S. T. Coleridge.

Classic Library of Famous Literature: Vol. 15, Occult Tales (Bodleian Society)

6 stories with 'Critical Analysis' and 'Biographical Dictionary' by the compiler: "The Metempsychosis," Dr. Robert McNish; "The Devil and Tom Walker," Washington Irving; "The Life Magnet," Alvey A. Adee; "What Was It?" Fitz-James O'Brien; "The Time Machine," H. G. Wells; "The Four-Fifteen Express," Amelia B. Edwards. Despite the title this is actually almost a science-fiction anthology!

DE CAMP, L(YON) SPRAGUE (27 Nov 1907–) U.S. writer, mainly of fiction and popularized science with special interests in history, technology and language. He graduated from Calif. Inst. of Technology with a B.S. in Aeronautical Engineering, then obtained his M.S. in Engineering and Economics from Stevens Inst. of Technology, New Jersey, 1933. He worked as editor, article writer, instructor and patent engineer, and spent a year as Principal of the School of Inventing and Patenting of the International Correspondence Schools. He has been a free-lance writer since 1937. He has travelled extensively in North America, Europe, Asia, Africa and the Pacific, and has studied several languages, speaking some "after a fashion."

In the science fiction and fantasy fields he has written many stories, and is particularly noted for his own style of whacky humour which assisted Campbell in giving *Unknown* its peculiar flavor. Many of his stories and articles were featured in *ASF* and *Unknown* from the late 1930's, and he later appeared in most magazines of the field. Sam Moskowitz's profile of de Camp was published in *AS*, Feb 1964, and is a chapter in his *Seekers of Tomorrow*, 1966. De Camp has taken a keen interest in R. E. Howard's writings, and has edited and completed a number of fragments found in Howard's effects; he worked on Gnome Press's hardcover Howard collections of the early 1950's and the more recent Lancer paperback series. He often collaborated with Fletcher Pratt; their works include the *Gavagan's Bar* series, in which Pratt was mainly responsible for the final writing. A number of de Camp's short stories have been translated into Italian, and together with some by C. M. Kornbluth made up an issue of *Urania* (#334, 1964).

As a result of his original research in many fields, including linguistics, phonetics, and history of imaginative fiction, de Camp has published numerous articles in both the sf and other magazine fields. Many of these have later been incorporated into books. From 1948 to 1956 he wrote 76 radio scripts for the Voice of America, mostly on current developments in science. Nonfiction books outside the scope of this *Encyclopedia* are *Inventions and Their Management* (with A. K. Berle, editions 1937-51), *The Evolution of Naval Weapons* (1947), *Inventions, Patents and Their Management* (with A. K. Berle, 1959), *The Heroic Age of American Invention* (1961), and also some works in a juvenile series for

Golden Press.

In recent years he has written little science fiction but has concentrated on historical novels, which have been extremely well received: *An Elephant for Aristotle* (Doubleday, 1958; Dobson, 1966), *The Bronze God of Rhodes* (D'day, 1960; Bantam, 1963, pa), *The Dragon of the Ishtar Gate* (D'day, 1961; Lancer, 1968, pa), and *The Arrows of Hercules* (D'day, 1965). His *The Ancient Engineers* covers the history of technology in the classical world and the practical aspects of ancient civilization. Books in collaboration with his wife Catherine include *Ancient Ruins and Archaeology* (D'day, 1964, 294 pp., illus., $5.95), outlining the magic and facts of 12 ancient sites; *Spirits, Stars and Spells* (Canaveral, 1966, 348 pp., $5.95), on the profits and perils of magic; and *The Day of the Dinosaur* (D'day, 1968, $6.95).

Series

Black, Johnny. An intelligent bear. All in *ASF*: "The Command" (Oct 1938); "The Incorrigible" (Jan 1939); "The Emancipated" (Mar 1940); "The Exalted" (Nov 1940). A film was once mooted.
Gavagan's Bar [with F. Pratt]. In *F&SF*: "Gavagan's Bar—1. Elephas Frumenti & 2. The Gift of God" (Win/Spr, 1950); "The Better Mousetrap" (Dec 1950); "More Than Skin Deep" (Apr 1951); "Beasts of Bourbon" (Oct 1951); "The Rape of the Lock" (Feb 1952); "The Ancestral Amethyst" (Aug 1952); "The Black Ball" (Oct 1952); "The Green Thumb" (Feb 1953); "The Untimely Toper" (July 1953); "One Man's Meat" (Sep 1953); "The Weissenbroch Spectacles" (Nov 1954). In *WT*: "When the Night Wind Howls" (Nov 1951); "Where To, Please?" (Sep 1952); "Caveat Emptor" (Mar 1953). In *FU*: "Ward of the Argonaut" (Jan 1959); "Bell, Book and Candle" (Oct 1959).
Poseidonis [or Pusadian]. "The Tritonian Ring" (*2CSAB*, Win 1951); "The Stronger Spell" (*Fantasy Fiction*, Nov 1953); "The Owl and the Ape" (*Imagination*, Nov 1951); "The Eye of Tandyla" (*FA*, May 1951); "The Hungry Hercynian" (*Universe*, Dec 1953); "Ka the Appalling" (*FU*, Aug 1958). The first four appeared as *The Tritonian Ring*.
Shea, Harold (or The Mathematics of Magic) [with F. Pratt]. "The Roaring Trumpet" (*Unknown*, May 1940); "The Mathematics of Magic" (*Unknown*, Aug 1940); "The Castle of Iron" (*Unknown*, Apr 1941); "The Wall of Serpents" (*Fantasy Fiction*, June 1953); "The Green Magician" (*Beyond*, No. 9, 1954). The first two were published as *The Incomplete Enchanter*, the third as *The Castle of Iron*, and the last two as *The Wall of Serpents*.
Viagens Interplanetarias. Stories in the era 2088-2168 or thereabouts, when Brazil dominates Earth and has interstellar commerce with Krishna, Vishnu and other worlds. An outline of the stories is given in an article in the amateur magazine *New Frontiers* (Dec 1959), where the dating herewith is given. Many appeared in *The Continent Makers* [denoted by *C.M.*]

2088: "The Inspector's Teeth" (*ASF*, Apr 1950; *C.M.*); 2114: "Finished" (*ASF*, Nov 1949; *C.M.*); 2115: "Summer Wear" (*SS*, May 1950; *C.M.*); 2117: "The Galton Whistle" (*Future*, July 1951; *C.M.*); 2117: "The Colorful Character" (*TWS*, Dec 1949; *Sprague de Camp's New Anthology*); 2120: "The Animal Cracker Plot" (*ASF*, July 1949; *C.M.*); 2122: "Calories" (*Ten Story*, Spr 1951; *S. de C.'s New Anthology*); 2137: "Perpetual Motion" (*Future*, Aug 1950; *C.M.*); 2138: "The Queen of Zamba" (*ASF*, sr2, Aug 1949; *Cosmic Manhunt*); 2143: "The Hand of Zei" (*ASF*, sr4, Oct 1950; *The Search for Zei & The Hand of Zei*); 2147: "Git Along" (*ASF*, Aug 1950; *C.M.*); 2150: "The Virgin of Zesh" (*TWS*, Feb 1953); 2153: "The Continent Makers" (*TWS*, Apr 1951; *C.M.*); 2168: "The Tower of Zanid" (*SFS*, sr4, May 1958; book); ? : *Rogue Queen* (book—see below).

Fiction

Carnelian Cube, The [with F. Pratt] (Gnome, New York, 1948, 230 pp., $3.00) (Lancer, 73-662, 1967, 222 pp., pa 60¢)
Strange writings on a cube transport an archaeologist into alternate versions of 1939.
Castle of Iron, The [with F. Pratt] (*Unknown Worlds*, Apr 1941) (Gnome, 1950, 224 pp., $2.50) (*Il castello d'accaiao* [Italian], Fantascienza: 4, 1961, pa) (Pyramid: F722, 1962, 159 pp., pa 40¢)
Second of the Harold Shea series books; adventures in the world

of Ariosto's *Orlando Furioso*.
Conan See HOWARD, R. E. (*Conan* series—Gnome cloth and Lancer paperback titles)
Conan of the Isles [pa] See HOWARD, R. E.
Conan the Adventurer [pa] See HOWARD, R. E.
Conan the Avenger [pa] See HOWARD, R. E.
Conan the Freebooter [pa] See HOWARD, R. E.
Conan the Usurper [pa] See HOWARD, R. E.
Conan the Wanderer [pa] See HOWARD, R. E.
Continent Makers and Other Tales of the Viagens, The [C] (Twayne, New York, 1953, 272 pp., $2.95)
Sf, 8 stories of the "Viagens Interplanetarias" series (which see for original printings): "The Inspector's Teeth"; "Summer Wear"; "Finished"; "The Galton Whistle" ("Ultrasonic God"); "The Animal-Cracker Plot"; "Git Along!"; "Perpetual Motion" ("Wide-Open Planet"); "The Continent Makers."
Cosmic Manhunt ("The Queen of Zamba," *ASF*, sr2, Aug 1949) (Ace: D-61, 1954, 128 pp., pa 35¢; with *Ring Around the Sun*) (*Menschenjagd im Kosmos* [German], *UG*: 82, 1958) (*A Planet Called Krishna*, Compact: F311, 1966, 158 pp., pa 3/6)
Fantastic adventure on Krishna when an Earthly detective seeks a client's runaway daughter.
Divide and Rule (*Unknown*, sr2, Apr 1939) —revised: (Fantasy, Reading, 1948, 231 pp., $3.00) (Lancer: 72-768, 1964, 160 pp., pa 50¢)
A whacky adventure story in which mankind is split into feudal states and ruled by kangaroolike "Hoppers." Both book editions also contain "The Stolen Dormouse" (*ASF*, sr2, Apr 1941), one of de Camp's best sf stories—love and intrigue between members of future social classes.
Floating Continent, The [pa] See *Search for Zei, The*
Genus Homo [with P. S. Miller] (*SSS*, Mar 1941) —revised: (Fantasy, Reading, 1950, 225 pp., $3.00, jacket—E. Cartier) (*Le regne du gorille* [French], Hachette Le RF, 1951) (*Gorilla sapiens* [Italian], *Urania*: 13, 1953) (*Die Neuen Herrscher* [German], *TS*: 40, 1960) (Berkley: G-536, 1961, 157 pp., pa 35¢)
People in a buried bus awaken after millions of years; interplay of characters in a bizarre world where evolved apes have replaced humanity.
Glory That Was, The (*SS*, Apr 1952) (Avalon, New York, 1960, 223 pp., $2.95)
Foreword by R. A. Heinlein. An eccentric archaeologist re-creates Periclean Athens as the setting for various adventures.
Goblin Tower, The [pa] (Pyramid: T1927, 1968, 253 pp., pa 75¢)
A king escapes the executioner, and travels in a world of sword and sorcery.
Gun for Dinosaur, A [C] (Doubleday, New York, 1963, 359 pp., $4.50) (D'day SF B.C., 1963, $1.90)
Sf, 14 stories originally published 1952-57: "A Gun for Dinosaur"; "Aristotle and the Gun"; "The Guided Man"; "Internal Combustion"; "Cornzan the Mighty"; "Throwback"; "Judgment Day"; "Gratitude"; "A Thing of Custom"; "The Egg"; "Let's Have Fun"; "Impractical Joke"; "In-Group"; "New Arcadia."
Hand of Zei, The (Avalon, New York, 1963, 222 pp., $2.95) (abr., Ace: F-249, 1963, 113 pp., pa 40¢; with *The Search for Zei* [de Camp])
The second half of the original title story (*ASF*, sr4, Oct 1950). The fulfilment of Barnevelt's quest amid the pirates of Krishna.
Incomplete Enchanter, The [with F. Pratt] (Holt, New York, 1942, 260 pp., $2.50) (Oxford, Toronto, $3.00) (Prime, Philadelphia, 1950, 326 pp., $2.50) (Pyramid: G-530, 1960, 192 pp., pa 35¢; F-723, 1962, pa 40¢; X1928, 1968, pa 60¢) (*Am Kreuzweg der Welten* [German], *UZ*: 529, 1967)
First of Harold Shea series books; a combination of "The Roaring Trumpet" (*Unknown*, May 1940) and "The Mathematics of Magic" (*Unknown*, Aug 1940). Adventures in the land of the Norse gods and in the world of Spenser's *Faerie Queene*.
Land of Unreason, The [with F. Pratt] (*Unknown*, Oct 1941) —revised: (Holt, 1942, 260 pp., $2.50) (Oxford, Toronto, $3.00)
Whacky variations on Shakespeare's *Midsummer Night's Dream*.
Lest Darkness Fall (*Unknown*, Dec 1939) (Holt, 1941, 379 pp., illus., $2.50) —revised: (Prime, Philadelphia, 1949, 233 pp., $3.00)

(abr., Galaxy SF Novel: 24, 1955, 125 pp., pa 35¢) (Heinemann, London, 1955, 230 pp., 12/6) (Pyramid: F-817, 1963, 174 pp., pa 40¢) (*Das Mittelalter findet nicht statt* [German], *TS*: 95, 1965)

An American thrown back in time to Rome tries to prevent the fall of the Dark Ages.

Planet Called Krishna, A [pa]　See *Cosmic Manhunt*
Return of Conan, The　See HOWARD, R. E. [actually by NYBERG, B.]
Rogue Queen (Doubleday, New York, 1951, 222 pp., $2.75) (Dell: 600, 1952, 192 pp., pa 25¢) (Pinnacle, 1954, 160 pp., pa 2/-) (*Le Amazzoni di Autinid* [Italian], *GRF*: 1, 1960) (Ace: F-333, 1965, 189 pp., pa 40¢)

A different angle on alien sex on a world visited by the Viagens Interplanetarias.

Search for Zei, The (Avalon, 1962, 224 pp., $2.95) (Ace: F-249, 1963, 143 pp., pa 40¢; with *The Hand of Zei* [de Camp]) (*The Floating Continent*, Compact: F321, 1966, 158 pp., pa 3/6)

The first half of "The Hand of Zei" (*ASF*, sr4, Oct 1950). Dirk Barnevelt is sent to Krishna to bring home his company's explorer-founder, but instead he saves the Princess Zei from pirates.

Solomon's Stone (*Unknown*, June 1942) (Avalon, 1956, 224 pp., $2.75) (*La gemme di Salomone* [Italian], *Cosmo*: 78, 1961)

A fake evocation calls up a real and uncontrollable demon who throws the hero into a world of wish-fulfilment.

Sprague de Camp's New Anthology [Editor–H. J. Campbell] [C] (Hamilton, London, 1953, 159 pp., 7/6; Panther: 92, pa 1/6)

Sf, 6 stories: "Calories"; "The Colorful Character"; "Juice"; "Proposal"; "The Saxon Pretender"; "The Space Clause."

Stolen Dormouse, The [n]　See *Divide and Rule*
Tales From Gavagan's Bar [with F. Pratt] [C] (Twayne, 1953, 228 pp., $3.00)

Fantasy, 23 stories of the Gavagan's Bar series (which see for original appearances; some in this collection are original): "The Gift of God"; "Corpus Delectable"; "The Better Mousetrap"; "Elephas Frumenti"; "Beasts of Bourbon"; "The Love-Nest"; "The Stone of the Sages"; " 'Where To, Please?' "; "The Palimpsest of St. Augustine"; "More Than Skin Deep"; "No Forwarding Address"; "When the Night Wind Howls"; "My Brother's Keeper"; "A Dime Brings You Success"; "The Rape of the Lock"; "All That Glitters"; "Here, Putzi!"; "Gin Comes in Bottles"; "The Black Ball"; "The Green Thumb"; "Caveat Emptor"; "The Eve of St. John"; "The Ancestral Amethyst."

Tales of Conan　See HOWARD, R. E.
Tower of Zanid, The (*SFS*, sr4, May 1958; *SFS* [Brit.], sr4, No. 3, 1958) (Avalon, 1958, 220 pp., $2.75) (*La torre di Zanid* [Italian], *GRF*: 6, 1961) (Airmont: SF2, 1963, 128 pp., pa 35¢)

A sort of sequel to *Cosmic Manhunt*, set on Krishna. Involved and fantastic career of a human adventurer trying to regain his lost kingship of Zamba.

Tritonian Ring, The [C] (Twayne, 1953, 262 pp., $2.95) (Paperback: 53-618, 1968, 224 pp., pa 60¢)

1 novel and 3 short stories (pa has novel only); all in the Poseidonis series: "The Tritonian Ring" (n); "The Stronger Spell"; "The Owl and the Ape"; "The Eye of Tandyla."

Undesired Princess, The (*Unknown*, Feb 1942) (FPCI, Los Angeles, 1951, 248 pp., $3.00) (in *Fantasy Twin* [double binding, pub. Crawford, W.], 1953)

A rollicking fantastic adventure. The book editions also contain the humorous fantasy "Mr. Arson" (*Unknown*, Dec 1941).

Wall of Serpents [with F. Pratt] (Avalon, 1960, 223 pp., $2.95)

Last of the Harold Shea series books. A combination of "Wall of Serpents" (*Fantasy Fiction*, June 1953) and "The Green Magician" (*Beyond*, No. 9, 1954); adventures first in the world of the *Kalevala* and then in Irish mythology-cum-history.

Wheels of If, The [C] (Shasta, Chicago, 1949, 223 pp., $3.00, jacket–H. Bok)

Fantasy, 7 stories: "The Wheels of If"; "The Merman"; "The Contraband Cow"; "Hyperpilosity"; "The Gnarly Man"; "The Warrior Race"; "The Best-Laid Scheme."

Nonfiction
Conan Reader, The (Mirage, Baltimore, 1968, 149 pp., $4.00; 1500 copies)

13 essays, all but the first (original) adapted from appearances in *Amra* [amateur journal]: "Conan's Ghost"; "Memories of R.E.H."; "The Trail of Tranicos"; "Hyborian Technology"; "Pirettes"; "Conan and Matho"; "Conan and Pizarro"; "Conan's Great-Grandfather"; "Conan's Imitators"; "Pratt's Parallel Worlds"; "Knights and Knaves in Neustria"; "El-Ron and the City of Brass"; "An Exegesis of Howard's Hyborian Tales."

Lands Beyond [with W. Ley] (Rinehart, New York, 1952, 346 pp., illus., $4.75) (Clarke Irwin, Toronto, $6.00) (British ed. was limited release of U.S. ed.)

Outlines man's earliest searchings for the marvelous just over the horizon. It won the 1953 International Fantasy Award for nonfiction.

Lost Continents (*Other Worlds*, sr9, Oct 1952) (Gnome, 1954, 362 pp., illus., $5.00)

The Atlantis theme in history and science—discussion of the scientific tales of Aristotle and others, and how through time they have been embellished and enlarged. Prime Press had planned to publish it in 1952.

Science-Fiction Handbook (Hermitage, New York, 1953, 328 pp., $3.50) (McLeod, Toronto, $4.00)

A valuable reference work for the aspiring author, magnificently covering the U.S. science fiction field from the viewpoint of writers and their potential markets; written brilliantly and with humour. Chapters are: "The World of Imaginative Fiction"; "The Origins of Imaginative Fiction"; "Modern Imaginative Fiction"; "Markets and Editors"; "Readers and Fans"; "Writers of Imaginative Fiction"; "Preparation for a Science-Fiction Career"; "Where Do You Get Those Crazy Ideas?"; "Plotting an Imaginative Story"; "Writing an Imaginative Story"; "Selling an Imaginative Story"; "Being an Imaginative-Fiction Writer"; plus Notes, Bibliography and Index.

Anthologies
Fantastic Swordsmen, The [pa] (Pyramid: R1621, 1967, 204 pp., pa 50¢)

8 stories of fantastic adventure, with introduction "Tellers of Tales": "Black Lotus," R. Bloch; "The Fortress Unvanquishable Save for Sacnoth," Lord Dunsany; "Drums of Tombalku," R. E. Howard & L. S. de Camp; "The Girl in the Gem," John Jakes; "Dragon Moon," H. Kuttner; "The Other Gods," H. P. Lovecraft; "The Singing Citadel," M. Moorcock; "The Tower," Luigi de Pascalis.

Spell of Seven, The [pa] (Pyramid: R-1192, 1965, 192 pp., pa 50¢, illus.–V. Finlay)

'Heroic' fantasy, 7 stories with compiler's introduction "Wizards and Warriors": "Bazaar of the Bizarre," Fritz Leiber; "The Dark Eidolon," Clark A. Smith; "The Hoard of the Gibbelins," Lord Dunsany; "The Hungry Hercynian," L. S. de Camp; "Kings in Darkness," Michael Moorcock; "Mazirian the Magician," Jack Vance; "Shadows in Zamboula," Robert E. Howard.

Swords and Sorcery [pa] (Pyramid: R-950, 1963, 186 pp., pa 50¢, illus.–V. Finlay)

'Heroic' fantasy, 8 stories with compiler's introduction: "The Valor of Cappen Varra," Poul Anderson; "Distressing Tale of Thangobrind the Jeweller," Lord Dunsany; "Shadows in the Moonlight," Robert E. Howard; "The Citadel of Darkness," Henry Kuttner; "When the Sea King's Away," Fritz Leiber; "The Doom That Came to Sarnath," H. P. Lovecraft; "Hellsgarde," C. L. Moore; "The Testament of Athammaus," Clark A. Smith.

DE CASTRO, A. (pseud)　See DANZIGER, G. A. de C.

DE CHAIR, SOMERSET (22 Aug 1911–) British M.P. and author. He was born at Sunningdale, Berks., and educated at Balliol College, Oxford (B.A.). He was the Member of Parliament for S. W. Suffolk 1935-45, and S. Paddington 1950-51. As a writer his works include *The Impending Storm, The Golden Carpet, Napoleon's Memoirs*, etc.

Fiction
Teetotalitarian State, The (Falcon, London, 1947, 175 pp., 8/6)
　Amusing satire of bookmakers' government of the future.

DE LA MARE, COLIN British, son of Walter De La Mare.
Anthologies
Ghost Book, The See *They Walk Again*
They Walk Again (Dutton, New York, 1931, 469 pp., $2.50)
(Faber, London, 1931, 469 pp., 7/6; 1932, 3/6; 1947) (*The Ghost Book: They Walk Again*, Dutton, 1937, 469 pp.) (Dutton, 1942, 469 pp., $2.50)

18 stories with introduction by Walter De La Mare: "Keeping His Promise," A. Blackwood; "The Electric King," Lord Dunsany; "The Ghost Ship," R. Middleton; "A Tough Tussle," A. Bierce; "Afterward," Edith Wharton; "Powers of the Air," J. D. Beresford; "Father Girdlestone's Tale," R. H. Benson; "The Magic Formula," L. P. Jacks; "A Visitor From Down Under," L. P. Hartley; "Caterpillars," E. F. Benson; "The Voice in the Night," W. H. Hodgson; "The Beckoning Fair One," O. Onions; "On the Brighton Road," R. Middleton; "The Story of a Disappearance and an Appearance," M. R. James; "All Hallows," W. De La Mare; "The Monkey's Paw," W. W. Jacobs; "Green Tea," J. S. Le Fanu; "Wood of the Dead," A. Blackwood. This anthology is notable in that it revived interest in the writings of W. H. Hodgson and caused others of his works to reappear.

DE LA MARE, WALTER J(OHN) (25 Apr 1873—22 June 1956) British poet and novelist. Of Huguenot descent, he was educated at St. Paul's, London. During 1889-1908 he was engaged in business in London, but had already published poems and prose, some under the pseudonym "Walter Ramal." In 1901 his *Songs of Childhood* appeared, followed in 1904 by the novel *Henry Brocken*. For 20 years he was an official of the Anglo-American Co., then a civil list pension allowed him to devote himself to literature. He gradually found a growing audience for his delicate and highly individual work; *The Return* (1910) won the Polignac Prize. From 1912 to 1920 he wrote many poems, and his *Collected Poems, 1901-18* appeared in 1920. His novel *Memoirs of a Midget* (1921) showed him to be a master of fantasy and symbolism; *Stuff and Nonsense* (1927) is a fantastic poem; and *The Traveller* (1946) is a long philosophical poem. *The Walter De La Mare Omnibus* (Collins, 1933, 926 pp., 7/6) consists of his novels *Henry Brocken*, *The Return*, and *Memoirs of a Midget*.
Fiction [Incomplete—other titles in Bleiler *Checklist*]
Beginning and Other Stories, A [C] (Faber, London, 1955, 256 pp., 12/6)

13 stories: "The Quinqunx"; "The Princess"; "The Cartouche"; "The Guardian"; "The Face"; "An Anniversary"; "Odd Shop"; "The Stranger"; "Neighbours"; "Bad Company"; "Music"; "The Picture"; "A Beginning."
Best Stories of Walter De La Mare [C] (Faber, 1942, 397 pp., 8/6; 1954, 6/-) (Ryerson, Toronto, $2.75)

16 stories: "All Hallows"; "The Almond Tree"; "Crewe"; "The House"; "An Ideal Craftsman"; "Miss Duveen"; "Miss Miller"; "Missing"; "The Nap"; "The Orgy: An Idyll"; "Physic"; "The Picnic"; "Seaton's Aunt"; "The Trumpet"; "The Vats"; " 'What Dreams May Come'."
Broomsticks and Other Tales [C] (Knopf, New York, 1925, 334 pp., illus.–Bold, $2.50; 1942, $3.00) (Constable, London, 1925, 378 pp., 10/6; 1933, 5/-) (Ryerson, Toronto, 1942, $3.75)

12 stories: "Alice's Grandmother"; "The Bowl"; "Dutch Cheese"; "Lovely Myfanwy"; "Lucy"; "Maria-Fly"; "Miss Jemina"; "A Nose"; "Pigtails Ltd."; "The Thief"; "Three Sleeping Boys of Warwickshire"; "Visitors."
Collected Stories [chosen by E. Wagenknecht] [C] (Knopf, 1950, 467 pp., $4.50)

24 stories, with introduction by E. Wagenknecht: "All Hallows"; "Almond Tree"; "The Bowl"; "Cape Race"; "The Connoisseur"; "The Creature"; "Ideal Craftsman"; "In the Forest"; "Lispet, Lispett and Vaine"; "Miss Duveen"; "Missing"; "The Nap"; "The Orgy: An Idyll"; "Physic"; "The Riddle"; "Seaton's Aunt"; "Strangers and Pilgrims"; "The Talisman"; "Three Friends"; "The Tree"; "The Trumpet"; "The Vats"; "The Wharf"; "The Willows."
Connoisseur and Other Stories, The [C] (Knopf, 1926, 309 pp., $2.50) (Collins, London, 1926, 364 pp., 10/6; 1930, 3/6; pocket ed., 1929, 2/6, 3/6)

9 stories: "All Hallows"; "The Connoisseur"; "Disillusioned"; "Lost Track"; "Missing"; "Mr. Kempe"; "The Nap"; "Pretty Poll"; "The Wharf."
Ghost Stories [C] (Folio Society, London, 1956, 234 pp., lithographs–B. Freedman, 21/-)

7 stories: "Out of the Deep"; "The House"; "Revenant"; "The Green Room"; "Bad Company"; "The Quincunx"; "An Anniversary."
Nap and Other Stories, The [C] (Nelson, London, nd [1936], 197 pp., 1/6) (Nelson, Toronto, 50¢)

6 stories: "The Bowl"; "Maria-Fly"; "Selina's Parable"; "The Nap"; "All Hallows"; "An Ideal Craftsman."
On the Edge [C] (Faber, 1930, 289 pp., illus.–E. Rivers, 10/6; 1932, 3/6) (Knopf, 1931, 314 pp., $3.00)

8 stories: "At First Sight"; "Crewe"; "Green Room"; "An Ideal Craftsman"; "The Orgy: An Idyll"; "The Picnic"; " 'A Recluse' "; "The Willows."
Return, The (Putnam, New York & London, 1911, 354 pp.) (Knopf, 1922, $2.50) (Collins, London, 1926, 313 pp., 3/6; 1932, vi+309 pp., 2/6) (Penguin: 38, 1935, 254 pp., 6d) (Faber, 1946, 248 pp., 8/6; 1955, 248 pp.) (Ryerson, Toronto, $2.75) (Pan: 270, 1954, 221 pp., pa 2/-)

A fight against evil by a man who awakens after a sleep on a gravestone and finds himself controlled by an 18th Century suicide.
Riddle and Other Tales, The [C] (Knopf, 1923, 290 pp., $2.50) (S. Blount, London, 1923, 303 pp., 7/6) (Faber, 1935, 280 pp., 3/6) (Ryerson, Toronto, $1.35)

15 stories: "The Almond Tree"; "Bird of Travel"; "The Bowl"; "Count's Courtship"; "The Creatures"; "Lispet, Lispett and Vaine"; "Looking-Glass"; "Miss Duveen"; "Out of the Deep"; "The Riddle"; "Seaton's Aunt"; "Selina's Parable"; "Three Friends"; "The Tree"; "The Vats."
Some Stories [C] [pa] (Faber, 1962, 192 pp., pa 6/-)

8 stories: "Missing"; "Physic"; "The Picture"; "The Trumpet"; "The Nap"; "The Wharf"; "The Princess"; "The Almond Tree."
Wind Blows Over, The [C] (Macmillan, New York, 1936, 321 pp., $2.50) (Ryerson, Toronto, $2.00) (Faber, 1936, 326 pp., 8/6; 1940, 5/-)

12 stories: "Cape Race"; " 'A Froward Child' "; "The House"; "In the Forest"; "Miss Miller"; " 'Nest of Singing Birds' "; "Physic"; "A Revenant"; "Strangers and Pilgrims"; "The Talisman"; "The Trumpet"; " 'What Dreams May Come'."

DE MAUPASSANT, GUY (5 Aug 1850–1893) Noted French author whom Anatole France called "The Prince of Story Tellers." His short stories have appeared world-wide. He led an unhappy life that ended in poverty and madness. Such stories as "The Necklace" and "A Piece of String" are unforgettable—many were darkened by the same impending tragedy and pre-occupation with human miseries that overshadowed his own life. In the weird field he is primarily noted for his short story "The Horla," which is considered one of the best of its type and has seen many reprintings. A translation by G. A. England appeared in *The Scrap Book* (June 1911) and in *FFM* (Sep 1942). The story also appears in *The Private Life of Guy de Maupassant*, R. Kirkbridge (Sears, 1932; Fell, 1947; Panther, 1961, pa), but the main theme of this book is a reconstruction of De Maupassant's life.
Fiction [Incomplete—other titles in Bleiler *Checklist*]
Allouma and Other Tales [C] (Holland Pub. Co., New York, 1895, 127 pp.)

Fantasy, 11 stories: "Allouma"; "Diary of a Madman"; "False Gems"; "Father and Son"; "In the Frozen Sky"; "In the Moonlight"; "A Repulse"; "Solitude"; "The Spectre"; "Terror"; "Two Little Soldiers."

DE PINA, (ROBERT) ALBERT (? –1957) U.S. author. He made no lasting impression on the science fiction field. He appeared primarily in *Planet Stories*, where he had five stories; of these he was most proud of "The Silver Plague" (Spr 1945). He also collaborated with H. Hasse. He was a traveller, lecturer, novelist in other fields, and a screenplay writer who sold a scientifilm script *I Captured the Sun*.

DE QUEIROZ, ECA
Fiction
Mandarin and Other Stories, The [C] [Trans. from Portuguese—Richard F. Goldman] (Bodley Head, London, 1966, 186 pp., 21/-)

4 stories with translator's note, author's note about "The Mandarin," and prologue: "The Mandarin" (with the help of the Devil a clerk acquires a fortune); "Peculiarities of a Fair-Haired Girl"; "A Lyric Poet"; "José Matias."

DE REYNA, JORGE (pseud) See DETZER, D.

DE RICHTER, CHARLES French author.
Fiction
Fall of the Eiffel Tower, The (*WS*, sr3, Sep 1934) (*La Menace invisible* [French], Les Editions de France, Paris, 1937)

A man who controls termites, etc., is a world menace. *Note:* This was probably serialised in a French magazine or paper prior to its *Wonder Stories* appearance.

DE ROUEN, REED R. U.S. author whose life has been more exciting than many people's fiction. He fought in the Spanish Civil War, and has travelled around the world a number of times. He has acted and lived in Britain, but prefers to live in Spain. He took 8 years to write *The Heretic*, a novel set in a Chicago war veterans' hospital and dealing with three men—one who fought in World War I, another from World War II, and the last in the Cold War.
Fiction
Split Image (Wingate, London, 1955, 283 pp., 11/6) (Panther: 763, 1958, 160 pp., pa 2/-) (Digit: R728, 1963, 160 pp., 2/6)

An attempt to convey that Christianity has failed and Science is the new religion. There is involved intrigue when space travellers are healed on Dextar, Earth's Image.

DE SADE, MARQUIS
Fiction
Eugenie de Franval and Other Stories [C] [Trans. from French—Margaret Crosland] (N. Spearman, London, 1965, 183 pp., 18/-)

8 stories and translator's introduction (4 pp.): "Eugenie de Franval"; "The Horse-Chestnut Flower"; "The Chastised Husband"; "Florville and Coirval"; "The Husband Who Played Priest"; "Emilie de Tourville"; "Room for Two"; "The Self-Made Cuckold."

DE VAUCOULEURS, GERARD (1918–) French astronomer. From 1943-49 he studied physics at the Sorbonne and at U. of Paris; he went to Australia in 1951 as research fellow at the Australian National University to undertake comprehensive study of the galaxies of the Southern Hemisphere. His *Discovery of the Universe* ([French], 1951; Faber, 1957; Macmillan, 1957) is a good outline of the history of astronomy up to 1956. His works on Mars are of topical interest: *The Planet Mars* (Faber, 1950; 2nd ed., 1951), and *Physics of the Planet Mars* (Faber, 1954; Macmillan, 1955), fundamentally a reference work.

DE VET, CHARLES V. (28 Oct 1911–) U.S. author. He has had over 30 stories in the sf magazines since first appearing in 1950.
Fiction
Cosmic Checkmate [with Katherine MacLean] [pa] ("Second Game," *ASF*, n'te, Mar 1958) —enlarged: (Ace: F-149, 1962, 96 pp., pa 40¢; with *King of the Fourth Planet*)

An Earthman plays in a great intrigue against Velda, a world of sexual anomalies.

DE WOHL, LOUIS (1903–61)
Fiction
Second Conquest (Lippincott, Philadelphia, 1954, 239 pp., $3.00) (Longmans, Toronto, $3.50) (*Die Erde liegt hinter uns* [German], ?, 1954)

Romantic theology—the struggle between God and the Devil to take over the Martians.
Strange Daughter (Lawson, London, 1946, 195 pp., 9/6)

Weird novel of astrology and black magic; two superminds fighting to the finish.

DEE, ROGER (pseud) See AYCOCK, R. D.

DEEGAN, JON J. Probably a pseudonym for a British writer or writers.
Series
Corridors of Time. Panther pa trilogy: *Corridors of Time* (1953); *Beyond the Fourth Door* (1954); *Exiles in Time* (1954).
Old Growler. In *Authentic*: "Reconnoitre Krellig II" (No. 2, 1951); "Old Growler" (No. 4, 1951); "Old Growler and Orbis" (No. 9, 1951; [German], TN: 31, 1968, pa); "Planet of Power" (No. 14, 1951); "The Singing Spheres" (No. 23, 1952). Panther paperbacks: *Underworld of Zello* (1952; [German], Zimmerman, 1960, and *T*: 238, 1962); *Amateurs in Alchemy* (1952); *Antro the Life-Giver* (1953; [German], *T*: 273, 1963); *The Great Ones* (1953). The last two also had hard-cover editions at 6/-.

DEEPING, (GEORGE) WARWICK (28 May 1877–20 Apr 1950) British novelist. He was qualified as a doctor, but first wrote poetry and then produced a series of historical novels successful enough for him to abandon medicine. He wrote some 60 novels from 1903 until his death, the most noted being *Sorrell and Son* (1925). His writing was very much for the sentimental and all too human narrative.
Fiction [Incomplete—other titles in Bleiler *Checklist*]
Man Who Went Back, The (Knopf, New York, 1940, 382 pp., $2.50) (Cassell, London, 1940, 347 pp., 9/-) (Grosset, New York, 1942, 382 pp., 85¢) (McClelland, Toronto, 98¢) (*FFM*, Dec 1947)

A return by supernatural means to Roman Britain, and adventures there.
Short Stories of Warwick Deeping, The [C] (Cassell, London, 1930, 992 pp., 8/6)

Omnibus of 51 stories. Not listed in Bleiler *Checklist* but contains some weird and fantasy: "Wilmer's Wife"; "Two Men"; "The Pool of the Satyr"; "Old Tagus"; "That Vulgar Person"; "The Immortals"; "The Harmless Satyr"; "Tom Silver's Bus"; "Poet and Peasant"; "Gustave"; "Sand Dunes"; "The First Wrinkle"; "Shipwreck and Shrew"; "Caleban"; "Noise"; "Six Months to Live"; "Sennen Climbs a Wall"; "Rachel in Search of Reality"; "Ridicule"; "The Great Sahara Bridge"; "The Blue Tulip"; "A Red Blind"; "The Three Trees"; "The Red Van"; "Stockings"; "Sappho"; "The Black Cat"; "The Other Woman"; "What About It"; "Contraband"; "Heritage"; "Discord"; "Restitution"; "At the 'Golden Palace' "; "The Hesperides"; "Elizabeth"; "The Man Who Came Back"; "The Child"; "Paternity"; "The Strange Case of Sybil Carberry"; "The Cave"; "Precious Stones"; "Barron's Broken Head"; "In the Snow"; "Laughing Sickness"; "The Man With the Red Tie"; "Escape"; "The Sand Pit"; "The Liars"; "The Broken Violin."

DEFOE, DANIEL (1659–26 Apr 1731) English preacher, merchant, soldier, secret service agent, pamphleteer and author—one of the most remarkable figures in literature. His industry was prodigious: he began his literary career in 1694, and no less than 550 works are attributed to him. *Robinson Crusoe* (1719) brought him immortality, and is the only English novel that Pantomime has adopted. His short story "The Apparition of One Mrs. Veal" is the first realistic ghost story in the language, and is a familiar story among many of the older weird anthologies.

deFORD, MIRIAM ALLEN (Mrs. Maynard Shipley) (21 Aug 1888–) U.S. writer and literary figure. Born in Philadelphia, she has lived all over the U.S.A., with 43 years in or near San Francisco. She was educated at Wellesley College, Temple U. (A.B., 1911) and U. of Pennsylvania (graduate work in English). She has been a staff feature writer on two newspapers, a labour journalist for 38 years, and has done a considerable amount of public relations work, public speaking, and editorial work. She is now contributing editor to *The Humanist* (the organ of the American Humanist Association). She is author of seven books, mostly biography and history, but including one novel and one reference work (*Who Was When? A Dictionary of Contemporaries*). Her true crime book *The Overbury Affair* won the non-fiction 'Edgar' award of the Mystery Writers of America for 1961. She has also been a major contributor to series of large literary biographical dictionaries, such as *20th Century Authors*, and she did 25 "Little Blue Books" in the Haldeman-Julius series, mostly biographies and Latin translations. Her magazine work includes articles on sociological, criminological and literary subjects as well as stories in general magazines and in the mystery, true crime, science fiction and fantasy fields. She has had over 30 sf and fantasy stories; these have appeared in most sf magazines, currently in *F&SF*, *GSF*, *If* and *AS*. She also has had a number of stories anthologised, including original stories in *Star Science Fiction No. 4* and *6* [F. Pohl].

Anthology

Space, Time and Crime [pa]   (Paperback: 52-502, 1964, 174 pp., pa 50¢; 52-622, 1968, pa 50¢)

Sf with a mystery slant—13 stories with compiler's introduction: "Crisis, 1999," F. Brown; "Criminal Negligence," J. F. McComas; "The Talking Stone," I. Asimov; "The Past and Its Dead People," R. Bretnor; "The Adventure of the Snitch in Time," M. Reynolds & A. Derleth; "The Eyes Have It," James McKimmey; "Public Eye," A. Boucher; "The Innocent Arrival," Poul & Karen Anderson; "Third Offense," F. Pohl; "The Recurrent Suitor," Ron Goulart; "Try and Change the Past," F. Leiber; "Rope's End," Miriam A. deFord; "Or the Grasses Grow," Avram Davidson.

DeGRAEFF, ALLEN (pseud)
Anthology
Human and Other Beings [pa]   See CONKLIN, G.

DEHAN, RICHARD (pseud)   See GRAVES, CLOTILDE I. M.

DEIGHTON, LEN   British author. After writing cookery books he wrote his first spy novel, the very successful *The Ipcress File* (about an unromantic hard-working agent; a reaction against the glamorous James Bond school). His later spy novels have been more conventional. He recently left this field to write a novel on confidence tricksters, *Only When I Larf*, sold direct to Sphere books for 1968 publication to coincide with the film of the book.

Fiction

Billion-Dollar Brain   (Cape, London, 1966, 412 pp., 20/-) (*Melbourne Herald*, sr9, 23 Apr 1966) (Penguin: 2662, 1966, 255 pp., pa 5/-; 1967, pa 5/-)

A spy novel of a Texan millionaire waging war against Communism in the near future. *Film:* British, 1968, with Michael Caine as the tough insubordinate secret agent.

DEL REY, LESTER   (2 June 1915–)   U.S. author and editor. His full name is Ramon Felipe San Juan Mario Silvio Enrico Alvarez-del Rey. In his early years he led a very hard life and tried many occupations. He was always interested in science fiction; as the result of an argument with a girl friend he wrote "The Faithful." Upon its acceptance by J. W. Campbell for *Astounding* (Apr 1938) he began to write other stories. After a time further success followed, with such stories in *ASF* as "The Smallest God" (Jan 1940), "The Stars Look Down" (Aug 1940) and "Nerves" (Sep 1942). There were also contributions to *Unknown*. New interest in his work was stimulated by the publication by Prime Press of his collection . . . *And Some Were Human* in 1948, and the written-to-order story "Over the Top" for the 'prophecy' issue of *ASF* (Nov 1949). Sales to Winston's 'Adventures in SF' juvenile book series followed. A story commissioned by New York publisher John Raymond led to del Rey becoming editor of Raymond's *Space Science Fiction*, *Science Fiction Adventures* and *Fantasy Fiction (Magazine)*. He proved to be a superior editor, but conflict with the publisher over policy resulted in his resignation in 1953.

Del Rey has used the pseudonyms "Philip St. John" and "Erik Van Lhin." He has written little magazine fiction since 1956, but has, however, written a number of thought-provoking articles, such as a series on various aspects of immediate space flight for the

late *Fantastic Universe*, and some more general ones in *Amazing Stories* 1960-61. He was a regular guest on the "Long John Nebel Show" from WOR, New York. Short novels include "For I Am a Jealous People," *Star Short Novels* [Pohl] (1954), and "Badge of Infamy" (*Satellite*, June 1957). Sam Moskowitz's profile of del Rey was published in *AS* (Apr 1963) and as a chapter in Moskowitz's *Seekers of Tomorrow* (1966). In mid-1968 del Rey joined the staff of Galaxy Publications and became Managing Editor of *Galaxy Science Fiction* and *If* as of the June issues.

Fiction

. . . And Some Were Human [C]   (Prime, Philadelphia, 1948, 331 pp., illus.–S. Levin, $3.00) (*–y algunos eran humanos* [Spanish], Nebula: 37, 1957, pa [omits "Helen O'Loy"]) (Ballantine: 552, 1961, 160 pp., pa 35¢ [8 stories marked †])

Sf, 12 stories and Foreword: *Today and Yesterday:* "Hereafter, Inc."†; "The Day Is Done"†; "Forsaking All Others"†; "The Coppersmith." *Tomorrow and Tomorrow:* "The Luck of Ignatz"†; "The Faithful"; "Dark Mission"†; "Helen O'Loy"†. *And Always:* "The Stars Look Down"; "The Renegade"†; "The Wings of Night"†; "Nerves."

Attack From Atlantis   (Winston, Philadelphia, 1953, 207 pp., $2.00) ([Japanese], GingaShobô 'Adv. in SF' 10, 1956)

Juvenile, one of the Adventures in SF series. The crew of an atomic submarine reach a subsea Atlantean city.

Badge of Infamy [pa]   See *Sky Is Falling, The*

Battle on Mercury [as Erik Van Lhin]   (Winston, 1953, 207 pp., $2.00) (*Stere di fuoco* [Italian], *Urania*: 46, 1954) ([Japanese], GingaShobô: 13, 1956) (*Die Elektriden des Merkur* [German], AWA, 1957; *T*: 192, 1961)

Juvenile, one of the Adventures in SF series. Depicts alien life —energy creatures and silicone monsters—within the Solar System.

Day of the Giants   ("When the World Tottered," *FA*, Dec 1950) (Avalon, New York, 1959, 224 pp., $2.75) (*Epope a di giganti* [Italian], *Cosmo*: 83, 1961) (Airmont: SF5, 1964, 128 pp., pa 40¢)

A fantastic adventure in Asgard, with Odin, Thor, etc., joining Earthmen to fight the frost giants.

Eleventh Commandment, The [pa]   (Regency: RB113, 1962, 159 pp., pa 50¢) (*L'undicesimo comandamento* [Italian], *GRF*: 41, 1964)

A powerful story about a future America utterly controlled by the 'American Catholic Eclectic Church,' with the 11th commandment being "Be fruitful and multiply." It is told from the viewpoint of an exile.

Infinite Worlds of Maybe, The   (Holt, New York, 1966, 192 pp., $3.95, lib. $3.59) (Faber, London, 1968, 150 pp., 16/-) (*Die Weltenspringer* [German], TN: 8, 1968, pa)

Juvenile.

Marooned on Mars   (Winston, 1952, 210 pp., $2.00) (*Il clandestino del-l'astronave* [Italian], *Urania*: 2, 1952) (Hutchinson, London, 1954, 220 pp., 7/6) (*Im Banne der Marswelt* [German], AWA, 1955; *T*: 203, 1962) ([Japanese], GingaShobô: 6, 1956) (*Mars er Malet* [Danish], Skrifola: F11, 1958, pa) (Paperback: 52-415, 1967, 158 pp., pa 50¢)

Juvenile, one of the Adventures in SF series. A young stowaway on the first Mars expedition makes friends with the Martians. It won the 1951 Boy's Award for Teen-Age Fiction.

Mission to the Moon   (Winston, 1956, 207 pp., $2.00) (*Destinazione Luna* [Italian], *Urania*: 167, 1957) (*Kapplöoning Till Manen* [Swedish], Wennerberg: R6, 1958, pa)

Juvenile, one of the Adventures in SF series. The first voyage to the Moon, and what the scientists found there; a sequel to *Step to the Stars*.

Moon of Mutiny   (Holt Rinehart & Winston, New York, 1961, 217 pp., $2.85) (Faber, London, 1963, 184 pp., 15/-)

Juvenile. Third of series, sequel to *Step to the Stars* and *Mission to the Moon*. The exploration of the Moon, with Fred Halpern becoming hero. Moon mining activities are well explained.

Mortals and Monsters [C] [pa]   (Ballantine: U2236, 1965, 188 pp., pa 50¢) (Tandem: T88, 1967, 192 pp., pa 3/6)

Sf, 12 stories: "And the Truth"; "The Years Draw Nigh"; "And

It Comes Out Here"; "The Seat of Judgment"; "The Dwindling Years"; "No Place Like Home"; "Lady of Space"; "Instinct"; "Return Engagement"; "The Course of Logic"; "Spawning Ground"; "Recessional."

Nerves (*ASF*, n'te, Sep 1942) (in . . . *And Some Were Human* [del Rey], 1948 [not in pa]) —enlarged: (Ballantine, 1956, 153 pp., $2.00; #151, pa 35¢; U2344, 1966, pa 50¢) (*Atomalarm* [German], *UG*: 59, 1956) (*Nervios* [Spanish], Nebula: 39, 1957, pa [with "Helen O'Loy"]) ([Japanese], Hayakawa: 3014, 1959, pa) (*Alarm in de atoomcentrale* [Dutch], Spectrum, Utrecht & Amsterdam, 1967)

A doctor's suspenseful trials in an atomic power plant disaster; vividly written. *Note:* The expansion was from 32,000 words to 54,000; the Spanish edition is probably the original novelette.

Outpost of Jupiter (Holt Rinehart Winston, 1963, 191 pp., $2.95) (Gollancz, London, 1964, 191 pp., 12/6) (*Epidemie auf Ganymed* [German], *T*: 543, 1967)

Juvenile. The hero is marooned with a struggling colony on Ganymede, faced with plague and hostile beings.

Police Your Planet [as Erik Van Lhin] (*SFA*, sr4, Mar 1953) (Avalon, 1956, 224 pp., $2.50) (*Attentat auf den Mars* [German], *UG*: 85, 1958)

Crooked Martian politics; a tough crime novel with Earth versus colonists.

Prisoners of Space (Westminster, New York, 1968, 143 pp., $3.75)

Juvenile. Two children born on the Moon explore a forbidden tunnel and find a living creature.

Robots and Changelings [C] [pa] (Ballantine: 246, 1957, 175 pp., pa 35¢)

11 stories: "The Pipes of Pan"; "Little Jimmy"; "The Coppersmith"; "No Strings Attached"; "The Still Waters"; "Kindness"; "Stability"; "The Keepers of the House"; "Uneasy Lies the Head"; "The Monster"; "Into Thy Hands."

Rocket From Infinity (Holt, 1966, 191 pp., $3.95, lib $3.67)

Intrigue in the asteroid belt; a boy and a girl encounter a mysterious rocket ship.

Rocket Jockey [as Philip St. John] (Winston, 1952, 207 pp., $2.00) (*Die Jagd der Astronauten* [German], AWA, 1954; *T*: 240, 1962) (*Rocket Pilot*, Hutchinson, 1955, 216 pp., 7/6) ([Japanese], GingaShobō: 17, 1956)

Juvenile, one of the Adventures in SF series. Planetary adventure of a teenage pilot.

Rocket Pilot See *Rocket Jockey*

Rockets to Nowhere [as Philip St. John] (Winston, 1954, $2.00) (*Razzi verso il nulla* [Italian], *Urania*: 67, 1955) (*Satellite No. 1* [French], Hachette Le RF, 1956) ([Japanese], GingaShobō: 5, 1956)

Juvenile, one of the Adventures in SF series. A teenager discovers a secret colony on the Moon; written with a quiet realism.

Runaway Robot, The (Westminster, New York, 1965, 176 pp., $3.50) (Gollancz, London, 1967, 176 pp., 15/-) (*Der unschuldige Roboter* [German], Pabel, 1967, pa)

Juvenile. A boy's robot companion tries to return to Earth with him.

Scheme of Things, The [pa] (Belmont: B50-682, 1966, 157 pp., pa 50¢)

A man seeks the reason for his memories of other lives.

Siege Perilous [pa] (Lancer: 73-468, 1966, 157 pp., pa 60¢)

Martians in human form capture a U.S. space station.

Sky Is Falling and Badge of Infamy, The [C] [pa] (Magabook: 1, 1963, 158 pp., pa 50¢)

Two short novels in the first of a short-lived paperback series. First story is an enlargement of the same title (*Satellite*, June 1957); second is enlargement of "No More Stars" [by "Charles Satterfield"] (*Beyond*, July 1954).

Step to the Stars (Winston, 1954, 210 pp., $2.00) (Hutchinson, 1956, 216 pp., 10/6) (*Der Schritt ins All* [German], *UG*: 56, 1956) ([Japanese], GingaShobō: 21, 1956) (*Noi verso le stelle* [Italian], *GRF*: 10, 1961) (Paperback: 52-955, 1966, 160 pp., pa 60¢)

Juvenile, one of the Adventures in SF series. The problems of a

lad trying to work with mature men on the first space station. Sequel is *Mission to the Moon*.

Tunnel Through Time (Westminster, 1966, 153 pp., $3.50) (Scholastic: TX1065, 1967, 160 pp., pa 50¢)

Juvenile.

Anthology

Year After Tomorrow, The [with Cecile Matschat & Carl Carmer] (Winston, 1954, 339 pp., illus.–M. Hunter, $3.00)

Juvenile sf, 9 stories, one of the Adventures in SF series. Foreword by L. del Rey: "The Luck of Ignatz," L. del Rey; "The Master Minds of Mars," Carl H. Claudy; "By Virtue of Circumference," Peter Van Dresser; "The Red Death of Mars," R. M. Williams; "The Land of No Shadow," C. Claudy; "Plum Duff," P. Van Dresser; "Kindness," L. del Rey; "Tongue of the Beast," C. Claudy; "Rocket to the Sun," P. Van Dresser. The 6 stories by Claudy and Van Dresser originally appeared in *The American Boy*; some by Claudy also had other appearances (check author).

Nonfiction

Mysterious Earth, The (Chilton, Philadelphia, 1960, 214 pp., $2.95) (Mayflower, 1960, 24/-) (Ambassador, Toronto, $3.95)

The International Geophysical Year and its discoveries are used to show that our planet is still full of mystery and scientific adventure. There are some inaccuracies (see P. S. Miller, *ASF*, Jan 1961).

Mysterious Sea, The (Chilton, 1961, 198 pp., $2.95) (Ambassador, $3.75)

Similar to *The Mysterious Earth*.

Rockets Through Space (Winston, 1957, 118 pp., quarto, illus.–James Heugh, $3.95; rev. 1960, $3.95) (Premier: d93, 1960, 192 pp., pa 50¢)

Juvenile. Step-by-step development of the subject for the younger folk, but oversimplified for high school ages. The pa ed. does not have the original illustrations.

Space Flight (Golden Press, 1959, 56 pp., illus.–J. Polgreen) (Bailey, 1959, 5/-)

In the Golden Library of Knowledge series. Subtitled "The Coming Exploration of the Universe."

DELANY, SAMUEL R(AY) (1 Apr 1942–) U.S. author. He grew up in New York City's Harlem. He attended the Bronx High School of Science and then City College, where he was poetry editor of *The Promethean* for a term. His poetry and prose have won many awards. When he was 19 he wrote his first work, *The Jewels of Aptor*. He wrote *The Einstein Intersection* while travelling in Europe. He is married to the poet Marilyn Hacker.

Series

Toromon trilogy. Overall title was "The Fall of the Towers"; it took two years to write. All are Ace paperbacks: *Captives of the Flame*, *The Towers of Toron*, and *City of a Thousand Suns*.

Fiction

Babel-17 (Ace: F-388, 1966, 173 pp., pa 40¢) (SF B.C. [S.J.], 1968)

An intricate novel set in a complex world with violent action and strange characters. It won the 1966 Nebula Award of the SFWA.

Ballad of Beta-2, The [pa] (Ace: M-121, 1965, 96 pp., pa 45¢; with *Alpha Yes, Terra No!*)

Strange events on a generations-long space trip to the stars.

Captives of the Flame [pa] (Ace: F-199, 1963, 147 pp., pa 40¢; with *The Psionic Menace*) (Rewritten as *Out of the Dead City*, Sphere: 28835, 1968, 143 pp., 5/-)

First of Toromon trilogy. A changed future Earth has an island empire fighting to sustain its economy. The revised version is also part of a later printing of the whole trilogy.

City of a Thousand Suns [pa] (Ace: F-322, 1965, 156 pp., pa 40¢)

Last of Toromon trilogy; involved intrigue.

Einstein Intersection, The (Ace: F-427, 1967, 142 pp., pa 40¢) (Gollancz, London, 1968, 159 pp., 21/-)

Love and adventure in the far future with the world intersecting a universe of different rules. Good characterisation. It won the 1967 Nebula Award of the SFWA.

Empire Star [pa] (Ace: M-139, 1966, 102 pp., pa 45¢; with *The Tree Lord of Imeten*)

Adventure through many worlds.

Jewels of Aptor, The [pa] (Ace: F-173, 1962, 156 pp., pa 40¢; with *Second Ending*) (Ace: G-706, 1968, 159 pp., pa 50¢) (Gollancz, London, 1968, 189 pp., 25/-)

Involved intrigue in the future; the adventures of four people and the use of power-wielding "jewels." The 1968 Ace ed. is the original unabridged form, which was cut by a third for the 1962 edition.

Nova (Doubleday, New York, 1968, 279 pp., $4.95)

The conflict of two families in the Pleiades Federation and the Draco Empire, the fortune of the latter being based on a super-rare element used in space ships. Part appeared as "House A-Fire" (*AS*, short n, July 1968)

Out of the Dead City [pa] See *Captives of the Flame*

Towers of Toron, The [pa] (Ace: F-261, 1964, 140 pp., pa 40¢; with *The Lunar Eye*) (Sphere: 28843, 1968, 140 pp., pa 5/-)

Middle of the Toromon series. Intrigue and mystification in the manoeuvring of various aspects of the Toromon establishment.

DELL, JEFFREY
Fiction
News for Heaven (J. Cape, London, 1944, 189 pp., 7/6) (Consul: 1290, 1964, 190 pp., pa 3/6)

Fantasy satire on Marco Polo revisiting Earth from Heaven.

DEMAITRE, EDMUND
Fiction
Liberation of Manhattan, The [with M. J. Appleman] (Doubleday, New York, 1949, 223 pp., illus.–P. Galdone, $2.75)

Satire of the Soviet invasion of New York and liberation of "oppressed" Manhattanites.

DENNIS, CLIFFORD E.
Fiction
King Joker (Willoughby, Hamburg, N.J., 1967, 169 pp., $4.95)

DENNIS, GEOFFREY (POMEROY) (20 Jan 1892–) British novelist and essayist. He holds M.A. in Modern History, Oxford; is co-founder of the Oxford Poetry Series; and was associated with the League of Nations in Geneva 1920-37. Besides some fiction, he wrote *Coronation Commentary* (1937), which caused quite a stir. He served in both wars and was general editor of a four-volume history of World War II. A fantasy besides that below is *Harvest in Poland* (Knopf, New York, 1925).
Fiction
End of the World, The (Simon & Schuster, New York, 1930, 3+170 pp., $2.50) (Musson, Toronto, $3.00) (Eyre Spottiswoode, London, 1930, 224 pp., 8/6; 1948, 8/6)

A discursive consideration of the many ways, both natural and supernatural, by which man can end; a combination of scientific and poetic imagination, and a masterpiece of English style. It was awarded the 1930 Hawthornden Prize.

DENNIS, NIGEL (FORBES) (1912–)
Fiction
Cards of Identity (Vanguard, New York, 1955, 379 pp., $3.75) (Penguin: 1468, 1960, 302 pp., pa 3/6) (Signet: P2432, 1964, 272 pp., pa 60¢)

The manipulation of personalities at the Identity Club.

DENT, LESTER (1905–11 Mar 1959) U.S. author. He is best known for his 'Doc Savage' novels, which appeared under the pseudonym "Kenneth Robeson" in Street & Smith's *Doc Savage*. This magazine ran from January 1933 to Summer 1949. Many sf collectors included *Doc Savage* in their collections, and although Dent did not write all the novels, ardent followers could recognize those he did write. In recent years the novels have been appearing as paperbacks. Dent also wrote under his own name and under the pseudonym "Tim Ryan."

Series
Doc Savage. Following is a list of the Bantam reprints, with dates of original magazine appearance. All are by Kenneth Robeson except Nos. 15 and 21 by Norman A. Danberg [ND] and No. 25 by Alan Hathway [AH]. There is a boxed set. For other publishing information, see the *PAPERBACK LISTING*.
1964
1. *The Man of Bronze* (Mar 1933) (Street & Smith, 1933)
2. *The Thousand-Headed Man* (July 1934)
3. *Meteor Menace* (Mar 1934)
1965
4. *The Polar Treasure* (June 1933)
5. *Brand of the Werewolf* (Jan 1934)
6. *The Lost Oasis* (Sep 1933)
7. *The Monsters* (Apr 1934)
8. *The Land of Terror* (Apr 1933) (Street & Smith, 1933)
9. *The Mystic Mullah* (Jan 1935)
1966
10. *The Phantom City* (Dec 1933)
11. *Fear Cay* (Sep 1934)
12. *Quest of Qui* (July 1935)
13. *Land of Always-Night* (Mar 1935)
14. *The Fantastic Island* (Dec 1935)
1967
Nos. 1, 5, 6, 7, 9, 10, 11, 12, 13 were reprinted
15. *Murder Melody* (Nov 1935) [ND]
16. *The Spook Legion* (Apr 1935)
17. *The Red Skull* (Aug 1933)
18. *The Sargasso Ogre* (Oct 1933)
19. *Pirate of the Pacific* (July 1933)
20. *The Secret in the Sky* (May 1935)
1968
21. *Cold Death* (Sep 1936) [ND]
22. *The Czar of Fear* (Nov 1933)
23. *Fortress of Solitude* (Oct 1938)
24. *The Green Eagle* (July 1941)
25. *The Devil's Playground* (Jan 1941) [AH]
26. *Death in Silver* (Oct 1934)
27. *The Mystery Under the Sea* (Feb 1936)
28. *The Deadly Dwarf* ("Repel," ? 1937)
29. *The Other World* (Jan 1940)
30. *The Flaming Falcons* (June 1939)
31. *The Annihilist* (Dec 1934)

Bleiler lists the Street & Smith book editions of *The Man of Bronze* and *The Land of Terror* but omits a third, *Quest of the Spider* (yet to appear in the Bantam series). All three were translated into French in 1939.

DERLETH, AUGUST W(ILLIAM) (24 Feb 1909–4 July 1971) U.S. author, editor, anthologist and publisher. Born in Sauk City, Wisconsin, he started writing at the age of 13, had his first piece published at 15, and eventually had over 100 books published. Around 4,000 shorter pieces have appeared in some 400 different magazines in the U.S.A., England and elsewhere. His interest in stories of the supernatural was shown when, as a student at the U. of Wisconsin, he wrote his B.A. thesis on "The Weird Tale in English Since 1890." In 1938 he was awarded a Guggenheim Fellowship to enable him to continue writing his *Sac Prairie* sagà, comprising some 50 books of all types depicting the growth and development of the Sac Prairie country. Other works included mystery novels, short story and poetry collections, a book on fiction writing, and many notable weird and science fiction anthologies. About 150 of his supernatural stories (many under pseudonyms) appeared in the late *Weird Tales*, including a number with Mark Schorer as co-author.

An ardent follower of H. P. Lovecraft, he was unable to persuade any existing publisher to bring out an omnibus volume of Lovecraft's works, so in December 1939 he and Donald Wandrei formed Arkham House for that purpose. The result, *The Outsider and Others*, is now one of the most treasured items among fantasy collectors. Later Wandrei withdrew from the venture because of war service. Derleth then produced many titles until the early 1950's, when he slowed down to one or two titles per year. The press still continues with its books eagerly awaited by enthusiasts of the weird genre. Derleth was also Director of other imprints: Mycroft & Moran, and Stanton & Lee, specializing in detective and general fiction, respectively. Beginning with Winter 1948 he edited and published the magazine *Arkham Sampler*, featuring material slanted to enthusiasts of the weird. However, there was not enough support for it and it ceased with the eighth issue, Autumn 1949. The chap-book *Arkham House: The First 20 Years* gives full details of every Arkham book for this period. Followers of H. P. Lovecraft owe Derleth a great debt for the number of this author's works he has produced in hard covers; he also completed the novel *The Lurker at the Threshold* from fragments left by Lovecraft, as well as a number of short stories collected as *The Survivor and Others*. His own appreciation is *H.P.L.: A Memoir*.

In his own right Derleth was noted in the detective field for his series set around that master of deduction, Mr. Solar Pons. In the poetry field, he was editor of *Hawk and Whippoorwill* (two issues per year), which began in Spring 1960. A full bibliographic coverage of his books is *100 Books by August Derleth* (Arkham, 1962).

Series

Harrigan, Tex. "McIlvaine's Star" (*If*, July 1952); "A Corner for Lucia" (*WT*, May 1953); "Invasion From the Microcosm" (*Orbit*, No. 1, 1953); "A Traveller in Time" (*Orbit*, No. 2, 1954); "The Ungrateful House" (*Orbit*, July/Aug 1954); "The Thinker and the Thought" (*Orbit*, Sep/Oct 1954); "The Penfield Misadventure" (*Orbit*, Nov/Dec 1954); "The Martian Artifact" (*Saturn*, July 1957). Mooted to appear as *Harrigan's File*.

Pons, Solar. Books, published by Mycroft & Moran [not covered in *Fiction*]: *In Re: Sherlock Holmes* (1945); *The Memoirs of Solar Pons* (1951); *Three Problems of Solar Pons* (1952); *The Return of Solar Pons* (1958); *The Reminiscences of Solar Pons* (1961). Short stories, with M. Reynolds as co-author: "The Adventure of the Snitch in Time" (*F&SF*, June 1953); "The Adventure of the Ball of Nostradamus" (*F&SF*, June 1955). Both appeared in *The Science-Fictional Sherlock Holmes* [Council of Four], 1960, 1968.

Trail of Cthulhu. All in *WT*: "The Trail of Cthulhu" (Mar 1944); "The Watcher From the Sky" (July 1945); "The Testament of Claiborne Boyd" (Mar 1949); "The Keeper of the Key" (May 1951); "The Black Island" (Jan 1952). Compiled as *The Trail of Cthulhu*.

Fiction

Beast in Holger's Woods, The (Crowell, New York, 1968, 194 pp., illus.–Susan Bennett, $3.95)

Juvenile fantasy.

Colonel Markesan and Less Pleasant People [with M. Schorer] [C] (Arkham, Sauk City, Wis., 1966, 285 pp., $5.00, jacket–F. Utpatel)

17 stories, written mostly in 1931 (some adapted for TV): "Spawn of the Maelstrom"; "The Pacer"; "The Lair of the Star-Spawn" (*Mag. Horror*, Win 1966/67); "Colonel Markesan"; "The Return of Andrew Bentley"; "Eyes of the Serpent"; "In the Left Wing"; "The Carven Image"; "The Woman at Loon Point"; "Death Holds the Post"; "Laughter in the Night"; "The Vengeance of Ai"; "Red Hands"; "They Shall Rise"; "The Horror From the Depths"; "The Occupant of the Crypt"; "The House in the Magnolia."

Lonesome Places [C] (Arkham, Sauk City, Wis., 1962, 198 pp., $3.50, jacket–C. J. Laughlin [photo] & C. Gore)

18 stories: "The Lonesome Place"; "Pikeman"; "Kingsridge 214"; "The Ebony Stick"; " 'Sexton, Sexton, on the Wall' "; "The Closing Door"; "A Room in a House"; "Potts' Triumph"; "Twilight Play"; "The Disc Recorder"; "Hector"; " 'Who Shall I Say Is Calling?' "; "The Extra Child" ("The Fifth Child"); "The Place in the Woods"; "Hallowe'en for Mr. Faulkner"; "House–With Ghost"; "The Slayers and the Slain"; "The Dark Boy."

Lurker at the Threshold, The See LOVECRAFT, H. P.

Mask of Cthulhu, The [C] (Arkham, 1958, 201 pp., $3.50, jacket–R. Taylor; 2,051 copies) (Consul: HS1036, 1961, 175 pp., pa 2/6)

Weird, 6 stories in the manner of Lovecraft (5 from *WT*), and introduction: "The Return of Hastur"; "The Whippoorwills in the Hills"; "Something in Wood"; "The Sandwin Compact"; "The House in the Valley"; "The Seal of R'lyeh".

Mr. George and Other Odd Persons [C] ([by Stephen Grendon], Arkham, Sauk City, Wis., 1963, 239 pp., $4.00) (Belmont: L92-594, 1964, 176 pp., pa 50¢) (*When Graveyards Yawn*, Tandem: T30, 1965, 176 pp., pa 3/6)

17 stories, all originally published under the Stephen Grendon byline, most from *WT*, and Introduction by A. Derleth: "Mr. George"; "Parrington's Pool"; "A Gentleman From Prague"; "The Man on B-17"; "Blessed Are the Meek"; "Mara"; "The Blue Spectacles"; "Alannah"; "Dead Man's Shoes"; "The Tsantsa in the Parlor"; "Balu"; "The Extra Passenger"; "The Wind in the Lilacs"; "Miss Esperson"; "The Night Train to Lost Valley"; "Bishop's Gambit"; "Mrs. Manifold."

Not Long for This World [C] (Arkham, 1948, x+221 pp., $3.00, jacket–R. Clyne; 2,067 copies) (Ballantine: 542, 1961, 159 pp., pa 35¢ [22 stories marked †])

Weird, 33 stories with Foreword: "The Shadow on the Sky"†; "Birkett's Twelfth Corpse"†; "The White Moth"†; "Nellie Foster"†; "Wild Grapes"†; "Feigman's Beard"†; "The Drifting Snow"†; "The Return of Sarah Purcell"†; "Logoda's Heads"†; "The Second Print"†; "Mrs. Elting Does Her Part"†; "A Little Knowledge"; "Mrs. Bentley's Daughter"†; "Those Who Seek"†; "Mr. Berbeck Had a Dream"†; "The Tenant"; "The Lilac Bush"†; " 'Just a Song at Twilight' "; "A Matter of Sight"†. *Chronicles of the City States*: "Lesandro's Familiar"; "Prince Borgia's Mass"; "The Bridge of Sighs"; "A Cloak for Messer Lando"; "A Dinner at Imola." "Mrs. Lannisfree"†; "After You, Mr. Henderson"†; "Baynter's Imp"; "The Lost Day"†; "A Collector of Stones"†; "The God-Box"† (mistitled "The Gold-Box" in the pa.); "Saunder's Little Friend"†; "He Shall Come."

Someone in the Dark [C] (Arkham, 1941, 335 pp., $2.00, jacket–F. Utpatel; 1,115 copies)

Weird, 16 stories with introduction "When the Night and the House Are Still": *Not Long for This World*: "Glory Hand"; "Compliments of Spectro"; "A Gift for Uncle Herman"; "McGovern's Obsession"; "Three Gentlemen in Black"; "Muggridge's Aunt"; "Bramwell's Guardian"; "Joliper's Gift"; "Altimer's Amulet." *A House With Somebody in It*: "The Shuttered House"; "The Sheraton Mirror"; "The Wind From the River"; "The Telephone in the Library"; "The Paneled Room." *Visitors From Down Under*: "The Return of Hastur"; "The Sandwin Compact."

Something Near [C] (Arkham, 1945, 274 pp., $3.00, jacket–R. Clyne; 2,054 copies) (*Cuento del Mas Allá* [Spanish (Argentine)], Acmé, 1951)

Weird, 21 stories: "A Thin Gentleman With Gloves"; "Mr. Ames' Devil"; "A Wig for Miss Devore"; "Mrs. Corter Makes Up Her Mind"; "Pacific 421"; "Headlines for Tod Shayne"; "No Light for Uncle Henry"; "Lansing's Luxury"; "Carousel"; "Lady Macbeth of Pimley Square"; "Here, Daemos!"; "McElwin's Glass"; "An Elegy for Mr. Danielson"; "The Satin Mask"; "Motive"; "The Metronome"; "The Inverness Cape"; "The Thing That Walked on the Wind"; "Ithaqua"; "Beyond the Threshold"; "The Dweller in Darkness."

Survivor and Others, The [C] See LOVECRAFT, H. P.

Trail of Cthulhu, The [C] (Arkham, 1962, 284 pp., $4.00)

The 5 stories of the title series, with first retitled "The House on Curwen Street" and concluding with "A Note on the Cthulhu Mythos."

When Graveyards Yawn [pa] See *Mr. George and Other Odd Persons*

Anthologies

Beachheads in Space (Pellegrini & Cudahy, New York, 1952, xii+320 pp., $3.95) (Weidenfeld Nicolson, London, 1954, 224 pp., 9/6 [7 stories marked *]) (Berkley: G-77, 1957, 190 pp., pa 35¢ [7 stories marked p]) (FSB: 1073, 1964, 219 pp., pa 3/6 [7 stories marked p1]) (*From Other Worlds*, FSB: 1107, 1964, 184 pp., pa 3/6 [6 stories marked p2])

Sf, 14 stories and introduction: *Prologue*: "The Star"p1, D. H. Keller. *Exploration*: "Man From Outside"p2, J. Williamson;

"Beachhead" ("You'll Never Go Home Again!")*,p1, C. D. Simak; "The Years Draw Nigh"*,p,p1, Lester del Rey; "Metamorphosite"*,p,p1, E. F. Russell; "The Ordeal of Professor Klein" p1, L. S. de Camp; "Repetition" p,p1, A. E. van Vogt. *Invasion:* "Breeds There a Man"*,p,p2, I. Asimov; "Meteor"p2, J. B. Harris; "And the Walls Came Tumbling Down"*,p,p2, John Wyndham; "The Blinding Shadows"*,p, Donald Wandrei; "The Metamorphosis of Earth"*,p2, C. A. Smith; "The Ambassadors From Venus"p2, K. F. Crossen. *Epilogue:* "To People a New World"p,p1, N. Bond.

Beyond Time and Space (Pellegrini Cudahy, 1950, 704 pp., $4.50) (Berkley: G-104, 1958, 174 pp., pa [8 stories marked †])

Sf, 32 stories, subtitled "A Compendium of SF Through the Ages" (pa—stories of more contemporary vintage): *Introduction:* "Atlantis," Plato; "A True History," Lucian. *The Social Scientists:* "Utopia," Sir T. More; "The Phalanstery of Theleme," F. Rabelais; "The City of the Sun," G. D. Campanella; "The Man in the Moone," F. Godwin; "Laputa," J. Swift; "Somnium," J. Kepler; "The New Atlantis," F. Bacon. "The Three Men of Potu," L. Holberg; "The Thousand-and-Second Tale of Scheherazade," E. A. Poe; "Dr. Ox's Experiment," J. Verne; "Pausodyne," G. Allen; "A Tale of Negative Gravity," F. R. Stockton; "The Blindman's World," E. Bellamy; "The Battle of the Monsters," M. Robertson; "The New Accelerator," H. G. Wells; "The Noise in the Night," W. H. Hodgson; "Space," J. Buchan; "When the Green Star Waned," N. Dyalhis; "The Revolt of the Pedestrians," D. H. Keller; "The Flying Men"†, O. Stapledon; "A Voyage to Sfanomoë"†, C. A. Smith; "Colossus"†, D. Wandrei; "The Lotus Eaters," S. G. Weinbaum; "Fessenden's World"†, E. Hamilton; "The Seesaw"†, A. E. van Vogt; "Wingless Victory," H. F. Heard; "When the Bough Breaks," L. Padgett; "Wanted—An Enemy," F. Leiber; "Humpty Dumpty Had a Great Fall"†, F. B. Long; "Minority Report"†, T. Sturgeon; "The Long Watch"†, R. Heinlein; "The Exiles," R. Bradbury.

Dark Mind, Dark Heart (Arkham, 1962, 249 pp., $4.00) (Mayflower: 1655, 1963, 222 pp., pa 3/6; 1966, pa 5/-)

Subtitled "New Horror Stories"; 17 items with compiler's introduction: "Under the Horns," R. Bloch; "Come Back, Uncle Ben," J. P. Brennan; "The Church in High Street," J. Ramsey Campbell; "Hargrave's Fore-Edge Book," Mary Eliz. Counselman; "Miss Esperson," Stephen Grendon; "The Habitants of Middle Islet," W. H. Hodgson; "The Grey God Passes," R. E. Howard; "The Aquarium," C. Jacobi; "The Man Who Wanted to Be in the Movies," John Jakes; "In Memoriam," D. H. Keller; "Witches' Hollow," H. P. Lovecraft; "The Ideal Type," Frank Mace; "The Firing Chamber," John Metcalfe; "The Green Vase," Dennis Roidt; "Xelucha," M. P. Shiel; "The Animals in the Case," H. R. Wakefield; "Caer Sidhi," George Wetzel.

Dark of the Moon: Poems of Fantasy and the Macabre (Arkham, 1947, xvi+418 pp., $3.00; 2,634 copies)

A compilation containing such verse as: "Sonnets of the Midnight Hours," D. Wandrei; "Psychopompos," H. P. Lovecraft; "The Hashish-Eater," C. A. Smith; "A Dracula in the Hills," "The Paper in the Gate-Legged Table," Amy Lowell; "The Haunted House," T. Hood; "The Goblin Market," Christina Rossetti; "The City of the Dreadful Night," J. Thomson; "Solomon Kane's Homecoming," R. E. Howard. Other writers include R. Burns, Wm. Blake, S. Coleridge, R. H. Barham, E. A. Poe, C. Kingsley, D. G. Rossetti, J. W. Riley, W. de la Mare, R. Frost, V. Starrett, C. Rosenberger, F. B. Long, A. Derleth, Leah B. Drake, D. Quick, D. Rimel.

Far Boundaries (Pellegrini Cudahy, 1951, x+292 pp., $2.95) (McLeod, Toronto, $3.95) (Consul: 1443, 1965, 233 pp., pa 3/6) (Sphere: 28924, 1967, 219 pp., pa 3/6)

Sf, 20 stories [Consul ed has no table of contents; Sphere ed omits 3rd story]: *I. Primitives:* "From a Private Mad-House," H. Repton; "Missing One's Coach: An Anachronism," Anon.; "Tale of a Chemist," Anon.; "The Last American," J. A. Mitchell. *II. Mid-Period Pieces:* "Infinity Zero," D. Wandrei; "Frankenstein Unlimited," H. A. Highstone; "Open, Sesame!" S. Grendon; "Tepondicon," C. Jacobi; "The Fear Planet," R. Bloch. *III. The Contemporary Scene:* "De Profundis," M. Leinster; "Invasion," F. B. Long; "Dear Pen Pal," A. E. van Vogt; "Time to Rest," J. B. Har-

ris; "An Ounce of Prevention," P. Carter; "The Song of the Pewee," Stephen Grendon; "And Lo! The Bird," N. S. Bond; Vignettes of Tomorrow—"The One Who Waits" and "Holiday," R. Bradbury; "The Man Who Rode the Saucer," K. Holmes; "Later Than You Think," F. Leiber.

Fire and Sleet and Candlelight (Arkham, 1961, 236 pp., $4.00)

Some 256 poems by such familiar writers as R. Bloch, J. P. Brennan, Lin Carter, S. A. Coblentz, Leah B. Drake, R. E. Howard, F. B. Long, Lilith Lorraine, Dorothy Quick, C. A. Smith, V. Starrett, and D. Wandrei, as well as 77 other authors.

From Other Worlds See *Beachheads in Space*
New Worlds for Old See *Worlds of Tomorrow*
Night Side, The (Rinehart, New York, 1946, viii+372 pp., illus.— L. B. Coye, $3.50) (FSB: 1657, 1966, 270 pp., pa 5/- [19 stories marked †])

Weird, 23 stories and compiler's foreword: "The Colour out of Space"†, H. P. Lovecraft; "The First Sheaf"†, H. R. Wakefield; "The Moon-Caller"†, MacKinlay Kantor; "The Extra Passenger"†, S. Grendon; "Bethmoora," Lord Dunsany; "The Smoking Leg"†, J. Metcalfe; "The Exalted Omega," Arthur Machen; "Cheese"†, A. E. Coppard; "Mr. Minchin's Midsummer"†, Margery Lawrence; "Mimsy Were the Borogoves"†, H. Kuttner; "The Eerie Mr. Murphy"†, H. Wandrei; "The Smiling People"†, R. Bradbury; "The Face in the Mirror"†, Denys V. Baker; "Professor Pfaff's Last Recital"†, Alan Nelson; "Seaton's Aunt," W. de la Mare; "The Mask of Medusa"†, N. Bond; "One Head Well Done"†, John D. Swain; "Joshua"†, R. Creighton-Buck; "Enoch"†, R. Bloch; "Sammy Calls a Noobus"†, Henry A. Norton; "The Night Wire"†, H. F. Arnold; "The Three Marked Pennies"†, Mary Eliz. Counselman; "Nightmare," Marjorie Bowen.

Night's Yawning Peal (Arkham & Pellegrini Cudahy, 1952, 288 pp., $3.00) (Consul: 1368, 1965, 160 pp., pa 3/6)

Weird, 15 stories and compiler's foreword [Consul pa omits last story]: "Mr. George," S. Grendon; "The Loved Dead," C. M. Eddy Jr.; "The Sign," Lord Dunsany; "The La Prello Paper," C. Jacobi; "The Gorge of the Churels," H. R. Wakefield; "Dhoh," M. W. Wellman; "The Churchyard Yew," J. S. Le Fanu; "Technical Slip," J. Beynon Harris; "The Man Who Collected Poe," R. Bloch; "Hector," Michael West; "Roman Remains," A. Blackwood; "A Damsel With a Dulcimer," M. Ferguson; "The Suppressed Edition," Richard Curle; "The Lonesome Place," A. Derleth; "The Case of Charles Dexter Ward," H. P. Lovecraft.

Other Side of the Moon, The (Pellegrini Cudahy, 1949, 416 pp., $3.75) (Grayson, London, 1956, 238 pp., 10/6 [11 stories marked *]) (McLeod, Toronto, $5.00) (Berkley: G-249, 1959, 172 pp., 35¢ [10 stories marked p]) (Panther: 1541, 1963, 144 pp., pa 2/6 [10 stories marked p1]) (Mayflower: 6740, 1966, 159 pp., pa 3/6 [10 stories marked p2])

Sf, 20 stories [Panther and Mayflower eds are complementary]: "The Appearance of Man"*,p1 (play), J. D. Beresford; "The Star"p1, H. G. Wells; "The Thing on Outer Shoal"p,p2, P. S. Miller; "The Strange Drug of Dr. Caber"p2, Lord Dunsany; "The World of Wulkins"p2, F. B. Long; "The City of the Singing Flame"*,p2, C. A. Smith; "Beyond the Wall of Sleep"*,p1, H. P. Lovecraft; "The Devil of East Lupton"*,p,p1, M. Leinster; "Conqueror's Isle"p,p2, N. S. Bond; "Something From Above"*,p,p2, D. Wandrei; "Pillar of Fire"*,p1, R. Bradbury; "The Monster"p1, G. Kersh; "Symbiosis"*,p,p2, W. F. Jenkins; "The Cure"p,p1, L. Padgett; "Vault of the Beast"p1, A. E. van Vogt; "The Earth Men"p2, R. Bradbury; "Original Sin"*,p,p2, S. P. Wright; "Spiro"*,p,p1, E. F. Russell; "Memorial"*,p,p1, T. Sturgeon; "Resurrection"*,p,p2, A. E. van Vogt.

Outer Reaches, The (Pellegrini Cudahy, 1951, 342 pp., $3.95) (Berkley: G-116, 1958, 174 pp., pa 35¢ [10 stories marked †]) (Consul: 1267, 1963, 173 pp., pa 2/6 [first 8 stories]; *The Time of Infinity*, Consul: 1268, 1963, 205 pp., pa 2/6 [remaining 9 stories])

Sf, 17 stories (favorite s-f tales chosen by their authors) and compiler's foreword: "Interloper," P. Anderson; "Death Sentence"†, I. Asimov; "This Is the Land"†, N. S. Bond; "Ylla"†, R. Bradbury; "The Green Cat"†, C. Cartmill; "Git Along!" L. S. de Camp; "Service First," D. H. Keller; "Shock," H. Kuttner; "The

Ship Sails at Midnight," F. Leiber; "The Power," M. Leinster; "The Critters"†, F. B. Long; "Pardon My Mistake"†, F. Pratt; "Goodnight, Mr. James"†, C. D. Simak; "The Plutonian Drug"†, C. A. Smith; "Farewell to Eden"†, T. Sturgeon; "Co-Operate—or Else!"†, A. E. van Vogt; "Finality Unlimited," D. Wandrei.

Over the Edge (Arkham, Sauk City, Wis., 1964, 297 pp., $5.00, jacket–F. Utpatel) (Gollancz, London, 1967, 297 pp., 28/-)

Weird, 18 stories and compiler's introduction: "The Crew of the Lansing," Wm. H. Hodgson; "The Last Meeting of Two Old Friends," H. R. Wakefield; "The Shadow in the Attic," H. P. Lovecraft; "The Renegade," J. Metcalfe; "Told in the Desert," C. A. Smith; "When the Rains Came," F. B. Long; "The Blue Flame of Vengeance" [a last Solomon Kane story], R. E. Howard; "Crabgrass," Jesse Stuart; "Kincaid's Car," C. Jacobi; "The Patchwork Quilt," A. Derleth; "The Old Lady's Room," J. Vernon Shea; "The North Knoll," J. P. Brennan; "The Huaco of Señor Perez," Mary E. Counselman; "Mr. Alucard," David A. Johnstone; "Casting the Stone," John Pocik; "Aneanoshian," Michael Bailey; "The Stone on the Island," J. Ramsey Campbell.

Portals of Tomorrow (Rinehart, 1954, 371 pp., $3.75) (Clarke Irwin, Toronto, $4.25) (D'day SF B.C., 1954, 214 pp., $1.15) (Cassell, London, 1956, 214 pp., 12/6)

Sf, 16 stories and compiler's introduction; subtitled "The Best of Science-Fiction and Fantasy"; also appendix [not in B.C. and Cassell eds.] listing best collections and fantastic stories of 1953: "The Hypnoglyph," J. Anthony; "Testament of Andros," J. Blish; "The Playground," R. Bradbury; "Gratitude Guaranteed," R. G. Bretnor & K. Neville; "Rustle of Wings," F. Brown; "The Other Tiger," A. C. Clarke; "Civilized," M. Clifton & A. Apostolides; "Stickeney and the Critic," Mildred Clingerman; "The Word," M. Clingerman; "Hermit on Bikini," John Langdon; "Jezebel," M. Leinster; "D.P. From Tomorrow," M. Reynolds; "The Altruists," I. Seabright; "Potential," R. Sheckley; "Eye for Iniquity," T. L. Sherred; "Kindergarten," C. D. Simak.

Sleep No More (Rinehart, 1944, 374 pp., $2.50) (Armed: r-33, 1944, 384 pp., pa np) (Panther: 1770, 1964, 189 pp., pa 3/6; 1965, pa 3/6 [12 stories marked p]) (*Stories From Sleep No More*, Bantam: H3425, 1967, 148 pp., pa 60¢ [9 stories marked p1])

Weird, 20 stories: "Count Magnus"p,p1, M. R. James; "Cassius"p,p1, H. S. Whitehead; "The Occupant of the Room"p,p1, A. Blackwood; "The Return of the Sorcerer"p,p1, C. A. Smith; "Johnson Looked Back"p1, T. Burke; "The Hand of the O'Mecca"p,p1, H. Wandrei; "He Cometh and He Passeth By"p,p1, H. R. Wakefield; "Thus I Refute Beelzy"p1, J. Collier; "The Mannikin"p,p1, R. Bloch; "Two Black Bottles," W. B. Talman; "The House of Sounds"p, M. P. Shiel; "The Cane," C. Jacobi; "The Horror in the Burying Ground"p, Hazel Heald; "The Kennel," M. Level; "The Yellow Sign"p, R. Chambers; "The Black Stone"p, R. E. Howard; "Midnight Express," A. Noyes; "A Gentleman From Prague," S. Grendon; "The Black Druid"p, F. B. Long; "The Rats in the Walls," H. P. Lovecraft.

Sleeping and the Dead, The (Pellegrini Cudahy, 1947, 518 pp., $3.75) (FSB: 943, 1963, 254 pp., pa 3/6 [15 stories marked †]; and *The Unquiet Grave*, FSB: 982, 1964, 254 pp., pa 3/6 [remaining 15 stories, unmarked])

Weird, 30 stories and compiler's introduction: "A View From a Hill"†, M. R. James; "Glory Hand"†, A. Derleth; "The Lady's Maid's Bell"†, Edith Wharton; "The Shadows," H. S. Whitehead; "Out of the Eons"†, Hazel Heald; "The Jar"†, R. Bradbury; "The Bully of Chapelizod"†, J. S. Le Fanu; "Over the River"†, P. S. Miller; "Carnaby's Fish," C. Jacobi; "The Painted Mirror," D. Wandrei; "The Double Shadow," C. A. Smith; "The Ocean Leech"†, F. B. Long; "Amina"†, Edward L. White; "Farewell Performance"†, H. R. Wakefield; "One Way to Mars," R. Bloch; "Out of the Picture," A. Machen; "The Canal," E. Worrell; "The Postman of Otford"†, Lord Dunsany; "Death, Dumb, and Blind," C. M. Eddy Jr.; "Spider-Bite," R. S. Carr; "Brenner's Boy," J. Metcalfe; "Mr. Lupescu," A. Boucher; "Masquerade"†, H. Kuttner; "Seventh Sister," Mary E. Counselman; "In Amundsen's Tent," J. M. Leahy; "Man in a Hurry," Alan Nelson; "The Last Pin," H. Wandrei; "The Doll"†, A. Blackwood; "The Tool"†, W. F. Harvey;

"The Dreams in the Witchhouse"†, H. P. Lovecraft.

Stories From Sleep No More See *Sleep No More*

Strange Ports of Call (Pellegrini Cudahy, 1948, 393 pp., $3.75) (Berkley: G-131, 1958, 173 pp., pa 35¢ [10 stories marked †])

Sf, 20 stories selected for their literary quality, and compiler's introduction: "The Cunning of the Beast"†, N. S. Bond; "The Worm," D. H. Keller; "The Crystal Bullet"†, D. Wandrei; "The Thing From Outside," G. A. England; "At the Mountains of Madness," H. P. Lovecraft; "Mars on the Ether," Lord Dunsany; "The God-Box," H. Wandrei; "Mr. Bauer and the Atoms"†, F. Leiber; "The Crystal Egg," H. G. Wells; "John Jones' Dollar," H. S. Keeler; "Call Him Demon"†, H. Kuttner; "Master of the Asteroid"†, C. A. Smith; "A Guest in the House"†, F. B. Long; "The Lost Street," C. Jacobi & C. D. Simak; "Forgotten"†, P. S. Miller; "Far Centaurus"†, A. E. van Vogt; "The Green Hills of Earth," R. A. Heinlein; "Thunder and Roses," T. Sturgeon; "Blunder"†, P. Wylie; "The Million Year Picnic"†, R. Bradbury.

Time of Infinity, The [pa] See *Outer Reaches, The*

Time to Come (Farrar Strauss & Young, New York, 1954, 311 pp., $3.50) (Berkley: G-189, 1958, 152 pp., pa 35¢ [10 stories marked †])

Sf and fantasy, 12 stories (all new) and compiler's foreword: "Butch"†, P. Anderson; "The Pause"†, I. Asimov; "Keeper of the Dream"†, C. Beaumont; "No Morning After"†, A. C. Clarke; "The Blight," A. J. Cox; "Hole in the Sky"†, I. Cox; "Jon's World"†, P. K. Dick; "The White Pinnacle"†, C. Jacobi; "Winner Take All"†, R. Rocklynne; "Paradise II"†, R. Sheckley; "Phoenix"†, C. A. Smith; "Daxbr Baxbr," Evelyn Smith.

Travellers by Night (Arkham, 1967, 261 pp., $4.00)

14 new macabre stories: "The Cicerones," Robert Aickman; "Episode on Cain Street," J. P. Brennan; "The Cellars," J. Ramsey Campbell; "The Man Who Rode the Trains," Paul A. Carter; "A Handful of Silver," Mary E. Counselman; "Denkirk," David Drake; "The Wild Man of the Sea," W. H. Hodgson; "The Unpleasantness at Carver House," C. Jacobi; "The Terror of Anerly House School," Margery Lawrence; "The Horror From the Middle Span," H. P. Lovecraft; "Not There," J. Metcalfe; "Family Tree," Frank D. Thayer; "Death of a Bumblebee," H. R. Wakefield; "The Crater," Donald Wandrei.

Unquiet Grave, The [pa] See *Sleeping and the Dead, The*

When Evil Wakes (Souvenir, London, 1963, 288 pp., 21/-) (Ryerson, Toronto, $4.50) (Corgi: GN7107, 1965, 223 pp., pa 3/6)

Weird, 16 stories with compiler's "A Cautionary Word," and ending with notes: "The Eye and the Finger," D. Wandrei; "The Feasting Dead," J. Metcalfe; "Death Waters," F. B. Long; "An Invitation to the Hunt," George Hitchcock; "The Tsanta in the Parlour," S. Grendon; "Moonlight–Starlight," Virginia Layefsky; "The Kite," C. Jacobi; "Sweets to the Sweet," R. Bloch; "A Thin Gentlemen With Gloves," Simon West; "The Horror at Red Hook," H. P. Lovecraft; "The Triumph of Death," H. R. Wakefield; "The Lips," H. S. Whitehead; "A Piece of Linoleum," D. H. Keller; "The Seed From the Sepulchre," C. A. Smith; "Canavan's Back Yard," J. P. Brennan; "The Shuttered Room," H. P. Lovecraft & A. Derleth.

Who Knocks? (Rinehart, 1946, ix+391 pp., $2.50, jacket–Audrey Johnson, illus.–L. B. Coye) (Panther: 1769, 1964, 191 pp., pa 3/6 [12 stories marked †])

20 Masterpieces of the Spectral, with compiler's foreword: "The Shadows on the Wall"†, Mary E. W. Freeman; "Running Wolf," A. Blackwood; "Old Martin"†, A. E. Coppard; "Alannah," S. Grendon; "The Shunned House," H. P. Lovecraft; "The Lake"†, R. Bradbury; "The Seventeenth Hole at Duncaster"†, H. R. Wakefield; "The Ankardyne Pew," W. F. Harvey; "It"†, T. Sturgeon; "The Phantom Farmhouse"†, S. Quinn; "Squire Toby's Will"†, J. S. Le Fanu; "Negotium Perambulans"†, E. F. Benson; "The Intercessor"†, May Sinclair; "The Dear Departed," Alice-Mary Schnirring; "The House of the Nightmare"†, E. L. White; "A Reversion to Type," Edgar L. Hampton; "The Follower"†, Lady C. Asquith; "The Ravel 'Pavane' "†, H. S. Whitehead; "The Ghosts of Steamboat Coulee," A. J. Burks; "The Woman at Seven Brothers," W. D. Steele.

Worlds of Tomorrow (Pellegrini Cudahy, 1953, 351 pp., $3.95)

(Weidenfeld Nicolson, London, 1955, 224 pp., 9/6 [15 stories marked *]) (Berkley: G-163, 1958, 172 pp., pa 35¢ [10 stories marked p]) (FSB: 794, 1963, 160 pp., pa 2/6 [10 stories marked p1]; and *New Worlds for Old*, FSB: 842, 1963, 126 pp., pa 2/6 [remaining 9 stories, marked p2])

Sf, 19 stories and compiler's introduction: "The Tinkler"p1, P. Anderson; "The Smile"*,p2, R. Bradbury; "The Fires Within"*,p,p2, Arthur C. Clarke; "Superiority"*,p1, A. C. Clarke; "McIlvaine's Star"*,p,p1, August Derleth; "Brothers Beyond the Void"*,p,p1, P. W. Fairman; "Beautiful, Beautiful, Beautiful!"p1, Stuart Friedman; "The Dead Planet"*,p,p1, E. Hamilton; "Like a Bird, Like a Fish"*,p1, H. B. Hickey; "The Gentleman Is an EPWA"p,p2, C. Jacobi; "The Enchanted Forest"*,p,p2, F. Leiber; "The Great Cold"*,p,p2, F. B. Long; "From Beyond"*,p2, H. P. Lovecraft; "Line to Tomorrow"*,p2, L. Padgett; "The Business, as Usual"p,p2, M. Reynolds; "The Gardener"*,p1, Marg. St. Clair; "The Martian and the Moron"*,p,p2, T. Sturgeon; "Null-P"*,p,p1, Wm. Tenn; "Strange Harvest"*,p1, D. Wandrei.

Nonfiction

Arkham House: The First 20 Years 1939–1959 (Arkham, 1959, 54 pp., $1.00)

A history and full details on every book published by this firm.

H.P.L.: A Memoir (Argus, New York, 1945, 122 pp., $2.50)

Title essay on H. P. Lovecraft, by A. Derleth. Also articles: "The Cats of Ulthar"; "The Festival"; "The Gardens of Yin"; "To Pan"; "Rudis Indigestague Moles"; "Does Vulcan Exist?"; Bibliography.

Some Notes on H. P. Lovecraft See LOVECRAFT, H. P. L. (nonfiction)

DERN, DOROTHY L.
Fiction

Doctor's Secret, The (Pageant, New York, 1954, 116 pp., $2.50)

A doctor discovers a means to recreate life.

DESMOND, HUGH
Fiction

Fear Rides the Air (Wright Brown, London, 1953, 160 pp., 6/6)

A group has fearful experiences, and escapes beyond Earth's attraction.

Terrible Awakening, The (Wright Brown, 1949, 220 pp., 7/6)

Humans flee to another planet, and find they are not the first there.

D'ESPERANCE, E.
Fiction

Northern Lights and Other Psychic Stories [C] (G. Redway [Office of 'Light'], London, 1901, 288 pp.)

10 stories and introduction (14 pp.): "Northern Lights"; "Benno, the Vagabond"; "The Warning Spirit"; "Hans Hauptmann's Warning"; "Pepi"; "The Mill Stream"; "Harald Arnhult"; "Together"; "Strange Excursions"; "The Light of Pentraginny."

DETZER, DIANE (13 May 1930–) Diane Detzer de Reyna.
Fiction

Alien World [as Adam Lukens] (Avalon, New York, 1963, 192 pp., $2.95)

Drama between human and humanoid races on the planet "Nightmare Hollow."

Conquest of Life [as Adam Lukens] (Avalon, 1960, 221 pp., $2.95) (*L'uomo rigenerato* [Italian], *Cosmo*: 158, 1964)

A future Earth in which women outnumber men and "reclaimed" men are purchased.

Eevalu [as Adam Lukens] (Avalon, 1963, 192 pp., $2.95)

The winged people of the planet Eevalu and their culture come in conflict with an Earth colony.

Glass Cage, The [as Adam Lukens] (Avalon, 1962, 223 pp., $2.95) (*Gehasst, gehetzt, gefangen* [German], *UZ*: 360, 1963) (*La città de cristallo* [Italian], *Cosmo*: 152, 1964)

Unusual future crime story with the murder of a freak being.

Planet of Fear, The (Avalon, New York, 1968, 190 pp., $3.50)

Return of the Starships, The [as Jorge de Reyna] (Avalon, 1968, 192 pp., $3.50)

In a future Earth of crowded cities, a telepathic girl forecasts the return of the starships.

Sea People, The [as Adam Lukens] (Avalon, 1959, 221 pp., $2.95) (*Dipartimento scienze spaziali* [Italian], *Urania*: 246, 1960) (*Die Anderen* [German], *T*: 207, 1962)

Invalided space serviceman encounters problems of the sea people on the planet "Skywash."

Sons of the Wolf [as Adam Lukens] (Avalon, 1961, 224 pp., $2.95) (Consul: 1207, 1963, 158 pp., pa 3/6) (*Magier, Menschen, Wölfe* [German], *UZ*: 366, 1963) (*I figli del lupo* [Italian], *Cosmo*: 129, 1963)

Medieval werewolves reappear in 2346 and find trouble in a bizarre future.

World Within, The [as Adam Lukens] (Avalon, 1962, 222 pp., $2.95) (*Welt hinter Spiegeln* [German], *UZ*: 385, 1964)

Mystery in a galactic future—mirrors swallow up people.

DEVAULX, NOEL
Fiction

Tailor's Cake, The [trans.–B. Askwith] [C] (*L'Auberge Parpillon*, Gallimard, Paris, 1945) (Wingate, London, 1946, 107 pp., 7/6)

Fantasy stories.

DEXTER, WILLIAM (pseud) See PRITCHARD, W. T.

DICK, KAY (29 July 1915–) British free-lance writer, born in London. She has worked mostly for publishers and book-selling firms. "Kay Dick" was once thought to be a pseudonym of J. Scott, but is listed in *Contemporary Authors* as a real person.
Anthology

Uncertain Element, The (Jarrolds, London, 1950, 280 pp., 10/6)

An anthology of fantastic conceptions; 21 stories: "Out of the Deep," W. de la Mare; "One Sunny Afternoon," W. Sansom; "The Tallow Candle," J. Shearing; "Tyme Tryeth Troth," F. Baker; "Magicians in London," O. Blakeston; "Enoch Soames," M. Beerbohm; "The Empty Schoolroom," Pamela H. Johnson; "The Secret Commonwealth," J. Heath-Stubbs; "The Duchess and the Doll," Edith Pargeter; "The Shirt of Nessus," Ethel C. Mayne; "The Man Who Stole a Tiger," Olivia Manning; "The Threepenny Piece," J. Stephens; "Edinburgh 1827," Norah Lofts; "God Almighty's Nephew," J. E. Morpurgo; "Beckwith's Case," M. Hewlett; "Follies: Active, Passive and Various," J. Curling; "Nuts in May," A. Graves; "The Stratagem," A. Crowley; "The Poet, the Hangman and the Solicitor," D. Wright; "The Zenith," P. H. Newby; "The Jolly Corner," H. James. Bibliography of the Fantastic by Anne Renier-Cliff.

DICK, PHILIP K(ENDRED) (16 Dec 1928–) U.S. author. He was born in Chicago and now lives in Berkeley, Calif. He first appeared in the sf field in 1952 and has now written about 100 stories; since 1955 he has concentrated mainly on books, with a number appearing as Ace paperbacks. He is now considered to be one of the most important writers in the field, and each new novel is viewed with interest by thoughtful readers. His first hard-cover book appearance in the U.S. was *Time Out of Joint*, although his *Solar Lottery* had a hard-cover edition (retitled) in England soon after the Ace edition appeared. His short story "Foster, You're Dead" (*Star SF No. 3* [Pohl], 1954) was translated into Russian and published in *Ogonek*, one of the largest-circulation magazines in the Soviet Union. Dick won the 1963 Hugo novel award with *The Man in the High Castle*, while his *The Three Stigmata of Palmer Eldritch* caused considerable comment.
Fiction

Clans of the Alphane Moon [pa] (Ace: F-309, 1964, 192 pp., pa 40¢)

Adventure on the moon of the Alpha System.

Cosmic Puppets, The [pa] ("A Glass of Darkness," *Satellite*, Dec 1956) (Ace: D-249, 1957, 127 pp., pa 35¢; with *Sargasso of Space*) (*La città sostituita* [Italian], *Urania*: 280, 1962)

Galactic beings use the inhabitants of an American town as pawns in their fight.

Counter Clock World [pa] (Berkley: X1372, 1967, 160 pp., pa 60¢) (Sphere: 29564, 1968, 160 pp., pa 5/-)

A future projection of the present Black Power movement, set in a banal plot with reverse-time fantasy.

Crack in Space, The [pa] (Ace: F-377, 1966, 190 pp., pa 40¢)

Human deep-freezing and a pleasure satellite run by a two-headed mutant lead to fast action in an election campaign. Derived from "Cantata 140" (*F&SF*, short n, July 1964).

Do Androids Dream of Electric Sheep? (Doubleday, New York, 1968, 210 pp., $3.95)

A world of falling population, sublethal fallout dust, concealed androids, and mechanical pets.

Dr. Bloodmoney, or, How We Got Along After the Bomb [pa] (Ace: F-337, 1965, 222 pp., pa 40¢)

A vivid description of a way of life after the Bomb; well characterised.

Dr. Futurity [pa] ("Time Pawn," *TWS*, Sum 1954) expanded: (Ace: D-421, 1960, 138 pp., pa 35¢; with *Slavers of Space*) (*Il dottor futuro* [Italian], *GRF*: 30, 1963)

U.S. doctor of 2000 AD is shanghaied to the far future where he becomes involved in a time tangle.

Eye in the Sky [pa] (Ace: D-211, 1956, 255 pp., pa 35¢; H-39, 1968, pa 60¢) (*L'occhio nel cielo* [Italian], *Urania*: 201, 1959) ([Japanese], Hayakawa: 3012, 1959,)

People caught in the beam of a 'bevatron' undergo fantastic adventures resulting from their thoughts.

Game-Players of Titan, The [pa] (Ace: F-251, 1963, 191 pp., pa 40¢) (*Torneo mortal* [Spanish], Nebula: 106, 1965, pa)

A battle of wits between Earth's remaining humans and the beings of Titan.

Ganymede Takeover [with R. Nelson] [pa] (Ace: G-637, 1967, 157 pp., pa 50¢)

Aliens from Ganymede find Earth hard to hold.

Handful of Darkness, A [C] (Rich Cowan, London, 1955, 224 pp., 10/6) (*Eine Handvoll Dunkelheit* [German], *TS*: 76, 1963 [probably abridged]) (Panther: 2108, 1966, 186 pp., pa 3/6 [7th & 8th stories omitted])

Sf, 15 stories: "Colony"; "Impostor"; "Expendable"; "Planet for Transients"; "Prominent Author"; "The Builder"; "The Little Movement"; "The Preserving Machine"; "The Impossible Planet"; "The Indefatigable Frog"; "The Turning Wheel"; "Progeny"; "Upon the Dull Earth"; "The Cookie Lady"; "Exhibit Piece."

Man in the High Castle, The (Putnam, New York, 1962, 239 pp., $3.95) (D'day SF B.C., 1962) (Popular: SP250, 1964, 191 pp., pa 50¢; 60-2289, 1968, pa 60¢)

Winner of the 1963 Hugo Award for best novel. An "if" story: the U.S.A. was conquered by Japan and Germany in World War II; the effect on this world if the Allies won.

Man Who Japed, The [pa] (Ace: D-193, 1956, 160 pp., pa 35¢; with *The Space-Born*) (*Planetas morales* [Spanish], Cenit: 6, 1960, pa)

An extrapolated society reflecting our current advertising religiosity and lip service to moral standards.

Martian Time-Slip [pa] ("All We Marsmen," *Worlds of Tomorrow*, sr3, Aug 1963) —enlarged: (Ballantine: U2191, 1964, 220 pp., pa 50¢)

Mental disruption among human colonists in the Martian frontier society, with glimpses of native Martians.

Now Wait for Last Year (Doubleday, 1967, 214 pp., $3.95) (Macfadden: 60-352, 1968, 224 pp., pa 60¢)

An addictive hallucinogenic drug gives time travel, and complications arise.

Penultimate Truth, The (Belmont: 92-603, 1964, 174 pp., pa 50¢) (Cape, London, 1967, 254 pp., 25/-)

In a future war some people move underground, and are fed false news.

Simulacra, The [pa] (Ace: F-301, 1964, 192 pp., pa 40¢, cover & illus.–E. Emsh)

A complicated story with sub-plots that ultimately join; it includes a telekinetic piano player and the idea of giving super-

weapons to Hitler's Germany.

Solar Lottery [pa] (Ace: D-103, 1955, 188 pp., pa 35¢ [with *The Big Jump*]; D-340, 1959, pa 35¢; G-718, 1968, pa 50¢) (*World of Chance*, Rich Cowan, 1956, 160 pp., 9/6; SF B.C. [S.J.], 1957, 4/6; Panther: 785, 1959, 156 pp., pa 2/6) (*Griff nach der Sonne* [German], *AW*: 7, 1958; *TE*: 47, 1964) (*Loteria solar* [Spanish], Cenit: 4, 1960, pa) (*Loterie solaire* [French], Galaxie Bis: 7, 1968, pa)

Intrigue in our future when the quiz shows take over in politics.

Three Stigmata of Palmer Eldritch, The (Doubleday, 1965, 278 pp., $4.95) (D'day, Toronto, $5.95) (D'day SF B.C., 1965, $1.20) (Cape, 1966, 278 pp., 21/-) (Macfadden: 60-240, 1966, 191 pp., pa 60¢)

Some ideas from "The Days of Perky Pat" (*AS*, Dec 1963). The promotion of Chew-Z, which causes hallucinations and from which the user can create the world he wishes.

Time Out of Joint (Lippincott, Philadelphia, 1959, 221 pp., $3.50) (*NW*, sr3, Dec 1959) (SF B.C. [S.J.], 1961, 5/6) (*Zeit ohne Grenzen* [German], Zimmermann, 1962) (Belmont: 92-618, 1965, 175 pp., pa 50¢)

The hero finds himself in the centre of a colossal piece of play-acting, and tries to break out.

Unteleported Man, The [pa] (*Fan*, Dec 1964) (Ace: G-602, 1966, 100 pp., pa 50¢; with *The Mind Monsters*)

A man combats the intrigue of giant industrial combines by using a space-ship instead of electronic transit.

Variable Man, The [C] [pa] (Ace: D-261, 1956, 255 pp., pa 35¢) (*Guerra con Centauro* [Spanish], Cenit: 14, 1961 pa) (*Krieg der Automaten* [German], *T*: 322-323 [as one issue, 4 stories, omitting last], 1964)

Sf, 1 short novel and 4 novelettes: "The Variable Man" (*Space SF*, n, Sep 1953); "Second Variety"; "The Minority Report"; "Autofac"; "A World of Talent."

Vulcan's Hammer [pa] (*Future SF*, No. 29, 1956) (Ace: D-457, 1960, 139 pp., pa 35¢; with *The Skynappers*) (*Vulkans Hammer* [German], *T*: 395, 1965)

Computers give power over government in the future, and conflict arises.

World Jones Made, The [pa] (Ace: D-150, 1956, 192 pp., pa 35¢ [with *Agent of the Unknown*]; F-429, 1967, pa 40¢) (*Geheim projekt Venus* [German], *AW*: 8, 1958; *TE*: 73, 1965) (*El tiempo doblade* [Spanish], Cenit: 3, 1960, pa) (Sidgwick Jackson, London, 1968, 192 pp., 18/-)

A man can see a year into the future, and his effect on society is more than mild.

World of Chance See *Solar Lottery*

Zap Gun, The [pa] ("Operation Plowshare," *Worlds of Tomorrow*, sr2, Nov 1965) (Pyramid: R1569, 1967, 176 pp., pa 50¢)

An answer to today's armament race turns sour when Earth is found defenseless to aliens.

DICKENS, CHARLES (JOHN HUFFAM) (7 Feb 1812–9 June 1870) English literary figure noted both as writer and editor. Although his early life was one of "hard times," he became so honoured in his lifetime that he was buried in Westminster Abbey. He was one of the greatest novelists to be attracted by sensational murder themes and the drama of mystery—his *Bleak House*, *Martin Chuzzlewit* and *Oliver Twist* (with its brutal scenes of the underworld) rank among the finest mystery stories ever penned. In the weird field his notable short stories include "The Trial for Murder," "The Story of the Bagman's Uncle," and "No. 1 Branch Line: the Signalman." Many of these have been reprinted in old weird anthologies. Bleiler lists some books.

DICKHOFF, ROBERT ERNST
Nonfiction

Agharta (Humphries, Boston, 1951, 106 pp., $2.50)

Written as "truth" by the leader of the American Buddhist Society. Tells of the vast underground city "Agharta," a network of tunnels leading to Antarctica, etc., visits by beings from Mars and Venus, maps of Atlantis and Lemuria . . .

DICKINSON, PETER
Fiction
Weathermonger, The (Gollancz, London, 1968, 160 pp., 18/-)

Juvenile—a youth and his sister escape from a future England, which is under a strange spell, and find France normal; they return to combat the menace.

DICKINSON, WILLIAM CROFT (28 Aug 1897–1963) Scottish historian. He was born at Leicester, the son of a minister, and studied at U. of St. Andrews and U. of London. He was librarian at the London School of Economics 1933-44, then Professor of Scottish History at U. of Edinburgh from 1944. He was Trustee of the National Library of Scotland 1944-60.
Fiction
Dark Encounters [C] (Harvill Press, London, 1963, 192 pp., 18/-) (Collins, Toronto, $4.25)

Short story collection; no further information.

DICKSON, CARTER (pseud) See CARR, J. D.

DICKSON, GORDON R(UPERT) (1 Nov 1923–) U.S. science fiction author. He was born in Edmonton, Alberta, the son of a mining engineer; he came to the U.S.A. when 13. In 1939 he entered the U. of Minnesota. He served in World War II 1943-46, and upon his return finished his B.A. with a major in writing. He re-established the Minneapolis Fantasy Society and became a friend of Poul Anderson, with whom he has often collaborated. He has had over 100 stories in all magazines of the field since 1950. His "Home From the Shore" (*GSF*, n'te, Feb 1963) was reprinted in Merril's *Year's Best SF (8th)* (1963), and his "Soldier, Ask Not" won the 1965 Hugo for best short fiction and was later expanded into a novel.
Series
Dorsai. Warrior race. "Dorsai!" (*ASF*, sr3, May 1959; pa as *The Genetic General*); "Soldier, Ask Not" (*GSF*, Oct 1964, pa); "Warrior" (*ASF*, Dec 1965).
Hoenig, Robby. Juvenile books published by Holt: *Secret Under the Sea*; *Secret Under Antarctica*; *Secret Under the Caribbean*.
Hoka. See ANDERSON, P. (co-author)
Fiction
Alien From Arcturus [pa] (Ace: D-139, 1956, 150 pp., pa 35¢; with *Atom Curtain*) (*Fremde vom Arcturus* [German], *UTR*: 3, 1957; *T*: 341, 1964)

Earth controlled by galactic commerce seeks to break its isolation; delightful characterisation of the alien "Peep."
Alien Way, The [pa] (Bantam: F2941, 1965, 184 pp., pa 50¢)

Opening section is based on "The Hard Way" (*ASF*, n'te, Jan 1963). An Earthman in an alien brain seeks to learn the mores of the alien race.
Delusion World [pa] ("Perfectly Adjusted," *Science Fiction Stories*, July 1955) —enlarged: (Ace: F-119, 1961, 100 pp., pa 40¢; with *Spacial Delivery* [Dickson]) (*Planet der Phantome* [German], *T*: 249, 1962)

Feliz Gebrod is caught between two human societies occupying the same city without being able to see each other.
Earthman's Burden See ANDERSON, P. (co-author)
Genetic General, The [pa] ("Dorsai!" *ASF*, sr3, May 1959) (Ace: D-449, 1960, 159 pp., pa 35¢ [with *Time to Teleport*, Dickson]; F-426, 1967, pa 40¢) (Digit: R437, 1961, 156 pp., pa 2/-) (*Il mercenario di Dorsai* [Italian], *GRF*: 23, 1962)

Runner-up for the 1960 Hugo award for best novel. The adventures of a lad in his rise as a mercenary soldier in the tradition of his race, and the heritage he reaches. The future galactic culture is well depicted. Sequel is *Soldier Ask Not*.
Mankind on the Run [pa] (Ace: D-164, 1956, 151 pp., pa 35¢; with *The Crossroads of Time*) (*Hetzjagd im All* [German], *AW*: 1, 1958; *TE*: 58, 1965) (*La razza sensa fine* [Italian], *Urania*: 204, 1959)

The involved mankind of a future era; the psi element is somewhat unbelievable.
Mission to Universe [pa] (Berkley: F1147, 1965, 175 pp., pa 50¢) (*Mission im Universum* [German], *T*: 500, 1967)

Commander and crew of an exploring spaceship encounter many adventures.
Naked to the Stars [pa] (*F&SF*, sr2, Oct 1961) —enlarged: (Pyramid: F682, 1961, 159 pp., pa 40¢) (*Gewalt zwischen den Sternen* [German], Winther, 1967, pa)

A future mercenary officer after ordinary service becomes contacts officer, for liaison with aliens, etc.
Necromancer (Doubleday, New York, 1962, 191 pp., $2.95) (D'day, Toronto, $3.50) (D'day SF B.C., 1962, $1.20) (Mayflower: 0799, 1963, 190 pp., pa 3/6) (*No Room for Man*, Macfadden: MB50-179, 1963, 158 pp., pa 50¢; 50-329, 1966, pa 50¢)

A kind of superman story, with a puzzled hero involved in a cosmic tangle in a van Vogtian plot (like *The World of Null-A*).
No Room for Man [pa] See *Necromancer*
Planet Run See LAUMER, K. (co-author)
Secret Under Antarctica (Holt Rinehart Winston, New York, 1963, 139 pp., $3.25)

Juvenile, second of Robby Hoenig series. Kidnapping by a would-be dictator who wants to reverse the wanderings of the continents.
Secret Under the Caribbean (Holt, 1964, 143 pp., $3.50, lib. $3.75)

Juvenile, third of Robby Hoenig series.
Secret Under the Sea (Holt, 1960, 121 pp., $2.95, illus.–J. Ann Stover) (Hutchinson, London, 1962, 142 pp., 12/6, illus.)

Juvenile, for 8-12 years, first of Robby Hoenig series. A boy's adventures, with his pet dolphin Balthasar, in a marvellous underwater setting from which the plot grows.
Soldier, Ask Not [pa] (*GSF*, short novel, Oct 1964) —enlarged: (Dell: 8090, 1967, 222 pp., pa 60¢)

One of the Dorsai stories, set in the author's canvas from our time to the far future. A ruthless man seeks to destroy the culture of the fanatic "Friendly" worlds.
Space Swimmers, The [pa] (Berkley: X1371, 1967, 160 pp., pa 60¢) (Sidgwick, London, 1968, 180 pp., 18/-)

A story of an intricately structured multi-dimensional universe, with psionically gifted individuals; social and racial overtones.
Space Winners (Holt, 1965, 217 pp., $3.50) (Faber, London, 1967, 186 pp., 16/-)

Juvenile; three U.S. students to be educated by a galactic federation are cast away with a furry extraterrestrial on an alien world.
Spacial Delivery [pa] ("The Man in the Mailbag," *GSF*, Apr 1959) —enlarged: (Ace: F-119, 1961, 123 pp., pa 40¢; with *Delusion World* [Dickson]) (*Regierungspost für Dilba* [German], *T*: 260, 1963)

Intrigue and adventure on Dilba for an Earthman amid the rugged individualistic native humanoids, who are over nine feet tall and built like bears.
Time to Teleport [pa] ("No More Barriers," *SF Stories*, Sep 1955) (Ace: D-449, 1960, 96 pp., pa 35¢; with *The Genetic General* [Dickson]) (*La era del teleporte* [Spanish], Cenit: 71, 1964, pa)

A mutant threat to a highly developed future society.

DIFFIN, CHARLES WILLARD U.S. author. His sf was very popular in the early *ASF*, some of his better known stories being "Pirate Planet" (sr4, Nov 1930), "Dark Moon" (May 1931) and sequels. A recent reprint was "The Dog That Laughed" (*Strange Tales*, Sep 1931; *Mag. Horror*, Sum 1967). He also had some fantasy stories in the adventure magazine *Top Notch*.

DIKTY, T(HADDEUS) E(UGENE) (16 June 1920–) U.S. anthologist. He and E. F. Bleiler compiled the annual *Best Science Fiction Stories* series from 1949 through 1954; Dikty continued the series alone from 1955 through 1957. He is married to author Julian May (1931–).
Anthologies [see also BLEILER, E. F. (co-anthologist)]
Best Science Fiction Stories and Novels 1955, The (F. Fell, New York, 1955, 544 pp., $4.50) (*5 Tales From Tomorrow*, Crest: s-197, 1956, 176 pp., pa 35¢; d597, 1963, pa 50¢; D996, 1967, pa 50¢ [5 stories marked †])

Sf, 20 stories, Book Index, and Introduction "The S-F Year," T. E. Dikty: "The Cold Equations"†, T. Godwin; "Of Course," C. Oliver; "Dominions Beyond," Ward Moore; "Guilty as Charged," A. Porges; "Careless Love" (as "Push-Button Passion" in pa)†, A. C. Friborg; "Memento Homo," W. M. Miller; "Mousetrap," A. Norton; "Christmas Trombone," R. E. Banks; "One Thousand Miles Up," F. M. Robinson; "How-2"†, C. D. Simak; "Heirs Apparent," R. Abernathy; "John's Other Practice," W. Marks; "The Inner Worlds," Wm. Morrison; "The Will," W. M. Miller; "Felony," J. Causey; "The Littlest People," R. E. Banks; "One Way Street," J. Bixby; "Axolotl" (as "Deep Space" in pa)†, R. Abernathy; "Exile"†, E. B. Cole; "Nightmare Blues" ("Operation Syndrome"), F. Herbert. The S-F Book Index (E. Kemp) lists every book in or near the sf/fantasy field published in 1954. This anthology is the first of the combined form of the previously separate series *The Best Science-Fiction Stories* and *Year's Best Science Fiction Novels* (see Bleiler, E. F.).

Best Science Fiction Stories and Novels 1956 (F. Fell, 1956, 242 pp., $3.50) (*6 From Worlds Beyond*, Crest: s-258, 1958, 160 pp., pa 35¢ [6 stories marked †])

Sf, 13 stories, Book Index (E. Kemp), and introduction "The S-F Year" (T. E. Dikty): "Jungle Doctor"†, Robert F. Young; "Judgment Day," L. S. de Camp; "The Game of Rat and Dragon"†, Cordwainer Smith; "The Man Who Always Knew," A. Budrys; "Dream Street"†, F. M. Robinson; "You Created Us"†, T. Godwin; "Swenson, Dispatcher," R. De W. Miller; "Thing," P. Janvier; "I Do Not Love Thee, Dr. Fell"†, R. Bloch; "Clerical Error," M. Clifton; "A Canticle for Leibowitz," W. M. Miller; "The Cyber and Justice Holmes," F. Riley; "The Shores of Night" (expansion of "Sea Change")†, T. N. Scortia.

Best Science Fiction Stories and Novels, 9th Series (Advent, Chicago, 1958, 258 pp., $3.50) (D'day SF B.C., 1958, 258 pp., $1.15) Book Club and Advent editions were the same; both were printed by Doubleday, with a few hundred being distributed by Advent.

Sf, 12 stories, Book Index (E. Kemp), and introduction "The S-F Year" (T. E. Dikty): "2066: Election Day," M. Shaara; "The Mile-Long Spaceship," Kate Wilhelm; "The Last Victory," T. Godwin; "Call Me Joe," P. Anderson; "Didn't He Ramble," C. Oliver; "The Queen's Messenger," J. J. McGuire; "The Other People," L. Brackett; "Into Your Tent I'll Creep," E. F. Russell; "Nor Dust Corrupt," J. McConnell; "Nightsound," A. Budrys; "The Tunesmith," L. Biggle, Jr.; "Hunting Machine," Carol Emshwiller.

Every Boy's Book of Outer Space Stories (Fell, 1960, 283 pp., $3.95)

Sf, juvenile, 11 stories, jacket is Cape Canaveral photo: " '. . . And a Star to Steer Her By!' " L. Correy; "Sitting Duck," O. Saari; "Blind Man's Buff," M. Jameson; "Gypsy," P. Anderson; "The Canal Builders," R. Abernathy; "Star of Wonder," Julian May; "The Reluctant Heroes," F. M. Robinson; "That Share of Glory," C. M. Kornbluth; "Men Against the Stars," M. W. Wellman; "Man in the Sky," A. Budrys; "A Rover I Will Be," R. Courtney & F. Robinson.

5 Tales From Tomorrow [pa] See *Best Science Fiction Stories and Novels 1955*

Great Science Fiction About Mars (F. Fell, 1966, 187 pp., $3.95) (McLeod, Toronto, $4.95)

7 stories and compiler's introduction with table comparing Earth and Mars: "The Sound of Bugles," R. M. Williams; "Nonstop to Mars," J. Williamson; "The First Martian," A. E. van Vogt; "Via Etherline," Eando Binder; "Tin Lizzie," R. Garrett; "Under the Sand Seas," Oliver E. Saari; "Omnilingual," H. B. Piper.

Great Science Fiction Stories About the Moon (F. Fell, 1967, 221 pp., $4.50)

7 stories, 3 features, and introduction "Earth's Natural Satellite" (T. E. Dikty): "Table of Comparisons: Earth and the Moon"; "Significant Events in Lunar Exploration"; "Moon Prospector," William B. Ellern; "The Reluctant Heroes," Frank M. Robinson; "Glimpses of the Moon," W. West; "The Pro," E. Hamilton; "Honeymoon in Hell," F. Brown; "Via Death," Eando Binder; "Trends," I. Asimov; Glossary (of space terms).

Imagination Unlimited See BLEILER, E. F. (co-anthologist)

6 From Worlds Beyond [pa] See *Best Science Fiction Stories and Novels 1956*

DIMMOCK, (FREDERICK) HAYDN (15 Dec 1895–26 Apr 1955) British journalist and editor. In 1913 he went to *The Scout* as office boy and by 1915 was assistant editor; after service in World War I he returned as editor and served until retirement in June 1954. He was Press Secretary to the Boy Scouts' Association 1940-47, and during his life did much for the Scouting movement. In the sf field he edited the weekly magazine *Scoops* for its 20 issues in 1934.

DINES, GLEN (19 Nov 1925–) U.S. author and illustrator. Born in Casper, Wyoming, he attended U. of Washington, the Art Center School in Los Angeles, and took his B.A. and M.A. from Sacramento State College. He was a staff artist on the Pacific edition of *Stars and Stripes* during the war. He is now a professional author and illustrator.
Fiction
Mysterious Machine, The (Macmillan, New York, 1957, 140 pp., $2.75)
Juvenile; an 11-year-old inventor helps a man constructing a mysterious machine.

DINESEN, ISAK (pseud) See BLIXEN, K.

DINESEN, THOMAS (1892–)
Fiction
Twilight on the Betzy (Putnam, London, 1952, 219 pp., 10/6)
Weird; set on a ship.

DINGWALL, E(RIC) J(OHN) British anthropologist. M.A., D.Sc. (London), Ph.D. He was Hon. Assistant Keeper of Printed Books at the British Museum, and was attached to the Ministry of Information and the Foreign Office 1941-45. From 1922 to 1927 he was a research officer for the Society of Psychical Research, investigating many mediums throughout the world. He also studied social and religious conditions in Trinidad, Haiti, etc. He has written many books dealing with ghosts and related events and has contributed to many British and foreign publications. The listing below is probably not complete.
Nonfiction
Four Modern Ghosts [with Trevor H. Hall] (Duckworth, London, 1958, 111 pp., 15/-, photos)
Introduction. Chapters: I. "The Yorkshire Museum Ghost"; II. "Harry Price and Rosalie"; III. "Runcorn Poltergeist"; IV. "The Ousedale Haunt"; Index.
Haunting of Borley Rectory, The (Society Psychical Research, London, 1956, 181 pp., 16/-)
Results of research into the haunting of this noted house.
Some Human Oddities (Home & Van Thal, London, 1947, 198 pp., 15/-, illus.)
Subtitled "Studies in the Queer, the Uncanny, and the Fanatical."
Unknown–Is It Nearer?, The [with J. Langdon-Davies] (Cassell, London, 1956, 174 pp., 10/6) (Signet: Ks336, 1956, 160 pp., pa 35¢; T3723, 1968, 176 pp., pa 75¢)
A good introduction to serious consideration of the psi/psychic field. Evidence pro and con on all aspects of ESP from telepathy to ghosts and poltergeists is presented and discussed lucidly.

DISCH, THOMAS M(ICHAEL) (2 Feb 1940–) U.S. science fiction author. Comparatively new to the field, he has had over 30 stories since first appearing in *Fantastic* with "The Double Timer" (Oct 1962). He has since been published in most sf magazines, and his writing is highly regarded in some quarters.
Fiction
Camp Concentration (*NW*, sr4, July 1967) (Hart-Davis, London, 1968, 177 pp., 25/-)
Experiments with a new drug in a mysterious barracks; intellectual powers are heightened, but death results.
Echo Round His Bones [pa] (*NW*, sr2, Dec 1966) (Berkley:

X1349, 1967, 144 pp., pa 60¢)

Intrigue about living in "interspace" and the saving of Earth.

Genocides, The (Berkley: F1170, 1965, 143 pp., pa 50¢) (Whiting & Wheaton, London, 1967, 192 pp., 18/-) (*De uitroeiers* [Dutch], Meulenhoff, Amsterdam, 1967) (Panther: 24204, 1968, 188 pp., pa 5/-)

Earth is smothered by an alien plant and humanity is exterminated.

Mankind Under the Leash [pa] (Ace: G-597, 1966, 140 pp., pa 50¢; with *Planet of Exile*)

Expansion of "White Fang Goes Dingo" (*If*, Apr 1965)—alien life forms take humans as pets, but some are rejected and revolt.

One Hundred and Two H Bombs [C] [pa] (Compact: F327, 1966, 192 pp., 3/6)

Sf, 14 stories and introduction: "102 H Bombs" (*Fan*, n'te, Mar 1965); "The Sightseers"; "Final Audit"; "The Vamp"; "Utopia? Never!"; "The Return of the Medusae"; "The Princess' Carillon"; "Genetic Coda"; "White Fang Goes Dingo"; "The Demi-Urge"; "Dangerous Flags"; "Invaded by Love"; "Bone of Contention"; "Leader of the Revolution."

Under Compulsion [C] (Hart-Davis, 1968, 220 pp., 25/-)

17 stories: "The Roaches"; "Come to Venus Melancholy"; "Linda and Daniel and Spike"; "Flight Useless, Inexorable the Pursuit"; "Descending"; "Nada"; "Now Is Forever"; "The Contest"; "The Empty Room"; "The Squirrel Cage"; "The Number You Have Reached"; "1–A"; "Fun With Your Head"; "The City of Penetrating Light"; "Moon Dust, the Smell of Hay, and Dialectical Materialism"; "Thesis on Social Forms and Social Controls in the U.S.A."; "Casablanca."

DISRAELI, BENJAMIN (21 Dec 1804–19 Apr 1881) British statesman, novelist, poet, and general writer. He was of Jewish descent but his father had him baptized a Christian, which permitted him to later hold political office. Articled first as a solicitor, his whole attention was not engaged by the law. His *Vivian Grey* (1826) brought him into literary prominence. His first attempts to enter Parliament failed and it was not until 1847 that he became a permanent member. He became leader of the Conservative opposition in the House of Commons, and was twice Prime Minister (1868 and 1874-1880). He was created Earl of Beaconsfield in 1876. Although his literary creations are not considered great, they played a part in the thought of the 19th century.

Fiction

Popanilla and Other Tales [C] (Knopf, New York, 1934, 367 pp.)

Fantasy, 8 stories (with "A Note on the Tales" by Philip Guedalla): "Popanilla"; "Ixion in Heaven"; "The Infernal Marriage"; "The Rise of Iskander"; "The Carrier-Pigeon"; "The Consul's Daughter"; "Walstein: or, A Cure for Melancholy"; "A True Story."

DIVINE, ARTHUR DURHAM (27 July 1904–) South African writer, born at Cape Town. He has been a war correspondent, foreign correspondent and feature writer for the *Sunday Times* and the Thomson newspapers, and has also contributed to *SEP*, *John Bull*, etc. Besides science fiction (for which he uses the pseudonym "David Divine"), he has written many other books, (some under the pseudonym "David Rame"), including *Wine of Good Hope*, *The King of Fassarai*, *The Golden Fool*, *Boy on a Dolphin*, *Tunnel From Calais*, and *The Nine Days of Dunkirk*.

Fiction

Atom at Spithead [as David Divine] (R. Hale, London, 1953, 186 pp., 9/6; 1955, 160 pp., pa 2/-) (Macmillan, New York, 1953, 186 pp., $2.75)

One man thinks an atom bomb could be smuggled in and used against a British naval review.

DIVINE, DAVID (pseud) See DIVINE, A. D.

DIXON, RICHARD

Anthology

Destination: Amaltheia [pa] (Foreign Languages Pub. House, Moscow, *ca.* 1963, 420 pp., pa np)

Sf, 7 stories by Russian authors, translated into English (authors' biographies on cover flaps): "The Astronaut," Valentina Zhuravlyova; "Over the Abyss," Alexander Belayev; "The Maxwell Equations," Anatoly Dnieprov; "The Valley of the Four Crosses," Igor Zabelin; "The Golub-Yavan," Kirill Stanyukovich; "Flying Flowers," Mikhail Vasilyev; "Destination: Amaltheia," Arkady & Boris Strugatsky.

DOCTOROW, E. L. (1931–)

Fiction

Big as Life (Simon & Schuster, New York, 1966, 218 pp., $4.95)

Two immense figures tower over the New York skyline, and panic strikes the city.

DODGSON, CHARLES LUTWIDGE See CARROLL, L.

DOGBOLT, BARNABY (pseud) See SILVETTE, H.

DOHERTY, G(EOFFREY) D(ONALD) (17 Feb 1927–) British school teacher, Senior English Master at the Pundswick Grammar School, Manchester.

Anthologies

Aspects of Science Fiction (J. Murray 'Albemarle Library for Schools,' London, 1959, 281 pp., 5/6, no jacket)

Sf, 12 stories, designed for use by students: *Space:* "Pictures Don't Lie," Kath. McLean; "The Cold Equations," T. Godwin. *Time and the Fourth Dimension:* "A Sound of Thunder," R. Bradbury; "He Walked Around the Horses," H. B. Piper. *Invasion:* "Zero Hour," R. Bradbury. *Other Worlds:* "The Crystal Egg," H. G. Wells; "Dormant," A. E. van Vogt. *Realism:* "The Sea Raiders," H. G. Wells. *Warfare:* "Dumb Show," B. W. Aldiss. *Catastrophe:* "The Nine Billion Names of God," A. C. Clarke. *The World of Tomorrow:* "Panel Game," B. W. Aldiss. *Humour:* "The Man in Asbestos: An Allegory of the Future," S. Leacock. Glossary. Further reading (in categories above). Exercises.

Second Orbit (Murray, 1965, 218 pp., 8/6)

Sf, 10 stories, selected for use in schools, with compiler's introduction: "The Star," H. G. Wells; "And Now the News," T. Sturgeon; "The Prize of Peril," R. Sheckley; "Trainee for Mars," H. Harrison; "With These Hands," C. M. Kornbluth; "Allamagoosa," E. F. Russell; "Outside," B. W. Aldiss; "The Veldt," R. Bradbury; "Common Time," J. Blish; "The Star," A. C. Clarke. Ends with balanced list of further reading and a set of exercises.

Stories From Science Fiction (Nelson, London, 1966, 213 pp., 7/-, no jacket but printed illus. cover—R. Micklewright)

11 stories with introduction by compiler; finishing with questions on the stories: "Who Can Replace a Man?" B. W. Aldiss; "The Golden Apples of the Sun," R. Bradbury; "Etaoin Shrdlu," F. Brown; "Hunting Problem," R. Sheckley; "Sunjammer," A. C. Clarke; "Rescue Operation," H. Harrison; "The Lord of the Dynamos," H. G. Wells; "The Asteroids, 2194," J. Wyndham; "Flowers for Algernon," D. Keyes; "The Man Who Tasted Ashes," A. Budrys; "The Subliminal Man," J. G. Ballard.

DOLBIER, MAURICE

Fiction

Half-Pint Jinni and Other Stories, The [C] (Random House, New York, 1948, 242 pp., $2.50) (Random, Toronto, $3.00)

Fantasy, 8 stories: "The Half-Pint Jinni"; "True-Bill and False-Beak"; "Moon Quest"; "The Fable of the Sensitive Prince"; "Very Like a Camel"; "No Marvel Too Great"; "Meeting of the Power"; "Before Its Time."

DOLD, ELLIOTT U.S. artist. He was educated at William and Mary College, Virginia; obtained an art scholarship; and then did scenic painting and commercial advertising. After World War I he worked in the magazine field and was instrumental in having Harold Hersey publish *Miracle, Science and Fantasy*. His illness at that time caused this magazine to cease after two issues which he illustrated and in which his only sf story appeared. He illustrated Hersey's book of verse *Night* and was chief artist for *Astounding Stories* 1934-38. He was considered to be one of the best sf artists.

DOLE, STEPHEN H. U.S. scientist, head of the human engineering group at Rand Corp.
Nonfiction
Habitable Planets for Man (Blaisdell, New York, 1964, 160 pp., $5.75)

Report of the RAND study for the U.S. Air Force which defines criteria for worlds comfortable for man, and works out the number within 100 light years. P. S. Miller (*ASF*, Nov 1964) feels the criteria are ultraconservative. Supporting data and tables are given. See also *Planets for Man*, by Dole and Asimov.
Planets for Man [with I. Asimov] (Random, New York, 1964, 242 pp., $4.95)

Popularized version of *Habitable Planets for Man*.

DOLLENS, MORRIS SCOTT (14 Apr 1920–) U.S. amateur artist. At present he is a tape recorder technician, but has done photography, art work, writing, and electronics. He has produced some effective and original artistic creations within the science-fantasy field, but little for the professional magazines. His artwork has been featured in such amateur magazines as *Fantasy Advertiser* (early 1950's).
Artwork
Approach to Infinity (Privately published by F. J. Ackerman, Los Angeles, *ca.* 1951, 15 photographic prints [not reproductions] 10 in. x 8 in., $3.75, spiral wire binding)

The artist's conception of our relation to the Universe, photographed directly from his original paintings exhibited at Los Angeles' leading art theatre. The introduction explains the meaning behind the paintings. The prints were also available unbound. Roy A. Squires published a booklet (same title) covering most of this material in June 1952 as a supplement to the amateur magazine *Fantasy Advertiser*.
Fantasy in Art (Publisher and price understood to be same as for *Approach to Infinity* above)

A collection of paintings and prize-winning photo-montages of sf, fantasy and astronomical subjects. Full data on the first edition is unknown, but the second had fourteen photographic prints 10 x 8¼ inches.

DOMINIK, HANS (1872–1946) One of the foremost German sf writers, particularly noted for his *Atlantis* (E. Keils, 1925). He had a number of novels published up to 1955. For listing see Transgalaxis *Katalog* (Bingenheimer), 1960.

DONLEAVY, J(AMES) P(ATRICK) (23 Apr 1926–) Irish writer and playwright. He was born in New York City, but attended Trinity College, Dublin. He has contributed to *Atlantic*, *New Yorker*, *Holiday*, etc.
Fiction
Meet My Maker the Mad Molecule [C] (Atlantic-Little Brown, Boston, 1964, 178 pp., $4.75) (Little, Toronto, $5.75)

27 stories, some probably fantasy. Most are wild, funny, sad, etc.

DONNELL, A. J. U.S. artist. He was one of the group who with L. A. Eshbach formed Fantasy Press (Reading, Penna.). He did most of the Fantasy Press jackets and illustrations until he left the firm in 1950.

DONNELLY, IGNATIUS (3 Nov 1831–1 Jan 1901) U.S. author and politician. He was born in Philadelphia of Irish parents. He studied law and migrated to Minnesota, where he had an active political career. He became lieutenant-governor at 28 and was one of the founders of the Populist party. He is noted in the sf field for his *Atlantis: The Antediluvian World* which has had many editions and converted the lost continent from a speculation to a cult. In *The Great Cryptogram* he promulgated the theory that Francis Bacon wrote the Shakespearian plays. His three novels of sf interest are *Caesar's Column*, *Dr. Huguet* and *The Golden Bottle*; he is most noted for the first-named, which had a recent reissue. A recent book about him was *Donnelly, the Portrait of a Politician*, M. Rudge (U. Chicago, 1962).

Fiction [Incomplete–see above]
Caesar's Column (F. J. Schulte, Chicago, 1890, 367 pp., under pseudonym "Edmund Boisgilbert") (Harvard U., 1960, 27+313 pp., $4.50) ([Swedish], Bonggren, 1891) ([German], 1893 and 1902)

The Harvard edition has a 27-page introduction by Prof. Walter B. Rideout of Northwestern University. This is a rousing story giving Donnelly's Utopian views, and is one of the better Utopian novels. It depicts a society of stratified corruption set in 1988; naturally the book is dated by its Victorian ancestry.
Nonfiction
Atlantis: The Antediluvian World (originally 1882) –modern revision, Egerton Sykes: (Harper, New York, 1949, xix+355 pp., $4.50) (Musson, Toronto, $5.00) (Sidgwick Jackson, London, 1950, 18/-) (Xanadu, 1963, 355 pp., pa $1.65)

A classic, and the source of much 'Atlantean' writing. It attempts to prove a close relationship between Grecian and Mayan, Egyptian and Peruvian cultures (most of which is pure conjecture), all based on Plato's report of a legend which originated in Egypt.

DONOVAN, D. J.
Fiction
Adventure of Starbeem and Re-Koil, The (House of Ideas, Spencer, Ohio, 1967, quarto, $2.50, illus.–E. A. Skrocki)
Juvenile.

DONOVAN, DICK (pseud) See MUDDOCK, J. E. P.

DONSON, CYRIL
Fiction
Born in Space (R. Hale, London, 1968, 191 pp., 18/-)
The emancipation of enslaved Earthmen, and a hero who faces treachery.

DORNBERGER, WALTER (1895–) German general, formerly Commanding Officer of Peenemünde Rocket Research Institute.
Nonfiction
V-2 [Trans.–J. Cleugh & G. Halliday] ([German], Bechtle, Esslingen, 1952) (Hurst Blackett, London, 1954, 264 pp., 16/-, illus.) (Viking, New York, 1954, 281+xvi pp., $5.00, illus.) (Panther: 747, 1958, 192 pp., pa 2/6) (Ballantine: 273K, 1958, 237 pp., pa 50¢)

The history of the Peenemünde project. It does not cover the scientific problems raised and solved; W. Ley's *Rockets, Missiles and Space Travel* is better in this regard. However, the work is fascinating and is an indispensable supplement to the Ley classic.

DOUGLAS, BRYAN
Anthology
Great Stories of Mystery and Imagination [pa] (Fontana: 1324, 1966, 224 pp., pa 3/6)

8 stories—some on which the ABC TV show was based: "Room 13," "Lost Hearts," "The Tractate Middoth," M. R. James; "The Body Snatcher," R. L. Stevenson; "The Phantom Lover," Vernon Lee; "The Fall of the House of Usher," E. A. Poe; "The Canterville Ghost," O. Wilde; "Carmilla," S. Le Fanu.

DOUGLAS, DRAKE
Nonfiction
Horror! (Macmillan, New York, 1966, 309, illus., $6.95) (*Horrors!*, John Baker, London, 1967, 326 pp., illus., 30/-)

A volume of research into both the literature of horror and its translation into films. Introduction and chapters: "The Vampire"; "The Werewolf"; "The Monster"; "The Mummy"; "The Walking Dead"; "The Schizophrenic"; "The Phantom"; "The Creators of Horror" (3 chapters). 8 pages of illustrations. Epilogue; Further Reading; List of Horror Films.
Horrors! See *Horror!*

DOUGLAS, Sir GEORGE
Fiction
New Border Tales, The [C] (Walter Scott Pub. Co., London, New-

castle-on-Tyne & New York, 1904, 284 pp.)

Fantasy, 12 stories: "The Chief Mourner"; "An Exodus From Rat Hall"; "The Brither Stanes"; "John Buncle"; "A Dark Page From a Family History"; "The Pot of Gold"; "The Nabob"; "Will Winter and Rob Scott"; "The Resurrectionist"; "The Broken Trysts"; "A Match Not Made in Heaven"; "A Death-Bed Vigil."

DOYLE, (Sir) A(RTHUR) CONAN (22 May 1859–7 July 1930) British author, creator of Sherlock Holmes. Doyle was a physician, and practiced from 1882 to 1890. Meanwhile his literary career started with his first Sherlock Holmes novel, *A Study in Scarlet* (1887). He did not immediately follow with further Holmes, but turned to historical novels. He contributed Holmes' exploits to *Strand Magazine*, and when these appeared in book form as *The Adventures of Sherlock Holmes* (1893) their success was sensational. In a later book he killed off the great detective—or so he thought—but popular acclaim forced him to write about Holmes through the years; the final book was *The Case Book of Sherlock Holmes* (1927). [See also J. D. CARR.] Interest in Sherlock Holmes is still maintained, especially by such bodies as the Baker Street Irregulars. Doyle in his own right loved to work with the police and solved many mysteries for them.

In the sf field Doyle is noted for his Professor Challenger stories, the first of which, *The Lost World*, is considered a classic. Of his short stories, "The Great Keinplatz Experiment" is probably the most noted and has seen numerous reprintings in anthologies. Sam Moskowitz's profile of Doyle was published in *Satellite* (Feb 1959) and in *Science-Fantasy* (Aug 1959), and was a chapter in Moskowitz's *Explorers of the Infinite* (1963). Biographies of Doyle include *The Man Who Was Sherlock Holmes*, Michael & Molly Hardwick (Murray, London, 1964, 10/6); *Conan Doyle*, Hesketh Pearson (Guild: 224, 1946, pa); *The Life of Sir Arthur Conan Doyle*, J. D. Carr (Pan: GP20, 1958, pa). Adrian Conan Doyle compiled *Sir Arthur Conan Doyle Centenary, 1859–1959* (J. Murray, London, 1968, 137 pp., 60/-) to celebrate the centenary of this writer's birth. It is a miscellany of articles, illustrations, newspaper clippings and photographs covering the whole range of his life and works and interests.

Fiction [Complete except for *The Mystery of Cloomber* (1895) and *The Parasite* (1895). *Strange Secrets* (Told by A. C. Doyle and Others) is covered as an ANONYMOUS ANTHOLOGY. All his works have seen separate French translation and have also been collected by Laffont (12 volumes); some Swedish titles are not given here as their original titles are unknown.]

Black Doctor and Other Tales of Terror and Mystery, The [C] (Doran, New York, 1925, 279 pp., 90¢)

13 stories: "The Horror of the Heights" (*FFM*, Dec 1947); "The Leather Funnel"; "The New Catacomb"; "The Case of Lady Sannox"; "The Terror of Blue John Gap"; "The Brazilian Cat"; "The Lost Special"; "The Beetle-Hunter"; "The Man With the Watches"; "The Japanned Box"; "The Black Doctor"; "The Jew's Breastplate"; "The Nightmare Room."

Captain of the Polestar and Other Tales, The [C] (Longmans Green, London, 1890, 315 pp., 6/-) (G. Munro, New York, 1894, 263 pp.) (Longmans, New York, 1913, $2.00) (E. Nash, London, 1912, 327 pp., 4/6) (Longmans, London, 1933, 315 pp., 3/6; New York, $1.50) (Murray, London, 1934, 315 pp., 3/6)

Original British edition—10 stories: "The Captain of the 'Pole Star' "; "The Great Keinplatz Experiment"; "J. Habakuk Jephson's Statement"; "The Man From Archangel"; "That Little Square Box"; "The Ring of Thoth"; "John Huxford's Hiatus"; "Cyprian Overbeck Wells" (as "A Literary Mosaic" in some later eds.); "Elias B. Hopkins" (as "The Parson of Jackman's Gulch" in some later eds.); "John Barrington Cowles." This collection has had over a dozen varied editions both in cloth and paper bindings. Many of the stories also appeared later in *The Great Keinplatz Experiment*.

Conan Doyle Stories, The [C] (Murray, London, 1929, 1939, 1940, 1945, 1949, 1951, 1956, 1960 1202 pp., 20/-)

Omnibus vol. of 76 stories from earlier collections (not all fantasy): *Tales of the Ring* (6 stories); *Tales of the Camp* (6) [was *The Croxley Master and Other Tales of the Ring and Camp*]; *Tales of*

Pirates (6), *Tales of Blue Water* (6) [from *The Dealings of Captain Sharkey*]; *Tales of Terror* (6) [first part of *The Black Doctor*]; *Tales of Mystery* (7) [second part of *The Black Doctor*]; *Tales of Twilight and the Unseen* (12) [from *The Great Keinplatz Experiment*, 2nd ed.]; *Tales of Adventure* (6) [first part of *The Man From Archangel*]; *Tales of Medical Life* (9) [second part of *The Man From Archangel*]; *Tales of Long Ago* [from *The Last of the Legions*, omitting the last story].

Danger! and Other Stories [C] (J. Murray, 1918, 246 pp., 6/-; 1929, 310 pp., 7/6; 1931, 246 pp., 6/-; 1934, 3/6) (Doran, 1931, 310 pp.) (Burt, New York, 75¢)

10 stories (one in 4 parts): "Danger!"; "One Crowded Hour"; "A Point of View"; "The Fall of Lord Barrymore"; "The Horror of the Heights"; "Borrowed Scenes"; "The Surgeon of Gaster Fell"; "How It Happened"; "The Prisoner's Defence"; "Three of Them: 1. 'A Chat About Children, Snakes and Zebus,' 2. 'About Cricket,' 3. 'Speculations,' 4. 'The Leatherskin Tribe'." "Danger!" is a prediction of submarines versus merchant marine; "The Horror of the Heights" tells of predatory monsters in the stratosphere that destroy the first aviators to go above 20,000 ft.

Dealings of Captain Sharkey, The [C] (Doran, 1925, 9+260 pp., 90¢)

13 stories: *Tales of Pirates:* "Captain Sharkey"; "How the Governor of Saint Kitt's Came Home"; "The Dealings of Captain Sharkey With Stephen Craddock"; "The Blighting of Sharkey"; "How Copley Banks Slew Captain Sharkey"; "The 'Slapping Sal' "; "A Pirate of the Land" ("One Crowded Hour"). *Tales of Blue Water:* "The Striped Chest"; "The Captain of the 'Polestar' "; "The Fiend of the Cooperage"; "Jelland's Voyage"; "J. Habakuk Jephson's Statement"; "That Little Square Box."

Doings of Raffles Haw, The [C] (J. W. Lovell, New York, 1891, 134 pp.) (Cassell, London, 1910, 6d; 1912, 256 pp.; 1920, 2/-; 1925, 2/6)

3 stories: "The Doings of Raffles Haw"; "The Red-Headed League"; "The Boscombe Valley Mystery." The title story deals with the effects of transmuting lead into gold and how this corrupts the inventor.

Great Keinplatz Experiment, The [C] (Rand McNally, New York & Chicago, 1895?, 7+232 pp.)

7 stories: "The Great Keinplatz Experiment"; "The Captain of the 'Polestar' "; "J. Habakuk Jephson's Statement"; "John Huxford's Hiatus"; "A Literary Mosaic"; "John Barrington Cowles"; "The Ring of Thoth."

Great Keinplatz Experiment and Other Tales of Twilight and the Unseen, The [C] (Doran, 1925, 254 pp., 90¢; Garden City, 1937)

12 stories: "The Great Keinplatz Experiment"; "A Literary Mosaic"; "The Ring of Thoth"; "The Brown Hand"; "The Usher of Lea House School"; "B.24"; "Playing With Fire"; "The Los Amigos Fiasco"; "How It Happened"; "Lot No. 249"; " 'De Profundis' "; "The Lift."

Great Stories [selected by J. D. Carr] [C] (J. Murray, 1959, 256 pp., 12/6)

No further information, but may contain some sf or fantasy.

Land of Mist, The (Doran, 1926, 285 pp., $2.00) (Hutchinson, London, 1926, 294 pp., 7/6; 1927, 3/6; 1931, 2/6) (*Das Nebelland* [German], Wille, 1926) (Burt, New York, 1927, 285 pp., 75¢) (in *The Professor Challenger Stories* [Doyle], 1952) (Consul: 1212, 1963, 223 pp., pa 3/6)

A novel of spiritualism and ghost hunting.

Last Galley: Impressions and Tales, The [C] (Smith Elder, London, 1911, 298 pp., frontis., 6/-; 1912, 3/6) (Doubleday Page, New York, 1911, 321 pp., frontis.) (J. Murray, 1934, 298 pp., 3/6)

18 stories: "The Last Galley"; "The Contest"; "Through the Veil"; "An Iconoclast"; "Giant Maximin"; "The Coming of the Huns"; "The Last of the Legions"; "The First Cargo"; "The Home-Coming"; "The Red Star"; "The Silver Mirror"; "The Blighting of Sharkey"; "The Marriage of the Brigadier"; "The Lord of Falconbridge"; "Out of the Running"; " 'De Profundis' "; "The Great Brown-Pericord Motor"; "The Terror of Blue John Gap."

Last of the Legions and Other Tales of Long Ago, The [C] (Doran, 1925, 224 pp., 90¢)

13 stories: "The Last of the Legions"; "The Last Galley"; "Through the Veil"; "The Coming of the Huns"; "The Contest"; "The First Cargo"; "An Iconoclast"; "Giant Maximin"; "The Red Star"; "The Silver Mirror"; "The Home-Coming"; "A Point of Contact"; "The Centurion."

Lost World, The (Hodder & Stoughton, London, 1912, 309 pp., 6/-; illus. 10/6) (Doran, 1912, $1.50) (*Die verlorene Welt* [German], Scherl, 1926) (Murray, 1934, 319 pp., 3/6) (Triangle Books, New York, 1943, 309 pp., 49¢) (*El mundo perdido* [Spanish (Argentine)], Acme, 1945) (Pan: 100, 1949, 224 pp., pa 2/-; 1953, pa 2/-) (in *The Lost World and The Poison Belt*, Eyre 'Century Library 12,' London, 1950, 291 pp., 7/6; 1958, 7/6; Collins, Toronto, 1950, $1.35; McClelland, Toronto, 1958, $1.50) (in *The Professor Challenger Stories* [Doyle], 1952) ([Japanese], Koyama-Shoten, 1953) (Permabooks: 279, 1954, 200 pp., pa 25¢) (*En Försvunnen Värld* [Swedish], Bonnier, 1955) (Pyramid: PR-15, 1959, 192 pp., pa 35¢; G-514, 1960, pa 35¢; F-713, 1962, pa 40¢) (J. Murray, 1960, 214 pp., 3/6) (Berkley: F1162, 1965, 176 pp., pa 50¢)

The first and more recent editions of this noted classic in which Prof. Challenger and party find a prehistoric world on a plateau in the wilds of South America. *Films:* 1. First National, 1925, with Wallace Beery as Prof. Challenger; 2. Irwin Allen, 1960, released by 20th Century Fox, colour, Cinemascope, with Claude Rains, Michael Rennie, Fernando Lamas and Jill St. John.

Lost World and the Poison Belt, The See *Lost World, The*
Man From Archangel and Other Tales of Adventure, The [C] (Doran, 1925, 256 pp., 90¢; 1929, 3+307 pp.) (Garden City, New York, 1937, 256 pp.)

15 stories: *Tales of Adventure:* "Debut of Bimbashi Joyce"; "The Surgeon of Gaster Fell"; "Borrowed Scenes"; "The Man From Archangel"; "The Great Brown-Pericord Motor"; "The Sealed Room." *Tales of Medical Life:* 9 stories not listed.

Maracot Deep and Other Stories, The [C] (Doubleday Doran, 1929, 3+307 pp., $2.00) (Burt, 1930, 75¢) (J. Murray, 1930, 310 pp., 7/6; 6/-; 2/-) (Title story [Japanese], Sogen-sha, 1957; Hayakawa: 3039, 1962, pa) (Title story, Murray, 1961, 153 pp., pa 3/-; 1968, pa 3/6; Norton, New York, 1968, 119 pp., $4.95, intro. J. D. Carr)

Sf, 1 novel and 3 short stories: "The Maracot Deep" (*SEP*, sr4, 18 Oct 1927; in *The Treasury of SF Classics* [Kuebler], 1954)—men descend to the ocean floor in a steel sphere, are trapped, and then rescued by a man of Atlantis; "Spodegue's Drooper"; "The Disintegration Machine" (*FFM*, Jan 1951); "When the World Screamed."

My Friend the Murderer and Other Mysteries and Adventures [C] (Lovell Coryell, New York, 1893, 288 pp.) (Donohue, Chicago, 1912?, 159 pp.)

5 stories: "My Friend the Murderer"; "The Silver Hatchet"; "The Gully of Bluemansdyke"; "The Parson of Jackman's Gulch"; "A Night Among the Nihilists."

Poison Belt, The (Hodder Stoughton, 1913, viii+199 pp., illus. 3/6; 1915, 208 pp., 2/-, 1/-) (Doran, 1913, 252 pp., illus.) ([Swedish], Geber, 191?) (*Scoops*, sr6, 5 May 1934) (in *The Lost World and The Poison Belt* [Doyle], 1950) in *The Professor Challenger Stories* [Doyle], 1952) (Macmillan, 1964, 158 pp., illus.–W. P. du Bois, $4.50, intro.–J. D. Carr, epilogue–H. Shapley) (Berkley: F1203, 1966, 158 pp., pa 50¢)

Set three years after *The Lost World*. Professor Challenger discovers the Earth is going to pass through a zone of poisonous "ether," and takes steps to observe the event. The Macmillan and Berkley eds. contain the further Prof. Challenger short stories "The Disintegration Machine" and "When the Earth Screamed," and also 6½-p. introduction "The Many-Sided Conan Doyle," John D. Carr, and 6½-p. article following the main story "On Lethal Clouds," Harlow Shapley.

Professor Challenger Stories, The [C] (J. Murray, 1952, 577 pp., 15/-)

Sf, 5 stories: "The Lost World"; "The Poison Belt"; "The Land of the Mist"; "The Disintegration Machine" (inventor with a matter-transmitter); "When the World Screamed" (Earth is a cos-

mic sea-urchin ploughing through the ether).

Ring of Thoth, The [C] [pa] (Murray: 8, 1968, 190 pp., pa 5/-)

8 stories: "The Ring of Thoth"; "The Brown Hand"; "Playing With Fire"; "B 24"; "Lot 249"; "The Usher of Lee House School"; "The Striped Chest"; "J. Habakuk Jephson's Statement."

Round the Fire Stories [C] (McClure, New York, 1908, 3+356 pp., illus.) (Smith Elder, 1908, 382 pp., 6/-; 1911, 3/6) (Murray, 1934, 372 pp., 3/6)

17 stories: "The Leather Funnel"; "The Beetle Hunter"; "The Man With the Watches"; "The Pot of Caviare"; "The Japanned Box"; "The Black Doctor"; "Playing With Fire"; "The Jew's Breastplate"; "The Lost Special"; "The Club-Footed Grocer"; "The Sealed Room"; "The Brazilian Cat"; "The Usher of Lea House School"; "The Brown Hand"; "The Fiend of the Cooperage"; "Jelland's Voyage"; "B.24."

Round the Red Lamp [C] (Appleton, New York, 1894, 307 pp., 1910; 1921, $2.00) (Methuen, 1903, 6d; 1912, 224 pp., 1/-; 1922, 2/-) (Elder Smith, 1915, 336 pp., 3/6) (Murray, 1934, 328 pp., 3/6)

15 stories: "Behind the Times"; "His First Operation"; "A Straggler of '15"; "The Third Generation"; "A False Start"; "The Curse of Eve"; "Sweethearts"; "A Physiologist's Wife"; "The Case of Lady Sannox"; "A Question of Diplomacy"; "A Medical Document"; "Lot No. 249"; "The Los Amigos Fiasco"; "The Doctors of Hoyland"; "The Surgeon Talks."

DRAKE, ALEXANDER W(ILSON) (1843–4 Feb 1916) U.S. art director. He studied and practiced wood engraving, and oil and water colour painting. He was a wood engraver 1865-70, and Head of Art Dept. of *Scribner's Monthly* 1870-81, remaining with this magazine when it became *The Century*. He was identified with many important art movements in the U.S.A. for the last 25 years of his life.

Fiction
Three Midnight Stories [C] (Century, New York, 1916, 117 pp., illus., $5.00; 500 copies)

3 stories: "The Yellow Globe"; "The Curious Vehicle"; "The Loosened Cord." Also contains a brief biography of the author and a number of tributes to him.

DRAKE, (HENRY) BURGESS (1894–)
Fiction
Children of the Wind See *Hush-a-by Baby*
Hush-a-by Baby (Falcon, London, 1954, 352 pp., 12/6) (*Children of the Wind*, Lippincott, Philadelphia, 1954, 352 pp., $3.50)

Told by a child poltergeist who has a twin sister, both 'kindled' into being by the childless wife of a British politician.

Woman and the Priest, The (Davies, London, 1955, 223 pp., 12/6)

The story of the struggle between the Church and malignant forces of evil on an island off the coast of France.

DRAKE, LEAH BODINE (1914–1964) U.S. poet, born in Chanute, Kansas. She had much verse published by *Weird Tales* and also appeared in the Derleth verse anthologies *Dark of the Moon* and *Fire and Sleet and Candlelight*.

Fiction
Hornbook for Witches, A [C] (Arkham, Sauk City, Wisc., 1950, 70 pp., $2.10; 553 copies)

Supernatural verse. Listed in Derleth's *Arkham House: The First 20 Years*.

This Tilting Dust [C] (Golden Quill, Francestown, N.H., 1956, $2.00)

More realistic verse than the above, but containing much fantasy poetry. It won the $1,250 Borestone Mountain Poetry Award.

DRING, NAT(HANIEL)
Fiction
Earth Is Your Spaceship, The (Space Age Press, Fort Worth, 1967, 118 pp., $2.95; pa $1.89)

The planet Trojan (next out from Mars) is threatened by a comet, and some Trojans visit Earth and stay.

DROKE, MAXWELL (1896–1957) U.S. author, columnist, editor and publisher. In 1941 he became the founder and publisher of *Quote*, a weekly digest. He was editor of *The Messenger*, sent by Protestant churches to men in the armed services 1943-45. His books include *The Speaker's Handbook of Humor* (1956).
Nonfiction
You and the World to Come (Harper, New York, 1959, 203 pp., $3.50)
This does not deal with fantastic inventions but instead follows the threads of sociological trends into the immediate future—working wives, senior citizens, dwindling families, increased leisure, the schooled generation, etc.—all viewed with with gently humorous profundity.

DRURY, ALLEN (2 Sep 1918–) U.S. author and journalist; a Washington correspondent for 15 years. He has had one story published in *F&SF*: "Something" (Oct 1960).
Fiction
Advise and Consent (Doubleday, New York, 1959, 616 pp., $5.75) (Collins, London, 1960, 628 pp., 21/-) (Pocket Books: GC-952, 1961, pa 95¢) (Corgi: EN1239, 1962, 624 pp., pa 7/6)
Set in the near (but unspecified) future, this novel gives a picture of the U.S. Senate and how it operates, with the machinations of the President to further his own ends. It was at the top of the *New York Times* best-seller list and was awarded the Pulitzer Prize. It is the first of a planned tetralogy; the others are to be *A Shade of Difference, Capable of Honor* and *Preserve and Protect*.
Shade of Difference, A (Doubleday, 1962, 603 pp., $6.95) (D'day, Toronto, $7.95) (M. Joseph, London, 1963, 784 pp., 30/-)
A novel on black extremism—a lengthy, complicated and lurid tale of the plotting of a young African princeling hastening independence for his remote country, and a conservative black U.S. delegate to the United Nations.

DRYASDUST (pseud) See HALIDOM, M. Y.

DU BOIS, THEODORA (McCORMICK) (14 Sep 1890–) Noted U.S. detective writer with over 20 books to her credit. Her *Murder Strikes an Atomic Unit* (Doubleday, 1946) touches on superscience.
Fiction
Armed With a New Terror (Houghton Mifflin, Boston, 1936, 266 pp., $2.00) (Heineman, London, 1937, 7/6) (T. Allen, Toronto, $2.25)
Weird adventure novel. Published in England serially as "Woman Accused."
Devil's Spoon, The (Stokes, New York, 1930, 312 pp., $2.50) (Jarrolds, London, 1931, 312 pp., 7/6) (*FFM*, June 1948)
A spirit takes over a man's body and tries to obtain his wife's love, and also makes a trip to stop the Devil controlling Earth.
Sarah Hall's Tea God (Doubleday, 1952, 11+250 pp., $2.75)
Amusing fantasy, with Sarah taking a cruise with a god.
Solution T-25 (Doubleday, 1951, 218 pp., $2.75) (D'day SF B.C., 1953?) (Kemsley: CT411, 1952, 190 pp., pa 1/6)
A world dominated by the Russians, and their final overthrow.

DU MAURIER, DAPHNE (13 May 1907–) British novelist. She is the granddaughter of artist and novelist George Du Maurier and daughter of noted actor George Du Maurier, and is married to Lt. Gen. Sir Frederick A. M. Browning, treasurer to the Duke of Edinburgh. She is noted for her *Rebecca* (1938) and *Frenchman's Creek* (1942), as well as more recent novels. She has also written about her family in *George* (1934) and *The Du Mauriers* (1937).
Fiction
Apple Tree, The [C] (Gollancz, London, 1952, 264 pp., 10/6, & Longmans, Toronto, $2.25) (*Kiss Me Again, Stranger*, Doubleday, New York, 1953, 319 pp., illus., $3.50, & ? , 1956, pa 35¢)
British ed. has 6 stories, titles not known. U.S. ed., 8 stories as follows, with over half fantasy: "The Apple Tree" (short novel); "The Birds"; "Kiss Me Again, Stranger"; "Little Photographer"; "Monte Verita"; "No Motive"; "Old Man"; "Split Second."
Kiss Me Again, Stranger [C] See *Apple Tree, The*

DUCHACEK, IVO DUKA (27 Feb 1913–) U.S. educator, born in Prostejov, Czechoslovakia. He was in the Czech diplomatic service in Paris and London, 1939-45, and was a member of the Czech parliament 1945-48. Since 1949 he has been a professor at City College of N.Y. He lectured at Yale 1949-51 and was Editor-in-Chief, U.S. Dept. of State and U.S. Information Agency, 1949-54. He is known for his pseudonym "Ivo Duka," as whom he has collaborated with Helena Kolda.
Fiction [as Ivo Duka]
Martin and His Friend From Outer Space [with Helena Kolda] (Harper, New York, 1955, 95 pp., illus., $2.50)
Juvenile—a boy builds a telepathic helmet and dates a beauty via matter transmitter.

DUFF, DOUGLAS V(ADER) (1901–) British author. He was born at Rosario de Santa Fe, Argentina, and was educated on H.M.S. *Conway*. He was the only known survivor of the Cunard ship *Thracia* in 1917, and was a former staff officer to Lord Cunningham of Hyndhope. He became an Officer of the Crown of Rumania, and a Knight of the Order of the Holy Sepulchre. He has contributed to *Blackwood's, Cornhill, Quarterly Review*, etc., and his works include *Sword for Hire* (Murray) and *Palestine Unveiled* (Blackie).
Fiction
Man From Outer Space, The (Blackie, London, 1953, 224 pp., illus., 6/-)
Juvenile—a formidable being is conquered and his awful threat nullified.

DUKA, IVO (pseud) See DUCHACEK, I. D.

DUKE, MADELAINE (ELIZABETH) (21 Aug 1925–) British physician, wife of Dr. Alexander Macfarlane and formerly Baroness de Hartog of the distinguished Dutch family. A further novel is *The Sugar Cube Trap* on juvenile drug addiction.
Fiction
Claret, Sandwiches and Sin (FSB:1564, 1966, 143 pp., pa 3/6) (Doubleday, New York, 1966, 192 pp., $3.95) (Collins, Toronto, $5.00)
An organisation sets out to remove political tensions in a future world—by quiet assassination.

DUMAS, ALEXANDRE (24 July 1802–5 Dec 1870) Great French novelist. He started as a clerk in Paris in 1823, but soon turned to literature and drama. A prodigious worker, he was the supreme craftsman and one of the masters of the art of narrative. His output has no parallel in French literature: historical novels, romances, plays, etc., poured from his pen. He is most noted for his D'Artagnan romances, which began with *The Three Musketeers*. His novels appeared in 15 volumes from Methuen, 1900-05.
Fiction [Incomplete—other titles in Bleiler *Checklist*]
Wolf Leader, The [trans.–A. Allinson] (originally 1857) –(Vol. 15 of *The Novels of Alexandre Dumas*, Methuen, London, *ca.* 1903, 115 pp., illus.) (*WT*, sr8, Aug 1931) (Prime, Philadelphia, 1950, 235 pp., illus.–M. Bláine, editor–L. S. de Camp)
A weird novel about werewolves.

DUNCAN, BRUCE
Fiction
Mirror Image [pa] (Belmont: B60-081, 1968, 90 pp., 60¢; with *Father of Lies*)
Aliens begin replacing the crew of a nuclear submarine with robot impostors.

DUNCAN, DAVID (17 Feb 1913–) U.S. author. He was born in Billings, Montana, received B.A., U. of Montana in 1935, and has been a social worker and a labour economist. He has been a freelance writer since 1946, and has written such diverse books as *The Bramble Bush* (psychological suspense), *Wives and Husbands* (examination of an artists' colony), and *The Serpent's Egg* (novel on American labour). He first touched on sf with his *The Shade of Time*, which concerned atomic displacement. He has done a number of screen plays, including an adaptation of H. G. Wells' *The Time Machine*; he has written for such TV shows as "Studio One," "Men Into Space" and "The Outer Limits." A story in *GSF* was "The Immortals" (Oct 1960).

Fiction

Another Tree in Eden See *Beyond Eden*

Beyond Eden (Ballantine, New York, 1955, 169 pp., $2.00; #102, pa 35¢) (*L'albero della vita* [Italian], *Urania*: 125, 1956) (*La fuente del Eden* [Spanish], Nebula: 27, 1956, pa) (*Another Tree in Eden*, Heinemann, London, 1956, 192 pp., 12/6) (*Unternehmen Neptun* [German], Weiss, 1957, pa)

An enormous atom-powered salt water distillation plant inadvertently produces a life stimulant.

Dark Dominion (*Collier's*, sr4, 2 Apr 1954) (Ballantine, 1954, 206 pp., $2.50; #56, pa 35¢) (*Everybody's* [English magazine], sr, late 1954) (*Den Svarta Planeten* [Swedish], Lindqvist, 1954) (Heinemann, 1955, 234 pp., 10/6) (*Il pianeta nero* [Italian], *Urania*: 84, 1955) ([Japanese], Gengen-sha: SF6, 1956) (*El planeta negro* [Spanish], Nebula: 16, 1956 pa) (Consul: SF1021, 1961, 221 pp., pa 2/6)

The building of the first satellite rocket, with technical problems and the drama of launching.

Madrone Tree, The (Macmillan, New York, 1949, 230 pp., $3.00) (Macmillan, Toronto, $3.40) (Gollancz, London, 1950, 230 pp., 8/6)

A suspense novel of fantasy and horror.

Occam's Razor (Ballantine: 230, 1957, 165 pp., pa 35¢; 1957, $2.75) (Gollancz, 1958, 200 pp., 12/6) (SF B.C. [S.J.], 1959, 5/6) (*Missile senza tempo* [Italian], *Urania*: 198, 1959) (*Le rasoir d'Occam* [French], Denoël: PF38, 1960) (FSB: 646, 1962, 160 pp., pa 2/6)

A slightly strange man and woman emerge from a parallel world and cause consternation and havoc in ours.

Shade of Time, The (Random, New York, 1946, 244 pp., $2.00) (Random, Toronto, $2.50) (Grey Walls, London, 8/6)

DUNCAN, RONALD (6 Aug 1914–) British poet and playwright, M.A. Cambridge, 1936. He was a founder of the English Stage Company.

Fiction

Last Adam, The (Dobson, London, 1953, 95 pp., 7/6)

The last man on Earth, with an unusual punch line.

DUNN, ALAN (11 Aug 1900–) U.S. writer. He has had some material in *The New Yorker*.

Fiction

Is There Intelligent Life on Earth? (Simon & Schuster, New York, 1960, quarto, 118 pp., illus., $3.50)

Subtitled "A Report to the Congress of Mars." A satirical mingling of text and cartoons that examines the lives and peculiar customs of our fellow Earthmen through the eyes of an invisible expedition from Mars. It is a refreshing work lampooning various sf hallmarks, and will please both lovers and detesters of sf.

DUNNE, JOHN WILLIAM (1875–24 Aug 1949) British Army officer and airplane pioneer. He built several of the first British planes 1905-13. He wrote some excellent children's fairy tales but is primarily noted for his *An Experiment With Time*.

Nonfiction

Experiment With Time, An (A. & C. Black, London, 1926, 204 pp., 10/6) (Macmillan, New York, 1927, 208 pp., $2.50) (Black, 1929, 2nd ed.) (Faber, London, 3rd ed., 1934, 288 pp., 5/-) (Ryerson, Toronto, $1.75) (Macmillan, New York, 4th ed., 1938, 297 pp., $2.00; new ed. 1949, 254 pp., $2.00) (Faber, 1950, 8/6; 1953, 254 pp.) (*Le temps et le rêve* [French], *ca.* 1946)

The noted work on the theory of "serialism." The author undertook to explain prophetic dreams by positing that we move along Time as a fourth dimension. The editions noted above may not be complete; this work was continually revised up till the author's death.

New Immortality, The (Faber, London, 1938, 157 pp.)

No information.

Serial Universe, The (Faber, 1934, 241 pp., illus., 10/6) (Ryerson, $3.50) (Macmillan, 1938, 240 pp., illus., $2.00) (Faber, 1941, 8/6) (Ryerson, $2.75) (Macmillan, 1948, 243 pp., $2.50)

No information.

DUNSANY, LORD [Edward John Moreton Drax Plunkett] (24 July 1878–25 Oct 1957) Irish poet, dramatist and author; the 18th Baron Dunsany since 1439. He served in the Coldstream Guards in the Boer War and World War I. He was Byron Professor of English Literature at the U. of Greece, in Athens. Apart from his strenuous literary life, Lord Dunsany ranged the world in pursuit of his favorite recreations—shooting and big-game hunting, etc.—and he was also in the top flight of chess players. A great student and lover of nature, he wrote much on the countryside he understood so well: the lovely vales of Kent where he was born, and Ireland.

Many of his stories and plays are fantasies, dealing with the supernatural and its beings; his style is simple, yet deals in the paradoxes of human existence. He received his early acclaim as a dramatist with *Glittering Gates* (produced in Dublin, 1909); among others are *The Gods of the Mountain* (1911), *If* (1921), and *The Laughter of the Gods* (1933). A biography is *Lord Dunsany–King of Dreams*, Hazel Littlefield (Exposition, New York, 1959, 148 pp., $5.00). Much of his fiction is of particular interest to the fantasy field; *The Pipes of Pan* and such other books as his tales of Jorkens and his cronies of the Billiard Club are especially notable. His short stories have been reprinted in such magazines as *FFM* and *AFR*, and many are included in fantasy anthologies.

Fiction [Incomplete; covers majority of Dunsany's collections, with other titles listed in Bleiler *Checklist*]

Book of Wonder, The [C] (Heineman, London, 1912, 97 pp., illus.–S. H. Sime, quarto, 6/-; 1919, 107 pp., 7/6) (J. W. Luce, Boston, 1915, 134 pp., illus.–S. H. Sime, $1.75) (Modern Library, New York, 1918, 234 pp., 95¢) (Elkin Mathews, London, 1920, 108 pp., illus.–S. H. Sime)

These editions have varying contents, and the listing below is an overall coverage; those in the Mathews 1920 ed. are marked †. Some editions include all stories in *Time and the Gods*. 34 stories: "The Bride of the Man-Horse"†; "Cave of Kai"; "Chu-Bu and Sheemish"†; "Coming of the Sea"; "The Coronation of Mr. Thomas Shap"†; "The Distressing Tale of Thangobrind the Jeweller"†; "Dreams of a Prophet"†; "For the Honour of the Gods"; "The Hoard of the Gibbelins"†; "The House of Sphinx"†; "How Nuth Would Have Practised His Art Upon the Gnoles"†; "How One Came, As Was Foretold, to the City of Never"†; "The Injudicious Prayers of Pombo the Idolater"†; "Jest of the Gods"; "Journey of the King"; "King That Was Not"; "Land of Time"; "Legend of the Dawn"; "The Loot of Bombasharna"†; "Men of Yarnith"; "Miss Cubbidge and the Dragon of Romance"†; "Mlideen"; "Night and Morning"; "The Probable Adventure of the Three Literary Men"†; "The Quest of the Queen's Tears"†; "Relenting of Sarnidac"; "Secret of the Gods"; "Sorrow of Search"; "South Wind"; "Time and the Gods"; "Usury"; "Vengeance of Men"; "When the Gods Slept"; "The Wonderful Window"; Epilogue.

Dreamer's Tales, A [C] (J. W. Luce, 1910, 194 pp., illus.–S. H. Sime, $1.75) (G. Allen, London, 1910, 262 pp., 6/-) (Modern Library, 1919, 194 pp., 95¢) ([Spanish], ? , 1945)

16 stories: "Poltarnees, Beholder of Ocean"; "Blagdaross"; "The Madness of Andelprutz" (*AFR*, No. 9, 1949); "Where the Tides Ebb and Flow"; "Bethmoora"; "Idle Days on the Yann"; "The Sword and the Idol"; "The Idle City"; "The Hashish Man" (*FFM*, Dec 1945); "Poor Old Bill"; "The Beggars"; "Carcassonne"; "In Zaccarath"; "The Field"; "The Day of the Poll"; "The Unhappy Body."

Fifty-One Tales (M. Kennerley, New York, 1915, 138 pp.) (Elkin Mathews, 1915, 111 pp., 3/6) (Little, Boston, 1917, $1.65)

51 stories: "The Assignation"; "Charon"; "The Death of Pan"; "The Sphinx at Gizeh"; "The Hen"; "Wind and Fog"; "The Raft Builders"; "The Workman"; "The Guest"; "Death and Odysseus"; "Death and the Orange"; "The Prayer of the Flowers"; "Time and the Tradesman"; "The Little City"; "The Unpasturable Fields"; "The Worm and the Angel"; "The Songless Country"; "The Latest

Thing"; "The Demagogue and the Demi-Monde"; "The Giant Poppy"; "Roses"; "The Man With the Golden Ear Rings"; "The Dream of King Karna-Vootra"; "The Storm"; "A Mistaken Identity"; "The True History of the Hare and the Tortoise"; "Alone the Immortals"; "A Moral Little Tale"; "The Return of Song"; "Spring in Town"; "How the Enemy Came to Thlunrana"; "A Losing Game"; "Taking Up Piccadilly"; "After the Fire"; "The City"; "The Food of Death"; "The Lonely Idol"; "The Sphinx in Thebes (Massachusetts)"; "The Reward"; "The Trouble in Leafy Green Street"; "Furrow Maker"; "Lobster Salad"; "The Return of the Exiles"; "Nature and Time"; "The Song of the Blackbird"; "The Messengers"; "The Three Tall Sons"; "Compromise"; "What Have We Come To"; "The Tomb of Pan"; "The Poet Speaks With Earth."

Five Plays [C] (G. Richards, London, 1914, 111 pp.) (M. Kennerley, New York, 1915, 116 pp.) (Putnam, London, 1920; 1925, 111 pp.; 1931)

Fantastic plays: "The Gods of the Mountain"; "The Golden Doom"; "King Argimenes and the Unknown Warrior"; "The Glittering Gate"; "The Lost Silk Hat."

Fourth Book of Jorkens, The [C] (Arkham, Sauk City, Wisc., 1948, 194 pp., $3.00; 3,118 copies) (Jarrolds, London, 1948, 176 pp., 9/6; 1950, 8/-; nd, pa np)

33 stories: "Making Fine Weather"; "Mgamu"; "The Haunting of Halahanstown"; "The Pale Green Image"; "Jorkens Leaves Prison"; "The Warning"; "The Sacred City of Krakovlitz"; "Jorkens Practices Medicine and Magic"; "Jarton's Disease"; "On the Other Side of the Sun"; "The Rebuff" (*Avon SF Reader*, No. 2, 1951); "Jorkens' Ride"; "The Secret of the Sphinx"; "The Khamseen"; "The Expulsion"; "The Welcome"; "By Command of Pharaoh"; "A Cricket Problem"; "A Life's Work"; "The Ingratiating Smile"; "The Last Bull"; "The Strange Drug of Dr. Caber"; "A Deal With the Devil"; "Strategy at the Billiards Club"; "Jorkens in Witch Wood"; "Lost"; "The English Magnifico"; "The Cleverness of Dr. Caber"; "Fairy Gold"; "A Royal Dinner"; "A Fight With Knives"; "Out West"; "In a Dim Room."

Jorkens Borrows Another Whisky [C] (M. Joseph, London, 1954, 256 pp., 12/6) ([German] ?)

34 stories: "The Two Way War"; "A Nice Lot of Diamonds"; "Letting Bygones Be Bygones"; "The Lost Invention"; "On Other Paths"; "The Partner"; "Poulet a la Richelieu"; "A Walk in the Night"; "One Summer's Evening"; "A Friend of the Family"; "An Eccentricity of Genius"; "Influenza"; "The Unrecorded Test Match"; "Idle Tears"; "Among the Neutrals"; "An Idyll of the Sahara"; "The Devil Among the Willows"; "A Spanish Castle"; "The New Moon"; "The Gods of Clay"; "A Rash Remark"; "The Story of Jorkens' Watch"; "The Track Through the Wood"; "Snow Water"; "The Greatest Invention"; "The Verdict"; "A Conversation in Bond Street"; "The Reward"; "Which Way?"; "A Desperado in Surrey"; "Misadventure"; "A Long Memory"; "An Absentminded Professor"; "Greek Meets Greek."

Jorkens Has a Large Whisky [C] (Putnam, London, 1940, 323 pp., 8/-) (McClelland, Toronto, $3.00)

26 stories: "Jorkens' Revenge"; "Jorkens Retires From Business"; "Jorkens Handles a Big Property"; "The Invention of Dr. Caber"; "The Grecian Singer"; "The Jorkens Family Emeralds"; "A Fishing Story"; "Jorkens in High Finance"; "The Sign"; "The Angelic Shepherd"; "The Neapolitan Ice"; "The Development of the Rillswood Estate"; "The Fancy Man"; "The Lion and the Unicorn"; "A Doubtful Story"; "Jorkens Looks Forward"; "Jorkens Amongst the Ghosts"; "Elephant Shooting"; "African Magic"; "Jorkens Consults a Prophet"; "A Matter of Business"; "The Invention of the Age"; "The Sultan, the Monkey and the Banana"; "Pundleton's Audience"; "The Fight in the Drawing Room"; "The Ivory Poacher."

Jorkens Remembers Africa [C] (Longmans Green, New York & Toronto, 1934, 303 pp., $2.50) (*Mr. Jorkens Remembers Africa*, Heinemann, 1934, 299 pp., 7/6; 1937, 3/6)

21 stories: "At the End of the Universe"; "An August in the Red Sea"; "Bare Truth"; "Black Mamba"; "The Club Secretary" (*F&SF*, July 1956); "Correct Kit"; "Curse of the Witch"; "Earth's Secret"; "Escape From the Valley"; "Golden Gods"; "How Ryan

Got Out of Russia"; "In the Garden of Memories"; "Lost Romance"; "Mystery of the East"; "Ozymandias"; "Pearly Beach"; "Persian Spell"; "Slugly Beast"; "Stranger Than Fiction"; "Walk in Lingham"; "What Jorkens Has to Put Up With."

Last Book of Wonder, The [C] (J. W. Luce, 1916, 213 pp., illus.– S. H. Sime, $1.75) (*Tales of Wonder*, E. Mathews, London, 1917, 187 pp., illus.–S. H. Sime)

19 stories: "A Tale of London"; "Thirteen at Table"; "The City on Mallington Moor"; "Why the Milkman Shudders When He Perceives the Dawn"; "The Bad Old Woman in Black"; "The Bird of the Difficult Eye"; "The Long Porter's Tale"; "The Bureau D'Echange de Maux"; "A Story of Land and Sea"; "The Loot of Loma"; "A Tale of the Equator"; "A Narrow Escape"; "The Watch Tower"; "The Secret of the Sea"; "How Plash-Goo Came to the Land of None's Desire"; "The Three Sailors Gambit"; "How Ali Came to the Black Country"; "The Exiles Club"; "The Three Infernal Jokes."

Last Revolution, The (Jarrolds, 1951, 200 pp., 9/6)

Revolt of machines—a cynical attack on our modern civilization.

Little Tales of Smethers and Other Stories, The [C] (Jarrolds, 1952, 232 pp., 10/6) ([German] ?)

26 stories (many fantasy, but described as modern detective stories): "The Two Bottles of Relish"; "The Shooting of Constable Slugger"; "An Enemy of Scotland Yard"; "The Second Front"; "The Two Assassins"; "Krieglut's Disguise"; "The Mug in the Gambling Hell"; "The Clue"; "Once Too Often"; "An Alleged Murder"; "The Waiter's Story"; "A Trade Dispute"; "The Pirate of the Round Pond"; "A Victim of Bad Luck"; "The New Master"; "A New Murder"; "A Tale of Revenge"; "The Speech"; "The Lost Scientist"; "The Unwritten Thriller"; "In Ravancore"; "Among the Bean Rows"; "The Death-Watch Beetle"; "Murder by Lightning"; "The Murder in Netherby Gardens"; "The Shield of Athene."

Man Who Ate the Phoenix, The [C] (Jarrolds, 1949, 223 pp., 9/6; 1951, 6/-)

41 stories: "The Man Who Ate the Phoenix"; "The Widow Flynn's Apple Tree"; "Where Everyone's Business Is Known"; "The Rose By-Pass"; "An Old Man's Tale"; "How the Tinker Came to Skavangur"; "The Opal Arrow-Head"; "The Sultan's Pet"; "The Descent of the Sultan of Khash"; "The Policeman's Prophecy"; "The Wind in the Wood"; "The Tiger's Skin"; "The Finding of Mr. Jupkens"; "The Awful Dream"; "Mrs. Mulger"; "The Choice"; "Rose Tibbets"; "Little Snow White Up to Date"; "The Return"; "The Mad Ghost"; "The Cause"; "The Cut"; "The Sleuthing of Lily Bostum"; "The Possibility of Life on the Third Planet"; "Old Emma"; "How Abdul Din Saved Justice"; "The First Watch-Dog"; "The Chess Player, the Financier and Another"; "The Honorary Member"; "The Experiment"; "Down Among the Kingcups"; "The Gratitude of the Devil"; "The After-Dinner Speech"; "The Je-Ne-Sais Quoi"; "Poseidon"; "A Near Thing"; "Ardor Canis"; "A Lapse of Memory"; "Forty Years On"; "The Iron Door"; "The Great Scoop."

Mr. Jorkens Remembers Africa See *Jorkens Remembers Africa*

Plays for Earth and Air [C] (Heinemann, London, 1937, viii+163 pp., 6/-)

10 plays: *Plays for Earth:* "Fame Comes Late"; "A Matter of Honour"; "Mr. Sliggen's Hour"; "The Pumpkin." *Plays for Air:* "The Use of Man"; "The Bureau de Change"; "The Seventh Symphony"; "Golden Dragon City"; "Time's Joke"; "Atmospherics."

Seven Modern Comedies [C] (Putnam, New York & London, 1929, 204 pp., $2.00)

"Atlanta in Wimbledon"; "The Raffle"; "The Journey of the Soul"; "In Holy Russia"; "His Sainted Grandmother"; "The Hopeless Passion of Mr. Bunyon"; "The Jest of Hahalaba."

Strange Journeys of Colonel Polders, The (Jarrolds, 1950, 208 pp., 6/-)

A challenge on transmigration—and the Colonel finds himself living as an animal for a few minutes. He passes through many creatures, and finishes as a flea.

Sword of Welleran and Other Stories, The [C] (G. Allen, 1908, 242 pp., illus.–S. H. Sime, 6/-) (J. W. Luce, 1916, 177 pp., illus.–

Sime, $1.75)

12 stories: "The Sword of Welleran"; "The Fall of Babbul-kind"; "The Kith of the Elf-Folk"; "The Highwayman"; "In the Twilight"; "The Ghosts"; "The Whirlpool"; "The Hurricane"; "The Fortress Unvanquishable, Save by Sacnoth"; "The Lord of Cities"; "The Doom of La Traviata"; "On the Dry Land." See also the next entry.

Sword of Welleran and Other Tales of Enchantment, The [C] (Devin-Adair, New York, 1954, 181 pp., illus.–R. Barrell, $3.00)

15 stories selected from the earlier volume (next above) and other collections, but unfortunately without the original exquisite Sime drawings: "Bethmoora"; "Bride of the Man-Horse"; "Distressing Tale of Thangobrind the Jeweller"; "East and West"; "Exiles' Club"; "The Hen"; "Idle Days on the Yan"; "The Kith of the Elf-Folk"; "Poltarnees, Beholder of Ocean"; "The Return"; "Story of Land and Sea"; "The Sword of Welleran"; "Three Sailors Gambit"; "Widow Flynn's Apple Tree"; "Wonderful Window."

Tales of Three Hemispheres [C] (J. W. Luce, 1919, 147 pp., $1.75) (Unwin, London, 1920, 147 pp., 6/-)

14 stories: "The Last Dream of Bwona Khubla"; "The Postman of Otford" (*FFM*, Sep 1944); "The Prayer of Boob Aheera"; "East and West"; "A Pretty Quarrel"; "How the Gods Avenged Meoul Ki Ning"; "The Gifts of Gods"; "The Sack of Emeralds"; "The Old Brown Coat"; "An Archive of the Older Mysteries"; "A City of Wonder." *Beyond the Fields We Know* [Publisher's Note, written by Dunsany as introduction to the "Three Tales"]: *First Tale*–"Idle Days on the Yann"; *Second Tale*–"A Shop in Go-By Street"; *Third Tale*–"The Avenger of Perdondaris."

Tales of War [C] (Little Brown, Boston, 1918, 166 pp.) (Talbot, Dublin, 1918) (Unwin, 1918, 156 pp., 5/-) (Putnam, 1922, 156 pp., 3/6)

32 stories: "The Prayer of the Men of Daleswood"; "The Road"; "An Imperial Monument"; "A Walk to the Trenches"; "A Walk in Picardy"; "What Happened on the Night of the Twenty-Seventh"; "Standing To"; "The Homing Plane"; "England"; "Shells"; "Two Degrees of Envy"; "The Master of No Man's Land"; "Weeds and Wire"; "Spring in England and Flanders"; "The Nightmare Countries"; "Spring and the Kaiser"; "Two Songs"; "The Punishment"; "The English Spirit"; "An Investigation Into the Causes and Origin of War"; "Lost"; "The Last Mirage"; "A Famous Man"; "The Oases of Death"; "Anglo-Saxon Tyranny"; "Memories"; "The Movement"; "Nature's Cad"; "The Home of Herr Schnitzelhaaset"; "A Deed of Mercy"; "Last Scene of All"; "Old England." *Note:* This listing is for the Talbot and the Unwin editions; in the other editions "The Homing Plane" is omitted and "Splendid Traveller" is added.

Tales of Wonder [C] See *Last Book of Wonder, The*

Time and the Gods [C] (Heinemann, London, 1906, 179 pp., illus., 6/-) (J. W. Luce, 1913, 219 pp., illus.–S. H. Sime, $1.75) (Putnam, 1923, 232 pp., illus.–Sime, 7/6)

20 stories: "Cave of Kai"; "Coming of the Sea"; "Dreams of a Prophet"; "For the Honour of the Gods"; "Jest of the Gods"; "Journey of the King"; "King That Was Not"; "Land of Time"; "Legend of the Dawn"; "Men of Yarnith"; "Mlideon"; "Night and Morning"; "Relenting of Sarnidac"; "Secret of the Gods"; "Sorrow of Search"; "South Wind"; "Time and the Gods"; "Usury"; "Vengeance of Men"; "When the Gods Slept."

Travel Tales of Mr. Joseph Jorkens, The [C] (Putnam, New York & London, 1931, 304 pp., $2.00 & 7/6)

13 stories: "Charm Against Thirst"; "Daughter of Rameses"; "Drink at a Running Stream"; "Electric King"; "How Jembu Played for Cambridge"; "King of Sahara"; "Large Diamond"; "Mrs. Jorkens"; "Our Distant Cousins"; "Queer Island"; "The Showman"; "Tale of Abu Laheeb"; "Witch of the Willows."

Unhappy Far Off Things [C] (Elkin Mathews, London, 1919, x+84 pp., 5/-) (Little Brown, Boston, 1919, 3+104 pp.)

1 sonnet and 12 stories telling "something of the wrongs that the people of France had suffered": "A Dirge of Victory" (sonnet); "The Cathedral of Arras"; "A Good War"; "The House With Two Storeys"; "Bermondsey Versus Wurtemburg"; "On an Old Battle-Field"; "The Real Thing"; "A Garden of Arras"; "After Hell"; "A Happy Valley"; "In Bethune"; "In an Old Drawing Room"; "The Homes of Arras."

Nonfiction

Sirens Wake, The (National Book Association & Hutchinson, London, *ca.* 1945, 128 pp.)

36 essays, including such titles as "Back to Europe With Jorkens"; "Better Fifty Years of Europe?"; "The Battle of Britain"; "In the Land of the Hittites"; "Africa at Peace," etc.

DUTHIE, ERIC
Anthologies

Stirring Stories for Boys (Odhams, London, 1967, 320 pp., illus., 11/6)

19 stories, mostly adventure, of which the following are of sf or fantasy interest: "See Luna and Die," John K. Cross; "Jorkens Practises Medicine and Magic," Lord Dunsany; "Little Tales of Tomorrow" (from *The Other Side of the Sky*), Arthur C. Clarke.

Tall Short Stories (Simon & Schuster, New York, 1959, 406 pp., $5.00) (Faber, London, 1959, 367 pp., 15/- [omits stories marked by *]) (Ace: Star K-113, 1960, 352 pp., pa 50¢)

48 stories, many fantasy: *I. The Natural Liar:* "A. V. Laider," M. Beerbohm; "A Funny Thing," H. E. Bates; "The Open Window," Saki. *II. The Air of Truth:* "Mrs. Jorkens," Lord Dunsany; "The Misadventures of a Matrimonial Swindler," K. Capek; "Entrance Fee," A. Woolcott; "Flurry at the Sheep Dog Trial," E. Knight; "Astonished Father," B. Glemser; "The Woman in the Case," A. Chekhov; "The Contraption," R. Davies; "Song at Twilight," W. Gibbs; "The Window," G. de Maupassant"; "Idle Tears," Lord Dunsany; "The B.B.I.," A. J. Alan. *III. The Wolf Strain: A Ferocious Pack:* "The Troll," T. H. White; "The Unicorn in the Garden," J. Thurber; "Fallen Star," J. Collier; "Another American Tragedy," J. Collier; "Earth to Earth," R. Graves; "On Guard," E. Waugh; "Two Bottles of Relish," Lord Dunsany. *IV. The Hyperbolist:* "The Great French Duel,"* M. Twain; "Guest of the Redshields," Christina Stead; "The Background," Saki; "Pigs Is Pigs,"* E. P. Butler; "A Cross Section," A. P. Herbert; "How the Brigadier Slew the Fox," A. C. Doyle; "The Awful Fate of Melpomenus Jones," S. Leacock; "Maxims at Fifty Thousand Feet,"* A. Buchwald; "The Golden Scilens," Sir J. Squire. *V. Science Fiction Surpassed:* "The Vanishing Man," R. Hughes; "No Strings Attached," R. Bradbury; "Elixir of Love," C. S. Forester; "Do Insects Think?" R. Benchley; "The Truth About Pyecraft," H. G. Wells; "God and the Machine," N. Balchin. *VI. Life, the Great Tall Story:* "I'll Always Call You Schnorrer, My African Explorer,"* S. J. Perelman; "The Extraordinary Cabman," G. K. Chesterton; "The Perfect Game," G. K. Chesterton; "The Rightful Heir," A. Marshall; "The Bus," A. Marshall; "The Man With the Heart in the Highlands," W. Saroyan. *VII. Upside Down–Inside Out:* "The Carmanship of Godfrey Plaste," S. Potter; "Quigley 873," F. Sullivan; "The Honest Man and the Devil," H. Belloc; "Mr. Havlena's Verdict," K. Capek; "If Grant Had Been Drinking at Appomattox," J. Thurber; "Love Is a Fallacy,"* M. Shulman (from *Dobie Gillis*).

DUTOURD, JEAN (14 Jan 1920–)
Fiction

Dog's Head, A (*Une tête de chien*, Gallimard, Paris) [Trans.–R. Chancellor]: (Lehman, London, 1951, 143 pp., 8/6) (Longmans, Toronto, $2.00) (Lion: 196, 1954, 128 pp., pa 25¢) (Avon: H102, 1963, 128 pp., pa 45¢)

Satirical fantasy about a man born with a spaniel's head; well done in the best classical manner.

DWIGHT, HARRISON GRISWOLD (16 Aug 1875–24 Mar 1959)
American writer, born at Constantinople, Turkey.
Fiction

Emperor of Elam and Other Stories, The [C] (Doubleday Page, New York, 1920, ix+387 pp., $2.00)

Fantasy, 14 stories: "Like Michael"; "Henrietta Stackpole, Rediviva"; "The Pagan"; "White Bombazine"; "Unto the Day"; "Mrs. Derwall and the Higher Life"; "The Bathers"; "Retarded Bombs"; "Susannah and the Elder"; "The Emerald of Tamerlane" (in collaboration with John Taylor); "Studio-Smoke"; "Behind

the Door"; "The Bald Spot"; "The Emperor of Elam."
Stamboul Nights [C] (Doubleday Page, New York, 1922, vxii+
371 pp., $2.00, 95¢)

Fantasy, 14 stories: "The Leopard of the Sea"; "Mortmain";
"Mehmish"; "The Glass House"; "The House of the Giraffe";
"The Golden Javelin"; "His Beatitude"; "The Place of Martyrs";
"Under the Arch"; "For the Faith"; "Mill Valley"; "The Regi-
cide"; "The River of the Moon"; "In the Pasha's Garden."

DWYER, JAMES FRANCIS (22 Apr 1874–1952) Australian author, born at Camden, N.S.W. He travelled extensively in Australia, the Middle East and North Africa, including crossing the Sahara to Timbuktoo in 1935. He wrote many fantastic adventure
novels, a number of which appeared in *Blue Book*, *Short Stories*,
etc.; he also contributed to *Collier's*, *Delineator*, etc. Novels listed
by Bleiler run from *The White Waterfall* (1912) to *The City of
Cobras* (1938), which appeared in *BB* as "Caravan Treasure."
Others appearing only in *BB* include "The Spotted Panther"
(1913), a borderline lost-race story, and its sequel "The Treasure
of Vanished Men." Two of his short stories were reprinted in the
Avon Fantasy Reader: "The Cave of the Invisible One" (1937;
AFR, No. 14, 1950), and "The Phantom Ship of Dirk Van
Tromp" (*AFR*, No. 18, 1952).
Fiction [Incomplete—other titles in Bleiler *Checklist*]
Breath of the Jungle [C] (McClurg, Chicago, 1915, 356 pp.)

12 stories, adventure, borderline fantasy: "The Bronze Tiger";
"The Soul Trapper"; "The Red Face of Feerish Ali"; "A Jungle
Graduate"; "The Phantom Ship of Dirk Van Tromp"; "The White
Tentacles"; "The Three Who Fled"; "The Black Horsemen of Mir
Jehal"; "The Orang Outang Fight on the Papuan Queen"; "The
Blind Dog of El Corib"; "The Golden Woman of Kelantan"; "The
Little Gold Ears of Sleth."

DYALHIS, NICTZIN British weird writer. He had a number of
noted stories in *Weird Tales* 1925-40. These included "The Sapphire Goddess" (*WT*, Feb 1934; *Worlds of Weird* [Margulies],
1965, pa); "The Sea Witch" (*WT*, Dec 1937, July 1953; *Weird
Tales* [Margulies], 1964, pa); "The Red Witch" (*WT*, Apr 1932;
Mag. Horror, Jan 1968); and two covering the adventures of Hul
Jok—"When the Green Star Waned (*WT*, Apr 1925, Jan 1929)
and "The Oath of Hul Jok" (*WT*, Sep 1928).

DYE, CHARLES (1927–1960?) U.S. sf author. He was in the
U.S. Army Air Force in World War II, and began writing after an
air crash. His first appearance was "The Last Orbit" (*AS*, Feb
1950). He wrote about 20 stories in the field 1950-54, most of
which appeared in the Lowndes magazines.
Fiction
Prisoner in the Skull (Abelard, New York, 1952, 256 pp., $2.50;
London, 1960, 9/6) (*NW*, sr3, Dec 1954) (Corgi: S486, 1957, 219
pp., pa 2/6) (*Le vasche del sonno* [Italian], *Cosmo*: 142, 1963)

EAGER, EDWARD (McMAKEN) U.S. author noted for the ju-
venile fantasy tetralogy listed below. Another novel, *The Well-
Wishers*, may be fantasy.
Series
'Children' tetralogy. *Half Magic*; *Knight's Castle*; *Magic by the
Lake*; *The Time Garden*. They were illustrated by N. M. Bodecker,
and published in alphabetical order.

Fiction [all juvenile]
Half Magic (Harcourt, New York, 1954, 217, illus., $2.75) (Mac-
millan, London, 1954, 185 pp., illus., 7/6; 1960, 12/6)

First of tetralogy: A group of children learn the strict rules of
magic, and have an amulet which annoyingly grants precisely half
of one's wish.
Knight's Castle (Harcourt, 1956, 183 pp., illus., $2.75) (Macmil-
lan, 1956, 197 pp., illus., 11/6)

Second of tetralogy: The children go to the world of *Ivanhoe*
and have grand sport applying logical magic to Scott's events.
Magic by the Lake (Harcourt, 1957, 183 pp., illus., $2.95) (*Magic
or Not*, Macmillan, 1959, 190 pp., illus., 12/6; Longmans, Toronto, $3.50)

Third of the journeys of the children into strictly logical adven-
tures in magic.
Magic or Not See *Magic by the Lake*
Seven-Day Magic (Harcourt, 1962, 156 pp., illus.–N. M. Bodeck-
er, $3.25) (Macmillan, 1963, 156 pp., illus., 12/6)
Time Garden, The (Harcourt Brace, 1958, 188 pp., illus., $3.00)
(Longmans, Toronto, $3.50) (Macmillan, 1959, 185 pp., illus.,
12/6)

Conclusion of the tetralogy; it involves a sundial reading "Anything Can Happen When You've All the Time in the World."
Well-Wishers, The (Harcourt, 1960, 191 pp., $3.25) (Macmillan,
1961, 191 pp., illus., 12/6) (Longmans, Toronto, $3.75)

EARLEY, GEORGE W(HITEFORD) (15 Feb 1927–) U.S. aero-
space administrative engineer.
Anthology
Encounters With Aliens (Sherbourne, Los Angeles, 1968, 244 pp.,
$4.95)

Sf, 12 stories, introduction by Ivan T. Sanderson, and editor's
preface: "The Four-Faced Visitors of Ezekiel," Arthur W. Orton;
"The Cave of History," T. Sturgeon; "The Uninvited Guest," C.
Anvil; "Something in the Sky," Lee Correy; "Albatross," M. Reynolds; "The Other Kids," Robert F. Young; "The Grantha Sighting," A. Davidson; "The Tie That Binds," George Whitley; "The
Venus Papers," R. Wilson; "Minister Without Portfolio," M. Clingerman; "Fear Is a Business," T. Sturgeon; "Ringer," G. C. Edmondson.

EARNSHAW, BRIAN
Fiction
Planet in the Eye of Time (Hodder & Stoughton, London, 1968,
192 pp., 21/-)

Adventure thriller with a journey through time to the Cruci-
fixion.

EASSON, ROBERT (WATSON) (10 Apr 1941–)
Fiction
Bird, the Ghoul, and in the Name of My Friend, The (Vantage,
New York, 1968, 66 pp., $2.50)

EASTWOOD, WILFRED
Nonfiction [editor]
Science and Literature (Macmillan, London, 1957, 296 pp., 6/-)

Subtitled "The literary relations of science and technology—an
anthology."
Science and Literature: Second Series (Macmillan, 1960, 290 pp.,
8/-)

EATON, EVELYN (SYBIL MARY) (1902–)
Fiction
King Is a Witch, The (Cassell, London, 1965, 263 pp., 25/-)
Borderline fantasy.

EBERS, GEORG MORITZ (1837–1898)
Fiction
Elixir and Other Tales, The [C] (W. S. Gottsberger, New York,
1890, 261 pp.)

Fantasy, 3 stories: "The Elixir"; "The Greylock, a Fairy Tale";
"The Nuts, a Christmas Story."

ECHARD, MARGARET
Fiction
Dark Fantastic (Doubleday, New York, 1947, 312 pp., $2.50) (McClelland, Toronto, $2.75) (Invincible Press, Sydney, 1948, 288 pp., 9/6)

A good combination murder and ghost story set in Indiana after the Civil War.

ECKSTROM, JACK DENNIS
Fiction
Time of the Hedrons (Avalon, New York, 1968, 190 pp., $3.50)

EDDISON, E(RIC) R(UCKER) (1882–1945) English civil servant. In addition to several minor works he wrote what some authorities consider to be three of the most remarkable romances in the English language: *The Worm Ouroboros*, *Mistress of Mistresses*, and *A Fish Dinner in Memison*. Out of print for many years, the first-named reappeared in 1952 and 1962, and since late 1967 Ballantine has been reprinting them all.
Series
Zimiamvian trilogy. *Mistress of Mistresses*; *A Fish Dinner in Memison*; *The Mezentian Gate*. This trilogy does *not* include *The Worm Ouroboros*; its only connection is in the use of the name "Lessingham" in the introduction and early chapters. The series was written in reverse order, with *Mistress of Mistresses* starting where *The Mezentian Gate* finishes; *A Fish Dinner in Memison* occurs during the time span of the latter.
Fiction
Fish Dinner in Memison, A (Dutton, New York, 1941, 3+349 pp., illus., $3.50; 998 copies) (Ballantine: U7064, 1968, 319 pp., pa 95¢)

The story of two worlds, ours and one in another dimension— "Zimiamvia." The differences in character of the two places are intermingled.
Mezentian Gate, The (Elek, London, 1958, xxiv+248 pp., frontis. & decorations–K. Henderson, 30/-)

Last of the Zimiamvian trilogy. It covers all but two years of the 70 of this world's history, often synoptically but at critical points in close detail. The novel begins before the birth of King Mezentius and covers his career and death.
Mistress of Mistresses (Dutton, 1935, 643 pp., maps, $3.50) (Faber, London, 1935, 10/6) (Ballantine: U7063, 1968, 404 pp., pa 95¢)

Subtitled "A Vision of Zimiamvia." An important fantastic romance.
Styrbiorn the Strong (A. C. Boni, New York, 1926, 256 pp., $2.00) (J. Cape, London, 1926, 7/6)

Historical romance: a Viking saga of a character mentioned in ancient manuscripts.
Worm Ouroboros, The (J. Cape, London, 1922, 446 pp.; 1924, 446 pp.) (A. C. Boni, 1926, 445 pp., $3.00) (Dutton, 1952, 445 pp., $5.00) (Crown 'Xanadu,' New York, 1962, 445 pp., pa $1.95) (Ballantine: U7061, 1967, 520 pp., pa 95¢) [All editions illus.– Keith Henderson; eds. before 1952 have 4½-p. intro.–J. Stephens; the Dutton ed. has new 5-p. intro.–Orville Prescott]

A classic which took 30 years to write, it is noted as one of the greatest fantasy-romance-adventure stories of all time. It is set in the Age of Chivalry in a never-never land called Mercury.

EDGAR, KENNETH U.S. school teacher in the Pittsburgh area.
Fiction
Starfire, The [pa] (Boxwood, Pittsburgh, 1961, 174 pp., illus.– Edna Schimizzi, pa $1.95)

Juvenile. A brilliant 12-year-old builds a moon rocket and a matter transmitter, and with others takes a jaunt to assorted planets. The story was tested in schools in Monroeville, Pa., prior to open publication. Some of the science is not accurate.

EDMONDS, HARRY
Fiction [Incomplete]
Rockets (Operation Manhattan), The (McDonald, London, 1951, 286 pp., 9/6)

Adventure with a successful stratosphere rocket, and the destruction of New York, Chicago and other cities by a foreign power.

EDMONDS, HELEN (WOODS) (1901–Dec 1968) Author. She was born in Cannes and raised in California, and lived in Burma, Europe, Australia and New Zealand. She was married first to Donald Ferguson and then to Stuart Edmonds.
Fiction [as Anna Kavan]
Asylum Piece and Other Stories [C] (J. Cape, London, 1940, 212 pp., 7/6) (Nelson, Toronto, $2.50) (Doubleday, New York, 1946, 312 pp., $2.50)

27 stories: "Airing a Grievance"; "All Kinds of Grief Shall Arrive"; "Asylum Piece"; "At Night"; "Benjo"; "The Birds"; "The Birthmark"; "The Blackout"; "The Brother"; "Certain Experience"; "Changed Situation"; "The Enemy"; "Face of My People"; "The Gannets"; "Glorious Boys"; "Going Up in the World"; "Heavenly Adversary"; "I Am Lazarus"; "Just Another Failure"; "Machines in My Head"; "Now I Know Where My Place Is"; "Palace of Sleep"; "The Picture"; "The Summons"; "There Is No End"; "Unpleasant Reminder"; "Who Desired the Sea."
House of Sleep (Doubleday, 1947, 223 pp., $2.50) (*Sleep Has His House*, Cassell, London, 1948, 192 pp., 7/6)

Story of the astral plane; a penetrating insight into the subconscious world of dreams and shadows.
Ice (P. Owen, London, 1967, 158 pp., 30/-)

The narrator's compulsive search for a girl in a world where an ice age is approaching, after a nuclear war.
Sleep Has His House See *House of Sleep*

EDMONDSON, G. C. [José Mario Garry Ordonez Edmondson y Cotton] (11 Oct 1922–) U.S. author and translator. He was born in Guatemala, took his M.D. in Vienna, but has never practised. At present he is a translator for the U.S. Navy.
Series
Mad Friend. All in *F&SF*: "Misfit" (Feb 1959); " 'From Caribou to Carry Nation' " (Nov 1959); "The Galactic Calabash" (Jan 1960); "The Sign of the Goose" (Aug 1960); "The Country Boy" (May 1961); "The World Must Never Know" (Apr 1963); "The Third Bubble" (June 1964). Published as *Stranger Than You Think*.
Fiction
Ship That Sailed the Time Stream, The [pa] (Ace: M-109, 1965, 167 pp., pa 45¢; with *Stranger Than You Think* [Edmondson])

The fascinating adventures of a U.S. Navy yawl as it jumps around in time.
Stranger Than You Think [C] [pa] (Ace: M-109, 1965, 87 pp., pa 45¢; with *The Ship That Sailed the Time Stream* [Edmondson])

7 stories of the Mad Friend series (see above).

EDWARDS, DAVID (1945?–)
Fiction
Next Stop, Mars! (Greenwich, New York, 1960, 113 pp., $2.75)

Subtitled "A novel of the first spaceship voyage to the Red Planet."

EDWARDS, FRANK (ALLYN) (4 Aug 1908–1968?) U.S. radio commentator, TV personality, and collector of strange facts. He was born in Mattoon, Illinois. He was at one time a golf professional, and in 1953 was voted one of the top news broadcasters of the U.S. His nonfiction paperbacks include *Strange Fate*, *Stranger Than Science*, *Flying Saucers–Here and Now*, *Flying Saucers–Serious Business*, etc. Check the PAPERBACK Listing.
Nonfiction
Strange People (L. Stuart, New York, 1961, 287 pp., $4.95) (Burns MacEachern, Toronto, $6.25) (Popular: PC1046, 1965, 191 pp., pa 50¢) (Pan: X484, 1966, 236 pp., pa 3/6)

Brief unexplained and unexplainable stories of strange people.
Strange World (L. Stuart, 1964, 408 pp., $4.95) (Ace: K-206, 1965, 251 pp., pa 50¢)

Strange stories.

EDWARDS, GAWAIN (pseud) See PENDRAY, G. E.

EDWARDS, NORMAN (pseud) See CARR, T. or WHITE, T. E.

EELLS, ELSIE SPENCER (21 Sep 1880–) American author (Mrs. B. G. Eells). She was born in West Winfield, N.Y.; she has written a number of 'nature'-type fantasies.
Fiction
Magic Tooth and Other Tales From the Amazon, The [C] (Little Brown, Boston, 1927, 243 pp., $2.00)
    Fantasy, 26 stories (not listed in Bleiler *Checklist*): "The Magic Tooth"; "Karu and Rairu"; "Sura's Seeds"; "Why the Owl Rules the Night"; "The Children of the House of Dawn"; "When Cavillaca Ran Away"; "When the Sun Fell From the Sky"; "How Sleep Came"; "How Strike Came to the World"; "How the Great Flood Began"; "Why the Fox Has a Dark Tail"; "The Mother"; "The King"; "The Royal Prince"; "The Contests"; "How the Alligator Got His Scales"; "How the Races Obtained Their Colors"; "The Frog Witch"; "How the Fox Used His Wits"; "Sumé"; "The Story of Mandioca"; "The Son of Ulé"; "How the Tortoise Conquered His Enemies"; "The Flight of Tiri"; "The Story of the Flute"; "In the Days of the Amazon."

EENHOORN, MICHAEL
Anthology
Omnibus of American Mysteries, An (Juniper Press, New York, 1959, 383 pp., $2.95; pa $1.45)
    13 stories, mostly weird: "The Boarded Window," Ambrose Bierce; " 'Thou Art the Man'," E. A. Poe; "In the Fog," Richard H. Davis; "The Woman by the Fountain," F. Marion Crawford; "The Mysterious Card," Cleveland Moffet; "The Cut on the Lips," Thomas B. Aldrich; "Corpus Delicti," Melville D. Post; "Wieland" (abr.), Charles Brockden Brown; "The Upper Berth," F. Marion Crawford; "The Lost Room," Fitz-James O'Brien; "The Lady or the Tiger," Frank R. Stockton; "A Tale of Negative Gravity," F. R. Stockton.

EFREMOV, I. See YEFREMOV, I.

EGBERT, H. M. (pseud) See EMANUEL, V. R.

EGERTON, GEORGE (pseud) See BRIGHT, M. C. D.

EHRLICH, MAX (SIMON) (1909–) U.S. author.
Fiction
Big Eye, The (Doubleday, New York, 1949, 221 pp., $2.50) (Popular Lib.: 273, 1950, 223 pp., pa 25¢) (Boardman, London, 1951, 256 pp., 7/-; #154, 1954, 192 pp., pa 2/-) ([Japanese], Yûkei-sha, abr., 1951) (*L'oeil géant* [French], Hachette, ?) (*Het reuzenoog* [Dutch], Servire en Heineman, 's-Gravenhage, 1952) (*L'occhio gigante* [Italian], *Urania*: 39, 1954) (Bantam: A1860, 1958, 181 pp., pa 35¢) (Corgi: SS844, 1960, 252 pp., pa 2/6)
    A U.S. Book-of-the-Month Club selection; Earth's nations combine under the threat of world disaster.

EICHNER, HENRY M. (19 Oct 1909–24 Nov 1971) U.S. medical artist. Born in Cleveland, Ohio, he was interested in the sf/fantasy field from 1923. He graduated from Cleveland School of Art in 1929, then learned anatomy and techniques of medical art at Johns Hopkins Medical School 1930-31, and worked in this field from then on. He lived in Los Angeles from 1947. He did some covers and illustrations for the Los Angeles Science Fantasy Society's *Shangri L'Affaires* [amateur magazine], and did the only original cover to appear on the Mexican magazine *Los Cuentos Fantásticos* (No. 27). He illustrated the memorial edition for E. E. Evans, *Food for Demons* (Shroud, 1971); he also compiled a comprehensive nonfiction work on Atlantis.

EINSTEIN, CHARLES (2 Aug 1926–)
Fiction
Day New York Went Dry, The [pa] (Gold Medal: k1446, 1964, 160 pp., pa 40¢)

The pressures faced by politicians in a future water shortage crisis.

EISELEY, LOREN (COREY) (3 Sep 1907–) U.S. anthropologist, born in Lincoln, Nebraska. He took his B.A. at U. of Nebraska, and M.A. and Ph.D. at U. of Pennsylvania. He taught at U. of Kansas 1937-44, and was head of the Dept. of Sociology and Anthropology at Oberlin College 1944-47. Since 1947 he has been a professor at U. of Pennsylvania. He is noted for his *The Immense Journey*.
Nonfiction
Firmament of Time, The (Atheneum, New York, 1960, 184 pp., $3.50)
    Six lectures at U. of Cincinnati, autumn 1959, exploring the gradual growth of the knowledge of life. Sections: "How the World Became Natural"; "How Death Became Natural"; "How Man Became Natural"; "How Human Is Man?"; "How Natural Is 'Natural'?"; "How Life Became Natural." Some concepts of sf are actually survivals of attitudes of former centuries.

EISLER, ROBERT (1882–1949)
Nonfiction
Man Into Wolf (Routledge, London, 1951, 286 pp., 21/-) (Philosophical Lib., New York, 1952, 286 pp., $6.00)
    A full study of lycanthropy, sadism and masochism.

EKSTROM, KJELL M. (9 July 1920–) Swedish editor and translator, Ph.D. in literature. He has edited *Häpna* since its inception, and has done translations for it from English and German, e.g., *The Mouse That Roared* (L. Wibberley) and *Heliopolis* (E. Jünger). He was also editor of *Thriller-Magasinet*.

ELAM, RICHARD M. Jr. U.S. author.
Fiction
Super Science Stories See *Teen-Age Super Science Stories*
Teen-Age Science Fiction Stories [C] (Grosset, New York, 1954, 254 pp., illus.–H. Geer, $1.25)
    11 stories: "By Jupiter"; "The Day the Flag Fell"; "Hands Across the Deep"; "The Iron Moon"; "Lunar Trap"; "Project Ocean Floor"; "Red Sands"; "Sol's Little Brother"; "The Strange Men"; "Venusway"; "What Time Is It?"
Teen-Age Super Science Stories [C] (Lantern, 1957, 253 pp., illus.–F. E. Vaughan, $2.75, lib. $2.85; 1958, $1.50) (*Super Science Stories*, Lantern: 50526, 1967, 231 pp., pa 50¢)
    9 stories: "Expedition Pluto"; "First Man Into Space"; "Flight of the Centaurus"; "Ghost Ship of Space"; "Mercy Flight to Luna"; "Mystery Eyes Over Earth"; "Peril From Outer Space"; "Race Around the Sun"; "Space Steward."
Young Readers Science Fiction Stories [C] (Lantern, 1957, 191 pp., $2.50, lib. $2.85) (McLeod, Toronto, $2.95) (Lantern: 50096, 1964, 212 pp., pa 50¢)
    11 stories (those marked † from *Boys' Life*): "What Time Is It?"; "The Strange Men"; "Project Ocean Floor"; "Lunar Trap"†; "Red Sands"; "The Iron Moon"†; "Venusway"†; "By Jupiter"†; "Sol's Little Brother"; "The Day the Flag Fell"; "Hands Across the Deep."
Young Visitor to Mars (Lantern, 1953, 256 pp., illus.–C. H. Geer, $2.50) (McLeod, Toronto, $3.00) (Grosset & Dunlap, New York, 1956, $1.00) (*Jenseits der Erde* [German], Oetinger, 1957)
    Juvenile.
Young Visitor to the Moon (Criterion, New York, 1965, 191 pp., $2.95)
    Juvenile.

ELDER, JOSEPH
Anthology
Farthest Reaches, The (Trident, New York, 1968, 217 pp., $4.95)
    Sf, 12 stories, with 4½-page foreword: "The Worm That Flies," B. W. Aldiss; "Kyrie," P. Anderson; "Tomorrow Is a Million Years," J. G. Ballard; "Pond Water," J. Brunner; "The Dance of the Changer and the Three," Terry Carr; "Crusade," A. C. Clarke; "Ranging," J. Jakes; "Mind Out of Time," K. Laumer; "The In-

spector," James McKimmey; "To the Dark Star," R. Silverberg; "A Night in Elf Hill," N. Spinrad; "Sulwen's Planet," J. Vance.

ELDERSHAW, F. S. P. See ELDERSHAW, M. B.

ELDERSHAW, M. BARNARD Pseudonym for the collaboration of Flora Sydney Patricia Eldershaw and May Faith Barnard.
Fiction
Tomorrow and Tomorrow (Georgian House, Melbourne, 1947, 466 pp., 13/6) (Phoenix, London, 1949, 468 pp., 12/6) (Dent, U.S., $3.00)
Time travel—a writer in Australia 400 years hence describes life in the bad old days of 1920-50.

ELDRIDGE, PAUL (5 May 1888–) U.S. author and teacher, born in Philadelphia. He obtained his B.A. at Temple U., M.A. at U. of Pennsylvania, then Docteur de l'Universite at U. of Paris, 1913. He was a high school teacher of Romance languages in New York 1914-45. He has lectured at the Sorbonne and at U. of Florence. He married Sylvette de Lamar (a contributor to *Ghost Stories*).
Series
Wandering Jew. See VIERECK, G. S. (co-author)

ELG, STEFAN
Nonfiction
Beyond Belief [pa] (Tower: 43-672, 1967, 155 pp., pa 60¢)
Supposedly true accounts of the Impossible That Happened, with 20 chapters covering such aspects as Swedenborg, levitation, poltergeists, persistent legends of the headless body, etc.

ELLIK, RON(ALD D.) (28 Sep 1938–27 Jan 1968) U.S. sf fan and author. He served in the U.S. Marines and was a computer programmer. He died in an automobile accident the day before he was to have been married. He won the 1962 TAFF nomination and visited the English Eastercon; he won a Hugo in 1959 for his publication (with Terry Carr) of the news fan magazine *Fanac*. As Frederick Davies he had one story in the Ace *Man From UNCLE* series.
Nonfiction
Universes of E. E. Smith, The [with Bill Evans] (Advent, Chicago, 1966, 272 pp., illus.—Bjo, $6.00; 1968, pa $2.45)
Introduction by James H. Schmitz, bibliography by Al Lewis. A concordance to E. E. Smith's "Lensman" series (by Ellik) and "Skylark" series (by Evans).

ELLIN, STANLEY
Fiction
Blessington Method, The [C] (Random, New York, 1964, 185 pp., $3.95) (Signet: D2805, 1966, 127 pp., pa 50¢)
Fantasy and mystery, 10 stories with 4-p. intro.—J. Symonds: "The Blessington Method"; "The Faith of Aaron Menefee"; "You Can't Be a Little Girl All Your Life"; "Robert"; "Unreasonable Doubt"; "The Day of the Bullet"; "Beidenbauer's Flea"; "The Seven Deadly Virtues"; "The Nine-to-Five Man"; "The Question."
Quiet Horror [C] [pa] (Dell: D325, 1959, 224 pp., pa 35¢) (Signet: D2806, 1965, 175 pp., pa 50¢)
10 horror mystery stories: "The Specialty of the House"; "The Cat's Paw"; "Death on Christmas Eve"; "The Orderly World of Mr. Appleby"; "Fool's Mate"; "The Best of Everything"; "The Betrayers"; "The House Party"; "Broker's Special"; "The Moment of Decision."

ELLIOT, JOHN British TV script writer. See HOYLE, F. (co-author).

ELLIOTT, BRUCE U.S. sf writer appearing in the magazine field in the 1950's.
Fiction
Asylum Earth [pa] (*SS*, Oct 1952) (Belmont: B50-819, 1968, 157 pp., pa 50¢)

ELLIOTT, GEORGE Author, had 7 stories in *F&SF* Apr 1951 to Nov 1961.

Fiction
Among the Dangs [C] (Holt Rinehart Winston, New York, 1961, 255 pp., $3.95) (Secker Warburg, London, 1962, 255 pp., 18/-)
10 stories including some fantasy: "A Family Matter"; "Brother Quintillian and Dick the Chemist" "FAQ"; "Miss Cudahy of Stowes Landing"; "The NRACP"; "Children of Ruth" "The Beatification of Bobbysu Wilson" "Love Among the Old Folks"; "Hymn of the Angels"; "Among the Dangs" (1958, reprinted in Apr 1960 *F&SF*).

ELLIOTT, H(ARRY) CHANDLER (26 Aug 1909–) Naturalised U.S. physician, born in Toronto, Canada. B.A., U. of Toronto 1930, M.A. 1935. His specialty is neuroanatomy, which he has taught at U. of Nebraska School of Medicine.
Fiction
Reprieve From Paradise (Gnome, New York, 1955, 256 pp., $3.00) (*El rescate del paraiso* [Spanish], Nebula: 47, 1958, pa)
After an atomic war the world is run by Polynesians. The hero discovers a plot to turn the Earth on its axis and make Antarctica inhabitable.

ELLIOTT, WILLIAM J.
Fiction
Tomorrow's Spectacles (Swan, London, 1946, 188 pp., 5/-)
Funny novel about precognition.

ELLISON, HARLAN (27 May 1934–) U.S. author and editor. He went through all the stages of sf fandom, writing numerous articles for amateur magazines and publishing fanzines himself, notably *Dimensions*. He attended Ohio State University. He has had various occupations—runner for a bookie, "top man" in a carnival, truck driver, salesman, logger, and department store floorwalker. When he first came to New York he joined a gang of juvenile delinquents in order to gain experience of this side of life, about which he has since written. Since 1954 he has appeared frequently in the sf field, with over 50 stories. His non-sf fiction includes *Rumble* (Pyramid, 1958, pa). Around 1959 he was assistant editor for Hamling's *Rogue* magazine, and then was editor with Regency Books until October 1961. He won the 1966 Hugo for best short fiction with " 'Repent, Harlequin!' Said the Ticktockman" (*GSF*, Dec 1965), which has been reprinted several times. Ellison compiled a controversial anthology, *Dangerous Visions* (1967), of new stories on 'normally censored themes.'
Series
Kyben. "Life Hutch" (*If*, Apr 1954); "The Crackpots" (*If*, June 1956); *A Touch of Infinity*.
Fiction
Doomsman [pa] ("The Assassin," *Imagination*, Oct 1958) (Belmont: B50-779, 1967, 74 pp., pa 50¢; with *Telepower*)
A youth is trained as an assassin and sent to kill his own father.
Earthman, Go Home [pa] See *Ellison Wonderland*
Ellison Wonderland [C] [pa] (Paperback: 52-149, 1962, 191 pp., pa 50¢) (*Earthman, Go Home*, Paperback: 52-508, 1964, 191 pp., pa 50¢; 53-727, 1968, pa 60¢)
16 stories: "Commuter's Problem"; "Do-It-Yourself"; "The Silver Corridor"; "All the Sounds of Fear"; "The Sky Is Burning"; "Mealtime" ("A Case of Ptomaine"); "The Very Last Day of a Good Woman" ("The Last Day"); "Battlefield" ("His First Day at War"); "Deal From the Bottom"; "The Wind Beyond the Mountains" ("Savage Wind"); "The Forces That Crush" ("Are You Listening?"); "Nothing For My Noon Meal"; "Hadj"; "Rain, Rain, Go Away"; "In Lonely Hands."
From the Land of Fear [C] [pa] (Belmont: B60-069, 1967, 176 pp., pa 60¢)
Weird, 11 stories: "The Sky Is Burning"; "The Time of the Eye"; "Back to the Drawing Boards"; "Battle Without Banners"; "The Voice in the Garden"; "Life Hutch"; " 'We Mourn for Anyone . . .' "; "A Friend to Man"; "My Brother Paulie"; "Soldier"; "Soldier" [TV script].
I Have No Mouth and I Must Scream [C] [pa] (Pyramid: X1611, 1967, 175 pp., pa 60¢)
Weird, 7 stories, with introduction "The Mover, the Shaker," T.

Sturgeon; foreword "How SF Saved Me From a Life of Crime": "I Have No Mouth, and I Must Scream"; "Big Sam Was My Friend"; "Eyes of Dust"; "World of the Myth"; "Lonelyache"; "Delusion for a Dragon Slayer"; "Pretty Maggie Moneyeyes."

Love Ain't Nothing But Sex Misspelled [C] (Trident, New York, 1968, 382 pp., $5.95)

22 stories, with preface "Motherhood, Apple Pie and the American Way' (Ellison): "Pretty Maggie Moneyeyes"; "The Night of Delicate Terrors"; "What I Did on My Vacation This Summer by Little Bobby Hirschhorn, Age 27"; "Neither Your Jenny Nor Mine"; "Final Shtick"; "O Ye of Little Faith"; "Blind Bird, Blind Bird, Go Away From Me!"; "Riding the Dark Train Out"; "Delusion For a Dragon-Slayer"; "Daniel White For the Greater Good"; "Lonelyache"; "The Universe of Robert Blake"; "Mona at Her Windows"; "G.B.K.—A Many Flavored Bird"; "The Face of Helene Bournouw"; "The Resurgence of Miss Ankle-Strap Wedgie"; "Ernest and the Machine God"; "Battle Without Banners"; "Punky and the Yale Men"; "A Path Through the Darkness"; "A Prayer For No One's Enemy"; "All the Sounds of Fear."

Man With Nine Lives, The [pa] (Ace: D-413, 1959, 133 pp., pa 35¢; with *A Touch of Infinity* [Ellison])

Novel written from "The Sound of a Scythe" (*AS*, Oct 1959) and "Assassin" (*SFA*, Feb 1957), as "Travelogues Two; In Delpheron's Armada." The dramatic and intricately woven story of Cal Emory trying to obtain vengeance in a future society.

Paingod and Other Delusions [C] [pa] (Pyramid: R1270, 1965, 157 pp., pa 50¢)

Weird, 7 stories, with introduction: "Paingod"; " 'Repent, Harlequin!' Said the Ticktockman"; "The Crackpots"; "Bright Eyes"; "The Discarded" ("The Abnormals"); "Wanted in Surgery"; "Deeper Than Darkness."

Touch of Infinity, A [C] [pa] (Ace: D-413, 1959, 123 pp., pa 35¢; with *The Man With Nine Lives* [Ellison])

Sf, 6 stories: "Run For the Stars"; "Back to the Drawing Boards"; "Life Hutch"; "The Sky Is Burning"; "Final Trophy"; "Blind Lightning."

Anthology

Dangerous Visions (Doubleday, New York, 1967, xxxii+520 pp., illus.—Leo & Diane Dillon, $6.95) (D'day SF B.C., 1967, $2.80)

33 stories, all new; introductions by I. Asimov and Ellison: "Evensong," L. del Rey; "Flies," R. Silverberg; "The Day After the Day the Martians Came," F. Pohl; "Riders of the Purple Wage," P. J. Farmer; "The Malley System," Miriam A. deFord; "A Toy for Juliette," R. Bloch; "The Prowler in the City at the Edge of the World," H. Ellison; "The Night That All Time Broke Out," B. W. Aldiss; "The Man Who Went to the Moon—Twice," H. Rodman; "Faith of Our Fathers," P. K. Dick; "The Jigsaw Man," L. Niven; "Gonna Roll the Bones," F. Leiber; "Lord Randy, My Son," J. L. Hensley; "Eutopia," P. Anderson; "Incident in Moderan," "The Escaping," D. R. Bunch; "The Doll-House," J. Cross; "Sex and/or Mr. Morrison," Carol Emshwiller; "Shall the Dust Praise Thee?" D. Knight; "If All Men Were Brothers, Would You Let One Marry Your Sister?" T. Sturgeon; "What Happened to Auguste Clarot?" L. Eisenberg; "Ersatz," H. Slesar; "Go, Go, Go, Said the Bird," Sonya Dorman; "The Happy Breed," J. T. Sladek; "Encounter With a Hick," J. Brand; "From the Government Printing Office," K. Neville; "Land of the Great Horses," R. A. Lafferty; "The Recognition," J. G. Ballard; "Judas," J. Brunner; "Test to Destruction," K. Laumer; "Carcinoma Angels," N. Spinrad; "Auto-da-Fe," R. Zelazny; "Aye, and Gomorrah," S. R. Delany.

ELTON, JOHN (pseud) See MARSH, J.

ELWOOD, ROGER
Anthologies
Alien Worlds [pa] (Paperback: 52-320, 1964, 176 pp., pa 50¢; 53-667, 1968, pa 60¢)

Sf, 10 stories, with brief introduction: "Afternoon of a Fahn," E. F. Russell; "The Cosmic Poachers," P. K. Dick; "Dawn Invader," R. Sheckley; "The Last Monster," P. Anderson; "The Fear Planet," R. Bloch; "Singleminded," J. Brunner; "The Stars, My Brothers," E. Hamilton; "The Brain Stealers of Mars," J. W. Camp-

bell, Jr.; "The Man From Beyond," J. Wyndham; "Madness From Mars," C. D. Simak.

Human Zero, The [pa] See MOSKOWITZ, S. (co-anthologist)
Invasion of the Robots [pa] (Paperback: 52-519, 1965, 157 pp., pa 50¢)

Sf, 8 stories, with brief introduction: "Satisfaction Guaranteed," I. Asimov; "Piggy Bank," Henry Kuttner; "With Folded Hands," Jack Williamson; "Brother to the Machine," Richard Matheson; "The Defenders," Philip K. Dick; "Almost Human," Robert Bloch; "Into Thy Hands," Lester del Rey; "Boomerang," Eric F. Russell.

Strange Signposts [with S. Moskowitz] (Holt Rinehart & Winston, New York, 1966, 319 pp., $5.50)

Sf, 15 stories, with introduction "The Other Side of the Curtain—A Reflection of the Future": "The Last Man," Mary W. Shelley; "Mellonta Tauta," E. A. Poe; "Rappaccini's Daughter," N. Hawthorne; "Hans Schnap's Spy-Glass," Erckmann-Chatrian; "The Chronic Argonauts," H. G. Wells; "The Begum's Fortune," J. Verne; "Frank Reade Junior's Air Wander," Luis P. Senarens; "The Whisperer in Darkness," H. P. Lovecraft; "The Man Who Saw the Future," E. Hamilton; "Prowler of the Wastelands," Harl Vincent; "Skeleton Men of Jupiter," E. R. Burroughs; "Doodad," Ray Bradbury; "The Cosmic Express," J. Williamson; "Castaway," A. C. Clarke; "One Way to Mars," Robert Bloch.

Time Curve, The [pa] See MOSKOWITZ, S. (co-anthologist)

ELY, DAVID (1927–) U.S. writer, Fulbright scholar and newspaperman. The novel below is his second.

Fiction
Seconds (Pantheon [Random House], New York, 1963, 181 pp., $3.95) (Random, Toronto, $4.95) (S. Warburg, London, 1963, 252 pp., 18/-) (Signet: D2507, 1964, 159 pp., pa 60¢) (FSB: 1290, 1965, 159 pp., pa 3/6) (*Andra upplagan* [Swedish], Bonnier, 1965) (*Les doubles* [French], Stock, 1964) (*De tweede kans* [Dutch], Gottner, Haarlem, 1965)

Immortality of sorts is achieved; it starts like a daydream but ends as a nightmare.

Time Out [C] (Secker & Warburg, London, 1968, 238 pp., 30/-)

15 stories of which those marked † are of fantasy interest: "The Academy"; "Creatures of the Sea"; "The Sailing Club"; "An Angel of Mercy"; "The Interview"; "Countdown"†; "Time Out"†; "Neighbours"; "The Glory of G. O'D."†; "The Persecution of the Colonel"; "The Evening Guests"; "Dolley Madison in Peru"†; "Living in Sin"; "One Sunday After Church"; "The Human Factor"†. The title story is a novelette in which Britain, destroyed by a nuclear explosion, must be replaced . . . and the Great Powers do so.

EMANUEL, VICTOR ROUSSEAU (1879–5 Apr 1960) U.S. author. He wrote much sf and fantasy under the pseudonym "Victor Rousseau," and also had some books published as "H. M. Egbert." One of the old-time authors, he wrote some sf directly for the magazines, such as the early Clayton *ASF*. He had stories in both issues of *Miracle, Science and Fantasy*, and also had much fantasy, etc., published in *All-Story Weekly* and borderline magazines. He died almost unnoticed in New York.

Reprints include "The Eye of Balamok" (*ASW*, sr3, 17 Jan 1920; *FN*, May 1949); "The Seal Maiden" (originally 1913; *A. Merritt's Fantasy*, Feb 1950); "The Curse of Amen-Ra" (*Strange Tales*, Oct 1932; *Book of Weird Tales* [British], 1960; *Mag. Horror*, Fall 1967); "A Cry From Beyond" (*Strange Tales*, Sep 1931; *Mag. Horror*, Mar 1968). A story never reprinted was "World's End" (*Arg*, sr3, 6 July 1933), dealing with the survival of some people on a piece of Earth set in orbit by a catastrophe. His last original work was "Moon Patrol" (*TWS*, Oct 1941). Under the name H. M. Egbert he wrote two books not covered here: *Eric of the Strong Heart* (1925) and *Mrs. Aladdin* (1925).

Series
Surgeon of Souls. All in *WT*: "The Case of the Jailer's Daughter" (Sep 1926); "The Woman With the Crooked Nose" (Oct 1926); "The Tenth Commandment" (Nov 1926); "The Legacy of Hate" (Dec 1926); "The Mayor's Menagerie" (Jan 1927); "The Fetish of

the Waxworks" (Feb 1927); "The Seventh Symphony" (Mar 1927); "The Chairs of Stuyvesant Baron" (Apr 1927); "The Man Who Lost His Luck" (May 1927); "The Dream That Came True" (June 1927); "The Ultimate Problem" (July 1927).

Fiction

Apostle of the Cylinder, The See *Messiah of the Cylinder, The*
Draught of Eternity ("Draft of Eternity" [as V. Rousseau], *ASW*, sr4, 1 June 1918) ([as H. M. Egbert], J. Long, London, 1924, 254 pp., 7/6)

Love and adventure in the days when New York is in ruins.

Messiah of the Cylinder, The [as Victor Rousseau] (*Everybody's Mag*, sr4, June 1917) (McClurg, Chicago, 1917, 319 pp., illus., $1.35) (C. Brown, London, 1917, 319 pp.) (*The Apostle of the Cylinder*, Hodder & Stoughton, London, 1918, 319 pp., 6/-)

A classic which foresaw a world dominated by an atheistic socialist tyranny.

Sea Demons, The ([as V. Rousseau], *ASW*, sr4, 1 Jan 1916) ([as H. M. Egbert], J. Long, 1925, 254 pp., 7/6)

Strange sea creatures, much like bees socially, attack humanity; a British submarine finds their "queen" and thwarts the invasion.

EMERSON, CAROLINE D. (1891–)
Fiction
Magic Tunnel, The (Four Winds, New York, 1968, 122 pp., $3.95)

EMSH, ED See EMSHWILLER, E. A.

EMSHWILLER, CAROL Wife of E. A. Emshwiller. She has written a number of sf short stories appearing in *F&SF*, etc.

EMSHWILLER, EDMUND ALEXANDER (1925–) One of the leading contemporary U.S. science fiction artists, principally under the byline "Ed Emsh." Born in Lansing, Michigan, he grew up in the Midwest and in Washington, D.C. He served in the infantry in World War II, then majored in art and graduated from U. of Michigan. He married in 1949, went to Paris to study graphics for a year, then motorcycled through Europe with his wife Carol. He came to New York in 1950 and began sf work with illustrations for *Galaxy*. He has since done many covers for most of the sf magazines, including all of *Infinity*'s but the first. He is particularly noted for achievements in creating alien atmosphere, including such representations as his four-armed Santa Claus which has appeared on a number of *Galaxy* Christmas-time covers. Emshwiller prefers to work on fine arts and experimental movies; his first serious film won the top awards in the Creative Film Foundation International Contest for 1959, and his "Lifelines" was chosen as one of the 10 official U.S. entries for West Germany's 7th International Short Film Festival.

ENDORE, GUY S. (4 July 1900–12 Feb 1970) U.S. author, M.A. (Columbia). His fiction includes *Man From Limbo* and *King of Paris* (Book-of-the-Month Club choice). A short story is "Men of Iron" (1940; *F&SF*, Fall 1949). He wrote the screenplay for *Mad Love*, the 1935 Peter Lorre version of the oft-filmed *The Hands of Orlac*, and became a fast friend of its director, the late Karl Freund (d. 1969). He also collaborated on the adaptation of A. Merritt's *Burn, Witch, Burn!*, which reached the screen as *The Devil Doll*. His fantasy "The Day of the Dragon" (*Blue Book*, mid-1930's) was reprinted in *AFR* No. 2, 1950, and in *Tales of Terror* [Singer], 1967.

Fiction [Incomplete—other titles in Bleiler *Checklist*]
Furies in Her Body, The [pa] See *Methinks the Lady*
Methinks the Lady (Duell Sloan Pierce, New York, 1945, 282 pp., $2.50) (Collins, Toronto, $2.75) (*Damen bedyrar* [Swedish], Ljus, 1946) (Cresset, London, 1947, 279 pp., 10/6) (*The Furies in Her Body*, Avon: 323, 1951, 220 pp., pa 25¢) (*Nightmare*, Dell: D183, 1957, 256 pp., pa 35¢)

Weird novel of a female Jekyll and Hyde.
Nightmare [pa] See *Methinks the Lady*
Werewolf of Paris, The (Farrar Rinehart, New York, 1933, 325 pp., $2.00) (J. Long, London, 1934, 7/6) (Grosset, New York,

1935, 325 pp., 75¢) (Avon: 354, 1951, 189 pp., pa 25¢) (Ace: K-160, 1962, 223 pp., pa 50¢) (Panther: 1555, 1963, 222 pp., pa 3/6)

A blend of lycanthropy with sexual pathology.

ENEY, RICHARD HARRIS (13 Sep 1932–) U.S. sf fan. He was born in New London, Connecticut, graduated B.S. in zoology from George Washington U. in 1958, and became a medical laboratory technologist at Alexandria (Virginia) Hospital. He has since served as a U.S. civil servant in Viet Nam. He discovered science fiction in 1945 and fandom in 1948, and has since published many fan magazines and held various fan offices, including secretary of the 1963 World SF Convention in Washington, D.C.

Nonfiction
Fancyclopedia II (Published by the compiler, Alexandria (Va.), 1959, 190 pp., cardboard covers, mimeo, $1.25, 450 copies)

An updating of Jack Speer's notable *Fancyclopedia* of 1944, long unobtainable. It covers everything in fan and sf terminology from Null-A to Zombie.
Proceedings of the 21st World Science Fiction Convention: Discon [pa] (Advent, Chicago, 1965, 191 pp., illus.—photos, pa $3.50; 1966, $1.95)

Illustrated transcript of the 1963 sf convention in Washington, D.C.

ENGEL, LEONARD (1916–)
Fiction
World Aflame, The [with E. Piller] (Dial, New York, 1947, 126 pp., $2.00)

Nightmarish novel of the Russo-American War of 1950.

ENGLAND, GEORGE ALLAN (9 Feb 1877–26 June 1936) U.S. author, born at Fort McPherson, Nebraska. He went through Harvard, then to cure incipient tuberculosis he went to live in the Maine woods and started writing there. About 1905 he became one of Bob Davis's staff authors for the Munsey magazines. He travelled widely and organized many treasure hunting expeditions. Of interest to fantasy enthusiasts is his nonfiction *Isles of Romance* (1920) telling of places he has visited, often the locale of weird and fantastic stories by various writers. He is primarily remembered for his *Darkness and Dawn* trilogy and for *The Flying Legion*, a classic of its type. He mainly appeared in *ASW* from Dec 1905 to May 1919, and *Cavalier* July 1911 to Feb 1914. His "The Nebula of Death" (*People's Favourite Magazine*, sr, 10 Feb–10 May 1918) is one of the longest fantasies ever written; it tells of Earth entering a nebula whose gases halt photosynthesis; it is generally felt that it would have been an excellent short novel if condensed.

Series
Darkness and Dawn trilogy. "Darkness and Dawn" (*Cavalier*, sr4, Jan 1912; *FFM*, June 1940); "Beyond the Great Oblivion" (*Cavalier*, sr6, 4 Jan 1913; *FFM*, June 1941); "The Afterglow" (*Cavalier*, sr6, 14 June 1913; *FFM*, Dec 1941). Combined as one book in 1914, then issued by Avalon as the books *Darkness and Dawn*, *Beyond the Great Oblivion*, *The People of the Abyss*, *Out of the Abyss* and *The Afterglow*.

Fiction
Afterglow, The (Avalon, New York, 1967, 191 pp., $3.50)
Latter portion of the original title story.
Air Trust, The (Phil Wagner, St. Louis, 1915, 333 pp., illus.)
Two millionaires "corner" air and plan to sell it.
Beyond the Great Oblivion (Avalon, 1965, 190 pp., $3.25)
First portion of the title novel, in which Stern and his secretary find the ocean draining into the abyss, and fly over it.
Cursed (*ASW*, sr6, 11 Jan 1919) (Small Maynard, Boston, 1919, 349 pp., illus.)
An abused native woman curses the next generation of a ruthless sea-captain, and he is compelled to watch his son follow a course of evil.
Darkness and Dawn (Small Maynard, 1914, 672 pp., $1.35) (Avalon, New York, 1964, 191 pp., $2.95)
New York engineer Stern and his secretary survive after a pro-

longed sleep in a deserted world. First of *Darkness and Dawn* series, and a classic of its kind.

Elixir of Hate, The [n] (*Cavalier*, sr4, Aug 1911; *FFM*, Oct 1942; *A. Merritt's Fantasy*, Oct 1950)

A stolen youth elixir and its consequences.

Flying Legion, The (*ASW*, sr6, 15 Nov 1919) (McClurg, Chicago, 1930, 394 pp., frontis.) (*Air Wonder*, sr4, Jan 1930) (*FN*, Jan 1950)

A band of flyers have many adventures following a future air-emperor endeavouring to dominate the world.

Golden Blight, The (*Cavalier*, sr6, 18 May 1912) (H. K. Fly, New York, 1916, 350 pp., illus.) (*FN*, Mar 1949)

Capitalism is smashed by the unleashing of a gold-destroying "zeta" ray.

Out of the Abyss (Avalon, 1967, 189 pp., $3.25)

Part of the *Darkness and Dawn* trilogy; the couple escape from the abyss.

People of the Abyss, The (Avalon, 1966, 192 pp., $3.25)

Part of the *Darkness and Dawn* trilogy. It follows *Beyond the Great Oblivion*; the couple attempt to cross the abyss.

ENGLE, E(LOISE HOPPER) (12 Apr 1923–) U.S. author, born in Seattle, Washington. She was educated at George Washington U., and was a bookkeeper and clerk in Guam 1947-48. She became editor of the Honolulu magazine *Paradise of the Pacific* in 1959.
Fiction
Countdown for Cindy (Hammond, New York, 1962, 191 pp., $2.95) (Bantam: J2753, 1964, 122 pp., pa 40¢)

A frolicsome space opera.

ENNIS, FRED
Fiction
Tales of Ergo (The Author, Palmyra, New York, 1928, 196 pp., wraps)

Not a collection; the author travels with the spirit "Ergo" who explains physics and astronomy to him.

EPSTEIN, BERYL See EPSTEIN, S.

EPSTEIN, SAMUEL (1909–)
Nonfiction
Prehistoric Animals [with Beryl Epstein] (Franklin Watts, New York, 1957, 210 pp., illus., $3.95)

Story of animals from trilobites to mammals that inhabited the Earth before modern Man arrived.
Rocket Pioneers on the Road to Space, The See WILLIAMS, B. (co-author [wife])

ERCKMANN, EMILE (20 May 1822–14 Mar 1899) French author. The son of a bookseller, he went to Paris to study law, but did not continue. He began writing fiction with Alexandre Chatrian (18 Dec 1826–3 Sep 1890) under the byline "Erckmann-Chatrian." Chatrian was an usher in the college of Phalsbourg when Erckmann made his acquaintance in 1847. The pair achieved no success until 1859. Then they became noted as authors of romances and graphic narratives of the manners and customs of Germany. They also wrote a successful play.
Fiction [Usually as Erckmann-Chatrian] [Incomplete—other titles in Bleiler *Checklist*]
Bells: or, The Polish Jew See *Polish Jew, The*
Polish Jew and Other Tales, The [C] (*The Bells: or, The Polish Jew*, R. M. De Witt, New York, 1872, 33 pp. [title story only; a play]) (G. Munro, New York, 1884, 76 pp. [title story (play) plus "The Three Sisters of the Briars," Owen Landor]) (Ward Lock, London, nd [probably 1890], 229 pp., illus.–Renet)

11 stories (Ward Lock edition): "The Polish Jew" (play); "Aloriis' Dream"; "Messire Tempus"; "The Invisible Eye"; "The Comet"; "The Burgomaster in Bottle"; "A Lock of Black Hair"; "Les Talionis"; "The Inventor"; "Hans Schnapps' Spy Glass"; "Uncle Bernard's Shell."
Strange Stories [C] (Appleton, New York, 1880, 190 pp.)

6 stories: "The Mysterious Sketch"; "The Dean's Worth";

" 'Abraham's Offering' "; "The Three Souls"; "The Invisible Eye"; "The Wonderful Glass."
Wild Huntsman and Other Tales, The [C] (Ward Lock, nd, 184 pp., illus.–Schuler)

3 stories: "The Wild Huntsman"; "The Gypsies"; "The Murderer's Violin." Not listed in Bleiler *Checklist*.

ERCKMANN-CHATRIAN See ERCKMANN, E.

ERISMAN, ROBERT O. U.S. editor. He edited the science fiction magazines *Marvel Science Stories* (Aug 1938–Apr 1941; Nov 1950–May 1952), *Dynamic Science Stories* (Feb 1939, Apr-May 1939), and *Uncanny Stories* (Apr 1941).

ERLANGER, MICHAEL U.S. business executive who is also a painter, sculptor and traveller.
Fiction
Silence in Heaven (Atheneum, New York, 1961, 169 pp., $3.75)

Borderline sf, about the last 10 people on Earth and the search for other survivors; an allegory on the degradation of present trends projected into the future.

ERNST, MORRIS L. (23 Aug 1888–) U.S. lawyer and political figure. He was born in Uniontown, Alabama. He took his B.A. at Williams College in 1909, and Ll.B. New York Law School in 1912. He manufactured shirts and furniture 1909-15, then in 1915 became a member of Greenbaum, Wolff & Ernst, attorneys. He was active in government, being the personal representative of F. D. Roosevelt on a mission abroad during World War II; later he was on President Truman's Civil Rights Commission. He has written a number of books, mostly on civil liberties and public affairs.
Nonfiction
Utopia 1976 (Rinehart, New York, 1955, 305 pp., $3.50)

An optimistic outlook for the world of 1976, in which rust, moths and the common cold have been eliminated, there are no barriers to world-wide travel, etc.

ERNST, PAUL (FREDERICK) (1902–) U.S. author [not the same as the mainstream writer Paul Ernst, who is about 20 years older]. He appeared in the sf field 1931-39 with about 20 stories, some of which have been since reprinted in magazines and anthologies. He had the noted "Dr. Satan" series in *Weird Tales*, and his "The Way Home" (*WT*, Nov 1935) under the pseudonym "Paul Frederick Stern" is considered a near-classic. Ernst left the pulp field, had a number of stories in *Argosy* in the early 1940's, and eventually moved into the slick magazines. His most noted sf stories include "The Microscopic Giants" (*TWS*, Oct 1936; *SS*, May 1948), "Nothing Happens on the Moon" (*ASF*, Feb 1939), and "To Heaven Standing Up" (*Arg*, 5 Apr 1941; *Fan*, Nov 1961).
Series
Doctor Satan. All in *Weird Tales*: "Doctor Satan" (Aug 1935; *Startling Mystery*, Fall 1966); "The Man Who Chained the Lightning" (Sep 1935; *Startling Mystery*, Win 1967/68); "Hollywood Horror" (Oct 1935); "The Consuming Flame" (Nov. 1935); "Horror Insured" (Jan 1936); "Beyond Death's Gateway" (Mar 1936); "The Devil's Double" (May 1936); "Mask of Death" (Aug/Sep 1936).

ERNSTING, WALTER (13 June 1920–) German editor, translator and author, born in Koblenz. He engaged in public works service pre-war. In World War II he was in Air Force communications, serving in Poland, Norway, Lapland and Russia. He spent 1945-50 in a P.O.W. camp in Karaganda, Siberia; when freed he was too ill to work for some time. Early in 1952 he became a translator for the British occupation army, and renewed his acquaintance with English and American science fiction. Deciding to write professionally, he contacted publisher E. Pabel and began the *Utopia* magazines. He was translator and editor for these, besides writing many original stories under the pseudonym "Clark Darlton." Another pseudonym is "F. MacPatterson." After leaving Pabel at the end of 1957 he began the new series *Terra-Sonderband* for the publisher Heyne Moewig. He is now co-publisher of the *Perry*

Rhodan series, for which he also writes. Overall he has translated more than 100 novels and written more than 60 original works. He has also been active in the fan field as president of the SF Club Europa and later the Science-Fiction Union. He has compiled selections from *Galaxy* and many paperback selections for Heyne. Ernsting remains one of Germany's leading sf figures.

ERSKINE, JOHN (5 Oct 1879–2 June 1951) U.S. novelist, poet and essayist. He was also a brilliant teacher of English and a soloist with the New York Philharmonic. In fiction, he is noted for his versions of the legendary tales of Helen of Troy, Lancelot and Galahad, Adam and Lilith.
Fiction [Incomplete—other titles in Bleiler *Checklist*]
Private Life of Helen of Troy, The (Bobbs-Merrill, Indianapolis, 1925, 11+301 pp., $2.00) (Nash, London, 1925, 7/6) (Grosset, New York, 1927, 304 pp., $1.00) (Grayson, London, 1936, 304 pp., 2/6) ([Spanish], Dedalo, 1942) (Wingate, London, 1948, 224 pp., 8/6) (Popular Lib.: 147, 1948, 222 pp., pa 25¢) (Graphic Giant: G-216, 1956, 285 pp., pa 35¢)
    A retelling of the love intrigues of Helen of Troy.
Venus the Lonely Goddess (Morrow, New York, 1949, 155 pp., $2.75) (Collins, Toronto, $3.00) (Wingate, 1950, 175 pp., 7/6)
    The love life of the gods on Mt. Olympus.

ESENWEIN, J(OSEPH) BERG (15 May 1867–1 Nov 1946) U.S. editor, writer and speaker. He obtained his A.M., Lafayette College (1894), Ph.D., Richmond College (1896), and Litt.D., U. of Omaha (1896). His editorships included *Lippincott's Magazine* (Philadelphia) 1905-14, and *The Writer's Monthly* (Springfield, Mass.) from 1915. Throughout his life he lectured and wrote on educational, ethical and popular topics, and wrote books on writing, public speaking, etc. He also composed many songs and hymns.
Anthology
Adventures to Come (McLoughlin Bros., Springfield (Mass.), 1937, 13+187 pp., illus., 50¢)
    Sf, 9 stories (apparently juvenile): "A Man in the Moon Comes Down," B. Copeman; "A Life by Television," J. Arnold; "The Cruise of the S-900," R. Kent; "Twenty-Five Miles Aloft," R. Watson; "Science Steals a March," N. Richards; "Dawn Attack," B. Copeman; "Pirate of the Air," J. S. Bradford; "Six Hundred Fathoms," N. Leslie; "It's Going To Be True," B. Franthway. Considered by many to be the first actual science fiction anthology.

ESHBACH, LLOYD ARTHUR (1910–) U.S. author and book publisher. He was born in Palm, Penna., and moved to Reading when five. At the age of nine he became interested in sf, and started collecting seriously when 14; he now possesses one of the most comprehensive magazine collections. He sold his fourth attempt at writing to *AS*: "The Voice From the Ether" (May 1931). Thereafter he had a number of sf stories published in the 1930's. After the war he formed Fantasy Press, one of the first specialist sf and fantasy publishing houses, became its director, and in 1950 bought out his partners. In 1952 he began the specialist Polaris Press to reprint the lesser-known classics of interest to collectors, but this produced only two books. In late 1958 he sold his stock, including unbound books, to Martin Greenberg, and they were then included in Gnome Press's Pick-a-Book selections.
Fiction
Tyrant of Time, The [C] (Fantasy, Reading [Penna.], 1955, 255 pp., $3.00)
    Sf, 9 stories: "The Tyrant of Time" ("The Time Conqueror"); "The Meteor Miners"; "Spaceways Incident"; "The Light From Beyond" ("God of Light"); "The Place of Orchids" ("The God That Science Made"); "The City of Dread"; "Singing Blades"; "The Cauldron of Life" ("The Cauldron").
Nonfiction [editor]
Of Worlds Beyond: The Science of Science-Fiction Writing (Fantasy, 1947, 96 pp., $2.00) (Advent, Chicago, 1964, 104 pp., $3.50; pa $1.95) (Dobson 'Studies in SF' No. 1, London, 1965, 118 pp., 13/6)
    Essays on techniques of writing science fiction: "On the Writing

of Speculative Fiction," R. A. Heinlein; "Writing a Science Fiction Novel," J. Taine [E. T. Bell]; "The Logic of Fantasy," J. Williamson; "Complication in the Science Fiction Story," A. E. van Vogt; "Humor in Science Fiction," L. S. de Camp; "The Epic of Space," E. E. Smith, Ph.D.; "The Science of Science Fiction Writing," J. W. Campbell, Jr. The Advent and Dobson editions are indexed.

ESSOE, GABE
Nonfiction
Tarzan of the Movies (Citadel, New York, 1968, 208 pp., $8.95)
    Introduction (9 pp.) by Joan Burroughs Pierce; an account of the Tarzan films.

ESTIVAL, IVAN LEON
Fiction [as "Estival"]
Mandragora (Staples, London, 1952, 240 pp., 9/6)
    Time travel by means of mandrake root.

ETTINGER, ROBERT C(HESTER) W(ILSON) (4 Dec 1918–) U.S. physics lecturer and writer. He was born in Atlantic City, N.J., and educated at Wayne State U., Detroit (B.S., M.S., M.A.). He was a 1st lieutenant in World War II. He taught physics at Wayne State 1953–63, then transferred to Highland Park College, Michigan.
Nonfiction
Prospect of Immortality, The (Published by the author, Michigan, 1963, 78 pp., mimeo) (Doubleday, New York, 1964, 190 pp., $3.95)
    A condensation appeared in *Worlds of Tomorrow*, June 1963; the Doubleday version is better documented and better reasoned. It covers deep freezing people in liquid helium and then thawing them when medicine has advanced enough to cure them. The replacement of faulty organs by synthetic or mechanical ones is considered.

EVANS, BERGEN B. (19 Sep 1904–)
Nonfiction
Spoor of Spooks and Other Nonsense (Knopf, New York, 1954, 295 pp., $4.50)
    An intelligent analysis, full of humour and stimulating writing, of the evidence about hundreds of "facts" which are part of our modern folklore.

EVANS, BILL See ELLIK, R. (co-author)

EVANS, E(DWARD) EVERETT (30 Nov 1893–2 Dec 1958) U.S. writer. He made his reputation as a member of sf fandom, and was often termed "The Grand Old Man." In his later years he became a successful science fiction writer with such books as *The Planet Mappers*. Fantasy Press published two others, and a fourth, *Minds Across Space*, has yet to appear. He collaborated with E. E. Smith on "Masters of Space" (*If*, sr2, Nov 1961). A selection of Evans' forty or so short stories has been mooted as a memorial volume.
    Amongst his many fan activities he helped to form the National Fantasy Fan Federation and to put on the first Westercon, he was active in the Fantasy Amateur Press Association, and he was Director of the Los Angeles Science Fantasy Society. He published the amateur magazine *The Time-Binder*. From the Chicon in 1940, he rarely missed a World SF Convention. He married Thelma D. Hamm in 1953.
Fiction
Alien Minds (Fantasy, Reading, 1955, 223 pp., $3.00) (*Kampf der Telepathen* [German], *T*: 190, 1961)
    Sequel to *Man of Many Minds*, with adventure on the planet Estrella.
Man of Many Minds (Fantasy, 1953, 222 pp., $3.00, jacket–M. Hunter) (Pyramid: G-458, 1959, 192 pp., pa 35¢; X1891, 1968, pa 60¢) (*Gefahr von Simonides IV* [German], Zimmermann, 1960; *T*: 184, 1961) (*El hombre de muchas mentes* [Spanish], Cenit: 24, 1961, pa) (*Missione paranormale* [Italian], *Cosmo*: 101, 1962)

The adventures of an ESP-gifted secret service operator of the future; sequel is *Alien Minds*.

Planet Mappers, The (Dodd Mead, New York, 1955, 242 pp., $2.50) (Dodd, Toronto, $2.95)

Juvenile—the adventures of a family mapping planets 62 light-years from Earth. It won the Boys' Clubs of America annual award for the most enjoyable book.

EVANS, I(DRISYN) O(LIVER) (11 Nov 1894–) British author, born at Bloemfontein, South Africa. He was Executive Officer at the Ministry of Works 1919-56. Besides contributing to many magazines such as *The Motor, Cycling*, etc., he has written nonfiction books about such subjects as geology and astronomy—*The World of Tomorrow, Discovering the Heavens* (Roy, 1939) (interesting vignettes on the founders of astronomy), etc. In the sf field he is principally known for his editing and translating of the 'Fitzroy Edition' of the novels of Jules Verne, a series which began in 1958 and includes some not previously translated into English. Prior to this he edited *Jules Verne—Master of Science Fiction* (Sidgwick & Jackson, 1956; Rinehart, 1957), which gives 15 extracts from some of Verne's noted novels. More recently he wrote *Jules Verne and His Work* (Twayne, 1967, $4.00). Ace Books began reprinting his Fitzroy translations of Verne in 1968.

Anthologies

Science Fiction Through the Ages 1 [pa] (Panther: 2152, 1966, 156 pp., pa 3/6)

12 extracts; introduction and bibliography: "Secret Weapon" (from *Count Robert of Paris*), Walter Scott; "The Vanished Civilization" (from *Timaeus* and *Critias*), based on Plato; "Interplanetary Warfare" (from *A True Story*), Lucian; "The Moon-Voyage" (from *Somnium*), Johannes Kepler; "Utopian Science Fiction" (from *The New Atlantis*), Francis Bacon; "Satirical Science Fiction" (from *Gulliver's Travels*), Dean Jonathan Swift; "The Human Mutant" (from *The Life and Adventures of Peter Wilkins*), Robert Paltock; "Visitors From Outer Space" (from *Micromegas*), Voltaire; "The Recalcitrant Robot" (from *Frankenstein*), Mary Shelley; "The Menace of the Machine" (from *Erewhon*), Samuel Butler; "The Conquest of the Air" (*The Balloon Hoax*), Edgar Allan Poe; "Into the Unknown" (from *20,000 Leagues Under the Sea*), Jules Verne.

Science Fiction Through the Ages 2 [pa] (Panther: 2159, 1966, 173 pp., pa 3/6)

12 items with introduction and suggestions for further reading: "An Expostulation" [verse], C. S. Lewis; "The Atomic Bomb" (from *The World Set Free*), H. G. Wells; "Action at a Distance" (from *Ralph 124C41+*), H. Gernsback. The following are complete stories, except the last: "Refugee," A. C. Clarke; "The Feeling of Power," I. Asimov; "A Little Oil," E. F. Russell; "The Cold Equations," Tom Godwin; "The Flinties," I. O. Evans; "A Sound of Thunder," R. Bradbury; "He Walked Around the Horses," H. Beam Piper; "The Light," Poul Anderson; "Those About to Die—" (from *On the Beach*), Nevil Shute.

EVENING STANDARD London newspaper.

Anthologies

Evening Standard Book of Best Short Stories, The (Search Pub. [Denis Archer], London, 1933, 312 pp., 5/-)

30 stories, many weird: "The Portrait," A. Huxley; "The Pioneers of Pike's Peak," B. Tozer; "Used Car," H. R. Wakefield; "The Dream of Ah Lum," T. Burke; "Bare-Nuckle Lover," L. Golding; "Was He a Liar?" M. Arlen; "Bachelors," H. Walpole; "Beyond the Wall," E. S. Ambrose; "The Jar," L. Pirandello; "Another Shot in the Locker," M. Kent; "The Brother," J. Barbusse; "The Brutality of Briggs," S. T. Simon; "A Toy Tragedy," N. Lyons; "Hop-Frog," E. A. Poe; "Ghosts and Jossers," W. F. Harvey; "The Storm," L. A. G. Strong; "Abu Widn," E. R. Morrough; "Lost Treasure," C. Evans; "The Perfect Crime," Seamark; "Rouge et Noir," M. Joseph; "The Patient," M. Mander; "Buridan's Ass," A. Gittins; "The Disappearance of an Actor," K. Capek; "The Man in Grey," B. Fleming; "The Man Who Stole the Pelican," I. A. Williams; "The Smile of La Gioconda," M. Roberts; "Kerrigan and the Blackmailer," N. Gordon; "The Boccherini Min-

uet," C. Landon; "The Triangle," S. A. Wood; "The Case of Susan Wragge," B. Stacey.

Evening Standard Book of Best Short Stories: 2nd Series (Search, 1934, 288 pp., 3/6)

24 stories, many weird: "The Wood of the Dead," A. Blackwood; "Beattock for Moffat," R. B. Cunninghame Graham; "The Luck of Captain Fortune," M. Arlen; "Sherry," P. Fleming; "Paradise Lost," H. A. Manhood; "White Man's Magic," Capt. F. McDermott; "Mad Palace," T. Pratt; "Blazey's Funeral," R. H. Mottram; "Goose-Murder at Tutz," H. Fallada; "Submarine," Stella Benson; "The String of Glass," Ruth Alexander; "The Island," M. Baring; "The Inspiration of Mr. Budd," Dorothy L. Sayers; "Poor Man's Inn," R. Hughes; "Balalaika," F. B. Young; "The Sheik, the Sun, and the Sack," Sirdar Ikbal Ali Shah; "The Case of Mr. Ryalstone," Ex-Private X; "The Dutch Defence," E. Ambrose; "At the Fortunate Frog," C. Brisbane; "It Seemed So Easy," A. P. Garland; "Where Beauty Lies," Marg. Irwin; "The Victim," P. Gibbon; "The Wild Swan," Liam O'Flaherty; "Mrs. Vaudrey's Journey," M. Armstrong.

Evening Standard Book of Strange Stories, The (Hutchinson, London, 1934, 1020 pp., 3/6, 5/6, 7/6)

Weird, 88 stories: "A Tiger's Skin," W. W. Jacobs; "The Room on the Fourth Floor," R. Strauss; "The Book," Marg. Irwin; "Crack o' Whips," H. A. Manhood; "Nobody's House," "The Black Diamond Tree," A. M. Burrage; "The Strange Case of Mr. Todmorden," F. B. Austin; "Mary Ansell," M. Armstrong; "The Devil's Ape," B. Stacey; "Chailey's Folly," L. A. G. Strong; "Dusk Below Helvellyn," A. Marsden; "Crab-Apple Harvest," G. R. Preedy; "Query," Seamark; "He Fought a Ghost," L. Golding; "The Third Performance," A. Gittins; "The Screaming Plant," Hal Pink; "The Old Man," H. Horn; "Sunset Woman," C. P. Thompson; "Portrait of a Queen," Kathleen Rivett; "The Big Drum," Wm. Gerhard; "The Third Medal," A. T. Sheppard; "Chinese Girl," H. de Vere Stacpoole; "My Adventure at Chiselhurst," "The Hair," A. J. Alan; "Fear," "The Hand," G. de Maupassant; "The Song of Ho Ling," "The Hollow Man," T. Burke; "The Lighthouse on Shivering Sand," J. S. Fletcher; "The Secret of the Schwarztal," Francis Gribble; "The Pioneers of Pike's Peak," B. Tozer; "The Shade of Peterbee," M. Kent; "The Screaming Skull," F. M. Crawford; "The Two Horns," Jan Neruda; "The Second Awakening of a Magician," S. L. Dennis; "The Sphinx Without a Secret," O. Wilde; "The Vanishing Trick," C. Davy; "The Punishment of Shahpesh, the Persian, on Khipil, the Builder," G. Meredith; "Three Pennyworth of Luck," B. Murray; "An Experiment With Blood," L. C. S. Abson; "No. 1 Branch Line: The Signalman," C. Dickens; "The Lady, or the Tiger?" F. R. Stockton; "A Horseman in the Sky," A. Bierce; "Escape," E. H. L. Watson; "Squirrel in a Cage," E. M. Delafield; "The Albatross," H. Bolitho; "The Land of Green Ginger," "Ancient Lights," A. Blackwood; "The Thing in the Upper Room," A. Morrison; "A Pair of Hands," Sir A. Quiller-Couch; "Entirely Imaginary," Sir J. Squire; "Mrs. Adis," Sheila Kaye-Smith; "The Battle of Berkeley Square," M. Arlen; "A Man of Letters," S. Aumonier; "Henry," Phyllis Bottome; "The End of the Party," G. Greene; "Romanoff," Ethel Mannin; "Glasshouses," Martha McKenna; "Discipline," Lesley Storm; "The Dust That Was Barren," P. C. Wren; "Balalaika," F. B. Young; "Phantas," O. Onions; "The Mummy's Foot," T. Gautier; "The Unprincipled Affair of the Practical Joker," Dorothy L. Sayers; "The De Medici Cup," F. A. Kummer; "High Tide," E. Phillpotts; "Mrs. Raeburn's Waxwork," "Satan's Circus," Lady Eleanor Smith; "I Pagliacci," R. H. Mottram; "The Elixir of the Rev. Father Gaucher," A. Daudet; "The Story of Ming-Y," L. Hearn; "Nor the Jury," S. Jepson; "Man-Size in Marble," E. Nesbit; "The Tunnel," "The Bad Lands," J. Metcalfe; "The Misanthrope," "The Powers of the Air," J. D. Beresford; "Mrs. Amworth," E. F. Benson; "The Dancing Partner," J. K. Jerome; "Venus," M. Baring; "The Story of Young Chang," Ernest Bramah; "Primula," G. Moss; "The House on Big Faraway," N. Matson; "If a Man Might Tarry," Sir M. Pemberton; "Coroner's Inquest," M. Connelly; "Judith," Hjalmar Bergman; "The Taipan," W. S. Maugham.

Evening Standard Second Book of Strange Stories, The (Hutchinson, 1937, 1021 pp., 3/6)

Weird, 84 stories: "The Hazard of the Spanish Horses," G. B. Stern; "Man Not Overboard," R. W. Lardner; "All Fools Court," L. Hooper; "Air Lock A.G.75," S. Stokes; "The Shrine of the Poly Pir," Sheikh A. Abdullah; "My Adventure at Soissons," A. Dumas; "The Statue and the Bust," P. C. Wren; "Conversion," Phyllis Bentley; "The Magic of Hussein," R. Carol; "Lenoir and Keller," F. Boutet; "The Ace of Spades," A. M. Pushkin; "The Shuttlecock of the Ritz-Ritz," C. P. Thomson; "The Raiser of Spectres," A. de Sauviniere; "Reincarnation," J. Talland; "Rats," R. Connor; "Gabriel-Ernest," Saki; "The Man Who Died," E. Ambrose; "Wish Me Luck," H. A. Manhood; "Lives of Men," J. Hilton; "White Stockings," E. Wallace; "Remnant of '22," Kathleen Warren; "An Anecdote," G. R. Preedy; "Inciting to Riot," E. Walrond; "The Right Side," J. Collier; "Maher-Shalal-Hashbaz," Dorothy L. Sayers; "The Black Dog," R. N. Currey; "Wicked Captain Walshawe," S. Le Fanu; "Carlton's Father," E. Ambrose; "The Adventure of the Second Lieutenant Bubnov," I. Turgenev; "The Suitor of Selkirk," Anon.; "The Honest Finder," D. Kosztolanyi; "The Veiled Lady," Agatha Christie; "Love or Money," F. Stuart; "Co-ordination," E. M. Forster; "Shining Hat at Tarring Neville," T. H. White; "The Departure," S. Robinson; "Mrs. Langpool's Buffalo," J. Brophy; "The Chasm," D. W. Macarthur; "Marriott's Monkey," H. Jones; "A School Story," M. R. James; "Galley Trot Blind," J. Gloag; "Supper at Borgy's," M. Kent; "Postscript," E. Bennett; "Going to Market," A. Halper; "The First Autumn," E. Caldwell; "The Urn," L. Bromfield; "Death on the Straightaway," N. Matson; "Horse of Death," R. Strauss; "Derrick's Return," G. Morris; "Felipe," P. Fleming; "Spellbound," Phyllis Bottome; "Country Born," E. Linklater; "Oblivion," Helena L. Caperton; "The Snow," H. Walpole; "So You Won't Talk," M. Komroff; "Judgment in the Underworld," J. Lindsay; "Nice Work," P. Cheyney; "Painted Love," L. Golding; "Over the Hill," M. Fessier; "Doo-Doom Got to Hang," H. B. Deutsch; "The Diviner and the Poor Woman," P. Wheeler; "Like a Diamond in the Sky," W. R. Brooks; "Siamese Hands," M. Komroff; "The Horrible God," T. Burke; "The Yellow Cat," M. Joseph; "Quiet Corner," G. B. Stern; "Murder," S. Jameson; "Lum Lo's Idol," H. Peterson; "The Dwarf," M. Ayme; "The Ringed Word," T. O. Beachcroft; "The House in the Wood," J. H. Turner; "The Pleasant Husband," Marj. Bowen; "The Shadow and the Bone," T. Burke; "The Cook's Room," Pansie Pakenham; "Lady Harpton's Garden Party," Mrs. Violet Campbell; "Doctors," L. Biro; "A Drink From a Running Stream," Lord Dunsany; "Towers of Flame," Eliz. I. Folsom; "Reconstruction of Chilton Hills," P. Curtiss; "The Late Bernard," A. Arnoux; "The Bearer of the Message," F. Hopman; "Hide Your Eyes," E. Acheson; "Haunted Ground," O. La Farge; "Beauty in His Brain," D. Burnet.

EVERETT, (Mrs.) H. D. Another fantasy title is *Iras: A Mystery* (Harper, New York, 1896), under the pseudonym Theo. Douglas.
Fiction
Death Mask and Other Ghosts, The [C] (P. Allan, London, 1920, 321 pp., 6/-)
Weird, 14 stories: "The Death Mask" (often reprinted, e.g., *Mag. Horror*, Sep 1968); "Parson Clench"; "The Wind of Dunowe"; "Neville Nugent's Legacy"; "The Crimson Blind"; "Fingers of a Hand"; "The Next Heir"; "Anne's Little Ghosts"; "Over the Wires"; "A Water Witch"; "The Lonely Road"; "A Girl in White"; "A Perplexing Case"; "Beyond the Pale."

EVERTS, LILLIAN
Fiction
Journey to the Future (Farrar Strauss, New York, 1955, 104 pp., $3.00)
Poetry.

EWERS, HANS HEINZ (3 Nov 1871–12 June 1943) German author, born in Dusseldorf. His literary career began in 1901 with the publication of rhymed satires entitled *A Book of Fables*. He formed a literary vaudeville theatre, and travelled widely. He was interned in the U.S.A. when that country entered World War I. Not much is known of his later life except that he joined the Nazi

Party. He is noted for a set of weird novels (translated into English) on the life of Frank Braun: *The Sorcerer's Apprentice* ([German], 1907; Day, 1927); *Alraune* ([German], 1911; Day, 1929); *Vampire* ([German], 1922; Day, 1934). Several of his weird short stories are often reprinted.

EX-PRIVATE X (pseud) See BURRAGE, A. M.

FABRICANT, NOAH D. (1904–) U.S. physician.
Anthology
Great Science Fiction About Doctors [pa] See CONKLIN, G. (co-anthologist)

FABUN, DON U.S. former sf enthusiast, now Publication Editor for the Kaiser Aluminum & Chemical Corp. As a fan he edited the amateur magazine *Rhodomagnetic Digest* from Vol. 2 No. 5 (Mar 1951). He was also a founding member of "The Elves, Gnomes and Little Men's Chowder and Marching Society," a San Francisco Bay Area sf fan group.
Nonfiction
Dynamics of Change, The (Prentice-Hall, Englewood Cliffs [N.J.], 1967, 192 pp., illus., $6.95)
6 articles originally in *Kaiser Aluminum News*: "The Dynamics of Change"; "The Promised Land"; "Telemobility"; "Automation"; "The Leisure Masses"; "Foreseeing the Unforeseeable." The last suggests the possibilities of tomorrow.

FADIMAN, CLIFTON (PAUL) (15 May 1904–) U.S. essayist and literary critic. Obtaining his B.A. from Columbia U. in 1925, he worked at Simon & Schuster 1927-35, being an editor in the latter years. He was Book Editor of the *New Yorker* 1933-43, editor of the Reader's Club, and member of the Book-of-the-Month Club Board and the War Writers' Board. He has contributed regularly to popular journals such as *Holiday* and *Saturday Review*. His books of essays include *Party of One* (the title of his regular department in *Holiday*) (1955) and *Any Number Can Play* (1957). Anthologies other than those below are *The American Treasury* [with Charles Van Doren] and *Reading I've Liked*. He is well known on radio and TV as an M.C., etc.
Anthologies
Fantasia Mathematica (Simon & Schuster, New York, 1958, 298 pp., $4.95; 1962, pa $1.45) ([Japanese], Arechi Shuppan-Sha, 1959, [abr., 10 stories from *Imaginaries* section])
Sf and fantasy on mathematical themes. 57 items with compiler's introduction: *Odd Numbers:* "Young Archimedes," A. Huxley; "Pythagoras and the Psychoanalyst," A. Koestler; "Mother and the Decimal Point," R. Llewellyn; "Jurgen Proves It By Mathematics," J. B. Cabell; "Peter Learns Arithmetic," H. G. Wells; "Socrates and the Slave," Plato; "The Death of Archimedes," K. Capek. *Imaginaries:* "The Devil and Simon Flagg," A. Porges; "And He Built a Crooked House," R. A. Heinlein; "Inflexible Logic," R. Maloney; "No-Sided Professor," M. Gardner; "Superiority," A. C. Clark; "The Mathematical Voodoo," H. Nearing, Jr.; "Expedition," F. Brown; "The Captured Cross-Section," M. J. Breuer; "A. Botts and the Moebius Strip," W. H. Upson; "God and the Machine," N. Balchin; "The Tachypomp," E. P. Mitchell; "The Island of Five Colors," M. Gardner; "The Last Magician," B. Elliott; "A Subway Named Moebius," A. J. Deutsch; "The Universal Library," K. Lasswitz; "Postscript to 'The Universal Library'," W. Ley; "John Jones' Dollar," H. S. Keeler. *Fractions* [verse, most quite brief]: "A New Ballad of Sir Patrick Spens," A. T. Quiller-

Couch; "The Unfortunate Topologist," C. M. Kornbluth; "There Was Once a Breathy Baboon," A. Eddington; "Yet What Are All . . .," L. Carroll; "Twinkle, Twinkle, Little Star," R. Barton; "Mathematical Love," A. Marvell; "The Circle," C. Morley; "The Circle and the Square," T. Dekker; "Euclid Alone Has Looked on Beauty Bare," Edna St. V. Millay; "Euclid," V. Lindsay; "To Think That Two and Two Are Four," A. E. Houseman; "The Uses of Mathematics," S. Butler; "Arithmetic," C. Sandburg; "Threes (To Be Sung By Niels Bohr)," J. Atherton; "Plane Geometry," Emma Rounds; "He Thought He Saw Electrons Swift," H. Dingle; "Fearsome Fable," B. Elliott; "Bertrand Russell's Dream," G. H. Hardy; "For All Practical Purposes," G. S. Ogilvy; "Eternity: A Nightmare," L. Carroll; "An Infinity of Guests," G. Gamow; "Infinity," A. Eddington; "No Power on Earth," W. Whewell; "X + 1," E. A. Poe; "The Receptive Bosom," E. Shanks; "Leinbach's Proof," A. Schnitzler; "A Problem," from *The New Yorker*; "A Letter to Tennyson," from *The Mathematical Gazette*; "A Fable," from *The Mathematical Gazette*; 4 anonymous limericks: "There Was a Young Man From Trinity," "Relativity," "There Was an Old Man Who Said, 'Do'," "There Was a Young Fellow Named Fisk."
Mathematical Magpie, The (Simon & Schuster, 1962, 300 pp., $4.95; 1963, pa $1.75)

Cartoon by Abner Dean; introduction by compiler: *I. A Set of Imaginaries:* Cartoon by Alan Dunn; "The Feeling of Power," I. Asimov; "The Law," R. M. Coates; "The Appendix and the Spectacles," M. J. Breuer; "Paul Bunyan v. the Conveyor Belt," W. H. Upson; "The Pacifist," A. C. Clarke; "The Hermeneutical Doughnut," H. Nearing Jr.; "Star, Bright," M. Clifton; "FYI," J. Blish; "The Vanishing Man," Richard Hughes; "The Nine Billion Names of God," A. C. Clarke. *II. Comic Sections:* "Three Mathematical Diversions," R. Queneau; "The Wonderful World of Figures," Corey Ford; "A, B and C—The Human Element in Mathematics," S. Leacock; Cartoon by Johnny Hart; "A Note on the Einstein Theory," M. Beerbohm; "The Achievement of H. T. Wensel," H. A. Smith; "Needed: Feminine Math," Parke Cummings; Cartoon by A. Fruch; "Two Extracts," M. Twain; "Mathematics for Golfers," S. Leacock; "The Mathematician's Nightmare: The Vision of Professor Squarepunt," B. Russell; "Milo and the Mathemagician," Norton Juster. *III. Irregular Figures:* Cartoon by S. Steinberg; "Sixteen Stories," Sam Beckett; "O'Brien's Table," J. L. Synge; "The Abominable Mr. Gunn," R. Graves; "Coconuts," Ben A. Williams; "Euclid and the Bright Boy," J. L. Synge; "The Purse of Fortunatus," L. Carroll; Cartoon by S. Steinberg; "The Symbolic Logic of Murder," J. Reese. *IV. Simple Harmonic Motion:* Cartoon by J. Frankfort; "The Square on the Hypotenuse," music by Saul Chaplin, lyrics by Johnny Mercer; "The Ta Ta," music by Joseph C. Holbrooke, jingles by Sidney H. Sime. *V. Dividends and Remainders:* Cartoon by S. Steinberg; Apothems from G. C. Lichtenberg, S. J. Lee, G. Polya, L. Carroll, J. Renard, G. Orwell, J. v. Goethe, W. Churchill, J. B. Mencken, A. DeMorgan, Etienne B. de Condillac, B. Mortlock, Anon.; A Subset of Anecdotes from A. DeMorgan, Thomas J. Hogg, G. Gamow, W. W. R. Ball, S. Newcomb, E. Paul, A. J. Lohwater. A Little Nursery Mathematics from Iona & Peter Opie, F. Winsor, L. A. Graham. A Quadrinomial of Poems: "To a Missing Member of a Family Group of Terms in an Algebraic Formula," J. J. Sylvester; "Portrait of a Mathematician," C. Morley; "From *The Dunciad*," Alex. Pope; "Geometry," W. Wordsworth. Surd and Absurd: "Me," H. Schenck Jr.; Cartoon by L. Demare; "Song of the Screw," Anon.; "The Modern Hiawatha," author unknown; "The Loves of the Triangles," John H. Frere & G. Canning; "The Mathematician in Love," W. J. M. Rankine; "E = mc²," M. Bishop; "Engineer's Yell," author unknown; "Rhymes by Algebra," W. Whewell & S. Barr; "Note on Θ, Φ, and Ψ," M. Roberts; "A Song Against Circles," R. P. Lister; "Wockyjabber," H. Schenck Jr.; "Einstein: A Parody in the Manner of Edw-n Markh-m," L. Untermeyer; "Tending to Infinity," J. L. Synge; "The Superlative Degree," Ernest Elmo Calkins; "The Magic Box," W. R. Baker; "The Kiss Precise," F. Soddy; "The Kiss Precise (generalized)," T. Gossett; "The Hexlet," F. Soddy; "Short Cuts to Success," R. A. Knox. A Group of Limericks: "The Young Lady Named Bright," A. H. R. Buller, FRS; "There Was an Old Woman Who Said 'Do . . .' "; "Snip," J. Schenck Jr.; Cartoon by P. P. Porges; "The Young Man of Sid Sussex," A. C. Hilton; "Pun in Orbit," H. Schenck; "A Mathematician Confided"; "A Mathematician Named Klein." Three Random Points: "The Map of England and the Absolute," G. Santayana; "Cupid With an Adding Machine," Charles D. Rice; "The Miniver Problem," J. Struther & L. A. Graham.

FAGAN, (Hon. Mr. Justice) HENRY A(LLAN) (4 Aug 1889–) South African judge and author. He was born at Lulbagh. He holds B.A., LL.B., Hon. LL.D. degrees. He became professor of law at Stellenbosch, South Africa, in 1920. He was an M.P. of the Union of South Africa 1933-43, and was also with the Ministry of Education, Social Welfare and Native Affairs 1938-39. He was a Judge of the Supreme Court of South Africa 1943-59, and Chief Justice 1956-59. Besides *Ninya*, he has published a number of dramatic works, some poems and short stories.
Fiction
Ninya (J. Cape, London, 1956, 221 pp., illus.–H. Jones, 13/6; 1957, 9/6) (Clarke Irwin, Toronto, $2.25)
    Survivors of a crash have adventure on the Moon, with a new kind of world.

FAIRCLOUGH, PETER
Anthology
Three Gothic Novels [pa] (Penguin: EL36, 1968, 505 pp., pa 8/-)
    3 novels, 28-p. intro. essay—Mario Praz, suggested further reading and notes: "The Castle of Otranto," Horace Walpole; "Vathek," William Beckford; "Frankenstein," Mary Shelley.

FAIRLESS, MICHAEL (pseud) See BARBER, MARGARET

FAIRMAN, PAUL W. (1916–) U.S. author and editor. He first appeared in the sf/fantasy field with many stories in the Ziff-Davis magazines (*AS* and *Fan*) around 1951, and became one of their principal writers; many of his stories appeared under pseudonyms, including the house name "Ivar Jorgensen." He became the first editor of *If* in Mar 1952, but left after the Sep 1952 issue. He joined Browne's staff on the Ziff-Davis magazines, but left in June 1954 to free-lance. He returned to Ziff-Davis in Dec 1955 as managing editor, and became editor when Browne went to Hollywood in May 1956. Fairman began the magazines *Dream World* (Feb 1957) and the non-sf *Pen Pal* (1957), but these only lasted three and two issues respectively. He finally left Ziff-Davis in Sep 1958 to continue writing. His "Deadly City" (n'te, *If*, Mar 1953, as Jorgensen) was the basis of the film *Target—Earth* by Allied Artists, 1954, produced by Herman Cohen, with Virginia Grey and Richard Denning. Another, "The Cosmic Frame" (*AS*, May 1953), was filmed as *Invasion of the Saucer Men*, American International, 1955, with Steve Terrell and Gloria Castillo, with special effects by Paul Blaisdell.
Fiction
City Under the Sea [pa] (Digit: R672, 1963, 158 pp., pa 2/6) (Pyramid: R1162, 1965, 141 pp., pa 50¢)
    Novelisation of the TV series *Voyage to the Bottom of the Sea*.
Forgetful Robot, The [C] (Holt, New York, 1968, 164 pp., $3.75)
    Sf, 15 stories: "Lost in a Junkyard"; "Those Remarkable Ravencrafts"; "The Space Museum"; "The Gallant Lady"; "Long Hop"; "The Brown Package"; "Phantoms of Zark"; "Mastermind of Zark"; "The Minefield"; "The Pit"; "Robots Should Stick Together"; "Interlude in the Desert"; "Delenda Est Carthago"; "Not Born to Greatness"; "Culture for the Planets."
Golden Ape, The [by Adam Chase (pseud. with M. Lesser)] ("Quest of the Golden Ape," I. Jorgensen & A. Chase, *AS*, sr3, Jan 1957) (Avalon, New York, 1959, 221 pp., $2.95) (*La scimmia d'oro* [Italian], *Cosmo*: 45, 1960) (*Der Weisse Golt* [German], *T*: 180, 1960)
    Fantastic adventure with a young giant who commutes between worlds, fights duels and saves the heroine from perils.
I, the Machine [pa] (Lancer: 73-735, 1968, 205 pp., pa 60¢)
    One man against the machine that rules society.
Rest in Agony [pa] ([as I. Jorgensen], Monarch: 362, 1963, 125

pp., pa 35¢) ([as P. Fairman], Lancer: 74-905, 1967, 223 pp., pa 75¢)

World Grabbers, The [pa] (Monarch: 471, 1964, 126 pp., pa 40¢)

FALLAW, L. M.
Fiction
Ugglians, The (Philosophical Lib., New York, 1957, 90 pp., $3.00)

A stinging satire with the Central African ruler Ugg I "converting" the U.S.

FANE, BRON (pseud) See FANTHORPE, R. I.

FANTASTIC UNIVERSE U.S. sf magazine. For anthology completely derived therefrom, see SANTESSON, H.

FANTASY BOOK U.S. sf and fantasy magazine. For anthology completely derived therefrom, see CRAWFORD, W.

FANTHORPE, ROBERT LIONEL (9 Feb 1935–) British author and teacher. Born at Dereham, Norfolk, England, he attended Keswick College, Norwich (1961-63) and attained Distinctions in Advanced Main Theology in English and Merit. He was schoolmaster with Dereham Secondary Modern School 1958-61 and 1963-67, then Tutor Further Education, Gamlingay Village College 1967-69, and more recently Group Industrial Training Officer for Phoenix Timber Company, Essex.

A prolific writer for the British Spencer 'Badger' SF and Supernatural Series, he has had a number of his novels reprinted in the U.S.A. Better-known pen names include Lionel Roberts, Trebor Thorpe, Leo Brett, Bron Fane, and Pel Torro, while much of the work published under the house-names John E. Muller and Karl Zeigfreid was his.
Fiction
Alien From the Stars (Badger: SF14, 1959, 156 pp., pa 2/-) (Arcadia, New York, 1968, 189 pp., $3.50)
Asteroid Man (Badger: SF35, 1960, 142 pp., pa 2/-) (Arcadia, 1967, 191 pp., $3.25) (Ambassador, Toronto, $3.95)
Barrier 346 [as Karl Zeigfreid] (Badger: SF113, 1965, 158 pp., pa 2/6) (Arcadia, 1968, 191 pp., $3.50)
Beyond Time ([as J. E. Muller], Badger: SF71, 1962, 158 pp., pa 2/6) ([as Marston Johns], Arcadia, 1966, 188 pp., $3.25)
Blue Juggernaut [as Bron Fane] (*Juggernaut*, Badger: SF41, 1960, 142 pp., pa 2/-) (Arcadia, 1965, 190 pp., $2.95) (Ambassador, Toronto, $3.95)
Crimson Planet [as J. E. Muller] (Badger: SF60, 1961, 158 pp., pa 2/6) (Arcadia, 1966, 191 pp., $3.25)
Exit Humanity [as Leo Brett] (Badger: SF40, 1960, 142 pp., pa 2/-) (Arcadia, 1965, 192 pp., $2.95)
Face of X, The ([as L. Roberts], Badger: SF39, 1960, 141 pp., pa 2/-) ([as Robert Lionel], Arcadia, 1965, 192 pp., $2.95)
Frozen Planet [as Pel Torro] (Badger: SF42, 1960, 142 pp., pa 2/-) (Arcadia, 1967, 191 pp., $3.00)
Galaxy 666 [as Pel Torro] (Badger: SF86, 1963, 157 pp., pa 2/6) (Arcadia, 1968, 191 pp., $3.50)
Hand of Doom (Badger: SF44, 1960, 158 pp., pa 2/6) (Arcadia, 1968, 192 pp., $3.50)
Hyperspace (Badger: SF17, 1959, 157 pp., pa 2/-) (Arcadia, 1966, 188 pp., $3.25)
In-World, The [as Lionel Roberts] (Badger: SF37, 1960, 142 pp., pa 2/-) (Arcadia, 1968, 189 pp., $3.50)
Juggernaut See *Blue Juggernaut*
Lightning World [as Trebor Thorpe] (Badger: SF38, 1960, 142 pp., pa 2/-) (Arcadia, 1964, 189 pp., $2.95)
No Way Back [as Karl Zeigfreid] (Badger: SF107, 1964, 160 pp., pa 2/6) (Arcadia, 1968, 191 pp., $3.50)
Orbit One ([as J. E. Muller], Badger: SF69, 1962, 158 pp., pa 2/6; Pitt & Bond, Sydney, PB512, 1963, 130 pp., pa 3/6) ([as Mel Jay], Arcadia, 1966, 189 pp., $3.25)

In the 30th century, Earth colonists on a Sirian planet fight a giant computer.
Power Sphere [as Leo Brett] (Badger: SF95, 1963, 158 pp., pa

2/6) (Arcadia, 1968, 192 pp., $3.50)
Somewhere Out There [as Bron Fane] (Badger: SF92, 1963, 158 pp., pa 2/6) (Arcadia, 1965, 191 pp., $3.25)
Time Echo ([as Lionel Roberts], Badger: SF23, 1959, 157 pp., pa 2/-) ([as Robert Lionel], Arcadia, 1964, 192 pp., $2.95)
Venus Venture, The ([as J. E. Muller], Badger: SF62, 1961, 158 pp., pa 2/6; Vega: VSF11, 1965, 155 pp., pa 60¢) ([as Marston Johns], Arcadia, 1965, 191 pp., $3.25)
World of the Future [as Karl Zeigfreid] (*World of Tomorrow*, Badger: SF84, 1963, 158 pp., pa 2/6) (Arcadia, 1964, 189 pp., $2.95)

Wandering galactic warships fight each other, making trouble for Earth.
World of Tomorrow [by Karl Zeigfreid] [pa] See *World of the Future*
Zero Minus X [as Karl Zeigfreid] (Badger: SF81, 1962, 160 pp., pa 2/6) (Arcadia, 1965, 192 pp., $3.25)

FARJEON, ELEANOR (1881–) British author, sister of J. J. Farjeon. She is noted for her plays and children's works. With her brother Herbert she wrote the highly successful musical play *The Glass Slipper* (1946).
Fiction [Incomplete—other titles in Bleiler *Checklist*]
Ariadne and the Bull (M. Joseph, London, 1945, 208 pp., 8/6) (Ryerson, Toronto, $2.50)

Retelling of the story of Theseus and the Minotaur in a modern idiom, as a humorous fantasy.
Faithful Jenny Dove [C] (M. Joseph, London, 1963, 160 pp., 16/-)

5 stories, 4 of which deal with ghosts as likeable, chubby creatures who can do what they like amongst old playmates on Earth.

FARJEON, J(OSEPH) JEFFERSON (4 June 1883–6 June 1955) British author, brother of Eleanor Farjeon. He was noted for his mystery stories and plays, writing over 80 novels. He was one of the first to mingle romance with crime, and within his special field he was unusually versatile, with variety always his aim. He often used the pseudonym "Anthony Swift."
Fiction
Death of a World (Collins, London, 1948, 192 pp., 8/6; #205c, nd, pa 1/6) (Collins, Toronto, $2.25)

Well-written but dismal story in which an expedition from another world finds a dead Earth.

FARLEY, RALPH MILNE (pseud) See HOAR, R. S.

FARMER, PENELOPE (1939–)
Fiction
Magic Stone, The (Chatto Windus, London, 1965, 224 pp., illus. J. Kaufman, 16/-)

Two young girls jointly holding a magic stone receive "insight" —not really fantasy, but an off-trail juvenile.

FARMER, PHILIP JOSÉ (26 Jan 1918–) U.S. author. He was born in North Terre Haute, Indiana, moved to Peoria when two, and spent most of his life there. He was introduced to sf and fantasy at an early age through Burroughs, Oz, and the Gernsback magazines. He attended Bradley U. and U. of Missouri, and was an aviation cadet in World War II. He worked 11 years in a steel mill, then in a dairy, a brewery, and an earth-excavation firm. He received B.A. in creative writing at Bradley U., 1950. For two years he was a military electronics technical writer at Syracuse, N.Y., and later he worked for Motorola in the same capacity.

He won the 1953 Hugo award as most promising new sf author. He is particularly noted for his unusual treatments, especially in alien biology and sexuality in such stories as *The Lovers* and those in *Strange Relations*, etc. Sam Moskowitz's profile of Farmer was published in *AS*, Dec 1964, and then became a chapter in Moskowitz's *Seekers of Tomorrow*, 1966. What is now known as Farmer's "Riverworld" series was originally written as a long novel which won the Shasta Publishers' contest in the early 1950's, but Shasta folded before it could be published. Pocket Books, Inc.

paid Shasta for the paperback rights, but the work was never published. Those who read it in manuscript praised it highly.

Series

Carmody, Father John. All in *F&SF*: "Attitudes" (Oct 1953); "Father" (July 1955); "The Night of Light" (June 1957; enlarged as pa, 1966); "A Few Miles" (Oct 1960); "Prometheus" (Mar 1961). Not in chronological sequence.

Riverworld (originally a novel; see biog. above). In *Worlds of Tomorrow*: "The Day of the Great Shout" (Jan 1965); "Riverworld" (n'te, Jan 1966); "The Suicide Express" (short n, Mar 1966). In *If*: "The Felled Star" (sr2, July 1967).

World of Tiers. *The Maker of Universes*; *The Gates of Creation*; *A Private Cosmos*.

Fiction

Alley God, The [C] [pa] (Ballantine: F588, 1962, 176 pp., pa 50¢)

3 n'te: "The Alley Man" (*F&SF*, June 1959); "The Captain's Daughter" ("Strange Compulsion," *SF Plus*, Oct 1953); "The God Business" (*Beyond*, Mar 1954).

Cache From Outer Space [pa] (Ace: F-165, 1962, 139 pp., pa 40¢; with *The Celestial Blueprint* [Farmer]) (*Von Himmel fielen Teufel* [German], *UZ*: 394, 1964)

Celestial Blueprint, The [C] [pa] (Ace: F-165, 1962, 114 pp., pa 40¢; with *Cache From Outer Space* [Farmer])

Sf, 4 stories: "Rastignac the Devil" (*FU*, May 1954); "The Celestial Blueprint"; "They Twinkled Like Jewels"; "Totem and Taboo."

Dare [pa] (Ballantine: U2193, 1965, 159 pp., pa 50¢)

Earth colonists on another world; adventure story, with satyrs, "horsnells" and humans well depicted.

Day of Timestop, The [pa] See *Woman a Day, A*

Flesh (Beacon: 227, 1960, 160 pp., pa 35¢) (Doubleday, New York, 1968, 212 pp., $3.95)

A starship returns to Earth and finds a fertility cult ruling the U.S.—much overt sexual motive and meaning. The D'day version is a slight expansion of the original.

Gate of Time, The [pa] (Belmont: B50-717, 1966, 176 pp., pa 50¢)

Adventure and intrigue in a parallel universe where munitions and aircraft are crude.

Gates of Creation, The [pa] (Ace: F-412, 1966, 159 pp., pa 40¢) (*Tor der Schöpfung* [German], *UZ*: 587, 1968)

Second of World of Tiers series. Robert Wolff finds his wife kidnapped, and with his brothers and sister he seeks revenge on his father.

Green Odyssey, The (Ballantine: 210, 1956, 152 pp., pa 35¢; 1957, $2.75; U2345, 1966, 152 pp., pa 50¢) (*Die Irrfahrten des Mr. Green* [German], *TS*: 57, 1962; Heyne: 3127, 1968, pa)

A castaway spaceman has many adventures in saving others on an unusual world of endless lawn.

Inside Outside [pa] (Ballantine: U2192, 1964, 156 pp., pa 50¢) (*Binnenste buiten* [Dutch], Meulenhoff, Amsterdam, 1967) (*L'univers à l'envers* [French], Ed. Opta 'Classique': SF13 [½], 1968)

Intriguing idea of a world inside a sphere, trying to survive.

Image of the Beast, The [pa] (Essex House: 0108, 1968, 255 pp., pa $1.95)

A private detective seeks revenge for his murdered partner and becomes involved in erotic encounters. One of the most sexy works to appear in sf.

Lovers, The [pa] (*SS*, Aug 1952) —enlarged: (Ballantine: 507K, 1961, 160 pp., pa 35¢) (*Les amants étrangers* [French], Ed. Opta 'Classique': SF13 [½], 1968)

An Earthman on a mission to Alpha Centaurus is seduced by a native woman who seems human but has very strange biology. The magazine story caused quite a sensation because of its sexual content, but now would hardly raise any eyebrows.

Maker of Universes [pa] (Ace: F-367, 1965, 191 pp., pa 40¢) (*Kampf der Weltenmacher* [German], *UZ*: 541, 1967)

First of World of Tiers series. A fascinating and fantastic adventure on a many-levelled world with creatures similar to those in Earth folklore.

Night of Light [pa] (Berkley: F1248, 1966, 160 pp., pa 50¢)

Enlargement of story in *F&SF*, June 1957. John Carmody, on the planet Dante's Joy, decides to stay awake during the long night and fight the planet's religion.

Private Cosmos, A [pa] (Ace: G-724, 1968, 192 pp., pa 50¢)

Third of World of Tiers series; further adventures of 'Kickaha.'

Strange Relations [C] (Ballantine: 391K, 1960, 190 pp., pa 35¢) (Gollancz, London, 1964, 189 pp., 15/-) (*Extranos parientes* [Spanish], Galaxia: 18, 1964, pa) (Panther: 2092, 1966, 187 pp., pa 3/6)

Sf, 5 stories: "Mother"; "Daughter"; "Father"; "Son" ("Queen of the Deep," *Arg*, Mar 1954); "My Sister's Brother" ("Open to Me, My Sister"). Graphic stories each dealing with the interrelation between a Terran and a strange person or creature of another world.

Tongues of the Moon [pa] (*AS*, n'te, Sep 1961) —enlarged: (Pyramid: R1055, 1964, 143 pp., pa 50¢)

Communist factions and others fight to survive on the Moon when Earth is destroyed.

Woman a Day, A [pa] (Beacon: 291, 1960, 160 pp., pa 35¢) (*The Day of Timestop*, Lancer: 73-715, 1968, 192 pp., pa 60¢)

Revision of "Moth and Rust" (*SS*, June 1953). A post-atomic-holocaust world with conflicting societies, fascinating and well depicted, and not overly sexual. A sequel to *The Lovers*.

FARNOL, JEFFERY (10 Feb 1878–9 Aug 1952) American novelist. His first literary success was *The Broad Highway* (1910), published in England after rejection by American publishers. He is mainly remembered for his swashbuckling romantic novels. A fantasy title in addition to that below was *Voices From the Dust* (Little Brown, Boston, 1932).

Fiction

Shadow and Other Stories, The [C] (Little Brown, Boston, 1929, 306 pp., $2.50) (Low, London, 1929, 313 pp., 7/6; 1930, 4/-; 1931, 2/-)

Fantasy, 17 stories: "The Shadow"; "Captain Hector"; "Retribution"; "The Heir"; "Black Coffee"; "Upon a Day"; "A Boy and the Man"; "An Episode"; "Jasper Railton"; "The Cupboard"; "Fortune's Fool"; "A Change of Mind"; "Journey's End"; "The Great Quietude"; "Sir Pertolepe the Red"; "The Divine Phyllidia"; "A Woman's Reason."

FARRERE, CLAUDE Better known name of Charles Bargone (1876–1957), noted French author. Translations into English include the novels below and *Thomas the Lambkin*, a tale of piracy; the novels below have also been translated into German.

Fiction

House of the Secret, The (*La Maison des Hommes Vivants*, Librairie des Annales, Paris, 1911) —[Trans.—A. Livingston] (Dutton, New York, 1923, 234 pp., $3.50, 500 copies; 1925, $2.00; 1928, 75¢) (*FFM*, Feb 1946)

A man gives his life for love to a family of three men who have the secret of continued survival.

Useless Hands (*Les condamnés à mort*, L'Illustration éditeur, Paris, 1920, limited ed.—300 Japan imperial, 500 Hollande Van Gelder; Flammarion, 2nd ed., 1921) —[Trans.—Elisabeth Abbott] (Dutton, 1926, 300, $2.00)

A pseudoscientific romance of the future.

FAST, HOWARD (MELVIN) (11 Nov 1914–) U.S. author, born in New York City. He studied at the National Academy of Design. He was founder and editor of *Reader's Scope*, 1943, and was a lecturer at U. of Indiana in 1947. He was a founder of the Progressive Party in 1948, and received the International Peace Prize in 1954. His works include *The Children* (1935), *Citizen Tom Paine* (1943), the best seller *Spartacus* (1951), *Moses, Prince of Egypt* (1958), and *April Morning* (1961), a reconstruction of the Battle of Lexington. He first appeared in the sf field with "Wrath of the Purple," *AS*, Oct 1932. He has contributed regularly to *F&SF*, beginning with "Of Time and Cats" (Mar 1959).

Fiction

Edge of Tomorrow, The [C] [pa] (Bantam: A2254, 1961, 120 pp., pa 35¢; F3309, 1966, 121 pp., pa 50¢) (Corgi: SS1107, 1962,

125 pp., pa 2/6) (*Au seuil du futur* [French], Gerard, Verviers [Belgium], 1962) (*Die neuen Menschen* [German], Goldmann, 1963, 1966 pa) (*Al borde del futuro* [Spanish], Galaxia: 19, 1964, pa)

Sf, 7 stories: "The First Men"; "The Large Ant" ("The Big Ant"); "Of Time and Cats"; "Cato the Martian"; "The Cold, Cold Box"; "The Martian Shop"; "The Sight of Eden." All but the second story originally appeared in *F&SF*.

Hunter and the Trap, The (Dial, New York, 1967, 214 pp., $4.50)

FAST, JULIUS (1918–)
Anthology
Out of This World [pa] (Penguin [U.S.]: 537, 1944, 245 pp., pa 25¢)

Weird, 14 stories: "Evening Primrose," J. Collier; "Laura," Saki; "Sam Small's Tyke," E. Knight; "Satan and Sam Shay," R. Arthur; "A Disputed Authorship," J. K. Bangs; "Mr. Mergenthwirker's Lobblies," N. S. Bond; "A Vision of Judgment," H. G. Wells; "Thus I Refute Beelzy," J. Collier; "The King of the Cats," S. V. Benét; "The Canterville Ghost," O. Wilde; "My Friend Merton," J. Fast; "And Adam Begot," A. Oboler; "The Club Secretary," Lord Dunsany; "The Scarlet Plague," J. London.

FATE U.S. magazine dealing with the occult and the unorthodox. A number of paperbacks have been selected from its pages, including *Beyond the Strange*; *Fate Stranger Than Fiction*; *Fate's Strangest Mysteries*; *Strange and the Unknown*; *Strange But True*; *Strange Fate*; *Strange World of the Occult*.

FAUCETTE, JOHN M(ATTHEW) Jr. (15 Sep 1943–) U.S. freelance writer.
Fiction
Age of Ruin [pa] (Ace: H-103, 1968, 114 pp., pa 60¢; with *Code Duello*)

A journey in a war-wrecked world.
Crown of Infinity [pa] (Ace: H-51, 1968, 129 pp., pa 60¢; with *The Prism*)

A sweeping space-opera of galactic conquest.

FAURE, RAOUL C(OHEN) (10 Sep 1909–) American novelist. He was born in Cairo, Egypt, and educated in Paris. Trained for business, he worked first in London and then in Egypt. He grew dissatisfied with the business world and became a writer. He travelled in the U.S., Mexico and Central America, settling down in Sausalito, Calif., and marrying an American girl. His first novel was *The Spear in the Sand*.
Fiction
Mister St. John (Harper, New York, 1947, 279 pp., $2.75)

Story of a doctor given a chance to relive his life.

FAUST, FREDERICK (29 May 1892–12 May(?) 1944) One of the most prolific U.S. authors, he wrote under many pseudonyms, especially "Max Brand." He was killed at Salerno, Italy, while a war correspondent. He was called "The King of the Pulp Writers," regularly receiving top rates. It was estimated that in the 20 or so years up to 1940 he had published 25 million words in books, stories and scenarios. He wrote the books and motion pictures about "Dr. Kildare." Post-war reprints of interest include "The Smoking Land" ([as George Challis], *Arg*, sr6, 29 May 1937; *A. Merritt's Fantasy*, Feb 1950); "Devil Ritter" (as Max Brand, *ASW*, 13 July 1918; *FN*, May 1949); "That Receding Brow" (as Brand, *ASW*, 15 Feb 1919; *FN*, Mar 1950). The Rev. D. C. Richardson compiled *The Fabulous Faust Fanzine* (1949), and then wrote the book *Max Brand: The Man and His Works* (FPCI, 1952).

FAVENC, ERNEST
Fiction
Last of Six: Tales of the Austral Tropics, The [C] (Bulletin Newspaper Co., Sydney, 1893, 141 pp., pa 1/-)

Fantasy, 17 stories: "The Last of Six"; "A Cup of Cold Water"; "A Haunt of the Jinkarras"; "The Rumford Plains Tragedy"; "Spirit-Led"; "Tranter's Shot"; "The Spell of the Mas-Hantoo"; "The Track of the Dead"; "The Mystery of Baines' Dog"; "Pompey"; "Malchook's Doom: A Nicholson River Story"; "The Cook and the Cattle-Stealer"; "The Parson's Blackboy"; "A Lucky Meeting"; "The Story of a Big Pearl"; "The Missing Super"; "That Other Fellow."

FAWCETT, F. DUBREZ
Fiction
Hole in Heaven (Sidgwick Jackson, London, 1954, 224 pp., 9/6) (*Il varco di Satano* [Italian], *Urania*: 150, 1957)

Three souls fight for one body, and a new entity appears. This was to have been the beginning of a new series edited by Angus Wilson.

FEAGLES, ANITA
Fiction
Thor and the Giants (Young Scott, New York, 1968, $3.95)

Juvenile.

FEARING, KENNETH (28 July 1902–26 June 1961) U.S. poet and novelist. He graduated from U. of Wisconsin in 1924 and freelanced until he received a Guggenheim fellowship in 1936 (renewed in 1939). Originally noted for his verse, he later was acclaimed for his novels. Among his novels is *Clark Gifford's Body* (Random, 1942).
Fiction
Loneliest Girl in the World, The (Harcourt Brace, New York, 1951, 238 pp., $3.00) (Lane, London, 1952, 224 pp., 10/6) (McLeod, Toronto, $3.75)

A curious blend of sf and detective; of particular appeal to those interested in acoustics and cybernetics.

FEARN, JOHN RUSSELL (5 June 1908–Sep 1960) British author of science fiction, westerns and mysteries. His writing ambitions were born early, but he was unable to become a full-time writer until the mid-1930's. After World War II he was a cotton salesman until he returned to full-time writing in 1950 as "Vargo Statten." He lived most of his life in Blackpool. A quite prolific writer, he entered the sf field with "The Intelligence Gigantic" (*AS*, sr2, June 1933). In the 1930's he was most noted for his extravaganzas featured in the Tremaine *ASF*, such as "Brain of Light" (May 1934), "Earth's Mausoleum" (May 1935), "Mathematica" (Feb 1936) and sequel, and "Red Heritage" (Jan 1938). His "Liners of Time" was a noted serial in *AS*. He used the pseudonym "Thornton Ayre" on "Penal World," a story emulating Weinbaum's style, in *ASF*, Oct 1937. He later began his famous "Golden Amazon" series under the Ayre pseudonym.

Fearn published approximately 120 novels, most appearing as British paperbacks or as supplements to the *Toronto Star Weekly*. Under the pseudonym "Vargo Statten" he wrote 51 paperback books and also edited the now extinct *Vargo Statten Science Fiction Magazine* (later *British Space Fiction Magazine*). Other pseudonyms included "Volsted Gridban" (a house name previously used by E. C. Tubb), "Astron Del Martia" (primarily remembered for *The Trembling World*), "L. F. Rose" (for *The Hell Fruit*), and "C. G. Holt" (for *Cosmic Exodus*). The last two were fine stories doomed to obscurity because of their cheap format as part of the Pearson's Tit-Bits SF Series. About 20 of Fearn's "Vargo Statten" novels were translated into French for the Le Fleuve Noir *Anticipation* series; a number appeared in the Italian magazines *Cosmo* and *Urania*; he was also translated into German and Danish.

Fearn had a long and illustrious career in the American sf magazines until he chose to bow out in the latter 1940's and continue with the old-style sf in Britain. Entering this easier, less-demanding market was a mistake that was fatal to his reputation, so that he died in complete eclipse. His "Vargo Statten" paperbacks of the 1950's (published by Scion) were dismissed as juvenile space-opera by many, but contain a vast range of pseudo-scientific plot ideas which for sheer escapism are unrivalled. Selling five million copies, they served as an admirable introduction for teen-agers and others who had never heard of sf. Philip Harbottle of England has compiled a very comprehensive bibliography of Fearn's works and

has found a number of previously unknown pseudonyms. Ron Graham of Sydney has bought the copyrights of most Fearn material and was planning a reprint paperback series.
Series
Drew, Clayton. All paperbacks, published in 1950: *Emperor of Mars*; *Warrior of Mars*; *Red Men of Mars*; *Goddess of Mars*.
Golden Amazon. In *FA* [as Thornton Ayre]: "The Golden Amazon" (July 1939); "The Amazon Fights Again" (June 1940); "The Golden Amazon Returns" (Jan 1941); "Children of the Golden Amazon" (Apr 1943). All were published in the Swedish *JVM* 1943-46. Novels appearing in *Toronto Star Weekly* (first date): *The Golden Amazon* (1944; World's Work, 1944, 117 pp., 5/-; Harlequin, 1953, 192 pp., pa 35¢); *The Golden Amazon Returns* (3 Nov 1945; World's Work, 1948, 133 pp., 5/-; *The Deathless Amazon*, Harlequin, 1955, 160 pp., pa 35¢); *The Golden Amazon's Triumph* (27 Apr 1946; World's Work, 1953, 192 pp., 8/6; Harlequin, 1958, 160 pp., pa 35¢); "Diamond Quest" (*Sunday Star Ledger*, 16 Mar 1947; *The Amazon's Diamond Quest*, World's Work, 1953, 175 pp., 7/6); *The Amazon Strikes Again* (21 Feb 1948; World's Work, 1954, 175 pp., 7/6); *Twin of the Amazon* (13 Nov 1948; World's Work, 1954, 159 pp., 7/6); "Conquest of the Amazon" (2 Apr 1949); "Lord of Atlantis" (8 Oct 1949); "Triangle of Power" (13 May 1950); "The Amethyst City" (3 Mar 1951); "Daughter of the Amazon" (1 Dec 1951); "Quorne Returns" (25 Oct 1952); "The Central Intelligence" (22 Aug 1953); "The Cosmic Crusaders" (2 Feb 1955); "Parasite Planet" (27 Aug 1955); "World out of Step" (17 Nov 1956); "The Shadow People" (6 Apr 1957); "Kingpin Planet" (19 Oct 1957); "World in Reverse" (26 Apr 1958); "Dwellers in Darkness" (29 Nov 1958); "World in Duplicate" (16 May 1959); "Standstill Planet" (26 Mar 1960); "Ghost World" (17 Dec 1960); "Earth Divided" (24 June 1961).
Fiction [Also check the PAPERBACK section for Fearn's many novels as Vargo Statten, Volsted Gridban (not all Fearn's), other pseudonyms, and under his own name.]
Amazon Strikes Again, The See *Golden Amazon* series
Amazon's Diamond Quest, The See *Golden Amazon* series
Deathless Amazon, The [pa] See *Golden Amazon* series
Golden Amazon, The See *Golden Amazon* series
Golden Amazon Returns, The See *Golden Amazon* series
Golden Amazon's Triumph, The See *Golden Amazon* series
Intelligence Gigantic, The (*AS*, sr2, June 1933) (World's Work, Tadsworth, 1943, 100 pp., 5/-)
In A.D. 2064 a superhuman intelligence seeks to dominate mankind.
Liners of Time (*AS*, sr4, May 1935) (World's Work, 1947, 156 pp., 5/-)
Melodrama of time travel and intrigue; sequel was "Zagribud" (see *Science Metropolis*).
Other Eyes Watching [as Polton Cross] [pa] (*SS*, Spr 1946) (Pendulum 'Spacetime Series 2,' London, 1946, 120 pp., pa 2/-)
A power-drunk scientist seeks to use the machines of a 4th-dimension super-world to dominate Earth.
Science Metropolis [as Vargo Statten] (Scion, 1952, 128 pp., pa 1/6)
Earth in peril from Jovian super-science. Abridged from "Zagribud" (*AS*, sr3, Dec 1937), the sequel to *Liners of Time*. The Fearn enthusiast P. Harbottle considers the abridging to have ruined any merit the original had.
Twin of the Amazon See *Golden Amazon* series

FEIFFER, JULES (26 Jan 1929–) U.S. cartoonist and writer, noted for sharp social commentary.
Nonfiction
Great Comic Book Heroes, The (Dial, New York, 1965, 189 pp. [127 pp. comics], $9.95) (Penguin, England, 1967, 189 pp., 70/-)
A study of the comics field, with aspects of autobiography, social comment and philosophy.

FELSEN, (HENRY) GREGOR (16 Aug 1916–) U.S. author.
Fiction
Boy Who Discovered the Earth, The (Scribner's, New York, 1955,

140 pp., $2.25)
Juvenile; a boy from a flying saucer changes places with an Earth boy, to enjoy the wonders of Earth. A good idea, but unnecessarily cute.

FENN, WILLIAM W(ALLACE) (1862–6 Mar 1932) U.S. theologian, born in Boston, Massachusetts.
Fiction
'Twixt the Lights: or, Odd Tales for Odd Times [C] (Henry J. Drane, London, 1893, vol. 1 – 415 pp., vol. 2 – 431 pp.)
Volume 1—13 stories of fantasy interest and 8 essays (marked †): "Was It a Dream? or What?"; "Rainbow Weather"†; "A Club Story"; "Shakespeare and the Art of Painting"†; "The Last of the Highwaymen"; "Idle Dials"†; "A Change in the Cast"; "A Bygone Story"; "Sketchers' Skies"†; "The Hooded Figure"; "The 'Murmuring Surge' "†; "The Bed That Could Not Be Moved"; "Reclaimed by Right"; "The Old House on the Cliff"; "The First Flight"†; "A Righteous Reparation"; "Thrice Warned"; "Alone With the Stars"†; "A New 'Flying Dutchman' "; "On the Wing"†; "A Midsummer Night's Dream—and Reality." *Volume 2*—13 stories, 11 essays (marked †): "Can a Blind Man See a Ghost?"†; "The Lady in the Lavender"; "Hopeful Doctors"†; "An Adventure—Quite in the Dark"; "Sight and Memory in Relation to Art"†; "The Phantom Fares"; "Our Weather-Eye"†; "A Dressmaker's Drama"; "The Hidden Voice"; "Night Whimsies"†; "A Very Peculiar Case"; "The 'Bump of Locality' "†; "The Key of the Tree"; "The Inverell Mystery"; "Canvas Under Canvas"†; "The Ghost in the Gallery"; "By the Avon in April"†; "In a Pit-Box"; "The Holly and the Hearth"†; "Midnight Courage"†; "The Doubt About Owen Clove"; "Woodland Harvest"†; "The Living Picture"; "A Balcony at Lucerne." *Volume 2*—contents not known.
Woven in Darkness [C] (Kelly & Co., London, 1885, vol. 1 – 451 pp., vol. 2 – ?)
Volume 1—11 stories of fantasy interest and 6 essays (marked †): "A Blind Man's Notions About Ghosts"†; "In the Room With the Arras"; "The Love of Landscape"†; "The Haunted Rock"; "A Dangerous Secret"; "The Little Pill"; "The Hand on the Latch"; "Red-Hot Friendships"†; "Held at Bay"; "The Living Likeness"; "The First Fire"†; "The Legend of the Light"; "The Face at the Window"; "Following the Brush"†; "The Marble Hands"; "Why Go Away?"†; "The Ghost on the Chain Pier." *Volume 2*—contents not known.

FENNER, PHYLLIS REID (29 Oct 1899–)
Anthology
Ghosts, Ghosts, Ghosts (Watts, New York, 1952, 281 pp., illus.– M. deV. Lee, $2.50) (Chatto Windus, London, 1953, 223 pp., illus.–Lee, 8/6)
Juvenile; one of the 'Terrific Triple Titles' series. 12 stories: "Jimmy Takes Vanishing Lessons," W. R. Brooks; "Spooks of the Valley," L. C. Jones; "Not Quite Martin," L. Wilson; "Dead Men on Parade," I. Crump; "The House of the Ocean Born Mary," Marion Lowndes; "Fiddler, Play Fast, Play Faster," Ruth Sawyer; "The Water Ghost of Harrowby Hall," J. K. Bangs; "The Golden Pitcher," Bertha L. Gunterman; "Prince Godfrey Frees Mountain Dwellers and Little Shepherds From a Savage Werewolf and From Witches," Halina Gorska; "Cobbler, Cobbler, Mend My Shoe," J. Struther; "The Devil and Daniel Webster," S. V. Benét; "The Cobra's Hood," R. S. Holland.

FENNERTON, WILLIAM
Fiction
Lucifer Cell, The (Atheneum, New York, 1968, 306 pp., $5.95)

FENTON, ROBERT W.
Nonfiction
Big Swingers, The (Prentice-Hall, New York, 1967, 258 pp., $6.95)
A sort of double-image biography of E. R. Burroughs and his Tarzan, covering titbits of both. With photos of movie Tarzans.

FERMAN, EDWARD L(EWIS) (6 Mar 1937–) Son of Joseph W.

Ferman, he became editor of *F&SF* as of January 1966.

Anthologies

Best From Fantasy and Science Fiction, 15th Series, The (Doubleday, New York, 1966, 248 pp., $4.50) (Gollancz, London, 1967, 256 pp., 22/6)

14 stories: "The Doors of His Face, The Lamps of His Mouth," Roger Zelazny; "Rake," Ron Goulart; "The History of Dr. Frost," Roderic C. Hodgins; "Four Ghosts in Hamlet," Fritz Leiber; "Keep Them Happy," Robert Rohrer; "A Murkle For Jesse," Gary Jennings; "Eyes Do More Than See," Isaac Asimov; "The House That the Blakeneys Built," A. Davidson; "The Eight Billion," Richard Wilson; "Something Else," Robert J. Tilley; "Aunt Millicent at the Races," Len Guttridge; "Sea Bright," Hal R. Moore; "Hog Belly Honey," R. A. Lafferty; "No Different Flesh," Zenna Henderson.

Best From Fantasy and Science Fiction, 16th Series, The (Doubleday, 1967, 264 pp., $4.50) (Gollancz, 1968, 256 pp., 25/-)

13 stories, with 6 Gahan Wilson cartoons and 4 short poems: "Matog," Joan P. Basch; "A Few Kindred Spirits," J. Christopher; "The Age of Invention," N. Spinrad; "Apology to Inky," R. M. Green Jr.; "Luana," Gilbert Thomas; "And Madly Teach," L. Biggle; "The Key," I. Asimov; "The Seven Wonders of the Universe," Mose Millette; "We Can Remember It for You Wholesale," P. K. Dick; "Experiment in Autobiography," Ron Goulart; "The Adjusted," K. Bulmer; "Three for Carnival," John Shepley; "The Moment of the Storm," R. Zelazny.

Best From Fantasy and Science Fiction, 17th Series, The (Doubleday, 1968, 260 pp., $4.50)

13 stories, 4 Gahan Wilson cartoons, and introduction: "Cyprian's Room," Monica Sterba; "Out of Time, Out of Place," George Collyn; "Van Goom's Gambit," Victor Contoski; "Bumberboom," A. Davidson; "Fill in the Blank," R. Goulart; "Balgrummo's Hell," Russell Kirk; "Corona," S. R. Delaney; "The Inner Circles," F. Leiber; "Problems of Creativeness," T. M. Disch; "Encounter in the Past," Robert Nathan; "The Sea Change," Jean Cox; "The Devil and Democracy," Brian Cleeve; "Randy's Syndrome," B. W. Aldiss.

Once and Future Tales From the Magazine of Fantasy and Science Fiction (Harris-Wolfe, Jacksonville [Ill.], 1968, 366 pp., $5.95)

9 stories, introduction by Judith Merril: "The Manor of Roses," T. B. Swann; "End of the Line," Chad Oliver; "The Fifteenth Wind of March," Frederick Bland; "Journey of Ten Thousand Miles," Will Mohler; "Fruiting Body," Rosel G. Brown; "Open to Me, My Sister," P. J. Farmer; "The Case of the Homicidal Robots," M. Leinster; "When You Care, When You Love," T. Sturgeon; "The Masculinist Revolt," Wm. Tenn.

FERMAN, JOSEPH WOLFE (8 June 1906–) U.S. publisher. Born in Lida, Lithuania, he received his B.C.S. at N.Y.U. in 1927, was married in 1931 and has one son. He was at *American Mercury* from 1926, being Director 1940-56 and Vice-President 1944-50. He was Director of Jonathan Press 1942-56, and has been Director of Fantasy House Inc. since 1949 and Vice-President of Mercury Publications since 1954. He is noted in the sf/fantasy field as the publisher of *The Magazine of Fantasy and Science Fiction*, which he also edited Dec 1964-Dec 1965.

Anthology

No Limits [pa] (Ballantine: U2220, 1964, 192 pp., pa 50¢; 1968, pa 50¢)

Sf, 9 stories originally in *F&SF*: "The Education of Tigress Macardle," C. M. Kornbluth; "All the Colors of the Rainbow," Leigh Brackett; "Now Let Us Sleep," A. Davidson; "Vengeance for Nikolai," W. M. Miller Jr.; "Seat of Judgment," L. del Rey; "Buy Jupiter!" I. Asimov; "And Then She Found Him," A. Budrys; "Before the Talent Dies," H. Slesar; "The Comedian's Children," T. Sturgeon.

FERNANDEZ FLOREZ, WENCESLAS (1892–) Spanish author, born in Galicia. His first major novel was *Volvoreta*. Others followed, including *Las siete columnas* (Earth is deprived of the seven mortal sins, and disaster results) and *El ladrón de glandulas* (The Glands-Stealer). He has also written some notable short stories. He

became a member of the Spanish Academy in December 1944.

Fiction

Laugh and the Ghosts Laugh With You [C] (*Fantasmas*) –Trans. –H. Baerlein: (Brit. Tech. & General Press, London, 1951, 176 pp., 12/6)

Ghost, 7 stories: "Twentieth Century"; "The Highway"; "The Ghost"; "What the Dead Men Think"; "My Wife"; "The Demeanour of a Corpse"; "The Case of the Defunct Pedroso."

FESSIER, MICHAEL (1907–) U.S. author. He has had some short stories in *F&SF*.

Fiction

Clovis (Dial, New York, 1948, 7+189 pp., $2.00) (Longmans, Toronto, $2.50) (Allan Wingate, London, 1949, 160 pp., 7/6)

A tale of an intelligent parrot.

Fully Dressed and in His Right Mind (Knopf, New York, 1935, 216 pp., $1.00) (Gollancz, London, 1935, 207 pp., 6/-) (Ryerson, Toronto, $2.25) (Lion: 214, 1954, 126 pp., pa 25¢)

A nymph turns a city upside down.

FEZANDIE, CLEMENT U.S. author.

Series

Hackenshaw, Dr. This had 43 numbered episodes in *Science & Invention*, beginning with "The Secret of Artificial Respiration" (May 1921) and running to "A Journey to the Center of the Earth" (sr4, concluding Sep 1925). The series continued with 2 stories in *Amazing*: "Minor Inventions" (June 1926) and "The Secret of the Invisible Girl" (July 1926).

Fiction

Through the Earth (*St. Nicholas Magazine*, sr4, Jan 1898) (Century, New York, 1898, 238 pp., illus.)

A great tube through the Earth is used once by a volunteer and then it collapses.

FIELD, EUGENE (2 Sep 1850–4 Nov 1895) U.S. writer and newspaper columnist. He was born in St. Louis. Upon his father's death he used his inheritance to tour England and southern Europe, and married upon his return at the age of 23. He then worked for 8 years on newspapers in St. Joseph, St. Louis, Kansas City and Denver. In 1883 he went to the *Chicago Morning News* (later *Record*) and became one of the first American newspaper columnists. His principal books are collections of his short stories and half a dozen volumes of verse; his "Little Boy Blue" and "Wynken, Blynken and Nod" remain classics among poems for children. A fantasy published in a limited edition was *The Temptation of Friar Gonsol* (Woodward & Lothrop, Washington, D.C., 1900, 40 pp.; 310 copies).

Fiction

Holy Cross and Other Tales, The [C] (Scribner's, New York, 1896, 293 pp.)

16 stories, some fantasy: "The Holy Cross"; "The Rose and the Thrush"; "The Pagan Seal-Wife"; "Flail, Trask, and Bisland"; "The Touch in the Heart"; "Daniel and the Devil"; "Methuselah"; "Felice and Petit–Poulain"; "The River"; "Franz Abt"; "Mistress Merciless"; "The Platonic Bassoon"; "Hawaiian Folk-Tales"; "Lute Baker and His Wife Em"; "Joel's Talk With Santa Claus"; "The Lonesome Little Shoe."

Second Book of Tales [C] (Scribner's, New York, 1896, 314 pp., illus.; 1907, 314 pp., frontis.)

Contains some juvenile fantasy, some articles, some stories in rural settings, and one weird tale, "The Werewolf."

FIELD, FRANCIS J.

Nonfiction [compiler]

Rocket and Jet Posts 1928-1955 (Published by compiler, 1956, 30 pp., 50¢)

An authoritative survey of the growth of rocketry on the basis of rocket and jet stamps, with photographic illustrations. False and faked items are also considered. It covers only 27 years; the compiler considers that there is no reliable record of the practice of message carrying by the Chinese rocket engineers of old or by the war-rockets of 150 years ago.

FINLAY, VIRGIL (WARDEN) (1914–18 Jan 1971) U.S. fantasy artist whose work in that field is quite distinctive. Self-taught, by 1933 he was a professional portrait and gallery painter. In 1935 he sold his first illustration to *Weird Tales*; his work in that magazine brought him to the notice of A. Merritt, editor of *American Week-ly*. He was invited to join Merritt's staff and was feature fiction illustrator there for three years. He then free-lanced and his work became a feature of *Famous Fantastic Mysteries* and *Fantastic Novels* 1941-43; these magazines published three portfolios of his art, in 1941, 1943 and 1949. During World War II he became a sergeant in the Army Corps of Engineers and did posters and illustrations for the Morale Services. As a gallery painter he has appeared in the Metropolitan Museum of Art in New York City, the Memorial Gallery in Rochester, and other noted museums.

His work in the sf/fantasy field included 20 covers for *Weird Tales* (8 out of the 11 issues for 1939), 24 for *FFM* and *FN*, 9 of the 12 covers for *Fantastic Universe* in 1957, a number of covers for other magazines, and some book jackets. He won the 1953 Hugo award as best interior artist. He illustrated the Borden memorial edition of A. Merritt's *The Ship of Ishtar*; he did some work for Gernsback's *Radio Electronics* and was a feature of the Ziff-Davis magazines for a number of years. Besides the portfolios mentioned above, one with some 15 drawings was published by Russell Swanson (Nova Press, *ca.* 1953, $2.00). At the time of his death Finlay was working with Don Grant to prepare a book covering his career in sf and fantasy. Sam Moskowitz's profile of Finlay was published in the Nov 1965 *Worlds of Tomorrow*.

FINN, RALPH LESLIE (1912–) British author, born in London and educated at London U. He was a feature writer for *People* 1941-45 and *Cavalcade* 1946-48, editor for *Weekly Sporting Review* 1953-54, senior copywriter for L.N.P. 1955-58, and has been joint copy chief at Everetts Advertising since 1958. He has contributed to *Courier, Evening News, Sunday Despatch*, etc. His books include *My Greatest Game, World Cup* (1954), *Red Roses, The Ants Came*, and two low-class sf paperbacks.
Fiction
Time Marches Sideways (Hutchinson, London, 1950, 224 pp., 9/6)
   A variant on time travel, set in London.

FINNEY, CHARLES G(RANDISON) (1 Dec 1905–) U.S. novelist. He enlisted in the army and served in China (1927-30). Upon discharge he went to Tucson where he has been ever since as proof-reader for the *Arizona Daily Star*. He only writes after work. He is especially noted for his *The Circus of Dr. Lao*; another book is *Past the End of the Pavement* (1939).
Fiction
Circus of Dr. Lao, The (Viking, New York, 1935, 154 pp., illus.–B. Artzybasheff, $2.00) (Argus, New York, 1945, 154 pp., illus.–Artzybasheff, $5.00) (Grey Walls, London, 1948, 151 pp., illus.–Fish, 15/-) (In *The Circus of Dr. Lao* [anthology, R. Bradbury], 1956, pa) (Compass: C82, 1961, 160 pp., illus.–B. Artzybasheff, pa $1.25) (Bantam: F2755, 1964, 119 pp., pa 50¢) (Penguin: 2537, 1966, 126 pp., pa 3/6)
   A peculiar but entrancing commentary on unusual animals in a special circus, where the spectator also learns about himself. Fish's illustrations are generally considered as good as the Artzybasheff originals. *Film: The Seven Faces of Dr. Lao*, MGM, 1963.
Ghosts of Manacle, The [pa] (Pyramid: R1042, 1964, 159 pp., pa 50¢)
   8 uncanny stories (4 from *F&SF*): "The Iowan's Curse"; "The Horsenaping of Hotspur"; "The Life and Death of a Western Gladiator"; "The Gilashrikes"; "The Black Retriever"; "The Captivity"; "The Door"; "The End of the Rainbow."
Magician out of Manchuria [pa] See *Unholy City, The*
Unholy City, The (Vanguard, New York, 1937, 167 pp., $2.00) (*Unholy City & Magician out of Manchuria*, Pyramid: X1818, 1968, 221 pp., pa 60¢)
   Fantastic adventure in the nightmare city of Heilar-Wey with its ghoulish pleasures and zany riots. *Magician out of Manchuria* tells of the exotic travels of the hero and a Queen of remarkable talents.

FINNEY, JACK Pseud. of Walter Braden Finney (1911–). U.S. author and free-lance journalist. He was born in Milwaukee, Wisc. His first story was published when he was 35, he later took a special prize in the 2nd Annual Contest of *Ellery Queen's Mystery Magazine*, and has since made a name for himself in *Collier's*, etc. His non-sf books *Five Against the House* and *The House of Numbers* are noted novels and have both been translated world-wide.
Fiction
Body Snatchers, The (*Collier's*, sr3, 10 Dec 1954) (Dell First Editions: 42, 1955, 191 pp., pa 25¢; B204 [as *Invasion of the Body Snatchers*], 1961, pa 35¢; 0674, 1967, pa 60¢) (Eyre Spottiswoode, London, 1955, 192 pp., 10/6) (*Gli invasati* [Italian], *Urania*: 118, 1956) (Beacon, 1956, 191 pp., pa 2/-) ([Japanese], Hayakawa: 3001, 1957, pa) (*Hemmelig Invasion* [Danish], Skrifola: F9, 1958, pa) (*Unsichtbare Parasiten* [German], Heyne, 1962, pa; *TN*: 20, 1968)
   A thriller of the American school, in which alien life forms are absorbed into the human host. *Film:* As *Invasion of the Body Snatchers*, Allied Artists, 1956, produced by Walter Wanger, directed by Don Siegel, starring Kevin McCarthy and Dana Wynter. The 1961 Dell paperback used the movie title. This film has no connection with the earlier film *The Body Snatchers*, starring Karloff and Lugosi and based on the story by R. L. Stevenson.
Clock of Time, The [C] See *Third Level, The*
I Love Galesburg in the Springtime [C] (Simon & Schuster, New York, 1963, 224 pp., $3.95) (Eyre Spottiswoode, 1965, 224 pp., 16/-) (Pan: 02021, 1968, 172 pp., pa 3/6)
   10 stories: " 'I Love Galesburg in the Springtime' "; "Love, Your Magic Spell Is Everywhere"; "Where the Cluetts Are"; "Hey, Look at Me!"; "A Possible Candidate for the Presidency"; "Prison Legend"; "Time Has No Boundaries"; "The Intrepid Aeronaut"; "The Coin Collector"; "The Love Letter."
Invasion of the Body Snatchers See *Body Snatchers, The*
Third Level, The [C] (Rinehart, New York, 1956, 256 pp., $3.00) (D'day SF B.C., 1957, $1.15) (*The Clock of Time*, Eyre Spottiswoode, London, 1958, 189 pp., 13/6; SF B.C. [S.J.], 1960, 5/6; Panther: 1193, 1961, 156 pp., pa 2/6) (Dell: D-274, 1959, 192 pp., pa 35¢) ([Japanese], Hayakawa 'Tales of Menace 3,' 1961, pa)
   Sf, 12 stories, many originally published in *Collier's* and some reprinted in *F&SF*: "The Third Level" (*Collier's*, 1951; *F&SF*, Oct 1952); "Such Interesting Neighbors"; "I'm Scared"; "Cousin Len's Wonderful Adjective Cellar"; "Of Missing Persons"; "Something in a Cloud"; "There Is a Tide . . ." (*Collier's*, 1952; *F&SF*, Sep 1954); "Behind the News"; "Quit Zoomin' Those Hands Through the Air" (*Collier's*, 1951; *F&SF*, Dec 1952); "A Dash of Spring"; "Second Chance"; "Contents of the Dead Man's Pocket."
Woodrow Wilson Dime, The (Simon & Schuster, 1968, 190 pp., $4.95)
   Greatly enlarged version of "The Other Wife" (*SEP*, 30 Jan 1960); a man finds a passport to a parallel world where he is married to a glamorous redhead, but his wife in this world still draws him.

FINNEY, WALTER BRADEN See FINNEY, J.

FIRBANK, ARTHUR A. RONALD (1886–1926) Another of fantasy interest besides that below is *Inclinations* (G. Richards, London, 1924).
Fiction
Extravaganzas [C] (Coward-McCann, New York, 1935, 204 pp., $2.00) (Longmans, Toronto, $2.25)
   2 fantasy stories: "The Artificial Princess"; "Concerning the Eccentricities of Cardinal Pirelli."

FIRSOFF, V(ALDEMAR) A(XEL) English amateur astronomer. He was written some nonfiction of popular interest: *Our Neighbour Worlds* (Hutchinson, 1952; Philosophical Library, 1953); *Strange World of the Moon* (Hutchinson, 1959; Basic Books, 1960); *Surface of the Moon* (Hutchinson, 1961); *Exploring the Planets* (Sidgwick Jackson, 1964); *Life Beyond the Earth* (Hutchinson, 1963; Basic Books, 1964).

FIRTH, VIOLET MARY (1890–1946) British author, better known under her pseudonym "Dion Fortune," which she used on all works except some on psychology and mysticism. She wrote a number of occult and black magic novels besides nonfiction about the psychic. Her works have been translated into many languages. She founded the Society of Inner Light, and bequeathed her estate to it.

Fiction [as Dion Fortune]

Demon Lover, The (N. Douglas, London, [1927], 286 pp., 7/6) (Aquarian, London, 1958, 15/-)

Stirring weird novel of black magic and the occult.

Goat-Foot God, The (Williams & Norgate, London, 1936, 383 pp., 7/6)

Black magic and the search for the god Pan.

Inner Light, The See *Sea Priestess, The*

Moon Magic (Aquarian, 1956, 241 pp., 16/-)

Subtitled "Being the Memoirs of a Mistress of the Art." Sequel to *The Sea Priestess*; magic and mystery of the old gods and their power in the world today.

Sea Priestess, The (Dion Fortune, London, 1938, 316 pp., 7/6) (Aquarian, 1957, 316 pp., 16/-) (*The Inner Light* [publisher, etc., unknown])

Weird and occult. Sequel is *Moon Magic*.

Secrets of Dr. Taverner, The (N. Douglas, 1926, 253 pp., 7/6) (Llewellyn Publishers, St. Paul [Minn.], 1962, 234 pp., $4.95, jacket–H. Bok)

11 stories (1962 ed. also has introduction "The Work of a Modern Occult Fraternity," Gareth Knight, 15 pp.): "Blood-Lust"; "The Return of the Ritual"; "The Man Who Sought"; "The Soul That Would Not Be Born"; "The Scented Poppies"; "The Death Hound"; "A Daughter of Pan"; "The Subletting of the Mansion"; "Recalled"; "The Sea Lure"; "The Power House."

Winged Bull, The (Williams & Norgate, 1935, 323 pp., 7/6) (Kyle, New York, 1935, $3.00)

Weird novel.

FISCHER, LEONARD
Fiction

Let Out the Beast [pa] (Export: KN18A, 1950, 159 pp., pa 25¢)

The world after a catastrophe; man reverts to savagery to survive.

FISCHER, MARJORIE
(1903?–1961) U.S. author and anthologist. Prior to her death she won the 1960 Lippincott Prize for *Mrs. Sherman's Summer*. With R. Humphries she compiled two notable weird anthologies.

Anthologies

Pause to Wonder [with R. Humphries] (J. Messner, New York, 1944, 572 pp., $3.00) (Smithers, Toronto, $4.00) (Sun Dial, New York, 1947, $1.00) (Blue Ribbon, Toronto, $1.79)

Weird, 74 stories and 8 poems: "Reason" (poem), R. Hodgson; "A Haunted House," Virginia Woolf; "The Philosophy of Relative Existences," F. R. Stockton; "Birth," L. O'Flaherty; "The Curious Case of Benjamin Button," F. S. Fitzgerald; "Strong But Quirky," I. Shapiro; "The Man That Stopped," F. O'Connor; "A Man and His Boots," W. B. Yeats; "Off the Ground" (poem), W. de la Mare; "The Rime of True Thomas," J. Buchan; "The Haunted Man," R. Bates; "A Horseman in the Sky," A. Bierce; "The Bowmen," A. Machen; "Before the Battle at Lake Trasimenus," Livy; "Private Martin Passy," Wm. March; "Ballad of the Buried Sword," E. Rhys; "The Perfect Game," G. K. Chesterton; "The Canterville Ghost," O. Wilde; "The Rival Beauties," W. W. Jacobs; "The Dong With the Luminous Nose" (poem), E. Lear; "A Haunted House," Pliny; "The Transferred Ghost," F. R. Stockton; "How a Beautiful Maiden Changed Into a Frog and Leaped Upon the Face of the Moon," C. E. S. Wood; "An Imperfect Conflagration," A. Bierce; "The Phantom Fence Rider of San Miguel," H. Yelvington; "Old Christmas," R. Helton; "The Real Right Thing," H. James; "The Quick and the Dead," F. P. Dunne; "Lady Into Fox," D. Garnett; "Charley Lambert," J. M. Synge; "The Bold Dragoon; or, The Adventure of My Grandfather," W. Irving; "The Vixen" (poem), W. W. Gibson; "A Blazing Starre Seene in the West," Anon.; "The

Last Laugh," D. H. Lawrence; "Dionysius and the Pard," G. Household; "Story of Pygmalion," Ovid; "The Chaser," J. Collier; "King Cheops' Daughter" (9½ lines), Herodotus; "Nelly Trim" (poem), Sylvia T. Warner; "The Story of the Siren," E. M. Forster; "The Unicorn in the Garden," J. Thurber; "How Mount Shasta Was Made and How Grizzly Bears Came to Be," C. E. S. Wood; "The Wisdom of the King," W. B. Yeats; "Orpheus and Eurydice," Virgil; "A True Account of the Tryals and Confessions of Several Witches, in New England, etc.," C. Mather; "The Witch of Coos" (poem), R. Frost; "Extract From Captain Stormfield's Visit to Heaven," M. Twain; "Colonel Sterett Relates Marvels," A. H. Lewis; "A True Story," Lucian; "Macavity: The Mystery Cat" (poem), T. S. Eliot; "Private Roger Jones, Wm. March; "Tall Tales of the G.I.'s," Sergeant B. Davidson; "The Elks," J. Caesar; "Sacre du Printemps," L. Bemelmans; "The Elf in Algiers," J. Steinbeck; "Lord Deliver Us," D. Cowie; "The Voice of God," Winifred Holtby; "The Judgement Seat," W. S. Maugham; "The Sensitive Goldfish," Christina Stead; "Panic: The Orson Welles Broadcast That Hoaxed America" (play form), O. Welles; "The Soul of Laploshka," H. H. Munro (Saki); " 'No Trouble at All'," L. Bemelmans; "Welsh Incident" (poem), R. Graves; "The Angry Street: A Bad Dream," G. K. Chesterton; "Artist Unknown," H. Broun; "A Miracle of St. Scothinus," Anon.; "The Saint," Antonia White; "The Silence of God" (poem), O. Sitwell; "A Miracle of St. Goar," Anon.; "Building the Church'," J. M. Synge; "Private Edward Romano," Wm. March; "Blessed Patrick of the Bells," Lady Gregory; "How Caedmon Learned to Sing," Bede; "King O'Toole and St. Kevin," S. Lover; "The Man Who Could Work Miracles," H. G. Wells; "A Shepherd and a Shepherdess," Eliz. Goudge; "The Case of Prometheus," M. Beerbohm; "The Road From Colonus," E. M. Forster; "Mr. Valiant Summoned," J. Bunyan; "Philemon and Baucis," Ovid; "The Fairy Goose," L. O'Flaherty; "The Passing Strange" (poem), J. Masefield.

Strange to Tell [with R. Humphries] (J. Messner, New York, 1946, 532 pp., $3.75) (Smithers, Toronto)

Weird, 68 stories: "The Unicorn," R. Maria Rilke; "The Wardrobe," T. Mann; "Adventure With a Handbag," I. Bunin; "To Saragossa or Back to the Pond," F. Caballero; "The Specter's Wedding," Guy de Pourtales; "The Virgin as Nun," G. Keller; "Nils Punctual and His Clocks," G. Scott; "The Haunted House," L. Pirandello; "The New Melusina," J. W. von Goethe; "The Princess on the Pea," H. C. Andersen; "The Waterwitch Lurley," H. Heine; "The Spirit of Madame de Genlis," N. Leskov; "The Devil Turned Pleader," Grimm Bros.; "The Ashald Who Made the Princess Say You Lie," S. Undset; "Federigo," P. Merrimee; "A Voyage to the Moon," Cyrano de Bergerac; "Lord Arnaldos," Anon.; "The Story of the Haunted Ship," W. Hauff; "The Big Gravel-Sifter," A. Strinberg; "Perseus and Andromeda," J. Lafourge; "About Theseus," P. Nizan; "Woman and Cat," P. Verlaine; "Bluebeard's Daughter," L. Couperus; "A Domestic Drama," G. Clemenceau; "The Waterman," J. W. von Goethe; "Dr. Ox's Experiment," J. Verne; "The Man With a National Face," M. Gorki; "Tortoises for Luck," L. Pirandello; "The Musical Conductor's Story," K. Capek; "The Writer," M. Gorki; "The Hunter Gracchus," F. Kafka; "The Stranger," M. Proust; "The Djinns," V. Hugo; "The Avenging Film," M. Bontempelli; "Two Actors for One Role," T. Gautier; "Gambling Hanzel," Grimm Bros.; "The Wondrous Wonder, the Marvellous Marvel," Afanasiev; "Makar's Dream," V. Korolenko; "Voyage to the Region of the Prodigies," L. A. Holberg; "How a Muzhik Fed Ten Russian Officials," M. E. Saltykov; "The Elk, When Captured Asleep," L. Da Vinci; "The Beyond," A. Averchenko; "The Wolf in the Kennels," Krylov; "A Trip to Paris," I. Silone; "Bontche Schweig," I. L. Perez; "God's Breath," S. Asch; "The Apparition," A. Zweig; "The First Miracle," Azorin; "The Three Hermits," L. Tolstoi; "A Convent Tragedy," John the Hermit; "The Milk White Doe," Anon.; "By the Light of the Lanterns," P. MacOrlan; "The Isle of Liberty," P. de Moncrieff; "The Master of the Atom," R. G. de la Serna; "The Death of Oedipus," Jean R. Bloch; "The City Coat of Arms," F. Kafka; "Plato's Dream," Voltaire; "The Hunter in Black," V. Hugo; "Mr. Maillochin Was Going Home," Y. & J. Boisyvon; "Faithful Peter," L. Feuchtwanger; "Hindenburg's March Into London," Munch; "Laughs Under the Heel," L. Besnard; "Penitent 43," L. Aragon; "Sonnet VII," J. Cassou; "From the Trial of Joan of Arc," Anon.; "The Miracle of Twelfth Night," G. de Pourtales; "Story for the Little Children of Poilus," Colette; "In the North," E. Verhaeren.

FISHER, MARY A. (1839– ?) American novelist, given a one-line mention in *A Dictionary of North American Authors*, W. Stewart Wallace, 1951. The Bleiler *Checklist* gives a further title to that below: *Among the Immortals, in the Land of Desire* (Shakespeare, New York, 1916).
Fiction
Ghost in the Garret and Other Stories, The [C] (Aberdeen, New York, 1910, 147 pp.)
   Fantasy, 7 stories: "The Ghost in the Garret"; "The Sealed Jar"; "The Work of the Woman"; "The Man With an Idea"; "Minerva Knowlton"; "How It Came Back"; "Helen Hamilton's Hero."

FISHER, PHILIP M. U.S. author. He was noted for his fantasy fiction appearing in the Munsey magazines of the 1920's. Reprints of interest are: "The Devil of the Western Sea" (*Arg*, 5 Aug 1922; *FFM*, Apr 1940); "Fungus Isle" (*Arg*, 27 Oct 1923; *FFM*, Oct 1940); "The Ship of Silent Men" (*ASW*, 3 Jan 1920; *FFM*, Feb 1941); "Beyond the Pole" (*Munsey's Magazine*, May 1924; *FFM*, June 1942).

FISHER, VARDIS (31 Mar 1895–) U.S. novelist. He was born of Mormon converts, but is an atheist. He took his B.A. from U. of Utah, and M.A. and Ph.D. at U. of Chicago; his doctoral thesis was on George Meredith. He has been outspoken about the Communist conspiracy and other things. His long novel on the history of Mormonism, *The Children of God* (1939), won the 1939 Harper novel prize. He is primarily noted for his *Testament of Man* series covered below.
Series
Testament of Man. Twelve novels depicting the spiritual and social history of the human race, from the first glimmerings of intelligence to the complex problems of our own day. The first five are prehistoric and thus of sf interest, but the whole series is given for completeness:
Darkness and the Deep (Caxton, Caldwell [Idaho], 1943) (Vanguard, New York, 1943) (Methuen, London, 1944) (Pyramid, 1960, 1962, 1965, pa)
   Man in the earliest beginnings of prehistory.
Golden Rooms, The (Vanguard, 1944, Armed: 733, nd, pa) (Methuen, 1947) (Pyramid, 1960, 1962, pa)
   The first big advance: the discovery of fire.
Intimations of Eve (Vanguard, 1946) (Methuen, 1947) (Pyramid, 1961, 1965, pa)
   A matriarchal society of cavemen.
Adam and the Serpent (Vanguard, 1947) (Pyramid, 1961, pa)
   The struggle to overthrow the matriarchy.
Divine Passion, The (Vanguard, 1948) (Pyramid, 1959, 1963, pa)
   The domination of the priesthood.
Valley of Vision, The (Abelard, New York, 1951) (Caxton De-Luxe, 1951) (Swallow, Denver, 1960, pa $1.95) (Pyramid, 1961, 1963, pa)
   The struggle between powerful passionate Solom and the prophet Ahijah.
Island of the Innocent, The (Abelard, 1952) (Swallow, 1960, pa $1.95) (Pyramid, 1961, 1963, pa)
   Greek and Jew in the time of the Maccabees—persecution and massacre.
Jesus Came Again (Swallow, 1956; 1960, pa) (Pyramid, 1962, pa)
   Sin and salvation in the 1st Century A.D.
Goat for Azazel, A (Swallow, 1956) (Pyramid, 1962, pa)
   A Roman searches for the answer to the riddle of gentle Christianity.
Passion Within, The (*Peace Like a River*, Swallow, 1957) (Pyramid, 1960, 1963, pa)
   Lust and renunciation at the dawn of the Christian era.
My Holy Satan (Swallow, 1958) (Pyramid, 1960, 1963, pa)

A man caught in the Inquisition.
Orphans in Gethesemane (Swallow, 1960, $10.00) (*For Passion, for Heaven* (Pt I), Pyramid, 1962, pa; *The Great Confession*, Pyramid, 1962, pa)
   A long personal story of a man searching for meaning in the present day.

FISK, NICHOLAS (10 Oct 1923–) British free-lance writer.
Fiction
Space Hostages (H. Hamilton, London, 1967, 160 pp., 16/-) (Collins, Toronto, $3.50)
   Juvenile; children are kidnapped and left in a space ship by a crazy space officer.

FITZGERALD, F(RANCIS) SCOTT (KEY) (24 Sep 1896–21 Dec 1940) Noted U.S. author.
Fiction
This Side of Paradise (Scribner's, New York, 1920, 305 pp., $2.00; 1921; 1922; 1948; 1951, $3.00; 1954 [final on original plates]) (Burt, New York, 1920, 305 pp.; 1923, 75¢) (Collins, London, 1921, 292 pp.) (Grey Walls, London, 1948, 269 pp., 8/6; 1950) (Dell: D140, 1948, 288 pp., pa 25¢; ? , 1954, pa 25¢) (Grosset, New York, 1957, 305 pp., $1.00) (Penguin: #1867, 1963, 256 pp., pa 3/6)
   Contains strangely resolved supernatural elements.

FITZGERALD, WILLIAM See JENKINS, W. F.

FITZGIBBON, CONSTANTINE (ROBERT LOUIS) (8th June 1919–) U.S. author, born in Lenox, Mass. He has written five novels and some other serious works.
Fiction
Iron Hoop, The (Knopf, New York, 1949, 268 pp., $3.00) (McClelland, Toronto, $3.25) (Cassell, London, 1950, 220 pp., 9/-) (*Le circle de fer* [French], Ed. du Temps Présent, 1950)
   Life in an occupied city during World War III.
When the Kissing Had to Stop (Norton, New York, 1960, 248 pp., $3.95) (Cassell, 1960, 256 pp., 16/-) (Bantam: F2255, 1961, 230 pp., pa 50¢) (*Wenn alle Küsse enden* [German], Th. Knaur, 1961) ([Japanese], Ronsô-sha, 1961) (Pan: G543, 1962, 252 pp., pa 2/6; X816, 193, pa 3/6) (*Nous n'irons plus au bois* [French], Calmann-Lévy, 1962)
   A Communist-backed politician seeks to rid Britain of U.S. nuclear bases, in order to form a dictatorship. Depicts a decaying society strangled in its own forms and formalities.

FLAGG, FRANCIS (pseud) See WEISS, G. H.

FLEMING, IAN (LANCASTER) (28 May 1908–12 Aug 1964) British author. He was foreign manager of the *Sunday Times*, and had served on the staff of Reuters in London, Berlin and Moscow, had been partner in a stockbroking firm, and had been special correspondent for *The Times* in Russia in the spring of 1939. During World War II he served in British Naval Intelligence, being personal assistant to the Director. He spent some time in Jamaica. As an author he had a vast following for his stories of James Bond, secret service agent, all of which were reissued in the mid-1960's by Pan Books, and some of which have been made into notable films starring Sean Connery.
Fiction
Moonraker (Macmillan, New York, 1955, 220 pp., $2.75) (J. Cape, London, 1955, 256 pp., 10/6) (Clarke Irwin, Toronto, $2.10) (Pan: 392, 1956, 185 pp., pa 2/-; 1959, 190 pp., pa 2/6; X234, 1963, pa 3/6) (*Too Hot to Handle*, Permabooks: M3070, 1957, 185 pp., pa 25¢) (*Attentat!* [Swedish], Bonnier, 1956, pa) (Signet: S1850, 1960, 175 pp., pa 35¢; D2053, 1963, 175 pp., pa 50¢)
   A mystery connected with the launching of a British long-range rocket; one of the James Bond series.
Too Hot to Handle [pa] See *Moonraker*

FLEMING, ROSCOE
Fiction
Man Who Reached the Moon, The (Golden Bell Press, Denver, 1958, $3.00)
Sf poetry volume, with some arresting and often inspiring works on sf themes.

FLES, BARTHOLD (1902–) U.S. anthologist and professional translator.
Anthology
Saturday Evening Post Fantasy Stories [pa] (Avon: 389, 1951, 126 pp., pa 25¢)
9 stories: "The Enemy Planet," D. V. Gallery; "The Child Who Believed," Grace Amundson; "Scene for Satan," N. Langley; "Doomsday Deferred," W. F. Jenkins; "The Eternal Duffer," Willard Temple; "Note on Danger B," G. Kersh; "The Terrible Answer," P. Gallico; "The Voice in the Earphones," W. Schramm; "Doctor Hanray's Second Chance," C. Richter.

FLETCHER, GEORGE U. (pseud) See PRATT, F.

FLINT, HOMER EON (189?–1924) U.S. author. He died mysteriously in his early 30's, his body being found at the bottom of a canyon. He was a noted pulp fiction writer for the Munsey magazines. Some of his stories were "The Lord of Death" (*ASW*, 10 May 1919; *FFM*, Dec 1939); "The Man in the Moon" (*ASW*, 4 Oct 1919) and sequel; "The Greater Miracle" (*ASW*, 14 May 1921), which was his own favourite. He often collaborated with Austin Hall, and the pair are known for *The Blind Spot*. Also of interest was "The Nth Man" (*ASQ*, Spr 1928). Prime Press had planned to publish the collection *The Planeteer and Other Stories*, but the firm died and the book never appeared.
Fiction
Blind Spot, The See HALL, A. (co-author).
Devolutionist and the Emancipatrix, The [pa] (Ace: F-355, 1965, 191 pp., pa 40¢)
In "The Devolutionist" (*Arg*, 23 July 1921) voyagers go to a world of Capella; in "The Emancipatrix" (*Arg*, Sep 1921) voyagers to Arcturus find a human race dominated by bees.
Lord of Death and the Queen of Life, The [pa] (Ace: F-345, 1965, 143 pp., pa 50¢)
In "Lord of Death" (*ASW*, 10 May 1919; *FFM*, Dec 1939) voyagers go to Mercury and find relics of a war-prone civilization; in "The Queen of Life" (*ASW*, 16 Aug 1919) voyagers to Venus find an advanced and overcrowded society.

FODOR, NANDOR See CARRINGTON, H. (co-author)

FONTENAY, C(HARLES) L(OUIS) (17 Mar 1917–) U.S. newspaperman. Born in São Paulo, Brazil, he came to the U.S. when less than a year old, and was reared in Union City, Tennessee. He became a newspaper reporter in 1936, and Associated Press editor in Nashville in 1940. His military service, 1942-46, was spent in Guadalcanal, Russell Island and the New Hebrides, in the Army Air Force. In 1946 he joined *The Nashville Tennessean* and is now a rewrite man. His principal hobby is painting—he obtained national publicity by winning an award for a canvas on which he had cleaned his brushes. He now lives in Madison, Tenn. In the sf field he was a regular contributor to *If* from his first story there ("Disqualified," Sep 1954), and has also appeared in other magazines, including *F&SF*.
Fiction
Day the Oceans Overflowed, The [pa] (Monarch: 443, 1964, 128 pp., pa 40¢)
Hydrogen power plants explode and cause vast flooding.
Rebels of the Red Planet [pa] (Ace: F-113, 1961, 143 pp., pa 40¢; with *200 Years to Christmas*) (*El planeta rojo* [Spanish], Cenit: 40, 1962, pa) (*Die Marsrebellen* [German], *T*: 325, 1964)
Complicated intrigue, with a telepathic mutant fighting against a space combine.
Twice Upon a Time [pa] (Ace: D-266, 1958, 152 pp., 35¢; with *The Mechanical Monarch*) (*Legion der Zeitlosen* [German], *TS*:

20, 1959; Zimmermann, 1962) (*Den Udödlige Legion* [Danish], Skrifola 'Lommeromanen P79,' 1959) (*Kontraspion I Rymden* [Swedish], Wennerberg: R13, 1959, pa) (*Detrás de las estrellas* [Spanish], Cenit: 8, 1961, pa)
The problems of a space-rover who remains young while his wife ages.

FORD, CHARLES HENRI
Anthology
Night With Jupiter and Other Fantastic Stories, A (Vanguard, New York, 1945, 128 pp., illus., $3.00) (D. Dobson, London, 1947, 128 pp., illus., 8/6)
15 stories: "A Night With Jupiter," H. Miller; "Tatuana," M. Asturias; "Dead Eye Dick Rides Again," C. Perry; "Hebdomeros," G. Di Chirico; "Dark Sugar," P. Childs; "Once the Soft Silken Damage Done," M. O'Reilly; "The Buzzard," R. J. Sender; "The Watermelons," L. Poch; "The Guardian Toad," Lydia Cabrera; "White Rabbits," Leonora Carrington; "Impressions of Africa," R. Roussell; "Bluey," P. Bowles (age 9); "Dream of Mobile," H. Miller; "Ms. Found in an Iceberg," Alva N. Turner; "The Sisters," L. Carrington. Illustrations are of all kinds, such as by Pavel Tchelitchew, one or more illus. from a child's alphabet, and other illus. from various sources.

FORD, GARRET (pseud) See CRAWFORD, W. L.

FORD, JAMES L(AUREN) (25 July 1854–26 Feb 1928) American novelist, born in St. Louis, Mo. His other works include *The Literary Shop and Other Tales* (1894) and *Forty-Odd Years in the Literary Shop* (autobiography, 1921).
Fiction
Hypnotic Tales and Other Tales [C] (George H. Richmond, New York, 1894, 220 pp., illus.)
26 stories: *Hypnotic Tales:* "Introduction" (fiction); "The Landlord's Tale"; "The Fiddler's Tale"; "The Spiritualist's Tale"; "The Detective's Tale"; "The Boston Girl's Tale"; "The Representative Business Man's Tale"; "The Rich Presbyterian's Tale"; "The Genial's Tale"; "The Chaperon's Tale"; "The Schoolboy's Tale." *Other Tales:* "The Bunco-Steerer's Christmas"; "Aladdin"; "John Coppertug's Fall"; "The Assemblyman's Bride"; "The Deserted House"; "Two Old Crones"; " 'Lish' Pogram's Thanksgiving Hog"; "Beanville Journalism"; "The Stockbroker's Christmas Gift"; "In the '400' and Out"; "The Evolution of the Humorist"; "The Curiosities' Christmas"; "At the Chromo-Literary Reception"; "The Master Thief"; "An Undiplomatic Diary."

FOREST, JEAN-CLAUDE French comic-strip artist.
Fiction
Barbarella [Trans. from French by Richard Seaver] (Grove, New York, 1966, 68 pp., $5.95; 1968, pa $1.50)
Adult comic strip. *Film:* Paramount, 1968, directed by Roger Vadim, starring Jane Fonda with David Hemmings, John Philip Law, Milo O'Shea and Anita Pallenberg; screenplay by R. Vadim and Terry Southern. The film has much brutality, nudity and uninhibited sexuality, but is considered by some to be a logical extrapolation to the world of 40,000 A.D.

FORESTER, CECIL S(COTT) (28 Aug 1899–2 Apr 1966) British novelist and general writer. He was born in Cairo, and in his later years lived in California with annual visits to London. His newspaper work included covering Spain 1936-37 and Prague during the Nazi conquest of Czechoslovakia. During World War II he was a propagandist in both Great Britain and the U.S.A. His first novel, *Payment Deferred* (1926), is considered a pioneer ironic murder novel. He is also noted for *The African Queen* (1935). His later *The Happy Return* (1937) was the forerunner of his popular Horatio Hornblower series. The last Hornblower story, in which the hero dies, was left to be published after Forester's death. Of science fictional interest is his short novel "If Hitler Had Invaded England" (*SEP*, sr3, 16 Apr 1960; *Melbourne Herald*, sr7, 28 May 1960). He appeared in *F&SF* (June 1956) with "Payment Anticipated" (1951).

Fiction
Peacemaker, The (Little Brown, Boston, 1934, 310 pp., $2.00) (Heinemann, London, 1934, 341 pp., 7/6; 1935, 3/6) (*FFM*, Feb 1948)
A pacifist's anti-magnetic ray causes disruption in London.

FORSTER, E(DWARD) M(ORGAN) (1 Jan 1879–7 June 1970). British author. He was educated at King's College, Cambridge, and has received Companion of Honour, Hon. LL.D. Aberdeen, Hon. Litt.D. Liverpool and other universities. On his 90th birthday he received the Order of Merit from Queen Elizabeth II. He is noted for his classic novel *A Passage to India*. Among his other works was the libretto for Benjamin Britten's opera *Billy Budd*. A recent study of him is *E. M. Forster*, by Norman Kelvin (Southern Illinois U., 1967, $4.95).
Fiction
Celestial Omnibus and Other Stories, The [C] (Sidgwick Jackson, London, 1911, 163 pp., 3/6) (Knopf, New York, 1923, 163 pp., $2.00)
Fantasy, 6 stories: "The Story of a Panic"; "The Other Side of the Hedge"; "The Celestial Omnibus" (*Fan*, Nov/Dec 1952); "Other Kingdom"; "The Curate's Friend"; "The Road From Colonus." Collected into the volume *Collected Tales*.
Collected Short Stories [C] See *Collected Tales*
Collected Tales [C] (Knopf, New York, 1947, 308 pp., $2.75) (*Collected Short Stories*, Sidgwick Jackson, 1948, 246 pp., 10/6; Nelson, Toronto, $3.00; Penguin: 1031, 1954, 222 pp., pa 2/-; 1956; 1961, 3/6)
The 12 stories in *The Celestial Omnibus* and *The Eternal Moment*, in the same order.
Eternal Moment and Other Stories, The [C] (Sidgwick Jackson, 1928, 185 pp., 5/-) (Harcourt Brace, New York, 1928, 245 pp., $2.50) (Grosset 'Universal LUL 172,' 1964, 245 pp., pa $1.65)
Fantasy, 6 stories: "The Machine Stops"; "The Point of It"; "Mr. Andrews"; "Co-ordination"; "The Story of the Siren"; "The Eternal Moment." Collected into the volume *Collected Tales*.

FORT, CHARLES (HOY) (9 Aug 1874–3 May 1932) U.S. author of an unusual type. For 26 years he kept notes on earthquakes, comets, and all sorts of "supernatural" and apparently inexplicable events, amassing 40,000 cuttings which he used to form his own unorthodox and provocative theories of such phenomena, and which he compiled as the four original works below. Three are primarily astronomical in nature (not that Fort 'believed in' astronomy), and the fourth, *Wild Talents*, deals with witchcraft, magic and poltergeist phenomena. Before writing these books he wrote a forgotten novel *The Outcast Manufacturers* (Dodge, 1909). The Fortean Society was founded after his death to preserve his notes, widen the scope of Fortean inquiry, and foster the Fortean viewpoint; Tiffany Thayer was its secretary for many years. Robert Barbour Johnson had an article on Fort in *If*, July 1952, and Miriam A. DeFord had a biographical piece in *F&SF*, Jan 1954. Sam Moskowitz covered Fort's work in *AS*, June 1965.
Nonfiction
Book of the Damned, The (Boni Liveright, New York, 1919, 298 pp., $1.90; 3rd ed. 1931, $2.50) (in *The Books of Charles Fort*, 1941) (*Le livre des damnés* [French], Ed. des Deux Rives, 1955) (Ace: K-156, 1962, 287 pp., pa 50¢; H24, 1967, pa 60¢)
Books of Charles Fort, The [C] [published for the Fortean Society, with introduction by T. Thayer] (Holt, New York, 1941, xxvi+1125 pp., $4.00) (Oxford, Toronto, $5.00)
Collection of the four books in this listing.
Lo! (C. Kendall, New York, 1931, 411 pp., $2.50) (Gollancz, London, 1931, 351 pp., 15/-) (*ASF*, sr8, Apr 1934) (in *The Books of Charles Fort*, 1941) (Ace: K-217, 1965, 284 pp., pa 50¢)
New Lands (Boni Liveright, 1923, 249 pp., $3.00) (in *The Books of Charles Fort*, 1941) (Ace: H73, 1968, 222 pp., pa 60¢)
Wild Talents (C. Kendall, 1932, 13+342 pp., $3.00) (in *The Books of Charles Fort*, 1941) (Ace: H88, 1968, 222 pp., pa 60¢)

FORTUNE U.S. periodical.
Nonfiction
Fabulous Future, The (Dutton, New York, 1956, 206 pp., illus., $3.50) (Smithers, Toronto, $4.25)
Noted contributors to *Fortune*, such as D. Sarnoff, J. Von Neumann, A. Stevenson, R. E. Sherwood, etc., were asked to speculate on what changes 1980 would bring. From the sf angle, the result seems to err on the side of caution.

FORTUNE, DION (pseud) See FIRTH, V. M.

FOSTER, C. E. (1919–)
Fiction
Journey to the Future (Exposition, New York, 1966, 204 pp., $5.00)

FOSTER, RICHARD (pseud) See CROSSEN, K. F.

FOULDS, ELFRIDA VIPONT (BROWN) (1902–)
Fiction
Ghosts' High Noon [as Elfrida Vipont] (H. Z. Walck, New York, 1967, 167 pp., $3.75)
Juvenile ghost story.
Terror by Night [as Elfrida Vipont] (H. Hamilton, London, 1968, vi+154 pp., 16/-)
10 linked stories of the supernatural: "Thwaite How"; "The Welcome Guests"; "The Door in the Wall"; "Mary's House"; "The Grey Lady"; "The Devil's Bird"; "The Power of the Dog"; "Susanna and the Wreckers"; "The Man With the Murderous Face"; "The Night That Never Was on Sea or Land."

FOWLER, SYDNEY (pseud) See WRIGHT, S. F.

FOWLES, JOHN (1926–)
Fiction
Magus, The (Little Brown, Boston, 1966, 582 pp., $7.95; Toronto, $8.95) (J. Cape, London, 1966, 617 pp., illus., 30/-) (Pan: 02032, 1968, 570 pp., pa 8/6)
Black magic, telepathy, adventures in time, and hideous pagan rites. *Film:* Blazer Films for 20th Century Fox, 1968; produced by Kinberg and John Kohn, directed by Guy Green, Panavision and Eastmancolor, starring Michael Caine, Anthony Quinn, Anna Karina and Candice Bergen.

FOX, GARDNER F(RANCIS) (20 May 1911–) U.S. science fiction author. Born in Brooklyn, he went through college and law school and began a law career, but then left to write. He appeared in *Planet Stories* 1945-50 with around a dozen stories, and more recently has done a number of novels for Ace Books. He is married with two children.
Series
Craig, Commander [as Bart Somers]. Space-opera paperbacks: *Beyond the Black Enigma* (1965; 1968); *Abandon Galaxy!* (1967).
Fiction
Arsenal of Miracles, The [pa] (Ace: F-299, 1964, 156 pp., pa 40¢; with *Endless Shadow*)
Pair seek ancient alien ruins for a weapon to save their empire.
Druid Stone, The [as Simon Majors] (Paperback: 52-488, 1967, 157 pp., pa 50¢)
Escape Across the Cosmos [pa] (Paperback: 52-273, 1964, 160 pp., pa 50¢; 52-635, 1968, pa 50¢)
Adventure; a doctor produces a "superman" to fight an interdimensional menace.
Hunter out of Time [pa] (Ace: F-354, 1965, 126 pp., pa 40¢)
Dramatic attempt to save Earth when alien superbeings seek to destroy mankind.
Thief of Llarn [pa] (Ace: F-399, 1966, 158 pp., pa 40¢)
Sequel to *Warrior of Llarn*; the hero achieves his aims by making several seemingly impossible thefts.
Warrior of Llarn [pa] (Ace: F-307, 1964, 160 pp., pa 40¢, cover—F. Frazetta)
Adventure seeking a princess' heritage. Sequel is *Thief of Llarn*.

FRANCE, ANATOLE (16 Apr 1844–12 Oct 1924) French author, whose real name was Jacques Anatole Thibault. A dominant figure in French literature, he was noted as an incurable sceptic, an opponent of church and state, and an active writer for progressive causes. A noted work is *Sur la pierre blanche* (Calmann-Lévy, 1903).

Fiction [Incomplete—other titles in Bleiler *Checklist*]

Penguin Island [Trans.–E. W. Evans, from *L'ile des pingouins*, 1908] (J. Lane, New York & London, 1909, 345 pp., 6/-) (Penguin: 617, 1948, 293 pp., pa 2/-) (*Die Insel der Pinguine* [German], Aufbau V., 1953) (Bantam: FC13, 1958, 239 pp., pa 50¢; SC247, 1965, pa 75¢)

A near-sighted bishop blesses penguins and they become "human."

Revolt of the Angels, The (*La revolte des anges*) (J. Lane, 1914, 348 pp., 6/-) (*Anglarnas uppror* [Swedish], Tiden, 1958) ([Trans. –Mrs. Wilfrid Jackson] Crown, New York, 1962, 348 pp., pa $1.45)

A "guardian angel" loses faith in God through reading scientific treatises, and organises a revolt against Heaven.

FRANK, BRUNO (13 June 1887–20 June 1945) American author. Born in Stuttgart, Germany, he saw service in World War I on the Western Front and in Russia. Following the rise of Hitler he left Germany and lived in Switzerland and elsewhere in Europe until 1937, when he moved to the U.S.A. His works include *The Days of the King* (1927), and *Lost Heritage*; he was primarily noted for his accurate historical novels.

Fiction

Magician and Other Stories, The [C] (Viking, New York, 1946, 7+271 pp., $2.50) (Macmillan, Toronto, $3.00)

Fantasy, 10 stories: "The Suitcase"; "Sixteen Thousand Francs"; "The Moon Watch"; "The Golden Beetle"; "Pantomime"; "An Adventure in Venice"; "The Concert"; "The Unknown Woman"; "The Magician"; "Chamfort Rehearses His Death" (fragment of novel).

FRANK, PAT (HARRY HART) (5 May 1907–) U.S. author and government official. He was educated at U. of Florida. He was Special Assistant, American Ministry to Australia, representing U.S. on Allied Political Warfare Council 1942-43. He was attached to the O.W.I. in Istanbul 1943-44 and to the U.N. Mission in Korea 1952-53. He has contributed to *SEP*, *Red Book*, *American Weekly*, etc.; his non-sf novels include *The Long Way Round*, *An Affair of State* and *Hold Back the Night*.

Fiction

Alas, Babylon (Lippincott, Philadelphia, 1959, 254 pp., $3.50) (Constable, London, 1959, 254 pp., 15/-) (Bantam: F2054, 1960, 279 pp., pa 50¢; HP70, 1964, 279 pp., pa 60¢) (*Ay, Babilonia* [Spanish], Galaxia: 40, 1965, pa)

An isolated area in Florida survives a nuclear war. The hero, with a group of mixed whites and blacks, fights through to life in a new pattern.

Forbidden Area ("Seven Days to Never," *New York Daily News*, sr, ?) (Lippincott, 1956, 252 pp., $3.50) (D'day SF B.C., 1956) (Bantam: A1553, 1957, 214 pp., pa 35¢) (*Seven Days to Never*, Constable, 1957, 252 pp., 15/-; Pan, 1959, 219 pp., pa 2/6) (*De fatale zeven dagen* [Dutch], Prisma, Utrecht & Antwerp, 1958)

Russian saboteurs land by submarine; all-out atomic war is averted by a hair's breadth.

Mr. Adam (Lippincott, 1946, 252 pp., $2.75) (Longmans, Toronto, $3.00) (Armed: 1217, nd, pa) (Gollancz, London, 1947, 191 pp., 8/6) (*Stackars Adam* [Swedish], Centrum, 1947) (*Mister Adam* [French], Ed. du Madrigal, 1947) (abr., *Reader's Digest*, 1947?) (Pocket Books: 498, 1948, 231 pp., pa 25¢; 2498, 1955, 204 pp., pa 25¢) ([Japanese], Hayakawa Shôbô, 1951) (*Adam und die Frauen* [German], K. Desch, 1952) (Panther: 688, 1957, 192 pp., pa 2/-)

All men except one are sterilized by a cosmic catastrophe. Logically developed, and can be read as a satire on American bureaucrats.

Seven Days to Never See *Forbidden Area*

FRANKAU, GILBERT (21 Apr 1884–4 Nov 1952) British novelist and short story writer. After leaving Eton in 1904 he entered the family cigar business. He served in World War I, received a commission, and was invalided out. He was married three times. He used his war experiences and his personal life as background for some of his books. One of his daughters, Pamela, is also a writer. He is most noted for *The Guns* (verse, 1916) and *The Love Story of Aliette Brunton* (1922). His older fantasy novel *The Seeds of Enchantment* (Doubleday, 1921) first appeared in *Popular Magazine* (sr7, 7 Feb 1920). His autobiography is *Self-Portrait* (1940).

Fiction

Unborn Tomorrow (MacDonald, London, 1953, 302 pp., 12/6)

In the distant future civilization has reverted to the 17th Century style because of a beam which detonates all explosives.

FRANKAU, PAMELA (3 Jan 1908–) British novelist and short story writer, younger of two daughters of Gilbert Frankau by his first wife. She began her literary career at 18, writing her first novel, *Marriage of Harlequin* (1927), under great difficulties. In World War II she served in the A.T.S., rising to major. She married Marshall Dill, Jr., and has lived in the U.S.A. since 1945. She is noted for *The Devil We Know* (1939) and *A Democrat Dies* (U.S.: *Appointment With Death*) (1940). Her autobiography is *I Find Four People* (1935). *Some New Planet* (J. Lane, London, 1937) was her only pre-war fantasy. Her *The Offshore Light* (1951) has fantasy overtones, with a man's dream of a perfect island displacing his belief in reality.

Fiction

Bridge, The (Heinemann, London, 1957, 299 pp., 16/-) (Harper, New York, 1957, 303 pp., $3.75) (Reprint Society [World Books], London, 1958, 250 pp.) (*Bron* [Swedish], Bonnier, 1958) (FSB: 137, 1959, 288 pp., pa 3/6)

The 'Bridge' runs between Earth and the upper and lower regions; the story is a series of flashbacks of a man reliving the crucial episodes of his life.

FRANKE, HERBERT

Fiction

Golden Casket, The [C] See BAUER, W.

FRANKLIN, H(OWARD) BRUCE (28 Feb 1934–) U.S. scholar, Associate Professor of English at Stanford University. He wrote *The Wake of the Gods; Melville's Mythology*, and is a contributor to *New England Quarterly*, *Studies in English Literature*, *Nineteenth-Century Fiction* and other scholarly journals.

Anthology

Future Perfect (Oxford U., New York, 1966, 401 pp., $6.50; GB241, 1968, pa $2.25)

Introduction; *Hawthorne and Poe*: Nathaniel Hawthorne and Poe: "The Birthmark," "The Artist of the Beautiful," "Rappaccini's Daughter," N. Hawthorne. Edgar Allan Poe and Science Fiction: "A Tale of the Ragged Mountains," "The Facts in the Case of M. Valdemar," "Mellonta Tauta," E. A. Poe. *Explorations*: 1. Automata! Herman Melville and Science Fiction: "The Bell-Tower," H. Melville. Man as Machine: "Dr. Materialismus," Frederic J. Stimson. 2. Marvelous Inventions. "The Atoms of Chladni," J. D. Whelpley. 3. Medicine Man. "Was He Dead?" Silas W. Mitchell. 4. Into the Psyche. Thomas Wentworth Higginson and His Dreamer: "The Monarch of Dreams," T. W. Higginson. Ambrose Bierce and Science Fiction: "A Psychological Shipwreck," A. Bierce. Edward Bellamy and Science Fiction: "To Whom This May Come," E. Bellamy. *Space Travel*: "The Blindman's World," E. Bellamy. Fitz-James O'Brien and Science Fiction: "The Diamond Lens," F.-J. O'Brien. Dimensional Speculation as Science Fiction: "Four-Dimensional Space," Anon.; "Mysterious Disappearances," A. Bierce; "From Four-Space," Arthur E. Bortwick (para. only). *Time Travel*: Beyond the Past: "Christmas 200,000 B.C.," Stanley Waterloo. Mark Twain and Science Fiction: "From the 'London Times' of 1904," M. Twain. The Perfect Future: "In the Year Ten Thousand," Wm. Harben.

FRANKLIN, JAY (pseud) See CARTER, J. F.

FRASER, HELEN
Fiction
Fulfilment at Noon (Hutchinson, London, 1950, 251 pp., 9/6; 1952, 6/-)
  A novel of ancient Egypt.

FRASER, J. T. U.S. senior scientist at General Precision Inc.
Nonfiction
Voices of Time, The (Braziller, New York, 1966, 710 pp., $12.50)
  A massive study of the problems of time—27 original essays by international specialists.

FRASER, PHYLLIS (MAURINE) (1915–)
Anthology
Great Tales of Terror and the Supernatural See WISE, H. A. (co-anthologist)

FRASER, Sir RONALD (ARTHUR) (3 Nov 1888–) British writer and public servant. He was educated at St. Paul's, served in World War I and was wounded and disabled for further service. He took part in Anglo-Argentine negotiations in 1933, and was Commercial Minister at H. H. Embassy in Paris 1944-49. He was President of the Caledonian Society of France 1946-53, K.B.E. 1949, and also Companion of the Order of Orange Nassau. He has written many novels beginning with *The Flying Draper* (1924) and including *Bell From a Distant Temple* and *Flight of Wild Geese*.
Fiction [Incomplete; see also Bleiler *Checklist*]
Beetle's Career (J. Cape, London, 1951, 160 pp., 8/6)
  A scientist invents a world-dominating weapon which has a highly therapeutic ray as a by-product.
Jupiter in the Chair (Cape, 1958, 192 pp., 15/-) (Clarke Irwin, Toronto, $3.25)
  Sequel to *A Visit From Venus*.
Trout's Testament (Cape, 1960, 3+191 pp., 15/-)
Visit From Venus, A (Cape, 1958, 188 pp., 15/-) (Clarke Irwin, Toronto, $3.25)
  Venerians visit Earth and vice versa; mild satire on interplanetary communication. Sequel is *Jupiter in the Chair*.

FRASER, WILLIAM
Fiction
Eye of a God and Other Tales of East and West, The [C] (Doubleday & McClure, New York, 1899, 260 pp.)
  Fantasy, 6 stories: "The Eye of a God"; " 'King for a Day' "; "Djalma"; "God and the Pagan"; "His Passport"; "The Conversion of Sweet Grass."

FRAYN, MICHAEL (8 Sep 1933–) British free-lance writer.
Fiction
Very Private Life, A (Viking, New York, 1968, 132 pp., $4.50) (Collins, London, 1968, 192 pp., 22/6)
  A young girl in the distant future where humanity is divided into insiders, who are well cared for, and outsiders, who get along as best they can.

FRAZEE, (CHARLES) STEVE (1909–) U.S. author. He was born in Salida, Colorado and educated at Western State College. He became president of Western Writers of America in 1954, and vice-pres. in 1962; he is also in the Colorado Author's League. A most versatile writer, he has produced many sf, mystery and western stories; he won the Ellery Queen Mystery Award in 1954 and appeared in *Best American Detective Stories* (1954). His novels include *Shining Mountains*, *Hellsgrin*, *Cry Coyote*, *High Cage* and *Rendezvous*; he has also written six movie and ten TV scripts. Some sf novelettes of interest are "Dragon Fire" (*Fantasy Mag*, Feb 1953), "Flying Saucers Do Exist" (*Space SF*, Aug 1957) and "Geoff the Djinn" (*Cosmos*, July 1954).
Fiction
Sky Block, The (Rinehart, New York, 1953, 247 pp., $2.75)

(Clarke Irwin, Toronto, $2.75) (Lion: LL3, 1954, 192 pp., pa 35¢) (Bodley Head, London, 1955, 192 pp., 9/6) (*Spärrade Skyar* [Swedish], Berghs, 1955) (Pyramid: PG-13, 1958, 192 pp., pa 35¢) (Mayflower: 8014, 1964, 143 pp., pa 2/6)
  Suspense story; only sf in that it describes an electronic weather control device operated by enemy agents.

FRAZETTA, FRANK U.S. artist. He is best known for cover paintings for E. R. Burroughs paperbacks. He has also done artwork for the comic strips *Ace McCoy*, *Johnny Comet*, *Flash Gordon* and *Li'l Abner*, and for numerous comic book features including *Buck Rogers* and *White Indian*. He created the movie serial and comic book hero "Thunda."

FREAS, FRANK KELLY U.S. artist. He is one of the most important artists in the science fiction field, and is known principally for his cover work on *ASF*, where he first appeared in Oct 1953. He has also illustrated other sf magazines. He won Hugo awards for artwork in 1955, 1958 and 1959, and was runner-up in 1960. His wife helps him on much of his work.
Fiction [artwork]
Frank Kelly Freas: A Portfolio (Advent, Chicago, 1957, 38 pp., 8½ in. x 11 in., $1.50)
  Two-colour covers, biographical sketch, and 16 black & white plates reprinted from magazine illustrations.

FREEDMAN, RUSSELL
Nonfiction
Two Thousand Years of Space Travel (Collins, London, 1965, 256 pp., 12/6)
  Juvenile; a history of space flight, sf and speculation on man's efforts to explore space, from the Greek discourses through Galileo, the Great Lunar Hoax, Verne, Oberth, Goddard, etc., to today.

FREKSA, FRIEDRICH (1882–) German author.
Fiction
Druso (*Druso oder die Gestohlene Menschenwelt*, Herman Reckendorf, Berlin, 1931) ([Trans.–F. Pratt] *WS*, sr3, May 1934) (*Druso* [French] [Trans.–G. H. Gallet], Hachette, Le RF: 73, 1960)
  Invaders from outer space dominate Earth; originally recommended by C. A. Brandt.

FRENCH, ALICE (19 Mar 1850–9 Jan 1934) American novelist and short-story writer, born at Andover, Mass. She never married. She began writing for the literary magazines of the East in the 1880's, continuing until she was nearly 70. She received an Hon. Litt.D. from U. of Iowa in 1911. She always used the pseudonym "Octave Thanet." A fantasy besides that below was *The Missionary Sheriff* (Harper, New York, 1897).
Fiction [as Octave Thanet]
Otto the Knight and Other Trans-Mississippi Stories [C] (Houghton Mifflin, New York, 1891, 348 pp.)
  Fantasy, 10 stories: "The Conjured Kitchen"; "The Day of the Cyclone"; "First Mayor"; "Governor's Prerogative"; "Loaf of Peace"; "Mortgage on Jeffy"; "Otto the Knight"; "Plumb Idiot"; "Sis' Chaney's Black Silk"; "Trusty No. 49."

FRENCH, JOSEPH LEWIS (16 Aug 1858–14 Dec 1936)
Anthologies
Best Ghost Stories, The (Boni Liveright, New York, 1919, 217 pp.)
  Not in the Bleiler *Checklist*. 12 stories and introduction "The Fascination of the Ghost Story," A. B. Reeve: "The Apparition of Mrs. Veal," D. Defoe; "Canon Alberic's Scrapbook," M. R. James; "The Haunted and the Haunters," E. Bulwer-Lytton; "The Silent Woman," L. Kompert; "Banshees"; "The Man Who Went Too Far," E. F. Benson; "The Woman's Ghost Story," A. Blackwood; "The Phantom Rickshaw," R. Kipling; "The Rival Ghosts," R. Matthews; "The Damned Thing," A. Bierce; "The Interval," V. O'Sullivan; "Dey Ain't No Ghosts," W. P. Butler; some American

ghosts.

Best Psychic Stories, The (Boni Liveright, 1920, 299 pp.)

Weird, 18 stories and articles with introduction by Dorothy Scarborough: "When the World Was Young," J. London; "The Return," A. Blackwood; "The Second Generation," A. Blackwood; "Joseph: A Story," Katherine Rickford; "The Clavecin, Briges," G. W. Edwards; "Ligeia," E. A. Poe; "The Sylph and the Father," Elsa Barker; "A Ghost," L. Hearn; "The Eyes of the Panther," A. Bierce; "Photographing Invisible Beings," W. T. Stead; "The Sin-Eater," Fiona Macleod; "Ghosts in Solid Form," G. Bolton; "The Phantom Armies Seen in France," H. Carrington; "The Portal of the Unknown," A. J. Davis; "The Supernormal Experiences," St. J. D. Seymour; "Nature-Spirits, or Elementals," Nizida; "A Witches' Den," Helena Blavatsky; "Some Remarkable Experiences of Famous Persons," W. F. Prince.

Ghost Story Omnibus, The (Dodd Mead, New York, 1933, 365 + 292 pp., $2.00) (McClelland, Toronto, $2.25) (Tudor, New York, $1.19)

24 stories: those in *Great Ghost Stories* and *Ghosts Grim and Gentle*, in the same order.

Ghosts Grim and Gentle (Dodd Mead, 1926, 292 pp., $2.00) (in *The Ghost Story Omnibus*)

12 stories: "A Psychical Invasion," A. Blackwood; "On the Stairway," Kath. F. Gerould; "Maese Perez, the Organist," G. A. Becquer; "The Feast of Redgauntlet," Sir W. Scott; "The Ghost of Fear," H. G. Wells; "The Tall Woman," P. A. de Alarcon; "The Dead Valley," R. A. Cram; "The Tractate Middoth," M. R. James; "The Ghost-Ship," R. Middleton; "The Canterville Ghost," O. Wilde; "The Middle Toe of the Right Foot," A. Bierce; "On the River," G. de Maupassant.

Great Ghost Stories (Dodd Mead, 1918, 365 pp., $2.00) (in *The Ghost Story Omnibus*)

12 stories: "The House and the Brain," Lord E. Bulwer-Lytton; "The Roll-Call of the Reef," A. T. Quiller-Couch; "The Open Door," Mrs. Marg. Oliphant; "The Deserted House," E. T. A. Hoffman; "The Mysterious Sketch," Erckmann-Chatrian; "Green Branches," Fiona Macleod; "The Four-Fifteen Express," Amelia B. Edwards; "The Werewolf," H. B. Marryat; "The Withered Arm," T. Hardy; "Clarimonde," T. Gautier; "The Stalls of Barchester Cathedral," M. R. James; "What Was It?" F.-J. O'Brien.

Masterpieces of Mystery—Vol. 2, Ghost Stories (Doubleday Page, 1921, 241 pp.) (Garden City Pub. Co., New York, 1937, 241 pp., $2.29)

9 stories: "The Listener," A. Blackwood; "Number 13," M. R. James; "Joseph: A Story," Katherine Rickford; "The Horla," Guy de Maupassant; "The Beast With Five Fingers," W. F. Harvey; "Sister Maddelena," R. A. Cram; "Thrawn Janet," R. L. Stevenson; "The Yellow Cat," W. D. Steele; "Letter to Sura," Pliny the Younger.

Masterpieces of Mystery—Vol. 3, Mystic-Humorous (Doubleday Page, 1921, 265 pp.) (Garden City Pub. Co., 1937, 265 pp., $2.29)

11 stories: "May Day Eve," A. Blackwood; "The Diamond Lens," F.-J. O'Brien; "The Mummy's Foot," T. Gautier; "Mr. Bloke's Item," M. Twain; "A Ghost," L. Hearn; "The Man Who Went Too Far," E. F. Benson; "Chan Tow the Highrob," C. B. Fernald; "The Inmost Light," A. Machen; "Secret of Goresthorpe Grange," A. C. Doyle; "The Man With the Pale Eyes," G. de Maupassant; "The Rival Ghosts," Brander Matthews.

Masterpieces of Mystery—Vol. 4, Riddle Stories (Doubleday Page, New York, 1920, 258 pp.) (Garden City Pub. Co., 1937, 258 pp., $2.29)

9 stories, many of weird interest: "The Mysterious Card," Cleveland Moffett; "The Great Valdez Sapphire," Anon.; "The Oblong Box," E. A. Poe; "The Birth-Mark," N. Hawthorne; "A Terribly Strange Bed," W. Collins; "The Torture by Hope," Villiers de L'Isle Adam; "The Box With the Iron Clamps," Florence Marryat; "My Fascinating Friend," William Archer; "The Lost Room," F.-J. O'Brien.

Tales of Terror (Small Maynard, Boston; 1925, 224 pp., $2.50) (Burt, New York, 1934, 231 pp., 75¢)

9 stories: "The Horla," G. de Maupassant; "A Terrible Night,"

W. C. Russell; "The Torture by Hope," Villiers de L'Isle Adam; "What Was It?" F.-J. O'Brien; "The Mark of the Beast," R. Kipling; "The Temple of Isis," R. Marsh; "The Pit and the Pendulum," E. A. Poe; "The Vampire," B. Stoker (from *Dracula*); "The Avengers," A. C. Doyle.

FRENCH, PAUL (pseud) See ASIMOV, I.

FRIEDBERG, GERTRUDE U.S. author and teacher, graduate of Barnard College. She has written short stories for *F&SF*, *Atlantic Monthly*, *Harper's*, *Esquire* and *New World Writing*. Her play *Three Cornered Moon* was produced in 1933 with Ruth Gordon in the lead and later adapted as a film starring Claudette Colbert. Married with two children, she enjoys substitute teaching of mathematics in the New York public schools.

Fiction

Revolving Boy, The (Doubleday, New York, 1966, 191 pp., $3.95) (Gollancz, London, 1967, 191 pp., 18/-) (Ace: H-58, 1968, 192 pp., pa 60¢) (*Ruf aus dem Weltraum* [German], Goldmann, 1967; 084, 1967, pa)

A lad born in orbit shows unusual inclinations. The story has some wide gaps in logic but was well received.

FRIEDMAN, BRUCE JAY

Fiction

Black Humour [pa] (Corgi: FN7268, 1965, 174 pp., pa 5/-)

13 stories and extracts showing macabre and sick humour.

FRIEND, OSCAR J(EROME) (8 Jan 1897–1963) U.S. author and literary agent. As a science fiction editor he worked on the Standard magazines: *Thrilling Wonder Stories* Aug 1941–Fall 1944, *Startling Stories* July 1941–mid 1944, *Captain Future* 1940-44. His fiction included many detective, western and sf stories, with a number under the pseudonym "Owen Fox Jerome," such as *The Hand of Horror* (Clode, 1927). In later years he was head of Otis Kline Associates literary agency. Some works of interest include "The Water World" (*SS*, May 1941; [Swedish], *Jules Verne Magasinet*, Nos. 28-39, 1942) and "Today Is Forever" (*AS*, June 1958). His "Roar of the Rocket" (*TWS*, Apr 1940) appeared as an Australian paperback, while "The Molecule Monsters" was the title story in an anonymous Australian paperback.

Fiction

Kid From Mars, The (*SS*, Sep 1940) (Fell, New York, 1949, 270 pp., $2.50, jacket—Finlay) ([Swedish], *JVM*, Nos. 6-19, 1942) (Kemsley: CT401, 1951, 190 pp., pa 1/6) (*Un martien sur la Terre* [French], Gallimard Le RF, 1953) (*Mann vom Mars in besonderer Mission*, [German], Weiss, 1956, pa; *T*: 228, 1962)

A young man from Mars in human form visits Hollywood.

Star Men, The (Avalon, New York, 1963, 221 pp., $2.95)

Anthologies

From Off This World See MARGULIES, L. (co-anthologist)

Giant Anthology of Science Fiction See MARGULIES, L. (co-anthologist)

My Best Science Fiction Story See MARGULIES, L. (co-anthologist)

FRITCH, CHARLES E. U.S. author and editor. His short, piquant O. Henryesque stories have been in many sf magazines since his first appearance with "The Wallpaper" (*OW*, Mar 1951). He edited the irregular and now defunct sf and fantasy magazine *Gamma*, mid-1963–Sep 1965.

FROST, CONRAD

Fiction

Evidence Before Gabriel (F. Aldor, London, 1947, 255 pp., 9/6)

Fantasy.

FULLER, JOHN G.

Nonfiction

Interrupted Journey, The (Dial Press, New York, 1966, xvi+302 pp., $5.95)

Subtitled "Two Lost Hours 'Aboard a Flying Saucer'"; the

story of two Americans, Betty and Barney Hill of Portsmouth, N.H., who on the night of 19 Sep 1961 sighted a flying saucer . . . and then found they had lost two hours. Under psychotherapy and hypnosis they give an account of meeting intelligent humanoids, etc.

FULLERTON, (JOHN) CHARLES (MARK) (1924–) British author. He served with the 60th Rifles during World War II; later he joined a Far Eastern shipping firm and finally an advertising agency. His book *If Chance a Stranger* describes the experiences of an English soldier in a Japanese prisoner-of-war camp.
Fiction
Man Who Spoke Dog, The (Harvill, London, 1959, 159 pp., illus. 12/6)
A man has the gift of understanding dog talk, and thereby builds a commercial empire.

FUMENTO, ROCCO (12 Feb 1923–)
Fiction
Devil by the Tail (McGraw, New York, 1954, 250 pp., $3.50) (Chatto, London, 1955, 239 pp., 12/6)
An old man is regarded as the Devil by his neighbours, and refuses to die.

FUQUA, ROBERT (pseud) See TILLOTSON, J. W.

FURMAN, A(BRAHAM) L(OUIS) (1902–)
Anthologies
Fourth Mystery Companion, The (Lantern, New York, 1946, 396 pp., $2.75) (McLeod, Toronto, $3.50)
19 stories: "White Carnations," Q. Patrick; "The Painted Nail," G. H. Cox; "Traitors Trail," H. Pentecost; "The Unbelievable Baroness," Eliz. S. Holding; "A Triumph in Theory," L. Paul; "The Tenth Clue," D. Hammett; "The Saint Sits In," L. Charteris; "The White Cat," R. Kent; "The Level Crossing," F. W. Crofts; "The Case of the Calico Dog," Mignon Eberhart; "Prelude to Murder," W. C. Brown; "Fog Over Hong Kong," V. Starrett; "The Adventure of the Bearded Lady," E. Queen; "Twice-Trod Path," Wm. Irish; "Tomorrow We Die," F. Owen; "The Important Point," Wm. McHarg; "The Secret of the Ruins," S. Rohmer; "Halloween Assassin," F. Skerry; "Library Book," C. Woolrich. Also biographies of authors.
Ghost Stories [pa] See *Teen-Age Ghost Stories*
More Ghost Stories [pa] See *More Teen-Age Ghost Stories*
More Teen-Age Ghost Stories (Lantern, New York, 1967, 189 pp., $2.95) (*More Ghost Stories*, Lantern: 50593, 1968, 152 pp., pa 50¢)
8 stories: "Hit and Run Ghost," Carl H. Rathjen; "The Ghosts of the F.F.'s," Flora R. Collier; "The Abominable Snowman," Ursula R. Johnson; "The Haunted Fairground," Diana Meyers; "The Skeleton Hotel," Kay Haugaard; "The Haunted Ruins," Reg Granger; "The Ghost at the Sliding Glass Door," Nancy MacRobert; "The Long Night," Molly Webster.
More Teen-Age Haunted Stories (Lantern Press, New York, 1967, 189 pp., $2.95)
9 stories: "The Secret in the Lost Gunboat," Roger Jackson; "The Gay Ghostess," Carl H. Rathjen; "The Riddle of Roundtree Schoolhouse," Audrey Wendland; "The Photo Phantom," Nancy MacRoberts; "The Ghost Played at Midnight," Ludmilla Bollow; "Cave of the Lost," Agnes Staudy; "The Haunted Canyon," Margaret & George Ogan; "The Haunted Elevator," Wilna Bednarz; "Ghost by Daylight," Irna Schmidt.
Mystery Companion, The (Gold Label, New York, 1943, 11+348 pp., $2.75) (McLeod, Toronto, $3.50)
19 stories: "Active Duty," R. Sale; "The Body in the Ostrich Cage," V. Starrett; "The Sword of God," H. Hode; "The Greek Poropulos," E. Wallace; "Bond of Reunion," C. Carmer; "Believe It or Die," P. Ketchum; "Yours Truly, Jack the Ripper," R. Bloch; "The Street of the Little Candles," J. F. Cooke; "The Blackout Murders," A. V. Elston; "You're Killing Me," D. Clark; "If the Dead Could Talk," C. Woolrich; "America's Most Famous Murder," G. L. Porter; "The Judge Finds the Body," G. Homes; "The

Phantom Slayer," F. Leiber; "Tears of the Virgin," T. G. Springer; "Me and His Majesty and Trouble," J. C. Stacey; "Death in a Gray Mist," F. Owen; "A Pair of Gloves," C. Carmer; "The Man in the Cask," V. Starrett.
Outer Space Stories [pa] See *Teen-Age Outer Space Stories*
Second Mystery Companion (Gold Label, 1944, 11+410 pp., $2.75) (McLeod, Toronto, $3.50)
16 stories: "The Bedchamber Mystery," C. S. Forester; "Delayed Verdict," A. V. Elston; "The Question Mark," Margery Allingham; "Ghosts Don't Make No Noise," R. Sale; "Post Mortem," C. Woolrich; "The Chop-Sticks of Confucius," V. Starrett; "The Master of the Murder Castle," J. B. Martin; "The Riddle of the Whirling Lights," S. Palmer; "Death by Accident," F. Cockcrell; "The Man Who Amazed Fish," F. Owen; "There Are More to Die," P. Ketchum; "Radio Patrol," L. T. White; "Scoundrels by Night," R. Kent; "The Fluted Arrow," W. B. Mowery; "Steve Takes a Hand," H. B. Cave; "Connoisseur of Murder," J. C. Stacey.
Teen-Age Ghost Stories (Lantern, New York, 1961, 189 pp., $2.95) (McLeod, Toronto, $3.50) (*Ghost Stories*, Lantern: PB50092, 1965, 163 pp., pa 50¢)
8 stories: "Ghost Alarm," Carl Henry Rathjen; "Ghost of Black John," Wm. MacKellar; "Dark Haugaard," Anon.; "The Ghost of Old Stone Fort," Harry H. Kroll; "Valley of No Return," Willis Lindquist; "Mystery of the Ghost Junk," James B. Moore; "The Haunted Pavilion," Patricia McCune; "The Haunted Tumbler," Diana Myers.
Teen-Age Outer Space Stories (Lantern, 1962, 190 pp., $2.95) (McLeod, Toronto, $3.50) (*Outer Space Stories*, Lantern: 50260, 1965, 173 pp., pa 50¢)
Juvenile, 8 stories (some from *Boys' Life*): "Sign Among the Stars," Lee Priestley; "Crash Alert," Clinton Pearl; "A New Game," A. M. Lightner; "Flying Teacup," Fred Gohman; "Rocket Rider," Charles Coombs; "Shake Hands With the Man in the Moon," Capt. Burr Leyson; "Moon Gold," Seth Harmon; "Space Secret," Clinton Pearl.
Third Mystery Companion (Gold Label, 1945, 395 pp., $2.75) (McLeod, Toronto, $3.50)
21 stories: "The Calling Card of Mr. Engle," L. Paul; "The Unloaded Gun," A. V. Elston; "The Experts," M. Lord; "The Kiskadee Bird," E. S. Holding; "Face in the Dark," H. Pentecost; "Wet Saturday," J. Collier; "One Chance in a Million," W. Payne; "Death Had a Pencil," R. Sale; "The Phantom of the Subway," C. Woolrich; "The Mark of the Mast," S. Rohmer; "The Third Ladder," P. Ketchum; "Hangin' Crazy Benny," L. T. White; "The Old Man in the Window," Marg. Allingham; "The Long Still Streets of Evening," F. Owen; "Crystal Evidence," D. B. Chidsey; "The Simple Art of Murder," R. Chandler; "The Riddle of the Blue Blood Murders," S. Palmer; "Ways That Are Dark," T. G. Springer; "The Case of the Turkey Point," H. Bloomfield; "The Witness," W. Brandon; "Murder at the Opera," V. Starrett.

FYFE, H(ORACE) B(ROWNE) (30 Sep 1918–) U.S. author. He was born in Jersey City, educated at Stevens Academy and Columbia U., and has lived mostly in New Jersey. He served in France and Germany in the infantry, winning the Bronze Star. He married and returned to college, graduating in 1950 with a B.S. in writing. He has worked as a laboratory assistant and draftsman, but is now writing full-time. He is very interested in photography. His first sf appearance was with "Locked Out" (*ASF*, Feb 1940), but he did not sell to this field again until after the war, with "Sinecure 6," (*ASF*, Jan 1947). He has now had about 50 stories published in various sf magazines. A novella of interest is "Moonwalk" (*Space SF*, Nov 1952).
Series
Bureau of Slick Tricks. All in *ASF*: "The Bureau of Slick Tricks" (Dec 1948); "Special Jobbery" (Sep 1949); "Compromise" (Dec 1950); "Implode and Peddle" (Nov 1951); "Bluff-Stained Transaction" (Mar 1952).
Fiction
D-99 [pa] (Pyramid: F794, 1962, 144 pp., pa 40¢) (*D-99* [Spanish], Cenit: 59, 1963, pa)

Intrigue; an ultra-secret department operates to rescue Earthmen imprisoned by aliens.

GADDIS, VINCENT H. (1913–)
Nonfiction
Mysterious Fires and Lights (McKay, New York, 1967, 280 pp., $5.50) (Dell: 6244, 1968, 236 pp., pa 75¢)
Well-organized and documented review of oddities, including UFO's, freak lightning, fireballs, electrically charged humans, etc.

GAIL, OTTO WILLI (1896–1956) German author.
Fiction
By Rocket to the Moon (Sears, New York, 1930, 303 pp., $2.50)
Juvenile. A newspaper reporter stows away on a flight to the Moon; a grim struggle against nature, realistically related.
Shot From the Moon, The [n] (*Der Stein vom Mond*, Bergstadt, 1926) –Trans. by F. Currier: (*WSQ*, Spr 1930)
Sequel to *The Shot Into Infinity*.
Shot Into Infinity, The [n] (*Der Schuss ins All*, Bergstadt, Breslau, 1925) –Trans. by F. Currier: (*WSQ*, Fall 1929) (*SFQ*, Win 1941)
A noted interplanetary novel. Sequel was *The Shot From the Moon*.

GAINES, WILLIAM M. U.S. publisher, noted for his comic magazine *Mad*. Gaines has edited a number of book collections from *Mad*.

GAITE, FRANCIS (pseud) See COLES, M.

GALAXY SCIENCE FICTION (formerly *Galaxy Magazine*) U.S. sf magazine. For anthologies derived completely therefrom, see GOLD, H.L., and POHL, F.

GALBRAITH, ALEXANDER (1924–) British author, better known as "Sandy Wilson." Graduate of Oxford (B.A.). He has contributed to *Elizabethan Magazine*, and also wrote *The Boy Friend* and *Who's Who for Beginners* (in collaboration).
Fiction [as Sandy Wilson]
This Is Sylvia: Her Lives and Loves (Dutton, New York, 1955, 125 pp., $2.50)
Fantasy satire about a theatrical cat.

GALLANT, JOSEPH (1907–1957) U.S. teacher. He was born in Poland and came to the U.S. at age three. Educated at CCNY and Columbia U., he taught English in New York high schools for nearly 30 years. He edited a number of texts and anthologies for high schools and was consultant for several Prentice-Hall English texts; he was also editor of *New York Teacher*. A note from Mrs. Gallant explains that his sf and science essay anthology for high school English grew out of his conviction that the artificial separation of the sciences and the humanities in education ought to be bridged as early as the secondary school.
Anthology
Stories of Scientific Imagination (Oxford Book Co., New York, 1954, 152 pp., pa 70¢)
Sf, 9 stories: "The Black Pits of Luna," R. A. Heinlein; "Planet Passage," D. A. Wollheim; "In Value Deceived," H. B. Fyfe; "Peril of the Blue World," R. Abernathy; "Propagandist," M. Leinster; "Symbiosis," W. F. Jenkins; "Conqueror's Isle," N. S. Bond; "The White Army," D. Dresser; "A Connecticut Yankee in King Arthur's Court" (excerpt), M. Twain.

GALLANT, ROY (1924–) U.S. popular science writer for children. He is noted for his many "Exploring" books: *Exploring the Moon* (1955), *Exploring Mars* (1956), *Exploring the Universe* (1956, rev. 1968), *Exploring the Planets* (1958).

GALLET, GEORGES H(ILAIRE) (1902–) French professional journalist and editor. He was born in Paris, with family ties in the west of France (Vendee and Poitou). He was a veteran of Dunkirk in 1940 and was on a ship sunk in the North Sea. His interest in science fiction stemmed from his maternal grandfather, a great admirer of Verne and Wells, and he was one of the first in Europe to become an enthusiast of sf when it appeared under that name, *ca.* 1927. He completed scientific studies equivalent to M.Sc., spent a short time in banking and a few years as commercial and technical manager of a large printing plant, and then his interest in sf led him into journalism. At present he is one of the best-known science commentators in France; he has a weekly column in a number of French and foreign papers, and also does radio broadcasts.
He dreamed of uniting science and science fiction in a weekly magazine of general nature, *Conquêtes*, of which one experimental issue appeared in Sep 1939. But the war intervened, and circumstances made him wait until 1950 before he could launch sf in France, in the form of the book series *Le Rayon Fantastique* (published by Hachette, Paris, the largest French publisher); the series ended in 1965 with just over 100 books. He has written several science books, including *A l'assaut de l'espace* (*ca.* 1954), in which he prophesied the approaching conquest of space. Recently he and Prof. Leonid Sedov collaborated on an important work on *Astronautics* which is to be part of an important illustrated science encyclopedia; Prof. Sedov covered only the Russian aspects and Gallet wrote the remainder.
Anthologies
Escales dans l'infini (Hachette Le RF, Paris, 1954, 256 pp., 192 fr.)
Sf, 10 stories: "Odysee Martienne," S. G. Weinbaum; "La Girafe bleue," L. S. de Camp; "Shambleau," C. L. Moore; "Touristes des temps future" ["Pawley's Peepholes"], J. Wyndham; "Colin-Maillard" ["Blind Man's Buff"], J. U. Giesy; "L'Homme-machine d'Ardathia," F. Flagg; "La bete du vide," ["A Beast of the Void"], R. Z. Gallun; "Trois lignes de vieux Français," A. Merritt; "Station interplanetaire No. 1," M. W. Wellman; "Le sourire du sphinx" ["The Smile of the Sphinx"], W. F. Temple.
Quatre pas dans l'étrange (Hachette Le RF: 79, 1961)
4 stories: "La Force Mysterieuse" (abr.), J. H. Rosny [Ainé; "Par la malle de nuit" ["With the Night Mail"], R. Kipling (first in French 1927); "L'eternel Adam," J. Verne (1910); "R.U.R.," K. Capek (first in French 1924).

GALLICO, PAUL (WILLIAM) (26 July 1897–) U.S. sportswriter, short story author and screenwriter. He is the son of a concert pianist from Trieste. He served in the U.S. Navy in World War I, and received B.S. from Columbia in 1921. His reputation as a sportswriter increased through the years, and by 1936 he was reported to be the highest paid in this field in New York. Many of his books are collections on sport, which he endeavours to study from the inside. Two of his novels have fantasy aspects: *The Snow Goose* (1941) and *The Abandoned* (1950; British title: *Jennie*). He discusses personal aspects of his writings in *Confessions of a Story Teller* (M. Joseph, 1961).
Fiction
Foolish Immortals, The (Doubleday, New York, 1953, 224 pp., $2.50) (M. Joseph, London, 1954, 288 pp., 12/6; 1955, 6/-)
Eternal youth.
Man Who Was Magic, The (Heinemann, London, 1967, 20/-) (Pan: 02194, 1968, 191 pp., pa 5/-)
Juvenile; a fable in which a boy with a talking dog arrives at the city Mageia, where all magic is no mystery.
Too Many Ghosts (*SEP*, sr?, 7 Nov 1959) (Doubleday, 1960, 288 pp., $3.95) (Doubleday, Toronto, $4.50) (M. Joseph, 1961, 272 pp., 16/-) (Cardinal: C426, 1961, 278 pp., pa 35¢) (Pan: M144, 1966, 267 pp., pa 5/-)

Routine story of ghosts haunting Paradine Hill, and how they were laid.

GALLUN, RAYMOND Z(INKE) (22 Mar 1910–) U.S. author, born in Beaver Dam, Wisconsin. He formed his own philosophy of life at an early age. He first studied law, then left it in 1931 to write full-time. He travelled widely, and was in Europe when World War II began. As an amateur astronomer he has always endeavoured to be accurate in his sf writing, though not many of his stories are considered classics. One of the older sf writers, he is particularly remembered for his "Old Faithful" series in *ASF*; his postwar appearances are in line with the modern trend in sf writing. Some stories of interest are "Godson of Almarlu" (*ASF*, Oct 1936), "Masson's Secret" (*ASF*, Sep 1939), "Passport to Jupiter" (*SS*, Jan 1951; [German], *T*: 37, 1961, *TE*: 164, 1967), "Ten to the Stars" (*SFA*, Mar 1953), "Legacy From Mars" (*SFA*, July 1953).
Series
Old Faithful. All in *ASF*: "Old Faithful" (Dec 1934); "The Son of Old Faithful" (July 1935); "Child of the Stars" (Apr 1936).
Fiction
People Minus X (Simon & Schuster, New York, 1957, 186 pp., $3.00) (Ace: D-291, 1958, 160 pp., pa 35¢; with *Lest We Forget Thee, Earth*) (*Quando espolose Selene* [Italian], *Cosmos*: 16, 1958) (*Menschen Minus X* [German], Dörner'sche, 1959; *T*: 134, 1960; TN: 27, 1968, pa)
   People who die can be reconstructed, but not quite the same—i.e., "minus X." A story of intrigue and the duplication of people as living microminiatures.
Planet Strappers, The [pa] (Pyramid: G-658, 1961, 157 pp., pa 35¢) (*Sternenfieber* [German], *TS*: 66, 1963; *TE*: 169, 1967)
   The struggles of a group of Earthmen to attain a new way of life in the Solar System.

GALOUYE, DANIEL F(RANCIS) (1920–) U.S. author and newspaperman. He was raised in Louisiana and obtained his B.A. in journalism from Louisiana State U. in 1941. He had a brief venture in newspaper and book editing. During the war he was a naval test pilot and one of the world's first rocket pilots. Postwar he married and returned to the newspaper profession. In the sf field his first appearance was in *Imagination* with "Rebirth" (Mar 1952). He had a number of stories in this and the other Hamling magazines, including such dramatic novellas as "Tonight the Sky Will Fall" (May 1952) and its sequel; "The Day the Sun Died" (Oct 1955); and "The Fist of Shiva" (May 1953; [German], *T*: 482, 1966). He has also appeared in *Galaxy SF* since 1954, a noted novelette being "The City of Force" (Apr 1959), and more recently in other magazines, e.g., "Descent Into the Maelstrom" (*Fan*, Apr 1961). His stories are very popular in Germany, where a number of collections of them have appeared, including *UZ*: 557 (1967) and *TS*: 131 (1968). In 1965-67 latent war injuries forced him to stop writing and leave his position as associate editor of the *New Orleans States-Item*; however he has since resumed writing.
Fiction
Counterfeit World See *Simulacron-3*
Dark Universe (Bantam: J2266, 1961, 154 pp., pa 40¢) (Gollancz, London, 1962, 188 pp., 15/-) (Sphere: 37435, 1967, 175 pp., pa 5/-) (*Percezione infinita* [Italian], *Cosmo*: 104, 1962) (*Dunkels Universum* [German], Goldmann, 1962, 1965 pa) (*Mundo tenebroso* [Spanish], Nebula: 89, 1963, pa) (SF B.C. [S.J.], 1963, 6/-)
   The story of nuclear war survivors living underground with the sense of sight unknown; describes their new religion, the development of hearing as the primary sense, and how vision is rediscovered. Very original, rated one of the best novels of 1961.
Last Leap and Other Stories of the Super-Mind, The [C] [pa] (Corgi: GS7043, 1964, 172 pp., pa 3/6) (*Das Gericht der Telepathen* [German], *T*: 408, 1965, abr.)
   Sf, 7 stories: "The Last Leap"; "Kangaroo Court"; "Sanctuary"; "Deadline Sunday"; "Fighting Spirit"; "Jebaburba"; "Seeing-Eye Dog."
Lords of the Psychon [pa] (Bantam: J2555, 1963, 153 pp., pa 40¢) (*Les seigneurs des sphères* [French], Denoël: PF87, 1965,

pa) (*Die gefangene Erde* [German], Goldmann, 1965, 1965 pa)
   The last humans on Earth fight invading spheres of force.
Lost Perception, The (Gollancz, 1966, 190 pp., 16/-) (SF B.C. [S.J.], 1966) (*A Scourge of Screamers*, Bantam: F3585, 1968, 172 pp., pa 50¢) (Corgi: GS7819, 1968, 173 pp., pa 3/6) (*Weltraumschiff "Nina" meldet* [German], Goldmann: 087, 1968, pa)
   The world is afflicted by a sickness causing people to scream. There are aliens disguised as men, and the world suffers a short atomic war.
Project Barrier [C] (Gollancz, 1968, 208 pp., 25/-)
   5 novelettes: "Shuffle Board"; "Recovery Area"; "Rub-a-Dub"; "Reign of the Teleguppets"; "Project Barrier."
Scourge of Screamers, A [pa] See *Lost Perception, The*
Simulacron-3 [pa] (Bantam: J2797, 1964, 152 pp., pa 40¢) (*Counterfeit World*, Gollancz, 1964, 159 pp., 15/-; SF B.C. [S.J.], 1965, 6/-) (*Welt am Draht* [German], Goldmann, 1965, 1965 pa) (*Simulacron 3* [French], Galaxie: Bis 8, 1968, pa)
   Complicated intrigue, with people controlling artificial worlds, and an analogue computer originally intended for market research.

GALSWORTHY, JOHN (14 Aug 1867–31 Jan 1933) English novelist, dramatist and man of letters. Born in comfortable circumstances, he showed no literary bent during schooling at Harrow and at New College, Oxford, where he graduated with honors in law. Writing under the pseudonym "John Sinjohn," he published his first novel, *Jocelyn* in 1898. The heartening reception given *Villa Rubein* (1900) influenced him to change from law to literature. He wrote many novels of interest before what was to become known as *The Forsyte Saga* began with *The Man of Property* in 1906. He met Joseph Conrad on a sea voyage and they remained friends until Conrad's death. Galsworthy refused knighthood after World War I, but accepted the Order of Merit in 1929. He received the 1932 Nobel Prize for Literature.
Fiction
Caravan [C] (Heinemann, London, 1925, 950 pp., 10/6) (Scribner, New York, 1925, 760 pp., $2.50, leather $4.00)
   56 stories, some of fantasy interest: "Acme"; "The Apple Tree"; "Black Godmother"; "Blackmail"; "The Bright Side"; "The Broken Boot"; " 'Cafard' "; "The Choice"; "Compensation"; "Conscience"; "The Consummation"; "Courage"; "Defeat"; " 'The Dog It Was That Died' "; "Expectations"; "A Feud"; "The First and the Last"; "Fisher of Men"; "The Grey Angel"; "Had a Horse"; "A Hedonist"; "Japanese Quince"; "Juryman"; "A Knight"; "Late-299"; "A Long-Ago Affair"; "Man of Devon"; "The Man Who Kept His Form"; "Manna"; "The Miller of Dee"; "Mother Stone"; "The Neighbors"; "Nightmare Child"; "Once More"; "The Pack"; "Peace Meeting"; "Philanthropy"; "A Portrait"; "The Prisoner"; "Quality"; "Recruit"; "Reversion to Type"; "Salta Pro Nobis"; "Salvation of a Forsythe"; "Santa Lucia"; "Silence"; "A Simple Tale"; "Spindle-Berries"; "A Stoic"; "Strange Thing"; "Stroke of Lightning"; "Timber"; "Two Looks"; "Ultima Thule"; "Virtue"; "A Woman."

GAMOW, GEORGE (4 Mar 1904–20 Aug 1968) Noted U.S. astronomer and science populariser. Born in Odessa, Russia, he taught and did research at Leningrad, Göttingen, Copenhagen and Cambridge before coming to the U.S. in 1934, when he settled in the chair of theoretical physics at George Washington U. A vigorous participant in a dozen branches of science from astronomy to fundamental biology to nuclear physics, he has written these books, recognised as the best of their type: *Biography of the Earth* (Viking, 1941; Macmillan, 1942; Signet, 1948, pa), rewritten as *A Planet Named Earth* (Viking, 1963); *The Birth and Death of the Sun* (Viking, 1940; Macmillan, 1941; Penguin-US, 1945, pa; Mentor, 1960, pa), rewritten as *A Star Called the Sun* (Viking, 1964); *The Creation of the Universe* (Viking, 1952, revised 1961; Macmillan, 1952, revised 1962; Compass, 1956, pa; Mentor, 1959, pa); *The Moon* (Abelard-Schuman, 1953, revised 1959); *1, 2, 3 .. Infinity* (Viking, 1947; Macmillan, 1947; Mentor, 1953, pa); *Thirty Years That Shook Physics* (Doubleday, 1966). The last-named outlines noted theories. Prof. Gamow was a winner of the UNESCO Kalinga prize for popularization of science. His fiction of interest to the sf field is *Mr. Tompkins in Wonderland* (Univ. Press, Cambridge, 1929) and *Mr. Tompkins Explores the Atom* (Macmillan, New York, 1944); both recently appeared as *Mr. Tompkins in Paperback* (Cambridge Univ. Press, 1967, $4.50); a collaboration with Martynas Ycas was *Mr. Tompkins Inside Himself* (Viking, 1967, $6.95). These are fictionalized science lessons.

GANDON, YVES (1899–) French author.
Fiction
Last White Man, The (*Après les hommes*, Paris, ? ; Laffont, Paris, 1963) –Translation: (Cassell, London, 1948, 254 pp., 9/6) (*Der letzte Weisse* [German], Port, 1948)
Future chemical warfare, and the effects of a toxin which only kills whites.

GANPAT (pseud) See GOMPERTZ, M. L.

GANTZ, KENNETH F. U.S. editor and author. He is editor of *The Air University Quarterly Review*, the Air Force's professional journal of strategy and techniques. He has also edited such nonfiction as *The U.S. Air Force Report on the Ballistic Missile*; *Man in Space* (Duell, 1959; Hollis & Carter, 1960); and *Nuclear Flight* (1960).
Fiction
Not in Solitude (Doubleday, New York, 1959, 240 pp., $3.50) (D'day SF B.C., 1959, $1.20) (Berkeley: Y582, 1961, 192 pp., pa 40¢) (Dobson, London, 1966, 240 pp., 21/-)
Exciting and plausible story of the first people to reach Mars and the conditions they are likely to encounter.

GARDNER, ALAN
Fiction
Escalator, The (Muller, London, 1963, 288 pp., 18/-) (Consul: 1411, 1965, 218 pp., pa 3/6)
A Polaris sub bound for NATO handover is hijacked by determined nuclear disarmers.

GARDNER, ERLE STANLEY (17 July 1889–11 Mar 1970) American detective-story writer. Admitted to the California Bar in 1921, he practiced law, mainly in trial work, for 22 years. He began writing in 1921, and by 1928 was turning out more than a million words per year in the pulp field. Noted for his book series about "Perry Mason" (later on TV), he also wrote under the name "A. A. Fair." In the fantasy field his short story "Rain Magic" (*Arg*, 20 Oct 1928) was reprinted in *Fantastic*, Apr 1963.

GARDNER, GERALD B(ROSSEAU) (1884–) British author. He was a tea planter in Ceylon 1900-09, then a rubber planter in Borneo and Malaya. He later worked in Customs in Malaya, retiring in 1936. A self-proclaimed witch (or warlock), he is Director of Witches Mill Museum. His books include one on Malay weapons and a novel, *High Magics Aid* (Atlantis Book Shop).
Nonfiction
Meaning of Witchcraft, The (Rider, London, 1954, 163 pp., 12/6)
A penetrating survey of the 'old religion' in ancient, medieval and modern history, by a genuine witch who has taken part in the occult ceremonies.
Witchcraft Today (Rider, London, 1954, 163 pp., 12/6) (Pedigree, 1960, 191 pp., pa 3/6) (Arrow: 926, 1966, 192 pp., pa 2/6)
Secrets of the witch cult, revealed by a practising devotee.

GARDNER, MARTIN (1914–)
Nonfiction
Ambidextrous Universe, The (Basic Books, New York, 1964, 294 pp., $5.95)
Exceptionally lucid explanation of the complex problems of the odd- or even-ness and right- or left-handedness of the universe.
Fads and Fallacies in the Name of Science See *In the Name of Science*
In the Name of Science (Putnam, New York, 1952, 320 pp., $4.00) (*Fads and Fallacies in the Name of Science*, Dover, New York, 1957, 363 pp., pa $1.50; Ballantine: 446K, 1960, pa 50¢)

A running account of some of the brands of alleged science, hoaxes, fads and theories which have been taken up by the public in recent years. Reviewed by P. S. Miller in *ASF*, Apr 1953.

GARDNER, MAURICE B. U.S. author, born in Portland, Maine, and still living there. When he was ten years of age his father died and he had to curtail his education. He is a machinist with the Boston & Maine Railroad, habitually working the 3 to 11 pm shift and writing in the morning. His hobbies are writing and reading.
Series
Bantan. A South Pacific imitation of Tarzan: *Bantan of the Islands* (*Bantan–God-Like Islander*, Meador, Boston, 1936; rev. 1957); *Bantan and the Island Goddess* (Meador, 1942); *Bantan Defiant* (Greenwich, New York, 1955); *Bantan Valiant* (Meador, 1957); *Bantan's Island Peril* (Meador, 1959); *Bantan Incredible* (Forum, Boston, 1960); *Bantan Primeval* (Forum, 1961); *Bantan Fearless* (Forum, 1963).

GARDNER, THOMAS S(AMUEL) (31 July 1908–11 Nov 1963) U.S. science fiction enthusiast, born in Kingsport, Tennessee. He was senior chemist at Hoffmann-La Roche, Inc., New Jersey, from 1946. He wrote a few stories for the magazines in the 1930's, including "The Insect World" (*WS*, Apr 1935; *Tales of Wonder*, Aut 1941) and "The Last Woman" (*WS*, Apr 1932; *SS*, Win 1944). For some years he did the annual review of the sf and fantasy magazine field for *Science-Fiction Times*.

GARIS, HOWARD ROGER (25 Apr 1873–5 Nov 1962) U.S. author. He is best known as the creator of the "Uncle Wiggily" series of children's stories, about the rheumatic old rabbit with the top-hat and full-dress suit and his retinue of "humanized" woodland creatures. At the height of their popularity these were syndicated in 100 newspapers, and the best of the 15,000 short stories were collected into 75 books. Garis was also one of the ghost writers in the Edward Stratemeyer Syndicate, which produced low-priced hard-cover books for youngsters; he wrote the first 35 of the "Tom Swift" series [see APPLETON, V.]. Other of his sf work appeared in *Argosy*; a recently reprinted example was "Professor Jonkin's Cannibal Plant" (Aug 1905; *Fan*, May 1963).

GARNER, ALAN British author. He is considered one of the most outstanding of today's writers for children. He won the 1968 *Guardian* Award for Children's Fiction with his fourth novel, *The Owl Service*, a non-fantasy which took four years to write.
Fiction
Elidor (Collins, London, 1965, 160 pp., 13/6) (Puffin: PS317, 1967, 171 pp., pa 3/6) (H. Z. Walck, New York, 1967, 185 pp., $3.75)
Juvenile—four children enter a strange and weird world where castles are holding out against evil, and do their bit to help.
Moon of Gomrath, The (Collins, 1963, 160 pp., illus., 12/6) (Collins, Toronto, $2.75) (H. Z. Walck, 1967, 184 pp., $3.75) (Ace: G-753, 1968, 157 pp., pa 50¢)
Juvenile—sequel to *The Weirdstone of Brisingamen*.
Weirdstone: A Tale of Alderley, The See *Weirdstone of Brisingamen, The*
Weirdstone of Brisingamen, The (Collins, 1960, 224 pp., maps, 12/6) (Collins, Toronto, $2.50) (*The Weirdstone: A Tale of Alderley*, F. Watts, New York, 1961, 224 pp., $2.95) (Puffin: PS193, 1963, 236 pp., pa 4/-) (Ace: G-570, 1966, 192 pp., pa 50¢)
Juvenile—fantasy along the lines of Tolkien, laid in modern England; sequel is *The Moon of Gomrath*.

GARNER, ROLF (pseud) See BERRY, B.

GARNETT, DAVID (9 Mar 1892–) British author and publisher. He was born into a family with a great tradition in English literature and publishing: his father (Edward) was probably the most celebrated publisher's reader in English publishing history, and his mother (Constance) was noted for her translations of Tolstoy and other Russian writers. He began book-selling in a small way, but gave it up after the success of his first book, *Lady Into Fox*. He was a partner in founding the Nonesuch Press, and was Literary Editor of the *New Statesman*, to which he contributed for six years. In the Second World War he was a flight-lieutenant in the R.A.F.V.R., and wrote up his experiences as *War in the Air*. He has been a director of Rupert Hart-Davis since its inception. His fiction includes *The Grasshoppers Come* (1931) and *A Terrible Day* (1932).

Fiction [Incomplete—other titles in Bleiler *Checklist*]

Lady Into Fox (Knopf, New York, 1923, 97 pp., illus.–R. A. Garnett) ([Swedish], Geber, 1924) (Armed: p-1, nd, 96 pp., pa) (Penguin-U.S.: 615, 1946, 135 pp., pa 35¢; with *A Man in the Zoo* [Garnett])

The transformation of a beautiful woman into a vixen, and the effect upon her doting husband. In 1923 it won the Hawthornden Prize and the James Tait Black Memorial Award.

Man in the Zoo, A (Knopf, New York, 1924, 118 pp.) (Penguin-U.S.: 615, 1946, pa 35¢; with *Lady Into Fox* [Garnett])

A man offers himself as a specimen of *Homo Sapiens*.

GARNETT, EDWARD (1868–19 Feb 1937) English author, second son of the late Dr. Richard Garnett. He married Constance Black, a well-known translator of Russian. He wrote the play *The Trial of Jeanne d'Arc* (1931) and edited *Letters From Conrad 1895 to 1924* and *Letters From John Galsworthy 1900-1932*.

Fiction

Papa's War and Other Satires [C] (G. Allen & Unwin, London, 1919, 120 pp., 5/-)

Fantasy, 22 stories: "Papa's War"; "The Lord Twatsi Awakes"; "A Week in Paris"; "The All-Highest"; "The Psychic War Map"; "Truth's Welcome Home"; "Holy Russia"; "A Mathematical Certainty"; "History of the War to End War"; "Creatures of Blood"; "The Ravine of Victory"; "A Page From Rabelais"; "The Liberals Who Lost Their Trousers"; "The Last Straw"; "The Orchestrated Press"; "The Decline of the Coshlings"; "The Nemesis of the Capitalists"; "The Council-Chamber"; "Lord Luxborough's Lecture"; "Christianity in Action"; "Voice of the Guns"; "The Anniversary."

GARNETT, RICHARD (27 Feb 1835–13 Apr 1906) Noted British critic, librarian and man of letters. He began as a clerk at the British Library Museum; in 1875 he became Assistant Keeper of the Printed Books, and was later Chief Keeper at the British Museum. He was granted LL.D. (Hon.) at Edinburgh. He was the author of distinguished contributions to the *Encyclopedia Britannica* and the *Dictionary of National Biography*; his most noted work is the one covered below.

Fiction

Twilight of the Gods [C] (1888) (J. Lane, London, 1903, 327 pp., 6/-; 1924) (Lane, intro.–T. E. Lawrence, 1924, 299 pp., illus.–Henry Keen, 21/-) (Knopf, New York, 1926, 304 pp., $3.00) (Watts 'Thinker's Library No. 81,' London, 1940, 118 pp.,; 1949, 2/6; 9 stories marked †) (Penguin: 586, 1947, 183 pp., pa 1/6)

Bleiler does not list the 1888 edition, known to have only 16 stories; the 1903 and 1924 Lane editions have 28 stories: "The Twilight of the Gods"†; "The Potion of Lao-Tsze"; "Abdalla the Adite"†; "Ananda the Miracle Worker"†; "The City of Philosophers"†; "The Demon Pope"†; "The Cupbearer"; "The Wisdom of the Indians"; "The Dumb Oracle"†; "Duke Virgil"; "The Claw"; "Alexander the Ratcatcher"†; "The Rewards of Industry"; "Madam Lucifer"; "The Talismans"; "The Elixir of Life"; "The Poet of Panopolis"; "The Purple Head"; "The Firefly"; "Pan's Wand"; "A Page From the Book of Folly"; "The Bell of Saint Euschemon"†; "Bishop Addo and Bishop Gaddo"†; "The Philosopher and the Butterflies"; "Truth and Her Companions"; "The Three Palaces"; "New Readings in Biography"; "The Poison Maid." Themes from ancient, medieval and oriental lore.

GARNETT, EILEEN J. (1893–) U.S. author, editor and publisher, the better-known name of Eileen Jeannette Lyttle. She edits and publishes *Tomorrow*, a review of psychical research, the field in which most of her books appear. She is also President of the Parapsychology Foundation. Her books include *Adventures in the*

Supernormal (Creative Age, New York, 1949; 1968, pa).

Nonfiction

Beyond the Five Senses (Lippincott, Philadelphia, 1957, 384 pp., $4.95)

Anthology of articles from *Tomorrow*, touching on spirits and poltergeists, hypnosis, precognition, ESP, and other related manifestations.

Sense and Nonsense of Prophecy, The (Creative Age, New York, 1950, 279 pp., $2.75) (McClelland, Toronto, $3.25)

A witty sketch of the borderlines of ESP and the supernormal; sensible scientific evaluation describing phenomena the author has encountered.

GARRETT, RANDALL (PHILLIPS) U.S. author, a regular contributor to the sf magazines since 1951. He has used many pseudonyms, such as David Gordon and Darrel T. Langart, and has also collaborated with Robert Silverberg (often as "Robert Randall") and with Larry M. Janifer as "Mark Phillips."

Series

Bupp, Walter. (Bupp pseud. as both author and first-person narrator.) All in *ASF*: "Card Trick" (Jan 1961); "Modus Vivendi" (Sep 1961); "The Right Time" (Dec 1963); "Psi for Sale" (Sep 1965).

Darcy, Lord. A detective in an alternate time where magic is real. All in *ASF*: "A Case of Identity" (Sep 1964); "The Muddle of the Woad" (June 1965); "Too Many Magicians" (sr4, Aug 1966; book, 1967).

Hale, Leland. Interstellar adventurer. "To Make a Hero" (*Infinity*, Oct 1957); "Respectfully Mine" (*Infinity*, Aug 1958); "Drug on the Market" (*FU*, Feb 1960).

Malone, Kenneth J. [by Mark Phillips–pseud with L. M. Janifer]. Secret service agent. All in *ASF*: "That Sweet Little Old Lady" (sr2, Sep 1959) [*Brain Twister*]; "Out Like a Light" (sr3, Apr 1960) [*The Impossibles*]; "Occasion for Disaster" (sr4, Nov 1960) [*Supermind*].

Nidor [by Robert Randall]. See SILVERBERG, R. (co-author)

Fiction

Anything You Can Do . . . [as Darrel T. Langart] (*ASF*, sr2, May 1962) (Doubleday, New York, 1963, 192 pp., $3.50; Toronto, $4.00; D'day SF B.C., 1963, $1.20) (Mayflower: 0238, 1963, 190 pp., pa 3/6) (*Die fremde Macht* [German], Goldmann, 1963)

The Nipe, a monstrous extraterrestrial, becomes a master criminal and a super-human is required to fight it.

Brain Twister [by Mark Phillips–pseud. with L. M. Janifer] [pa] ("That Sweet Little Old Lady," *ASF*, sr2, Sep 1959) (*Die Lady mit dem 6. Sinn* [German], *UG*: 165, 1962) (Pyramid: F-783, 1962, 144 pp., pa 40¢)

First of Malone series; the search for a telepath to help find a spy results in many misadventures.

Dawning Light, The [by Robert Randall] See SILVERBERG, R. (co-author)

Impossibles, The [by Mark Phillips–pseud. with L. M. Janifer] [pa] ("Out Like a Light," *ASF*, sr3, Apr 1960) (*Die Geisterbande* [German], *UG*: 162, 1962) (Pyramid: F-875, 1963, 157 pp., pa 40¢)

Second of Malone series; his opponents are a gang of teleporting juvenile delinquents.

Pagan Passions [with Larry M. Harris] [pa] (Beacon: 263, 1959, 158 pp., pa 35¢)

A sex fantasy; the return of the Greek pantheon after 3,000 years of oblivion.

Shrouded Planet, The [by Robert Randall] See SILVERBERG, R. (co-author)

Supermind [by Mark Phillips–pseud. with L. M. Janifer] [pa] (enlarged from "Occasion for Disaster," *ASF*, sr4, Nov 1960) (Pyramid: F-909, 1963, 192 pp., pa 40¢) (*I dominatori dei pensiero* [Italian], *Cosmo*: 141, 1963)

Third of Malone series; Malone and his cronies in more psionic troubles.

Too Many Magicians (*ASF*, sr4, Aug 1966) (Doubleday, 1967, 260 pp., $4.95) (MacDonald, London, 1968, 260 pp., 25/-)

One of the Lord Darcy series—a pleasant blend of spies, magic, and a locked-room murder.

Unwise Child (Doubleday, New York, 1962, 215 pp., $2.95, jacket—Powers) (D'day, Toronto, $4.00) (D'day SF B.C., 1962) (Mayflower: 9220, 1963, 192 pp., pa 3/6) (*Das elektronische Genie* [German], Goldmann, 1963, 1965 pa) (*Il robot minorenne* [Italian], *GRF*: 35, 1963)

A thoughtful novel about a super-robot with self-determination.

GARRISON, CHARLES M.
Fiction
Murder on the Moon [as Charles MacDaniel] (Vantage, New York, 1968, 224 pp., $3.95)

GARTMANN, HEINZ (1917—) German engineer, born in Dessau. Dipl.—Ing. Since 1950 he has been writing in technical journals. He has written a number of nonfiction books, including the translated *Science as History* (Hodder & Stoughton, 1960), a recommended layman's guide to science which describes technological progress from steam engine to satellite, and also *Space Travel* (Batsford Low, 1962). He edited the German learned journal *Weltraumfahrt* 1950-59, and is a fellow of various interplanetary societies, including British and U.S.
Nonfiction
Man Unlimited [Trans.—R. & C. Winston] (Pantheon, New York, 1957, 214 pp., illus., $4.50)

Subtitled "Technology's Challenge to Human Endurance." It discusses the stresses imposed on man by his newest inventions and the body's ability to adapt to and withstand such strains.
Men Behind the Space Rockets, The (*Traümer, Forscher, Konstrukteure*, Econ-Verlag, Dusseldorf, 1955) [Trans.—E. Wareing & M. Glenny]: (Weidenfeld Nicolson, London, 1955, 185 pp., illus., 18/-) (Ambassador, Toronto, $4.00) (McKay, New York, 1956, 185 pp., illus., $3.95)

The author describes the early researches of eight men between 1856 and 1912, including Ganswindt, Tscolovski (Tsiolkovsky), Goddard, and Oberth. He knew some of them personally. Wartime V2 developments are also covered.

GARVER, RONALD G.
Nonfiction (?)
Saucer People (Meador, Boston, 1957, 132 pp., $3.00)

GARVIN, RICHARD M(cCLELLAN) (4 Aug 1934—) U.S. free-lance writer and bookstore owner.
Fiction
Fortec Conspiracy, The [with E. G. Addeo] (Sherbourne, Los Angeles, 1968, 181 pp., $3.95)

An alien ship crashes on Earth and infects mankind with a deadly disease.
Talbot Agreement, The [with E. G. Addeo] (Sherbourne, 1968, 255 pp., $4.95)

Espionage in the near future; U.S. agents in China strive to nullify a brilliant weapon.

GARY, ROMAIN (1914—) Polish-born Frenchman. He is a general fiction author, particularly known for *The Roots of Heaven* and *The Ski Bums*.
Fiction
Hissing Tales [C] [Trans. from French—R. Howard] (Harper & Row, New York, 1964, 186 pp., $4.95) (M. Joseph, London, 1964, 186 pp., 18/-)

Includes two sf stories: "Decadence"; "New Frontiers"; remainder are of marginal interest.

GASKELL, ELIZABETH (29 Sep 1810—12 Nov 1865) English novelist, born Elizabeth Stevenson. She married a young minister, William Gaskell, in 1832 and did little writing until her first son died in 1845. She then anonymously wrote *Mary Barton* (1848), and its literary success encouraged her to continue writing. Her most famous work is *Cranford* (1853); she also wrote a valuable biography of Charlotte Bronte, whom she knew intimately. One of her most noted weird short stories is "The Squire's Story," often reprinted in anthologies.
Fiction
Cousin Phyllis [C] (? , London, 1865; ? , London, 1867, 304 pp.) (Putnam, New York, 1906, 727 pp., frontis.) (Everyman, London, 1906, 325 pp.)

Fantasy, 11 stories (Putnam ed.): "Cousin Phyllis"; "The Crooked Branch"; "Crowley Castle"; "Curious If True"; "A Dark Night's Work"; "The Grey Woman"; "Lois the Witch"; "Right at Last"; "Shah's English Gardener"; "Six Weeks at Heppenheim"; "Two Fragments of Ghost Stories."

GASKELL, JANE (7 July 1941—) Better-known name for British author Jane Lynch, considered to be a new literary discovery. She is the great-great-great-great niece of Mrs. Gaskell who wrote the immortal *Cranford*. Daughter of a newspaperman, she wrote *Strange Evil* long-hand in school exercise books. Her second book was fantasy, but the third, *Attic Summer* (1962), was not. She worked on *Argosy*; a free-lance feature in *Harper's Bazaar* resulted in a job with the London *Daily Express* where she became a feature writer.
Fiction
Atlan (Hodder & Stoughton, London, 1965, 286 pp., 25/-) (Sphere: 37818, 1966, 1968, 286 pp., pa 5/-) (Paperback: 55-738, 1968, 287 pp., pa 95¢)

Intrigue, turmoil, witchcraft and sorcery in Atlantis. Middle of the Atlantis trilogy, preceded by *The Serpent* and followed by *The City*.
City, The (Hodder & Stoughton, 1966, 190 pp., 21/-) (Sphere: 37826, 1966, 1968, 191 pp., pa 5/-) (Paperback: 64-019, 1968, 176 pp., pa 75¢)

Last of the Atlantis trilogy; further adventures of Princess Cija as she returns to her homeland.
King's Daughter, The (Hutchinson, London, 1958, 280 pp., 15/-)

Fantasy in a period when the world has no moon; knights and castles with a touch of magic.
Serpent, The (Hodder & Stoughton, 1963, 445 pp., 21/-) (Sphere: 37834, 1966, 479 pp., pa 5/-) (Paperback: 55-693, 1968, 477 pp., pa 95¢)

First of Atlantis trilogy; imaginative fantasy adventure in prehistoric times. Princess Cija is married off to a semihuman conqueror.
Strange Evil (Hutchinson, 1957, 256 pp., 12/6)

A struggle between good and evil in a fairy country. The writing is inexperienced but creates a good atmosphere.

GATCH, TOM Jr.
Fiction
King Julian (Vantage, New York, 1955, 187 pp., $2.75)

A novel of royalty in the contemporary U.S. as it would be had George Washington accepted the crown.

GATLAND, KENNETH W(ILLIAM) (1924—) British science writer. He is F.R.A.S., Vice-Chairman of the British Interplanetary Society 1957-60, and editor of *Space Flight* since 1959. He is a contributing editor for *The Aeroplane* and *Astronautics*, and also contributes to *Missiles & Rockets*. His nonfiction books include *Development of the Guided Missile* (2nd ed., Iliffe, 1954; Philosophical Lib., 1954), *Space Travel* [with A. M. Kunesch] (Wingate, 1953; Philos., 1953), *The Inhabited Universe* (Wingate, 1957; McKay, 1958), and *Project Satellite* [editor] (Wingate, 1958).

GAUGHAN, JACK U.S. artist. He began as an amateur and has developed into one of the better-known of present-day sf artists, with work in most magazines. He won the 1967 and 1968 Hugo awards as Best Professional Artist.

GAUTIER, THÉOPHILE (31 Aug 1811—23 Dec 1872) French litterateur , critic, and poet. About 1836 he became assistant editor of *La Presse*, for which he wrote criticism of drama and fine arts until 1854. He was extolled as an original and brilliant writer. One of his noted books was about an attempt to kidnap Napoleon from St. Helena in 1821 using a submarine; its appearances were: "Les deux étoiles," *La Presse*, sr, 20 Sep-15 Oct 1848; Librairie de

Tarride, Bruxelles, 1848, 2 vols.; *Partie carrée*, Lescou, Paris, 1851; *La Belle-Jenny*, Lévy, Paris, 1865. The idea was later used by Paul Féval (1817-87) in *Jean Diable* (Dentu, Paris, 1863) and by Capitaine Danrit in *Evasion d'Empereur* (*ca.* 1905). Other works include *Jettatura* (Lévy, 1857; *Avatar* (Lévy, 1857; Vizetelly, London, 1888), a malevolent change of souls for romantic purposes; *Spirite* (Charpentier, Paris, 1866; Appleton, New York, 1877). He is best known for his classic *Mademoiselle de Maupin* (1835).

Fiction [Incomplete—other titles in Bleiler *Checklist*]
One of Cleopatra's Nights [C] (*Une nuit de Cléopâtre*, 1845) Trans.–Lafcadio Hearn: (B. Worthington, New York, 1882, 220 pp.) (Brentano's, New York, 1900, 388 pp.; 1915, 388 pp., $2.00; 1927, 388 pp.) (Modern Library, New York, *ca.* 1948, 125 pp.)

Noted: 6 stories: "One of Cleopatra's Nights"; "Clarimonde"; "Arria Marcella" (1852); "The Mummy's Foot" (1863); "Omphale: A Rococo Story" (1845); "King Caudaule" (1847).

GAWSWORTH, JOHN (29 June 1912–) British author and anthologist. His real name is T. I. F. Armstrong, but he is best known as Gawsworth. He is noted as a poet, essayist, and bibliographer. Besides the anthologies herewith, he has edited Best Short Story collections of both M. P. Shiel and T. Burke. Other books include *Ten Contemporaries* and *Poems 1930:32*. As Armstrong he has written short stories. He has also been a publisher, operating the Twyn Barlwun Press, which has issued works by A. Machen, Edith Sitwell, Edmund Blunden, Herbert Palmer, and W. H. Davies.

Anthologies
Crimes, Creeps and Thrills (E. H. Samuel, London, 1936, 575 pp., illus., 2/6) (E. Grant, London, 1937, 2/6)

Weird, 45 stories: "The Shadow," E. H. Visiak; "Hunger," P. Lindsey; "The Eyes of Obi," E. E. Page; "The Uncharted Islands," E. H. Visiak & J. Gawsworth; "The Woman With the Bundle," K. Hare; "The Skull," A. L. Davis; "The Rattlesnake," J. Rowland; "Chinese Mask," J. St. C. Muriel; "The Ninth Year," R. E. Page; "Sacrifice," S. Dewes; "Broken," H. Yalden; "The Hand," R. Middleton; "The Falls Scandal," M. P. Shiel & F. Armstrong; "Eccentric Lady Tullswater," R. Middleton; "The Execution of Damiens," H. H. Ewers; "Murray's Child," R. Middleton & G. Dundas; "The Cat-Lovers," E. H. W. Meyerstein; "The Tube of Radium," R. E. Page; "Coincidence," F. Carter; "The Woman Avenge," E. Jepson; "High Politics," G. R. Mallock; "The Signet Ring," F. Marsden; "The House Opposite," O. Blakeston; "My Friend Trenchard," E. O'Duffy; "Boxbug Paints His Kitchen," E. H. W. Meyerstein; "On Lighthouse Rock," J. Lindsey; "Secret Service Work," E. Jepson; "Gilmartin," Mary F. McHugh; "Decision," J. St. C. Muriel; "Death for the Gander," Simon; "The Case of the Absconding Financier," E. Jepson; "Really Was a Bluetit," E. H. W. Meyerstein; "Helping Mummy," Norah C. James; "The Jingling Telephone," R. E. Page & K. Jay; "Carson," E. H. Visiak; "The Ride," Mary F. McHugh; "A Whistling Woman, and a Crowing Hen," E. H. W. Meyerstein; "Summer Harvest," H. MacLaren; "Cruelty in Sunlight," P. Henderson; "The Lost Meadow," E. Jepson; "The Disappearance," Simon; "The 'Master'," M. P. Shiel & F. Armstrong; "The Announcement," N. Barker; "The Fakir of Teheran," F. Carter; "The Shifting Growth," E. Jepson & J. Gawsworth.

Full Score [as T. I. Fytton Armstrong] (Rich Cowan, London, 1933, 295 pp., 7/6)

Weird, 26 stories: "Aha," S. Graham; "The Irreverence of Fod," S. Leslie; "Luigi of Catanzaro," L. Golding; "Dark Lot of One Saul," M. P. Shiel; "The Chemise of Margarita Pareja," L. Hearn; "The Secret Land," W. Ewart; "The Coffin," C. Evans; "Nikaldon," L. A. Pavey; "Gold Like Glass," F. Carter; "A Wonderful Woman," A. Machen; "X," M. Whitaker; "The Gardener," J. Lindsey; "In the Night," P. Henderson; "Metamorphosis," A. Wareham; "The Exorciser," F. Marsden; "Last Days in High Germany," H. Palmer; "Kitchener at Archangel," S. Graham; "A Pilgrimage," W. Ewart; "What Is There to Say?" R. Davies; "The Fur Coat," C. Duff; "The Fluke Cannon," R. L. Megroz; "Finding," J. Lindsey; "Innocence," H. E. Bates; "A Suet Pudding," T. E. Powys; "Above the River," J. Gawsworth; "A Postscript to 'Above the River'," A. Machen.

Masterpieces of Thrills (Daily Express, London, 1936, 735 pp., illus.)

60 stories: "Kali," Dr. M. R. Anand; "Death's Door," N. Barker; "Sluice Gates," "The Grim Case of Mrs. John," O. Blakeston; "Felo de Se," J. Brownson; "The Grey Room," R. Burford; "Spells by Night," "Bergamask's Revenge," "Fine Hands," "The Fetch," "The Mannikin's Tale," F. Carter; "Judgment," S. Dewes; "What Happened to Larry?" R. Dewsbury; "A Mysterious Coincidence," C. Duff; "A Man of Spirit," R. Dundas; "The Cherries," L. Durrell; "The Upstairs Room," "Sprigge," W. Ewart; "A Stele From Atlantis," "The Woman of Leadenhall Street," "First and Last Woman," L. G. Gibbon; "The Dark Wood," H. Gore; "5,000 Enemy Planes Over London," S. Graham; "Whither Thou Goest. . .," J. Greenidge; "The Man Upstairs," "Charlie," "Strange Idyll," F. Gregg; "Dr. Samson Gregory," "The Superintendent's Story," N. Harman; "The Mother," P. Henderson; "Melodrama," J. Lindsey; "Mrs. Biggadyke's 'Unconscious'," A. M. Ludovici; "The String Game," M. Magill; "The Secret Chapel," "The Companion," "Duty," "Shillings," F. Marsden; "Second Sight," "The Folkema," "The Crossword," "Hengo," "Death Pages Mr. Startle," E. H. W. Meyerstein; "The Failure," R. Middleton; "Busman's Holiday," "The Road to Freedom," "Lost Tribes," J. L. Mitchell; "Kametis and Evelpis," J. L. Mitchell & F. Armstrong; "Ghost of Fleur-de-Lis Court," K. Myer; "Murder Most Foul," E. O'Duffy; "Dr. Todor Karadja," "The Mystery of the Red Road," "The Hanging of Ernest Clark," M. P. Shiel & J. Gawsworth; "The Flying Worm," "Borderlines," by 'Simon'; "The Traveller," Gay Taylor; "Red Foam," Hedda Veseley & R. L. Megroz; "A Good Reprisal," "In the Mangrove Hall," E. H. Visiak; "The Mist Rider," G. West; "A Shawl From the East," P. Whitehouse.

Strange Assembly (Unicorn, London, 1932, 334 pp., 7/6)

Weird, 14 stories with compiler's prologue: "The Flying Cat," M. P. Shiel; "The Vivisector Vivisected," Sir Ronald Ross; "The Black Lad," Frederick Carter; "The Franc-Tireur's Escape," Herbert E. Palmer; "The Gift of Tongues," A. Machen; "A Fellside Tragedy," Hubert Crackenthorpe; "The Mask," Francis Marsden; "Ilya Vilka," Stephen Graham; "The Journey," Rhys Davies; "A Fragment," Stephen Hudson; "Londoners," Wilfred Ewart; "The Harrying of the Dead," F. Carter; "A Night in Venice," M. P. Shiel; "The Rose Garden," A. Machen.

Thirty New Tales of Horror (Hutchinson, London, 1935, 2/6)

Listed in the Bleiler *Checklist*, this is considered by some authorities to be the title *New Tales of Horror* (listed under ANONYMOUS ANTHOLOGIES).

Thrills, Crimes and Mysteries (Associated Newspapers Ltd, London, nd, 864 pp.)

Not listed in the Bleiler *Checklist*. 63 stories, many weird: "The Skeleton," Frederick Carter; "The Vivisector Vivisected," Sir Ronald Ross; "The Gift of Tongues," A. Machen; "The Purchester Instrument," M. P. Shiel; "A Fellside Tragedy," Hubert Crackanthorpe; "The Invalid," Nugent Barker; "The Wrong Turning," R. Middleton; "The Flying Cat," M. P. Shiel; "The Old Lawyer's Tale," Charles Duff; "Rescued," E. H. Visiak; "Torture," A. Machen; "The Last Adventure," R. Middleton; "A Woman, a Dog, and a Walnut Tree," E. H. W. Meyerstein; "The Death Dance," M. P. Shiel; "The Mask," Francis Marsden; "The Cry of a Century," R. Middleton & Edgar Jepson; "At the Eleventh Hour," M. P. Shiel; "What the East Wind Brought," Anthony M. Ludovici; "I Am a Murderer," E. H. Visiak & A. Vesselo; "The Miracle of the Octagon Room," Eimar O'Duffy; "Gold Like Glass," Fred. Carter; "The Place of Pain," M. P. Shiel; "The Mills of Hell," Herbert De Hamel; "Kitchener at Archangel," Stephen Graham; "The Captain," F. Marsden; "Drake's Drum," A. Machen; "The Harrying of the Dead," F. Carter; "The Bath," E. H. W. Meyerstein; "The Glass Panel," E. O'Duffy; "A Suet Pudding," T. F. Powys; "Superintendent Deering's Dilemma," Oswell Blakeston; "The Strangeness of Joab Lashmere," E. Wallace; "December," R. L. Megroz; "The Flying Pig," Malachi Whitaker; "A Shot at Goal," Dorothy L. Sayers; "The Disappearance of George Wake," R. L. Megorz; "The Six," N. Barker; "A Document From the Russian," S. Graham; "The Triptych," E. H. W. Meyerstein; "The Funspot-

Street Affair," T. Burke; "You Wouldn't Understand," John Lindsey; "Superintendent Deering Puts a Question," O. Blakeston; "Statement of a Scholar," E. H. W. Meyerstein; "There Was a Man Dwelt by a Churchyard," M. R. James; "Mr. Parsons' Revenge," Simon Dewes; "Miss Kitten's Case," E. O'Duffy; "The Fear From the Lake," O. Blakeston; "The Second Gong," Agatha Christie; "The Pageant," E. H. W. Meyerstein; "Whessoe," N. Barker; "Orpheus," L. A. G. Strong; "Tom Mackie's Trial," Hugh MacDiarmid; "Encounter at Night," Mary F. McHugh; "The Coffin," Caradoc Evans; "The Fluke Cannon," R. L. Megroz; "The Legacy," E. H. Visiak; "The Solution," O. Blakeston; "The Shopwalker's Wife," G. R. Malloch; "Flat to Let," Marcus Magill; "The Rival Poets," E. H. W. Meyerstein; "The Friendly Creature," Rhys Davies.

Twenty Tales of Terror (Susil Gupta, Calcutta, 1945)

Listed in the Bleiler *Checklist*; no further information.

GAYLE, HENRY K. (1910–) Canadian author. He was born in Leeds, Yorkshire, but now resides in Niagara Falls, Canada, where he is employed by the National Dept. of Defence of Canada. He served with the R.A.F. in World War II and saw action in India and Burma.
Fiction
Spawn of the Vortex (Comet, New York, 1957, 148 pp., $3.00)

An army of metallic monsters thrown up from the Pacific deeps by an undersea atomic bomb moves towards the coast of California.

GEIER, CHESTER S. (4 Apr 1921–) U.S. author and editor. He began writing when he saw the success of his friend William Hamling in the sf field, and set up an office with him in 1945. Geier mainly appeared in the Ziff-Davis magazines of the 1940's, under both his own name and a number of pseudonyms, including "Guy Archette," and also house names. Probably his most noted story is the novel "Forever Is Too Long" (*FA*, Mar 1947). He fostered the Shaver Mystery after it was dropped from *Amazing Stories*, forming the Shavery Mystery Club for which he edited the *Shaver Mystery Magazine*. He has since been managing editor of *Fate*.

GEIGLEY, VANCE A(CTON) (10 Oct 1907–) U.S.
Fiction
Will It End This Way? (Vantage, New York, 1968, 295 pp., $4.50)

GEIS, RICHARD E(RWIN) (19 July 1927–) U.S. author, primarily of sex novels. As a fan, he is editor and publisher of *Science Fiction Review* (formerly *Psychotic*), one of the most important of the U.S. amateur magazines and winner of the 1969 Hugo.

GELULA, ABNER J. (1906–) U.S. newspaper reporter and writer. For several years he worked as a reporter, news editor, and picture editor on New York and Atlantic City newspapers. He was one of the first radio hams, and has been connected with *Radio World*, Gernsback's *Experimenter Magazine*, and *Radio Magazine*. He made history when his short story "Automaton" (*AS*, Nov 1931) was purchased by Universal Pictures soon after publication, but estimated costs caused it never to be produced. After the war it was supposedly reconsidered during the revival of interest in sf films. Others of his prewar stories were quite good, but his last appearance in the field, "The Whistling Death" (*AS*, June 1939), did not find much favour.

GENTRY, CURT
Fiction
Last Days of the Late, Great State of California (Putnam's, New York, 1968, 384 pp., $6.95)

In 1969 California is hit by an earthquake as foretold by Edgar Cayce; bizarre cults and bewildering politics develop.

GEORGE, BRIAN
Fiction
Atom of Doubt (Methuen, London, 1959, 221 pp., 15/-) (FSB:

196, 1961, 160 pp., pa 2/6) (Horwitz: FH28, 1962, 162 pp., pa 4/6)

Amusing borderline sf—a slapdash research chemist stumbles on what appears to be a sex stimulant.

GEORGE, PETER (1924–1 June 1966) British author, born in Wales. He was a navigator in the R.A.F. during World War II, rejoined in 1951, and retired as Flight Lieutenant in 1962. Under the pseudonym "Peter Bryant" he wrote *Two Hours to Doom* (*Red Alert*), which was turned into the very successful film *Dr. Strangelove* in 1964. In 1963 he brought a lawsuit against E. L. Burdick and J. H. Wheeler on grounds that their *Fail-Safe* was based on his work. In seven other novels ending with *Commander-1* he expressed fear of the atomic bomb; he shot himself while working on the ninth, *Nuclear Survivors*.
Fiction
Commander-1 (Heinemann, London, 1965, 253 pp., 21/-) (Dell: 1430, 1966, 251 pp., pa 75¢) (Pan: X524, 1966, 222 pp., pa 3/6)

After a nuclear war started by powers other than Russia and the U.S.A.; the lives of certain small groups are followed.
Dr. Strangelove, or, How I Learned to Stop Worrying and Love the Bomb [pa] (Corgi: SN1453, 1963, 145 pp., pa 2/6) (Bantam: F2679, 1964, 145 pp., pa 50¢; S3856, 1968, pa 75¢) (*Docteur Folamour: Comment j'ai appris a ne plus M'en faire et a aimer la bombe* [French], Ed. France-Empire, 1964, illus.–film)

The serious treatment of the earlier *Two Hours to Doom* is turned into a burlesque comedy proposing that only a government of idiots could start a nuclear war. *Film:* Directed by Stanley Kubrick, with Peter Sellers playing the President of the U.S.A., a British aide of the crackpot general, and the Nazi scientist.
Red Alert [pa] See *Two Hours to Doom*
Two Hours to Doom [as Peter Bryant] (Boardman, London, 1958, 192 pp., 10/6) (*Red Alert*, Ace: D-350, 1959, 191 pp., pa 35¢; F-210, 1963, pa 40¢) (Corgi: SN1091, 1961, 189 pp., pa 2/6) (*Bei Rot: Alarm!* [German], *UZ*: 300, 1961) (*Operation undergäng* [Swedish], Geber, 1961) (*Het fatale commando* [Dutch], Spectrum, Utrecht & Antwerp, 1963)

Action story of a U.S. Air Force general who believes in preventive war but starts World War III.

GERBER, RICHARD Professor of English at U. of Zurich.
Nonfiction
Utopian Fantasy: A Study of English Utopian Fiction Since the End of the Nineteenth Century (Routledge & Kegan Paul, London, 1955, xii+162 pp., 16/-)

The author is mainly concerned with about 100 British utopian novels of the first half of the 20th Century, with utopian writings before this from Plato to Bellamy. He covers imaginative fiction that looks forward. Not many American works are considered; however, for the period covered British works in this genre were far ahead of the American in skill and solidity. The book is not as well written as Penzoldt's *The Supernatural in Fiction* but its content seems sounder and more mature. It discusses the rise of utopian humanism, the conflict between the arcadian and scientific versions of utopia, and the impact of Darwinian evolution on utopian writing. [See L. S. de Camp, *SF Stories*, Sep 1957, p. 112.]

GERNSBACK, HUGO (16 Aug 1884–19 Aug 1967) U.S. publisher. He is known as one of the 'fathers of science fiction' because he founded *Amazing Stories* in April 1926 as the first sf magazine. Born in Luxembourg, at an early age he taught himself the intricacies of telephone and electrical communication systems. He invented a battery on which he was refused patents in France and Germany. In Feb 1904 he emigrated to the U.S.A. and began a venture which eventually became the world's first mail-order radio house. He designed the first home radio set in history, the Telimco Wireless. His *Telimco* catalogue evolved into the first radio magazine, *Modern Electrics*, which was very successful. Other magazines followed—*Electrical Experimenter* (1913, changed to *Science and Invention* in 1920) and *Radio News* (1919). The science fiction which he published in *Science and Invention* aroused such interest that he started *Amazing Stories* in 1926; this title is still appearing, though it left Gernsback's control in 1929. In 1927 he began publishing *Amazing Stories Annual* and this evolved into *Amazing Stories Quarterly*, but a financial setback caused him to relinquish control of his sf magazines in 1929. Because of great reader support, however, he soon returned to the sf field with the new magazines *Science Wonder Stories, Air Wonder Stories, Wonder Stories Quarterly* and *Amazing Detective Tales*. He also published the cheap paper-covered *Science Fiction* series and sets of these appeared in 1929 and 1932. All these magazines led chequered careers, some lasting only brief periods, until he sold his last magazine, *Wonder Stories* (the continuation of *Science Wonder*) in 1936.

After some 17 years away from the sf field, Gernsback returned in 1953 with the short-lived *Science Fiction Plus*. He maintained his radio magazine publishing through the years and celebrated 50 years of publishing with the Apr 1958 issue of *Radio-Electronics*, still a leader in its field. Another magazine, *Sexology*, is also a leader in its field. For many years he produced for limited distribution an annual special Christmas-card booklet, noted for its strong bias toward his predictions of the future. He patented some 80 inventions. The Grand Duchess Charlotte of Luxembourg created him an "Officer of the Oaken Crown" on 23 Jan 1954 for his service to science. He had his body donated to the Cornell U. School of Medicine for study and research.

His writing included the noted novel *Ralph 124C 41+*. He was instrumental in forming the Science Fiction League in 1934, an important event in sf fan history; it was the first such organization to be formed by a magazine. The amateur magazine *Science-Fiction Times* dedicated its 18th Anniversary Issue (1 Sep 1959) to him, and also published the special booklet "Hugo Gernsback: Father of Science Fiction," written by Sam Moskowitz, as a free supplement to that issue. This article later appeared in *AS* Sep 1960 and was a chapter in Moskowitz's *Explorers of the Infinite* in 1963. The science fiction field has honored Gernsback by giving his name to the "Hugo Awards" presented by the annual World Science Fiction Convention for the best performances in the field.

Series

Baron Munchausen's Scientific Adventures. Further adventures of this famed character of world literature; originally published in *Electrical Experimenter* (first date given) and later reprinted in *Amazing Stories* (second date given): 1. "How to Make a Wireless Acquaintance" (May 1915; Feb 1928); 2. "How Munchausen and the Allies Took Berlin" (June 1915; Feb 1928); 3. "Munchausen on the Moon" (July 1915; Mar 1928); 4. "The Earth as Viewed From the Moon" (Aug 1915; Mar 1928); 5. "Munchausen Departs for the Planet Mars" (Oct 1915; Apr 1928); "Munchausen Lands on Mars" (Nov 1915; Apr 1928); 7. "Munchausen Is Taught Martian" (Dec 1915; May 1928); "Thought Transmission on Mars" (Jan 1916; May 1928); 9. "Cities of Mars" (Mar 1916; June 1928); 10. "The Planets at Close Range" (Apr 1916; June 1928); 11. "Martian Amusements" (June 1916; July 1928); 12. "How the Martian Canals Are Built" (Nov 1916; July 1928); 13. "Martian Atmosphere Plants" (Feb 1917; July 1928).

Fiction

Ralph 124C 41+ (*Modern Electrics*, sr12, Apr 1911) (Stratford, Boston, 1925, 293 pp., $2.15; 5,000 copies) (*ASQ*, Win 1929) (Fell, New York, 1950, 207 pp., $2.50) (Kemsley: CT406, 1952, 190 pp., pa 1/6) (*Ralph 124C41+* [German], *UG:* 52, 1957) (Crest: s226, 1958, 142 pp., pa 35¢) ([French], *Satellite:* No. 96 bis [special], 1962)

Gernsback's noted novel, now principally of historic interest in the sf field. Although it had a melodramatic plot and old-fashioned writing, it described many inventions now in daily use.

GESTON, MARK S(YMINGTON) (20 June 1946–) U.S. author. He was born in Atlantic City, N.J., graduated from Alvington High School, and became an honors history major at Kenyon College in Ohio.

Fiction

Lords of the Starship [pa] (Ace: G-673, 1967, 156 pp., pa 50¢)

The story of a huge spaceship constructed over a span of generations in a war-torn world.

GHOSE, ZULFIKAR

Fiction

Statement Against Corpses [C] See JOHNSON, B. S. (co-author)

GIBBON, PERCEVAL (4 Nov 1879–30 May 1926) English novelist and short-story writer. He was in British, French and American merchant shipping, and then was a journalist and war correspondent in much of Africa, America and Europe. He was a major of Royal Marines 1918-19. His novels include *Souls in Bondage, Salvator* and *Margaret Harding*.

Fiction

Vrouw Grobellar's Leading Cases [C] (Blackwood, Edinburgh & London, 1905, 320 pp., 6/-) (T. Nelson, London & Edinburgh, 1918, 286 pp., 1/6)

Fantasy, 17 stories (not in Bleiler *Checklist*): "Unto the Third Generation"; "The Dream-Face"; "The Avenger of Blood"; "The Hands of the Pitiful Woman"; "Piet Naude's Trek"; "Like Unto Like"; "Counting the Colors"; "The King of the Baboons"; "Morder Drift"; "A Good End"; "Vasco's Sweetheart"; "The Peruvian"; "Tagalash"; "The Home Kraal"; "The Sacrifice"; "The Coward"; "Her Own Story."

GIBBONS, GAVIN (1922–)

Nonfiction

Coming of the Space Ships, The (N. Spearman, London, 1957, 188 pp., 13/6) (Citadel, New York, 1958, 188 pp., $3.50)

A flying saucer book; the author attributes them to other inhabitants of the Solar System, gives other 'facts,' and even grades the various types of UFO's.

On Board the Flying Saucers [pa] (Paperback: 53-585, 1967, 192 pp., pa 60¢)

They Rode in Space Ships (Spearman, London, 1957, 217 pp., 16/-) (Citadel, 1957, $3.50)

A critical coverage of the stories of those who claim contact with flying saucer visitors, such as Daniel Fry and T. Bethurum.

GIBBS, HENRY

Fiction

Pawns in Ice (Jarrolds, London, 1948, 222 pp., 9/6)

Veterans of the next war meet in the future.

GIBBS, LEWIS (pseud) See COVE, J. W.

GIBBS, Sir PHILIP (HAMILTON) (1 May 1877–10 Mar 1962) English author and journalist. At 21 he was an editor with Cassell & Co, and later entered journalism. He was literary editor of several periodicals, and a war correspondent with the British Army 1915-1918. He wrote numerous novels and was a noted commentator on the European scene. A fantasy title besides that below is *Darkened Rooms* (Doubleday, 1929).

Fiction

Out of the Ruins and Other Little Novels [C] (Doubleday Doran, New York, 1928, 350 pp., $2.50) (Hutchinson, London, 1927, 287 pp., 7/6; 1930, 5/-, 3/6)

Fantasy, 9 stories: "Out of the Ruins"; "The Wandering Birds"; "The Beating of Wings"; "The Supernatural Lady"; "The House on the Hill"; "The Fortunate Face"; "The School of Courage"; "The Sign of the Crooked Cross"; "The Shock of Success."

GIBSON, WALTER B. U.S. author and editor. He created "The Shadow," master of disguise, first in magazine and book appearances and later in radio, motion pictures and television. *The Shadow* magazine appeared from Nov 1931 to Sum 1949; Gibson tells in "Me and My Shadow" (introduction to the book below) how he wrote 24 novels a year, each of about 60,000 words, for seven years, and in all 283 novels in 15 years. The more recent paperback series is covered herewith. Gibson also edited the short-lived juvenile *Fantastic Science Fiction* which had two issues in 1952.

Series

Shadow, The. [Paperbacks published by Belmont; first title by Gibson, remainder under Maxwell Grant pseud]: *Return of the Shadow* (1963); *The Shadow Strikes* (1964); *Shadow Beware*

(1965); *Cry Shadow!* (1965); *The Shadow's Revenge* (1965); *Mark of the Shadow* (1966); *Shadow—Go Mad!* (1966); *Night of the Shadow* (1966).

Fiction

Weird Adventures of the Shadow, The [as Maxwell Grant] [C] (Grosset & Dunlap, New York, 1966, 216 pp., 7¼ x 10¼ in., $3.95)

Three "Shadow" stories, with introduction "Me and My Shadow": "The Grove of Doom" (1933); "Voodoo Death" (1944); "Murder by Moonlight" (1943).

GIESY, J(OHN) U(LRICH) (6 Aug 1877–1948) U.S. physiotherapist who wrote as a sideline. He was a very popular writer for the Munsey magazines 1914-34, appearing in both *Argosy* and *All-Story Weekly*, often in collaboration with B. Smith. He is principally remembered for the trilogy below, but is also noted for *All For His Country* (1915, not sf) and for the Semi-Dual series in the Munsey magazines.

Series

Palos trilogy: *Palos of the Dog Star Pack*; *The Mouthpiece of Zitu*; *Jason, Son of Jason* [see entries below].

Fiction

Jason, Son of Jason (*Arg*, sr6, 16 Apr 1921; *FN*, May 1948) (Avalon, New York, 1966, 192 pp., $3.25)

Last of Palos trilogy.

Mouthpiece of Zitu, The (*ASW*, sr5, 5 July 1919; *FFM*, Nov 1942) (Avalon, 1966, 192 pp., $3.25)

Second of Palos trilogy.

Palos of the Dog Star Pack (*ASW*, sr5, 13 July 1918; *FFM*, Oct 1941) (Avalon, 1966, 192 pp., $3.25)

First of Palos trilogy. Jason Croft uses the occult for an interstellar journey and encounters fantastic adventures on a world of Sirius.

GILBERT, Sir WILLIAM SCHWENCK (18 Nov 1836–29 May 1911) English dramatist and librettist. He took his B.A. at U. of London, 1857, and qualified for the bar, but was not successful. Becoming an author, he wrote many plays, and later formed his famous partnership with Arthur Sullivan. He wrote clever, witty and dramatic librettos for the 'Gilbert and Sullivan' operettas; this collaboration had many ups and downs, and lasted some 20 years. Gilbert was knighted in 1907.

Fiction

Foggerty's Fairy and Other Tales [C] (Routledge, London, 1890, 366 pp.; 1892, 2/-; 1894, 1/-)

19 stories, some of fantasy flavour: "Foggerty's Fairy"; "An Elixir of Love"; "Johnny Pounce"; "Little Mim"; "The Triumph of Vice"; "My Maiden Brief"; "Creatures of Impulse"; "Maxwell and I"; "Actors, Authors and Audiences"; "Angela"; "Wide Awake"; "A Stage Play"; "The Wicked World"; "The Finger of Fate"; "A Tale of a Dry Plate"; "The Burglar's Story"; "Unappreciated Shakespeare"; "Comedy and Tragedy"; "Rosencrantz and Guildenstern."

GILCHRIST, ROBERT MURRAY (6 Jan 1868–4 Apr 1917) English novelist. Born in Sheffield, he spent many summers in Derbyshire and lived for a time in the remote part of High Peak studying the country folk. He contributed to the *National Observer* in W. C. Henley's day, and published about 30 titles from *Passion the Plaything* (1890) to *Honeysuckle Rogue* (1916).

Fiction

Stone Dragon and Other Tragic Romances, The [C] (Methuen, London, 1894, 208 pp., 6/-)

Fantasy, 14 items: "The Stone Dragon"; "The Manuscript of Francis Shackerly"; "Midsummer Madness"; "The Lost Mistress"; "Witch In-Grain"; "The Noble Courtesan"; "The Writings of Althea Swarthmoor"; "The Return"; "The Basilisk"; "Dame Inowslad"; "Excerpts From Pliny Witherton's Journal: Also a Letter of Crystall's"; "My Friend"; "Roxana Runs Lunatick"; "The Pageant of Ghosts."

GILES, RAYMOND

Fiction

Night of the Warlock [pa] (Paperback: 53-677, 1968, 160 pp., pa 60¢)

A warlock's dying whisper spreads a net of evil to endanger a beautiful woman.

GILLIATT, PENELOPE

Fiction

One by One (Atheneum, New York, 1965, 189 pp., $3.95) (Secker & Warburg, London, 1965, 18/-) (Panther: 2234, 1967, 157 pp., pa 3/6)

Twenty years from now a plague hits London, with 10,000 dying in three weeks. Couples stop making love, but one has a life to live.

GILLINGS, WALTER (1911–) British editor. He has been interested in the sf field since the early 1930's, when he tried to begin a British magazine. He had no success until 1937, when he started *Tales of Wonder*. The first British sf magazine, it ran for nearly five years until forced to stop because of World War II. After the war Gillings re-entered the sf field as editor of *Fantasy*, published by Temple Bar, but it survived only three issues. He then edited *Fantasy Review* 1947-50; one of the best amateur magazines of its type, it had 18 issues, was printed, and covered the sf/fantasy field with articles, book reviews, etc. With fan support, Gillings and E. J. Carnell formed Nova Publications; with this backing Gillings edited *Science-Fantasy*, incorporating some of the departments from his amateur magazine. Pressure of business as a professional journalist forced him to resign after two issues, and the magazine was taken over by Carnell. Gillings also acted as an authors' agent, and published some articles under the pseudonym "Thomas Sheridan." In June 1960, after recovering from a serious slipped disc, he began a new and specialised press service to help editors. During his illness he wrote his first novel. He is also interested in setting up a "newspaper" for the blind using tape recordings.

GILLMORE, INEZ HAYNES (Inez Haynes Irwin) (2 Mar 1873–) U.S. novelist, born in Rio de Janeiro. The Gillmore surname is from her first husband, she is also known as Irwin from her second husband. Her early novels concerned families of self-reliant young people. Her second book, *Maida's Little Shop* (1910), has been followed by many other "Maida" novels. She was an executive of many writers' societies.

Fiction

Angel Island (Holt, New York, 1914, 351 pp., $1.35) (*FFM*, Feb 1949)

Winged women are caught by shipwrecked mariners, and a settlement is begun.

GILLON, DIANA (PLEASANCE) (1 Sep 1915–)

Fiction

Unsleep, The [with Meir Gillon] (Barrie Rockliff, London, 1961, 246 pp., 16/-) (Smithers, Toronto, $3.75) (Ballantine: F571, 1962, 207 pp., pa 50¢) (FSB: 811, 1963, 223 pp., pa 3/6; #1578, 1966, 317 pp., pa 3/6)

'Sta-wake,' a drug to keep one awake all the time, and its effects on a couple in a future world of "Better Harmony."

GILLON, MEIR (SELIG) (11 Aug 1907–)

Fiction

Unsleep, The See GILLON, D. (co-author)

GILMAN, ROBERT CHAM (pseud) See COPPEL, A.

GILMORE, ANTHONY (pseud) See BATES, HARRY

GILZIN, KARL U.S.S.R. lecturer at the Moscow Aviation Institute. He has had the following nonfiction translated: *Travel to Distant Worlds* (Foreign Languages Publishing House, Moscow, 1957); *Sputniks and After* (MacDonald, 1959).

GINSBURG, MIRRA
Anthology
Last Door to Aiya [Edited and translated by Mirra Ginsburg] (S. G. Phillips, New York, 1968, 192 pp., $4.95)

Subtitled "A selection of the best new science fiction from the Soviet Union." 9 stories with editor's introduction: "The World in Which I Disappeared," A. Dneprov; "The New Signal Station," S. Gansovsky; "The Golden Lotus, a Legend," M. Greshnov; "My Colleague," V. Grigoriev; "Vanya," V. Grigoriev; "Last Door to Aiya," E. Parnov & M. Yemstev; "Homer's Secret," A. Poleshchuk; "The White Cone of the Alaid," A. Strugatsky & B. Strugatsky; "Out in Space," I. Varshavsky. Recommended by P. S. Miller.

GIRONELLA, JOSÉ MARIA (1917–) Spanish author, born in Gerona. He is noted for his trilogy of novels about the Spanish Civil War, the first of which, *The Cypresses Believe in God*, won the Thomas More Association Medal for 1955.
Fiction
Phantoms and Fugitives [C] (*Los Fantasmas de Mi Cerebro*, 1958) Trans.–T. B. Fontsere: (Sheed Ward, New York, 1964, 177 pp., $3.95)

Stories of fantasy interest, including: "Twilight"; "Fugitives"; "The Death of the Sea" (reprinted in *Vintage Anthology of Science Fantasy* [C. Cerf], 1966, pa); "The Red Egg"; "Miracle in the Village."

GIRVAN, WAVENEY British author. He was responsible for publishing the British editions of *The Flying Saucers Have Landed* and *Is Another World Watching?*
Nonfiction
Flying Saucers and Common Sense (F. Muller, London, 1955, 160 pp., 10/6) (Citadel, New York, 1956, 160 pp., $3.50)

An account of the stories behind the books, articles, broadcasts, sightings and rumours of flying saucers. One of the better books on the subject.

GIUNTA, JOHN (1920?–6 Nov 1970) U.S. science fiction illustrator, comic magazine artist, editor and active science fiction fan for over 30 years. He never married, and died nearly penniless.

He became professionally known to sf fans for his work in *Astonishing* and *Super Science Stories* when Alden H. Norton edited them in the early 1940's. He did several covers and interiors for *Weird Tales* and the majority of the interior illustrations for *Venture Science Fiction* Jan 1957–Jan 1958. His work appeared in most sf magazines, including *Galaxy SF*, *If* and *Satellite SF*. As Art Editor of *Saturn* he often did all the illustrations for an issue.

An active fan, he had illustrations in many of the amateur magazines of the late 1930's, including several of his own. He entered the comics field in the early 1940's and work with Fawcett Publications for a time. He edited a number of comic magazines and was highly respected in this regard.

GLASGOW, ELLEN (ANDERSON GHOLSON) (22 Apr 1874–21 Nov 1945) U.S. novelist. She started writing unknown to her family. Her novels are considered of high literary standard; they run from *The Descendant* (1897) to *A Certain Measure* (1943). Her autobiography is *The Woman Within* (1954).
Fiction
Shadowy Third and Other Stories, The [C] (Doubleday Page, New York, 1923, 3+291 pp.)

7 stories: "The Shadowy Third" (*FN*, June 1951); "Dare's Gift"; "The Past"; "Whispering Leaves"; "A Point in Morale"; "The Difference"; "Jordan's End."

GLASKIN, G(ERALD) M(ARCUS) (16 Dec 1923–) Australian author. He lives in Perth, West Australia, where he was born, the eldest of seven children. After a state school education and several jobs he enlisted in the Royal Australian Navy in 1941. While a rating on the armed merchant cruiser *Kanimbla* he suffered an accident, and while recovering he began writing professionally, producing some 12 short stories. In 1943 he worked for a soap manufacturing firm in Sydney, but then joined the R.A.A.F. for

navigator training. He graduated from Winnipeg, his irregular entry into this service gaining but slight reproof from the R.A.A.F. liaison officer in Canada. However, he did not see active service, as the war in Europe was ending. He wrote *A World of Their Own* (400,000 words cut to 160,000), then went to Singapore in motor merchandising. He later changed to stockbrokering, and produced *A Minor Portrait* during a long convalescence. Following his success with *A Change of Mind*, written in Singapore, he decided to write full-time and returned to Perth. Later novels have included *A Lion in the Sun*, *A Waltz Through the Hills*, and *The Beach of Passionate Love*; he has also published a collection of short stories and a nonfiction work about North Australia.
Fiction
Change of Mind, A (Barrie Rockliff, London, 1959, 232 pp., 15/-) (*Melbourne Herald*, sr11, 9 Apr 1960) (*Sydney Morning Herald*, sr18, 25 June 1960) (Ace [British]: H489, 1961, 188 pp., pa 2/6) (*Billets de logement* [French], Denoël: PF53, 1961)

Exchange of personality between two men and the consequent complications; it is treated seriously and not like a Thorne Smith fantasy. It has been bought by a British film company.

GLEMSER, BERNARD (1908–) British author, living in the U.S.A. For some years he worked with the BBC in London. During the war he was attached to the Intelligence Branch of the R.A.F. in the U.S., being Editor of Publications of the British Information Service in New York and cultural officer at the British Embassy in Washington. He has used the pseudonym "Robert Crane." His works include *Strangers in Florida*, *The Radar Commandos* and *All About the Human Body*.
Fiction
Hero's Walk [as Robert Crane] (*Collier's*, sr ?) (Ballantine, New York, 1954, 196 pp., $2.50; #71, pa 35¢) (Ambassador, Toronto, $2.25) (Cresset, London, 1954, 223 pp., 10/6) (*L'occhio invisible* [Italian], *Urania*: 91, 1955) (*Stemmen uit het heelal* [Dutch], Prisma, Utrecht & Antwerp, 1955) (*Ojne I Verdensrummet* [Danish], Skrifola: P6, 1958)

Future world politics with an invasion by the "Ampiti." It was adapted as the TV play "The Voices" (1954).

GNAEDINGER, MARY U.S. editor. She was noted for her editorship of *Famous Fantastic Mysteries* and *Fantastic Novels*. She began these magazines in the late 1930's to reprint fantasy from the Munsey magazines, and they met with considerable success. Late in 1941 they were combined under the *FFM* title. Frank A. Munsey sold *FFM* to Popular Publications in 1943; Gnaedinger remained editor and changed the reprint policy to suit the new owner. She recommended *FN* in 1948, and then edited *A. Merritt's Fantasy*; both of these ceased by mid-1951, while *FFM* remained in the sf field until mid-1953.

GODWIN, FRANCIS (1562–1633) English bishop of Llandaff (1601-17) and of Hereford (1617-33). A scholar, he wrote several learned books; however he is most noted for his *The Man in the Moone*, one of the very early classics of science fiction. The foreword of the 1959 edition below gives a brief review of Godwin and the history of the story.
Fiction
Man in the Moone, The [by "Domingo Gonsales"] (Joshua Kirton & Thomas Warren, London, 1638) (John Lever, London, 1768) (in *Smith College Studies in Modern Languages XIX*, Oct 1937, pp. 1-48, introduction–Grant McColley) (Nagram–c/o *Hereford Times*, Hereford, 1959, iv+48+iii pp., pa 5/-)

A story of space travel in the early 17th Century; Gonsales trains wild swans which take him to the Moon. The 1959 edition is the first solo edition since the 18th century, and presents frontispieces of both the early editions noted. The text is from the 1638 edition (of which only 4 copies are known) and the original pagination (126) is shown.

GODWIN, TOM (1915–) U.S. author. He grew up in the American West, has been a prospector, and now lives in Nevada. He first appeared in the sf field with "The Gulf Between" (*ASF*, short n,

Oct 1953), but is best known for his much-anthologised "The Cold Equations" (*ASF*, Aug 1954), the poignant story of a girl stowaway having to give up her life to save a space colony.

Fiction

Space Barbarians, The [pa] (Pyramid: R993, 1964, 169 pp., pa 50¢)

Sequel to *The Survivors*. The Ragnarokians, let down by Earth, fight a new menace with the aid of telepathic aliens.

Space Prison [pa] See *Survivors, The*

Survivors, The (Expansion of "Too Soon to Die," *Venture*, Mar 1957) (Gnome, New York, 1958, 190 pp., $3.00) (*Space Prison*, Pyramid: G-480, 1960, 158 pp., pa 35¢; F-774, 1962, pa 40¢) (*I superstiti di Ragnarok* [Italian], *Urania*: 229, 1960) (*Sie starben auf Ragnarok* [German], *TS*: 34, 1960) (*Prision espacial* [Spanish], Cenit: 21, 1961, pa)

Captives in an interstellar war are marooned on the hell-planet Ragnarok; they struggle to survive and be revenged.

GOLD, H(ORACE) L(EONARD) (26 Apr 1914–) U.S. author and editor. He was born in Montreal, Canada; his family moved to the Bronx, N.Y., when he was two, and later to Providence, Rhode Island. After high school he had to begin working. He was introduced to fantasy through *The Wizard of Oz*; later he discovered the Burroughs books and then *Amazing Stories* (which he couldn't afford to buy regularly). His first sale to the sf field was "Inflexure" (*ASF*, Oct 1934), under the pseudonym "Clyde Crane Campbell." Although he sold a number of stories, he found making a living hard in the years 1935-38 and moved from one job to another. In 1938 he began selling to *ASF* again, under his own name, and later appeared in *Unknown* with "Trouble With Water" (Mar 1939; 1948 reprint issue), probably his best-remembered story. His novel "None But Lucifer" was revised by L. S. de Camp and appeared in *Unknown*, Sep 1939.

Gold worked a while on the staff of the Standard magazines, then joined Magazine House where he created two true-detective magazines, writing much of the material for them. He formed a partnership with K. F. Crossen and they worked on comic books and other material until Gold was drafted. He spent two years as a combat engineer, seeing action in the Philippines. In 1950 World Editions was looking for a new magazine field to enter, and Gold was able to begin *Galaxy Science Fiction*. This magazine was most successful, and in its early years was rated with *ASF* and *F&SF* as the best in the sf field, though it has since not been so highly commended. Gold also began a companion novel series, *Galaxy Science Fiction Novels*, and edited the short-lived fantasy magazine *Beyond*. More recently he edited *If* when it was purchased by his publisher. Illness forced him to leave these editorial posts at the end of 1961. He edited many anthologies of *Galaxy* stories.

Fiction

Old Die Rich and Other Science Fiction, The [C] (Crown, New York, 1955, 250 pp., $3.00) (Dobson, London, 1965, 250 pp., 18/-)

Sf, 12 stories: "The Old Die Rich"; "Trouble With Water"; "No Charge for Alterations"; "Don't Take It to Heart"; "Man of Parts"; "Love in the Dark"; "The Man With English"; "The Biography Project"; "At the Post"; "Hero"; "And Three to Get Ready"; "Problem in Murder."

Anthologies

Bodyguard and Four Other Short Novels From Galaxy (Doubleday, New York, 1960, 312 pp., $3.95) (D'day SF B.C., 1960, $1.20) (Permabooks: M4252, 1962, 273 pp., pa 35¢)

Sf, 5 short novels; introduction—F. Pohl: "Bodyguard," C. Grimm; "How-2," C. D. Simak; "Delay in Transit," F. L. Wallace; "The City of Force," D. F. Galouye; "Whatever Counts," F. Pohl.

Fifth Galaxy Reader, The (Doubleday, 1961, 260 pp., $3.95) (D'day SF B.C., 1961, $1.20) (Pocket Books: 6163, 1963, 241 pp., 35¢)

Sf, 15 stories; introduction—H. L. Gold: "Inside John Barth," W. W. Stuart; "The Last Letter," F. Leiber; "Perfect Answer," L. J. Stecher; "Double Dare," R. Silverberg; "Pastoral Affair," C. A. Stearns; "Black Charlie," G. R. Dickson; "$1,000 a Plate," J. McKenty; "Take Wooden Indians," A. Davidson; "The Bitterest

Pill," F. Pohl; "This Side Up," R. E. Banks; "The Eel," Miriam A. DeFord; "A Feast of Demons," W. Morrison; "Nightmare With Zeppelins," F. Pohl & C. M. Kornbluth; "We Never Mention Aunt Nora," P. Flehr; "When the People Fell," Cordwainer Smith.

Five Galaxy Short Novels (Doubleday, 1958, 287 pp., $3.95) (D'day, Toronto, $4.50) (Permabooks: M4158, 1960, 292 pp., pa 35¢)

Sf, 5 short novels: "Tangle Hold," F. L. Wallace; "World Without Children," D. Knight; "Wherever You May Be," J. E. Gunn; "Mind Alone," J. T. McIntosh; "Granny Won't Knit," T. Sturgeon.

Fourth Galaxy Reader, The (Doubleday, 1959, 264 pp., $3.95) (D'day SF B.C., 1959, $1.20) (Permabooks: M4184, 1960, 239 pp., pa 35¢)

Sf, 15 stories: "I Am a Nucleus," S. Barr; "Name Your Symptom," J. Harmon; "Horror Howce," Marg. St. Clair; "Man of Distinction," M. Shaara; "The Bomb in the Bath-Tub," T. N. Scortia; "What's He Doing in There?" F. Leiber; "You Were Right, Joe," J. T. McIntosh; "The Gentlest Unpeople," F. Pohl; "The Hated," P. Flehr; "Kill Me With Kindness," R. Wilson; "Or All the Seas With Oysters," A. Davidson; "The Gun Without a Bang," F. O'Donnevan; "Man in a Quandary," L. J. Stecher Jr.; "Blank Form," A. Sellings; "The Minimum Man," R. Sheckley.

Galaxy Reader of Science Fiction (Crown, New York, 1952, 566 pp., $3.50) (Grayson, London, 1953, 254 pp., 9/6 [13 stories marked *])

Sf, 8 novelettes, 25 short stories, with introduction by H. L. Gold: *I. It Happened Tomorrow:* "Honeymoon in Hell," F. Brown; "Coming Attraction," F. Leiber; "Rule of Three," T. Sturgeon; "Third From the Sun"*, R. Matheson; "The Last Martian," F. Brown. *II. Sooner Than You Think:* "Jaywalker," R. Rocklynne; "The Reluctant Heroes," F. Robinson; "A Little Journey," R. Bradbury; "Venus Is a Man's World," W. Tenn. *III. The Worlds We Made:* "Beyond Bedlam," W. Guin; "The Stars Are the Styx"*, T. Sturgeon; "Inside Earth"*, P. Anderson; "I, the Unspeakable," W. Sheldon. *IV. Aren't You an Extraterrestrial?:* "The Pilot and the Bushman"*, Sylvia Jacobs; "Judas Ram," S. Merwin; "Hostess," I. Asimov; "Betelgeuse Bridge"*, Wm. Tenn; "Cabin Boy," D. Knight; "Field Study"*, P. Phillips. *V. Let's Build Somebody:* "Goodnight, Mr. James"*, C. D. Simak; "Syndrome Johnny," C. Dye; "Made to Measure"*, Wm. C. Gault. *VI. Not Around the Corner:* "Ask Me Anything," D. Knight; "If You Was a Moklin," M. Leinster; "Man of Destiny"*, J. Christopher; "Susceptibility"*, J. D. MacDonald. *VII. The End of History and Beyond:* "The Waker Dreams," R. Matheson; "Common Denominator"*, J. D. MacDonald; "Second Childhood," C. D. Simak. *VIII. About Time:* "Don't Live in the Past," D. Knight; "The Biography Project"*, D. Dell; "Dark Interlude"*, M. Reynolds & F. Brown; "The Other Now," M. Leinster.

Galaxy Science Fiction Omnibus See *Second Galaxy Reader of Science Fiction*

Mind Partner and Eight Other Novelets From Galaxy Science Fiction (Doubleday, 1961, 263 pp., $3.95, jacket—Mel Hunter) (Permabooks: M4287, 1963, 241 pp., pa 35¢)

Sf, 9 novelettes and compiler's introduction: "Mind Partner," Christopher Anvil; "The Lady Who Sailed the Soul," Cordwainer Smith; "The Stentorii Luggage," Neal Barrett Jr.; "Snuffles," R. A. Lafferty; "The Sly Bungerhop," Wm. Morrison; "Blacksword," A. J. Offutt; "The Civilization Game," C. D. Simak; "The Hardest Bargain," Evelyn E. Smith; "With Redfern on Capella XII," Charles Satterfield.

Second Galaxy Reader of Science Fiction (Crown, 1954, 504 pp., $3.50) (*Galaxy Science Fiction Omnibus*, Grayson, 1955, 350 pp., 13/6, jacket—H. Johns [20 stories marked *])

Sf, 31 stories (including 12 novelettes): *I. Tomorrow's The Day:* "The Year of the Jackpot," R. Heinlein; "A Bad Day for Sales"*, F. Leiber; "The Misogynist"*, J. E. Gunn; "Saucer of Loneliness"*, T. Sturgeon; "Teething Ring," J. Causey; "A Gleeb for Earth"*, C. Schafhauser. *II. The Wild Black Yonder:* "Hallucination Orbit"*, J. T. McIntosh; "The C-Chute"*, I. Asimov; "Junkyard"*, C. D. Simak; "Problem on Balak"*, R. Dee. *III. Adapt or Die!:* "Surface Tension," J. Blish; "Specialist," R. Sheckley; "Four in One"*, D. Knight; "Caretaker"*, J. Schmitz; "Lost Memory"*, P. Phillips. *IV. Worlds of Others:* "Not Fit for Children"*, Evelyn Smith; "Student Body"*, F. L. Wallace; "Lover When You're Near Me," R. Matheson. *V. It's All in the Mind:* "Command Performance," W. Miller Jr.; "Star Bright"*, M. Clifton; "Warm"*, R. Sheckley; "Unready to Wear," K. Vonnegut Jr. *VI. Blueprint for Chaos:* "Tiger by the Tail," A. E. Nourse; "Self Portrait," B. Wolfe; "The Snowball Effect"*, Kath. MacLean. *VII. Time and Time Again:* "Pillar to Post"*, J. Wyndham; "Minimum Sentence"*, T. Cogswell; "A Game for Blondes," J. D. MacDonald. *VIII. The Nth Generation:* "University," P. Phillips; "Tea Tray in the Sky"*, Evelyn E. Smith; "A Pail of Air"*, F. Leiber.

Sixth Galaxy Reader, The (Doubleday, 1962, 240 pp., $3.95, jacket—Roger Zimmerman)

Sf, 14 stories and introduction "How to Write Science Fiction": "The Nuse Man," Margaret St. Clair; "Success Story," Earl Goodale; "A Husband for My Wife," Wm. M. Stuart; "Insidekick," J. F. Bone; "Love Called This Thing," A. Davidson & Laura Goforth; "Lex," W. T. Haggart; "License to Steal," Louis Newman; "True Self," Elizabeth M. Borgese; "Flower Arrangement," Rosel G. Brown; "Thing of Beauty," D. Knight; "A Personnel Problem," H. L. Gold; "The Number of the Beast," F. Leiber; "The Ifth of Oofth," Walter S. Tevis Jr.; "The Genius Heap," J. Blish.

Third Galaxy Reader, The (Doubleday, 1958, 262 pp., $3.95, jacket—A. Renshaw) (D'day, Toronto, $4.25) (D'day SF B.C., 1958, $1.20) (Permabooks: M4172, 1960, 235 pp., pa 35¢)

Sf, 15 stories and compiler's introduction "Program Notes": "Limiting Factor," T. R. Cogswell; "Protection," R. Sheckley; "The Vilbar Party," Evelyn E. Smith; "End as a World," F. L. Wallace; "Time in the Round," F. Leiber; "Help! I Am Dr. Morris Goldpepper," A. Davidson; "A Wind Is Rising," F. O'Donnevan; "Ideas Die Hard," I. Asimov; "Dead Ringer," L. del Rey; "The Haunted Corpse," F. Pohl; "The Model of a Judge," Wm. Morrison; "Man in the Jar," D. Knight; "Volpla," W. Guin; "Honorable Opponent," C. D. Simak; "The Game of Rat and Dragon," Cord. Smith.

Weird Ones, The (Belmont: L92-541, 1962, 173 pp., pa 50¢) (Dobson, 1965, 173 pp., 15/-) (Corgi: GS7592, 1967, 190 pp., pa 3/6)

Sf, 7 stories (none previously in book form) with compiler's preface: "Small Lords," F. Pohl; "Sentiment, Inc." P. Anderson; "Name Your Tiger," M. Lesser; "Iron Man," Eando Binder; "The Hunted Ones," M. Reynolds; "Hail to the Chief," Sam Sackett; "Impractical Joke," L. S. de Camp.

World That Couldn't Be and Eight Other Novelets From Galaxy, The (Doubleday, 1959, 288 pp., $3.95) (D'day, Toronto, $4.50) (Permabooks: M4197, 1961, 260 pp., pa 35¢)

Sf, 9 novelettes: "One for the Books," R. Matheson; "An Eye for a What?" D. Knight; "A Woman's Place," M. Clifton; "Brightside Crossing," A. E. Nourse; "Mezzerow Loves Company," F. L. Wallace; "Once a Greech," Evelyn E. Smith; "A Gun for Dinosaur," L. S. de Camp; "The Music Master of Babylon," E. Pangborn; "The World That Couldn't Be," C. D. Simak.

GOLDING, LOUIS (Nov 1895—9 Aug 1958) English novelist. He wrote many books before *Magnolia Street* (1931) established him. He later wrote a series of interlinked but independent novels in a contemporary history of Europe: *Mr. Emmanuel* (1939), *The Glory of Elsie Silver* (1944), *The Dangerous Places* (1952), *To the Quayside* (1953). His fantasy novels other than that below are *The Miracle Boy* (Knopf, 1927; 1944, pa) and *The Pursuer* (Farrar & Rinehart, 1936).

Fiction

Doomington Wanderer, The [C] (Gollancz, London, 1934, 286 pp., 7/6)

22 stories, many of fantasy interest (not in Bleiler *Checklist*): "Miss Pomfret and Miss Primrose"; "Black Frailty"; "The Doomington Wanderer"; "The Man in the White Tie"; "The Last Troubador"; "The Vicar of Dunkerly Briggs"; "Wimpole's Woe"; "No More Apple-Blossom"; "The Haunted Cinema"; "But the Gods Will Not Have It"; "The Window of Broken Magic"; "Bishops and Poets"; "The Inn"; "Little Grocer With Yellow Hair"; "The Tat-

tooed Bird"; "The Bondage of Jack"; "Bare-Knuckle Lover"; "The Call of the Hand"; "Pompeii in Massachusetts"; "Divinity in Deauville"; "In Ararat"; "In and Out of the Window."

Honey for the Ghost (Dial, New York, 1949, 383 pp., $3.00) (Hutchinson, London, 1949, 448 pp., 12/6; 1950, 6/-)

A witch buys the soul of a sick man. Recommended by A. Boucher.

GOLDING, WILLIAM (GERALD) (17 Sep 1911—) British author. He is particularly noted for his novel *Lord of the Flies*, which has been used as an English textbook and has been made into a film. A literary criticism of his works is *William Golding—A Critical Study*, by Mark Kinkead-Weekes and Ian Gregor (Faber, 1967, 35/-).

Fiction

Brass Butterfly, The (Faber, London, 1958, 80 pp., 10/6)

Dramatised version of the short novel "Envoy Extraordinary," originally published in *Sometime, Never* [Anonymous Anthology], 1956.

Inheritors, The (Faber, 1955, 233 pp., 12/6; 1961, 6/-; 1963, 282 pp., 8/6; 1964, pa 6/6) (Harcourt Brace World, New York, 1962, 233 pp., $4.50; 1963, pa $1.65) (Cardinal: GC787, 1964, 213 pp., pa 75¢)

An idealization of the life of the last of the Neanderthal people, depicting them as a sort of noble savage.

Lord of the Flies (Faber, 1954, 248 pp., 12/6; 1958, pa 5/-; [school ed. notes by I. Gregor & M. Kinkead-Weekes] 1962, xii+ii+263 pp., 6/6, 4/-; 1963, 248 pp., illus.—film, 6/-; [Ed. by F. W. Nelson] 1963, pa 6/-; 1967, 223 pp., pa 3/6) (Coward-McCann, New York, 1955, 243 pp., $3.50) (*Der Herr der Fliegen* [German], S. Fischer, 1957) (Capricorn: CAP-14, 1959, 256 pp., $1.25) (Penguin: 1471, 1960, 192 pp., pa 2/6)

An unusual story of a plane load of English school boys cast away on a tropical island, and the society they develop. A pessimistic view of mankind. *Film:* British, 1963, distributed by British Lion; directed by Peter Brook; score by Raymond Leppard, ironic and evocative.

Spire, The (Faber, 1964, 223 pp., 18/-) (Harcourt, 1964, 214 pp., $3.95; 1965, pa $1.35)

Compelling subjective account of the obsession of a man driven by his fantasies to truly superhuman endeavour.

GOLDSMITH, CELE (1933—) U.S. editor. She was born in Scranton, Pa., and educated at Vassar (B.A., 1955). She joined Ziff-Davis as Assistant Editor of *Amazing Stories* and *Fantastic* (1956-57), became Managing Editor (1957-58), and was Editor 1958 to June 1965, when Sol Cohen became publisher. For a period in the early 1960's she and Norman Lobsenz had both magazines and presented quite interesting material, but the standard lapsed toward the end of her editorship. In mid-1964 she married, becoming Cele G. Lalli.

GOLDSTON, ROBERT C. (1927—) U.S. author. He was born in Brooklyn but spent most of his early life in the Midwest. He served in the Army in Germany 1945-47, and studied at Columbia U. He has sailed a schooner on the Great Lakes, and has worked as a book designer for several firms. He now lives in Europe with his wife and daughter. His first novel was *The Eighth Day*.

Fiction

Catafalque, The (Rinehart, New York, 1958, 314 pp., illus.—Gretchen Seltzer, $3.95) (Clarke Irwin, Toronto, $4.75) (Popular: 75-1260, 1968, 272 pp., pa 75¢)

Weird-supernatural.

Eighth Day, The (Rinehart, 1956, 345 pp., $3.95) (Clarke Irwin, $4.75)

A novel of miracles performed by a French monk.

Nonfiction

Satan's Disciples [pa] (Ballantine: F581, 1962, 189 pp., pa 50¢)

A modern history of Satanism and witchcraft from the Middle Ages to the present day.

GOLL, REINHOLD WEIMAR
Fiction
Spaceship to Planet Veta (Westminster, New York, 1962, 160 pp., illus.–G. O. James, $2.95) (Ryerson, $3.75)
    Juvenile.
Through Space to Planet T (Westminster, 1963, 156 pp., illus.–G. O. James, $3.25) (Ryerson, $3.95)
    Juvenile.
Visitors From Planet Veta, The (Westminster, 1961, 116 pp., illus.–G. O. James, $2.95)
    Juvenile.

GOMPERTZ, MARTIN L(OUIS) (ALAN) (1886–29 Sep 1951) Noted fantasy author under the pseudonym "Ganpat." He lived for many years in India and became thoroughly acquainted with that country. He is remembered primarily for some excellent fantasy adventures set in Tibet and little-known regions of Central Asia. His more important novels were written 1923-39; these include *Harilek* (Houghton Mifflin, 1923; Blackwood), *Snow Rubies* (Houghton Mifflin, 1925; Blackwood, 1925), *The Voice of Dashin* (Hodder & Stoughton, 1926), and *Mirror of Dreams* (Doubleday, 1928). A number of others are also listed in the Bleiler *Checklist*. Gompertz also wrote two travel books.

GONSALES, DOMINGO See GODWIN, F.

GOOD, I(RVING) J(OHN) U.S. mathematician and statistician.
Nonfiction
Scientist Speculates, The (Heinemann, London, 1962, 413 pp., 50/-) (Basic Books, New York, 1963, 413 pp., $6.95)
    A collection of partly-baked ideas that raise more questions than answers, in sections such as "Ideas About Ideas," "Information About Information," "Minds, Meaning and Cybernetics," "Psi," etc. Reviewed by P. S. Miller (*ASF*, Dec 1963, p. 86).

GOODCHILD, GEORGE (1888–) A fantasy besides that below was *The Monster of Grammont* (Mystery League Inc., New York, 1930).
Fiction
Dr. Zils Experiments (Ward Lock, London, 1953, 206 pp., 9/6; 1954, 6/-)
    Five men and one woman survive an experiment. Written in the form of a film scenario.

GOODRICH, CHARLES
Fiction
Genesis of Nam, The (Dorrance, Philadelphia, 1957, 136 pp., $2.00)
    A pleasing allegory on the creation of an interstellar Eden.

GOODRICH-FREER, ADELA M.
Anthology
Professional and Other Psychic Stories, The (Hurst Blackett, London, 1900, 288 pp.)
    Not listed in Bleiler *Checklist*. Somewhat oddly, the author has "(Miss X)" noted after her name. 7 stories: "A Professional Person," "Another Professional Person," "A Dead Man's Evidence," A. Goodrich-Freer; "The History of Malcolm Mackenzie," Olive Birrell; "Alice and Alicia," Christabel Coleridge; "A Closed Door," M. E. Bramston; "The Haunting of White Gates," G. M. Robins.

GOODWIN, HAROLD LELAND U.S. science writer. He is the author of *The Science Book of Space Travel* (Cardinal, 1956, pa).
Series
Rick Brant–Science-Adventure Stories [by John Blaine, pseudonym of H. L. Goodwin and P. J. Harkins]. This juvenile series began in 1947 and is published by Grosset & Dunlap, New York, originally at 95¢, then $1.00, with most recent titles $1.50. The books have no dust-jackets, but the covers are printed with coloured illustrations.
    Rick Brant, the teenage son of scientist Hartson Brant, lives with his parents, sister Barby and friend Don Scott (Scotty) on Spindrift Island off the New Jersey coast. He is mechanically and scientifically inclined and is a confirmed inventor. His father has laboratories staffed by scientists on the island, a map of which is on the end covers of the books.
    The titles run: 1. *The Rocket's Shadow* (1947); 2. *The Lost City* (1947); 3. *Sea Gold* (1947); 4. *100 Fathoms Under* (1947); 5. *The Whispering Box* (1948); 6. *The Phantom Shark* (1949); 7. *Smuggler's Reef* (1950); 8. *The Caves of Fear* (1951); 9. *Stairway to Danger* (1952); 10. *The Golden Skull* (1954); 11. *The Wailing Octopus* (1956); 12. *The Electronic Mind Reader* (1957); 13. *The Scarlet Lake Mystery* (1958); 14. *The Pirates of Shan* (1958); 15. *The Blue Ghost Mystery* (1960); 16. *The Egyptian Cat Mystery* (1961); 17. *The Flaming Mountain* (1962); 18. *The Flying Stingaree* (1963); 19. *The Ruby Ray Mystery* (1964); 20. *The Veiled Raiders* (1965); 21. *Rocket Jumper* (1966); 22. *The Deadly Dutchman* (1967); 23. *Danger Below!* (1968).
    Rick Brant's Science Projects (Grosset, 1960, 247 pp., $1.95) is not a novel in the series, but apparently is adventure stories.

GORDON, ISABEL S.
Anthology
Armchair Science Reader, The [with Sophie Sorkin] (Simon & Schuster, New York, 1959, 832 pp., $7.95)
    Anthology of 175 items—stories, articles, essays, poems, etc.—concerning science (not technical). The science fiction is concentrated in Part I, with a few other scattered titles elsewhere. *I. Science Sparks the Imagination:* Man Among the Stars: "Invasion From Mars," H. Koch (script of O. Welles 1938 broadcast); "Flight to Malacandra," C. S. Lewis (from *Out of the Silent Planet*); "Our Distant Cousins," Lord Dunsany. Man Upon the Seas: "The Nautilus Reaches the Pole," J. Verne (from *20,000 Leagues Under the Sea*); "A Descent into the Maelstrom," E. A. Poe. Man and His Earth: "John Thomas' Cube," J. Leimert; "In Hiding," Wilmar H. Shiras; "Creative Evolution," G. B. Shaw (from preface to *Back to Methuselah*); "Split Cherry Tree," Jesse Stuart; "Cabinet Decision," N. Balchin (from *Who Is My Neighbour*); "Dr. Southport Vulpes's Nightmare," B. Russell (from *Nightmares of Eminent Persons*); "The Portable Phonograph," W. Van T. Clark; "By the Waters of Babylon," S. V. Benét. *In other parts:* "Laputan Projects," J. Swift (from *Gulliver's Travels*); "Machines to Do Our Work," E. Bellamy (from *Looking Backward*); "In Bondage to a Central Authority," A. Huxley (from *Brave New World*); "The Machine Stops," E. M. Forster; "The Morning of the Day They Did It," E. B. White. The whole book is of interest, and is recommended by P. S. Miller for sampling.

GORDON, REX (pseud) See HOUGH, S. B.

GOREY, EDWARD
Fiction
Doubtful Guest, The (Doubleday, New York, 1957, 32 pp., $2.00)
    An extraterrestrial moves in on an Edwardian family. The book content is slight: 28 lines of verse and 16 full-page illustrations; it has some macabre limericks.

GOTLIEB, PHYLLIS (FAY) (25 May 1926–) Canadian author. She was born and educated in Toronto, with a Master's in English from the U. of Toronto. She is married to the Director of the Institute of Computer Science at the U. of Toronto; they have three children. She has written a number of stories for the sf magazines, and her verse appears regularly in Canadian literary periodicals.
Fiction
Sunburst [pa] (*AS*, sr3, Mar 1964) (Gold Medal: k1488, 1964, 160 pp., pa 40¢) (Coronet: F117, 1966, 160 pp., pa 3/6)
    Mutant children buck authority.

GOTTLIEB, HINKO
Fiction
Key to the Great Gate, The [Trans. from Serbo-Croat by F. Bolman & Ruth Morris] (Simon & Schuster, New York, 1948, viii+178 pp., illus.–S. Fischer, $2.75) (Musson, Toronto, $3.00)

A prisoner of the Nazis uses mystical powers. Writing after being freed from Nazi camps, Gottlieb convincingly portrays the cruelty and stupidity of Nazi tyranny.

GOUDGE, ELIZABETH (DE BEAUCHAMP) (24 Apr 1900–)
British author. Among her works are *The Middle Window* (Duckworth, 1935) and the noted *Green Dolphin Street* (Coward McCann, 1944).
Fiction
Little White Horse, The (Coward McCann, New York, 1947, 280 pp., illus.–C. Walter Hodges, $2.50) (Longmans, Toronto, $3.00) (U. of London Press, 1946, 286 pp., illus.–Hodges, 6/-) (Clarke Irwin, Toronto, $1.80)
Fairy magic.

GOULART, RON(ALD JOSEPH) (13 Jan 1913–) U.S. author.
He was educated at the U. of California, and is a part-time writer of advertising copy. In recent years he has been a prolific author of science fiction, with about 50 stories published. His fiction has also appeared in such magazines as *Show*, *Gentlemen's Quarterly* and *Alfred Hitchcock's Mystery Magazine*.
Fiction
Sword Swallower (Doubleday, New York, 1968, 181 pp., $4.95)
An agent seeks the reason for kidnapping on a super-resort.

GOULD, ARTHUR LEE (pseud) See LEE, A. S. G.

GOULD, MAGGY
Fiction
Dowry, The (Morrow, New York, 1949, 244 pp., $2.75) (Collins, Toronto, $3.50) (Wingate, London, 1950, 244 pp., 9/6)
Horror tale of a man who has a curse laid on him.

GOURAUD, AMIEE CROCKER
Fiction
Moon-Madness and Other Fantasies [C] (Broadway Pub. Co., New York, 1910, 91 pp., frontis.)
8 stories: "Our Lady of Red Lips"; "Paula Loved Pearls"; "The Dance of the Cobra"; "The Painted Mrs. Perry"; "Kava the Faithful"; "Betty and Buddha"; "Mrs. Pepper in Paris"; "Moon-Madness." *Note:* Bleiler *Checklist* erroneously lists author as Gourand.

GOURLAY, REGINALD
Fiction
Necklace of Pandura, The [C] (Broadway Pub. Co., New York, 1907, 121 pp.)
Not given in the Bleiler *Checklist*. 9 items: "The Necklace of Pandura, or, The Cord, the Poison and the Shadow"; "The Capture of Tom Dare"; "Every Year" (a Tale of Northern Quebec); "Satanism and the Black Mass (Le Misse Noir) in Paris"; "Even If I Am Dead" (s); "Never Alone" (s); "A Match by Mishap"; "Rural Culture" (a comedieeta); " 'Unknown Forces'."

GOUSCHEV, SERGEI Russian reporter.
Nonfiction
Russian Science in the 21st Century See VASSILIEV, M. (co-author)

GOVE, PHILIP BABCOCK (27 June 1902–)
Nonfiction
Imaginary Voyage in Prose Fiction, The (Holland [N. Spearman], London, 1961, 445 pp., 63/-) (Burns MacEachern, Toronto, $14.50)
Subtitled "A history of criticism and a guide for its study with an annotated checklist of 215 imaginary voyages from 1700 to 1800."

GOWANS, ADAM L(UKE)
Anthology
Famous Ghost Stories by English Authors (Gowans & Grey, London, 1912, 220 pp., 1/-; 1919, 225 pp., 2/-)
The Bleiler *Checklist* does not give the first edition. 11 stories:

"To Be Taken With a Grain of Salt," C. Dickens; "The Old Nurse's Story," Mrs. Gaskell; "The Tapestried Chamber," Sir W. Scott; "The Haunted and the Haunters," Lord Lytton; "The Haunted Ships," A. Cunningham; "No. 1 Branch Line: The Signalman," C. Dickens; "The Mysterious Bride," J. Hogg; "A True Relation of the Apparition of One Mrs. Veal the Next Day After Her Death to One Mrs. Bargrave at Canterbury, the 8th of September 1705," D. Defoe; "The Bagman's Story," C. Dickens; "Mary Burnet," J. Hogg; "Telling Winter Stories," C. Dickens.

GOWLAND, JOHN STAFFORD (1898–)
Fiction
Beyond Mars (Gryphon, London, 1956, 191 pp., 9/6)
Antigravity, a trip to the Moon, and further adventures.

GRAHAM, KENNETH W. (3 Mar 1859–6 July 1932) English
story writer. Reared by relatives, he went to work in the Bank of England, rising to Secretary in 1898. He combined banking and literature. He married in 1899. His son Alastair, for whom *The Wind in the Willows* was written, died in an accident at 20. Graham's health broke down and he retired to live at Blewbury. Other fantasy titles besides that below were *Dream Days* (J. Lane, London, 1899) and *The Golden Age* (Stone & Kimball, Chicago, 1895).
Fiction
Wind in the Willows, The [C] (Scribner, New York, 1908, 302 pp., frontis.; 1933) (Methuen, London, 1961, 256 pp., illus.–E. Shepard, pa 3/6; many eds. to 1967) (Avon: SS4, 1965, 224 pp., pa 60¢) (Lancer: 12-404, 1967, 253 pp., pa 60¢)
Juvenile—not strictly a collection, but the continuing adventures of Rat, Mole, Badger and Toad—12 chapters: "The River Bank"; "The Open Road"; "The Wild Wood"; "Mr. Badger"; "Dulce Domum"; "Mr. Toad"; "The Piper at the Gates of Dawn"; "Toad's Adventures"; "Wayfarers All"; "The Further Adventures of Toad"; " 'Like Summer Tempests Came His Tears' "; "The Return of Ulysses."

GRAHAM, ROGER P(HILLIPS) (1909–1965) U.S. author, bet-
ter known to the science fiction and fantasy field by his pseudonym "Rog Phillips." He was born in Spokane, Wash., graduated from Gonzaga U., Spokane, and also studied at U. of Washington in Seattle. He was in power plant engineering until World War II, when he became a shipyard welder. After the war he became a full-time writer, and wrote some 3 million words under 20 pseudonyms. He is primarily remembered for some notable stories in the Ziff-Davis magazines in the mid-1940's, which did much to raise their standard, and also for his column "The Club House" which ran in *Amazing Stories* 1948-53 and was one of the best of its kind in reviewing fan magazines and covering fan affairs. It was later revived in *Universe SF*. He was married to Mari Wolf for a time. In 1956 he married Honey Wood. Stories of interest include "Atom War" (*AS*, May 1946) and sequel; "So Shall Ye Reap" (*AS*, Aug 1947) and sequel; "M'Bong-Ah" (*AS*, Feb 1949; [German], *UZ*: 91, 1957); "The Cyberene" (*Imagination*, Sep 1953); "The Cosmic Junkman" (*Imagination*, Dec 1953; [German], *UZ*: 62, 1956); a German collection appeared as *T*: 429 (1965).
Series
Baker, Lefty [as Rog Phillips]. "Squeeze Play" (*AS*, Nov 1947); "The Immortal Menace" (*AS*, Feb 1949); "The Insane Robot" (*FA*, Nov 1949); "But Who Knows Huer or Huen?" (*Fan*, Nov 1961).
Fiction (as Rog Phillips)
Involuntary Immortals, The (enlarged from *FA*, Dec 1949) (Avalon, New York, 1959, 223 pp., $2.75) (*Der Club der Unsterblichen* [German], *T*: 297, 1963)
An immortal thinks herself unique, but then finds many others.
Time Trap [pa] (Century: 116, 1949, 158 pp., pa 25¢) (*Piege dans le temps* [French], Le Fleuve Noir: A30, 1954, pa) (*Trappola nel tempo* [Italian], *Urania*: 82, 1955) (Atlas: SFL8, 1956, 114 pp., pa 2/6) (*Die Zeitfalle* [German], Zimmermann, 1958; *T*: 111, 1960)
Time intrigue.

World of If [pa] (Century: B13, 1951, 126 pp., pa 35¢) (*Welten der Wahrscheinlichkeit* [German], Zimmermann, 1960)

Worlds Within [pa] (Century: 124, 1950, 159 pp., pa 25¢) (Export: MDS142, 1950, 160 pp., pa 25¢) (*La porta sui mondi* [Italian], *Urania*: 101, 1955) (*Unsichtbare Welten* [German], *AW*: 10, 1958)

GRANT, DONALD (METCALF) (1927–) U.S. publisher. He was born in Providence, Rhode Island, and took his A.B. at U. of Rhode Island in 1949. Publishing, bookselling and related printing are his full-time work, under the name The Grandon Company. Many of the works produced are of sf/fantasy interest, but usually in small editions. He was co-founder of Buffalo Book Co. in 1946; this published J. Taine's *The Time Stream*. Grant also worked on *333, A Bibliography of the Science-Fantasy Novel*, 1953 [see CRAWFORD, J. H.]. More recently he published the H. H. Heins' notable *Golden Anniversary Bibliography of Edgar Rice Burroughs*. Other books include several by R. E. Howard, such as *A Gent From Bear Creek* and *Red Shadows*.

GRANT, (Mrs.) JOAN (MARSHALL) (12 Apr 1907–) British author, daughter of J. F. Marshall, C.B.E. She has written a number of fantasy/historical novels, including *So Moses Was Born* (1952); her autobiography is *Time Out of Mind* (1956). Her fiction includes *Eyes of Horus* (Methuen, 1942) and *Life as Carola* (1939).
Fiction [Incomplete—other titles in Bleiler *Checklist*]
Return to Elysium (Methuen, London, 1947, 317 pp., 9/6)
An interesting story of occult power development, set in ancient Greece.
Winged Pharaoh (A. Barker, London, 1937, 382 pp., 10/6) (Methuen, 1940, 393, 5/-) (Harper, New York, 1938, 382 pp., $2.50) (Saunders, Toronto, $3.00; $1.98) (FSB: 11, 1958, 255 pp., pa 2/6)
First-person novel of a co-ruler of ancient Egypt before its glory was dimmed; it is of rare literary value and has a spiritual quality seldom found in modern fiction.

GRANT, MAXWELL (pseud) See GIBSON, W. B.

GRAVES, CLOTILDE INEZ MARY (1863–1932)
Fiction [as Richard Dehan]
Off Sandy Hook and Other Stories [C] (Stokes, New York, 1915, 327 pp., $1.25)
Fantasy, 24 stories: "Off Sandy Hook"; "Gemini"; "A Dish of Macaroni"; " 'Freddy et Cie' "; "Under the Electrics"; " 'Valcourt's Grin' "; "The Evolution of the Fairest"; "The Revolt of Rustleton"; "A Dyspeptic's Tragedy"; "Renovation"; "The Breaking Place"; "A Lancashire Daisy"; "A Pitched Battle"; "The Tug of War"; "Gas! Air Side!"; "A Spirit Elopement"; "The Widow's Mite"; "Susanna and Her Elders"; "Lady Clanbevan's Baby"; "The Duchess's Dilemma"; "The Child"; "A Hindered Honeymoon"; " 'Clothes—and the Man' "; "The Devil and the Deep Sea."
Under the Hermés, and Other Stories [C] (Dodd Mead, New York, 1917, vii+341 pp.)
Fantasy, 18 stories: "Under the Hermés"; "Brother Nightingale"; "Peter"; "The Compleat Housewife"; "The Queen of Ruatava"; "The Mortality of the Divine Emilie"; "The Jest"; "A Speaking Likeness"; "A Game of Faro"; "The Vengeance of the Cherry-Stone"; "Apamé"; "White Man's Magic"; "Utukuluk"; "How Yamko Married 14 Wives"; "The Tooth of Tuloo"; "The Great Beast of Kafue"; "The Judgment of Big Man"; "The Vengeance of Ounaka."

GRAVES, ROBERT (26 July 1895–) British poet and novelist. He served as an officer in the Royal Welsh Fusiliers where, under the influence of Siegfried Sassoon, he began to write poetry in earnest. Three volumes had been published by 1917, while he was still on active service. After serving as Professor of English at U. of Cairo, he separated from his wife and went to Majorca. There he and Laura Riding conducted the Seizin Press until the Spanish Civil War forced them to leave the island. Later he returned there.
He is noted for *I, Claudius* and its sequel *Claudius the God*

(both 1934), which are magnificent reconstructions of Roman life. He and George Orwell were hailed in 1949 in the *Times Literary Supplement* as the two living masters of the plain prose style. His short story "The Shout" (1926) has been reprinted in *F&SF* (Apr 1952, May 1959) and also in his *Collected Short Stories* (Cassell, London, 3rd ed., 1966). A story in *Punch*, to which he regularly contributes, was "An Appointment for Candlemas" (1954; *F&SF*, Oct 1955).
Fiction
Golden Fleece, The (Cassell, London, 1944, 371 pp., 12/6; 1951, 7/6) (*Hercules, My Shipmate*, Creative Age, New York, 1945, 465 pp., illus., $3.00; Cassell, Toronto, $3.25; Grosset, New York, 1957, $1.25; Universal: UL19, 1957, 467 pp., pa $1.25; Pyramid: S1346, 1966, 463 pp., pa 85¢)
A retelling of the story of Jason and the Golden Fleece.
Hercules, My Shipmate See *Golden Fleece, The*
Seven Days in New Crete (Cassell, 1949, 288 pp., 9/6) (McClelland, Toronto, $3.00) (*Watch the North Wind Rise*, Creative Age, 1949, 290 pp., $3.00; Avon: V2075, 1964, 254 pp., pa 75¢) (*Kärlek Pa Nya Kreta* [Swedish], Tiden, 1950)
A utopian future world with poets and magicians the only intellectuals.
Watch the North Wind Rise See *Seven Days in New Crete*

GRAY, CURME
Fiction
Murder in Millennium VI (Shasta, Chicago, 1952, 249 pp., $3.00)
Sf detective story, set in a matriarchy 6,000 years in the future. It is given an extended review in D. Knight's *In Search of Wonder*.

GRAY, NICHOLAS STUART
Fiction
Down in the Cellar (Dobson, London, 1961, 205 pp., illus.—E. Ardizzone, 12/6) (McClelland, Toronto, $2.50)
Juvenile with an element of magic.
Grimbold's Other World (Faber, London, 1963, 158 pp., illus.—Charles W. Stewart, 19/-)
Juvenile—a foundling named Muffler and his mysterious cat Grimbold enter the dangerous world of magic.
Mainly in Moonlight [C] (Faber, London, 1965, 159 pp., illus.—C. W. Stewart, 21/-) (Meredith, New York, 1967, viii+182 pp., $3.50)
12 stories of sorcery and magic for children (U.S. ed. subtitled "Ten Stories of Sorcery and the Supernatural," omits 3rd and 6th): "The Sorcerer's Apprentice"; "The Reluctant Familiar"; "The Hunting of the Dragon"; "Mainly in Moonlight"; "A Letter to My Love"; "The Star Beast"; "A Message in a Bottle"; "According to Tradition"; "The Silver Ship"; "The Lady's Quest"; "The Man Who Sold Magic"; "The Thunder Cat."
Over the Hills to Fabylon (Dobson, 1968, 206 pp., illus.—author, 21/-)
Fairy tale of a city with magic.
Seventh Swan, The (Dobson, 1962, 252 pp., illus.—Joan J. Farjeon, 15/-)
Juvenile adventure based on the legend of the "Wild Swans." It is also in play form (Dobson, 1962, 10/6; pa 5/-).
Stone Cage, The (Dobson, 1963, 246 pp., illus.—author, 15/-)
Fairy story of the girl who as a prisoner in a high tower lets down her hair for her lover. There is also a trip to the Moon, etc. It is also in play form (Dobson, 1963, 10/6; pa 5/-).

GRAYSON, CHARLES (1905–)
Anthology
Golden Argosy, The [with V. H. Cartmell] (Dial, New York, 1947, 11 + 656 pp., $3.75; rev. 1955) (Longmans, Toronto, $4.50) (Bantam: F1441, 1956, 403 pp., pa 50¢, 1960 [25 stories marked †])
40 stories, many fantasy, selected from *Argosy*: "I'm a Fool"†, S. Anderson; "The Happy Hypocrite," M. Beerbohm; "The Devil and Daniel Webster"†, S. V. Benét; "The Damned Thing," A. Bierce; "The Chink and the Child"†, T. Burke; "Paul's Case"†, Willa Cather; "Back for Christmas"†, J. Collier; "Youth," J. Con-

rad; "The Bar Sinister," R. H. Davis; "The Red-Headed League"†, A. C. Doyle; "A Rose for Emily"†, W. Faulkner; "Old Man Minick"†, Edna Ferber; "The Rich Boy," F. S. Fitzgerald; "The Celestial Omnibus"†, E. M. Forster; "The Three Strangers"†, T. Hardy; "The Outcasts of Poker Flat," B. Harte; "The Killers," E. Hemingway; "The Gift of the Magi"†, O. Henry; "The Gioconda Smile"†, A. Huxley; "The Monkey's Paw," W. W. Jacobs; "The Man Who Would Be King," "The Incarnation of Krishna Mulvaney"†, R. Kipling; "Champion"†, R. Lardner; "To Build a Fire," J. London; "The Fly"†, Katherine Mansfield; "Rain"†, W. S. Maugham; "Big Blonde," Dorothy Parker; "The Murders in the Rue Morgue," "The Gold-Bug"†, E. A. Poe; "Flowering Judas"†, Katherine A. Porter; "Tobermory"†, Saki; "The Leader of the People"†, J. Steinbeck; "Markheim," "A Lodging for the Night"†, R. L. Stevenson; "The Lady, or, the Tiger?"†, F. R. Stockton; "Monsieur Beaucaire"†, B. Tarkington; "The Secret World of Walter Mitty"†, J. Thurber; "The Jumping Frog"†, M. Twain; "The Other Wise Man"†, H. Van Dyke; "Chickamauga," T. Wolfe.

GREEN, JOSEPH L(EE) (14 Jan 1931–) U.S. free-lance writer.
Series
Refuge. Encounters with natives on an alien world. All in *NW*: "Initiation Rites" (Apr 1962); "The Colonist" (Aug 1962); "Life-Force" (Nov 1962); "Transmitter Problem" (Dec 1962); "The Old-Man-in-the-Mountain" (June 1963); "Refuge" (July 1963).
Fiction
Loafers of Refuge, The (Ballantine: U2233, 1965, 160 pp., pa 50¢) (Gollancz, London, 1965, 176 pp., 15/-) (Pan: X651, 1967, 175 pp., pa 3/6)
Chapters I and II as in the series above, but stories 3 to 5 rearranged. Psi communication, and relations between human colonists and natives on a new world.

GREEN, ROGER (GILBERT) L(ANCELYN) (2 Nov 1918–) British author; M.A., B.Litt. (Oxon). He was Deputy Librarian at Merton College, Oxford, 1945-50, and William Noble Research Fellow in English at Liverpool U., 1950-52. He has contributed to the *Times Literary Supplement*, *Books and Bookman* and *Quarterly Review*, etc. He has had many books on literature, and has also translated *Two Satyr Plays* (Penguin, 1957, pa). More recently he wrote *C. S. Lewis*, examining the writings of that author (Bodley Head, 1963, 7/6).
Fiction
From the World's End (Edmund Ward, London, 1948, 128 pp., 7/6)
Weird story set in the Welsh mountains.
Nonfiction
Into Other Worlds (Schuman, London, 1957, 190 pp., 16/-) (Abelard-Schuman, New York, 1958, 190 pp., $3.75)
A digest of fiction dealing with voyages into space, from Lucian to C. S. Lewis. It is somewhat similar to P. Moore's *Science and Fiction* (1957), but freer with quotations, some being quite long. It has literary interest.

GREENBERG, MARTIN (1918–) U.S. anthologist and publisher. He married in 1941. He was in the U.S. Army 1942-45, becoming a corporal and winning 5 battle stars in the European campaign. In 1948 he was one of the founders of Gnome Press, specializing in science fiction and fantasy, and became its president. In 1958 he bought out the stock of Fantasy Press, and later that of Fantasy Publishing Co. Inc., and with these and Gnome Press works he began his very successful Pick-A-Book plan for low-priced books.
Anthologies
All About the Future (Gnome, New York, 1955, 374 pp., $3.50)
Sf, 6 stories and 4 nonfact articles (by Wellen), with compiler's foreword and introductions "Where To?" R. A. Heinlein, and "Let's Not," I. Asimov: "The Midas Plague," F. Pohl; "Un-Man," P. Anderson; "Granny Won't Knit," T. Sturgeon; "Natural State," D. Knight; "Hobo God," M. Jameson; "Blood Bank," W. M. Miller; "Excerpts From *Encyclopedia of Galactic Culture*: 'Origins of Galactic Etiquette,' 'Origins of Galactic Law,' 'Origins of Galactic Slang,' 'Origins of Galactic Medicine,' " edited by E. Wellen.

Coming Attractions (Gnome, 1957, 254 pp., $3.50)
Nonfiction, 11 articles with introduction by D. W. Batteau: "A Letter to the Martians," W. Ley; "How to Learn Martian," C. F. Hockette; "Language for Time Travellers," L. S. de Camp; "Geography for Time Travellers," W. Ley; "Time Travel and the Law," C. M. Kornbluth; "Space Fix," R. S. Richardson; "Space War," W. Ley; "Space War Tactics," M. Jameson; "Fuel for the Future," J. Hatcher; "How to Count on Your Fingers," F. Pohl; "Interplanetary Copyright," D. F. Reines.
Crucible of Power, The See *Five Science Fiction Novels*
Five Science Fiction Novels (Gnome, 1952, 13 + 282 pp., $3.50) (*The Crucible of Power*, Bodley Head, London, 1953, 236 pp., 8/6 [3 novels marked †])
Sf, 5 novels: "But Without Horns"†, N. W. Page (*Unknown*, June 1940); "Destiny Times Three," F. Leiber (*ASF*, sr2, Mar 1945); "Crisis in Utopia"†, N. L. Knight (*ASF*, sr2, July 1940); "The Chronicler," A. E. van Vogt (*ASF*, sr2, Oct 1946); "The Crucible of Power"†, J. Williamson (*ASF*, Jan 1939). Some have since seen further reprinting.
Journey to Infinity (Gnome, 1951, 381 pp., $3.50) ([German], 8 SF Stories, Heyne Anthologien 8, 1964, pa [stories marked †])
Prepublication title: "Men Everlasting"—it attempts sf history of Man. Sf, 12 stories with introduction by F. Pratt: "False Dawn," A. B. Chandler; "Atlantis," E. E. Smith; "Letter to a Phoenix"†, F. Brown; "Unite and Conquer"†, T. Sturgeon; "Breakdown"†, J. Williamson; "Dance of a New World"†, J. D. MacDonald; "Mother Earth"†, I. Asimov; "There Shall Be Darkness"†, C. L. Moore; "Taboo"†, F. Leiber; "Overthrow," C. Cartmill; "Barrier of Dread," Judith Merril; "Metamorphosite"†, E. F. Russell.
Men Against the Stars (Gnome, 1950, 351 pp., $2.95) (Grayson, London, 1951, 256 pp., 8/6 [8 stories marked †]) (Pyramid: G-234, 1957, 191 pp., pa 35¢; F852, 1963, pa 40¢ [9 stories marked p])
Sf, 12 stories arranged as the story of the future conquest of space; foreword by the compiler, and introduction by W. Ley: "Trends"†, I. Asimov; "Men Against the Stars"†p, M. W. Wellman; "The Red Death of Mars"†p, R. M. Williams; "Locked Out," H. B. Fyfe; "The Iron Standard"†p, L. Padgett; "Schedule"p, H. Walton; "Far Centaurus"†p, A. E. van Vogt; "Cold Front"p, H. Clement; "The Plants"p, M. Leinster; "Competition"†p, E. M. Hull; "Bridle and Saddle"†, I. Asimov; "When Shadows Fall"†p, L. R. Hubbard.
Robot and the Man, The (Gnome, 1953, 251 pp., $2.95) (Grayson, 1954, 224 pp., 9/6) (*Die Roboter und wir* [German], *TS*: 50, 1962 [7 stories marked †; omitted ones were in *Utopia* mag.])
Sf, 10 stories: "Mechanical Answer," J. D. MacDonald; "Self-Portrait," B. Wolfe; "Deadlock"†, L. Padgett; "Robinc"†, H. H. Holmes; "Burning Bright"†, J. Browning; "Final Command"†, A. E. van Vogt; "Though Dreamers Die"†, L. del Rey; "Rust"†, J. Kelleam; "Robots Return," R. M. Williams; "Into Thy Hands"†, L. del Rey.
Travellers of Space (Gnome, 1951, 400 pp., illus.–E. Cartier, $3.95)
Sf, 14 stories, with compiler's foreword and introduction by W. Ley: "Rocketeers Have Shaggy Ears," K. Bennett; "Christmas Tree," C. S. Youd; "The Forgiveness of Tenchu Taen," F. A. Kummer; "Episode on Dhee Minor," H. Walton; "The Shape of Things," R. Bradbury; "Columbus Was a Dope," L. Monroe; "Attitude," H. Clement; "The Ionian Circle," Wm. Tenn; "Trouble on Tantalus," P. S. Miller; "Placet Is a Crazy Place," F. Brown; "Action on Azura," R. Osborne; "The Rull," A. E. van Vogt; "The Double Dyed Villains," P. Anderson; "Bureau of Slick Tricks," H. B. Fyfe. Cartier's work is 16 full-page illus. of "Life on Other Worlds," with related description "The Interstellar Zoo," D. Kyle. There is also a science fiction dictionary.

GREENE, GRAHAM (2 Oct 1904–) British author. He was educated at Berkhamsted and Balliol College, Oxford. His first book was *Bubbling April* (verse, 1925). He was sub-editor on *The Times* 1926-30. His first novel (*The Man Within*, 1929) and later ones showed clearly the influence of such authors as Stevenson, Conrad

and Woolf. After other books he became widely know with his *Brighton Rock* (1938); he then won the 1940 Hawthornden Prize with *The Power and the Glory*. With Dorothy Craigie he has written many juveniles. His script for the film *The Third Man* (1949) helped give him the mantle of being one of the world's finest writers of suspense thrillers. His *Our Man in Havana* (Heinemann, 1958) is listed as a tale of the future in the I. F. Clarke bibliography *The Tale of the Future* (1961).
Fiction
Nineteen Stories [C] (Heinemann, London, 1947, 231 pp., 8/6) (Viking, New York, 1949, 247 pp., $2.75) (Lion: LL31, 1955, 192 pp., pa 35¢)

19 stories; 6 considered fantasy; 8 of these stories originally appeared in *The Basement Room* (Cresset): "The Basement Room"; "The End of the Party"; "I Spy"; "The Innocent"; "A Drive in the Country"; "Across the Bridge"; "Jubilee"; "Brother"; "Proof Positive" (fantasy, *F&SF*, Aug 1952); "A Chance for Mr. Lever"; "The Hint of an Explanation" (fantasy); "The Second Death" (fantasy); "A Day Saved" (fantasy); "A Little Place Off the Edgware Road" (fantasy); "The Case for the Defence"; "When Greek Meets Greek"; "Men at Work"; "Alas, Poor Maling" (fantasy); "The Other Side of the Border."

GREENE, J(OSEPH) I(NGHAM) (1897–)
Series
Dig Allen [juvenile books published by Golden Press, New York, $1.00]: *Journey to Jupiter* (1961; [Dutch], De Geillistreerde pers, Amsterdam, 1964), *Lost City of Uranus* (1962), *Robots of Saturn* (1962).

GREENER, LESLIE English author and archaeologist, now living in Tasmania. In World War II he was a prisoner of war in Singapore. He then spent 10 years as a journalist in Sydney, following which he became Head of Adult Education in Hobart, Tasmania. Since about 1955 he has been concentrating on archaeology and has made a number of visits to Egypt in this connection.
Fiction
Moon Ahead! (Viking, New York, 1951, 256 pp., illus.–W. Pene du Bois, $2.50) (Bodley Head, London, 1952, 192 pp., illus.–du Bois, 9/6) (Puffin: PS107, 1957, 160 pp., pa 2/6) (*Flug ins Ungewisse* [German], Ueberreuther, 1954)

Juvenile; an Australian and an American boy go with their parents on the first trip to the Moon. Well-written and scientifically accurate.

GREENFIELD, IRVING A. (22 Feb 1928–) U.S. free-lance writer.
Fiction
Waters of Death [pa] (Lancer: 73-672, 1967, 157 pp., pa 60¢)
Intrigue with a food crisis and a rebellion of sea farmers.
Nonfiction
UFO Report, The [pa] (Lancer: 73-624, 1967, 141 pp., pa 60¢)

GREENFIELD, LOUIS
Anthology
Rue Morgue No. 1 See STOUT, R. (co-anthologist)

GREGORY, FRANKLIN (1901–) U.S. newspaperman and author. He studied journalism at U. of Iowa. He wrote eight novels before selling *Cipher of Death* (1934), and has published a number of others since. He has written a number of shorter works for magazines, of which sf/fantasy includes "The Poisonous Soul" (*Ten Story*, n'te, Spr 1951) and "The Screaming Shapes" (*AS*, n, Aug 1950). He has also worked in public relations in the Far East.
Fiction
White Wolf, The (Random, New York, 1941, 271 pp., $2.00) (Macmillan, Toronto, $2.50) (*FFM*, Aug 1952)

Set in the modern U.S.A.; a girl unconsciously becomes a werewolf.

GRENDON, STEPHEN (pseud) See DERLETH, A. W.

GREY, CHARLES (pseud) See TUBB, E. C.

GRIFFITH, GEORGE (? –4 June 1906) British author. The son of a country clergyman, he had a venturesome life, going around the world six times. In his travels he journeyed once across the Rockies, three times over the Andes, three times around the Horn; he found the source of the Amazon River system, and he flew in a balloon to France. He was a very popular writer in his day, but his works are now almost forgotten. Those of sf/fantasy adventure interest include *The Angel of the Revolution* (1893), *Olga Romanoff* (1894), *Valdar* (1895), *The Virgin of the Sun* (1898) and *The Honeymoon in Space* (1901).
Fiction
Gambles With Destiny [C] (F. V. White, London, 1899, viii+232 pp., 6/-)

5 stories (all sf or fantasy), not listed in the Bleiler *Checklist*: "Hellville U.S.A."; "The Great Crellin Comet"; "A Corner in Lightning"; "A Genius for a Year"; "The Plague-Ship 'Tupisa'."

GRIFFITH, MARY (ca. 1800–1877) U.S. author. She was from Charles Hope, New Jersey. She was noted as a writer on agricultural subjects and on moral and social reform.
Fiction
Three Hundred Years Hence (First part of *Camperdown; or, News From Our Neighborhood: Being Sketches* [by "an Author of Our Neighborhood"], Carey Lea & Blanchard, Philadelphia, 1836, 9 + 300 pp.) (Prime Press 'American Utopian Novel No. 2,' Philadelphia, 1950, 131 pp., $2.50, no jacket, 500 copies)

An anticipation of Bellamy and Wells. The hero goes into a deep sleep in a deep chamber and awakens in the utopian states of Pennsylvania, New Jersey and New York.

GRIFFITHS, JOHN
Fiction
Survivors, The (Collins, London, 1965, 156 pp., 16/-)
Interplay of personalities in problems of survival in a World War III shelter project in a disued Cornish copper mine.

GRILLOT DE GIVRY, EMILE (1870–)
Nonfiction
Pictorial Anthology of Witchcraft, Magic and Alchemy [Trans.–J. C. Locke] (Houghton, New York, 1931, 395 pp., $10.00) (Harrap, London, 1931, 42/-) (Univ. Books, New York, 1958, quarto, $10.00)

A volume containing 400 quite horrible illustrations and many useful spells.
Picture Museum of Sorcery, Magic and Alchemy [Trans.–J. C. Locke] (Univ. Books, 1963, 376 pp., illus., $17.50)

Includes sections on the Jewish and Christian Cabbalists, Astrology and the Macrocosm and Microcosm, Metoposcopy, Physiognomy, Cheiromancy, etc. It has a wealth of curious and beautiful pictures.

GRIMSHAW, BEATRICE (? –30 June 1953) Adventure writer who has had some works of fantasy interest. The Bleiler *Checklist* gives the novel *The Sorcerer's Stone* (Winston, Philadelphia, 1914; London, nd), but her *The Candles of Katara* is a non-weird collection.
Fiction
Valley of Never Come Back, The [C] (Hurst & Blackett, London, nd, 287 pp.)

Not listed in Bleiler *Checklist*, but some stories tend to fantasy. 9 stories: "The Valley of Never Come Back"; "Lost Wings"; "The Island Grave"; "Isles of Peace"; "Under the She-Dagon"; "The Woman in the Cage"; "Peak of the Moon"; "Something Lost"; "The Long, Long Day."

GRINNELL, DAVID (pseud) See WOLLHEIM, D. A.

GRONER, AUGUSTA
Fiction
City of the Dead (*Mene Tekel: a tale of strange happenings*

[Trans.—Grace I. Colbron], Duffield, New York, 1912, 243 pp., $1.20) (*FFM*, Apr 1948)

An archaeologist deciphers past writings to foil a hoax.

Mene Tekel: a tale of strange happenings See *City of the Dead*

GROOM, PELHAM
Fiction

Purple Twilight, The (T. Werner Laurie, London, 1948, 282 pp., 8/6; 1956, 6/-)

A story leading naturally up to a trip to Mars and the nature of its inhabitants.

GROULING, THOMAS E(DWARD) (9 June 1940–) U.S. English instructor.
Fiction

Project 12 (Vantage, New York, 1962, 109 pp., $2.75)

A simple story of an attempt at Cape Canaveral to put a man into space, doomed to disaster by internecine jealousies and hostilities.

GROVES, J(OHN) W(ILLIAM) (6 Nov 1910–) British novelist; his first connection with science fiction was the publication of the story "The Sphere of Death" in *AS* (Oct 1931).
Fiction

Shellbreak (R. Hale, London, 1968, 190 pp., 18/-)

A man awakens in the future with the secret of collapsing a force shell around a great city; he helps rebels against the city's dictators.

GROVES, JAY (VOELKER) (4 Aug 1922–) U.S. economics instructor.
Fiction

Fireball at the Lake: A Story of Encounter With Another World (Exposition, New York, 1967, 65 pp., $3.00)

GRUBB, DAVIS U.S. author and anthologist. He wrote *The Night of the Hunter*.
Fiction

One Foot in the Grave [pa] See *Twelve Tales of Suspense and the Supernatural*

Twelve Tales of Suspense and the Supernatural [C] (Scribner, New York, 1964, 175 pp., $3.95) (Crest: d814, 1965, 144 pp., pa 50¢) (*One Foot in the Grave*, Arrow: 925, 1967, 186 pp., pa 3/6)

12 stories, of which 8 are reprinted from *Collier's, Cavalier, WT,* etc.: "Busby's Rat"; "The Rabbit Prince"; "Radio"; "One Foot in the Grave"; "Moonshine"; "The Man Who Stole the Moon"; "Nobody's Watching!"; "The Horsehair Trunk"; "The Blue Glass Bottle"; "Wynken, Blynken and Nod"; "Return of Verge Likens"; "Where the Woodbine Twineth."

GUERARD, ALBERT JOSEPH (1914–)
Fiction

Night Journey (Knopf, New York, 1950, 357 pp., $3.00) (McClelland, Toronto, $3.50) (Longmans, London, 1951, 356 pp., 10/6)

An indictment of ideological wars, showing the future with both sides losing; a chronicle of terror, betrayal and confusion, often quite effective.

GUIEU, JIMMY French author. He has had a number of novels in the *Anticipation* series of Le Fleuve Noir, some of which have been translated into Italian for *I Romanzi di Urania* (later *Urania*), and also into German.
Nonfiction

Flying Saucers From Another World (*Les Soucoupes Volantes Viennent d'un Autre Monde*, Editions du Fleuve Noire, Paris, 1954) [Trans.—C. Ashleigh]: (Hutchinson, London, 1956, 248 pp., illus., 12/6)

The British edition has only 10 of the 20 original extraordinary illustrations.

GUIN, WYMAN (WOODS) (1 Mar 1915–) U.S. science fiction author. He has had a number of stories published, mainly in *Galaxy Science Fiction*.

Fiction

Living Way Out [C] [pa] (Avon: S298, 1967, 208 pp., pa 60¢)

Sf, 7 stories: "A Man of the Renaissance"; "My Darling Hecate"; "The Delegate From Guapanga"; "The Root and the Ring"; "Trigger Tide"; "Volpla"; "Beyond Bedlam."

GUINN, ROBERT M. (1911–) U.S. publisher. Born in Mount Vernon, N.Y., he attended New York U. 1930-32. He is married, and has worked mostly in the advertising business. He has been President and Director of The Guinn Co. since 1941 and of Galaxy Publishing Corp. since 1951. The latter firm took over the publishing of *Galaxy SF* from World Pub. Co., and later purchased *If*. Guinn is also Director of The Barmaray Corp.

GUNDRAN, OLIVE (1912–)
Fiction

Mysterious Stranger (Comet Press 'Milestone,' New York, 1958, 56 pp., $2.00)

GUNN, JAMES E(DWIN) (11 July 1923–) U.S. author and English instructor, born in Kansas City, Mo. of a family steeped in printer's ink: his grandfather was a country editor, his father was a printer, two uncles were pressmen and a third was a proofreader. Graduating from U. of Kansas with a B.S. in Journalism, he served three years in the U.S. Navy in World War II, after which he studied speech and drama at Northwestern U., obtaining his M.A. in English in 1951. He began writing in 1947, when he wrote a full-length play, followed by features and scripts for local newspapers and radio. In 1948 he began writing sf and sold 9 out of 10 stories; they were published under the pseudonym "Edwin James." His M.A. thesis, a critical analysis of science fiction, was published in *Dynamic SF* (Mar 1953, June 1953, Oct 1953, Jan 1954). He has been an editor for a publisher of paperback reprints, assistant director of Civil Defense in Kansas City, and managing editor of K.U. Alumni Publications. He now serves at Univ. of Kansas as administrator to the Chancellor for University Relations and as an instructor in English. Four of his stories have been dramatised over NBC radio and one was dramatised on TV's Desilu Playhouse ("The Cave of Night," *GSF*, Feb 1955). His stories have been reprinted in various countries; a German translation not mentioned below is "The Sine of the Magus" (*Beyond*, short novel, May 1954), published in *UZ*: 491, 1966.
Fiction

Future Imperfect [C] [pa] (Bantam: J2717, 1964, 137 pp., pa 40¢)

Sf, 10 stories: "The Misogynist"; "The Last Word"; "Little Orphan Android"; "The Stilled Patter"; "Skin Game"; "Every Day Is Christmas"; "The Girls Who Were Really Built"; "Survival Policy"; "Tsylana"; "Feeding Time."

Immortals, The [pa] (Bantam: J2484, 1962, 154 pp., pa 40¢; H3915, 1968, pa 60¢) (*Il rosso fiume dell'eternità* [Italian], *Cosmo*: 144, 1963) (*Der Gammastoff* [German], Goldmann, 1964, 1964 pa)

A "novel" in parts originally published as follows: I. "New Blood" (*ASF*, Oct 1955); II. "Donor" (*Fan*, Nov 1960); III. "Medic" ("Not So Great an Enemy," *Venture*, July 1957); IV. "Immortal" (rev. of "The Immortals," *Star SF No. 4* [Pohl], 1958). Immortals fight to stay alive.

Joy Makers, The (Bantam: A2219, 1961, 160 pp., pa 35¢) (Gollancz, London, 1963, 191 pp., 15/-) (SF B.C. [S.J.], 1964, 6/-) (*Wächter des Glücks* [German], Pabel: 290, 1966, pa)

Combination of: "The Unhappy Man" (*FU*, Feb 1955); "The Naked Sky" (*SS*, Fall 1955); "Name Your Pleasure" (*TWS*, Win 1955). Story of a future civilization based on hedonism and synthetic bliss.

Star Bridge See WILLIAMSON, J. (co-author)

Station in Space [C] [pa] (Bantam: A1825, 1958, 156 pp., pa 35¢)

Sf, 5 stories: "The Cave of Night"; "Hoax"; "The Big Wheel"; "Powder Keg"; "Space Is a Lonely Place."

This Fortress World (Gnome, New York, 1955, 216 pp., $3.00) (Ace: D-223, 1957, 190 pp., pa 35¢; with *The 13th Immortal*)

(*Von Mauen Ungeben* [German], *UG*: 60, 1959)
The power of a future church and one man's fight against it.

GUNN, NEIL M(ILLER) (8 Nov 1891–) Scottish novelist. He worked in Civil Service and for some years his job took him all over the Highlands. He started writing as a pastime. His sixth novel, *Highland River* (1937), was awarded the James Tait Black Memorial Prize. He writes mainly about Scotland. Of fantasy interest is *The Green Isle of the Great Deep* (Faber, 1944).
Fiction
Well at World's End, The (Faber, London, 1951, 295 pp., 12/6)
The story of the quest for the well.

GUNTER, ARCHIBALD CLAVERING (25 Oct 1847–Feb 1907) American novelist, playwright and publisher, as well as one-time railway civil engineer, chemist and stockbroker. He wrote a number of books and also edited *Gunter's Magazine*.
Fiction
City of Mystery, The [C] (Ward Lock, London, 1904, 275 pp., 5/-)
3 stories of weird interest, set in Paris of the 1720's (not listed in Bleiler *Checklist*): "Secret From Italy"–story of a wizard and dealer of the black arts; "The Mystery of the Garden Pavilion"–ghost story; "The Agent of D'Argenson"–a story of punishment.

GUNTHER, GOTTHARD German philosopher, now residing in the U.S.A. He was a lecturer in logic and the philosophy of history at Leipzig U. in 1939. Because of Hitler he left Germany and went to South Africa as Carnegie Lecturer at U. of Capetown, Stellenbosch. He arrived in the U.S.A. in 1940, and until 1944 was a lecturer and assistant professor at Colby College, Waterville, Maine. Since 1945 he has been engaged in research on non-Aristotelian logic and its applications to problems of history. He was living in Richmond, Va., in the early 1950's. He has published two books: *Grundzüge Einer Neuen Theorie des Denkens in Hegels Logik* (New Elements in Thinking in Hegel's Logic) and *Christliche Metaphysik* (Christian Metaphysics). He is of interest to the sf field because of articles in the sf magazines. Of five articles in *Startling Stories* 1953-55, three were on seetee and logic: "The Seetee Mind" (Spr 1954), "The Soul of a Robot" (Win 1954), and "The Thought Translator" (Spr 1955). He has also appeared in *ASF*.
Anthology
Überwindung von Raum und Zeit (K. Rauch, Dusseldorf, 1952, 239 pp., DM9.80)
The first book anthology of U.S. sf writers in German. The stories were translated by O. Schrag and E. Klein (1 story). 7 stories, with afterword by the compiler: "Flucht" ["Desertion"], C. D. Simak; "Einbruch der Nacht" ["Nightfall"], I. Asimov; "Wer da?" ["Who Goes There?"], J. W. Campbell; "Die Lotusesser" ["The Lotus Eaters"], S. G. Weinbaum; "Zeit und wieder Zeit" ["Time and Time Again"], H. B. Piper; "Wiedererweckung" ["The Monster"], A. E. van Vogt; "Mimsy Were the Borogoves," L. Padgett.

GUTHRIE, ELLEN JANE EMMA
Fiction
Tales of the Covenanters [C] (Hamilton Adams, London, & Thomas D. Morrison, Glasgow, 1888, 303 pp.)
Fantasy of 6 stories: "A Tale of Bothwell Bridge"; "The Laird of Culzean"; "Peden's Stone"; "The Murder of Inchdarnie"; "The Laird of Lag"; "The Suitor's Seat."

GUTHRIE, THOMAS A(NSTEY) (8 Aug 1856–10 Mar 1934) British novelist and playwright, known under his pseudonym "F. Anstey." He was educated at King's College, London, and Trinity Hall, Cambridge, and was called to the bar in 1880. His reputation began with the humorous fantasy *Vice-Versa* (Appleton, 1882); this was followed by many other novels and collections both within and outside the fantasy field. His best play was *The Man From Blankley's* (1901).
Fiction [as F. Anstey] [Incomplete—other titles in Bleiler *Checklist*]
Black Poodle, and Other Tales, The [C] (Longmans Green, Lon-

don, 1884, 269 pp., illus.) (Lovell, New York, 1896, 264 pp., illus.)
Fantasy, 10 stories: "Accompanied on the Flute"; "The Black Poodle"; "The Curse of the Catafalques"; "Farewell Appearance"; "The Return of Agamemnon"; "The Siren"; "The Story of a Sugar Prince"; "Toy Tragedy"; "The Undergraduate's Aunt"; "The Wraith of Barnium."
Brass Bottle, The (Appleton, New York, 1900, 355 pp., frontis.) (*Bronsflaskan*, [Swedish], Fahlcrants, 1901) (in *Humour and Fantasy* [Anstey], 1931) (Penguin: 542, 1946, 227 pp., pa 1/6) (Penguin [U.S.], 1953, pa 35¢)
Djinns raise merry hell with modern Londoners.
Humour and Fantasy [C] (J. Murray, London, 1931, 1174 pp., 8/6) (Dutton, New York, 1931, 1175 pp., $2.50)
6 books: *Vice Versa*; *The Tinted Venus*; *A Fallen Idol*; *The Talking Horse*; *Salted Almonds*; *The Brass Bottle*.
Talking Horse, The [C] (J. W. Lowell, New York, 1891, 298 pp.) (Smith Elder & Co., New York, 1892, 320 pp.)
10 stories (Smith Elder edition): "The Talking Horse"; "The Good Little Girl"; "A Matter of Taste"; "Don: The Story of a Greedy Don"; "Taken by Surprise"; "Paleface and Redskin"; "Shut Out"; "Tommy's Hero"; "A Canine Ishmail"; "Marjory."

H

HAAS, CHARLES
Fiction
Adel Hitro (Vantage, New York, 1962, 93 pp., $2.95)
A dictator using laser power throws all red-headed people into concentration camps.

HABER, HEINZ (1913–) German scientist, specializing in space medicine. He has been a physicist and astronomer in the U.S. Air Force School of Space Medicine, and now works in the Dept. of Engineering at the U. of California. He has contributed many articles to popular nonfiction collections on space technology, etc. A work of interest is *Stars, Men and Atoms* (Washington Square, 1966, pa).
Nonfiction
Men in Space (*Menschen, Raketen und Planeten* [German], Blüchert, 1955) (Bobbs-Merrill, Indianapolis, 1953, 291 pp., illus.–J. Milord, $3.75) (Sidgwick Jackson, London, 1953, 291 pp., illus.–Milord, 30/-)
The first book on the physiology of man in space, covering experimentation on weightlessness, lack of oxygen, etc.

HADFIELD, JOHN British anthologist. In the general field he has had such books as *A Book of Beauty* and *A Book of Britain*.
Anthology
Chamber of Horrors, A (Studio Vista, London, 1965, 320 pp., 37 illus., 28/-) (Little Brown, Boston, 1965, 320 pp., illus., $7.95) (Fontana: 1484, 1967, 285 pp., pa 5/-)
23 stories, plus verse and drawings, and compiler's introduction: *I. The Bells of Hell:* Lines by O. Wilde, John Webster, Shakespeare, and from 'The Book of Job'; "Recipe for Villainy" [excerpt], Thomas Middleton; "Exercise" [verse], George Crabbe; "Hell," "Satan" [v], John Milton; "Innocents' Song" [v], Charles Causey; "The Hunted Beast," T. F. Powys; "Captain Murderer," Charles Dickens; "Tailpiece" [v], Harry Graham. *II. Seeds of Destruction:* "Saturn" [v], Hesiod; "The Small Assassin," R. Bradbury; "Berenice," E. A. Poe; "Mr. Loveday's Little Outing," Evelyn Waugh; "Randolf's Party" [short], John Lennon; "Imitation of Things to Come" [play], Shakespeare; "The Tender Age," John

Collier; "More Spinned Against," John Wyndham. *III. Love and Death:* Lines by W. E. Henley and O. Wilde; "Necessity" [v], Harry Graham; "The Abyss," Leonid Andreyev; "A Woman Seldom Found," Wm. Sansom; "The Monk," M. G. Lewis; "Fair Elenor" [v], Wm. Blake; "Porphyria's Lover" [v], R. Browning; "At the Draper's" [v], Thomas Hardy; "An Actor of Parts," P. S.; "O Amiable Death," Shakespeare. *IV. Unquiet Minds:* Lines by J. Webster, J. Dryden, E. A. Poe and Anon.; "The Spectre-Smitten," Samuel Warren; "The Valley of Vain Desires" [v], John A. Symonds; "The Desire to Be a Man," Villiers de L'Isle Adam; "Minotaur" [v], M. Ayrton; "The Yellow Wall-Paper," Charlotte P. Gilman; "Bianca" [v], Arthur Symons; "Meeting With a Double" [v], George D. Painter; "Drugged" [v], W. de la Mare; "Miss Cornelius," W. F. Harvey; "Munny to the Rescue," Angus Wilson; "A Little Place off the Edgware Road," Graham Greene; "The Horrors of Sleep" [v], Emily Bronte. *V. Apparitions:* 'Revelation of St. John'; "Green Teas," J. S. Le Fanu; "The Upper Berth," F. M. Crawford; "William and Mary," Roald Dahl; "Skirmish," C. D. Simak. *VI. The Dance of Death:* "The Dance of Death" [v], C. Baudelaire; "The Mansions of the Dead" [v], John A. Symonds; "Holy-Day for Ghosts" [v], J. Dryden & N. Lee; "Thou Shell of Death" [v], Cyril Tourneur; "A Tough Tussle," A. Bierce; "The Ultimate Fear," Shakespeare; "The Living Death" [v], O. Wilde; "Envoi" [short], D. B. Wyndham Lewis.

HADFIELD, ROBERT L.
Nonfiction
Phantom Ship and Other Ghost Stories, The (G. Bles, London, 1937, 218 pp.)

Though listed by Bleiler as fiction, this title is nonfiction about ghosts and weird legends of the sea. It has bibliography, appendix and index.

HADLEY, ARTHUR T. U.S. journalist and author. As a 22-year-old U.S. Army captain in the invasion of Germany, he commanded the world's first propaganda unit, patrolling behind enemy lines with appeals to surrender. After the war he attended Yale (of which his grandfather was president); his thesis was on "fear in battle." In 1949 he joined *Newsweek* as a military correspondent, and later became White House correspondent. He then spent three years as an executive editor of the *New York Herald Tribune*. He is particularly noted for his satire *The Joy Wagon*. His later work *The Nation's Safety and Arms Control* (1961) was abridged as a series of articles in the *Melbourne Herald* from 16 Sep 1961.
Fiction
Joy Wagon, The (Viking, New York, 1958, 223 pp., $3.50) (Berkley: G-466, 1960, 158 pp., pa 35¢)

A comedy about the electronic computer that runs for President of the U.S.A. This work has sold more than 150,000 copies.

HADLEY, FRANKLIN T.
Fiction
Planet Big Zero [pa] (Monarch: 431, 1964, 126 pp., pa 40¢)
Adventure in a future galactic war.

HAGGARD, H(ENRY) RIDER (22 June 1856–14 May 1925) British author. He spent part of his younger life in South Africa. He then became a barrister in London in 1884, but was never very active in that profession. On the great success of his *King Solomon's Mines* (1885) he abandoned law completely and began writing full-time. He left a legacy of some 75 books in many fields. His autobiography was *The Days of My Life* (1926). Other works about him include J. E. Scott's *A Bibliography of the Works of Sir Henry Rider Haggard* (Elkin Mathews, Herts., 1948, 258 pp., 42/-); *The Cloak That I Left*, by his daughter, Lilias Rider Haggard (Hodder Stoughton, London, 1951, 18/-), giving a wealth of detail on his life; and a recent critical biography by the American academic Morton Cohen, *Rider Haggard: His Life and Works* (Hutchinson, 1960; Macmillan, 2nd ed., 1968, 45/- [new preface covering more recent films and books]). A brief review is also given by Malcolm Elwin in the MacDonald 1948 edition of *She*. Haggard's noted *She* and *King Solomon's Mines* have each had sequels and parodies by other writers.

Series
Quatermain, Allan. This character first appeared in *King Solomon's Mines* and then in a sequel *Allan Quatermain* in which he met his death. However, the author then donned the cloak of an editor discovering manuscripts of Quatermain's adventures, and these then appeared. The overall total was 15 books—in the main these covered lost races in different settings, and each had its own set of thrills. Most of these are covered below.

She. In series order: *Wisdom's Daughter*; *She and Allan*; *She*; *Ayesha*.

Zulu trilogy. *Marie* (1912; MacDonald, 1959); *Child of the Storm*; *Finished* (1916). Only the middle novel is covered below and in the Bleiler *Checklist*, but all embrace the magic of African witchdoctors and cover the early days of King Chaka's great power up to the last of the Zulu empire. The unforgettable character of Zikali the Witch-Doctor appears in all these novels. Allan Quatermain is also in them.

Fiction
[The following is a reasonably comprehensive coverage, but does not attempt to list all of the multitude of editions of *King Solomon's Mines* and *She*, nor the many cheap editions of the 1900's, nor the translations.

Longmans (London) published the following sets not listed within particular entries:

Romances (Uniform Edition, 1933, illus., 3/6): 1. *Allan Quatermain*; 2. *Allan's Wife and Other Tales*; 3. *Nada the Lily*; 4. *Black Heart and White Heart and Other Stories*; 5. *Montezuma's Daughter*; 6. *Pearl Maiden*; 7. *She*; 8. *The People of the Mist*; 9. *The World's Desire*; 10. *Lysbeth*; 11. *Cleopatra*; 12. *Swallow*.

Novels (Uniform Edition, 1933, 3/6): 1. *Mr. Meeson's Will*; 2. *Beatrice*; 3. *Joan Haste*; 4. *Stella Fregelius*; 5. *The Witch's Head*; 6. *Colonel Quaritch V.C.*

In the 1930's McKinley, Stone & Mackenzie (U.S.A.) also produced many titles in a uniform edition.]

Allan and the Holy Flower (Longmans Green, New York, 1915, 384 pp., illus., $2.00) (*The Holy Flower*, Ward Lock, London, 1915, 368 pp., illus.–M. Greiffenhagen, 6/-; 1917, 1/-; 1920, 320 pp., 2/-; 1926, 3/6) (MacDonald, London, 1954, 304 pp., illus.–H. Cowles, 8/6)

Allan and the Ice Gods (Doubleday Page, New York, 1927, 316 pp., $2.00) (Hutchinson, London, 1927, 287 pp., 7/6; 1928, 3/6; 1929, 2/6; 1930, 252 pp., 1/-; 1936, 2/6) (Grosset, New York, 1929, 75¢) (*FFM*, Apr 1947)
Subtitled: "A tale of beginnings."

Allan Quatermain (*Longman's Mag.*, sr8, Jan 1887) (Longmans, London, 1887, 335 pp., illus.–C. H. M. Kerr; 1904, 6/-) (Harper, New York, 1887, 310 pp., illus.) (Franklin News, Philadelphia, 1887, 270 pp., illus.) (Lovell, New York, 1887, 226 pp.) (MacDonald, 1949, 304 pp., illus.–H. Cowles, 8/6) (U. London 'Pilot Book,' 1950, 207 pp., illus., 2/9) (Hodder & Stoughton, London, 1951, 256 pp., pa 2/-; 1958, pa 2/6) (Royal Giant: 18, nd, 170 pp., pa 50¢ [½ book]) (Collins, London, 1955, 318 pp., illus.–W. Nickless, 5/-) (Nelson, London, 1956, 280 pp., illus., 4/-) (*Allan Quatermain & King Solomon's Mines*, Globe, New York, 1956, 336 pp., illus., $2.40) (Ballantine: X743, 1963, 222 pp., pa 60¢) (Hodder: 118, 1966, 255 pp., pa 3/6)
Sequel to *King Solomon's Mines*—the death of Allan.

Allan the Hunter: A Tale of Three Lions (*A Tale of Three Lions*, Lovell, New York, 1887, 58 pp.) (Lothrop, Boston, 1898, 111 pp., illus.) (in *Allan's Wife and Other Tales* [Haggard], certain editions)

Allan's Wife and Other Tales [C] (S. Blackett, London, 1889, 331 pp., illus.–M. Greiffenhagen & C. H. M. Kerr) (Munro, New York, 1889, 177 pp., pa) (Griffith Farrar Okeden & Welsh, London, *ca*. 1890, 331 pp., illus.–Greiffenhagen & Kerr) (Longmans, New York, $1.75) (MacDonald, 1951, 240 pp., illus.–H. Cowles, 8/6)

The title story is one of the lesser in the Quatermain series. The MacDonald ed. has 4 stories: "Allan's Wife"; "Hunter Quatermain's Story"; "A Tale of Three Lions"; "Long Odds."

Ancient Allan, The (*Cassell's Mag.*, sr7, Mar 1919) (Longmans Green, New York, 1920, 298 pp., illus.–A. Morrow, $2.00) (Cassell, London, 1920, 310 pp., 8/6; 1922, 246 pp., 2/-; 1925, 312 pp., 2/6) (*FFM*, Dec 1945)

Allan and Lady Ragnall mentally journey back and relive their lives in ancient Babylon.

Ayesha, the Return of She (Ward Lock, 1905, 384 pp., illus.–M. Greiffenhagen, 6/-; 1916, 1/-; 1917, 1/-; 1926, 317 pp., 3/6) (Doubleday, 1905, 359 pp., illus.) (Grosset Dunlap, 1905, 359 pp., illus.) (Garden City, New York, 1923, 95¢) (MacDonald, 1956, 304 pp., illus.–H. Cowles, 10/6) (Collins, 1957, 352 pp., illus.–W. Nickless, 5/-) (Icon: F14, 1964, 288 pp., pa 3/6) (Lancer: 74-899, 1967, 350 pp., pa 75¢)

Mystical fantasy set in bleak Tibet.

Belshazzar (S. Paul, London, 1930, 285 pp., 7/6; 1931, 3/6) (Doubleday, 1930, 306 pp., $1.00)

A picture of life at the courts of ancient Babylon and Egypt; historical rather than fantasy. This was Haggard's last book.

Benita, an African Romance (Cassell, 1906, 3+334 pp., illus.–G. Browne; 1920, 250 pp., 2/-; 1926, 310 pp., 2/6) (*The Spirit of Bambatse*, Longmans Green, New York, 1906, 329 pp.) (Chariot, 1952, pa 2/-)

Black Heart and White Heart and Other Stories [C] (Longmans, London, 1900, 426 pp., illus.–C. H. M. Kerr, 6/-; 1903, 3/6) (*Black Heart and White Heart and The Wizard*, Hodder Stoughton, 1924, 318 pp., 2/-)

The 1900 & 1903 editions contain the title story plus *Elissa* and *The Wizard*, q.v.

Child of Storm (Mameena) (Cassell, 1913, 364 pp., colour frontis. & illus.–A. C. Michael, 6/-; 1925, 311 pp., 2/6) (Longmans, New York, 1913, $2.00) (MacDonald, 1952, 256 pp., illus.–H. Cowles, 8/6)

Cleopatra (*Illustrated London News*, sr?, 1889) (Longmans, London, 1889, 316 pp., illus.–M. Greiffenhagen & R. C. Woodville; 1893) (Longmans, New York, 1927, $1.75) (Longmans, London, 1927, 352 pp., 3/6) (MacDonald, 1958, 273 pp., illus.–H. Cowles, 10/6) (Hodder: 620, 1963, 256 pp., pa 4/6) (Pocket Books: 7025, 1963, 290 pp., pa 50¢)

Subtitled "Being an Account of the Fall and Vengeance of Harmachis"; a tremendous novel of an attempt to dethrone Cleopatra and install the last rightful pharaoh in Egypt.

Elissa: The Doom of Zimbabwe. Black Heart and White Heart (Longmans Green, New York, 1900, 246 + 105 pp., illus., $2.00) [see also *Black Heart and White Heart*]

A story of Elissa, the ancient colony of Solomon which produced the gold of Ophir.

Eric Brighteyes (Longmans, London, 1891, 319 pp., illus.–Lancelot Speed; 3rd ed., 1893) (Harper, 1891, 319 pp.) (Harrap, London, 1925, 319 pp., 2/6) (MacDonald, 1949, 304 pp., illus.–Speed & H. Cowles, 8/6)

A retelling of an Icelandic saga.

Favourite Novels of H. Rider Haggard, The [C] See *Works of H. Rider Haggard, The*

Five Adventure Novels [C] (Dover, New York, 1951, 800 pp., $3.95)

5 novels: *She*; *Maiwa's Revenge*; *Allan Quatermain*; *Allan's Wife*; *King Solomon's Mines*.

Ghost Kings, The See *Lady of the Heavens, The*

Heart of the World (Longmans Green, New York, 1895, 347 pp.) (Longmans, London, 1896, 347 pp., illus.; 1897) (Hodder Stoughton, 1920, 323 pp.; 1928, 302 pp.) (Harrap, 1926, 302 pp., 2/6) (MacDonald, 1954, 304 pp., illus.–H. Cowles, 8/6)

Adventure about a lost city built entirely beneath a lake.

Heu-Heu, or, The Monster (Hutchinson, 1924, 286 pp., 7/6; 1925, 3/6) (Doubleday, 1924, 265 pp., $2.00) (Grosset, 1926, 75¢)

An Allan Quatermain story.

Holy Flower, The See *Allan and the Holy Flower*

Ivory Child, The (Cassell, 1916, 352 pp., colour frontis.–A. C. Michael, 6/-; 1926, 312 pp., 2/6) (Longmans, New York, 1916, 377 pp., illus.–Michael, $2.00) (MacDonald, 1958, 274 pp., illus.–H. Cowles, 10/6)

An Allan Quatermain story.

Jess (*The Cornhill Mag.*, sr12, May 1886) (Smith Elder, London,

1887, 336 pp.; 1905, 378 pp., 3/6) (Harper, 1887, 281 pp.) (Lovell, 1887, 242 pp.) (Newnes, London, 1899, 192 pp., illus.–M. Greiffenhagen, 6d) (Donohue Hennebery, Chicago, nd, 274 pp.)

A novel of South African life.

King Solomon's Mines (Cassell, 1885, 320 pp.; 1905, 318 pp., illus.–R. Flint; 1915, 350 pp., 3/6) (Lovell, 1886, 195 pp.) (Harper, 1887, 274 pp.) (Longmans, New York, 1901; 1926, $1.75) (Armed: 795, nd, 319 pp., pa) (Dell: 433, 1950, 192 pp., pa 25¢) (Royal Giant: 18, nd, 149 pp., pa 50¢ [½ book]) (Pan: 163, 1951, 191 pp., pa 1/6) (Ward Lock, 1951, quarto, 96 pp., text & illus. from MGM film, 8/6) (Collins, 1955, 236 pp., illus.–W. Nickless, 5/-) (MacDonald, 1956, 240 pp., illus.–H. Cowles, 10/6) (Nelson, 1956, 278 pp., 5/-; 1956, 286 pp., 5/-) (C. Windus, London, 1956, 143 pp., illus., 4/9) (Thames, London, 1956, 214 pp., 2/6) (*Allan Quatermain & King Solomon's Mines*, Globe, New York, 1956, 336 pp., illus., $2.40) (*King Solomon's Mines & She*, Modern Library, New York, 1957, 266 + 361 pp., $1.65) (abr., Longmans, London, 1961, 4/6; 5/6) (Blackie, London, 1961, 240 pp., 10/6) (Ballantine: X733, 1963, 190 pp., pa 60¢) (Puffin: PS111, 1966, 256 pp., pa 3/6)

The famous lost-race novel. *Films*: (1) English, 1927, more or less faithfully reproduced, with Paul Robeson in the leading role, and also Sir Cedric Hardwicke. (2) MGM, 1950, with Stewart Granger and Deborah Kerr.

Lady of the Heavens, The (Authors & Newspapers Assoc., New York & London, 1908, 342 pp.) (*The Ghost Kings*, Pearson's, sr9, Oct 1907; *Gunter's Mag.*, about the same time; Cassell, 1908, 384 pp., 6/-; 1909, 1/-; 1932, 379 pp., 1/-; 1935, 304 pp., 2/6)

Kipling aided in compounding the plot: a white maiden in whom is embodied a divine spirit comes to a strange land where wizards and witches live, each under his own tree. At least one copy of this book exists, at the Library of Congress copyright depository.

Lost Civilizations [C] (Dover, 1953, 776 pp., $3.95)

3 novels: *Montezuma's Daughter*; *Eric Brighteyes*; *Cleopatra*.

Love Eternal (Cassell, 1918, 344 pp., illus.–A. C. Michael, 6/-; 1921, 240 pp., 2/-) (Longmans, New York, 1918, 368 pp., $2.00)

A young man in communication with the dead is haunted by the spirit of a woman.

Mahatma and the Hare, a Dream Story, The (Longmans Green, London, 1911, 176 pp., illus.–W. T. Horton & H. M. Brown, 2/6) (Holt, New York, 1911, 165 pp., illus.–Horton & Brown, $1.00)

Maiwa's Revenge (*Harper's Monthly*, sr, 1888) (Harper, 1888, 157 pp.) (Longmans, London, 1888, 216 pp.; 1923, 5/-) (Longmans, New York, 1920, illus.–M. Greiffenhagen, $1.25)

A native's terrible revenge.

Missionary and the Witch Doctor, The (Paget Lit. Agency, New York, 1920, 64 pp., 12 copies for copyright purposes)

An almost mythical edition; however it has been republished as "Little Flower" in *Smith and the Pharaohs* [C].

Montezuma's Daughter (*The Graphic* [weekly], sr, 1 Jul–17 Nov 1893) (Longmans, 1893, 325 pp., illus.; [US], $1.75) (Newnes: 96, London, nd–ca. 1910, 186 pp., pa 6d) (Harrap, 1925, 255 pp., 255 pp., 2/6) (MacDonald, 1948, 334 pp., illus.–H. Cowles, 8/6)

The fall of the Aztec empire in Mexico.

Moon of Israel: A Tale of the Exodus (*Cornhill Mag.*, sr10, Jan 1918) (J. Murray, London, 1918, 328 pp., 7/-; 1921, 3/6, 2/-; 1926, 316 pp., 3/6; 1934, 2/6) (Longmans, New York, 1918, 502 pp., $2.00)

A tale of the Exodus, containing much about ancient Egyptian magic and vividly describing the plagues.

Morning Star (*Cavalier*, sr8, Nov 1909) (Cassell, 1910, 320 pp., 6/-; 1912, 1/-; 1920, 242 pp., 2/-; 1926, 256 pp., 1/-) (Longmans, New York, 1910, 308 pp., illus.–A. C. Michael, $2.00) (*FFM*, Feb 1950)

An imprisoned queen is magically spirited away while her ka (or double) takes her place and marries the usurping pharaoh.

Nada the Lily (*Illustrated London News*, sr, 1891) (Longmans, London, 1892, 295 pp., illus.) (Hodder Stoughton 1914, 321 pp.) (Longmans, New York, 1918, $1.75) (MacDonald, 1949, 304 pp., illus.–H. Cowles, 8/6) (Thames, 1956, 247 pp., 3/6) (Collins,

1958, 320 pp., illus.—W. Nickless, 5/6)

Pagan superstition, with witchcraft and occult forces rampant; the terrible pack of the Wolf Brethren.

People of the Mist, The (Longmans, London, 1894, 343 pp.; 1911, 343 pp.; 1928, 355 pp., 3/6) (Longmans, New York, 1894, 357 pp., $1.75) (Hodder Stoughton, 1921, 318 pp., 2/-) (Pearson, 1926, 351 pp., 2/6) (MacDonald, 1951, 375 pp., illus.—J. Matthew, 8/6)

A lost-race story; the raiding of a hidden jungle slave-camp and the search for a lost city which has a living monster god.

Queen of the Dawn: A Love Tale of Old Egypt (Hutchinson, 1925, 287 pp., 7/6; 1927, 3/6; 1928, 2/-; 1920, 2/-) (Doubleday Page, 1925, 307 pp., $2.00) (Grosset, 1927, 307 pp., 75¢)

Historical fantasy of ancient Egypt.

Queen Sheba's Ring (*Gunter's Mag.*, sr?, Nov 1909) (Nash, London, 1910, 319 pp., colour frontis.—C. Cuneo, 6/-; 1913, 319 pp., 2/-; 1920, 3/6) (Doubleday Page, 1910, 326 pp., illus.—S. Schow) (Unwin, 1922, 316 pp., 2/6; 1923, 2/-) (Nash Grayson, 1925, 315 pp., 2/6; 1930, 3/6; 1932, 2/6) (Murray, 1926, 319 pp., 2/-) (MacDonald, 1953, 256 pp., illus.—G. Whittam, 8/6) (Thames, 1956, 214 pp., 3/6)

Lost race adventure in northern Central Africa.

Red Eve (Hodder Stoughton, 1911, 296 pp., illus.—A. C. Michael, 6/; 1921, 305 pp., 2/-; 1929, 296 pp., 2/-) (Doubleday Page, 1911, 351 pp.)

Splendid historical fantasy set in Europe at the time of the Black Death. Dying souls are taken to the fantastic figure of "Murgh of the Death."

She: A History of Adventure (*The Graphic* [weekly], sr, 2 Oct 1886–8 Jan 1887) (Lovell, 1887, 227 pp.) (Longmans, London, 1887, 317 pp.; 1890, illus.—M. G. & C. Kerr) (Grosset Dunlap, 1926, 302 pp., illus.—film) (Armed: 881 [abr.], nd, pa) (MacDonald, 1948, 320 pp., 8/6, introduction—H. Cowles, special intro.—M. Erwin) (Dell: 339 [abr.], 1949, 192 pp., pa 25¢; 1339 [rewritten by D. Ward], nd, 192 pp., pa 25¢) (Hodder: 119, 1949, 255 pp., pa 2/-; C119, 1953, 256 pp., pa 2/-; 1961, pa 3/6; #1808, 1968, 255 pp., pa 5/-) (Collins, 1957, 320 pp., illus.—W. Nickless, 5/6) (*She & King Solomon's Mines*, Modern Library, 1957, 316 + 266 pp., $1.65) (Lancer: 72-614, 1961, 256 pp., pa 50¢; 72-925, 1965, pa 50¢; 72-140, 1966, pa 50¢) (Pyramid: X1403, 1966, 238 pp., pa 60¢) (Airmont: CL146, 1967, pa 60¢)

The classic, set in Africa, of an immortal woman inspired by an immortal love. It has appeared in so many editions that it is doubtful that an accurate record can ever be compiled. *Film:* RKO, 1935, directed by Merian C. Cooper, with Randolph Scott. The locale was changed. There apparently was also a silent film in the mid-1920's.

She and Allan (Longmans, New York, 1920, 392 pp., illus.—M. Greiffenhagen, $2.00) (Hutchinson, 1921, 303 pp., 8/6; 1922, 302 pp., 3/6; 1924, 2/-; 1933, 1/-) (MacDonald, 1960, 288 pp., illus.—H. Cowles, 10/6) (Arrow: 587, 1960, 288 pp., pa 2/6)

Allan journeys to the land of Kor and meets the woman known as She.

Smith and the Pharaohs and Other Tales [C] (Arrowsmith, Bristol, 1920, 320 pp., 7/6; 1923, 3/6) (Longmans, New York, 1921, 316 pp., $2.00)

6 stories: "Smith and the Pharaohs" (*The Strand*, sr3, Dec 1912) [reincarnation of Egyptian mummies]; "Magepa the Buck"; "The Blue Curtains"; "Little Flower"; "Only a Dream"; "Barbara Who Came Back."

Spirit of Bambatse, The See *Benita*

Stella Fregelius: A Tale of Three Destinies (Longmans Green, New York, 1903, 361 pp., $1.75; [London], 1904, 372 pp., 6/-; 1906, 3/6) (Hodder Stoughton, 1923, 316 pp., 2/-)

Has spectral aspects.

Swallow: A Tale of the Great Trek (Longmans, London, 1899, 248 pp., 6/-; 1901, 3/6) (Longmans, New York, 1899, $2.00) (Hodder Stoughton, 1919, 244 pp., 2/-)

The great Boer Trek of the 19th Century, in South Africa.

Tale of Three Lions, A See *Allan the Hunter*

Three Adventure Novels [C] (Dover, 1960, 636 pp., $2.00) (McClelland, Toronto, $2.20)

3 novels: *King Solomon's Mines*; *She*; *Allan Quatermain*.

Treasure of the Lake (Doubleday Page, 1926, 312 pp., $2.00) (Hutchinson, 1926, 288 pp., 7/6; 1928, 3/6; 1929, 256 pp., 2/6) (Grosset, 1928, 312 pp., 75¢)

Supernatural events baffle Allan Quatermain.

Virgin of the Sun, The (Doubleday Page, 1922, 294 pp., frontis., $2.00) (Cassell, 1922, 308 pp., 7/6; 1923, 3/6; 1928, 2/6; 1931, 317 pp., 1/-)

Adventure with supernatural overtones in a great and ancient South American kingdom.

Wanderer's Necklace, The (Cassell, 1914, 340 pp., illus.—A. C. Michael, 6/-; 1916, 1/-) (Longmans, New York, 1914, illus.—Michael, $2.00) (*FFM*, Apr 1953)

A romance of the Northland and the court of Theodora, Empress of the Byzantine Empire.

When the World Shook (Cassell, 1919, 355 pp., 7/; 1921, 272 pp., 2/-; 1930, 2/6) (Longmans, New York, 1919, 407 pp., illus., $2.50) (Skeffington, London, ?)

Crystal sarcophagi containing the last king and princess of Atlantis are discovered. The former hopes to reverse the catastrophe he caused that sank Atlantis.

Wisdom's Daughter (Doubleday Page, 1923, 383 pp., $2.00) (Hutchinson, 1923, 288 pp., 7/6; 1924, 3/6; 1925, 302 pp., 2/-) (Grosset, 1927, 383 pp., 75¢)

Subtitled: "The Life and Love Story of She-Who-Must-Be-Obeyed." It is the final volume in the *She* tetralogy, but covers Ayesha's birth and early youth in ancient Egypt. It is full of magic and adventure.

Witch's Head, The (Hurst & Blackett, London, 1885, 3 vol.) (? , 1886, illus.—C. Kerr) (Hodder Stoughton, 1914, 324 pp., 7d; 1920, 2/-; 1927, 2/-) (Longmans, New York, $1.75) (Pearson, 1925, 352 pp., 2/6)

The evil influence of the severed head of an African witch.

Wizard, The (? , Bristol, 1896) (Longmans, New York, 1896, 293 pp., illus.—C. Kerr, $2.00) (Arrowsmith, 1933, 248 pp., 3/6) (? , London, 1940, illus.—N. Whittaker)

A missionary and a witch doctor struggle for spiritual supremacy over an African tribe.

Works of H. Rider Haggard, The [C] (W. J. Black, New York, 1928, 728 pp., illus., $2.98) (*The Favourite Novels of H. Rider Haggard*, Blue Ribbon, New York, 1928, 728 pp., illus., $1.00)

5 novels: *Cleopatra*; *She*; *King Solomon's Mines*; *Allan Quatermain*; *Maiwa's Revenge*.

World's Desire, The [with Andrew Lang] (Longmans, London, 1890, 316 pp., illus.; 1894, illus.—M. Greiffenhagen) (Harper, 1890, 274 pp.) (Hodder Stoughton, 1920, 260 pp., 2/-; 1924) (MacDonald, 1953, illus.—G. Whittam, 8/6)

Magic and fantasy—a great romance of ancient Egypt and Helen of Troy.

Yellow God, The (Cupples & Leon Co., New York, 1908, 320 pp.) (Cassell, 1909, 360 pp., illus.—A. C. Michael, 6/-; 1909, 352 pp.; 1912; 1915, 356 pp., 2/-; 1920, 245 pp.)

A lost-race story, with a wicked queen who mummifies her lovers. The theme of this book is said to have been plagiarised by P. Benoit in his *L'Atlantida*.

HAGGARD, J. HARVEY (30 Nov 1913–) U.S. science fiction author. He had a number of stories in the field starting in 1930, but has made only occasional appearances since World War II. His "World Reborn" was the first novel in *Future Fiction* (Nov 1939). One story has been reprinted: "Children of the Ray" (*WS*, Mar 1934; *FSM*, Spr 1950). All told, he had 30 stories published.

Series

Earthguard. All in *WS*: "Through the Einstein Line" (Nov 1933); "Evolution Satellite" (sr2, Dec 1933); "An Episode on Io" (Feb 1934).

HAGGARD, WILLIAM (pseud) See CLAYTON, R.

HAILEY, ARTHUR (5 Aug 1920–) Canadian author.

Fiction

In High Places (Doubleday, New York, 1962, 415 pp., $4.95) (M.

Joseph, London, 1962, 397 pp., 18/-) (Corgi: FN1339, 1963, 376 pp., pa 5/-) (Bantam: S2526, 1962, 376 pp., pa 75¢)

A near-future story about political intrigues around the Canadian Prime Minister who is instrumental in the U.S. and Canada joining militarily.

HAINING, PETER (ALEXANDER) (2 Apr 1940–) British editor and anthologist. He was co-editor (with A. V. Sellwood) of *Devil Worship in Britain* (Corgi, 1964, pa).
Anthologies
Beyond the Curtain of Dark [pa] (FSB: 1634, 1966, 320 pp., pa 5/-)

Weird, 24 stories: "Lizzie Borden Took an Axe," R. Bloch; "The Snail Watcher," Patricia Highsmith; "Chickamauga," A. Bierce; "At Last the True Story of Frankenstein," Harry Harrison; "The Horla," Guy de Maupassant; "Fever Dream," R. Bradbury; "The Other Celia," T. Sturgeon; "The Oval Portrait," E. A. Poe; "The Monster Maker," W. C. Morrow; "Come and Go Mad," Fredric Brown; "The Survivor," "The Ancestor," H. P. Lovecraft & A. Derleth; "The Mortal Immortal," Mary Shelley; "Dr. Heidegger's Experiment," N. Hawthorne; "By These Presents," H. Kuttner; "Whosit's Disease," Henry Slesar; "King Pest," E. A. Poe; "Mayaya's Little Green Men," Harold Lawlor; "For the Blood Is Life," F. M. Crawford; "The Human Chair," Edogawa Rampo; "The Fortunes of Sir Robert Ardagh," J. S. Le Fanu; "Return to the Sabbath," R. Bloch; "The Will of Luke Carlowe," Clive Pemberton; "Eyes Do More Than See," I. Asimov.
Craft of Terror, The [pa] (FSB: 1678, 1966, 188 pp., pa 3/6)

15 extracts from Gothic horror novels, editor's introduction, and a 2½-page bibliography of rare horrors: "The Monk," Matthew Lewis; "Ferdinand, Count Fathom," Tobias Smollett; "The Castle of Otranto," Horace Walpole; "The Old English Baron," Clara Reeve; "Vathek," Wm. Beckford; "Caleb Williams," Wm. Godwin; "Wieland, or, The Transformation," Charles B. Brown; "Melmoth the Wanderer," Charles Maturin; "The Last Man," Mary Shelley; "The Cult of Zanoni," Edward Bulwer-Lytton; "The Feast of Blood," Thomas Prest; "The Mysteries of Paris," Eugene Sue; "The House by the Churchyard," J. S. Le Fanu; "The Elixir of Life," Wm. H. Ainsworth; "Metzengerstein," E. A. Poe.
Dr. Caligari's Black Book (Allen, London, 1968, 190 pp., 21/-)

13 stories ["An Excursion into the Macabre in Thirteen Acts"] and 1½-page introduction: "The Second Awakening of a Magician," S. L. Dennis; "The Jar," R. Bradbury; "Satan's Circus," Lady Eleanor Smith; "The Last Seance," Agatha Christie; "Mrs. Eltring Plays Her Part," A. Derleth; "The Third Performance," A. Gittins; "The Waxwork," A. M. Burrage; "The Sorcerer's Apprentice," R. Bloch; "The Dwarf," M. Ayme; "The Demon King," J. B. Priestley; "The Horror in the Museum," Hazel Heald; "Farewell Performance," H. R. Wakefield; "The End of a Show," B. Pain.
Evil People, The (Leslie Frewin, London, 1968, 252 pp., 25/-)

Weird, 13 stories and introduction: "The Nocturnal Meeting," W. Harrison Ainsworth; "The Peabody Heritage," H. P. Lovecraft; "The Witch's Vengeance," W. B. Seabrook; "The Snake," D. Wheatley; "Prince Borgia's Mass," A. Derleth; "Secret Worship," A. Blackwood; "The Devil-Worshipper," Francis Prevot; "Archives of the Dead," Basil Copper; "Mother of Serpents," R. Bloch; "Cerimarie," Arthur J. Burks; "The Witch," Shirley Jackson; "Homecoming," R. Bradbury; "Never Bet the Devil Your Head," E. A. Poe.
Future Makers, The (Sidgwick Jackson, London, 1968, 191 pp., 18/-)

Sf, 8 stories with compiler's introduction: "The Weapon Too Dreadful to Use," I. Asimov; "Abreaction," T. Sturgeon; "The Piper," R. Bradbury; "The Eternal Now," M. Leinster; "Columbus Was a Dope," R. A. Heinlein; "Castaway," A. C. Clarke; "The Hour of Battle," R. Sheckley; "Equator," B. W. Aldiss.
Gentlewomen of Evil, The (R. Hale, London, 1967, 254 pp., 25/-) (Taplinger, New York, 1967, 254 pp., illus., $4.50)

Subtitled: "An anthology of rare supernatural stories from the pens of the Victorian Ladies." 13 stories and compiler's intro. (with some original magazine illus.): "The Transformation," Mary Shelley; "The Open Door," Mrs. Margaret Oliphant; "The Italian's

Story," Catherine Crowe; "The Ghost," Mrs. Henry Wood; "The Old Nurse's Story," Elizabeth C. Gaskell; "The Phantom Coach," Amelia B. Edwards; "The Lifted Veil," Mary Ann Evans [George Eliot]; "Eveline's Visitant," Mary Eliz. Braddon; "Sandy the Tinker," Charlotte E. Riddell; "A Tale of a Gas Light Ghost," Anon.; "Eyes of Terror," Mrs. L. T. Meade; "At the Dip of the Road," Mary L. Molesworth; "The Gorgon's Head," Miss Gertrude Bacon.
Hell of Mirrors, The [pa] (FSB: 1423, 1965, 189 pp., pa 3/6)

Weird, 14 stories with compiler's introduction: "The Werewolf," Frederick Marryat; "Ligeia," "The Black Cat," E. A. Poe; "Young Goodman Brown," N. Hawthorne; "Schalken the Painter," J. S. Le Fanu; "The Middle Toe on the Right Foot," "The Damned Thing," A. Bierce; "The Squaw," Bram Stoker; "Who Knows?" "The Drowned Man," Guy de Maupassant; "The Caterpillar," "The Hell of Mirrors," Edogawa Rampo [Japanese writer]; "The Knocking in the Castle," Henry Slesar; "The Fanatic," Arthur Porges.
Legends for the Dark [pa] (FSB: 2094, 1968, 127 pp., pa 3/6)

Weird, 10 stories and 1½-page introduction: "Solomon's Demon," Arthur Porges; "The Altar," R. Sheckley; "Here Daemos," A. Derleth; "The Academy of Pain," Basil Copper; "Floral Tribute," R. Bloch; "The Secret of the Vault," Wesley Rosenquest; "The Ordeal of Doctor Trifulgas," J. Verne; "A Night With Hecate," Edward W. Ludwig; "Beyond the Wall of Sleep," H. P. Lovecraft; "The Scythe," Ray Bradbury.
Midnight People, The (L. Frewin, London, 1968, 255 pp., 30/-)

18 stories of vampires, with 2½-page introduction: "Fritz Haarmann–'The Hanover Vampire'," M. Summers; "The Vampire of Croglin Grange," Augustus Hare; "The Vampyre," John Polidori; "The Storm Visitor," Thomas P. Prest; "Three Young Ladies," B. Stoker; "An Episode in Cathedral History," M. R. James; "Bat's Belfry," A. Derleth; " 'And No Bird Sings'," E. F. Benson; "The Believer," S. Horler; "Drifting Snow," S. Grendon; "When It Was Moonlight," M. W. Wellman; "Over the River," P. S. Miller; "Drink My Blood," R. Matheson; "Pillar of Fire," R. Bradbury; "Dr. Porthos," Basil Copper; "The Living Dead," R. Bloch; "The Girl With Hungry Eyes," F. Leiber; "Postscript," M. Summers.
Summoned From the Tomb [pa] (Brown Watson: R968, 1966, 160 pp., pa 3/6)

Horror, 10 stories with brief introduction: "Hell on Earth," R. Bloch; "Guests From Gibbet Island," Washington Irving; "The Judge's House," B. Stoker; "The Bully of Chapelizod," J. S. Le Fanu; "The Curse," I. Jorgenson; "The Coffin-Maker," Alexander Pushkin; "Purple Eyes," Clive Pemberton; "A Watcher by the Dead," A. Bierce; "The Whippoorwills in the Hills," A. Derleth; "Hop Frog," E. A. Poe.
Where Nightmares Are [pa] (Mayflower: 9504, 1966, 174 pp., pa 3/6)

Weird, 14 stories and introduction: "Moxon's Master," A. Bierce; "The Body Snatchers," R. L. Stevenson; "The Man That Was Used Up," E. A. Poe; "Night," Guy de Maupassant; "Rappaccini's Daughter," N. Hawthorne; "What Was It?" F.-J. O'Brien; "The Familiar," J. S. Le Fanu; "The Trial for Murder," C. Dickens; "The Spectre Bridegroom," W. Irving; "Thrawn Janet," R. L. Stevenson; "The Cask of Amontillado," E. A. Poe; "An Occurrence at Owl Creek," A. Bierce; "The White Cat of Drumgunniol," J. S. Le Fanu; "Passeur," R. W. Chambers.

HALACY, D(ANIEL) S(TEPHEN) Jr. (1919–) U.S. writer, born in Charleston, S.C. After graduation from Phoenix College and Arizona State U., he worked in the aircraft industry. He served in World War II and the Korean War as an Air Force navigator. Since Korea he has specialized in technical writing in the aircraft and electronic fields; he has freelanced since 1962. He also taught writing at Phoenix College for ten years. He now lives in Glendale, Calif., is married, and has two daughters.
Fiction
Rocket Rescue (W. W. Norton, New York, 1968, 192 pp., $3.95)

Story of telepathic twins—one in the Space Squadron and the other in the misfits of Rocket Rescue.

HALDANE, CHARLOTTE (FRANKEN) (1898–) British author

and newspaper correspondent. She was born in Sydenham, London, and educated in Belgium, Germany and France. She was a member of the St. Pancras Borough Council 1939-42. She has been a foreign correspondent for the *Daily Herald* in China and the *Daily Sketch* in Russia, and now contributes to numerous newspapers and journals. Her works include biographies of Marcel Proust and Mozart; fantasies besides the one below are *Man's World* (C. Windus, 1926), in which war is abolished and birth and parenthood are regimented, and *Melusine; or, The Devil Take Her!* (Barker, 1936).

Fiction

Shadow of a Dream (Weidenfeld Nicolson, London, 1952, 287 pp., 12/6) (Roy, New York, 1953, 287 pp., $2.50)

ESP and other psi phenomena are the basis for protesting Great Britain's fraudulent mediums act.

HALE, EDWARD EVERETT (3 Apr 1822–10 June 1909) U.S. author. He was active for half a century in raising the tone of American life as a writer, editor, clergyman and abolitionist. A voluminous contributor to newspapers and magazines, he is remembered mainly for his *The Man Without a Country* (1863); other works caused the formation of "Lend-a-Hand" societies, etc. Much of his writing lies in the field of sf and fantasy; in particular *The Brick Moon* had the first mention of an artificial Earth satellite. One of the first "if . . ." (alternate worlds) stories was "Hands Off" (originally anon., *Harper's*; *F&SF*, Feb 1952). Reprinted earlier was "The Good-Natured Pendulum" (*AS*, May 1933). He is covered by Moskowitz in the article "The Real Earth Satellite Story" (*Satellite*, June 1957).

Fiction [Incomplete—other titles in Bleiler *Checklist*]

Brick Moon and Other Stories, The [C] (Little Brown, Boston, 1899, 369 pp., frontis.)

8 stories: "The Brick Moon" (*The Atlantic Monthly*, sr4, Oct 1869); "Crusoe in New York"; "Bread on the Waters"; "The Lost Palace"; "99 Linwood Street"; "Ideals"; "Thanksgiving at the Polls"; "The Survivor's Story." The title story tells of Earth scientists building a 200-ft brick satellite launched by flywheels.

His Level Best and Other Stories [C] (Roberts Bros., Boston, 1872, 293 pp.)

8 stories, including the first book appearance of "The Brick Moon"; other stories of fantasy interest are "A Tale of a Salamander"; "The Queen of California" (lost race).

HALIDOM, M. Y. Pseudonym used on later appearances of "Wonder Club" stories, supplanting earlier pseudonym "Dryasdust." The "Halidom" byline was used on many other weird and fantasy titles, such as *The Weird Transformation* (L. T. Burleigh, London, 1904); *The Poet's Curse* (Greening, London, 1911)—horror follows desecration of Shakespeare's coffin; *Zoe's Revenge* (Greening, 1908)—life-size doll built around the skeleton of a murdered girl. The latter two books are not in the Bleiler *Checklist*.

Fiction

Spirit Lovers and Other Stories, The [C] (Simpkin, London, 1903, 192 pp., 6/-)

Fantasy, 3 stories: "The Spirit Lovers"; "The Dream of Toughyarn"; "The Pigmy Queen."

Tales of the Wonder Club [C] ([by Dryasdust] Harrison, London, 1899, 402 pp., illus.) ([by Halidom] Burleigh, London, new rev. ed., 1903, 316 pp., illus.–John Jellicoe & Val Prince after designs by author, 6/-)

Introduction "A Peep at the Wonder Club" and 9 Chapters: I. "The Phantom Flea—The Lawyer's Story"; II. "The Spirit Lovers—The Doctor's Story"; III. "The Mermaid Palace; or, Captain Toughyarn's Dream"; IV. "The Headless Ladye—The Artist's First Story"; V. "The Demon Guide; or, The Gnome of the Mountain—The Geologist's Story"; VI. "The Landlord's Daughter's Story—The Pigmy Queen: A Fairy Tale"; VII. "The Haunted Stage Box—The Tragedian's Story"; VIII. "The Spirit Leg—The Analytical Chemist's Story"; IX. "Lost in the Catacombs—The Antiquary's Story."

Tales of the Wonder Club II [C] ([by Dryasdust] Harrison, 1900, 388 pp., illus.) ([by Halidom] T. Burleigh, new rev. ed., 1904, 318

pp., illus.–J. Jellicoe & V. Prince, 6/-)

6 stories: "Buried Alive—The Landlord's Story"; "Der Scharfrichter—The Artist's Second Story"; "The Three Pauls—The Artist's Third Story"; "The Waxen Image—The Hostess's Story"; "The Chieftain's Destiny"; "A Tale of the French Revolution—The Barber's Story."

Tales of the Wonder Club III [C] ([by Dryasdust] Harrison, 1900, 274 pp. [see note below], illus.) ([by Halidom] T. Burleigh, new rev. ed., 1905, 158 pp. + 144 pp., illus.–J. Jellicoe & V. Prince, 6/-)

Note: The Dryasdust volumes II and III were apparently issued together, as III continues the pagination of II: pages 389 to 662. Both editions of III contain the same basic material but entirely rearranged. Dryasdust Vol. III: "The Gypsy Queen" (play); "The Last of the Wonder Club"—the varying fortunes of its members and the destruction by fire of "Ye Headless Ladye." The Halidom Vol. III places "The Last of the Wonder Club" first (158 pp.), and gives the non-fantasy "The Gypsy Queen" its own title and pagination (144 pp.). These may thus have also been issued separately.

HALIFAX, (LORD) CHARLES L(INDLEY) W(OOD) (7 June 1839–19 Jan 1934) British author, Second Viscount Halifax, father of the late Great Earl Halifax.

Nonfiction

Further Stories From Lord Halifax's Ghost Book (G. Bles, London, 1937, 182 pp., 8/6) (S. J. R. Saunders, Toronto, $2.50) (*Lord Halifax's Ghost Book, Vol. 2*, G. Bles, 1946)

Ghost stories: "Shrieks in the West Room at Flesbury"; "The Shrouded Watcher." *Apparitions:* "The Ghostly Passenger"; "The Fawn Lady of Burton Agnes"; "The Page Boy of Hayne"; "The Ghost of Lord Conyers Osborne"; "The Ghost of Lady Carnavon"; "The Ghost of Bishop Wilberforce"; "The Ship in Distress"; "The Widow in the Train"; "Killed in Action"; "The Troubled Spirit of Tintern Abbey"; "Labedoyere's Doom." *Haunted Houses:* "Exorcism of St. Donat's Castle"; "What the Gardener Saw"; "Three in a Bed"; "The Simla Bungalow"; "The Cardinal of Waverley Abbey." *Ghostly Guardians:* "Someone by His Side"; "Bishop King's Escape"; "Two Friends." *Dreams and Portents:* "The Spanish Knife"; "Turn to the Right"; "President Lincoln's Dream"; "John Arthington's Escape"; "Two Submarines"; "Fighting Rooks and the Black Mouse"; "Lord Decies' Ring"; "The Death of Lord Hastings"; "The Rustling Lady of Lincoln." *Some Curious Stories:* "The Bloody Hand"; "The 'Tweenie"; "Warning for a Submarine"; "The Restless Dead"; "The Countess of Belvedere." *Note:* Vol. 2 is a reprint of the above without "The 'Tweenie'," but adding the following two stories: "Lord Lytton and a Horoscope"; "Colonel P's Ghost Story." These are the final two stories in the entry below, except they are omitted in the 1946 edition (Vol. 1).

Lord Halifax's Ghost Book (G. Bles, 1936, 243 pp., 8/6) (S. J. R. Saunders, $3.00) (Fontana: 603, 1961, 287 pp., pa 3/6; 1964, pa 3/6) (*Lord Halifax's Ghost Book, Vol. 1*, G. Bles, 1946, 3/6; 1968, pa 3/6)

Ghost stories [also see note, preceding entry]: "The Harper of Inverary"; "The Man in the Iron Cage"; "The Secret of Glamis"; "The Grey Man of Wrotham"; "The Haunting of Hinton Ampner"; "The Death of Lord Tyrone"; "The Passenger With the Bag"; " 'Marche!' "; "The Man in a Silk Dress"; "The Strange Experience of the Reverend Spencer Nairne"; "The Renishaw Coffin"; "The Butler in the Corridor"; "The Telephone at the Oratory." *Haunted Rooms:* "The Strangling Woman"; " 'Here I Am Again!' "; "Head of a Child"; "The Woman in White." *Prophetic and Other Dreams:* "The Corpse Downstairs"; "The Murderer's Dream"; "The Mad Butler"; "Lady Goring's Dream"; "The Sexton of Chilton Polden"; "The Last Appearance of Mr. Bullock"; "The Corpse That Rose"; "The Footsteps at Haverholme Priory." *Mr. Dundas's Stories:* " 'I Will Pay You All To-Morrow' "; "The Haunted Bungalow." *Apparitions:* "The Monk of Bolton Abbey"; "The Gentleman With the Latch-Key"; "The Bordeaux Diligence"; "The Appearance of Mr. Birbeck"; "The Vampire Cat"; "Lord Lytton and a Horoscope"; "Colonel P's Ghost Story."

HALL, AUSTIN (*ca.* 1882–1933)

HALL, AUSTIN (*ca.* 1882–1933) U.S. author. After some newspaper and electrical work, he took to life in the open; he began writing when one of the cowboys working with him asked him to write a story. He started writing for a living, and was forced to "churn out" westerns although his love was for the fantastic. He was noted for his camera-like memory. He is known for his collaboration with H. E. Flint—*The Blind Spot*, the sequel to which he wrote alone. Fantasy fiction not covered below includes "The Man Who Saved the Earth" (*Arg*, 13 Dec 1919; *AS*, Apr 1926; *AS Annual*, 1927; *FFM*, Feb 1940); "Almost Immortal" (*ASW*, 7 Oct 1916; *FFM*, Nov 1939; *Mag. Horror*, Sum 1966). His "The Rebel Soul" is covered under *Into the Infinite*.

Fiction

Blind Spot, The [with H. E. Flint] (*Arg*, sr6, 14 May 1921) (*FFM*, incomplete, sr3, Mar 1940) (*FN*, July 1940) (Prime, Philadelphia, 1951, 293 pp., illus.–H. Bok, $3.00) (Museum, London, 1953, 254 pp., 10/6) (Ace: G-547, 1964, 318 pp., pa 50¢)

The noted classic about another world; it is somewhat ponderous in its action. The sequel is *The Spot of Life*.

Into the Infinite [n] (*ASW*, sr6, 12 Apr 1919) (*FFM*, sr4, Oct 1942)

Good men fight to drive the evil from a man with two souls. This is the sequel to "The Rebel Soul" (*ASW*, 30 June 1917; *FFM*, Aug 1940), and the whole was to have been published by Prime Press under the title *The Rebel Soul*.

People of the Comet ("Hop O' My Thumb," *WT*, sr2, Sep 1923) (Griffin, Los Angeles, 1948, 131 pp., $2.00, jacket–Gaughan) (*La comète rouge* [French–Belgian], *Bravo* [mag.], Bruxelles, 23 Nov 1950–15 Feb 1951)

Super-beings reveal that our solar system is an atom in a larger universe, with comets as its ions.

Spot of Life, The [pa] (*Arg*, sr5, 13 Aug 1932) (*FFM*, Feb 1941) (Ace: F-318, 1964, 187 pp., pa 40¢)

Further adventures in the world of *The Blind Spot*. It was to have been published by Prime Press about 1950.

HALL, D. W. See BATES, H. (co-author)

HALL, MANLY P(ALMER)
Fiction

Shadowy Forms: A Collection of Occult Stories [C] (Hall Pub., Los Angeles, 1925, 165 pp., $2.00)

12 stories and 2¼-p. introduction: "Black Hat Sorcery"; "The Witch Doctor"; "The Teapot of Mandarin Wong"; "Silver Souls"; "The Third Eye"; "The Spirit of the Snows"; "The Lota of the Great God, Shiva"; "The Temple of Sin"; "The Dance of the Veils"; "The Emerald Tablet"; "Your God and My God"; "The Cave of Apes." Not in Bleiler *Checklist*.

Ways of Lonely Ones; A Collection of Mystical Allegories, The [C] (Phoenix, Los Angeles, 1934, 89 pp., illus., $1.50)

Fantasy, 8 stories and introduction: "Nature's Homage"; "The Maker of the Gods"; "The Master of the Blue Cape"; "The Face of Christ"; "The Guardian of the Light"; "The One Who Turned Back"; "The Glory of the Lord"; "The Last of the Shamans."

HALL, STEVE
Fiction

Midnight Club. All in *Science-Fantasy*: "Beginner's Luck" (Aug 1962); "Weekend Trip" (Oct 1962); "Hole in the Dyke" (Apr 1963); "Party Piece" (Aug 1963).

HALL, T(REVOR) H(ENRY)
British author. He is interested in ghost lore; he wrote *Four Modern Ghosts* (1958) with E. J. Dingwall.

Nonfiction

New Light on Old Ghosts (Duckworth, London, 1965, 142 pp., illus., 25/-)

HALLAM, (SAMUEL BEHONI) ATLANTIS
U.S. author. He had five stories published in the sf magazine *Spaceway* 1953-54.

Fiction

Star Ship on Saddle Mountain (Macmillan, New York, 1955, 182 pp., $2.50)

Juvenile, about a boy captured by Saturnians, and his life on that planet.

HALLE, LOUIS J(OSEPH)
(17 Nov 1917) U.S. author, professor, and authority on international affairs.

Fiction

Sedge (Praeger, New York, 1963, 118 pp., $3.50) (Burns MacEachern, Toronto, $4.25)

A subtle dissertation on an imaginary utopia: a self-sufficient principality which cut itself off from the world for centuries; a satire on our crowded, nervous world.

HAMILTON, ALEX(ANDER)
British author and anthologist.

Fiction

Beam of Malice [C] (D. McKay, New York, 1967, 222 pp., $4.50) (Corgi: GN7812, 1968, 190 pp., pa 3/6)

Weird, 15 stories: "The Baby Sitters"; "What's Your Problem"; "The Jinx"; "The Words of the Dumb"; "Only a Game"; "Dodensraum"; "Last Resource"; "A Glutton for Punishment"; "To Start a Hare"; "The Attic Express"; "Recall"; "Kiss of Death"; "Breakaway"; "Many a Slip"; "Searchlight."

Anthology

Cold Embrace, The [pa] (Corgi: GN75-8, 1966, 188 pp., pa 3/6)

Weird, 18 stories (all by women authors) and introduction: "The Cold Embrace," M. E. Braddon; "Open End," Shena MacKay; "The Lottery," Shirley Jackson; "The Demon Lover," Eliz. Bowen; "The Seance," Agatha Christie; "The Werewolf," Marie de France; "The Country Gentleman," Margaret Irwin; "The King Is Dead," Mary Coleridge; "Akin to Love," Christianna Brand; "John Charrington's Wedding," E. Nesbit; "Heartburn," Hortense Calisher; "The Cenotaph," Scheherezade; "Three Miles Up," Eliz. Jane Howard; "The Confessor," Marguerite de Navarre; "The Press Gang," Janet Frame; "Judgment Day," Flannery O'Connor; "The Doom of the Griffiths," Eliz. Gaskell; "Poor Girl," Eliz. Taylor.

HAMILTON, COUNT ANTHONY
Fiction

Fairy Tales and Romances [C] (Henry G. Bohn, 1849, 562 pp.)

5 stories of the supernatural, translated from the French by M. Lewis, H. T. Ryde and C. Kenney, and originally written around the end of the 17th century: "Zeneyda"; "The Story of the May-Flower"; "The Ram"; "The Enchanter Faustus"; "The Four Facardins." The last, a long and complex Arabian Nights style fantasy, was mainly written by M. G. Lewis and has an alternate ending by M. de Levis; it was later reissued (Printed for the Lutetian Society, 1899, 286 pp., 680 copies).

HAMILTON, EDMOND
(21 Oct 1904–) U.S. science fiction author. He was born in Youngstown, Ohio, and had his schooling in Pennsylvania. He majored in physics with the intention of becoming an electrical engineer; however, he was side-tracked into fiction writing, and has remained an author ever since. A reader of science fiction and fantasy since he was 12, in the 1930's he became a prolific writer for the sf/fantasy magazines. His first appearance was in *Weird Tales* with "The Monster-God of Mamurth" (Aug 1926; *Mag. Horror*, Win 1966-67); this was followed by many sf space stories in the same magazine, usually in an interstellar locale. Some of these in his "Interstellar Patrol" series were much admired by A. Merritt, who backed Hamilton in endeavouring to publish them in book form in the early 1930's. It was only comparatively recently that these did appear, as Ace paperbacks. In his younger days Hamilton knocked around with Jack Williamson. In the pre-war period he became known as "World-Saver Hamilton" for the numerous stories in which he employed this theme.

Late in the 1930's Standard Magazines conceived the idea of a science fiction magazine built around a novel featuring the same character in each issue, and commissioned Hamilton to write his "Captain Future" novels. He kept these running for some four years in the magazine *Captain Future* (with some exceptions), and continued them in *Startling Stories* in 1945-46 and again in

1950-51.

Hamilton is noted also for his fantastic adventure stories; he personally considers E. R. Burroughs to be one of the most underrated writers in the whole fantasy field. Since World War II Hamilton has not been so prolific a writer, but his work has become generally more noteworthy. He married another noted sf writer, Leigh Brackett, at the end of 1946.

Novels of interest, not covered below, include: "The Hidden World" (*WSQ*, Fall 1929; *FSM*, Spr 1950); "Locked Worlds" (*ASQ*, Spr 1929; *AS*, July 1968); "The Three Planeteers" (*SS*, Jan 1940); "Forgotten World" (*TWS*, Win 1946; *FSM*, Fall 1954). A weird short story also has been reprinted: "The Three From the Tomb" (*WT*, Feb 1932; *Startling Mystery*, Spr 1968). Many of his lighter post-war novels appeared in *Imagination* and *Imaginative Tales*, a number under house pseudonyms. In the British *American Fiction* series he had two small collections: *Murder in the Clinic* and *Tiger Girl*; a German collection is *Kinder der Sonne*, T: 545, 1967, containing "The Comet Doom"; "Sunfire"; "Babylon in the Sky"; "Devolution."

Sam Moskowitz's profile of Hamilton appeared in *AS*, Oct 1963, and was a chapter in Moskowitz's *Seekers of Tomorrow* (1966).

Series

Captain Future. [Note that this is a full listing, and not all stories were by Hamilton.] In *Captain Future*: "Captain Future and the Space Emperor" (Win 1940); "Calling Captain Future" (Spr 1940); "Captain Future's Challenge" (Sum 1940); "The Triumph of Captain Future" (Fall 1940); "Captain Future and the Seven Space Stones" (Win 1941); "Star Trail to Glory" (Spr 1941); "The Magician of Mars" (Sum 1941); "The Lost World of Time" (Fall 1941); "The Quest Beyond the Stars" (Win 1942); "Outlaws of the Moon" (Spr 1942); "The Comet Kings" (Sum 1942); "Planets in Peril" (Fall 1942); "The Face of the Deep" (Win 1943); "Worlds to Come" (by "Brett Sterling" [J. Samachson]) (Spr 1943); "The Star of Dread" (by "Brett Sterling" [E. Hamilton]) (Sum 1943); "Magic Moon" (by "Brett Sterling" [E. Hamilton]) (Win 1944); "Days of Creation" (by "Brett Sterling" [J. Samachson]) (Spr 1944). In *Startling Stories*: "Red Sun of Danger" (by "Brett Sterling" [E. Hamilton]) (Spr 1945); "Outlaw World" (Win 1946); "The Solar Invasion" (by Manly Wade Wellman) (Fall 1946; 1968, pa [see M. W. WELLMAN]). Series continued as novelettes, still in *SS*: "The Return of Captain Future" (Jan 1950); "Children of the Sun" (May 1950); "The Harpers of Titan" (Sep 1950); "Pardon My Iron Nerves" (Nov 1950); "Moon of the Unforgotten" (Jan 1951); "Earthmen No More" (Mar 1951); "Birthplace of Creation" (May 1951). A number of the early novels were serialised in the Swedish magazine *Jules Verne Magasinet*, and in the early 1960's some were reprinted in the German *Utopia-Grossband* magazine series.

Interstellar Patrol (or Federation of Suns). Adventures in the remote future. All in *Weird Tales*: "Crashing Suns" (sr2, Aug 1928); "The Star Stealers" (Feb 1929; *AFR*, No. 6, 1948); "Within the Nebula" (May 1929); "Outside the Universe" (sr4, July 1929); "The Comet Drivers" (Feb 1930); "The Sun People" (May 1930); "The Cosmic Cloud" (Nov 1930). All but "The Sun People" were reprinted as *Crashing Suns* and *Outside the Universe*.

Starwolf (Morgan Chane). Ace paperbacks: *The Weapon From Beyond*; *The Closed Worlds*; *World of the Starwolves*.

Fiction

Battle for the Stars (*Imagination*, June 1956 [as Alexander Blade]) —enlarged: (Dodd Mead, New York, 1961, 206 pp., $2.95) (D'day SF B.C., 1961) (Mayflower: 0480, 1963, 190 pp., pa 3/6) (Paperback: 52-311, 1964, 159 pp., pa 50¢; 52-609, 1967, pa 50¢) (*Die Heimat der Astronauten* [German], Heyne, 1964, pa) (*La spedizione della v Flotta* [Italian], *Urania*: 381, 1965)

Adventure in future power politics, with Earth as the bone of contention.

Beyond the Moon [pa] See *Star Kings, The*

City at World's End (*SS*, July 1950) —enlarged: (Fell, New York, 1951, 239 pp., $2.75) (Museum, London, 1952, 192 pp., 9/6) (*Ville sous globe* [French], Hachette: Le RF, 1952) (*SOS, die Erde erkaltet* [German], Weiss, 1952, 1957 pa; T: 211, 1962)

(*Galaxy SF Novel*: 18, 1953, 129 pp., pa 35¢) (*Agonia della Terra* [Italian], *Urania*: 23, 1953) (Corgi: T58, 1954, 221 pp., pa 2/-) (Crest: s184, 1956, 160 pp., pa 35¢; s494, 1961, pa 35¢; L758, 1964, pa 45¢)

A town is hit by a "super-bomb" and is hurled, with its inhabitants, to the Earth of a future era.

Closed Worlds, The [pa] (Ace: G-701, 1968, 156 pp., pa 50¢)

Second of "Starwolf" series—Morgan Chane comes to grips with a relict science of an ancient race on a forbidden world.

Crashing Suns [pa] (Ace: F-319, 1965, 192 pp., pa 40¢)

5 stories of the "Interstellar Patrol" series: "Crashing Suns"; "The Star Stealers"; "Within the Nebula"; "The Comet Drivers"; "The Cosmic Cloud."

Doomstar [pa] (Belmont: B50-657, 1966, 158 pp., 50¢)

A man seeks the source of a terrible weapon which can change a sun.

Fugitive of the Stars [pa] (*Imagination*, Dec 1957) —revised: (Ace: M-111, 1965, 116 pp., pa 45¢; with *Land Beyond the Map*)

Typical Hamilton space-opera.

Haunted Stars, The (Dodd Mead, 1960, 192 pp., $3.00) (Dodd, Toronto, $3.50) (D'day SF B.C., 1960, $1.20) (Pyramid: F-698, 1962, 159 pp., pa 50¢) (*Gli incappuciati di ombra* [Italian], *Urania*: 331, 1964) (*Das Gestirn der Ahnen* [German], *TS*: 84, 1964) (H. Jenkins, London, 1965, 174 pp., 12/6)

Fast-paced and well-written space-opera of a man conquering the universe.

Horror on the Asteroid [C] (P. Allan, London, 1936, 256 pp., 2/6)

Sf & weird, 6 stories—one of this publishers' *Creeps Library*, and now comparatively scarce: "Horror on the Asteroid"; "The Accursed Galaxy"; "The Man Who Saw Everything"; "The Earth-Brain''; ''The Monster-God of Mamurth''; ''The Man Who Evolved."

Monsters of Juntonheim, The [pa] See *Yank at Valhalla, A*

Outside the Universe [pa] (*WT*, sr4, July 1929) (Ace: F-271, 1964, 173 pp., pa 40¢)

Fourth story (second book) of "Interstellar Patrol" series. A somewhat dated, slow-moving tale of a journey to another galaxy with its many perils.

Star Kings, The (*AS*, Sep 1947) (Fell, 1949, 262 pp., $2.50) (*Beyond the Moon*, Signet: 812, 1950, 167 pp., pa 25¢) (Museum, 1951, 219 pp., 8/6) (*Les rois des étoiles* [French], Hachette: Le RF, 1951; *Les rois des étoiles & Retour aux étoiles*, Ed. Opta 'Classique SF: 12,' 1968) (*Herrscher im Weltenraum* [German], Weiss, 1952; *T*: 418-9, 1965) (*Guerra nella galassia* [Italian], *Urania*: 14, 1953) (*Los reyes de las estrellas* [Spanish], Nebula: 14, 1955, pa) (Paperback: 53-538, 1967, 190 pp., pa 60¢)

Grand space-opera with a modern Earthman involved in dramatic intrigue and adventure in the far future among the stars. Two lesser sequels were: "Kingdoms of the Stars" (*AS*, Sep 1964) and "The Shores of Infinity" (*AS*, Apr 1965). These also appeared in German as *UZ*: 571 (1968). These with two other short stories written by Hamilton at the request of the publisher form the four stories in the French *Retour aux étoiles* (the latter two have thus never appeared in English).

Star of Life, The (*SS*, Jan 1947) (Dodd Mead, 1959, 192 pp., $2.95) (Dodd, Toronto, $3.50) (D'day SF B.C., 1959, $1.20) (Crest: s329, 1959, 187 pp., pa 35¢) (*La stella della vita* [Italian], *Urania*: 236, 1960) (*Das Gestirn des Lebens* [German], *T*: 374-5, 1965)

The hero, frozen in space for many years, revives and finds himself in the midst of a struggle between the much-mutated races of humanity.

Sun Smasher, The [pa] ("Starman Come Home," *Universe*, Sep 1954) (Ace: D-351, 1959, 110 pp., pa 35¢; with *Starhaven*) (*Im Banne der Vergangenheit* [German], *UG*: 128, 1960; *TE*: 118, 1966)

A young book salesman finds himself the heir to a stellar empire and with knowledge of an omnipotent weapon.

Tharkol, Lord of the Unknown [pa] ("The Prisoner of Mars," *SS*, May 1939) (World Distributors: WFC, 1950, 160 pp., pa 1/6)

Intrigue with the Martians who invade Earth for its water.

Valley of Creation, The [pa] (*SS*, July 1948) (Lancer: 72-721, 1964, 159 pp., pa 50¢; 73-577, 1967, pa 60¢) (*Das Tal der Schöpfung* [German], *T*: 436, 1966)

Mercenaries fight a group in telepathic partnership with animals.

Weapon From Beyond, The [pa] (Ace: G-639, 1967, 158 pp., pa 50¢)

First of "Starwolf" series—Morgan Chane, raised by humanoids on a world dedicated to piracy, is cast out to find his place in interstellar society.

World of the Starwolves [pa] (Ace: G-766, 1968, 158 pp., pa 50¢)

Third of "Starwolf" series.

Yank at Valhalla, A [pa] (*SS*, Jan 1941) (*En Yankee Far Till Valhall* [Swedish], *JVM*: 19-33, 1943) (*The Monsters of Juntonheim*, World Distributors: WFC, 1950, 160 pp., pa 1/6) (*Unternehmen Walhalla* [German], *UG*: 75, 1958)

Adventure and intrigue, with a U.S. airman amongst the Norse Gods.

HAMILTON, PETER Scottish editor and publisher of *Nebula Science Fiction* for 41 issues 1952-59. At one stage he he planned a companion *American SF* to appear in the spring of 1954, to reprint U.S. material of a less sophisticated nature, but this was never published.

HAMLING, WILLIAM L(AWRENCE) (14 June 1921–) U.S. science fiction author and editor. As a fan he produced the high-class pre-war amateur magazine *Stardust*; his first professional writing appearance was in *Amazing Stories*, collaborating with M. Reinsberg on "War With Jupiter" (May 1939). During World War II he was a lieutenant in the infantry; upon his return he set up a writing office with his friend C. S. Geier. After having some stories in the Ziff-Davis magazine, in mid-1946 he joined their staff as associate editor. He later became managing editor for three years until the end of 1950. Early in 1951 he bought *Imagination* from R. A. Palmer. Operating as Greenleaf Publishing Co., he published *Imagination* and its later companion *Imaginative Tales* (later retitled *Space Travel*) until September 1958. In October 1955 he began the non-sf men's magazine *Rogue*; this is still running, but is no longer published by Hamling.

Hamling is married to Frances Yerxa, the widow of sf writer Leroy Yerxa.

HAMMETT, (SAMUEL) DASHIELL (27 May 1894–10 Jan 1961) U.S. author, founder of the "hard-boiled" school of detective fiction. He was born Samuel Dashett. He worked at a variety of occupations, including eight years as a Pinkerton detective. He served in World War I (and later in World War II). His first detective book was *Red Harvest* (1929). He reached his peak with *The Maltese Falcon* (later filmed), while his *The Thin Man* (1932), not considered one of his best works, was a sensationally successful Hollywood film, with William Powell and Myrna Loy; it had many film sequels and also became a successful TV series. After World War II Hammett was connected with left wing activities, and even served a jail sentence for contempt of court in this regard in 1951.

Anthologies

Creeps by Night (John Day, New York, 1931, 15+525 pp., $2.50) (*Modern Tales of Horror*, Gollancz, London, 1932, 448 pp., 5/-) (Blue Ribbon, New York, 1936, 525 pp., $1.00) (McClelland, Toronto, $1.29) (World Pub. Co., New York, 1944, 525 pp., $1.00) (Belmont: 230, 1961, 141 pp., pa 35¢ [10 stories marked †]) (*The Red Brain*, Belmont: 239, 1961, 141 pp., pa 35¢ [10 stories not marked]; FSB: 1328, 1965, 159 pp., pa 3/6) (FSB: 1438, 1966, 141 pp., pa 3/6 [same 10 stories marked †])

Weird, 20 stories, a number reprinted from *WT*, with introduction: "A Rose for Emily"†, Wm. Faulkner; "Green Thoughts," J. Collier; "The Ghost of Alexander Perks, A.B.," R. D. Frisbie; "The House"†, A. Maurois; "The Kill," Peter Fleming; "Ten O'Clock." Philip MacDonald; "The Spider"†, Hanns H. Ewers; "Breakdown" L. A. G. Strong; "The Witch's Vengeance"†, W. B. Seabrook; "The Rat," S. F. Wright; "Faith, Hope and Charity," Irvin S. Cobb; "Mr. Arcularis"†, C. Aiken; "The Music of Erich

Zann," H. P. Lovecraft; "The Strange Case of Mrs. Arkwright"†, Harold Dearden; "The King of the Cats"†, S. V. Benét; "The Red Brain," D. Wandrei; "The Phantom Bus," W. Elwyn Backus; "Beyond the Door"†, Paul Suter; "Perchance to Dream"†, Michael Joyce; "A Visitor From Egypt"†, F. B. Long.

Modern Tales of Horror See *Creeps by Night*
Red Brain, The [pa] See *Creeps by Night*

HAMPDEN, JOHN (6 Feb 1898–) British author and teacher. He has been an English master and a university professor; pre-war he was an editor for T. Nelson (publishers). He has written many books of various types. Since 1941 he has been associated in many capacities with the British Council, and since 1959 has been Books and Periodicals adviser to this cultural body.

Anthology

Ghost Stories (Dent 'Everyman Library: 952,' London, 1939, 366 pp., 2/-; 3/-; 1951, 366 pp.; 1958, 384 pp., 8/6; 1961, pa 5/-)

18 stories and compiler's introduction: "Wandering Willie's Tale," Sir W. Scott; "Ligeia," E. A. Poe; "The Signalman," C. Dickens; "The Watcher," J. S. Le Fanu; "The Dream Woman," W. W. Collins; "The Middle Toe of the Right Foot," A. Bierce; "A Wicked Voice," V. Lee; "Count Magnus," M. R. James; "Running Wolf," A. Blackwood; "The Tomb of Sarah," F. G. Loring; "All Hallows," W. de la Mare; "The Extra Hand," H. M. Tomlinson; "The Beast With Five Fingers," W. F. Harvey; "A Daughter of Rameses," Lord Dunsany; "Mrs. Lunt," Sir H. Walpole; "The Buick Saloon," Ann Bridge; "The White Road," E. F. Rozman; "The Earlier Service," Margaret Irwin.

HAMPTON, LOU
Fiction
Ghosts of My Study [C] (Authors & Publishers Corp., New York, 1927, 284 pp., $2.00)

Ghost, 16 stories: "Pursued"; "After"; "Surprise Island"; "The Prairie Cabin"; "The Mysterious Gift of the Hermit of Kanawha"; "The Hidden Continent"; "What the Closet Revealed"; "The Change"; "An Interstellar Voyage"; "Her Lover–the Ghost"; "The Darkened Days"; "Heir to the Plantation"; "In the Days of the Monster Plants"; "The Ghost of the Old House"; "The Turn of Fate"; "A Day Dream at Eventide."

HANLON, JON
Anthologies [Selections from magazines of 1930's]
Death's Loving Arms and Other Terror Tales [pa] (Corinth: CR147, 1966, 159 pp., pa 60¢)

5 stories [last is novel] and compiler's intro. (abr. version of first issue of *Terror Tales*): "Death's Loving Arms," Hugh B. Cave; "Vampire Meat," Frederick C. Painton; "Blood Magic," G. T. Fleming-Roberts; "From Out of the Shadows," Frances B. Middleton; "Village of the Dead," Wyatt Blassingame.

House of Living Death and Other Terror Tales, The [pa] (Corinth: CR143, 1966, 160 pp., pa 60¢)

4 stories [first is novel] and compiler's intro. (abr. version of 2nd issue of *Terror Tales*): "The House of Living Death," Arthur L. Zagat; "Blood Hunter," Charles R. Wayne; "Dead Man's Bride," Wyatt Blassingame; "Hands Beyond the Grave," Henry T. Sperry.

Stories From Doctor Death and Other Terror Tales [pa] (Corinth: CR129, 1966, 159 pp., pa 60¢)

10 stories and compiler's intro. (selections from *Doctor Death*): "The Beast That Talked," Damascus Blount; "The Black Orchids," Arthur J. Burks; "The Electric Ostrich," Harvey A. Tampa; "The Skeleton Screams," O'Casey Holt; "I Am Dead!" Harold Ward; "Lake of Fear," Robert C. Blackmon; "The Man Who Didn't Exist," A. J. Burks; "Web of Terror," Michael Crowley; "Caged Horror," A. L. Zagat; "When the Buzzards Fed," R. C. Blackmon.

HANNA, W. C.
Fiction
Tandar Saga, The (Arcadia, New York, 1964, 190 pp., $2.95)

People of Tandar rove the galaxy looking for unoccupied inhabitable planets.

HANSEN, L(OUISE) TAYLOR U.S. author. She appeared in the sf field first with the story "What the Sodium Lines Revealed" (*ASQ*, Win 1929), and was noted for the following stories: "The Man From Space" (*AS*, Feb 1930); "The Prince of Liars" (*AS*, Oct 1930); "The Undersea Tube" (*AS*, Nov 29; reprint May 1961). A mysterious figure, she once appeared at a meeting of the Los Angeles Science Fantasy Society in 1939 and told F. J. Ackerman that she had placed these stories for her brother, a world traveller, who had written them. The mystery remains unsolved, but a series of many "Scientific Mystery" articles in *AS* 1941-48 under this name showed an amazing range of exploratory and archaeological knowledge.

HANSMAN, WILLIAM (DONALD) (13 Feb 1913–)
Fiction
A.G. Man, The (Vantage, New York, 1968, 193 pp., $3.95)

HARDEN, JOHN (22 Aug 1902–) U.S. newspaperman and public relations man. For many years he worked with various newspapers in various capacities; he turned to public relations, and in that field has had his own firm at Greensboro (N.C.) since 1958. Besides the work below he has also written *The Devil's Tramping Ground and Other North Carolina Mystery Stories* (1928).
Nonfiction
Tar Heel Ghosts (U. of North Carolina, 1954, 178 pp., illus.–L. McAlister, $3.00) (Oxford, 24/-)
Largely covers routine hauntings with but few provocative cases.

HARDIE, JOHN LIPP
Anthologies [There are understood to be a number more in the "Seven" paperback series.]
Seven More Strange Stories [pa] (Art & Educational Pub., Glasgow, *ca.* 1948, pa 1/3)
7 stories: "A Watcher by the Dead," A. Bierce; "Strange Adventures of a Private Secretary," A. Blackwood; "Mr. Higginbotham's Catastrophe," N. Hawthorne; "Sir Dominick Sarsfield," J. S. Le Fanu; "The Black Tom Cat," Captain Marryat; "The Accident," O. Onions; "The Facts in the Case of M. Valdemar," E. A. Poe.
Seven Strange Stories [pa] (Art & Educational, *ca.* 1948, 80 pp., 1/3)
7 stories: "Dr. Heidegger's Experiment," N. Hawthorne; "The Haunted and the Haunters," Lord Lytton; "Schalken the Painter," J. S. Le Fanu; "A Terribly Strange Bed," W. W. Collins; "The Werewolf," Capt. Marryat; "The Cask of Amontillado," "The Tell-Tale Heart," E. A. Poe.
Strange Stories–The Last Seven [pa] (Art & Educational, *ca.* 1948, 80 pp., 1/3)
7 stories: "The Sire de Maletroit's Door," R. L. Stevenson; "Keeping His Promise," A. Blackwood; "The Girl on the Bridge," Davis Tindall; "The Diamond Lens," F.-J. O'Brien; "The Squire's Story," Mrs. Gaskell; "The Masque of the Red Death," E. A. Poe; "The Middle Toe of the Right Foot," A. Bierce.
Twenty-Two Strange Stories (Art & Educational, Glasgow, 1945, 280 pp., 8/6)
22 stories: "The Cosy Room," A. Machen; "Dr. Heidegger's Experiment," N. Hawthorne; "Running Wolf," A. Blackwood; "The Facts in the Case of M. Valdemar," E. A. Poe; "The Monkey's Paw," W. W. Jacobs; "The Haunted and the Haunters," Lord Lytton; "A Night at a Cottage," R. Hughes; "The Spectre Bridegroom," W. Irving; "Schalken the Painter," J. S. Le Fanu; "Markheim," R. L. Stevenson; "The Squire's Story," Mrs. Gaskell; "The Three Strangers," T. Hardy; "A Singular Passage in the Life of the Late Henry Harris, D.D.," R. H. Barham; "The Story of Mary Ancel," W. M. Thackeray; "The Accident," O. Onions; "A Terribly Strange Bed," W. Collins; "The Mirror," Sir W. Scott; "The Upper Berth," F. M. Crawford; "The Werewolf," Capt. Marryat; "Because of the Dollars," J. Conrad; "The Diamond Lens," F.-J. O'Brien; "A Watcher by the Dead," A. Bierce.

HARDING, LEE (1937?–) Australian author. He had a number of short stories in the British sf magazines of the early 1960's;

some were reprinted in the U.S. As "Leo" Harding he was prominent in fan affairs in Victoria in the early 1950's, and edited a number of Australian amateur magazines; he left this type of activity in 1955. He made his early career in photography, both portraits and commercial projects, then changed to photo-journalism and fiction writing. He covered the filming of Nevil Shute's *On the Beach* with the Stanley Kramer film unit in Melbourne, and did a similar job for the film *The Sundowners* in New South Wales. He helped establish *Australian Science Fiction Review* in 1966 and contributed to it.

HARGREAVES, Sir GERALD
Fiction
Atlanta–A Story of Atlantis (Hutchinson, London, *ca.* 1946, 216 pp.)
A fantasy play in three acts, with music and illustrations by author. Based on the legend of Atlantis, it is set a few years after the Greeks return from the sack of Troy, the farthest colony of Atlantis. Atlanta, daughter of King Atlas and heir to the throne of Atlantis, is wrecked on the Greek coast and encounters Zeno (Achilles).

HARGREAVES, REGINALD See BENJAMIN, L. S. (co-anthologist)

HARKER, KENNETH British author. He graduated from Durham U. as a physicist. After contributing fact and fiction to various publications he decided in 1962 to become a full-time writer.
Fiction
Symmetrians, The [pa] (Compact: F308, 1966, 160 pp., pa 3/6)
The breeding of a race for physical perfection, and the revolt against it.

HARKINS, PETER J.
Series
Rick Brant [as John Blaine] See GOODWIN, H. L. (co-author)

HARMON, JIM U.S. author. He has written about 40 stories appearing in many sf magazines since 1954. His book *The Great Radio Heroes* (1967, 1968 pa) includes coverage of Superman, the Green Hornet, etc.

HARNESS, CHARLES L(EONARD) (29 Dec 1915–) U.S. patent attorney in Connecticut, associated with American Cyanamid Company. He wrote a number of sf stories for the magazines around the beginning of the 1950's and a few since.
Fiction
Flight Into Yesterday (*SS*, May 1949) –enlarged: (Bouregy Curl, New York, 1953, 256 pp., $2.75) (*The Paradox Men*, Ace: D-118, 1955, 187 pp., pa 35¢; with *Dome Around America*; Faber, London, 1964, 256 pp., 18/-, intro.–B. W. Aldiss; Queenswood, Toronto, $3.95; SF B.C. [S.J.], 1966; FSB: 1769, 1967, 158 pp., pa 3/6)
Set towards the end of civilization, with many involved plot twists. This story took two years to write.
Paradox Men, The [pa] See *Flight Into Yesterday*
Ring of Ritornel, The (Gollancz, London, 1968, 221 pp., 25/-) (Berkley: X1630, 1968, 191 pp., pa 60¢)
Galactic wanderings and a conception of circular time, involving mythological creatures, feudal society, anti-matter, etc.
Rose, The [C] [pa] (Compact: F295, 1966, 189 pp., pa 3/6) (Sidgwick, London, 1968, 191 pp., 18/-)
Sf, one novel and two short stories: "The Rose" (*Authentic*, n, Mar 1953); "The Chess Players"; "The New Reality." The title story is of interest as it has not yet been published in the U.S.A; it outlines the growth of a man to a superman, with the sacrifice of 'art' to defeat 'science.'

HARNEY, W. E. (BILL)
Fiction
Tales From the Aborigines [C] (R. Hale, London, 1965, 189 pp., 21/-)

23 stories, 11 verses, Author's Note, intro. and epilogue; subdivided into four parts of which *Tales of Fantasy* covers "giants striding" and "little men" and also the Lightning Totem, and *Tales of Imagination* is a series on the Evil One. Stories from the environment of aboriginal camplife, told and retold from the beginning of their time.

HARPER, C. ARMITAGE
Anthology
American Ghost Stories (Houghton, New York, 1928, 287 pp., $2.50) (Jarrolds, London, 1929, 288 pp., 7/6)

16 stories: "The Specter Bridegroom," W. Irving; "Ligeia," E. A. Poe; "Ghost of Dr. Harris," N. Hawthorne; "What Was It?" F.-J. O'Brien; "Ghost Story," M. Twain; "Transferred Ghost," F. R. Stockton; "Ghost Story," J. C. Harris; "Rival Ghosts," B. Matthews; "The Damned Thing," A. Bierce; "Eyes," Edith Wharton; "The Water Ghost of Harrowby Hall," J. K. Bangs; "Shadows on the Way," M. E. W. Freeman; "The Upper Berth," F. M. Crawford; " 'Dey Ain't No Ghosts'," E. P. Butler; "The Woman at Seven Brothers," W. D. Steele; "Hand," T. Dreiser.

HARPER, WILHELMINA (1884–)
Anthology
Ghosts and Goblins (Dutton, New York, 1964, 250 pp.; rev. 1965, $4.50)

Juvenile, 32 stories: "The Ghosts of Forefather's Hill," Raymond M. Alden; "Schippeitaro," Anon.; "Tomson's Halloween," Margaret Baker; "The Conjure Wives," Frances G. Wickes; "Wait Till Martin Comes," F. G. Wickes; "Witch Cat," "The Witch of Willowby Wood," Rowena Bennett; "The Giant Ghost," Elizabeth Sechrist; "Halloween," Molly Capes; "Theme in Yellow," Carl Sandburg; "Tcha the Sleeper," Arthur B. Chrisman; "The Wonderful Lamb," Nandor Pogany; "The Enchanted Cow," Mary G. Davis; "The Witch's Shoes," Frances J. Olcott; "Someone," Walter de la Mare; "The Witch of Lok Island," Elsie Masson; "Witches' Ride," Lupe De Osma; "The Goblin of the Pitcher," Alida S. Malkus; "The Ghost Wife," Charles Eastman; "The Old Hag of the Forest," Seumas MacManus; "The Woodman and the Goblins," J. B. Esenwein; "The Great White Bear," "The Wishing Well," Maude Lindsay; "The Hungry Old Witch," Charles J. Finger; "The Shadow People," Francis Ledwidge; "The Witch in the Wintry Wood," Aileen Fisher; "Here We Go!" Maria Leach; "The Ghosts of Kahlberg," Bernard Henderson; "The Old Witch," "Teeny-Tiny," "Tamlane," Joseph Jacobs; "A Halloween Story," Margaret Widdemer.

HARRE, T(HOMAS) EVERETT (17 Dec 1884–deceased [date unknown]) U.S. newspaperman, born in Marietta, Pa. He was on the staff of the *Philadelphia Press* 1905-7, and was then Associate Editor of *Hampton's* 1909-11, during which time he and another writer obtained the serial rights for Peary's trip to the North Pole. He has two fantasy novels listed in the Bleiler *Checklist*.
Anthology
Beware After Dark (Macaulay, New York, 1929, 461 pp., $2.50) (Gold Label, New York, 1931, 461 pp., $1.00) (Emerson, New York, 1942, 1945, 461 pp., $2.50)

Subtitled: "The world's most stupendous tales of mystery, horror, thrills and terror." The Emerson editions have no copyright credit. 21 stories, with compiler's introduction: "Negotium Perambulans," E. F. Benson; "Back There in the Grass," Gouverneur Morris; "The Mollmeit of the Mountain," Cynthia Stockley; "Fishhead," I. S. Cobb; "The Fountain of Gold," L. Hearn; "The Shadowy Third," Ellen Glasgow; "Lukundoo," E. L. White; "Rappaccini's Daughter," N. Hawthorne; "Lazarus," L. Andreyeff; "The Lame Priest," S. Carleton; "The Call of Cthulhu," H. P. Lovecraft; "Novel of the White Powder," A. Machen [spelt "Macken" on all contents pages]; "The Devils of Po Sung," B. Morgan; "The Isle of Voices," R. L. Stevenson; "The Sunken Land," G. W. Bayly; "Two Spinsters," E. P. Oppenheim; "The Monster-God of Mamurth," E. Hamilton; "Huguenin's Wife," M. P. Shiel; "The Coconut Pearl," Beatrice Grimshaw; "The Quest of the Tropic Bird," J. F. Wilson; "The Striding Place," Gertrude Atherton. Recommended by such reviewers as C. A. Brandt and A. Boucher.

HARRIS, CLARE WINGER (1891–) U.S. science fiction and fantasy writer of the late 1920's. The first woman writer for *Amazing Stories*, she won third prize in Gernsback's first cover contest. She is best known for her "Miracle of the Lily" (*AS*, Apr 1928). She had one notable collaboration with M. J. Breuer: "A Baby on Neptune" (*AS*, Nov 1929). Most of her short stories were collected as the book below.
Fiction
Away From the Here and Now [C] (Dorrance, Philadelphia, 1947, 365 pp., $2.50)

Sf and fantasy, 11 stories: "A Runaway World"; "The Fate of the Poseidonia"; "A Certain Soldier"; "The Diabolical Drug"; "The Miracle of the Lily"; "A Baby on Neptune"; "The Artificial Man"; "The Menace of Mars"; "The Evolutionary Monstrosity"; "The Fifth Dimension"; "The Ape Cycle." This contains only one or two stories of note.

HARRIS, FRANK (1854–26 Aug 1931) British and U.S. novelist, critic and biographer. He was born in Ireland, and as a youth went steerage to the U.S. He was admitted to the bar in Kansas in 1875. Later he was editor of *The Saturday Review* and *Vanity Fair*; he also bought and edited *Pearson's Magazine*. A strange, bombastic, violent, prejudiced type despised by Shaw and others, he was an inspired literary scout. In his last years he lived in obloquy because of the scandal resulting from *My Life and Loves* (published only in Germany). After his death his almost complete biography of G. B. Shaw was published. His fiction includes *Pantopia* (Panurge, ca. 1930) and *Unpath'd Waters* (M. Kennerley, 1913).
Fiction
Veils of Isis, The [C] (Doran, New York, 1915, 312 pp.)

Not listed in the Bleiler *Checklist*. 10 stories, with only the first being fantasy: "The Veils of Isis"; "The Yellow Ticket"; "The Ugly Duckling"; "A Daughter of Eve"; "Isaac and Rebecca"; "A French Artist"; "A Fool's Paradise"; "Within the Shadow"; "A Miracle and No Wonder"; "A Prostitute"; " 'The Kiss'."

HARRIS, JOHN (WYNDHAM PARKES LUCAS) B(EYNON) (10 July 1903–10 Mar 1969) British sf author, connected with the field for nearly 40 years. In 1930 he won an *Air Wonder Stories* competition with the slogan "Future Flying Fiction" (which was never used). His experience ranged from farming to advertising to reading for the bar. He contributed to *Wonder Stories* in the early 1930's under his own name; many of these stories were reprinted in *Tales of Wonder* under his "John Beynon" pseudonym. His two pre-war books appeared under this byline. In World War II he served with the Royal Signals, and was in London during the Blitz. After the war he adopted the pseudonym "John Wyndham." He was one of Britain's foremost sf writers for some years, with his novels making a good impression outside the field. He was the longest-writing British author in the sf and fantasy fields.
Series [as John Wyndham]
Troon. Career of a family in the conquest of space. All in *NW*: "For All the Night" (Apr 1958; "The Troons of Space," *Fan*, Nov 1958); "Idiot's Delight" (June 1958; "The Troons of Space: The Moon A.D. 2044," *Fan*, Dec 1958); "The Thin Gnat-Voices" (July 1958; "The Troons of Space: Mars A.D. 2094," *Fan*, Jan 1959); "Space Is a Province of Brazil" (Sep 1958; "The Troons of Space: Venus A.D. 2144," *Fan*, Feb 1959); "The Emptiness of Space" (Nov 1960; *AS*, Jan 1961). The first four were published in the 1959 edition of *The Outward Urge*, with later editions adding the fifth.
Fiction [all by John Wyndham unless otherwise stated]
Chocky (*AS*, n'te, Mar 1963) —enlarged: (Ballantine: U6119, 1968, 221 pp., pa 75¢) (M. Joseph, London, 1968, 184 pp., 21/-)

An invisible alien something attaches itself to a young lad.

Chrysalids, The See *Re-Birth*

Consider Her Ways and Others [C] (M. Joseph, London, 1961, 223 pp., 15/-) (Penguin: 2231, 1965, 190 pp., pa 3/6) (*I raconti del tiempo* [Italian], *Urania*: 304, 1963)

6 stories (Italian edition has three stories marked †, plus "The

Wheel"): "Consider Her Ways"† (n'te, from *Sometime, Never* [Anon.], 1956); "Odd"†; "Oh, Where, Now, Is Peggy Macrafferty?"; "Stitch in Time"; "Random Quest"†; "A Long Spoon."

Day of the Triffids, The (*Collier's*, sr5, 6 Jan 1951) (Doubleday, New York, 1951, 6+222 pp., $2.50; Doubleday 'Dolphin' C130, ca. 1960, 233 pp., pa 95¢) (M. Joseph, 1951, 302 pp., 10/6; 1958, 12/6) (*De Triffids komen* [Dutch], Breughel, Amsterdam, 1951; Spectrum, Utrecht, 1962; De Geillustreerde pers, Amsterdam, 1967) (*Revolt of the Triffids*, Popular: 411, 1952, 224 pp., pa 25¢) (*L'orrenda invasione* [Italian], *Urania*: 3, 1952) (D'day SF B.C., ca. 1953) (*Triffidernas Uppror* [Swedish], Eklund, 1953) (Penguin: 993, 1954, 272 pp., pa 2/-; 1958, pa 2/6; 1968, pa 4/-) (*Die Triffids* [German], Süddeutscher, 1955; Heyne, 1960, pa) (*Revolte des Triffids* [French], Fleuve Noire: A68, 1956, pa) (*El dia de los trifidos* [Spanish—Argentine], Minotauro: 7, 1956, pa) (*Da Trifitterne Kom* [Danish], Skrifola: F3, 1957, pa) (Abr.: Hutchinson, London, 1960, 208 pp., illus.—A. Breeze, 6/-) (Horwitz: H993, 1961, 272 pp., pa 5/6) (Crest: D531, 1962, 191 pp., pa 50¢; d741, 1964, pa 50¢; R1049, 1967, pa 60¢) (in *The John Wyndham Omnibus*, 1964, 1965)

Catastrophe strikes the Earth after the arrival of mobile plants (the Triffids), when everyone is blinded; a derivative of Wells' "Country of the Blind." The story received the second International Fantasy Award, in 1952, and was serialized as a BBC radio play about 1957. *Film:* British Security Pictures, 1963, colour and cinemascope, starring H. Keel and Nicole Maurey. It was well liked by E. J. Carnell (*NW*, June 1963), but was apparently banned in Australia.

Infinite Moment, The [C] [pa] (Ballantine: 546, 1961, 159 pp., pa 35¢)

6 stories about time (most from *Consider Her Ways*): "Consider Her Ways"; "Odd"; "How Do I Do"; "Stitch in Time"; "Random Quest"; "Time Out."

Jizzle [C] (Dobson, London, 1954, 251 pp., 11/6; 1963, 15/-) (SF B.C. [S.J.], 1961, 5/6) (FSB: 730, 1962, 191 pp., pa 2/6; 1308, 1965, pa 3/6)

Sf and fantasy, 15 stories (those marked † appear in *Tales of Gooseflesh and Laughter*): "Jizzle"† (*Collier's*, 8 Jan 1949, as J. Beynon; *F&SF*, Feb 1952); "Technical Slip"; "A Present From Brunswick"†; "Chinese Puzzle"†; "Esmeralda"; "How Do I Do?"; "Una"†; "Affair of the Heart"; "Confidence Trick"†; "The Wheel"†; "Look Natural, Please!"; "Perforce to Dream"; "Reservation Deferred"; "Heaven Scent"†; "More Spinned Against"†.

John Wyndham Omnibus, The [C] (M. Joseph, 1964, 532 pp., 25/-) (Simon & Schuster, New York, 1965, 532 pp., $5.95)

Three novels: *The Day of the Triffids; The Kraken Wakes; The Chrysalids.*

Kraken Wakes, The (M. Joseph, 1953, 288 pp., 10/6; 1958, 12/6) ("The Things From the Deep," *Everybody's* [British mag.], sr?) (*Out of the Deeps*, Ballantine, 1953, 182 pp., $2.00; #50, pa 35¢; #545, 1961, pa 35¢; U2814, 1965, pa 50¢) (*Vidundret Vaknar* [Swedish], Eklund, 1954) (*Il risveglio dell' abisso* [Italian], *Urania*: 35, 1954; 307 bis, 1963) (SF B.C. [S.J.], 1955, 4/6) (Penguin: 1075, 1955, 240 pp., pa 2/6; 1956, pa 2/6; 1961, pa 3/6; 1964, pa 3/6) (*Kraken acecha* [Spanish], Nebula: 13, 1955, pa) ([Japanese], Gegen-sha SF:4, 1956) (*Le peril vient de la mer* [French], Gallimard: Le RF, 1958) (Abr. & intro—S. S. Moody: Longmans Green, London, 1961, 162 pp., 5/6) (*Kolonie im Meer* [German], Goldmann, 1961, 1962 pa) (in *The John Wyndham Omnibus*, 1964, 1965) (*Invasie uit de ruimte* [Dutch], Spectrum, Utrecht, 1967)

A novel of interstellar invaders in the ocean's depths, and their effect on mankind. It has been a radio play scripted by J. K. Cross for the BBC (and used in Australia).

Midwich Cuckoos, The (M. Joseph, 1957, 239 pp., 13/6) (Ballantine, 1958, 247 pp., $3.50; #299K, 1959, 189 pp., pa 35¢; *Village of the Damned*, 453K, 1960, pa 35¢; U2840, 1966, pa 50¢) (T. Allen, Toronto, 1958, $4.00) (*Les coucous de Midwich* [French], Denoël: PF28, 1959, pa) ([Japanese], Hayakawa: 3017, 1959, pa) (*I figli della invasione* [Italian], *Urania*: 200, 1959) (Penguin: 1440, 1960, 220 pp., pa 2/6—two editions, one with photograph as cover; 1967, pa 3/6) (*Operatie Koekoek* [Dutch], Spectrum,

Utrecht, 1963) (Abr. & intro.—L. Fuller: Longmans, 1964, 133 pp., 7/6) (*Es geschah am Tage X* [German], 1965, pa)

After a UFO lands, women become pregnant and produce unusual children; Russia and England overcome the danger using vastly different methods. *Film:* M.G.M., 1960, as *Village of the Damned*, starring George Sanders and Barbara Shelley. It differs from the book in some respects, but the photography and production are well handled, with the children being simply fantastic and conveying perfectly their non-human characteristics.

Out of the Deeps See *Kraken Wakes, The*

Outward Urge, The [by J. Wyndham & Lucas Parkes] (M. Joseph, 1959, 192 pp., 13/6) (Collins, Toronto, $3.25) (Ballantine: 341K, 1959, 143 pp., pa 35¢; U2809, 1965, pa 50¢) (SF B.C. [S.J.], 1961, 5/6) (Penguin: 1544, 1962, 187 pp., pa 3/-)

The conquest of the Solar System over 150 years, from manned orbit to landing on Venus, linked by successive members of the Troon family. See *Troon* series. *Note:* Lucas Parkes is a pseudonym of J. B. Harris and was added to the book merely for sales value.

Planet Plane [as John Beynon] ("Stowaway to Mars," British newspaper sr, 1935) (Newnes, London, 1936, 248 pp., 3/6) (*Passagere clandestine pour Mars* [French], Hachette: Le RF, 1951) (*Stowaway to Mars*, Nova: 1, 1953, 128 pp., pa 1/6) (*Avventura su Marte* [Italian], *Urania*: 49, 1954) (*Fripassagerare Till Mars* [Swedish], Lindqvist, 1955, pa)

Space adventure. After the 1936 book edition the story was abridged and serialised as "The Space Machine." The 1953 Nova edition was a modernised story; it was the first of a projected Nova SF Novel Series which did not continue. The original story had a sequel: "Sleeper of Mars" (*Tales of Wonder*, No. 2, 1938).

Re-Birth (Ballantine, 1955, 185 pp., $2.00; #104, pa 35¢; 423K, 1960, pa 35¢; U2820, 1965, pa 50¢) (*The Chrysalids*, M. Joseph, 1955, 239 pp., 10/6; Penguin: 1308, 1958, 200 pp., pa 2/6; 1967, pa 3/6; 1968, pa 4/-; Hutchinson, 1964, 200 pp., illus.—P. Edwards, 6/-; in *The John Wyndham Omnibus*, 1964, 1965) (*Las crisálidas* [Spanish], Nebula: 31, 1956, pa) (*I transfigiurati* [Italian], *Urania*: 149, 1957) (*Den Stora Hemsökelsen* [Swedish], Eklund, 1958) (*Les transformes* [French], Le Fleuve Noir: A123, 1958, pa) (in *A Treasury of Great SF* [Boucher], 1959) (*De getekenden* [Dutch], Spectrum, Utrecht, 1959) (*Wem gehört die Erde* [German], Goldmann, 1960, 1963, pa) (Horwitz: H1308, 1961, 198 pp., pa 5/-)

After an atomic war and the end of 20th century civilization, mutant telepaths develop in a back-to-God society.

Revolt of the Triffids [pa] See *Day of the Triffids*

Secret People, The [as John Beynon] (*Passing Show* [Brit. mag.], sr, July-Sep 1935) (Newnes, 1935, 256 pp., 7/6; 1936, 2/6) (*FFM*, Apr 1950) (*Le onde del Sahara* [Italian], *Urania*: 56, 1954) ([as J. B. Harris], Lancer: 72-701, 1964, 175 pp., pa 50¢; 71-155, 1967, pa 50¢)

Adventure with a hidden underground race in the Sahara desert.

Seeds of Time, The [C] (M. Joseph, 1956, 253 pp., 12/6) (*Semillas del tiempo* [Spanish], Nebula: 51, 1958, pa) (Penguin: 1385, 1959, 222 pp., pa 2/6) (*Le temps casse* [French], Denoël: PF34, 1959, pa) (*Die Kobaltblume* [German], Goldmann, 1960, 1962 pa) (Horwitz: H1385, 1961, 220 pp., pa 5/-)

10 stories of off-trail sf (stories marked † appeared in *Tales of Gooseflesh and Laughter*): "Chronoclasm"; "Time to Rest"; "Meteor"; "Survival"; "Pawley's Peepholes"; "Opposite Number"†; "Pillar to Post"; "Dumb Martian"; "Compassion Circuit"†; "Wild Flower"†. *Note:* The Spanish edition omits "Opposite Number"; the German edition's title is that of the last story, and this edition omits "Survival" and "Compassion Circuit."

Stowaway to Mars [pa] See *Planet Plane*

Tales of Gooseflesh and Laughter [C] [pa] (Ballantine: 182, 1956, 150 pp., pa 50¢; U2832, 1966, pa 50¢)

Sf and fantasy, 11 stories: "Jizzle"; "A Present From Brunswick"; "Chinese Puzzle"; "Una"; "Confidence Trick"; "The Wheel"; "Heaven Scent"; "More Spinned Against"; "Opposite Number"; "Compassion Circuit"; "Wild Flower."

Trouble With Lichen, The (M. Joseph, 1960, 190 pp., 13/6) (Ballantine: 449K, 1960, 160 pp., pa 35¢) (*L'herbe a vivre* [French],

Denoël: PF 54, 1961) (SF B.C. [S.J.], 1962, 5/6) (*Il lichene chinese* [Italian], *Urania*: 286, 1962) (Penguin: #1986, 1963, 204 pp., pa 3/6) (*Dificultades con los liquenos* [Spanish], Galaxia: 41, 1965, pa)

Two scientists independently find means to prolong life; the story deals with the psychological implications, but neglects some aspects of the question.

Village of the Damned See *Midwich Cuckoos, The*

HARRIS, LARRY M. (pseud) See JANIFER, L. M.

HARRISON, G. B.
Fiction
Fires of Arcadia, The (Harcourt Brace, New York, 1965, vi+153 pp., $3.95)

An uninhibited Arcadian romp when an experimental biologist breeds satyrs.

HARRISON, HARRY (12 Mar 1925–) U.S. author, editor and commercial artist. He was born in Stamford, Connecticut. He was the editor of the last numbers of *Science Fiction Adventures* (first series), and was to have been the editor of *Rocket Stories* from its fourth issue (1953), but the magazine folded. In 1956 he became Art Manager of *Picture Week* for a period. More recently he was Editor-in-Chief of the British magazine *Impulse*, Nos. 8 to 12 (Oct 1966–Feb 1967). He then edited *Amazing Stories* and *Fantastic* for about a year starting in late 1967.

As a science fiction writer Harrison first appeared with "Rock Diver" (*Worlds Beyond*, Feb 1951). A later story of note was "Web of the Norns" [with Kath. MacLean] (*Fantasy Fiction*, Nov 1953; *Science-Fantasy*, Apr 1958). Since 1958 he has become quite a regular writer in the field and has made a name for robust adventure sf. He is a member of the Hydra Club in New York, speaks fluent Esperanto, and has lived in Europe.

Series
dinAlt, Jason. All in *ASF*: "Deathworld" (sr3, Jan 1960; paperback); "The Ethical Engineer" (sr2, July 1963; *Deathworld 2*); "The Horse Barbarians" (sr3, Feb 1968; *Deathworld 3*).

Fiction
Bill, the Galactic Hero ("The Starsloggers," *GSF*, Dec 1964) (Doubleday, New York, 1965, 185 pp., $3.50) (*NW*, sr3, Aug 1965 [first 3 sections of book]) (Gollancz, London, 1965, 160 pp., 16/-) (Berkley: F1186, 1966, 143 pp., pa 50¢)

An unwilling hero in a lightweight farce and satire on perennial military idiocies.

Deathworld [pa] (*ASF*, sr3, Jan 1960) (Bantam: A2160, 1960, 154 pp., pa 25¢) (*Planet des falschen Zaubers* [German], *UG*: 141, 1961) (*Mundo muerto* [Spanish], Nebula: 37, 1962, pa) (*Mondo maledetto* [Italian], *Cosmo*: 115, 1963) (Penguin: 1095, 1963, 158 pp., pa 3/-; 1966, pa 3/6) (*Die Todeswelt* [German], Heyne: 3067, 1966, pa) (*Doodstrijd op Pyrrus* [Dutch], Meulenhoff, Amsterdam, 1967)

First of "Jason dinAlt" series. A realistic fight for survival by colonists on a tough planet, with nature fighting back.

Deathworld 2 [pa] ("The Ethical Engineer," *ASF*, sr2, July 1963) –enlarged: (Bantam: F2838, 1964, 151 pp., pa 50¢) (*Il pianeta dei damnati* [Italian], *Cosmo*: 135, 1963) (*L'ingegnere etico* [Italian], *GRF*: 37, 1964) (*The Ethical Engineer*, Gollancz, 1964, 176 pp., 15/-) (*Mundo verto* [Spanish], Galaxie: 42, 1965, pa) (*Die Sklavenwelt* [German], Heyne: 3069, 1966, pa)

Second of "Jason dinAlt" series. Captured by Mikah, an ethical fanatic, Jason crashes the ship on a planet of primitive ethics and fights their way out of many traps.

Deathworld 3 [pa] ("The Horse Barbarians," *ASF*, sr3, Feb 1968) (Dell: 1849, 1968, 188 pp., pa 60¢)

Third of "Jason dinAlt" series. On the planet Felicity, Jason tries to undermine a society of people born only to attack and kill.

Ethical Engineer, The See *Deathworld 2*

Make Room! Make Room! (*Impulse*, sr3, Aug 1966) (Doubleday, 1966, 213 pp., $3.95) (Berkley: X1416, 1967, 208 pp., pa 60¢) (Penguin: 2664, 1967, 224, pa 4/6)

An outline of the ignorance and stupidity of man breeding himself into extinction; set in 1995, but not too different from today.

Man From P.I.G., The [pa] (*ASF*, n'te, July 1967) –enlarged: (Avon: ZS136, 1968, 120 pp., pa 60¢)

A pig farmer and police agent of the future, with his "porcine interstellar guard"!

Plague From Space (Doubleday, 1964, 207 pp., $3.95) (D'day, Toronto, $4.75) (Gollancz, London, 1966, 207 pp., 18/-) (*Die Pest kam von den Sternen* [German], *TS*: 108, 1966) (Bantam: F3640, 1968, 154 pp., pa 50¢)

The fight against a viral epidemic with no antibody reaction.

Planet of the Damned ("Sense of Obligation," *ASF*, sr3, Sep 1961) (Bantam: J2316, 1962, 135 pp., pa 40¢) (*Sense of Obligation*, Dobson, London, 1967, 135 pp., 16/-)

A shanghaied agent fights to save the planet Dis from obliteration.

Sense of Obligation See *Planet of the Damned*

Stainless Steel Rat, The [pa] (Pyramid: F672, 1961, 158 pp., pa 40¢) (*Il titano d'acciaio* [Italian], *Cosmo*: 112, 1962) (*Agenten im Kosmos* [German], Heyne: 3083, 1966, pa) (FSB: 1605, 1966, 158 pp., pa 3/6)

The adventures of Slippery Jim DiGriz, a future con man, and how he was forced to join the Special Corps. Written from "The Stainless Steel Rat" (*ASF*, Aug 1957) and "The Misplaced Battleship" (*ASF*, Apr 1960).

Technicolor Time Machine, The ("The Time Machined Saga," *ASF*, sr3, Mar 1967) (Doubleday, 1967, 190 pp., $3.95) (Faber, London, 1968, 190 pp., 21/-) (Berkley: X1640, 1968, 174 pp., 60¢)

A movie company out to make a Viking epic on the cheap goes on location to the Orkney Islands of 1,000 A.D.

Two Tales and Eight Tomorrows [C] (Gollancz, 1965, 191 pp., 16/-) (Bantam: F3722, 1968, 147 pp., pa 50¢) (*Bruder im All* [German], Goldmann: 097, 1968, pa)

10 stories: "The Streets of Ashkelon"; "Portrait of an Artist"; "Rescue Operation"; "Captain Bedlam"; "Final Encounter"; "Into My Manifold Rooms"; "The Pliable Animal"; "Captain Honario Harpplayer, R.N."; "According to His Abilities"; "I Always Do What Teddy Says."

War With the Robots [C] [pa] (Pyramid: F771, 1962, 158 pp., pa 40¢; X1898, 1968, pa 60¢) (*Die Roboter rebellieren* [German], Goldmann, 1964, 1964 pa) (Dobson, 1967, 158 pp., 18/-) (SF B.C. [S.J.], 1968)

Sf, 8 stories with author's introduction, and introductory comment on each story: "Simulated Trainer" ("Trainee for Mars"); "The Velvet Glove"; "Arm of the Law"; "The Robot Who Wanted to Know"; "I See You" ("Robot Justice"); "The Repairman"; "Survival Planet"; "War With the Robots."

Nonfiction
Collected Editorials From Analog [Editor for] See CAMPBELL, J. W.

Anthologies
All About Venus See ALDISS, B. W. (co-anthologist)
Apeman, Spaceman See STOVER, L. E. (co-anthologist)
Backdrop of Stars (Dobson, 1968, 222 pp., 25/-) (*SF: Author's Choice*, Berkley: S1567, 1968, 224 pp., pa 75¢)

Sf, 13 stories with introduction: "Judas Danced," B. W. Aldiss; "The Last of the Deliverers," Poul Anderson; "Founding Father," I. Asimov; "End-Game," J. G. Ballard; "Tiger Ride," J. Blish & D. Knight; "Consumer's Report," T. R. Cogswell; "Proposal," L. S. de Camp; "Sail On! Sail On!" P. J. Farmer; "Missing Link," Frank Herbert; "Myths My Great-Granddaughter Taught Me," Fritz Leiber; "Syndrome Johnny," Katherine MacLean; "Day Million," Frederik Pohl; "Retaliation," Mack Reynolds.

Best SF: 1967 [with B. W. Aldiss] [pa] (Berkley: S1529, 1968, 256 pp., pa 75¢) (*Year's Best Science Fiction*, Sphere: 43311, 1968, 207 pp., pa 5/-)

15 stories, with "Credo"–J. Blish; introduction–H. Harrison; afterword–"Knights of the Paper Spaceship"–B. W. Aldiss: "Hawksbill Station," R. Silverberg; "Ultimate Construction," C. C. Shackleton; "1937 A.D.!" John T. Sladek; "Fifteen Miles," B. Bova; "Blackmail," F. Hoyle; "The Vine," Kit Reed; "Interview With a Lemming," J. Thurber; "The Wreck of the Ship 'John B',"

F. M. Robinson; "The Left-Hand Way" ("Navel Engagement," from Australian amateur mag.), A. B. Chandler; "The Forest of Zil," K. Neville; "The Assassination of John Fitzgerald Kennedy Considered as a Downhill Motor Race," J. G. Ballard; "Answering Service," F. Leiber; "The Last Command," K. Laumer; "Mirror of Ice," Gray Wright; "Pretty Maggie Moneyeyes," H. Ellison.
Farewell Fantastic Venus See ALDISS, B. W. (co-anthologist)
Nebula Award Stories 1967 See ALDISS, B. W. (co-anthologist)
Nebula Award Stories 2 See ALDISS, B. W. (co-anthologist)
SF: Author's Choice [pa] See *Backdrop of Stars*
Year's Best Science Fiction [pa] See *Best SF: 1967*

HARRISON, HELGA
Fiction
Catacombs (Chatto Windus, 1962, 223 pp., 18/-)

HARRISON, MICHAEL British author, who also uses the pseudonym "Quentin Downes."
Fiction
Brain, The (Cassell, London, 1953, 287 pp., 10/6)
An atomic bomb cloud assumes the shape of a human brain, and becomes intelligent.
Higher Things (MacDonald, London, 1945, 187 pp., 8/6)
The invention of a gravity nullifier, and the resultant power of flying.

HART, EDWARD (1854– ?)
Fiction
Silica Gel Pseudomorph and Other Stories, The [C] (Chemical Pub. Co., Easton [Penna.], 1924, 175 pp., $1.50)
20 stories of fantasy interest: "The Silica Gel Pseudomorph"; "Peep-Chick Mountain"; "Round Valley"; "Mont L'Hery"; "Death Valley"; "The Professor's Story"; "My Friend Zahn"; "Just Samuel Jones"; "Fat and Lean"; "Woozy"; "The Hermit"; "Sandy's Story"; "The Hoboes"; "Jumping Steel"; "All the Way From Melbourne"; "A Defense of the Wealthy"; "The Skin of the Bear"; "A Visit From the Wileys"; "In the Days of the Roses"; "The Red Devil."

HARTLEY, L(ESLIE) P(OLES) (30 Dec 1895–) British author. He graduated from Balliol College in 1922. He has reviewed many novels and short stories. He is a bachelor, and enjoys sculling. His published works began with *Night Fears* (1924). He has received the James Tait Black Memorial Prize and also the Heinemann Foundation Award. Two of his books of slight fantasy content are *Sixth Heaven* (Putnam, 1946; Doubleday, 1947) and *The White Wand and Other Stories* (H. Hamilton, 1954). Other fiction includes *The Killing Bottle* (Putnam, 1932). His ghost stories have been favorably compared with Henry James.
Fiction
Collected Short Stories of L. P. Hartley, The [C] (H. Hamilton, London, 1968, viii+626 pp., 42/-)
41 stories and 3¾-p. intro.–Lord David Cecil: *Simonetta Perkins* (1925). *The Travelling Grave* (1951, 12 stories): "A Visitor From Down Under"; "Podolo"; "Three, or Four, for Dinner"; "The Travelling Grave"; "Feet Foremost"; "The Cotillon"; "A Change of Ownership"; "The Thought"; "Conrad and the Dragon"; "The Island"; "Night Fears"; "The Killing Bottle." *The White Wand* (1954, 14 stories): "The White Wand"; "Apples"; "A Summons"; "A Tonic"; "A Condition of Release"; "Witheling End"; "Mr. Blandfoot's Picture"; "The Price of the Absolute"; "A Rewarding Experience"; "W.S."; "The Two Vaynes"; "Monkshood Manor"; "Up the Garden Path"; "Hilda's Letter." *Two for the River* (1961, 14 stories): "Two for the River"; "Someone in the Lift"; "The Face"; "The Corner Cupboard"; "The Waits"; "The Pampas Clumps"; "Won by a Fall"; "A Very Present Help"; "A High Dive"; "The Crossways"; "Per Far L'Amore"; "Interference"; "Naughts and Crosses"; "The Pylon."
Facial Justice (H. Hamilton, London, 1960, 256 pp., 16/-) (Collins, Toronto, $3.75) (Doubleday, New York, 1961, 263 pp., $3.50) (D'day SF B.C., 1961, $1.20) (Penguin: 2455, 1966, 220 pp., pa 4/6)

A girl rebels against life in a stereotyped future after World War III.
Travelling Grave and Other Stories, The [C] (Arkham, Sauk City [Wis.], 1948, 235 pp., $3.00; 2,047 copies) (J. Barrie; London, 1951, 288 pp., 8/6; 1956, 10/6) (Barker: D20, 1959, 192 pp., pa 2/6 [9 stories marked †])
Weird, 12 stories: "A Visitor From Down Under"†; "Podolo"†; "Three, or Four, for Dinner"; "The Travelling Grave"†; "Feet Foremost"†; "The Cotillon"; "A Change of Ownership"†; "The Thought"†; "Conrad and the Dragon"†; "The Island"; "Night Fears"†; "The Killing Bottle"†.

HARTLIB, SAMUEL (? –1662) English author.
Fiction
Description of the Famous Kingdome of Macaria, A (London, 1st 1641, reprinted in the *Harleian Miscellany* Vol. I, 1744) ("A facsimile edition," intro.–Richard H. Dillon, Wallace Kibbee, Corte Madera [Calif.], 1961, 5 pp. intro. + 18 pp. text, 490 copies)
Title continues: "showing its excellent Government, wherein the Inhabitants live in great Prosperity, Health and Happiness: the King obeyed, the Nobles honoured, and all good Men respected: Vice punished, and virtue rewarded. An Example to Other Nations in a Dialogue between a Scholar and a Traveller." This is one of the many utopian works referred to in the *Cambridge Bibliography of English Literature* and the *Cambridge History of English Literature*. It was influenced by V. Andreae's *Christianopolis* (1619). Not listed in the Bleiler *Checklist*.

HARVEY, ALEXANDER (25 Dec 1868–20 Nov 1949) American editor and author, born in Brussels, Belgium. He was associate editor of *Current Opinion* 1905-22 and *American Monthly* 1922-29.
Fiction
Toe and Other Tales, The [C] (M. Kennerley, New York, 1913, 251 pp., $1.25)
11 stories of fantasy interest (not in Bleiler *Checklist*): "The Toe"; "The Raft"; "The Fools"; "The Finishing Touch"; "The Finger of Fate"; "The Measure of All Things"; "The Mustache"; "Miss Dix"; "The Forbidden Floor"; "The Frou-Frou"; "The Golden Rat."

HARVEY, FRANK
Fiction
Air Force! [C] [pa] (Ballantine: 329K, 1959, 142 pp., pa 35¢)
8 stories set in the 'near future,' with supersonic flight, manned Earth satellites, and the Air Force on the frontiers of space: "Orbit Flight"; "Panic on Runway 6"; "Test Jump"; "Runaway Prop"; "Jinx Jet"; "100 Miles Up"; "Moon Shot"; "Destruct Button."

HARVEY, W(ILLIAM) F(RYER) (1885–1937) British author. He took a medical degree at Leeds. His natural ill-health was worsened by service in World War I, during which he received the Albert Medal for gallantry in saving a life at sea. In the weird field his most noted stories are "The Beast With Five Fingers" and "August Heat," both of which have appeared in numerous anthologies; the former was also the basis for a film of the same title–Warner Bros., 1947, directed by Robert Florey and starring Peter Lorre. Harvey's *Midnight Tales* is a posthumous selection of his older stories by M. Richardson; other fiction includes *Midnight House and Other Tales* (1910).
Fiction
Arm of Mrs. Egan and Other Stories, The [C] (Dent, London, 1951, 256 pp., 10/6) (*The Arm of Mrs. Egan and Other Strange Stories*, Dutton, New York, 1952, 256 pp., $2.50)
16 stories; four are fantasy: "The Arm of Mrs. Egan"; "Account Rendered"; "The Flying Out of Mrs. Barnard Hollis"; "The Habeas Corpus Club."
Arm of Mrs. Egan and Other Strange Stories, The [C] See *The Arm of Mrs. Egan and Other Stories*
Beast With Five Fingers, The [C] (Dent, 1928, 228 pp., 6/-; 1932, 3/6; 'Aldine 10,' 1962, 200 pp., pa 5/-) (Dutton, 1928, 228 pp.,

$2.50) (Guild: 4, 1941, 128 pp., pa) (*Die Bestie mit den fünf Fingern* [German], Diogenes, 1964)

Weird, 20 stories: "The Beast With Five Fingers"; "Midnight House"; "The Dabblers"; "Unwinding"; "Mrs. Ormerod"; "Double Demon"; "The Tool"; "The Heart of the Fire"; "The Clock"; "Peter Levisham"; "Miss Cornelius"; "The Man Who Hated Aspidistras"; "Sambo"; "The Star"; "Across the Moors"; "The Follower"; "August Heat"; "Sarah Bennet's Possession"; "The Ankardyne Pew"; "Miss Avenal."

Midnight Tales [selected by M. Richardson] [C] (Dent, 1946, 200 pp., 8/6)

Weird, 20 stories and introduction: "Midnight House"; "The Dabblers"; "Unwinding"; "Mrs. Ormerod"; "Double Demon"; "The Tool"; "The Heart of the Fire"; "The Clock"; "Peter Levisham"; "Miss Cornelius"; "The Man Who Hated Aspidistras"; "Sambo"; "The Star"; "The Follower"; "August Heat"; "Sarah Bennet's Possession"; "Miss Avenal"; "The Beast With Five Fingers."

Moods and Tenses [C] (Blackwell, London, 1933, 223 pp., 5/-)

17 stories and introduction "The Double Eye": *Part I:* "The Dabblers"; "Full Circle"; "Mrs. Ormerod"; "Pelly's Gambit"; "The Follower." *Part II:* "The King Who Could Not Grow a Beard"; "Dung, Worm-Casts, Snow and Ice"; "The Man Who Hated Aspidistras." *Part III:* "The Ivory House"; "The Two Llewellyns"; "Death of a God"; "London Calling"; "Double Demon." *Part IV:* "Autumn Love"; "Hypocrites"; "Jimmy's Aunt"; "Shepherde and Kings."

HASSE, HENRY U.S. science fiction author and fan. He was well known in pre-war U.S. fan circles; he has worked in many occupations, and in 1947 was living in Hollywood. He had a number of stories in the sf magazines up to the early 1950's. He collaborated with R. Bradbury on a number of occasions, including Bradbury's first story: "Pendulum" (*SSS*, Nov 1941; *FFM*, June 1953). He wrote some amusing skits on sf with A. Fedor: "The End of Tyme" (*WS*, Nov 1933) and a sequel. Probably his most unusual story was "He Who Shrank" (*AS*, Aug 1936). He had a number of stories in *Planet*, and has had a few in the 1960's in *Amazing* and *Fantastic*.
Fiction
Stars Will Wait, The (Avalon, New York, 1968, 191 pp., $3.50)

HASSON, JAMES
Fiction
Bid Time Return (Macmillan, London, 1960, 243 pp., 16/-)
Concerns longevity.

HATCH, GERALD U.S. author. He was born in Brooklyn, N.Y. and attended Erasmus Hall in Brooklyn. For many years he was a court reporter. He has written over 30 novels under various pseudonyms; the only sf is the one below. His hobbies are book collecting, hi-fi and the study of electronics.
Fiction
Day the Earth Froze, The [pa] (Monarch: 354, 1963, 125 pp., pa 35¢)

HATHAWAY, LOUISE
Fiction
Enchanted Hour, The [C] (J. J. Newbegin, San Francisco, 1940, 128 pp., $1.50; 500 copies)
Foreword and 3 stories: "The Enchanted Hour"; "In the Shadow of the Pyramid"; "Mars Meets Earth."

HAUFF, WILHELM (29 Nov 1802–18 Nov 1827) German short-story writer and novelist. Taking his Ph.D. at U. of Tübingen in 1824, he became a private tutor to a Stuttgart family and began his writing career with fairy stories to entertain his charges. He was very productive during his three-year writing period before he died of typhoid. A fantasy in addition to those below was *The Wine-Ghosts of Bremen* (White & Allen, New York & London, 1889; 500 copies).

Fiction
Caravan Tales and Some Others [Adapted and retold–J. G. Hornstein] [C] (Stokes, New York, 1912, 337 pp., illus.–Norman Ault)

Weird, 7 stories: "Caliph Stork"; "The Death Ship"; "Little Mook"; "The False Prince"; "The Golden Whistle, or, The Fortunes of Said"; "The Wonder Child"; "The Rusty Key."
Tales [C] (G. Bell, London, 1890, 342 pp.)

Weird, 3 stories: "The Caravan"; "The Sheik of Alexandria and His Slaves"; "The Inn in the Spessart."

HAUSER, HEINRICH (1901–) German author and sea traveller. He wrote many high-class novels in his youth, including *Bitter Waters* (Gerhart Hauptmann Prize winner, 1929); he also took motion pictures throughout the world before the war. He left Germany in 1939 and lived in New York State, where he wrote his controversial *The German Talks Back* (1945), published soon after the defeat of Germany. He wrote some science fiction which was published in *Amazing Stories*: the highly regarded "Agharti" (June 1946) and the lesser "Titan's Battle" (Mar 1947). He returned to his homeland soon afterwards, and has since translated many German novels. He has also written some original material, including work on German politics. A recent sf novel is *Gigant Hirn* (Weiss, 1958; Goldmann, 1962).

HAWKES, JACQUETTA (1910–) British archaeologist, O.B.E., M.A., and wife of author J. B. Priestley. She has written, lectured and broadcast on archaeology. She has worked for UNESCO, been Vice-President of the Council for British Archaeology 1949-52, and served with the Government Film Institute 1950-55. Her book *A Land* has been very highly commended. She has written *Man and the Sun* (Random, 1963, $5.00), a discussion of man's past, present and future.
Fiction
Fables [C] See *Woman as Great as the World, A*
Providence Island (Random, New York, 1959, 239 pp., $3.50) (C. Windus, London, 1959, 251 pp., 16/-) (Grey Arrow: G89, 1961, 199 pp., pa 3/6)

An expedition finds an island inhabited by the Magdalenians, descendants of Stone Age society with developed psi powers.
Woman as Great as the World and Other Fables, A [C] (Random, New York, 1953, 184 pp., $2.75) (*Fables*, Cresset, London, 1953, 164 pp., 15/-)

Fantasy, 18 stories: "The Nature of a Red Admiral"; "The City of the Cats"; "The Fountain"; "The Poet, the Woman, and the Wall"; "Land, Water, and Wind"; "The Couple Who Lived and the Couple Who Died"; "The Three Women"; "The Weevil and the Chestnut Tree"; "Export and Die"; "A Woman as Great as the World"; "Elopdatery"; "The Woodpeckers and the Starlings"; "The Great Fish"; "Other Island"; "Death and the Standard of Living"; "The Garden Seat"; "The Unites"; "The Fossil Fish and the Swimming Fish."

HAWKINS, JOHN
Fiction
Ark of Fire [n] (*American Weekly*, sr, *ca.* 1937-38) (*FFM*, Mar 1943)

A despot moves Earth into an orbit swinging nearer to the Sun. A graphic novel of the last days of Man on Earth (except for a chosen few), it was very well received when first published.

HAWTHORNE, JULIAN (22 June 1846–14 July 1934) U.S. novelist, journalist and biographer. He was born in Boston, the son of Nathaniel Hawthorne. He was trained as an engineer, but after 1871 he was exclusively an author. He lived in Europe at various times, and also in Jamaica, as well as in a number of parts of the U.S. From 1915 he lived in California. He wrote a considerable amount of fantasy which has not been reprinted (see the Bleiler Checklist), and he edited the following anthology series of fantasy interest: *Library of the World's Best Mystery and Detective Stories* (Review of Reviews Co., New York, 1906, 6 vols., frontis.)—selections from American authors (J. Hawthorne, F. M. Crawford,

A. Bierce, E. A. Poe, etc.), English-Scottish (R. Kipling, A. C. Doyle, etc.), English-Irish (J. O'Brien, E. Bulwer-Lytton, etc.), and European writers; *Lock and Key Library: Classic Mystery and Detective Stories* (Review of Reviews, 1909, 10 vols., frontis.)— selections both modern and old from all countries.

Fiction [Incomplete—other titles in Bleiler *Checklist*]
David Poindexter's Disappearance and Other Tales [C] (Appleton, New York, 1888, 210 pp.) (Chatto & Windus, London, 1888, 332 pp.)

    Fantasy; U.S. ed. has 5 stories, British adds 2 more, as noted: "David Poindexter's Disappearance"; "Ken's Mystery"; " 'When Half-Gods Go, the Gods Arrive' "; " 'Set Not Thy Foot on Graves' "; "My Friend Paton." British ed. adds: "Dr. Carajo's Patient"; "A Strange Friend."
Ellice Quentin and Other Stories [C] (Chatto & Windus, London, 1885, 359 pp.)

    Fantasy, 5 stories: "Ellice Quentin"; "The Countess's Ruby"; "A Love in Spite of Himself"; "Kildhurm's Oak"; "The New Endymion."
Laughing Mill and Other Stories, The [C] (Macmillan, London, 1879, 326 pp.)

    Fantasy, 4 stories: "The Laughing Mill"; "Calbot's Rival"; "Mrs. Gainsborough's Diamond"; "The Christmas Guest, a Myth."
Six Cent Sam's [C] (Price-McGill, St. Paul, 1893, 332 pp.)

    Fantasy, 14 stories: "Mr. Dunton's Invention"; "Greaves' Disappearance"; "Raxworthy's Treasure"; "The John North Mystery"; "A Model Murder"; "The Symposium"; "The Author's Story"; "The Virtuoso's Story"; "The Electrical Engineer's Story"; "The Captain's Story"; "The Unseen Man's Story"; "The Swarthy Man's Story"; "The Irishman's Story"; "My Own Story."

HAWTHORNE, NATHANIEL (4 July 1804–19 May 1864) U.S. novelist. His early life was a long apprenticeship for a comparatively brief period of literary activity; though he never once doubted that he must become an author, he was 33 before his first collection appeared, and 46 before he wrote a successful novel. He was in turn a customs officer, surveyor, and American Consul at Liverpool; he also travelled in Italy. After a number of "Twice Told Tales" he wrote his noted *The Scarlet Letter* and a number of other novels of importance in American literature. A scholarly analysis is *The Light and the Dark*, Richard H. Fogle (U. of Oklahoma Press, 1964, 234 pp., $5.00).

Fiction [Incomplete—other titles in Bleiler *Checklist*]
Celestial Railroad and Other Stories, The [C] [pa] (Signet: CP153, 1963, 301 pp., pa 60¢)

    Selections from *Twice-Told Tales* (both series) and *The Snow Image*, written 1832-1851. With "Afterword" by R. P. Blackmur, "Selected Bibliography," and "Note on Text." 18 stories: "Roger Malvin's Burial"; "My Kinsman, Major Molineux"; "The Wives of the Dead"; "The Gray Champion"; "Wakefield"; "The Ambitious Guest"; "Young Goodman Brown"; "The Minister's Black Veil"; "The Maypole of Merry Mount"; "The Great Carbuncle"; "Dr. Heidegger's Experiment"; "Lady Eleanor's Mantle"; "Egotism, or, the Bosom Serpent"; "The Celestial Railroad"; "The Birthmark"; "Rappaccini's Daughter"; "The Snow Image: A Childish Miracle"; "Ethan Brand."
Twice-Told Tales [C] (American Stationers, Boston, 1837, 334 pp., 1st Series) (Ticknor Reed & Fields, 1851, 2nd Series; 1865, 2 vols. [probably both series]) (Crowell, New York, 1900, 2 vols.) (Scott Foresman, New York, 1903, 542 pp.) (Dent 'Everyman Library,' 1911; Dutton, 1911, 357 pp.) (Washington: W580, 1961, 430 pp., pa 50¢) (Airmont: CL66, 1965, 288 pp., pa 60¢)

    Above are some editions of these noted Series. Paperback contents unknown. *Vol. 1* (1st Series): "The Gray Champion"; "Sunday at Home"; "The Wedding Knell"; "The Minister's Black Veil"; "The May-Pole at Merry Mount"; "The Gentle Boy"; "Mr. Higginbotham's Catastrophe"; "Little Annie's Ramble"; "Wakefield"; "A Rill From the Town Pump"; "The Great Carbuncle"; "The Prophetic Pictures"; "David Swan"; "Sights From a Steeple"; "The Hollow of the Tree Hill"; "The Vision of a Fountain"; "Fancy's Show Box"; "Dr. Heidegger's Experiment." *Vol. 2* (2nd Series): "Legends of the Province House"; "The Haunted Mind";

"The Village Uncle"; "The Ambitious Guest"; "The Sister Years"; "Snow Flakes"; "The Seven Vagabonds"; "The White Old Maid"; "Peter Goldthwaite's Treasure"; "Chippings With a Chisel"; "The Shaker Burial"; "Night Sketches"; "Endicott and the Red Cross"; "The Lily's Quest"; "Foot-Prints on the Seashore"; "Edward Fane's Rosebud"; "The Threefold Destiny."

HAWTON, HECTOR (1901–) British author. He has been Managing Director of the Rationalist Press Assoc. and Editor of *Humanist* and *The Rationalist Annual*; his works include *Philosophy for Pleasure*.
Fiction
Operation Superman (Ward Lock, London, 1951, 224 pp., 8/6; 1953, 6/-)

HAY, GEORGE
Anthology
Hell Hath Fury (N. Spearman, London, 1963, 240 pp., 15/-)

    Fantasy, 7 stories from the U.S. magazine *Unknown*: "Hell Hath Fury," Cleve Cartmill; "The Bleak Shore," Fritz Leiber; "The Frog," P. Schuyler Miller; "The Refugee," Jane Rice; "The Devil's Rescue," L. Ron Hubbard; "The Cloak," Robert Bloch; "The Extra Bricklayer," A. M. Phillips.

HAYNES, DOROTHY K.
Fiction
Thou Shalt Not Suffer a Witch [C] (Methuen, London, 1949, 208 pp., illus.–M. Peake, 9/6) (S. J. R. Saunders, Toronto, $2.50)

    26 stories: "The Head"; "The Gay Goshawk"; "Thou Shalt Not Suffer a Witch"; "The Bean-Night"; "Paying Guests"; "Changeling"; "Gas"; "Delirium"; "Music in the Memory"; "Such a Beautiful Life"; "Class"; "Pentecost–A Flashback"; "Tinker's Child"; "Miss Vestal Visits"; "The Memory"; "Good Bairns"; "Whuppittie Scoorie"; "The Nest"; "Thist"; "The Trap"; "Miss Poplar"; "Double Summer Time"; "Windfall"; "No Cakes and Honey"; "The Return of the Ritchies"; "A Story at Bedtime" (*F&SF*, June 1951).

HAYNES, JOHN ROBERT (pseud) See WILDING, P.

HAZLITT, HENRY (28 Nov 1894–) U.S. author and journalist, specializing in economics. He was born in Philadelphia. For many years his "Business Tides" column ran in *Newsweek*. Among his works is *The Foundations of Morality* (Van Nostrand, 1964).
Fiction
Great Idea, The (Appleton, New York, 1951, 374 pp., $3.50) (Collins, Toronto, $4.50) (*Time Will Run Back*, Benn, London, 1952, 256 pp., 15/-)

    A sociological novel set in a communist world of the future; the dictator's son restores freedom and the market economy, in the belief that he is improving communism.
Time Will Run Back See *Great Idea, The*

HEALY, RAYMOND J(OHN) (1907–) U.S. publisher and anthologist. He was born in Brooklyn, N.Y.; one maternal forebear was a captain with Ethan Allen. Healy has been in the book-publishing business in a number of capacities since he was 17, and is now head of Healy-Mittenthal Associates, a group of publisher's representatives. He and J. F. McComas compiled the science-fiction anthology *Adventures in Time and Space* (1946), one of the first and among the best to appear in this field. Besides other anthologies he has also done some quiz books.
Anthologies
Adventures in Time and Space [with J. F. McComas] (Random, New York, 1946, 997 pp., $3.00; 2nd ed. omitting last 5 stories in list below, 1953) (Grayson, London, 1952, 326 pp., 9/6 [11 stories marked †]) (Bantam: P44, 1954, 160 pp., pa 25¢; F3102, 1966, 181 pp., pa 50¢ [8 stories marked p1] (*More Adventures in Time and Space*, Bantam: 1310, 1955, 142 pp., pa 25¢; F3261, 1966, pa 50¢ [7 stories marked p2) (*Famous Science Fiction Stories*, Modern Library: G31, New York, 1957, 997 pp., $2.95; Random, Toronto, $3.45) ([Japanese], Gegensha & Tokyo-Life-Sha,

abr., 1957)

Sf, 33 stories and 2 articles (other editions as noted above): "Requiem"p1, R. A. Heinlein; "Forgetfulness," D. A. Stuart; "Nerves," L. del Rey; "The Sands of Time"†, P. S. Miller; "The Proud Robot"p2, L. Padgett; "Black Destroyer"p1, A. E. van Vogt; "Symbiotica," E. F. Russell; "Seeds of the Dusk"†, R. Z. Gallun; "Heavy Planet"p2, L. Gregor; "Time Locker"†,p1, L. Padgett; "The Link"†,p2, C. Cartmill; "Mechanical Mice"†,p1, M. G. Hugi; "V2—Rocket Cargo Ship" (art.), W. Ley; "Adam and No Eve"†,p2, A. Bester; "Nightfall"†,p2, I. Asimov; "A Matter of Size"†, H. Bates; "As Never Was"p1, P. S. Miller; "Q.U.R.," A. Boucher; "Who Goes There?" D. A. Stuart; "The Roads Must Roll"†,p2, R. Heinlein; "Asylum," A. E. van Vogt; "Quietus"p1, R. Rocklynne; "The Twonky"†, L. Padgett; "Time-Travel Happens" (art.), A. M. Phillips; "Robot's Return"p1, R. M. Williams; "The Blue Giraffe," L. S. de Camp; "Flight Into Darkness"†, W. Marlowe; "The Weapons Shop," A. E. van Vogt; "Farewell to the Master"p1, H. Bates; "Within the Pyramid"p2, R. D. Miller; "He Who Shrank," H. Hasse; "By His Bootstraps," A. MacDonald; "The Star-Mouse," F. Brown; "Correspondence Course," R. F. Jones; "Brain," S. F. Wright.

Famous Science Fiction Stories See *Adventures in Time and Space*

More Adventures in Time and Space [pa] See *Adventures in Time and Space*

New Tales of Space and Time (Henry Holt, New York, 1951, 294 pp., $3.50) (Weidenfeld Nicolson, London, 1952, 279 pp., 10/6) (Pocket Books: 908, 1952, 273 pp., pa 25¢; Cardinal: C319, 1958, 273 pp., pa 35¢)

Sf, 10 original stories optimistically slanted to man's future, with introduction—A. Boucher [and "Why Science Fiction?" G. Heard, only in British ed.] : "Here There Be Tygers," R. Bradbury; "In a Good Cause—," I. Asimov; "Tolliver's Travels," F. Fenton & J. Petracca; "Bettyann," K. Neville; "Little Anton," R. Bretnor; "Status Quondam," P. S. Miller; "B + M—Planet 4," G. Heard; "You Can't Say That," C. Cartmill; "Fulfillment," A. E. van Vogt; "The Quest for Saint Aquin," A. Boucher. The 1952 pa cover by Charles Frank was awarded first prize in a contest by Pocket Books Inc. at the Art Students League, New York City; it was much better than the original book jacket.

9 Tales of Space and Time (Holt, 1954, 307 pp., $3.50) (Weidenfeld Nicolson, 1955, 272 pp., 9/6)

Sf of 9 original stories (some later reprinted): "The Idealists," J. W. Campbell; "Shock Treatment," J. F. McComas (*F&SF*, Apr 1956); "Genius of the Species," R. Bretnor (*F&SF*, June 1956); "Overture," K. Neville [sequel to "Bettyann"]; "Compound B," David H. Fink; "The Chicken or the Egg-Head," F. Fenton; "The Great Devon Mystery," R. J. Healy; "Balaam," A. Boucher; "Man of Parts," H. L. Gold.

HEARD, H(ENRY) F(ITZGERALD) [GERALD] (6 Oct 1889—14 Aug 1971) British author, essayist and philosopher. He was educated at Cambridge, taking a degree in history and doing post-graduate work in philosophy. Born H. F. Heard, he used the initials for his mystery and weird fiction, and "Gerald" on other occasions. He spent five years as a popular science commentator for the BBC before moving to California in 1937. He has contributed to such organs as *Harper's Magazine*, *The New Statesman*, and the *New York Times Book Review*. In 1946 he won the Ellery Queen award for the best mystery of the year with "President of the U.S.A., Detective." A disciple of the Vedanta cult, from 1920 he published several studies on theology and the history of morals. At the time of his death he resided in Southern California and was the last survivor of the famous scientist-philosopher group that included Bernard Shaw, Bertrand Russell, and Aldous and Julian Huxley. Sam Moskowitz wrote a critical survey of Heard which was published in *Fantastic* (Aug 1960) and *Science-Fantasy* (Dec 1961).

Fiction

Black Fox, The (Cassell, London, 1950, 234 pp., 9/6) (Harper, New York, 1951, 275 pp., $3.00)

Supernatural; recommended by *F&SF* as outstanding.

Doppelgangers, The (Vanguard, New York, 1947, 281 pp., $2.75) (Cassell, 1948, 256 pp., 9/6) (SF B.C. [S.J.], 1965, 6/-) (Ace: M-142, 1966, 253 pp., pa 45¢)

A world culture of 1997, and the "psychological" struggle between two factions, complicated by a third.

Gabriel and the Creatures (Harper, 1952, 244 pp., illus.—Susanne Suba, $3.50)

A dynamic new concept of the evolution of animals, written within the framework of a fantasy allegory.

Great Fog and Other Weird Tales, The [C] (Vanguard, 1944, 238 pp., $2.50) (*Weird Tales of Terror and Detection*, Sun Dial, New York, 1946, 238 pp., $1.00; Blue Ribbon, Toronto, $1.29) (Cassell, 1947, 234 pp., 8/6)

Fantasy, 9 stories: "The Crayfish"; "The Great Fog"; "Wingless Victory"; "Vindicae Flammae"; "Eclipse"; " 'The Swap' "; "Dromenon"; "The Cat 'I Am' "; "The Rousing of Mr. Bradegar." Note: *Weird Tales of Terror and Detection* omits "Vindicae Flammae" and "Eclipse" and adds "Despair Deferred."

Lost Cavern and Other Tales of the Fantastic, The [C] (Vanguard, 1948, 262 pp., $3.00) (Cassell, 1949, 267 pp., 9/6; 1951, 4/6)

4 stories: Fantasy—"The Cup"; "The Chapel of Ease." Sf—"The Lost Cavern"; "The Thaw Plan." The philosophy is quite good, but this collection is not as notable as *The Great Fog*.

Murder by Reflection (Vanguard, 1942, 9+283 pp., $2.00)

Excellent borderline sf horror story.

Reply Paid (Vanguard, 1942, 3+274 pp., $2.00) (Lancer: 72-754, 1964, 158 pp., pa 50¢)

A straight mystery, but with the same characters as *A Taste for Honey*.

Taste for Honey, A (Vanguard, 1941, 234 pp., $2.00) (Cassell, 1942, 153 pp., 7/6) (Avon: 108, 1946, 186 pp., pa 25¢) (Penguin: 1624, 1961, 156 pp., pa 2/6) (Lancer: 72-752, 1964, 142 pp., pa 50¢; 73-647, 1967, pa 60¢)

Noted horror-mystery; not sf.

Weird Tales of Terror and Detection See *Great Fog and Other Weird Tales, The*

Nonfiction

Is Another World Watching? See *Riddle of the Flying Saucers*

Riddle of the Flying Saucers: Is Another World Watching? (Carroll, London, 1950, 160 pp., illus., 10/6) (S. J. R. Saunders, Toronto, $2.75) (*Is Another World Watching? The Riddle of the Flying Saucers*, Harper, 1951, xiv+183 pp., $2.75; Musson, Toronto, $3.00; rev., Bantam: 1079, 1953, 182 pp., pa 35¢)

A review of UFO's; generally conceded to be one of the best, possibly as good as D. F. Keyhoe.

HEARN, LAFCADIO (27 June 1850—26 Sep 1904) U.S. writer, translator and traveller. He was born on the Ionian island of Santa Maura. He had a tempestuous youth, and as a child lost the sight of his left eye. He went to the U.S. and, after some time in semi-starvation, was taught to set type and read proof. He began to get a name for macabre write-ups of news stories. He translated Gautier in 1882 as his first book, then wrote his first novel, *Chita: A Story of the Last Island*. He went to Japan in 1890, married there, and even became a Japanese subject. Just prior to his death he was appointed to the Chair of English Literature at the Imperial University of Tokyo. Henry Goodman has edited *Selected Writings of Lafcadio Hearn* (Citadel, 1949), which includes much fantasy; H. E. Wedeck's *Mortal Hunger* (Sheridan, 1947) is a biography. The Bleiler *Checklist* gives only *Fantastics*, but most of the remainder of those below have fantasy leanings and are listed for reference.

Fiction and Essays, etc.

Fantastics [Edited by Charles Woodward Hutson] [C] (Houghton Mifflin, Boston, 1914, 242 pp.; 550 copies)

Compiler's introduction. *In the Item:* "All in White"; "The Little Red Kitten"; "The Night of All Saints"; "The Devil's Carbuncle"; "Les Coulisses"; "The Stranger"; "Y Porqué"; "A Dream of Kites"; "Hereditary Memories"; "The Ghostly Kiss"; "The Black Cupid"; "When I Was a Flower"; "Metempsychosis"; "The Undying One"; "The Vision of the Dead Creole"; "The Name on the Stone"; "Aphrodite and the King's Prisoner"; "The Fountain of Gold"; "A Deadlove"; "At the Cemetery Aida El Vomito"; "The Idyll of a French Snuff Box"; "Spring Phantoms"; "A Kiss Fantastical"; "The Bird and the Girl"; "The Tale of a Fan"; "A Legend, the Gypsy's Story"; "The One Pill Box." *In the Times Democrat:* "A River Reverie"; " 'His Heart Is Old' "; "MDCCCLIII"; "Hiouen-Thsang"; "L'amour Apres la Mort"; "The Post-Office."

Gleanings in Buddha Fields [C] (Houghton Mifflin, New York, 1897, 296 pp., $2.00)

11 chapters, essays on life in Japan: "A Living God"; "Out of the Street"; "Notes of a Trip to Kyoto"; "Deist"; "About Faces in Japanese Art"; "Ningyo-no-Haka"; "In Osaka"; "Buddhist Allusions in Japanese Folksong"; "Nirvana"; "The Rebirth of Katsugoro"; "Within the Circle."

In Ghostly Japan [C] (Little Brown, Boston, 1899; 1919, 241 pp., illus.)

14 items: "Fragment"; "Furisode"; "Incense"; "A Story of Divination"; "Silkworms"; "A Passional Karma"; "Footprints of the Buddha"; "Uluation"; "Bits of Poetry"; "Japanese Buddhist Proverbs"; "Suggestion"; "Ingwa-Banashi"; "Story of a Tengu"; "At Yaidzu."

Japanese Fairy Tales [by L. Hearn, Grace James, Prof. Basil Hall Chambers, et al.] [C] (Boni Liveright, New York, 1918, 160 pp.)

"Chin-Chin Kobakama"; "The Goblin Spider"; "The Boy Who Drew Cats"; "The Silly Jelly Fish"; "The Hare of Inaba"; "Shippeitaro"; "The Matsuyama Mirror"; "My Lord Bab-O-Rice"; "The Serpent With Eight Heads"; "The Old Man and the Devils"; "The Tongue-Cut Sparrow"; "The Wooden Bowl"; "The Tea Kettles"; "Urashema"; "Green Willow"; "The Flute Reflections"; "The Spring Lover and the Autumn Lover"; "Momotaro."

Japanese Miscellany, A [C] (Little Brown, 1901, 305 pp., illus.)

Strange Stories: "Of a Promise Kept"; "Of a Promise Broken"; "Before the Supreme Court"; "The Story of Kwashin Koji"; "The Story of Umetsu Chubei"; "The Story of Kogi the Priest." *Folklore Gleanings:* "Dragon Flies"; "Buddhist Names of Plants and Animals"; "Songs of Japanese Children." *Studies Here and There:* "On a Bridge"; "The Case of Udai"; "Beside the Sea"; "Drifting Otokichis Daruma"; "In a Japanese Hospital."

Karma and Other Stories [C] (Harrap, New York, 1921, 205 pp., frontispiece of Hearn)

8 stories: "Karma"; "A Ghost"; "The First Muezzin"; "China and the Western World"; "Chin-Chin Kobakama"; "The Goblin Spider"; "The Old Woman Who Lost Her Dumpling"; "The Boy Who Drew Cats."

Kotto [C] (Macmillan, New York, 1902, illus.—Gengiro Yeto)

Old Stories: "The Legend of Yureé-Dake"; "In a Cup of Tea"; "Common Sense"; "Tkeryô"; "Shiryô"; "The Story of O. Kamé"; "Story of a Fly"; "Story of a Pheasant"; "The Story of Chûgorô."

"A Woman's Diary"; "Neiké-Gane"; "Tereflies"; "A Drop of Dew"; "Gaki"; "A Matter of Custom"; "Revery"; "Pathological"; "In the Dead of the Night"; "Kusa-Hibari"; "The Eater of Dreams."

Kwaidan [C] (Houghton Mifflin, 240 pp., illus.)

"The Story of Mimi-Nashi"; "Hoichi O Shidori"; "The Story of O-tee: Ubazakura"; "Diplomacy"; "Of a Mirror and a Bell"; "Jikirinki"; "Mujina"; "Rokuro-Kubi"; "A Dead Secret"; "Yuki-Onna"; "The Story of a Voyage: Jiu-Roku-Zakura"; "The Dream of Akinosuké: Riki-Baka Hi-Mawari Horai." *Insect Studies:* "Butterflies"; "Mosquitoes"; "Ants."

Kwaidan [Translated and annotated by R. Tanabe, Professor in the Peeresses' School] [C] (Hokuseido, Tokyo, 1923, 335 pp., illus.)

"The Story of the Tutor of Tottori"; "A Legend of Tzumo"; "A Queer Tale, the Return of the Dead"; "Ingua-Banaski"; "Reconciliation"; "The Screen Maiden"; "Of a Promise Kept"; "Of a Promise Broken"; "The Story of Kwasen Koyi"; "The Story of Umétsu Chûbei"; "The Story of Kogi the Priest"; "A Legend of Yuree-Daki"; "Common Sense"; "The Story of Mimi-Nashi-Hoichi"; "Ashidori"; "The Story of O-tei: Ubazakura"; "Diplomacy"; "Mujina"; "A Dead Secret"; "The Dream of Akinosuké: Yuki-Onna Jiki-Nin-ki"; "The Story of a Voyage."

Shadowings [C] (Little Brown, 1900, 268 pp., illus.) (? , London, 1900)

Stories From Strange Books: "The Reconciliation"; "A Legend of Fugen Bosatsu"; "The Screen Maiden"; "The Corpse Rider"; "The Sympathy of Benten"; "The Gratitude of Samebits." *Japanese Studies:* "Séme"; "Japanese Female Names"; "Old Japanese Songs." *Fantastics:* "Noctilucae"; "A Mystery of Crowds"; "Gothic Horror"; "Levitation"; "Nightmare Touch"; "Readings From a Dream Book"; "In a Pair of Eyes."

Some Chinese Ghosts [C] (Roberts Bros., Boston, 1887) (Little Brown, 1906, 203 pp., $2.00) (Modern Library, New York, 1927, 206 pp., 95¢) (New Collectors, New York, 1948, $2.00)

6 stories, with introduction—M. Komroff (1927 ed.): "The Soul of the Great Bell"; "The Story of Ming-Y"; "The Legend of Tchi-Niu"; "The Return of Yen-Tchin-King"; "The Tradition of the Tea Plant"; "The Tale of the Porcelain God." Notes and glossary.

Stray Leaves From Strange Literatures [C] (James R. Osgood, 1884) (Houghton Mifflin, 1893, 225 pp.)

Stray Leaves: "The Book of Thoth"; "The Fountain Maiden"; "The Bird Wife." *Tales Retold From Indian and Buddhist Literature:* "The Making of Tilottama"; "The Brahman and His Brahmini"; "Bakawale"; "Natalika"; "The Corpse Demon"; "The Lion"; "The Legend of the Monster Misfortune"; "A Parable Buddhistic"; "Pundari, Yamaraja, the Lotos of Faith." *Runes From the Kalewala:* "The Magical Words"; "The First Magician"; "The Healing of Wainamoinen." *Stories of Moslem Lands:* "Boutimar the Dove"; "The Son of a Robber, a Legend of Love"; "The King's Justice." *Traditions Retold From the Talmud:* "A Legend of Rabba"; "The Mocker"; "Esther's Choice"; "The Dispute in the Halacha"; "Rabbi Yochanan Ben Zachai"; "A Tradition of Titus."

HEATH, THOMAS EDWARD
Fiction

Tales in Prose and Verse and Dramas [C] (King Sell & Olding, London, 1906, 259 pp., illus.—T. E. Heath & T. Hasted Heath)

12 short stories, plays & verse written 1863-1881 and published here posthumously. The following are ghost stories: "The Story of the Gunner's Mate"; "The Lone House on the Moor"; "The Ghost My Uncle Saw"; "A Tale of Old Sully House"; "The Spectre Bridegroom" (play); "Ararat Lodge."

HECHT, BEN (28 Feb 1893–18 Apr 1964) U.S. novelist and dramatist, of Russian parentage. Besides writing newspaper columns he collaborated on plays and motion pictures, the latter being his main interest in his later years. In 1944 he published his controversial *A Guide to the Bedevilled*. His autobiography is *Child of the Century* (1954).

Fiction [Incomplete—other titles in Bleiler *Checklist*]

Book of Miracles, A [C] (Viking, New York, 1939, 465 pp., $2.75) (Macmillan, Toronto, $3.00) (Nicholson, London, 1940, 328 pp., 8/-) (Sun Dial, New York, 1941, 465 pp., $1.00) (Blue Ribbon, Toronto, $1.39)

7 stories: "Adventures of Professor Emmett"; "Death of Eleazer"; "Heavenly Choir"; "Little Candle"; "Lost Soul"; "Missing Idol"; "Remember Thy Creator." Most of these are contained in Hecht's *Collected Stories* (Crown, 1945).

HEDGES, (Mrs.) DORIS
Fiction

Dumb Spirit (A. Barker, London, 1952, 224 pp., 9/6) (McClelland, Toronto, $2.50)

Hilarious story of a man in a dog's body.

HEINLEIN, ROBERT A(NSON) (7 July 1907–) U.S. science fiction author, one of the most noted in the field, both for his accomplished style and for occasional controversial themes. Born in Butler, Missouri, he attended Kansas City public schools and the U. of Missouri. He then attended the U.S. Naval Academy (Annapolis, Md.), graduated in 1929, and served with the fleet until 1934; he retired because of physical disability. He worked in politics, silver mining and real estate until World War II. During the war he served in aeronautical engineering with the U.S. Navy, writing numerous aviation reports.

From his very first appearance in the sf field—"Lifeline" (*ASF*, Aug 1939.)—he became an important writer; he was one of the authors who made J. W. Campbell's *Astounding Science Fiction* (now *Analog*) so outstanding in the early 1940's. He appeared consistently in *ASF* until 1942, when war work ended his writing. Some of his work appeared under pseudonyms, including "Anson MacDonald" and "Lyle Monroe," the latter used for most of his stories outside of Campbell's *ASF* and *Unknown*. Most of his early stories under his own name (and some later ones) were written to fit into his *Future History* framework, in which he very meticulously worked out a political and technological history of the next few centuries. Besides sf, he also wrote some fantasy which appeared in *Unknown*.

When he resumed writing after the war, he was the first sf author to make consistent sales to the *Saturday Evening Post*, starting in 1947; he later reappeared in the sf magazines. He began a series of juvenile books for Scribner's in 1947 and averaged around one a year until 1958; some of the later titles were serialised in various of the "Big Three" sf magazines (*GSF*, *ASF*, *F&SF*) prior to book publication. Heinlein wrote the story and was technical adviser for the film *Destination: Moon* (produced by George Pal, 1950). His 1957 lecture at the U. of Chicago, "Science Fiction: Its Nature, Faults and Virtues," was published in *The Science Fiction Novel* [Symposia] (Advent, 1959). Sam Moskowitz's comprehensive profile of Heinlein was published in *AS* (June 1961) and is a chapter in Moskowitz's *Seekers of Tomorrow* (1966). A careful and detailed study of Heinlein was recently made by A. Panshin: *Heinlein in Dimension* (Advent, 1968). Heinlein is a master of modern science fiction and each new novel he writes is always received with more than ordinary interest.

Series

Future History. Stories set within the author's "Future History" chart, first published in *ASF*, Mar 1941, and reprinted (with revisions) in *The Man Who Sold the Moon* etc. The stories were compiled as books each covering a particular era. The five books originally planned were *The Man Who Sold the Moon*, *The Green Hills of Earth*, *"If This Goes On—"* (published as *Revolt in 2100*), *Methuselah's Children* and *The Endless Frontier*. The last-named never appeared, but the comparatively recent *Orphans of the Sky* is essentially part of the series, containing two of the three stories (one was never written) originally intended for *The Endless Frontier*. The "Future History" has recently been compiled in one volume as *The Past Through Tomorrow* (1967). The original chart listed a number of proposed stories; Heinlein in his postscript to *Revolt in 2100* discusses why he never wrote them.

Fiction

Assignment in Eternity [C] (Fantasy, Reading [Penna.], 1953, 256 pp., $3.00) (Museum, London, 1954, 224 pp., 9/6) (Signet: 1161, 1954, 192 pp., pa 25¢; D2587, 1964, pa 50¢; P3163, 1967, pa 60¢) (*Cita en la eternidad* [Spanish], Nebula: 12, 1955, pa) (*Assignment in Eternity*, Digit: D368, 1960, 156 pp., pa 2/- [2 stories marked p1]) (*Lost Legacy*, Digit: D386, 1960, 156 pp., pa 2/- [2 stories marked p2])

Sf, 4 stories: "Gulf"p1 (*ASF*, sr2, Nov 1949); "Elsewhen"p1 ("Elsewhere," as Caleb Saunders, *ASF*, Sep 1941); "Lost Legacy"p2 ("Lost Legion," as Lyle Monroe, *SSS*, Nov 1941); "Jerry Was a Man"p2 (*TWS*, Oct 1947; *WS Annual*, 1953). *Note:* The Spanish edition has only the first and last stories; "Gulf" appeared in German as *Am Rande des Abgrunds*, *UG*: 127, 1960; *TE*: 115, 1966.

Between Planets ("Planets in Combat," *BB*, sr2, Sep 1951) (Scribner's, New York, 1951, 222 pp., illus., $2.50; 1960, $3.50; #SL-67, 1962, pa $1.45) (*Zwischen den Planeten* [German], Weiss, 1955; *T*: 494-5, 1967) (Gollancz, London, 1968, 222 pp., 18/-)

Juvenile. A boy born in space and schooled on Earth is summoned to Mars but winds up on Venus in the midst of a revolt.

Beyond This Horizon (*ASF*, sr2, Apr 1942, as Anson MacDonald) (Fantasy, 1948, 242 pp., illus.—R. Breck, jacket—A. J. Donnell, $3.00) (abr., *2CSAB*, Win 1952) (Grosset & Dunlap, New York, 1952, 192 pp., $1.00) (*L'enfant de la science* [French], Gallimard: Le RF, 1953) (*Oltre l'orrizzonte* [Italian], *Urania*: 15,

1953) (Signet: S1891, 1960, 158 pp., pa 35¢; D2539, 1964, pa 50¢) (*Más allá del horizonte* [Spanish], Galaxia: 1, 1963, pa; *Horizontes futuros*, Nebula: 114, 1965, pa) (Panther: 23488, 1967, 206 pp., pa 5/-) (in *A Robert Heinlein Omnibus*, 1966)

A plausible future world employing controlled genetics.

Citizen of the Galaxy (*ASF*, sr4, Sep 1957) (Scribner's, 1957, 302 pp., $2.95; 1961, $3.50) (*Bewohner der Milchstrasse* [German], Weiss, 1958; Heyne, 1965, pa) (*Ciudadano de la Galaxia* [Spanish], Nebula: 54, 1958, pa) (*Vintergatans Son* [Swedish], Sv. Läraretidn., 1961) (*Cittadino della Galassia* [Italian], *Cosmo*: 161, 1964)

A slave brought up by a beggar has many adventures amid the galactic worlds before finding his true heritage.

Day After Tomorrow, The [pa] See *Sixth Column*

Door Into Summer, The (*F&SF*, sr3, Oct 1956) (Doubleday, New York, 1957, 188 pp., $2.95) (D'day SF B.C., 1958, $1.20) ([Japanese], Kodan-sha: 4, 1958) (*Puerta al verano* [Spanish], Nebula: 52, 1958, pa) (Signet: S1639, 1959, 159 pp., pa 35¢; D2443, 1964, pa 50¢) (*La porta sull'estate* [Italian], *Urania*: 197, 1959) (Panther: 1021, 1960, 160 pp., pa 2/6) (*Tür in die Zukunft* [German], Goldmann, 1963; #075, 1967, pa) (Gollancz, 1967, 190 pp., 21/-)

A refreshing story in the tradition of Wells' *The Sleeper Wakes* with the hero moving between 1970 and 2000 to obtain vengeance.

Double Star (*ASF*, sr3, Feb 1956) (Doubleday, 1956, 186 pp., $2.95) (D'day, Toronto, $3.50) (D'day SF B.C., 1956, $1.20) (Signet: S1444, 1957, 159 pp., pa 35¢; D2419, 1964, 128 pp., pa 50¢) (*Intriga estelar* [Spanish], Nebula: 35, 1957, pa) (*Stella doppia* [Italian], *Cosmo*: 7, 1957) (M. Joseph, London, 1958, 208 pp., 13/6) (*Double étoile* [French], Hachette: Le RF, 1958, pa) (SF B.C. [S.J.], 1959, 5/6) (Panther: 1120, 1960, 158 pp., pa 2/6; 1963, 127 pp., pa 2/6; 25022, 1968, 143 pp., pa 3/6) (*Doppelleben im Kosmos* [German], Weiss, 1961; Heyne, 1965, pa; *Doppelganger auf zwei Planeten*, UG: 176, 1962) (*Dubbelstjärna* [Swedish], Biblioteksf., 1961) (*Estrella doble*, [Spanish], Cenit: 47, 1963, pa)

Winner of the 1956 Hugo for best novel. Amid great intrigue, actor Lorenzo Smythe is moulded into the famous interplanetary politician John J. Bonforte.

Farmer in the Sky (abr., "Satellite Scout," *Boys' Life*, sr3, Aug 1950) (Scribner's, 1950, 216 pp., illus.—C. Geary, $2.50) (S. J. R. Saunders, Toronto, $3.25) (*Pioniere im Weltall* [German], Weiss, 1951) (*Nybyggare I Rymden* [Swedish], Sv. Läraretidn., 1957) (Gollancz, 1963, 216 pp., illus.—Geary, 12/6) (Pan: X713, 1967, 174 pp., pa 3/6) (Dell: 2518, 1968, 221 pp., pa 50¢)

Juvenile. A Boy Scout in the colonization of Ganymede.

Farnham's Freehold (*If*, sr3, July 1964) (Putnam, New York, 1964, 315 pp., $4.95) (Longmans, Toronto, $4.50) (D'day SF B.C., 1964, $1.20) (Signet: T2704, 1965, 256 pp., pa 75¢; 1968, pa 75¢) (Dobson, 1965, 315 pp., 21/-) (Corgi: FS7577, 1967, 254 pp., pa 5/-) (*Die Reise in die Zukunft* [German], Heyne, 3087, 1967, pa)

A family group is projected forward in time by a nuclear bomb; they fight to survive in a well-depicted future civilization dominated by the black race.

Glory Road (*F&SF*, sr3, July 1963) (Putnam, 1963, 288 pp., $3.95) (D'day SF B.C., 1963, $1.20) (Avon: V2102, 1964, 288 pp., pa 75¢; V2202, 1967, pa 75¢) (FSB: 1300, 1965, 256 pp., pa 3/6; 2250, 1968, pa 5/-)

Fantasy. A hired hero on a perilous quest with a near-immortal woman has dramatic adventures amid the Twenty Universes.

Green Hills of Earth, The [C] (Shasta, Chicago, 1951, 256 pp., $3.00) (Signet: 943, 1952, 176 pp., pa 25¢; S1537, 1958, pa 35¢; D2348, 1963, pa 50¢; T3193, 1967, pa 75¢) (Sidgwick Jackson, London, 1954, 224 pp., 9/6) (*Los negros fosos de la luna* [Spanish], Nebula: 3, 1955, pa) (Pan: 377, 1956, 189 pp., pa 2/-; X679, 1967, pa 3/6) ([Japanese], Gengen-sha: SF16, 1957; Hayakawa: 3037, 1962, pa) (in *Robert Heinlein Omnibus*, 1958) (Digit: R583, 1962, 160 pp., pa 2/6) (*Die grünen Hugel der Erde* [German], Goldmann, 1964, 1964 pa) (in *A Robert Heinlein Omnibus*, 1966) (*Les vertes collines de la Terre* [French], Ed. Opta 'Classique SF: 10' [½], 1967) (in *The Past Through Tomorrow* [Heinlein], 1967)

Second book in the "Future History" series. Sf, 10 stories (*SEP* dates given): "Delilah and the Space-Rigger"; "Space Jockey" (26 Apr 1947); "The Black Pits of Luna" (10 Jan 1948); "Gentlemen, Be Seated!"; "Ordeal in Space"; "It's Great to Be Back!" (26 July 1947); "The Green Hills of Earth" (8 Feb 1947); " '—We Also Walk Dogs' "; "Logic of Empire"; "The Long Watch." *Note:* Japanese version has 8 stories, omitting 4th and 8th. "The Black Pits of Luna" was in German in *Utopia-Magazin* No. 2, 1956.

Gulf [n]   See *Assignment in Eternity*

Have Space Suit—Will Travel   (*F&SF*, sr3, Aug 1958) (Scribner's, 1958, 276 pp., $2.95) (S. J. R. Saunders, Toronto, $3.50) (*Egen rymddräkt finnes* [Swedish], Sv. Läraretidn., 1959) (*Piraten im Weltenraum* [German], Weiss, 1960; *T*: 510-1, 1967)

Juvenile. A boy wins a space-suit, and his resulting adventures in company with a professor's daughter include the defeat of "bad" aliens with the help of another alien.

Heinlein Triad, A [C]   See *Three by Heinlein*

Lost Legacy [pa]   See *Assignment in Eternity*

Man Who Sold the Moon, The [C]   (Shasta, 1950, 299 pp., $3.00; 1955, $3.00) (Signet: 847, 1951, 167 pp., pa 25¢; S1644, 1959, 159 pp., pa 35¢; D2358, 1963, pa 50¢ [all Signet eds., 4 stories marked †]) (Sidgwick Jackson, 1953, 256 pp., 9/6) (*De man die de maan verkocht* [Dutch], Servire, 's-Gravenhage, 1953) (*Mannen Som Salde Manen* [Swedish], Eklund, 1954) (Pan: 327, 1955, 252 pp., pa 2/-; X227, 1963, 238 pp., pa 3/6) (*El hombre que vendio la Luna* [Spanish], Nebula: 6, 1955, pa) (*L'homme qui vendio la Lune* [French], Gallimard: Le RF, 1958; Ed. Opta 'Classique: SF10' [½], 1967) (in *Robert Heinlein Omnibus*, 1958) (in *A Robert Heinlein Omnibus*, 1966) (in *The Past Through Tomorrow* [Heinlein], 1967)

First book in the "Future History" series. Sf, 6 stories: "Life-Line"; "Let There Be Light"†; "The Roads Must Roll"†; "Blow-ups Happen"; "The Man Who Sold the Moon"† [n'te]; "Requiem"†. The title n'te also appeared as an issue of *American SF Magazine* [Australian], Aug 1952 [nd], and also in *A Treasury of Great SF* [Boucher], 1959. The Spanish ed. omits "Blowups Happen" and "Requiem"; the former is included in the Nebula [Spanish] ed. of W. F. Jenkins' *The Murder of the U.S.A.* The French Gallimard ed. consists only of the title n'te and "Requiem," while the Classique ed. is the full 6 stories.

Menace From Earth, The [C]   (Gnome, New York, 1959, 255 pp., $3.50) (Ambassador, Toronto, $3.95) (Signet: D2105, 1962, 189 pp., pa 50¢; 1964, pa 50¢) (Dobson, 1966, 255 pp., 21/-) (Corgi: 07860, 1968, 189 pp., pa 3/6)

Sf, 8 stories: "The Year of the Jackpot" (*GSF*, Mar 1952); "By His Bootstraps" (*ASF*, Oct 1941); "Columbus Was a Dope"; "The Menace From Earth"; "Sky Lift"; "Goldfish Bowl"; "Project Nightmare"; "Water Is for Washing." *Note:* "By His Bootstraps" has also been titled "The Time Gate," and is so included in Galaxia No. 7 ([Spanish], 1964, pa).

Methuselah's Children   (*ASF*, sr3, July 1941) (Gnome, 1958, 188 pp., $3.00) (Signet: S1752, 1959, 160 pp., pa 35¢; D2191, 1962, pa 50¢; D2621, 1965, pa 50¢) (*I figli di Matusalemme* [Italian], *Urania*: 262, 1961) (*Die Ausgestossen der Erde* [German], Goldmann, 1963; #079, 1967, pa) (Gollancz, 1963, 192 pp., 15/-) (SF B.C. [S.J.], 1964, 6/-) (*Los hijos de Matusalen* [Spanish], Nebula: 107, 1965, pa) (Pan: X526, 1966, 191 pp., pa 3/6) (in *The Past Through Tomorrow* [Heinlein], 1967)

Fourth of the "Future History" series. A race bred for longevity conflicts with the rest of mankind and flees to the stars.

Moon Is a Harsh Mistress, The   (*If*, sr5, Dec 1965) (Putnam, 1966, 383 pp., $5.95) (Dobson, 1967, 25/-) (Berkley: N1601, 1968, 302 pp., pa 95¢)

Winner of 1967 Hugo award for best novel. A fascinating narrative of the computer-led rebellion of a lunar penal colony, in good tactical detail.

Orphans of the Sky   (Gollancz, 1963, 160 pp., 13/6) (SF B.C. [S.J.], 1964, 6/-) (Putnam, 1964, 187 pp., $3.50) (D'day SF B.C., 1964, $1.20) (Signet: D2618, 1965, 128 pp., pa 50¢; P3344, 1968, pa 60¢) (Mayflower: 6705, 1965, 111 pp., pa 2/6) (*Die*

lange Reise [German], *UG*: 90, 1959; Heyne: 3101, 1967, pa) (*Verdwaald tussen de sterren* [Dutch], Meulenhoff, Amsterdam, 1967)

Last of the "Future History" series. 2 stories: "Universe" (*ASF*, n'te, May 1941; Dell: 36, 1951, 54 pp., pa 10¢); "Common Sense" (*ASF*, n'te, Oct 1941). A generations-long voyage to the stars aboard a vast space-ship whose inhabitants think the ship is the entire universe; the characters include the twin-headed 'Mutie,' Joe-Jim Gregory. *Note:* The *UG* German version is probably "Universe" only, as is the Italian *Urania*: 378 (1965).

Past Through Tomorrow, The [C]   (Putnam, 1967, 667 pp., $5.95) (Longmans, Toronto, $6.95) (D'day SF B.C., 1967, $2.30)

The "Future History" stories from "Life-Line" through "Methuselah's Children." 21 stories, with introduction by D. Knight: *The Man Who Sold the Moon; The Green Hills of Earth; Revolt in 2100; Methuselah's Children.* A revised time chart is given; the volume omits "Let There Be Light" but includes a new story, "Searchlight."

Podkayne of Mars   (*If*, sr3, Nov 1962) (Putnam, 1963, 191 pp., $3.50) (Longmans, Toronto, $4.25) (Avon: G1211, 1964, 159 pp., pa 50¢; S335, 1968, pa 60¢) (*Bürgerin des Mars* [German], Goldmann, 1964, 1964 pa)

Juvenile. A 16-year-old girl from Mars takes a vacation trip to Earth via Venus, and is caught up in melodramatic adventures.

Puppet Masters, The   (*GSF*, sr3, Sep 1951) (Doubleday, 1951, 219 pp., $2.75) (*Il terrore dalla sesta luna* [Italian], *Urania*: 5, 1952) (D'day SF B.C., 1953) (Signet: 980, 1952, 175 pp., pa 25¢; D2366, 1963, pa 50¢; P2863, 1966, pa 60¢) (Museum, 1953, 191 pp., 9/6) (*Marionettes humaines* [French], Hachette: Le RF, 1954) (*Titan invade la Tierra* [Spanish], Nebula: 1, 1955, pa) ([Japanese], Gengen-sha: SF2, 1956) (*Weltraummollusken erobern die Erde* [German], Weiss, 1957; Heyne, 1965, pa) (*Universets Parasitter* [Danish], Skrifola: Lommeroromanen P75, 1959, pa) (Panther: 1001, 1960, 190 pp., pa 2/6) (in *Three by Heinlein*, 1965; *Heinlein Triad*, 1966) (*De marionetten zijn onder ons* [Dutch], Bruna, Utrecht & Antwerp, 1967 [in *SF Omnibus*])

Fast-moving variation on the flying saucer theme, with alien invaders becoming parasites on human beings.

Red Planet, The   (Scribner's, 1949, 211 pp., illus.—C. Geary, $2.50; 1961, $3.50; SL-100, 1964, pa $1.25) (S. J. R. Saunders, Toronto, $3.25, pa $1.55) (*La planete rouge* [French], Hachette, 1952) (*Der Rote Planet* [German], Weiss, 1952; *T*: 454-5, 1966) ([Japanese], Kodan-sha: World's Science Adv. Series No. 7, 1956) (Gollancz, 1963, 211 pp., 12/6; 1967, 15/-) (Pan: X712, 1967, 173 pp., pa 3/6)

Juvenile. Three teen-age colonists on Mars get involved in a revolt against the colonial proprietors.

Revolt in 2100 [C]   (Shasta, 1953, 317 pp., $3.50) (Signet: 1194, 1955, 192 pp., pa 25¢; D2638, 1965, pa 50¢; P3563, 1958, pa 60¢) ([Japanese], Gengen-sha: SF15, 1956) (Digit: D235, 1959, 159 pp., pa 2/-) (Gollancz, 1964, 305 pp., 16/-) (*Revolt im Jahre 2100* [German], Goldmann, 1964, 1964 pa) (SF B.C. [S.J.], 1965, 6/-) (Pan: M172, 1966, 253 pp., pa 5/-) (in *The Past Through Tomorrow* [Heinlein], 1967)

Third in the "Future History" series. 3 stories: " 'If This Goes On—' " (enlarged from *ASF*, sr2, Feb 1940); "Coventry" (*ASF*, July 1940); "Misfit" (*ASF*, Nov 1939). The second story is a direct sequel to the first. "Coventry" also saw German translation in *Utopia-Magazin*: 11 (1958).

Robert Heinlein Omnibus [C]   (SF B.C. [S.J.], 1958, 5/6)

Double binding of *The Man Who Sold the Moon* and *The Green Hills of Earth.*

Robert Heinlein Omnibus, A [C]   (Sidgwick Jackson, 1966, 158 pp., 256 pp., 224 pp., 30/-)

A binding of *Beyond This Horizon; The Man Who Sold the Moon; The Green Hills of Earth.*

Rocket Ship Galileo   (Scribner's, 1947, 212 pp., illus., $2.00) (*Endstation Mond* [German], Weiss, 1951; *T*: 462-3, 1966) ([Japanese], Kodan-sha: World's Science Adv. Series No. 1, 1956)

Juvenile; the first of Heinlein's juvenile series for Scribner's. A scientist and his nephew and two other boys fly the first piloted rocket ship to the Moon, and discover anachronistic Nazis.

Rolling Stones, The ("Tramp Space Ship," *Boys' Life*, sr4, Sep 1952) (Scribner's, 1952, 276 pp., illus.–C. Geary, $2.50) (S. J. R. Saunders, Toronto, $3.25)

Juvenile; teen-age twins and their family go adventuring in an old space ship to Mars and the asteroids.

6 X H [pa] See *Unpleasant Profession of Jonathan Hoag, The*

Sixth Column (*ASF*, sr3, Jan 1941, as Anson MacDonald) (Gnome, 1949, 256 pp., $2.50, jacket–E. Cartier) (*The Day After Tomorrow*, Signet: 882, 1951, 160 pp., pa 25¢; S1577, 1958, 144 pp., pa 35¢; D2649, 1965, pa 50¢; Mayflower: A36, 1962, 159 pp., pa 2/6) (*Sjätte Kolonnen* [Swedish], Eklund, 1953) (*Sixieme Colonne* [French], Hachette, 1951) (*La sesta colonna* [Italian], *GRF*: 24, 1962) (*El dia de pasado mañana* [Spanish], Galaxia: 37, 1965, pa)

The U.S.A. is conquered by Asians and then freed by the use of scientific "miracles."

Space Cadet (Scribner's, 1948, 242 pp., illus.–C. Geary, $2.50; 1961, $3.50) (*Weltraum-Piloten* [German], Weiss, 1952; *T*: 502-3, 1967) (*Rymdkadetten* [Swedish], Sv. Läraretidn., 1956) (Gollancz, 1966, 240 pp., 16/-)

Juvenile; adventures of a boy in training in a space academy.

Star Beast, The ("Star Lummox," *F&SF*, sr3, May 1954; [Australian], sr3, No. 4, 1955) (Scribner's, 1954, 282 pp., illus.–C. Geary, $2.50; 1962, $3.50) (*La bestia estelar* [Spanish], Nebula: 10, 1955, pa) (*Das Ultimatum von den Sternen* [German], *TS*: 114, 1966)

Juvenile; a pet brought back from another world grows up and brings a threat of destruction upon the Earth.

Starman Jones (Scribner's, 1953, 305 pp., illus.–C. Geary, $2.50) (S. J. R. Saunders, Toronto, $3.25) (Sidgwick Jackson, 1954, 305 pp., illus., 7/6) (*Abenteuer im Sternenreich* [German], Weiss, 1954; *T*: 486-7, 1966) (*Varning För Okänd Planet* [Swedish], Lindqvist, 1954) (*Jones, el hombre estelar* [Spanish], Nebula: 9, 1955, pa) (Puffin: PS267, 1966, 250 pp., pa 4/6) (Dell: 8246, 1967, 252 pp., pa 60¢)

Juvenile; an interstellar space-liner becomes lost, and a young crewman wins the chance to be the astrogator.

Starship Troopers ("Starship Soldier," *F&SF*, sr2, Oct 1959) –enlarged: (Putnam, 1959, 309 pp., $3.95) (FSB: 299, 1961, 224 pp., pa 2/6; 1803, 1967, 222 pp., pa 5/-) (Signet: D1987, 1961, 208 pp., pa 50¢; D2381, 1963, pa 50¢) (*Fanteria dello spazio* [Italian], *Urania*: 276, 1962) (Berkley: S1560, 1968, 208 pp., pa 75¢)

Juvenile; winner of the 1960 Hugo award for best novel. It describes the training of a lad for the "Mobile Infantry" (space marines) and his adventures in the Bug War. The story caused wide controversy, as some consider it to glorify war.

Stranger in a Strange Land (Putnam, 1961, 408 pp., $4.50) (D'day SF B.C., 1961, $1.70) (Avon: V2056, 1962, 414 pp., pa 75¢; V2191, 1967, pa 75¢) (FSB: 1282, 1965, 400 pp., pa 5/-; 2124, 1968, pa 7/6) (Berkley: N1571, 1968, 414 pp., pa 95¢)

An Earthman born on Mars and raised by Martians returns to Earth and founds a religious cult, employing his unusual Martian senses and powers. Winner of the 1962 Hugo award for best novel, it is a controversial story depicting a sexually open society. The writing fades considerably in the last half.

Three By Heinlein [C] (Doubleday, 1965, 426 pp., $5.95) (D'day SF B.C., 1965, $1.90) (*A Heinlein Triad*, Gollancz, 1966, 426 pp., 21/-)

3 novels: *The Puppet Masters*; *Waldo*; *Magic, Inc.*

Time for the Stars (Scribner's, 1956, 244 pp., $2.75) (D'day SF B.C., 1957, $1.20) (*Von Stern zu Stern* [German], Weiss, 1957; *T*: 470-1, 1966) (*La hora de las estrellas* [Spanish], Nebula: 45, 1958, pa) (Gollancz, 1963, 244 pp., 12/6) (S. J. R. Saunders, Toronto, $3.75) (Pan: 02028, 1968, 190 pp., pa 3/6)

Juvenile; rivalry between twins, one of whom is aboard an interstellar exploratory ship and is in telepathic communication with his brother on Earth.

Tunnel in the Sky (Scribner's, 1955, 273 pp., $2.50) (*Tunnel zu den Sternen* [German], Weiss, 1956; *T*: 438-9, 1966) (*Tunnel en el espacio* [Spanish], Nebula: 22, 1956, pa) (Gollancz, 1965, 273 pp., 15/-) (Pan: 02029, 1968, 222 pp., pa 5/-)

Juvenile; an examination in solo survival: any planet, any cli-

mate, any terrain, any weapons.

Universe [pa] See *Orphans of the Sky*

Unpleasant Profession of Jonathan Hoag, The [C] (Gnome, 1959, 256 pp., $3.50) (*6 X H*, Pyramid: G-642, 1961, 191 pp., pa 35¢; F-910, 1963, pa 40¢) (Dobson, 1964, 256 pp., 18/-) (Burns MacEachern, Toronto, $3.95) (SF B.C. [S.J.], 1965, 6/-) (Penguin: 2510, 1966, 221 pp., pa 4/-)

Sf & fantasy, 6 stories: "The Unpleasant Profession of Jonathan Hoag" (*Unknown*, short n, Oct 1942, as John Riverside); "The Man Who Travelled in Elephants"; " 'All You Zombies' "; "They"; "Our Fair City"; " 'And He Built a Crooked House'."

Waldo & Magic, Inc. (Doubleday, 1950, 219 pp., $2.50) (*Waldo: Genius in Orbit*, Avon: T261, 1958, 191 pp., pa 35¢) ("Waldo" in *A Treasury of Great SF* [Boucher], 1959) (*Waldo, o dell' impossible* [Italian], *GRF*: 20, 1962) (Pyramid: F859, 1963, 191 pp., pa 40¢; X1286, 1966, pa 60¢; X1758, 1968, pa 60¢) (*Waldo y Magic, Inc.* [Spanish], Nebula: 99, 1964, pa) (both in *Three By Heinlein*, 1965; *Heinlein Triad*, 1966) (Signet: T3690, 1968, pa 75¢)

2 novels, recommended: "Waldo" (*ASF*, Aug 1942, by Anson MacDonald)—a physical weakling invents "waldoes" and learns about "the other world"; "Magic, Inc." ("The Devil Makes the Law," *Unknown*, Sep 1940)—a fight against extortion in a world where magic works.

Waldo: Genius in Orbit [pa] See *Waldo & Magic, Inc.*

Worlds of Robert A. Heinlein, The [C] [pa] (Ace: F-375, 1966, 189 pp., pa 40¢)

Sf, 5 stories and author's intro.–"Pandora's Box": "Blowups Happen"; "Searchlight"; "Life-Line"; "Solution Unsatisfactory"; "Free Men" (new).

Anthology

Tomorrow the Stars (Doubleday, 1951, 249 pp., $2.95) (Signet: 1044, 1953, 207 pp., pa 25¢) (Berkley: S1426, 1967, 224 pp., pa 75¢)

Sf, 14 stories and compiler's introduction: "I'm Scared," J. Finney; "The Silly Season," C. M. Kornbluth; "The Report on the Barnhouse Effect," K. Vonnegut; "The Tourist Trade," Bob Tucker; "Rainmaker," J. Reese; "Absalom," H. Kuttner; "The Monster," L. del Rey; "Jay Score," E. F. Russell; "Betelgeuse Bridge," Wm. Tenn; "Survival Ship," Judith Merril; "Keyhole," M. Leinster; "Misbegotten Missionary," I. Asimov; "The Sack," W. Morrison; "Poor Superman" ("Appointment in Tomorrow"), F. Leiber.

HEINS, (Rev.) HARDY HENRY (1923–) U.S. Lutheran minister. He was born on Long Island, attended Queens County public schools, and took degrees at Hartwick College and Gettysburg Theological Seminary. In the early 1950's he did much work with displaced persons. He has had over 18 years with three churches in upstate New York. He is married and has a teen-aged daughter. He has written *Throughout All the Years*, a bicentennial history of the Hartwick (N.Y.) schools, and *Numeral Cancellations of the British Empire* a postal history published in England. He has been collecting and studying E. R. Burroughs for over 30 years; besides the work below he wrote the preface to R. A. Lupoff's *Edgar Rice Burroughs: Master of Adventure* (Canaveral, 1965).

Nonfiction

Golden Anniversary Bibliography of Edgar Rice Burroughs, A (Grant, West Kingston [R.I.], 1964, 418 pp., $10.00, 1,000 copies)

Revised from the first mimeo edition of Sep 1962. It lists books and stories, editions and their varying contents, and is enriched with information about Burroughs. It gives forgotten articles by Burroughs, and has a rich final section of magazine illustrations and publisher's announcements. The whole is a masterpiece of bibliography.

HELD, SERGE SIMON French author.

Fiction

Death of Iron, The (*La mort du fer*, A. Fayard, Paris, 1931, 311 pp.) –[Trans.–F. Pratt]: (*WS*, sr3, Sep 1932; *WS Annual*, 1952)

Chaos is caused by iron rusting away rapidly.

HELM, THOMAS
Nonfiction
Monsters of the Deep (Dodd Mead, New York, 1962, 232 pp., $4.00)
    Includes discussion of prehistoric sea-monsters, some still living.

HELVICK, JAMES (pseud) See COCKBURN, C.

HEMING, JOHN (WINTON) (1900–1953) Australian writer. He wrote immense amounts—at least 25 million words—of popular fiction, articles, plays, and radio scripts under many names; asked how many short stories he had written, he said he had no idea, perhaps 2,000 or so. He achieved some prominence in the Australian sf field by writing a number of paperback novels for Currawong Publishers, Sydney, after the wartime ban (May 1940) on the importing of sf (as well as other material) of U.S. origin. His first novel was *The Living Dead*; this was followed by a number of others, including *Time Marches Off* (pseudonym "Paul de Wreder") (see listing in Paperback Appendix). He left the sf field in the mid-1940's.

HEMMING, NORMA (KATHLEEN) (28 July 1927–14 July 1960) English science fiction writer and fan. She was born in Ilford, Essex, and emigrated to Australia in 1949. She joined Sydney sf circles and became prominent in their activities in the early 1950's. She wrote a number of stories for the British magazines: "Loser Take All" (*Science-Fantasy*, Win 1951/52); "Dwellers in Silence" (*NW*, Sep 1956); "Call Them Earthmen" (*SFA* [Brit.], Oct 1959); "Debt of Lassor" (*Nebula*, Aug 1958). In the Australian field she had one story each in *Future Science Fiction* and *Popular Science Fiction*, as well as a story in each of the last seven issues of *Thrills Incorporated*.

HENDERSON, PHILLIP (RICHARD) (1906–) British author, editor and anthologist. He has written a number of literary works since 1930, and many articles for the British Council.
Anthology
Shorter Novels of the 18th Century (Dent 'Everyman,' 1948; 1953, 6/-) (Dutton, New York, 1954, 278 pp., pa $1.65)
    3 novels: "Rasselas, Prince of Abyssinia," Samuel Johnson; "The Castle of Otranto," Horace Walpole; "Vathek, an Arabian Tale," William Beckford.

HENDERSON, ZENNA (1 Nov 1917–) U.S. school teacher. She was born in Tucson, Arizona. She became a teacher because the nearest state college trained only teachers at that time. During World War II she taught at one of the desert Relocation camps where the Japanese-Americans of the West Coast were held. In 1955 she went to France to teach at a U.S. Air Force base north of Paris, then returned to teaching in Arizona. As a science-fiction writer she is primarily noted for her "People" series, on the trials of human-like aliens living in the world of today.
Series
People. All in *F&SF*: "Ararat" (Oct 1952); "Gilead" (Aug 1954); "Pottage" (Sep 1955); "Wilderness" (Jan 1957); "The Last Step" (Feb 1958); "Captivity" (June 1958); "Jordan" (Mar 1959); "And a Little Child" (Oct 1959); "Return" (Mar 1961); "Shadow on the Moon" (Mar 1962); "Deluge" (Oct 1963); "No Different Flesh" (May 1965); "Angels Unawares" (Mar 1966); "Troubling of the Water" (Sep 1966); "The Indelible Kind" (Dec 1968). The first 8 stories appeared as *Pilgrimage*; the remainder, with modifications and new material, appeared as *The People: No Different Flesh*.
Fiction
Anything Box, The [C] (Doubleday, New York, 1965, 205 pp., $3.95) (Gollancz, London, 1966, 205 pp., 18/-) (SF B.C. [S.J.], 1967)
    Sf and fantasy, 14 stories: "The Anything Box"; "Subcommittee"; "Something Bright"; "Hush"; "Food to All Flesh"; "Come On, Wagon!"; "Walking Aunt Daid"; "The Substitute"; "The Grunder"; "Things"; "Turn the Page"; "Stevie and the Dark"; "And a Little Child . . ."; "The Last Step."
People: No Different Flesh, The [C] (Gollancz, London, 1966,

223 pp., 21/-) (Doubleday, New York, 1967, 236 pp., $4.50) (Avon: S328, 1968, 221 pp., pa 60¢) (*Aufbruch ins All* [German], Goldmann: 088, 1968, pa)
    6 stories: "No Different Flesh"; "Deluge"; "Angels Unawares"; "Troubling of the Water"; "Return"; "Shadow on the Moon." This comprises most of the later-published stories of the "People" series, but chronologically it precedes the stories in *Pilgrimage*; the stories of Marnie and Timmy are worked in by the addition of material wherein they are recounted to Merus.
Pilgrimage; the Book of the People [C] (Doubleday, 1961, 239 pp., $3.50) (D'day, Toronto, $4.00) (*Wo ist unsere Welt* [German], Goldmann, 1961, 1964 pa) (Gollancz, 1962, 239 pp., 16/-) (Avon: G1185, 1963, 255 pp., pa 50¢; S243, 1966, 60¢) (SF B.C. [S.J.], 1963, 5/9) (Panther: #1971, 1965, 208 pp., pa 3/6)
    Novelisation of the first 8 stories of the "People" series. The descendants of the survivors of a crashed space ship from another world gather to find their heritage on Earth.

HENNEBERG, CHARLES (1899–1959) Stories under this name were actually written by Charles Henneberg zu Irmelshausen Wasungen and his wife Nathalie in collaboration. Charles was born in Germany and had an active and varied career. He met his future wife, a Russian journalist, when he was in the French Foreign Legion, stationed at Homs, Syria. After marriage they spent four years in the Arabian desert. During the war Charles fought under General de Gaulle, and was subsequently appointed Directeur des Medailles Militaires. His widow is carrying on the science-fantasy novels under the by-line Nathalie Charles-Henneberg. Charles Henneberg had a number of stories in the French *Fiction*, of which the following were translated by Damon Knight and appeared in *F&SF*: "The Blind Pilot" (Jan 1960); "The Non-Humans" (June 1960); "Moon Fishers" (Apr 1962). These were also in Knight's *13 French SF Stories* (Bantam, 1965, pa; Corgi, 1965, pa). Novels in "Le Rayon Fantastique" series were: *La rosee du soleil* (1959); *Les dieux verts* (1961); *Le forteresse perdue* (1962) [the last two by Nathalie]. Henneberg was also translated into Italian for *Urania* No. 92 (1955).

HEPWORTH, (Rev.) GEORGE HUGHES (4 Feb 1833–7 June 1902) American Unitarian clergyman, editor and author, born at Boston, Mass. His sermons in the *New York Herald* were published in four volumes 1894-1904.
Fiction [Incomplete—other titles in Bleiler *Checklist*]
Queerest Man Alive and Other Stories, The [C] (R. F. Fenno, New York, 1897, 256 pp.)
    Fantasy, 6 stories: "The Queerest Man Alive"; "Yegor's Portrait"; "A Little Mouse"; "For Tom's Sake"; "The Flirt"; "Klang and Klung."

HERBERT, BENSON (1912–) British author and editor. He has M.Sc. for radio research. He began writing when he was 13 years old—first poetry and then science essays and fantastic fiction. Before the war he was noted for the short story "The World Without" (*WS*, Feb 1931) and sequel, as well as the book below. In the war years he wrote some interplanetary novels published in paperback by Messrs. Lloyd Cole, London. He then began his own publishing firm, Utopian Publications Ltd., whose works included *American Fiction*, *Strange Tales* and *New Frontiers*; he selected and edited the material for these in conjunction with Walter Gillings. He has also written a book of verse, *This Mighty Isle*, and derived the new philosophy Brüllism (from Bronte and Dunne).
Fiction
Crisis!–1992 ("The Perfect World," *WS*, sr3, Oct 1935) (Richards, London, 1936, 286 pp., 5/6)
    The marvels of a world intruding into the Solar System and visited by Earth scientists.

HERBERT, FRANK (1920–) U.S. author and newspaperman. He was educated at U. of Washington. He has been a working writer for about 20 years, and has also been a TV cameraman, radio news commentator, oyster diver, jungle survival instructor, lay analyst, and teacher of creative writing. He was editor of several Washington State newspapers and was later with the Santa Rosa (Calif.) *Press-Democrat*. He began free-lancing in the 1960's. His fiction has appeared in *Collier's*, *Esquire* and various sf magazines. His *Dragon in the Sea* was a very highly regarded first novel in the sf field, while his *Dune* is an epic highly regarded by some and poorly by others.

Fiction

Destination: Void [pa] ("Do I Wake or Dream?" *GSF*, Aug 1965) (Berkley: F1249, 1966, 190 pp., pa 50¢) (Penguin: 2689, 1967, 219 pp., pa 4/6)

Technical and psychological drama in a star ship when organic brains break down and a computer must be used for control.

Dragon in the Sea, The ("Under Pressure," *ASF*, sr3, Nov 1955) (Doubleday, New York, 1956, 192 pp., $2.95) (D'day, Toronto, $3.50) (D'day SF B.C., 1956) (*21st Century Sub*, Avon: T-146, 1956, 190 pp., pa 35¢; G1092, 1961, pa 50¢) (*Atom-U-Boot S1881* [German], *UK*: 26, 1958; Heyne: 3091, 1967, pa) ([Japanese], Hayakawa: 3006, 1958, pa) (*Smg "RAM" 2000* [Italian], *Urania*: 194, 1959) (Gollancz, 1960, 206 pp., 13/6) (SF B.C. [S.J.], 1961, 5/6) (Penguin: 1886, 1963, 219 pp., pa 3/6) (Avon: S290, 1967, 189 pp., pa 60¢)

Sf suspense novel; a psychologist joins the four-man crew of a deep-sea sub-tug to find which one is a saboteur.

Dune (Chilton: 5077, Philadelphia, 1965, 412 pp., $5.95) (Gollancz, 1966, 430 pp., 30/-) (Ace: N-3, 1967, 544 pp., pa 95¢) (FSB: 2176, 1968, 510 pp., pa 10/6) (*Der Wüstenplanet* [German], Heyne: 3108-9, 1967, pa)

Winner of the 1966 Hugo award for best novel. It combines "Dune World" (*ASF*, sr3, Dec 1963) and "The Prophet of Dune" (*ASF*, sr5, Jan 1965). The novel concerns an involved vendetta and the ecology of a desert planet where water is the key. The book ed. includes appendices, maps and a who's who; the supplement explains the history and purpose of the Bene Gesserit, and although not necessary, it enables the finer points of the story to be better understood.

Eyes of Heisenberg, The [pa] ("Heisenberg's Eyes," *GSF*, sr2, June 1966) (Berkley: F1283, 1966, 158 pp., pa 50¢) (Sphere: 45179, 1968, 157 pp., pa 5/-) (*Revolte der Unsterblichen* [German], Heyne: 3125, 1968, pa)

Elite human immortals and genetic engineering.

Green Brain, The [pa] ("Greenslaves," *AS*, n'te, Mar 1965) —enlarged: (Ace: F-379, 1966, 160 pp., pa 40¢)

Earth becomes dominated by an unusual mutant life form.

Heaven Makers, The [pa] (*AS*, sr2, Apr 1967) (Avon: S319, 1968, 159 pp., pa 60¢)

An immortal uses Earth as a stage for entertaining his race.

Santaroga Barrier, The [pa] (*AS*, sr3, Oct 1967) (Berkley: S1615, 1968, 255 pp., pa 75¢)

An investigation of an isolated community with its potent 'Jaspers' food.

21st Century Sub [pa] See *Dragon in the Sea, The*

HERING, HENRY A(UGUSTUS) (1864– ?) British author.
Fiction
Adventures and Fantasy [C] (Wright Brown, London, 1930, 288 pp., 7/6; 1932, 3/6)

15 stories: "Major Butterfield's Adventure"; "Mr. John Jude's Diary"; "An Episode in Polydore"; "The Disintegrated Greengrocer"; "Hunt the Tiger"; "Marmaduke Dulcimer"; "Codicil-Forger"; "Silas P. Cornu's System"; "Psyche's Experience Exchange"; "Psyche's Liquid Thought"; "The Late Eugene Aram"; "The Telepather"; "The Vanished Prime Minister"; "Mr. Broadbent's Information"; "The Crew of the Flying Dutchman."

HERON, E. and H. (pseud) See PRICHARD, K. & HESKETH

HERRMAN, PAUL (1905–) German geographer.
Nonfiction
Conquest by Man (Harper, New York, 1955, 455 pp., illus., $6.00)

A book in the same category as W. Ley & L. S. de Camp's *Lands Beyond*, covering some of the same ground but drawing on many

other sources, especially German and Scandinavian, and delving into many other by-roads. It makes no mention of the Zimbabwe ruins, but includes a coverage of the Viking habitation of Greenland and the Greek opening of the Black Sea country.

HERSEY, HAROLD (1892–) U.S. editor and publisher. He became interested in science fiction in his youth. After war service he became editor of Street & Smith's *Thrill Book*. He worked with Margaret Sanger in her birth control movement, and in 1926 he became Supervising Editor of all the Macfadden publications. He also had much to do with the founding of the Clayton *Astounding Stories* (later *ASF*) and published the short-lived *Miracle, Science and Fantasy*. He was associated with many old-time authors. He told his story in *Pulpwood Editor* (1937) and in the article "Looking Backward Into the Future" (*Golden Atom* [amateur magazine], 1954/55).

HERSEY, JOHN (17 June 1914–) U.S. author and editor. He was born of American parents at Tientsin, China; he took his B.A. at Yale in 1936. He has been a writer for *Time*, the *New Yorker*, etc., and an editor of *Life*. He was awarded a Pulitzer Prize in 1945.
Fiction
Child Buyer, The (Knopf, New York, 1960, 258 pp., $4.00) (Penguin: 2152, 1965, 262 pp., pa 4/6)

Subtitled as a "Novel in the Form of Hearings Before the Standing Committee on Education, Welfare and Public Morality of a Certain State Senate Investigating the Conspiracy of Mr. Wissey Jones With Others to Purchase a Male Child." It is set in our immediate future and concerns "progressive education"; it is science-fictional in its points but would be improved if written according to sf's principles.

White Lotus (Knopf, New York, 1965, 683 pp., $6.95) (Random, Toronto, $8.50) (Bantam: Q3095, 1966, 692 pp., pa $1.25) (Corgi: EN7568, 1967, 704 pp., pa 7/6)

A lengthy parable of slavery and racial conflict set in an alternate probability time stream where white America is subject to raids by the dominant yellow race.

HESKY, OLGA
Fiction
Purple Armchair, The (Blond, London, 1961, 232 pp., 15/-) (Mayflower: 7166, 1963, 221 pp., pa 3/6)

An unusual extrapolation of social trends, competently treated, based on a visitor from outer space who looks like a purple armchair.

HESSE, HERMAN (2 July 1877–9 Aug 1962) German author, particularly noted for the Nobel Prize novel covered below. An early translated work, *Steppenwolf* (London, 1929), is based on lycanthropy (not listed in the Bleiler *Checklist*).
Fiction
Magister Ludi (*Das Glasperlenspiel* [German], 1945) –[Trans.– M. Savill]: (Aldus, London, 1949, 502 pp., 15/-) (Holt, New York, 1949, $5.00)

A Nobel Prize novel; a philosophical romance attempting to give a design for an ideal way of life. Intellectuals of the Castalian Order aim at coordination of all arts and sciences, with music and mathematics as their basis.

HEUER, KENNETH (1927–)
Nonfiction
End of the World, The (Rinehart, New York, 1953, 220 pp., illus.–C. Bonestell, $3.00) (Gollancz, London, 1953, 159 pp., 8/6) (*The Next 50 Billion Years*, Viking, New York, 1957, 144 pp., $3.00)

A collection of superstitious and pseudo-religious ideas from the past concerning the world's end, plus some chapters on the scientific likelihood of the Earth's destruction. Bonestell's plates, originally published in *Collier's*, July 1947, appear in black and white but are still worth having.

Men of Other Planets (Pellegrini & Cudahy, New York, 1951, 165 pp., illus., $3.00; 2nd ed., 1954, 160 pp., $3.00) (Gollancz, 1951,

165 pp., illus., 12/6)
Based only on scientific guesswork, this shows no imagination for anything but life based on the carbon-water cycle.
Next 50 Billion Years, The See *End of the World, The*

HEUVELMANS, BERNARD Belgian zoologist, jazz musician and columnist. His wife is the fantasy writer Monique Watteau.
Nonfiction
On the Track of Unknown Animals (*Sur la piste des animaux ignores*, ?) —Trans.—R. Garrett: (Hill & Wang, New York, 1959, 558 pp., illus., $6.95) (Hart-Davis, London, 1959, 558 pp., illus., 35/-)
This covers the many strange animals met in Ley's zoological works, but documents the reports more fully and goes further. Are there many creatures still unknown? What animals have survived practically unchanged since the time of the mammoths or before? It is one of the most comprehensive and challenging works of its kind.

HEYNE, WILLIAM P. (1910–)
Fiction
Tales of Two Futures (Exposition, New York, 1958, 160 pp., $3.00)
Subtitled: "A novel of life on Earth and the planet Paliades in 1975." A mixture of the Bible, angels, and modern sf.

HEYWOOD, ROSALIND British ESP enthusiast. Urged by Guy Wint and Chatto & Windus (British publishers) to do a book on ESP, she wrote *The Sixth Sense*, followed by *The Infinite Hive*. Mrs. Heywood also contributed the section "ESP and the Changing Mental Climate" to *Science and ESP*, edited by Dr. J. R. Smythe (Routledge & Kegan Paul).
Nonfiction
ESP, A Personal Memoir See *Infinite Hive, The*
Infinite Hive, The (Chatto Windus, London, 1964, 224 pp., 25/-) (Clarke Irwin, Toronto) (*ESP, A Personal Memoir*, Dutton, New York, 1964, 224 pp., $4.50)
Sixth Sense, The (Chatto Windus, 1964, 224 pp., 21/-)
Recounts the history and researches of inexplicable phenomena in the realm of psi. It is well indexed and has an appendix recording the explanations and hypotheses of some of the groups and other researchers.

HICHENS, ROBERT S(MYTHE) (14 Nov 1864–20 July 1950) English author. He studied music in his youth, and for a while was on the staff of the London *World* as music critic. He first wrote short stories for *Pall Mall Magazine*. He travelled a great deal; a visit to North Africa inspired him to write the very successful *The Garden of Allah* (1904), which has been a play and a film. He wrote over 50 novels, and was considered a master hand at blending the exotic and the emotional. He died in Zurich, Switzerland.
Fiction [Incomplete—other titles in Bleiler *Checklist*]
Black Spaniel and Other Stories, The [C] (Stokes, New York, 1905, 280 pp., illus.—A. Forestier) (Methuen, London, 1905, 318 pp., 6/-)
The only story of note is "The Black Spaniel," a well-written weird long novelette.
Bye-Ways [C] (Dodd Mead, New York, 1897, 3+356 pp.; 1914, 356 pp.) (Collins, London, 1907, 320 pp., 7d) (Methuen, London, 1916, 326 pp., 2/-)
10 stories (one sectionalised): "The Charmer of Snakes"; "A Tribute of Souls—Prelude: I. The Stranger by the Burn, II. The Soul of Dr. Wedderburn, III. The Soul of Kate Walters, IV. The Soul of Hugh Fraser, V. The Return of the Grey Traveller" [written with Lord Frederick Hamilton]; "An Echo in Egypt"; "The Face of the Monk"; "The Man Who Intervened"; "After Tomorrow"; "A Silent Guardian"; "A Boudoir Boy"; "The Tee-To-Tum."
Snake-Bite and Other Stories [C] (Doran, New York, 1919, 337 pp.) (Cassell, London, 1919, 351 pp.; 1920, 246 pp., 2/6)
6 stories: "Snake-Bite"; "The Lost Faith"; "The Hindu"; "The Lighted Candles"; "The Nomad"; "The Two Fears."

Tongues of Conscience [C] (Stokes, [1900], 368 pp.)
Contains only one weird story, the noted "How Love Came to Professor Guildea." It is often anthologized and recently was in *Fear*, July 1960.

HICKEY, T. EARL
Fiction
Time Chariot, The (Avalon, New York, 1966, 191 pp., $3.25)
Whacky and uncomplicated story of the finding of a time machine.

HICKS, CLIFFORD B. (10 Aug 1920–) U.S. author, born in Marshalltown, Iowa.
Fiction
First Boy on the Moon (Winston, Philadelphia, 1959, 120 pp., illus., $2.95)
Juvenile; two boys stow away on a rocket piloted by the father of one.

HIGGINSON, THOMAS WENTWORTH (22 Dec 1823–9 May 1911) American Unitarian clergyman, critic and poet. Devoted to the anti-slavery cause, he commanded the first regiment of freed slaves in the service of the United States in the Civil War. H. Bruce Franklin considered his story "The Monarch of Dreams" quite extraordinary and reprinted it in *Future Perfect* (1966).
Fiction
Tales of the Enchanted Isles of the Atlantic [C] (Macmillan, London & New York, 1898, 259 pp.)
Juvenile fantasy, 20 stories—an imitation of *The Wonder Book*: "The Story of Atlantis"; "Taliessin of the Radiant Brow"; "The Swan-Children of Lir"; "Usheen in the Island of Youth"; "Bran the Blessed"; "The Castle of the Active Door"; "Merlin the Enchanter"; "Sir Lancelot of the Lake"; "The Half-Man"; "King Arthur at Avalon"; "Maelduin's Voyage"; "The Voyage of St. Brendan"; "Kirwan's Search for Hy-Brasail"; "The Isle of Satan's Hand"; "Antillia, the Island of the Seven Cities"; "Harald the Viking"; "The Search for Norumbega"; "The Guardians of the St. Lawrence"; "The Island of Demons"; "Bimini and the Fountain of Youth."

HIGH, PHILIP E(MPSON) (28 Apr 1914–) British sf writer. He has been a commercial traveller, insurance agent, bus driver, reporter, and salesman, among other things, trying to find a position which would also allow him to write, particularly sf, which he discovered when 13. After collecting many rejection slips, in 1956 he became a regular contributor to the British field. He wrote a guest editorial for *New Worlds*: "Why Explain S-F?" (Apr 1962). He is interested in literature, psychology and drama, is married and has one daughter, and lives in Canterbury, Kent.
Fiction
Invader on My Back (R. Hale, London, 1968, 192 pp., 18/-) (Ace: H-85, 1968, 146 pp., pa 60¢; with *Destination: Saturn*)
A struggle against alien invaders, and the mystery of why people can't look up.
Mad Metropolis, The [pa] (Ace: M-135, 1966, 142 pp., pa 45¢; with *Space Captain*)
An attempt to regain control of the "mother" computer of a huge future city.
No Truce With Terra [pa] (Ace: F-275, 1964, 110 pp., pa 40¢; with *The Duplicators*)
Invasion of an electronic life form, with help from humanoid aliens.
Prodigal Sun, The [pa] (Ace: F-255, 1964, 192 pp., pa 40¢) (Compact: F273, 1965, 190 pp., pa 3/6)
Raised on an alien planet, a man returns to a corrupt Earth with a secret mission.
Reality Forbidden (Ace: G-609, 1967, 151 pp., pa 50¢; with *Contraband From Otherspace*) (R. Hale, London, 1968, 176 pp., 16/-)
Rebellion against a world under the control of dream machines.
These Savage Futurians [pa] (Ace: G-623, 1967, 134 pp., pa 50¢; with *The Double Invaders*)
Future factions fight each other after civilization's collapse.

Time Mercenaries, The (Ace: H-59, 1968, 118 pp., 60¢; with *Anthropol*) (Dobson, London, 1968, 118 pp., 18/-)

Fascinating adventure of a modern submarine crew transferred to the future to save the world.

Twin Planets [pa] (Paperback: 52-392, 1967, 159 pp., pa 50¢) (Dobson, London, 1968, 159 pp., 18/-)

Rebellious factions on a planet similar to Earth, with aliens and an Earth-grown superman playing roles.

HIGHAM, CHARLES (18 Feb 1931–) British literary figure, now living in Sydney, Australia. The oldest son of Sir Charles F. Higham, he was born in London and educated at Cranleigh. He was assistant to the education manager at Macmillan & Co., publishers, 1952-54. Since 1955 he has been a book critic for the *Sydney Morning Herald*, and in Aug 1961 began the "Talking of Books" column in Saturday issues. Besides the weird anthologies below, his books include *A Distant Star* (verse, 1951), *Spring and Death* (verse, 1954), *The Earthbound & Other Poems* (verse, 1959), *They Came to Australia* (anthology, with Alan Brissenden, 1961), *The Big Beat* (1961). With Michael Wilding he compiled *Australians Abroad: An Anthology* (Cheshire, Melbourne, 1967). He has contributed to the *Inter-Literary Annual*, *Australian Poetry* (Angus & Robertson), *P.E.N. Anthology*, etc.; some of his poems have appeared in other languages.

Anthologies

Curse of Dracula and Other Terrifying Tales, The [pa] (Horwitz: PB111, Sydney, 1962, 130 pp., pa 3/9)

Weird, 6 stories: "The Curse of Dracula," Bram Stoker; "The Mummy's Foot," Theophile Gautier; "The Unknown Island," H. T. W. Bousfield; "A Watcher by the Dead," Ambrose Bierce; "Man-Size in Marble," E. Nesbit; "El Verdugo," Honore de Balzac.

Nightmare Stories [pa] (Horwitz: PB117, 1962, 130 pp., pa 3/9)

Weird, 9 stories [authors not given on title page]: "The Mummy's Curse," James Workman; "The Ghost of a Hand," J. Sheridan Le Fanu; "Sir Dominick's Bargain," J. S. Le Fanu; "To Be Taken With a Grain of Salt," C. Dickens; "A Horseman in the Sky," Ambrose Bierce; "The Suitor of Selkirk," Anon.; "How the Third Floor Knew the Potteries," Amelia B. Edwards; "Whistler's Mother," D. W. Preston; "The Cask of Amontillado," Edgar A. Poe.

Spine-Tingling Tales [pa] (Horwitz: PB98, 1962, 162 pp., pa 3/9)

Weird, 6 stories: "Blood and Roses," S. Le Fanu; "The Devil of the Marsh," H. B. Marriott-Watson; "The Unquiet Grave," F. M. Mayor; "The Tapestried Chamber," Sir W. Scott; "The Phantom Coach," Amelia B. Edwards; "The Judge's House," B. Stoker.

Tales of Horror [pa] (Horwitz: PB104, 1962, 160 pp., pa 3/9)

Weird, 8 stories (no table of contents): "The Death Mask," Mrs. H. D. Everett; "The Invisible Eye," Mm. Erckmann-Chatrian; "The Middle Toe of the Right Foot," A. Bierce; "Berenice," E. A. Poe; "The Haunted Station," Hume Nisbet; "Schalken the Painter," J. S. Le Fanu; "The Horla," Guy de Maupassant; "The Reptile," Augustus Muir.

Tales of Terror [pa] (Horwitz: PB93, 1961, 194 pp., pa 4/6)

Weird, 10 stories: "The Screaming Skull," "The Upper Berth," F. Marion Crawford; "The Body Snatcher," R. L. Stevenson; "The Monkey's Paw," W. W. Jacobs; "The Ace of Spades," A. M. Pushkin; "The Dead Hand," Wilkie Collins; "The Signalman," C. Dickens; "The Tell-Tale Heart," E. A. Poe; "Dracula's Guest," "The Squaw," B. Stoker.

Weird Stories [pa] (Horwitz: PB82, 1961, 127 pp., pa 3/9)

Weird, 9 stories: "The Black Cat," "The Case of M. Valdemar," E. A. Poe; "The Werewolf," F. Marryat; "Vendetta," Fear," "The Hand," G. de Maupassant; "A Terribly Strange Bed," "The Dream Woman," W. W. Collins; "Wicked Captain Walshawe," S. Le Fanu.

HILL, DOUGLAS (ARTHUR) (6 Apr 1935–) Canadian poet, critic, editor and historian.

Nonfiction

Supernatural, The [with Pat Williams] (Aldus, London, 1965, 350 pp., illus., 63/-) (Hawthorn, New York, 1966, 350 pp., illus., $12.50) (Signet: Q3256, 1967, 240 pp., pa 95¢)

About half devoted to history and current practices of magic and witchcraft, and half to discussion of supernatural beings believed to inhabit darkness, history of spiritualism, and coverage of cults and factions.

Anthologies

Devil His Due, The (Hart-Davis, London, 1967, 156 pp., 25/-)

Weird, 8 stories: "The Eastern Windows," Keith Roberts; "Devil of a Drummer," Hilary Bailey; "A Long Spoon," John Wyndham; "Anthropologic Demonography," Ramsay Wood; "Return Visit," E. C. Tubb; "The Atheist's Bargain," Tom Disch & John Sladek; "The Shrine of Temptation," Judith Merril; "The Singing Citadel," M. Moorcock.

Way of the Werewolf [pa] (Panther: 2149, 1966, 143 pp., pa 3/6)

Weird, 8 stories and introduction: "The Phantom Farmhouse," Seabury Quinn; "Gabriel-Ernest," Saki; "Running Wolf," A. Blackwood; "Wolves Don't Cry," Bruce Elliott; "The Galoup," Claude Seignolle; "The Refugee," Jane Rice; "The White Wolf of the Hartz Mountains," Frederick Marryat; "Cain's Lupus Sapiens," Alex Hamilton.

Window on the Future (Hart-Davis, London, 1966, 159 pp., 21/-)

Sf, 7 stories: "The Subliminal Man," J. G. Ballard; "The Disposal Unit Man," David Alexander; "Wasted on the Young," John Brunner; "Categorical Imperative," Arthur Sellings; "The Facts of Life," Martin Hillman; "Sense of Proportion," E. C. Tubb; "The Circulation of the Blood," Brian W. Aldiss.

HILL, ERNEST (14 July 1915–)

Fiction

Pity About Earth [pa] (Ace: H-56, 1968, 132 pp., pa 60¢; with *Space Chantey*)

A future newspaper, and intrigue and adventure on an alien world.

HILLEGAS, MARK R.

Nonfiction

Future as Nightmare: H. G. Wells and the Anti-Utopians, The (Oxford U. Press, 1967, 200 pp., $5.75)

A critical study of dystopian science fiction.

HILTON, JAMES (9 Sep 1900–20 Dec 1954) British author. He was obscure until his *Lost Horizon* was acclaimed throughout the English-speaking world. He lived in the U.S.A. after 1935. He was a gifted raconteur, and became a familiar figure to U.S. audiences with his articles, book reviews and motion picture dramatisations. He is noted for his *Good-Bye, Mr. Chips* and *Random Harvest*, both of which were made into excellent films.

Fiction

Lost Horizon (W. Morrow, New York, 1933, 3+277 pp., $2.50) (Macmillan, London, 1933, 281 pp., 7/6) (Macmillan, Toronto, $2.25) (Pocket Books: 1, 1939, 181 pp., pa 25¢; 1945, 239 pp., pa 25¢; 1952, 169 pp., pa 25¢; 1956, 169 pp., pa 25¢; 1959, pa 25¢) (Grosset, New York, 1943, $1.00) (Macmillan, Toronto, 75¢) (*Les horizons perdus* [French–Swiss], Jeheber, Geneve, 1943) (*Horizontes perdidos* [Spanish], Molino, 1944) (Armed, nd, 182 pp., pa) (World 'Tower Book," 1947, 277 pp., pa 49¢) (Pan: 2, 1947, 192 pp., pa 2/-; 1953, pa 2/-; 1957, pa 2/-; G330, 1960, 186 pp., pa 2/6; X558, 1966, pa 3/6) (*Bla Manen* [Swedish], Bonnier, 1948) ([Japanese], Kanto-sha, 1950) (Washington: RE108, 1964, 236 pp., pa 60¢)

A romance in Shangri-La, a valley paradise in Tibet; awarded the Hawthornden Prize in 1939. *Film:* Columbia, 1937, directed by Frank Capra, with Ronald Colman and Jane Wyatt.

HINE, AL

Fiction

Bewitched [pa] (Mayflower: 0551, 1965, 157 pp., pa 3/6)

Based on the TV series—a light fantasy of the lovely witch Samantha and her marriage with human Darrin Stephens.

HINE, MURIEL Pseudonym of Mrs. Sydney Coxon (Muriel Coxon).

Fiction

Seven Lovers and Other Stories, The [C] (J. Lane, London, 1927,

293 pp., 7/6; 1932, 3/6) (Appleton, New York, 1928, 283 pp.; $2.00)

7 stories, of which only one, "The Wishing Ball," is fantasy (ghost).

HINGLEY, RONALD (FRANCIS) (1920–) British writer. M.A. and Ph.D., he has been Lecturer in Russian at Oxford U. since 1955. He contributes to the *Sunday Times*, *Punch*, *Soviet Survey*, etc. His works include *Chekhov*; *Russian for Beginners*; *Soviet Prose*.

Fiction

Up Jenkins! (Longmans Green, London, 1956, 226 pp., 12/6)

Brilliant satirical political fantasy of England split by civil war into North and South sections with an "iron curtain" between.

HINTON, C(HARLES) HOWARD (1853–1907) A fantasy in addition to those below was *An Episode of Flatland* (Sonnenschein, London, 1907).

Fiction

Scientific Romances: First Series [C] (Sonnenschein, London, 1886, 229 pp., illus.) (Allen Unwin, London, 1925, 229 pp., 6/-)

4 stories: "What Is the Fourth Dimension?"; "The Persian King. A Plane World"; "A Picture of Our Universe"; "Casting Out the Self."

Scientific Romances: Second Series [C] (Sonnenschein, London, 1902, 177 pp.) (Allen Unwin, 1925, 231 pp., 6/)

4 stories: "The Education of the Imagination"; "Many Dimensions"; "Stella"; "Unfinished Communication."

HIRSCH, WALTER U.S. sociologist. His doctoral dissertation (Northwestern U.) is *American Science Fiction: 1926-50—A Content Analysis* (available on interlibrary loan, or microfilm or Xerox from University Microfilms, Ann Arbor, Mich.). [From report in the *American Journal of Sociology*, Mar 1958.]

HITCHCOCK, ALFRED (JOSEPH) (13 Aug 1899–) Noted film producer and anthologist. He was born in London, the son of a poultry dealer. He attended U. of London at night, studying art, navigation, political science and economics. At 20 he went to work with Famous Players-Lasky Co. (now Paramount Pictures) as a writer; in rapid succession he became script writer, art director, and producer. In 1923 he became assistant director of Gainsborough Studios, and full director two years later. With his reputation established, in 1938 he hit the U.S.A. with his maddeningly uncertain mysteries. He has the ability to make uncommon things happen to common people on a believable basis. These days he is world renowned for his spine-chilling TV series. Strange to say, his crime library consists only of the annual *Famous Trials* which covers British murder cases. His anthologies have been appearing for over 20 years; many open their titles with "Alfred Hitchcock Presents:." In recent years a number have been translated into German. A recent book about him is *Hitchcock*, by Francois Truffaut in collaboration with Helen G. Scott (Secker Warburg, 1967, 250 pp., £5), discussing how each film was made, and related aspects.

Anthologies

Note: Most titles beginning *Alfred Hitchcock Presents:* are given below as *A.H.P.:* etc. However, in the *PAPERBACK* section (Vol. 3), titles are given alphabetically with *Alfred Hitchcock Presents:* omitted.

Alfred Hitchcock Presents: A Baker's Dozen of Suspense Stories [pa] (Dell: 3626, 1963, 192 pp., pa 50¢)

No further information.

A.H.P.: Bar the Doors [pa] See *Bar the Doors*

A.H.P.: Fear and Trembling [pa] See *Fear and Trembling*

A.H.P.: 14 of My Favourites in Suspense [pa] See *A.H.P.: My Favourites in Suspense*

A.H.P.: 14 Suspense Stories to Play Russian Roulette By [pa] See *Suspense*

A.H.P.: A Hangman's Dozen [pa] (Dell: 3428, 1962, 222 pp., pa 50¢) (Mayflower: 1964, 222 pp., pa 2/6)

Weird & horror, 15 stories and compiler's preface: "Bomb

#14," Jack Ritchie; "The Forgiving Ghost," C. B. Gilford; "The Children of Noah," R. Matheson; "An Attractive Family," Robert Arthur; "Let the Sucker Beware," Charles Einstein; "Fair Game," John Cortez; "The Curious Facts Preceding My Execution," Richard Stark; "Your Witness," Helen Nielson; "Blackout," Richard Deming; "The October Game," Ray Bradbury; "Stop Calling Me 'Mister'," Jonathan Craig; "The Last Escape," Jay Street; "Not a Laughing Matter," Evan Hunter; "Most Agreeably Poisoned," Fletcher Flora; "The Best-Friend Murder," Donald E. Westlake.

A.H.P.: Hold Your Breath [pa] See *Hold Your Breath*

A.H.P.: More of My Favourites in Suspense [pa] See *A.H.P.: My Favourites in Suspense*

A.H.P.: More Stories for Late at Night [pa] See *A.H.P.: Stories for Late at Night*

A.H.P.: More Stories My Mother Never Told Me [pa] See *A.H.P.: Stories My Mother Never Told Me*

A.H.P.: My Favourites in Suspense (Random, New York, 1959, 502 pp., $4.95) (Reinhardt, London, 1960, 560 pp., 18/-) (*A.H.P.: 14 of My Favourites in Suspense*, Dell: F125, 1960, 286 pp., pa 50¢ [14 stories marked p1]) (*A.H.P.: More of My Favourites in Suspense*, Dell: F130, 1961, 287 pp., pa 50¢; 3260, 1964, pa 50¢ [7 stories marked p2]) (*I skräckens paradis* [Swedish], Wahlström & Widstrand, 1961) ([Part I], Pan: X177, 1962, 269 pp., pa 3/6 [first 12 stories only]) ([Part II], Pan: X271, 1963, 269 pp., pa 3/6 [last 10 stories])

22 stories with compiler's preface (repeated in both Dell pa eds.): "The Birds"p1, Daphne Du Maurier; "Man With a Problem"p1, Donald Honig; "They Bite"p1, A. Boucher; "The Enemy"p1, Charlotte Armstrong; "The Inexperienced Ghost"p1, H. G. Wells; "Sentence of Death"p1, Thomas Walsh; "Spring Fever"p1, Dorothy Salisbury Davis; "The Crate at Outpost 1"p1, Matthew Gant; "My Unfair Lady"p1, Guy Cullingford; "Composition for Four Hands" [n'te] p2, Hilda Lawrence; "New Murders for Old"p1, Carter Dickson; "Terrified"p1, C. B. Gilford; "The Duel"p1, Joan Vatsek; "Four O'Clock"p1, Price Day; "Too Many Coincidences"p1, Paul Eiden; "Of Missing Persons"p2, Jack Finney; "Island of Fear"p2, William Sambrot; "Getting Rid of George"p2, Robert Arthur; "Treasure Trove"p2, F. T. Jesse; "The Body of the Crime"p2, Wilbur D. Steele; "A Nice Touch"p2, Mann Rubin; "The Blank Wall" [n], Elisabeth S. Holding.

A.H.P.: Once Upon a Dreadful Time [pa] (Dell: 6622, 1964, 192 pp., pa 50¢)

16 stories with foreword "Department of the Departed," A. Hitchcock: "A Little Push From Cappy Fleers," Gilbert Ralston; "The Safe Street," Paul Edien; "No One on the Line," R. Arthur; "Antique," Hal Ellson; "Suspicion Is Not Enough," Richard Hardwick; "A Family Affair," Talmage Powell; "Granny's Birthday," F. Brown; "Third Party in the Case," Philip Ketchum; "Hill Justice," John Falkner"; "If This Be Madness," Lawrence Block; "Anatomy of an Anatomy," D. E. Westlake; "A Cool Swim on a Hot Day," Fletcher Flora; "By the Sea, by the Sea," Hal Dresner; "Bodies Just Won't Stay Put," Tom McPherson; "The Dagerfield Saga," C. B. Gilford; "Number One Suspect," R. Deming.

A.H.P.: 16 Skeletons From My Closet [pa] (Dell: 8011, 1963, 221 pp., pa 50¢) (Mayflower: 8011, 1964, 221 pp., pa 3/6)

16 stories with compiler's introduction: "Ghost Story," Henry Kane; "Where Is Thy Sting?" James Holding; "The Butler Who Didn't Do It," Craig Rice; "Christmas Gift," Robert Turner; "The Man at the Table," C. B. Gilford; "Death of Another Salesman," Donald Honig; "Man With a Hobby," R. Bloch; ". . . Said Jack the Ripper," R. Arthur; "A Gun With a Heart," Wm. Logan; "Assassination," Dion Henderson; "A Little Sororicide," R. Deming; "The Man Who Got Away With It," Lawrence Treat; "Secret Recipe," Charles Mergendahl; "Daddy-O," David Alexander; "The Crime Machine," Jack Ritchie; "Homicide and Gentlemen," Fletcher Flora.

A.H.P.: Stories for Late at Night (Random, 1961, 469 pp., $5.95) (Reinhardt, 1962, 500 pp., 20/-) (*A.H.P.: 12 Stories for Late at Night*, Dell: 9178, 1962, 223 pp., pa 50¢ [12 stories marked p1]) (*A.H.P.: More Stories for Late at Night*, Dell: 5815, 1962, 207 pp., pa 50¢; 1967, pa 50¢ [11 stories marked p2]) ([Part I], Pan: X344, 1964, 285 pp., pa 3/6 [15 stories—first 16 except 6th])

([Part II], Pan: X456, 1965, 237 pp., pa 3/6 [7 stories—last 7 including novel])

24 stories, including 2 n'te and 1 novel (Reinhardt and Pan eds. omit 2 stories, by Dahl and Morris): "Death Is a Dream"p1, R. Arthur; "It's a Good Life"p2, Jerome Bixby; "The Whole Town's Sleeping"p1, R. Bradbury; "Lady's Man"p2, Ruth Chatterton; "Evening Primrose"p1, J. Collier; "The Sound Machine"p2, R. Dahl; "The Cocoon"p2, John B. L. Goodwin; "Vintage Season" [n'te] p1, C. L. Moore; "Pieces of Silver"p2, Brett Halliday; "The Whistling Room"p2, Wm. H. Hodgson; "Told for the Truth"p2, Cyril Hume; "The Ash Tree"p1, M. R. James; "Side Bet"p1, W. F. Jenkins; "Second Night Out"p1, F. B. Long; "Our Feathered Friends"p1, Phillip MacDonald; "The Fly"p2, George Langelaan; "Back There in the Grass"p1, Gouverneur Morris; "The Mugging"p2, Edward L. Perry; "Finger! Finger!"p2, Margaret Roman; "A Cry From the Penthouse"p2, Henry Slesar; "The People Next Door"p2, Pauline Smith; "D-Day"p1, Robert Trout; "The Man Who Liked Dickens"p1, Evelyn Waugh; "The Iron Gates" ("Taste of Fears") [n], Margaret Millar.

A.H.P.: Stories My Mother Never Told Me (Random, 1963, 401 pp., $5.95) (Random, Toronto, $6.50) (Reinhardt, 1964, 448 pp., 20/-) (*A.H.P.: More Stories My Mother Never Told Me*, Dell: 5816, 1966, 190 pp., pa 50¢ [contents unknown]) ([Part I], Pan: X581, 1966, 255 pp., pa 3/6 [first 16 stories below]) ([Part II], Pan: M250, 1967, 236 pp., pa 5/- [last 10 stories below])

26 stories (listed from Pan pa eds.) and introduction: "The Child Who Believed," Grace Amundson; "Just a Dream," Robert Arthur; "The Wall-to-Wall Grave," Andrew Benedict; "The Wind," R. Bradbury; "Congo," Stuart Cloete; "Witch's Money," J. Collier; "Dip in the Pool," R. Dahl; "The Secret of the Bottle" [n'te], G. Kersh; "I Do Not Hear You, Sir," A. Davidson; "The Arbutus Collar," Jeremiah Digges; "A Short Trip Home," F. S. Fitzgerald; "An Invitation to the Hunt," G. Hitchcock; "The Man Who Was Everywhere," E. D. Hoch; "The Summer People," Shirley Jackson; "Adjustments," George Mandel; "The Children of Noah," R. Matheson; "The Idol of Flies" [n'te], Jane Rice; "Courtesy of the Road," Mack Morriss; "Remains to Be Seen," Jack Ritchie; "The Man Who Sold Rope to the Gnoles," I. Seabright; "Lost Dog," H. Slesar; "Hostage," Don Stanford; "Natural Selection," Gilbert Thomas; "Simone," Joan Vatsek; "Smart Sucker," Richard Wormser; "Some of Your Blood" [n], T. Sturgeon.

A.H.P.: Stories Not for the Nervous (Random, 1965, 363 pp., $5.95) (Reinhardt, 1966, 384 pp., 20/-) (Dell: 8288, 1966, 188 pp., pa 50¢) ([Part I], Pan: 02195, 1968, 187 pp., pa 5/- [stories not known])

24 stories with introduction "A Brief Message From Our Sponsor": "To the Future," R. Bradbury; "River of Riches," G. Kersh; "Levitation," J. P. Brennan; "Miss Winters and the Wind," Christine N. Govan; "View From the Terrace," Mike Marmer; "The Man With Copper Fingers," Dorothy L. Sayers; "The Twenty Friends of William Shaw," R. E. Banks; "The Other Hangman," Carter Dickson; "Don't Look Behind You," Fredric Brown; "No Bath for the Browns," Margot Bennet; "The Uninvited," Michael Gilbert; "Dune Roller," Julian May; "Something Short of Murder," H. Slesar; "The Golden Girl," Ellis Peters; "The Boy Who Predicted Earthquakes," Marg. St. Clair; "Walking Alone," Miriam A. DeFord; "For All the Rude People," Jack Ritchie; "The Dog Died First," Bruno Fischer; "Room With a View," Hal Dresner; "Lemmings," R. Matheson; "White Goddess," I. Seabright; "The Substance of Martyrs," Wm. Sambrot; "Call for Help," R. Arthur; "Sorry, Wrong Number," Lucille Fletcher & Allan Uilma.

A.H.P.: Stories That Scared Even Me (Random, 1967, 463 pp., $6.95) (Reinhardt, 1967, 413 pp., 25/-)

19 stories with introduction (1 p.) and acknowledgment: "Fishhead," I. S. Cobb; "Camera Obscura," B. Copper; "A Death in the Family," Miriam A. DeFord; "Men Without Bones," G. Kersh; "Not With a Bang," D. Knight; "Party Games," John Burke; "X Marks the Pedwalk," F. Leiber; "Curious Adventures of Mr. Bond," N. Barker; "Two Spinsters," E. P. Oppenheim; "The Knife," R. Arthur; "The Cage," Ray Russell; "It," T. Sturgeon; "Tough Town," Wm. Sambrot; "The Troll," T. H. White; "Evening at the Black House," Robert Somerlott; "One of the Dead,"

Wm. Wood; "The Master of the Hounds," A. Budrys; "The Candidate," H. Slesar; "The Body Snatchers" [n], J. Finney.

A.H.P.: Stories They Wouldn't Let Me Do on TV (Simon Schuster, New York, 1956, 372 pp., $3.95) (Reinhardt, 1957, 373 pp., 18/-) (*A.H.P.: 12 Stories They Wouldn't Let Me Do on TV*, Dell: D231, 1958, 224 pp., pa 35¢; F206, 1961, pa 50¢; #3645, 1962, pa 50¢ [first 12 stories in same order]) (*A.H.P.: 13 More Stories They Wouldn't Let Me Do on TV*, Dell: D281, 1959, 224 pp., pa 35¢ [remaining 13 stories]) (Pan: X71, 1960, 378 pp., pa 3/6; M251, 1967, pa 5/-)

25 stories (both Brit. ed. have all stories): "Being a Murderer Myself," Arthur Williams; "Lukundoo," Edward L. White; "A Woman Seldom Found," Wm. Sansom; "The Perfectionist," Margaret St. Clair; "The Price of the Head," John Russell; "Love Comes to Miss Lucy," Q. Patrick; "Sredni Vashtar," Saki; "Love Lies Bleeding," Philip MacDonald; "The Dancing Partner," Jerome K. Jerome; "Casting the Runes," M. R. James; "The Voice in the Night," Wm. H. Hodgson; "How Love Came to Professor Guildea" [n'te], Robert S. Hichens; "The Moment of Decision," Stanley Ellin; "A Jungle Graduate," James F. Dwyer; "Recipe for Murder," C. P. Donnel, Jr.; "Nunc Dimittis," Roald Dahl; "The Most Dangerous Game," Richard Connell; "The Lady on the Grey," John Collier; "The Waxwork," A. M. Burrage; "The Dumb Wife," Thomas Burke; "Couching at the Door," D. K. Broster; "The October Game," R. Bradbury; "Water's Edge," Robert Bloch; "The Jokester," Robert Arthur; "The Abyss," Leonid Andreyev.

A.H.P.: 13 More Stories They Wouldn't Let Me Do on TV [pa] See *A.H.P.: Stories They Wouldn't Let Me Do on TV*
A.H.P.: 12 Stories for Late at Night [pa] See *A.H.P.: Stories for Late at Night*
A.H.P.: 12 Stories They Wouldn't Let Me Do on TV [pa] See *A.H.P.: Stories They Wouldn't Let Me Do on TV*
Alfred Hitchcock's Fireside Book of Suspense (Simon & Schuster, 1947, 367 pp., $3.50)

Weird, 27 stories and compiler's essay "Quality of Suspense": "The Second Class Passenger," P. Gibbons; "The News in English," G. Greene; "Leiningen Versus the Ants," C. Stephenson; "If You Don't Get Excited," E. Corle; "Fire in the Galley Stove," W. Outerson; "The Liqueur Glass," Phyllis Bottome; "Alarm Bell," D. Henderson; "The Room on the Fourth Floor," R. Strauss; "With Bated Breath," R. Santee; "Flood on the Goodwins," A. D. Divine; "Sunset," S. H. Small; "The House of Ecstasy," R. M. Farley; "The Hangman Won't Wait," J. D. Carr; "Second Step," Margery Sharp; "After-Dinner Story," W. Irish; "The Tunnel," J. Metcalfe; "Triggers in Leash," A. V. Elston; "Blue Papers," A. P. Terhune; "Three Good Witnesses," H. Lamb; "R.M.S. Titanic," H. Baldwin; "Ringed World," T. O. Beachcroft; "Yours Truly, Jack the Ripper," R. Bloch; "Baby in the Icebox," J. M. Cain; "Two Bottles of Relish," Lord Dunsany; "Smee," Ex-Private X; "His Brother's Keeper," W. W. Jacobs; "Elementals," S. V. Benét.

Alfred Hitchcock's Ghostly Gallery (Reinhardt, 1966, 262 pp., 21/-) (Puffin: PS319, 1967, 223 pp., pa 5/-)

Subtitled "Eleven Spooky Stories for Young People"; with introduction by compiler: "The Waxwork," A. M. Burrage; "Miss Emmeline Takes Off," Walter Brooks; "The Valley of the Beasts," A. Blackwood; "The Haunted Trailer," R. Arthur; "The Upper Berth," F. M. Crawford; "The Wonderful Day," R. Arthur; "The Truth About Pyecraft," H. G. Wells; "Housing Problem," H. Kuttner; "In a Dim Room," Lord Dunsany; "Obstinate Uncle Otis," R. Arthur; "The Isle of Voices," R. L. Stevenson.

Alfred Hitchcock's Haunted Houseful (Random, 1961, 208 pp., $3.95) (Reinhardt, 1962, 288 pp., 16/-) (FSB: 1471, 1966, 189 pp., pa 5/-)

Weird & horror, 9 stories (listing from FSB ed.) and introduction: "The Mystery of Rabbit Run," Jack Bechdolt; "Jimmy Takes Vanishing Lessons," Walter R. Brooks; "Let's Haunt a House," M. W. Wellman; "The Wastwych Secret," Constance Savery; "The Water Ghost of Harrowby Hall," John K. Bangs; "The Red-Headed League," Sir Arthur C. Doyle; "The Mystery in Four-and-a-Half Street," Donald & Louise Peattie; "The Forgotten Island," Elizabeth Coatsworth; "The Treasure in the Cave," Mark Twain.

Alfred Hitchcock's Monster Museum (Random, 1965, 207 pp., $3.95)

Weird, 13 stories, intended for young readers: "The Day of the Dragon," Guy Endore; "The King of the Cats," S. V. Benét; "Slime," J. P. Brennan; "The Man Who Sold Rope to the Gnoles," Idris Seabright; "Henry Martindale, Great Dane," Miriam A. De-Ford; "The Microscopic Giants," Paul Ernst; "The Young One," J. Bixby; "Doomsday Deferred," W. F. Jenkins; "Shadow, Shadow on the Wall," T. Sturgeon; "The Desrick on Yandro," M. W. Wellman; "The Wheelbarrow Boy," Richard Parker; "Homecoming," Ray Bradbury.

Alfred Hitchcock's Witches' Brew [pa] (Dell: 9613, 1965, 192 pp., pa 50¢)

13 stories and compiler's introduction: "Premonition," Charles Mergendahl; "A Shot From the Dark Night," Avram Davidson; "I Had a Hunch, and . . .," Talmage Powell; "A Killing in the Market," R. Bloch; "Gone as by Magic," Richard Hardwick; "The Big Bajoor," Borden Deal; "The Gentle Miss Bluebeard," Nedra Tyre; "The Guy That Laughs Last," Philip Tremont; "Diet and Die," Wenzell Brown; "Just for Kicks," Richard Marsten; "Please Forgive Me," Henry Kane; "A Crime Worthy of Me," Hal Dresner; "When Buying a Fine Murder," Jack Ritchie.

Bar the Doors [pa] (Dell: 143, 1946, 192 pp., pa 25¢) (*A.H.P.: Bar the Doors*, Dell: F166, 1962, 192 pp., pa 50¢; 0436, 1965, pa 50¢; Mayflower: 0436, 1963, 192 pp., pa 2/6)

Weird, 14 stories (1962 ed. has 13, omitting "Couching at the Door") with compiler's introduction "Speaking of Terror": "Pollock and the Porroh Man," H. G. Wells; "The Storm," McKnight Malmar; "Moonlight Sonata," A. Woollcott; "The Half-Pint Flask," DuBose Heyward; "The Kill," Peter Fleming; "The Upper Berth," F. M. Crawford; "Midnight Express," A. Noyes; "The Damned Thing," A. Bierce; "Couching at the Door," Dorothy K. Broster; "The Metronome," A. Derleth; "The Pipe-Smoker," Martin Armstrong; "The Corpse at the Table," Samuel H. Adams; "The Woman at Seven Brothers," W. D. Steele; "The Book," Margaret Irwin.

Behind the Locked Door and Other Strange Tales [pa] (FSB: 1773, 1967, 160 pp., pa 5/-)

Weird, 14 stories: "The Crime Machine," Jack Ritchie; "Perfect Pitcher," A. Porges; "Diminishing Wife," Michael Zuroy; "You Can't Blame Me," H. Slesar; "Behind the Locked Door," O. H. Leslie; "All the Needless Killing," Bryce Walton; "IQ–184," Fletcher Flora; "Death Begins at Forty," Richard Hardwick; "Adventures of the Sussex Archers," A. Derleth; "These Daisies Told," A. Porges; "Antique," Hal Ellson; "The Sweater," R. O. Lewis; "Upside Down World," J. Ritchie; "Lady With a Hobby," R. E. Banks.

Fear and Trembling [pa] (Dell: 264, 1948, 192 pp., pa 25¢) (*A.H.P.: Fear and Trembling*, Dell: 2495, 1963, 192 pp., pa 50¢)

13 stories and compiler's foreword "Forms of Fear": "Cassius," H. S. Whitehead; "The Tarn," H. Walpole; "Little Memento," J. Collier; "Oh, Whistle, and I'll Come to You, My Lad," M. R. James; "One Summer Night," A. Bierce; "Telling," Eliz. Bowen; "The Jar," R. Bradbury; "The Bad Lands," J. Metcalfe; "Ghost Hunt," H. R. Wakefield; "Skule Skerry," J. Buchan; "The Red Room," H. G. Wells; "The Sack of Emeralds," Lord Dunsany; "The Night Reveals," C. Woolrich.

Graveyard Man, The [pa] (NEL: 2281, 1968, 95 pp., pa 3/6)

10 stories with brief introduction: "The Cemetery Man," C. B. Gilford; "Spook House," Clark Howard; "Poltergeist," W. S. Hartman; "A Killing in the Market," R. Bloch; "Never Marry a Witch," C. B. Gilford; "A Shot From the Dark Night," A. Davidson; "Murder Delayed," H. Slesar; "Shoot a Friendly Bullet," Lawrence Treat; "The Man in the Lobby," Wm. Link & R. Levinson; "The Shunned House," R. E. Alter.

Guaranteed Rest in Peace [pa] (FSB: 1656, 1966, 223 pp., pa 5/-)

20 stories, selected by Peter Haining from issues of *Alfred Hitchcock's Mystery Magazine* of the previous five years: "The Awful Experiment," Michael Zuroy; "A Hint of Henbane," Frederik Pohl & C. M. Kornbluth; "Dig We Must," Jeff Heller; "Guaranteed Rest in Peace," Bryce Walton; "Top-Flight Aquarium," Wm. Link & R. Levinson; "Deadly Shade of Blue," Jack Sharkey;

"Mr. Kang vs. the Demon," Maxwell Trent; "A Change for the Better," Arthur Porges; "The Thing in the Closet," Don Tothe; "Countdown," David Ely; "Ruby Martinson and the Great Coffin Caper," H. Slesar; "Walk Up Through Death," Andrew Benedict; "The Green Heart," J. Ritchie; "The Adventure of the Haunted Library," A. Derleth; "Bully Boy," Leo R. Ellis; "The Egg Head," Rog Phillips; "Prolonged Visit," Hal Dresner; "Beauty and the Beasts," Allen K. Lang; "Requiem for Grandma," Marvin Karp; "The Crazy Wine," Alex Austin.

Hold Your Breath [pa] (Dell: 206, 1947, 192 pp., pa 25¢) (*A.H.P.: Hold Your Breath*, Dell: 3658, 1963, 192 pp., pa 50¢; Mayflower: 3658, 1964, 192 pp., pa 2/6)

Weird, 9 stories and compiler's foreword "And More Suspense": "Taboo," G. Household; "The Cone," H. G. Wells; "Up Periscope," Alec Hudson; "The Greatest Thing in the World," Norman K. Mailer; "Footfalls," W. D. Steele; "Midnight Rendezvous," Margaret Manners; "Action," C. E. Montague; "Philomel Cottage," Agatha Christie; "Dygartsbush," Walter D. Edmonds.

Late Unlamented, The [pa] (FSB: #1978, 1967, 128 pp., pa 3/6)

Subtitled "And Other Tales of Evil"; 12 stories: "The Late Unlamented," Jonathan Craig; "The Telltale Eye," A. Porges; "Ghost of a Chance," Carroll Mayers; "The Madness Machine," Leo R. Ellis; "A Witch for the Burning," C. B. Gilford; "Haunted Hall," Donald Honig; "The End of an Era," Richard Levinson & Wm. Link; "Until Death Do Us Part," Carroll Mayers; "The China Cottage," A. Derleth; "Death by Misadventure," Wenzell Brown; "When This Man Dies," Lawrence Block; "Sheriff Peary's Cosa Nostra Caper," Richard Hardwick.

Meet Death at Night [pa] (FSB: #1869, 1967, 160 pp., pa 5/-)

Weird, 12 stories: "Keeper of the Crypt," C. Howard; "The Nightmare," D. A. Coleman; "Meet Death at Night," C. B. Gilford; "Dead Giveaway," Leo R. Ellis; "The Amateur Philologist," A. Derleth; "Mirror, Mirror," Pauline K. Prilucik; "Death, the Black-Eyed Denominator," Ed Lacy; "She Loved Funerals," Hilda Cushing; "Avery's Ghost," J. M. Gilmore; "For Money Received," Fletcher Flora; "Drawer 14," Talmage Powell; "The 79 Murders of Martha Gibbs," Joseph Csida.

Suspense [pa] (Dell: 92, 1945, 192 pp., pa 25¢) (*A.H.P.: 14 Suspense Stories to Play Russian Roulette By*, Dell: 3632, 1964, 208 pp., pa 50¢; Mayflower: 3632, 1964, 208 pp., pa 3/6)

14 stories and compiler's preface "The Quality of Suspense" (1945 and 1964 eds. are same except for first story): "Leiningen Versus the Ants," C. Stephenson (1945 ed. only); "Never Kill for Love," C. B. Gilford (1964 ed. only); "The Liqueur Glass," Phyllis Bottome; "Flood on the Goodwins," A. D. Divine; "R.M.S. Titanic," H. Baldwin; "Blue Murder," W. D. Steele; "The House of Ecstasy," R. M. Farley; "Fire in the Galley Stove," Capt. W. Outerson; "The Lady or the Tiger?" F. Stockton; "An Occurrence at Owl Creek Bridge," A. Bierce; "The Second Step," Margery Sharp; "The Blue Paper," A. P. Terhune; "The Baby in the Ice Box," J. M. Cain; "The Room on the Fourth Floor," R. Strauss; "Elementals," S. V. Benét.

Suspense Stories [pa] (Dell: 367, 1949, 192 pp., pa 25¢)

13 stories and compiler's preface "Long Live Suspense": "The Mask," F. T. Jesse; "Accident," Agatha Christie; "The Case for the Defence," G. Greene; "Roman Holiday," Robert Lewis; "Revenge," Samuel Blas; "The Snake," J. Steinbeck; "Long Shadow on the Lawn," Mary Deasy; "The Night," R. Bradbury; "The Rocking-Horse Winner," D. H. Lawrence; "The Warden," Georges Carousso; "Leviathan," Ellis St. Joseph; "Breakdown," Louis Pollock; "The Fool's Heart," Eugene M. Rhodes.

This Day's Evil [pa] (FSB: 1723, 1967, 204 pp., pa 5/-)

Weird/mystery, 18 stories: "Lucky Catch," Ed Lacy; "The Adventure of the Intersia Box," A. Derleth; "Pousse Cafe," Robert Sheckley; "How to Stop Smoking," H. Slesar; "Get-Away," Borden Deal; "The Travelling Arm," Jack Ritchie; "The Missing Bow," Arthur Porges; "The Pulque Vendor," Hal Ellson; "Flora Africana," De Firbes; "Never Hang Another," W. Walton; "The Alibi-Makers," M. Rubin; "This Day's Evil," J. Craig; "The Sound of Murder," D. Westlake; "I Still Scream," F. Swann; "The Painless Method," J. Street; "Deduct One Wife," C. B. Gilford; "Fiesta Time," D. Campbell; "Where the Finger Points," Jack Ritchie.

HOAR, ROGER SHERMAN (8 Apr 1887–1963) U.S. physicist, better known under the pseudonym "Ralph Milne Farley" which he used on most of his science fiction and fantasy. He began writing as a sports reporter for the *Boston Daily Post*, and then taught geodetics and railroad surveying as a means of getting to college. He took three degrees at Harvard, and has taught ballistics as well as other engineering and mathematical subjects. He served as a Wisconsin state senator. He was head of the Legal and Patent Dept. of the Bucyrus-Erie Co. 1921-54, and thereafter was a patent engineer.

He wrote a considerable amount of fiction for such magazines as *Argosy*, which printed most of his "Radio Man" series as well as novels such as "The Golden City" (sr5, 15 May 1933; *FFM*, Dec 1942). He was responsible for R. A. Palmer being appointed editor of *Amazing Stories* in 1938. As a member of the Milwaukee Fictioneers, Hoar was associated with Stanley G. Weinbaum, collaborating with him on some occasions, and completing "Revolution in 1950" (*AS*, sr2, Oct 1938). He appeared in most sf magazines before World War II; his novel "Dangerous Love" (from *Mind Magic*) was reprinted by Utopian Publications during the war. He was not very active in the field after the war.

Series [as Ralph Milne Farley]

Radio Man. "The Radio Man" (*Arg*, sr4, 28 June 1924; *FFM*, sr3, Dec 1939; book and pa); "The Radio Beasts" (*Arg*, sr4, 21 Mar 1925; *FN*, Jan 1941; pa); "The Radio Planet" (*Arg*, sr6, 26 June 1926; *FFM*, Apr 1942; pa); "The Radio Man Returns" (*AS*, June 1939); "The Radio Minds of Mars" (*Spaceway*, sr, June 1955 [only one part appeared]). Other "Radio" stories, not part of the series, include: "The Radio Menace"; "The Radio War"; "The Radio Flyers" (*Arg*, sr5, 11 May 1929); "The Radio Gun-Runners" (*Arg*, sr6, 22 Feb 1930).

Fiction [as Ralph Milne Farley]

Earthman on Venus, An [pa]   See *Radio Man, The*

Hidden Universe, The (*AS*, sr2, Nov 1939) (FPCI, Los Angeles, 1950, 134 pp., $2.00) (in *Strange Worlds* [double binding])

A commercial "boss" reduces men to 1/72 inch and speeds their time sense 32 to 1. The book also contains "We, the Mist" ("The Living Mist," *AS*, Aug 1940)—an evil gaseous entity is defeated by the power of good.

Immortals, The [pa]   (*Arg*, sr6, 17 Nov 1934) (Popular, 1946, 46 pp., pa 1/-)

Omnibus of Time, The [C]   (FPCI, 1950, 16+315 pp., $3.50)

Sf, 14 stories, extracts, etc.: "The Man Who Met Himself"; "Time for Sale"; "Rescue Into the Past"; "The Immortality of Alan Whidden"; "The Time-Wise Guy"; "A Month a Minute"; "The Invisible Bomber"; "The Time Traveller"; "I Killed Hitler"; (missing first chapter of) "The Radio War"; (extract from) "The Golden City"; (extract from) "The Hidden Universe"; "Stranded in Time"; "The Man Who Lived Backwards"; "The Revenge of the Great White Lodge"; "The Man Who Could Turn Back the Clock"; "The End of the World"; "After Math" [13-page discussion about time].

Radio Beasts, The [pa]   (*Arg*, sr4, 21 Mar 1925) (*FN*, Jan 1941) (Ace: F-304, 1964, 191 pp., pa 40¢)

Second of "Radio Man" series.

Radio Man, The (*Arg*, sr4, 28 June 1924) (*FFM*, sr3, Dec 1939) (FPCI, 1948, 177 pp., $2.50) (*An Earthman on Venus*, Avon: 285, 1950, 125 pp., pa 25¢) (in *Strange Worlds* [double binding])

First of "Radio Man" series; fantastic adventures on Venus.

Radio Planet, The [pa]   (*Arg*, sr6, 26 June 1926) (*FFM*, Apr 1942) (Ace: F-312, 1964, 224 pp., pa 40¢)

Third of "Radio Man" series.

Strange Worlds (FPCI, 1952, 311 pp., $3.00)

Double binding of *The Radio Man* and *The Hidden Universe*.

HODDER-WILLIAMS, (JOHN) CHRISTOPHER (1926–) British author. He is the elder son of Ralph Hodder-Williams, chairman of Hodder & Stoughton (publishers). He developed interests in electronics, music and writing after serving with the Royal Signals in the Middle East. At first composing took pride of place, and TV audiences in Britain are familiar with the credit line "Music by Hodder-Williams." He wrote his first novel in 1957 and submitted

it under a pseudonym to his father's firm; it was accepted, and *The Cummings Report* (by "James Brogan") was widely acclaimed as a thriller. Much of his work since has been in the sf field.

Fiction

Chain Reaction (Hodder & Stoughton, London, 1959, 224 pp., 15/-) (Corgi: GS7484, 1966, 190 pp., pa 3/6)

Mystery thriller on the spread of atomic radiation through food, and what happens to man; a warning to humanity.

Egg-Shaped Thing, The (Hodder & Stoughton, 1967, 249 pp., 21/-) (Putnam, New York, 1967, 252 pp., $4.95) (D'day SF B.C., 1967, $1.70)

Industrial espionage and a detective investigation leading to a fourth-dimensional terror.

Fistful of Digits (Hodder & Stoughton, 1968, 288 pp., 25/-)

The consequences of an obsession with machinery; the story is inclined to lose touch with reality.

Main Experiment, The (Hodder & Stoughton, 1964, 224 pp., 18/-) (Putnam, 1965, 250 pp., $4.95) (D'day SF B.C., 1965, $1.20) (Ballantine: U6049, 1966, 238 pp., pa 75¢) (Corgi: GN7390, 1966, 190 pp., pa 3/6)

Typical British mystery with psionics and other weird events at a research laboratory.

HODGES, C. WALTER (1909–)

Fiction

Flying House   See *Sky High*

Sky High (Coward McCann, New York, 1947, 112 pp., illus.—author, $2.50) (Longmans, Toronto, $3.00) (*Flying House*, Benn, London, 1961, 120 pp., illus., 6/-)

Subtitled "The story of a house that flew." A not-so-juvenile fairy tale.

HODGSON, WILLIAM HOPE (15 Nov 1877–17 Apr 1918) British author. Son of an Essex clergyman, he left home as a youngster and spent eight years at sea, voyaging around the world three times. He received the Royal Humane Society's medal for saving a life at sea. He and his wife were living in the south of France when World War I broke out; he returned to England and was granted a commission in the 171st Brigade of the Royal Field Artillery. His brigade saw much fighting in France and did splendid work at Ypres; Hodgson was later killed after volunteering as an observation officer.

The majority of his writings deal with aspects of the sea; many are of a weird nature, and he was favourably reviewed in the weird field when he was writing. However, he appeared to be forgotten until his short story "The Voice in the Night" was reprinted in the 1931 anthology *They Walk Again* [Colin de la Mare], causing renewed interest in his writings; this resulted in some reprinting in *Famous Fantastic Mysteries* and in the Arkham House collections covered below. A critical article and bibliography of Hodgson's works is given by A. L. Searles in *Fantasy Commentator* [amateur magazine], Sep 1944; this mentions a number of small volumes not covered herewith. Hodgson's *Captain Gault* (1917) is a non-weird collection dealing with ships and sail.

Fiction

Boats of the "Glen Carrig," The (Chapman Hall, London, 1907, 312 pp., 6/-) (Holden Hardingham, London, 1920, 252 pp., 2/6) (abr., *FFM*, June 1945) (in *The House on the Borderland* [Hodgson], 1946)

The adventures of some ship survivors, with magnificent descriptions of the flat land, the storm, the sea of weeds, and weirdly menacing landscapes.

Carnacki, the Ghost Finder [C]   (*Idler*, sr5, Jan 1910) (*Carnacki, the Ghost Finder, and poem*, P. R. Reynolds, New York, 1910, 14 pp., 25¢) (E. Nash, London, 1913, 288 pp., 6/-; 1914, 2/-) (Holden Hardingham, 1920, 248 pp., 2/6) (Mycroft Moran, Sauk City [Wisc.], 1948, 241 pp., $3.00)

The Reynolds ed. was a small board-bound brochure giving synopses of the episodes; the Mycroft & Moran ed. has 9 stories (listed), including 3 (listed last) that were in Hodgson's effects and had not been previously published: "The Thing Invisible"; "The Gateway of the Monster"; "The House Among the Laurels"; "The

Whistling Room" (*Magazine of Horror*, June 1965); "The Searcher of the End House"; "The House of the Invisible"; "The Haunted Jarvee"; "The Find"; "The Hog."
Deep Waters [C] (Arkham, Sauk City [Wisc.], 1967, 300 pp., jacket—F. Utpatel, $5.00)

13 macabre stories about the sea: "The Sea Horses"; "The Derelict"; "The Thing in the Weeds"; "From the Tideless Sea"; "The Island of the Ud"; "The Voice in the Night"; "The Adventure of the Headland"; "The Mystery of the Derelict"; "The Shamraken Homeward-Bounder"; "The Stone Ship"; "The Crew of the Lancing"; "The Habitants of Middle Islet"; "The Call in the Dawn."

Ghost Pirates, The (S. Paul, London, 1909, 276 pp., frontis.—S. H. Sime, 6/-) (H. Hardingham, 1920, 248 pp., 2/6) (abr., *FFM*, Mar 1944) (*Super Science* [Canadian], Aug 1944) (in *The House on the Borderland* [Hodgson], 1946)

Weird beings from a ghost ship destroy an ill-fated ship and its crew. *Note:* Magazine version cut by 10,000 words.

House on the Borderland, The [C] (Chapman Hall, 1908, xii+300 pp., 6/-) (H. Hardingham, 1921, 252 pp., 2/6) (*The House on the Borderland and Other Novels*, Arkham, Sauk City [Wisc.], 1946, 650 pp., $5.00; 3014 copies) (Ace: D553, 1962, 159 pp., pa 35¢)

The title novel was considered by Lovecraft to be perhaps Hodgson's greatest work—the story of a lone house in Ireland enveloped by hideous forces from other worlds and besieged by weird monstrosities from an abyss beneath. The Arkham edition contains four novels: *The Boats of the "Glen Carrig"*; *The House on the Borderland*; *The Ghost Pirates*; *The Night Land*.

Luck of the Strong, The [C] (E. Nash, 1916, 318 pp., 6/-) (H. Hardingham, 1920, 250 pp., 2/6)

8 stories and 2 poems: "The Pirates" (poem); "Capt. Gunbolt Charity and the Painted Lady"; "Capt. Jat—The Island of the Ud"; "Capt. Jat—The Adventure of the Headland"; "The Getting Even of 'Parson' Guyles"; "D.C.O. Cargunka—The Adventure With the Claim Jumpers"; "D.C.O. Cargunka—The Bells of the 'Laughing Sally' "; "We Two and Bully Dunkan"; "The Stone Ship"; "The Ship" (poem).

Men of the Deep Waters [C] (E. Nash, 1914, 304 pp., 7/6) (H. Hardingham, 1921, 250 pp., 2/6)

7 supernatural sea stories, with opening poem "The Story of the Great Bull Whale" and foreword "On the Bridge": "The Sea Horses"; "The Derelict" (*FFM*, Dec 1943; *AFR*, No. 4, 1947); "My House Shall Be Called the House of Prayer" [not fantasy]; "From the Tideless Sea"; "The Captain of the Onion Boat" [not fantasy]; "The Voice in the Night" (*AFR*, No. 1, 1947); "Through the Vortex of the Cyclone" [not fantasy].

Night Land, The (E. Nash, 1912, 584 pp., 6/-) (H. Hardingham, abr., 1921, 254 pp., 2/6) (in *The House on the Borderland* [Hodgson], 1946)

A world of total darkness millions of years in the future, peopled with monstrous beasts and the remnants of humanity living in metal pyramids; an extraordinary love tale with a bold youth journeying through the country; a masterpiece of imaginative writing.

HOFFMAN, LEE (14 Aug 1932–) U.S. author. She was very active and well known in s-f fan circles before becoming a professional writer.
Fiction
Telepower [pa] (Belmont: B50-779, 1967, 85 pp., pa 50¢; with *Doomsman*)

HOFFMANN, E(RNST) T(HEODOR) A(MADEUS) (24 January 1776–24 July 1822) German author, one of the most remarkable and original of German story tellers. He studied law and held minor appointments until he became counsellor of the royal court of judicature at Berlin. His health was undermined by dissipation, leading to his death. His gifted and versatile mind led him to cultivate music, poetry and letters; he is primarily noted for his successful use of the magical and demoniac elements in fiction. His best-known novels are *The Serapion*, *Brethren* and *The Devil's Elixir*. Some collections are listed below for interest although full publishing information is not available.

Fiction
Best Tales of Hoffmann, The [Editor—E. F. Bleiler] [C] [pa] (Dover: 21793, 1967, xxxiii+419 pp., $2.50) (Constable, 1968, pa 19/-)

10 stories and 28½-p. intro.—E. F. Bleiler: "The Golden Flower Pot"; "Automata"; "A New Year's Eve Adventure"; "Nutcracker and the King of Mice"; "The Sand-Man"; "Rath Krespel"; "Tobias Martin, Master Cooper, and His Men"; "The Mines of Falun"; "Signor Formica"; "The King's Betrothed."

Devil's Elixir, The (*Die Elixiere des Teufels* [German]) (Blackwood, Edinburgh, 1824, 2 vol.) ([Trans.—R. Taylor] John Calder, London, 1963, xii+324 pp., illus.—Hellmuth Weissenborn [line drawings], 30/-)

Calder edition has 4½-p. intro.—Ronald Taylor. The story of Medardus the Monk who is tempted by the Devil and falls into a life of sin and degradation.

Hoffman's Strange Stories [C] (Burnham Bros., Boston, 1855, 444 pp.)

Weird, 12 stories with intro. "Life of Hoffman": "The Cooper of Nuremberg"; "The Lost Reflection"; "Antonia's Song"; "The Walled-Up Door"; "Berthold, the Madman"; "Coppelius, the Sandman"; "Salvator Rosa"; "Cardillac the Jeweller"; "The Pharo-Bank"; "Fascination"; "The Agate Heart"; "The Mystery of the Deserted House."

Weird Tales of E. T. W. Hoffmann, The [C] [Trans.—J. T. Bealby] (Scribner, New York, 1885, 2 vol.; 1923, 2 vol. in 1, $3.00)

10 stories: "The Cremona Violin"; "Signor Formica"; "The Sandman"; "The Entail"; "Arthur's Hall"; "The Doge and the Dogess"; "Master Martin the Cooper"; "Mademoiselle De Scuderi"; "Gambler's Luck"; "Master Johannes Wacht." *Note:* The author sometimes used the name "Wilhelm," hence the "W." in the title.

Weird Tales of Hoffmann, The [C] [Editor—Christopher Lazare] (? , illus.—Richard Lindner)

10 stories: "Mademoiselle De Scuderi"; "Don Juan"; "Antonio's Song"; "The Golden Pot"; "The Doubles"; "The Vow"; "The Fermata"; "Berthold the Madman"; "Salvatore Rosa"; "The Legacy."

HOGAN, ROBERT J. (189?–17 Dec 1963) U.S. author. He created the "G-8" pulp novels, appearing in the Popular Publications magazine *G-8 And His Battle Aces*, 1933-44, and recent reprints. One of the top writers of pulp flying stories, he was reported to write about 200,000 words a month. After *G-8* ceased he wrote westerns and other fiction, and then finally wrote for TV.

HOGG, JAMES (24 Nov [?] 1770–21 Nov 1835) British author. An eccentric protégé of Sir Walter Scott, he is mainly remembered for the novel below.
Fiction
Private Memoirs and Confessions of a Justified Sinner, The (originally 1825) (A. M. Philpott, London, 1924, 287 pp., 5/-, introduction—T. Earle Welby) (Cresset, London, 1947, 230 pp., 9/6) (Chanticleer, New York, 1949, 230 pp., $2.00)

A nearly forgotten classic which gives a terrifying picture of the Devil's subtle conquest of a self-righteous man; a masterpiece of the supernatural.

Winter Evening Tales [C] (Oliver, Edinburgh, 1820, 2 vols.) (Leavitt & Allen, New York, 1873, 2 vols.—297 pp., 289 pp.)

Vol. I—14 stories: "The Renowned Adventures of Basil Lee"; "Adam Bell"; "Duncan Campbell"; "An Old Soldier's Tale"; "Highland Adventures"; "Halbert of Lyne"; "The Long Pack"; "A Peasant's Funeral"; "Dreadful Story of Macpherson"; "Story of Two Highlanders"; "Maria's Tale"; "Singular Dream"; "Love Adventures of Mr. George Cochrane." *Country Dreams and Apparitions:* I. "John Gray of Middleholm."

Vol. II—8 stories: "The Bridal of Polmwood"; "King Gregory"; "The Shepherd's Calendar." *Country Dreams and Apparitions:* II. "Connel of Dee"; III. "The Wife of Lochmaben"; IV. "Cousin Mattie"; V. "Welldean Hall"; VI. "Tibby Johnston's Wraith."

HOKE, HELEN L. (1903–) Mrs. Franklin Watts.
Anthology
Spooks, Spooks, Spooks . . . (F. Watts, New York, 1966, 213 pp., illus.–W. R. Lohse, $3.95)
22 stories and 2 verses: "Jamie's Ghost House," Marion Garthwaite; "Witch Wood," Anna E. Bennett; "The Hag" (verse), Robert Herrick; "The Ghost Village," Erick Berry; "The King O' the Cats," Joseph Jacobs; "The Demon at Green Knowe," Lucy M. Boston; "The Burning Ship," M. Jagendorf; "Sop-Doll," Richard Chase; "The Ghostly Hitchhiker," Maria Leach; "Caleb Thorne's Day," Eliz. Coatsworth; "The Shadow People," Francis Ledwidge; "Witch Girl," Eliz. Coatsworth; "The First Spell," Josephine Lee; "The Devil's Thoughts," Samuel T. Coleridge; "The King and the Merman," Thomas D. Leekley; "The Ghosts of the Mohawk," Anna L. Curtis; "The Black Thing," Madelaine L'Engle; "The Ride-by-Nights" (verse), Walter de la Mare; "The Tinker of Tamlacht," Seumas MacManus; "The Battle With the Bogles," Sorche NicLeodhas; "Mungo," Geoffrey Palmer; "Suppose You Met a Witch," Ian Serraillier; "The Spooky Thing," William O. Steele; "The Conjure Wives," Frances G. Wickes.

HOLBERG, LUDWIG (1684–1754) Danish author
Fiction
Journey of Niels Klim to the World Underground (Latin edition, 1741) (French, 1741) (English, 1742) (*Journey to the World Underground*, T. North, London, 1828) (*Niels Klim's Journey Under the Ground*, Saxton Pierce, Boston, 1845, 190 pp., illus.) (abr., *Arkham Sampler*, sr2, Sum 1949) (*Le Voyage souterrain de Nicolas Klim* [French], Nouvelle Bibliotheque, Neuchatel [Switz.], 1954) (U. Nebraska 'Bison Book BB-102,' 1961, 31+236 pp. [intro.], pa $1.40)
A successor to Swift's *Gulliver*, and an old classic. Klim, a typical young scholar of his time, explores a cave and falls through to the world inside the Earth; he has trouble with intelligent trees and is expelled to "Firmament," the inner surface. The author satirises society by exaggerating human foibles and making the hero unable to explain the logic of human society to non-humans.
Journey to the World Underground See *Journey of Niels Klim to the World Underground*
Niels Klim's Journey Under the Ground See *Journey of Niels Klim to the World Underground*

HOLDEN, R(ICHARD) C(ORT)
Fiction
Snow Fury (Dodd Mead, New York, 1955, 186 pp., $3.00) (D'day SF B.C., 1955) (Permabooks: M-3034, 1956, 194 pp., pa 25¢) (*Nell'inferno di neve* [Italian], *Urania*: 117, 1956) (*Todlicher Schnee* [German], *AW*: 11, 1959) (*Nieve mortal* [Spanish], Constelacion, 1964, pa)
Scientific mystery of the type done by Taine. Horrible events occur and mystery builds up well, but the ending could be better.

HOLDING, ELISABETH SANXAY (1890–7 Feb 1955) U.S. author. She was a successful writer for over 30 years, starting with the romantic novel and then, since 1929, creating a series of psychological suspense stories of murder upon which it could almost be said the modern murder novel was based. Some of note are *The Obstinate Murderer* (1938), *Lady Killer* (1942), and *The Virgin Huntress* (1951). Some of her short stories appeared in *F&SF*: "Friday the Nineteenth" (Sum 1950); "Shadow of Wings" (July 1954); "The Strange Children" (Aug 1955). Her short novel "The Blank Wall" was reprinted in *Alfred Hitchcock Presents: My Favourites in Suspense* (1959, not in pa ed.).
Fiction
Miss Kelly (Morrow, New York, 1947, 125 pp., illus.–M. S. Johnson, $2.00; 1955, $2.50) (McClelland, Toronto, $2.35) (M. Joseph, London, 1948, 128 pp., illus., 7/6)
A cat understands and speaks human language but knows better than to reveal her talents—until dramatic events force her to do so.

HOLE, (DOROTHY) CHRISTINA (STANLEY) (1896–) British

writer and editor. She was educated at St. Bernard's Convent, Slough, and privately in France. She is very interested in folklore, and became editor of the journal of the Folk-Lore Society. She has worked on folklore catalogues, and has written much nonfiction, such as *Haunted England*, *English Folk-Heroes*, and *Witchcraft in England* (1947; Collier, 1968, pa).
Nonfiction
Mirror of Witchcraft, A (Chatto Windus, London, 1957, 260 pp., 4 plates, 21/-) (Pedigree, 1960, 245 pp., pa 3/6)

HOLLAND, W. BOB
Anthologies
Haunted Hotel and 25 Other Ghost Stories, The [Anon.] [pa] See [pa] See *Twenty-Five Ghost Stories*
Permabook of Ghost Stories [pa] See *Twenty-Five Ghost Stories*
Twenty-Five Ghost Stories (J. S. Ogilvie, New York, 1904, 255 pp. [no authors listed]) (Hartsdale House, New York, 1941?, illus.–F. J. Russell [no authors listed]) (World, New York, 1942, 255 pp., 59¢ [no authors listed]) (*Twenty-Five Great Ghost Stories*, [Anon.], Avon: nn, 1943, 190 pp., pa 25¢ [authors listed]) (*The Haunted Hotel and 25 Other Ghost Stories*, [Anon.], Avon: 6, nd, 256 pp., pa 25¢ [authors listed] [this ed. adds "The Haunted Hotel," W. W. Collins, but has same cover and intro. as previous Avon ed.]) (*Permabook of Ghost Stories*, Permabooks: P94, 1950, 188 pp., pa 35¢ [credits compiler but not authors]) (*20 Great Ghost Stories* [Anon.], Avon: 630, 1955, 127 pp., pa 25¢ [omits stories marked *])
25 stories: "The Black Cat," E. A. Poe; "The Flayed Hand," G. de Maupassant: "The Vengeance of a Tree," Eleanor Lewis; "The Parlor-Car Ghost," 'A Lady'; "Ghost of Buckstown Inn," Arnold M. Anderson; "The Burglar's Ghost," 'A Constabulary Officer'; "A Phantom Toe," Anon.; "Mrs. Davenport's Ghost," Fred F. Schrader; "The Phantom Woman," from Traditional; "The Phantom Hag," G. de Maupassant; "From the Tomb," G. de Maupassant; "Sandy's Ghost," 'A Witness'; "The Ghosts of Red Creek," S.T.; "The Spectre Bride,"* Folk story from Lakes region; "How He Caught the Ghost," Anon.; "Grand-Dame's Ghost Story," C.D.; "A Fight With a Ghost," Q.E.D.; "Colonel Halifax's Ghost Story," S. Baring-Gould; "The Ghost of the Count,"* A Spinster; "The Old Mansion," A Sportsman; "A Misfit Ghost,"* from Traditional; "An Unbidden Ghost,"* from a letter; "The Dead Woman's Photograph," from Traditional; "The Ghost of a Live Man," A Traveller; "The Ghost of Washington,"* Anon.
Twenty-Five Great Ghost Stories [pa] See *Twenty-Five Ghost Stories*
20 Great Ghost Stories [pa] See *Twenty-Five Ghost Stories*

HOLLEDGE, JAMES Australian.
Nonfiction
Flying Saucers Over Australia [pa] (Horwitz: 36, 1965, 130 pp., pa 5/-)
Compilation of unidentified flying object visitations, including a number in Australia.

HOLLY, J. HUNTER (pseud) See HOLLY, JOAN C.

HOLLY, JOAN C. (25 Sep 1932–) U.S. psychologist and science fiction author. She was born in Lansing, Mich., and graduated from Michigan State U. in 1954 with a B.A. in psychology. She received the Hinman superior student scholarship. Apart from sf (where she uses the pseudonym "J. Hunter Holly") and psychology, her main interests lie in the study of American folklore, anthropology, philosophy and the arts.
Fiction [as J. Hunter Holly]
Dark Enemy, The (Avalon, New York, 1965, 190 pp., $3.25)
A search for a controlled telepath to help cure psychopaths.
Dark Planet, The (Avalon, 1962, 224 pp., $2.95) (*Das grosse Sterben* [German], *UZ*: 396, 1964)
Earth is invaded and most people are killed by virus; Earth's case is taken to a Galactic Tribunal.
Encounter (Avalon, 1959, 224 pp., $2.75) (*L'altra faccia di Mr. Kiel* [Italian], *Urania*: 247, 1960) (*Der geheimnis volle Fremde*

[German], *UG*: 149, 1961) (Monarch: 240, 1962, 142 pp., pa 35¢)

Men strive to pierce the defenses of Ezekiel, a mind-eating alien.

Flying Eyes, The [pa] (Monarch: 260, 1962, 140 pp., pa 35¢)

Melodrama with menacing aliens who require atomic radiation.

Green Planet, The [pa] (Avalon, 1960, 222 pp., $2.95) (Monarch: 213, 1961, 143 pp., pa 35¢) (*Der grüne Planet* [German], *T*: 206, 1962) (*Pianeta verde* [Italian], *Cosmo*: 94, 1962)

Thirteen persons exiled from Earth find mystery and sudden death on the planet Korath.

Grey Aliens, The (Avalon, 1963, 192 pp., $2.95) (Mayflower: 3255, 1964, 125 pp., pa 2/6) (*Il regno delle ombre* [Italian], *Cosmo*: 155, 1964) (*Die fremde Schatten* [German], *T*: 535, 1967)

A story of mysticism—bodiless shadows wield massive cosmic forces and can dissolve human beings.

Mind Traders, The (Avalon, 1966, 192 pp., $3.25) (Macfadden: 60-291, 1967, 143 pp., pa 60¢)

What have mind-controlling Regans to do with vanishing Terrans?

Running Man, The [pa] (Monarch: 342, 1963, 142 pp., pa 35¢) (*Von Grauen gejagt* [German], *UZ*: 400, 1964) (*L'uomo che correva* [Italian], *Urania*: 333, 1964)

Extraterrestrial intelligences dominate the Earth sect 'Heralds of Peace.'

Time Twisters, The [pa] (Avon: G1231, 1964, 160 pp., pa 50¢)

An alien invasion of Earth.

HOLM, JOHN C(ECIL) (1904–) U.S. playwright.
Fiction

McGarrity and the Pigeons (Rinehart, New York, 1947, 239 pp., illus.–R. Frankenberg, $2.75) (Clarke Irwin, Toronto)

A whimsical account of the horse that could talk to birds.

HOLMES, CLARA H.
Fiction

Floating Fancies Among the Weird and Occult [C] (F. T. Neely, London & New York, 1898, 248 pp.)

Fantasy, 11 stories: "Nordhung Nordjansen"; "In the Beyond"; "The Tragedy of the Gnomes"; "An Unfair Exchange"; "Limitations"; "A Tale of Two Pictures"; "A Nineteenth Century Ghost"; "What Became of the Money?" "His Friend"; "A Tale of the X-Ray"; "An Averted Tragedy."

HOLMES, DAVID C. U.S. Navy captain.
Nonfiction

Search for Life on Other Worlds, The [pa] (Bantam: SA2, 1967, 184 pp., pa 75¢)

A discussion of the possibilities of life on other worlds, with such topics as "Are Flying Saucers Visitors From Space?" "Star Talk," "Are We Unique?" "The Orbital Stargazer," and "Life in the Solar System."

HOLZER, HANS W. (1920–) Noted U.S. ghost hunter.
Nonfiction

Ghosts I've Met (Bobbs-Merrill, Indianapolis, 1965, 308 pp., $5.00) (Jenkins, London, 1966, 25/-) (Smithers, Toronto, $5.75) (Ace: H-16, 1966, 253 pp., pa 60¢)

Ghosts of the Golden West (Bobbs-Merrill, 1968, 220 pp., $5.00)

Lively Ghosts of Ireland, The (Bobbs-Merrill, 1967, 182 pp., illus.–C. Buxhoeveden, $5.00) (T. Allen, Toronto, $6.25) (Ace: H-47, 1968, pa 60¢)

Yankee Ghosts (Bobbs-Merrill, 1966, 199 pp., $5.00) (T. Allen, Toronto, $6.25) (Ace: K-272, 1967, 191 pp., pa 50¢)

'True' ghost stories from the northeastern United States.

HOOD, THOMAS (23 May 1799–3 May 1845) English poet, humorist and editor. The son of a London bookseller, he was the cleverest punster in an age when puns were fashionable, and he was yet able to instill deep feeling in his writings. A weird work published posthumously was *The Haunted House* (Lawrence & Bullen, London, 1896).

Fiction

National Tales [C] (W. H. Ainsworth, London, 1827, 2 vols.)

Vol. I—14 stories, some fantasy: "The Spanish Tragedy"; "The Miracle of the Holy Hermit"; "The Widow of Galicia"; "The Golden Cup and the Dish of Silver"; "The Tragedy of Seville"; "The Lady in Love With Romance"; "The Eighth Sleeper of Ephesus"; "Madeline"; "Masetto and His Mare"; "The Story of Michel Argenti"; "The Three Jewels"; "Geronimo and Ghisola"; "The Fall of the Leaf"; "Baranga."

Vol. II—11 stories: "The Exile"; "The Owl"; "The German Knight"; "The Florentine Kinsmen"; "The Carrier's Wife"; "The Two Faithful Lovers of Sicily"; "The Venetian Countess"; "A Tale of the Harem"; "The Chestnut Tree"; "The Fair Maid of Ludgate"; "The Three Brothers."

HOOPES, NED E.
Anthology

Speak of the Devil [pa] (Dell: 8184, 1967, 205 pp., pa 60¢)

17 stories and 2-p. intro.: "The Devil and Tom Walker," Washington Irving; "The Devil and Daniel Webster," Stephen V. Benét; "The Painter's Bargain," William M. Thackeray; "The Devil and the Old Man," John Masefield; "The Devil and the Deep Sea," Rudyard Kipling; "Satan and Sam Shay," Robert Arthur; "The Friendly Demon," Daniel Defoe; "The Devil in the Belfry," Edgar Allan Poe; "Young Goodman Brown," Nathaniel Hawthorne; "The Lightning-Rod Man," Herman Melville; "The Devil," Guy de Maupassant; "Madam Lucifer," "The Demon Pope," Richard Garnett; "Little St. Michael," Laurence Housman; "The Demon Lover," Elizabeth Bowen; "The Devil, George and Rosie," John Collier; "Dance With the Devil," Betsy Emmons."

HOPKINS, R(OBERT) THURSTON (1884–23 May 1958) British author, well known as a ghost hunter. He wrote features for many leading newspapers, such as the *London Evening News*, as well as for the Press Association and Reuters, from 1912 to 1940. He had many books published from 1916 on. Ghost works other than those covered below include *Ghosts Over England* (1953)—experiences of many people, including R. Kipling and G. K. Chesterton, and *Adventures with Phantoms* (Quality, 1947, 176 pp., 10/6)—ghost-lore and ghostly adventures.

Fiction

Cavalcade of Ghosts See in Nonfiction section below.

Horror Parade [C] [pa] (Mitre, 1945, 63 pp., pa 1/-)

5 stories: "The Vampire of Woolpit Grange"; "The Haunted Ring"; "The Scarlet Girdle"; "The Strange Blooming of the Spotted Rampion"; "Fortune What She Wills."

Weird and Uncanny Stories [C] [pa] (Mitre, *ca*. 1945, 32 pp., pa 1/-)

4 stories: "The Release of Wedderburn's Ghost"; "Sir Ralph Agincourt Armour"; "A Ghost Takes Up the Feud"; "The Pool of Death."

Nonfiction

Cavalcade of Ghosts (World's Work, England, 1956, 245 pp., illus.–R. Broomfield, 17/6) (abr., Panther: 1502, 1963, 219 pp., pa 3/6)

Part I: True Ghost Stories– 13 stories by the compiler, and "Only Dreamers Die," F. D. Gardner; "The Powers of Darkness," Nancy Price; "Parson Rudall's Ghost," S. Baring-Gould.

Part II: Fictitious Ghost Stories– 9 stories: "The Man With the Roller," "The Indian Lampshade," C. G. Swan; "The Glass Staircase," "The Restless Dead," Anon.; "The Man With the Crumpled Ear," "Shadrach, Meshach, and Abed-Nego," C. A. L. Brownlow; "Old Bodet's Ghost," "Haunted Hands," "The Middle of the Thetford Vampire," M. Saltmarsh.

World's Strangest Ghost Stories, The (World's Work, England, 1955, 237 pp., illus.–R. Broomfield, 15/-; 'Cedar': 57, 1958, 317 pp., pa 5/-)

Compilations of true ghost stories in 24 chapters: "A Sheaf of True Dreams"; "Some Faces in the Dark"; "Some Surprising Dreams About Racehorses"; "Dreams and the Whipsnade Lions"; "The Phantom Leper of Brandon Warren"; "Telepathic Visions and Intuitions"; "Jeanne d'Arc, the Dynamic Dreamer"; "Is There a Perfect Apparition?"; "London Ghosts, Spectres, and Revenants"; "The Brown Lady and the Naked Ghost of Rattlesden"; "Some Unusual Wraiths"; "Wilfred Pickles and the Missing Lady"; "Dead Men in the Darkness"; "Fulmerston, Dreamer and Revenant"; "Ghosts of the Great"; "George Bernard Shaw's Itinerant Ghost Story"; "The Devil on Beachy Head"; "The Brotherhood of Firewalkers"; "Jack the Ripper and Witchcraft"; "A Witch Is Born"; "A Muster of Devonshire Witches"; "My One and Only Witch"; "Scotland Yard and the 'Black Magic' Murder"; "My Psychic Cat."

HOPLEY, GEORGE (pseud) See WOOLRICH, C.

HORNIG, CHARLES D. (25 May 1916–) U.S. science-fiction editor. Born in Jersey City, he discovered the sf magazines with the Sep 1930 *Amazing*. As one of the early fans he produced the high-class amateur magazine *The Fantasy Fan* in the 1930's. Hugo Gernsback selected him to be managing editor of *Wonder Stories* from Aug 1933. He helped Gernsback establish the Science Fiction League and was its assistant secretary. In 1939 he began *Science Fiction* magazine and followed it with the companions *Future Fiction* and *Science Fiction Quarterly*; however, he did not have much success with these and left them in 1941. That year he was classified as a conscientious objector, and later did forestry work in lieu of military service.

HORSEMAN, ELAINE
Fiction
Hubbles and the Robot, The (Chatto Windus, London, 1968, 176 pp., 21/-)
   A robot programmed to cope with an inconvenient old house acts like a Victorian housemaid.
Hubble's Bubble (Chatto, 1964, 220 pp., 15/-)
   Juvenile—a boy and his sister find a book of spells, and their experimenting leads to extraordinary adventures.

HORWOOD, HAROLD
Nonfiction
Conquest of Time, The (Sayani, Slough Lane, London, 1959, 104 pp., illus., 15/-)
   A fascinating sequel to J. W. Dunne's *Experiment With Time*, taking that work much further and proving that precognition can be produced "on demand" for specified future events. It was favourably reviewed by occult journals.

HOTSON, CORELIA (HINKLEY)
Fiction
Shining East, The (Vantage, New York, 1965, 107 pp., $2.00)
   A story of life after death.

HOTTINGER, MARY German compiler. See *GENERAL* section: GERMANY

HOUGH, RICHARD ALEXANDER (5 May 1922–) British author and editor. He was general manager of Bodley Head (publishers) 1947-55, and has been editor with Hamish Hamilton since 1958. He has contributed articles to *The Guardian*, *The New Yorker*, *History Today*, etc.; his books include *The British Grand Prix* and *The Fleet That Had to Die*.
Fiction [as "Bruce Carter"]
Into a Strange Lost World See *Perilous Descent Into a Strange Lost World, The*
Perilous Descent Into a Strange Lost World, The (Bodley Head, London, 1952, 179 pp., illus., 8/6) (*Into a Strange Lost World*, Crowell, New York, 1952, 196 pp., $2.50) ([Japanese], Kodansha 'World's Science Adventure 9,' 1956) (H. Hamilton, London, 1962, illus., 6/-)
   Juvenile—young flyers find a 17th Century English cavern world.

HOUGH, S(TANLEY) B(ENNETT) (25 Feb 1917–) British author, born in Preston, Lancashire. He writes under his own name

and under the pseudonyms "Rex Gordon" (mainly for science fiction) and "Bennett Stanley." His works include *Frontier Incident*, *The Primitives*, and such exciting dramas as *Moment of Decision* and *Mission in Guemo*.
Fiction [as Rex Gordon, unless otherwise indicated]
Beyond the Eleventh Hour (Hodder & Stoughton, London, 1961, 190 pp., 15/-)
   A gloomy and disturbing picture of the near future: atomic war starts in Nepal in 1962 and spreads over the whole world.
Extinction Bomber [as S. B. Hough] (Bodley Head, 1956, 11/6) (WDL: W419, 1958, 190 pp., pa 2/6)
   A story of the very near future, and the possibility of a bomber starting World War III.
First on Mars [pa] See *No Man Friday*
First Through Time [pa] (Ace: F-174, 1962, 160 pp., pa 40¢) (*The Time Factor*, Gibbs Phillips, London, 1964, 125 pp., 16/-; Panther: #1921, 1965, 121 pp., pa 3/6) (*Caverna nel temp* [Italian], *Urania*: 383, 1965) (*Der Zeitfaktor* [German], Goldmann, 1966; 1966 pa)
   A straightforward adventure; an astronaut rides ahead in time to investigate the future.
First to the Stars [pa] (Ace: D-405, 1959, 190 pp., pa 35¢) (*The Worlds of Eclos*, Consul: SF1050, 1961, 160 pp., pa 2/6) (*Im Kosmos verschollen* [German], *T*: 69, 1963)
   A flight to Mars goes astray and the crew (one man and one woman) are carried to a far star.
No Man Friday (Heinemann, London, 1956, 201 pp., 13/6) (*First on Mars*, Ace: D-233, 1957, 192 pp., pa 35¢) (Corgi: S569, 1958, 222 pp., pa 2/6) ([Japanese], Hayakawa: 3004, 1958, pa) (*Prigionero del silenzio* [Italian], *Urania*: 168, 1958) (*Robinson en Marte* [Spanish], Nebula: 63, 1960, pa) (*Der Mars-Robinson* [German], *TS*: 79, 1964)
   The solitary survivor of the first Mars expedition adapts to living on that planet; highly recommended by reviewers.
Paw of God, The [pa] See *Utopia Minus X*
Time Factor, The See *First Through Time*
Utopia Minus X [pa] (Ace: F-416, 1966, 190 pp., pa 40¢) (*The Paw of God*, Tandem: T107, 1967, 189 pp., pa 3/6)
   The return of a space traveller after 200 years causes havoc on a utopian Earth.
Utopia 239 (Heinemann, 1954, 208 pp., 12/-) (Consul: SF1063, 1961, 222 pp., pa 2/6) (*Utopia 239* [Italian], *Cosmo*: 18, 1958)
   An anarchic ideal state emerges in Britain after an atomic war.
Worlds of Eclos, The [pa] See *First to the Stars*

HOUSE, BRANT U.S. editor and anthologist of wide interests. His works include *Lincoln's Wit*, *Crimes That Shocked America* and *Great Trials of Famous Lawyers*.
Nonfiction
Strange Powers of Unusual People [pa] (Ace: K-176, 1963, 189 pp., pa 50¢; K-224, 1965, pa 50¢)
   One of the "Strange Facts" series, outlining the powers of 11 people, from levitation to curing cancer.

HOUSEHOLD, GEOFFREY (30 Nov 1900–) British novelist and short story writer. He was a first class graduate in English literature from Oxford, has lived in many parts of the world, and speaks Spanish fluently. He is noted for his many romantic novels about spying and international intrigue, of which *Rogue Male* (1939) is probably the best. A juvenile-slanted fantasy is *The Spanish Cave* (Little Brown, 1936; Comet, 1948, pa; Penguin, 1963, pa).
Fiction [Incomplete]
Tales of Adventurers [C] (Atlantic-Little Brown, Boston, 1952, 247 pp., $3.00) (McClelland, Toronto, $3.75) (M. Joseph, London, 1952, 224 pp., 12/6)
   13 stories, most devoted to crime and espionage, but including two fantasies: "Debt of Honor"; "The Pejemuller."

HOUSMAN, LAURENCE (18 July 1865–20 Feb 1959) English dramatist, novelist and illustrator. He wrote many plays which, however, were censored at some times because they represented Biblical personages or living members of the Royal Family. His

published works began with *The Writings of William Blake* (1893).
Fiction [Incomplete—other titles in Bleiler *Checklist*]
All-Fellows and the Cloak of Friendship [C] (Harcourt, New York, 1923, illus., $2.00)

16 stories, some of fantasy interest (not in Bleiler *Checklist*): "The Cloak of Friendship"; "Damien, the Worshipper"; "The Heart of the Sea"; "The House of Rimmon"; "Inside Out"; "The Story of Bunder-Bunder, the Jail Bird"; "King's Evil"; "Little St. Michael"; "The Love-Child"; "The Lovely Messengers"; "The Merciful Drought"; "The Staff of Life"; "The Tree of Guile"; "The Troubling of the Waters"; "Truce of God"; "When Pan Was Dead."

Ironical Tales [C] (J. Cape, London, 1926, 224 pp., 6/-) (Doran, New York, 1927, 266 pp., $2.50)

Fantasy, 30 stories: "A Blind World"; "The Perfect One"; "Educating Our Masters"; "Blind Knowledge"; "Joy in Heaven"; "The Real Temptation of St. Anthony"; "The Turn of the Worm"; "The Merchant and the Robber"; "The King's Pleasure"; "The King's Jester"; "The King and the Philosopher"; "The Poet and His Mistress"; "The King and His Word"; "The Rose and the Thorn"; "The Man Who Sold His Soul"; "Father and Son"; "The Prince and His Two Mistresses"; "Two Kings and Their Queens"; "A Heart of Stone"; "The Mirror and the Mistress"; "The Wise Penny and the Foolish Pound"; "Winkiboo"; "The Talking Horse"; "Means to an End"; "A Landlord and His Rent"; "The Family Fairy"; "Kill or Cure"; "Blind Love"; "Lady Into George Fox"; "A Side-Wind."

Strange Ends and Discoveries [C] (J. Cape, London, 1948, 189 pp., 8/6) (Clarke Irwin, Toronto, $2.25)

Fantasy, 24 stories and introduction: "The Distorting Mirror"; "The Great Adventure"; "The Return Journey"; "The Impossible Penitent"; "The Finishing Touch"; "The Fall of the Sparrow"; "The New Dispensation"; "Vessels of Clay"; "The Catch of the Cherub"; "Improved Relations"; "The Cry of the Parrot"; "An Unexplained Miracle"; "The Flag of Peace"; "A Striking Incident"; "Hidden Identity"; "Weighed in the Balance"; "Changa-Ranga"; "Dead Man's Lane"; "The Widow"; "The Return of the Prodigal"; "Oranges and Lemons"; "Maggie's Bite"; "Camouflage"; "Little Pear-Blossom."

What Next? Provocative Tales of Faith and Morals [C] (J. Cape, London, 1938, 336 pp., 8/6) (Nelson, Toronto, $2.50)

Fantasy, 31 stories and preface: "A God and His Makers"; "The Man Who Did Not Pray"; "The Eye-Opener"; "The Watchers"; "Hidden Identity"; "Good Succour"; "The Catch of the Cherub"; "The Fall of the Sparrow"; "Improved Relations"; "The Cry of the Parrot"; "A Strange Coincidence"; "The Devil Help Us!"; "Happy Despatch"; "A Clean Conscience"; "The Flag of Peace"; "Sea-Change"; "An Unexplained Miracle"; "Their Own Image"; "The Tuppenny Twins"; "Aunt Jane's Tea-Blend"; "A 'Don't-Tell' Tale"; "Sweets to the Sweet"; "A Shocking Recovery"; "Happy Deliverance"; "The King's Dream"; "The Beginning of Wisdom"; "The Twinkling of an Eye"; "Little Pear-Blossom"; "Uncovenanted Mercies"; "Food for Babies"; "The Distorting Mirror."

HOWARD, DANA British author of the flying saucer type books *Diane—She Came From Venus* (Regency, London, 1956) and *My Flight to Venus* (Regency, nd).

HOWARD, ELIZABETH JANE (26 Mar 1923–) British author, born in London.
Fiction
We Are for the Dark [with R. Aickman] [C] (Cape, London, 1951, 285 pp., 10/6) (Clarke Irwin, Toronto, $2.25) (Mayflower: 9438, 1965, 174 pp., pa 3/6)

6 ghost stories (pa omits one, not known which): "Perfect Love"; "The Trains"; "The Insufficient Answer"; "Three Miles Up"; "The View"; "Left Luggage."

HOWARD, HAYDEN
Fiction
Eskimo Invasion [pa] (Ballantine: U6112, 1967, 380 pp., pa 75¢)

An unusual novel of what would happen if Eskimos began grow-

ing to maturity—and multiplying—much faster than normal. Rewritten from stories in *GSF*: "Death and Birth of the Angakok" (Apr 1965); "The Eskimo Invasion" (June 1966); "Who Is Human?" (Aug 1966); "Too Many Esks" (Oct 1966); "The Modern Penitentiary" (Dec 1966); "Our Man in Peking" (Feb 1967); "The Purpose of Life" (Apr 1967).

HOWARD, IVAN U.S. anthologist.
Anthologies
Escape to Earth [pa] (Belmont: L92-571, 1963, 173 pp., pa 50¢)

Sf, 6 stories: "Escape to Earth," M. Banister; "We Are Alone," R. Sheckley; "Doomsday's Color-Press," R. F. Jones; "A Big Man With the Girls," J. MacCreigh & J. Merril; "Temple of Despair," M. C. Pease; "'If the Court Pleases'," N. Loomis.
Novelets of Science Fiction [pa] (Belmont: L92-567, 1963, 173 pp., pa 50¢; B50-770, 1967, pa 50¢)

8 stories: "Ultrasonic God," L. S. de Camp; "The Chapter Ends," P. Anderson; "'A' As in Android," M. Lesser; "... And the Truth Shall Make You Free," C. D. Simak; "Night Fear," F. B. Long; "I Am Tomorrow," L. del Rey; "Testament of Andros," J. Blish; "The Possessed," A. C. Clarke.
Rare Science Fiction [pa] (Belmont: L92-557, 1963, 173 pp., pa 50¢)

8 stories: "Let's Have Fun," L. S. de Camp; "Do It Yourself," M. Lesser; "In Human Hands," A. Budrys; "Protective Camouflage," C. V. De Vet; "Asylum," Alice Bullock; "Quick Freeze," R. Silverberg; "Luck, Inc.," J. Harmon; "Ripeness," M. C. Pease.
6 and the Silent Scream [pa] (Belmont: L92-564, 1963, 173 pp., pa 50¢) (Consul: 1298, 1964, 206 pp., pa 2/6)

Sf, 6 stories: "Vulcan's Hammer," [short novel], P. K. Dick; "Riddle of the Deadly Paradise," F. B. Long; "The Ear-Friend," R. E. Banks; "Peace on Earth," I. Cox Jr.; "Ask a Foolish Question," R. Sheckley; "Children of Fortune," D. A. Jourdan.
Things [pa] (Belmont: L92-582, 1964, 157 pp., pa 50¢) (Mayflower: 7815, 1965, 173 pp., pa 3/6) (*Cosas* [Spanish], Galaxia: 27, 1964, pa)

Sf, 6 stories: "The Gift of the Gods," R. F. Jones; "Turn of a Century," J. Blish; "Courier of Chaos," P. Anderson; "Mind of Tomorrow," L. del Rey; "In the Beginning," D. Knight; "Little Green Man," N. Loomis.
Way Out [pa] (Belmont: L92-575, 1963, 173 pp., pa 50¢)

Sf, 7 stories: "Ennui," M. Lesser; "Knowledge Is Power," H. B. Fyfe; "Snail's Pace," A. Budrys; "'X' for 'Expendable'," Wm. C. Bailey; "Blood Lands," A. Coppel; "Blunder Enlightening," D. Dryfoos; "Honorable Enemies," P. Anderson.

HOWARD, ROBERT E(RVIN) (22 Jan 1906–12 June 1936) U.S. fantasy author. He was born in Peaster, Texas, the son of a doctor. He is noted for his many stories of fantastic adventure which were featured in *Weird Tales*, where he first appeared when he was 18. He lived most of his life as a bachelor in Cross Plains, Texas; he was so attached to his mother, an invalid in her last years, that when she was about to pass away he took his own life.

Howard was a friend of H. P. Lovecraft and E. Hoffman Price; the latter freely acknowledged Howard's assistance with the beginning of his writing career. Howard wrote a number of series stories about adventurous characters, of which the most notable was the "Conan" series. This appeared as a book series in the 1950's and has recently been revised with fresh material (fragments completed, etc.) to appear as a paperback series which has sold extremely well. L. S. de Camp assisted in preparing both book and paperback series; Lin Carter and Björn Nyberg also helped.

Howard used the pseudonyms "Patrick Howard" (on verse), "Patrick Ervin" (in *Magic Carpet* and *Strange Detective Stories*), and "Sam Walser" (in *Spicy Adventure Stories*). He also wrote a number of westerns, of which "A Man-Eating Jeopard" is probably the best remembered. A collection of westerns is *A Gent From Bear Creek* (H. Jenkins, London, 1937; D. M. Grant, West Kingston [R.I.], 1965), about the character Breckinridge Elkins; Grant published a further Elkins collection as *The Pride of Bear Creek* (1966).

Interest in Howard's writings became such that the "Hyborian

Legion" was formed in Nov 1955, comprising fans of Howard's and other "sword and sorcery" fiction. The amateur magazine *Amra*, devoted to facts and fancies concerning Howard's work and associated types of fantastic adventure, was started in 1957 as the organ of the Hyborian Legion, and is still being published by G. H. Scithers. Glenn Lord has been publishing *The Howard Collector* at intervals since Summer 1961, presenting such material as indexes of verse and fiction, articles on series, and Howard's letters and verse. R. A. W. Lowndes has reprinted many Howard stories in his *Magazine of Horror*.

Series

Note: The last "King Kull" story and the "Bran Mak Morn" and "Turlogh O'Brien" series are in a pseudo-historical setting in the era of the Picts.

Allison, James. "The Garden of Fear" (*Marvel Tales*, July 1934; in *The Garden of Fear* Crawford, 1946, pa; *Fan*, May 1961); "The Valley of the Worm" (*WT*, Feb 1934; in *Skull-Face*, 1946).

Bran Mak Morn. "Kings of the Night" (*WT*, Nov 1930; *Mag. Horror*, May 1968); "Worms of the Earth" (*WT*, Nov 1932; *Mag. Horror*, July 1968). Both were in *Skull-Face*.

Conan. For convenience, the books in this series are here given numbers, and thereafter referred to by number. The published order of the Gnome Press books was: (1) *Conan the Conqueror*; (2) *The Sword of Conan*; (3) *King Conan*; (4) *The Coming of Conan*; (5) *Conan the Barbarian*; (6) *Tales of Conan* [revised and completed by L. S. de Camp]. Some Conan stories also appeared in (7) *Skull-Face and Others*. The Lancer paperback series in chronological story sequence is: (8) *Conan*; (9) not yet published; (10) *Conan the Freebooter*; (11) *Conan the Wanderer*; (12) *Conan the Adventurer*; (13) not yet published; (14) *Conan the Warrior*; (15) *Conan the Usurper*; (16) *Conan the Conqueror*; (17) *Conan the Avenger*; (18) not yet published; (19) *Conan of the Isles*.

The sequence of the stories, including recently completed fragments, etc., is as follows (date of *Weird Tales* printing unless otherwise noted; numbers for books, as above): "The Hyborian Age" [article] (*Phantagraph* [U.S. amateur mag.], 1936; booklet, 1938; in 4, 7, 8, and *King Kull*); "The Thing in the Crypt" (by Carter & de Camp, in 8); "The Tower of the Elephant" (Mar 1933; in 4, 7, 8); "The Hall of the Dead" (completed by de Camp: *F&SF*, Feb 1967; in 8); "The God in the Bowl" (*Space SF*, Sep 1952; in 4, 8); "Rogues in the House" (Jan 1934; in *Terror by Night* [Thomson], 1934; in 4, 7, 8); "The Hands of Nergal" (by Howard & Carter, in 8); "Chains of Shamballah" (by Carter & de Camp, in 8); "The Blood-Stained God" (*FU*, Apr 1956; in 6); "The Frost-Giant's Daughter" [many versions (from de Camp, 1957)] (a. Title as given, ms with literary agent; b. Retitled "Gods of the North," hero changed to Amra of Akbitana, in *The Fantasy Fan* [amateur mag.], Mar 1934; *FU*, Dec 1956; c. Rewrite of 'a' by de Camp, *Fantasy Mag.*, Aug 1953; d. Version of 'c' in book 4); "Queen of the Black Coast" (May 1934; *AFR* No. 8, 1948; in 4); "Hawks Over Shem" (by de Camp from Howard's "Hawks Over Egypt," *FU*, Oct 1955; in 6, 10); "Black Colossus" (June 1933; in 5, 10); "Shadows in the Moonlight" (Apr 1934; in 5, 10; in *Swords and Sorcery* [de Camp], 1963); "The Road of the Eagles" (rewritten by de Camp; as "Conan, Man of Destiny," *FU*, Dec 1955; in 6, 10); "A Witch Shall Be Born" (Dec 1934; *AFR* No. 10, 1949; in 5, 10); "Black Tears" (by de Camp & Carter, in 11); "Shadows in Zamboula" (Nov 1935; in 5, 7, 11; in *Spell of Seven* [de Camp], 1965, pa); "The Devil in Iron" (Aug 1934; in 5, 11); "The Flame Knife" (in 6, 11); "The People of the Black Circle" (sr3, Sep 1934; in 2, 12; *Fan*, Jan 1967); "The Slithering Shadow" (Sep 1933; in 2, 12); "Drums of Tombalku" (completed by de Camp, in 12); "The Pool of the Black One" (Oct 1933; in 2, 12); "Red Nails" (sr3, July 1936; in 2, 14); "Jewels of Gwahlur" (Mar 1935; in 3, 14); "Beyond the Black River" (sr2, May 1935; in 3, 14); "The Treasure of Tranicos" (rev. by de Camp, as "The Black Stranger," *Fantasy Mag.*, Mar 1953; in 3, 15); "Wolves Beyond the Border" (completed by de Camp, in 15); "The Phoenix on the Sword" (Dec 1932; in 3, 7, 11); "The Scarlet Citadel" (Jan 1933; in 3, 7, 15); "Conan the Conqueror" ("The Hour of the Dragon," sr5, Dec 1935; in 1, 16; also as British ed. and Ace pa ed.); "The Return of Conan" (by B. Nyberg & de Camp; as "Conan the Vic-

torious," *FU*, Sep 1957; Gnome, 1957; in 17); "Conan of the Isles" (by de Camp & Carter, in 19).

An amusing take-off on Conan was P. Anderson's "The Barbarian" (*F&SF*, May 1956).

Kane, Solomon. In *Weird Tales*: "Red Shadows" (Aug 1928); "Skulls in the Stars" (Jan 1929; *Mag. Horror*, June 1965); "Rattle of Bones" (June 1929; *Mag. Horror*, Nov 1965); "The Moon of Skulls" (sr2, June 1930); "The Hills of the Dead" (Aug 1930); "The Footfalls Within" (Sep 1931); "Wings in the Night" (July 1932). *Verse:* "The One Black Stain"; "Solomon Kane's Homecoming." The 3rd, 5th and 7th appeared in *Skull-Face* (1946), and all are given in *Red Shadows* (1968).

King Kull. In *Weird Tales*: "The Shadow Kingdom" (Aug 1929); "The Mirrors of Tuzun Thune" (Sep 1929); "Kings of the Night" (Nov 1930; *Mag. Horror*, May 1968); "The King and the Oak" (verse). All except the 3rd are in *The Coming of Conan* and *King Kull*; all except the verse appear in *Skull-Face*.

O'Brien, Turlogh. In *Weird Tales*: "The Gods of Bal-Sagoth" (Oct 1931; "The Blonde Goddess of Bal-Sagoth," *AFR*, No. 12, 1950); "The Dark Man" (Dec 1931).

Skull-Face. In *Weird Tales*: "Skull-Face" (sr3, Oct 1929; book; *FFM*, Dec 1952); "The Haunter of the Ring" (June 1934); "Dig Me No Grave" (Feb 1937).

Fiction

Almuric [pa] (*WT*, sr3, May 1939) (Ace: F-305, 1964, 157 pp., pa 40¢)

Fantastic adventure on another planet.

Always Comes Evening [Compiled by Glenn Lord] [C] (Arkham, Sauk City [Wisc.], 1958, 86 pp., $3.00, jacket–F. Utpatel)

Introduction by Dale Hart, and 66 poems (46 new to book form). The poems include such ballads as "Solomon Kane's Homecoming," and are interesting as footnotes to Howard's career.

Coming of Conan, The [C] (Gnome, New York, 1953, 224 pp., $3.00)

8 stories; intro.–L. S. de Camp; article "The Hyborian Age." (Howard) running through book between stories; Howard's letter to P. Schuyler Miller; H.P.L.'s letter to Donald Wollheim; article "An Informal Biography of Conan the Cimmerian," J. D. Clark & P. S. Miller. The stories include 3 of King Kull and 5 of Conan: "The Shadow Kingdom"; "The Mirrors of Tuzun Thune"; "The King and the Oak"; "The Tower of the Elephant"; "The God in the Bowl"; "Rogues in the House"; "The Frost-Giant's Daughter"; "Queen of the Black Coast."

Conan [R. E. Howard, L. S. de Camp & L. Carter] [C] [pa] (Lancer: 73-685, 1967, 221 pp., pa 60¢; 74-958, 1968, pa 75¢)

Introduction–L. S. de Camp; Letter from R. E. Howard to P. S. Miller; "The Hyborian Age–Part 1" (Howard); 7 stories: "The Thing in the Crypt"; "The Tower of the Elephant"; "The Hall of the Dead"; "The God in the Bowl"; "Rogues in the House"; "The Hand of Nergal"; "Chains of Shamballah."

Conan of the Isles [L. S. de Camp & Lin Carter] [pa] (Lancer: 73-800, 1968, 189 pp., pa 60¢)

An additional novel in the "Conan" series; not by Howard, but included here for completeness. Introduction by L. S. de Camp.

Conan the Adventurer [R. E. Howard & L. S. de Camp] [C] [pa] (Lancer: 73-526, 1966, 224 pp., pa 60¢)

4 stories, intro.–de Camp: "The People of the Black Circle"; "The Slithering Shadow"; "Drums of Tombalku"; "The Pool of the Black One."

Conan the Avenger [R. E. Howard, B. Nyberg & L. S. de Camp] [pa] ("Conan the Victorious," *FU*, Sep 1957, by B. Nyberg & L. S. de Camp) –expanded: (*The Return of Conan*, Gnome, 1957, 191 pp., $3.00) (Lancer: 73-780, 1968, 192 pp., pa 60¢)

Intro.–de Camp; "The Return of Conan" (novel); "The Hyborian Age, Part 2," Howard.

Conan the Barbarian [C] (Gnome, 1955, 224 pp., $4.00)

5 stories: "Black Colossus"; "Shadows in the Moonlight"; "A Witch Shall Be Born"; "Shadows in Zamboula"; "The Devil in Iron."

Conan the Conqueror ("The Hour of the Dragon," *WT*, sr5, Dec 1935) (Gnome, 1950, 255 pp., $2.75) (Ace: D-36, 1954, 131 pp., pa 35¢; with *Sword of Rhiannon*) (Boardman, London, 1954, 255 pp., 9/6) (Lancer: 73-572, 1967, 224 pp., pa 60¢)

Introduction, and map of the world of Conan. A colourful fantastic adventure worthy to stand with Burroughs and Tolkien.

Conan the Freebooter [R. E. Howard & L. S. de Camp] [C] [pa] (Lancer: 74-963, 1968, 223 pp., pa 75¢)

Intro.–de Camp; 5 stories: "Hawks Over Shem"; "Black Colossus"; "Shadows in the Moonlight"; "The Road of the Eagles"; "A Witch Shall Be Born."

Conan the Usurper [R. E. Howard & L. S. de Camp] [C] [pa] (Lancer: 73-599, 1967, 256 pp., pa 60¢)

Intro.–de Camp; 4 stories: "The Treasure of Tranicos"; "Wolves Beyond the Border"; "The Phoenix on the Sword"; "The Scarlet Citadel."

Conan the Wanderer [R. E. Howard, L. S. de Camp & L. Carter] [C] [pa] (Lancer: 74-976, 1968, 222 pp., pa 95¢)

Intro.–de Camp; 4 stories: "Black Tears"; "Shadows in Zamboula"; "The Devil in Iron"; "The Flame Knife."

Conan the Warrior [editor–L. S. de Camp] [C] [pa] (Lancer: 73-549, 1967, 222 pp., pa 60¢)

Intro.–de Camp; 3 stories: "Red Nails"; "Jewels of Gwahlur"; "Beyond the Black River."

Dark Man and Others, The [C] (Arkham, Sauk City [Wisc.], 1963, 284 pp., $5.00)

Fantasy, 15 stories, with introduction by A. Derleth: "The Voice of El-Lil"; "Pigeons From Hell"; "The Dark Man"; "The Gods of Bal-Sagoth"; "People of the Dark"; "The Children of the Night"; "The Dead Remember"; "The Man on the Ground"; "The Garden of Fear"; "The Thing on the Roof"; "The Hyena"; "Dig Me No Grave"; "The Dream Snake"; "In the Forest of Villefere"; "Old Garfield's Heart."

Etchings in Ivory [C] (Glenn Lord, Pasadena [Calif.], 1968, vi+ 26 pp., $1.25)

Prose poems, with 6-p. introduction by Don Fryer: "Proem"; "Flaming Marble"; "Skulls and Orchids"; "Medallions in the Moon"; "The Gods That Men Forgot"; "Bloodstones and Ebony."

King Conan [C] (Gnome, 1953, 255 pp., $3.00)

Intro.–de Camp; 5 stories: "Jewels of Gwahlur"; "Beyond the Black River"; "The Treasure of Tranicos"; "The Phoenix on the Sword"; "The Scarlet Citadel."

King Kull [with Lin Carter] [C] [pa] (Lancer: 73-650, 1967, 223 pp., pa 60¢)

Edited by Glenn Lord; prolog and (final) epilog from "The Hyborian Age"; 13 stories: "Exile of Atlantis"; "The Shadow Kingdom"; "The Altar and the Scorpion"; "Black Abyss"; "Delcarde's Cat"; "The Skull of Silence"; "Riders Beyond the Sunrise"; "By This Axe I Rule!"; "The Striking of the Gong"; "Swords of the Purple Kingdom"; "Wizard and Warrior"; "The Mirrors of Tuzun Thune"; "The King and the Oak."

Red Shadows [C] (D. M. Grant, West Kingston [R.I.], 1968, 381 pp., illus.–J. Jones, $6.00)

12 stories and 3 poems, including all "Solomon Kane" works: "Skulls in the Stars"; "The Right Hand of Doom"; "Red Shadows"; "Rattle of Bones"; "The Castle of the Devil"; "The Moon of Skulls"; "The One Black Stain" [verse]; "Blades of the Brotherhood"; "The Hills of the Dead"; "Hawk of Basti"; "The Return of Sir Richard Grenville" [verse]; "Wings in the Night"; "The Footfalls Within"; "The Children of Asshur"; "Solomon Kane's Homecoming" [verse].

Return of Conan, The [by B. Nyberg & L. S. de Camp] See *Conan the Avenger*

Skull-Face and Others [C] (Arkham, 1946, 501 pp., jacket–H. Bok; 3,000 copies)

Weird, 23 stories, with "Memoriam" by H. P. Lovecraft and a study by E. Hoffman Price: "Which Will Scarcely Be Understood" (Prologue); "Wolfshead"; "The Black Stone"; "The Horror From the Mound"; "The Cairn on the Headland"; "Black Canaan"; "The Fire of Asshurbanipal"; "A Man-Eating Jeopard"; "Skull-Face"; "The Hyborian Age" (article); "Worms of the Earth"; "The Valley of the Worm"; "Skulls in the Stars"; "Rattle of Bones"; "The Hills of the Dead"; "The Shadow Kingdom"; "Wings in the Night"; "The Mirrors of Tuzun Thune"; "Kings of the Night"; "The Phoenix on the Sword"; "The Scarlet Citadel"; "The Tower of the Ele-

phant"; "Rogues in the House"; "Shadows in Zamboula"; "Lines Written in the Realization That I Must Die" (Epilogue).

Sword of Conan, The [C] (Gnome, 1952, 251 pp., $2.75)

4 "Conan" stories: "The People of the Black Circle"; "The Slithering Shadow"; "The Pool of the Black One"; "Red Nails."

Tales of Conan [with L. S. de Camp] [C] (Gnome, 1955, 219 pp., $3.00)

4 stories, not published by Howard, but revised and completed by de Camp; intro.–P. S. Miller: "The Blood-Stained God"; "Hawks Over Shem"; "The Road of the Eagles"; "The Flame-Knife."

Wolfshead [C] [pa] (Lancer: 73-721, 1968, 190 pp., pa 60¢)

Weird, 7 stories: "The Black Stone"; "The Valley of the Worm"; "Wolfshead"; "The Fire of Asshurbanipal"; "The House of Arabu"; "The Horror From the Mound"; "The Cairn on the Headland."

HOWELLS, WILLIAM DEAN (1 Mar 1837–11 May 1920) U.S. author. The son of a country editor, he gained experience in his father's and other country newspaper offices. He was U.S. consul in Venice 1861-65 and studied Italian literature while in that position. He later worked up to being editor of *Atlantic Monthly* 1872-81, and became president of the American Academy of Art and Letters. He wrote numerous books, including lives of Abraham Lincoln and Rutherford B. Hayes.

Fiction [Incomplete—other titles in Bleiler *Checklist*]

Questionable Shapes [C] (Harper, New York, 1903, 219 pp., frontis.; London, 1903, 222 pp., 6/-)

3 stories: "His Apparition"; "The Angel of the Lord"; "Though One Rose From the Dead."

Traveler From Altruria, A (Harper, New York, 1894, 318 pp.) (Sagamore: S16, 1957, 211 pp., pa $1.35)

Utopian novel.

Anthology

Shapes That Haunt the Dusk [with Henry M. Allen] (Harper, New York & London, 1907, 301 pp.)

Weird, 10 stories: "The Christmas Child," Georg Schock; "The White Sleep of Auber Hurn," Richard Rice; "In Tenebras," Howard Pyle; "The Little Room," Madalene Yale Wynne; "The Bringing of the Rose," Harriet Lewis Bradley; "Perdita," Hildegarde Hawthorne; "At La Glorieuse," M. E. M. Davis; "A Faded Scapular," F. D. Millet; "At the Hermitage," E. Levi Bowen; "The Reprisal," H. W. McVickar.

HOWELLS, WILLIAM (WHITE) (27 Nov 1908–) Noted U.S. authority on the sciences of humanity. He also gives a perspective on man's religions in *The Heathens*.

Nonfiction

Back of History (Doubleday, New York, 1954, 384 pp., illus., $5.00)

A view of the sciences of humanity from pre-human times to the dawn of written history; the gradual growth of culture and language through the ages.

Mankind So Far (Doubleday, 1944, 319 pp., illus., $3.00) (McClelland, Toronto, $6.00) (Sigma, London, 1947, 319 pp., illus., 16/-)

Man's thinking and culture in the prehistoric era.

HOYLE, FRED (24 June 1915–) British astronomer and science-fiction author. He was educated (M.A.) at St. John's College, Cambridge. He has been on the staffs of Mt. Wilson and Palomar Observatories, and is now Plumian Professor of Astronomy and Experimental Philosophy at Cambridge. His science-fiction novels are always of interest, with extrapolations from accurate present-day science.

Fiction

A for Andromeda [with J. Elliot] (Souvenir, London, 1962, 206 pp., 15/-) (*Melbourne Herald*, sr12, 7-21 Apr 1962 [omitting 20th]) (Harper, New York, 1962, 191 pp., $3.50) (Corgi: YS1300, 1963, 174 pp., pa 3/-; GS7348, 1966, pa 3/6) (Crest: d773, 1964, 205 pp., pa 50¢) (*A de Andromeda* [Spanish], Constelacion: 1, 1964, pa) (*"A" comme Andromède* [French], Le

Fleuve Noire: A281, 1966, pa) (*A wie Andromeda* [German] [includes sequel], Goverts, Stuttgart, 1967)

A radio-telescope picks up signals from a great computer in Andromeda, but it appears to have malignant intentions. The BBC TV play (7 parts) was considered a failure because of poor characterisation. The sequel is *Andromeda Breakthrough*.

Andromeda Breakthrough [with J. Elliot] (Souvenir, 1964, 192 pp., 16/-) (Harper, 1964, 192 pp., $3.50) (D'day SF B.C., 1965, $1.20) (Corgi: GS7347, 1966, 190 pp., pa 3/6) (Crest: R1080, 1967, 192 pp., pa 60¢) (*Andromède revient* [French], Le Fleuve Noire: A282, 1966, pa) ([German]—see *A for Andromeda*)

Sequel to *A for Andromeda*. The world suffers havoc as men struggle against the Andromeda computer. The 7-part BBC TV play was well characterised and quite dramatic.

Black Cloud, The (Heinemann, London, 1957, 251 pp., 15/-; 'Windmill,' 1960, 5/6) (Harper, 1957, 251 pp., $2.95) (D'day SF B.C., 1958, 201 pp., $1.20) (*Die Schwarze Wolke* [German], Kiepenheuer & Witsch, 1958; Heyne, 1964, pa) ([Japanese], Hosei Univ. Press, 1958) (*Det Svarta Molnet* [Swedish], Bonnier, 1958) (Signet: S1673, 1959, 191 pp., pa 35¢; P3384, 1968, pa 60¢) (*De donkere wolk* [Dutch], Hollandia, Baarn, 1959) (Penguin: 1466, 1960, 219 pp., pa 2/6; 1963, pa 3/-; 1968, pa 4/-) (*La nuee de l'Apocalypse* [French], Le Club Français du Livre, 1962; *Le nuage noir*, Dunod, 1962) (Perennial: P37, 1965, 214 pp., pa 50¢)

A dark cloud blots out our Sun, and proves to be intelligent; correct technically. *Note*: The French editions appeared two months apart, from the same translation; Dunod is a scientific publisher.

Element 79 [C] (New American Library, New York, 1967, 189 pp., $4.50) (D'day SF B.C., 1967, $1.70) (Signet: P3463, 1968, 143 pp., pa 60¢)

Sf, 15 stories: "Zoomen" (*F&SF*, Mar 1967); "Pym Makes His Point"; "The Magnetosphere"; "A Play's the Thing"; "Cattle Trucks"; "Welcome to Slippage City"; "The Ax"; "Agent 38"; "The Martians"; "Shortsighted"; "A Jury of Five"; "Blackmail" (*F&SF*, Feb 1967); "Element 79"; "The Judgment of Aphrodite"; "The Operation."

Fifth Planet [with Geoffrey Hoyle] (Harper, 1963, 218 pp., $3.50) (Heinemann, 1963, 218 pp., 16/-) (D'day SF B.C., 1964, $1.20) (Crest: d812, 1965, 192 pp., pa 50¢) (Penguin: 2244, 1965, 220 pp., pa 3/6) (*La cinquième planète* [French], Dunod, 1965)

Russia and the West send ships out to a fast-approaching star; both crews join forces to face strange phenomena on "Achilles."

October the First Is Too Late (Heinemann, 1966, 200 pp., 18/-) (Harper & Row, 1966, 190 pp., $3.95) (D'day SF B.C., 1966, $1.20) (SF B.C. [S.J.], 1967) (Crest: R1155, 1968, 160 pp., pa 60¢) (Penguin: 2886, 1968, 175 pp., pa 4/-)

As part of an experiment, future people duplicate parts of the world from 1966 and other times.

Ossian's Ride (Harper, 1959, 207 pp., $3.00; P60A, 1965, 181 pp., pa 50¢) (Heinemann, 1959, 252 pp., 15/-) (D'day SF B.C., 1959, $1.20) (*Caraghs Gata* [Swedish], Bonnier, 1960) (Berkley: G495, 1961, 153 pp., pa 35¢; X1506, 1968, pa 60¢) (FSB: 317, 1961, 189 pp., pa 2/6; 2051, 1967, pa 3/6) (*Das Geheimnis der Stadt Caragh* [German], Kiepenheuer, 1962; Heyne: 3061, 1966, pa)

A mysterious power appears in Ireland, and the hero takes a Hitchcock type of journey to find out about it.

Nonfiction

Encounter With the Future [pa] (Simon & Schuster, New York, 1968, xviii+108 pp., pa $1.95)

A 'Credo Perspective' book planned & edited by Ruth N. Anshen, with introduction explaining the series. 4 chapters: "The State of Things"; "The Anatomy of Doom"; "Reflections and Reminiscences"; "Astronomical Studies, Problems and Speculations."

Frontiers of Astronomy (Heinemann, 1955, 360 pp., illus., 25/-) (Harper, 1955, 360 pp., illus., $5.00) (*Das grenzenlose All* [German], Kiepenheuer, 1957) (Mentor: MD200, 1957, 317 pp., pa 50¢)

A comprehensive summary of the rich astronomical discoveries

of recent years; radio astronomy, etc.

Man in the Universe (Columbia U. Press, New York, 1966, 81 pp., $3.50)

5 essays, including one on the author's dissatisfaction with Heisenberg's uncertainty principle and with our physical concepts of the direction of Time. Hoyle uses these ideas in *October the First Is Too Late*.

Nature of the Universe, The (*Harper's Magazine*, 1950?) (Blackwell, London, 1950, 121 pp., 5/-; 1952, 112 pp., 6/-; 1960, vii+103 pp., illus., 8/6) (Harper, 1950, 142 pp., $2.50) (Signet: ?, 1954, 128 pp., pa 35¢; P2331, 1963, 124 pp., pa 60¢) ([German], ?)

A popularization of the New Cosmology; new ideas on the theory of the expanding universe, and Hoyle's theory of continuous creation. The British 3rd ed. includes a new chapter on the origin of the planets based on Alfvén's theory.

Of Men and Galaxies (U. Washington Press, Seattle, 1964, 73 pp., $2.95) (Heinemann, 1965, 12/6)

3 philosophical essays: "Motives and Aims of the Scientist"; "An Astronomer's View of Life"; "Extrapolations into the Future."

HOYLE, GEOFFREY (12 Jan 1941–) Son of Fred Hoyle.
Fiction
Fifth Planet See HOYLE, F. (co-author)

HUBBARD, L(AFAYETTE) RON(ALD) (1911–) U.S. author. He began his writing career in 1934 and became noted in adventure fiction before writing science fiction. His first sf story was "The Dangerous Dimension" (*ASF*, July 1938). His fiction has appeared under six pen-names (two used for sf were "Rene Lafayette" and "Kurt Von Rachen") in over 72 publications. He has been a member of the Explorers Club of New York and the Authors League of America. In World War II he served with the U.S. Navy as commanding officer of escort vessels in both the Atlantic and Pacific.

Hubbard is mainly remembered for his classic *Final Blackout* (originally in *ASF*); his postwar emulation of the same theme in "The End Is Not Yet" (*ASF*, sr3, Aug 1947) was not anywhere near as successful. Many of his fantasy novels were featured in *Unknown* and helped make that magazine uniquely famous; most later appeared as books; those not reprinted were "The Ultimate Adventure" (Apr 1939), "The Ghoul" (Aug 1939), and "The Case of the Friendly Corpse" (Aug 1941).

In 1950 Hubbard left the fiction field to devote himself to "dianetics," a new form of psychotherapy based on his research into the human mind. After several years, in which he published several monographs on this subject, he formed his "scientology" foundation which now has branches world-wide. This school of mental therapy, operating as a "religion," has been banned in certain places because of its alleged harm to its patients.

Series

Conquest of Space. [as R. Lafayette] All in *SS*: "Forbidden Voyage" (Jan 1949); "The Magnificent Failure" (Mar 1949); "The Incredible Destination" (May 1949); "The Unwilling Hero" (July 1949); "Beyond the Black Nebula" (Sep 1949); "The Emperor of the Universe" (Nov 1949); "The Last Admiral" (Jan 1950).

Kilkenny Cats. [as K. Von Rachen] All in *ASF*: "The Idealists" (July 1940); "The Kilkenny Cats" (Sep 1940); "The Traitor" (Jan 1941); "The Mutineers" (Apr 1941); "The Rebels" (Feb 1942).

Methuselah, Doc. [as R. Lafayette] All in *ASF*: "Old Doc Methuselah" (Oct 1947); "The Expensive Slaves" (Nov 1947); "Her Majesty's Aberration" (Mar 1948); "The Great Air Monopoly" (Sep 1948); "Plague" (Apr 1949); "A Sound Investment" (June 1949); "Ole Mother Methuselah" (Jan 1950).

Fiction

Death's Deputy (*Unknown*, Feb 1940) (FPCI, Los Angeles, 1948, 167 pp., $2.50) (in *From Death to the Stars* [double binding], 1953) (*Le Bras de la mort* [French], Hachette, 1951) (*L'uomo che no poteva morire* [Italian], *Urania*: 37, 1954)

A notable fantasy based on the idea of an accident-prone.

Fear & Typewriter in the Sky (Gnome, New York, 1951, 9+256 pp., $2.75) (*Typewriter in the Sky & Fear*, Kemsley: CT409, 1952, 190 pp., pa 1/6) (*Le quattro ore di Satana* ("Fear") [Italian], *Urania*: 89, 1955; *La trama fra le nubi* ("Typewriter in the Sky") [Italian], *Urania*: 105, 1955) (*Fear* only, Galaxy SF Novel: 29, 1957, 125 pp., pa 35¢)

"Fear" (*Unknown*, July 1940) is a famous weird psychological story. "Typewriter in the Sky" (*Unknown*, sr2, Nov 1940) is a swashbuckling adventure in which the hero is "written into" his friend's story.

Final Blackout (*ASF*, sr3, Apr 1940) (Hadley, Providence, 1948, 154 pp., $3.00)

Hubbard's masterpiece; the classic about a lieutenant who becomes dictator of England after a devastating world war.

From Death to the Stars (FPCI, 1953, $3.00)

Double binding of *Death's Deputy* and *The Kingslayer*.

Kingslayer, The (FPCI, 1949, 208 pp., $3.00) (*2CSAB*, Win 1950) (in *From Death to the Stars* [double binding]) (*Rebell der Milchstrasse* [German], *UZ*: 105, 1957)

Space-opera with a trick ending. The book editions also include two short stories: "The Beast" and "The Invaders."

Return to Tomorrow [pa] ("To the Stars," *ASF*, sr2, Feb 1950) (Ace: S-66, 1954, 157 pp., pa 25¢) ([Japanese], Gengen-sha: SF1, 1956) (Panther: 692, 1957, 144 pp., pa 2/-) (*Retour a demain* [French], Le Fleuve Noir: A98, 1957) (*Aterkomst Till Morgondagen* [Swedish], Wennerbergs: R1, 1957, pa) (*Gefungen in Raum und Zeit* [German], Zimmermann, 1957; *T*: 60, 1959) (*Retorno al domani* [Italian], *Urania*: 147, 1957)

Adventure among the stars and the effect on spacemen of the Einsteinian time dilatation.

Science-Fantasy Quintet (FPCI, 1953, $3.50)

Double binding of *Triton* (2 stories) and E. E. Repp's *The Radium Pool* (made up from 3 stories).

Slaves of Sleep (*Unknown*, July 1939) (Shasta, Chicago, 1948, 206 pp., $3.00) ([Dutch], ?) (*Versklavte Seelen* [German], *UZ*: 391, 1963) (Lancer: 73-573, 1967, 175 pp., pa 60¢)

A modern man has adventures in the world of the Arabian Nights; sequel was "The Masters of Sleep" (*FA*, Oct 1950).

Triton ("The Indigestible Triton," *Unknown*, Apr 1940) (FPCI, 1949, 172 pp., $3.00) (in *Science-Fantasy Quintet* [double binding], 1953)

A Thorne Smith type of fantasy, with Neptune and other gods; the book ed. also contains "The Battle of the Wizards" (*Fantasy Book*, No. 5, 1949).

Typewriter in the Sky [pa] See *Fear & Typewriter in the Sky*

HUDSON, W(ILLIAM) H(ENRY) (4 Aug 1841–18 Aug 1922) British naturalist and writer. He was born at Quilmes, near Buenos Aires, and remained on the Argentine pampas until 1874. He called himself a field naturalist and the charms of wild-life appealed most to his observing mind, but he was not without an understanding of simple human joys and sorrows. His writings include memorable pictures of South America when he was a youth, such as *The Purple Land* (1885); the collection *Tales of the Pampas* (Knopf, 1916) gives 6 stories of possible interest. Another fiction work was *A Little Boy Lost* (Duckworth, 1905). His collected works were published in London in 24 vols. (1922-23).

Fiction

Crystal Age, A (T. F. Unwin, London, 1887, iv+287 pp. [anonymous]) (Duckworth, London, 1913, 316 pp.) (Dutton, New York, 1906, 1916, 1922) (Dent, London, 1922, limited ed.) (Armed: g-196, nd, 256 pp., pa) (Doric, New York, 1950, 182 pp., $1.50)

One of the classics—a matriarchal Golden Age in which all work in fields with plants, animals and men is wonderfully developed, but machinery is abolished. The Bleiler *Checklist* does not mention the anonymous first edition.

Green Mansions (Putnam, New York, 1904, 315 pp.) (Duckworth, 1904, 315 pp., 6/-) (Knopf, New York, 1916, 350 pp.) (Modern Library, New York, 1920, 289 pp.; 1944, 284 pp., $2.50) (Dutton, 1923, 323 pp.) ([Swedish], 1928) (Pocket Books: 16, 1938, 291 pp., pa 25¢) (Random, New York, 1944, 303 pp., colour illus.—E. M. Kauter, $3.95) (Armed: c-71, nd, 285 pp., pa) (Heritage, New York, 1944, 246 pp., illus., $1.95; 1956,

$5.00) (Bantam: 63, 1946, 275 pp., pa np; F-1878, 1959, 297 pp., pa 50¢; HP103, 1965, pa 60¢) (Guild: 420, 1950, 216 pp., pa 1/6) (Dodd, New York, 1949, 261 pp., $2.75) (Dent, 1951, 323 pp., 8/6)

Fantastic adventure in South America. *Film:* M.G.M., 1958, colour, directed by Mel Ferrer, with Audrey Hepburn; not particularly successful.

HUGHES, PENNETHORNE
Nonfiction

Witchcraft [pa] (Penguin: A745, 1965, 236 pp., pa 5/-)

A review of the history of witchcraft from its pre-classical origins until modern times.

HUGHES, RICHARD (ARTHUR WARREN) (1900–)
Fiction

Moment of Time, A [C] (Chatto Windus, London, 1926, 243 pp., 7/-)

21 stories: "Lochivarovic"; "The Stranger"; "Locomotive Llwyd"; "Poor Man's Inn"; "A Moment of Time"; "She Caught Hold of the Tow"; "The Vanishing Man"; "Monoculism"; "Jungle"; "The Cart"; "The Swans"; "The Ghost"; "Cornelius Katie"; "The Sea"; "Leaves"; "Martha"; "The Chest"; "The Devil Stick"; "A Night at a Cottage"; "The Victorian Room and James"; "The Diary of a Steerage Passenger."

HUGHES, RILEY
Fiction

Hills Were Liars, The [pa] (All Saints Press, AS-230, 1963, 216 pp., pa 50¢)

The story of eight men's efforts to preserve the Church after the breakdown of a war-torn civilisation.

HUGHES, WALTER LLEWELLYN (15 June 1910–) British author, born in Bilston, England. He uses the pseudonym "Hugh Walters."
Series [by Hugh Walters]
Godfrey, Chris. Juvenile book series; see Fiction listing.
Fiction

Blast-Off at 0300 See *Blast Off at Woomera*

Blast Off at Woomera (Faber, London, 1957, 202 pp., 12/6) (*Blast-Off at 0300*, Criterion, New York, 1958, 187 pp., $3.50)

First of Chris Godfrey series. A combination of circumstances lets a boy fly to the Moon, where he finds non-terrestrial life and Russian intrigue.

Destination Mars (Faber, 1963, 160 pp., 15/-) (Criterion, 1964, 160 pp., $3.50)

Sixth of Chris Godfrey series.

Domes of Pico, The (Faber, 1958, 196 pp., 13/6) (*Menace From the Moon*, Criterion, 1959, 191 pp., $3.50)

Second of Chris Godfrey series. A neutron stream from the Moon causes atomic piles to run wild, and must be stopped.

Expedition Venus (Faber, 1962, 160 pp., 13/6) (Criterion, 1963, 191 pp., $3.50)

Fifth of Chris Godfrey series. A journey to Venus to find an antidote to nasty fingers.

First on the Moon See *Operation Columbus*

Journey to Jupiter (Faber, 1965, 159 pp., 15/-) (Criterion, 1966, 190 pp., $3.50)

Ninth of Chris Godfrey series.

Menace From the Moon See *Domes of Pico, The*

Mission to Mercury (Faber, 1965, 158 pp., 16/-) (Criterion, 1965, 189 pp., $3.50)

Eighth of Chris Godfrey series.

Moon Base One (Faber, 1961, 189 pp., 13/6) (*Outpost on the Moon*, Criterion, 1962, 191 pp., $3.50)

Fourth of Chris Godfrey series. A mystery is cleared up by a joint East-West expedition to establish a permanent lunar base.

Operation Columbus (Faber, 1960, 191 pp., 13/6) (*First on the Moon*, Criterion, 1961, 192 pp., $3.50) (Tempo: T13, 1962, 192 pp., pa 50¢)

Third of Chris Godfrey series. The first major landing on the Moon, seeking to discover the secret of the Domes.

Outpost on the Moon See *Moon Base One*
Spaceship to Saturn (Faber, 1967, 160 pp., 16/-) (Criterion, 1967, 190 pp., $3.95)
Tenth of Chris Godfrey series.
Terror by Satellite (Faber, 1964, 159 pp., 13/6) (Criterion, 1964, 159 pp., $3.50)
Seventh of Chris Godfrey series.

HUGI, MAURICE G. (1904–1947) British science fiction author. He first appeared in *Scoops* and then had three stories in *Tales of Wonder*. "The Mechanical Mice" appeared under his name (*ASF*, Jan 1941) but was actually written by E. F. Russell [see the Day *Index*]. After World War II he returned to sf with "The Mill of the Gods" (*NW*, No. 1, 1946).

HULL, E(DNA) M(AYNE) U.S. author. Daughter of the late J. T. Hull, Canadian newspaper editor and wheat pool executive, she married A. E. van Vogt in 1939 and has helped him considerably in his writing. In her own right she has written the "Artur Blord" series, a number of fantasy stories for *Unknown*, and the novel "The Winged Man" (*ASF*, sr2, May 1944).
Series
Blord, Artur. Space intrigue with an interstellar businessman. All in *ASF*: "Abdication" (Apr 1943); "Competition" (June 1943); "The Debt" (Dec 1943); "The Contract" (Mar 1944); "Enter the Professor" (Jan 1945); "Bankruptcy Proceedings" (Aug 1946). All except the first were published in *Planets for Sale*.
Fiction
Out of the Unknown [C] See VAN VOGT, A. E.
Planets for Sale [C] (F. Fell, New York, 1954, 192 pp., $2.75) (*Sterne der Macht* [German], *UG*: 42, 1956)
Old-fashioned space-opera; the last five of the "Artur Blord" series.
Winged Man, The See VAN VOGT, A. E.

HUME, CYRIL (16 Mar 1900–) American novelist, born at New Rochelle, N.Y. He left Yale before taking a degree. His first book, *Wife of a Centaur* (1923), was not generally well regarded but became a successful movie. Since 1930 he has written screenplay adaptations, and he occasionally appeared in *SEP* and *Collier's*. A fantasy in addition to those below was *The Golden Dancer* (Doran, New York, 1926).
Fiction
Myself and the Young Bowman and Other Fantasies [C] (Doubleday, New York, 1932, 166 pp., $2.50; 1500 copies)
Fantasy, 23 items, all verse except 6 marked as fiction: "Myself and the Young Bowman" (fiction); "To a Mocking-Bird at Night"; "Paragon"; "To Elaine in Avalon"; "In the Chinese Manner"; "Forrester" (fiction); "In a Tuscan Garden"; "Rain-Val d'Arno"; "Triple Rhymes for April"; "Madre Crudele"; "The Frogs and the Stork" (fiction); "Summer Storm"; "Two Lyrics From a Masque of Harlequin"; "Lane in Vermont"; "The Tree of Knowledge" (fiction); "Ode to Pan"; "Alter Ego"; "Berkshire Water"; "Progress in Arcadia" (fiction); "Uther's Blood"; "Song for Camelot"; "Dialogue"; "Godmother's Gift" (fiction).
Street of the Malcontents and Other Stories [C] (Doran, New York, 1927, 331 pp., $2.50)
Fantasy, 14 stories: "Elisaveth, a Story of Roumania"; "Street of the Malcontents"; "Cowards of Conscience"; "The Shout"; "Coffinwood"; "Loyalty"; "The Tower in the Winds"; "Count Pizziccheria's China Teeth"; "The Head"; "Atlantis' Exile" (*FFM*, Dec 1947); "Told for the Truth"; "Suttee à la Mode"; "In the Dark of the Moon"; "Fantasy in the First Person."

HUME, FERGUS (8 July 1859–13 July 1932) Australian novelist who moved to England. He was noted for many mystery and detective stories. Writing over 100 novels, he was contemporary with A. Conan Doyle, but did not achieve the same renown. He is probably most noted for his *The Mystery of a Hansom Cab*, first published in Melbourne, which sold more than half a million copies during his lifetime. He has not been reprinted in recent years but his fantastic works are listed in the Bleiler *Checklist*.

Fiction
Chronicles of Fairy Land [C] (Griffith, London, 1892, 6/-) (Lippincott, Philadelphia & London, 1911, 191 pp.)
Fantasy, 9 stories (not in Bleiler *Checklist*): "King Oberon's Library"; "The Red Elf"; "Shadowland"; "The Water-Witch"; "Moon Fancies"; "The Rose-Princess"; "Sorrow-Singing"; "The Golden Goblin"; "The Enchanted Forest."
Dwarf's Chamber and Other Stories, The [C] (Ward Lock & Bowden, London, 1896, 386 pp.)
Fantasy, 9 stories (not in Bleiler *Checklist*): "The Dwarf's Chamber"; "Miss Jonathan"; "The Dead Man's Diamonds"; "The Tale of the Turquoise Skull"; "The Green-Stone God and the Stockbroker"; "The Jesuit and the Mexican Coin"; "The Rainbow Camellia"; "The Ivory Leg and the Twenty-Four Diamonds"; "My Cousin From France."

HUMPHRIES, ROLFE (20 Nov 1894–) U.S. anthologist.
Anthologies
Pause to Wonder See FISCHER, M. (co-anthologist)
Strange to Tell See FISCHER, M. (co-anthologist)

HUNT, DOUGLAS
Nonfiction
Handbook on the Occult, A (Arthur Barker, London, 1967, 219 pp., 21/-)
The author feels there is no such thing as the Supernatural, but occultism is that study of certain unknowns which in no way implies belief in unnatural or supernatural explanations. He examines authenticated observations concerning hauntings, astral projection, hypnosis, telepathy, clairvoyance, levitation, black magic, etc.

HUNT, VIOLET (1866–16 Jan 1942) British biographer and novelist. Daughter of the noted painter Alfred William Hunt, she did not follow his occupation but instead became a well-known novelist, hostess and journalist, having a weekly column in the *Pall Mall Gazette*. She was an active worker for women's suffrage. Her works run from *The Maiden's Progress* (1894) to *The Wife of Rosetti* (1932), but are nearly forgotten now.
Fiction
More Tales of the Uneasy [C] (Heinemann, London, 1925, 317 pp., 7/6)
4 stories: "The Night of No Weather"; "The Cigarette Case of the Commander"; "Love's Last Leave"; "The Corsican Sisters."
Tales of the Uneasy [C] (Heinemann, 1911, 319, 6/-)
9 stories: "The Barometer"; "Blue Bonnet"; "The Coach"; "The Memoir"; "The Operation"; "The Prayer"; "The Telegram"; "The Tiger-Skin"; "The Witness."

HUNTER, ALAN (Feb 1923–) British science-fiction artist. He worked as a technical illustrator in a drawing office, and was self-taught in the sf field. He mainly appeared with interior illustrations in *New Worlds*, but also painted the first two covers for *Nebula*. He organised the Fantasy Art Society.

HUNTER, EVAN [pseud. of S. A. Lombino] (1926–) U.S. author. He majored in art, taking his B.A. in New York; after he served in the U.S. Navy he changed to writing. He has been equally at home in both the science fiction and mystery fields; his best-selling novel *The Blackboard Jungle* (on juvenile delinquency) was made into an outstanding motion picture. Other mysteries include *Second Ending* and *Strangers When We Meet*, and (under the pseudonym "Ed McBain") the "Eighty-Seventh Precinct" series. He appeared in the sf magazines with a number of stories in the mid-1950's. In addition to "Evan Hunter," he has used the pseudonyms "Hunt Collins" and "Richard Marsten" for sf stories. In recent years he has left the sf field to concentrate on general fiction; his books include *Mothers and Daughters*. A recent collection is *Happy New Year, Herbie* (Constable, London, 1965, 206 pp., 25/-), containing 11 stories of which only one is sf or fantasy: "Million Dollar Maybe" (*AS*, Dec 1953).
Fiction
Danger: Dinosaurs! [as Richard Marsten] (Winston, Philadelphia,

1953, 209 pp., $2.00) (*L'era del dinosauro* [Italian], *Urania*: 64, 1954) ([Japanese], GingaShobo 'Adv. in SF 18,' 1956)

Juvenile, one of Winston's "Adventures in SF" series; time travel into the past, with uranium hunting as a sideline.

Find the Feathered Serpent [as Evan Hunter] (Winston, 1952, 207 pp., $2.00)

Juvenile, one of the "Adventures in SF" series; time travel to the Mayan Empire in search of Kulkulcan.

Last Spin, The [as Evan Hunter] [C] (Constable, London, 1960, 218 pp., 13/6) (Corgi, GN1021, 1961, 220 pp., pa 3/6)

15 stories, including 3 fantasy: "The Fallen Angel"; "Silent Partner"; "Robert."

Rocket to Luna [as Richard Marsten] (Winston, 1952, 211 pp., $2.00) (Hutchinson, London, 1954, 232 pp., 7/6) ([Japanese], GingaShobo 'Adv. in SF 9,' 1956) (*Rakete ab zum Mond* [German], AWA, 1954; *T*: 196, 1961)

Juvenile, one of Winston's "Adventures in SF" series; senior students journey from a satellite space station to the Moon.

Tomorrow and Tomorrow [pa] See *Tomorrow's World*
Tomorrow's World [as Hunt Collins] (Avalon, New York, 1956, 223 pp., $2.50) (*Tomorrow and Tomorrow*, Pyramid: G214, 1956, 190 pp., pa 35¢; G654, 1961, pa 35¢) ([Japanese], Hayakawa: 3018, 1959, pa) (*Morgen en overmorgen* [Dutch], Nederlandsche Keurboekerij, Amsterdam, 1959)

Elaboration of "Malice in Wonderland" (*If*, Jan 1954 [as Evan Hunter]); a future in which drug-addict cults seek to control the U.S.A.

HUNTER, MEL (1929–) U.S. science fiction artist. He became prominent in the field in the 1950's. He had no formal training; his occupational background was in advertising copy writing and production engineering. Barely heard of in 1952, he emerged in 1953 as one of the best sf cover artists, and has done covers for *Galaxy*, *If* and *F&SF*, as well as some book jackets. Mostly he works on interplanetary themes, where his detail is meticulously accurate; his work is favourably compared with that of Chesley Bonestell.

HUNTING, GARDNER (1872–21 Nov 1958) U.S. author. He is noted particularly for *The Vicarion* (1926), a best-seller in its day. He was a reporter, advertising man, editor of newspapers and magazines, playwright (*The Cave of the Bottomless Pool*, 1909) and film executive. He revised *The Vicarion* as *Naked Yesterdays or The Scarlet Eye* but the manuscript was lost. At one time C. Beaumont and F. J. Ackerman collaborated on adapting *The Vicarion* as a possible TV series, but it was never taken up.

HURD, DOUGLAS
Fiction
Send Him Victorious [with Andrew Osmond] (Collins, London, 1968, 287 pp., 25/-)

An ingenious and swift story of action and intrigue. If a coup d'etat were attempted in Britain, how would the Government and the Throne cope?

HURLEY, RICHARD J.
Anthology
Beyond Belief [pa] (Scholastic Book Service, New York, 1966, 188 pp., wraps, pa 45¢)

Sf, 8 stories: "The Hardest Bargain," Evelyn E. Smith; "The Invasion," Robert Willey [W. Ley]; "It's Such a Beautiful Day," I. Asimov; "The Man Who Lost the Sea," T. Sturgeon; "Phoenix," C. A. Smith; "Third From the Sun," R. Matheson; "Keyhole," M. Leinster; "History Lesson," A. C. Clarke.

HURWOOD, BERNHARDT J.
Nonfiction
Monsters and Nightmares [pa] (Belmont: B50-735, 1967, 156 pp., pa 50¢)

38 true ghost and horror stories (one in 4 parts), with epilogue.
Strange Talents [pa] (Ace: K-276, 1967, 189 pp., pa 50¢)
Terror by Night [pa] (Lancer: 72-656, 1963, 127 pp., pa 50¢)

Vampires, Werewolves and Ghouls [pa] (Ace: H-83, 1968, 158 pp., pa 60¢)
Anthology
Monsters Galore [pa] (Gold Medal: d1544, 1965, 224 pp., pa 50¢)

Weird, 23 items and introduction: "The Eyes of the Panther," A. Bierce; "The Dreadful Visitor" (from *Varney the Vampyre*), Thomas P. Prest; "The Monster-Maker," Wm. C. Morrow; "Mohammed Bux and the Demon," adapted by B. J. Hurwood; "Count Magnus," M. R. James; "The Purple Terror," Fred M. White; "The Werewolf" (from *The Phantom Ship*), Frederick Marryat; "The Wer-Bear" (from *The History of Hrolfekraka*), Sir Walter Scott; "Jikininki," Lafcadio Hearn; "The Vampire Cat of Nabeshima," from the Japanese, adapted by Hurwood; "The Corpse at the Inn" ("The Demon Who Changed Its Skin," from *Liao Chai*), Pu Sung Ling, adapted by Hurwood; "The Guest and the Striges," from the Greek, adapted by Hurwood; "A Vatanuan Cannibal Tale," from the Melanesian, adapted by Hurwood; "Four Siberian Demon Tales," from the Siberian, adapted by Hurwood; "An Irish Vampire," R. S. Breen; "Peter Kürten–the Monster of Dusseldorf," B. J. Hurwood; "The Mark of the Beast," R. Kipling; "The Were-Tiger," Sir Hugh Clifford; "Johannes Cuntius, a Citizen of Pentsch," Henry More; "Hungary's Female Vampire," Dean Lipton; "Sawney Beane, the Man Eater of Eastlothian," Capt. Charles Johnson; "Stubbe Peeter," from the Gaelic, adapted by Hurwood.

HUXLEY, ALDOUS (LEONARD) (26 July 1894–22 Nov 1963) British novelist and essayist. He was nearly blind in his youth and spent most of his life fighting incipient blindness. He took his degree in 1915, and worked on the staff of *Athenaeum* in the late 1920's. He lived in Italy and France, and more recently in the U.S.A. He was very interested in Vedanta and the other mystic religions, in which field he had the anthology *The Perennial Philosophy* (1945). One of his most successful later books was *The Devils of Loudun* (1952). In his last years he discussed present-day trends in the light of the "forecasts" in his classic *Brave New World*. A memorial volume is *Aldous Huxley 1894–1963*, edited by Julian Huxley, with contributions from his distinguished contemporaries.

All of his fiction books are listed below except *Time Must Have a Stop* (Harper, 1944) and *Eyeless in Gaza* (Chatto, 1936); the latter is listed in the Bleiler *Checklist* but is not a fantasy. *Aldous Huxley–A Study of the Major Novels*, Peter Bowering (U. of London 'Athone Press,' 1968, x+242 pp., 45/-), is an evaluation of Huxley's nine major novels from *Crome Yellow* (1921) through to *Island* (1962); sf works covered are *Brave New World*, *After Many a Summer*, and *Island*.

Fiction
After Many a Summer (*Harper's Magazine*, sr, 1938) (Chatto Windus, London, 1939, 314 pp., 8/3; 1942, 314 pp., 4/6) (*After Many a Summer Dies the Swan*, Harper, New York, 1939, 356 pp., $2.50; Sun Dial, New York, 1941, $1.00) (*Efter manga somrar* [Swedish], Wahlström & Widstrand, 1940) (Macmillan, Toronto, 1942, $2.25) (*Jouvence* [French], Plon, ?) (*After Many a Summer Dies the Swan*, Avon: 388, 1951, pa 25¢; AT435, 1952, 250 pp., pa 35¢; T75, 1954, pa 35¢; VS1, 1964, 254 pp., pa 75¢) (Vanguard Lib: 16, *ca.* 1952, 3/6) (Penguin: 1049, 1955, 251 pp., pa 2/6) (*Viejo muere el cisne* [Argentine–Spanish], Losada, 1957) (*Nach vielen Sommern* [German], S. Fischer, 1959, pa)

Received the James Tait Black Memorial Award, 1939. A multimillionaire discovers an 18th Century remedy for old age.
Ape and Essence (Harper, 1948, 205 pp., $2.50) (C. Windus, 1949, 153 pp., 9/6; 1951, 160 pp., 7/6) (*Apa och ande* [Swedish], Wahlström, 1949) (*Temps futurs* [French], Plon, 1951) (*Affe und Wesen* [German], Steinberg, 1951) ([Japanese], Hayakawa Shobo, 1951) (Bantam: A1793, 1958, 152 pp., pa 35¢; HC262, 1964, pa 60¢)

A decadent U.S. society and its sexual mores, after an atomic war.
Brave New World (C. Windus, 1932, limited autog. ed., 30/-; 1932; 1934, 305 pp., 3/6; 1950, 213 pp., 6/-) (Doubleday, New York, 1932, 311 pp., limited ed., $10.00; $2.50) (Garden City,

New York, 1932, $1.00) (*Du sköna nya värld* [Swedish], Wahlström, 1932) (*Le meilleur des mondes* [French], Plon, 1933) (*Un mundo feliz* [Spanish], Miracle, 1934) (*Het Soma-paradijs* [Dutch], Contact, Amsterdam, 1934; *Heerlijke nieuwe wereld*, Contact, 1956) (Sun Dial, New York, 1937, 311 pp., 89¢) (Macmillan, Toronto, $1.00) (Zodiac, London, 1948, 213 pp., 7/6) (*Wackere neue Welt* [German], Steinberg, 1950; S. Fischer, 1953, pa) (Vanguard Lib: 2, 1952, 214 pp., 3/6) (Bantam: A1071, 1953, 266 pp., pa 35¢; A1369, 1955, 177 pp., pa 35¢; AC-1, 1959, pa 35¢; HC206, 1964, pa 60¢; SY4172, 1968, pa 75¢) ([Japanese], Mikaso Shobo 'Lib. World's Contemp. Literature 1,' 1954) (excerpts in *Treasury of SF Classics* [Kuebler], 1954) (*Admirabel Mundo* [Portuguese], ?) (Penguin: 1052, 1955, 201 pp., pa 4/-; 1958, pa 4/-; 1966, pa 5/6)

The noted classic of a "controlled" future Earth, with incubated babies, etc.

Heaven and Hell (Harper, 1956, 103 pp., $2.00) (Clarke Irwin, Toronto, $1.60)

The author theorises that there is a real physical-psychological basis for the "sense of wonder" that is inherent in the human race.

Island (Harper, 1962, 334 pp., $5.00) (C. Windus, 1962, 286 pp., 18/-) (*Ön* [Swedish], Wahlström, 1962) (*Ile* [French], Plon, 1963) (Bantam: S2695, 1963, 295 pp., pa 75¢; N3481, 1968, pa 95¢) (Penguin: 2193, 1964, 297 pp., pa 4/6; 1966, pa 5/-)

The slight plot is merely a foundation for long discussions and explanations of a utopian society founded a century ago, reflecting the author's views on how people should live. It is comparable with *Brave New World* in such ways as having a euphoric drug; the society postulated sounds pleasant, but can happiness be obtained by decree?

Nonfiction

Brave New World Revisited (Harper, 1958, 147 pp., $3.00) (C. Windus, 1959, 164 pp., 12/6) (*Retour au meilleur des mondes* [French], Plon, ?) (Bantam: F2124, 1960, 116 pp., pa 50¢) (Perennial: P23, 1965, 118 pp., pa 50¢)

Twenty-six years after *Brave New World*, Huxley sees the regimented world he envisioned taking shape faster than he expected —already two samples in our time (Nazi Germany and Soviet Russia). He argues simply from facts, such as propaganda under dictatorships and techniques of brainwashing. He is not convincing in the later chapters. A documentation of his future is given in *The Next Hundred Years* (Harrison Brown, ed., 1957); the chapter on drugs "Revisited" appeared as "Chemical Persuasion" (*F&SF*, Apr 1959).

HUXLEY, JULIAN (22 June 1887–) British biologist, science writer, and statesman; elder brother of Aldous. He has lectured and done much work in biology and allied fields, and was biology editor of the *Encyclopedia Britannica* (14th ed.). He has also written a number of brilliant scientific, social and philosophical books and essays; he collaborated with H. G. Wells. He was the first Director-General of UNESCO (1946-48), and was knighted in 1958. His only sf story has been "The Tissue-Culture King" (*AS*, Aug 1927; in *Great SF by Scientists* [Conklin], 1962, pa).

Nonfiction

Evolution in Action (Chatto Windus, London 1953, 160 pp., plates, 9/6) (Clarke Irwin, Toronto, $2.25) (Harper, New York, 1953, 182 pp., $2.75) (Signet, 1957, 141 pp., pa 50¢)

The author reaches back to the beginning of the Universe and traces the threads which have led to the evolution of Man and his societies.

HYAMS, EDWARD (SOLOMON) (30 Sep 1910–) British author. He was born in London and educated at Lycee-Jaccard and Lausanne University. He has contributed to *New Statesman, Lilliput, Illustrated London News*, etc. His nonfiction includes works on vineyards and strawberry cultivation, while fiction (not sf) includes *The Wings of Morning, Into the Dream* and *Taking It Easy*.

Fiction

Astrologer, The (Longmans Green, London, 1950, 244 pp., 9/6) (Longmans, New York, $2.50) (Longmans, Toronto, $2.25) (*Det star i stjärnorna* [Swedish], Skoglund, 1950)

Astrological forecasting with a sound scientific basis is taken up by governments for their own ends.

998 See *Sylvester*

Stories and Cream [C] (Longmans Green, 1954, 242 pp., 11/6) (Longmans, Toronto, $2.25)

Satirical stories with some fantasy.

Sylvester (Longmans Green, 1951, 198 pp., 10/6) (Longmans, Toronto, $2.25) (*998*, Pantheon, New York, 1952, 11+207 pp., $2.75) (*Weltraum ohne Tränen* [German], die Arche, 1954)

Typical English satire about a fantastic super-super radar. *Film:* "You Know What Sailors Are," J. Arthur Rank, 1953, colour, with Akim Tamiroff and Donald Sinden; the fantasy was cut down.

HYNAM, JOHN CHARLES (10 June 1915–) British schoolmaster. He is better known in the British sf field by his pseudonym "John Kippax," under which he has had over 30 stories. He was one of the authors featured (under his own name) in the 100th issue of *New Worlds*. He has had four TV plays accepted. He has been a jazz musician.

Fiction

Thunder of Stars, A See MORGAN, D. (co-author)

HYND, LAVINIA

Fiction [as Lavinia Leitch]

Vampire and Other Stories, A [C] (Christopher Pub. House, Boston, 1927, 231 pp., $2.00)

Weird, 10 stories: "A Vampire"; "Her Stratagem"; "Lots of Room"; "Thoughts Are Things"; "The Neighbor's Cat"; "Honest Jane"; "His Wife's Absences"; "Growing Pains"; "Duty"; "Clothing a Lily."

HYNE, C(HARLES) J(OHN) CUTCLIFFE (WRIGHT) (11 May 1865–10 Mar 1944) British novelist and short story writer; B.A. and M.A. from Cambridge. Potboilers, boys' books and advice to readers kept him going until he hit on the idea of "Captain Kettle." C. A. Pearson started a 6d magazine (*Pearson's Magazine*) and wanted a series with a central character like Sherlock Holmes; from this Captain Kettle began to appear regularly. Aside from this series not much of Hyne's work has survived.

Fiction [Incomplete—other titles in Bleiler *Checklist*]

Adventures of a Solicitor, The [as Weatherby Chesney] [C] (J. Bowden, London, 1898, 268 pp., 4 illus.–George Hutchinson, 2/6)

Much sought after by collectors of detective fiction; not listed in the Bleiler *Checklist*. 18 adventures of Edward Dale, solicitor; all except the first two are either sf or weird: "The Muggler"; "The Sorceress"; "The Mechanical Burglar"; "The Ghost of Farnley Abbey"; "The Supreme Court"; "A Maker of Thumbs"; "The Dried Pirate"; "The Trance"; "The Rain-Maker"; "The End of England"; "The Witch"; "The Renewer of Youth"; "The Crimson Beast"; "Pluck by Proxy"; "The Seven Fluttering Hearts"; "Branded by Kisses"; "The Men From Mars"; "The Streaked Heads."

Atoms of Empire [C] (Macmillan, New York & London, 1904, 311 pp., 6/-)

16 stories, with the following sf: "The Fire" (destruction of London); "The Mummy of Thomson-Pratt" (a revived mummy gives court scandal, not history); "The Lizard" (a prehistoric lizard revives).

Lost Continent, The (Harper, New York, 1900, 352 pp.) (Hutchinson, London, 1900, 368 pp., 6/-; '9d Library,' 1905, 188 pp., pa 6d) (*FFM*, Dec 1944)

Adventure and intrigue in doomed Atlantis; the hero fights the usurping Empress.

Man's Understanding [C] (Ward Lock, London, 1933, 287 pp., 7/6; 1934, 3/6; 1936, 2/6)

Contains among others 8 sf stories: "Caterpillars"; "The Island That Was Seldom There"; "The Aero-Service Restaurant Enquiry"; "The Gentleman on the Mat"; "The Eeel"; "My Mermaid and the Giants"; "Dragons"; "Tribute for the Emperor Solomon."

Red Herrings [C] (Methuen, London, 1918, 237 pp., 6/-)

Contains among others 3 fantasy stories: "The McTodd Plug"; "The Man Who Once Made Diamonds"; "Og-Star."
Rev. Captain Kettle, The [C] (Hutchinson, London, 1936, 256 pp., 2/6)

Includes one sf short story about Kettle: "Ice Age Woman."

I

IGGULDEN, JOHN M. (1917–) Australian author, born at Brighton, Victoria. He gave up his position as general manager of an engineering company to become a novelist. With the novel below, and a second one, *The Storms of Summer* (Chapman Hall, 1960), with an Australian setting, he became one of Australia's top contemporary writers. In 1959 he became the Australian National Gliding Champion.
Fiction
Breakthrough (Chapman Hall, London, 1960, 240 pp., 16/-) (FSB: 873, 1963, 221 pp., pa 3/6)

The overthrow of a dictator who can control people's actions by radio; original and well-written.

IMBERT, ENRIQUE ANDERSON
Fiction
Other Side of the Mirror, The [Trans. & intro.–Isabel Reade] [C] (Southern Illinois U. Press, 1966, 226 pp., $5.95) (MacDonald, London, 1968, 226 pp., 30/-)

31 short stories, a blend of the fantastic and the real with irony as a principal characteristic: "Light Pedro"; "The Determined Goblins"; "The Ghost"; "Blackout in New York"; "The Air and the Man"; "Alejo Zaro, Lost in Time"; "The Prodigal Son"; "Ash Moon"; "The Death of the Water"; "Fantomas Saves Mankind"; "The Crime in the Attic"; "The Politician"; "The Path"; "The Hands"; "Situations"; "The Magic Book"; "The Voyage"; "The Wall"; "The General Makes a Lovely Corpse"; "Mishina"; "The Lesson"; "A Saint in the New World"; "In the Aconquija Mountains"; "The Queen of the Wood"; "Tsanta"; "The Tired Bullet"; "The Kiss"; "Taste of Lipstick"; "The Electric Bulb"; "Patrick O'Hara, the Liberator"; "More Situations."

INCE, RICHARD BASIL
Fiction
At the Sign of Sagittarius [C] (Faber & Gwyer, London, 1926, 11+255 pp., 6/-) (J. Day, New York, 1927)

Fantasy, 8 stories: "The Beard"; "The Faith of Fanu"; "The Good Deeds of Dean Ensfrid"; "The Penitent"; "The Return"; "The Royal Limp"; "St. Orphitus"; "The Thanatists."

INGREY, DEREK
Fiction
Pig on a Lead (Faber, London, 1963, 252 pp., 21/-)

The life of the last three people in England—two men and a boy—told by the boy.

INSTITORIS, HENRICUS Medieval author.
Nonfiction
Malleus Malificarum [with Jakob Sprenger] (originally 1489) (John Rodker, England, 1928, 324 pp., 35/-) (Pushkin, London, 1948, 278 pp., 15/-) (Anglo Books, New York, 1951, 278 pp., $3.50) (Folio Society, London, 1968, 221 pp., 28/6)

One of the most noted works on witchcraft, for its time a classic. The 1948 and 1951 eds. have introduction, bibliography and notes by M. Summers. The 1968 ed. is edited and introduced by Pennethorne Hughes.

IONESCO, EUGENE French author.
Fiction
Colonel's Photograph, The [C] (Faber, London, 1967, 177 pp., 25/-)

7 stories of near fantasy: "Oriflamme"; "The Colonel's Photograph"; "The Stroller in the Air"; "A Victim of Duty"; "Rhinoceros"; "The Slough"; "Spring, 1939."

IRVING, WASHINGTON (1783–1859) American literary figure. He had little formal education; apprenticed to the law, he never practiced much. He travelled extensively and his first essays, gay and witty, appeared in 1807. By 1815 he was well known in England and Sir Walter Scott persuaded him to have his *Sketch Book of Geoffrey Crayon* published in London in 1819-20. This contained the famous story of Rip Van Winkle. After living in England and touring widely in Europe he returned to America in the early 1830's, and found himself both famous and criticized for spending his talents on European themes.
Fiction
Legend of Sleepy Hollow and Other Stories, The [C] [pa] (Washington Square: W581, 1962, 165 pp., pa 60¢) (Airmont: CL50, 1964, 190 pp., pa 50¢) (Lancer: 13-453, 1968, 319 pp., pa 60¢)

There are a number of variants. The Airmont ed. has 18 stories and articles and includes "English Writers on America" as the 5th item in *The Sketch Book* selections, but does not have the *Alhambra* items. The Lancer ed. has 19 items and includes the *Alhambra* pieces. From *The Sketch Book* (1820): "The Author's Account of Himself"; "The Legend of Sleepy Hollow"; "Rip Van Winkle"; "The Specter Bridegroom"; "The Broken Heart"; "The Wife"; "The Voyage"; "Traits of Indian Character"; "The Pride of the Village"; "The Angler." From *Tales of a Traveller* (1824): "The Adventure of the German Student"; "The Devil and Tom Walker." From *The Alhambra* (1832): "The Adventure of the Mason"; "The Governor and the Notary." From *A Tour of the Prairies* (1835): "Grand Prairie—A Buffalo Hunt." From *Sketches in Paris in 1825*: "The Field of Waterloo." From *Wolfert's Roost and Other Papers*: "The Creole Village." From *Knickerbocker's History of New York, Book IV* (1809): "The Chronicles of the Reign of William the Testy." From *Crayon Miscellany*: "The Legend of Don Munio Sancho de Hinojosa." The Washington edition has 22 stories and articles; it adds two stories from *The Sketch Book*, two further *Sketches in Paris*, one item from *A Tour of the Prairies* and one from *Crayon Miscellany*, and one item each from the further works *Astoria* and *Oliver Goldsmith*.

IRWIN, (Mrs.) CONSTANCE U.S. professional writer, teacher of library science at U. of Iowa, and amateur historian and archaeologist.
Nonfiction
Fair Gods and Stone Faces (St. Martin's Press, New York, 1963, 346 pp., $7.50)

A plausible case for early contacts between the Old World—primarily Carthage and Phoenicia—and Central America and Peru. (Reviewed by P. S. Miller, *ASF*, Sep 1963.)

IRWIN, MARGARET (190?–) British historical novelist. She was educated at Oxford, and encouraged to write by her uncle, S. T. Irwin. She became the wife of artist John Robert Monsell. She has had many works, from *Still She Wished for Company* (1924; Argentine, 1950) to the present day, but is most noted for her brightly tapestried historical novels starting with *The Gay Galliard* (1941), and others including a trilogy on Queen Elizabeth starting with *Young Bess* (1945).
Fiction [Incomplete—other titles in Bleiler *Checklist*]
Bloodstock and Other Stories [C] (Chatto, London, 1953, 206 pp., 8/6) (Clarke Irwin, Toronto, $1.75) (Harcourt Brace, New York, 1954, $3.00)

11 stories, with fantasy (4 stories) grouped as *Uncanny Stories*: "The Book" (*FFM*, Dec 1951); "Monsieur Seeks a Wife" (*FFM*, Oct 1951); "Mistletoe"; "The Earlier Service" (*F&SF*, Dec 1951).
Madame Fears the Dark [C] (Chatto Windus, 1935, 276 pp., 7/6)

7 stories and 1 play, including 4 fantasy: "The Book"; "The

Earlier Service"; "Monsieur Seeks a Wife"; "The Curate and the Rake."

IVIE, LARRY U.S. artist. In the sf field he has appeared in *ASF*, *Galaxy*, *Amazing*, *Fantastic* and *If*. He has also done newspaper advertising illustrations for fantasy and horror movies. He edited *Castle of Frankenstein* and has contributed to several similar publications. He has done scripts and artwork for the comics publications *Suspense*, *Alarming Adventures*, *Classics Illustrated* and *Private Strong*. Creator of *Altron Boy*, he has done some hardcover illustrations for E. R. Burroughs.

J

JACKS, L(AWRENCE) P(EARSALL) (9 Oct 1860–17 Feb 1955) British philosopher, essayist and editor. He took his M.A. at U. of London in 1886. He started in the ministry, but with the foundation of the *Hibbert Journal* in 1902 he became its editor, retiring in 1947. He also was professor of philosophy at Manchester College, Oxford, and was later Principal of the College, 1915-31. His work was often religious in nature; his imaginary industrial city "Smokeover" allowed him to criticize life through the mouths of its fictitious inhabitants. The list below includes all of his fiction except *The Last Legend of Smokeover* (1939) and *Mad Shepherds* (1924).

Fiction

All Men Are Ghosts [C] (Williams Norgate, London, 1913, 360 pp., 5/-; 1917, 254 pp., 2/6; 1927, 2/6)

7 stories (some sectionalised): "Panhandle and the Ghosts: I. Panhandle Lays Down a Principle, II. Panhandle Narrates His History and Describes the Haunted House, III. Panhandle's Remarkable Adventure"; "The Ghost Appears"; "The Magic Formula"; "All Men Are Ghosts: I. Dr. Pyecraft Becomes Confused, II. The Hole in the Water Skin, III. Dr. Pyecraft Clears His Mind"; "The Professor's Mare"; "Farmer Jeremy and His Ways"; "White Rose."

Legends of Smokeover, The [C] (Hodder Stoughton, London, 1921, 324 pp., 12/6)

5 stories on Smokeover and Its Smoke: I. "The Legend of Rumbelow, the Betting Man"; II. "The Legend of the Mad Millionaire"; III. "The Legend of Margaret Wolfstone"; IV. "The Legend of Professor Ripplemark"; V. "The Legend of the League."

Magic Formula and Other Stories, The [C] (Harper, New York & London, 1927, 367 pp., 7/6)

12 stories: "The Magic Formula"; "A Psychologist Among the Saints"; "White Roses"; "The Hole in the Water-Skin"; "The Poor Man's Pig"; "Farmer Jeremy and His Ways"; "A Gravedigger Scene"; "The Professor's Mare"; "The Chest of Cedar"; "Bracketed First"; "The Self Deceivers"; "Made Out of Nothing."

JACKSON, BIRDSALL

Fiction

Pipe Dreams and Twilight Tales [C] (Paumanok Press, Rockville [N.Y.], 1936, 234 pp., $2.50)

Not in Bleiler *Checklist*. Fantasy, 15 stories and 14 verses (marked "v"), with introduction: "To My Pipe" (v); "Petruchio in Plainsville"; "The Realization"; "Dry Goods"; "Son of Father Abraham"; "The Antagonists"; "The Old Meeting House"; "The Mysterious Disappearance of Old Mayhew"; "The Two Admirals"; "The Wicked King and the Good Queen"; "Little Cherry and Uncle Joel"; "The Life Saver"; "Romeo Goes to Court"; "A Bedtime Fable" (v); "The Dream of Power" (v); "The White Man and the Red Man" (v); "The Dream of Gold" (v); "Don Quixote of the Ink Pot" (v); "Gloria Mundi" (v); "The Cruise of the Graduates"; "Sister Liza's Boy" (v); "The Romance of the 'Dorothy' "; "The Fox Hunt"; "The Boat Race" (v); "The Kidnappers" (v); "The

Yellow Covered Days" (v); "Under the Cherry Tree" (v); "The Master's First Day" (v); "When Me an' Jim Went Fishin' " (v).

JACKSON, CHARLES LORING (1847– ?)

Fiction

Gold Point and Other Strange Stories, The [C] (Stratford Co., Boston, 1926, 275 pp., $2.00)

Weird, 12 stories: "The Gold Point"; "The Moth"; "An Uncomfortable Night"; "Mr. Smith"; "The Cube"; "Sister Hannah"; "Linden"; "The Travelling Companion"; "Lot 13"; "An Undiscovered Isle in the Far Sea"; "The Three Nails"; "A Remarkable Case."

JACKSON, SHIRLEY (14 Dec 1919–8 Aug 1965) U.S. novelist and short-story writer. She was born in San Francisco; she later moved east and attended Syracuse U., where she met her husband-to-be, Stanley Edgar Hyman, literary critic and *New Yorker* staff writer. She was a practising amateur witch, specialising in small-scale magic. Her books began with *The Road Through the Wall* (1948). She is especially remembered for her short story "The Lottery," which first appeared in *The New Yorker* in 1948 and has since been often anthologised and on TV.

Fiction

Bird's Nest, The (Farrar Strauss, New York, 1954, 276 pp., $3.50) (M. Joseph, London, 1955, 240 pp., 12/6) (*Lizzie*, Signet, 1957, pa)

Come Along With Me [C] (Viking, New York, 1968, 243 pp., $5.95)

Unfinished novel, 16 stories, and 3 lectures: "Come Along With Me" [novel]; "Janice"; "Tootie in Peonage"; "A Cauliflower in Her Hair"; "I Know What I Love"; "Beautiful Stranger"; "The Summer People"; "Island"; "A Visit"; "The Rock"; "A Day in the Jungle"; "Pajama Party"; "Louisa, Please Come Home"; "The Little House"; "The Bus"; "Experience and Fiction" [lecture]; "The Night We All Had Grippe"; "Biography of a Story" [lecture]; "The Lottery"; "Notes for a Young Writer" [lecture].

Hangsaman [pa] (Ace: K-185, 1964, 191 pp., pa 50¢)

Haunting of Hill House, The (Viking, 1959, 246 pp., $3.95) (M. Joseph, 1960, 205 pp., 15/-) (Popular: K6, 1962, 174 pp., pa 40¢) (FSB:848, 1963, 190 pp., pa 2/6)

The rooms of a house are somewhat strange in dimensions. It is a sort of ghost story, but not in the normal pattern. The characters never become credible; however, the story shows the author's unique sense of the persuasiveness of evil. *Film*: *The Haunting*, M.G.M., 1963, following the story closely; it was highly regarded by P. S. Miller, *ASF*, Jan 1964.

Lizzie See *Bird's Nest, The*

Lottery, The [C] (Farrar Strauss, 1949, 306 pp., $2.75) (Clarke Irwin, Toronto, $3.00) (Gollancz, London, 1950, 306 pp., 10/6) (Lion: 14, 1950, 238 pp., pa 25¢) (Avon: T449, 1960, 222 pp., pa 35¢; S197, 1965, 219 pp., pa 60¢)

Subtitled "The Adventures of James Harris." 25 stories and 1 poem: "The Intoxicated"; "The Demon Lover"; "Like Mother Used to Make"; "Trial by Combat"; "The Villager"; "My Life With R. H. Macy"; "The Witch"; "The Renegade"; "After You, My Dear Alphonse"; "Charles"; "Afternoon in Linen"; "Flower Garden"; "Dorothy and My Grandmother and the Sailors"; "Colloquy"; "Elizabeth"; "A Fine Old Firm"; "The Dummy"; "The Seven Types of Ambiguity"; "Come Dance With Me in Ireland"; "Of Course"; "Pillar of Salt"; "Men With Their Big Shoes"; "The Tooth"; "Got a Letter From Jimmy"; "The Lottery"; "Epilogue" (poem).

Sundial, The (Farrar Strauss, 1958, 245 pp., $3.75) (M. Joseph, 1958, 256 pp., 15/-) (Ace: K-166, 1963, 192 pp., pa 50¢; H-96, 1968, pa 60¢)

The story of the end of the world as seen by a somewhat mad household.

We Have Always Lived in the Castle (Viking, 1962, 224 pp., $3.95) (M. Joseph, 1963, 190 pp., 18/-) (Popular: M2041, 1963, 173 pp., pa 60¢; 60-2137, 1968, pa 60¢) (FSB: 1289, 1965, 158 pp., pa 3/6)

A powerful and ingeniously developed novel of dark powers.

JACKSON, (Sir) THOMAS GRAHAM (21 Dec 1835–7 Nov 1924)
Fiction
Six Ghost Stories [C] (J. Murray, London, 1919, 243 pp., 6/-)
6 stories: "The Lady of Rosemount"; "The Ring"; "A Romance of the Piccadilly Tube"; "The Eve of St. John"; "Pepina"; "The Red House."

JACOB, PIERS ANTHONY DILLINGHAM (6 Aug 1934–) U.S. science fiction author, better known under his pseudonym "Piers Anthony." He was born in England, but had all his schooling in the U.S.A. He served in the Army and had other occupations. He wrote sf for 8 years before his first sale in 1962; he has since had a number of novels and short stories published. His first sf novel was submitted in lieu of a conventional thesis for his B.A. in creative writing. In 1968 his *Sos the Rope* won the $5,000 SF Novel Award sponsored by *F&SF*, Pyramid Books and Kent Productions.
Fiction [as Piers Anthony]
Chthon [pa] (Ballantine: U6107, 1967, 252 pp., pa 75¢)
The hero is doomed to a weird prison world for life, for love of a 'minionette.' It took seven years to write.
Omnivore [pa] (Ballantine: 72014, 1968, 221 pp., pa 75¢)
How three survived on a fungus planet, and why.
Ring, The [with R. Margroff] [pa] (Ace: A-19, 1968, 254 pp., pa 75¢)
The effects of an ingenious method of reforming criminals.
Sos the Rope [pa] (*F&SF*, sr3, July 1968) (Pyramid: X1890, 1968, 157 pp., pa 60¢)
Nomads and "crazies" intrigue in a post-atomic-war society.

JACOBI, CARL (1908–) U.S. author and editor. He was born in Minneapolis and still lives there; he was educated at the U. of Minnesota, studying both geology and writing. The latter became his vocation and he has been an editor on both *Midwest Media* and *Minnesota Quarterly*. A contest-winning story, "Mive," introduced him to readers of *Weird Tales* (Jan 1932). He has since had many stories published in magazines both in the U.S. and abroad, including *Short Stories*, *MacLean's Magazine*, *The Toronto Star*, *Thrilling Mystery* and others in the sf/fantasy field.
Fiction
Portraits in Moonlight [C] (Arkham, Sauk City [Wisc.], 1964, 213 pp., $4.00, jacket–F. Utpatel)
Sf and weird, 14 stories: "Portrait in Moonlight"; "Witches in the Cornfield"; "The Martian Calendar"; "The Corbie Door"; "Tepondicon"; "Incident at Galloping Horse"; "Made in Tanganyika"; "Matthew South and Company"; "Long Voyage"; "The Historian"; "Lodana"; "The Lorenzo Watch"; "The La Prello Paper"; "The Spanish Camera."
Revelations in Black [C] (Arkham, 1947, 272 pp., $3.00, jacket– R. Clyne; 3,082 copies)
21 stories: "Revelations in Black"; "Phantom Brass"; "The Cane"; "The Coach on the Ring" ("The Haunted Ring"); "The Kite" ("Satan's Kite"); "Canal"; "The Satanic Piano"; "The Last Drive"; "The Spectral Pistol" ("The Phantom Pistol"); "Sagasta's Last"; "The Tomb From Beyond"; "The Digging at Pistol Key"; "Moss Island"; "Carnaby's Fish"; "The King and the Knave" ("The Devil Deals"); "Cosmic Teletype"; "A Pair of Swords"; "A Study in Darkness" ("Spawn of Blackness"); "Mive"; "The Writing on the Wall" ("The Cosmic Doodler"); "The Face in the Wind."

JACOBS, W(ILLIAM) W(YMARK) (8 Sep 1863–1 Sep 1943) English short-story writer. Educated in private schools, he worked in the Civil Service. Upon the success of his first book, *Many Cargoes* (1896), he began to write full time and became noted for his lusty sea stories. His most important weird story is the spine-chilling "The Monkey's Paw," a regular reprint in weird anthologies. Collections of possible fantasy interest besides those below include *Odd Craft* (Scribner, 1903) and *Short Cruises* (Scribner, 1907).
Fiction
Lady of the Barge, The [C] (Dodd, New York, 1902, 300 pp., illus., $2.00)
Fantasy, 12 stories: "Adulteration Act"; "Bill's Paper Chase";

"Captain Rogers"; "Cupboard Love"; "Golden Venture"; "In the Library"; "The Lady of the Barge"; "Mixed Proposal"; "The Monkey's Paw"; "Three at Table"; "Tiger's Skin"; "The Well."
Night Watches [C] (Scribner, New York, 1914, 247 pp., illus., $2.00)
Fantasy, 10 stories: "Back to Back"; "Easy Money"; "His Other Self"; "Keeping Watch"; "Stepping Backwards"; "Three Sisters"; "The Understudy"; "The Unknown"; "The Vigil"; "The Weaker Vessel."

JAEGER, C(YRIL) K(AREL) British writer, born in Bradford, Yorkshire. He also wrote *Angels on Horseback* (1940).
Fiction
Man in the Top Hat, The (Grey Walls, London, 1949, 264 pp., 10/6)
Considered to be a somewhat silly fantasy.

JAKES, JOHN (WILLIAM) (31 Mar 1932–) U.S. author, born in Chicago. He began writing fantasy in high school and persisted at it until *The Magazine of Fantasy and Science Fiction* bought his first story during his initial year at college. He has now sold over 200 stories to many magazines, including *Playboy*, *Manhunt*, and *Saint Mystery*, as well as the sf magazines. His novels include mysteries, westerns and historicals, under his own name and pen names. He has worked for Abbott Laboratories. He now lives in Dayton, Ohio.
Series
Brak the Barbarian. All in *Fan*: "Devils in the Walls" (May 1963); "Witch of the Four Winds" (sr2, Nov 1963); "When the Idols Walked" (sr2, Aug 1964); "The Girl in the Gem" (Jan 1965); "The Pillars of Chambalor" (Mar 1965); "The Silk of Shaitan" (Apr 1965). The last two form chapters in *Brak the Barbarian*.
Fiction
Brak the Barbarian [pa] (Avon: S363, 1968, 173 pp., pa 60¢)
Adventures of Brak in the Courts of the Conjurer and with the Ghosts of Stone, among others, on his way to fabled Khurdisan.
When the Star Kings Die [pa] (Ace: G-656, 1967, 160 pp., pa 50¢)
In the fight against deathless overlords their medical recuperation centre is captured.

JAMES, HENRY (15 Apr 1843–28 Feb 1916) U.S. author. However, he spent most of his life in England and Europe. He retained his American citizenship until July 1915 when he became a British subject in protest against America's failure to enter the war. Once termed the novelist who wrote like a psychologist, he had a style meticulously cautious and precise, using long sentences; he left a rich literary legacy. His indirect way of approaching characters and action was eminently suited to the ghost field. H. Montgomery Hyde's *Henry James at Home* (Methuen, 1968, 36/-), through access to family papers and letters, etc., throws new light on the personality of James and his wide circle of friends.
Fiction [Incomplete—other titles in Bleiler *Checklist*]
Ghostly Tales of Henry James, The [C] (Editor–Leon Edel, Rutgers Univ. Press, New Brunswick [N.J.], 1948, 766 pp., $5.00) (Grosset 'Universal': VL-161, 1963, 433 pp., pa $2.25 [10 stories marked †])
18 stories and essay "Henry James's Ghost," L. Edel: "The Romance of Certain Old Clothes"†; "De Grey: A Romance"†; "The Last of the Valerii"; "The Ghostly Rental"†; "Sir Edmund Orme"†; "Nona Vincent"; "The Private Life"; "Sir Dominick Ferrand"; "Owen Wingrave"†; "The Altar of the Dead"; "The Friends of the Friends"† (*F&SF*, July 1953); "The Turn of the Screw"†; "The Real Right Thing"†; "The Great Good Place"; "Maud-Evelyn"; "The Third Person"†; "The Jolly Corner"†.
Short Stories of Henry James, The [C] (Random House, New York, 1945, 644 pp., $3.00) (Random, Toronto, $4.00) (Modern Library, New York, 1948, 644 pp., $2.45) (Random, Toronto, $2.95)
17 stories, including many of this writer's ghost stories: "The Altar of the Dead"; "The Beast in the Jungle"; "The Birthplace"; "Brooksmith"; "A Bundle of Letters"; " 'Europe' "; "Four Meet-

ings"; "The Great Good Place"; "The Jolly Corner"; "The Liar"; "Louisa Pallant"; "The Middle Years"; "Mrs. Medwin"; "The Pupil"; "The Real Thing"; "The Tone of Time"; "The Tree of Knowledge."

Turn of the Screw, The (in *Two Magics* [James], Macmillan, New York & London, 1898) (Penguin, 1946, pa) (Dell: 800, 1954, 121 pp., pa 25¢; D181, 1957, pa 25¢) (World Distributors: W937, 1960, 143 pp., pa 2/6) (*Otra vuelta de tuerca* [Argentine—Spanish], Emecé, ?) (*The Turn of the Screw & The Aspern Papers*, Dent 'Everyman 1012,' 1964, 299 pp., pa 6/-) (in many anthologies, including *Treasury of Great Short Stories* [Peck], 1965, pa) (Oxford, Canada, 1967, 146 pp., $1.50, pa 95¢) (F. Watts, New York, 1967, quarto, 182 pp., $6.95; lib. $4.95) (*The Turn of the Screw & Other Stories*, Scholastic: TK650, 1966, 316 pp., pa 60¢) (Airmont: CL155, 1967, 127 pp., pa 50¢) (*The Turn of the Screw & Daisy Miller*, Lancer: 13-433, 1968, 284 pp., pa 60¢)

The Oxford and Watts editions have a critical essay by Robert Heilman and notes and questions prepared by Arthur Livingston. This is one of the most widely read American macabre stories: the Victorian tale of a governess and two innocent children who, she alleges, are in danger of possession by the ghosts of a a dead servant and his dead love. *Play and film:* The story was the basis of W. Archibald's play *The Innocents* (Coward McCann, 1950), and was filmed under this title about 1961 in Britain. Produced by Jack Clayton, the film starred Deborah Kerr with Pamela Franklin and Martin Stephens as the children, and was most striking and effective.

JAMES, JOHN
Fiction
Votan (Cassell, London, 1966, 233 pp., 21/-) (Longmans, Toronto, $4.75) (New American Library, New York, 1967, vi+233 pp., $5.00)

Based on German mythology—an earthy and humorous fantasy of an adventurer in 2nd century Germany.

JAMES, M(ONTAGU) R(HODES) (1 Aug 1862–12 June 1936) Noted British ghost story writer. Brilliant from his early years, he developed a keen interest in classical archaeology and took part in excavations in Cyprus. At Cambridge he became Dean of King's College and later its provost. He was director of the FitzWilliam Museum at Cambridge for 15 years, securing many precious manuscripts for it. In 1918 he was given the Crown appointment of Provost of Eton College. His short story "Casting the Runes" was filmed by Columbia in Britain in 1958 as *Curse of the Demon*; directed by Jacques Tourneur and starring Dana Andrews and Peggy Cummins, it is considered to be a fine production. A selection of James' ghost stories appeared as an Armed Services edition.
Fiction
Best Ghost Stories of M. R. James, The [C] (World 'Tower Book,' Cleveland, 1944, 319 pp., 49¢; 1946, 49¢)

23 stories: "Casting the Runes"; "Canon Alberic's Scrap-Book"; "Lost Hearts"; "The Mezzotint"; "The Ash-Tree"; "Number 13"; "Martin's Close"; "Two Doctors"; "The Haunted Doll's House"; "A View From the Hill"; "A Warning to the Curious"; "Rats"; "Wailing Well"; "The Treasure of Abbot Thomas"; "A School Story"; "The Rose Garden"; "Count Magnus"; " 'Oh, Whistle and I'll Come to You, My Lad' "; "The Residence at Whitminster"; "The Diary of Mr. Poynter"; "A Neighbor's Landmark"; "The Tractate Middoth"; "Stories I Have Tried to Write."
Collected Ghost Stories of M. R. James, The [C] (Arnold, London, 1931, 647 pp., 8/6; 1943; 1944; 1947, 647 pp., 7/6) (Longmans Green, New York, 1931, $3.00)

31 stories from his smaller collections, running in order: *Ghost Stories of an Antiquary*, *More Ghost Stories of an Antiquary*, *A Thin Ghost*, *A Warning to the Curious*; plus: "There Was a Man Who Dwelt by a Churchyard"; "Rats"; "After Dark on the Playing Fields"; "Wailing Well"; "Stories I Have Tried to Write."
Five Jars, The [C] (Arnold, 1922, 172 pp., 6/-)

Weird, 8 stories: "The Discovery"; "The First Jar"; "The Second Jar"; "The Small People"; "Danger to the Jars"; "The Cat, Wag, Slim and Others"; "The Bat Ball"; "Wag at Home."

Ghost Stories of an Antiquary [C] (Arnold, 1904, 270 pp., illus., 6/-; 1910; 1917, 2/-; 1920) (Penguin: 91, 1937, 256 pp., pa; 1959, 153 pp., pa 2/6; 1960, pa 2/6) (Pan: 266, 1953, 159 pp., pa 2/-)

8 stories: "Canon Alberic's Scrap-Book"; "Lost Hearts"; "The Mezzotint"; "The Ash-Tree"; "Number 13"; "Count Magnus"; " 'Oh, Whistle and I'll Come to You, My Lad' "; "The Treasure of Abbot Thomas."
More Ghost Stories of an Antiquary [C] (Arnold, 1911, 282 pp., 6/-; 1919, 274 pp., 5/-; 1920; 1924, 274 pp.; 1927, 5/-) (Pan: 359, 1955, 160 pp., pa 2/-) (Penguin: 1347, 1959, 152 pp., pa 2/6)

7 stories: "A School Story"; "The Rose Garden"; "The Tractate Middoth"; "Casting the Runes"; "The Stalls of Barchester Cathedral"; "Martin's Close"; "Mr. Humphreys and His Inheritance."
Selected Ghost Stories of M. R. James [C] [pa] (Armed: 0-28, 1944, 352 pp., pa)

20 stories: "Casting the Runes"; "Canon Alberic's Scrap-Book"; "Lost Hearts"; "The Mezzotint"; "The Ash-Tree"; "Number 13"; "Martin's Close"; "The Haunted Dolls' House"; "A Warning to the Curious"; "Rats"; "Wailing Well"; "The Treasure of Abbot Thomas"; "A School Story"; "The Rose Garden"; "Count Magnus"; " 'Oh, Whistle and I'll Come to You, My Lad' "; "Residence at Whitminster"; "The Diary of Mr. Poynter"; "A Neighbour's Landmark"; "The Tractate Middoth."
Thin Ghost and Others, A [C] (Arnold, 1919, 152 pp., 7/6; 1920, 152 pp.; 1925, 152 pp.) (Longmans Green, 1919)

5 stories: "The Residence at Whitminster"; "The Diary of Mr. Poynter"; "An Episode of Cathedral History"; "The Story of a Disappearance and an Appearance"; "Two Doctors."
Warning to the Curious and Other Ghost Stories, A [C] (Arnold, 1925, 200 pp., 5/-; 1927, 5/-)

6 stories: "The Haunted Dolls' House"; "The Uncommon Prayer-Book"; "A Neighbour's Landmark"; "A View From a Hill"; "A Warning to the Curious"; "An Evening's Entertainment."

JAMESON, MALCOLM (21 Dec 1891–16 Apr 1945) U.S. naval officer and science fiction author. He died after an eight-year writing career which had been initiated when cancer of the throat forced him to give up a more active life. His health was severely bad throughout these years, but he nevertheless left a legacy of good fiction. His "Bullard" series grew out of his own experiences as an officer in the U.S. Navy from 1916 till his retirement in 1927; he later had much to do with the development of modern naval ordnance. He first appeared in sf with "Eviction by Isotherm" (*ASF*, Aug 1938). Besides his stories in *ASF* he had a number in *Unknown* and other magazines.
Series
Bullard. Space navy. All in *ASF*: "Admiral's Inspection" (Apr 1940); "White Mutiny" (Oct 1940); "Slacker's Paradise" (Apr 1941); "Devil's Powder" (June 1941); "Bullard Reflects" (Dec 1941); "Brimstone Bill" (July 1942); "The Bureaucrat" (Apr 1944); "Orders" (Dec 1945). Most appear in *Bullard of the Space Patrol*.
Fiction
Atomic Bomb [pa] ("The Giant Atom," *SS*, Win 1944) (Bond-Charteris, 1945, 128 pp., pa 25¢) ([Swedish], *JVM*: 38–47, 1945)

An atomic fire gets out of control. The paperback is quite scarce.
Bullard of the Space Patrol [Editor—Andre Norton] [C] (World, Cleveland, 1951, 255 pp., $2.50; 1955 [Junior Library], 206 pp., $1.00, jacket—V. Finlay)

First ed.: 7 stories of the "Bullard" series, omitting "Devil's Powder" and with "Slacker's Paradise" retitled "Blockade Runner." Second ed.: 6 stories, omitting also "The Bureaucrat."
Tarnished Utopia [pa] (*SS*, Mar 1943) (Galaxy SF Novel: 27, 1956, 126 pp., pa 35¢)

A man and a girl sleep into a future era and fight a despotic ruler.

JAMESON, (MARGARET) STORM (1897–) Pseudonym of Mrs. Guy Chapman.

Fiction [Incomplete—other titles in Bleiler *Checklist*]
Moment of Truth, The (Macmillan, London, 1949, 176 pp., 7/6; [U.S.] $2.50) (Canada, $2.25)

A future England under Communist domination.

JANIFER, LAURENCE M(ARK) (17 Mar 1933–) U.S. author and editor. This is the writing name for Larry Mark Harris. The 'Janifer' name is of Polish origin, and was changed by Harris' paternal grandfather on arriving in the U.S.A. Laurence Janifer was an editor with the Scott Meredith Literary Agency 1952-57 and has been a free-lance writer ever since. He has written in collaboration with Randall Garrett under the pseudonym Mark Phillips.
Fiction
Brain Twister [by Mark Phillips] [pa] See GARRETT, R. (co-author)
Bloodworld [pa] See *You Sane Men*
Impossible? [C] [pa] (Belmont: B50-810, 1968, 159 pp., pa 50¢)

16 stories, with introduction "But First" by the author: "Charley de Milo"; "The Question" [with D. Westlake]; "The Man Who Played to Lose"; "Fire Sale"; "Obey That Impulse!"; "Lost in Translation"; "Expatriate"; "Excerpts From the Galactic Almanack—Music"; "Wizard" "Elementary" [with Michael Kurland]; "Sight Gag"; "Sword of Flowers"; "Three Excerpts"; "Replace That Horse"; "In the Bag"; "Love Story."
Impossibles, The [by Mark Phillips] [pa] See GARRETT, R. (co-author)
Pagan Passions [by L. M. Harris & R. Garrett] [pa] See GARRETT, R. (co-author)
Piece of Martin Cann, A [pa] (Belmont: B50-811, 1968, 141 pp., pa 50¢)

The medical and mental treatment of a patient, delving into his thought processes. (One reviewer considers Brunner's *The Whole Man* to be of wider theme and to have better possibilities.)
Slave Planet [pa] (Pyramid: F840, 1963, 142 pp., pa 40¢)

Galactic agencies fight each other to free a native population.
Supermind [by Mark Phillips] [pa] See GARRETT, R. (co-author)
Target: Terra [with J. Treibich] [pa] (Ace: H-91, 1968, 104 pp., pa 60¢; with *Proxima Project*)

Wacky story of the misadventures of a satellite crew and how there may, or may not, have been a Third World War.
Wonder War, The [pa] (Pyramid: F863, 1964, 128 pp., pa 40¢)

The "Overdogs" endeavour to control galactic civilization, and get involved in a struggle on an earthlike planet.
You Sane Men [pa] (Lancer: 72-789, 1965, 159 pp., pa 50¢) (*Bloodworld*, Lancer: 73-752, 1968, 159 pp., pa 60¢)

Study of a man from a society that is insane by the standards of other worlds.
Anthology
Masters' Choice (Simon & Schuster, New York, 1966, 350 pp., $5.95) (Jenkins, London, 1968, 327 pp., 25/-) (*Masters' Choice 1*, Tandem: PB380, 1968, 175 pp., pa 3/6 [first 10 stories]; *Masters' Choice 2*, Tandem: PB381, 1968, 160 pp., pa 3/6 [remaining 8 stories])

18 stories and preface: "Liar!" I. Asimov; "The Veldt," R. Bradbury; "It's a *Good* Life," J. Bixby; "The Golem," A. Davidson; "Helen O'Loy," L. del Rey; "The Cold Equations," T. Godwin; "The Dwindling Sphere," W. M. Hawkins; "Requiem," R. Heinlein; "Theory of Rocketry," C. M. Kornbluth; "Don't Look Now," H. Kuttner; "Seven-Day Terror," R. A. Lafferty; "Coming Attraction," F. Leiber; "Politics," M. Leinster; "Memento Homo," W. M. Miller; "The Bright Illusion," C. L. Moore; "And Now the News," T. Sturgeon; "The Custodian," Wm. Tenn; "The New Accelerator," H. G. Wells.

JANVIER, THOMAS ALLIBONE (16 July 1849–18 June 1913) American journalist and writer, born in Philadelphia. From 1871-1880 he was a journalist with a number of Philadelphia papers. His wife was the author and painter Catharine Ann Drinker. He used much of the old and quaint as background for his writings.
Fiction [Incomplete—other titles in Bleiler *Checklist*]
In Great Waters [C] (Harper, New York, 1901, 222 pp.)

Fantasy, 4 stories: "The Wraith of the Zuyder Zee"; "A Duluth Tragedy"; "The Death-Fires of Les Martiques"; "A Sea Upcast."

JARDINE, JACK OWEN (10 Oct 1931–) U.S. radio creative director and free-lance writer. He wrote a paperback series under the pseudonym "Larry Maddock," and combined with his former wife Julie Ann Jardine to write two novels under the pseudonym "Howard L. Cory."
Series
Agent of T.E.R.R.A. [as Larry Maddock]. Ace paperbacks: *The Flying Saucer Gambit*; *The Golden Goddess Gambit*; *The Emerald Elephant Gambit*.
Fiction
Emerald Elephant Gambit, The [as Larry Maddock] [pa] (Ace: G-644, 1967, 158 pp., pa 50¢)

Third of T.E.R.R.A. series—'Empire' time-travel intriguers in the Indus civilization in 1481 B.C.
Flying Saucer Gambit, The [as Larry Maddock] [pa] (Ace: G-605, 1966, 159 pp., pa 50¢)

First of T.E.R.R.A. series—Hannibal Fortune and his alien assistant save Earth from the tyranny of 'Empire.'
Golden Goddess Gambit, The [as Larry Maddock] [pa] (Ace: G-620, 1967, 158 pp., pa 50¢)

Second of T.E.R.R.A. series—Hannibal Fortune travels back to 1800 B.C. to thwart a renegade's attempt to create a civilization before its due time.
Mind Monster, The [with J. A. Jardine, as Howard L. Cory] [pa] (Ace: G-602, 1966, 146 pp., pa 50¢ [with *The Unteleported Man*])

Adventures of a Terran who becomes a ruler on an alien world.
Sword of Lankor, The [with J. A. Jardine, as Howard L. Cory] [pa] (Ace: F-373, 1966, 158 pp., pa 40¢)

Fantastic adventure on an alien planet during its Bronze Age.

JARDINE, JULIE ANN (6 Feb 1926–)
Fiction
Mind Monsters, The [as H. L. Cory] See JARDINE, J. O. (co-author)
Sword of Lankor, The [as H. L. Cory] See JARDINE, J. O. (co-author)

JAVOR, F. A.
Fiction
Rim-World Legacy, The [pa] (Signet: P3183, 1967, 144 pp., pa 60¢)

Interstellar mystery thriller.

JAY, MEL
Fiction
Orbit One See FANTHORPE, R. L.

JENKINS, ALAN C(HARLES)
Anthology
Thin Air: An Anthology of Ghost Stories (Blackie, London, 1966, 412 pp., 15/-; 1967, 15/-)

30 stories and 1½-p. compiler's intro.: "The Treasure of Abbot Thomas," M. R. James; "Running Wolf," Algernon Blackwood; "The Ghost of Glam," Andrew Lang; "The Haunted Mosque," S. L. Sadhu; "The Canterville Ghost," Oscar Wilde; "The Whistling Ghosts," Sir Arthur Grimble; "The Ghost in the Ring," Elliott O'Donnell; "A Phantom of the Seas," Warren Armstrong; "The Unforgiving Garden," Frances Hayley Bell; "The Monkey's Paw," W. W. Jacobs; "The Inexperienced Ghost," H. G. Wells; "The Ghost of a Saint," W. H. Barrett; "My Own True Ghost Story," Rudyard Kipling; "The Death Watch," Charles Downing; "The Open Window," Saki (H. H. Munro); "An Apparition," Guy de Maupassant; "The Spectre Bridegroom," Washington Irving; "Sambo," W. F. Harvey; "William Wilson," Edgar Allan Poe; "The Ghost Ship," Richard Middleton; "A Little Ghost," Hugh Walpole; "The Signalman," Charles Dickens; "The House with the Brick-Kiln," E. F. Benson; "A Pair of Hands," Sir Arthur Quiller-Couch; "Phantas," Oliver Onions; "The Coat," A. E. D. Smith; "The Sto-

ry of Admetus," Roger Lancelyn Green; "The Stranger," Ambrose Bierce; "The Haunted Forest," Geoffrey Palmer & Noel Lloyd; "Full Fathom Five," Alexander Woolcott.

JENKINS, WILL(IAM) F(ITZGERALD) (16 June 1896–) U.S. author. Often called "the dean of science fiction," he is better known in the sf field by his pseudonym "Murray Leinster." No other writer has been in the sf field so long; he started in 1919 a month or so before the late R. K. Cummings, and his works still appear after half a century. A Virginian born in Norfolk, he has been writing since his teens. At 17 he sold a number of stories to *Smart Set*, and when 21 he became a complete free lance, and has been one ever since except for two periods in the World Wars when he served with the Army. He has made a successful living, selling well over a thousand stories and numerous books and being included in many anthologies. Much of his work is not sf, and in fact he was well established in other fields before his "The Runaway Skyscraper" appeared in *Argosy* (22 Feb, 1919; reprinted in *AS*, June 1926, Feb 1966). Through the years he has appeared in practically all the sf magazines.

Jenkins usually writes a very workmanlike story, easy to read, with ordinary people applying themselves to remove apparently insurmountable difficulties. At times his stories have reached the status of classics; one such, "The Mad Planet," was later revised with its sequels into the book *Forgotten Planet*. Stories of particular interest include: "Dead City" (*TWS*, Sum 1946; *FSM*, July 1953; in *Twists in Time* [Leinster], 1960, pa); "Doomsday Deferred" [as Jenkins] (*SEP*, 24 Sep 1949; *Best SF Stories, 1950* [Bleiler & Dikty]; *SEP Fantasy Stories* [Bles], 1951, pa); "First Contact," (*ASF*, May 1945; many anthologies) [the classic of humanity meeting an alien race in space]; "Symbiosis' [as Jenkins] (*Collier's*, 14 June 1947); "Things Pass By" (*TWS*, Sum 1945; *FSM*, Win 1955); "The Other World" (*SS*, Nov 1949; *6 Great Short Novels of SF* [Conklin], 1954, pa; [German], *UZ*: 92, 1957). He generally uses the name Jenkins in the non-sf magazines.

He won the 1956 Hugo for best novelette with "Exploration Team" (*ASF*, Mar 1956; part of *Colonial Survey* [Leinster], 1957; in *The Hugo Winners* [Asimov], 1962). The entire Fall 1968 issue of *Most Thrilling SF* was taken up by his novels "Long Ago, Far Away" (see *Four From Planet 5*) and "Planet of Dread" (*Fan*, May 1962). Sam Moskowitz's profile of Jenkins was published in *AS*, Dec 1961, and forms a chapter in Moskowitz's *Seekers of Tomorrow* (1966).

Series [as Murray Leinster unless otherwise stated]
Burl. "The Mad Planet"; "The Red Dust"; "Nightmare Planet." [See *Forgotten Planet*.]
Gregory, Bud [by William Fitzgerald]. All in *TWS*: "The Gregory Circle" (Apr 1947); "The Nameless Something" (June 1947); "The Deadly Dust" (Aug 1947); "The Seven Temporary Moons" (Feb 1948). The first three were revised as *Out of This World*.
Kenmore, Joe. Juvenile—a lad going into space: *Space Platform*; *Space Tug*; *City on the Moon*.
Master of Darkness. All in *Arg*: "The Darkness on Fifth Avenue" (30 Nov 1929; *Fan*, Mar 1962; *Startling Mystery*, Sum 1967); "The City of the Blind" (28 Dec 1929); "The Storm That Had to Be Stopped" (1 Mar 1930); "The Man Who Put Out the Sun" (14 June 1930).
Med Service. Calhoun and the being Murgatroyd. "Ribbon in the Sky" (*ASF*, June 1957); "Med Service" (*ASF*, Aug 1957) (*The Mutant Weapon*); "The Grandfathers' War" (*ASF*, Oct 1957); "Pariah Planet" (*AS*, July 1961) (*This World Is Taboo*); "The Hate Disease" (*ASF*, Aug 1963); "Med Ship Man" (*GSF*, Oct 1963); "Plague on Kryder II" (*ASF*, Dec 1964); "Quarantine World" (*ASF*, Nov 1966). Published in books as noted, with the 3rd, 5th (retitled) and 6th in *Doctor to the Stars*, and the first and the last two in *S.O.S. From Three Worlds*.
Rendell, Kim. All in *TWS*: "The Disciplinary Circuit" (Win 1946); "The Manless Worlds" (Feb 1947); "The Boomerang Circuit" (June 1947). Rewritten as *The Last Space Ship*.
Fiction [as Murray Leinster unless otherwise stated]
Aliens, The [C] [pa] (Berkley: G-410, 1960, 144 pp., pa 35¢;

F1139, 1965, pa 50¢)
Sf, 5 stories: "The Aliens"; "Fugitive From Space"; "Anthropological Note"; "Skit-Tree Planet"; "Thing From the Sky" [new].
Black Galaxy, The [pa] (*SS*, Mar 1949) (Galaxy SF Novel: 20, 1954, 127 pp., pa 35¢) (*Die schwarze Galaxis*, [German], *UG*: 63, 1957; *TE*: 84, 1966) (*La galaxie noire* [French], Ed. Satellite Club Satellite No. 3, 1958)
Sequel to "The Story of Rod Cantrell" (*SS*, Jan 1949); the hero fights galactic marauders.
Brain-Stealers, The [pa] ("The Man in the Iron Cap," *SS*, Nov 1947) (Ace: D-79, 1954, 139 pp., pa 35¢; with *Atta*) (Badger: SF33, 1960, 141 pp., pa 2/-) (*Vampire aus dem All* [German], *T*: 200, 1961) (*Les voleurs de cerveaux* [French], Fleuve Noir: A66, 1956, pa)
One man's great fight against alien creatures who control Earthmen by telepathy.
Checkpoint Lambda [pa] ("Stopover in Space," *AS*, sr2, June 1966) (Berkley: F1263, 1967, 143 pp., pa 50¢) (in *Murray Leinster Omnibus*, 1968)
Space pirates invade a stationary ship used as a navigational checkpoint, with comets imminent.
City on the Moon (Avalon, New York, 1957, 224 pp., $2.75) (Ace: D-277, 1958, 151 pp., 35¢; with *Men on the Moon*) (*Die Mondstadt* [German], *UK*: 23, 1957; *TE*: 126, 1967) (*La ciudad de la Luna* [Spanish], Cenit: 32, 1962, pa) (*La citta sulla Luna* [Italian], Fantascienza: 5, 1962, pa)
Juvenile, third of the Joe Kenmore series (see *Space Platform*). Details of lunar life are ingenious but plot is rather inadequate.
Colonial Survey (Gnome, New York, 1956, 185 pp., $3.00) (*The Planet Explorer*, Avon: T202, 1957, 171 pp., pa 35¢) (*Bordman greift ein* and *Abenteuer auf Loren II* [German], *UZ*: 108 & 110, 1958; *Der Planeteninspektor*, Heyne: 3098, 1967, pa) (*Constanti solare* [Italian], *Urania*: 182, 1958)
The following four stories from *ASF* rewritten into continuity: "Solar Constant" ("Critical Difference," July 1956); "Sand Doom" (Dec 1955); "Combat Team" ("Exploration Team," Mar 1956); "The Swamp Was Upside Down" (Sep 1956). The protagonists of the original stories are merged into one man, Bordman of "Sand Doom." "Exploration Team" won the 1956 Hugo for best novelette.
Creatures of the Abyss [pa] (Berkley: G-549, 1961, 143 pp., pa 35¢) (*Die Lauscher in der Tiefe* [German], *T*: 490, 1967)
Beings at the bottom of the Luzon Deep try to take over the world.
Destroy the U.S.A. See *Murder of the U.S.A., The*
Doctor to the Stars [C] [pa] (Pyramid: F987, 1964, 176 pp., pa 50¢) (*Un dottore fra le stelle* [Italian], Cosmo: 154, 1964) (*Der Weltraumarzt auf dem Kriegspfad* [German], *T*: 405, 1965)
Three of the "Med Service" series: "The Grandfathers' War"; "Tallien Three" ("The Hate Disease"); "Med Ship Man."
Duplicators, The [pa] ("Lord of the Uffts," *Worlds of Tomorrow*, Feb 1964) —enlarged: (Ace: F-275, 1964, 143 pp., pa 40¢; with *No Truce With Terra*) (*La terra degli Uffts* [Italian], *Urania*: 339, 1964) (*Die Revolution der Uffts* [German], *T*: 426, 1965)
Adventure story, with the galactic economy in danger of ruin by matter duplicators.
Fight for Life [pa] ("The Laws of Chance," *SS*, Mar 1947; *FSM*, Spr 1954) (Crestwood 'Prize 10,' nd, 118 pp., pa 25¢) (*Gesetz des Zufalls* [German], *UZ*: 125, 1958; *TE*: 154, 1967)
The laws of probability are used to their utmost limits in making weapons to rid the U.S.A. of an invader.
Forgotten Planet, The (Gnome, 1954, 177 pp., $2.50) (*Il pianeta dimenticato* [Italian], *Urania*: 88, 1955) (Ace: D-146, 1956, 175 pp., pa 35¢ [with *Contraband Rocket*]; D-528, 1961, pa 35¢) (*Der vergessene Planet* [German], *UG*: 62, 1956; *TE*: 68, 1965) (*Den Glemte Planet* [Danish], Skrifola: F12, 1958, pa) (*La planète oubliee* [French], Ditis, 1960)
A connected rewriting of the "Burl" series: "The Mad Planet" (*Arg*, 12 June 1920; *AS*, Nov 1926; *Tales of Wonder*, Spr 1939; *FN*, Nov 1948); "The Red Dust" (*Arg*, 2 Apr 1921; *AS*, Jan 1927; *Tales of Wonder*, Win 1939; *FN*, May 1949); "Nightmare Planet" (*SF Plus*, June 1953). The first two stories were originally set

30,000 years in Earth's future (and stand exceedingly well on their own); for the book the locale was made an alien planet which was originally sterile but then seeded with terrestrial life. The story follows the fight to live of the distant descendants of survivors of a space ship crash.

Four From Planet 5 [pa] ("Long Ago, Far Away," *AS*, Sep 1959; *Most Thrilling SF*, July 1968) (Gold Medal: s937, 1959, 160 pp., pa 35¢; K1397, 1964, pa 40¢) (*Die Kinder vom fünften Planeten* [German], *TS*: 70, 1963) (*Cuatro en el planeta cinco* [Spanish], Nebula: 96, 1964, pa)

Four children from the Fifth Planet come from the distant past (when their world is about to disintegrate) to Earth as advance scouts.

Gateway to Elsewhere [pa] ("Journey to Barkut," *Fantasy Book*, sr2 [unfinished], No. 7, 1950; *SS*, Jan 1952) (Ace: D-53, 1954, 139 pp., pa 35¢; with *Weapon Shops of Isher*) (*Guerra a los Djinns* [Spanish], Nebula: 29, 1956, pa)

Enjoyable fantastic adventure set in the land of the djinns.

Get Off My World [C] [pa] (Belmont: B50-676, 1966, 157 pp., pa 50¢)

3 sf novelettes: "Second Landing" (*TWS*, Win 1954); "White Spot" (*SS*, Sum 1955); "Planet of Sand" (*FFM*, Feb 1948).

Greks Bring Gifts, The [pa] (Macfadden: 50-224, 1964, 143 pp., pa 50¢; 50-418, 1968, pa 50¢)

The apparently altruistic Greks come to Earth.

Invaders of Space [pa] (Berkley: F1022, 1964, 144 pp., pa 50¢) (*Freibeuter des Alls* [German], *UZ*: 465, 1965) (*L'astronef pirate* [French], Fleuve Noir: A314, 1967, pa) (Tandem: T201, 1968, 141 pp., pa 3/6) (in *Murray Leinster Omnibus*, 1968)

Routine space-opera.

Land of the Giants [pa] (Pyramid: X1846, 1968, 156 pp., pa 60¢)

Based on the U.S. ABC TV series created and produced by Irwin Allen. A supersonic flight ends up on a monstrous world with 70-foot human giants.

Last Space Ship, The (Fell, New York, 1949, 239 pp., $2.50) (Kemsley: CT404, 1952, 190 pp., pa 1/6) (Galaxy SF Novel: 25, 1955, 126 pp., pa 35¢) (*Le dernier astronef* [French], Hachette: Le RF, 1953) (*Das letzte Raumschiff* [German], *UG*: 79, 1958; *TE*: 131, 1967) (*L'ultima astronave* [Italian], *Urania*: 307, 1963)

Connected rewrite of the "Kim Rendell" series; a space-opera with the hero and girl using matter transmitters to fight the tyranny of a decadent civilization.

Men Into Space [pa] (Berkley: G461, 1960, 142 pp., pa 35¢)

Based on the TV series; 6 episodes follow Ed McCauley from a young first lieutenant riding an Aerobee into space until he is a colonel leading the First Martian Expedition.

Miners in the Sky [pa] (Avon: G1310, 1967, 127 pp., 50¢)

The fight to survive among the lawless mining asteroids.

Monster From Earth's End, The [pa] (Gold Medal: s832, 1959, 176 pp., pa 35¢) (Muller: GM433, 1960, 159 pp., pa 2/-) (*L'incubo sul fondo* [Italian], *Urania*: 294, 1962) (*Monster vom Ende der Welt* [German], *UZ*: 549, 1967)

An invisible monster from Antarctica gets loose in a U.S. advance supply base, and turmoil reigns.

Monsters and Such [C] [pa] (Avon: T345, 1959, 174 pp., pa 35¢)

Sf, 7 stories: "The Lonely Planet"; "If You Was a Moklin"; "The Castaway"; "Proxima Centauri"; "Nobody Saw the Ship"; "The Trans-Human"; "De Profundis."

Murder Madness (*ASF*, sr4, May 1930) (Brewer Warren, Chicago, 1931, 298 pp., $2.00) (FPCI, Los Angeles, 1949, 298 pp., $2.75) (in *Quadratic* [double binding], see CRAWFORD, W. L.)

Not strictly sf. A would-be tyrant uses a madness-inducing drug to dominate civilization. The FPCI ed. is a photolith copy of the 1931 ed.

Murder of the U.S.A., The [as Will F. Jenkins] (Crown, New York, 1946, 172 pp., $2.00) (*Destroy the U.S.A.*, Ambassador, Toronto, 1946, $2.35; Newsstand: 141, 1950, 156 pp., pa 25¢) (Quinn: H62, 1947, 127 pp., pa 25¢) (*Assassinat des Etats-Unis* [French], Hachette: Le RF, 1951) (*Atentado a los EE.UU.* [Spanish], Nebula: 28, 1956, pa)

Very credible story of atomic missile attack on the U.S.A., and detective work to discover the aggressor. First published in *Argosy*.

Murray Leinster Omnibus, A [C] (Sidgwick Jackson, London, 1968, 160 + 144 + 143 pp., 30/-)

3 novels: *Operation Terror*; *Checkpoint Lambda*; *Invaders of Space*.

Mutant Weapon, The [pa] ("Med Service," *ASF*, Aug 1957) (Ace: D-403, 1959, 93 pp., pa 35¢; with *The Pirates of Zan* [Leinster]) (*Der Weltraumarzt* [German], *TS*: 49, 1962)

Second of the "Med Service" series. Calhoun and the being Murgatroyd help a planet's surviving colonists expel murderous invaders.

Operation: Outer Space (Fantasy, Reading, 1954, 208 pp., $3.00; 'Golden SF Library,' 1957, pa $1.00) (Grayson, London, 1957, 190 pp., 10/6) (Signet: S1346, 1957, 160 pp., pa 35¢) (*Al di la del sole* [Italian], *Cosmo*: 6, 1957) (*Operation espace* [French], Le Fleuve Noir: A120, 1958, pa) (*Safari Mellem Stjerner* [Danish], Skrifola: P14, 1958, pa) (*Fernsehstudio Galaxis* [German], *UG*: 83, 1958; *TE*: 137, 1967)

Exploration of outer space; the first flight outside the Solar System.

Operation Terror [pa] (Berkley: F694, 1962, 160 pp., pa 50¢) (*Terrorstrahlen* [German], *T*: 366, 1964) (Tandem: T200, 1968, 160 pp., pa 3/6) (in *Murray Leinster Omnibus*, 1968)

The onslaught of creatures from space armed with a terrifying paralysis ray.

Other Side of Here, The [pa] ("The Incredible Invasion," *ASF*, sr5, Aug 1936) —revised: (Ace: D-94, 1955, 134 pp., pa 35¢; with *One Against Eternity*) (*L'altra dimensione* [Italian], *Urania*: 99, 1955) (*Ataque desde la 4a dimension* [Spanish], Nebula: 32, 1956, pa) (*L'autre cote du monde* [French], Le Fleuve Noir: A116, 1958, pa) (*Invasion aus einer anderen Welt* [German], *T*: 94, 1959)

The U.S.A. is invaded from another dimension.

Other Side of Nowhere, The [pa] ("Spaceman," *ASF*, sr2, Mar 1964) —revised: (Berkley: F918, 1964, 142 pp., pa 50¢)

A mutiny aboard a gigantic spaceship.

Out of This World (Avalon, 1958, 221 pp., $2.75) (*L'uomo che vedeva gli atomi* [Italian], *Urania*: 217, 1959) (*Fuera de este mundo* [Spanish], Cenit: 25, 1962, pa)

First three of the "Bud Gregory" series, about an unschooled hillbilly genius with an intuitive grasp of superscience.

Pirates of Zan, The [pa] ("The Pirates of Ersatz," *ASF*, sr3, Feb 1959) (Ace: D-403, 1959, 163 pp., pa 35¢; with *The Mutant Weapon* [Leinster]) (*Pirattenflotte über Darth* [German], Zimmermann, 1962; *T*: 284, 1963)

A rollicking tale of a youth trying to break away from a life of piracy and become an electronics expert, with circumstances dictating otherwise.

Planet Explorer, The [pa] See *Colonial Survey*

S.O.S. From Three Worlds [C] [pa] (Ace: G-647, 1967, 140 pp., pa 50¢)

Three stories of the "Med Service" series: "Plague on Kryder II"; "Ribbon in the Sky"; "Quarantine World."

Sidewise in Time [C] (Shasta, Chicago, 1950, 211 pp., $3.00) (*Bivi nel Tempo* [Italian], *Urania*: 52, 1954 [first 2 stories only]) (*Den Stora Tidbavningen* [Swedish], *Hapna*, sr2, May/June 1957) (*Kortslutning i Universet* [Danish], Skrifola: F15, 1958, pa [1st & 5th stories only])

Sf, 6 stories: "Sidewise in Time" (*ASF*, n'te, June 1934; [German] *UZ*: 500, 1966); "Proxima Centauri" (*ASF*, n'te, Mar 1935; *Hapna*, sr2, Dec 1958); "A Logic Named Joe"; "De Profundis"; "The Fourth-Dimensional Demonstrator"; "The Power."

Space Captain [pa] ("Killer Ship," *AS*, sr2, Oct 1965) (Ace: M-135, 1966, 112 pp., pa 45¢; with *The Mad Metropolis*) (*Captain Trent und die Piraten* [German], *UZ*: 514, 1966)

Space captain beats pirates by capturing their ships and hunting their hideout.

Space Gypsies [pa] (Avon: G1318, 1967, 128 pp., pa 50¢)

Earthmen meet midget humanoids and help fight alien slug creatures.

Space Platform (Shasta, 1953, 223 pp., illus., $2.50) (Pocket Books: 920, 1953, 167 pp., pa 25¢) (*Projekt Raumstation* [German], *UK*: 16, 1957; *TE*: 96, 1966) (*Plattaform spaziale* [Italian], *Cosmo*: 1, 1957) (Belmont: 92-625, 1965, 157 pp., pa 50¢)

Juvenile; first of "Joe Kenmore" series. Sabotage hampers the placement of a platform in Earth orbit.

Space Tug (Shasta, 1953, 223 pp., $2.50) (Pocket Books: 1037, 1955, 154 pp., pa 25¢) (*Zwischen Erde und Mond* [German], *UG*: 49, 1957; *TE*: 97, 1966) (Belmont: B50-632, 1965, 147 pp., pa 50¢; B50-846, 1968, pa 50¢)

Juvenile; second of "Joe Kenmore" series. The enemy continues action against the manned space station.

Talents, Incorporated [pa]   (Avon: G1120, 1962, 159 pp., pa 50¢) (*Talente—GmbH* [German], *T*: 432, 1966)

Old-style sf. A group of human "predicters" enable the hero to save a world from both its insipid politicians and from invaders.

This World Is Taboo [pa]   ("Pariah Planet," *AS*, July 1961) (Ace: D-525, 1961, 127 pp., pa 35¢) (*Der Weltraumarzt u. d. Seuche von Dara* [German], *TS*: 52, 1962) (*Mundo prohibido* [Spanish], Cenit: 38, 1962, pa)

A "Med Service" story; Calhoun irons out the antagonism between the worlds of Weald and Dara.

Time Tunnel [pa]   (Pyramid: R1043, 1964, 140 pp., pa 50¢) (*Der Tunnel in die Vergangenheit* [German], *T*: 457, 1966)

Time travel links the age of Napoleon to today.

Time Tunnel, The [pa]   (Pyramid: R1522, 1967, 143 pp., pa 50¢)

One of the stories from the TV series (not connected with the preceding entry of the same title). The saving of a town from flood waters.

Timeslip! [pa]   (Pyramid: R1680, 1967, 140 pp., pa 50¢)

Second book from the TV series; repercussions of an incident in the Mexican-American war.

Tunnel Through Time (Westminster, Philadelphia, 1966, 153 pp., $3.50)

Juvenile. Two lads go back through an intermittent time tunnel to find one boy's father, and have adventures with dinosaurs, savages, etc.

Twists in Time [C] [pa]   (Avon: T389, 1960, 160 pp., pa 25¢)

Sf, 7 stories: "Rogue Star" (new); "Dear Charles"; "Dead City"; "Sam, This Is You"; "The Other Now"; "The Fourth-Dimensional Demonstrator"; "The End."

Wailing Asteroid, The [pa]   (Avon: T483, 1961, 143 pp., pa 35¢; G1306, 1966, 143 pp., pa 50¢) (*El asteroide iloroso* [Spanish], Cenit: 19, 1961, pa) (*L'asteroide abbandonato* [Italian], *Urania*: 289, 1962) (*Der Ruf des Asteroiden* [German], *T*: 416, 1965)

Old-fashioned in writing and plot—an armed robot asteroid gives a warning to Earth, and is used by the inventor of a new type of space ship.

War With the Gizmos [pa]   ("The Strange Invasion," *Satellite*, Apr 1958) (Gold Medal: s751, 1958, 156 pp., pa 35¢) (*Gefährliche Invasion* [German], *UZ*: 130, 1958) (Muller: GM368, 1960, 159 pp., pa 2/-; nn, nd, pa 3/-) (*Questo e un Gizmo* [Italian], *Urania*: 284, 1962)

Admirably portrayed alien invaders in a routine and old-fashioned story.

Anthology

Great Stories of Science Fiction (Random House, New York, 1951, 321 pp., $2.95) (Cassell, London, 1953, 318 pp., 15/-) (SF B.C. [S.J.], 1955, 6/-)

12 stories with introduction by C. Fadiman and compiler's "Let's Call It a Hobby": "The Fascinating Stranger," M. Fessier; "Liquid Life," R. M. Farley; "Symbiosis," W. F. Jenkins; "Number Nine," C. Cartmill"; "Blind Alley," M. Jameson; "In Hiding," Wilmar H. Shiras; "No Woman Born," C. L. Moore; "The Strange Case of John Kingman," M. Leinster; "The Impossible Highway," O. J. Friend; "Open Secret," L. Padgett; "The Chronokinesis of Jonathan Hull,'" A. Boucher; "The Chromium Helmet," T. Sturgeon.

JENKS, TUDOR (7 May 1857–11 Feb 1922) American author and editor, born in Brooklyn. He wrote a number of books for young people, and was assistant editor of *St. Nicholas* 1887-1902.

Fiction

Imaginations: Truthless Tales [C]   (Century, New York, 1894, 230 pp., illus.)

Fantasy, 19 stories, magnificently illustrated: "Prehistoric Photography"; "The Tongaloo Tournament"; "The Dragon's Story"; "A Duel in the Desert"; "The Sequel"; "A Lost Opportunity"; "The Astrologer's Niece"; "The Astrologer's Niece Marries"; "The Winning of Vanella"; "The Professor and the Patagonian Giant"; "The Prince's Councilors"; "Teddy and the Wolf"; "Little Plunkett's Cousin"; "Professor Chipmunk's Surprising Adventure"; "The Satchel"; "Good Neighbors"; "Anthony and the Ancients"; "A Yarn of Sailor Ben's"; "The Statue."

JENS, WALTER   German author, professor at U. of Tübingen. Probably his best known work is *Nein Die Welt der Angeklaglen* ([French], Plon, 1950; Rowohlt, 1954; Spanish ed.), in the vein of Orwell's *1984*.

Fiction

Blind Man, The (*Der Blind*, Rowohlt, Hamburg, 1953) [Trans.—M. Bullock]: (Macmillan, New York, 1954, 92 pp., $2.50) (Deutsch, London, 1954, 119 pp., 8/6)

A short novel of German mysticism.

JENSEN, AXEL   Norwegian author.

Fiction

Epp [Trans.—Oliver Stallybrass]   (C. Windus, London, 1967, 116 pp., 18/-)

A dismal future—a cell world where people live alone in apathy. The protagonist complacently disregards his fellow man as he feeds a carnivorous plant and writes reports on his neighbours.

JEROME, JEROME K(LAPKA) (2 May 1859–11 June 1927) English humorist and playwright. He was born in Welsall. He began as a clerk but later became editor of *Idler* in 1892. Then he launched his own paper but a damage suit forced him to sell it. He began to write plays in earnest, and was most noted for *The Passing of the Third Floor Back*, which was introduced in 1908 and ran for seven years in Britain and America. His humorous book *Three Men in a Boat* (1889) was exceedingly successful and was later filmed.

Fiction [Incomplete—other titles in Bleiler *Checklist*]

Told After Supper [C]   (Leadenhall Press & Simpkin Marshall Hamilton & Kent, London, 1891, 169 pp., illus.—Kenneth M. Skeaping) (Altemus, Philadelphia, 1891, 169 pp., illus.—Skeaping)

Introductory – "How the Stories Came to Be Told"; "Teddy Biffle's Story – Johnson and Emily, or, The Faithful Ghost"; "Interlude – The Doctor's Story"; "Mr. Coombe's Story – The Haunted Mill, or, The Ruined Home"; "Interlude"; "My Uncle's Story – The Ghost of the Blue Chamber"; "S Persona"; "Explanation"; "My Own Story." *Note:* All the above except "Mr. Coombe's Story" are in *Funny Ghost Stories* (Told After Supper) (Little Blue Book No. 1170).

JESSE, F(RYNIWYD) TENNYSON (1889–6 Aug 1958) British novelist, dramatist and criminologist. She was the grand-niece of the poet Tennyson, and daughter of a clergyman. She worked on many newspapers and even did war reporting in World War I. She married playwright Harold Marsh Harwood and the pair produced many noted plays. She wrote some acutely perceptive modern studies on real crimes. Probably her most noted work was *The Saga of San Demetrio*.

Fiction

Solange Stories, The [C]   (Macmillan, New York, 1931, 182 pp., $1.75) (Heinemann, London, 1931, 285 pp., 7/6)

5 stories: "Black Veil"; "The Canary"; "Lot's Wife"; "The Pedlar"; "The Reprieve." *Note:* A further "Solange" story was "The Railway Carriage" (1950; *F&SF*, Feb 1951).

JESSUP, MORRIS K.   U.S. astronomer; instructor in astronomy and mathematics at U. of Michigan and at Drake U. He helped erect and operate the largest refracting telescope in the Southern Hemisphere in South Africa for the U. of Michigan, and did much research there. He has also explored in the headwaters of the Amazon and in Central America.

Nonfiction

Case for the UFO, The (Citadel, New York, 1955, 320 pp., illus., $3.50) (Arco, London, 1955, 239 pp., illus., 15/-) (Bantam: A1374, 1955, 208 pp., pa 35¢)

A disappointing book which does not give much fresh evidence on "Unidentified Flying Objects" as being space craft; the evidence is taken from a jumble of scientific observations.

Expanding Case for the UFO, The (Citadel, 1959, 253 pp., $3.75) (Arco, 1957, 16/-)

Suggests among other things that the Moon is a base for UFO activity and that the world's pygmies have a common—and startling—origin.

UFO and the Bible (Citadel, 1956, 126 pp., $2.50)

Concerning the thesis that present times are the Latter Days of biblical prophecy and that Christ was a saucer-visitant.

UFO Annual (Citadel, 1956, 379 pp., $4.95) (Arco, 1956, 375+4 pp., 16/-)

A large scrapbook (135,000 words) of undigested Forteana— newspaper clipping and personal narratives of flying saucers and also other phenomena.

JOHANNESSON, OLOF (1908–) Pseudonym of Hannes Alfvén, Swedish cosmologist.

Fiction

Great Computer, The See *Tale of the Big Computer, The*

Tale of the Big Computer, The ([Swedish], Albert Bonniers, Stockholm, 1966) Trans.—Naomi Walford: (Coward-McCann, 1968, 126 pp., $4.00) (*The Great Computer*, Gollancz, London, 1968, 126 pp., 21/-)

Future history of the evolution of life on Earth through the age of humans and the 'Symbiotic Age' to the beginning of the true Computer Age. In 1967 it was produced as an opera for the Royal Swedish Opera.

JOHN, JASPER British author. He used the pseudonym "Rosalia Muspratt" for the weird collection *Tales of Terror* (Old Royalty Book Pub., London, 1931, 167 pp., 2/6) [no further information].

Fiction

Sinister Stories [C] (H. Walker, London, 1930, 171 pp., illus., 2/6)

20 stories: "The Sense of Smell"; "The Human Blood Hound"; "The Dual Personality"; "A Dreadful Decision"; "The Spirit of Stonehenge"; "The Shivering Tree of Wandor Hall"; "A Fratricide"; "The Seeker of Souls"; "The Secret of the Red Loom"; "The Suicide of Clive Grantham"; "Hair From the Harem"; "The Will of the Witch Doctor"; "Ellen the Fair"; "The Chateau of Horror"; "A Castle in the Air"; "The Man With the Cut Throat"; "Lovers of Long Ago"; "The Swan Song"; "The Hound From Hell"; "The Black Ben."

JOHNS, KENNETH (pseud) See NEWMAN, J.

JOHNS, MARSTON U.S. house pseudonym.

Fiction

Beyond Time See FANTHORPE, R. L.

Space Void ([as John E. Muller], Badger: SF34, 1960, 141 pp., pa 2/-) (Arcadia, New York, 1965, 192 pp., $3.25) (Ambassador, Toronto, $3.95)

Venus Venture, The See FANTHORPE, R. L.

JOHNS, W(ILLIAM) E(ARL) (5 Feb 1893–June 1968) British author. He joined the Royal Flying Corps in World War I and continued in the R.A.F. until 1930. As Captain W. E. Johns he was noted worldwide for his "Biggles" stories which he began in 1932 when he was editor of a flying magazine. The fame of Biggles is such that he has been translated into 14 other languages. Johns has written much non-fiction, thrillers, and science fiction, although the sf is not as notable as the juvenile fiction of writers predominantly in the sf field. Recent juvenile sf books include *Kings of*

Space; *Return to Mars*; *Now to the Stars*; *The Edge of Beyond* (Hodder & Stoughton, 1958); *Death Rays of Ardilla* (Hodder, 1959); *The Quest for the Perfect Planet* (Hodder, 1961).

JOHNS, WILLY (pseud?)

Fiction

Fabulous Journey of Hieronymus Meeker (Little, Boston, 1954, 370 pp., $3.50) (McClelland, Toronto, $4.00)

Adventures of the crew of the "Jeemarad" bound for Venus but deflected by a comet.

JOHNSON, B. S.

Fiction

Statement Against Corpses [with Zulfikar Ghose] [C] (Constable, London, 1964, 204 pp., 21/-)

Weird, 14 stories (first 9 by Johnson, last 5 by Ghose): "Clean Living Is the Real Safeguard"; "Perhaps It's These Hormones"; "Statement"; "Kindly State Your Motive"; "Broad Thoughts From a Home"; "On Supply"; "Never Heard It Called That Before"; "Sheela-na-gig"; "Only the Stones"; "Godbert"; "Amy"; "The Corpses"; "The Departure"; "The Zoo People."

JOHNSON, GEORGE CLAYTON

Fiction

Logan's Run [with William Nolan] (Dial, New York, 1967, 133 pp., $3.50) (Gollancz, London, 1968, 134 pp., 21/-)

A not-too-distant future, with LSD parlors, unlimited sex, etc. A complex conspiracy develops.

JOHNSON, JAMES W.

Nonfiction

Utopian Literature: A Selection [pa] (Random House: T-96, 1968, pa $1.95)

JOHNSON, JOSEPHINE W.

Fiction

Sorcerer's Son and Other Stories, The [C] (Simon & Schuster, New York, 1965, 219 pp., $4.50)

14 stories: "The Sorcerer's Son"; "The Garden"; "The Glass Pigeon"; "Christmas Morning in May"; "Penelope's Web"; "Story Without End"; "Night Flight"; "The Rented Room"; "Fever Flower"; "Alexander to the Park"; "The Heirs"; "Coney Island in November"; "The Author"; "The Glass Mountain."

JOHNSON, L. P. V.

Fiction

In the Time of the Thetans (Macmillan, London, 1961, 274 pp., 15/-)

Struggles of Earthmen against the menace of the Thetans, aliens from Mars resembling large starfish.

JOHNSON, RAY W. (1900–)

Fiction

Astera: The Planet That Committed Suicide (Exposition, New York, 1960, 27 pp., $2.00)

JOHNSON, ROSSITER (27 Jan 1840–3 Oct 1931) Noted U.S. editor of many U.S. encyclopedias, dictionaries, etc. The "Little Classics" series appeared for some 18 volumes from Osgood, 1874-81, and was reprinted by Houghton Mifflin in 1900. Bleiler lists Volume 2, *Stories of Intellect* and Volume 8, *Mystery*, upon which no information is available. The one listed below is not mentioned by Bleiler.

Fiction

Little Classics Volume 3: Tragedy (J. R. Osgood, Boston, 1875, 205 pp.)

7 stories: "Murders in the Rue Morgue," E. A. Poe; "The Lawson Tragedy," J. W. De Forest; "The Iron Shroud," Wm. Mudford; "The Bell Tower," H. Melville; "The Kathayan Slave," Emily C. Judson; "The Story of La Roche," Henry McKenzie; "The Vision of Sudden Death," Thomas De Quincy.

JOKAI, MOR (19 Feb 1825–5 May 1904) Hungarian novelist. He studied law but disliked it and entered the literary field, where he was hailed as a rising young author. He supported Kossuth in the ill-fated Revolution of 1848, and was for a time a fugitive from the Austrian imperium. His rights restored, he later took active interest in Hungarian political affairs and was also one of the most popular European novelists at the turn of the century. Bleiler lists two works of possible interest, *Timar's Two Worlds* (Blackwood, London, 1888, 3 vols.) and *Told by the Death's Head* (Saalfield, Akron, 1902).

Fiction

Tales From Jokai [C] (Jarrold, London, 1904, xlvi+275 pp., 6/-)

9 stories, some fantasy: "The Celestial Slingers"; "The Compulsory Diversion"; "The Sheriff of Caschau"; "The Justice of Soliman"; "Love and the Little Dog"; "The Red Starosta"; "The City of the Beast"; "The Hostile Skulls"; "The Bad Old Times."

JONES, CHARLOTTE R(OSALIE)

Fiction

Hypnotic Experiment of Dr. Reeves and Other Stories, The [C] (Bliss Sands & Foster, London; Brentano's, New York, 1894, 95 pp.)

Fantasy, 5 stories: "The Hypnotic Experiment of Dr. Reeves"; "An International Courtship"; "One Woman's History Out of Many"; "Miss Cameron's Art Sale"; "A Complex Question."

JONES, CONSTANCE B(RIDGES) See JONES, GUY PEARCE

JONES, D(ENNIS) F(ELTHAM) British author. He was a commander in the Royal Navy throughout World War II. He has worked at various times as a radio operator, bricklayer and market gardener, and also in the fields of architecture and geology. He now lives in Cornwall.

Fiction

Colossus (Hart-Davis, London, 1966, 246 pp., 25/-) (Longmans, Toronto, $4.75) (Putnam, New York, 1967, 256 pp., $4.95) (D'day SF B.C., 1967, $1.70) (Berkley: X1455, 1967, 233 pp., pa 60¢) (Pan: 02110, 1968, 221 pp., pa 5/-)

The master computers of the U.S.A. and the U.S.S.R. combine to rule the world.

Implosion (Putnam, New York, 1968, 286 pp., $5.95) (D'day SF B.C., 1968, $1.70)

Most of England's women become sterile; the fertile ones are taken to special breeding areas.

JONES, DUPRE

Fiction

Adventures of Gremlin, The (Lippincott, Philadelphia, 1966, 112 pp., illus.–E. Gorey, $3.95)

Fairy tale—in the kingdom of Etaoin live a deserted boy and girl.

JONES, EWART C.

Fiction

How Now Brown Cow (Home & Van Thal, London, 1947, 142 pp., 7/6) (McClelland, Toronto, $2.25)

A lady turned into a cow cuts cute capers.

JONES, GLYN

Fiction

Blue Bed and Other Stories, The [C] (J. Cape, London, 1937, 245 pp., 7/6) (Nelson, Toronto) (Dutton, New York, 1938, 245 pp., $2.00)

Fantasy, 9 stories: "The Blue Bed"; "Cadi Hughes"; "Eben Isaac"; "Eden Tree"; "I Was Born in Ystrad Valley"; "The Kiss"; "Knowledge"; "Port-y-rhyd"; "Wil Thomas."

JONES, GONNER

Fiction

Dome, The (Faber, London, 1968, 239 pp., 25/-)

Future city controlled by a living brain—"the Dome."

JONES, GUY PEARCE and CONSTANCE B(RIDGES)

Fiction

Peabody's Mermaid (*Cosmopolitan*, sr2, Oct 1945) (Random, New York, 1946, 242 pp., illus., $2.50) (M. Joseph, London, 1947, 191 pp., 9/6) (Sun Dial, New York, 1947, 242 pp., illus., $1.00) (Blue Ribbon, Toronto, $1.29) (Pocket Books: 503, 1948, 148 pp., pa 25¢) (*En Flicka Pa Kroken* [Swedish], Wahlström & Widstrand, 1949)

The amusing result of a man finding a mermaid. *Film:* Universal-International, 1948, starring William Powell and Ann Blyth.

There Was a Little Man (Random, 1948, 245 pp., $2.50) (Random, Toronto, $3.00)

A humorous novel about a leprechaun.

JONES, Sir HAROLD SPENCER (29 Mar 1890–3 Nov 1960) The Astronomer Royal, 1933-55. He was educated at Jesus College, Cambridge, winning many prizes. As an astronomer he was Chief Assistant at Greenwich 1913-23, H. M. Astronomer at Cape of Good Hope 1923-33, and then Astronomer Royal. He was connected in various capacities with many learned astronomical societies, etc., of international scope, and received many notable medals. He wrote many works, including *General Astronomy*, the 4th ed. of which (1961) was almost completed prior to his death. His main work of interest to sf is covered below.

Nonfiction

Life on Other Worlds (English Univ. Press, Kent, 1940, 259 pp., 7/6) (Mentor: M39, 1949, 160 pp., pa 35¢; MD144, 1956, pa 50¢; MP440, 1962, 160 pp., pa 60¢) (Macmillan, New York, rev. 1954, 259 pp., illus., $3.00) (Hodder & Stoughton, London, rev. 1959, 251 pp., illus., pa 3/6)

A noted work on the possibilities of extra-terrestrial life.

JONES, JACK

Nonfiction

Fantasy Films and Their Fiends (Compiler?, 1964, 131 pp., 8½ x 11 in., $2.00)

A compilation of over 1200 films of horror, sf and fantasy, covering title, producer or distributor, release year, principal cast and story line. There is also a biographical section on over 250 fantasy film stars and a guide for nearly 150 silent serials.

JONES, LOUIS C(LARK) (28 June 1908–) U.S. educator and society executive. He was born in Albany, N.Y., and took his A.M. at Columbia in 1931 and Ph.D. in 1941. He has been an instructor in English at various universities, was assistant professor at New York State College of Teachers 1934-46, and since 1946 has been executive director of the New York State Historical Association. He is a specialist in folk museums, U.S. folklore, etc., including supernatural happenings. He founded the Farmers Museum Folklore Archive, which contains thousands of songs, beliefs and stories of the people of New York State, collected by state college students. He edited the *Quarterly* of the New York Folklore Society 1945-50 and also *New York History*.

Nonfiction

Spooks in the Valley (Houghton, New York, 1948, illus.–Erwin Austin, $2.50)

Subtitled "Ghost Stories for Boys and Girls." A group of weird legends and folk tales; entertaining reading and something of Americana.

Things That Go Bump in the Night (Hill & Wang, New York, 1959, 208 pp., illus.–E. Austin, $3.75) (Copp, Toronto, $4.25)

Ghost stories, many legendary and some supposed to be factual. Over 200 stories in the form of a flowing narrative. Chapters are: "Introducing the Dead"; "Why They Return"; "Haunted Houses"; "Violence and Sudden Death"; "Haunted History"; "The Ghostly Hitchhiker."

JONES, MARGARET

Fiction

Day They Put Humpty Together Again, The (Collins, London, 1968, 224 pp., 21/-) (*Transplant*, Stein & Day, New York, 1968, 224 pp., $5.95)

A surgeon unites the head and brain of an artist friend with the body of a lecherous petty criminal, producing a fight between art and lust.

Transplant See *Day They Put Humpty Together Again, The*

JONES, MERVYN (1922–) British author. He was educated at Abbotsholme School, Derbyshire, and at New York University. He has contributed to *New Statesman*, New York *Herald-Tribune* and *Observer*, and his works include *No Time to Be Young* (1952) and *The Last Barricade* (1953).

Fiction

On the Last Day (Cape, London, 1958, 268 pp., 15/-)

During World War III the Allies strive to build the first intercontinental missile.

JONES, NEIL R(ONALD) (29 May 1909–) U.S. author. He was born in Fulton, N.Y. From his early years he had literary leanings, winning local essay prizes and then writing in school magazines. After writing articles on stamps he tried science fiction and sold his first six stories, but later found it harder to sell. The first story he wrote was "The Electrical Man" (*Scientific Detective*, May 1930), for which he wrote an unpublished sequel; but his second story, "The Death's Head Meteor" (*Air Wonder*, Jan 1930), was the first to be published. Jones is primarily remembered for his "Professor Jameson" series, one of the longest in the sf field, appearing 1931-1950 in three different magazines. He was regularly featured in most sf magazines until the early 1940's, when military service took him overseas 1942-45. He met his wife-to-be in London and married 15 months after the war. By 1941 he had written two novels—*The Cosmic Veil* and *The Outlawed World*—but neither has been published. He has not written much since World War II, aside from a few stories in the two series listed below. Practically all his stories are set against a single consistent "history of the future," which he outlines in an article in the amateur magazine *The Fanscient*, Sum 1948. After the war he invented "Interplanetary," a disc-and-counters game which has proved quite popular. He now works with the New York Dept. of Labor. His hobby is book-binding, which he uses on his sf collection.

Series

Durna Rangue. An infamous fantastic cult. "Little Hercules" (*ASF*, Sep 1936); "Durna Rangue Neophyte" (*ASF*, June 1937); "Invisible One" (*SSS*, Sep 1940); "Captives of the Durna Rangue" (*SSS*, Mar 1941); "Priestess of the Sleeping Death" (*AS*, Apr 1941); "Vampire of the Void" (*Planet*, Spr 1941); "The Citadel in Space" (*2CSAB*, Sum 1951). The reading sequence is 4, 2, 5, 3, 1, 6, 7. As a prelude to these stories Jones introduced the character Nez Hulan in "The Asteroid of Death" (*WSQ*, Fall 1931), and followed with "The Moon Pirates" (*AS*, sr2, Sep 1934); later this character joined the Durna Rangue.

Jameson, Professor. A man's brain in a robot body touring the universe. In *Amazing*: "The Jameson Satellite" (July 1931; Apr 1956); "Planet of the Double Sun" (Feb 1932; Nov 1962); "The Return of the Tripeds" (May 1932); "Into the Hydrosphere" (Oct 1933); "Time's Mausoleum" (Dec 1933); "The Sunless World" (Dec 1934); "Zora of the Zoromes" (Mar 1935); "Space War" (July 1935); "Labyrinth" (Apr 1936); "Twin Worlds" (Apr 1937); "On the Planet Fragment" (Oct 1937); "The Music Monsters" (Apr 1938). In *Astonishing*: "The Cat Men of Aemt" (Aug 1940); "Cosmic Derelict" (Feb 1941); "Slaves of the Unknown" (Mar 1942); "Doomsday on Ajiat" (Oct 1942). In *Super Science Stories*: "The Metal Moon" (Sep 1949); "Parasite Planet" (Nov 1949); "World Without Darkness" (Mar 1950); "The Mind Masters" (Sep 1950); "The Star Killers" (Aug 1951). This sf series lasted longer than any other, and had the most wordage. There was a drop in quality after the war.

Fiction

Doomsday on Ajiat [C] [pa] (Ace: G-719, 1968, 159 pp., pa 50¢)

Fifth in the "Prof. Jameson" series. 4 stories: "In the Meteoric Cloud"; "The Accelerated World"; "The Metal Moon"; "Doomsday on Ajiat." The first two were accepted by a magazine which then ceased publication; this is thus their first appearance.

Planet of the Double Sun [C] [pa] (Ace: F-420, 1967, 123 pp., pa 40¢)

First of "Prof. Jameson" series. 3 stories: "The Jameson Satellite"; "Planet of the Double Sun"; "The Return of the Tripeds."

Space War [C] [pa] (Ace: G-650, 1967, 158 pp., pa 50¢)

Third of "Prof. Jameson" series. 3 stories: "Zora of the Zoromes"; "Space War"; "Labyrinth."

Sunless World, The [C] [pa] (Ace: G-631, 1967, 189 pp., pa 50¢)

Second of "Prof. Jameson" series. 3 stories: "Into the Hydrosphere"; "Time's Mausoleum"; "The Sunless World."

Twin Worlds [C] [pa] (Ace: G-681, 1967, 157 pp., pa 50¢)

Fourth of "Prof. Jameson" series. 3 stories: "Twin Worlds"; "On the Planet Fragment"; "The Music Monsters."

JONES, RAYMOND F. (1915–) U.S. author. He was born in Salt Lake City. He made his name in *ASF* in the late war years. He is not now a regular contributor to the sf field, but still appears occasionally. He has had meteorological experience which he sometimes uses in his stories, and he also holds a "ham" (amateur) radio operator's licence. Some of his notable fiction includes: "Fifty Million Monkeys" (*ASF*, Oct 1943); "Forecast" (*ASF*, May 1946); "The Toymaker" (*ASF*, Sep 1946); "I Tell You Three Times" (*ASF*, Feb 1951); "The Colonists" (*If*, June 1954); "The Unlearned" (*If*, Aug 1954). His juvenile novels were among the best in the Winston "Adventures in SF" book series, and his notable *This Island Earth* was made into a high-class film.

Fiction

Alien, The [pa] (Galaxy SF Novels: 6, 1951, 160 pp., pa 35¢) (*Das Erbe der Hölle* [German], *TS*: 14, 1959) (Belmont: B50-708, 1966, 157 pp., pa 50¢)

A member of a super-race is brought back to life, with consequent turmoil.

Cybernetic Brains, The (*SS*, Sep 1950) (Avalon, New York, 1962, 223 pp., $2.95) (*I cervelli cibernetici* [Italian], *Cosmo*: 103, 1962)

A fight against a welfare state which uses human brains in the control circuits of super-computers.

Deviates, The [pa] See *Secret People, The*

Man of Two Worlds [pa] See *Renaissance*

Non-Statistical Man, The [C] [pa] (Belmont: L92-588, 1964, 158 pp., pa 50¢; B50-820, 1968, pa 50¢) (Brown-Watson: R904, 1965, 192 pp., pa 3/6) ([German], first 2 stories: *T*: 534, 1967)

Sf, 4 stories: "The Non-Statistical Man"; "The Moon Is Death"; "The Gardener"; "Intermission Time."

Planet of Light (Winston, Philadelphia, 1953, 211 pp., $2.00) (*Pionjär I Rymden* [Swedish], Wennerbergs: R4, 1957, pa)

Juvenile, one of the "Adventures in SF" series. A family represents Earth in a bid to join the galactic federation; sequel to *Son of the Stars*.

Renaissance (*ASF*, sr4, Aug 1944) (Gnome, New York, 1951, 255 pp., $2.75) (*Renaissance* [French], Ed. Satellite Club Satellite: 4, 1959) (*Man of Two Worlds*, Pyramid: F941, 1963, 268 pp., pa 40¢) (*Der Mann zweier Welten* [German], *TS*: 130, 1968, pa)

The story of two worlds: the remnants of a self-destroyed Earth, and Kronweld, the strangely tortured world in another plane.

Secret People, The (Avalon, 1956, 224 pp., $2.50) (*Experiment Genetik* [German], *WF*: 6, 1958) (*The Deviates*, Beacon: 242, 1959, 160 pp., pa 35¢) (*Il popolo segreto* [Italian], *Cosmo*: 73, 1961)

Mutants populate Earth after an atomic war; one man secretly breeds beneficial mutants to take over as Man slowly dies out.

Son of the Stars (Winston, 1952, 210 pp., $2.00) (Hutchinson, London, 1954, 216 pp., 7/6) ([Japanese], GingaShobo 'Adv. in SF 1,' 1955) (*Rymdens Son* [Swedish], Wennerbergs: R3, 1957, pa) (*Sohn der Sterne* [German], AWA, 1957; *T*: 246, 1962)

Juvenile, one of the "Adventures in SF" series. A flying saucer survivor is befriended by young people, but comes up against adult prejudices. Sequel is *Planet of Light*. The German AWA edition also contains the sequel, probably abridged.

This Island Earth (Shasta, Chicago, 1952, 220 pp., $3.00) (D'day SF B.C., 1953) (*Universum Ockuberat* [Swedish], Lindqvist,

1954) (Boardman, London, 1955, 9/6) (*Il cittadino dello spazio* [Italian], *Urania*: 96, 1955) (*Insel zwischen den Sternen* [German], *UG*: 37, 1956) (*Les survivants de l'infini* [French], Gallimard: Le RF, 1956) (*Esta isla la Tierra* [Spanish], Nebula: 41, 1957, pa)

Extension of the *TWS* novelettes "The Alien Machine" (June 1949); "The Shroud of Secrecy" (Dec 1949); "The Greater Conflict" (Feb 1950). Super-beings pull strings on Earth to gain help in fighting an intergalactic enemy. The German ed. was adapted by W. Ernsting to follow the film version. *Film:* U.S., Universal-International, 1955, wide-screen, starring Jeff Morrow, Faith Domergue and Bart Roberts, directed by Joe Newman and produced by W. Allan. After starting like the novel the story changes somewhat; it is quite high-class with good space ship effects.

Toymaker, The [C] (FPCI, Los Angeles, 1951, 287 pp., $3.00) (*Les imaginos* [French], Ed. Métal, 1955)

Sf, 6 stories: "The Model Shop"; "The Deadly Host"; "Utility"; "Forecast"; "The Toymaker"; "The Children's Hour."

Year When Stardust Fell, The (Winston, 1958, 203 pp., $2.50) (*Sternenstaub* [German], *UG*: 124, 1960)

Juvenile, one of the "Adventures in SF" series. A comet makes all machinery useless.

JONES, ROBERT WEBSTER
Fiction

Light Interviews With Shades [C] (Dorrance, Philadelphia, 1922, 151 pp., $1.50)

Fantasy, 19 stories: "Bluebeard Tells Why He Killed Wives"; "Queen Elizabeth Discloses Why She Never Married"; "John Paul Jones and a Grogless Navy"; "Joshua Advises Daylight Saving"; "King Solomon's Family Vacation Trip"; "Brigham Young Endorses Woman Suffrage"; "Hippocrates on Modern Doctors"; "Methuselah Gives Longevity Secrets"; "Jesse James Talks on Tipping"; "Shakespeare Mentions Movies"; "Adam Condemns Present Fashions"; "Captain Kidd Speaks on Tag Days"; "Alfred the Great Tries to Find Prosperous King"; "Old King Cole Gives Views on Prohibition"; "King Henry VIII Admits Some Matrimonial Mistakes"; "Don Quixote Says He 'Wasn't So Crazy as Some Modern Reformers' "; "Pharaoh Solves the Servant Problem"; "Nero Discusses Jazz"; "Lord Bacon Muses on Ciphers."

JONES, TUPPER (1909?–)
Fiction

Building of the Alpha One, The (Exposition, New York, 1956, 80 pp., $3.00)

Tales in verse of the first space station.

JORDAN, ELIZABETH G(ARVER) (9 May 1867–24 Feb 1947)
American critic, novelist and playwright. She never married. After editing *Harper's Bazaar* for a time, she became literary adviser for Harper & Bros. 1913-18. She contributed numerous essays and short stories to English and American magazines, and received the Cross of Honour.
Fiction

Tales of the Cloister [C] (Harpers, New York, 1901, 252 pp.)

Fantasy, 10 stories: "From out of the Old Life"; "The Surrender of Sister Philomene"; "As Told to May Iverson"; "Her Audience of Two"; "The Girl Who Was"; "Belonging to the Third Order"; "Under the Black Pall"; "Between Darkness and Dawn"; "The Ordeal of Sister Cuthbert"; "Saint Ernesta and the Imp."

JORGENSEN, IVAR U.S. house pseudonym.
Fiction

Rest in Agony [pa] (Monarch: 362, 1963, 125 pp., pa 35¢)
Starhaven See SILVERBERG, R.
Ten From Infinity [pa] (Monarch: 297, 1963, 139 pp., pa 35¢) (*Il decimo androide* [Italian], *Cosmo*: 140, 1963) (*Zehn aus dem All* [German], *UZ*: 409, 1964)

Aliens use androids to study Earth before conquest.

JOSEPH, M(ICHAEL) K(ENNEDY) (9 July 1914–)
Fiction

Hole in the Zero, The (Gollancz, London, 1967, 191 pp., 21/-) (Dutton, New York, 1968, 192 pp., $3.95) (SF B.C. [S.J.], 1968)

People travel into the 'beyond' from stations at the edge of the universe.

JOSLIN, SESYLE
Fiction

Night They Stole the Alphabet, The (Harcourt, New York, 1968, $3.95)

Juvenile fantasy.

JOURDAIN, E(LEANOR) F(RANCES) (1863–1924)
Nonfiction

Adventure, An See MOBERLY, C. A. E. (co-author)

JUDD, CYRIL (pseud) See MERRIL, J. or KORNBLUTH, C. M.

JUENGER, ERNST (29 Mar 1895–) German novelist. He volunteered for the army when 19 years old, and was an officer of the Wehrmacht in Paris in World War II. He has always been fond of French culture. Besides the fantasy below he wrote *Heliopolis* (1949), a political utopia story about a strange city and its troubles.
Fiction

Glass Bees, The (*Gläserne Bienes*, E. Klett, Stuttgart, 1957) (Noonday, New York, 1961, 149 pp., $3.75; #204, pa $1.65)

The story of an ex-cavalryman hero and the society in which he moves when he comes into contact with the industrial wizard Zapparoni and his robot bees.

On the Marble Cliffs (*Auf den Marmorklippen*, ca. 1942) (French trans., Gallimard, 1942) Trans.–Stuart Hood: (Lehmann, London, 1947, 120 pp., 7/6) (New Directions, New York, 1948, v+8+120 pp., $2.50)

An imaginary civilized country is slowly invaded by barbarians. An allegory with an anti-Hitler bias.

JUNG, CARL GUSTAV (28 July 1875–6 June 1961) Noted Swiss medical psychologist and psychiatrist. He was Chief Assistant at Burgholzi, Zurich, 1905-09; professor at the Hochschule, 1933-39; and professor at Basle, 1944 on. His publications range from clinical treatises to works of touching simplicity and humanity. He formulated various hypotheses on human life, some of which will be debated for many years to come.
Nonfiction

Flying Saucers (*Ein moderner Mythus* [German], Rascher, Zurich, 1958) Trans.–R. F. C. Hull: (Routledge & K. Paul, London, 1959, 184 pp., illus., 14/-)

Subtitled "A modern myth of things seen in the skies."

JUSTER, NORTON
Fiction

Phantom Tollbooth, The (Collins, London, 1962, 256 pp., illus.–Jules Feiffer, 15/-) (Puffin: PS236, 1965, 214 pp., pa 4/-)

Juvenile fantasy.

K

KAFKA, FRANZ (3 July 1883–3 June 1924) Czech author of Jewish ancestry. During most of his life he was solitary, ill and unhappy. When he died he left three allegorical novels and other writings which were not appreciated until some years later. These

works are now hailed as a perfect expression of the profound despair and moral depression that gripped Europe after World War I. Kafka is noted for his *Metamorphosis*. His short story "In the Penal Colony" was reprinted in *Timeless Stories for Today and Tomorrow* [Bradbury] (1952, pa); *Selected Stories* is a general collection of interest. Books about Kafka include *Kafka's Prayer*, Paul Goodman (Vanguard, 1941), an analysis of his writings, *Franz Kafka*, Max Brod (Germany, 1937; Schocken, 1947), a biography, and more recently, *Franz Kafka: A Critical Study of His Writings* [trans.—F. Unger; 1968], *Kafka: The Torment of Man*, R. M. Albérés & Pierre de Boisdeffre (Philosophical Lib., 1968, $4.75), and *Kafka Versus Kafka* M. Carrouges (U. of Alabama, $6.50).
Fiction
Castle, The (M. Secker, London, 1930, 450 pp., 7/6) (Knopf, New York, 1930, 340 pp., $2.50; 'definitive edition, with added material,' 1954, 481 pp., $4.50) (Secker & Warburg, 'definitive edition, with added material,' 1953, 451 pp., 15/-); (Penguin: 1235, 1957, 298 pp., pa 3/6; 1962, pa 6/-?)
   Classic allegorical novel.
Metamorphosis (Parton, London, 1937, 74 pp., 3/6 [trans.—A. L. Loyd]) (Vanguard, New York, 1946, 98 pp., $2.75) (in *Man Into Beast* [Spectorsky], 1947, and in *Worlds of Wonder* [Pratt], 1952) (*FFM*, June 1953) (Schocken; U.S., 1968, $4.50, pa $1.95)
   Symbolic story of the metamorphosis of a travelling salesman into a cockroach.
Metamorphosis and Other Stories [C] [pa] (Penguin: 1572, 1968, 218 pp., pa 4/-)
   An abridgement of *Selected Stories of Franz Kafka* [trans.—Willa & E. Muir]. 6 stories: "Metamorphosis"; "The Great Wall of China"; "Investigations of a Dog"; "The Burrow"; "In the Penal Settlement"; "The Giant Mole."
Selected Stories of Franz Kafka [trans.—Willa & E. Muir] [C] (Modern Library, New York, 1952, 328 pp., $1.25)
   16 stories and Introduction—Philip Rahv: "The Judgment"; "The Metamorphosis"; "In the Penal Colony"; "The Great Wall of China"; "A Country Doctor"; "A Common Confusion"; "The New Advocate"; "An Old Manuscript"; "A Fratricide"; "A Report to an Academy"; "The Hunter Gracchus"; "A Hunger Artist"; "Investigations of a Dog"; "The Burrow"; "Josephine the Singer"; "Or the Mouse Folk."
Trial, The (V. Gollancz, London, 1937, 285 pp., 7/6) (Ryerson, Toronto, $2.00) (Knopf, 1937, 297 pp., $2.50) (Penguin: 907, 1953, 256 pp., pa 2/-; 1966, pa 3/6) (Folio Society, London, 1967, 219 pp.)
   A weird and haunting story of man's loneliness in an accusing, incomprehensible world controlled by implacable, irresponsible authorities.

KAHN, HERMAN (15 Feb 1922—) Director of the Hudson Institute [U.S.A.], a non-profit research organization devoted to the study of major problems affecting U.S. public policy, international development, defence and peace keeping.
Nonfiction
Year 2000, The [with Anthony J. Wiener] (Macmillan, New York, 1968, 431 pp., $9.95)
   A comprehensive and imaginative forecast of developments in science, technology, population and international power balances in the year 2000. First volume of 'The Commission of the Year 2000' sponsored by the American Academy of Arts and Sciences and others.

KAHN, JOAN
Anthology
Edge of the Chair, The (Arlington, London, 1968, 551 pp., 42/-)
   Weird, 35 stories, with intro. (1½ pp.) by editor: "The Sixth Capsule, or, Proof of Circumstantial Evidence," Edmund Pearson; "Fool's Mate," S. Ellin; "The Axeman Wore Wings," Robert Tallent; "Stone From the Stars," Valentina Zhuravleva; "The Queen of Spades," A. Pushkin; "Billy: The Seal Mission," Stewart Alsop & Thomas Braden; "A Watcher by the Dead," A. Bierce; "Tea Party," Harold Pinter; "Death Draws a Triangle," Edward H. Bier-

stadt; "The Net," R. M. Coates; "Prisoner of the Sand," Antoine de Saint-Exupery; "The End of the Party," G. Greene; "The Last Inhabitant of the Tuileries," Andre Castelot; "Jesting Pilot," L. Padgett; "Shattering the Myth of John Wilkes Booth's Escape," Wm. G. Shepherd; "A Piece of Steak," J. London; "The Game of Murder," Gerd Gaiser; "On the Killing of Eratosthenes the Seducer," Kathleen Freeman; "The Adventure of the Clapham Cook," Agatha Christie; "The Last Night of the World," R. Bradbury; " 'They'," R. Kipling; "The Chair," John B. Martin; "Old Fags," S. Aumonier; ". . . Dead Men Working in the Cane Fields," Wm. Seabrook; "How the Brigadier Lost His Ear," Sir A. C. Doyle; "Dry September," Wm. Faulkner; "Rattenbury and Stoner," F. T. Jesse; "Sing a Song of Sixpence," J. Buchan; "The Murder in Le Mans," Janet Flanner; "Sleeping Beauty," J. Collier; "The Shadow of the Shark," G. K. Chesterton; "A Small Buried Treasure," J. Fischer; "The Horla," Guy de Maupassant; "Scrawns," Dorothy L. Sayers.

KANER, HYMAN British author and publisher. He also wrote some paper-covered items during World War II.
Fiction
People of the Twilight (Kaner, Llandudno, 1946, 188 pp., illus., 8/6)
   Travel to a parallel world where time is exceedingly faster than on Earth.
Sun Queen, The (Kaner, 1946, 204 pp., 8/6)
   A novel of life on the Sun.

KANTOR, MacKINLAY (4 Feb 1904—) U.S. author. His *Long Remember* is considered one of the great novels about the American Civil War.
Fiction
If the South Had Won the Civil War [pa] (expansion from *Look*, 22 Nov 1960) (Bantam: A2241, 1961, 113 pp., pa 35¢)
   An alternate time-track history of the U.S. from 12 May 1863 to the present—starting with the death of Grant when thrown from his horse, and ending with the Presidents of the United States, Confederate States and Texas meeting to face the threat of a Russia that never sold Alaska.

KAPP, COLIN (1929?—) British science-fiction writer, employed as a technical assistant in a leading electronics research laboratory. He was interested in sf from his youth, and graduated through the U.S. magazines to the British field as a writer in 1958. Probably his most noted short story is "Lambda 1" (*NW*, n'te, Dec 1962), which became the title of an anthology edited by E. J. Carnell. His wife is both his typist and his critic.
Fiction
Dark Mind, The [pa] See *Transfinite Man*
Transfinite Man [pa] ("The Dark Mind," *NW*, sr3, Nov 1963) (Berkley: F974, 1964, 160 pp., pa 50¢) (*The Dark Mind*, Corgi: GS7160, 1965, 158 pp., pa 3/6)
   A powerful novel of a 'man' who can't die and his fight against a colossus.

KARIG, WALTER (1898—) U.S. novelist and journalist. After military service overseas in World War I, in 1921 he joined the *Newark Evening News* and stayed for 21 years. During this period he wrote the "Nancy Drew" books for girls and the "X-Bar-X" books for boys. In World War II he served in various capacities with the U.S. Navy, and after the war was co-author and editor of the notable *Battle Report* series (6 vols., 1944-52) which gave a highly detailed account of the U.S. Navy. Since 1954 he has been Book Editor of the *Washington Post*. He has used many pseudonyms during his long writing career of over 40 years.
Fiction
Zotz! (Rinehart, New York, 1947, 265 pp., $2.75)
   Fantasy satire; a man acquires the power to kill by saying "zotz!"

KARINTHY, FRIGYES (1888-1938) Noted Hungarian writer of utopian novels.

Fiction
Voyage to Faremido and Capillaria [trans.–P. Tabori] (Living Books, New York, 1966, 127 pp., $3.75)
 Introduction by P. Tabori. Two short novels of an eventful imaginary world.

KARLOFF, BORIS (pseud) See PRATT, W. H.

KARP, DAVID (5 May 1922–) U.S. writer. He served in the U.S. Army in Leyte and Japan. In 1946 he resumed his education and graduated from the College of the City of New York in 1948. He has always been interested in creative writing, and since college he has done a great deal of it for radio and TV.
Fiction
Day of the Monkey, The (Gollancz, London, 1955, 383 pp., 15/-) (FSB: 154, 1959, 320 pp., pa, 3/6)
 Borderline fantasy; story in Africa with strange psychological implications.
Escape to Nowhere [pa] See *One*
One (Vanguard, New York, 1953, 311 pp., $3.50) (Copp, Toronto, $4.00) (Gollancz, 1954, 256 pp., 12/6) (*Escape to Nowhere*, Lion: LL10, 1955, 222 pp., pa 35¢) (Penguin: 1459, 1960, 220 pp., pa 2/6) (Universal: UL126, 1962, 311 pp., pa $1.65)
 A choice of the U.S. Book of the Month Club. It is similar to Orwell's *1984*, but not as good: a welfare state endeavours to press an individual into its mould.

KARP, MARVIN ALLEN U.S. anthologist.
Anthologies
Suddenly [with Irving Settel] [pa] (Popular: SP351, 1965, 144 pp., pa 50¢)
 Weird, 9 stories: "Heatburn," Hortense Calisher; "The Jar," R. Bradbury; "Torch Song," John Cheever; "Decadence," Romain Gary; "Pillar of Salt," Shirley Jackson; "Final Performance," Robert Bloch; "The White Quail," John Steinbeck; "The Aftertaste," Peter Ustinov; "23 Pat O'Brien Movies," Bruce J. Friedman.
Unhumans, The [pa] (Popular: SP405, 1965, 141 pp., pa 50¢)
 Weird, 9 stories: "Green Thoughts," J. Collier; "The Grey Ones," J. B. Priestley; "Mrs. Amworth," E. F. Benson; "Dearth's Farm," Gerald Bullett; "The Seed From the Sepulchre," C. A. Smith; "Moxon's Master," A. Bierce; "Tarnhelm," H. Walpole; "The Father-Thing," P. K. Dick; "The Thing on the Doorstep," H. P. Lovecraft.

KASTLE, HERBERT
Fiction
Reassembled Man, The [pa] (Gold Medal: K1494, 192 pp., pa 45¢)
 Aliens remake a man, giving him superhuman powers, including sexual.

KATCHA, VAHE
Fiction
Hook & An Eye for an Eye, The (Hart-Davis, London, 1961, 171 pp., 13/6)
 Two psychological horror thrillers.

KAVAN, ANNA (pseud) See EDMONDS, HELEN

KEDABRA, ABBY (pseud)
Anthology
Nine Witch Tales [pa] (Scholastic: TX1308, 1968, 112 pp., pa 50¢)
 9 stories and 1 poem: "Witch's Chant," William Shakespeare; "The Horned Witches," Geoffrey Palmer & Noel Lloyd; "The Huntsman and the Witch," Brothers Grimm; "The Cat Witch," Maria Leach; "Baba Yaga, the Forest Witch," Arthur Ransome; "The Bewitching Ointment," G. Palmer & N. Lloyd; "The Hungry Old Witch," Charles J. Finger; "The Young Witch-Horse," Moritz Jagendorf; "The Witch of Wandaland," G. Palmer & N. Lloyd; "The Hex and the Oxen," M. Jagendorf.

KEE, ROBERT (1920?–)
Fiction
Sign of the Times, A (Eyre Spottiswoode, London, 1955, 256 pp., 12/6) (McClelland, Toronto, $2.50)
 A regimented world of the near future.

KEEL, JOHN
Fiction
Jadoo (J. Messner, New York, 1957, 249 pp., $2.95) (Tower: 43-620, 1966, 188 pp., pa 60¢)
 Off-beat adventure, with black magic of the Orient and supernatural phenomena.

KEENE, DAY U.S. writer for Hollywood and TV. He has written a number of detective stories for Gold Medal paperbacks; he and Dwight Vincent wrote *Chautauqua* (1960), a serious novel on rural Iowa which was well received.
Fiction
World Without Women [with Leonard Pruyn] [pa] (Gold Medal: s975, 1960, 176 pp., pa 35¢; L1504, 1965, pa 45¢) (Muller: GM531, 1961, 158 pp., pa 2/6; nn, nd, pa 3/-)
 A switch on Pat Frank's *Mr. Adam*; a mysterious epidemic wipes out most women, and an estranged couple become involved in the resulting gang conflicts.

KEIGHTLEY, DAVID NOEL (25 Oct 1932–)
Anthology
Contact [as Noel Keyes] [pa] (Paperback: 52-211, 1963, 176 50¢; 52-837, 1965, pa 50¢)
 Sf, 12 stories with compiler's introduction: *Man the Discoverer:* "First Contact," Murray Leinster; "Intelligence Test," Harry Walton; "The Large Ant," Howard Fast; "What's He Doing in There?" Fritz Leiber; "Chemical Plant," Ian Williamson; "Limiting Factor," Clifford D. Simak; "The Fire Balloons," Ray Bradbury. *Man the Discovered:* "Invasion From Mars," Howard Koch; "The Gentle Vultures," Isaac Asimov; "Knock," Fredric Brown; "Specialist," Robert Sheckley; "Lost Memory," Peter Phillips.

KEITH, DONALD (pseud) See MONROE, D. & K.

KELLEAM, JOSEPH E(VERIDGE) (11 Feb 1913–) U.S. former Air Force contract officer, retired ranch owner, and author of irregular appearance in the sf field. He had three short stories in *ASF* 1939-42, and more recently appeared in *Amazing* in 1959 and 1960.
Fiction
Hunters of Space (*AS*, May 1960) (Avalon, New York, 1960, 223 pp., $2.95) (*Galassie in fiamme* [Italian], *Cosmo*: 108, 1962)
 Sequel to *The Little Men*. Jack Odin, with the help of the little folk, ranges the galaxy after the villainous Grim Hagen, who has kidnapped the Princess. *Note:* This story is tied into "Tani of Ekkis" (*ASQ*, Win 1930), by Aladra Septama, which could mean the older story was under a pseudonym.
Little Men, The ("Hunters Out of Time," *AS*, Feb 1959) (Avalon, 1960, 226 pp., $2.95) (*Le creature di opale* [Italian], *Cosmo*: 102, 1962)
 An old-fashioned story with the hero, Jack Odin, helping a beautiful girl and faithful dwarves in the lost world within the Earth. Sequel is *Hunters of Space*.
Overlords From Space [pa] (Ace: D-173, 1956, 146 pp., pa 35¢; with *The Man Who Mastered Time*) (*Das Geheimnis der Zaarlen* [German], *AW*: 4, 1958)
 A standard type—Earth slaves defeat alien overlords.
When the Red King Woke (Avalon, New York, 1966, 192 pp., $3.25)
 Globes engulf a pair and they have adventures in another world.

KELLER, DAVID H. (23 Dec 1880–13 July 1966) U.S. physician and noted science fiction and weird writer. He graduated from the University of Philadelphia medical school at the turn of the century. After general practice he specialised in psychoanalysis and through the years served at various state hospitals for the abnormal in Illinois, Louisiana, Tennessee and Pennsylvania. He did much medical writing, producing nearly 700 articles, a ten-volume set of books, and a more recent unpublished work on his life as a psychiatrist.

He wrote his first story when he was 14, but was 47 when a story was first accepted and paid for; before then he wrote for the pleasure of writing. After seeing *Amazing Stories* in 1926 he submitted "The Revolt of the Pedestrians" to H. Gernsback, and was favorably noticed upon its appearance in the Feb 1928 issue. He then initiated his noted "Taine" series with "The Menace," and later had some stories in *Weird Tales* which included the first of his "Overlord of Cornwall" series. Many a classic appeared from his typewriter until he was called to active duty in World War II, and served as Medical Professor on the faculty of the Army Chaplain's School at Harvard. Some of his fiction appeared prewar in the French periodical *Les Primaires* which an ardent follower, Professor Regis Messac, helped to found. This magazine began to serialise Keller's novel *The Eternal Conflict*, but the war intervened before it was completed. Other writings have included a family history, privately published in 1922; some poetry—*Songs of a Spanish Lover* (limited edition, 1924, under the pseudonym "Henry Cecil"); and a number of general stories for *Ten Story Book* in the 1930's under the pseudonym "Amy Worth."

Keller wrote numerous works—mostly before 1928—which lay unpublished but bound into volumes in his own library. He also wrote much for the amateur magazine field, and was often imposed upon in this respect. He is primarily noted for his simple style and characterisation of plain everyday people, with their actions and reactions under the impact of a new idea. His works are therefore worthy of study for anyone interested in writing styles.

Among his most notable stories is "The Thing in the Cellar" (*WT*, Mar 1932). This has seen at least 14 reprintings, has been translated, and was broadcast in Malaya. It also appeared as a pamphlet of the same title (Bizarre Series No. 2, *ca.* 1940, 32 pp.), also containing an interview of Keller by J. Schwartz and M. Weisinger, an afterword, and two poems: "Colophon" and "To You." Other notable stories include "A Piece of Linoleum" (*Ten Story Book*, Dec 1933 [as Amy Worth]), reprinted and broadcast in Sweden and Denmark; "Stenographer's Hands" (*ASQ*, Fall 1928; *Tales of Wonder*, No. 2, 1938; *AFR*, No. 2, 1947); "The Ivy War" (*AS*, May 1930; in *Best of SF* [Conklin], 1946; *Fan*, Sep 1967); "Revolt of the Pedestrians" (*AS*, Feb 1928; Dec 1966). Novels of interest not covered below include: "The Human Termites" (*Science Wonder*, sr3, Sep 1929; *Captain Future*, sr4, Win 1940); "The Conquerors" (*Science Wonder*, sr2, Dec 1930; *FSM*, Sum 1951) and sequel; "The Time Projector" (*WS*, sr2, July 1931 [with D. Lasser]); "The Metal Doom" (*AS*, sr3, May 1932; *Fan*, sr2, Nov 1967); "The Fireless Age" (*AS*, sr2, Aug 1937). Other pamphlets besides *The Thing in the Cellar* included "Men of Avalon," with C. A. Smith's "The White Sybil" under the latter title (Fantasy Pubs., Everett [Penna.] [W. Crawford], *ca.* 1935, 38 pp., pa 15¢)—now a collector's item; *The Thought Projector*, Science Fiction Series No. 2 (published by Gernsback, 1929); and more recently, *Figment of a Dream* (Anthem, 1962, 39 pp., illus.–D. Prosser, $2.00, limited autographed edition of 175 copies)—an allegorical fantasy.

Series

Loo, Wing. All in *WT*: "The Ambidexter" (Apr 1931); "The Cerebral Library" (May 1931)"; "The Steam Shovel" (Sep 1931). The middle story was also in the "Taine" series.

Overlord of Cornwall. "Battle of the Toads" (*WT*, Oct 1929); "Tailed Men of Cornwall" (*WT*, Nov 1929); "No Other Man" (*WT*, Dec 1929); "The Bride Well" (*WT*, Oct 1930); "The Thirty and One" (*Marvel*, Nov 1938); "Key to Cornwall" (*Stirring*, Feb 1941).

Taine. "The Menace" [4 stories: "The Menace," "The Gold Ship," "The Tainted Flood," "The Insane Avalanche"] (*ASQ*, Sum 1928; *ASQ*, Win 1933); "The Feminine Metamorphosis" (*Science Wonder*, Aug 1929); "Euthanasia Limited" (*ASQ*, Fall 1929); "A Scientific Widowhood" (*Scientific Detective*, Feb 1930); "Burning Water" (*Amazing Detective*, June 1930); "Menacing

Claws" (*Amazing Detective*, Sep 1930); "The Cerebral Library" (*AS*, May 1931); "The Tree of Evil" (*WS*, Sep 1934); "The Island of White Mice" (*AS*, Feb 1935); "Wolf Hollow Bubbles" (ARRA Printers [pamphlet], nd); "Hands of Doom" (*Ten Story Detective*, Oct 1947).

Fiction

Devil and the Doctor, The (Simon & Schuster, New York, 1940, 308 pp., illus., $2.50)

Dr. Jacob Hubler is visited by Robin Goodfellow (the Devil), who isn't such a bad sort, and is granted his dreams and desires; however, trouble follows.

Eternal Conflict, The ("Le Duel Sans Fin" [French], *Le Primaires*, sr?, July 1939 [6 parts published]) (Prime Press, Philadelphia, 1949, 191 pp., $3.50; 350 copies)

Portrayal of two conflicts: between the sexes, and within a woman's mind.

Guerre du Lierre, La [C] (*Les Hypermondes No. 1*, Barbaroux, Saint Lo [France], 1936; 2,000 copies)

3 stories: "La Guerre du Lierre" ("The Ivy War"); "Les Maines et la Machine" ("Stenographer's Hands"); "La Nourice Automatique" ("The Psychophonic Nurse"). All had been published in *Les Primaires*.

Homunculus, The (Prime, 1949, 160 pp., $3.00)

Delightful short fantasy on efforts to produce a parthenogenic baby.

Lady Decides, The (Prime, 1950, 139 pp., $3.50; 350 copies)

Readable story of a man with a dream.

Life Everlasting and Other Tales of Science, Fantasy and Horror [C] (Avalon, Newark, 1949, 394 pp., $3.50)

One novel and 10 short stories [selected by S. Moskowitz, with his introduction]: "Life Everlasting" (*AS*, sr2, July 1934); "The Boneless Horror"; "Unto Us a Child Is Born"; "No More Tomorrows"; "The Thing in the Cellar"; "The Dead Woman"; "Heredity"; "The Face in the Mirror"; "The Cerebral Library"; "A Piece of Linoleum"; "The Thirty and One."

Sign of the Burning Hart, The (Imprimerie de la Manche, Saint Lo [France], 1938, 164 pp., frontis.; 100 copies) (National Fantasy Fan edition, 1948, 166 pp., $2.50; 250 signed copies)

The noted fantasy, actually composed of four connected stories, which the author had submitted to a *Harper's Magazine* prize contest and withdrew from publication rather than change.

Solitary Hunters and The Abyss, The (New Era Pub. Co., Philadelphia, 1948, 265 pp., $3.00) (*Desert des spectres* [French], Fleuve Noir 'Series Angoisse' No. 5, 1955)

"The Solitary Hunters" (*WT*, sr 3, Jan 1934)—criminals are secretly fed to a gigantic insect; an old-style horror story with social overtones. "The Abyss" (original; reprinted in *Mag Horror*, sr2, Sep 1968)—adventures in the human mind; a chewing gum sends New Yorkers deep into primeval memory.

Tales From Underwood [C] (Pellegrini Cudahy, New York, 1952, x+352 pp., $3.95)

23 stories–sf, weird, psychiatric: *The Science-Fictioneer:* "The Worm"; "The Revolt of the Pedestrians"; "The Yeast Men"; "The Ivy War"; "The Door Bell"; "The Flying Fool"; "The Psychophonic Nurse"; "A Biological Experiment"; "Free as the Air." *The Fantaisiste:* "The Bridle"; "Tiger Cat"; "The God Wheel"; "The Golden Bough"; "The Jelly Fish"; "The Opium Eater." *The Psychiatrist:* "The Thing in the Cellar"; "Creation Unforgivable"; "The Moon Artist"; "The Dead Woman"; "The Door"; "The Perfumed Garden"; "The Literary Corkscrew"; "A Piece of Linoleum."

KELLEY, THOMAS P. Canadian author of the 1930's and early 1940's. He was a noted prizefighter as "Tommy Kelley" 1927-29. He wrote a number of novels serialised in *Weird Tales*; besides the one below there were "The Last Pharaoh" (sr4, May 1937) and "A Million Years in the Future" (sr4, Jan 1940). He also appeared in the Canadian magazines with original stories, including the unfinished serial "The Weird Queen" in *Eerie Tales*.

Fiction

I Found Cleopatra [pa] (*WT*, sr4, Nov 1938) (abridged, Export, 1946, 126 pp., pa 9d)

KELLINO, PAMELA (pseud) See MASON, P.

KELLY, FRANK K. (12 June 1914–) U.S. journalist and author. He was born in Kansas City, and has spent his life in journalism. He was a noted writer in the sf field in the early 1930's, when he wrote some 10 stories while in his late teens. These included: "Crater 17, Near Tycho" (*ASF*, June 1934); "Exiles of Mars" (*WSQ*, Sum 1932; *WS Annual*, 1950); "The Light Bender" (*WS*, June 1931; *FSM*, Sum 1950); "Red April, 1965" (*WS*, Mar 1932).

KELLY, ROBERT (24 Sep 1935–) U.S. poet.
Fiction
Scorpions, The (Doubleday, New York, 1967, 188 pp., $3.95) (D'day, Toronto, $4.75)
    A neurotic society woman convinces her psychiatrist that there is a race of ultraviolet people.

KELLY, WALT (25 Aug 1913–) U.S. cartoonist. He was an animator with Walt Disney 1935-41, then an artist in New York City 1941-48. He is now known worldwide for his "Pogo" comic strip. Regular Pogo collections from Simon & Schuster (New York, $1.00) and Musson (Toronto, $1.35) have included: *Pogo* (1951); *I Go Pogo* (1952); *Uncle Pogo So-So Stories* (1953); *The Pogo Papers* (1953); *The Pogo Stepmother Goose* (1954); *The Incompleat Pogo* (1954); *Pogo Peek-a-Book* (1954); *Potluck Pogo* (1955, reprint of daily comic strip); *The Pogo Sunday Book* (1956); *The Pogo Party* (1956); *Pogo's Sunday Punch* (1957); *Positively Pogo* (1957); *The Pogo Sunday Parade* (1958); *Fizzicle Pogo* (1958); *Pogo Sunday Brunch* (1959); *Ten Ever-Luvin' Blue-Eyed Years With Pogo* (1959, $4.95); [hereafter, $1.25] *Beau Pogo* (1960); *Pogo Extra* (Election special) (1960); *Pogo a la Sundae* (1961); *Gone Pogo* (1961); *Instant Pogo* (1962); *The Jack Acid Society Black Book of Pogo* (1962); *Pogo Puce Stamp Catalog* (1963); *Deck Us All With Boston Charlie* (1963); *The Return of Pogo* (1965); *The Pogo Poop Book* (1966); *Prehysterical Pogo (in Pandemonia)* (1967). Others include *Songs of Pogo* [with Norman Monath] (Simon & Schuster, 1956, $3.95). Australian reprints [selected] are *Potluck Pogo* and *I Go Pogo*. *Pogo Parade* (1953, 25¢) was a comic reprinting 11 of the old "Albert the Alligator" and "Albert and the Pogo" stories which appeared in *Animal Comics*, a magazine which saw 30-odd issues and ended in 1948. *Pogo Comicbook* was the best of its type, having 16 quarterly issues ending with the Apr/June 1954 issue.

KEMP, EARL (24 Nov 1929–) U.S. science-fiction and fantasy collector and prominent fan. He was born in Arkansas. He moved to Chicago and worked in the advertising, printing, and publishing fields. He was one of the founders of Advent:Publishers and was its manager until he moved to California in 1965. Until recently he was an editor with Greenleaf in San Diego. Early in 1960 he circulated the questionnaire "Who Killed Science Fiction?" to 108 writers, editors, artists and fans. The 70 replies were collected as the booklet of the same title (107 pp.) and sent only to the contributors and to members of the Spectator Amateur Press Society. (For general comment see P. S. Miller, *ASF*, Dec 1960.)
Nonfiction
Proceedings of the 20th World Science Fiction Convention—Chicon III [editor] [pa] (Advent, Chicago, 1963, 208 pp., illus., pa $3.50; 1966, $1.95)
    Transcript of the 1962 convention in Chicago.

KEMP, HAROLD (CURRY) (1896–)
Fiction
Mark of a Witch (Bles, London, 1959, 254 pp., 12/6) (Collins, Toronto, $2.75)
    Macabre mystery about the Witch of Fangmoor and a vile and ugly wooden doll.

KEMP, ROBERT (1908–) Scottish writer. He was born in the Orkney Islands and educated at Aberdeen University. He has worked for the Manchester *Guardian* and the BBC, but has now established himself as a playwright in Edinburgh.

Fiction
Malacca Cane, The (Duckworth, London, 1954, 167 pp., 8/6)
    A racy and delightful fantasy novel.

KENDALL, CAROL
Fiction
Gammage Cup, The [pa] (Voyager: AVB43, 1966, 221 pp., pa 60¢)
    Fantasy about the Minnipins, a race of little people in an isolated valley, with a group of rebels challenging authority.

KENNAWAY, JAMES (pseud) See PEEBLES, J. E.

KENNICOTT, DONALD (30 Sep 1881–) U.S. editor. He was born in Chicago, He was on the editorial staff of *Blue Book*, *Red Book* and *Green Book* 1910-29. In 1929 he became editor of *Blue Book* and held that position into the 1940's.

KEPPEL-JONES, ARTHUR
Fiction
When Smuts Goes (African Bookman, Cape Town, 1947, x+203 pp., 12/6)
    Subtitled: "History of South Africa from 1952 to 2010—first published in 2015." This is a grim picture of the future of South Africa and its eventual fall and regression to barbarism (written when the retirement of General Smuts was imminent).

KERBY, SUSAN ALICE (pseud) See BURTON, E.

KERNAHAN, COULSON
Fiction [Incomplete—other titles in Bleiler *Checklist*]
Book of Strange Sins, A [C] (Ward Lock & Bowden, London, 1894, 195 pp.) (Altemus, Philadelphia, 1895, 195 pp.)
    Fantasy, 7 stories: "The Lonely God"; "A Strange Sin"; "A Suicide"; "The Garden of God"; "The Apples of Sin"; "A Literary Gent"; "A Lost Soul."

KERR, GEOFFREY (1895–) British author and radio and film script writer. He has contributed to *Vanity Fair*, *Harper's Bazaar*, *Esquire*, etc., while his books include *Cottage to Let* and *Black Swans*. He collaborated with Robert Sherwood on the screen-play *The Ghost Goes West*.
Fiction
Under the Influence (M. Joseph, London, 1953, 238 pp., 10/6) (Collins, Toronto, $2.75) (Lippincott, Philadelphia, 1954, 251 pp., $3.50) (Pan: G138, 1958, 190 pp., pa 2/6) (Berkley: G-518, 1961, 189 pp., pa 35¢)
    Fun in ESP; a bank clerk becomes an involuntary telepathic detective.

KERRUISH, JESSIE D(OUGLAS) Another work is *Babylonian Nights' Entertainment* (1934).
Fiction
Undying Monster, The (Heath Cranton, London, 1922, 280 pp., 7/6) (Macmillan, New York, 1936, 256 pp., $2.00) (P. Allan, London, 1936, 256 pp., 3/6) (*Le Monstre immortel* [French], Les Editions de France, 1939) (*Il mostro immortale* [Italian], *Urania*: 85, 1955) (*FFM*, June 1946) (Award: A3515, 1968, pa 75¢)
    Fascinating novel of inherited inhibition. *Film*: 20th Century Fox, directed by John Brahm with Heather Angel and John Howard.

KERSH, GERALD (6 Aug 1911–5 Nov 1968) British author and journalist. He was born in Russia, lived many years in Britain, and went to the U.S.A. after World War II. His various occupations included baker, bouncer, wrestler and Coldstream Guardsman. He achieved publication in 1935 with a novel which had to be withdrawn because of several libel suits. He was a frequent contributor to leading magazines such as *SEP* and also wrote plays and movie scripts. He once estimated that he had written 5,000 articles and short stories. He was one of the most provocative of post-war writers. He is noted for his *Prelude to a Certain Midnight* (1947) and *Fowler's End*; probably his best known sf story was "What-

ever Happened to Corporal Cuckoo?"
Fiction
Brighton Monster, The [C] (Heinemann, London, 1953, 197 pp., 10/6)

12 stories: "The Brighton Monster"; "Frozen Beauty"; "The Copper Dahlia"; "White Horse With Wings"; "Ladies or Clothes"; "Judas Forgiven"; "The Epistle of Simple Simon"; "Note on Danger B"; "The Queen of Pig Island"; "Wealth of Nations"; "The Ape and the Mystery"; "Whatever Happened to Corporal Cuckoo?"
Great Wash, The See *Secret Masters, The*
Horrible Dummy and Other Stories, The [C] (Heinemann, 1944, 166 pp., 8/6)

23 stories: "The Undefeated"; "The Ten Old Tigers"; "Comrade Death"; "The Extraordinarily Horrible Dummy"; "Lunatic's Broth"; "A Ruby Worth £1100"; "The Stone"; "The Devil That Troubled the Chessboard"; "The Bitter Seas"; "The Drunk and the Blind"; "The Woman in the Mud"; "Shaggy Yellow Fog"; "The Battle of the Singing Men"; "The Musicians"; "A Bit of a Change"; "The Last Coin of Mr. Baer"; "Irongut and the Brown Mouse"; "Hairy Cohen"; "Dudelsack"; "Slaves"; "The Evil Destiny of Dr. Polacek"; "The White Flash"; "All That One Man Remembered."
Men Without Bones [C] (Heinemann, 1955, 194 pp., 12/6) (WDL: SF975, 1960, 156 pp., pa 2/6) (Paperback: 52-127, 1962, 223, pa 50¢)

Both British eds., 22 stories: "Men Without Bones"; "The Hack"; "The White-Washed Room"; "The Violin Maker"; "Femme Fatale"; "Gratitude"; "The Madwoman"; "The Life and Times of the Dog Basta"; "The Guardian"; "Carnival on the Downs"; "Elizabeth and Temptation"; "In a Misty Window"; "Memory of a Fight"; "The Fabulous Fido"; "The Tarleton Twins"; "The Charcoal Burner"; "The Sympathetic Souse"; "Incident in a Tavern"; "The End of a Wise Guy"; "The Dancing Doll"; "Buried Treasure"; "One Case in a Million."

U.S. pa ed., 13 stories: "Men Without Bones"; "The Shady Life of Annibal"; "The Ape and the Mystery"; "The Oxoxoco Bottle"; "Thicker Than Water"; "The Madwoman"; "The Terrible Ride of Colonel Tessier"; "The Dancing Doll"; "The Hack"; "Ladies or Clothes"; "In a Room Without Walls"; "Clock Without Hands"; "The Epistle of Simple Simon."
Nightshade and Damnation [C] [pa] (Gold Medal: R1887, 1968, 192 pp., pa 60¢)

Weird, 11 stories, introduction by Harlan Ellison: "The Queen of Pig Island"; "Frozen Beauty" "The Brighton Monster"; "Men Without Bones"; " 'Busto Is a Ghost, Too Mean to Give Us a Fright!' "; "The Ape and the Mystery"; "The King Who Collected Clocks"; "Bone for Debunkers"; "A Lucky Day for the Boar"; "Voices in the Dust of Anna"; "Whatever Happened to Corporal Cuckoo?"
On an Odd Note [C] [pa] (Ballantine: 268, 1958, 154 pp., pa 35¢)

Fantasy, 13 stories: "Seed of Destruction"; "Frozen Beauty"; "Reflections in a Tablespoon"; "The Crewel Needle"; "The Sympathetic Souse"; "The Queen of Pig Island"; "Prophet Without Honor"; "The Beggars' Stone"; "The Brighton Monster"; "The Extraordinarily Horrible Dummy"; "Fantasy of a Hunted Man"; "The Gentleman All in Black"; "The Eye."
Secret Masters, The ("The Mystery of the Third Compartment," *SEP*, sr5, 22 Nov 1952) (Ballantine, New York, 1953, 225 pp., $2.00; #28, pa 35¢) (*The Great Wash*, Heinemann, 1953, 246 pp., 12/6)

A formula-type save-the-world theme; the writing falls off towards the end.

KEY, ALEXANDER (1904–)
Fiction
Escape to Witch Mountain (Westminster, New York, 1968, 172 pp., illus.–L. Wisdom, $3.75)

Juvenile; two children of alien origin escape from a juvenile home and set out to return to their real home.
Forgotten Door, The (Westminster, 1965, 126 pp., $3.50) (Scho-

lastic: TX791, 1968, pa 45¢)

Juvenile; an inhabitant of a parallel continuum comes to Earth and communicates by telepathy.
Rivets and Sprockets (Westminster, Philadelphia, 1964, 160 pp., $3.95)

Juvenile—space and robot story, illustrated by author.

KEY, EUGENE GEORGE
Fiction
Mars Mountain (Fantasy Publications, Everett (Penna.), 1934, 142 pp., 2 illus.–I. E. G. Bjurkmann, 25¢; 6½ in. x 4¼ in., 400 copies)

3 stories: "Mars Mountain"; "Earth Sees Mars"; "Lake Tempest." The stories are of little merit and the book originally was not well received. It is now, however, a rare and sought-after item. It was the first hard-cover book from a specialty publisher. It is not listed in the Bleiler *Checklist*.

KEYES, DANIEL (9 Aug 1927–) U.S. author and editor. He helped edit the post-war *Marvel Stories* (from Aug 1950) and did much to raise its standard. Although he has not had much fiction published in the sf/fantasy field, he won the 1960 Hugo for best short story with "Flowers for Algernon" (*F&SF*, Apr 1959; reprinted in *The Hugo Winners* [Asimov], 1962). This story was the basis for his novel of the same title.
Fiction
Flowers for Algernon (Harcourt Brace World, New York 1966, 274 pp., $4.95) (Cassell, London, 1966, 274 pp., 25/-) (Bantam: S3339, 1967, 217 pp., pa 75¢; 1968, pa 75¢) (Pan: M02094, 1968, 238 pp., pa 5/-)

Moronic Charles Gordon is artificially brought up to genius level, and then reverts.
Touch, The (Harcourt, 1968, 215 pp., $4.75)

Borderline; humans under extraordinary stress due to radioactive contamination.

KEYES, NOEL (pseud) See KEIGHTLEY, D. N.

KEYHOE, DONALD E. (20 June 1897–) U.S. author. He is a retired Marine Corps officer and was formerly information chief of the U.S. Dept. of Commerce. He is noted for his books supporting the existence of "flying saucers."
Nonfiction
Flying Saucer Conspiracy, The (Holt, New York, 1955, 315 pp., $3.50) (Hutchinson, London, 1957, 248 pp., 15/-)

Another interesting and potentially controversial contribution to the literature of flying saucers.
Flying Saucers Are Real, The [pa] (Gold Medal: 107, 1950, 175 pp., pa 25¢) (Arrow, 1950, 192 pp., pa 2/-)

One of the first works on the occurrence of flying saucers.
Flying Saucers From Outer Space (Holt, 1953, 276 pp., $3.00) (Hutchinson, 1954, 270 pp., 10/6) (*Der Weltraum rückt uns näher* [German], Blan Valet, 1954) (Perma: Star 297, 1954, 241 pp., pa 25¢) (Arrow: 402H, 1955, 256 pp., pa 25¢)

A kind of 2nd edition of *The Flying Saucers Are Real*, with the author more than ever convinced that "saucers" are real and may carry visitors from other worlds.

KHOSROFIAN, HARRY (1924–)
Fiction
Fallen Star (Comet Press 'Milestone,' New York, 1959, 71 pp., $2.50)

KING, (WILLIAM BENJAMIN) BASIL (26 Feb 1859–22 June 1928) American novelist, short-story writer and spiritualist. An Episcopalian minister, he was rector at St. Luke's Procathedral, Halifax, 1881. His first novel, *Griselda* (1900), appeared when he was 41, but it was *The Inner Shrine*, anonymously published in *Harper's Magazine*, that drew attention to him. He learnt to typewrite before he went blind. He joined Sir A. C. Doyle and Sir Oliver Lodge in his belief in spiritualism.

Fiction [Incomplete—other titles in Bleiler *Checklist*]
Spreading Dawn: Stories of the Great Transition, The [C] (Harper, New York, 1927, 136 pp., $2.00)

Fantasy, 6 stories (not covered in Bleiler *Checklist*): "The Spreading Dawn"; "The Ghost's Story"; "Heaven"; "Abraham's Bosom"; "Going West"; "The Last Enemy."

KINGSMILL, HUGH (pseud) See LUNN, H. K.

KIP, LEONARD (13 Sep 1826–1906) U.S. author. He graduated from Trinity College, Hartford, in 1846. He was admitted to the bar and practised for the greater part of his life in Albany; he was president of Albany Institute for 10 years. His writing began with *California Sketches* (1850).
Fiction
Hannibal's Man and Other Tales [C] (Argus Co., Albany [N.Y.], 1878, 371 pp.)

6 stories: "Hannibal's Man"; "In Three Heads"; "The Ghost at Grantley"; "The Secret of Appolonius Septro"; "Prior Polycarp's Portrait"; "St. Nicholas and the Gnome." Four of these stories appeared in successive issues of *The Argus* of Albany, with the title story being published by Argus in 1873 (46 pp.). "Prior Polycarp's Portrait" was an original with "The Secret of Appolonius Septro," and was published well before 1878 anonymously under another title.

KIPLING, RUDYARD (30 Dec 1865–18 Jan 1936) English imperialist, poet and writer. He was born in Bombay and lived there until 6 years old when he was sent to England. He returned to India in 1883 and began his journalism career. He went to London, and after some success and marriage he moved to America, but returned in 1896. In this period he wrote some of his noted books such as *Many Inventions* (1893) and *Jungle Books* (1893-4). He was an observer in the Boer War, after which he wrote *Kim* (1901). He later associated himself with controversial matters, but helped as a propagandist during World War I, in which his only son died. He won many awards and held numerous honorary degrees.
Fiction [Incomplete—other titles in Bleiler *Checklist*]
Phantom Rickshaw, The [C] (H. Altemus, Philadephia, [1898], 243 pp., frontis.) (Caldwell, New York & Boston, 1899, 222 pp.) (Publisher's Guild, nd, 222 pp.) ([Spanish], La Nave, nd)

5 stories (Publisher's Guild ed.; contents vary in various other editions): "The Phantom Rickshaw"; "My Own True Ghost Story"; "The Strange Ride of Morrowbie Jukes"; "The Man Who Would Be King"; "The Funniest Story in the World."
Puck of Pook's Hill [C] (Doubleday & Page, New York, 1906, 277 pp., illus.) (Macmillan 'Papermac: P76,' London, 1967, 222 pp., pa 5/-)

Juvenile, 10 stories and 16 poems (not listed): "Weland's Sword"; "Young Men at the Manor"; "The Knights of the Joyous Venture"; "Old Men at Pevensey"; "A Centurion of the Thirtieth"; "On the Great Wall"; "The Winged Hats"; "Hal o' the Draft"; " 'Dymchurch Flit' "; "The Treasure and the Law."

KIPPAX, JOHN (pseud) See HYNAM, J.

KIRK, LAURENCE (pseud) See SIMSON, E. A.

KIRK, RUSSELL (AMOS) (19 Oct 1918–) U.S. author and lecturer. He was born in Plymouth, Mich.; received B.A., Michigan State College in 1940, M.A. at Duke, 1941, and D. Litt. at St. Andrews University in Scotland, 1952. He was Assistant Professor of the History of Civilization at Michigan State College 1946-53. He is well known as a leading exponent of conservative political philosophy and is a columnist for *National Review* and other publications.
Fiction
Lost Lake [pa] See *Surly Sullen Bell, The*
Old House of Fear (Fleet, New York, 1961, 256 pp., $3.95) (Gollancz, London, 1962, 16/-) (Copp, Toronto, $4.50) (Avon: G1262, 1965, 192 pp., pa 50¢)

Weird novel.

Surly Sullen Bell, The [C] (Fleet, 1962, 240 pp., illus., $4.50) (Paperback: 52-316, 1964, 159 pp., pa 50¢) (*Lost Lake*, Paperback: 52-365, 1966, 159 pp., pa 50¢)

Weird of 10 stories, foreword, and final "A Cautionary Note on the Ghostly Tale": "Uncle Isaiah"; "Off the Sand Road"; "Ex Tenebris"; "The Surly Sullen Bell"; "The Cellar of Little Egypt"; "Skyberia"; "Sorworth Place" (*F&SF*, Nov 1962); "Behind the Stumps" (*F&SF*, Dec 1962); "What Shadows We Pursue"; "Lost Lake."

KIRST, HANS HELLMUT (1914–) German author. He is noted for his Gunner Asch trilogy, a humorous satire about one man's revolt against the tenets of military life in Nazi Germany.
Fiction
No One Will Escape [pa] See *Seventh Day, The*
Seventh Day, The (*Keiner Kommt Davon* [German], Kurt Desch, München, 1957, 512 pp., DM16.80) Trans.–Richard Graves: (Doubleday, New York, 1959, 424 pp., $4.95) (Weidenfeld Nicolson, London, 1959, 412 pp., 18/-) (Ace: Star K110, 1960, 384 pp., pa 50¢) (*No One Will Escape*, WDL: N961, 1960, 446 pp., pa 5/6) (*Ingen Kommer Att Överleva* [Swedish], Horsta, 1958) (*Nadie escapara* [Spanish], Destino, 1959) (Pyramid: T1215, 1965, 382 pp., pa 75¢)

Some may not call this sf, but it predicts events that could happen tomorrow. It is an extensive and deadly earnest coverage of the days before the next world war, and depicts the characteristics of political manoeuvring between East and West today. Although weak in some ways, it is a compelling plea for peace.

KISSLING, (Mrs) DOROTHY HIGHT (RICHARDSON) (1904–)
Fiction [as Dorothy Langley]
Mr. Bremble's Buttons (Simon & Schuster, New York, 1947, 186 pp., $2.75) (Musson, Toronto, $3.00) (Heinemann, London, 1948, 185 pp., 7/6)

A whimsical and often humorous allegory about God.

KLASS, PHILIP (1920–) U.S. science fiction author and anthologist, better known under his pseudonym "William Tenn." In school he did not study literature and writing. Since World War II he has been a professional writer, with occasional work in other occupations such as salesman and purser. Since 1946 he has written over 50 stories published in most sf magazines. In recent years he has written few new stories, but interest in his writings has been renewed with the appearance of six volumes in a uniform edition from Ballantine in 1968.
Fiction [as William Tenn]
Human Angle, The [C] (Ballantine, New York, 1956, 152 pp., $2.00; #159, pa 35¢; U2190, 1964, pa 50¢; U6135, 1968, 153 pp., 75¢)

Sf, 8 stories: "Project Hush" (rev. from *GSF*); "The Discovery of Morniel Mathaway"; "Wednesday's Child"; "The Servant Problem"; "Party of the Two Parts"; "The Flat-Eyed Monster"; "The Human Angle"; "A Man of Family."
Lamp for Medusa, A [pa] ("Medusa Was a Lady," *FA*, Oct 1951) (Belmont: B60-077, 1968, 78 pp., pa 60¢; with *The Players of Hell*)

The gods of Greek mythology come to life for Percy Yuss.
Of All Possible Worlds [C] (Ballantine, 1955, 160 pp., $2.00; #99, pa 35¢; 407K, 1960, pa 35¢; U6136, 1968, 161 pp., pa 75¢) (M. Joseph, London, 1956, 255 pp., 12/6) (*Mundos posibles* [Spanish], Nebula: 71, 1961 pa) (Mayflower: 6532, 1963, 190 pp., pa 3/6; 1966, pa 3/6)

Sf, 7 stories: "Down Among the Dead Men"; "Me, Myself and I"; "The Liberation of Earth"; "Everybody Loves Irving Bommer"; "Flirgleflip"; "The Tenants"; "The Custodian."
Of Men and Monsters [pa] (Ballantine: U6131, 1968, 251 pp., pa 75¢)

The first portion appeared originally as "The Men in the Walls" (*GSF*, short n, Oct 1963)—mankind in degenerated tribal groupings in a land of giants, and how they were patched up into a new society.
Seven Sexes, The [C] [pa] (Ballantine: U6134, 1968, 238 pp., pa

75¢)

Sf, 8 stories and Author's Note: "Child's Play"; "The Malted Milk Monster"; "Errand Boy"; "The House Dutiful"; "Mistress Sary"; "Sanctuary"; "Venus and the Seven Sexes"; "Bernie the Faust."

Square Root of Man, The [C] [pa] (Ballantine: U6132, 1968, 221 pp., pa 75¢)

Sf, 9 stories and Author's Note: "Alexander the Bait"; "The Last Bounce"; "She Only Goes Out at Night"; "My Mother Was a Witch"; "The Jester"; "Confusion Cargo"; "Venus Is a Man's World"; "Consulate"; "The Lemon-Green Spaghetti-Lord Dynamite-Dribble Day" ("Did Your Coffee Taste Funny This Morrug?" *Cavalier*, 1967).

Time in Advance [C] [pa] (Bantam: A1786, 1958, 153 pp., pa 35¢) (*Tiempo anticipade* [Spanish], Nebula: 86, 1962, pa) (Gollancz, London, 1963, 153 pp., 15/-) (SF B.C. [S.J.], 1964, 6/-) (*Die Welt der Zukunft* [German], Pabel: 249, 1966, pa [omits 3rd story]) (Panther: 2037, 1966, 173 pp., pa 3/6)

Sf, 4 short novels: "Firewater" (*ASF*, Feb 1952); "Time in Advance" (*GSF*, Aug 1956); "The Sickness" (*Infinity*, Nov 1955); "Winthrop Was Stubborn" ("Time Waits for Winthrop," *GSF*, Aug 1957).

Wooden Stars, The [C] [pa] (Ballantine: U6133, 1968, 251 pp., pa 75¢)

11 stories with Author's Note: "Generation of Noah"; "Brooklyn Project"; "The Dark Star"; "Null-P"; "Eastward Ho!"; "The Deserter"; "Betelgeuse Bridge"; " 'Will You Walk a Little Faster?' "; "It Ends With a Flicker"; "Lisbon Cubed"; "The Masculinist Revolt."

Nonfiction [as Philip Klass]

UFO's–Identified (Random, New York, 1968, 290 pp., $6.95)

Anthology [as William Tenn]

Children of Wonder (Simon & Schuster, New York, 1953, 336 pp., $2.95) (D'day SF B.C., 1954) (*Outsiders: Children of Wonder*, Permabooks: P291, 1954, 355 pp., pa 35¢)

Sf, 19 stories and 1 poem (stories about children): "The Rocking-Horse Winner," D. H. Lawrence; "The Words of Guru," C. M. Kornbluth; "Baby Is Three," T. Sturgeon; "Small Assassin," R. Bradbury; "The Piper's Son," L. Padgett; "Miriam," T. Capote; "Adam and Eve and Pinch Me," A. E. Coppard; "Child's Play," Mary-Alice Schnirring; "The Open Window," Saki; "The End of the Party," Graham Greene; "The Idol of the Flies," Jane Rice; "That Only a Mother," Judith Merril; "Born of Man and Woman," R. Matheson; "Keyhole," M. Leinster; "Terminal Quest," P. Anderson; "The Origin of the Species" (new), Katherine MacLean; "In Hiding," Wilmar H. Shiras; "The Hatchery," A. Huxley; "Errand Boy," Wm. Tenn; "Nightmare for Future Reference" (verse), S. V. Benét.

Outsiders: Children of Wonder [pa] See *Children of Wonder*

KLEY, HEINRICH Noted German artist. At first he was a painter of unexceptional subjects—portraits, landscapes, city scenes, etc. In 1892 he began doing industrial scenes, and finally developed a highly individualised technique using as subject matter satire to near-obscenity, despair, cruelty and pain. A number of his drawings in the last phase were reprinted in early issues of *Fantastic* and *Coronet*.

Artwork

Drawings of Heinrich Kley, The (Dover, New York, 10½ in. x 7½ in., 1962, 128 pp., $1.85) (Imported into England by Constable, London, 15/-)

200 of his drawings.

More Drawings by Heinrich Kley (Dover, 10½ in. x 7½ in., 1962, 104 pp.) (Constable, 15/-)

158 of his drawings.

KLINE, OTIS ADELBERT (1891–24 Oct 1946) U.S. fantasy author and authors' agent. He was born in Chicago of Dutch ancestry. He was a song writer and music publisher before he began writing film scenarios and popular fiction in the early 1920's. His fiction was of all types and appeared in many magazines outside the fantasy field. He was one of the earliest contributors to *Weird*

Tales, with the novel "The Thing of a Thousand Shapes" (sr2, Mar 1923). Much of his fiction was fantastic adventure in the vein of E. R. Burroughs, with whom he had to compete; nevertheless he had many appearances in *Argosy* and other general fiction magazines. Probably his most successful novel was *The Call of the Savage* ("Jan of the Jungle" from *Argosy*), which was made into a film in which Dorothy Lamour wore her famous sarong and which was also adapted as a radio serial. Stories of interest besides those covered below include: "Race Around the Moon" (*TWS*, Aug 1939); "Spawn of the Comet" (*Arg*, 27 Sep 1930; *FN*, June 1951); "Satans of Saturn" (in collaboration with E. H. Price) (*Arg*, sr5, 2 Nov 1940). Kline was also a leading literary agent with world-wide connections, and handled the work of many noted authors, including H. G. Wells; the late O. J. Friend became the head of the agency, Otis Kline Associates, which continues to the present day.

Series

Dragoman. *Oriental Stories*: "The Man Who Limped" (Oct/Nov 1930); "The Dragoman's Revenge" (Feb/Mar 1931); "The Dragoman's Secret" (Apr/June 1931); "The Dragoman's Pet Slave Girl" (Sum 1931); "The Dragoman's Jest" (Win 1932 [with E. H. Price]); "The Dragoman's Confession" (Sum 1932). *Magic Carpet*: "The Dragoman's Pilgrimage" (Jan 1933). All except the 2nd and 5th were published as *The Man Who Limped*.

Grandon, Robert. Fantastic adventure on Venus: *The Planet of Peril*; *The Prince of Peril*; *The Port of Peril* [see book entries]. These are actually part of a larger series linked by the character Doctor Morgan; further novels are *The Swordsman of Mars* and *The Outlaws of Mars*.

Fiction [*Note:* Avalon editions are often abridged]

Call of the Savage, The ("Jan of the Jungle," *Arg*, sr6, 18 Apr 1931) (Clode, New York, 1937, 9+256 pp., $2.00) (McLeod, Toronto, $2.25) (*Jan of the Jungle*, Ace: F-400, 1966, 172 pp., pa 40¢)

Jan, raised in the South American jungle, has adventures with the descendants of Atlantis. The sequel is "Jan in India" (*Arg*, sr3, 12 Jan 1935).

Jan of the Jungle [pa] See *Call of the Savage, The*

Man Who Limped and Other Stories, The [C] [pa] (Saint Enterprises, 1946, 128 pp., pa 25¢)

5 stories of the "Dragoman" series, which see.

Maza of the Moon (*Arg*, sr4, 21 Dec 1929) (McClurg, Chicago, 1930, 341 pp., $2.00) (Grosset, New York, 1931, 75¢) (Ace: F-321, 1965, 144 pp., pa 40¢)

Fantastic adventure with beings on the Moon.

Outlaws of Mars (*Arg*, sr7, 25 Nov 1933) (Avalon, New York, 1961, 224 pp., $2.95, jacket—E. Emshwiller) (Ace: D-531, 1961, 158 pp., pa 35¢; G-693, 1967, pa 50¢)

Sequel to *The Swordsman of Mars*, with a different hero involved in Martian intrigue.

Planet of Peril, The (*Arg*, sr6, 20 July 1929) (McClurg, 1929, 358 pp., $2.00) (Avalon, 1961, 224 pp., $2.95, jacket—E. Emshwiller) (Ace: F-211, 1963, 160 pp., pa 40¢)

First of "Grandon" series—fantastic adventure on Venus, which has a mixture of advanced science, feudalism and monster-fighting.

Port of Peril, The ("Buccaneers of Venus," *WT*, sr6, Nov 1932) (Grandon, Providence [R.I.], 1949, 218 pp., illus.—J. A. St. John, $3.00) (Ace: F-294, 1964, 192 pp., pa 40¢)

Third of "Robert Grandon" series. The Grandon ed. has original magazine illustrations.

Prince of Peril, The (*Arg*, sr6, 2 Aug 1930) (McClurg, 1930, 322 pp., $2.00) (Avalon, 1962, 224 pp., $2.95, jacket—E. Emshwiller) (Ace: F-259, 1963, 174 pp., pa 40¢)

Second of "Grandon" series.

Swordsman of Mars, The (*Arg*, sr6, 7 Jan 1933) (Avalon, 1960, 218 pp., $2.95) (Ace: D-516, 1961, 174 pp., pa 35¢; G-692, 1967, pa 50¢) (*Lo spadaccino di Marte* [Italian], Fantascienza: 9, 1962, pa)

Fantastic adventure in which an Earth hero is transferred to Mars by telepathy and saves Martian civilization from destruction. A slightly connected later story is *Outlaws of Mars*.

Tam, Son of the Tiger (*WT*, sr6, June/July 1931) (Avalon, 1962, 222 pp., $2.95)

KNEALE, (THOMAS) NIGEL (1922–) British author and BBC writer. He was born in Lancaster and grew up on the Isle of Man, where for some time he was a law student. He received his diploma as a playwright after studying at the Royal Academy of Dramatic Art, London; he also acted in Shakespeare at Stratford-on-Avon. He now devotes himself entirely to writing. Besides scripting such BBC production as G. Orwell's *1984* and the "Quatermass" series, he has done screenplays for John Osborne's *Look Back in Anger* and *The Entertainer* in the U.S.A.

Series

Quatermass. BBC TV plays, with film and book derivatives: *The Quatermass Experiment*; *Quatermass II*; *Quatermass and the Pit*. The TV plays were high-class productions, very well presented.

Fiction

Quatermass and the Pit [pa] (Penguin: 1449, 1960, 188 pp., pa 2/6)

Third of series, script of BBC TV play, 6 parts, Dec 1958–Jan 1959. Prof. Quatermass investigates strange phenomena from a cylinder in a pit.

Quatermass Experiment, The [pa] (Penguin: 1421, 1959, 192 pp., pa 2/6)

First of series, script of BBC TV play, 6 parts, July-Aug 1953, later produced as a film. A ship takes three crewmen into space but only one returns, and he cannot immediately tell what happened; he finds his body is being used by an intelligent life cell. *Film:* Above title, Independent Film (British), 1955; released as *The Creeping Unknown* in the U.S. and Australia. It starred Brian Donlevy, Jack Warner, Marcia Dean and David K. Wood, and was produced by Anthony Hinds and directed by Val Guest, with screenplay by Richard Landau from the TV serial.

Quatermass II [pa] (Penguin: 1448, 1960, 174 pp., pa 2/6)

Second of series, script of BBC TV play, 6 parts, late 1955. Prof. Quatermass versus vaporous entities from space. *Film:* Above title, Hammer (British), 1956; also released as *Enemy From Space*; starring Brian Donlevy, produced by A. Hinds and directed by V. Guest.

Tomato Cain [C] (Collins, London, 1949, 256 pp., 8/6) (Collins, Toronto, $2.00) (Knopf, New York, 1950, 300 pp., $3.00) (Fontana: 561, 1961, 190 pp., pa 2/6)

29 stories, with foreword by Elizabeth Bowen: "Tomato Cain"; "Enderby and the Sleeping Beauty"; " 'Minuke' "; "Clog Dance for a Dead Farce"; "Essence of Strawberry"; "Lotus for Jamie"; " 'Oh, Mirror, Mirror' "; "God and Daphne"; "Jeremy in the Wind"; "The Excursion"; "Flo"; "The Putting Away of Uncle Quaggin"; "The Photograph"; "Chains"; "The Tarroo-Ushtey"; "Mrs. Mancini"; "Curphey's Follower"; "Quiet Mr. Evans"; "Tootie and the Cat Licenses"; "Peg"; "Zachary Crebbin's Angel"; "Bini and Bettine"; "The Stocking"; "Who– Me, Signor?"; "The Pond"; "They're Scared, Mr. Bradlaugh"; "The Calculation of M'Bambwe"; "Nature Study"; "The Patter of Tiny Feet." The book won the 1950 Somerset Maugham Award for new stories.

KNEBEL, FLETCHER (1 Oct 1911–) U.S. political journalist in Washington. His *Night of Camp David* (1965) is of sf interest; it deals with a U.S. President wishing to make an unusual alliance.

Fiction

Seven Days in May [with C. Bailey] (Harper & Row, New York, 1962, 341 pp., $4.95) (Bantam: N2640, 1963, 372 pp., pa 95¢) (*Zeven dagen in mei* [Dutch], Nieuwe Wieken, Amstelveen, 1963) (Corgi: FN1455, 1965, 372 pp., pa 5/-) (*Course à la maison blanche* [French], Fayard, 1965)

A novel of a possible future crisis; the Joint Chiefs of Staff plot to depose an unpopular U.S. President in 1974 and set up a military government.

KNIGHT, DAMON (FRANCIS) (20 Sep 1922–) U.S. science fiction and fantasy author, editor and book critic. He began collecting in those fields in 1933, and led a varied life until he became a writer. His editing work began when he assisted E. Jakobsson for a

while in editing *Super Science Stories* (2nd Series). He left in 1950 to become editor of *Worlds Beyond*, which was quite favourably received although the publisher cancelled it after three issues. In 1958 he returned to sf editing and worked on J. L. Quinn's *If* (Oct 1958–Feb 1959) in an endeavour to raise the magazine's circulation, but he could not save it from suspension; *If* was later bought by Guinn.

In the 1950's his critical book reviews were a feature of many magazines in the field, such as *Infinity*, *SF Stories* and *Future SF*; in April 1958 he joined *If* and continued the reviews there. Later he ran the book review column for *F&SF* (Apr 1959–Sep 1960), but often only covered one or two books per issue (the ones worth attention). He won a Hugo in 1956 for his book reviewing; many of his reviews were collected in his noted book *In Search of Wonder* (1956; rev. 2nd ed., 1967). Since 1959 his reviewing has virtually ceased.

Knight's own fiction has appeared in most magazines, with around 70 stories since the early 1940's (some under pseudonyms and in collaboration). One was dramatised on TV: "To Serve Man" (*GSF*, Nov 1950) on R. Serling's *Twilight Zone*. In recent years he has translated a number of French sf stories by such writers as C. Henneberg, Claude Veillot, Claude F. Cheinisse, Michael Ehrwein, and J.-H. Rosny aîné; a number of these appeared in *F&SF* and the anthology *13 French Science-Fiction Stories*. Since 1962 he has developed into a notable anthologist; among the more important of his compilations are the *Orbit* series of new stories.

Series

Thorinn. All in *GSF*: "The World and Thorinn" (Apr 1968); "The Garden of Ease" (June 1968); "The Star Below" (Aug 1968).

Fiction

A for Anything [pa] See *People Maker, The*

Analogue Men [pa] See *Hell's Pavement*

Beyond the Barrier ("The Tree of Time," *F&SF*, sr2, Dec 1963) (Doubleday, New York, 1963, 188 pp., $3.50) (D'day, Toronto, $4.00) (D'day SF B.C., 1964, $1.20) (Gollancz, London, 1964, 188 pp., 15/-) (Macfadden: 50-234, 1965, 142 pp., pa 50¢) (Corgi: GS7502, 1966, 123 pp., pa 3/6)

Outlandish things happen to a physics professor in travelling through time.

Far Out [C] (Simon & Schuster, New York, 1961, 199 pp., $3.95) (D'day SF B.C., 1961, $1.20) (Gollancz, 1962, 5+282 pp., 15/-) (Berkley: F616, 1962, 192 pp., pa 50¢) (Corgi: GS1439, 1963, 221 pp., pa 3/6)

13 stories, with introduction by A. Boucher: "To Serve Man"; "Idiot Stick"; "Thing of Beauty"; "The Enemy"; "Not With a Bang"; "Babel II"; "Anachron"; "Special Delivery"; "You're Another"; "Time Enough"; "Extempore"; "Cabin Boy"; "The Last Word."

Hell's Pavement [pa] (Lion: LL13, 1955, 192 pp., pa 35¢) (Miller: Banner 59, 1958, 160 pp., pa 2/-) (*Il fabbricanti di schiavi* [Italian], Cosmo: 39, 1959) (*Analogue Men*, Berkley: F647, 1962, 160 pp., pa 50¢; Sphere: 53031, 1967, 191 pp., pa 3/6)

A weird account of a terrifying mind-controlled society of 2134. Chapter I was originally "The Analogues" (*ASF*, Jan 1952), and the rest is based on "Turncoat" (*TWS*, Apr 1953; [German], *UZ*: 463, 1965).

In Deep [C] (Berkley: F760, 1963, 158 pp., pa 50¢) (Gollancz, 1964, 158 pp., 15/-) (SF B.C. [S.J.], 1964, 6/-) (Corgi: GS7399, 1966, 174 pp., pa 3/6)

Sf, 8 stories (both British eds. omit 3rd): "Four in One"; "An Eye for a What?"; "The Handler"; "Stranger Station"; "Ask Me Anything"; "The Country of the Kind"; "Ticket to Anywhere"; "Beachcomber."

Masters of Evolution [pa] ("Natural State," *GSF*, Jan 1954; in *All About the Future* [Greenberg], 1955) –expanded: (Ace: D-375, 1959, 96 pp., pa 35¢; with *Fire in the Heavens*)

City people are at loggerheads with country folk who see no good in machines and have a satisfactory way of life based on biological manipulation.

Mind Switch [pa] ("The Visitor at the Zoo," *GSF*, short n, Apr 1963) –enlarged: (Berkley: F1160, 1965, 144 pp., pa 50¢) (*The Other Foot*, Whiting & Wheaton, London, 1966, 159 pp., 18/-;

Corgi: 07994, 1968, 125 pp., pa 3/6)

The tribulations of a human transferred to an alien body.

Off Center [C] [pa] (Ace: M-113, 1965, 141 pp., pa 45¢; with *The Rithian Terror* [Knight])

Sf, 5 stories: "What Rough Beast"; "The Second-Class Citizen"; "Be My Guest"; "God's Nose"; "Catch That Martian."

Other Foot, The See *Mind Switch*

People Maker, The [pa] (Zenith: ZB-14, 1959, 159 pp., pa 35¢) (*A for Anything*, FSB: 382, 1961, 160 pp., pa 2/6) (Berkley: F1136, 1965, 160 pp., pa 50¢)

A peculiar story of lust and decadence in a world dominated by the "gismo," a matter-duplicating device that works on people. Part I was originally "A for Anything" (*F&SF*, Nov 1957), enlarged for this work. The Zenith version is badly cut; FSB ed. is the complete text.

Rithian Terror, The [pa] ("Double Meaning," *SS*, Jan 1953) (Ace: M-113, 1965, 111 pp., pa 45¢; with *Off Center* [Knight])

The fate of Earth hangs on detecting an alien infiltrator able to assume human form.

Sun Saboteurs, The [pa] ("The Earth Quarter," *If*, Jan 1955) —expanded: (Ace: F-108, 1961, 101 pp., pa 40¢; with *The Light of Lilith*)

Complex society of human refugees on a totally alien world.

Three Novels [C] (Doubleday, 1967, 189 pp., $3.95) (D'day SF B.C., 1967, $1.70) (Gollancz, 1967, 189 pp., 21/-) (SF B.C. [S.J.], 1968) (*Welt ohne Maschinen* [German], Goldmann: 092, 1968, pa)

3 novels: "Rule Golden" (*SFA*, May 1954); "Natural State" (*GSF*, Jan 1954; see also *Masters of Evolution*); "The Dying Man" ("Dio," *Infinity*, Sep 1957).

Turning On [C] (Doubleday, 1966, 180 pp., $3.50) (Gollancz, 1967, 159 pp., 18/-) (Ace: G-677, 1967, 160 pp., pa 60¢)

Collection of 14 stories (Ace ed. 13 stories, omitting "The Handler"): "Semper Fi" ("Satisfaction"); "The Big Pat Boom"; "Man in the Jar"; "The Handler"; "Many" ("An Ancient Madness"); "Auto-da-Fe"; "To the Pure"; "Eripmav"; "Backward O Time" ("This Way to the Regress"); "The Night of Lies"; "Maid to Measure"; "Collector's Item" ("The End of the Sea"); "A Likely Story"; "Don't Live in the Past."

Nonfiction

In Search of Wonder (Advent, Chicago, 1956, 180 pp., illus.—J. L. Patterson, $4.00; 1960, $4.00, pa $1.65; revised 2nd ed., 1967, 306 pp., $6.00; 1968, pa $2.45)

Introduction by A. Boucher; 2nd ed. considerably enlarged. A selection of book reviews from the 1950's, revised from the original magazine appearances. It is not scrappy but is grouped logically in chapters on individual authors or subjects. Knight lays down his critical principles, and the volume has a sense of dedication and consistency which must be unprecedented considering the scattered origin of most of the pieces.

Anthologies

Beyond Tomorrow (Harper & Row, New York, 1965, 333 pp., $4.50, lib. $4.00) (Longmans, Toronto, $5.50) (Gollancz, 1968, 21/-)

10 stories: "Twilight," D. A. Stuart; "The Mile-Long Spaceship," Kate Wilhelm; "Coventry," R. A. Heinlein; "The Seesaw," A. E. van Vogt; "Nightfall," I. Asimov; "Desertion," C. D. Simak; "The Deep Range," A. C. Clarke; "Brightside Crossing," A. E. Nourse; "The Million-Year Picnic," R. Bradbury; "Happy Ending," H. Kuttner.

Century of Great Short Science Fiction Novels, A (Delacorte, New York, 1964, 379 pp., $4.95) (Dell: 1158, 1965, 447 pp., pa 75¢) (Gollancz, London, 1965, 379 pp., 21/-) (Mayflower: 1168, 1968, np, pa 5/-)

6 novels, each with biographical introduction on the author: *Strange Case of Dr. Jekyll and Mr. Hyde*, R. L. Stevenson; *The Invisible Man*, H. G. Wells; *The Absolute at Large*, K. Capek; *Gulf*, R. A. Heinlein; *E for Effort*, T. L. Sherred; *Hunter, Come Home*, Richard McKenna.

Century of Science Fiction, A (Simon & Schuster, New York, 1962, 352 pp., $4.95) (D'day SF B.C., 1962, $1.90) (Dell: 1157, 1963, 384 pp., pa 75¢) (Gollancz, 1963, 352 pp., 21/-) (Pan: T19,

1966, 446 pp., pa 6/-)

26 stories, with compiler's introduction: *I. Robots:* A selection from "The Ideal," S. G. Weinbaum; "Moxon's Master," A. Bierce; "Reason," I. Asimov; "But Who Can Replace a Man?" B. W. Aldiss. *II. Time Travel:* A selection from *The Time Machine*, H. G. Wells; "Of Time and Third Avenue," A. Bester; "Sail On! Sail On!" P. J. Farmer; a selection from *Worlds of the Imperium*, Keith Laumer; "The Business, as Usual," M. Reynolds. *III. Space:* "What's It Like Out There?" E. Hamilton; "Sky Lift," R. A. Heinlein; "The Star," A. C. Clarke. *IV. Other Worlds and People:* "The Crystal Egg," H. G. Wells; "The Wind People," Marion Z. Bradley; "Unhuman Sacrifice," Katherine MacLean. *V. Aliens Among Us:* "What Was It?" Fitz-James O'Brien; "The First Days of May," Claude Veillot; "Day of Succession," T. L. Thomas; "Angel's Egg," E. Pangborn. *VI. Supermen:* "Another World," J. H. Rosny ainé; a selection from *Odd John*, O. Stapledon; "Call Me Joe," P. Anderson. *VII. Marvelous Inventions:* "From the London Times of 1904," M. Twain; a selection from *Twenty Thousand Leagues Under the Sea*, J. Verne; "You Are With It!" Will Stanton; "Cease Fire," Frank Herbert. Appendix—Suggested Reading.

Cities of Wonder (Doubleday, 1966, 252 pp., $4.50) (D'day, Toronto, $4.95) (Macfadden: 75-183, 1967, 251 pp., pa 75¢) (Dobson, 1968, 252 pp., 25/-)

Sf, 11 stories: "The Machine Stops," E. M. Forster; "Okie," J. Blish; "By the Waters of Babylon," S. V. Benét; "It's Great To Be Back!" R. A. Heinlein; "Forgetfulness," D. A. Stuart; "Dumb Waiter," W. M. Miller; "The Luckiest Man in Denv," C. M. Kornbluth; "Billenium," J. G. Ballard; "Jesting Pilot," H. Kuttner; "The Underprivileged," B. W. Aldiss; "Single Combat," R. Abernathy.

Dark Side, The (Doubleday, 1965, 241 pp., $4.50) (D'day SF B.C., 1965, $1.20) (Dobson, 1966, 241 pp., 21/-) (Corgi: GS7788, 1967, 172 pp., pa 3/6)

Sf and fantasy, 12 stories: "The Dark Ferris," R. Bradbury; "They," R. A. Heinlein; "Mistake Inside," J. Blish; "Trouble With Water," H. L. Gold; "C/o Mr. Makepeace," Peter Phillips; "The Golem," A. Davidson; "The Story of the Late Mr. Elvesham," H. G. Wells; "It," T. Sturgeon; "Nellthu," A. Boucher; "Casey Agonistes," Richard McKenna; "Eye for Iniquity," T. L. Sherred; "The Man Who Never Grew Young," F. Leiber.

First Flight [pa] (Lancer: 72-672, 1963, 160 pp., pa 50¢; 72-145, 1966, pa 50¢)

Sf, 10 stories (the first published story of each well-known author), with brief introduction: "The Isolinguals," L. S. de Camp; "The Faithful," L. del Rey; "Black Destroyer," A. E. van Vogt; "Life-Line," R. A. Heinlein; "Ether Breather," T. Sturgeon; "Loophole," A. C. Clarke; "Tomorrow's Children," P. Anderson; "That Only a Mother," Judith Merril; "Walk to the World," A. Budrys; "T," B. W. Aldiss.

Metal Smile, The [pa] (Belmont: B60-082, 1968, 158 pp., pa 60¢)

Sf, 11 stories and 1 verse: "The New Father Christmas," B. W. Aldiss; "Answer" (short), F. Brown; "Fool's Mate," R. Sheckley; "Quixote and the Windmill," P. Anderson; "Two-Handed Engine," H. Kuttner & C. L. Moore; "First to Serve," A. Budrys; "I Made You," W. M. Miller; "Monkey Wrench," G. R. Dickson; "Impostor," P. K. Dick; "Someday," I. Asimov; "Short in the Chest," Idris Seabright; "Nightmare Number Three" (verse), S. V. Benét.

Nebula Award Stories 1965 (Doubleday, 1966, 299 pp., $4.95) (D'day SF B.C., 1966, $1.20) (Gollancz, 1967, 254 pp., 25/-) (Pocket Books: 75275, 1967, 244 pp., pa 75¢)

1st volume of award-winning stories and runners-up selected by the Science Fiction Writers of America (British ed. titled *No. 1* rather than *1965*): "The Doors of His Face, the Lamps of His Mouth," Roger Zelazny; "Balanced Ecology," J. H. Schmitz; "'Repent, Harlequin,' Said the Ticktockman," H. Ellison; "He Who Shapes," R. Zelazny; "Computers Don't Argue," G. R. Dickson; "Becalmed in Hell," Larry Niven; "The Saliva Tree," B. W. Aldiss; "The Drowned Giant," J. G. Ballard.

One Hundred Years of Science Fiction (Simon & Schuster, 1968, $6.00)

21 stories with compiler's introduction: *I. Worlds of Tomor-*

row: "With the Night Mail," R. Kipling; "Mr. Murphy of New York," Thomas McMorrow; "New Apples in the Garden," Kris Neville; "Sanity," Fritz Leiber. *II. Aliens, on Earth and Elsewhere:* "The Shapes," J. H. Rosny aîné; "The Other Celia," T. Sturgeon; "Black Charlie," Gordon R. Dickson. *III. Other Dimensions:* "A Subway Named Möbius," A. J. Deutsch; "The Man Who Came Early," Poul Anderson; "The Other Now," Murray Leinster. *IV. Mutants and Monsters:* "Whatever Happened to Corporal Cuckoo?" Gerald Kersh; "The Mindworm," C. M. Kornbluth; "Nobody Bothers Gus," Algis Budrys. *V. Marvelous Inventions:* "The Ingenious Patriot," Ambrose Bierce; "The Equalizer," Norman Spinrad; "Splice of Life," Sonya Dorman; "Business as Usual, During Alterations," Ralph Williams. *VI. The Mysterious Universe:* "The Quest for St. Aquin," Anthony Boucher; "The Nine Billion Names of God," A. C. Clarke; "The Voices of Time," J. G. Ballard.

Orbit 1 (Putnam, New York, 1966, 192 pp., $3.50) (Berkley: F1291, 1966, 192 pp., pa 50¢) (Whiting & Wheaton, London, 1966, 192 pp., 18/-) (Panther: 2325, 1967, 156 pp., pa 3/6)

First of a series of original stories; 9 sf stories, with introduction: "Staras Flonderans," Kate Wilhelm; "The Secret Place," Richard McKenna; "How Beautiful With Banners," J. Blish; "The Disinherited," P. Anderson; "The Loolies Are Here," Allison Rice; "Kangaroo Court," Virginia Kidd; "Splice of Life," Sonya Dorman; "5 Eggs," Thomas M. Disch; "The Deeps," Keith Roberts.

Orbit 2 (Putnam, 1967, 255 pp., $4.95) (Berkley: S1448, 1967, 255 pp., pa 75¢) (Rapp & Whiting, London, 1968, 255 pp., 25/-)

10 stories: "The Doctor," Ted Thomas; "Baby, You Were Great," Kate Wilhelm; "Fiddler's Green," R. McKenna; "Trip, Trap," Gene Wolfe; "The Dimple in Draco," P. Latham; "I Give Her Sack and Sherry," "The Adventuress," Joanna Russ; "The Hole on the Corner," R. A. Lafferty; "The Wood Farm," Kit Reed; "Full Sun," Brian W. Aldiss.

Orbit 3 (Putnam, 1968, 224 pp., $4.95) (Berkley: S1608, 1968, 224 pp., pa 75¢)

9 stories with editor's comment prefacing each: "Mother to the World," R. Wilson; "Bramble Bush," R. McKenna; "The Barbarian," Joanna Russ; "The Changeling," Gene Wolfe; "Why They Mobbed the White House," Doris P. Buck; "The Planners," Kate Wilhelm; "Don't Wash the Carats," P. J. Farmer; "Letter to a Young Poet," James Sallis; "Here Is Thy Sting," John Jakes.

Orbit 4 (Putnam, 1968, 254 pp., $4.95)

9 original stories with editor's introduction to each: "Windsong," Kate Wilhelm; "Probable Cause," Charles L. Harness; "Shattered Like a Glass Goblin," Harlan Ellison; "This Corruptible," Jacob Transue; "Animal," Carol Emshwiller; "One at a Time," R. A. Lafferty; "Passengers," Robert Silverberg; "Grimm's Story," Vernor Vinge; "A Few Last Words," James Sallis.

Science Fiction Inventions [pa] (Lancer: 73-691, 1967, 253 pp., pa 60¢)

10 stories and introduction: "No, No, Not Rogov!" Cordwainer Smith; "Rock Diver," H. Harrison; "Private Eye," H. Kuttner & C. L. Moore; "The Snowball Effect," Katherine MacLean; "The Chromium Helmet," T. Sturgeon; "Employment," L. S. de Camp; "Dreaming Is a Private Thing," I. Asimov; "Invariant," J. Pierce; "Hunting Machine," Carol Emshwiller; "Committee of the Whole," F. Herbert.

Shape of Things, The [pa] (Popular: SP352, 1965, 206 pp., pa 50¢)

Sf, 11 stories originally appearing in *TWS* and *SS*, with introduction commending these two deceased magazines and their editors: "Don't Look Now," H. Kuttner; "The Box," J. Blish; "The New Reality," C. L. Harness; "The Eternal Now," M. Leinster; "The Sky Was Full of Ships," T. Sturgeon; "The Shape of Things," R. Bradbury; "The Only Thing We Learn," C. M. Kornbluth; "The Hibited Man," L. S. de Camp; "Dormant," A. E. van Vogt; "The Ambassadors," A. Boucher; "A Child Is Crying," J. D. MacDonald.

13 French Science-Fiction Stories [pa] (Bantam: F2817, 1965, 167 pp., pa 50¢) (Corgi: GS7312, 1965, pa 3/6)

13 stories originally translated by Knight [some from French *Fiction* magazine and some published in *F&SF*], with his intro-

duction: "Juliette," Claude F. Cheinisse; "The Blind Pilot," Charles Henneberg; "Olivia," "The Notary and the Conspiracy," Henri Damonti; "The Vana," Alain Doremieux; "The Devil's God-Daughter," Suzanne Malaval; "Moon-Fishers," "The Non-Humans," C. Henneberg; "After Three Hundred Years," Pierre Mille; "The Monster," Gerard Klein; "A Little More Caviar?" Claude Veillot; "The Chain of Love," Catherine Cliff; "The Dead Fish," Boris Vian. Afterword: "About the Authors."

Tomorrow X 4 [pa] (Gold Medal: d1428, 1964, 176 pp., pa 50¢) (Coronet: F124, 1967, 176 pp., pa 4/-)

Sf, 4 novelettes with brief introduction: "The Night of Hoggy Darn" (*If*, Dec 1958), R. M. McKenna; "The Sources of the Nile" (*F&SF*, Jan 1961), A. Davidson; "No Woman Born" (*ASF*, Dec 1944), C. L. Moore; "The Roads Must Roll" (*ASF*, June 1940), R. A. Heinlein.

Toward Infinity (Simon & Schuster, New York, 1968, 319 pp., $4.95)

Sf, 9 stories and 3-p. introduction: "The Man Who Lost the Sea," T. Sturgeon; "March Hare Mission," Ford McCormack; "The Earth Men," R. Bradbury; "Who Goes There?" Don A. Stuart; "In Hiding," Wilmar H. Shiras; "Not Final!" I. Asimov; "And Be Merry," Katherine MacLean; "The Witches of Karres," J. H. Schmitz; "Resurrection," A. E. van Vogt.

Worlds to Come (Harper & Row, New York, 1967, 337 pp., $4.95, lib. $4.43) (Gold Medal: R1942, 1968, 254 pp., pa 60¢)

Sf, 9 stories: "The Sentinel," A. C. Clarke; "Moonwalk," H. B. Fyfe; "Mars Is Heaven!" R. Bradbury; "The Edge of the Sea," A. Budrys; "The Martian Way," I. Asimov; "The Big Contest!" J. D. MacDonald; "Ordeal in Space," R. A. Heinlein; "That Share of Glory," C. M. Kornbluth; "Sunken Universe," J. Blish.

KNIGHT, ERIC (MOWBRAY) (10 Apr 1897–15 Jan 1943) British and U.S. novelist. He came to the U.S. in 1912, and served in World War I with the Canadian Light Infantry. He was originally interested in art, but, being colour blind, left it for writing and newspaper work. He is primarily remembered for *This Above All*.
Fiction
Flying Yorkshireman, The [C] See *Sam Small Flies Again*
Flying Yorkshireman, The [A] See BURNETT, W.
Sam Small Flies Again [C] (Harper, New York, 1942, 285 pp., $2.50) (Musson, Toronto, $2.75) (Cassell, London, 1943, 255 pp., 8/6; [Melbourne], 1945, 9/-) (Grosset, New York, 1943, 285 pp., $2.00) (Armed: g-187, nd, 318 pp., pa) (*The Flying Yorkshireman: Sam Small Flies Again*, World, New York, 1946, 285 pp., $1.00; Pocket Books: 493, 1948, 273 pp., pa 25¢)

The "Sam Small" saga of 10 stories: "All Yankees Are Liars"; "Strong in the Arms"; "Sam Small's Better Half"; "The Flying Yorkshireman"; "Sam Small's Tyke"; "Never Come Monday"; "Cockles for Tea"; "Mary Ann and the Duke"; "Constable Sam and the Ugly Tyke"; "The Truth About Rudolph Hess (or Sam Small Flies Again)." A Yorkshireman discovers that he can fly by willpower.

KNIGHT, NORMAN L(OUIS) (21 Sep 1895–) U.S. chemist and author. He was born in St. Joseph, Missouri, and graduated from the Junior College, St. Joseph, in 1918. He was drafted in July 1918 and served 8 months–4 months in France–but saw no action; he was in the 29th Field Artillery, 10th Division. He was appointed assistant observer in the Weather Bureau office in Davenport, Iowa, in 1919, later transferring to Washington, D.C. There he attended George Washington University for five years while still working, and graduated B.S. in Chemical Engineering in 1925. In August 1925 he transferred to the Insecticide and Fungicide Board (now the Pesticide Regulation Branch), and for many years analyzed insecticides, fungicides, rodenticides, herbicides, disinfectants, etc., at the Agricultural Research Center, Beltsville, Maryland.

In the science fiction field he wrote some notable fiction for *ASF* in the late 1930's and early 1940's, principally: "Frontier of the Unknown" (sr2, July 1937); "Crisis in Utopia" (sr2, July 1940; in *Five SF Novels* [Greenberg], 1952); "Fugitive From Vanguard" (Jan 1942). More recently Knight collaborated with James

Blish on further stories about underwater civilizations, etc., culminating in the book mentioned below.
Fiction
Torrent of Faces, A See BLISH, J. (co-author)

KNOWLES, VERNON (1899–) British writer. He was born in Adelaide, S. Australia, and was educated there and at the U. of W. Australia. He has written numerous books and contributed to various journals.
Fiction
Here and Otherwhere [C] (Robert Holden, London, 1926, 257 pp., illus.–Ralph Keene, 7/6)
   9 stories: "The Shop in the Off Street"; "The Birds"; "The Painter of Trees"; "The Land of Ideas"; "The Road to Tolbrisa"; "The Land of No More Tears"; "The Triumph of the Tree"; "A Conversation"; "A Set of Chinese Boxes."
Ladder, The (in *Silver Nutmegs* [Knowles], 1927) (Mandrake Press, London, 1929, 98 pp., 3/6)
Silver Nutmegs [C] (R. Holden, 1927, 202 pp., illus.–Eric Bailey, 7/6)
   7 stories: "The Ladder"; "The River and the Road"; "The Chimpanzee"; "The Gong of Transportation"; "The Great Onion"; "The City of All Cities"; "The Door With the Three Padlocks."
Street of Queer Houses and Other Tales, The [C] (Wells Gardner Darton, London, 1925, 225 pp., illus.–Helen Binyon, 6/-)
   15 stories: "The Street of Queer Houses"; "The Weeping God"; "A Matter of Characterization"; "The House of Yesterdays"; "The Three Gods"; "The Pendant"; "The Author Who Entered His MS."; "The Mask"; "The Man Who Was Troubled by His Shadow"; "The Book of the Thousand Answers"; "The Idealist"; "The Broken Statue"; "The House That Took Revenge"; "The Elizabethan Gown"; "Honeymoon Cottage."
Two and Two Make Five [C] (Newnes, London, 1935, 256 pp., 7/6)
   12 stories: "The Curious Activities of Basil Thorpenden"; "The First Coming"; "The Brief History of a Boy Who Was Different"; "The Two Selves"; "The Road to Tolbrisa"; "The Great Onion"; "The Birds"; "The Shop in the Off-Street"; "The Chimpanzee"; "The Gong of Transportation"; "The Painter of Trees"; "A Set of Chinese Boxes."

KNOX, CALVIN M. (pseud) See SILVERBERG, R.

KOCH, HOWARD (1902–) U.S. film producer. He wrote the radio script "Invasion From Mars" (from H. G. Wells' *War of the Worlds*) which O. Welles so dramatically presented in 1938. Koch had the story "Invasion From Inner Space" published in *Star SF No 6* [Pohl], 1959.

KOESTLER, ARTHUR (1905–) Author and journalist. He was born in Budapest and educated in Vienna. He was a Communist, and was arrested by General Franco's forces during the Spanish Civil War and sentenced to death; he was released through the intervention of the British government. He broke with the Communists and became noted for his novel *Darkness at Noon* on Party life. He now lives in France. A fantasy not covered below was *Twilight Bar: An Escapade in Four Acts* (Macmillan, New York, 1945).
Fiction
Age of Longing, The (Collins, London, 1951, 448 pp., 12/6) (Collins, Toronto, $3.00) (Macmillan, New York, 1951, 362 pp., $3.50) (Mayflower: B12, 1961, 320 pp., pa 3/6)
   A forecast of what living in France would be like in the near future, awaiting conquest from the East.

KOLDA, HELENA See DUCHACEK, I. D. (co-author)

KOOMOTER, ZENO (pseud) See MARNELL, J.

KOONTZ, DEAN R(AY) (9 July 1945–)
Fiction
Star Quest [pa] (Ace: H-70, 1968, 127 pp., pa 60¢; with *Doom*

of the Green Planet)

KORNBLUTH, C(YRIL) M. (1923–21 Mar 1958) U.S. science fiction and fantasy author. He was born in New York. An active sf fan in the 1937-40 era, he began writing professionally at the age of 15. He became a prolific writer in the early 1940's, when he is said to have used 18 or 19 pseudonyms (see Supplement for those publicly acknowledged), of which the most noted were S. D. Gottesman and Cecil Corwin. He graduated from the University of Chicago. During World War II he was an infantryman, taking part in the Battle of the Bulge and winning the Bronze Star. After the war he worked his way up to the position of editor of the Chicago office of Trans-Radio Press; he resigned in 1951 for full-time writing. In the years that followed he became one of sf's top creators, and at the time of his death was about to become consulting editor for the *Magazine of Fantasy and Science Fiction*.
   In the 1950's he wrote many notable short stories for *F&SF*, etc., collaborated with Judith Merril under the pseudonym Cyril Judd, and wrote many works with Frederik Pohl. The works with Pohl have been notable in the field, particularly *The Space Merchants*. In the collaborations with Pohl each author wrote alternate sections, instead of following the usual system of one author revising the work of the other. A pseudonym of interest, not used in science fiction, was Jordan Park (Pohl was associated with this on at least one occasion). Kornbluth's lecture at the University of Chicago, "The Failure of the SF Novel as Social Criticism," was published in *The Science Fiction Novel* (1959) [See SYMPOSIA]. It is understood that the initial "M." in Kornbluth's writing name stood for his wife Mary. After his death Mary G. Kornbluth compiled the anthology *Science Fiction Showcase* as a memorial volume.
Fiction
Best Science Fiction Stories [C] (Faber, London, 1968, 277 pp., 25/-)
   12 stories and 1 verse; introduction–Edmund Crispin: "The Unfortunate Topologist" (verse); "The Marching Morons"; "The Altar at Midnight"; "The Little Black Bag"; "The Mindworm"; "The Silly Season"; "I Never Ast No Favours"; "Friend to Man"; "The Only Thing We Learn"; "Gomez"; "With These Hands"; "Theory of Rocketry"; "That Share of Glory."
Christmas Eve See *Not This August*
Explorers, The [C] [pa] (Ballantine: 86, 1954, 145 pp., pa 35¢; F708, 1963, pa 50¢)
   Sf, 9 stories: "Gomez" (new); "The Mindworm"; "The Rocket of 1955"; "The Altar at Midnight"; "The Goodly Creatures"; "Friend to Man"; "With These Hands"; "That Share of Glory"; "Thirteen O'Clock."
Gladiator-at-Law See POHL, F. (co-author)
Gunner Cade [as Cyril Judd] See MERRIL, J. (co-author)
Marching Morons, The [C] [pa] (Ballantine: 303K, 1959, 158 pp., pa 35¢; F760, 1963, pa 50¢) (*Desfile de cretines* [Spanish], Galaxia: 26, 1964, pa)
   Sf and fantasy, 9 stories: "The Marching Morons"; "Dominoes"; "The Luckiest Man in Denv"; "The Silly Season"; "Ms. Found in a Chinese Fortune Cookie"; "The Only Thing We Learn"; "The Cosmic Charge Account"; "I Never Ast No Favors"; "The Remorseful."
Mile Beyond the Moon, A [C] (Doubleday, New York, 1958, 239 pp., $2.95, jacket–R. Charlip) (D'day, Toronto, $3.50) (D'day SF B.C., 1959, $1.20) (Macfadden: 40-100, 1962, 175 pp., pa 40¢; 50-288, 1966, pa 50¢ [11 stories marked †])
   Sf and fantasy, 15 stories: "Make Mine Mars"†; "The Meddlers"; "The Events Leading Down to the Tragedy"†; "The Little Black Bag"†; "Everybody Knows Joe"†; "Time Bum"†; "Passion Pills"; "Virginia"†; "The Slave"; "Kazam Collects"†; "The Last Man Left in the Bar"†; "The Adventurer"†; "The Words of Guru"†; "Shark Ship"†; "Two Dooms."
Mindworm and Other Stories, The [C] (M. Joseph, London, 1955, 256 pp., 12/6)
   Sf and fantasy, 12 stories: "The Mindworm"; "Gomez"; "The Rocket of 1955"; "The Altar at Midnight"; "The Little Black Bag"; "The Goodly Creatures"; "Friend to Man"; "With These

Hands"; "That Share of Glory"; "The Luckiest Man in Denv"; "The Silly Season"; "The Marching Morons."

Not This August (Doubleday, 1955, 190 pp., $2.95, jacket—M. Hunter) (*MacLean's* [Canada], sr3, 14 May 1955) (D'day SF B.C., 1956) (Bantam: A1492, 1956, 165 pp., pa 35¢) (*Christmas Eve*, M. Joseph, 1956, 207 pp., 10/6; Digit, 1957, 160 pp., pa 2/-; SF B.C. [S.J.], 1958, 5/6) (*Non sarà per Agosto* [Italian], *Urania*: 143, 1957) (*Nederlagets Tine* [Danish], Skrifola: P10, 1958, pa; P21 [double binding, with *The Naked Sun*], 1958, pa) ([Japanese], Hayakawa: 3007, 1958, pa)

The U.S. is conquered by the Soviet Union and China; daily life under Communist domination is realistically portrayed. A rebellion is attempted using a satellite loaded with nuclear weapons.

Outpost Mars [as Cyril Judd] See MERRIL, J. (co-author)
Search the Sky See POHL, F. (co-author)
Sin in Space [as Cyril Judd] See MERRIL, J. (co-author)
Space Merchants, The See POHL, F. (co-author)
Syndic, The (Doubleday, 1953, 223 pp., $2.95, jacket—P. Galdone) (D'day, Toronto, $3.25) (D'day SF B.C., 1954) (*SFA*, sr2, Dec 1953) (Bantam: 1317, 1955, 142 pp., pa 25¢) (*Schwarze Dynastie* [German], *UK*: 24, 1957; *TE*: 93, 1966) (*L'era della follia* [Italian], *Urania*: 72, 1955) (Faber, 1964, 223 pp., 18/-; intro. —E. Crispin) (Berkley: F1032, 1965, 144 pp., pa 50¢) (Queenswood, Toronto, 1964, $3.95) (SF B.C. [S.J.], 1966) (Sphere: 53171, 1968, 160 pp., pa 5/-)

The adventures of a spy in a future world in which gangsters are the government.

Takeoff (Doubleday, 1952, 218 pp., $2.75, jacket—A. Shilstone) (D'day SF B.C., 1953) (Bantam: P15, 1953, 149 pp., pa 25¢) (*Partida* [Spanish, Argentina], Fantaciencia: 1, 1956, pa) (*Start zum Mond* [German], *UG*: 76, 1958)

An sf detective story about a group building the first space ship. This novel was runner-up for the 1953 International Fantasy Award for fiction.

Wolfbane See POHL, F. (co-author)
Wonder Effect, The [C] [pa] See POHL, F. (co-author)

KORNBLUTH, MARY G. (BYERS) (1920–) Widow of C. M. Kornbluth. She is a fine ceramicist.
Anthology
Science Fiction Showcase (Doubleday, New York, 1959, 264 pp., $3.95) (D'day, Toronto, $4.50) (D'day SF B.C., 1960, $1.20) (Whiting & Wheaton, London, 1966, 264 pp., 21/-) (Mayflower: 112250, 1968, 204 pp., pa 5/-)

Sf, 12 stories: "Ticket to Anywhere," D. Knight; "That Low," T. Sturgeon; "Or the Grasses Grow," A. Davidson; "The Man Who Ate the World," F. Pohl; "The Long Remembering," P. Anderson; "The End of the Beginning," R. Bradbury; "A Work of Art," J. Blish; "The Cold Green Eye," J. Williamson; "Med Service," M. Leinster; "Expendable," P. K. Dick; "Mantage," R. Matheson; "Nightmare Number Four," R. Bloch.

KORSHAK, (ERLE) MELVIN (1923–) U.S. science fiction and fantasy fan. In his early days he bought and sold magazines, and was one of the Chicago group who helped put on the "Chicon" (World SF Convention) in 1940, and "Chicon II" in 1952. After the war he was a co-founder of Shasta Publishers, formed to publish *The Checklist of Fantastic Literature* by E. F. Bleiler (1948), for which Korshak wrote the preface. Shasta published a number of other books in the early 1950's, notably the first three of Heinlein's "Future History" series.

KRAFT, ROBERT (1870–1916) German author. He was one of the most important in the German pulp field, but is no longer well known as his works have been out of print since 1925. His best works include: *Die Nihilit-Expedition* (1909, lost race); *Die Arbeiten des Herkules* [The Labours of Hercules]; *Die Neue Erde* [The New Earth] (1910, Earth after sonic catastrophe).

KRAMER, NORA U.S. anthologist.
Anthologies
Arrow Book of Ghost Stories [pa] (Scholastic: TX232, 1963, 116 pp., pa 35¢, illus.—G. Wilde)

9 stories: "The King o' the Cats," Joseph Jacobs; "Jimmy Takes Vanishing Lessons," Walter R. Brooks; "The Woodman and the Goblins," J. B. Esenwein & Marietta Stockard; "The Wonderful Cat of Cobbie Bean," Barbee Oliver Carleton; "Teeny-Tiny," Joseph Jacobs; "The Conjure Wives," Frances G. Wickes; "Spook's Bones," Louis C. Jones; "Which Was Witch?" Elanore M. Jewett; "The Water Ghost," J. K. Bangs.

Arrow Book of Spooky Stories [pa] (Scholastic: TX331, 1962, 90 pp., pa 35¢)

11 stories: "Horace the Happy Ghost," Elizabeth Ireland; "Never Mind Them Watermelons," Maria Leach; "The Tinker and the Ghost," R. S. Boggs & Mary G. Davis; "The Lucky Man," Maria Leach; "The Stubbornest Man in Maine," Moritz Jagendorf; "Here We Go," Maria Leach; "The Friendly Ghost," Eliz. Yates; "The Dancing Jug," Lupe de Osma; "The Strange Visitor," Joseph Jacobs; "A Shiver of Ghosts," Cyril Birch; "The Ghostly Fisherman," Natalie S. Carlson.

KRASPEDON, DINO Brazilian writer.
Nonfiction
My Contact With Flying Saucers [trans. from Portuguese—J. B. Wood] (Spearman, London, 1959, 205 pp., 16/-)

First published in Brazil in 1958, where it was a bestseller, and then serialised in *Flying Saucer Review*; conversations with beings from outer space and allegedly factual descriptions of how saucers fly and overcome gravity.

KREISHEIMER, (Mrs) H. C.
Fiction
Whooping Crane, The (Pageant, New York, 1955, 89 pp., $2.50)
The future state of "Mazuria" is infiltrated by Communists.

KREMER, RAYMOND DE (1887–1964) Belgian author, considered by many to be his country's most important writer of fantasy and weird fiction. His first selection of weird tales appeared in 1925, but it was not until the 1930's that he confirmed his skillful talent for horror and associated fiction. He used such pen names as Jean Ray (mostly for works in French) and John Flanders (mostly for juveniles or works in Dutch). During World War II his most famous fantasy novel, *Malpertuis* was published; it has been compared to works of Hodgson or Ewers. Later several collections of his works appeared. In 1947 he edited an important anthology of fantasy tales that included such writers as A. Bierce, H. Heine and T. Ingoldsby. Interest in his writings was renewed with the publication of many of his works by Marabout (Belgium) in the early 1950's. The following stories appeared under the pseudonym "John Flanders" in *WT*: "Nude With a Dagger" (Nov 1934); "The Graveyard Duchess" (Dec 1934); "The Aztec Ring" (Apr 1935); "The Mystery of the Last Guest" (Oct 1935).
Fiction
Ghouls in My Grave [C] [pa] [as Jean Ray; trans.—Lowell Blair] (Berkley: F1071, 1965, 143 pp., pa 50¢)

Weird, 8 stories: "Gold Teeth"; "The Shadowy Street"; "I Killed Alfred Heavenrock"; "The Cemetery Watchman"; "The Mainz Psalter"; "The Last Traveler"; "The Black Mirror"; "Mr. Glass Changes Direction."

KRENKEL, ROY G. U.S. artist. He has illustrated for several of the science fiction magazines, including *ASF*. He won the 1963 Hugo as best artist of the year. He has become well known for his book jackets and paperback covers (Ace Books) for the works of E. R. Burroughs. He has had many illustrations in the amateur magazine *Amra*.

KREPPS, ROBERT W(ILSON) (11 Dec 1919–) U.S. author, better known under his pseudonym Geoff St. Reynard. He was born in Pittsburgh and has lived there with occasional excursions to California, Arizona and Mexico. He has his A.B. from U. of Pittsburgh. He sold his first story to *Unknown*, but *Fantastic Adventures* printed most of his fantasy 1944-51, including "Mistress of the Djinn" (Nov 1950); "The Usurpers" (Jan 1950); "Five Years in the Marmalade" (July 1949). The first two had sequels in other magazines. He also had some novelettes in *Imagination*, including "The Buttoned Sky" (Aug 1953; [German], *T*: 29, 1958), and has contributed to *SEP, Collier's, Argosy, Blue Book*, etc. Non-sf novels include *The Field of Night, In the Courts of the Lion, Tell It on My Drums, Earthshaker, Gamble My Last Game, Baboon Rock*.

KRESSING, HARRY (pseud)
Fiction
Cook, The (Random, New York, 1965, 244 pp., $4.95) (Random, Toronto, $6.25) (J. Cape, London, 1966, 244 pp., 21/-) (Panther: 2311, 1967, 223 pp., pa 5/-; 026037, 1968, pa 5/-)
Well-characterised fantasy on up-to-date exploration of the human psyche; a cook becomes dominant in a family.

KRIGE, UYS (1910-) South African author. He has a law degree, has travelled extensively, and has been an athlete and a coach to professional rugby and swimming teams. A war correspondent during World War II, he was taken prisoner in 1941 but escaped in 1943. He has broadcast in four languages for the BBC. His wife is a well-known South African actress.
Fiction
Dream and the Desert [C] (Collins, London, 1953, 223 pp., 10/6) (Collins, Toronto, $2.75) (Houghton, New York, 1954, 223 pp., $3.00)
Weird and fantastic short stories [no further information].

KRUSE, CLIFTON B. U.S. science fiction author. He wrote 19 stories for the sf magazines 1933-43; most appeared in *ASF*. His most unusual story was "Flight of the Typhoon" (*ASF*, Oct 1936).
Series
W62. Space ship. All in *ASF*: "W62 to Mercury" (Sep 1935); "A Princess of Pallis" (Oct 1935); "Stranger From Fomalhaut" (Jan 1936); "The W62's Last Flight" (May 1936).

KRUSS, JAMES (1926-)
Fiction
Talking Machine; an extraordinary story, The [told in English by Oliver Coburn] (Universe Books, New York, 1965, $3.95) (E. Ward, London, 1965, 18/-) (Burns MacEachern, Toronto, $4.95)
Juvenile.

KUBILIUS, WALTER (1918-) U.S. editor and author. He was an active science fiction fan in the early 1930's, when he helped found the International Scientific Association (which did not survive). Editor of an industrial paper, he wrote occasionally and had a number of stories published in the early 1940's in *Astonishing* and *Super Science Stories*. A few more stories appeared in the 1950's; his "The Other Side" (*Super Science Stories*, Apr 1951) was reprinted in Bleiler's *Best SF Stories 1952*.

KUEBLER, HAROLD W. U.S. anthologist and editor. He has been an editor for Ace Books westerns.
Anthology
Treasury of Science Fiction Classics, The (Hanover, New York, 1954, 694 pp., $2.95) (D'day SF B.C., 1954)
17 stories and excerpts, with introduction: *Worlds in Collision:* "The Conversation of Eiros and Charmion," E. A. Poe: "The Star," H. G. Wells; excerpts from *When Worlds Collide*, E. Balmer & P. Wylie. *The Great Adventure:* "The Maracot Deep," A. C. Doyle; "Round the Moon," J. Verne (sequel to *From the Earth to the Moon*); "The Last Terrestrials," O. Stapledon (from *Last and First Men*). *The World of the Future:* "The Machine Stops," E. M. Forster; "R.U.R." K. Capek (reading version); excerpts from *Brave New World*, A. Huxley. *Worlds in Conflict:* "The Invasion From Mars," H. Koch (radio script of *War of the Worlds*); *Edison's Conquest of Mars* (abr.), G. P. Serviss; "The Martians," O. Stapledon (from *Last and First Men*). *Adventures in Time: The Time Machine*, H. G. Wells; "The Curious Case of Benjamin Button," F. S. Fitzgerald; "The Rat," S. F. Wright. *Beyond Time and Space:*

"The Damned Thing," A. Bierce; "Mr. Strenberry's Tale," J. B. Priestley. Only recommended to recent enthusiasts who do not have the stories in other forms.

KURLAND, MICHAEL J. (1 Mar 1938-) See ANDERSON, C. (co-author)

KURTZMAN, HARVEY U.S. humorist. He was editor of *Mad* comic book for a period; the first three paperback selections from *Mad* are credited to him. Other cartoon books include *Harvey Kurtzman's Jungle Book* (Ballantine: 338K, 1959); *Help!* (Gold Medal: s1163, 1961); *Second Help!ing* (Gold Medal: s1225, 1962).

KUTTNER, HENRY (1914-3 Feb 1958) U.S. science fiction and fantasy author. He was born in Los Angeles. He became interested in the field through reading *Weird Tales*, and his first story in that magazine, "The Graveyard Rats" (Mar 1936), showed his admiration for Lovecraft. Except for a period of military service he spent most of his adult life as a free-lance writer. The depression stopped his formal education before he wished, and towards the end of his life he began studying for an advanced degree and consequently wrote less. After his appearance in *WT* he wrote for *TWS*, and then during the war he became a mainstay of *Astounding Science Fiction*, using various pseudonyms of which the most important was Lewis Padgett. In 1940 he married Catherine L. Moore, an author in her own right, and virtually every story after their marriage was a collaboration, with the pair using such pseudonyms as Lawrence O'Donnell.

Most of his better short stories and novels have now been reprinted in book form. The longer ones not yet reprinted include: "When New York Vanished" (*SS*, Mar 1939); "Lands of the Earthquake" (*SS*, May 1947); "Lord of the Storm" (*SS*, Sep 1947, as Keith Hammond); "The Mask of Circe" (*SS*, May 1948); "A God Named Kroo" (*TWS*, Win 1944; *FSM*, Sum 1954); "Wet Magic" (*Unknown*, Feb 1943). "Twonky" (*ASF*, Sep 1942, as Lewis Padgett) was filmed by United Artists in 1953, produced by Arch Oboler with Hans Conreid and Gloria Blondell. For *Thrilling Adventures* Kuttner wrote a Doc Savage sort of series (May-Sep 1941) under the house-name Charles Stoddard. He also wrote much in the mystery field, including *The Brass Ring* (1946, as Lewis Padgett), *The Day He Died* (1947, as Padgett), and *Man Drowning* (1952, as Kuttner). He then produced a notable series for Permabooks on the cases of the lay psychoanalyst Michael Gray: *The Murder of Eleanor Pope* (1956), *The Murder of Ann Avery* (1956), *Murder of a Mistress* (1957), *Murder of a Wife* (1958).

In his early years Kuttner wrote anything and everything, and it is only in his later writing (from the early 1940's) that he developed his own style and his work matured and became lasting. Sam Moskowitz's profile of Kuttner was published in *AS* (Oct 1962) and is a chapter in Moskowitz's *Seekers of Tomorrow* (1966). In 1958 Karen Anderson produced *Henry Kuttner: A Memorial Symposium*, giving critiques and reminiscences by prominent authors plus a complete bibliography.
Series
Baldy [as L. Padgett]. Mutants. All in *ASF*: "The Piper's Son" (Feb 1945); "Three Blind Mice" (June 1945); "The Lion and the Unicorn" (July 1945); "Beggars in Velvet" (Dec 1945); "Humpty Dumpty" (Sep 1953). Published as *Mutant*.
Elak of Atlantis. All in *WT*: "Thunder in the Dawn" (sr2, May 1938); "Spawn of Dagon" (July 1938); "Beyond the Phoenix" (Oct 1938); "Dragon Moon" (Jan 1941).
Gallegher, Galloway [as L. Padgett]. All in *ASF*: "Time Locker" (Jan 1943); "The World Is Mine" (June 1943); "The Proud Robot" (Oct 1943); "Gallegher Plus" (Nov 1943); "Ex Machina" (Apr 1948). Published as *Robots Have No Tails*.
Hogben. All in *TWS*: "Exit the Professor" (Oct 1947); "Pile of Trouble" (Apr 1948); "See You Later" (June 1949); "Cold War" (Oct 1949).
Hollywood on the Moon. All in *TWS*: "Hollywood on the Moon" (Apr 1938; *SS*, July 1949); "Doom World" (Aug 1938); "The Star

Parade" (Dec 1938); "The Energy Eaters"† (Oct 1939; *SS*, Sep 1950); "Suicide Squad" (Dec 1939); "The Seven Sleepers"† (May 1940); "Trouble on Titan" (Feb 1941); "Percy the Pirate" (Feb 1941). These are mainly about 'Tony Quade,' but the stories marked † are collaborations with A. K. Barnes and include the character 'Gerry Carlyle.'

Manx, Pete [as Kelvin Kent; by A. K. Barnes and H. Kuttner both separately and in collaboration]. All in *TWS*: "Roman Holiday" (Aug 1939; *SS*, Jan 1950); "World's Pharaoh" (Dec 1939; *FSM*, Sum 1951); "Science Is Golden" (Apr 1940; *FSM*, May 1953); "Knight Must Fall" (June 1940); "Comedy of Eras" (Sep 1940); "Man About Time" (Oct 1940); "The Greeks Had a War for It" (Jan 1941); "Hercules Muscles In" (Feb 1941); "Dames Is Poison" (June 1942; *FSM*, Fall 1954); "DeWolfe of Wall Street" (Feb 1943); "Grief of Bagdad" (June 1943); "Swing Your Lady" (Win 1944; *FSM*, Win 1955).

Fiction

Ahead of Time [C] (Ballantine, New York, 1953, 177 pp., $2.00; #30, pa 35¢; U2341, 1966, pa 50¢) (Weidenfeld Nicolson, London, 1954, 192 pp., 9/6) (FSB: 371, 1961, 160 pp., pa 2/6; 1964, pa 2/6; #1990, 1967, pa 3/6) (*Deja demain* [French], Gallimard, Le RF: 89, 1962)

Sf & fantasy, 10 stories (contents of French ed. unknown): "Or Else"; "Home Is the Hunter"; "By These Presents"; "De Profundis" ("The Visitors," C. H. Liddell); "Camouflage"; "Year Day" (new); "Ghost"; "Shock"; "Pile of Trouble"; "Deadlock."

Best of Kuttner 1 [C] [pa] (Mayflower: 0547, 1965, 286 pp., pa 5/-)

Sf, 15 stories: "Or Else"; "Year Day"; "Shock"; "See You Later"; "The Proud Robot"; "The Ego Machine"; "Juke-Box"; "Cold War"; "Call Him Demon"; "The Piper's Son"; "Absalom"; "Housing Problem"; "A Gnome There Was"; "The Big Night"; "Don't Look Now."

Best of Kuttner 2, The [C] [pa] (Mayflower: 0547, 1966, 288 pp., pa 5/-)

Sf, 14 stories: "The Voice of the Lobster"; "Masquerade"; "The Iron Standard"; "Endowment Policy"; "When the Bough Breaks"; "Line to Tomorrow"; "Clash by Night"; "A Wild Surmise"; "What You Need"; "The Twonky"; "Mimsy Were the Borogoves"; "The Devil We Know"; "Exit the Professor"; "Two-Handed Engine."

Beyond Earth's Gates [as L. Padgett, & with C. L. Moore] [pa] ("The Portal in the Picture," *SS*, Sep 1949) (Ace: D-69, 1954, 138 pp., pa 35¢; with *Daybreak—2250 A.D.*)

Tale of an evil theocratic world to which our Earth is "Paradise."

Bypass to Otherness [C] [pa] (Ballantine: 497K, 1961, 144 pp., pa 35¢) (Consul: 1269, 1963, 155 pp., pa 2/6)

Sf, 8 stories: "Cold War"; "Call Him Demon"; "The Dark Angel"; "The Piper's Son"; "Absalom"; "The Little Things"; "Nothing But Gingerbread Left"; "Housing Problem."

Chessboard Planet [pa] See *Tomorrow and Tomorrow & The Fairy Chessmen*

Creature From Beyond Infinity, The [pa] ("A Million Years to Conquer," *SS*, Nov 1940; *FSM*, Sep 1952) (Popular: 60-2355, 1968, 125 pp., pa 60¢)

Dark World, The [pa] (*SS*, Sum 1946; *FSM*, Win 1954) (Ace: 1965, 126 pp., pa 40¢) (Mayflower: 1657, 1966, 127 pp., pa 3/6)

Colorful and mystic novel written in the vein of Merritt.

Destination Infinity [pa] See *Fury*

Earth's Last Citadel [with C. L. Moore] [pa] (*Arg*, sr4, Apr 1943; *FN*, July 1950) (Ace: F-306, 1964, 128 pp., pa 40¢) (*Der Brunnen der Unsterblichkeit* [German], *T*: 450, 1966)

A struggle for the survival of the human race, against an irresistible alien.

Fairy Chessmen, The See *Tomorrow and Tomorrow & The Fairy Chessmen*

Far Reality, The [pa] See *Tomorrow and Tomorrow & The Fairy Chessmen*

Fury (*ASF*, sr3, May 1947, as L. O'Donnell) (Grosset Dunlap, New York, 1950, 186 pp., $1.00) (Dobson, London, 1954, 186 pp., 8/6) (SF B.C. [S.J.], 1955, 4/6) (*Destination Infinity*, Avon:

T-275, 1958, 192 pp., pa 35¢) (*Venus et le Titan* [French], Gallimard: Le RF, 1958) (*Gli immortali* [Italian], *Cosmo*: 10, 1958) (Digit: R413, 1960, 156 pp., pa 2/6) (*Alle Zeit der Welt* [German], *TS*: 53-54, 1962) (Mayflower: 2779, 1963, 190 pp., pa 3/6; 1966, pa 3/6)

A struggle on Venus, with immortality and an undersea civilization; sequel to "Clash by Night" (*ASF*, Mar 1943).

Gnome There Was, A [as L. Padgett] [C] (Simon & Schuster, New York, 1950, 276 pp., $3.00)

Sf, 11 stories: "A Gnome There Was"; "What You Need"; "The Twonky"; "The Cure"; "Exit the Professor"; "See You Later"; "Mimsy Were the Borogoves"; "Jesting Pilot"; "This Is the House"; "Rain Check"; "Compliments of the Author."

Line to Tomorrow [as L. Padgett] [C] [pa] (Bantam: 1251, 1954, 184 pp., pa 25¢)

Sf, 7 stories: "Line to Tomorrow"; "A Gnome There Was"; "What You Need"; "Private Eye"; "The Twonky"; "Compliments of the Author"; "When the Bough Breaks."

Mutant [as L. Padgett] [C] (Gnome, New York, 1953, 210 pp., $2.75) (Weidenfeld Nicolson, London, 1954, 224 pp., 9/6) (SF B.C. [S.J.], 1962, 5/6) (*Operazione apocalisse* [Italian], Biblioteca Economica Mondadori, 1955, pa) (Mayflower: B27, 1962, 192 pp., pa 2/6, by Kuttner) (Ballantine: F724, 1963, 191 pp., pa 50¢; U2859, 1968, pa 50¢) (*Mutante* [Spanish], Galaxia: 10, 1964, pa) (*Die Mutanten* [German], Heyne: 3065, 1966, pa)

Sf, 5 stories: the "Baldy" series (which see), plus epilogue as Chapter VI.

No Boundaries [with C. L. Moore] [C] (Ballantine, 1955, 149 pp., $2.00; #122, pa 35¢) (Consul: SF1025, 1961, 159 pp., pa 2/6)

Sf and fantasy, 5 stories: "Vintage Season"; "The Devil We Know"; "Home There's No Returning" (new); "Exit the Professor"; "Two-Handed Engine."

Return to Otherness [C] [pa] (Ballantine: F619, 1962, 240 pp., pa 50¢) (Mayflower: 7401, 1965, 288 pp., pa 5/-) (*Der verrückte Erfinder* [German], *T*: 444, 1966)

Sf, 8 stories (German ed. abridged): "See You Later"; "This Is the House"; "The Proud Robot"; "Gallegher Plus"; "The Ego Machine"; "Android"; "The Sky Is Falling"; "Juke-Box."

Robots Have No Tails [as L. Padgett] [C] (Gnome, 1952, 224 pp., $2.75) (*Der Stolze Roboter* & *Mir gehört die welt* [German], *UG*: 96 & 99, 1959) (*I robot nonhanno la coda* & *Mr. Gallegher, Supergenio* [Italian], *GRF*: 16 & 18, 1962)

Sf, 5 stories; the "Gallegher" series (which see).

Time Axis, The [pa] (*SS*, Jan 1949) (Ace: F-356, 1965, 142 pp., pa 40¢)

Battle for supremacy through time, with humans as pawns.

Tomorrow and Tomorrow & The Fairy Chessmen [as L. Padgett] (Gnome, 1951, 254 pp., $2.95) ([2nd only] *Chessboard Planet*, Galaxy SF Novel: 26, 1956, 124 pp., pa 35¢) (*La sacchiera sterminata* [Italian], *Cosmo*: 8, 1958) ([2nd only] *Gefahrliches schachspiel* [German], *UG*: 108, 1959) (*L'homme venu du futur* [French], Ed. des Deux Rives, 1957) ([1st only], Consul: 1265, 1963, 106 pp., pa 2/6) ([2nd only] *The Far Reality*, Consul: 1266, 1963, 155 pp., pa 2/6)

Two ultra-involved and mystifying novels from *ASF*: "Tomorrow and Tomorrow" (sr2, Jan 1947) and "The Fairy Chessmen" (sr2, Jan 1946).

Valley of the Flame [pa] ([by Keith Hammond, pseud.], *SS*, Mar 1946) (Ace: F-297, 1964, 156 pp., pa 40¢)

In the Amazon jungle a lost race, descended from jaguars, degenerates as "the flame" fades.

Well of the Worlds [pa] (*SS*, Mar 1952) ([as L. Padgett], Galaxy SF Novel: 17, 1953, 127 pp., pa 35¢) (Ace: F-344, 1965, 142 pp., pa 40¢)

An alternate-universe story, slow-moving but with a good climax.

KYFFIN-TAYLOR, (LADY) BESSIE

Fiction

From Out of the Silence [C] (Books Ltd.: London, [1920], 284 pp., 2/6; 1930)

Unusual selection of 7 stories: "Room No. 1"; "Two Little Red Shoes"; "Outside the House"; "The Winds in the Wood"; "The Twins"; "Sylvia"; "The Star Inn."

KYLE, DAVID A. U.S. science fiction and fantasy fan. Very active in fan affairs, he was co-founder (with M. Greenberg) of Gnome Press. He also designed several Gnome book jackets.

LA FARGE, OLIVER (HAZARD PERRY) (19 Dec 1901–2 Aug 1963) Noted U.S. author. He was educated at Harvard (A.M.). He was on many archaeological and ethnological expeditions to Arizona, Guatemala, etc., and lectured at Columbia University 1936-41. He published a number of works on American Indians, and was president of the Association on American Indian Affairs 1933-41 and again for some years from 1947.
Fiction
Pause in the Desert, A [C] (Houghton Mifflin, New York, 1957, 235 pp., $3.50) (T. Allen, Toronto, $4.00)
A notable collection of short stories, mainly from *The New Yorker*, but including one sf (from *F&SF*) and 3 fantasy stories [no further information].

LA SPINA, GREYE (BRAGG) (1880–) Noted U.S. writer for *Weird Tales*. Her father was a Methodist clergyman, but by the time she turned 21 she had become a freethinker. In 1898 she married Ralph Geissler (deceased 1900) and had one daughter; in 1910 she married Robert Rosario La Spina, Barone di Savuto. The title was not used in the U.S., but the author employed it on occasions as a nom de plume. Writing was no more than a hobby to her. Another hobby was weaving, for which she won blue ribbons. She published several one-act plays, and her short story "A Seat on the Platform" won a $2,500 prize. She has appeared in *Top Notch, Metropolitan, Photoplay, Black Mask, All-Story, Ten-Story Book, Action Stories, Saucy, Follies, Snappy, Breezy, Parisienne, Telling Tales, Love Romances, Modern Marriage, Love Stories, Thrill Book*, etc. She is particularly remembered by readers of *Weird Tales* for many thrilling stories. Two post-war reprints were "The Wax Doll" (*Thrill Book*, 1 Aug 1919 [as Isra Putnam]; *AFR*, No. 16, 1951) and "The Devil's Pool" (*WT*, June 1932; *Mag. of Horror*, Nov 1965).
Fiction
Invaders From the Dark (*WT*, sr3, Apr 1935) —revised: (Arkham, Sauk City [Wisc.], 1960, 168 pp., $3.50; 1,500 copies)
A story in the Gothic tradition: heroine Portia Differdale combats the Russian Princess Tchernova, a werewolf.
Shadow of Evil [pa] (Paperback: 52-334, 1966, 160 pp., pa 50¢)

LAFFERTY, R(APHAEL) A(LOYSIUS) (7 Nov 1914–) U.S. electrical engineer and sf author. He was born in Iowa, and moved to Oklahoma when four. He likes to describe himself as a correspondence school electrical engineer who has worked in that field most of his life. He began writing in the early 1960's and has had stories in most sf magazines and also such journals as *New Mexico Quarterly* and *Literary Review*.
Fiction
Past Master (Ace: H-54, 1968, 191 pp., pa 60¢) (Rapp & Whiting, London, 1968, 191 pp., 21/-)
An intriguing novel of assorted characters on the planet Astrobe, with a view of Sir Thomas More somewhat different from that of historians.

Reefs of Earth, The [pa] (Berkley: X1528, 1968, 144 pp., pa 60¢)
A crossbred alien family decides to depopulate Earth.
Space Chantey [pa] (Ace: H-56, 1968, 123 pp., pa 60¢; with *Pity About Earth*)
A space captain and crew have misadventures like those of the noted Greek seafarer, Odysseus.

LAFOREST-DIVONNE, PHILOMENE DE, COMTESSE
Fiction [as Claude Silve]
Eastward in Eden [Trans.–Evelyn Hatch] (Creative Age, New York, 1945, xv+271 pp., illus., $2.50) (McClelland, Toronto, $3.00) (Gollancz, London, 1948, 184 pp., 7/6)
Delightful tale of a little boy kidnapped to a never-never land.

LAFORGUE, JULES (1860–1887) French poet.
Fiction
Six Moral Tales [C] (Liveright, New York, 1928, 292 pp., $2.50)
Edited and translated by Frances Newman: "Hamlet, or, The Consequences of Filial Piety"; "Lohengrin, Son of Parsifal"; "The Miracle of the Roses"; "Pan and the Syrinx, or, The Invention of the Flute With Seven Reeds"; "Perseus and Andromeda, or, The Happiest One of the Triangle"; "Salome."

LAHMAN, DAMON U.S. author. Half Indian, he was born in a coal-mining region of West Virginia, later moving to Baltimore. He was a world roamer, travelling mainly in the U.S.A. and South America, and comments that most of his education came through his travels. An accident paralyzed him but he overcame the affliction; he then settled in College Park, Maryland, and still lives there.
Fiction
Stories in Fantasia [C] (Exposition, New York, 1967, 99 pp., $4.00)
Weird and macabre, 18 stories: "Captain Devilin's Last Voyage"; "Johnny Sellers"; "The Love Story of Mark Ring"; "Bluebeard of Linden"; "The Prank"; "Werewolves"; "The Doctor's Lesson"; "Idyll of Homer"; "My Great-Grandmother"; "The Story of the U.F.O."; "How Jim Forbes Won His Bride"; "The Wild Dog of the Dakotas"; "Commander Strob's Story"; "The Mystery in Space"; "Christmas, 1965"; "The Fate of Ann Smothers"; "My Brother's Strange Adventure"; "Deadlock."

LAING, ALEXANDER (KINNAN) (7 Aug 1903–) U.S. poet, novelist and educator. He was educated at Dartmouth College 1921-25 (A.B.) and 1932-33 (M.A.). He was interested in both radio and seafaring; he helped edit *Radio News* (1925-26) and *The Power Specialist* (1927-28), and later wrote a number of books on the sea. In 1930 he joined the faculty of Dartmouth College as tutorial adviser in English, was assistant librarian (1937-50), and became Professor of Belle Lettres in 1965. His writing style is best shown by its full use of the English language in *Clipper Ship Men* (1944). He has some books of fantasy interest with "Dr. Scarlett" as the leading character.
Fiction [Incomplete—other titles listed in Bleiler *Checklist*]
Cadaver of Gideon Wyck, The (Farrar Rinehart, New York, 1934, 376 pp., illus., $2.00) (Butterworth, London, 1934, 318 pp., 7/6; 1935, 318 pp., pa 2/6) (Grosset, New York, 1935, 384 pp., 75¢) (Armed: 685, nd, pa) (Collier: AS257X, 1962, 250 pp., pa 95¢)
A noted weird tale.
Anthologies
Great Ghost Stories of the World See *Haunted Omnibus, The*
Haunted Omnibus, The (Farrar Rinehart, New York, 1937, 848 pp., illus., $3.00) (Oxford, Toronto) (Cassell, London, 1937) (Garden City Pub. Co., New York, 1939, $1.79) (*Great Ghost Stories of the World: The Haunted Omnibus*, Blue Ribbon, New York, 1941, viii+485 pp., $1.00; Blue Ribbon, Toronto, $1.39 [27 stories])
41 stories: "August Heat," W. F. Harvey; "The Half Pint Flask," DuBose Heyward; "The Brahman, the Thief, and the Ghost," from the *Panchatantra* (Sanskrit); "The Treasure of Abbot Thomas," M. R. James; "The Yellow Wall Paper," Charlotte P.

Gilman; "The King of the World," A. E. Coppard; "Perez," W. L. George; "The Wendigo," A. Blackwood; "The Furnished Room," O. Henry; "The Screaming Skull," F. M. Crawford; "The Monkey's Paw," W. W. Jacobs; "The Horla," G. de Maupassant; "Laura," Saki; "The White People," A. Machen; "Concerning Phantoms," Pliny the Younger; "Markheim," R. L. Stevenson; "The Story of Ming-Y," L. Hearn; "The Beast With Five Fingers," W. F. Harvey; "Adam and Eve and Pinch Me," A. E. Coppard; "Where Their Fire Is Not Quenched," May Sinclair; "The Second Kalandar's Tale," Arabian Nights; "Full Fathom Five," A. Woollcott; "An Occurrence at Owl Creek Bridge," A. Bierce; "The Ghost-Ship," R. Middleton; "William Wilson," E. A. Poe; "The Feather Cloak of Hawaii," J. C. Andersen; "The Gentleman From America," M. Arlen. Following are omitted from the Blue Ribbon editions: "The Story of Glam the Grettissag and the Ghosts of Wulakai," Owen Lattimore; "Casting the Runes," M. R. James; "Man With Two Lives," A. Bierce; "The Open Window," Saki; "The Woman's Ghost Story," A. Blackwood; "The Haunted Hotel," Wilkie Collins; "Clorinda Walks in Heaven," A. E. Coppard; "The Grendel Episode," (*Beowulf*); "Green Thoughts," J. Collier; "The Tell Tale Heart," E. A. Poe; "A Visitor From Down Under," L. P. Hartley; "The Foghorn," Gertrude Atherton; "The Cherry Tree," A. E. Coppard; "Afterward," Edith Wharton.

LAMBERT, R. S. Canadian broadcaster.
Nonfiction
Exploring the Supernatural (A. Barker, London, 1954, 198 pp., 15/-)
    Subtitled "The Weird in Canadian Folklore—an assembly of queer happenings"—11 true ghost stories and 5-p. introduction. Includes: "The Shaking Tent of the Indian Medicine Man"; "Magic and Witchcraft in Quebec"; "The Fire-Spook of Caledonia Mills"; "Hauntings—East and West," etc.

LAMBOURN, RICHMAL CROMPTON (15 Nov 1890—) English author. She took B.A. Honours at U. of London in 1914 and was a a classics teacher at two schools before beginning to write in 1922. She is primarily noted for her "Just William" series of books about a boy aged 11 which began in 1922 and have continued to at least 1964 with 33 titles, including *William and the Moon Rocket* (1954) and *William and the Space Animal* (1956) of sf interest. She has written many other titles. Another fantasy besides that below is *Dread Dwelling* (Boni & Liveright, 1926). She always writes as Richmal Crompton.
Fiction [as Richmal Crompton]
Mists and Other Stories [C] (Hutchinson, London, 1928, 287 pp., 7/6)
    Fantasy and weird, 13 short stories: "The Bronze Statuette"; "The Visit"; "The Spanish Comb"; "Rosalind"; "Marlowes"; "The House Behind the Wood"; "Harry Lorrimer"; "The Little Girl"; "The Haunting of Greenways"; "The Oak Tree"; "Hands"; "The Sisters"; "Mist."

LAMPMAN, EVELYN SIBLEY (1907—)
Fiction
Rusty's Space Ship (Doubleday, New York, 1957, 240 pp., illus.—B. Krigstein, $2.95)
    Juvenile; the efforts of a fantastically inept extraterrestrial messenger to return an errant flying saucer to its owner.

LANDOLFI, TOMMASO (1908—)
Fiction
Gogol's Wife and Other Stories [C] (New Directions, New York, 1963, 183 pp., $4.00, pa $1.95) (McClelland, Toronto, $5.00, pa $2.35)
    8 stories: "Gogol's Wife"; "Dialogue on the Greater Harmonies"; "Two Old Maids"; "Wedding Night"; "The Death of the King of France"; "Giovanni and His Wife"; "Sunstroke"; "Pastorale." In the vein of Kafka, says A. Davidson's review in *F&SF*, Apr 1964.

LANDON, PERCEVAL (1869—1927) English barrister who be-

came a writer of plays and stories. He was also a special correspondent and spent some time in the East.
Fiction
Raw Edges [C] (Heinemann, 1908, 312 pp., illus.—Alberto Martini)
    A collection of 13 stories of which two are of interest: "Thurnley Abbey," one of the noted short English ghost stories and often reprinted, and "The Gyroscope," sf in which a huge gyroscope runs amok.

LANE, JANE (pseud) See DAKERS, E. (K.)

LANEY, FRANCIS TOWNER (30 Mar 1914—8 June 1958) U.S. fan noted in the early 1940's. He is primarily remembered for his editorship of *Acolyte* (14 issues, Fall 1942—Spr 1946), an amateur magazine dedicated to the memory of H. P. Lovecraft; it published much distinctive material by noted writers. Laney was active in the Fantasy Amateur Press Association but dropped out of the field some years before his death.

LANG, ALLEN KIM (31 July 1928—) U.S. science fiction author. He has had about 20 stories published in the sf magazines since his first appearance with "Guest Expert" (*Planet*, Jan 1941).
Fiction
Wild and Outside (Chilton, Philadelphia, 1966, 139 pp., $3.95) (Ambassador, Toronto, $5.50)
    A secret agent sets out to civilize a planet with quarterstaff and baseball bat.

LANG, ANDREW (31 Mar 1844—20 July 1912) Noted British literary figure. Roger Lancelyn Green gives an account of this writer and his works in *Andrew Lang* (Edmund Ward, Leicester, 1946, 15/-).
Fiction [Incomplete—other titles listed in Bleiler *Checklist*]
World's Desire, The See HAGGARD, H. R. (co-author)
Anthology
Dead Leman and Other Tales From the French, The [Trans.—A. Lang & P. Sylvester] (Swann Sonnenschein, London, 1889, 336 pp.)
    7 stories, with introduction: "The Dead Leman," T. Gautier; "How We Took the Redoubt," Prosper Mérimée; "The Taper," Leon Tolstoi; "These Lots To Be Sold," Edmund About; "A Conversion," Th. Bentzon; "The Etruscan Vase," P. Mérimée; "The Doctor's Story (a Grande Breteche)," H. de Balzac.

LANG, DANIEL (1913—)
Nonfiction
Man in the Thick Lead Suit, The (Oxford Univ. Press, 1954, 207 pp., $3.50) (Oxford, Toronto, $3.75)
    Essays on the human, personal side of spaceflight and nuclear research; originally published as a series in *The New Yorker*; recommended by A. Boucher.

LANGART, DARREL T. (pseud) Anagrammatical pseudonym of GARRETT, RANDALL, q.v.

LANGDON-DAVIES, JOHN
Nonfiction
Unknown—Is It Nearer?, The See DINGWALL, E. J. (co-author)

LANGE, JOHN FREDERICK (3 June 1931—) U.S. writer and philosophy teacher.
Series [as John Norman]
Gor. Paperbacks: *Tarnsman of Gor*; *Outlaw of Gor*; *Priest-Kings of Gor*. [Series continues after 1968.]
Fiction [as John Norman]
Outlaw of Gor [pa] (Ballantine: U6072, 1967, 254 pp., pa 75¢)
    Second of Gor series. Cabot seeks to clear his name after being made to appear a traitor by the 'Priest-Kings.'
Priest-Kings of Gor [pa] (Ballantine: 72015, 1968, 317 pp., pa 75¢)

Third of Gor series. Cabot seeks vengeance on the mysterious 'Priest-Kings'—and lives with them for a while.

Tarnsman of Gor [pa] (Ballantine: U6701, 1966, 219 pp., pa 75¢)

First of Gor series. Our hero Tarl Cabot is transferred from Earth to Gor, the Counter-Earth, and becomes a warrior amid fantastic adventures.

LANGELAAN, GEORGE (1908–) British journalist. He was born in Paris, and has worked for the Paris staff of A.P., U.P., I.N.S. and *The New York Times*. He wrote one of the most noted recent weird-horror stories: "The Fly" (*Playboy*, 1957; *Best SF* [Merril], 1958). This was filmed by 20th Century-Fox in 1958, produced and directed by Kurt Neumann, with Vincent Price and Herbert Marshall.
Fiction
Out of Time [C] [pa] (FSB: 1129, 1964, 190 pp., pa 3/6)

Fantasy, 10 stories, with brief preface but no table of contents: "The Fly"; "The Devil His Due"; "Armchair Detective"; "Past the Time Limit"; "Recession"; "The Lady From Nowhere"; "The Other Hand"; "The Miracle"; "The Drop of Forgetfulness"; "Parkson's Last Flight."

LANGLEY, DOROTHY (pseud) See KISSLING, D. H.

LANNING, GEORGE (1925–)
Fiction
Pedestal, The (Harper, New York, 1966, 198 pp., $4.50) (M. Joseph, London, 1967, 192 pp., 25/-) (Avon: S376, 1968, 158 pp., pa 60¢)

The narrator is haunted by a huge wooden pedestal impulsively bought at an auction.

LARGE, ERNEST C. British author. An sf work less known than those below is *Asleep in the Afternoon* (Holt, 1939).
Fiction
Dawn in Andromeda (J. Cape, London, 1956, 282 pp., 15/-)

"God" maroons five couples on an Andromedan planet without tools or personal memories, but retaining general knowledge; the story is of their rise to "civilized" ways.

Sugar in the Air (Cape, London, 1937, 447 pp., 7/6) (Nelson, Toronto, $2.00) (Scribner, New York, 1937, 447 pp., $2.50)

A young engineer joins a complex company and becomes involved in the complications of marketing 'Sunsap.' Considered by many to be a near-classic sf novel.

LARSEN, EGON (1904–) German writer. He was born in Munich as Egon Lehrburger; he now lives in London and has been the London representative of the Bavarian Radio Network since 1954. He has travelled worldwide on assignments for *The New York Times*, and during the war was engaged in secret propaganda work for the U.S. Office of Strategic Services. He has contributed many features to the BBC as a script writer and has narrated his own "Travelogue" series; he has also done some work for TV and documentary films. He has written a number of books on popular science, such as *Men Who Changed the World* and *Men Under the Sea*.
Fiction
You'll See (Rider, London, 1957, 176 pp., 16/-)

The world of 1982, with a benevolent though somewhat bureaucratic World Government in charge of mankind's fate.

LASKI, MARGHANITA (24 Oct 1915–) British novelist and critic. The granddaughter of Dr. Moses Gaster, a Chief Rabbi of England, she studied philology and took her B.A. at Somerville College, Oxford. She turned to journalism and has contributed to *Observer*, etc. Her first novel was *Love on the Super-Tax* (1944); other works include *The Patchwork Book* (an anthology for children), and *Mrs. Ewing, Mrs. Molesworth, and Mrs. Hodgson Burnett* (a critical study of their works). Her husband, John Howard, is now her publisher.
Fiction
Victorian Chaise-Longue, The (Cresset, London, 1953, 159 pp.,

8/6) (Houghton Mifflin, New York, 1954, 119 pp., $2.75) (Guild: 01, 1956, 159 pp., pa 2/-) (Ballantine: 441K, 1960, 125 pp., pa 35¢; 70005, 1968, pa 50¢) (Penguin: 1835, 1962, 160 pp., pa 4/-)

A horror story of twin lives in which Melanie Langdon of 1954 is transferred to the body of invalid Milly Baines of 1864.

LASSER, DAVID (20 Mar 1902–) U.S. engineer, writer and economist. He studied engineering at M.I.T. 1920-24, and was a technical writer with New York Edison Co. 1927-29. Then he became managing editor of the Gernsback science fiction magazines 1929-1933, and was the first president of the American Interplanetary Society (now the American Rocket Society). He has since been on various labour boards, etc., and has been Chief Economist with the International Union of Electrical Workers since 1950. He wrote one of the first nonfiction works on rocketry, *The Conquest of Space* (Penguin, New York, 1931; Hurst, London, 1932), and collaborated with D. H. Keller on the novel *The Time Projector* (*WS*, sr2, July 1931).

LASSWITZ, KURD (1848–1910) German professor. He spent most of his life at the Gymnasium Ernestinum in Gotha publishing learned works on philosophy and physics and consistently amusing himself by writing science fiction and fantasy which included much original thinking. Of his three novels, *Auf Zwei Planeten* (1897) is the most noted; it is a political utopia story covering spaceflight, the first satellite launching station and the first plausible working-out of interplanetary gravitational orbits. Banned by the Nazis as "demokratisch," it was reprinted in *AW*: 5 & 6, 1958; among other appearances it was serialised in a Spanish newspaper before World War I as "Entre dos planetas." Despite his popularity, not only in German but in almost all other European languages, not a word by Lasswitz appeared in English until the following short stories appeared in *F&SF* (translated by W., Ley): "When the Devil Took the Professor" (Jan 1953); "Aladdin's Lamp" (May 1953); "Psychotomy" (July 1955). His memory has been perpetuated by the Kurd Lasswitz Literary Achievement Award, given for the first time at the First European SF Convention at Zurich in 1959.

LATHAM, PHILIP (pseud) See RICHARDSON, R. S.

LAUGHLIN, CLARENCE JOHN
Nonfiction
Ghosts Along the Mississippi (Scribner, New York, 1948, 100 photos and text, $12.50)

Macabre photos of interest to specialists.

LAUMER, (JOHN) KEITH (9 June 1925–) U.S. military officer, diplomat and science fiction author. He was born in Syracuse, N.Y., and attended Philips U. in Enid, Oklahoma, and Coffeyville Junior College, Kansas. He went into the army in Aug 1943 and went to Europe for the finish of World War II and the occupation of Germany. Upon discharge he entered U. of Illinois in 1946 and studied architecture, took a year off in 1949 to study at U. of Stockholm (B.Sc.), and returned to Illinois and gained B.Sc. Arch. in 1952. He served in the U.S. Air Force 1953-56 as a first lieutenant on radar sites. He switched to the U.S. Foreign Service and served in Rangoon among other places. He resigned in 1958 and rejoined the U.S.A.F. in May 1960 as captain. He later served with Third Air Force H.Q. in London.

He began writing in 1959 and has now written well over 50 stories, becoming one of the more prolific writers of recent years. Besides regular sf he has written a number of novelized adaptations of TV series for paperback publication, such as *The Avengers* No. 5 (*The Afrit Affair*) and No. 7 (*The Gold Bomb*), and two in the *Invaders* series noted below. Laumer has also written a number of articles on model building and the book *How to Design and Build Flying Models* (Harper, 1960).
Series
Alternate Earths (the Imperium): *Worlds of the Imperium*; *The Other Side of Time*; *Assignment in Nowhere*.
Retief. Interplanetary administrative agent (troubleshooter!). The

stories marked "1" are included in *Envoy to New Worlds*; "2" in *Galactic Diplomat*; "3" in *Retief's War* (book form); "4" in *Retief and the Warlords*. In *Fan*: "Diplomat-at-Arms" (Jan 1960). All others in *If*: "The Frozen Planet" (Sep 1961; "Courier" in 2); "Gambler's World" (Nov 1961; "Palace Revolution" in 1); "The Yillian Way" (Jan 1962; "Protocol" in 1); "The Madman From Earth" (Mar 1962; "Policy" in 1); "Retief of the Red-Tape Mountain" (May 1962; "Sealed Orders" in 1); "Aide Memoire" (July 1962; in 1); "Cultural Exchange" (Sep 1962; in 1); "The Desert and the Stars" (Nov 1962; "Protest Note" in 2); "The Governor of Glave" (Nov 1963; "Native Intelligence," in 2); "The City That Grew in the Sea" (Mar 1964; "Wicker Wonderland" in 2); "The Prince and the Pirate" (Aug 1964; in 2); "The Castle of Light" (Oct 1964; in 2); "Retief, God-Speaker" (Jan 1965; "The Brass God" in 2); "Trick or Treaty" (Aug 1965); "Giant Killer" (Sep 1965); "Retief's War" (sr2, Oct 1965; as 3); "Dam Nuisance" (Mar 1965); "Truce or Consequences" (Nov 1966); "Forest in the Sky" (Feb 1967); "Retief, War Criminal" (Apr 1967); "Clear as Mud" (Aug 1967).

Fiction

Assignment in Nowhere [pa] (Berkley: X1596, 1968, 143 pp., pa 60¢)

A modern man travels in time to play Richard the Lion-Hearted. Related to *Worlds of the Imperium*.

Catastrophe Planet [pa] (Berkley: F1273, 1966, 158 pp., pa 50¢)

Adventure on an Earth ravaged by volcanic action and with a battle against an alien menace.

Day Before Forever & Thunderhead, The (Doubleday, New York, 1968, 164 pp., $3.95) (D'day, Toronto, $4.75)

Two short novels: "The Day Before Forever" (*F&SF*, July 1967); "Thunderhead" (*GSF*, Apr 1967).

Earthblood [with Rosel G. Brown] (*If*, sr4, Apr 1966) (Doubleday, 1966, 253 pp., $4.50) (D'day SF B.C., 1967, $1.70) (Berkley: S1544, 1968, 287 pp., pa 75¢)

A human born in mysterious circumstances goes to space in a zoo-ship, then turns pirate and seeks the story of his origin.

Enemies From Beyond [pa] (Pyramid: X1689, 1967, 159 pp., pa 60¢)

Second of "Invaders" series.

Envoy to New Worlds [C] [pa] (Ace: F-223, 1963, 134 pp., pa 40¢; with *Flight From Yesterday*) (*Botschafter im Kosmos* [German], *UZ*: 388, 1964)

Sf, 6 stories of the "Retief" series [noted as "1" in the series listing above].

Galactic Diplomat [C] (Doubleday, 1965, 227 pp., $3.95) (Berkley: X1240, 1966, 223 pp., pa 60¢) (*Diplomat der Galaxis* [German], *TS*: 115, 1966, pa)

Sf, 9 stories of the "Retief" series [noted as "2" in the series listing above].

Galactic Odyssey ("Spaceman," *If*, sr3, May 1967) (Berkley: X1447, 1967, 160 pp., pa 60¢) (*Galaktische Odyssee* [German], Heyne: 3132, 1968, pa) (Dobson, 1968, 160 pp., 18/-)

A fast-moving interstellar adventure with an amazing assortment of races and peoples.

Great Time Machine Hoax, The ("A Hoax in Time," *Fan*, sr3, June 1963) —enlarged: (Simon & Schuster, New York, 1964, 190 pp., $3.95) (Pocket Books: 50156, 1965, 176 pp., pa 50¢) (*Im Banne der Zeitmaschine* [German], *TS*: 111, 1966) (*L'ordinateur desordonne* [French], Denoël: PF93, 1966, pa)

A computer can make changes in time.

Greylorn [C] [pa] (Berkley: X1514, 1968, 192 pp., pa 60¢) (*The Other Sky*, Dobson, 1968, 191 pp., 21/-)

4 novelettes: "Greylorn" (*AS*, Apr 1959); "The Night of the Trolls"; "The Other Sky"; "The King of the City."

Invaders, The [pa] (Pyramid: R1664, 1967, 142 pp., pa 50¢) (*The Meteor Men* [by A. Lebaron], Corgi: GS7836, 1968, 127 pp., pa 3/6)

First of the TV series.

It's a Mad, Mad, Mad Galaxy [C] [pa] (Berkley: X1641, 1968, 160 pp., pa 60¢)

Sf, 5 stories: "The Body Builders"; "The Planet Wreckers"; "The Star-Sent Knaves"; "The War With the Yukks"; "Goober-

cality."

Meteor Men, The [pa] See *Invaders, The*

Monitors, The (Berkley: X1340, 1966, 160 pp., pa 60¢) (Dobson, London, 1968, 160 pp., 18/-)

A story of anti-conformity. Logical and benevolent aliens take over the Earth, with unexpected results.

Nine by Laumer [C] (Doubleday, 1967, 222 pp., $3.95) (Faber, 1968, 222 pp., 20/-)

9 stories: "A Trip to the City" ("It Could Be Anything"); "Cocoon"; "Dinochrome"; "Door-Step"; "Placement Test"; "The Long-Remembered Thunder"; "Hybrid"; "End as a Hero"; "The Walls."

Other Side of Time, The (*Fan*, sr3, Apr 1965) —revised: (Berkley: F1129, 1965, 160 pp., pa 60¢) (Dobson, London, 1968, 160 pp., 18/-)

Sequel to *Worlds of the Imperium*; the adventures of Brion Bayard in thwarting an invasion from another time line.

Other Sky, The [C] See *Greylorn*

Plague of Demons, A [pa] ("The Hounds of Hell," *If*, sr2, Nov 1964) —revised: (Berkley: F1086, 1965, 159 pp., pa 50¢) (Penguin: 2698, 1967, 170 pp., pa 3/6) (*Krieg auf dem Mond* [German], *TS*: 128, 1967)

Creatures masquerading as men take slaves to run robot war machines.

Planet Run [with G. R. Dickson] (Doubleday, 1967, 167 pp., $3.95) (Berkley: X1588, 1968, 143 pp., pa 60¢)

A crusty old star frontiersman seeks revenge against a ruthless despot.

Retief and the Warlords (Doubleday, 1968, 188 pp., $4.50)

Retief's War (*If*, sr3, Dec 1965) (Doubleday, 1966, 208 pp., $3.95) (Berkley: X1427, 1967, 175 pp., pa 60¢)

A Retief story, in which he endeavours to displace the dictatorship of the planet Quopp, a mechanic's delight.

Time Bender, The [pa] ("Axe and Dragon," *Fantastic*, sr3, Nov 1965) (Berkley: F1185, 1966, 160 pp., pa 50¢) (*Das grosse Zeitabenteuer* [German], *TS*: 143, 1968 pa)

Lawrence O'Leary uses psychic energies, and lands in 'Artesia,' where he has fantastic adventures—including some he can't control.

Trace of Memory, A [pa] (*AS*, sr3, July 1962) —enlarged: (Berkley: F780, 1963, 174 pp., pa 50¢) (Mayflower: 11329X, 1968, 188 pp., pa 5/-)

A space-and-time adventure with galactic intrigue as a man tries to reconstruct the past.

Worlds of the Imperium (*Fan*, sr3, Feb 1961) (Ace: F-127, 1962, 133 pp., pa 40¢ [with *Seven From the Stars*]; M-165, 1967, pa 45¢] (*I mondi dell'impero* [Italian], *GRF*: 39, 1964) (Dobson, London, 1967, 138 pp., 18/-)

Fantastic intrigue when a man is kidnapped from this Earth to kill his dictator "brother" on an alternate Earth.

LAW, WINIFRED Australian author.
Fiction
Rangers of the Universe (New Century, Sydney, 1945, 176 pp., illus.–D. Alderton, 5/6)

Juvenile (not listed in the Bleiler *Checklist*); sequel to *Through Space to the Planets*.

Through Space to the Planets (New Century, 1944, 174 pp., illus.–D. Alderton, 4/9)

Juvenile (not in Bleiler *Checklist*); a boy has strange and exciting adventures on a new planet; sequel is *Rangers of the Universe*.

LAWRENCE (pseud) See STEVENS, L. S.

LAWRENCE, D(AVID) H(ERBERT) (11 Sep 1885–2 Mar 1930) English novelist, poet, essayist and playwright. He was one of five children brought up in an atmosphere of poverty, brutality and drunkenness. Some of his best writing occurs in *Sons and Lovers* (1913) and *The Rainbow* (1915). He is now remembered as one of the early writers to break sexual taboos, primarily with his *Lady Chatterley's Lover*, originally written in 1926 and prohibited in many countries (thousands of copies were said to have been smuggled into England and the U.S.A.) until comparatively recent years.

Fiction

Woman Who Rode Away and Other Stories, The [C] (Secker & Warburg, London, 1928, 292 pp., 7/6) (Knopf, New York, 1928, 307 pp., $2.50)

11 stories: "Two Blue Birds"; "Sun"; "The Woman Who Rode Away"; "Smile"; "The Border Line"; "Jimmy and the Desperate Woman"; "The Last Laugh"; "In Love"; "The Man Who Loved Islands"; "Glad Ghosts"; "None of That."

LAWRENCE, HENRY LIONEL

Fiction

Children of Light, The (MacDonald, London, 1960, 192 pp., 12/6) (*Kinder des Lichts* [German], Heyne, 1962) (Consul: 1167, 1962, 191 pp., pa 2/6)

The consequences of atomic radiation.

LAWRENCE, MARGERY (pseud) See TOWLE, (Mrs.) A. E.

LAWSON, ROBERT (1892) Has also written *Mr. Wilmer* (Little Brown, 1945).

Fiction

Mr. Twigg's Mistake (Little Brown, Boston, 1947, 141 pp., illus.–author, $2.50) (McClelland, Toronto, $2.75)

A little boy feeds vitamin to a mole, who becomes as big as a bear.

LAWTON, CLIFF British artist. He was art editor of the magazine *Phantom* from Dec 1957 until it ceased in July 1958, but may have had an earlier interest in it. In 1960 he edited the only issue to appear of *A Book of Weird Tales* (F. J. Ackerman, associate editor), which printed material of U.S. origin.

LAYNE, STAN (1899–)

Nonfiction

I Doubted Flying Saucers (Meador, Boston, 1958, 177 pp., illus.–Elna L. Reynolds, $2.00)

LE FANU, J(OSEPH) SHERIDAN (28 Aug 1814–7 Feb 1873) Irish author. Born in Dublin, he entered Trinity College in 1833, and from 1839 he devoted himself to journalism. He bought three Dublin newspapers and merged them into *The Evening Mail*. Later he edited the *Dublin University Magazine* 1869-72. It was not until 1864 that he published his first novel, *Uncle Silas*, the success of which encouraged him to continue; some 12 other novels and shorter pieces followed between 1865 and 1875. His work is ranked with that of Lever as representing the best of the early 19th century Irish novelists.

"Green Tea" and "Carmilla" are the most noted of Le Fanu's supernatural short stories; they influenced M. R. James and other British writers. Reprints include "The Dead Sexton" (*F&SF*, Jan 1957; from *Once a Week*, 1871 Christmas Issue); however, "The Churchyard Yew" (*WT*, July 1947) credited to Le Fanu was written by another author. The recent French collection *Carmilla* (Denoël: PF42, 1960) contained "Carmilla," "Green Tea," and two other stories. A scholarly survey is *Sheridan Le Fanu* by Nelson Brown (Roy, 1953).

Fiction [Incomplete—other titles listed in Bleiler *Checklist*]

Best Ghost Stories [editor–E. F. Bleiler] [C] [pa] (Dover: T415, 1964, 467 pp., pa $2.00)

16 stories with editor's introduction (7 pp.): "Squire Toby's Will"; "Schalken the Painter"; "Madam Crowl's Ghost"; "The Haunted Baronet"; "Green Tea"; "The Familiar"; "Mr. Justice Harbottle"; "Carmilla"; "The Fortunes of Sir Robert Ardagh"; "An Account of Some Strange Disturbances in Aungier Street"; "The Dead Sexton"; "Ghost Stories of the Tiled House"; "The White Cat of Drumgunniol"; "An Authentic Narrative of a Haunted House"; "Sir Dominick's Revenge"; "Ultor de Lacy."

Diabolical Genius, The [editor–Michael Econhoorn] [C] [pa] (Juniper 'Forgotten Classics of Mystery': 3, New York, 1959, 384 pp., $2.95; pa $1.45)

3 novels: "Uncle Silas" (abr.); "The Inn of the Flying Dragon"; "Carmilla."

Green Tea and Other Ghost Stories [C] (Arkham, Sauk City [Wisc.], 1945, 367 pp., $3.00, jacket–R. Clyne; 2,026 copies)

14 stories, foreword–A. Derleth: "Schalken the Painter"; "Squire Toby's Will"; "Green Tea"; "Wicked Captain Walshawe of Wauling"; "Carmilla"; "The Sexton's Adventure"; "Madam Crowl's Ghost"; "Sir Dominick's Bargain"; "The Vision of Tom Chuff"; "Ultor de Lacy"; "Dickon the Devil"; "The House in Aungier Street"; "Mr. Justice Harbottle"; "The Familiar."

In a Glass Darkly [C] (R. Bentley, London, 1886, 471 pp.) (Nash & Grayson, London, 1923, 471 pp., 7/6) (Davies, London, 1929, 382 pp., illus.–E. Ardizzone, 12/6; 1931, 390 pp., 5/-) (J. Lehmann, London, 1947, 288 pp., 8/6, intro.–V. S. Pritchett)

5 stories: "Green Tea"; "The Familiar"; "Carmilla"; "Mr. Justice Harbottle"; "The Room in the Dragon Volant."

Madame Crowl's Ghost and Other Tales of Mystery [editor–M. R. James] [C] (G. Bell, London, 1923, 277 pp., 7/6)

12 stories: "The Child That Went With the Fairies"; "Dickon the Devil"; "Ghost Stories of Chapelizod"; "Madame Crowl's Ghost"; "Sir Dominick's Bargain"; "Squire Toby's Will"; "Some Strange Disturbances in Aungier Street"; "Stories of Lough Guir"; "Ultor de Lacy"; "Vision of Tom Chuff"; "White Cat of Drumgunniol"; "Wicked Captain Walshaw of Wauling."

Strange Adventure in the Life of Miss Laura Mildmay, A (Home & Van Thal, London, 1947, 108 pp., tinted frontis.–F. Kelly, 8/6) (McClelland, Toronto, $2.50)

A macabre novelette.

Uncle Silas (Tinsley Bros., London, 1864, 3 vols.) (Cresset, London, 1947, 480 pp., 8/6, intro.–Eliz. Bowen) (Penguin, 1947, 191 pp., pa 1/3) (Dufont, New York, 1948, 480 pp., $3.95, intro.–E. Bowen) (Blackie, London, 1963, 448 pp., 12/6) (Ryerson, Toronto, $2.75) (Corgi: FN7506, 1966, 382 pp., pa 5/-) (Dover: T1715, 1966, 436 pp., pa $2.00) (Paperback: 54-390, 1967, 351 pp., pa 75¢)

Noted psychological suspense story.

Wylder's Hand (London, 1864, 3 vols. in 1) (Gollancz, London, 1963, 387 pp., 18/-)

Supernatural novel.

LE QUEUX, WILLIAM (TUFNELL) (2 July 1864–13 Oct 1927) British author. Over a period of 40 years he wrote a great number of books in the fields of detection and mystery, espionage and intrigue, fantasy and science fiction. These included a number of serials in *Chamber's Journal*. He wrote material similar to H. R. Haggard's, and in the same period, so he was overshadowed to a great extent. Nevertheless, and even though none of his fantasy novels have seen recent reprinting, the following are of interest: *The Great War in England in 1897* (1894), *The Great White Queen* (1898), *The Unknown Tomorrow* (1910), and *Zoraida: A Romance of the Harem and the Great Sahara* (1895).

LEA, RICHARD

Fiction

Outward Urge, The (R. Cowan, London, 1947, 216 pp., 9/6)

Time travel to the days of the druids.

LEACOCK, STEPHEN (BUTLER) (30 Dec 1869–28 Mar 1944) Canadian author and educator; professor of political economy at McGill University. He was particularly noted for his unique brand of humor which appeared in such stories as "The Man in Asbestos," a takeoff of H. G. Wells' *The Time Machine*.

Fiction

Afternoons in Utopia [C] (Dodd Mead, New York, 1932, 221 pp., $2.00) (Lane, London, 1932, 240 pp., 5/-)

6 satirical utopia stories: "Utopia Old and New"; "Grandfather Goes to War"; "The Doctor and the Contraption"; "Rah! Rah! College, or, Tom Buncom at Shucksford"; "The Band of Brothers"; "A Fragment From Utopia."

Frenzied Fiction [C] (Lane, New York & London, 1918, 240 pp., 4/-; 1931, 3/6) (Dodd, ?, 527 pp., $2.00)

19 stories: "My Revelations as a Spy"; "Father Knickerbock-

er"; "A Fantasy"; "The Prophet in Our Midst"; "Personal Adventures in the Spirit World"; "The Sorrows of a Summer Guest"; "To Nature and Back Again"; "The Cave Man as He Is"; "Ideal Interviews"; "The New Education"; "The Errors of Santa Claus"; "Lost in New York"; "This Strenuous Age"; "The Old, Old Story of How Five Men Went Fishing"; "Back From the Land"; "The Perplexity Column as Done by Jaded Journalists"; "Simple Stories of Success, or, How to Succeed in Life"; "In Dry Toronto"; "Merry Christmas."

Iron Man and the Tin Woman, The [C] (Dodd Mead, 1929, 309 pp., $2.00) (Lane, 1929, 308 pp., 7/6)

48 humorous sketches with many of sf interest, including: "When Social Regulation Is Complete"; "Athletics for 1950"; "Astronomical Alarms"; "Uninvented Inventions"; "More Messages From Mars"; "Portents of the Future"; "Intimate Disclosures of a Wronged Woman."

Laugh With Leacock [C] [pa] (Corgi: GH736, 1959, 288 pp., pa 3/6)

8 short stories, plus numerous selections from books. Selections from *Literary Lapses*; *My Discovery of England*; *The Hohenzollerns of America*; *Over the Footlights*; *Winnowed Wisdom*; *Short Circuits*; *Moonbeams From the Larger Lunacy*; *Further Foolishness*. Five stories from *Nonsense Novels*: "Maddened by Mystery"; "Guido the Gimlet of Ghent"; "Gertrude the Governess"; "Soaked in Seaweed"; "The Man in Asbestos." Three stories from *Frenzied Fiction*: "The New Education"; "The Old, Old Story of How Five Men Went Fishing"; "Simple Stories of Success."

Nonsense Novels [C] (Lane, New York & London, 1911, 7+230 pp.) (Lane, 1921, 176 pp., 10/6; 1926, 231 pp., 2/6; 1932, 230 pp., 3/6) (Dodd Mead, 1922; 1929, 229 pp.) (Sun Dial, New York, 1929, 229 pp., $1.00)

10 stories: "Caroline's Christmas, or, The Inexplicable"; "Gertrude the Governess, or, Simple Seventeen"; "Guido the Gimlet of Ghent: A Romance of Chivalry"; "Hannah of the Highlands, or, The Laird of Loch Aucherlocherty"; "Hero in Homespun, or, The Life Struggle of Hezekiah Hayloft"; "Maddened by Mystery, or, The Defective Detective"; "Man in Asbestos: An Allegory of the Future"; " 'Q': A Psychic Pstory of the Psupernatural"; "Soaked in Seaweed, or, Upset in the Ocean"; "Sorrows of a Super Ghoul, or, The Memoirs of Marie Mushenough."

LEAHY, JOHN M(ARTIN) (1886–) U.S. author. He wrote a number of weird stories. Some appeared in *Weird Tales*, where he was mainly noted for "In Amundsen's Tent" (Jan 1928; *AFR*, No. 15, 1951) and the serial below. He also appeared in *Science & Invention* with "The Living Death" (sr9, Oct 1924).

Fiction

Drome (*WT*, sr5, Jan 1927) (FPCI, Los Angeles, 1952, 295 pp., illus.–author, $3.00) (Nelson, Toronto, $3.75)

A secret land inside the Earth.

LEARY, FRANCIS

Fiction

This Dark Monarchy (Dutton, New York, 1949, 316 pp., $3.00) (Evans Bros., London, 1950, 299 pp., 9/6)

Well-written Gothic horror story set in the 1800's.

LEBARON, A. (Pseud) See LAUMER, K.

LEBLANC, MAURICE (1864–6 Nov 1941) French author. He was noted as the Conan Doyle of France because of his Arsene Lupin stories. These began in 1907; Lupin, a modern Robin Hood and Dick Turpin, became the greatest character in all the sensational French police romances. In the science fiction and fantasy field Leblanc wrote four novels: *The Secret of Sarek* (Macaulay, London & New York, 1920), *The Secret Tomb* (Macaulay, 1923), *The Three Eyes* (Macaulay, 1921) and *The Tremendous Event* (Macaulay, 1922). The last two saw Japanese editions in 1953. Leblanc was made an Officer of the Legion of Honour.

LECKIE, PETER MARTIN (1890–)

Fiction

Summer in 3,000 [as Peter Martin] (Quality, London, 1946, 184 pp., 8/6)

An interesting story of a well-depicted future world, with the progressive ideal state of the World Island and the still bad old world of America. Highly rated by F. J. Ackerman.

LEE, ARTHUR STANLEY GOULD (31 Aug 1894–) British author. He has written *The Son of Leicester* (Gollancz, 1964), a biography of Sir Robert Dudley.

Fiction

Airplane in the Arabian Nights, An [as Arthur Lee Gould] (Laurie, London, 1947, 240 pp., 8/6)

A time fault places aviators in a harem.

LEE, CHRISTOPHER (1923?–) British actor. He is noted for his portrayals of monsters for Hammer Films, although of his 91 films up to 1968, only 15 were horror. He is trained as an opera singer and speaks seven languages. He is married and has one daughter.

Anthology

Christopher Lee's Treasury of Terror [pa] (Pyramid: R1498, 1966, np, pa 50¢)

Comic-book versions of 5 stories: "The Mark of the Beast," R. Kipling; "Wentworth's Day," H. P. Lovecraft & A. Derleth; "The Past Master," R. Bloch; "The Death of Halpin Frayser," A. Bierce; "Dracula's Guest," B. Stoker. The stories are adapted by Craig Tennis (1st, 3rd, 4th stories), Russ Jones (2nd), and E. Nelson Bridwell (5th). Artists are Johnny Craig (1st), Russ Jones (2nd), Alden McWilliams (3rd), and Frank Bolle (4th, 5th).

LEE, ELIZABETH British anthologist.

Anthologies

Horror Stories [pa] (Elek 'Bestseller,' 1961, 256 pp., pa 3/6)

No compiler is credited, but the entry is placed here because Lee compiled the sequel. 15 stories: "Moonlight Sonata," A. Woollcott; "The Novel of the Black Seal," A. Machen; "Mrs. Amworth," E. F. Benson; "The Upper Berth," F. M. Crawford; "The Dunwich Horror," H. P. Lovecraft; "Was It a Dream?" G. de Maupassant; "The Judge's House," B. Stoker; "The Trial for Murder," Charles Collins & C. Dickens; "The Man With a Malady," J. F. Sullivan; "Sawney Bean and His Family," Scottish traditional; "The Squaw," B. Stoker; "The Hair," A. J. Alan; "What Was It?" F.-J. O'Brien; "The Cone," H. G. Wells; "The Screaming Skull," F. M. Crawford.

More Horror Stories [pa] (Elek 'Bestseller,' 1962, 222 pp., pa 3/6)

10 stories: "The Dead Smile," F. M. Crawford; "Caterpillars," E. F. Benson; "Monstrous Regiment," H. R. Wakefield; "Telling," Eliz. Bowen; "The Veldt," R. Bradbury; "A Little Place off Edgware Road," Graham Greene; "Nowhere Without Her," Colin Evans; "The Sorcerer's Apprentice," Robert Bloch; "The Travelling Grave," L. P. Hartley; "The Murders in the Rue Morgue," E. A. Poe.

Spine Chillers: An Anthology of Mystery and Horror (Elek, London, 1961, 528 pp., 25/-) (Ryerson, Toronto)

39 stories: "The Pit and the Pendulum," "The Facts in the Case of M. Valdemar," "The Cask of Amontillado," "Berenice," Edgar A. Poe; "No. 1 Branch Line: The Signalman," C. Dickens; "The Trial for Murder," C. Dickens & Charles Collins; "A Terribly Strange Bed," Wilkie Collins; "The Case of Mr. Lucraft," Sir W. Besant & James Rice; "A Watcher by the Dead," A. Bierce; "The Screaming Skull," F. M. Crawford; "Man-Size in Marble," "John Charrington's Wedding," E. Nesbit; "The Mezzotint," M. R. James; "The Novel of the White Powder," A. Machen; "Pollock and the Porroh Man," "The Red Room," H. G. Wells; "Lukundoo," Edward L. White; "In the Tube," "At the Farmhouse," E. F. Benson; "When I Was Dead," "The Business of Madame John," Vincent O'Sullivan; "The Strange Adventures of a Private Secretary in New York," A. Blackwood; "Benlian," "Phantas," Oliver Onions; "Where Their Fire Is Not Quenched," May Sinclair; "The Voice in the Night," W. H. Hodgson; "The Bureau d'Echange de

Maux," Lord Dunsany; "That Dieth Not," H. R. Wakefield; "The Thing on the Doorstep," "Cool Air," "The Outsider," H. P. Lovecraft; "A Visitor From Down Under," L. P. Hartley; "A Rose for Emily," Wm. Faulkner; "The Cat Jumps," Eliz. Bowen; "Ghost of Honour," Pamela H. Johnson; "Catnip," "Enoch," Robert Bloch; "The Portobello Road," Muriel Spark; "Skeleton," R. Bradbury.

LEE, MARGUERITE DU PONT
Nonfiction
Virginia Ghosts (Virginia Book Co., Berryville [Va.], rev. ed. 1966, 255 pp., illus., $6.00; pa $3.00)

LEE, ROBERT C.
Fiction
Day It Rained Forever, The (Little, Boston, 1968, 178 pp., illus.— A. Fiorentino, $3.95)
Juvenile.

LEE, VERNON (pseud) See PAGET, V.

LEE, WALTER W. U.S. film executive. He was an honours graduate of Calif. Inst. of Technology, and is vice-president of Technical Communications, Inc., a firm specializing in films for industry. His own specialty is collecting data on science fiction and fantasy films; he has published *Science Fiction and Fantasy Film Checklist* (*ca.* 1958, $2.00)—a revised edition in three volumes is being published.

LEE, WAYNE CYRIL (2 July 1917–) U.S. ex-farmer, now a rural mail carrier.
Fiction
Doomed Planet [as Lee Sheldon] (Avalon, New York, 1967, 190 pp., $3.50)

LEEK, SYBIL Self-proclaimed modern witch.
Nonfiction
Diary of a Witch (Prentice-Hall, New York, 1968, 187 pp., $4.95)
Sketchy reminiscences of the author's life, and a tract for the old religion and astrology, etc.

LeGUIN, URSULA K(ROEBER) (21 Oct 1929–) U.S. science fiction author. She was born in Berkeley, Calif., the daughter of anthropologist A. L. Kroeber and author Theodora Kroeber. She attended college at Radcliffe and Columbia, and married C. A. LeGuin in Paris in 1951. They have three children and live in Portland, Oregon. Mrs. LeGuin is one of the more highly regarded contemporary sf writers.
Fiction
City of Illusions [pa] (Ace: G-626, 1967, 160 pp., pa 50¢)
A future Earth where alien ravagers do not allow science and skills.
Planet of Exile [pa] (Ace: G-597, 1966, 113 pp., pa 50¢; with *Mankind Under the Leash*)
Survivors of an Earth colony on a far world revolt against alien enslavement.
Rocannon's World [pa] (Ace: G-574, 1966, 117 pp., pa 50¢; with *The Kar-Chee Reign*)
A colorful action story of a strange world and its strange races in a galactic war. Based on "The Dowry of Angyar" (*AS*, short story, Sep 1964).
Wizard of Earthsea, A (Parnassus, New York, 1968, 205 pp., $3.95)
Juvenile—a young man suffers many trials as he learns the uses of sorcery in a world where it has a place.

LEIBER, FRITZ (REUTER) (Jr) (24 Dec 1910–) U.S. author and editor. He is now one of the foremost fantasy writers, and his work has always been of interest. Son of a noted Shakespearean actor, he was at one time an actor of repute and a member of his father's troupe. He has studied many sciences, and was editor of *Science Digest* for a period. His writing began with the appearance before World War II of some weird stories in *Weird Tales*; he then

had some stories published in *Unknown*, including the noted *Conjure Wife*. He wrote several novels for *ASF* in the mid-1940's and has since appeared quite regularly in most sf and fantasy magazines. His "Gray Mouser" series started in *Unknown* and was later featured in *Fantastic*, which devoted its entire Nov 1959 issue to Leiber's stories. Leiber won a Hugo at the 1959 World SF Convention for his novel *The Big Time* (so far not published in hardcover), and another Hugo in 1965 for *The Wanderer*. His "Gonna Roll the Bones" won a Hugo in 1968 for best novelette. Sam Moskowitz's profile of Leiber was published in *AS*, Dec 1963, and forms a chapter in Moskowitz's *Seekers of Tomorrow* (1966).
Series
Change War (or, "Snakes and Spiders" stories). "Try and Change the Past" (*ASF*, Mar 1958); "The Big Time" (*GSF*, sr2, Mar 1958; pa ed.); "A Deskful of Girls" (*F&SF*, Apr 1958); "Damnation Morning" (*Fan*, Aug 1959); "The Oldest Soldier" (*F&SF*, n'te, May 1960); "No Great Magic" (*GSF*, n'te, Dec 1963); "When the Change Winds Blow" (*F&SF*, Aug 1964); "Knight to Move" (*Broadside*, Dec 1965). A number were published in *The Mind Spider*.
Gray Mouser and Fafhrd. In *Unknown*: "Two Sought Adventure" (Aug 1939); "The Bleak Shore" (Nov 1940); "The Howling Tower" (June 1941); "The Sunken Land" (Feb 1942); "Thieves' House" (Feb 1943). "Adept's Gambit" (in *Night's Black Agents*, 1947; *Fan*, May 1964). "Dark Vengeance" (*Suspense*, Fall 1941). "The Seven Black Priests" (*Other Worlds*, May 1953). In *Fan*: "Lean Times in Lankhmar" (Nov 1959); "When the Sea-King's Away" (May 1960); "Scylla's Daughter" (May 1960); "The Unholy Grail" (Oct 1962); "The Cloud of Hate" (May 1963); "Bazaar of the Bizarre" (Aug 1963); "The Lords of Quarmall" (sr2, Jan 1964); "Stardock" (Sep 1965); "The Two Best Thieves in Lankhmar" (Aug 1968). "Adept's Gambit" was an original in *Night's Black Agents*, which also had "The Sunken Land." In book form the series includes *Two Sought Adventure* (first 7 of series, excluding "Adept's Gambit") and the Ace paperback series: *The Swords of Lankhmar*; *Swords Against Wizardry*; *Swords in the Mist* (some include new stories).
Fiction
Big Time, The [pa] (*GSF*, sr2, Mar 1958) (Ace: D-491, 1961, 129 pp., pa 35¢ [with *The Mind Spider* (Leiber)]; G-627, 1967, pa 50¢) (FSB: 1267, 1965, 127 pp., pa 3/6)
Winner of 1958 Hugo for best novel. Adventure mystery of strangely assorted men and women snatched to the far future by emissaries scheming to change the structure of time and history. Part of the "Change War" series.
Conjure Wife (*Unknown*, Apr 1943) (in *Witches Three* [Anon.], 1952) (Twayne, New York, 1953, 154 pp., $2.75) (Lion: 179, 1954, 192 pp., pa 25¢) (Berkley: F621, 1962, 176 pp., pa 50¢) (Award: A341, 1968, 188 pp., pa 60¢)
Suspenseful novel of present-day sorcery in a college faculty. *Film:* As *Burn, Witch, Burn*, American-International, 1962, starring Janet Blair and Peter Wyngard; a Julian Wintle and Leslie Parkyn production with screenplay by Richard Matheson and Charles Beaumont.
Destiny Times Three (*ASF*, sr2, Mar 1945) (in *Five SF Novels* [Greenberg], 1952) (Galaxy SF Novels: 28, 1957, 126 pp., pa 35¢) (*Welten des Grauens* [German], *T*: 400, 1965)
Atomic weapons and other possible Earths.
Gather, Darkness! (*ASF*, sr3, May 1943) (Pellegrini & Cudahy, New York, 1950, 240 pp., $2.75) (McLeod, Toronto, $3.75) (Grosset & Dunlap, New York, 1951, 256 pp., $1.00) (*A L'aube des tenebres* [French], Gallimard: Le RF, 1958) (Berkley: F679, 1962, 174 pp., pa 50¢) (FSB: 1548, 1966, 192 pp., pa 3/6)
A notable novel of a future Earth run by a religion using secret science for its miracles.
Green Millennium, The (Abelard, New York, 1953, 256 pp., $2.75) (Lion: LL7, 1954, 192 pp., pa 35¢) (Abelard-Schuman, London, 1960, 256 pp., 12/6) (*Il verde millennio* [Italian], *Cosmo*: 149, 1963) (Icon: SF3, 1964, 160 pp., pa 3/6)
A mystery placed in the next century, with extraterrestrials visiting Earth's degenerate society of sadism and cut-throat enterprise.

Mind Spider and Other Stories, The [C] [pa] (Ace: D-491, 1961, 127 pp., pa 35¢; with *The Big Time* [Leiber])

Sf & weird of 6 stories: "The Mind Spider"; "The Haunted Future" ("Tranquility, or Else!"); "Damnation Morning"; "The Oldest Soldier"; "Try and Change the Past"; "The Number of the Beast."

Night of the Wolf, The [C] [pa] (Ballantine: U2254, 1966, 221 pp., pa 50¢)

Sf, 3 short novels and 1 short story: "The Lone Wolf" ("The Creature From Cleveland Depths," *GSF*, Dec 1962); "The Wolf Pair" ("Night of the Long Knives," *AS*, Jan 1960); "Crazy Wolf" ("Sanity," short, *ASF*, Apr 1944); "The Wolf Pack" ("Let Freedom Ring," *AS*, Apr 1950).

Night's Black Agents [C] (Arkham, Sauk City [Wisc.], 1947, ix+237 pp., $3.00, jacket–R. Clyne; 3,084 copies) (Ballantine: 508K, 1961, 143 pp., pa 35¢)

Fantasy, 11 stories with foreword (pa: 10 stories, omitting "Adept's Gambit"): *Modern Horrors:* "Smoke Ghost"; "The Automatic Pistol"; "The Inheritance"; "The Hill and the Hole"; "The Dreams of Albert Moreland"; "The Hound"; "Diary in the Snow." *Transition:* "The Man Who Never Grew Young." *Ancient Adventures:* "The Sunken Land"; "Adept's Gambit."

Pail of Air, A [C] [pa] (Ballantine: U2216, 1964, 191 pp., pa 50¢)

Sf, 11 stories: "A Pail of Air"; "The Beat Cluster"; "The Foxholes of Mars"; "Pipe Dream"; "Time Fighters"; "The 64-Square Madhouse"; "Bread Overhead"; "The Last Litter"; "Rump-Titty-Titty-Tum-Tah-Tee"; "Coming Attraction"; "Nice Girl With Five Husbands."

Secret Songs, The [C] (Hart-Davis, London, 1968, 229 pp., 25/-)

11 stories with 4-p. intro.: "The Winter Flies"; "The Man Who Made Friends With Electricity"; "Rump-Titty-Titty-Tum-Tah-Tee"; "Marianna"; "Coming Attraction"; "The Moon Is Green"; "A Pail of Air"; "Smoke Ghost"; "The Girl With the Hungry Eyes"; "No Great Magic"; "The Secret Songs."

Shadows With Eyes [C] [pa] (Ballantine: 577, 1962, 128 pp., pa 35¢)

Weird, 6 stories (no table of contents, but gives credits): "A Bit of the Dark World"; "The Dead Man"; "The Power of the Puppets"; "Schizo Jimmie"; "The Man Who Made Friends With Electricity"; "A Deskful of Girls."

Ships to the Stars [C] [pa] (Ace: F-285, 122 pp., pa 40¢; with *The Million Year Hunt*) (*Tödlicher Mond* [German], *UZ*: 445, 1965–5 stories, omitting 2nd)

Sf, 6 stories: "Dr. Kometevsky's Day"; "The Big Trek"; "The Enchanted Forest"; "Deadly Noon"; "The Snowbank Orbit"; "The Ship Sails at Midnight."

Silver Eggheads, The [pa] (*F&SF*, n'te, Jan 1959) –enlarged: (Ballantine: F561, 1961, 192 pp., pa 50¢) (FSB: 1629, 1966, 192 pp., pa 5/-)

A satire on the future when automation has taken over the book industry and writers saved from the drudgery of their trade are free to be public figures.

Sinful Ones, The [pa] ("You're All Alone," *FA*, July 1950) (Universal: Giant G5, 1953, 319 pp., pa 50¢; double binding with *Bulls, Blood and Passion*, by David Williams [non-sf])

A solipsist world in which most people are constructs.

Swords Against Wizardry [C] [pa] (Ace: H-73, 1968, 188 pp., pa 60¢)

Fantasy, 4 loosely-connected stories of the "Gray Mouser" series: "In the Witch's Tent" (introductory); "Stardock" (the long climb of a mountain); "The Two Best Thieves in Lankhmar" (how to fence hot goods); "The Lords of Quarmall" (the Mouser and Fafhrd are separately hired as assassins by different contenders for the throne).

Swords in the Mist [C] [pa] (Ace: H-90, 1968, 190 pp., pa 60¢)

Fantasy, 6 stories of the "Gray Mouser" series (3rd and 5th are new): "The Cloud of Hate"; "Lean Times in Lankhmar"; "Their Mistress, the Sea"; "When the Sea-King's Away"; "The Wrong Branch"; "Adept's Gambit."

Swords of Lankhmar, The [pa] (Ace: H-38, 1968, 224 pp., pa 60¢)

A "Gray Mouser" story, based on "Scylla's Daughter"; the pair of rogues are hired to ensure safe delivery of grain and must outwit a witch with her entourage of trained rats.

Tarzan and the Valley of Gold [pa] (Ballantine: U6125, 1966, 317 pp., pa 75¢)

One of the "Tarzan" series, with preface by Hulbert Burroughs. After a slow start it achieves the same breathlessness as if written by Burroughs himself.

Two Sought Adventure [C] (Gnome, New York, 1957, 186 pp., $3.00)

The first 7 stories of the "Gray Mouser" series, excluding "Adept's Gambit."

Wanderer, The (Ballantine: U6010, 1964, 318 pp., pa 75¢) (Dobson, London, 1967, 364 pp., 25/-) (*Wanderer in Universum* [German], Heyne: 3096, 1967, pa)

Winner of the 1965 Hugo for best novel. The passage of a strange world through the Solar System causes havoc to the Earth and the Moon; the story alternates between the experiences of various people amid the resulting riots, pillage, earthquakes, etc.

LEIGHTON, PETER
Nonfiction
Moon Travellers (Oldbourne, London, 1960, 240 pp., 16/-)

A collection of various speculations on the Moon rather than a coverage of modern selenology. There are liberal quotations from the ancient world, including the most extravagant speculation interwoven with genuine scientific work.

LEINSTER, MURRAY (pseud) See JENKINS, W. F.

LEITCH, LAVINIA See HYND, LAVINIA

LEITCH, PATRICIA
Fiction
Treasure to the East (Gollancz, London, 1966, 128 pp., 15/-)

LEM, STANISLAW (1921–) Polish sf author, considered by many to be the leading representative of sf in the Communist world. He was born in Lwow; during World War II he worked as a mechanic, and later studied medicine and philosophy. His first work of fiction was *The Errors of Dr. Stefan T.*, which won a prize given by the city of Krakow, where he now lives. Lem is now one of the most widely translated sf writers in the world—his first sf novel, *The Planet of Death* (Astronauci), was a huge success, has sold some millions of copies with translations into 15 languages, including Russian, French and German. Other sf works include the novels *Guest in Space* (1952), *Eden, Return to the Stars, Solaris*, and *The Interrogation*, as well as the collections *The Star Diaries of Ijon Tichy, Moon Night, Invasion From Aldebaran, Cyberiad* and *Book of the Robots*. Nonfiction works include *Cybernetic Dialogues* and *Summa Technologiae*. His *The Planet of Death* was filmed in East Germany as *The Silent Star*.

LEMAITRE, JULES (27 Aug 1853–5 Aug 1914) French critic and playwright. He taught at various schools 1875-1883. Of his many plays, *The Pardon* (1895) was the most notable, but later his critical work overshadowed his plays. A fantasy collection, other than that below, is *Serenus & Other Tales of the Past and Present* (Selwyn & Blount, nd).
Fiction
On the Margins of Old Books [C] [Trans. from French–Clarence Stratton] (Coward McCann, New York, 1929, 322 pp., $1.00)

Not in the Bleiler *Checklist*; 36 stories, some of fantasy interest: "Among the Robbers"; "Beast of the Fields"; "The Confession of Eumaeus"; "A Critic"; "A Christmas Story"; "Daughter of the King"; "Dulcinea"; "The Eleven-Thousandth Virgin"; "First Impulse"; "The French Knight and a Dame of Constantinople"; "Good Woman . . . Though Thief"; "An Idealist"; "The Infant and the Good Mason"; "In the Wooden Horse"; "The Innocent Diplomacy of Helen"; "The Journal of the Duke of Bourgogne"; "The Journey of Little Hozael"; "The Later Story of Griselda"; "The Marquise de la Troche to the Countess de Guitaut"; "The Marriage of Telemachus"; "Mother and Daughter"; "The Opinions of Liette"; "Pallas—Son of Evander"; "Panurge Married"; "The Renegade"; "A Retreat"; "Saint Martha"; "Sarai"; "The School of Kings"; "The Second Life of the Seven Sleepers"; "Shadows Awaken"; "The Siren"; "Sister Anne"; "The Story of a Merveilleuse"; "Thersites"; "Two Sanctities: Diptych, the Virgin of the Angels, the Vow of Vivien."

LEMKIN, WILLIAM U.S. science fiction author. He was very popular in the pre-war *Amazing Stories*; his more notable stories were: "The Eclipse Special" (Dec 1930); "Vitamine Z" (Feb 1930); "Beyond the Stratosphere" (sr2, June 1936).

L'ENGLE, MADELEINE (Mrs. Hugh Franklin) (1918—)
Fiction
Wrinkle in Time, A (Farrar Strauss, New York, 1962, 211 pp., $3.25; 1968, $3.25?) (Ambassador, Toronto, $3.95) (Constable, London, 1963, 182 pp., 13/6)
Juvenile—a mathematician experimenting with the fifth dimension vanishes; his daughter and others search the galaxy.

LENGYEL, CORNEL (ADAM) (1915—)
Fiction
Atom Clock, The (FPCI, Los Angeles, 1951, 66 pp., $2.00; pa $1.00)
A dramatic play which won the 1950 Maxwell Anderson Award. A worker attempts rebellion against military control of atomic energy.

LEODHAS, SORCHE NIC (pseud) See ALGER, L. G.

LEONARDO DA VINCI (15 Apr 1452—2 May 1519)
Fiction
Deluge, The [with Robert Payne] (Twayne, New York, 1954, 99 pp., $3.00) (Lion: 233, 1955, 124 pp., pa 25¢)
Actually written by Payne (1911—) from notes, and is not particularly notable.

LERNET-HOLENIA, ALEXANDER MARIE (1897—) Viennese novelist.
Fiction
Count Luna [C] (Criterion, New York, 1956, 252 pp., $4.00) (*El conde Luna* [Spanish—Argentine], Isla, 1956)
2 novels: "Baron Bragge"; "Count Luna."

LEROUX, GASTON (1868—1927) French author. He was already a well-known journalist and popular author when in 1907 he turned his hand to the mystery detection novel with *Le Mystere de la chambre jaune*, the famous *Mystery of the Yellow Room*; many others followed. He wrote many fantasies [see the Bleiler *Checklist*], and one, *The Machine to Kill* (1935) was reportedly serialised (4 parts, 12 June 1936) but the magazine is unknown. However, Leroux is best remembered for his *The Phantom of the Opera* (1911), which has been filmed as follows: (1) Universal, 1925, silent, starring Lon Chaney; (2) Universal, 1943, starring Claude Rains; (3) British, 1962.

LEROY, GERARD See BUSSON, B. (co-author)

LESLIE, DESMOND (1921—) British film director. He has worked with Leinster Films Ltd., Coracle Films Ltd., New Dimension Sound & Vision Ltd., etc., has contributed to *Illustrated*, *Picture Post*, *Life*, *Vogue*, etc., and has composed some musical scores, such as *The Death of Satan* (ABC) and *Nude With Variations*.
Fiction
Amazing Mr. Lutterworth, The (Wingate, London, 1958, 215 pp., 13/6) (Smithers, Toronto, $2.50) (Digit: D315, 1960, 159 pp., pa 2/-)
Suspenseful science fiction.
Nonfiction
Flying Saucers Have Landed, The See ADAMSKI, G. (co-author)

LESLIE, Sir SHANE (29 Sep 1885—) Irish biographer and critic. He took his degree in 1907 and then went to Russia and became friendly with Tolstoi. He has been known for his unorthodox views—he even led a tramp's life for a time—and his works of all types are often controversial. He is best known for biographies, of which *The Skull of the Swift* is the most widely read.
Fiction
Ghost on the Isle of Wight, A (Benn, 1930; 500 copies)
Masquerades, Studies in the Morbid [C] (J. Long, London, 1924, 318 pp., 7/6)
21 stories: "The Pope's Temptation"; "Connemara"; "Inspiration"; "Balthasar the Cruel"; "A Saving Phantasm"; "Jealousy"; "The Drummer of Gordonmuir"; "The Supreme Complement"; "A Study in Smoke"; "The Missionary"; "Midir and Etain"; "Kathleen"; "John Saltus"; "Loaded Dice"; "At the High Tables"; "A Saint"; "Cannes"; "The Necrophiles"; "The Beau Geste"; "The Evil Eye"; "The Weird Gilly."
Shane Leslie's Ghost Book (Hollis Carter, London, 1955, 160 pp., 12/6) (Sheed Ward, New York, 1957, $3.00) (FSB: 1150, 1964, 191 pp., pa 3/6)
A routine ghost story, but mentions the Roman Catholic doctrine on ghosts, etc.

LESSER, MILTON (1928—) U.S. author. He began as a fan and ran his own amateur magazine, *Cepheid*. He served two years in the Korean War, finishing as a corporal. He majored in philosophy. For a period around the 1950's he appeared regularly in the science fiction magazines, but has been less frequent of late. He has used the pseudonyms "Stephen Marlowe" and (with P. W. Fairman) "Adam Chase."
Fiction
Earthbound (Winston, Philadelphia, 1952, 208 pp., $2.00) (Hutchinson, London, 1955, 224 pp., 7/6) ([Japanese], Ginga-Shobo 'Adv. in SF 3,' 1956)
Juvenile, one of the "Adventures in SF" series. A young lad unjustly expelled from Solar Academy becomes the dupe of space pirates.
Golden Ape [as Adam Chase] See FAIRMAN, P. W. (co-author)
Recruit for Andromeda [pa] ("Voyage to Eternity," *Imagination*, July 1953) (Ace: D-358, 1959, 117 pp., pa 35¢; with *The Plot Against Earth*) (*Verpflichtet für das Niemandsland* [German], *TS*: 27, 1960)
Draftees on a 'nowhere' journey; a test to find the smartest and ablest race.
Secret of the Black Planet [pa] (Belmont: 92-621, 1965, 157 pp., pa 50¢)
Title story (*AS*, June 1952) and sequel "Son of the Black Chalice" (*AS*, July 1952). Space intrigue, with a strong man coming to the fore.
Spacemen, Go Home (Holt Rinehart Winston, New York, 1961, 221 pp., $2.95)
Juvenile. Earth groups scheme to either bomb the Star Brain, the gigantic computer controlling the Galaxy, or convince it that mankind should not be grounded.
Stadium Beyond the Stars (Winston, 1960, 206 pp., $2.50)
Juvenile, one of the "Adventures in SF" series. A weak plot of intrigue in a space ship carrying young athletes from Earth to "Ophiuchus" for the Interstellar Olympics.
Star Seekers, The (Winston, 1953, 212 pp., $2.00) ([Japanese], GingaShobo 'Adv. in SF 7,' 1956) (*Die Weltensucher* [German], *T*: 475, 1966)
Juvenile, one of the "Adventures in SF" series. It uses Heinlein's "Universe" situation, with a ship taking six generations to reach Alpha Centauri.
Anthology
Looking Forward (Beechhurst, New York, 1953, 400 pp., $4.95) (Cassell, London, 1955, 400 pp., 15/-)
Sf, 20 stories and compiler's introduction "SF Comes of Age": *I. Today—and Yesterday:* "The Man From Outside," J. Williamson; "We Kill People," L. Padgett; "Win the World," C. Oliver; "The Little Creeps," W. M. Miller; "Highway," R. W. Lowndes; "Exile," E. Hamilton; "The Power," M. Leinster. *II. The Day*

After Tomorrow: "The Man in the Moon," M. Reynolds; "Production Test," R. F. Jones; "Lion's Mouth," S. Marlowe; "In This Sign," R. Bradbury; "Victory Unintentional," I. Asimov; "The Voyage That Lasted Six Hundred Years," D. Wilcox. *III. Imagination Unlimited:* "The Last Monster," P. Anderson; "The King of Thieves," J. Vance; "Man of Destiny," J. Christopher; "Lulungomeena," G. R. Dickson; "Ultima Thule," E. F. Russell; "Into Thy Hands," L. del Rey; "Transience," A. C. Clarke.

LETHBRIDGE, KATHARINE G(REVILLE)
Fiction
In Search of Thunder (Faber, London, 1966, 192 pp., 21/-)
Juvenile, sequel to *The Rout of the Ollafubs*; for lovers of 'Narnia' type stories.
Rout of the Ollafubs, The [C] (Faber, 1964, 189 pp., illus.—Pauline Baynes, 21/-) (Queenswood, Toronto, $4.65)
Juvenile, 7 stories: "The Rout of the Ollafubs"; "On Picking Up a Baby"; "The House That Had Learned to Keep Still"; "The Music Lesson"; "Ice Bear and Spun Bear"; "The Wishes."

LETHBRIDGE, T(HOMAS) C(HARLES)
Noted British archaeologist. He specializes in research on Britain's ancient gods, and has led expeditions for the Cambridge Antiquarian Society and the University Museum of Archaeology and Ethnology.
Nonfiction
Ghost and Ghoul (Routledge, London, 1961, 156 pp., illus., 18/-) (Doubleday, New York, 1962, 156 pp., illus., $3.75)
An exploration of the world of the supernatural with an attempt to explain it in terms of natural law; with personal experiences from archaeological tours. A portion was reprinted as "Ghost and Ghoul" (*Fan*, Jan 1963, 8 pp.).
Witches: Investigating an Ancient Religion (Routledge, 1962, 162 pp., illus., 21/-)

LEVEL, MAURICE
(1875–1926) French author.
Fiction [One other fantasy: *The Grip of Fear* (M. Kennerley, New York, 1911)]
Crises [Trans.—Alys E. Macklin] [C] (E. MacDonald, London, 1920, 239 pp., 6/-) (*Tales of Mystery and Horror*, McBride, New York, 1920, 303 pp., illus.—$2.00) (*Crises: Tales of Mystery and Horror*, A. M. Philpot, London, 1921, 239 pp., 6/-) (*Grand Guignol Stories*, Philpot, 1922, 237 pp., 3/-)
26 stories: "The Debt Collector"; "The Kennel"; "Who"; "Illusion"; "In the Light of the Red Lamp"; "A Mistake"; "Extenuating Circumstances"; "The Confession"; "The Test"; "Porissette"; "The Father"; "For Nothing"; "In the Wheat"; "The Beggar"; "Under Chloroform"; "The Man Who Lay Asleep"; "Fascination"; "The Bastard"; "That Scoundrel Miron"; "The Taint"; "The Kiss"; "The Maniac"; "The 10.50 Express"; "Blue Eyes"; "The Empty House"; "The Last Kiss."
Grand Guignol Stories [C] See *Crises*
Tales of Mystery and Horror [C] See *Crises*

LEVENE, MALCOLM
Fiction
Carder's Paradise (Hart-Davis, London, 1968, 180 pp., 25/-)
A 21st-century society with complete automation and sophisticated forms of artificial amusement.

LEVENE, PHILIP
Fiction
City of Hidden Eyes, The [with J. L. Morrissey] [pa] (World Distributors: SF973, 1960, 160 pp., pa 2/6) (*Silenciosa invasion* [Spanish], Cenit: 42, 1962, pa) (*Das Grauen kommt aus der Tiefe* [German], *UG*: 187, 1962) (*I meandri del silenzio* [Italian], *Cosmo*: 122, 1963)
Based on the BBC radio serial of the same title—a race of troglodytes threaten the upper world.

LEVIE, REX DEAN
(1937?–) U.S. writer and business worker, born in Salt Lake City, Utah. He has a B.A. in history and is working towards his M.A. He has been writing since he was 15. After

leaving school he worked as a beet hand, a student teacher, and a personnel specialist in the U.S. Army; he is now an estimator for a pipe manufacturer.
Fiction
Insect Warriors, The [pa] (Ace: F-334, 1965, 143 pp., pa 40¢)
A novel derived from giant-insect movies and an article by Dr. Clark Menninger on size problems; humans strive to live on a world where everything seems gigantic.

LEVIN, IRA
(1929–) U.S. author. He has written a noted mystery, *A Kiss Before Dying*.
Fiction
Rosemary's Baby (Random, New York, 1967, 245 pp., $4.95) (M. Joseph, London, 1967, 222 pp., 25/-) (Dell: 7509, 1968, 218 pp., pa 95¢) (Pan: 02115X, 1968, 205 pp., pa 5/-)
A couple move into a strange apartment with witches for neighbours; the wife's baby proves to be highly unusual.

LEVITT, ISRAEL MONROE
(19 Dec 1908–) U.S. astronomer. He is director of the Fels Planetarium in Philadelphia and is the inventor of the 'space clock' (developed by Hamilton Watch Co.). He has written some popular nonfiction, such as *A Space Traveler's Guide to Mars* (Holt, 1956; Gollancz, 1957), on Martian conditions, and *Target for Tomorrow* (Fleet, 1959), on space research.

LEWIN, LEONARD C.
Fiction
Report From Iron Mountain (Dial, New York, 1967, xxxii+109 pp., $5.00) (MacDonald, London, 1968, 141 pp., 18/-)
Enlarged from *Esquire*. Presented as nonfiction, purporting to be a secret high-level study, it is an oddly lucid outline of important theoretical problems of war and peace.

LEWIS, AL(BERT)
U.S. science fiction and fantasy collector. He is active in the bibliographic field, and compiled the *Index to the Science Fiction and Fantasy Magazines* covering the years 1961, 1962 and 1963.

LEWIS, BRIAN
British technical artist. Following technical school he enlisted in the R.A.F. for seven years, during which he first read science fiction. Most of his work has been in engineering draftsmanship, which has given him technical grounding for illustrating spaceship scenes. He now works for a leading radar company. He was a regular artist for the Nova magazines; his first cover for *New Worlds* was July 1957, and he did most of the following ones until a photo cover was adopted. Similarly, he painted *Science-Fantasy* covers from No. 26 (Dec 1957). He is an ardent follower of the U.S. artist Ed Emsh(willer), and although he does not emulate Emsh's style, there is some similarity in his ability to achieve an alien atmosphere in his paintings.

LEWIS, C(LIVE) S(TAPLES)
(29 Nov 1898–22 Nov 1963) British novelist, born in Belfast. After war service he lectured at University College from 1924. For a number of years before his death he was a Fellow of Magdalene College, Oxford, where he was Professor of Medieval and Renaissance English. He was widely noted for a number of popular books on religion, and often brought religious aspects into his science fiction writings, particularly in *That Hideous Strength*, the last novel of the trilogy which began with *Out of the Silent Planet*. His *Chronicles of Narnia* are a delightful series of fables for children in the vein of Lewis Carroll. He had two stories in *F&SF*—"The Shoddy Lands" (Feb 1956) and "Ministering Angels" (Jan 1958)—as well as several poems.
Walter Hooper edited Lewis' *Poems* (Bles, 1964; Harcourt, 1965). *Light on C. S. Lewis*, edited by Jocelyn Gibb (Bles, 1966, 16/-) is a collection of essays by a group of Lewis' friends and colleagues. He had extensive correspondence resulting from his broadcasts and writings; his brother made the selection *Letters of C. S. Lewis* (G. Bles, 1966, x+308 pp., 30/-).

Series

Narnia, The Chronicles of. Adventures of the Prevensie children: *The Lion, the Witch and the Wardrobe*; *Prince Caspian*; *The Voyage of the "Dawn Treader"*; *The Silver Chair*; *The Horse and His Boy*; *The Magician's Nephew*; *The Last Battle*. All editions, including Puffin, illus.–Pauline Baynes.

Ransom, Dr. *Out of the Silent Planet*; *Perelandra* (also titled *Voyage to Venus: Perelandra*); *That Hideous Strength* (also titled *The Tortured Planet*).

Fiction

Great Divorce, The (Bles, London, 1945, 118 pp., 7/6) (Macmillan, New York, 1946, 133 pp., $1.50) (S.J.R. Saunders, Toronto, $3.00)

A fantasy about Heaven and Hell.

Horse and His Boy, The (Bles, London, 1954, 10/6) (Macmillan, New York, 1954, 191 pp., $2.75) (Puffin: PS244, 1965, 188 pp., 3/6)

Fifth of *The Chronicles of Narnia*: the boy Shasta and the horse Bree run away from the cruel city of Calormen to adventure in another city, Tashbaan.

Last Battle, The (Lane, London, 1956, 184 pp., 9/6) (Macmillan, 1956, 174 pp., $2.75) (Puffin: PS205, 1964, 165 pp., pa 3/6)

Seventh and last of *The Chronicles of Narnia*: Jill and Eustace, the descendants of the first children, become involved in the fight between good and evil in Narnia.

Lion, the Witch, and the Wardrobe, The (Bles, 1950, 8/6) (Macmillan, 1950, 154 pp., $2.50) ([Swedish], Bonnier, 1959) (Puffin: PS132, 1959, 171 pp., pa 3/-)

First of *The Chronicles of Narnia*: Peter, Susan, Edmund and Lucy meet the White Witch, then Queen of Narnia, who needs them to help maintain her spell over the land.

Magician's Nephew, The (Lane, 1955, 8/6) (Macmillan, 1955, 167 pp., $2.75) ([Swedish], Bonnier, 1958) (Puffin: PS192, 1963, 171 pp., pa 3/-)

Sixth of *The Chronicles of Narnia*: the story of the original comings and goings from our world to Narnia—Polly and Digory of old London find their way to this enchanted realm.

Of Other Worlds [C] [Editor–W. Hooper] (Bles, London, 1966, 148 pp., 16/-) (Harcourt Brace & World, New York, 1967, 147 pp., $3.95)

13 assorted selections: Essays, lectures, an interview, an introduction, a polemic, 3 short stories, and 5 chapters of an unfinished novel. Stories: "The Shoddy Lands"; "Ministering Angels"; "Form of Things Unknown." Lecture: "On Science Fiction." Three pieces dealing with children's books and/or fairy tales. "On Criticism" (first appearance in print of a lecture). Discussion: "Unreal Estates" (with B. W. Aldiss and K. Amis), published in *SF Horizons* No. 2.

Out of the Silent Planet (Lane, London, 1938, 264 pp., 7/6; 1950, 5/-; 1951, 182 pp., 6/-) (Nelson, Toronto, $2.00) (Macmillan, New York, 1943, 174 pp., $2.75; #08688, 1965, 160 pp., pa 95¢; 1967, large print, $6.95) (*Der verstummte Planet* [German], Amundus Ed., 1948; *Jenseits des Schweigenden Sterne* [German], Rowohlt, 1958, pa) (Avon: 195, 1949, 159 pp., pa 25¢; T127, 1956, pa 35¢; T410, 1960, pa 35¢) (Pan: 213, 1952, 190 pp., pa 2/-; G403, 1960, pa 2/6; 02171, 1968, 206 pp., pa 5/-) (*Le silence de la Terre* [French], Hachette: Le RF, 1952; [with other 2 of trilogy] Ed. Opta 'Classique: SF8, 1967) (*Fuga a los espacio* [Spanish], Janes, 1949) (*Utflykt Fran Tyst Planet* [Swedish], FA-Press, 1955) ([Japanese], Gegen-sha 'SF 17,' 1957) (*Ver van de zwijgende planeet* [Dutch], Ten Have, Amsterdam, 1960) (Collier: AS207V, 1962, 160 pp., pa 95¢) (Oxford, New York, 1966, 184 pp., $1.50; notes & questions–M. Heery & D. King) (Longmans, London, 1966, xxxvi+196 pp., 6/6; intro.–D. Elloway)

First of "Dr. Ransom" series. Considered to be a science fiction classic: philosophical happenings on Mars, a world of harmony and peace—a plea for Christianity.

Perelandra (Lane, 1943, 256 pp., 8/6) (Macmillan, 1944, 238 pp.,$2.75; 1965, 222 pp., pa 95¢) (Avon: 270, 1950, 191 pp., pa 25¢; T157, 1957, pa 35¢) (*Voyage to Venus: Perelandra*, Pan: 253, 1953, 188 pp., pa 2/-; G404, 1960, 206 pp., pa 2/6; 02172, 1968, 187 pp., pa 5/-) (*Perelandra* [Spanish], Janes, 1949) (*Pere-*

landra [German], Hegner, 1957; Herder, 1959, pa) (*Reiss naar Venus* [Dutch], Ten Have, Amsterdam, 1961) (Collier: AS183V, 1962, 222 pp., pa 95¢) (*Voyage à Vénus* [French], [with other 2 of trilogy] Ed. Opta 'Classique: SF8,' 1967)

Second of "Dr. Ransom" trilogy. Venus as a Garden of Eden and an endeavour to save the Lady of Venus from corruption; admirable as Christian propaganda, but with a weak plot.

Pilgrim's Regress, The (Bles, London, 1943, 190 pp., 8/6)

Prince Caspian (Bles, 1951, 10/-) (Macmillan, 1951, 186 pp., $2.50) ([Swedish], Bonnier, 1961) (Puffin: PS173, 1962, 190 pp., pa 3/-)

Second of *The Chronicles of Narnia*: the Prevensie children return to Narnia to help Prince Caspian retain his throne in a civil war; Aslan the Lion also helps.

Screwtape Letters, The (Bles, London, 1942, 160 pp., 5/-) (Macmillan, 1943, 160 pp., $1.50; 1960, pa 75¢) (S.J.R. Saunders, Toronto, $2.00) (Fontana: 49B, 1955, 160 pp., pa 2/-) (*The Screwtape Letters & Screwtape Proposes a Toast*, Bles, 1961, 157 pp., 12/6; Macmillan, 1964, 185 pp., $3.50) (*Fran Helvetets Brevskola* [Swedish], Gleerup, 1955)

Letters from an older devil to a younger one advising the best way to win a wavering human soul, giving a glimpse of a spiritual hell as persuasive as any yet devised. *Screwtape Proposes a Toast* originally appeared in the *Saturday Evening Post*.

Silver Chair, The (Bles, 1953, 10/6) (Macmillan, 1953, 208 pp., $2.75) (Puffin: PS240, 1965, 206 pp., pa 3/6)

Fourth of *The Chronicles of Narnia*: Aslan the lion sends Jill Pole and Eustace Scrubb to the ruined city of the ancients to find their Prince and raise their self-confidence.

That Hideous Strength (Lane, 1945, 475 pp., 9/6; 1949, 9/6) (Nelson, Toronto, $2.75) (Macmillan, 1946, 459 pp., $3.00; 1949, $3.50; 1965, 382 pp., pa $1.50) (*Esa horrible tortaleza* [Spanish], Janes, 1949) (Pan: 321, 1955, 252 pp., pa 2/-; G421, 1960, pa 2/6; X266, 1965, pa 3/6; 02170, 1968, pa 5/-) (*The Tortured Planet* [abr.], Avon: T211, 1958, 254 pp., pa 35¢) (*Die böse Macht* [German], Hegner, 1958; Herder, 1960, pa) (Collier: B658V, 1962, 328 pp., pa $1.50) (*Cette hideuse puissance* [French], [with other 2 of trilogy] Ed. Opta 'Classique: SF8,' 1967)

Third of "Dr. Ransom" trilogy. More Christian propaganda.

Till We Have Faces (Bles, 1956, 320 pp., 15/-) (Harcourt Brace, 1956, 313 pp., $4.50) (*Det Rätta Ansiktet* [Swedish], Gleerup, 1958) (*Het wordend aangezicht* [Dutch], Ten Have, Amsterdam, 1958) (Eerdmans, 1964, 313 pp., pa $1.50)

A retelling of the myth of Psyche and Eros. (First written by Lucius Apuleius in *The Golden Ass*.)

Tortured Planet, The [pa] See *That Hideous Strength*

Voyage of the "Dawn Treader," The (Bles, 1952, 223 pp., 10/6) (Macmillan, 1952, 210 pp., $2.75) ([Swedish], Bonnier, 1963) (Puffin: PS229, 1965, 212 pp., pa 3/6)

Third of *The Chronicles of Narnia*: Edward and Lucy with odious cousin Eustace Scrubb journey through the picture of the ship "Dawn Treader" and find adventures with King Caspian.

Voyage to Venus: Perelandra [pa] See *Perelandra*

Nonfiction

World's Last Night, The (Harcourt Brace, 1960, 113 pp., $3.00) (Longmans, Toronto, $3.50)

Essays: various speculations on religious matters, life on other planets ("religion and rocketry"); also the essay "Screwtape Proposes a Toast." Full of interest and brilliantly expressed.

LEWIS, IRWIN

Fiction

Day New York Trembled, The [pa] (Avon: G1315, 1967, 144 pp., pa 50¢)

A nightmare with a drug to eliminate pain.

Day They Invaded New York, The [pa] (Avon: G1227, 1964, 160 pp., pa 50¢)

Aliens propose to conquer New York after creating chaos by distributing subway tokens too large to fit, turning all traffic lights green, etc. The same idea is in Lewis' short story "To Invade New York" (*ASF*, Aug 1963).

LEWIS, L. A.
Fiction
Tales of the Grotesque [C] (P. Allan, London, 1934, 244 pp., 2/6)

One of the *Creeps Library*; weird, 10 stories: "Lost Keep"; "Hybrid"; "The Tower of Moab"; "The Child"; "The Dirk"; "The Chords of Chaos"; "The Meerschaum Pipe"; "Haunted Air"; "The Iron Swine"; "Animate in Death."

LEWIS, M(ATTHEW) G(REGORY) (9 July 1775–10 May 1818) British writer, diplomat, and member of the House of Commons. After education at Westminster and Christ College, Oxford, he became an attaché to the British Embassy at The Hague. Literature attracted him from an early age; his *Ambrosio, or, The Monk* was his most noted success. From 1796 he sat six years in the House of Commons. He also wrote verse and plays in this time, including *Castle Spectre* produced at Drury Lane in 1798 under Sheridan's management. He had ample means, and social life later attracted him more than the pen, though his output was considerable.
Fiction [Incomplete—other titles in Bleiler *Checklist*]
Monk, The (J. Bell, London, 1796, 3 vols.) (London, 1806; 1835) ([Swedish], 1834) (Grove: E163, 1959, 445 pp., pa $2.45) (Elek, 1960, 256 pp., pa 3/6)

Noted Gothic drama.
Romantic Tales [C] (Chapman & Hall, London, 1848, 214 pp.) (Groombridge & Sons, London, 1857, 215 pp., 5/-)

3 novels adapted from the German and originally published about 1808 (frontispiece engraving illustrates first story): "My Uncle's Garret Window"; "The Anaconda"; "Amorassan—or, The Spirit of the Frozen Ocean."
Anthology
Tales of Wonder (J. Bell, London, 1801, 2 vols.) (Charles Tilt: 'Miniature Classical Library Vol. 6,' London, 1836, 136 pp., 1/6; 2¾ in. x 4¼ in.)

23 stories: "Bothwell's Bonny Jane"; "Sir Hengist"; "Alonzo the Brave and Fair Imogene"; "The Sword of Augantyr"; "King Hocho's Death Song"; "The Erl-King"; "The Erl-King's Daughter"; "The Water-King"; "The Cloud-King"; "The Fisherman"; "The Gay Gold Ring"; "The Grim White Woman"; "Glenfinlas; or Lord Ronald's Coronach"; "The Eve of Saint John"; "Frederick and Alice"; "The Wild Huntsmen"; "The Old Woman of Berkeley"; "Bishop Bruno"; "Painter of Florence, Part 1"; "Painter of Florence, Part 2"; "Donica"; "Rudiger."

LEWIS, OSCAR (5 May 1893–) U.S. writer. He began with stories for boys and later contributed articles and fiction to magazines; he has been an author and editor since 1925. He was secretary of the Book Club of California 1924-45 and was editor of its *News-Letter* 1933-46.
Fiction
Lost Years, The (Knopf, New York, 1951, 121 pp., $2.50) (in *A Treasury of Great SF* [Boucher], 1959)

A sensitive and touching alternate history studying the last years of an unassassinated Lincoln.

LEWIS, SINCLAIR (7 Feb 1885–10 Jan 1951) Noted U.S. author, best known for his social satires, such as *Babbitt*.
Fiction
It Can't Happen Here (Doubleday Doran, New York, 1935, 458 pp.) (Mayflower: 4128, 1965, 382 pp., pa 5/-)

A shocking picture of the U.S.A. in the grip of a despotic dictator. Written in the time of Huey Long and Adolf Hitler, the story is of particular interest in showing the change in American customs.

LEWIS, (PERCY) WYNDHAM (1884–7 Mar 1957) British novelist, essayist and artist (not to be confused with the humorist and essayist D. B. Wyndham Lewis). For many years he edited the *Blast*, a well known magazine. He lived eight years in the U.S.A. from 1940. His life was a mixture of phases of novelist, painter, sculptor, philosopher, draughtsman, critic, politician, etc., and he did notable work in each. He also wrote his autobiography.

Fiction
Childermass, The (Covici Friede, New York, 1928, 322 pp., $3.00) (Chatto Windus, London, 1928, 8/6) (*The Human Age—I. The Childermass*, Methuen, London, 1956, 401 pp., illus.–M. Ayrton, 25/-) (Jupiter: J8, 1966, 320 pp., pa 10/6)

First of trilogy, continued with *Malign Fiesta* and *Monstre Gai*.
Human Age, The (Methuen, 1955, 566 pp., illus.–M. Ayrton, 30/-) (*Monstre Gai*, Jupiter: J12, 1966, 254 pp., pa 6/6; and *Malign Fiesta*, Jupiter: J16, 1966, 240 pp., pa 6/6)

Methuen ed. noted as *Book 2. Monstre Gai* and *Book 3. Malign Fiesta*. Second and third parts of a trilogy, of which the first novel, *The Childermass*, had appeared 27 years earlier. Two characters enter an imaginary city inhabited by extraordinary beings. There is understood to be a fourth part which is not allowed to be published in the United Kingdom.
Malign Fiesta [pa] See *Human Age, The*
Monstre Gai [pa] See *Human Age, The*

LEY, ROBERT ARTHUR (1921–24 Sep 1968) British sf author. He is better known by the pseudonym "Arthur Sellings" used on all his fiction. He had some science training, but took a job with Customs. He was also a dealer in antiquarian books. Though he was interested in science fiction as a lad, it was not until 1953 that he began writing. His stories sold regularly, mainly to U.S. markets. A place in the first 18 in the *Sunday Observer*'s "AD 2500" literary contest eventually led to publication of the collection *Time Transfer*. All told he wrote over 30 stories from "The Haunting" (*Authentic*, Oct 1953) to one in *New Writings in SF 12* [Carnell], 1968.
Fiction [all as "Arthur Sellings"]
Long Eureka, The [C] (Dobson, London, 1968; 184 pp., 21/-)

Sf, 9 stories: "Blank Form"; "The Scene Shifter"; "One Across"; "The Well Trained Heroes"; "Homecoming"; "The Long Eureka"; "Verbal Agreement"; "Trade-In"; "Birthright."
Power of X, The (Dobson, 1968, 156 pp., 18/-)

Perfect duplication of items ("plying") is forbidden, and then a London art dealer makes an astonishing discovery.
Quy Effect, The (Dobson, 1966, 141 pp., 18/-) (Berkley: X1350, 1967, 144 pp., pa 60¢) (SF B.C. [S.J.], 1968)

A self-taught inventor blows himself up in an attempt to produce a super-conductor.
Silent Speakers, The See *Telepath*
Telepath [pa] (Ballantine: F609, 1962, 160 pp., pa 50¢) (*The Silent Speakers*, Dobson, 1963, 192 pp., 16/-; Panther: 1787, 1965, 127 pp., pa 2/6)

Well-written story with a slow, almost casual build-up of the awareness in the mind of the first human with latent but limited telepathic powers.
Time Transfer [C] (M. Joseph, London, 1956, 240 pp., 12/6) (Compact: F302, 1966, 189 pp., pa 3/6 [11 stories marked †])

Sf, 16 stories: "The Wordless Ones"†; "The Awakening"; "Soliloquy"; "Escape Mechanism"†; "Jukebox"†; "Categorical Imperative"†; "Pentagram"; "The Proxies"†; "From Up There"†; "A Start in Life"†; "Time Transfer"†; "The Haunting"; "Control Room"†; "The Age of Kindness"†; "The Figment"†; "The Transfer."
Uncensored Man, The (Dobson, 1964, 183 pp., 16/-) (SF B.C. [S.J.], 1965) (Berkley: X1379, 1967, 160 pp., pa 60¢)

A drug takes a man into another dimension where he meets "superior beings."

LEY, WILLY (2 Oct 1906–24 June 1969) U.S. writer, born in Berlin. He was one of the founders of the German Rocket Society, which was dissolved by the Nazis. Ley emigrated to the U.S. in 1935; attempts to interest the U.S. in rocket research failing, he became a free-lance writer. He called himself a "historian of science," and won Hugos in 1953 and 1956 for his article writing. He was science editor of the New York newspaper *PM* for almost the whole of its existence, 1940-48. In the science fiction field he began to appear with articles in *Astounding* in the late 1930's. He maintained a notable science department in *Galaxy Science Fic-*

tion from Mar 1952 until his death, winning a considerable following.

His first work was the small paper-backed *Die Fahrt ins Weltall* [Journey Into Space] (Hachmeister & Thal, 1926); his *Die Möglichkeit der Weltraumfahrt* [The Possibility of Interplanetary Travel] (1928) was one of the works that inspired Thea Von Harbou's *Die Frau im Mond* [The Girl in the Moon]. He became the foremost U.S. writer of popular articles on rocketry and many other sciences; he also lectured, and from 1947 was a consultant to the U.S. Dept. of Commerce's Office of Technical Services. At the time of his death he was Professor of Science at Fairleigh Dickinson University. In Oct 1958 he and his golf partner won a $10,000 "Brains and Brawn" TV jackpot.

Ley's most famous books are *Rockets, Missiles and Space Travel* and *The Conquest of Space*; the latter was magnificently illustrated by Chesley Bonestell and won the 1951 International Fantasy Award. The following year Ley's zoological work *Dragons in Amber* was runner-up for the same award. He wrote many articles for compendiums such as C. Ryan's *Across the Space Frontier*. A juvenile book series for Guild (Simon & Schuster) in 1957-58, illustrated by I. Polgreen, included *Man-Made Satellites*; *Space Pilots*; *Space Stations*; *Space Travel*. Other books not listed below include *Inside the Orbit of the Earth* (McGraw, 1968); *The Meteorite Craters* (Weybright & Talley, 1968); *Our Work in Space* (Macmillan, 1964); *Harnessing Space* (Macmillan, 1963). Articles of interest in the sf magazines include: "Power Plants" (*ASF*, sr3, Jan 1938); "Geography for Time Travellers" (*ASF*, July 1939); and the article series "Fantastic Hoaxes" (*FA*, Jan-Oct 1940), "Landscapes on Other World" (*AS*, Apr-Oct 1942), and "The Road to Space Travel" (*SS*, Mar-Sep 1949).

His only science fiction was written under the pseudonym "Robert Willey" and appeared in *ASF*: "At the Perihelion" (Feb 1937; "A Martian Adventure," *Great SF by Scientists* [Conklin], 1962); "Orbit XXIII/H" (Sep 1938); "Fog" (Dec 1940).

Nonfiction

Beyond the Solar System (Viking, New York, 1964, 108 pp., illus.–C. Bonestell, $6.50) (Macmillan, Toronto, $7.95)

Foreword by W. Von Braun. Typical Bonestell illustrations with Ley's text showing a strong sense of history. One reviewer found some current aspects not completely accurate.

Conquest of Space, The (Viking, New York, 1949, 168 pp., 48 illus.–[16 in full colour] –C. Bonestell, $3.95) (Sidgwick & Jackson, London, 1950, 160 pp., illus., 18/-) (Macmillan, Toronto, $5.50) (*Die Eroberung des Weltalls* [German], Frank'sche Verlagsbuchhandl, 1952)

Beautifully illustrated survey of the possibility of travel to the moon and planets, with exceptional artwork by Bonestell and very worthwhile commentary by Ley. It won the 1951 International Fantasy Award. The British edition had no appendix (and later eds. were more expensive). There were also Dutch and Japanese eds. There was a film of the same title, whose plot was only distantly related.

Days of Creation (Viking, 1952, x+275 pp., illus., $2.75) (McLeod, Toronto, $3.50)

A short biography of the universe, arranged like the first chapter of Genesis.

Dragons in Amber (Viking, 1951, viii+328 pp., illus.–Olga Ley, $3.75) (Macmillan, Toronto, $6.50) (Sidgwick & Jackson, 1951, 328 pp., illus., 21/-)

Winner of 2nd-place 1952 International Fantasy Award for nonfiction. In sections: *I. Records in Stone* (insects occluded in amber, etc.; the story of scientific detection). *II. The Last of Their Kind* (dramatic and pathetic stories of plants and animals narrowly escaping extinction; living fossils). *III. Wanderers Across the Planet* (the story of "adventive" fauna and flora).

Engineers' Dreams (Viking, 1954, 239 pp., illus., $3.50) (Phoenix, London, 1955, 192 pp., illus., 15/-)

Things that can be done as far as engineering is concerned but most of which may remain dreams because of political difficulties, e.g., the tunnel beneath the English Channel.

Exotic Zoology (Viking, 1959, 468, $4.95)

A compression of *The Lungfish, the Dodo and the Unicorn*

(1948), *Dragons in Amber* (1951) and *Salamanders and Other Wonders* (1955), created by combining chapters and shortening and revising material. It has five sections of three to six chapters each: *I. The Fauna of Myth* (the unicorn, the dragon of the Ishtar Gate, etc.). *II. Fossil Creatures. III. Mysteries of the Oceans. IV. Things on Isolated Islands* (dodo, etc.). *V. Witnesses of the Past* (fossils that didn't die).

Exploration of Mars, The [with W. Von Braun] (Viking, 1956, 176 pp., illus.–[16 in colour] –C. Bonestell, $4.95) (Sidgwick & Jackson, 1956, 184 pp., illus., 30/-) (*Project Mars*, Badger: SS4, 1962, 184 pp., illus., pa 2/6)

The authors give present knowledge and most accepted theories about Mars; they believe an expedition to Mars will be feasible once a space station is established. The pa ed. omits the colour frontispiece but has all other illustrations in black and white and gives the full text.

Lands Beyond See DE CAMP, L. S. (co-author)

Lungfish and the Unicorn, The See *Lungfish, the Dodo and the Unicorn, The*

Lungfish, the Dodo and the Unicorn, The (1st ed. *The Lungfish and the Unicorn*, Modern Age Books, New York, 1941, 305 pp., $2.75) (Viking, 1948, 361 pp., $3.75)

The 1st ed. was the Scientific Book Club selection for May 1941. It covers the curious ideas that were current when zoology was becoming a science—animals that are not and never were, etc.

Missiles, Moonprobes and Megaparsecs [pa] (Signet: P2445, 1964, 189 pp., pa 60¢)

On Earth and in the Sky (Doubleday, New York, 1967, 249 pp., $4.95) (Ace: H-55, 1968, 192 pp., pa 60¢)

First of projected series based on articles appearing as "For Your Information" in *Galaxy* since 1952. Sixteen chapters cover dinosaurs, fossil man, strange planets and various other subjects.

Project Mars [pa] See *Exploration of Mars, The*

Ranger to the Moon [pa] (Signet: P2668, 1965, 127 pp., pa 60¢)

Rockets See *Rockets, Missiles and Space Travel*

Rockets and Space Travel See *Rockets, Missiles and Space Travel*

Rockets, Missiles and Men in Space See *Rockets, Missiles and Space Travel*

Rockets, Missiles and Space Travel (1st ed. *Rockets*, Viking, 1944) (2nd ed. *Rockets and Space Travel*, Viking, 1947, 374 pp., illus., $4.50; Macmillan, Toronto; Chapman, London, 1949, 374 pp., illus., 18/-) (3rd ed. *Rockets, Missiles and Space Travel*, Viking, 1951, 436 pp., illus., $5.95; Macmillan, $6.50; Chapman [2nd Brit. ed.], 1951, 436 pp., illus., 30/-) (Viking, rev. ed., 1957, 528 pp., illus., $6.75) (*Rockets, Missiles and Men in Space*, Viking, 1968, $10.95)

The noted basic reference work on this subject. The 3rd ed. printed hitherto secret material; the 4th printing of the 1951 U.S. ed. had additional material by W. Von Braun, the 1957 ed. was further enlarged to complete the story of Peenemunde and the V-2 programme, etc., and the retitled 1968 edition was again updated. The book has a valuable bibliography. There have been Spanish (South American) and German editions.

Salamanders and Other Wonders (Viking, 1955, 293 pp., illus., $3.95) (Phoenix, 1956, 304 pp., illus., 16/-)

Subtitled "Still More Adventures of a Romantic Naturalist." Sections are: *Problems of the Past* (cave salamanders and high politics, the little people, Natura Artis Magistra, the abominable snowman, prelude to aviation); *Botanical Interlude* (three fabulous trees, the tree of death, the man-eating tree, the Emperor's Arcanum Magnum); *Survivors* (the case of the cahow, the Waldrapp of Switzerland, the furry old man of the sea, the old ones). Also includes geological table and index.

Satellites, Rockets and Outer Space [pa] (Signet: KS360, 1958, 128 pp., pa 35¢; P2218, 1962, 218 pp., pa 60¢)

Collection of 46 of Ley's short newspaper pieces; excellent for the uninformed layman. The later ed. is updated.

Watchers of the Skies (Viking, 1963, 528 pp., illus., $8.50) (Macmillan, Toronto, $10.50) (Sidgwick & Jackson, 1964, xiii+528 pp., 45/-)

Subtitled "An Informal History of Astronomy from Babylon to the Space Age." In parts: *1. A Science Grows Up. 2. The Solar*

System. This was well received by *Nature* (25 July 1964, p. 335), whose reviewer said that if the astrophysical section were extended the book would be in a class of its own.

LICATA, TONY
Anthology
Great Science Fiction [pa] (Three Star: 102, 1965, 128 pp., pa 60¢)

8 stories: "The Wind," Ray Bradbury; "Mouse," Fredric Brown; "The Golem," Avram Davidson; "Judgment Day," L. Sprague de Camp; "History Lesson," A. C. Clarke; "The Ruum," Arthur Porges; "Dark Mission," Lester del Rey; "A Better Rat Trap," Brad Steiger.

LIE, JONAS (LAURITZ IDEMIL) (6 Nov 1833–5 July 1908)
Norwegian novelist, playwright and poet. Speculation in lumber threw him into bankruptcy in 1868, but he repaid everything many years later. He became a noted figure in Norwegian literature, his best works being a number of sea masterpieces in the 1880's.
Fiction
Weird Tales From Northern Seas [Trans.–R. Nisbit] [C] (K. Paul Trench Truebner, London, 1893, 201 pp., illus.–L. Housman)

11 stories: "The Fisherman and the Draug"; "Jack of Sjoholm and the Gan-Finn"; "Tug of War"; " 'The Earth Draws' "; "The Cormorants of Andvaer"; "Isaac and the Parson of Bröno"; "The Wind-Gnome"; "The Huldrefish"; "Finn Blood"; "The Homestead Westward in the Blue Mountains"; "It's Me."

LIEBER, MAXIM U.S. editor.
He has edited *The American Century*, a general anthology published in Germany in English and sold overseas.
Anthologies
Ghosts, Ghouls and Other Nuisances [pa] (Seven Seas Books, Berlin, 1959, 272 pp., pa, about 2/6 sterling)

Weird, 11 stories: "Peter Rugg, the Missing Man," "Further Account of Peter Rugg," William Austin; "The Specter Bridegroom," Washington Irving; "The Fall of the House of Usher," E. A. Poe; "Rappaccini's Daughter," Nathaniel Hawthorne; "What Was It?" F.-J. O'Brien; "The Body-Snatcher," Robert L. Stevenson; "A Tale of Negative Gravity," Frank R. Stockton; "An Occurrence at Owl Creek Bridge," Ambrose Bierce; "A Double-Barreled Detective Story," Samuel L. Clemens [Mark Twain]. An Author's Who's Who.

Great Short Stories of the World See CLARK, B. H. (co-anthologist)

Great Stories of All Nations (Brentano's, New York, 1927, 1121 pp.) (Tudor, New York, 1934, 1132 pp., $1.35)

Selection of tales from many countries, including such stories as (Great Britain) "Markheim," R. L. Stevenson; "The Stolen Bacillus," H. G. Wells; and (U.S.) "Rappaccini's Daughter," N. Hawthorne; "The Cask of Amontillado," E. A. Poe. Most of the stories of weird flavour are also contained in the more direct weird anthologies. This work's first edition is not given in the Bleiler *Checklist.*

LIGHTNER, ALICE M. (11 Oct 1904–)
U.S. author (Mrs. Ernest Hopf). Born in Detroit, she was educated at Westover School and Vassar College, where she majored in music and English. After graduation she moved to New York to work on an engineering magazine, and more recently on the house organ of a major advertising agency. Following marriage she developed a serious interest in natural sciences and is now a member of the Lepidopterists' Society and the New York Entomological Society. Her earlier writing interests were drama and poetry, but while her son Christopher was growing up she formed an interest in science fiction and then began to write it.
Fiction
Doctor to the Galaxy (Norton, New York, 1965, 175 pp., $3.50, lib $3.28)

Well developed story.

Galactic Troubadours, The (Norton, 1965, 237 pp., $3.75, lib $3.48) (McLeod, Toronto, $4.50, lib $3.44)

Juvenile—a group of young people tour worlds where their songs and zest for living cause trouble.

Planet Poachers, The (Putnam, New York, 1965, 184 pp., illus., $3.50) (Longmans, Toronto, $4.25)

Space Ark (Putnam, 1968, 190 pp., illus.–D. McMains, $3.50)

Juvenile.

Space Olympics, The (Norton, 1967, 211 pp., $3.95, lib $3.73)

Juvenile.

Space Plague, The (Norton, 1966, 156 pp., $3.50, lib $3.28) (McLeod, Toronto, $3.45)

LIN, YU-T'ANG (YUTANG) (1895–)
Chinese-U.S. essayist. He was born in Amoy, and studied in Europe, taking Ph.D. at Leipzig. He founded and edited some literary journals in the 1930's, and was a student of Chinese affairs. His *My Country and My People* (1935) and *The Importance of Living* (1937) were best-sellers in the U.S. After nationwide tours he settled in New York. Following World War II he was connected with UNESCO. He was to have become chancellor of the new Chinese University at Singapore in 1954, but upon disagreement with the trustees he never took the position.
Fiction
Looking Beyond See *Unexpected Island, The*
Unexpected Island, The (Hutchinson, London, 1955, 351 pp., 15/-) (*Looking Beyond*, Prentice Hall, New York, 1955, 387 pp., $4.95)

The story of a refugee island and its people after four world wars.

LINDEGREN, CARL C.
Nonfiction
Cold War in Biology, The (Planarian Press, Ann Arbor [Mich.], 1966, 113 pp., $6.50)

Views of fundamental problems in biology presented in a simple, fascinating and intriguing way. (See *ASF*, Nov 1967, p. 167.)

LINDNER, ROBERT (1914–1956)
U.S. psychiatrist. He is noted for his *Rebel Without a Cause* (1944) dealing with the hypnoanalysis of a criminal psychopath.
Nonfiction
Fifty-Minute Hour, The [C] (Rinehart, New York, 1955, 293 pp., $3.50) (*The Jet-Propelled Couch and Other True Psychoanalytic Tales*, Secker Warburg, London, 1954, 272 pp., 15/-) (Bantam, 1956, 207 pp., pa 35¢) (Corgi: GG1137, 1962, 207 pp., pa 3/6)

5 'psychoanalytic tales' (true case histories). Of sf interest is "The Jet-Propelled Couch" (abr., *F&SF*, Jan 1956), the incredible story of the dream life of an atomic physicist who by mental power lives the life of a great man in a future era.

Jet-Propelled Couch and Other True Psychoanalytic Tales, The [C] See *Fifty-Minute Hour, The*

LINDSAY, DAVID (1876–1945)
Obscure British spiritualist primarily remembered for his *Voyage to Arcturus.*
Fiction [Incomplete—other titles in Bleiler *Checklist*]
Haunted Woman, The (Methuen, London, 1922, 197 pp., 6/-) (Gollancz 'Connoisseur's Lib. Strange Fiction,' London, 1947, 176 pp., 7/6; 1964, 21/-)

Voyage to Arcturus, A (Methuen, 1920, 308 pp., 8/6) (Gollancz 'Connoisseur's Lib. Strange Fiction,' 1946, 248 pp., 8/6, introduction–E. H. Visiak; 1963, 18/-) (Macmillan 'SF Classic,' 1963, 244 pp., $2.95, introduction–Loren Eiseley) (Ballantine: 73010, 1968, 287 pp., pa 95¢, intro.–L. Eiseley)

An extremely fascinating account of an incredibly different planet. From a conventional seance the story moves to Tormance, sole planet of the double suns of Arcturus. A strange force is experimenting with life forms. The adventures described exemplify ethical concepts made real by the demonic imagination of the author. It is understood that the 1920 edition sold only 596 copies, and the 1946 ed. was also small.

LINEBARGER, PAUL MYRON ANTHONY (15 July 1913–6 Aug 1966) U.S. professor, political scientist, military adviser, anthropologist, and noted sf author under the pseudonym "Cordwainer Smith." He was born in Milwaukee, Wisconsin. He attended the University of Nanking (1930), the National China Union School (1931), George Washington U. (A.B. 1933), and did graduate work at Oxford, American U. and U. of Chicago. Johns Hopkins granted him his M.A. in 1935 and Ph.D. in 1936. In 1955 he was awarded a certificate in psychiatry at the Washington School of Psychiatry, and he attended the Universidad Interamericana 1959-60. He taught as professor of Asiatic politics at Harvard, Duke and Johns Hopkins in America and the U. of Canberra in Australia. He spoke Chinese, German, French and Spanish, and could read Russian, Portuguese and Dutch. He was married and had two children.

Prof. Linebarger's career was as diverse and intensive as his education. He was private secretary to the legal advisor to the Government of China 1930-36, and wrote books on China from his observations. During World War II he was in the U.S. Army Intelligence Corps, attaining the rank of Lt. Col. and winning the Bronze Star. He helped found the Office of War Information and was on the Planning and Intelligence Board. He served as an advisor in the Korean War and to the British in the Malay campaign.

In the science fiction field he was known for many provocative and unusual stories under the pseudonym "Cordwainer Smith." The first to appear in print was "Scanners Live in Vain" (*Fantasy Book*, No. 6, 1950); it left an indelible impression on its readers, but it was some years before he became a regular writer and his distinctive and lyrical style of writing became better known. He left a legacy of about 30 stories.

Series [as Cordwainer Smith]
Instrumentality, The. "The Game of Rat and Dragon" (*GSF*, Oct 1955; *Best SF 3* [Crispin], 1958; *Six From Worlds Beyond*; *Best SF Stories & Novels 1956* [Dikty], 1956); "The Burning of the Brain" (*If*, Nov 1958); "The Lady Who Sailed the Soul" (*GSF*, Apr 1960); "A Planet Named Shayol" (*GSF*, Oct 1961); "Alpha Ralpha Boulevard" (*F&SF*, June 1961); "The Ballad of Lost C'mell" (*GSF*, Oct 1962); "The Boy Who Bought Old Earth" (*GSF*, Apr 1964); "The Store of Heart's Desire" (*If*, May 1964).
Fiction [as Cordwainer Smith]
Planet Buyer, The [pa] ("The Boy Who Bought Old Earth," *GSF*, Apr 1964) —enlarged: (Pyramid: R-1084, 1964, 156 pp., pa 50¢)

A boy bound by a planet's austere, cruel customs uses the family computer to become the richest human in the universe.
Quest of the Three Worlds [C] [pa] (Ace: F-402, 1966, 174 pp., pa 40¢)

Arranged in 4 parts: Part 1 – "On the Gem Planet" (*GSF*, Oct 1963); Part 2 – "On the Storm Planet" (*GSF*, Feb 1965); Part 3 – "On the Sand Planet" (*AS*, Dec 1965); Part 4 – "Three to a Given Star" (*GSF*, Oct 1965).
Space Lords [C] [pa] (Pyramid: R1183, 1965, 206 pp., pa 50¢; X1911, 1968, pa 60¢)

Sf, 5 stories with prologue and epilogue: "Mother Hitton's Littul Kittens"; "The Dead Lady of Clown Town"; "Drunkboat"; "The Ballad of Lost C'mell"; "A Planet Named Shayol."
Underpeople, The [pa] (Pyramid: X1910, 1968, 159 pp., pa 60¢)

A loosely-knit novel of the "Instrumentality" series. Chapters: 1. "Lost Music in an Old World"; 2. "Discourses and Recourses"; 3. "The Road to the Catmaster"; 4. "The Department Store of Hearts' Desires"; 5. Everybody's Fond of Money"; 6. "Tostig Amaral"; 7. "Birds, Far Underground"; 8. "His Own Strange Altar"; 9. "Counsels, Councils, Consoles and Consuls."
You Will Never Be the Same [C] [pa] (Regency: RB309, 1963, 156 pp., pa 50¢)

Sf, 8 stories: "No, No, Not Rogov!"; "The Lady Who Sailed the Soul"; "Scanners Live in Vain"; "The Game of Rat and Dragon"; "The Burning of the Brain"; "Golden the Ship Was—Oh! Oh! Oh!"; "Alpha Ralpha Boulevard"; "Mark Elf."

LINES, K(ATHLEEN) M(ARY)
Anthology
House of the Nightmare and Other Eerie Tales, The (Bodley Head, London, 1967, 208 pp., 21/-) (Farrar Strauss, New York, 1968, $3.95)

19 stories and 7 'true' stories, with 2-p. foreword by compiler: *From Imagination:* "The House of the Nightmare," E. L. White; "The Hauntings at Thorhallstead," Allen French; "His Own Number," Wm. Croft Dickinson; "Gabriel-Ernest," Saki; "Hand in Glove," Eliz. Bowen; "Mr. Fox," traditional; "Curfew," L. M. Boston; "John Bartine's Watch," A. Bierce; "The Monkey's Paw," W. W. Jacobs; "My Grandfather, Hendry Watty," Sir A. Quiller-Couch; "A School Story," M. R. James; "The Red Cane," E. F. Bozman; "A Diagnosis of Death," A. Bierce; "Bad Company," W. de la Mare; "Proof," Henry Cecil; "The Amulet," Thomas Raddall; "The Hair," A. J. Alan; "The Return of the Native," Wm. C. Dickinson; "The Earlier Service," Marg. Irwin. *From Life:* "Here I Am Again," Charles G. S–, Esq. (from *Lord Halifax's Ghost Book*); "The Man Who Died at Sea," Rosemary Sutcliffe; "The Wish Hounds," Kathleen Hunt; "The Man in the Road," F. M. Pilkington; "My Haunted Houses," M. Joyce Dixon; "In Search of a Ghost," Eric Roberts; "The Limping Man of Makin-Meang," Sir Arthur Grimble.

LINKLATER, ERIC (1899–) Scottish novelist. He took his M.A. at the U. of Aberdeen. In 1918 he was severely wounded while a private in the Black Watch. He was in the public relations division of the War Office in World War II, gaining experience which helped him write up the Korean campaign for the British Government. In 1954 he received the Order of the British Empire from Queen Elizabeth II. He has been a successful freelance writer with many novels and biographies, and is considered to be one of the most gifted of the less profound contemporary novelists. The title story of his *Sealskin Trousers* (Hart-Davis, 1947) is a fantasy dealing with were-seals; it was reprinted in *F&SF* (Apr 1952).
Fiction [Incomplete—other titles in Bleiler *Checklist*]
Sociable Plover and Other Stories and Conceits, A [C] , (Hart-Davis, London, 1957, 222 pp., illus.–R. Stone)

3 stories [and 2 'conceits']: "A Sociable Plover" (ghostly bird-haunting); "The Masks of Purpose" (massacre of Glencoe); "Escape Forever" (convicts' escape across Scotland).
Spell for Old Bones, A (J. Cape, London, 1949, 223 pp., 9/6) (Macmillan, New York, 1950, 223 pp., $2.50) (Clarke Irwin, Toronto, $2.25) (*Trolleri med gamla ben* [Swedish], Norstedt, 1951)

Light wit and epic grandeur of pre-Arthurian Britain.

LINTON, ELIZABETH LYNN (10 Feb 1822–14 July 1898) English novelist and essayist, born Eliza Lynn. Rebelling against her family, she went to London in 1845 to make her way as a journalist. After the failure of three novels, she went to Paris as a newspaper correspondent. In 1858 she married the engraver William James Linton at the request of his dying wife, but they were never compatible. She then used her husband's name on her writings. A fantasy in addition to that below is *Witch Stories* (Chapman & Hall, London, 1961).
Fiction
With a Silken Thread and Other Stories [C] (Tauchnitz, Leipzig, 1880, 352 pp.) (Chatto & Windus, London, 1880, 3 vols.; 1909, 405 pp.)

Fantasy, 7 stories (Tauchnitz ed.): "With a Silken Thread"; "The Countess Melusine"; "Mildred's Lovers"; "The Latest Tenants of Hangman's House"; "The Family at Fenhouse"; "The Best to Win"; "For Love."

LISSNER, IVAR (1909–) German writer. He was born in Riga and educated at various European universities. He has made expeditions into Mongolia, North Manchurian taiga, Northeast Australia and Polynesia. He edited *Kristall* (an illustrated magazine) 1949-56. Another translated work is *The Caesars*.
Nonfiction
Living Past, The [Trans. from German by J. M. Brownjohn] (J. Cape, London, 1957, 462 pp., 42/-) (Clarke Irwin, Toronto, $8.50) (Putnam, New York, 1957, 444 pp., illus., $5.95)

Well-written telescopic view of past civilizations, including such enigmatic ones as Crete, Mohenjo-Daro, Etruria and Tiahuanacu.

LISTER, STEPHEN (pseudonym)
Fiction
Hail Bohemia! (Davies, London, 1948, 170 pp., 8/6)
 A fantastic satire about an island where Christian enlightenment reigns.

LISTON, EDWARD J. U.S. physician, naturalised in 1927. After medical training in England he had hospital experience in Buenos Aires and San Francisco. He has been a general practitioner in California since 1927 except for 3 years as a flight surgeon in Texas. The book below was his first novel, though he had written privately for the stage.
Fiction
Bowl of Night, The (Coward-McCann, New York, 1948, 246 pp., $2.75) (Longmans, Toronto) (Jarrolds, London, 1950, 224 pp., 8/6)
 A doctor crashes in a South American jungle and finds romance—a lost-race story in the style of H. R. Haggard.

LIVINGSTON, BERKELEY (26 Nov 1908–) U.S. author, born in Chicago. He originally wanted to be a journalist but did not complete the course. After various jobs and a South Sea tour he began writing; he first appeared in the Ziff-Davis *South Sea Stories*. He later wrote about 50 stories for *AS* and *FA* from 1943-50 (some under house pseudonyms).

LIVINGSTON, HAROLD (4 Sep 1924–) U.S. author, born in Haverhill, Mass.
Fiction
Climacticon, The [pa] (Ballantine: 406K, 1960, 191 pp., pa 35¢)
 The use of a small machine that detects the emotional attitudes of girls.

LIVINGSTON, HERB (1916–) U.S. author. He has written under his own name and as "H. B. Hickey," the latter being mainly used for science fiction appearing in *AS* and *FA* from 1947 to the early 1950's. He has also written a western novel. He lives in California.

LLOYD, J.
Fiction
Tales From the Beyond [C] [pa] (Tandem: T56, 1966, 200 pp., pa 3/6)
 American Indian 'folk' stories.

LLOYD, NOEL
Fiction
Brew of Witchcraft, A [C] See PALMER, G. (co-author)
Ghosts Go Haunting [C] See PALMER, G. (co-author)
Moonshine and Magic [C] See PALMER, G. (co-author)

LOBSENZ, NORMAN (MITCHELL) (1919–) U.S. editor He was born in New York City and educated at New York U. (B.S., 1939) and the Graduate School of Journalism at Columbia Univ. (M.S., 1940). He did newspaper work in New York City; was managing editor of *Quick* 1951-53; then worked for Pines Pubs. in 1954 and Hillman Periodicals in 1955. He was editorial director of the Ziff-Davis magazines *Amazing* and *Fantastic* from Sep 1958 until they were sold in June 1965. He is married and has two sons.

LOCKE, WILLIAM J(OHN) (20 Mar 1863–15 May 1930) English novelist. Born in British Guiana, he was schooled in England and Trinidad and in 1884 graduated from Cambridge in mathematics. After teaching, he began to write; his first novel was *At the Gate of Samaria* (1895). A fantasy was *The Golden Journey of Mr. Paradyne* (Dodd Mead, New York, 1924), contained in the collection below. He wrote to entertain and was not a serious novelist.
Fiction
Stories Near and Far [C] (Dodd Mead, New York, 1927, 253 pp., $2.00) (Lane, London, 1927, 7/6; 1928, 3/6)
 Fantasy, 9 stories: "The Song of Oo-Oo"; "A Moonlight Effect"; "A Spartan of the Hills"; "Pontifex"; "An Echo of the Past"; "The Apostle"; "Ridet Olympus"; "The Golden Journey of

Mr. Paradyne"; "Roses."

LOCKRIDGE, NORMAN
Anthology
Bachelor's Quarters (Biltmore, New York, 1944, 764 pp., $3.00) (McLeod, Toronto, $2.98)
 83 stories (80 from *Two Worlds Quarterly/Monthly*, *Beau* and *Secret Memoirs*), introduction–J. Cournos. 17 stories are weird: "On the Brighton Road," T. Middleton; "Nymph and Shepherd," M. Frere; "Lumpy," S. Roth; "Mysterious Case of Mr. Perkins and Mr. Johnson," "Worcester Bowl," M. Armstrong; "Ambassador of Carpipedia," A. Huxley; "Miraculous Revenge," G. B. Shaw; "Finding Your Woman: In Paris," P. Morand; "Devil in a Summer House," W. Enscore; "His Sainted Grandmother," Lord Dunsany; "A Fragment," N. Douglas; "The Vampire," J. Neruda; "Apsethus and the Green Parrots," "Hermit and the Satyr," F. McCord; "Women Without Breasts," J. D. Radcliff; "Hyalis," A. Samain; "In the World Beyond," E. Pelin.

LOFTING, HUGH (14 Jan 1886–27 Sep 1947) English author. He was born in Maidenhead of English-Irish parentage. He was trained in civil engineering and built railways in West Africa and Canada before World War I. His "Dr. Dolittle" series began as illustrated letters to his children from the trenches of France during World War I. In 1967 they were the basis of the film starring Rex Harrison as Dr. Dolittle.
Series
Dr. Dolittle. Children's stories about a man who could talk with animals. All were originally published by Jonathan Cape, London. In 1967 the first five appeared as Dell 60¢ paperbacks and the first three and the fifth appeared as Puffin paperbacks. *The Story of Doctor Dolittle*; *The Voyages of Doctor Dolittle* (also called *Dr. Dolittle and the Pirates*); *Doctor Dolittle's Post Office*; *Doctor Dolittle's Circus*; *Doctor Dolittle's Zoo*; *Doctor Dolittle's Caravan*; *Doctor Dolittle's Garden*; *Doctor Dolittle in the Moon*; *Doctor Dolittle's Return*; *Doctor Dolittle and the Secret Lake*; *Doctor Dolittle and the Green Canary*; *Doctor Dolittle's Puddleby Adventure*.

LOFTS, NORAH (ROBINSON) (27 Aug 1904–) Mrs. Robert Jorisch.
Fiction
Devil's Own, The [as Peter Curtis] (Doubleday, New York, 1960, 239 pp., $3.50; 'Dolphin,' 1961, 279 pp., pa 95¢) (MacDonald, London, 1960, 15/-) (*The Witches*, Pan: X591, 1966, 254 pp., pa 3/6)
 Witchcraft and satanism; highly considered by A. Boucher. *Film:* As *The Witches*, by Hammer Films in Eastmancolor, starring Joan Fontaine, Kay Walsh, Alec McCowen; produced by Anthony N. Keys and directed by Cyril Frankel.
Witches, The [pa] See *Devil's Own, The*

LOMBINO, S. A. See HUNTER, E.

LONDON, JACK (12 Jan 1876–22 Nov 1916) U.S. novelist and short-story writer. He was born Jack Chaney but used his stepfather's name from childhood. He led a precarious life as a child and spent his youth in a variety of occupations, including a sealing trip to Japan and Siberia. An avid reader, he started some schooling, but went on the Klondike Gold Rush in 1896 with no luck. At one stage he contemplated suicide but was saved by the acceptance of the short story "A Thousand Deaths" (*Black Cat, ca.* 1898-99; *F&SF*, Sep 1967). He became famous with his *The Call of the Wild* (1903) and remained a best-selling writer for many years. He reported the Russo-Japanese War for the Hearst Newspapers. He was very interested in socialism. Recently his fragment *The Assassination Bureau* was completed by Robert L. Fish (McGraw, 1963, 184 pp., $4.50; pa $1.65; Deutsch, 1964, 18/-). The listing below includes all of London's fiction except *Hearts of Free* (1920) and *Human Drift* (1917); it includes most of his collections. Macmillan published 21 volumes of his works around 1919-20 in the 'Sonoma' edition at $1.75, illus.–R. M. Reay;

while more recently at least 7 volumes appeared in *The Bodley Head Jack London* edited and introduced by I. O. Evans (1964). Most are not sf.

Fiction

Before Adam (Macmillan, New York, 1906, 214 pp.; 1962, 172 pp., illus.–L. E. Fisher, $3.95) (Laurie, London, 1908, 308 pp., 6/-; 1910, 2/-) ([Swedish], Bohlin, 1918; Natur & Kultur, 1959) ([French], Juvennot) (Macmillan 'SF Classic,' 1963, 172 pp., illus. –L. E. Fisher, $3.95, intro.–W. Ley, epilogue–L. Eiseley)

Through racial memory the narrator dreams of his life as Big-Tooth, a member of a paleolithic tribe.

Children of the Frost [C] (Macmillan, New York & London, 1902, 3+263 pp.) (Bodley Head, 1964, 160 pp., 12/6) (Panther: 1954, 1965, 155 pp., pa 3/6)

10 stories: "In the Forests of the North"; "The Law of Life"; "Nam-Bok the Unveracious"; "The Master of Mystery"; "The Sunlanders"; "The Sickness of Lone Chief"; "Keesh, the Son of Keesh"; "The Death of Ligoun"; "Li Wan, the Fair"; "The League of the Old Men."

Iron Heel, The (Macmillan, New York, 1907, 354 pp.) (Everett, London, 1908, 292 pp., 6/-; 1930, 2/-) (Grosset Dunlap, New York, 1920, 354 pp.) (*Le talon de fer* [French], Crès, 1923, intro. –A. France) (*Die eiserne Ferse* [German], Büchergilde, 1928) (Penguin: 461, 1945, 219 pp., pa 9d) (Laurie, London, 1947, 292 pp., 6/-) (Sagamore, New York, 1957, 303 pp., pa $1.45) (McClelland, Toronto, $1.60) (Macmillan, New York, 1958, 303 pp., $3.75) (*Järnhälen* [Swedish], FIB, 1958) (Arco, London, 1966, 230 pp., 25/-, editor–I. O. Evans)

The adventures of a Victorian-type hero in the future (beginning in 1913). This is considered by many to be a classic, and is noted for London's forecasts, some of which have been wrong while others are of interest. For example, a war begins with a German attack on Honolulu. The story is said by some to forecast Nazism, etc.

Jacket, The See *Star Rover, The*

Moon-Face and Other Stories [C] (Macmillan, New York, 1906, 273 pp.; 1929) (Heinemann, London, 1906, 280 pp., 6/-)

8 stories: "All Gold Canyon"; "Amateur Night"; "Leopard Man's Story"; "Local Color"; "Minions of Midas"; "Moon-Face"; "Planchette"; "The Shadow and the Flash" (*FFM*, June 1948).

Night-Born, The [C] (Century, New York, 1913, 3+290 pp., $2.00)

10 stories: "The Night-Born"; "The Madness of John Harned"; "When the World Was Young"; "The Benefit of the Doubt"; "Winged Blackmail"; "Bunches of Knuckles"; "War"; "Under the Deck Awnings"; "To Kill a Man"; "The Mexican." The third story is actually the only fantasy.

Red One, The [C] (Macmillan, New York, 1918, 193 pp., frontis.) (Grosset, New York, 1918)

4 stories: "The Hussy"; "Like Argus of the Old Times"; "The Princess"; "The Red One."

Scarlet Plague, The (Macmillan, New York, 1915, 181 pp., illus. $1.00; 'Sonoma' ed., 1919) (Mills Boon, London, 1915, 153 pp.) (*La peste écarlate* [French], Crès, 1924) (*Röda Pesten* [Swedish], Bohlin, 1927) (*Scarlet Plague and Other Stories*, Staples, London, 1946, 100 pp., 6/-) (*FFM*, Feb 1949) (in *Out of This World*, Penguin, 1944; *Omnibus of SF* [Conklin], 1952; *Strange Travels in SF* [Conklin], 1953)

A classic of world disaster recounted by an old man. The British (Staples) ed. also has "Love of Life" and "The Unexpected."

Star Rover, The (Macmillan, New York, 1915, 329 pp.; 'Sonoma' ed., 1920; 1929, $1.75) (*The Jacket*, Mills Boon, 1915, 334 pp., 6/-; Arco, 1967, 279 pp., 25/-, editor–I. O. Evans) (*Le vagabond des étoiles* [French], Crès, 1925) (Macmillan 'SF Classic,' 1963, 336 pp., illus.–L. E. Fisher, $4.50, biog. intro. & epilogue–G. Murphy)

The mind of a "convict" roves the stars; supposedly based on the life of Ed Morrel [see letter, *FFM*, Aug 1947].

Strength of the Strong, The [C] (Macmillan, New York, 1914, 257 pp., frontis.) (Title story only, C. H. Kerr, Chicago, 1911, 30 pp., illus.)

7 stories: "Dream of Debs"; "Enemy of All the World"; "Sam-

uels"; "The Sea-Farmer"; "South of the Slot"; "The Strength of the Strong"; "Unparalleled Invasion."

When God Laughs and Other Stories [C] (Macmillan, 1911, 319 pp., $1.50) (Mills Boon, 1912, 320 pp., 6/-)

12 stories: "The Apostate"; "The Chinago"; "Created He Them"; "Curious Fragment"; " 'Francis Spaight' "; " 'Just Meat' "; "Make Westing"; "Nose for the King"; "Piece of Steak"; "Semper Idem"; "When God Laughs"; "Wicked Woman."

LONDON OBSERVER English newspaper.

Anthology

AD 2500 (Heinemann, London, 1955, 241 pp., 15/-)

Prize-winning stories from a contest. The emphasis of the stories was on humanity, not gadgets. 21 stories, intro.–N. Balchin: "Return of the Moon Man," E. L. Malpass; "Not for an Age," B. W. Aldiss; "The Right Thing," Wm. Andrew; "Jackson's Wrong Story," J. Bolsover; "Voice From the Gallery," Catherine Brownlow; "Walkabout," S. Earl; "The Shadow Play," E. D. Fitzpatrick; "Venus and the Rabbitt," E. M. Fitzpatrick; "The Place of the Tigress," Isobel Mayne; "Another Antigone," D. A. C. Morrison; "Spud Failure Definite," N. Peart; "The Three Brothers," Wm. M. Russell; "The Atavists," G. A. Rymer; "The Mission," A. Sellings; "Alpha in Omega," J. Stones; "The Blond Kid," H. Sutherland; "The Case of Omega Smith," G. Walsh; "The Machine That Was Lonely," R. Wills; "Hitch Hike to Paradise," G. Whybrow; "The Knitting," Marg. Wood; "Man Manifold," P. Young.

LONG, AMELIA REYNOLDS (1904–) U.S. detective writer. She occasionally appeared in the science fiction magazines before the 1940's. Her "The Mechanical Man" was part of No. 7 in the Gernsback SF Series. Her story "The Thought-Monster" was filmed as *Fiend Without a Face* in the U.S. by M.G.M. in 1958, produced by John Croydon and directed by Arthur Crabtree, with Marshall Thompson.

LONG, CHARLES R(USSELL) (1904–)

Fiction

Eternal Man, The (Avalon, New York, 1964, 191 pp., $2.95)

An Earth immortal becomes involved with a dictatorship, and comes up against alien immortals.

Infinite Brain (Avalon, 1957, 224 pp., $2.75) (*Il cervello infinito* [Italian], *Cosmo*: 69, 1961)

Complicated action and suspense on a world like Earth, 35 light years away.

LONG, FRANK B(ELKNAP) (27 Apr 1903–) U.S. science fiction and fantasy writer, most noted in the weird field. Of New England stock, he once commented that his direct maternal ancestor Edward Doty was the only apprenticed lad on the *Mayflower* and later the first man to fight a duel on the American continent. His paternal grandfather was a building contractor who erected the pedestal of the Statue of Liberty in 1883 and was the statue's first superintendent. Long was educated in New York public schools and the New York U. School of Journalism. His interests include anthropology, natural history, and many other sciences, and he has a scholarly interest in the Fine Art of Murder as defined by the noted authors of that genre.

He has written for a variety of markets since the 1920's, appearing continually in *Weird Tales*, for which his first story was "Death Waters," Dec 1924. He has also appeared in most sf magazines. He has sold some 500 stories in all fields, including mystery, adventure, and detective, and has written occasional articles and verse. A number of his weird and sf stories have been placed on records for the blind. His "Guest in the House" was on CBS-TV about 1954, while "A Visitor From Egypt" and several other stories have been dramatised on radio. Noted works not covered below include a number of short stories on the future of man in *ASF* in 1934; "Operation: Square Peg" [with I. W. Lande] (*Satellite*, Apr 1957); and "Mission to a Distant Star" (*Satellite*, Feb 1958), which was to have been the first sf in Margulies' 'Renown' books. He also wrote the 'story about the cover' for *Fantastic Universe* for a period, and was associate editor of *Satellite* in 1959.

Series

Carstairs, John. Botanical detective. All in *TWS*: "Plants Must Grow"† (Oct 1941); "Snapdragon"† (Dec 1941); "Plants Must Slay"† (Apr 1942); "Satellite of Peril"† (Aug 1942); "The Ether Robots" (Dec 1942); "The Heavy Man" (Apr 1943); "Wobblies in the Moon"† (June 1943). The stories marked † are in *John Carstairs: Space Detective.*

Fiction

. . . And Others Shall Be Born [pa] (Belmont: B50-809, 1968, 86 pp., pa 50¢; with *The Thief of Thoth*)

Reconstructed remnants of a galactic empire seek to colonize Earth.

Dark Beasts, The [pa] See *Hounds of Tindalos, The*

Goblin Tower, The [C] (Dragon-Fly Press, Cassia [Florida], 1935, 25 pp., $1.00; 100 copies) (New Collectors, Denver [Colo.], 1949, 30 pp., 50¢; 500 copies)

A collection of verse, some fantastic, of which about half appeared in *WT* 1925-34: "In Mayan Splendor"; "The White People"; "An Old Wife Speaketh It"; "Stallions of the Moon"; "Advice"; "The Goblin Tower"; "The Inland Sea"; "On Icy Kinarth"; "Great Ashtoreth"; "Night-Trees"; "The Horror on Dagoth Wold"; "The Abominable Snow Men"; "Pirate-Men"; "Subway"; "Sonnet"; "The Hashish Eater"; "The Ballad of Mary Magdalene"; "Ballad of Saint Anthony"; "From the Catullian Fount"; "The Prophet"; "Prediction"; "Walt Whitman." Cover and identical title-page illustration by Roy Hunt. The original edition was compiled by Barlow and Lovecraft and intended as a surprise for Long. It contains poems Long wrote between the ages 16-30. This edition is very rare. The reprint is marred by numerous bad typographical errors which affect about a third of the poems.

Horror From the Hills, The [C] (Arkham, 1963, 110 pp., $3.00) (Brown-Watson: R907, 1965, 159 pp., pa 3/6) (in *Odd Science Fiction*, Belmont: L92-/00, 1964, 141 pp., pa 50¢)

The Arkham ed. has only the short novel from *WT* (sr2, Jan 1931); the pa ed. also contains the stories "The Flame of Life" and "Giant in the Forest."

Hounds of Tindalos, The [C] (Arkham, Sauk City [Wisc.], 1946, 316 pp., $3.00, jacket–H. Bok; 2,602 copies) (Museum, London, 1950, 352 pp., 8/6, jacket–Powell) (Belmont: L92-569, 1963, 173 pp., pa 50¢ [9 stories marked 1]; *The Dark Beasts*, Belmont: L92-579, 1963, 141 pp., pa 50¢ [9 stories marked 2])

Weird, 21 stories: "A Visitor From Egypt"; "The Refugees"2; "Fisherman's Luck"1; "Death-Waters"2; "Grab Bags Are Dangerous"1; "The Elemental"1; "The Peeper"1; "Bridgehead"; "Second Night Out"; "The Dark Beasts"2; "Census Taker"2; "The Ocean Leech"2; "The Space-Eaters"1; "It Will Come to You"2; "A Stitch in Time"2; "Step Into My Garden"2; "The Hounds of Tindalos"1; "Dark Vision"1; "The Flame Midget"2; "Golden Child"1; "The Black Druid"1.

It Was the Day of the Robot (Belmont: 90-277, 1963, 141 pp., pa 40¢) (Dobson, London, 1964, 141 pp., 15/-) (*Cuando el robotse impuso* [Spanish], Cenit: 67, 1964, pa)

A fleeing couple search for refuge in a decadent 23rd century society.

John Carstairs: Space Detective [C] (F. Fell, New York, 1949, 7+265 pp., $2.50) (McLeod, Toronto, $3.35) (Kemsley: CT400, 1951, 192 pp., pa 1/6)

6 stories of the "John Carstairs" series [which see].

Journey Into Darkness [pa] (Belmont: B50-757, 1967, 156 pp., pa 50¢)

Invisible aliens menace Earth.

Lest Earth Be Conquered [pa] (Belmont: B50-726, 1966, 144 pp., pa 50¢)

Aliens on Earth.

Man From Genoa and Other Poems, A [C] (W. Paul Cook, Athol [Mass.], 1926, 31 pp.; 300 copies)

Long's first verse collection, privately printed and bound in blue cloth. It includes: "A Knight of La Mancha"; "The Marriage of Sir John de Mandeville"; "A Man From Genoa"; "A Sonnet for Seamen"; "Manhattan Skyline"; "In Hospital"; "The Magi"; "An Old Tale Retold"; and some others, a few of which were reprinted in *The Goblin Tower.*

Mars Is My Destination [pa] (Pyramid: F-742, 1962, 158 pp., pa 40¢) (*Marte es mi destino* [Spanish], Cenit: 57, 1963, pa)

Intrigue involving power combines on Mars.

Martian Visitors, The (Avalon, 1964, 192 pp., $2.95)

An engineer and some scientists meet the real Martians.

Mating Center, The [pa] (Chariot: 162, 1961, 160 pp., pa 50¢)

Mission to a Star ("Mission to a Distant Star," *Satellite*, Feb 1958) (Avalon, 1964, 192 pp., $2.95)

An agent tries to discover why seemingly noble geniuses from the stars prolong their visit to Earth.

Odd Science Fiction [pa] See *Horror From the Hills, The*

So Dark a Heritage [pa] (Lancer: 72-106, 1966, 175 pp., pa 50¢)

Space Station No. 1 [pa] (Ace: D-242, 1957, 157 pp., pa 35¢ [with *Empire of the Atom*]; D-544, 1962, pa 35¢) (*Rymdresenär Kidnappas* [Swedish], Wennerberg: R12, 1958, pa) (*Rumstation I Kaldar* [Danish], Skrifola 'Lommeromanen P72,' 1959, pa) (*Die Marsfestung* [German], *T*: 51, 1959)

Intrigue and adventure on a space station.

This Strange Tomorrow [pa] (Belmont: B50-663, 1966, 158 pp., pa 50¢)

An episodic story of intrigue about the future control of Earth and a space station.

Three Steps Spaceward (Avalon, 1963, 192 pp., $2.95)

Adventure on Titan, jungle covered and with savages and telepathic animals.

Woman From Another Planet [pa] (Chariot: CB123, 1960, 190 pp., pa 50¢)

Invasion of Earth by "android-women."

LONG, Mrs. GABRIELLE M(ARGARET) V(ERE) (CAMPBELL) (29 Oct 1886–23 Dec 1952) British historical novelist and short-story writer. The extent of her published work will probably never be known exactly, since she wrote about 150 books under 6 or possibly 10 pseudonyms. These ranged from *The Viper of Milan* (1906, as Marjorie Bowen) to *To Bed at Noon* (1951, as Joseph Shearing). Under the latter pseudonym she wrote many widely admired historical novels based usually on actual criminal cases; this by-line was a closely kept secret until 1942. Another pseudonym was George Preedy.

Fiction [Incomplete—for other titles as M. Bowen, see Bleiler *Checklist*]

Bishop of Hell and Other Stories, The [as Marjorie Bowen] [C] (Bodley Head, London, 1949, 230 pp., 8/6)

Weird, 12 stories with introduction–Michael Sadleir: "The Fair Hair of Ambrosine"; "The Crown Derby Plate"; "The Housekeeper"; "Florence Flannery"; "Elsie's Lonely Afternoon"; "The Bishop of Hell"; "The Grey Chamber"; "The Extraordinary Adventure of Mr. John Proudie"; "The Scoured Silk"; "The Avenging of Ann Leete"; "Kecksies"; "Ann Mellor's Lover."

Julia Roseing Rave [as Robert Paye] (E. Benn, London, 1933, 223 pp., 3/6) (Longmans, Toronto, $2.50)

A most unusual and unique story. Not in the Bleiler *Checklist.*

Sheep's Head and Babylon, and Other Stories of Yesterday and Today [as Marjorie Bowen] [C] (Bodley Head, 1929, 344 pp., 7/6)

18 items: *Stories of Yesterday:* "Sheep's Head and Babylon"; "A Matrimonial Entanglement"; "The Folding Doors"; "The Necromancers"; "The Pond"; "The Triumph of Mr. Westfield"; "Miranda"; "A Pose for Fanchon"; "Pat-a-too." *Of Today:* " 'Crowd –With Flags' "; "The Careful Youth"; "The Wall"; "The Prescription"; "Mrs. Hopeton at the Flower Show"; "False Pretences"; "An Appointment With Stiffkey"; "The Usual Thing"; "All the Same Price." Not in the Bleiler *Checklist.*

Anthologies [as Marjorie Bowen]

Great Tales of Horror (J. Lane, London, 1933, 415 pp., 7/6; 1935, 3/6)

Weird, 29 stories (many are also in *The Great Weird Stories* [Neale], 1929): "The Grey Chamber," Anon.; "The Murder of Squire Langton," M. Bowen; "Sir Dominick Sarsfield," J. S. Le Fanu; "The Queen of Spades," A. Pushkin; "The Two Sisters of Cologne," Anon.; "The Witch (St. John's Eve)," Gogol; "The Ghost of a Head," Anon.; "The Great Keinplatz Experiment," A.

C. Doyle; "The Woman's Ghost Story," A. Blackwood; "The Doppelganger," "The Dead Bride," Anon.; "The Tapestried Chamber," Sir W. Scott; "Almodoro's Cupid," W. W. Astor; "The Skull," Anon.; "The Magic Mirror," G. MacDonald; "The Red Room," H. G. Wells; "In Letters of Fire," G. Leroux; "The Legend of Dunblane," Anon.; "The Shining Pyramid," A. Machen; "A Night in an Old Castle," G. P. R. James.
More Great Tales of Horror (J. Lane, 1935, 431 pp., 8/6)
Weird, 26 stories: "Laird of Cassway," J. Hogg; "The Room With the Arras" (from *Woven in Darkness*), W. W. Fenn; "The Coffin Maker" [trans.—T. Keane], N. Poushkin; "Wicked Captain Walshawe of Wauling," S. Le Fanu; "Wooden Woman," A. Cunningham; "The Fatal Hour" [trans. from French—M. Bowen], Anon.; "Elie Anderson's Revenge" (from *The Odd Volume*), Anon.; "The Haunted Mill" (from *The Night Side of Nature*), Mrs. Cath. Crowe; "The Laird of Cool's Ghost" (18th century old chap book), Anon.; "The Sexton's Adventure," S. Le Fanu; "Ezra Peden," A. Cunningham; "The Suitor of Selkirk" (*The Odd Volume*), Anon.; "Hand on the Latch" (*Woven in Darkness*), W. W. Fenn; "Laird of Wineholm," J. Hogg; "Vision of Tom Chuff," S. Le Fanu; "Fairy Bride," Anon.; "Black Joe o' the Bow," J. Smith; "A Ghost in a Prison" (*The Night Side of Nature*), Mrs. Crowe; "The Accursed Portrait" [trans. from French—M. Bowen], Anon.; "Infernal Major Weir," R. Chambers; "Spectre Lovers," S. Le Fanu; "The Murder Hole," Anon.; "Perling Joan," J. G. Lockhart; "Ghost on the Chain Pier" (*Woven in Darkness*), W. W. Fenn; "Resurrection Men," D. M. Moir; "Ghost With the Golden Casket," A. Cunningham.

LONGSTRETH, T. MORRIS (1886–) U.S. author. He has contributed to many American magazines and has had over 40 books —novels, poetry, history, and biography.
Fiction
Time Flight (Macmillan, New York, 1954, 216 pp., $2.75)
Juvenile; the heroes go backward in time to Salem during the witchcraft trials.

LONNERSTRAND, STURE (13 Mar 1919–) Swedish journalist and author, B.A., U. of Lund. He has written much in various weekly newspapers about unidentified flying objects and parapsychology. He is the author of eight books, including a volume of verse, *Den Incentrala Blodsymfonien*. In 1954 he won the 15,000 crown first prize in the first Swedish Science Fiction Book Competition with *Rymhunden* [The Space Hound] (Bonnier, 1954), but this has been much criticised because of its similarity to van Vogt's *Voyage of the Space Beagle*. He later formed his own press to publish *Virus* (Symb, 1960). A translated short story was "Meeting Mr. Ipusido" (*Science-Fantasy*, No. 21, 1957). He is active in Swedish sf fan circles, publishing the first Swedish amateur magazine, *Futura*, and attending Stockholm conventions.

LOOMIS, NOEL (MILLER) (3 Apr 1905–) U.S. author, born in Wakita, Oklahoma. He attended Oklahoma University. He became a linotype machinist by trade, and has edited newspapers and taught Spanish. He has a huge file of clippings on pseudoscience. He began writing around 1935 and has sold a number of stories in many fields, often using the pseudonym "Benj. Miller." He has been president, secretary, and treasurer of Western Writers of America, and in 1959 became a member of the National Postal Committee.
Series
Prem, Orig [as Benj. Miller]. All in *TWS*: "Date Line" (Oct 1948); "A Horse on Me" (Dec 1948); "Monsters of the West" (Feb 1949); "On the House" (Apr 1949).
Fiction
City of Glass [pa] (*SS*, July 1942) ([Swedish], *Jules Verne Magasinet*, Nos. 3–18, 1944) (Columbia, 1955, 128 pp., pa 35¢) (*Die gläserne Stadt* [German], *UZ*: 53, 1955)
Adventurers return to Earth and find a huge time lapse. Sequel was "Iron Men," (*SS*, Win 1945).
Man With Absolute Motion, The ([by Silas Water], Rich Cowan, London, 1955, 206 pp., 9/6; Arrow: 795, 1964, 192 pp., pa 3/6;

1966, pa 3/6) (*Satellite*, Oct 1958) (*Jenseits der Sterne* [German], *AW*: 19, 1959)
A search for cosmic power when the Universe is running down.

LORD, BEMAN
Fiction
Day the Spaceship Landed, The (H. Z. Walck, New York, 1967, 64 pp., illus.—H. Berson, $3.25)
Juvenile—a little boy discovers a spaceship with aliens on a pre-official visit to Earth.

LORD, GLENN Noted U.S. authority on the writings of Robert E. Howard. He has published *The Howard Collector* at intervals since Summer 1961; he also edited the Howard collections *Wolfshead* (1968, pa) and *King Kull* (1967, with L. Carter).

LORENZEN, CORAL E. (1925–) U.S. enthusiast of flying saucers, UFO's, etc. Besides the book below, she has also written *Flying Saucer Occupants* (Signet, 1967, pa).
Nonfiction
Flying Saucers: The Startling Evidence of the Invasion From Outer Space [pa] See *The Great Flying Saucer Hoax*
Great Flying Saucer Hoax, The (William-Frederick, New York, 1962, 257 pp., $4.45) (*Flying Saucers: The Startling Evidence of the Invasion From Outer Space*, Signet: T3058, 1966, 278 pp., pa 75¢)
Not an exposure of this "legend"; however the author marshals her data and photographs quite cogently.

LORRAINE, LILITH (1894–) U.S. poet (Mrs. Mary M. Wright). She was born in Corpus Christi, Texas; educated at U. of Arizona and U. of California; and has been a teacher. As a poet she has done much to give science fiction verse a better understanding. She founded the Avalon World's Arts Academy and edited its official journal *Different* and the verse journal *Flame*. She ran a verse section in *Fantasy Book* from No. 3, and has had published one verse collection, *Let the Patterns Break* (over 500 poems). She has written some fiction, including "The Brain of the Planet" in the Gernsback *SF Series* (No. 5, 1929) and stories in *Wonder Stories Quarterly* (1930) and *Wonder Stories* (1935).

LOUGHLIN, RICHARD L. U.S.
Anthology
Journeys in Science Fiction [with Lilian M. Popp] (Globe Book Co., 1961, 655 pp., illus.—photos, no jacket but has design printed on cover, $3.52)
High-school text; 15 stories, 1 novel, 1 play: "Daedalus," T. Bullfinch (from *The Age of Fable*); "The Birthmark," N. Hawthorne; "A Descent Into the Maelstrom," E. A. Poe; "A Journey to the Center of the Earth" [novel], J. Verne; "Moxon's Master," A. Bierce; "A Tale of Negative Gravity," F. R. Stockton; "The Disintegration Machine," A. C. Doyle; "Aepyornis Island," H. G. Wells; "'Wireless'," R. Kipling; "Tobermory," Saki; "The Roads Must Roll," R. A. Heinlein; "Visit to a Small Planet" [play], G. Vidal; "Quit Zoomin' Those Hands Through the Air," J. Finney; "The Fun They Had," I. Asimov; "Triggerman," J. F. Bone; "The Report on the Barnhouse Effect," K. Vonnegut Jr.; "Daxbr Baxbr," Evelyn E. Smith. Also has Appendix "Check Your Understanding" and biographical sketches.

LOVECRAFT, H(OWARD) P(HILLIPS) (20 Aug 1890–15 Mar 1937) U.S. weird-story author of high literary standard. As a youth his main interest was science; at 16 he was contributing a monthly article on astronomy to the *Providence Tribune*. Poor health prevented him from attending college, and he supported himself by ghost writing and revising. He spent most of his life in Providence, Rhode Island, and was something of a recluse, though reported to be kind and generous by the few who met him personally. He was briefly married to Sonia Greene in the middle 1920's. He was very active in various amateur press associations, and conducted a huge correspondence with many literary acquaintances.
Lovecraft's first published story "The Alchemist" (written in

1908) appeared in *The United Amateur* in 1916, and from that time his work appeared in little magazines such as *The Vagrant* and *Home Brew*. However, he did not have a regular market until "Dagon" was published in *Weird Tales* (Oct 1923), after which he regularly appeared in that magazine. His only fantasy or sf stories to appear in the other main magazines were "The Colour out of Space" (*AS*, Sep 1927; *FFM*, Oct 1941); two novels, "At the Mountains of Madness" and "The Shadow out of Time," in *ASF* [see below]; and "The Challenge From Beyond," a round-robin story from the amateur *Fantasy Magazine* (1935; *Fan*, May 1960).

He enriched the field of fantastic literature with *The Necronomicon*—the tome diabolique—and the Cthulhu Mythos (see Series entry below). He was noted for his many revisions of other authors' weird stories, most of which were reprinted in some of his book collections. He collaborated with E. Hoffman Price, and his influence on other authors of his period was incalculable. He was also known for his long essay *Supernatural Horror in Literature*. Although only one of Lovecraft's books (*The Shadow Over Innsmouth*) was published in his lifetime, interest in him was revived and stimulated by August Derleth, one of his foremost followers, who with D. Wandrei established Arkham House in 1939 to publish Lovecraft's *The Outsider and Others*. Numerous other Lovecraft collections have appeared since, including many from Arkham House.

Derleth wrote about Lovecraft in *H.P.L.: A Memoir*. The British amateur magazine *Fantasy Review* examined Lovecraft in its Aug/Sep 1947 issue, and more recently he was profiled by Moskowitz in *Fantastic*, May 1960 (*Science-Fantasy*, Dec 1960). *Fresco*, the literary quarterly of U. of Detroit, devoted its Spr 1958 issue to a symposium on Lovecraft (edited by Steve Eisner); it gives excellent and comprehensive coverage, mostly of aspects of Lovecraft's strange life and work; it includes a bibliography, the story "The Music of Erich Zann," and appreciations and anecdotes by A. Derleth, D. H. Keller, F. Leiber, and others. Bibliographers are continually researching Lovecraft, producing such works as J. P. Brennan's *A Lovecraft Bibliography* and Jack Chalker's more recent *The New H. P. Lovecraft Bibliography* (Anthem Press, 1962, mimeo, 40 pp., quarto); the latter was updated as *Mirage on Lovecraft* (Anthem, 1965, 47 pp., $2.50). These show the vast quantity of Lovecraft's writings for both the amateur and professional presses. W. P. Cook's *H. P. Lovecraft: A Portrait* (Mirage, 1968, iv+66 pp., $2.50) reprints rambling remembrances of a 20-year friendship; it originally appeared in *Beyond the Wall of Sleep*.

A number of Lovecraft's stories have been translated into French in the following collections: Denoël 'Presence du Futur' series No. 4, *La Couleur tombee du ciel* (1954, pa); No. 5, *Dans l'abime du temps* (1954, pa); No. 16, *Par dela le mur du sommeil* (1956, pa); *Je suis d'ailleurs* (1961, pa); and from Deux-Rives, *Demons et merveilles* (1955, pa). Other foreign collections include the Argentine *El color que cayó del cielo* ([Spanish], Minotauro: 8, 1957, pa), the Italian magazine *Urania*: 310 (1963), and a German 1965 paperback from Heyne.

Series

Carter, Randolph. In *WT*: "The Unnamable" (July 1925); "The Statement of Randolph Carter" (Feb 1925; Aug 1937); "The Silver Key" (Jan 1929; *AFR* No. 3, 1947); "Through the Gates of the Silver Key" [with E. H. Price] (July 1934; *AFR* No. 17, 1951). In *Arkham Sampler*: "The Dream Quest of Unknown Kadath" (sr4, Win 1948; book). Most are contained in either *The Outsider and Others* or *Beyond the Wall of Sleep*.

Cthulhu Mythos. The background of the unseen weird world built up by Lovecraft as atmosphere for many of his stories. He attributed much of the information to a mythical book, *The Necronomicon* (see *Arkham Sampler* Win 1948), which he derived from R. W. Chambers' *King in Yellow* (other authors also had mythical works); he may also have got some ideas from A. Machen's writings. Stories in this framework appearing in *WT* are: "The Nameless City" (Nov 1938); "The Festival" (Jan 1925, Oct 1933); "The Call of Cthulhu" (Feb 1928); "The Case of Charles Dexter Ward" (sr2, May 1941); "The Dreams in the Witch-House" (July 1933); "The Whisperer in Darkness" (Aug 1931); "The Haunter of the Dark" (Dec 1936); "The Shadow Over Innsmouth" (Jan 1942);

"The Dunwich Horror" (Apr 1929); "The Thing on the Doorstep" (Jan 1937). Others are (see below): "The Colour Out of Space"; *The Shadow Out of Time*; *At the Mountains of Madness*. Derleth continued the pattern in completing *The Lurker at the Threshold* (originally a Lovecraft fragment) and in some stories on his own; D. Wandrei's *The Web of Easter Island* is in a similar vein.

Fiction

At the Mountains of Madness and Other Novels [C] (Arkham, Sauk City [Wisc.], 1964, xii+432 pp., jacket—L. B. Coye; 3,000 copies) (Gollancz, London, 1966, 432 pp., 30/-) (Panther: 025960, 1968, 300 pp., pa 5/-)

8 stories, selected and with introduction by A. Derleth (pa omits 2nd and 3rd stories): "At the Mountains of Madness" (abr. from *ASF*, sr3, Feb 1936; in full in *The Outsider* [Lovecraft], 1939); "The Case of Charles Dexter Ward" (abr. from *WT*, sr2, May 1941); "The Shunned House"; "The Dreams in the Witch House"; "The Statement of Randolph Carter"; "The Dream Quest of Unknown Kadath"; "The Silver Key"; "Through the Gates of the Silver Key" (with E. H. Price).

Best Supernatural Stories [edited—A. Derleth] [C] (World, Cleveland, 1945, 307 pp., 60¢; 2nd ed., 1945; 3rd ed., 1946 [both higher priced])

Weird, 14 stories; introduction—A. Derleth: "In the Vault"; "Pickman's Model"; "The Rats in the Walls"; "The Outsider"; "The Color Out of Space"; "The Music of Erich Zann"; "The Haunter of the Dark"; "The Picture in the House"; "The Call of Cthulhu"; "The Dunwich Horror"; "Cool Air"; "The Whisperer in Darkness"; "The Terrible Old Man"; "The Thing on the Doorstep."

Beyond the Wall of Sleep [collected by A. Derleth & D. Wandrei] [C] (Arkham, Sauk City [Wisc.], 1943, 458 pp., $5.00; 1,217 copies)

"By Way of Introduction," A. Derleth & D. Wandrei; "Autobiography: Some Notes on a Nonentity"; "The Commonplace Book"; "History and Chronology of the *Necronomicon*." *Prose Poems*: "Memory"; "What the Moon Brings"; "Nyarlathotep"; "Ex Oblivion." *Stories*: "The Tree"; "The Other Gods"; "The Quest of Iranon"; "The Doom That Came to Sarnath"; "The White Ship"; "From Beyond"; "Beyond the Wall of Sleep"; "The Unnameable"; "The Hound"; "The Moon-Bog"; "The Evil Clergyman"; "Herbert West—Reanimator"; "The Dream-Quest of Unknown Kadath"; "The Case of Charles Dexter Ward." *Revisions and Collaborations*: "The Crawling Chaos," "The Green Meadow," Elizabeth Berkeley; "The Curse of Yig," Zelia Brown-Reed Bishop; "The Horror in the Museum," "Out of the Eons," Hazel Heald; "The Mound," Zelia Bishop; "The Diary of Alonzo Typer," William Lumley; "The Challenge From Beyond" (round-robin tale; portions by H.P.L. and others; complete); "In the Walls of Eryx," with Kenneth Sterling. *Miscellany*: "Ibid"; "Sweet Ermengarde."

Selected Poems—

Early Poetry: "Providence"; "On a Grecian Colonnade in a Park"; "Old Christmas"; "New England Fallen"; "On a New England Village Seen by Moonlight"; "Astrophobos"; "Sunset"; "A Year Off"; "A Summer Sunset and Evening"; "To Mistress Sophia Simple." *The Ancient Track*: "The Ancient Track"; "The Eidolon"; "The Nightmare Lake"; "The Outpost"; "The Rutted Road"; "The Wood"; "Hallowe'en in a Suburb"; "Primavera"; "October"; "To a Dreamer"; "Despair"; "Nemesis." *Psychopompos* (narrative poem). *Fungi From Yuggoth* (complete cycle of 36 sonnets [listed in *Collected Poems*]). *Last Poems*: "Yule Horror"; "To Mr. Finlay, Upon His Drawing for Mr. Bloch's Tale 'The Faceless God' "; "To Clark Ashton Smith, Esq., Upon His Phantastick Tales, Verse, Pictures, and Sculptures"; "Where Once Poe Walked"; "Christmas Greetings to Mrs. Phillips Gamwell—1925"; "Brick Row"; "The Messenger."

Addenda: "The Cthulhu Mythology: A Glossary," Francis T. Laney; "An Appreciation of H. P. Lovecraft," W. Paul Cook.

Case of Charles Dexter Ward, The (abr., *WT*, sr2, May 1941) (in *Beyond the Wall of Sleep* [Lovecraft], 1943) (Gollancz, London, 1951, 160 pp., 9/6) (in *Night's Yawning Peal* [Derleth], 1952) (*Os mortos podem voltar* [Portuguese], Livros de Brazil, nd) (in *At the Mountains of Madness* [Lovecraft], 1964) (Panther: 1513,

1963, 127 pp., pa 2/6) (Belmont: 92-617, 1965, 141 pp., pa 50¢)
A rather laborious weird novel.

Collected Poems [C] (Arkham, 1963, x+134 pp., $4.00, jacket & illus.—F. Utpatel; 2,000 copies)

Foreword—A. Derleth. *Early Poems:* "Providence"; "On a Grecian Colonnade in a Park"; "Old Christmas"; "New England Fallen"; "On a New England Village Seen by Moonlight" "Astrophobos"; "Sunset"; "To Pan"; "A Summer Sunset and Evening"; "To Mistress Sophia Simple, Queen of the Cinema"; "A Year Off"; "Sir Thomas Tryout"; "Phaeton"; "August"; "Death"; "To the American Flag"; "To a Youth"; "My Favourite Character"; "To Templeton and Mount Monadnock"; "The Poe-et's Nightmare"; "Lament for the Vanished Spider"; "Regnar Lodbrug's Epicedium"; "Little Sam Perkins"; "Drinking Song From the Tomb." *The Ancient Track:* "The Ancient Track"; "The Eidolon"; "The Nightmare Lake"; "The Outpost"; "The Rutted Road"; "The Wood"; "The House"; "The City"; "Hallowe'en in a Suburb"; "Primavera"; "October"; "To a Dreamer"; "Despair"; "Nemesis"; "Yule Horror"; "To Mr. Finlay, Upon His Drawing for Mr. Bloch's Tale 'The Faceless God' "; "Where Once Poe Walked"; "Christmas Greeting to Mrs. Phillips Gamwell—1925"; "Brick Row"; "The Messenger"; "To Klarkash-Ton, Lord of Averoigne." *Psychopompos. Fungi From Yuggoth:* I. "The Book," II. "Pursuit," III. "The Key," IV. "Recognition," V. "Homecoming," VI. "The Lamp," VII. "Zaman's Hill," VIII. "The Port," IX. "The Courtyard," X. "The Pigeon-Flyers," XI. "The Well," XII. "The Howler," XIII. "Hesperia," XIV. "Star Winds," XV. "Antarktos," XVI. "The Window," XVII. "Memory," XVIII. "The Gardens of Yin," XIX. "The Bells," XX. "Night Haunts," XXI. "Nyarlathotep," XXII. "Azathoth," XXIII. "Mirage," XXIV. "The Canal," XXV. "St. Toad's," XXVI. "The Familiars," XXVII. "The Elder Pharos," XXVIII. "Expectancy," XXIX. "Nostalgia," XXX. "Background," XXXI. "The Dweller," XXXII. "Alienation," XXXIII. "Harbour Whistles," XXXIV. "Recapture," XXXV. "Evening Star," XXXVI. "Continuity."

Colour Out of Space, The [C] [pa] (Lancer: 73-425, 1964, 222 pp., pa 60¢; 73-608, 1967, pa 60¢)

Weird, 7 stories: "The Colour out of Space"; "The Picture in the House"; "The Call of Cthulhu"; "Cool Air"; "The Whisperer in Darkness"; "The Terrible Old Man"; "The Shadow out of Time."

Cry Horror! See *Lurking Fear, The*

Dagon and Other Macabre Tales [C] (Arkham, 1965, 413 pp., $6.50, jacket—L. B. Coye) (Gollancz, 1967, 413 pp., 30/-)

Weird, 33 short stories, 4 fragments, essay "Supernatural Horror in Literature," and complete list of Lovecraft's fiction in chronological order. Fragments: "Azathoth"; "The Descendant"; "The Book"; "The Thing in the Moonlight." Stories: "Dagon," "The Doom That Came to Sarnath"; "The Cats of Ulthar"; "The Strange High House in the Mist"; "The Temple"; "The Lurking Fear"; "The Festival"; "Herbert West—Reanimator"; "Imprisoned With the Pharaohs"; "The Tomb"; "Polaris"; "Beyond the Wall of Sleep"; "The White Ship"; "Arthur Jermyn"; "Celephais"; "From Beyond"; "The Tree"; "The Moon-Bog"; "The Nameless City"; "The Other Gods"; "The Quest of Iranon"; "The Hound"; "Hypnos"; "The Unnamable"; "He"; "The Horror at Red Hook"; "In the Walls of Eryx"; "The Evil Clergyman"; "The Beast in the Cave"; "The Alchemist"; "Poetry and the Gods"; "The Street"; "The Transition of Juan Romero."

Dark Brotherhood, The [C] (Arkham, 1966, 321 pp., $5.00, jacket—F. Utpatel)

Introduction by A. Derleth, who selected the contents; covers the last of hitherto uncollected material by or about Lovecraft. Contents of major interest [see R. W. Lowndes, *Mag. Horror*, Sum 1966] include: "The Dark Brotherhood," H. P. Lovecraft & A. Derleth; "Suggestions for a Reading Guide," H. P. Lovecraft; "The Lovecraft 'Books': Some Addenda and Corrigenda," William Scott Home; "To Arkham and the Stars," Fritz Leiber; "Through Hyper-Space With Brown Jenkin," F. Leiber; "Lovecraft and the New England Megaliths," Andrew E. Rothovius; "Howard Phillips Lovecraft: A Bibliography," Jack Chalker (more complete than earlier ones); "The Making of a Hoax," A. Derleth (on the birth

and continuing life of the *Necronomicon*); "Final Notes," A. Derleth. Of lesser interest are "The Loved Dead," "Deaf, Dumb, and Blind," "The Ghost-Eater," [3 stories] C. M. Eddy Jr.; "Walks With Lovecraft," C. M. Eddy Jr.; "The Cancer of Superstition," H. P. Lovecraft & C. M. Eddy Jr.; "Lovecraft's Illustrators," John E. Vetter. Of little interest are: "Alfredo," "What Belongs in Verse," "Six Poems—'Bells,' 'Oceanus,' 'Clouds,' 'Mother Earth,' 'Cindy'," H. P. Lovecraft; "Amateur Journalism: Its Possible Needs and Betterment," H. P. Lovecraft.

Dream-Quest of Unknown Kadath, The [pa] (in *Beyond the Wall of Sleep* [Lovecraft], 1943) (*Arkham Sampler*, sr4, Win 1948) (Shroud, New York, 1955, 107 pp., paper covers illus.—C. Nomberger, $1.25; 1,490 copies paper, 50 cloth)

A novel in the "Randolph Carter" series, where once again we meet the legendary figures of Cthulhu, Nyarlathotep, etc.

Dreams and Fancies [C] (Arkham, 1962, 174 pp., $3.50; 2,000 copies)

Introduction by A. Derleth; includes a collection of the most outstanding of Lovecraft's "Dreams and Fancies" as gleaned from his letters to various friends and acquaintances. Stories: "Memory"; "The Statement of Randolph Carter"; "Celephais"; "The Doom That Came to Sarnath"; "Nyarlathotep"; "The Evil Clergyman"; "The Thing in the Moonlight"; "The Shadow out of Time."

Dunwich Horror, The [C] [pa] (Bart House: 12, 1945, 186 pp., pa 25¢)

Weird, 3 stories: "The Dunwich Horror"; "The Shadow out of Time"; "The Thing on the Doorstep."

Dunwich Horror and Other Weird Tales, The [C] [pa] (Armed: 730, 1945, 382 pp., pa np)

Copyrighted 1939. Weird, 12 stories, introduction—A. Derleth: "The Dunwich Horror"; "In the Vault"; "The Rats in the Walls"; "Pickman's Model"; "The Music of Erich Zann"; "The Color out of Space"; "The Outsider"; "The Call of Cthulhu"; "The Whisperer in Darkness"; "The Shadow Over Innsmouth"; "The Moon-Bog"; "The Hound."

Dunwich Horror and Others [C] (Arkham, 1963, xx+431 pp., $5.00) (Lancer: 72-702, 1963, 158 pp., pa 50¢ [7 stories marked †])

Weird, 16 stories and introduction "H. P. Lovecraft and His Work," A. Derleth: "In the Vault"†; "Pickman's Model"†; "The Rats in the Walls"†; "The Outsider"; "The Colour out of Space"; "The Music of Erich Zann"†; "The Haunter of the Dark"†; "The Picture in the House"; "The Call of Cthulhu"; "The Dunwich Horror"†; "Cool Air"; "The Whisperer in Darkness"; "The Terrible Old Man"; "The Thing on the Doorstep"†; "The Shadow Over Innsmouth"; "The Shadow out of Time."

Haunter of the Dark, The [C] (Gollancz, 1951, 302 pp., 10/6) (Panther: 1474, 1963, 256 pp., pa 3/6)

Weird, 10 stories and introduction—A. Derleth: "The Outsider"; "The Rats in the Walls"; "Pickman's Model"; "The Call of Cthulhu"; "The Dunwich Horror"; "The Whisperer in Darkness"; "The Colour out of Space"; "The Haunter of the Dark"; "The Thing on the Doorstep"; "The Music of Erich Zann."

Lurker at the Threshold, The [completed by A. Derleth] (Arkham, 1945, 196 pp., $2.50, jacket—R. Clyne; 3,041 copies) (Hutchinson, London, 1948, 224 pp., 8/6)

This novel is actually by Derleth; it was evoked by the short essay "The Round Tower" (1,200 words) and other notes [see *Arkham Sampler*, Spr 1948, p. 49]. It deals with the familiar facets of the Cthulhu Mythos.

Lurking Fear, The [C] [pa] (Avon: 136, 1947, 223 pp., pa 25¢) (*Cry Horror!*, Avon: T-284, 1958, 191 pp., pa 35¢; WDL: HS853, 1959, 190 pp., pa 2/6)

Weird, 11 stories: "The Lurking Fear"; "The Colour out of Space"; "The Nameless City"; "Pickman's Model"; "Arthur Jermyn"; "The Unnamable"; "The Call of Cthulhu"; "The Moon-Bog"; "Cool Air"; "The Hound"; "The Shunned House."

Lurking Fear and Other Stories, The [C] [pa] (Panther: 1759, 1964, 208 pp., pa 3/6)

Weird, 13 stories (different from title above): "The Lurking Fear"; "The Shunned House"; "In the Vault"; "Arthur Jermyn"; "Cool Air"; "The Moon-Bog"; "The Nameless City"; "The Unnamable"; "The Picture in the House"; "The Terrible Old Man"; "The Hound"; "The Shadow Over Innsmouth"; "The Shadow Out of Time."

Marginalia [collected by A. Derleth & D. Wandrei] [C] (Arkham, 1944, 377 pp., $3.00, jacket–V. Finlay [from Oct 1937 *WT*]; 2,035 copies)

Foreword–A. Derleth & D. Wandrei. Collection of revisions, essays, etc.: *Revisions:* "Imprisoned With the Pharaohs," Houdini; "Medusa's Coil," Zelia Brown-Reed Bishop; "Winged Death," Hazel Heald; "The Man of Stone," H. Heald. *Essays, etc.:* "Notes on the Writing of Weird Fiction"; "Notes on the Writing of Interplanetary Fiction"; "Lord Dunsany and His Work"; "Heritage or Modernism: Commonsense in Art Forms"; "Some Backgrounds of Fairyland"; "Some Causes of Self-Immolation"; "A Guide to Charleston, South Carolina"; "Observations on Several Parts of North America." *Fiction:* "The Beast in the Cave"; "The Transition of Juan Romero." *Fragments:* "Azathoth"; "The Book"; "The Descendant"; "The Very Old Folk"; "The Thing in the Moonlight"; "Two Comments" (from *Fantasy Fan* and *Weird Tales*). *Appreciations:* "His Own Most Fantastic Creation," Winfield T. Scott; "Some Random Memories of H.P.L.," F. B. Long; "H. P. Lovecraft: An Appreciation," T. O. Mabbott; "The Wind That Is in the Grass: A Memory of H. P. Lovecraft in Florida," Robert Barlow; "Lovecraft and Science," Kenneth Sterling; "Lovecraft as a Formative Influence," A. Derleth; "The Dweller in Darkness," D. Wandrei. *Memorial Verse:* "To Howard Phillips Lovecraft," C. A. Smith; "H.P.L.," H. Kuttner; "Lost Dream," Emil Petaja; "To Howard Phillips Lovecraft," Francis Flagg; "Elegy: In Providence in the Spring," A. Derleth; "For the Outsider: H. P. Lovecraft," Charles E. White; "In Memoriam: H. P. Lovecraft," Richard Ely Morse.

Outsider and Others, The [collected–A. Derleth & D. Wandrei] [C] (Arkham, 1939, xiv+553 pp., $5.00, jacket–V. Finlay; 1,258 copies)

Weird, 36 stories and "Howard Phillips Lovecraft: Outsider" –A. Derleth & D. Wandrei: "Dagon"; "Polaris"; "Celephais"; "Hypnos"; "The Cats of Ulthar"; "The Strange High House in the Mist"; "The Statement of Randolph Carter"; "The Silver Key"; "Through the Gates of the Silver Key"; "The Outsider"; "The Music of Erich Zann"; "The Rats in the Walls"; "Cool Air"; "He"; "The Horror at Red Hook"; "The Temple"; "Arthur Jermyn"; "The Picture in the House"; "The Festival"; "The Terrible Old Man"; "The Tomb"; "The Shunned House"; "In the Vault"; "Pickman's Model"; "The Haunter of the Dark"; "The Dreams in the Witch-House"; "The Thing on the Doorstep"; "The Nameless City"; "The Lurking Fear"; "The Call of Cthulhu"; "The Colour out of Space"; "The Dunwich Horror"; "The Whisperer in Darkness"; "The Shadow Over Innsmouth"; "The Shadow out of Time"; "At the Mountains of Madness." Also contains essay "Supernatural Horror in Literature" (its first complete appearance). This was the first book from Arkham House, and is now one of the most valuable of the weird collectors' items.

Shadow out of Time, The [n] (*ASF*, June 1936) (in *The Outsider* [Lovecraft], 1936) (in *The Dunwich Horror* [Lovecraft], 1945, pa; 1963) (in *Portable Novels of Science* [Wollheim], 1945) (in *The Colour out of Space* [Lovecraft], 1964, pa; 1967, pa)

Mind transference and prehuman life.

Shadow Over Innsmouth, The (Visionary Press, Everett [Pa.], 1936, 13+158 pp., illus.–F. A. Utpatel, $1.00) (in *The Outsider* [Lovecraft], 1939) (*The Weird Shadow Over Innsmouth*, Bart House: 4, 1944, 190 pp., pa 25¢) (in *The Dunwich Horror and Others* [Lovecraft], 1963)

The original 1936 edition was the only Lovecraft book published in his lifetime; copies of this edition are now collectors' items. The 1944 Bart House pa was a collection of 5 weird stories: "The Weird Shadow Over Innsmouth"; "The Festival"; "He"; "The Outsider"; "The Whisperer in Darkness."

Shunned House, The (Recluse Press [W. Paul Cook], Athol [Mass.], 1928, 59 pp., np)

Originally written in 1924 and offered to *Weird Tales*, it was rejected by F. Wright; it was then offered to W. P. Cook, who printed it in 1928, with an introduction by F. B. Long. It was not bound at that time. R. H. Barlow found a few in 1936 and placed the work under copyright. For many years these were all that were known to be in circulation. More recently A. Derleth discovered 100 or so copies and these were bound for sale at $17.50. The story is reprinted in *At the Mountains of Madness* [Lovecraft], 1964.

Shuttered Room and Other Pieces, The [C] (Arkham, 1959, 313+xiv pp., illus.–photos, $5.00, jacket–R. Taylor; 2,500 copies)

Some fiction on which Lovecraft collaborated, and items about Lovecraft; foreword by A. Derleth. "The Shuttered Room" (completed by A. Derleth); "The Fisherman of Falcon Point" (completed by A. Derleth); *Juvenilia and Early Tales* (with Editorial Note): "The Little Glass Bottle"; "The Secret Cave"; "The Mystery of the Grave-Yard"; "The Mysterious Ship"; "The Alchemist"; "Poetry and the Gods"; "The Street."

"Old Bugs" (never before published); "Idealism and Materialism: A Reflection"; "The Commonplace Book" (annotated–A. Derleth & D. Wandrei); "Lovecraft in Providence," D. Wandrei; "Lovecraft as Mentor," A. Derleth; "Out of the Ivory Tower," R. Bloch; "Three Hours With Lovecraft," Dorothy C. Walter; "Memories of a Friendship," Alfred Galpin. *Four Poems:* "Homage to Lovecraft," Felix Stefanile; "H.P.L.," C. A. Smith; "Lines to H. P. Lovecraft," Joseph P. Brennan; "Revenants," A. Derleth. "The Barlow Tributes–'H.P.L.,' 'Anniversary,' 'Letter for Last Christmas to Frank Belknap Long'," Robert H. Barlow. "H. P. Lovecraft: The Books," "H. P. Lovecraft: The Gods," Lin Carter; "Addendum: Some Observations on the Carter Glossary," T. G. L. Cockcroft; "Notes on the Cthulhu Mythos," George T. Wetzel; "Lovecraft's First Book," Wm. L. Crawford. [Stories]: "Dagon"; "The Strange High House in the Mist"; "The Outsider."

Something About Cats and Other Pieces [collected–A. Derleth] [C] (Arkham, 1949, 306 pp., illus.–photos, $3.00, jacket–R. Clyne; 2,995 copies)

Weird revisions, essays, etc., with "Prefatory Note," A. Derleth: "Something About Cats" (originally "Cats and Dogs" [*Leaves*, Sum 1937], by Lewis Theobold [pseud. of H.P.L.]). *Revisions:* "The Invisible Monster," "Four O'Clock," Sonia Greene; "The Horror in the Burying Ground," Hazel Heald; "The Last Test," "The Electric Executioner," Adolphe De Castro; "Satan's Servants," R. Bloch (with notes). *Essays:* "The Despised Pastoral"; "Time and Space"; "Merlinus Redivivus"; "At the Root"; "The Materialist Today"; "Vermont: A First Impression"; "The Battle That Ended the Century" (with denials of H.P.L. as having authored the piece). *Notes and Drafts:* "The Shadow Over Innsmouth" (2 versions); "At the Mountains of Madness"; "The Shadow out of Time." *Poems:* "Phaeton"; "August"; "Death"; "To the American Flag"; "To a Youth"; "My Favorite Character"; "To Templeton and Mount Monadnock"; "The House"; "The City"; "The Poe-et's Nightmare" (includes "Aletheia Phrikodes"); "Sir Thomas Tryout"; "Lament for the Vanished Spider"; "Regnar Lodbrug's Epicedium." *Appreciations:* "A Memoir of Lovecraft," Rheinhart Kleiner; "Howard Phillips Lovecraft," Samuel Loveman; "Lovecraft as I Knew Him," Sonia H. Davis (the former Mrs. Lovecraft); "Addenda to *H.P.L.: A Memoir*," A. Derleth ("Lovecraft's Sensitivity," "Lovecraft's *Conservative*"); "The Man Who Was Lovecraft," E. Hoffman Price; "A Literary Copernicus," F. Leiber, Jr. *Memorial Poems:* "Providence: Two Gentlemen Meet at Midnight," A. Derleth; "H.P.L.," Vincent Starrett.

Survivor and Others, The [with A. Derleth] [C] (Arkham, 1957, 161 pp., $3.00, jacket–R. Clyne; 2,096 copies) (Ballantine: 629, 1962, 143 pp., pa 35¢)

7 notes or outlines of stories completed by A. Derleth: "The Survivor"; "Wentworth's Day"; "The Peabody Heritage"; "The Gable Window"; "The Ancestor"; "The Shadow out of Space"; "The Lamp of Alhazred." "The Shadow out of Space" is a parallel treatment of "The Shadow out of Time," and was drawn from the same notes; it also appeared in *Fantastic*, Feb 1962.

Three Tales of Terror [C] (Arkham, 1968, 134 pp., illus.–Lee Brown Coye, $7.50)

3 stories with 15 illustrations printed on coated paper: "The Colour out of Space"; "The Dunwich Horror"; "The Thing on the

Doorstep."
Weird Shadow Over Innsmouth, The See *Shadow Over Innsmouth, The*
Nonfiction
Selected Letters 1911–1924 [edited—A. Derleth & D. Wandrei] (Arkham, 1965, xxix+362 pp., $7.50)
   For the Lovecraft follower.
Selected Letters II, 1925–1929 (Arkham, 1968, 359 pp., $7.50)
   A further volume for Lovecraft enthusiasts.
Some Notes on H. P. Lovecraft [by A. Derleth] [pa] (Arkham, 1959, 42 pp., pa $1.25)
   An examination of some Lovecraft myths: 1. That Lovecraft died of starvation. 2. That Lovecraft committed suicide. 3. That Lovecraft was violently anti-Semitic. 4. That many of Lovecraft's manuscripts were lost. Also includes an explanation about unfinished manuscripts, comments on Lovecraft's writing habits, the Barlow journal of Lovecraft's visit to Florida in 1939, and four letters by Lovecraft to Derleth.
Supernatural Horror in Literature (*Recluse* [amateur mag.], 1920's) (*The Fantasy Fan* [amateur mag.], 1934) (in *The Outsider* [Lovecraft], 1939) (Abramson, New York, 1945, 106 pp., $2.50) (in *Dagon* [Lovecraft], 1965)
   Lovecraft's famous essay for lovers of the macabre. It was revised from its original appearance for *The Fantasy Fan*, and the first complete version was published in *The Outsider*. The Abramson edition has Introduction by A. Derleth, notes and index.

LOW, A(RCHIBALD) M(ONTGOMERY) (17 Oct 1888–13 Sep 1956) British professor and author. He invented the first guided missile (a flying bomb) in 1917, and later the first radio-controlled rocket. He was credited with over 200 inventions. He was a regular writer of scientific fact and also wrote some science fiction. For a time he was president of the British Interplanetary Society.
Fiction [Incomplete—other titles in Bleiler *Checklist*]
Adrift in the Stratosphere ("Space," *Scoops*, sr10, 19 Feb 1934) (Blackie, London, 1937, 224 pp., 2/-; 1956, 3/6) (*Steuerlos in der Stratosphäre* [German], F. Oetinger, 1955)
   Juvenile; some youths unexpectedly take a trip in a professor's rocket and have many adventures.
Satellite in Space (H. Jenkins, London, 1956, 191 pp., 10/6; 1958, 6/-) (Digit: R734, 1963, 160 pp., pa 2/6)
   Action between Earth satellites, one controlled by a German of Hitler's ideals; aliens from the Asteroid Belt enter the picture.
Nonfiction
It's Bound to Happen (Burke, London, 1950, 204 pp., 10/6) (*What's the World Coming To?*, Lippincott, Philadelphia, 1951, 214 pp., $3.00; Longmans, Toronto, $3.75)
   Brilliantly written portrayal of things to come.
What's the World Coming To? See *It's Bound to Happen*

LOWNDES, Mrs. BELLOC (1868–14 Nov 1947) English writer. After historical and fiction writing, she became established as a mystery writer with *The Lodger* (1913), a fictionalised representation of Jack the Ripper's murders. Her autobiographies *I, Too, Have Lived in Arcadia* (1942), *Where Love and Friendship Dwelt* (1943), *Merry Wives of Westminster* (1946), are considered one of the greatest memoir series of their time. A further fantasy is *From the Vasty Deep* (Doran, New York, 1921).
Fiction
Studies in Love and Terror [C] (Methuen, London, 1913, vii+299 pp., 6/-) (Scribner, New York, 1913, 3+299 pp.)
   Fantasy, 5 stories: "Price of Admiralty"; "The Child"; "St. Catherine's Eve"; "The Woman From Purgatory"; "Why They Married."

LOWNDES, ROBERT A(UGUSTINE) W(ARD) (4 Sep 1916–) U.S. author and editor. Born in Bridgeport, Conn., he graduated from Darien High School in 1933 and attended Stamford Community College, 1936. He began reading sf in 1928 and became an ardent fan in the 1930's. He tried unsuccessfully to start a chapter of the Science Fiction League and was very active in the fan affairs of the period. He was married in 1948, acquiring a stepson, and

was separated in 1968. He is very interested in history, politics, music, opera, astrology, spiritualism and Indian philosophy. He became a Catholic and adopted the name Augustine.
   Lowndes is primarily noted as an editor of science-fiction and weird magazines, but he has also contributed many stories to those fields, especially in the early 1940's (many under pseudonyms). His published work includes westerns, sports, detective and love-pulp fiction, as well as articles on psychology and spiritual development. He has used around 50 pseudonyms, including about 12 in sf/fantasy. For a time he was an authors' agent; he then became editor of *Future Science Fiction* with the Apr 1941 issue and *Science Fiction Quarterly* with the Spr 1941 issue. These lapsed during the war years, but he was able to restart them as of the May-June 1950 and May 1951 issues, respectively. Lowndes was managing editor of Columbia's entire pulp chain from 1940 to 1960, when the remaining magazines ceased, primarily through loss of the distributor. Lowndes' Columbia magazines included the short-lived *Dynamic Science Fiction*; his final two were *(Original) Science Fiction Stories* and *Future Science Fiction*. In Dec 1960 he was hired by Health Knowledge Inc. (Acme News) to edit *Real Life Guide*, a "sexology" type magazine, and *Exploring the Unknown*, dealing with psychic phenomena and the occult, etc. The former ceased early in 1967, while the latter continued until 1971. The following titles were added to his Health Knowledge chain: *Magazine of Horror*, 1963; *Startling Mystery Stories*, 1966; *Famous Science Fiction*, 1966; *World-Wide Adventure*, 1967; *Thrilling Western Magazine*, 1968; *Weird Terror Tales*, 1968; and *Bizarre Fantasy Tales*, 1970. All were essentially reprint magazines, though the first three used some new material. They are now all extinct. Lowndes became editor of the Avalon sf books from the first title, *Three to Conquer*, E. F. Russell, in Aug 1956, and edited all but four (in early 1958) up to early 1968; *The Day the World Stopped*, S. A. Coblentz, was the last Avalon book he edited.
Fiction
Believers' World (Avalon, New York, 1961, 224 pp., $2.95) (*Planet der Erleuchteten* [German], *UZ*: 364, 1963)
   Conflict in a hyperspatial three-planet system, originally colonized by Terra, where each has its own version of the "true word" based on the teachings of Ein (Einstein).
Duplicated Man, The See BLISH, J. (co-author)
Mystery of the Third Mine (Winston, Philadelphia, 1953, 201 pp., $2.00) ([Japanese], GingaShobo 'Adv. in SF 8,' 1955) (*La cintura degli asteroidi* [Italian], Fantascienza: 1, 1961, pa)
   Juvenile, one of the Adventures in SF series; melodrama among the miners of the asteroids.
Puzzle Planet, The [pa] (Ace: D-485, 1961, 119 pp., pa 35¢; with *The Angry Espers*) (*Das Rätsel Carolus* [German], *UZ*: 357, 1963)
   A human expedition on an alien planet, murder, and a denouement with the "natives."

LUBAN, MILTON (1909–10 Aug 1956) U.S. writer. He was a reviewer for the daily film-journal *Hollywood Reporter*, introducing the term "scientifilm" to its pages. He collaborated with K. F. Crossen on an original screen treatment, *Barrier to the Stars* (which apparently has never been sold).
Fiction
Spirit Was Willing, The (Greenberg, New York, 1951, 188 pp., $2.50)
   Ghosts get sued for alienation of affections—meant to be humorous, but does not compare with Thorne Smith.

LUDLAM, HARRY Author; he has written a biography of Bram Stoker.
Fiction
Coming of Jonathan Smith, The [pa] (Arrow: 838, 1956, 184 pp., pa 3/6)
Nonfiction
Mummy of Birchen Bowen and Other True Ghosts, The [C] (Foulsham, London, 1966, 159 pp., illus., 20/-) (Taplinger, New York, 1967, 159 pp., illus., $3.95)

LUDLOW, EDMUND (1898–)
Fiction
Coming of the Unselves, The (Exposition, New York, 1965, 194 pp., $4.50)

LUKENS, ADAM (pseud) See DETZER, DIANNE

LUM, PETER (1911–)
Nonfiction
Fabulous Beasts (Pantheon, New York, 1951, 7+256 pp., illus.– A. M. James, $3.75) (McClelland, Toronto, $5.00) (Thames, London, 1952, 15/-) (Longmans, Toronto, $3.00)
  Fascinating information on the legendary beasts of man's imaginings; well written but not well organized.

LUNDBERG, KNUD (1920–) Danish author.
Fiction
Olympic Hope, The [Trans. from Danish–Eiler Hansen & William Luscombe] (S. Paul, London, 1958, 172 pp., 12/6)
  The Olympic Games of 1996, with the use of science and drugs to aid the athletes.

LUNDWALL, SAM J. Swedish science-fiction bibliographer and publisher, and a noted figure in Swedish fan affairs for a number of years. He was to have edited the new s-f magazine *Alpha*, but after the first issue was prepared the financier backed out. Lundwall compiled a bibliography of Swedish books of sf and fantasy since 1830; this appeared duplicated in 1962, and lithographed in late 1963 titled *Bibliografi över Science Fiction och Fantasy*, 76 pp. In recent years he has become noted as a musician and popular composer.

LUNN, HUGH KINGSMILL (1889–15 May 1949) British author, better known under his pseudonym Hugh Kingsmill. He was also a biographer, literary critic, and anthologist. He spent some of his childhood in Switzerland. In World War I he served in the Royal Naval Division and was two years a prisoner of war in Germany. He devoted himself to writing until 1940, when he became a headmaster. He was adjudged a versatile, energetic, and entertaining author and critic.
Fiction [as Hugh Kingsmill]
Dawn's Delay, The [C] (Eyre Spottiswoode, London, 1948, 248 pp., 10/6) (Collins, Toronto, $3.25)
  4 stories: "The End of the World"; "Disintegration of a Politician"; "W.J."; "The Return of William Shakespeare." A 1924 edition with the same title is probably one of these stories retitled.
Return of William Shakespeare, The (Duckworth, London, 1929, 254 pp., 7/6) (Bobbs Merrill, Indianapolis, 1929, 320 pp., $2.50) (McClelland, Toronto, $2.00) (in *The Dawn's Delay* [Kingsmill], 1948)
  This author's most notable fantasy.

LUPOFF, RICHARD A(LLEN) (21 Feb 1935–) U.S. editor, author, fan, and amateur magazine publisher. An enthusiast of E. R. Burroughs, he became fiction editor for Canaveral Press and wrote the book below on Burroughs.
Fiction
One Million Centuries [pa] (Lancer: 74-892, 1967, 352 pp., pa 75¢)
  Fascinating adventures of a man in the far future among a number of possible future societies.
Nonfiction
Edgar Rice Burroughs: Master of Adventure (Canaveral, New York, 1965, 296 pp., $7.50) (Ace: N-6, 1968, 315 pp., pa 95¢)
  A running chronicle of Burroughs' writing career shown against the popular magazine fiction of the early and middle 20th century of which it was a part. (See P. S. Miller, *ASF*, June 1966, p. 148.) The Ace ed. has had certain aspects corrected.

LUTHER, RAY
Fiction
Intermind [pa] (Banner: B50-117, 1967, 144 pp., pa 50¢)

Through mind operation a spy checks into an unusual secret.

LYMINGTON, JOHN British author, possibly a pseudonym.
Fiction
Coming of the Strangers, The (Hodder Stoughton, London, 1961, 190 pp., 12/6) (Corgi: YS1267, 1963, 142 pp., pa 3/-)
  Unseen aliens terrorize a seaside resort.
Froomb! (Hodder Stoughton, 1964, 223 pp., 16/-) (Doubleday, 1966, 187 pp., $3.95) (D'day SF B.C., 1966, $1.20) (Hodder: 818, 1967, 191 pp., pa 3/6) (Macfadden: 60-287, 1967, 224 pp., pa 60¢)
Giant Stumbles, The (Hodder Stoughton, 1960, 160 pp., 12/6) (Corgi: SS1036, 1961, 157 pp., pa 2/6) (Hodder: 753, 1965, 157 pp., pa 2/6)
  Dramatic events after a scientist discovers the human race is in danger.
Green Drift, The (Hodder Stoughton, 1965, 191 pp., 16/-)
Grey Ones, The (Hodder Stoughton, 1960, 160 pp., 12/6) (Corgi: SS1227, 1962, 126 pp., pa 2/6)
Night of the Big Heat (Hodder Stoughton, 1959, 160 pp., 12/6) (Dutton, New York, 1960, 160 pp., $2.95) (Corgi: SS982, 1961, 157 pp., pa 2/6) (Hodder: 738, 1965, 126 pp., pa 2/6)
  A modern novel of human relationships; the sf element of a heat-ray attack and matter-transmitter invasion of monsters is kept in the background. It was made into a one-hour BBC teleplay about 1963.
Night Spiders, The [C] (Corgi: GS1540, 1964, 159 pp., pa 3/6) (Doubleday, New York, 1967, 192 pp., $3.95)
  Weird, 28 stories: "The Night Spiders"; "Battle of Wills"; "Easy With Music"; "Moving House"; "The Waking Ghost"; "The Hole in the World"; "The Forger's Gloves"; "The Long Caretaker"; "No Sale"; "Head Under Arm"; "Noises Off"; "Scratch in Time"; "Threepenny to Mars"; "Second Time Round"; "The Time Stopper"; "Mourning Train"; "Pie in the Sky"; "Then I Woke Up"; "The Televisitor"; "The Thief"; "The Space Traveller"; "The Locked Room"; "The Sky Ghost"; "Buttons in the Night"; "Gang Aft Agley"; "The Bad Thought"; "The Man on the Beam"; "The Man Behind Me."
Screaming Face, The (Hodder Stoughton, 1963, 160 pp., 12/6) (Corgi: GS7142, 1965, 159 pp., pa 3/6)
Sleep Eaters, The (Hodder Stoughton, 1973, 224 pp., 16/-) (Corgi: GS7066, 1964, 174 pp., pa 3/6)
  Invasion of Earth by mental forces from outer space.
Star Witches, The [pa] (Hodder: 737, 1965, 128 pp., pa 2/6)
Sword Above the Night, A [pa] (Hodder Stoughton, London, 1962, 158 pp., 12/6) (Corgi: SS1334, 1963, 126 pp., pa 2/6)
Ten Million Years to Friday (Hodder, 1967, 191 pp., 16/-)
  A machine which multiplies the speed of light brings back the world of many millions of years ago.

LYNCH, (JOHN GILBERT) BOHUN (1884–)
Fiction
Menace From the Moon (Jarrolds, London, 1925, 306 pp., 7/6)
  Sf, considered by some to be quite notable. Not listed in the Bleiler *Checklist* or I. F. Clarke's *The Tale of the Future*.
Anthologies
Best Ghost Stories (Small Maynard, Boston, 1924, 326 pp., $2.50) (*A Muster of Ghosts*, C. Palmer, London, 1924, 354 pp., 7/6)
  10 stories: "The Shadow of a Midnight," M. Baring; "The Thing in the Cellar," E. F. Benson; "The Willows," A. Blackwood; "The Old Nurse's Story," Mrs. Gaskell; "The Tractate Middoth," M. R. James; "Thurnley Abbey," Percival Landon; "The Fountain," Elinor Mordaunt; "Not on the Passenger-List," B. Pain; "The Fall of the House of Usher," E. A. Poe; "The Victim," May Sinclair.
Muster of Ghosts, A See *Best Ghost Stories*

LYTTLE, EILEEN JEANNETTE See GARRETT, E. J.

LYTTON, LORD See BULWER-LYTTON, E. G.